SWORDS OF SORROW™

THE COMPLETE SAGA

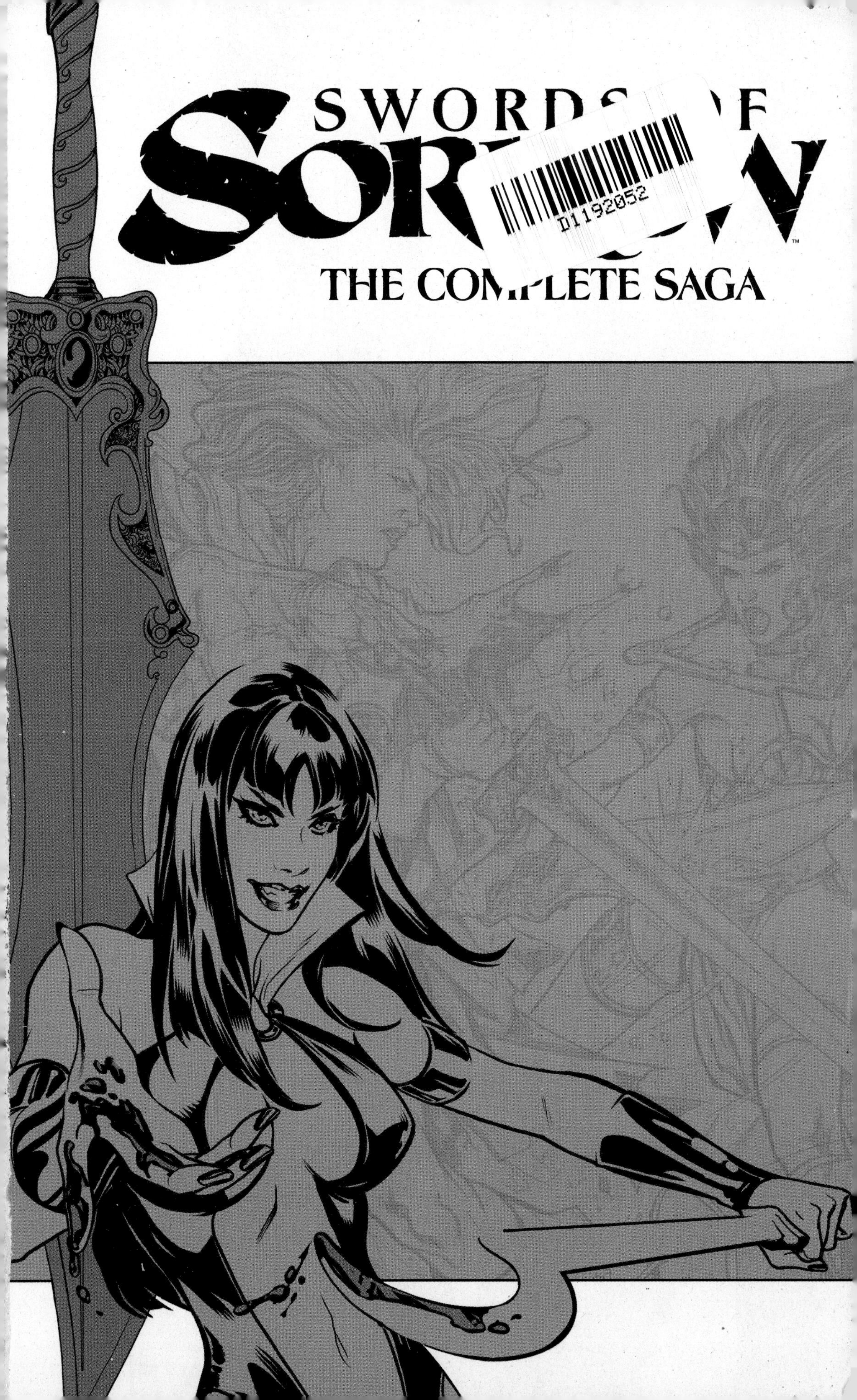

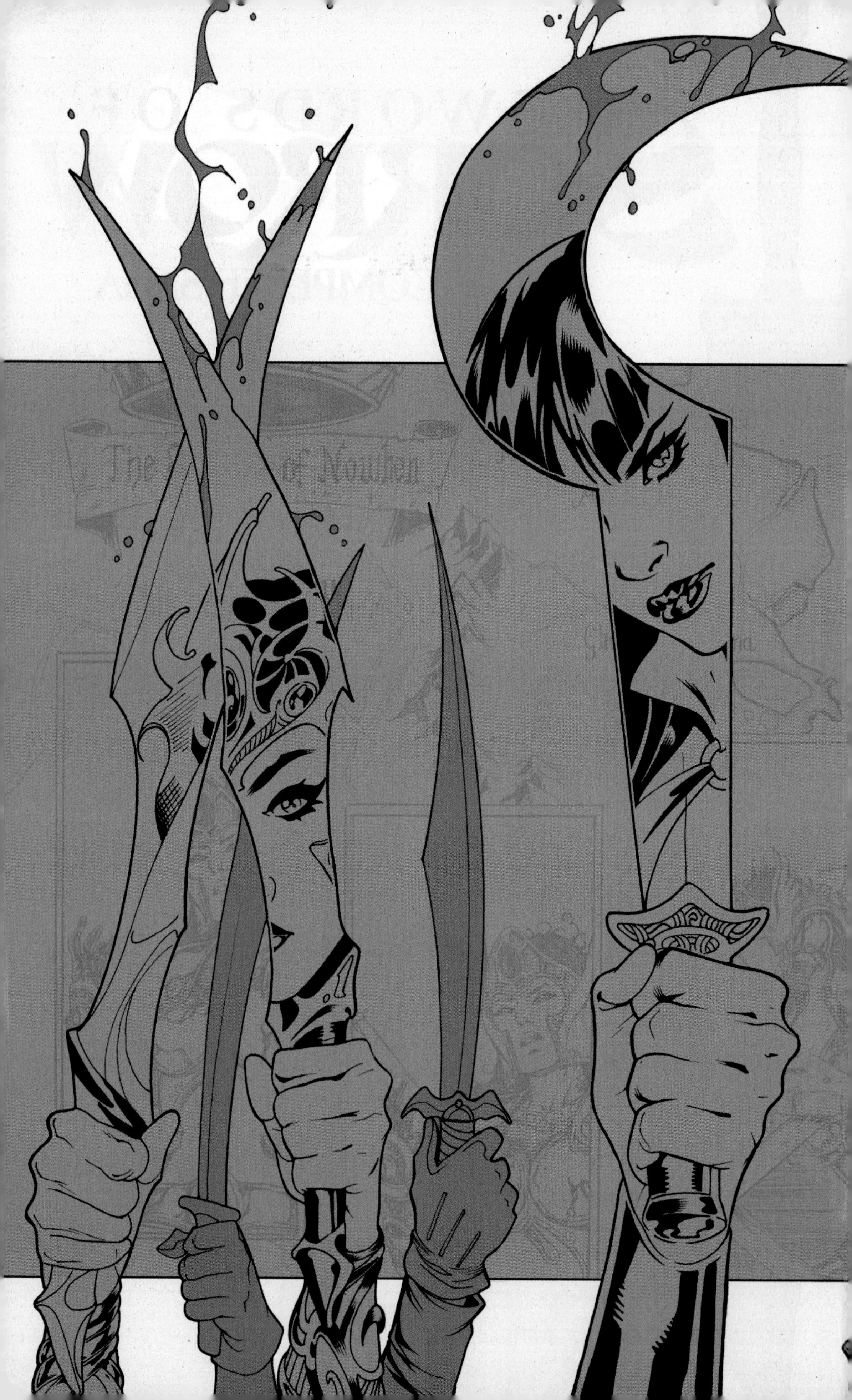

SWORDS OF SORROW

THE COMPLETE SAGA

story by GAIL SIMONE

written by GAIL SIMONE, EMMA BEBBY,
MARGUERITE BENNET, NANCY A. COLLINS,
MIKKI KENDALL, LEAH MOORE,
MAIRGHREAD SCOTT, ERICA SCHULTZ,
and G. WILLOW WILSON

illustrated by SERGIO DÁVILA, DAVE ACOSTA,
MIRKA ANDOLFO, RONILSON FREIRE,
FRANCESCO MANNA, ROD RODOLFO,
NOAH SALONGA, and CRIZAM ZAMORA

additional inks by ELISA FERRARI (Arancia Studio)

colored by JORGE SUTIL, SALVATORE AIALA
STUDIOS, INLIGHT STUSIOS, NANJAN JAMBERI,
VALENTINA PINTO, AGNES POZZA (Mad5),
DINEI RIBIERO, VINCENZO SALVO (Arancia Studio),
KRISTY SWAN, and CHIARA ZEPPEGNO

lettered by ERICA SCHULTZ

original series edits by JOSEPH RYBANDT, RACHEL
PINNELAS, MOLLY MAHAN, and HANNAH ELDER

additional collection edits by KEVIN KETNER

collection cover art by J. SCOTT CAMPBELL
collection cover colors by NEI RUFFINO

collection design by JASON ULLMEYER

SWORDS OF SORROW™: THE COMPLETE SAGA, VOLUME ONE.
Contains materials originally published in magazine form as Swords
of Sorrow #1-6, Swords of Sorrow: Black Sparrow & Lady Zorro,
Swords of Sorrow: Chaos! Prequel, Swords of Sorrow: Dejah Thoris
& Irene Adler #1-3, Swords of Sorrow: Masquerade & Kato, Swords
of Sorrow: Miss Fury & Lady Rawhide, Swords of Sorrow: Pantha &
Jane Porter,Swords of Sorrow: Red Sonja & Jungle Girl #1-3, and
Swords of Sorrow: Vampirella & Jennifer Blood #1-4, . Published by
Dynamite Entertainment. 113 Gaither Dr., STE 205, Mt. Laurel, NJ
08054. Swords of Sorrow is ™ & © 2016 Dynamite Characters, llc.
Vampirella ® and Pantha ® are ® & © 2016 Dynamite, All Rights
Reserved. Red Sonja ® & © 2016 Red Sonja, llc. All Rights Reserved.
John Carter, Dejah Thoris, Tars Tarkas, Warlord of Mars, Jane Porter,
and Edgar Rice Burroughs are ™ ERB, Inc. and used by permission.
Lady Zorro ®, and Lady Rawhide ™ are © 2016 Zorro Productions, Inc.
All Rights Reserved. Copyright © 2016 The Green Hornet, Inc. All
Rights Reserved. The Green Hornet, Black Beauty, Kato, and the hor-
net logos are trademarks of The Green Hornet, Inc. www.thegreen-
hornet.com. Jennifer Blood ™ and The Ninjettes™ are ™ & © 2016
Spitfire Productions, Inc. and Dynamite Characters, llc. Bad Kitty ™,
The Black Sparrow ™, Chastity ®, Jungle Girl ®, Masquerade ®, Miss
Fury ®, Mistress Hel ™, Purgatori ®, and Vanessa "Voodoo" Childe™
are ™ & © 2016 Dynamite Characters, llc. Dynamite, Dynamite
Entertainment & its logo are ® 2016 Dynamite. All Rights Reserved.
All names, characters, events, and locales in this publication are
entirely fictional. Any resemblance to actual persons (living or dead),
events or places, without satiric intent, is coincidental. No portion of
this book may be reproduced by any means (digital or print) without
the written permission of Dynamite Entertainment except for review
purposes. The scanning, uploading and distribution of this book via
the Internet or via any other means without the permission of the
publisher is illegal and punishable by law. Please purchase only
authorized electronic editions, and do not participate in or encourage
electronic piracy of copyrighted materials. **Printed in Canada.**

For media rights, foreign rights, promotions, licensing, and
advertising: marketing@dynamite.com

DYNAMITE.

Nick Barrucci, CEO / Publisher
Juan Collado, President / COO

Joe Rybandt, Senior Editor
Rachel Pinnelas, Associate Editor

Jason Ullmeyer, Design Director
Geoff Harkins, Graphic Designer
Chris Caniano, Digital Associate
Rachel Kilbury, Digital Assistant

Brandon Dante Primavera, Director of IT/Operations
Rich Young, Director of Business Development

Keith Davidsen, Marketing Manager
Kevin Pearl, Sales Associate

Online at www.DYNAMITE.com
On Facebook /Dynamitecomics
Instagram /Dynamitecomics
On Tumblr dynamitecomics.tumblr.com
On Twitter @Dynamitecomics
On YouTube /Dynamitecomics

ISBN-10: 1-60690-806-5
ISBN-13: 978-1-60690-806-8
First Printing
10 9 8 7 6 5 4 3 2 1

PEFC Certified
Printed on paper from
sustainably managed
forests and controlled
sources
www.pefc.org
PEFC/01-31-106

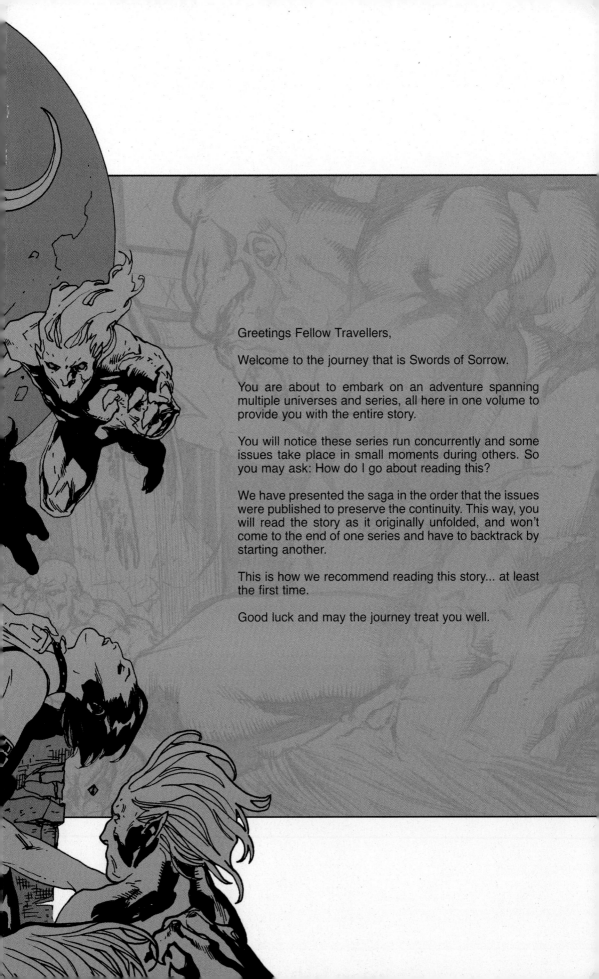

Greetings Fellow Travellers,

Welcome to the journey that is Swords of Sorrow.

You are about to embark on an adventure spanning multiple universes and series, all here in one volume to provide you with the entire story.

You will notice these series run concurrently and some issues take place in small moments during others. So you may ask: How do I go about reading this?

We have presented the saga in the order that the issues were published to preserve the continuity. This way, you will read the story as it originally unfolded, and won't come to the end of one series and have to backtrack by starting another.

This is how we recommend reading this story... at least the first time.

Good luck and may the journey treat you well.

HOW NICK BARRUCCI TRICKED ME INTO

So, I've been in the industry for a bit and written a bunch of comics, and I've noticed that the publisher of each company has a huge effect on not just the content they put out, but also the tone of the entire operation. Some are very businesslike, some are very creative, they all have imposed their demeanor on their respective companies, for good or ill (mostly good).

I've talked with numerous Dynamite creators, and we all say the same thing; Nick Barrucci knows what you want.

Seriously. That sounds a little sinister, but if you let it slip that you love, say, the Lone Ranger, sure enough, a year later, you get a call from Nick and he offers you that masked man exactly. And you find yourself scrambling your schedule around because damn, the Lone Ranger, right? And pretty soon you're thinking, he got me again.

I have until recently mostly written superhero comics, and I had a full schedule. Due to some weirdness, I agreed to write Red Sonja for Dynamite, but just six issues; even that was pushing it, time-wise. But Nick got me a tremendous artist in Walter Geovani, and I loved the character so much that I ended up doing six issues, then ANOTHER six issues, then a one-shot, then a four issue anthology, then another one-shot, then six MORE issues. Because damn, Red Sonja, right?

Anyway, my time with Sonja was sadly coming to an end, I had a lot of other commitments I had already agreed to do, when I get this call from Nick.

A SNEAKY call, y'all.

He calls me up to talk about this project they want to do and he wants to get my opinion.

Sure, happy to do it, I get calls about this stuff from publishers all the time.

They have this idea, see, they want to take nearly every female character they publish and do a big crossover featuring those ladies.

My first thought was, wow, that's really cool. I can't think of a major publisher that had ever done anything like that. And the few female-character-driven things they had done line-wide always had a name like GirlFrenzy or HotChicks or some other signpost saying, GUYS THOUGHT THIS UP.

So I was enthused, and we talked a little bit. And then it started to hit me. Dynamite has, bar none, the BEST stable of pulp heorines going. Wait. Wait a minute, I'm thinking. I start listing off the names in my head. Vampirella? Yes. Kato? You could have the new KATO! What about Jennifer Blood? What about Miss Fury? HEY! Lady ZORRO! Lady RAWHIDE!

And then it hit me, YOU COULD HAVE DEJAH THORIS AND RED SONJA in the same book!

That blew my mind.

See, we all have some incident, some hallelujah moment that made us fans of genre fiction. For me, a little girl who lived on a farm in very remote Oregon, it was finding a stack of comics and pulp novels at garage sales. That's where I first learned about many of these characters, and where I first fell in love with the worlds of Robert E. Howard and Edgar Rice Burroughs.

And whoever got to write this story got to bring characters from those two worlds together. For the first time in HISTORY.

THE MOST FUN ASSIGNMENT I EVER HAD

I was silent for a moment, then the ideas started flooding out right on the phone. You should have SONJA meet Tars Tarkas! Oh! And the Black Beauty gets stolen by Jungle Girl's tribe! Oh, man, you should get Irene Adler in there. OH! And Jane PORTER! And the Martians should invade Earth just after Orson Welles' War of the Worlds broadcast!

It just was too much fun to even contemplate.

When I've exhausted my brain pan after a bit, I finally ask, "By the way, Nick...who's WRITING this thing?"

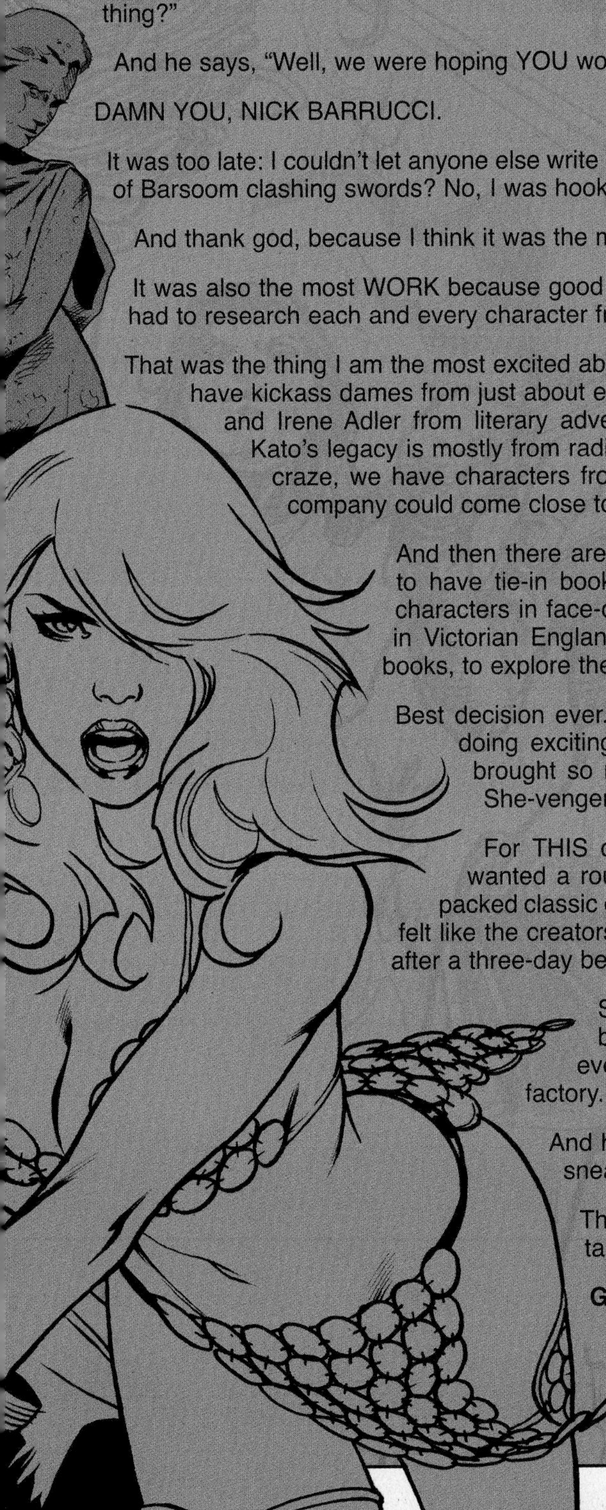

And he says, "Well, we were hoping YOU would, Gail."

DAMN YOU, NICK BARRUCCI.

It was too late: I couldn't let anyone else write it, now. Turn down the She-Devil and the Princess of Barsoom clashing swords? No, I was hooked way too deep.

And thank god, because I think it was the most fun I've ever had writing comics.

It was also the most WORK because good LORD, crossovers require a lot of coordination. I had to research each and every character from Masquerade to the Ninjettes.

That was the thing I am the most excited about, still. In this book, we were blessed enough to have kickass dames from just about every possible pulp tradition. We have Jane Porter and Irene Adler from literary adventure fiction, Miss Fury from newspaper strips, Kato's legacy is mostly from radio, we have the Chaos women from the 'Bad Girl' craze, we have characters from pulps, comics, novels, you name it. No other company could come close to putting this line-up together.

And then there are the mighty She-vengers. We decided it'd be fun to have tie-in books, one-shots and mini-series, and to put these characters in face-off situations – Irene Adler on Mars, Dejah Thoris in Victorian England – and have other female writers tackle those books, to explore the characters more fully.

Best decision ever. I went through and looked at writers who were doing exciting stuff in genre fiction and comics, and they all brought so much talent and energy! These were the mighty She-vengers and I couldn't have done this without them.

For THIS crossover, I didn't want the usual boring stuff. I wanted a rough and tumble, fun and sexy, scary and action-packed classic epic. Subtlety be damned, I wanted something that felt like the creators of all of these characters got together in a room after a three-day bender and just JAMMED.

So that's what we did. We assembled a team of the best writers and artists we could find and just threw every firecracker we could right into the gunpowder factory. I hope you like it.

And hey, Nick? If you ever do a sequel, CALL me, you sneaky bastard!

Thanks for reading our weird fantasy, our savage tale,

Gail Simone

I have a lot of people to thank. I've been part of lots of crossovers; I dearly love them. I love the puzzle of making them fit together and be worthy stories despite whatever meta-textual thing is going on. In this case, I didn't just have allies, I had WARRIORS.

First, huge thanks to Nick Barrucci and the whole crew at Dynamite. I can't even imagine what a nightmare it must have been to make this happen. Huge thanks to editors Joseph Rybandt, Rachel Pinnelas, Hannah Elder, and Molly Mahan. They did a great deal of the hard coordination work.

Most of these characters are owned by completely different companies. But they trusted us to take care of their babies, and that made an impossible task into a joyful one. Thank you to the licensors, you guys showed a lot of heart!

I have to thank all the amazing artists who worked so hard: fantastic cover artists like Tula Lotay, Robert Hack, J. Scott Campbell, Jenny Frison, and so many more.

And my final two thank-yous to the best collaborators ever:

First, to the SHE-VENGERS, the assassin writing squad of killer authors, who each rose to the occasion and gave us something great. Girls, I adore you, and you have MY Sword of Sorrow, should you ever need it. Mikki Kendall, G. Willow Wilson, Marguerite Bennett, Leah Moore, Mairghread Scott, Nancy Collins, and Emma Beeby each brought something wonderful to the table: comedy, horror, Victorian drama, I loved each of their books. And the final She-Venger, Erica Schultz, not only wrote a great book (and co-wrote another) herself, she also lettered the main series AND constantly jumped in to coordinate on so many small details, even logos and coloring. Erica, you are the best, and She-Vengers FOREVER!

Finally, my biggest thanks go out to Sergio Davila, who had to continually draw the impossible. I had one page that had more than two dozen individual heroines on it and he not only drew it, he made it look beautiful and full of life. He had to draw Mars, and 1940's Broadway and Hyrkania and swordfights and snipers and horses and giant white gorillas and honestly, I'm surprised he didn't jump out the nearest window. But nope, he just turned in page after page of beautiful stuff. A book like this could have been a cheesecake nightmare, but he never forgot that these amazing ladies are FIGHTERS. I dearly love him and can't wait to work with him again.

That's it, thank you, everyone, and BEWARE THE SHARD MEN (they totally suck!).

Hope you enjoy!
– Gail

THE BAD GUYS

The Prince

Bad Kitty

Chastity

Mistress Hel

Purgatori

THE GOOD GUYS

The Traveller

The Courier

Dejah Thoris

Red Sonja

Vampirella

Athena

Black Sparrow

Eva: Daughter of Dracula

Irene Adler

Jane Porter (Lady Greysoke)

Jennifer Blood

Jungle Girl (Jana)

Kato

Lady Rawhide

Lady Zorro

Masquerade

Miss Fury

Pantha

Red

Voodoo Childe

Woola

THE PLAYERS

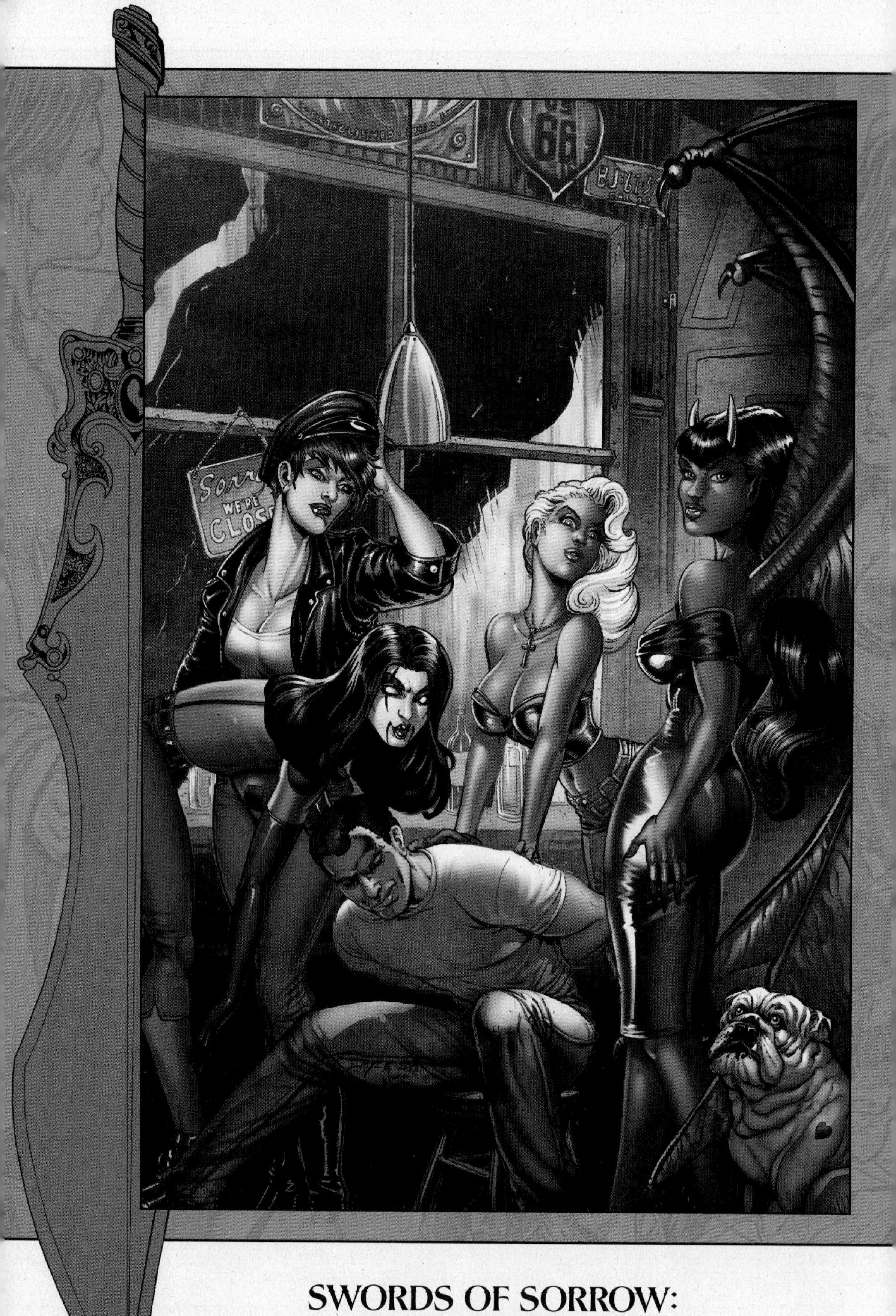
ESTABLISHED
66
WE'RE

SWORDS OF SORROW: CHAOS! PRELUDE

written by MAIRGHREAD SCOTT illustrated by MIRKA ANDOLFO
colored by CHIARA ZEPPEGNO and AGNESE POZZA (Mad5)
color supervision by MIRKA ANDOLFO lettered by ERICA SCHULTZ

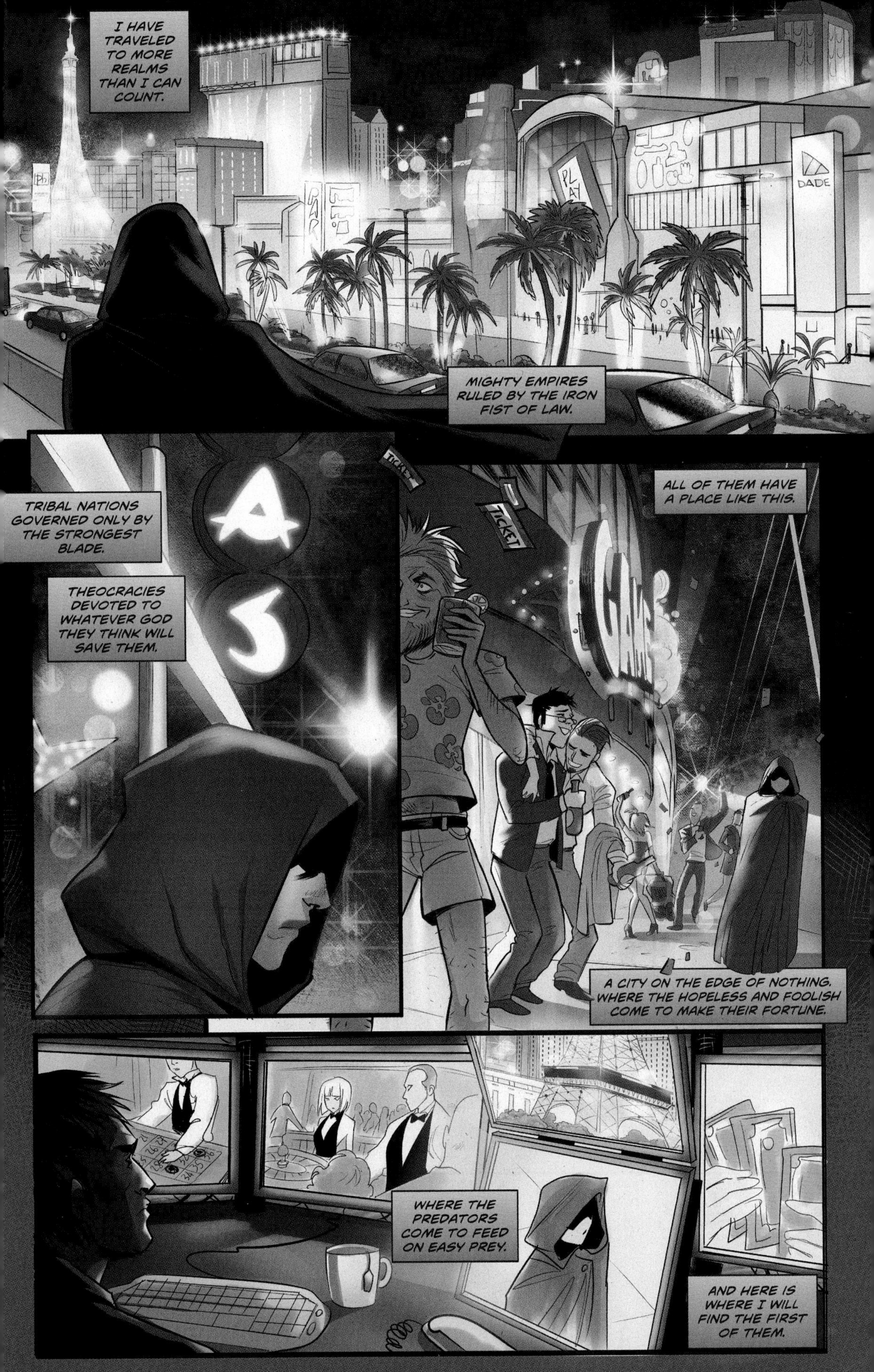
I HAVE TRAVELED TO MORE REALMS THAN I CAN COUNT.
MIGHTY EMPIRES RULED BY THE IRON FIST OF LAW.
TRIBAL NATIONS GOVERNED ONLY BY THE STRONGEST BLADE.
THEOCRACIES DEVOTED TO WHATEVER GOD THEY THINK WILL SAVE THEM.
ALL OF THEM HAVE A PLACE LIKE THIS.
A CITY ON THE EDGE OF NOTHING. WHERE THE HOPELESS AND FOOLISH COME TO MAKE THEIR FORTUNE.
WHERE THE PREDATORS COME TO FEED ON EASY PREY.
AND HERE IS WHERE I WILL FIND THE FIRST OF THEM.

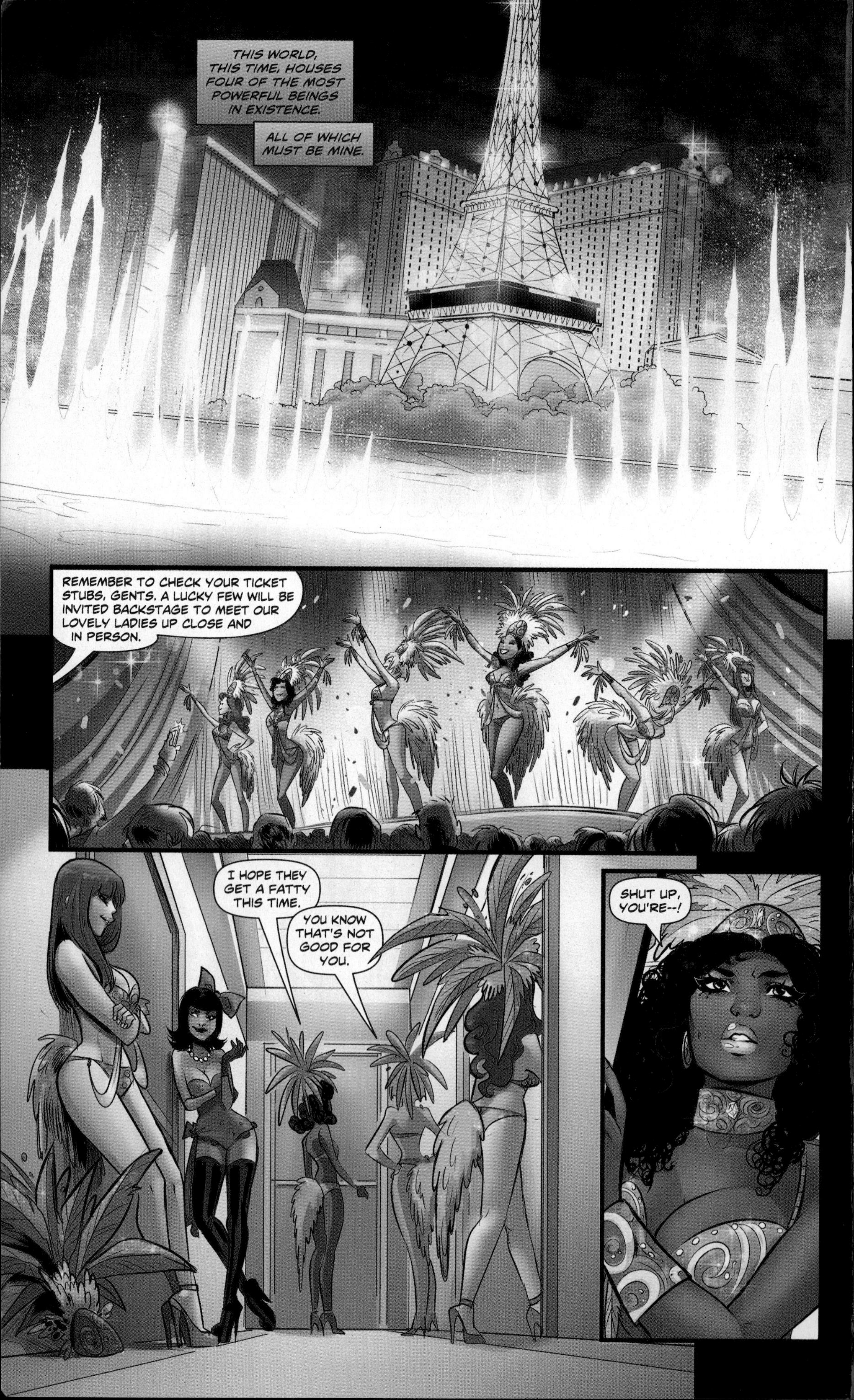
THIS WORLD, THIS TIME, HOUSES FOUR OF THE MOST POWERFUL BEINGS IN EXISTENCE.
ALL OF WHICH MUST BE MINE.
REMEMBER TO CHECK YOUR TICKET STUBS, GENTS. A LUCKY FEW WILL BE INVITED BACKSTAGE TO MEET OUR LOVELY LADIES UP CLOSE AND IN PERSON.
I HOPE THEY GET A FATTY THIS TIME.
YOU KNOW THAT'S NOT GOOD FOR YOU.
SHUT UP, YOU'RE--!

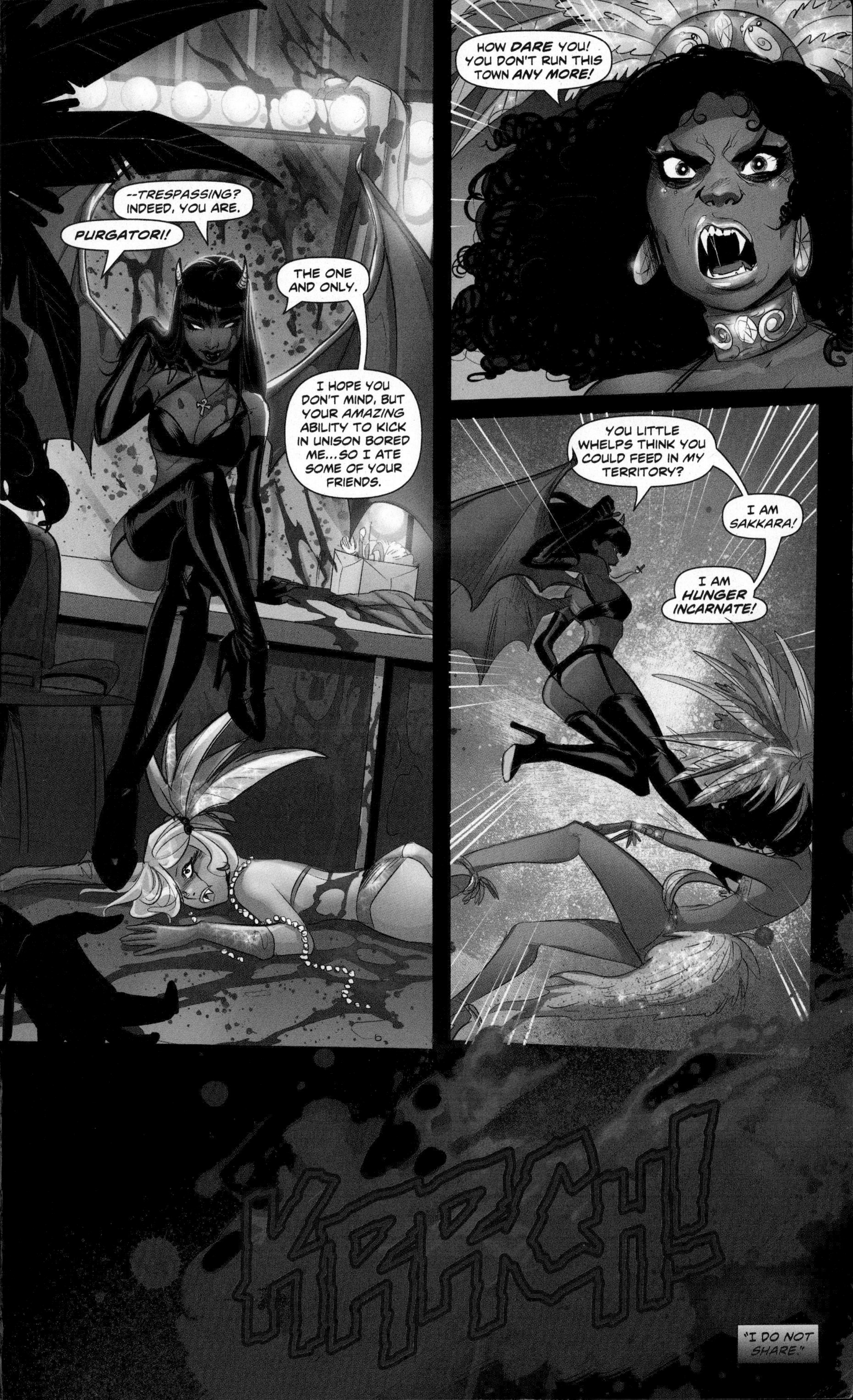
--TRESPASSING? INDEED, YOU ARE.
PURGATORI!
THE ONE AND ONLY.
I HOPE YOU DON'T MIND, BUT YOUR AMAZING ABILITY TO KICK IN UNISON BORED ME...SO I ATE SOME OF YOUR FRIENDS.
HOW DARE YOU! YOU DON'T RUN THIS TOWN ANY MORE!
YOU LITTLE WHELPS THINK YOU COULD FEED IN MY TERRITORY?
I AM SAKKARA!
I AM HUNGER INCARNATE!
KRRRCH!
"I DO NOT SHARE."

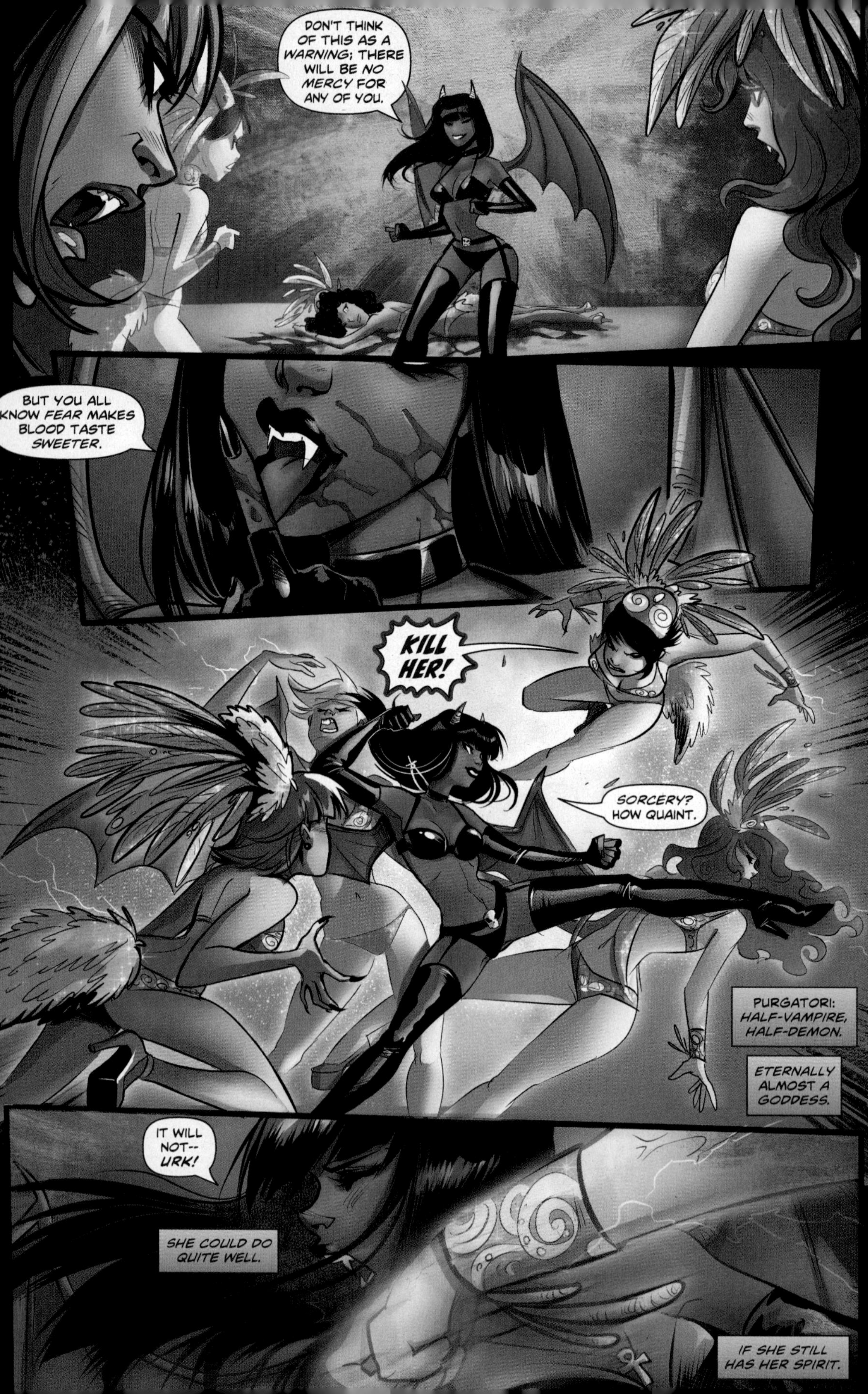
DON'T THINK OF THIS AS A WARNING; THERE WILL BE NO MERCY FOR ANY OF YOU.
BUT YOU ALL KNOW FEAR MAKES BLOOD TASTE SWEETER.
KILL HER!
SORCERY? HOW QUAINT.
PURGATORI: HALF-VAMPIRE, HALF-DEMON.
ETERNALLY ALMOST A GODDESS.
IT WILL NOT-- URK!
SHE COULD DO QUITE WELL.
IF SHE STILL HAS HER SPIRIT.

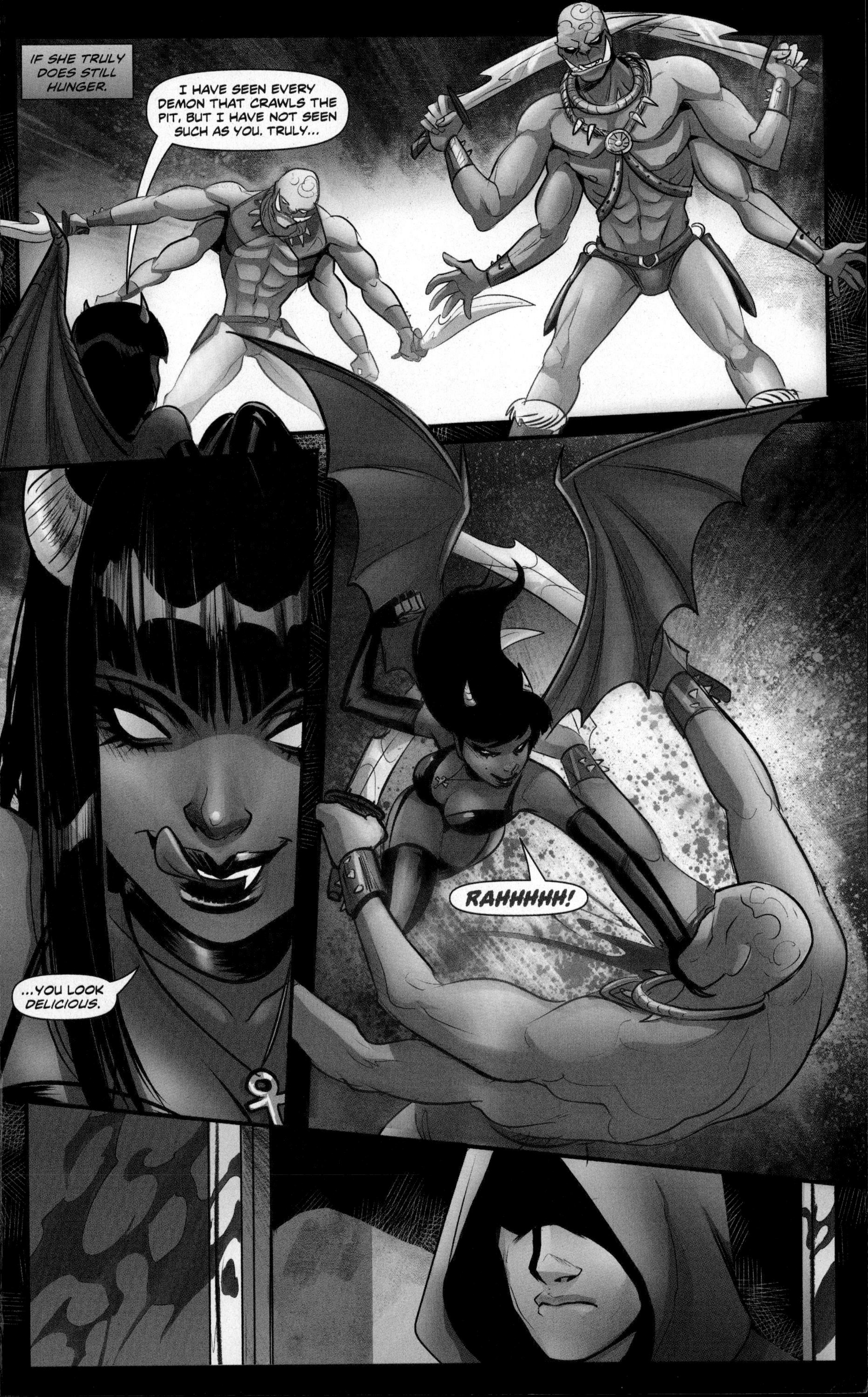
IF SHE TRULY DOES STILL HUNGER.
I HAVE SEEN EVERY DEMON THAT CRAWLS THE PIT, BUT I HAVE NOT SEEN SUCH AS YOU. TRULY...
...YOU LOOK DELICIOUS.
RAHHHHH!

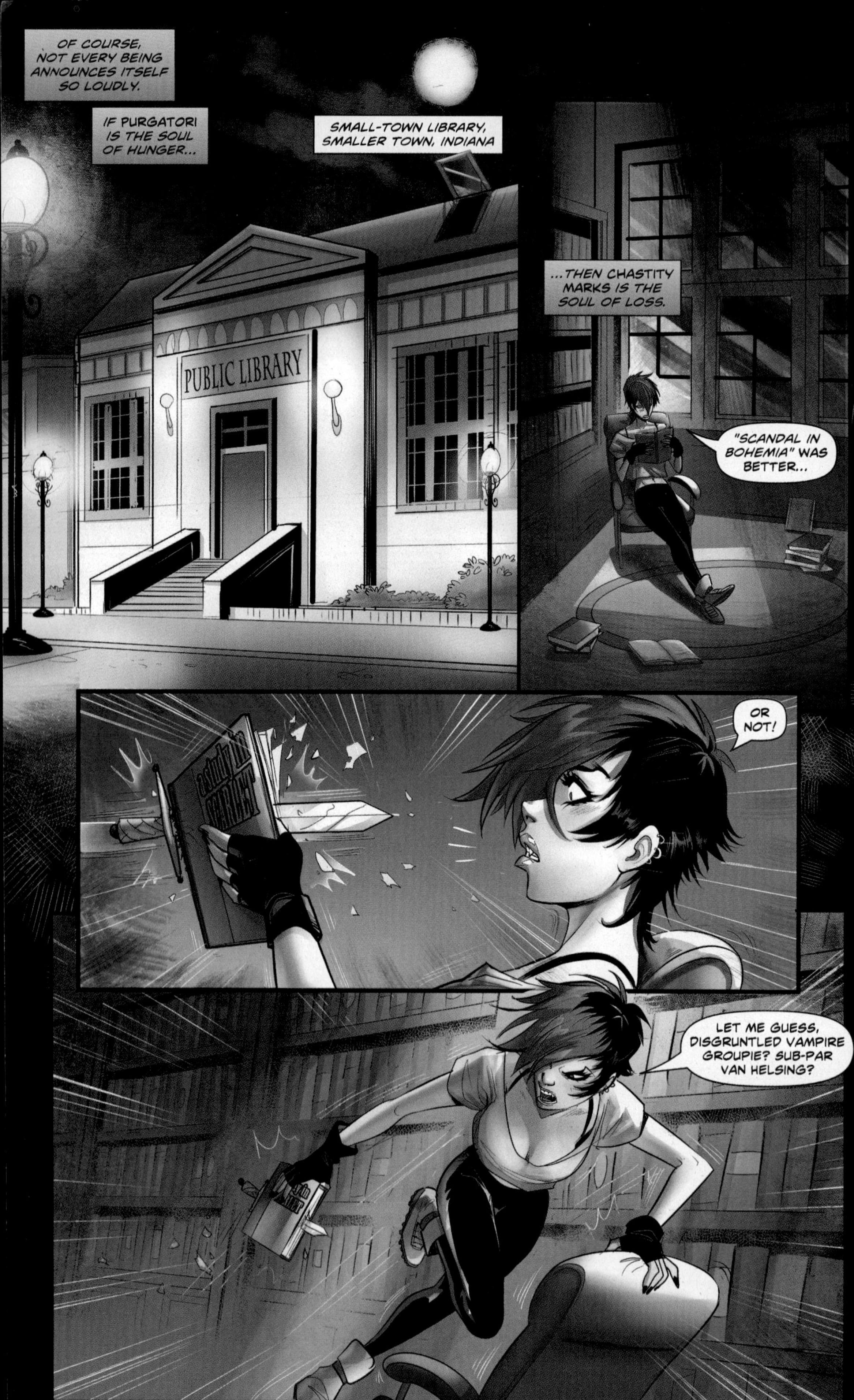
OF COURSE, NOT EVERY BEING ANNOUNCES ITSELF SO LOUDLY.
IF PURGATORI IS THE SOUL OF HUNGER...
SMALL-TOWN LIBRARY, SMALLER TOWN, INDIANA
PUBLIC LIBRARY
...THEN CHASTITY MARKS IS THE SOUL OF LOSS.
"SCANDAL IN BOHEMIA" WAS BETTER...
OR NOT!
LET ME GUESS, DISGRUNTLED VAMPIRE GROUPIE? SUB-PAR VAN HELSING?

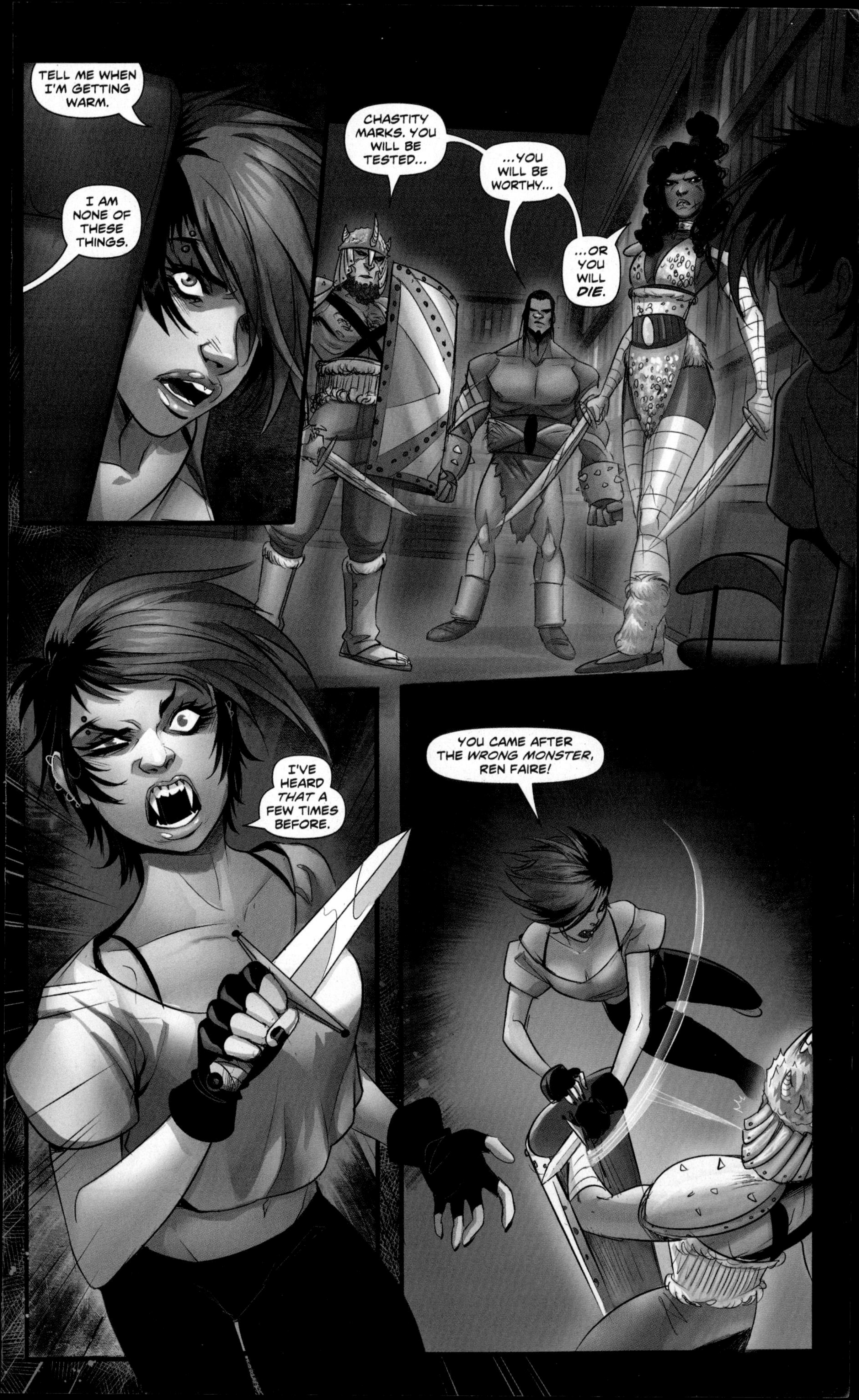
TELL ME WHEN I'M GETTING WARM.
I AM NONE OF THESE THINGS.
CHASTITY MARKS. YOU WILL BE TESTED...
...YOU WILL BE WORTHY...
...OR YOU WILL *DIE*.
I'VE HEARD *THAT* A FEW TIMES BEFORE.
YOU CAME AFTER THE *WRONG MONSTER*, REN FAIRE!

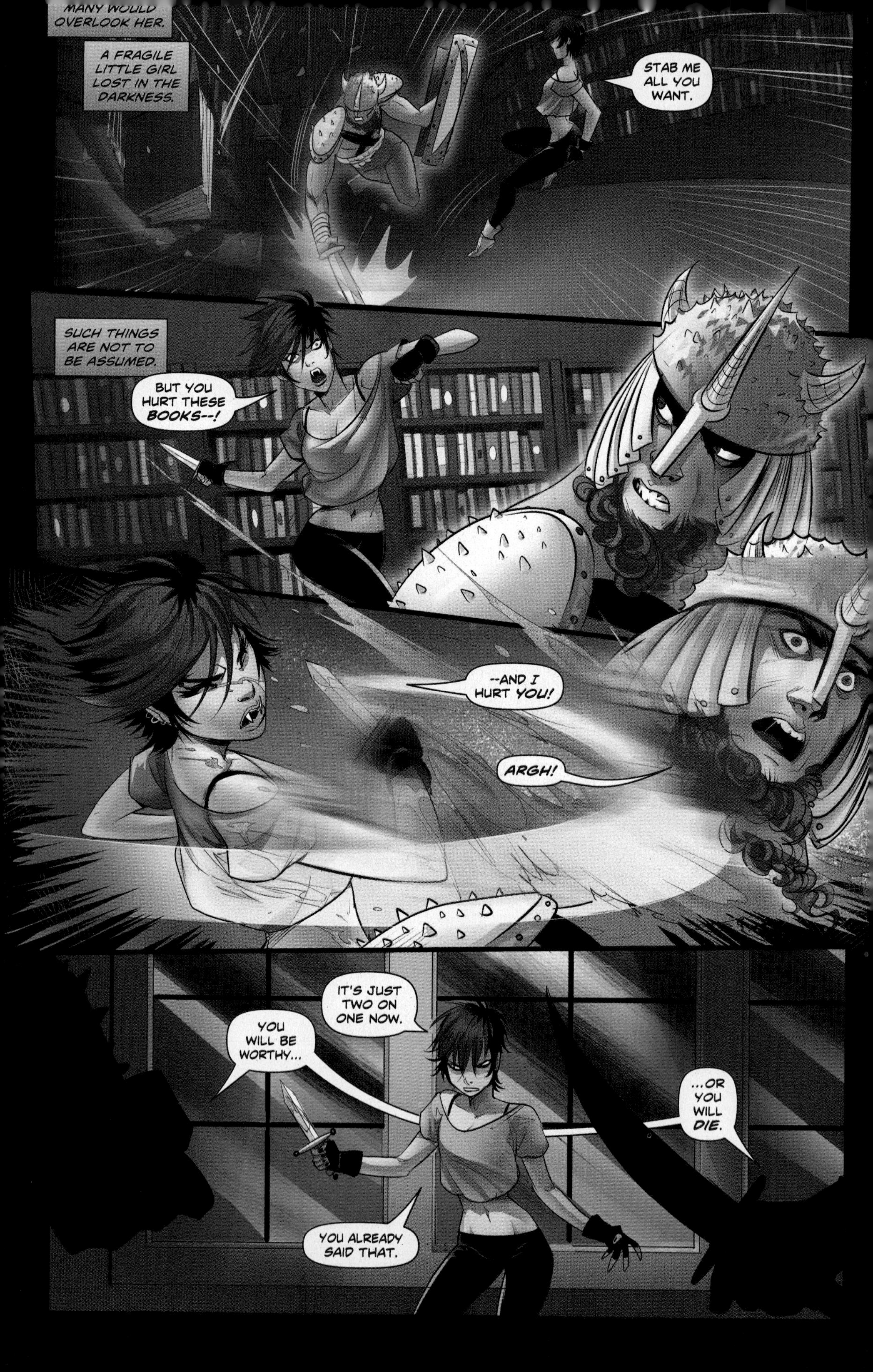
MANY WOULD OVERLOOK HER.
A FRAGILE LITTLE GIRL LOST IN THE DARKNESS.
STAB ME ALL YOU WANT.
SUCH THINGS ARE NOT TO BE ASSUMED.
BUT YOU HURT THESE BOOKS--!
--AND I HURT YOU!
ARGH!
IT'S JUST TWO ON ONE NOW.
YOU WILL BE WORTHY...
...OR YOU WILL DIE.
YOU ALREADY SAID THAT.

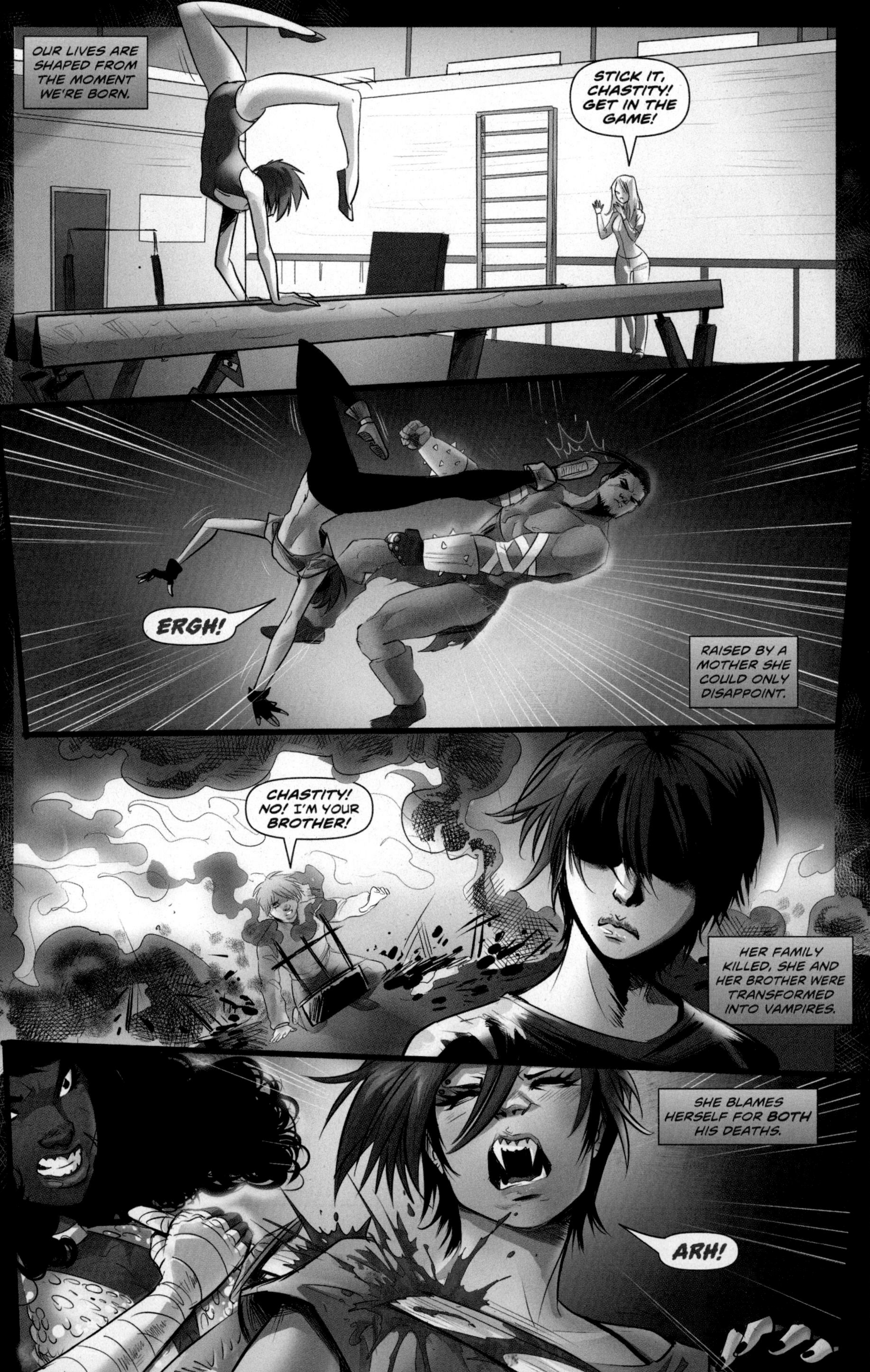
OUR LIVES ARE SHAPED FROM THE MOMENT WE'RE BORN.
STICK IT, CHASTITY! GET IN THE GAME!
ERGH!
RAISED BY A MOTHER SHE COULD ONLY DISAPPOINT.
CHASTITY! NO! I'M YOUR BROTHER!
HER FAMILY KILLED, SHE AND HER BROTHER WERE TRANSFORMED INTO VAMPIRES.
SHE BLAMES HERSELF FOR BOTH HIS DEATHS.
ARH!

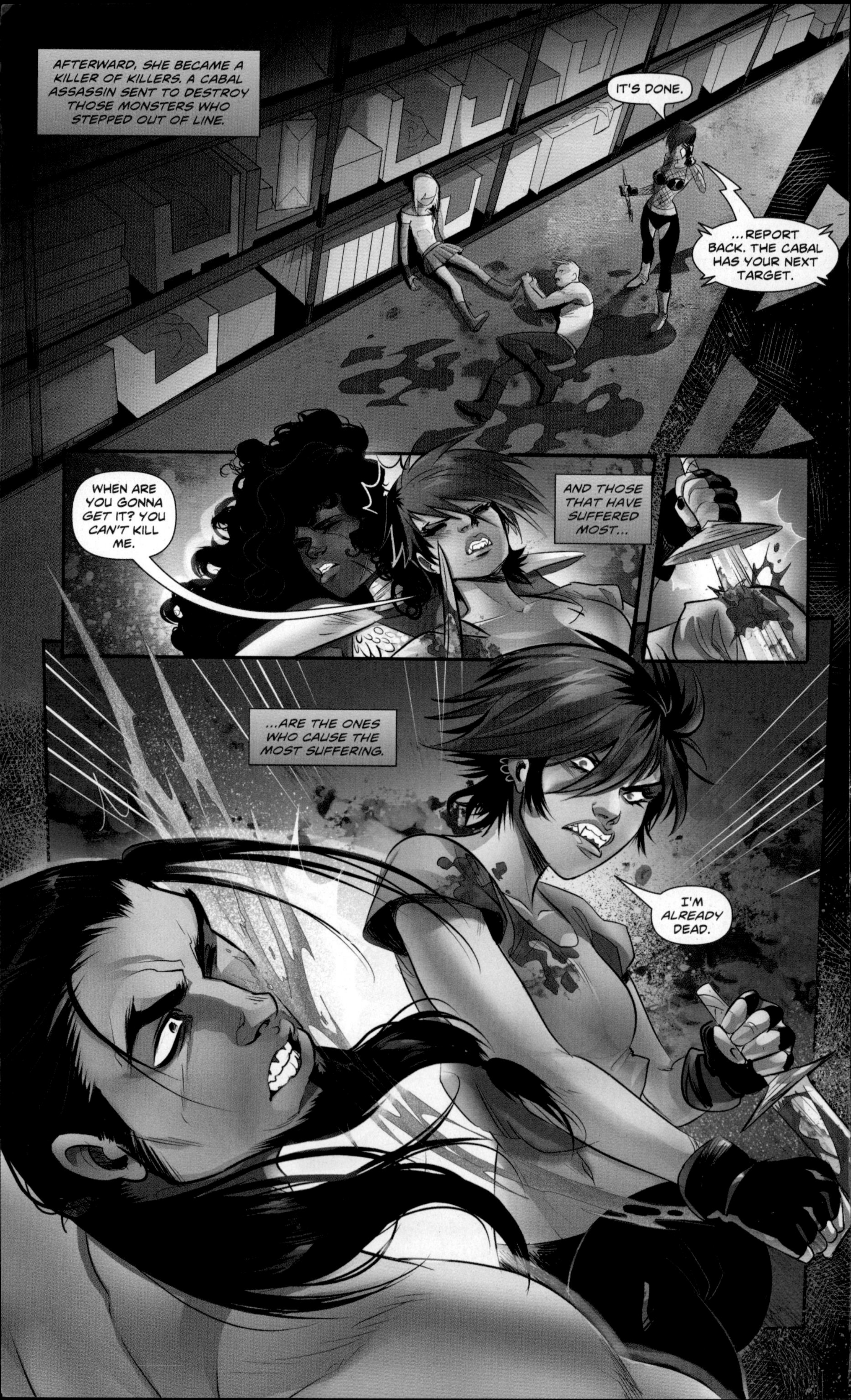
AFTERWARD, SHE BECAME A KILLER OF KILLERS. A CABAL ASSASSIN SENT TO DESTROY THOSE MONSTERS WHO STEPPED OUT OF LINE.
IT'S DONE.
...REPORT BACK. THE CABAL HAS YOUR NEXT TARGET.
WHEN ARE YOU GONNA GET IT? YOU CAN'T KILL ME.
AND THOSE THAT HAVE SUFFERED MOST...
...ARE THE ONES WHO CAUSE THE MOST SUFFERING.
I'M ALREADY DEAD.

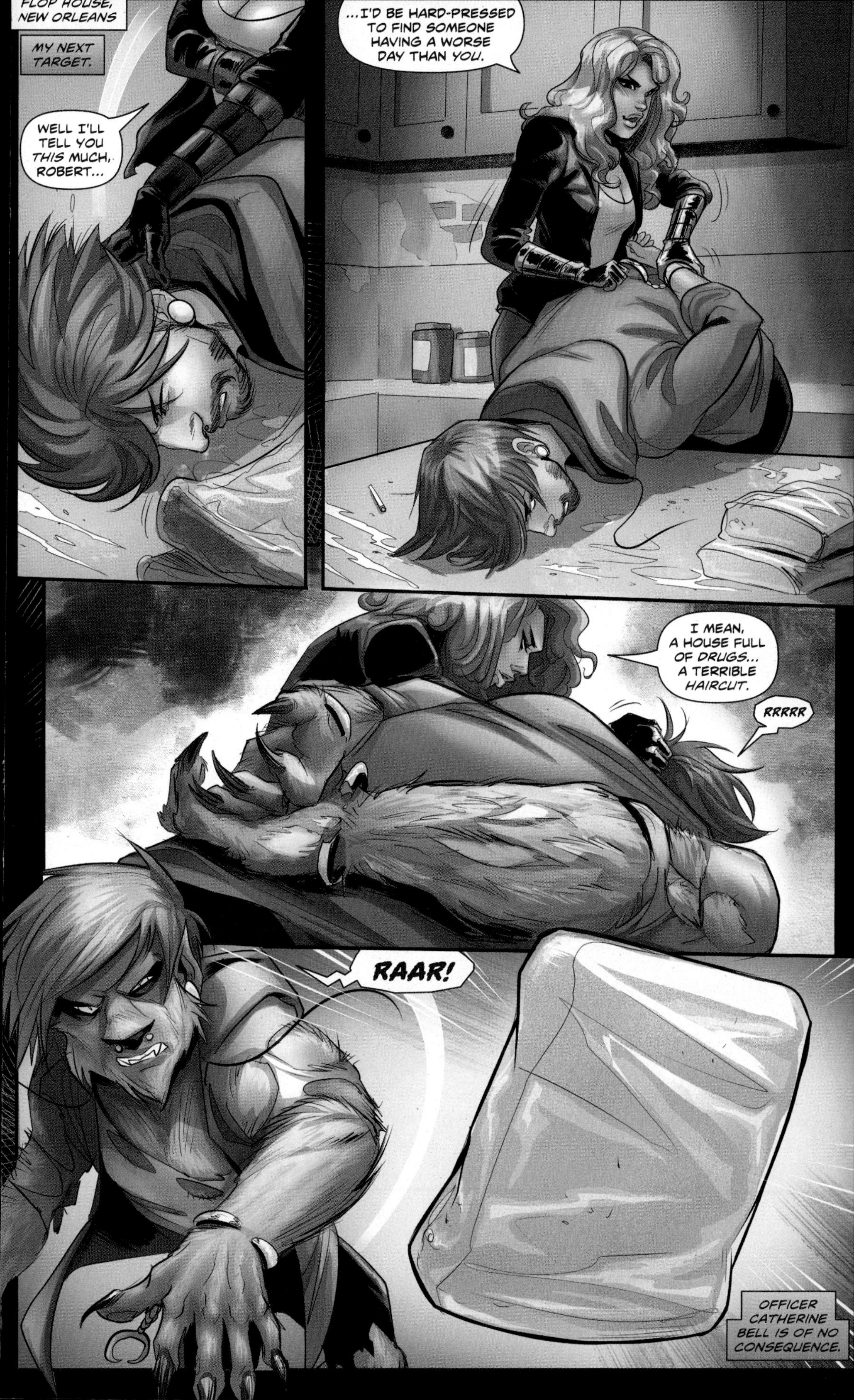
FLOP HOUSE, NEW ORLEANS
MY NEXT TARGET.
WELL I'LL TELL YOU *THIS* MUCH, ROBERT...
...I'D BE HARD-PRESSED TO FIND SOMEONE HAVING A WORSE DAY THAN *YOU*.
I MEAN, A HOUSE FULL OF DRUGS... A TERRIBLE *HAIRCUT*.
RRRRR
RAAR!
OFFICER CATHERINE BELL IS OF NO CONSEQUENCE.

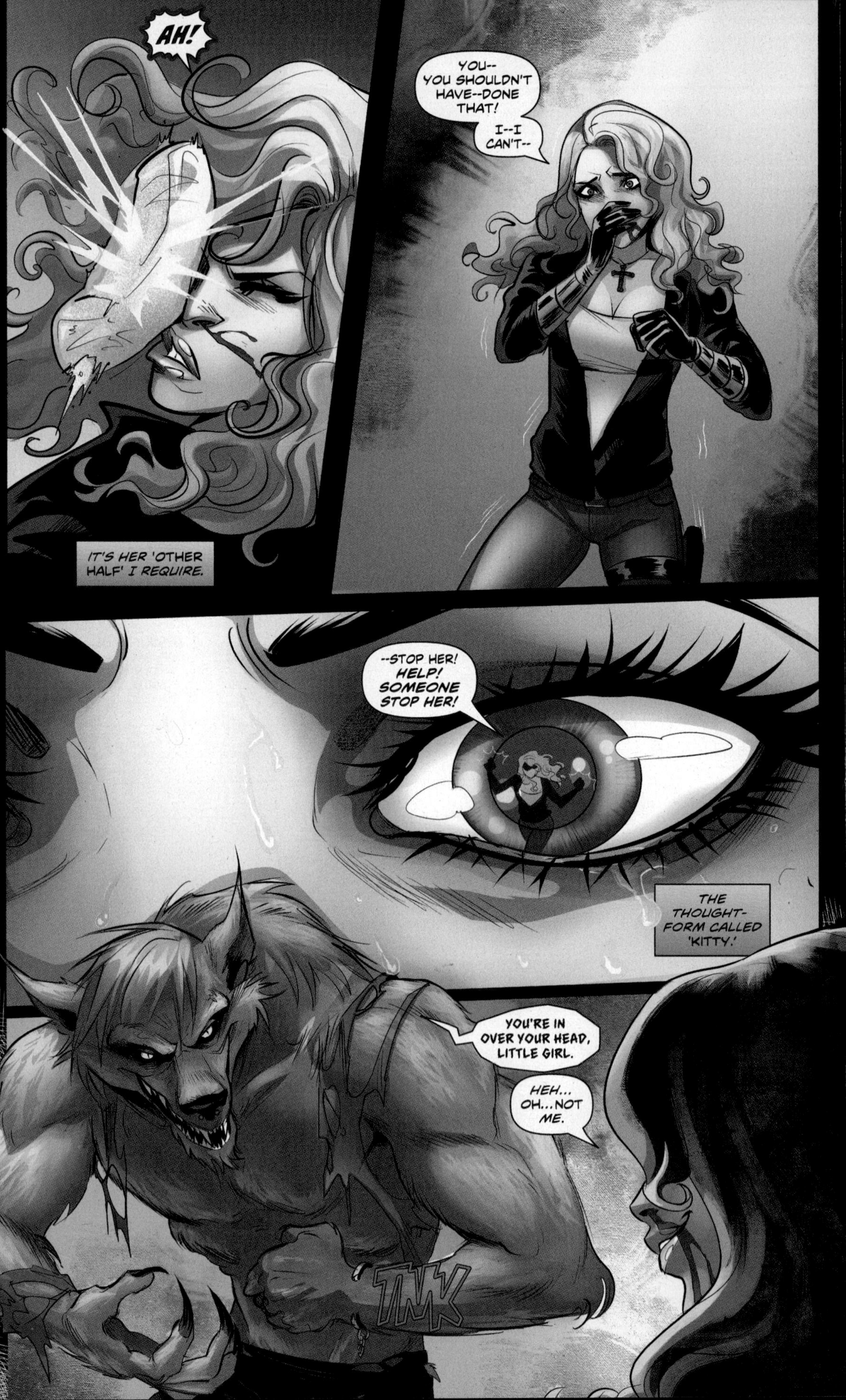
AH!
IT'S HER 'OTHER HALF' I REQUIRE.
YOU-- YOU SHOULDN'T HAVE--DONE THAT!
I--I CAN'T--
--STOP HER! HELP! SOMEONE STOP HER!
THE THOUGHT-FORM CALLED 'KITTY.'
YOU'RE IN OVER YOUR HEAD, LITTLE GIRL.
HEH... OH...NOT ME.
TNK

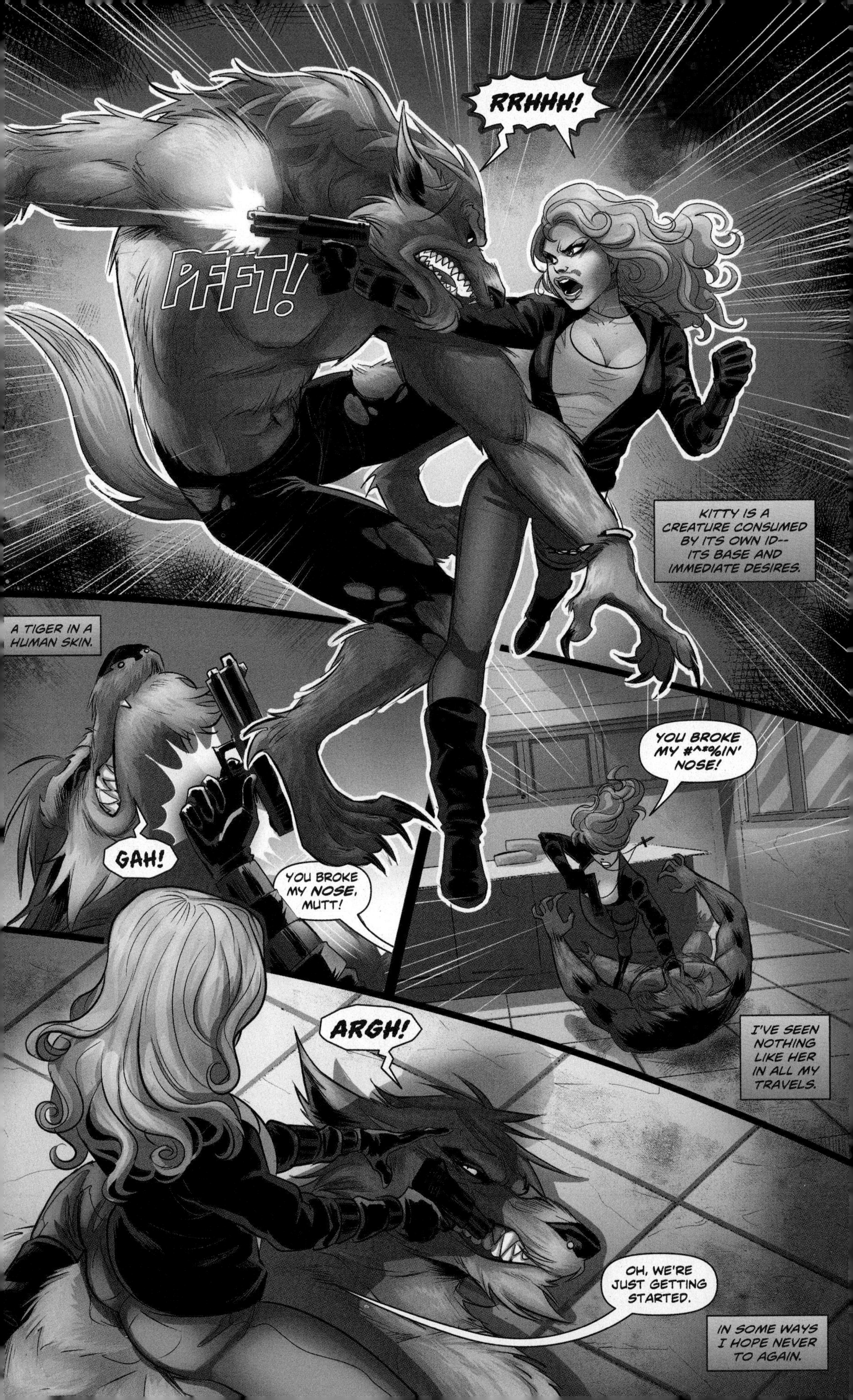
RRHHH!
PFFT!
KITTY IS A CREATURE CONSUMED BY ITS OWN ID-- ITS BASE AND IMMEDIATE DESIRES.
A TIGER IN A HUMAN SKIN.
GAH!
YOU BROKE MY NOSE, MUTT!
YOU BROKE MY #^*%IN' NOSE!
I'VE SEEN NOTHING LIKE HER IN ALL MY TRAVELS.
ARGH!
OH, WE'RE JUST GETTING STARTED.
IN SOME WAYS I HOPE NEVER TO AGAIN.

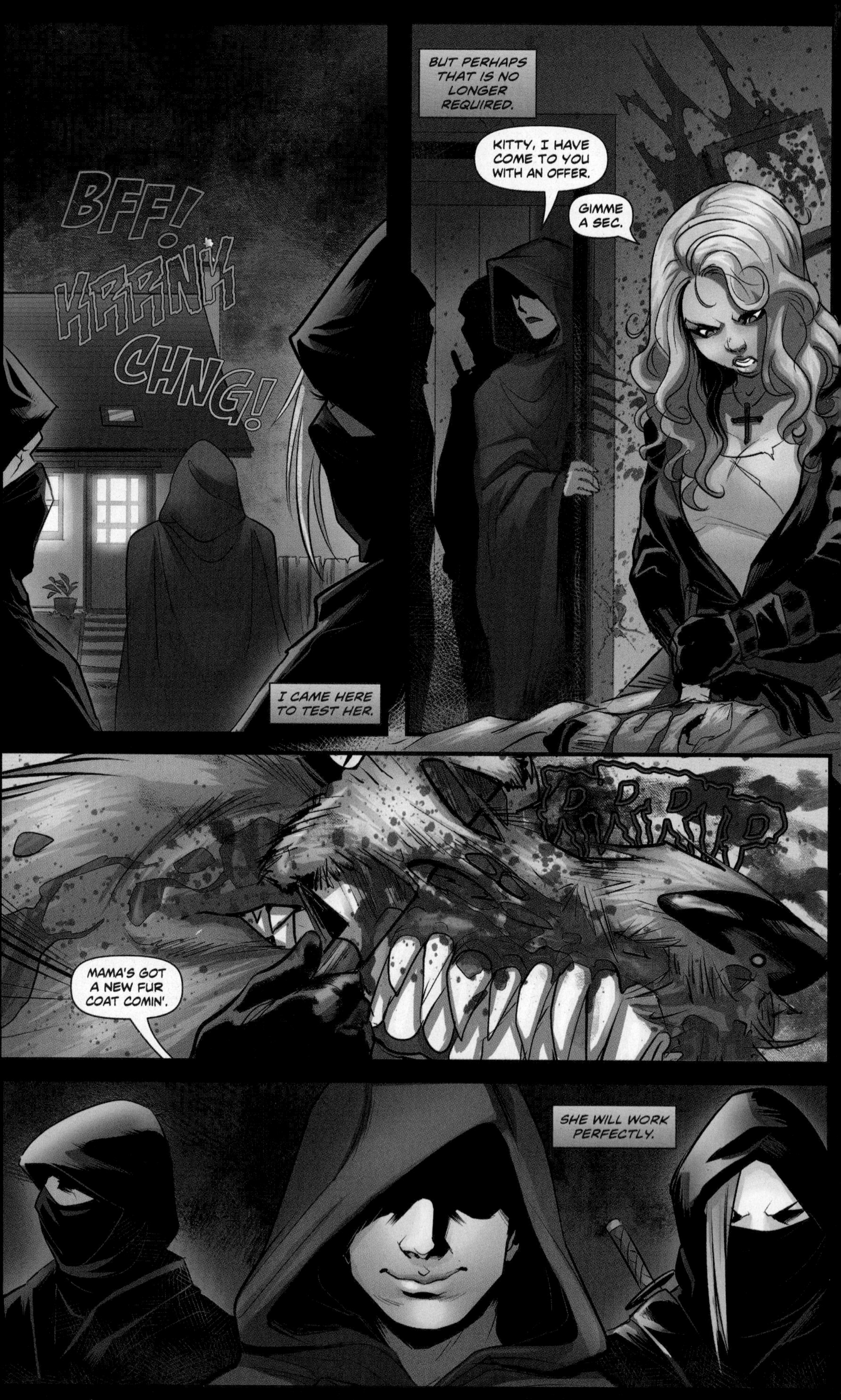
BFF!
KRRNK
CHNG!
I CAME HERE TO TEST HER.
BUT PERHAPS THAT IS NO LONGER REQUIRED.
KITTY, I HAVE COME TO YOU WITH AN OFFER.
GIMME A SEC.
MAMA'S GOT A NEW FUR COAT COMIN'.
SHE WILL WORK PERFECTLY.

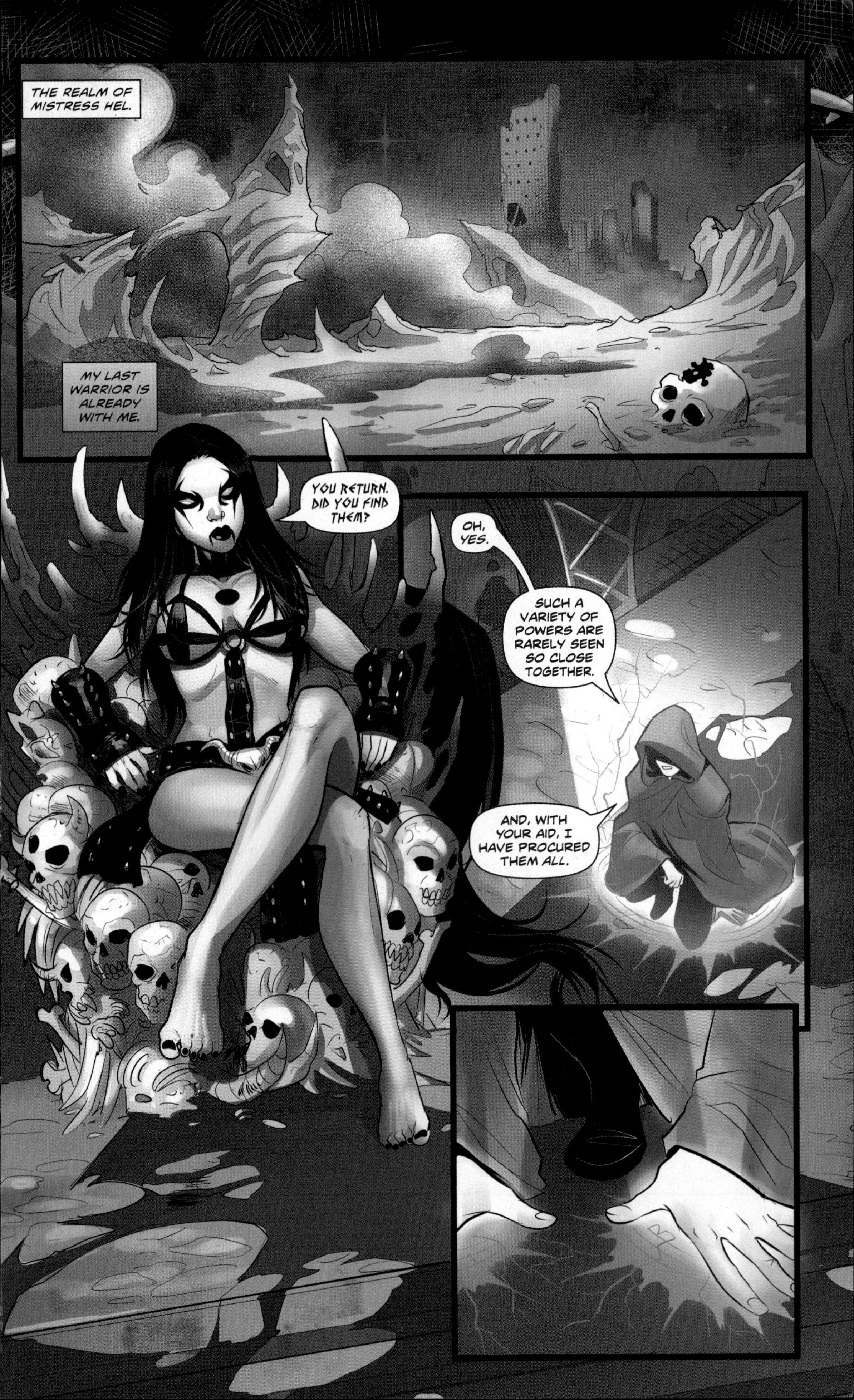
THE REALM OF MISTRESS HEL.
MY LAST WARRIOR IS ALREADY WITH ME.
YOU RETURN. DID YOU FIND THEM?
OH, YES.
SUCH A VARIETY OF POWERS ARE RARELY SEEN SO CLOSE TOGETHER.
AND, WITH YOUR AID, I HAVE PROCURED THEM ALL.

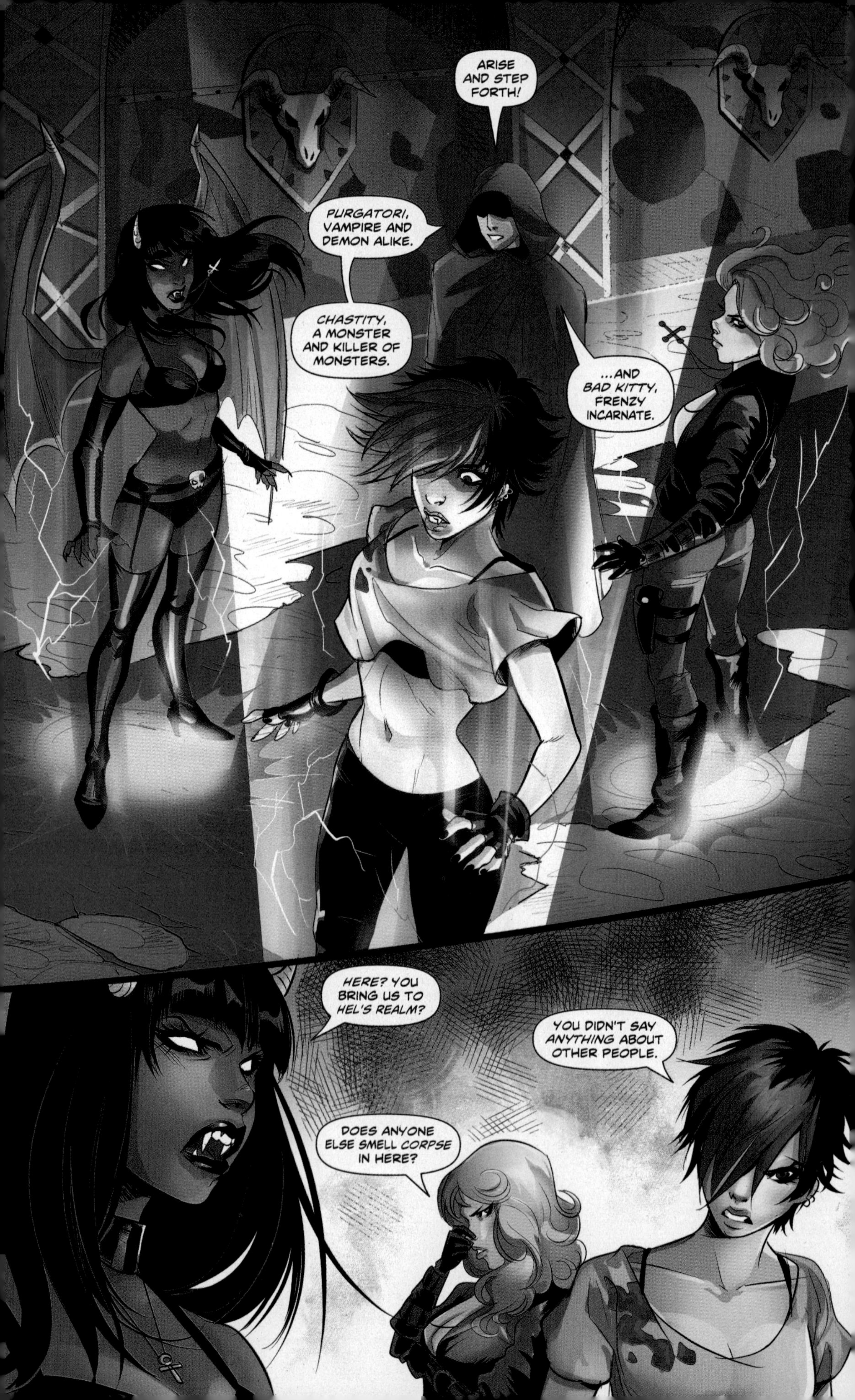
ARISE AND STEP FORTH!
PURGATORI, VAMPIRE AND DEMON ALIKE.
CHASTITY, A MONSTER AND KILLER OF MONSTERS.
...AND BAD KITTY, FRENZY INCARNATE.
HERE? YOU BRING US TO HEL'S REALM?
YOU DIDN'T SAY ANYTHING ABOUT OTHER PEOPLE.
DOES ANYONE ELSE SMELL CORPSE IN HERE?

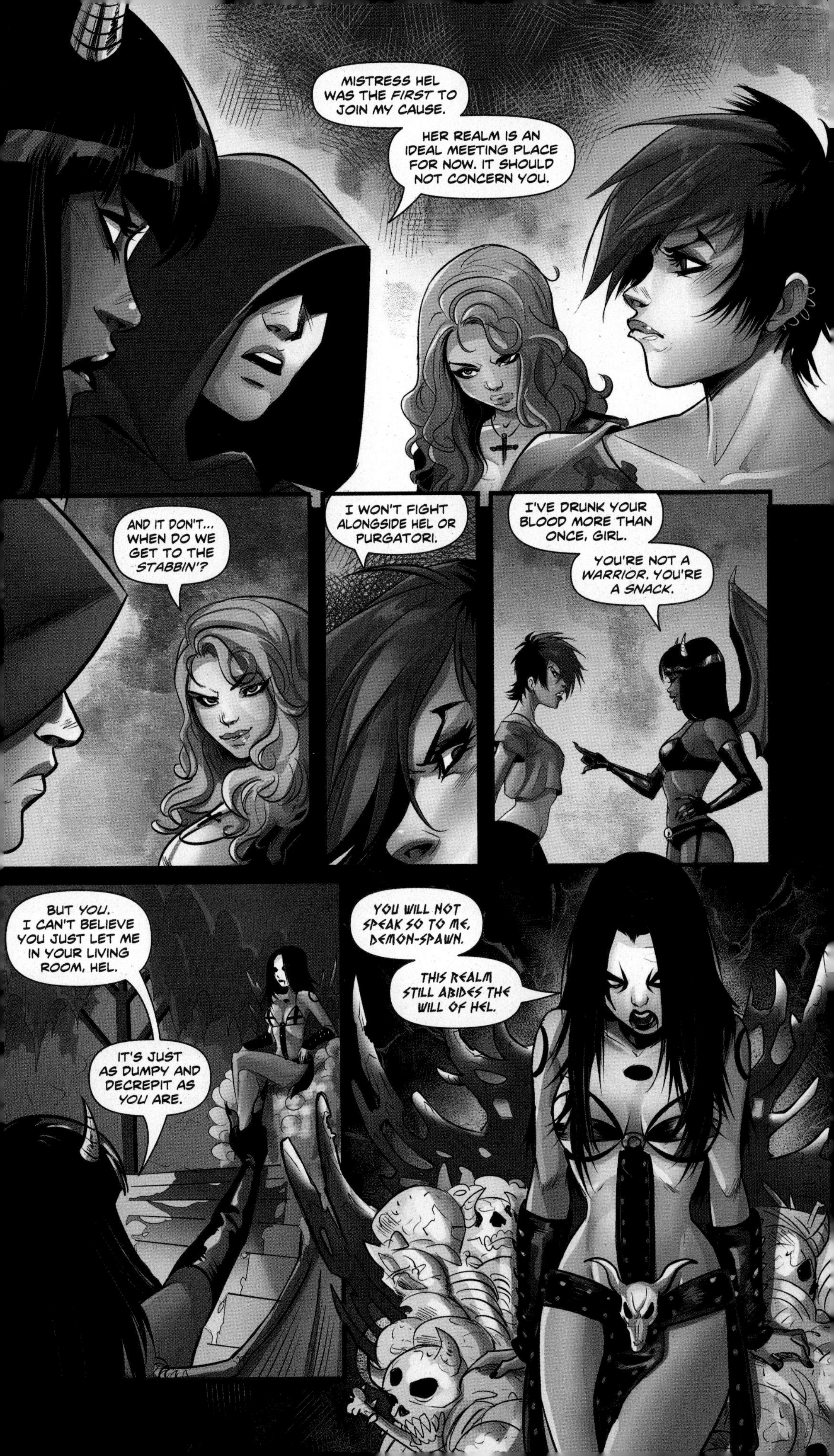

MISTRESS HEL WAS THE *FIRST* TO JOIN MY CAUSE.
HER REALM IS AN IDEAL MEETING PLACE FOR NOW. IT SHOULD NOT CONCERN YOU.
AND IT DON'T... WHEN DO WE GET TO THE *STABBIN'*?
I WON'T FIGHT ALONGSIDE HEL OR PURGATORI.
I'VE DRUNK YOUR BLOOD MORE THAN ONCE, GIRL.
YOU'RE NOT A *WARRIOR*. YOU'RE A *SNACK*.
BUT *YOU*. I CAN'T BELIEVE YOU JUST LET ME IN YOUR LIVING ROOM, HEL.
IT'S JUST AS DUMPY AND DECREPIT AS *YOU* ARE.
YOU WILL NOT SPEAK SO TO ME, DEMON-SPAWN.
THIS REALM STILL ABIDES THE WILL OF HEL.

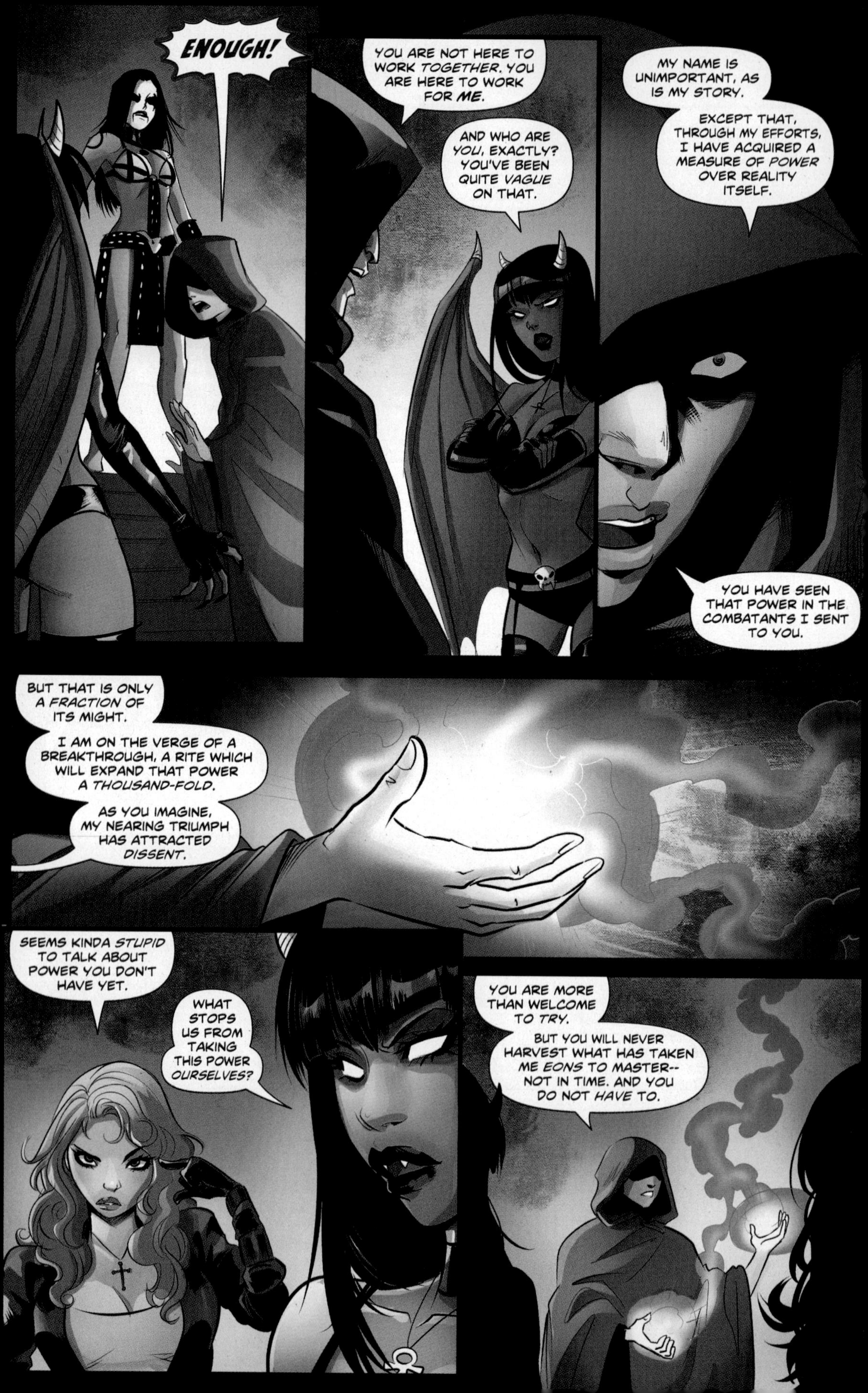
ENOUGH!
YOU ARE NOT HERE TO WORK TOGETHER. YOU ARE HERE TO WORK FOR ME.
AND WHO ARE YOU, EXACTLY? YOU'VE BEEN QUITE VAGUE ON THAT.
MY NAME IS UNIMPORTANT, AS IS MY STORY.
EXCEPT THAT, THROUGH MY EFFORTS, I HAVE ACQUIRED A MEASURE OF POWER OVER REALITY ITSELF.
YOU HAVE SEEN THAT POWER IN THE COMBATANTS I SENT TO YOU.
BUT THAT IS ONLY A FRACTION OF ITS MIGHT.
I AM ON THE VERGE OF A BREAKTHROUGH, A RITE WHICH WILL EXPAND THAT POWER A THOUSAND-FOLD.
AS YOU IMAGINE, MY NEARING TRIUMPH HAS ATTRACTED DISSENT.
SEEMS KINDA STUPID TO TALK ABOUT POWER YOU DON'T HAVE YET.
WHAT STOPS US FROM TAKING THIS POWER OURSELVES?
YOU ARE MORE THAN WELCOME TO TRY.
BUT YOU WILL NEVER HARVEST WHAT HAS TAKEN ME EONS TO MASTER-- NOT IN TIME. AND YOU DO NOT HAVE TO.

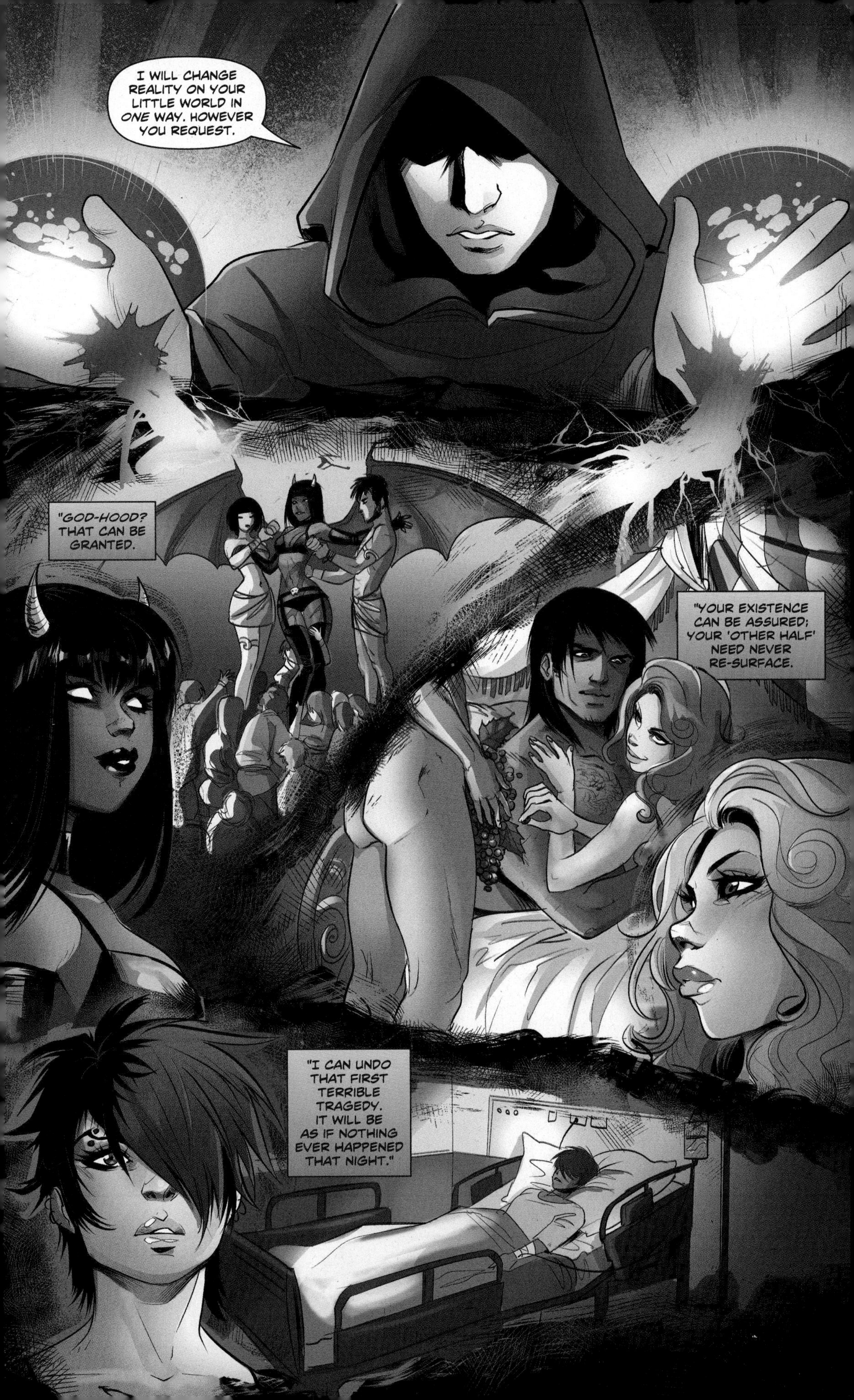
I WILL CHANGE REALITY ON YOUR LITTLE WORLD IN ONE WAY. HOWEVER YOU REQUEST.
"GOD-HOOD? THAT CAN BE GRANTED.
"YOUR EXISTENCE CAN BE ASSURED; YOUR 'OTHER HALF' NEED NEVER RE-SURFACE.
"I CAN UNDO THAT FIRST TERRIBLE TRAGEDY. IT WILL BE AS IF NOTHING EVER HAPPENED THAT NIGHT."

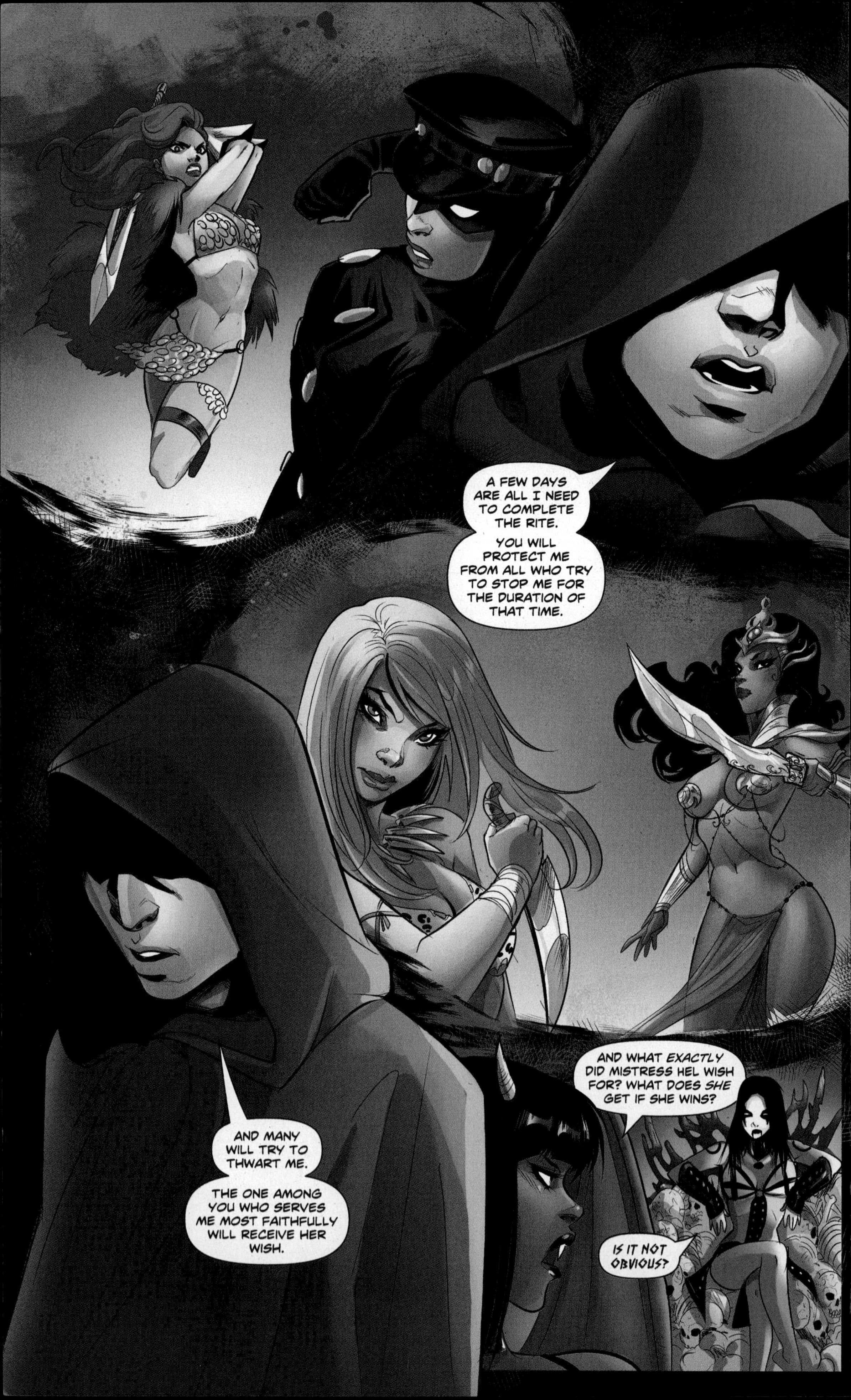
A FEW DAYS ARE ALL I NEED TO COMPLETE THE RITE.
YOU WILL PROTECT ME FROM ALL WHO TRY TO STOP ME FOR THE DURATION OF THAT TIME.
AND MANY WILL TRY TO THWART ME.
THE ONE AMONG YOU WHO SERVES ME MOST FAITHFULLY WILL RECEIVE HER WISH.
AND WHAT EXACTLY DID MISTRESS HEL WISH FOR? WHAT DOES SHE GET IF SHE WINS?
IS IT NOT OBVIOUS?

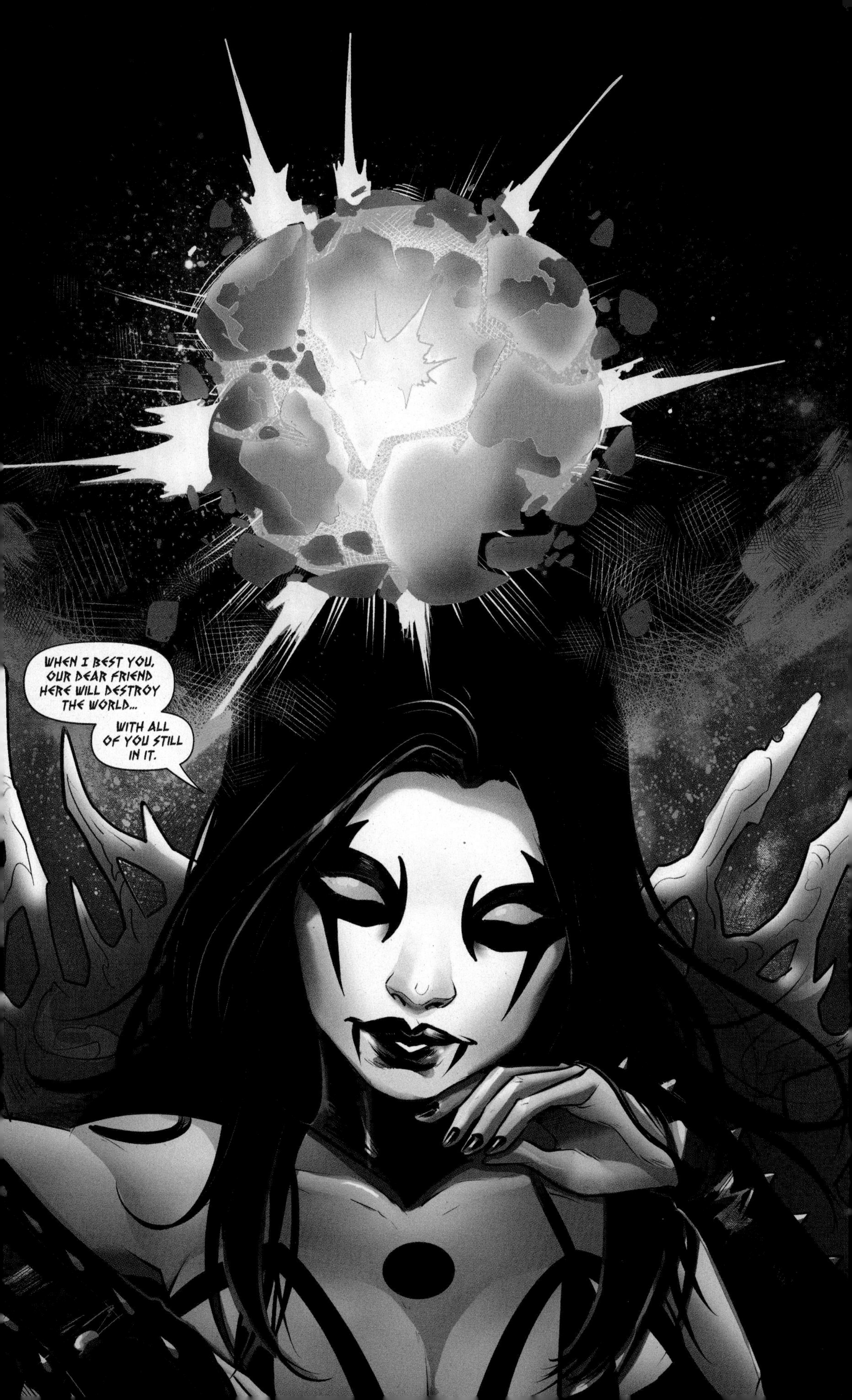
WHEN I BEST YOU, OUR DEAR FRIEND HERE WILL DESTROY THE WORLD...
WITH ALL OF YOU STILL IN IT.

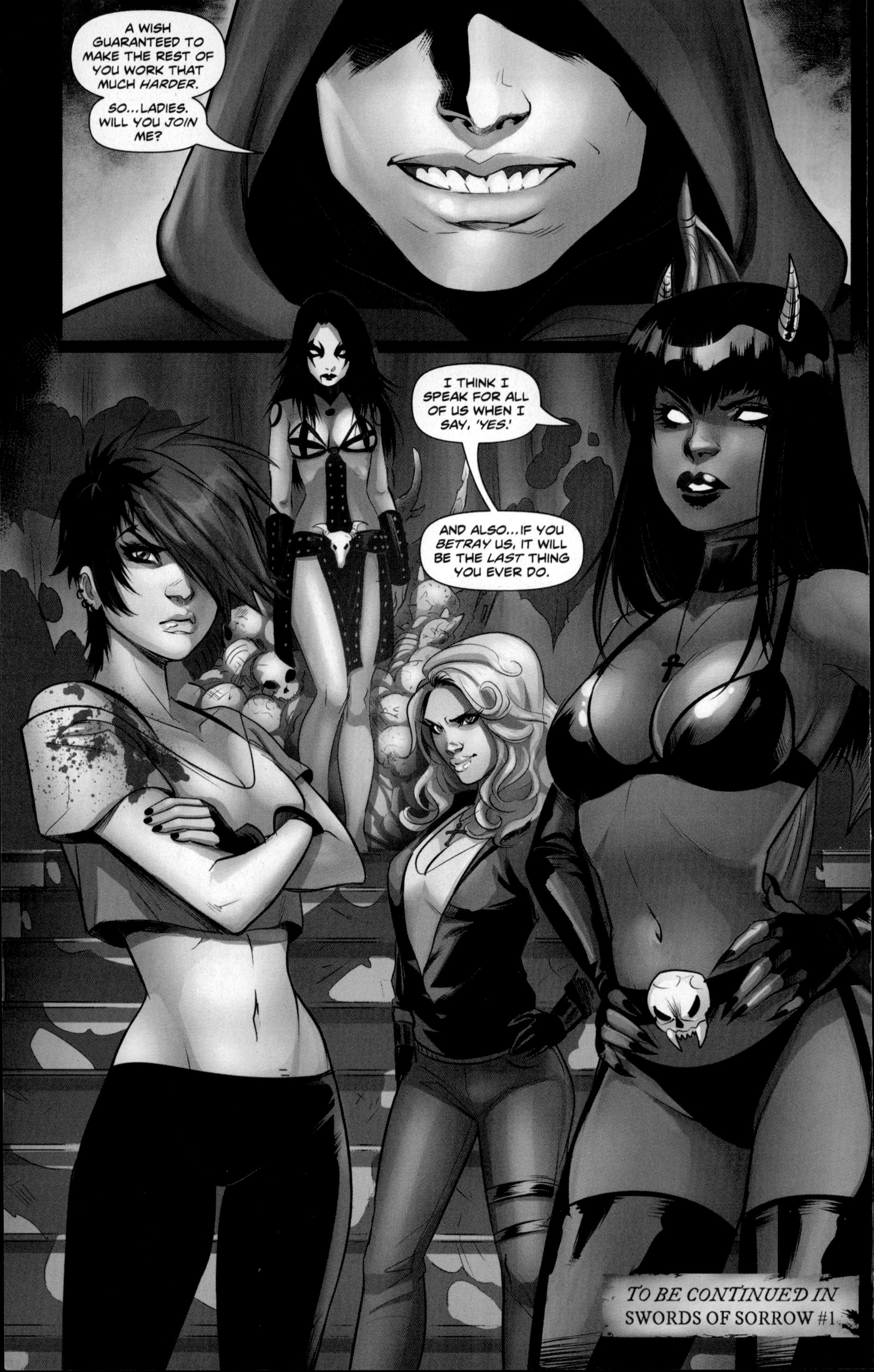
A WISH GUARANTEED TO MAKE THE REST OF YOU WORK THAT MUCH *HARDER.*
SO... LADIES. WILL YOU *JOIN* ME?
I THINK I SPEAK FOR ALL OF US WHEN I SAY, *'YES.'*
AND ALSO... IF YOU *BETRAY* US, IT WILL BE THE *LAST* THING YOU EVER DO.
TO BE CONTINUED IN
SWORDS OF SORROW #1

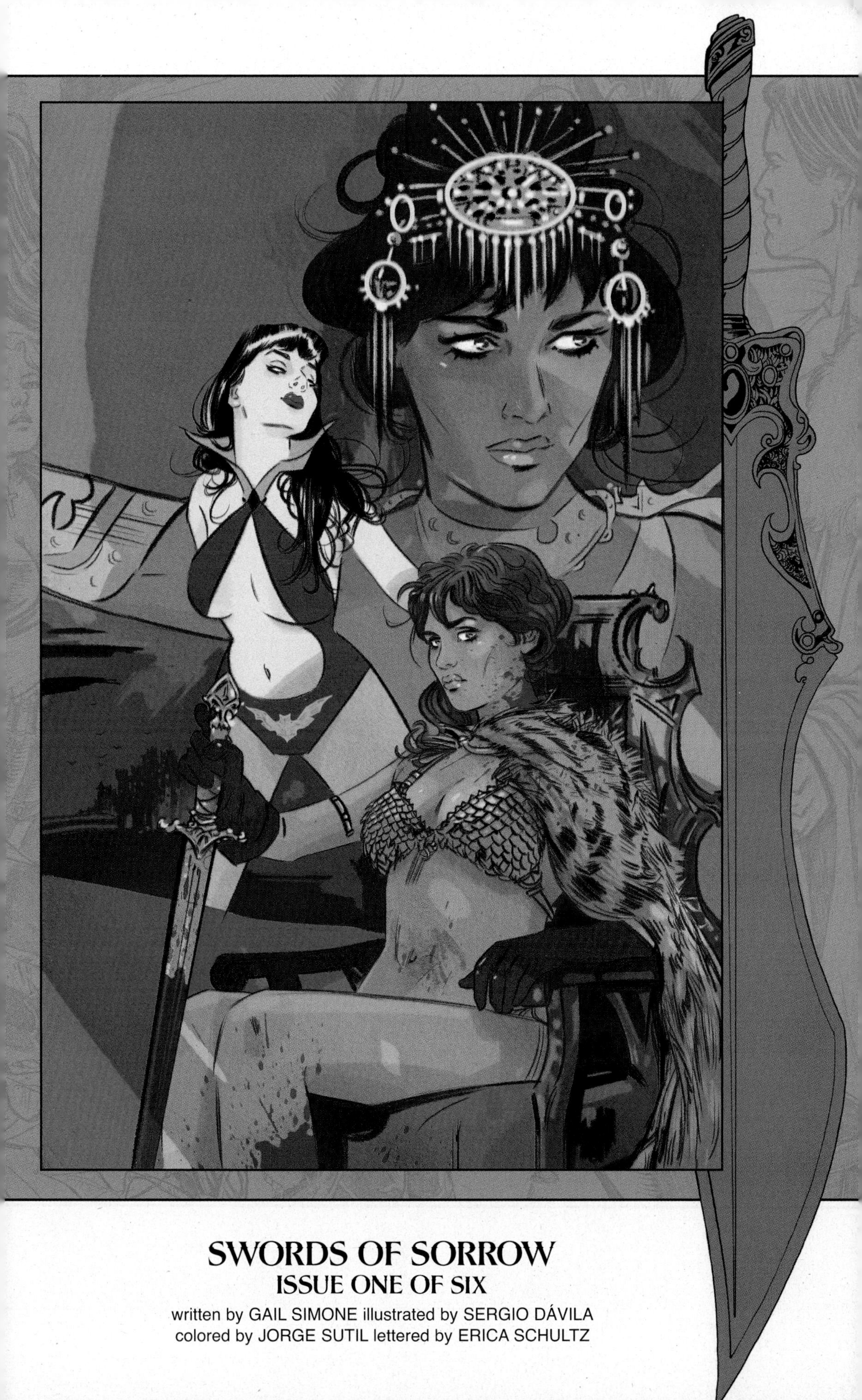

SWORDS OF SORROW
ISSUE ONE OF SIX

written by GAIL SIMONE illustrated by SERGIO DÁVILA
colored by JORGE SUTIL lettered by ERICA SCHULTZ

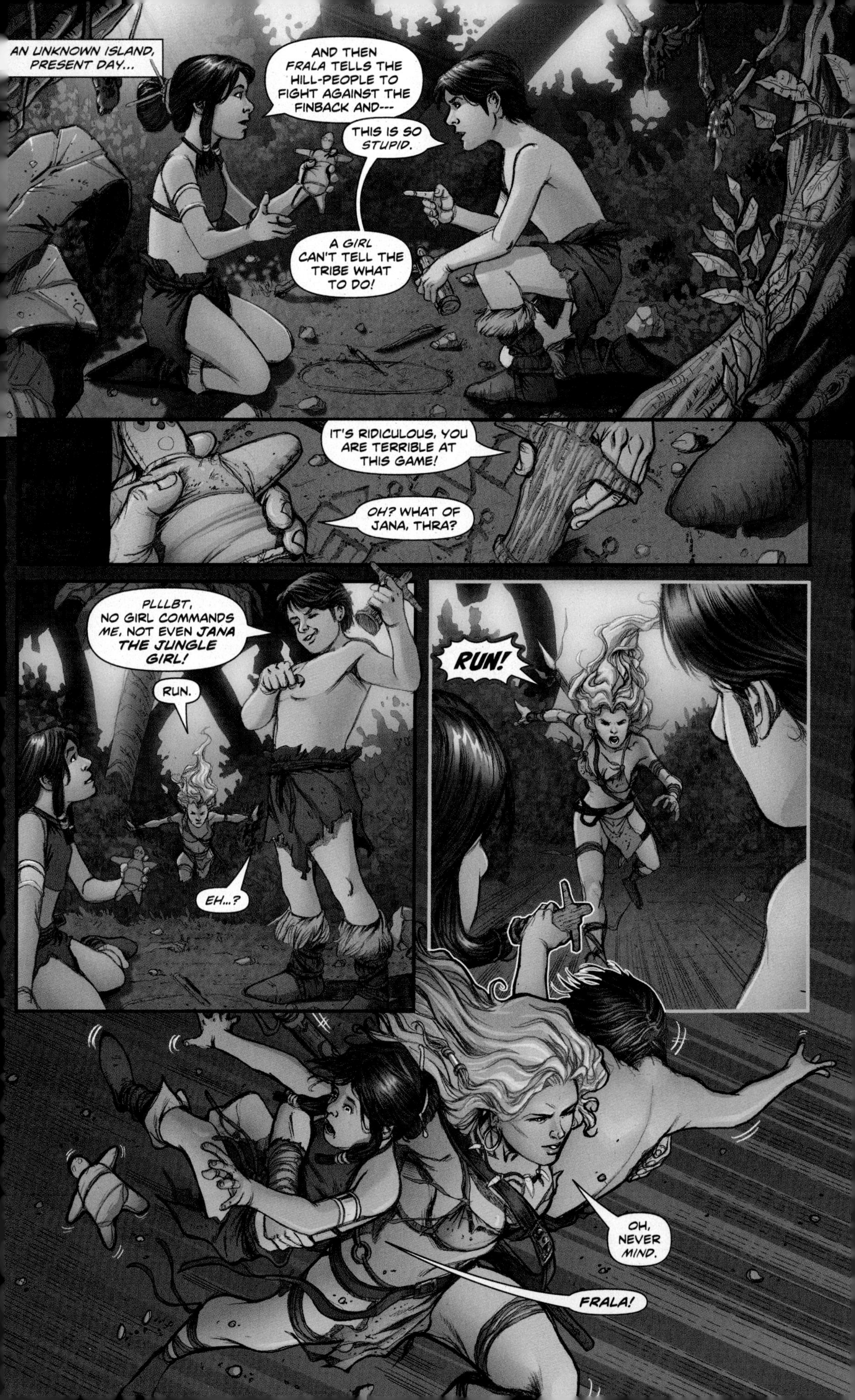
AN UNKNOWN ISLAND, PRESENT DAY...
AND THEN FRALA TELLS THE HILL-PEOPLE TO FIGHT AGAINST THE FINBACK AND---
THIS IS SO STUPID.
A GIRL CAN'T TELL THE TRIBE WHAT TO DO!
IT'S RIDICULOUS, YOU ARE TERRIBLE AT THIS GAME!
OH? WHAT OF JANA, THRA?
PLLLBT, NO GIRL COMMANDS ME, NOT EVEN JANA THE JUNGLE GIRL!
RUN.
EH...?
RUN!
OH, NEVER MIND.
FRALA!

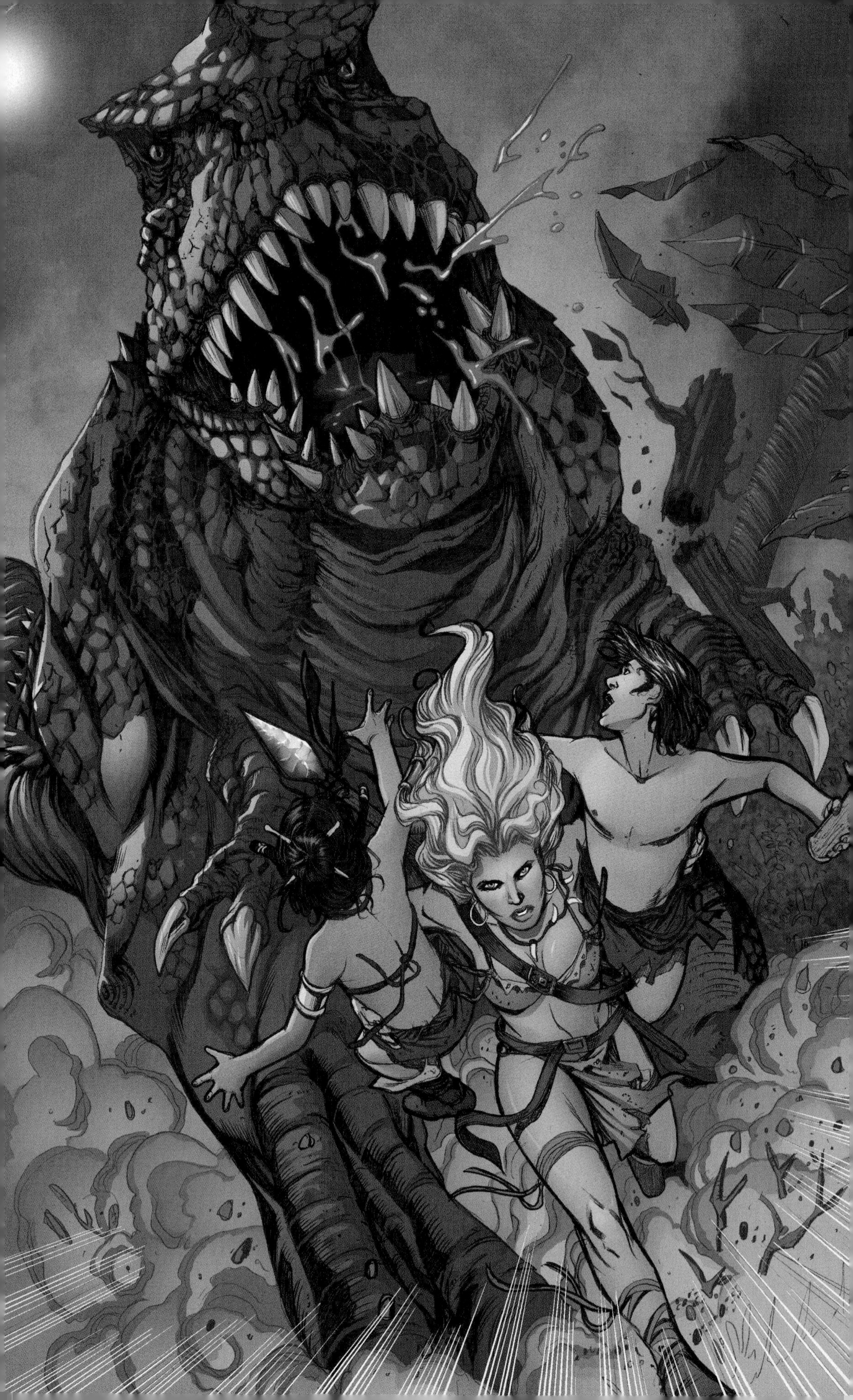

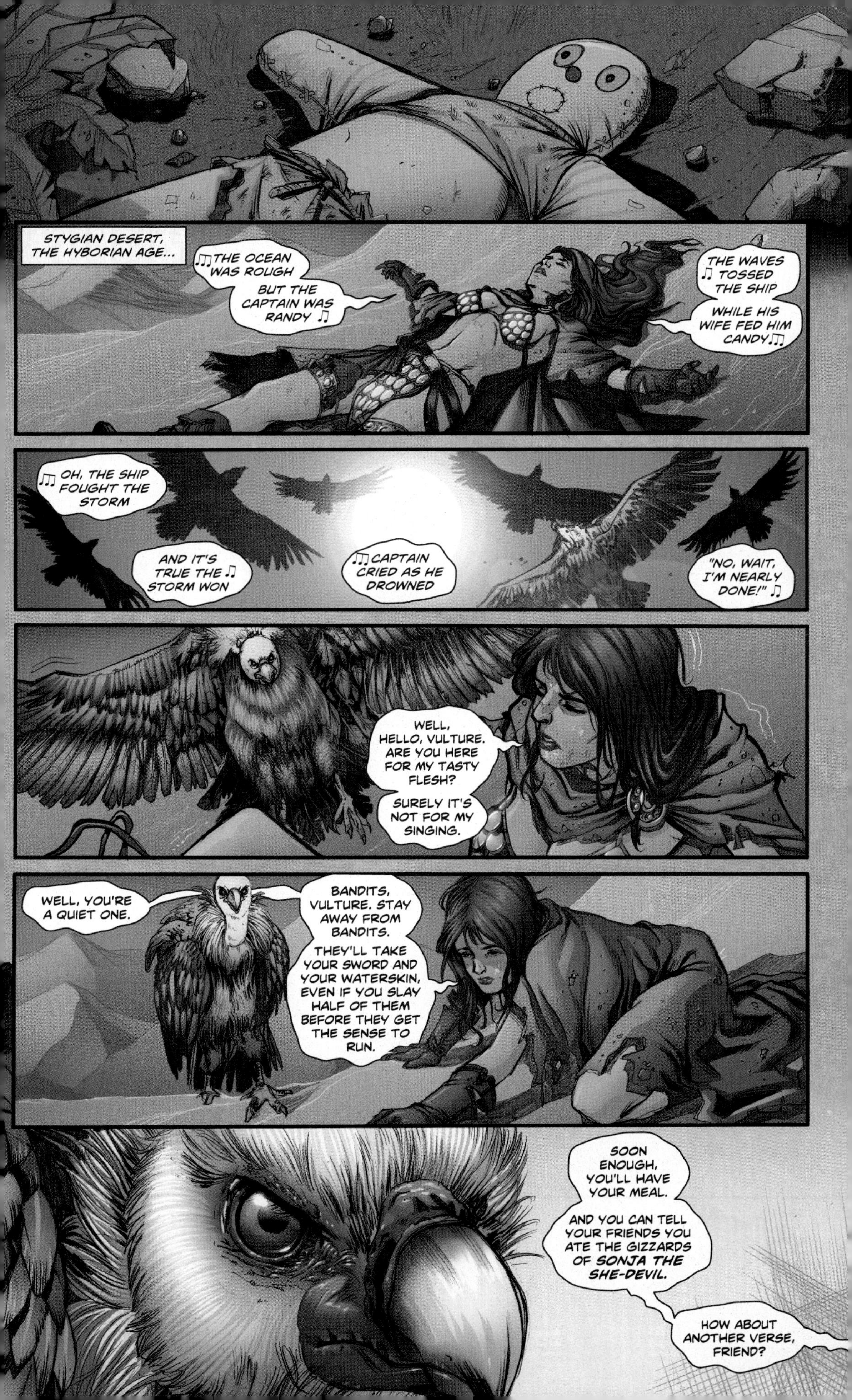
STYGIAN DESERT, THE HYBORIAN AGE...
♫THE OCEAN WAS ROUGH
BUT THE CAPTAIN WAS RANDY ♫
THE WAVES ♫ TOSSED THE SHIP
WHILE HIS WIFE FED HIM CANDY♫
♫ OH, THE SHIP FOUGHT THE STORM
AND IT'S TRUE THE ♫ STORM WON
♫CAPTAIN CRIED AS HE DROWNED
"NO, WAIT, I'M NEARLY DONE!" ♫
WELL, HELLO, VULTURE. ARE YOU HERE FOR MY TASTY FLESH?
SURELY IT'S NOT FOR MY SINGING.
WELL, YOU'RE A QUIET ONE.
BANDITS, VULTURE. STAY AWAY FROM BANDITS.
THEY'LL TAKE YOUR SWORD AND YOUR WATERSKIN, EVEN IF YOU SLAY HALF OF THEM BEFORE THEY GET THE SENSE TO RUN.
SOON ENOUGH, YOU'LL HAVE YOUR MEAL.
AND YOU CAN TELL YOUR FRIENDS YOU ATE THE GIZZARDS OF SONJA THE SHE-DEVIL.
HOW ABOUT ANOTHER VERSE, FRIEND?

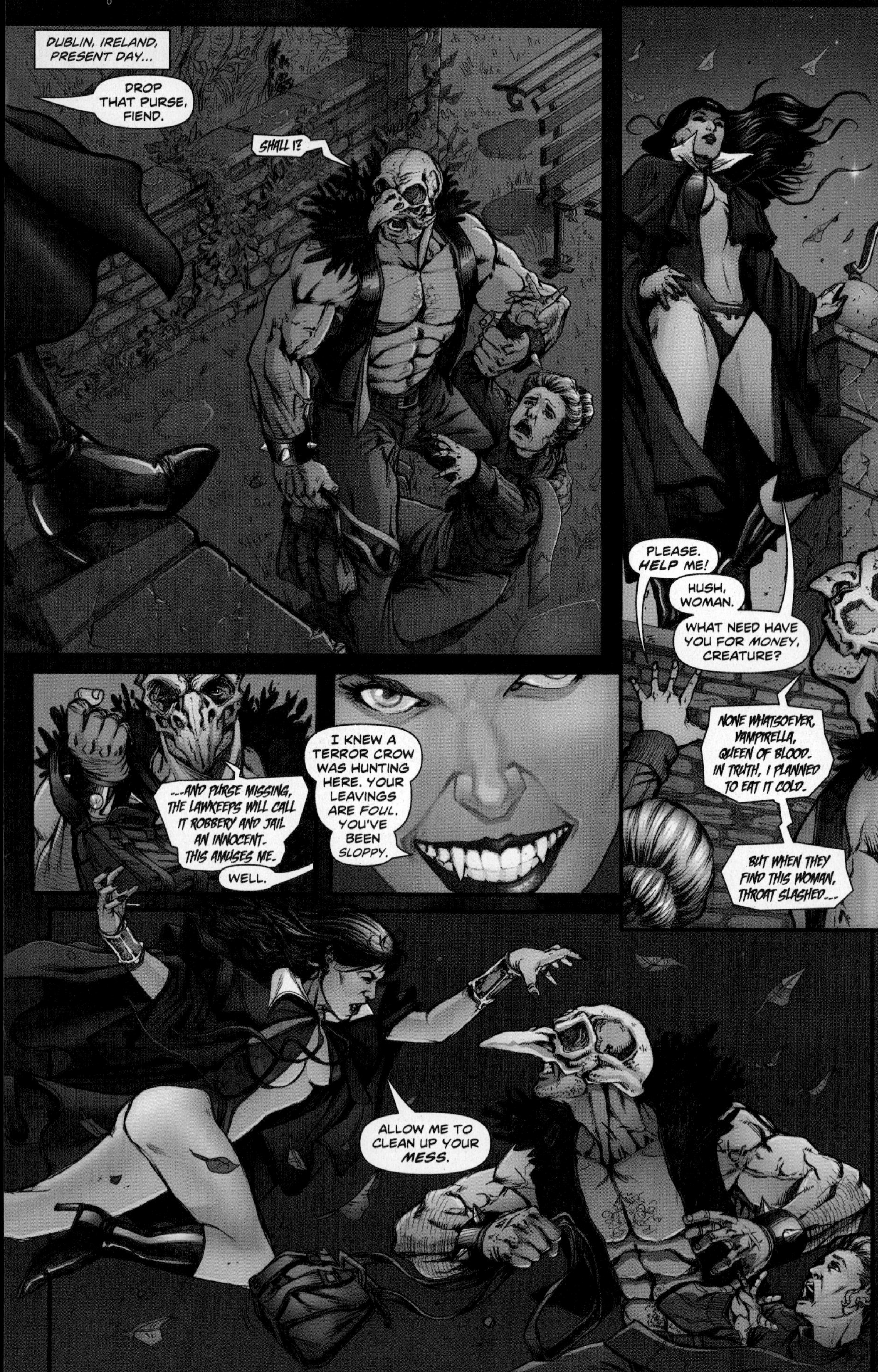
DUBLIN, IRELAND, PRESENT DAY...
DROP THAT PURSE, FIEND.
SHALL I?
PLEASE. HELP ME!
HUSH, WOMAN.
WHAT NEED HAVE YOU FOR MONEY, CREATURE?
NONE WHATSOEVER, VAMPIRELLA, QUEEN OF BLOOD. IN TRUTH, I PLANNED TO EAT IT COLD.
BUT WHEN THEY FIND THIS WOMAN, THROAT SLASHED...
---AND PURSE MISSING, THE LAWKEEPS WILL CALL IT ROBBERY AND JAIL AN INNOCENT. THIS AMUSES ME.
WELL.
I KNEW A TERROR CROW WAS HUNTING HERE. YOUR LEAVINGS ARE FOUL. YOU'VE BEEN SLOPPY.
ALLOW ME TO CLEAN UP YOUR MESS.

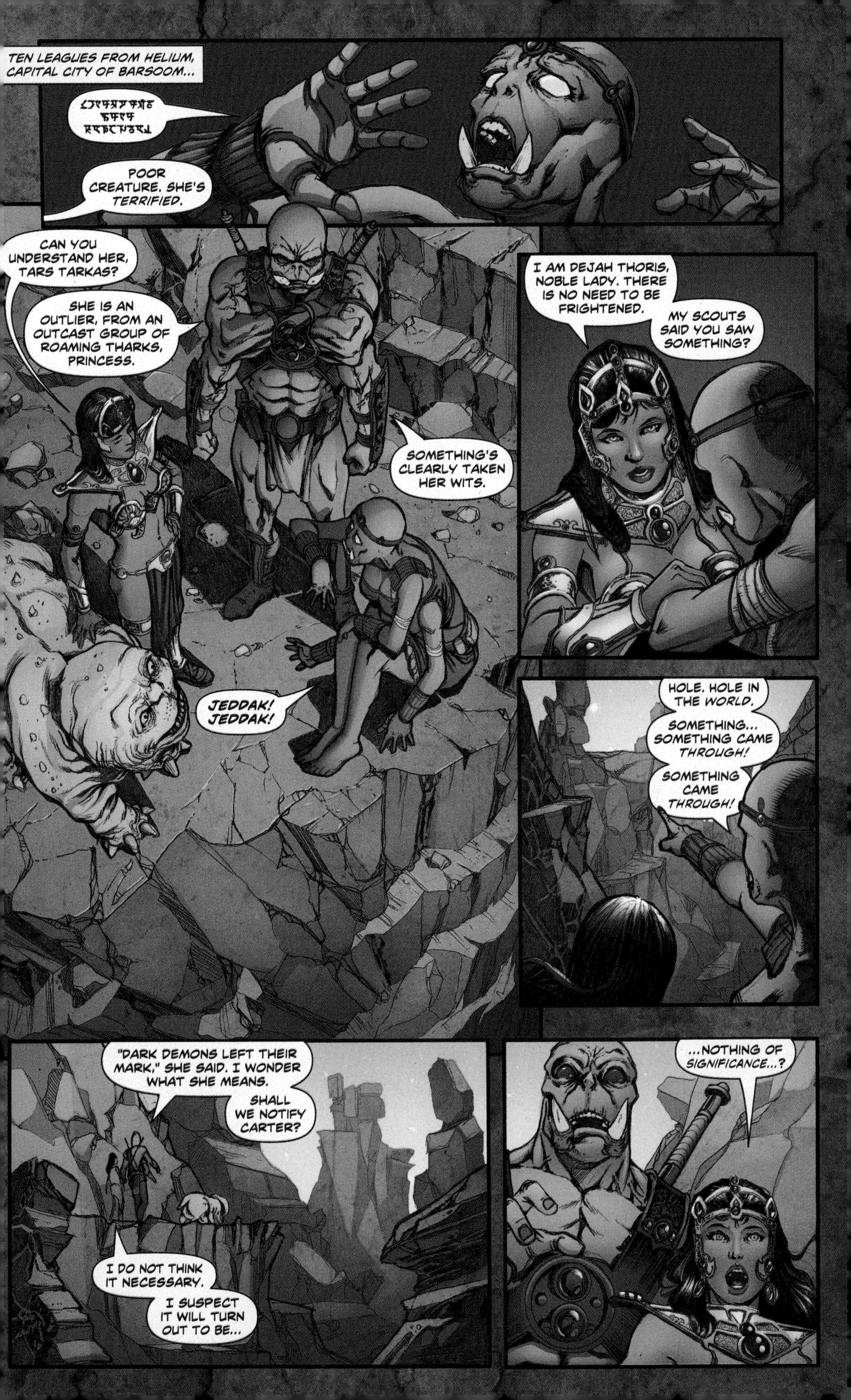

TEN LEAGUES FROM HELIUM, CAPITAL CITY OF BARSOOM...
POOR CREATURE. SHE'S *TERRIFIED*.
CAN YOU UNDERSTAND HER, TARS TARKAS?
SHE IS AN OUTLIER, FROM AN OUTCAST GROUP OF ROAMING THARKS, PRINCESS.
SOMETHING'S CLEARLY TAKEN HER WITS.
JEDDAK! JEDDAK!
I AM DEJAH THORIS, NOBLE LADY. THERE IS NO NEED TO BE FRIGHTENED.
MY SCOUTS SAID YOU SAW SOMETHING?
HOLE. HOLE IN THE *WORLD*.
SOMETHING... SOMETHING CAME *THROUGH!*
SOMETHING CAME *THROUGH!*
"DARK DEMONS LEFT THEIR MARK," SHE SAID. I WONDER WHAT SHE MEANS.
SHALL WE NOTIFY CARTER?
I DO NOT THINK IT NECESSARY.
I SUSPECT IT WILL TURN OUT TO BE...
...NOTHING OF *SIGNIFICANCE*...?

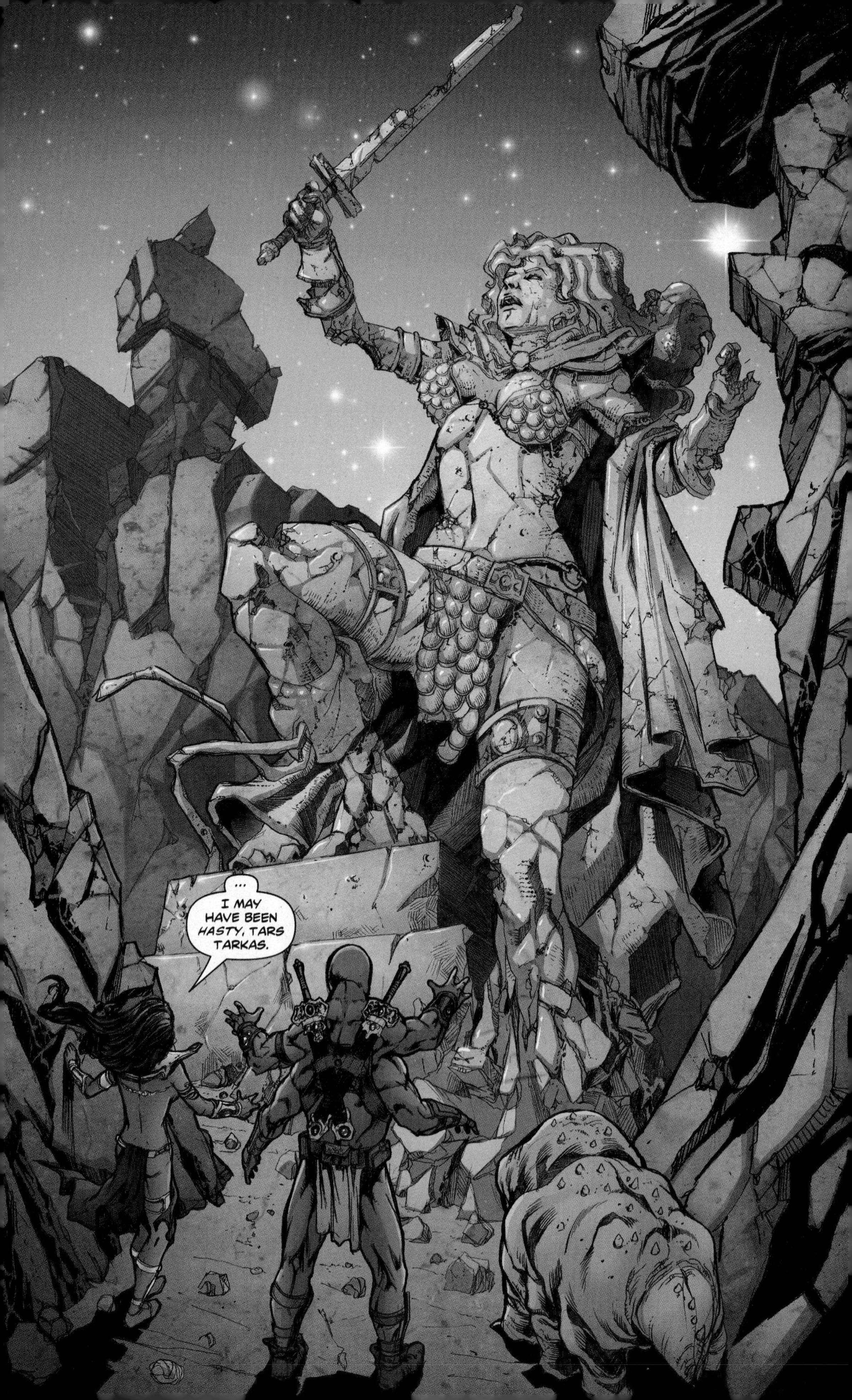
... I MAY HAVE BEEN HASTY, TARS TARKAS.

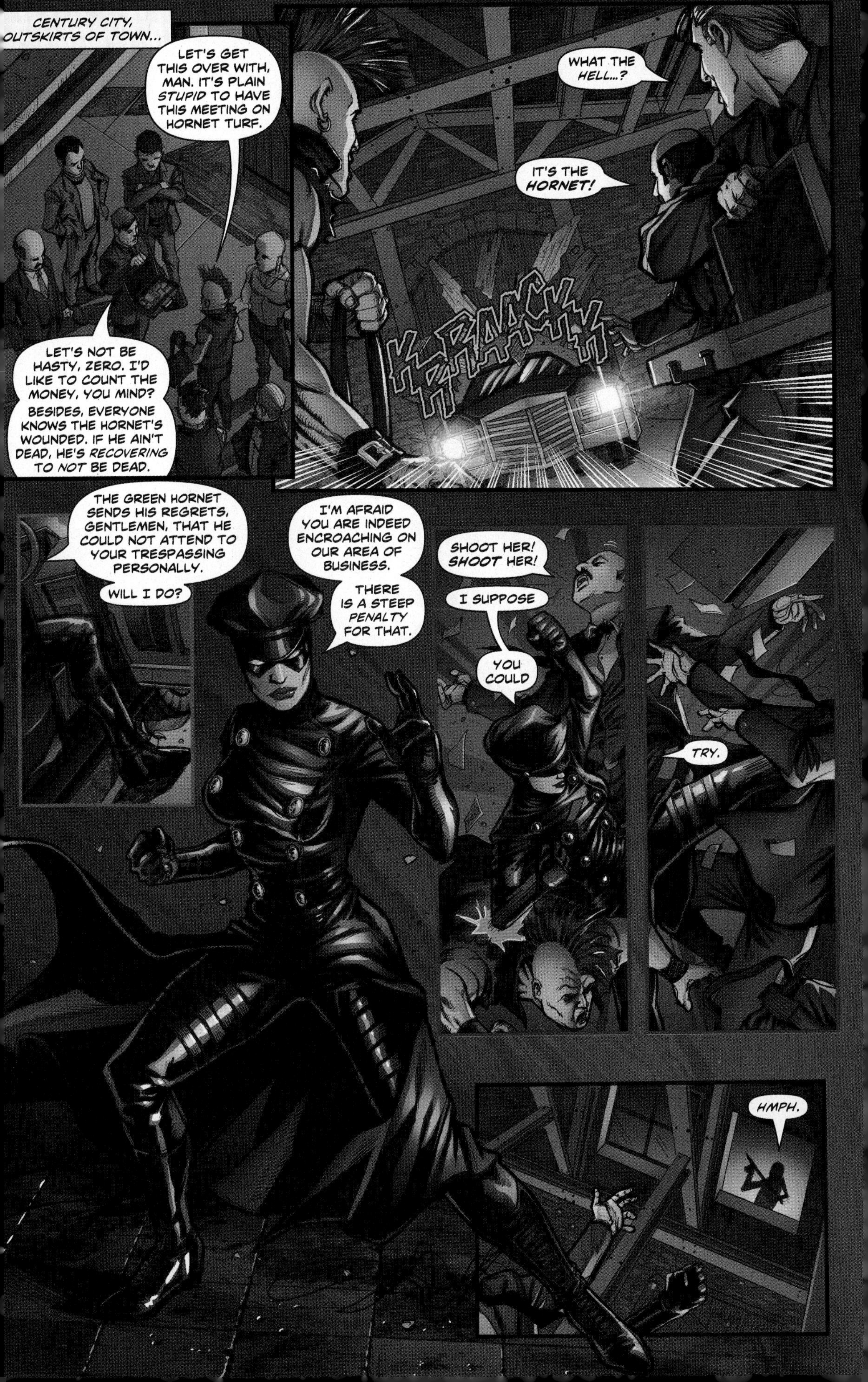
CENTURY CITY, OUTSKIRTS OF TOWN...
LET'S GET THIS OVER WITH, MAN. IT'S PLAIN STUPID TO HAVE THIS MEETING ON HORNET TURF.
LET'S NOT BE HASTY, ZERO. I'D LIKE TO COUNT THE MONEY, YOU MIND?
BESIDES, EVERYONE KNOWS THE HORNET'S WOUNDED. IF HE AIN'T DEAD, HE'S RECOVERING TO NOT BE DEAD.
WHAT THE HELL...?
IT'S THE HORNET!
KRAACK
THE GREEN HORNET SENDS HIS REGRETS, GENTLEMEN, THAT HE COULD NOT ATTEND TO YOUR TRESPASSING PERSONALLY.
WILL I DO?
I'M AFRAID YOU ARE INDEED ENCROACHING ON OUR AREA OF BUSINESS.
THERE IS A STEEP PENALTY FOR THAT.
SHOOT HER! SHOOT HER!
I SUPPOSE
YOU COULD
TRY.
HMPH.

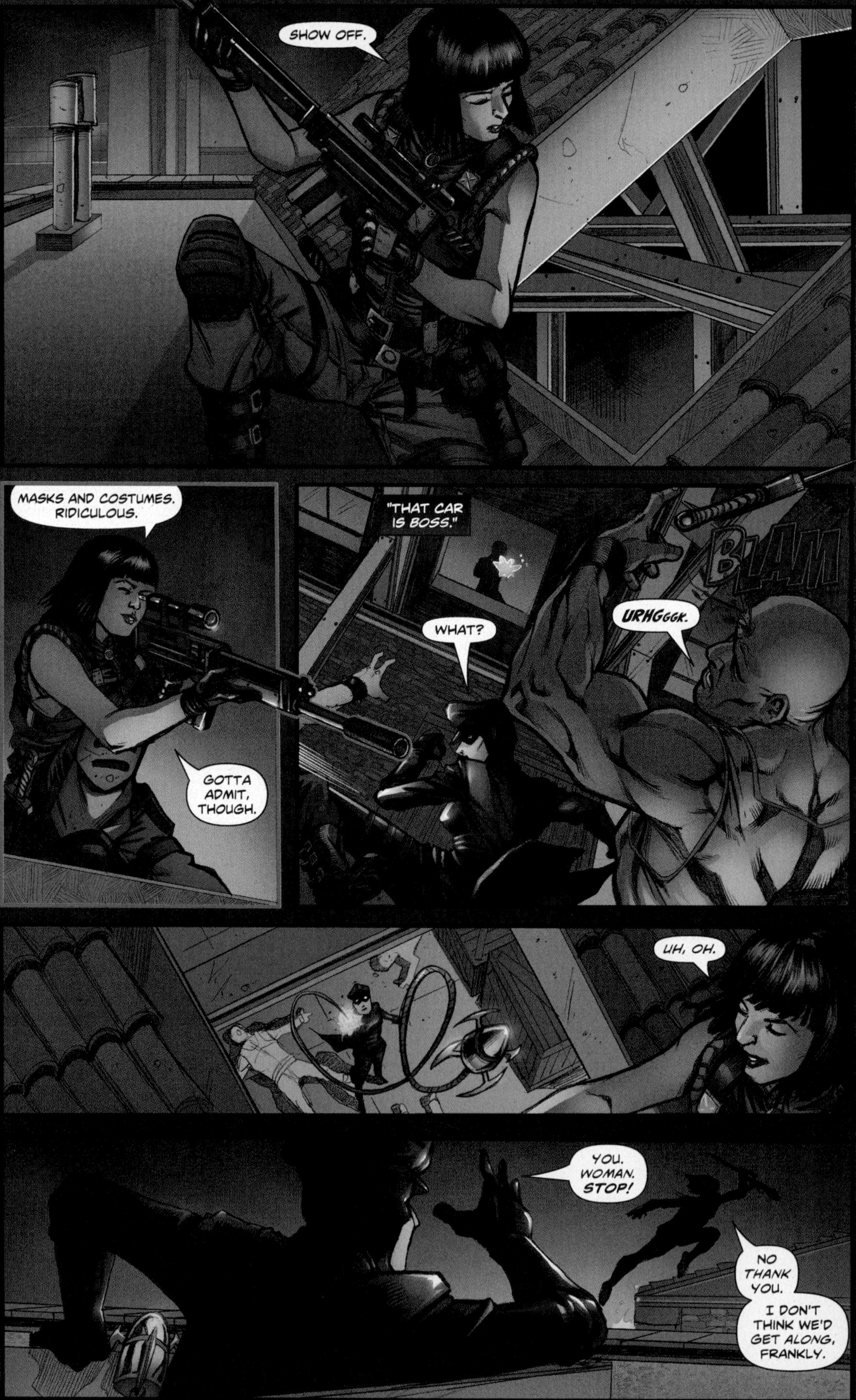
SHOW OFF.
MASKS AND COSTUMES. RIDICULOUS.
GOTTA ADMIT, THOUGH.
"THAT CAR IS BOSS."
WHAT?
BLAM
URHGGGK.
UH, OH.
YOU. WOMAN. STOP!
NO THANK YOU.
I DON'T THINK WE'D GET ALONG, FRANKLY.

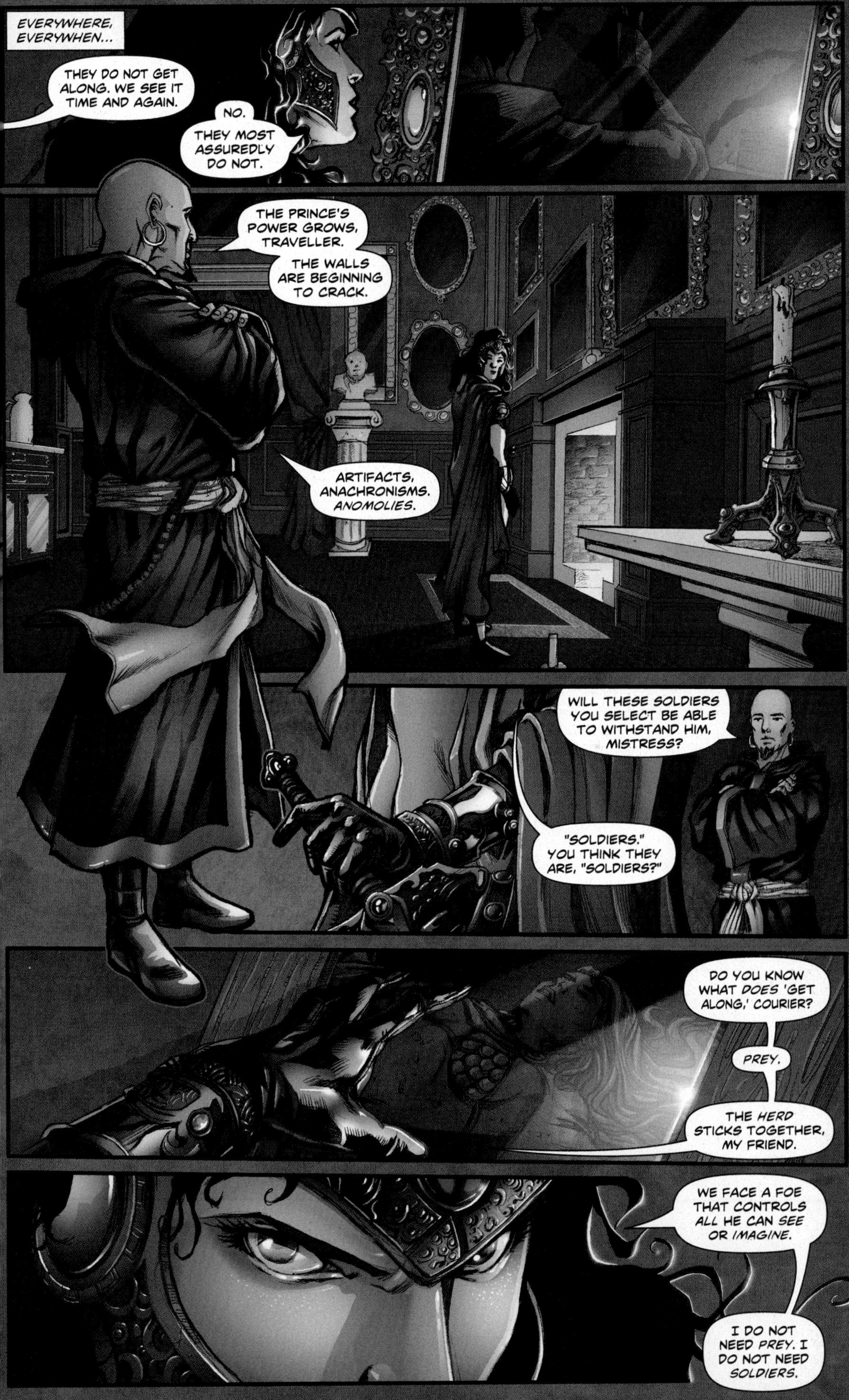
EVERYWHERE, EVERYWHEN...
THEY DO NOT GET ALONG. WE SEE IT TIME AND AGAIN.
NO. THEY MOST ASSUREDLY DO NOT.
THE PRINCE'S POWER GROWS, TRAVELLER.
THE WALLS ARE BEGINNING TO CRACK.
ARTIFACTS, ANACHRONISMS. ANOMOLIES.
WILL THESE SOLDIERS YOU SELECT BE ABLE TO WITHSTAND HIM, MISTRESS?
"SOLDIERS." YOU THINK THEY ARE, "SOLDIERS?"
DO YOU KNOW WHAT DOES 'GET ALONG,' COURIER?
PREY.
THE HERD STICKS TOGETHER, MY FRIEND.
WE FACE A FOE THAT CONTROLS ALL HE CAN SEE OR IMAGINE.
I DO NOT NEED PREY. I DO NOT NEED SOLDIERS.

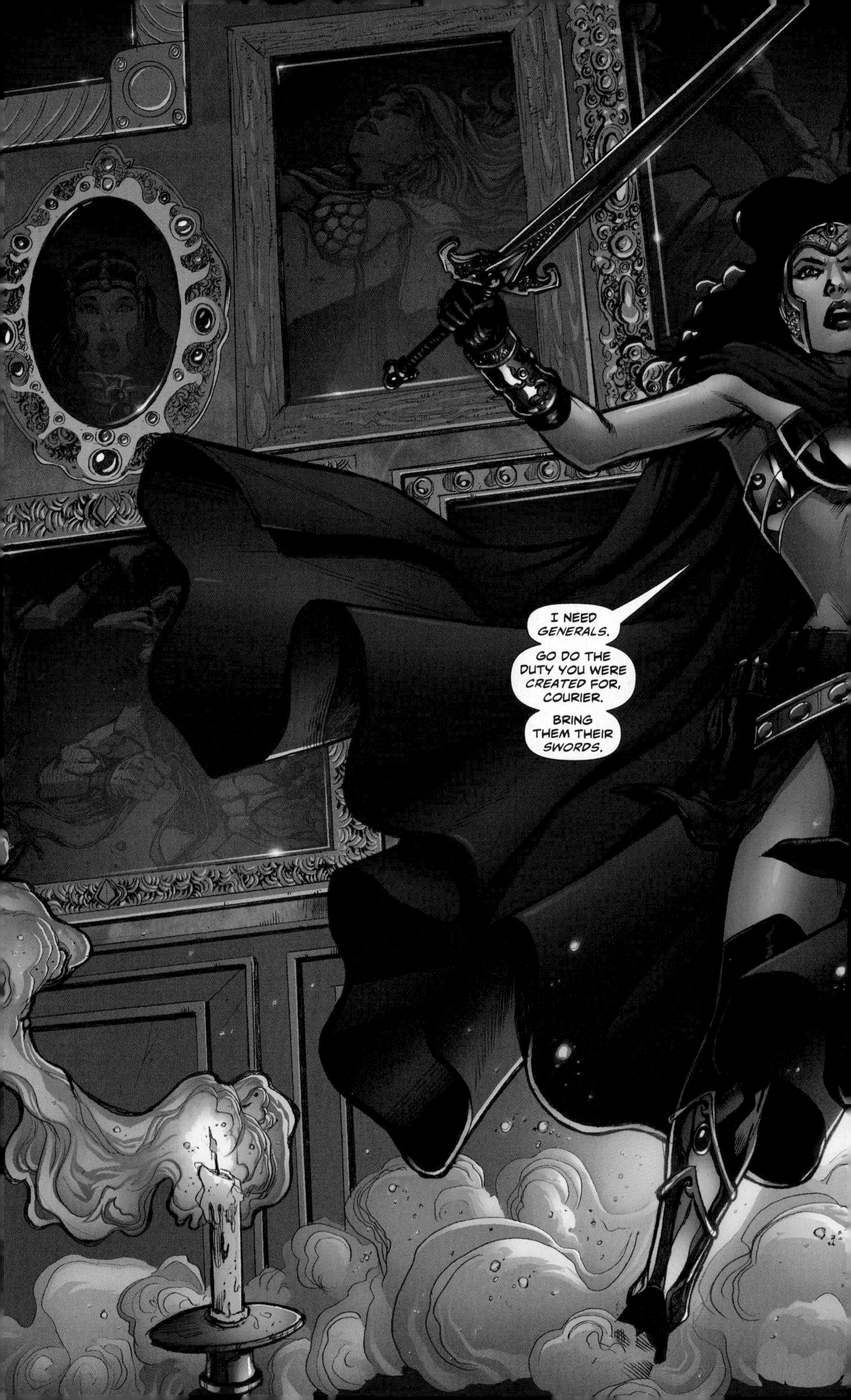
I NEED GENERALS.
GO DO THE DUTY YOU WERE CREATED FOR, COURIER.
BRING THEM THEIR SWORDS.

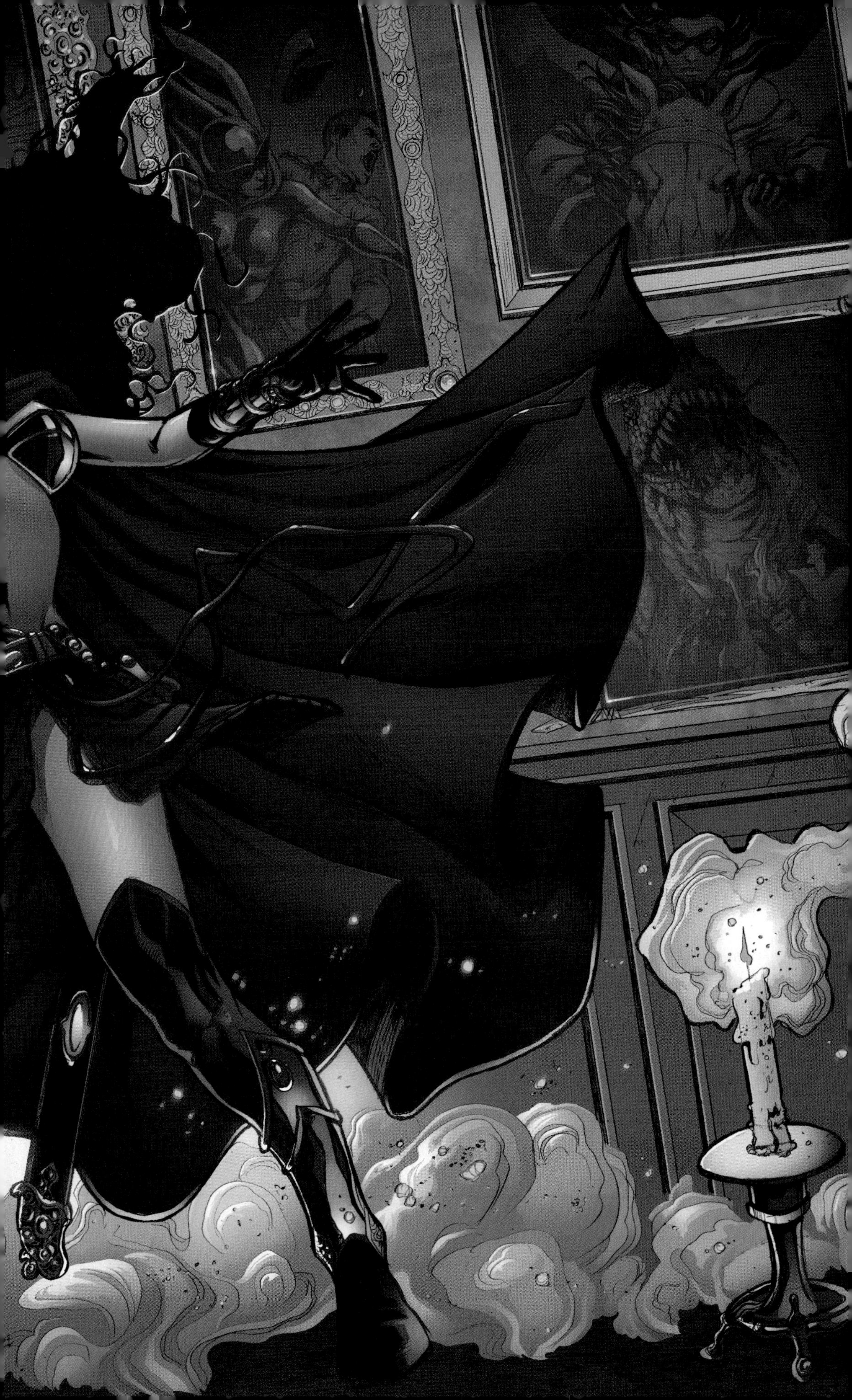

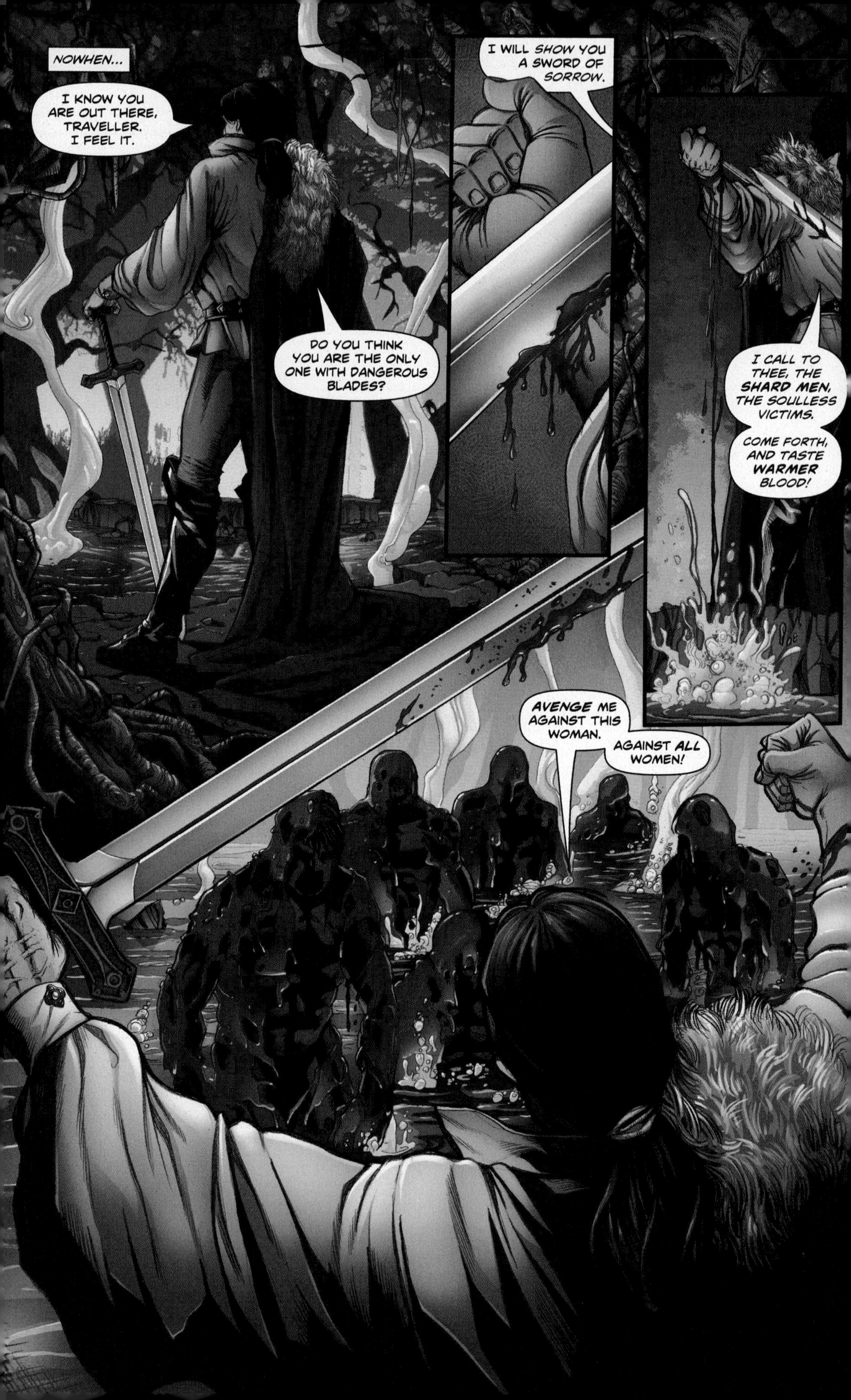

NOWHEN...
I KNOW YOU ARE OUT THERE, TRAVELLER. I FEEL IT.
DO YOU THINK YOU ARE THE ONLY ONE WITH DANGEROUS BLADES?
I WILL SHOW YOU A SWORD OF SORROW.
I CALL TO THEE, THE SHARD MEN, THE SOULLESS VICTIMS.
COME FORTH, AND TASTE WARMER BLOOD!
AVENGE ME AGAINST THIS WOMAN.
AGAINST ALL WOMEN!

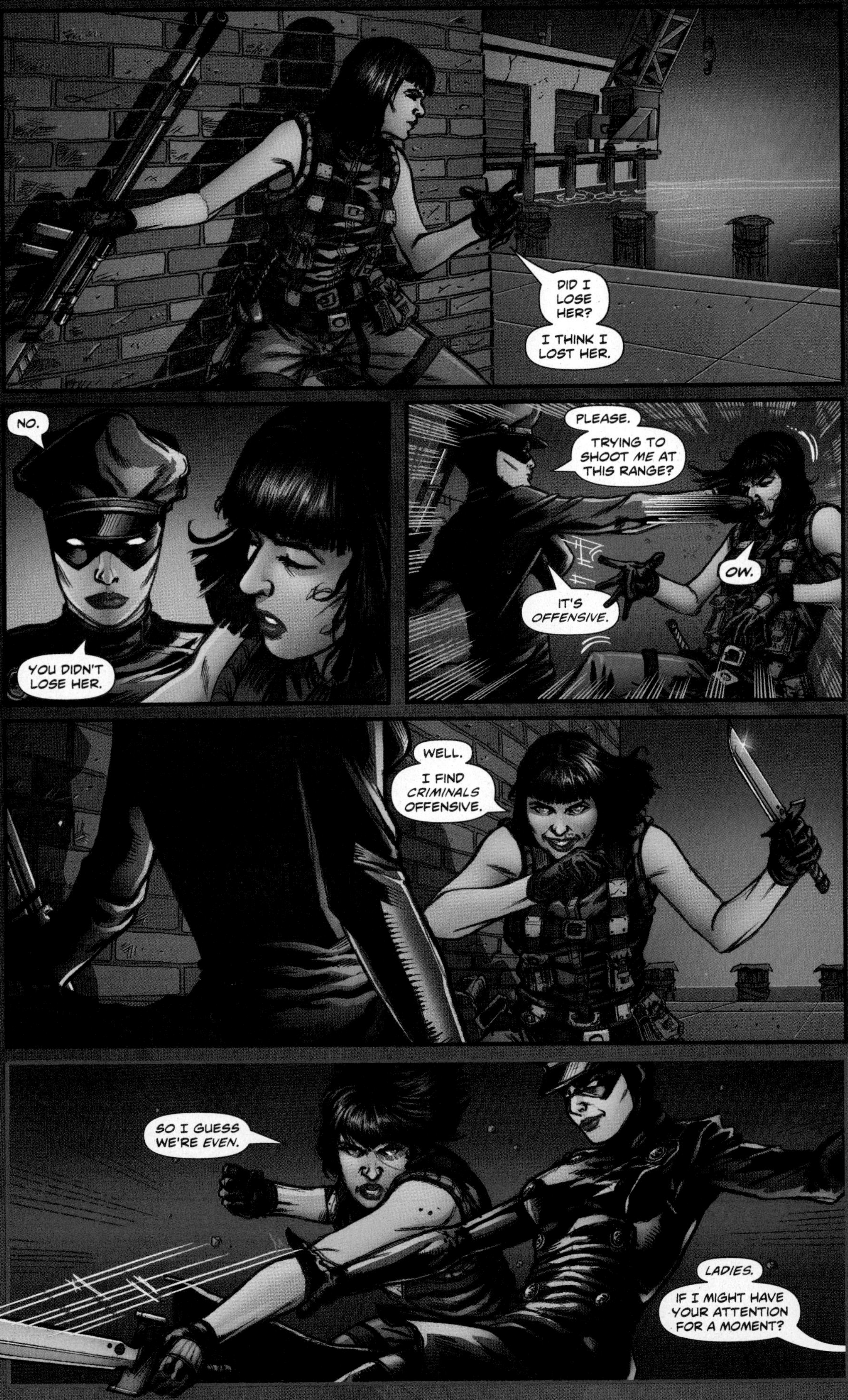

DID I LOSE HER?
I THINK I LOST HER.
NO.
YOU DIDN'T LOSE HER.
PLEASE.
TRYING TO SHOOT *ME* AT THIS RANGE?
IT'S *OFFENSIVE.*
OW.
WELL.
I FIND *CRIMINALS* OFFENSIVE.
SO I GUESS WE'RE *EVEN.*
LADIES.
IF I MIGHT HAVE YOUR ATTENTION FOR A MOMENT?

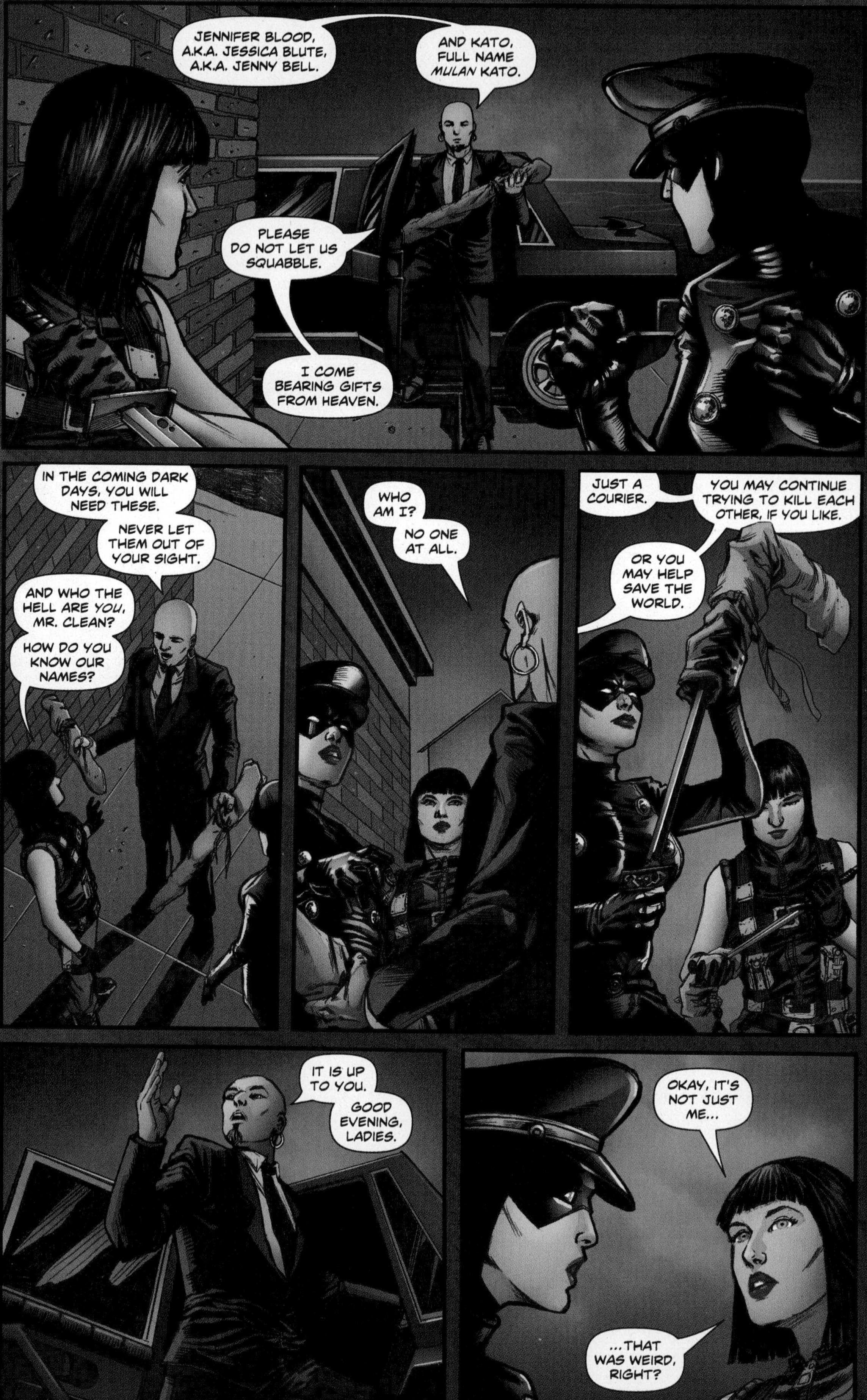
JENNIFER BLOOD, A.K.A. JESSICA BLUTE, A.K.A. JENNY BELL.
AND KATO, FULL NAME *MULAN KATO.*
PLEASE DO NOT LET US SQUABBLE.
I COME BEARING GIFTS FROM HEAVEN.
IN THE COMING DARK DAYS, YOU WILL NEED THESE.
NEVER LET THEM OUT OF YOUR SIGHT.
AND WHO THE HELL ARE *YOU,* MR. CLEAN?
HOW DO YOU KNOW OUR NAMES?
WHO AM I?
NO ONE AT ALL.
JUST A COURIER.
YOU MAY CONTINUE TRYING TO KILL EACH OTHER, IF YOU LIKE.
OR YOU MAY HELP SAVE THE WORLD.
IT IS UP TO YOU.
GOOD EVENING, LADIES.
OKAY, IT'S NOT JUST ME...
...THAT WAS WEIRD, RIGHT?

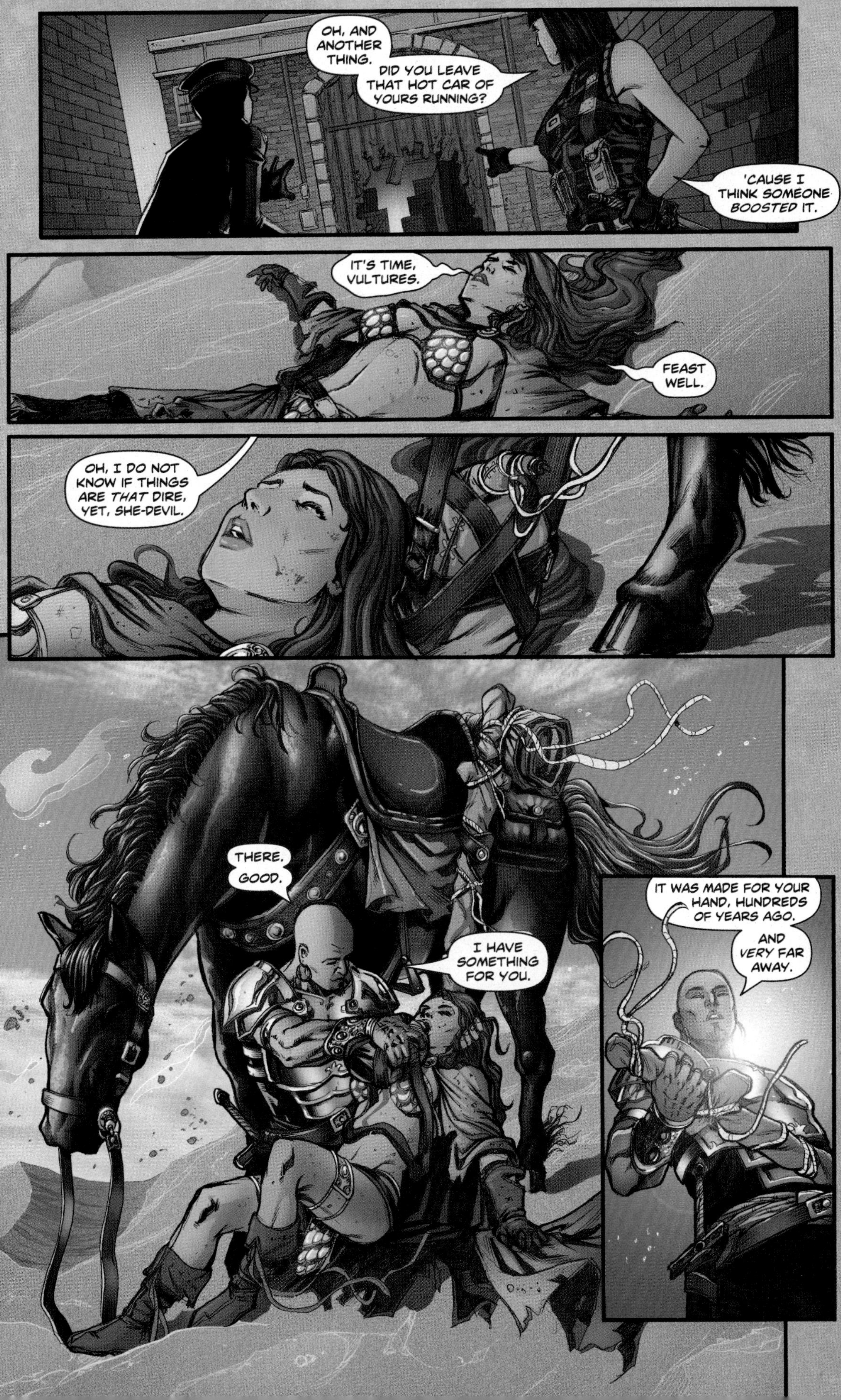
OH, AND ANOTHER THING.
DID YOU LEAVE THAT HOT CAR OF YOURS RUNNING?
'CAUSE I THINK SOMEONE BOOSTED IT.
IT'S TIME, VULTURES.
FEAST WELL.
OH, I DO NOT KNOW IF THINGS ARE *THAT* DIRE, YET, SHE-DEVIL.
THERE. GOOD.
I HAVE SOMETHING FOR YOU.
IT WAS MADE FOR YOUR HAND, HUNDREDS OF YEARS AGO.
AND *VERY* FAR AWAY.

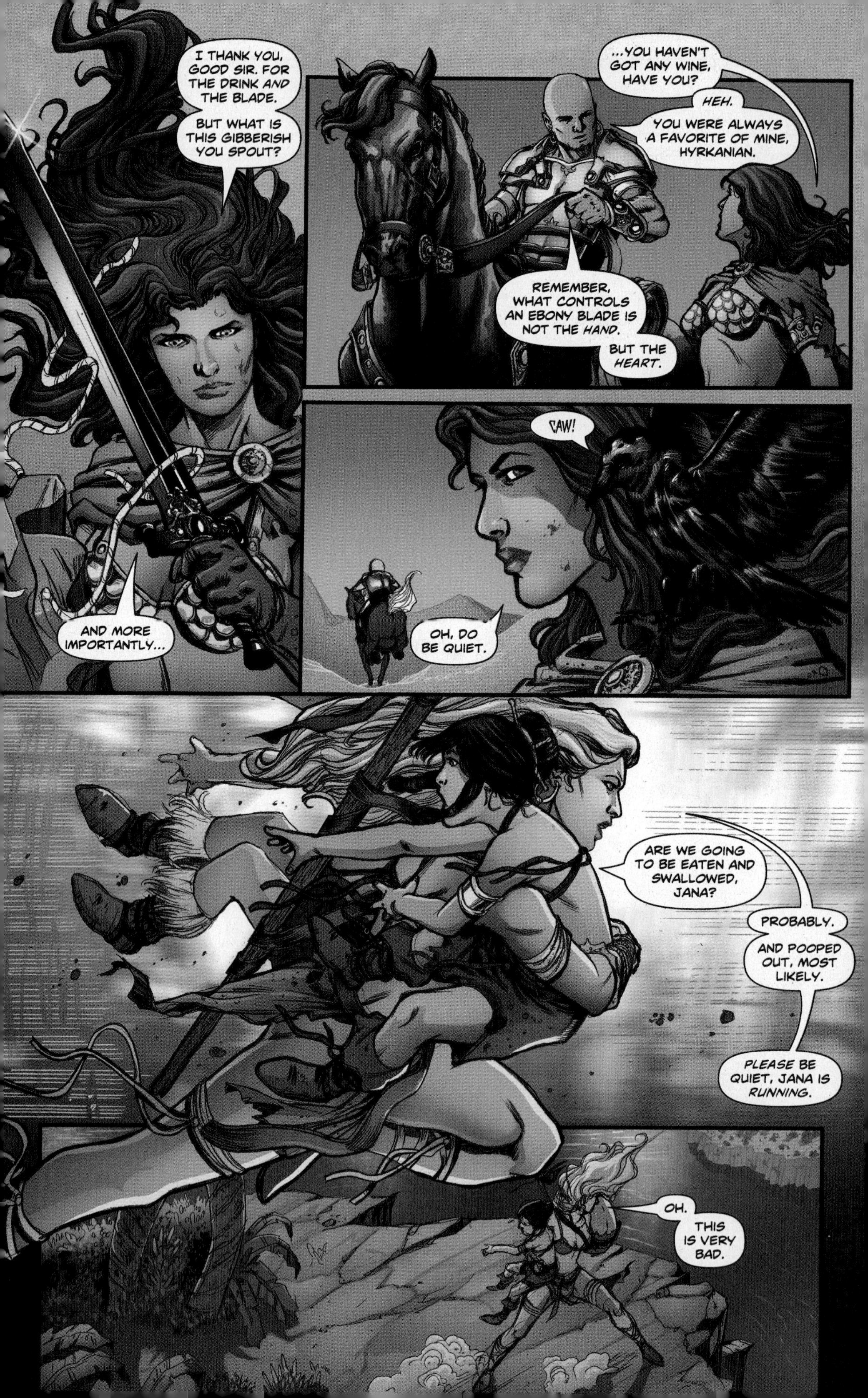
I THANK YOU, GOOD SIR. FOR THE DRINK *AND* THE BLADE.
BUT WHAT IS THIS GIBBERISH YOU SPOUT?
...YOU HAVEN'T GOT ANY WINE, HAVE YOU?
HEH.
YOU WERE ALWAYS A FAVORITE OF MINE, HYRKANIAN.
REMEMBER, WHAT CONTROLS AN EBONY BLADE IS NOT THE *HAND*.
BUT THE *HEART*.
AND MORE IMPORTANTLY...
CAW!
OH, DO BE QUIET.
ARE WE GOING TO BE EATEN AND SWALLOWED, JANA?
PROBABLY.
AND POOPED OUT, MOST LIKELY.
PLEASE BE QUIET, JANA IS RUNNING.
OH.
THIS IS VERY BAD.

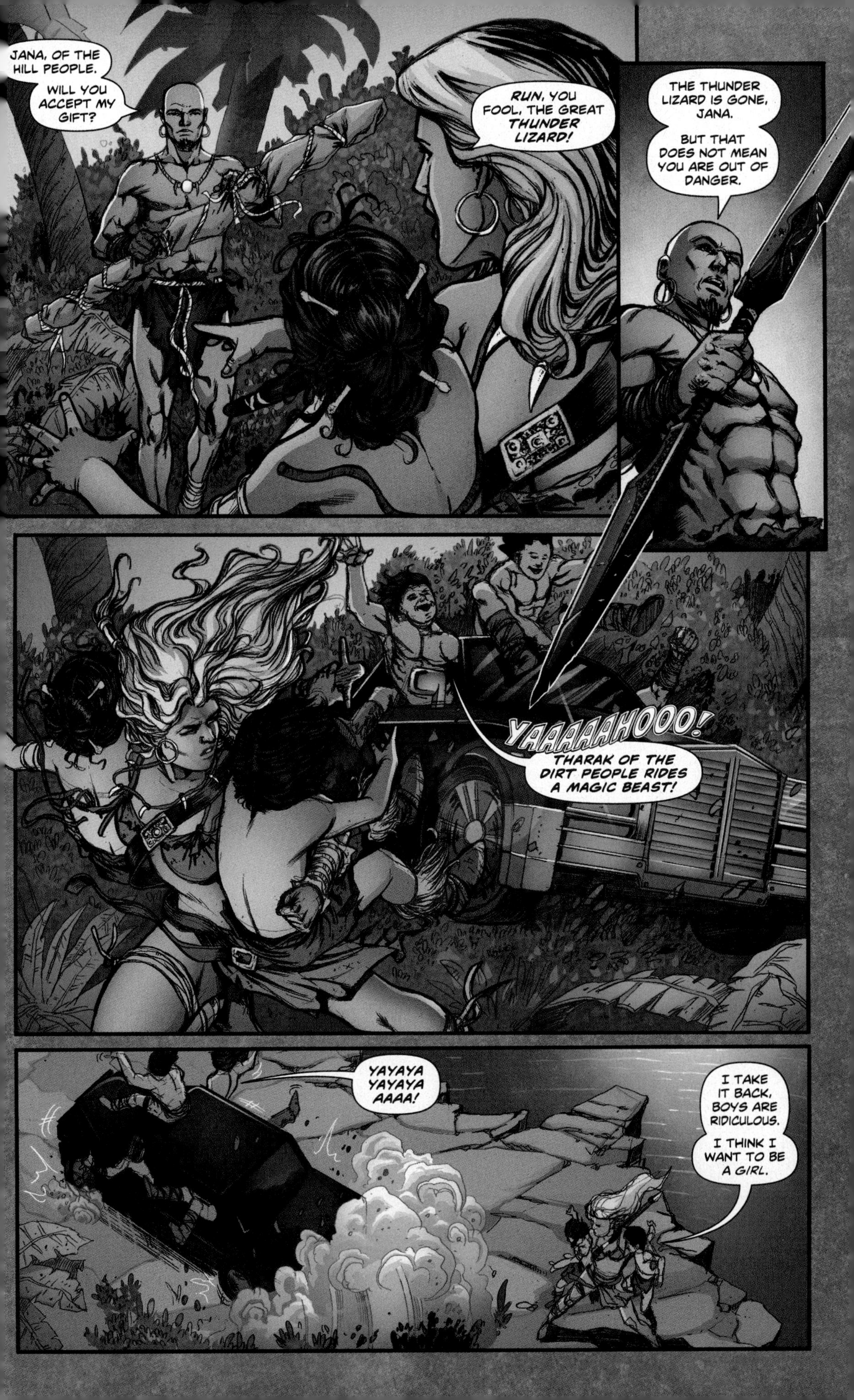
JANA, OF THE HILL PEOPLE.
WILL YOU ACCEPT MY GIFT?
RUN, YOU FOOL, THE GREAT THUNDER LIZARD!
THE THUNDER LIZARD IS GONE, JANA.
BUT THAT DOES NOT MEAN YOU ARE OUT OF DANGER.
YAAAAAHOOO!
THARAK OF THE DIRT PEOPLE RIDES A MAGIC BEAST!
YAYAYA YAYAYA AAAA!
I TAKE IT BACK, BOYS ARE RIDICULOUS.
I THINK I WANT TO BE A GIRL.

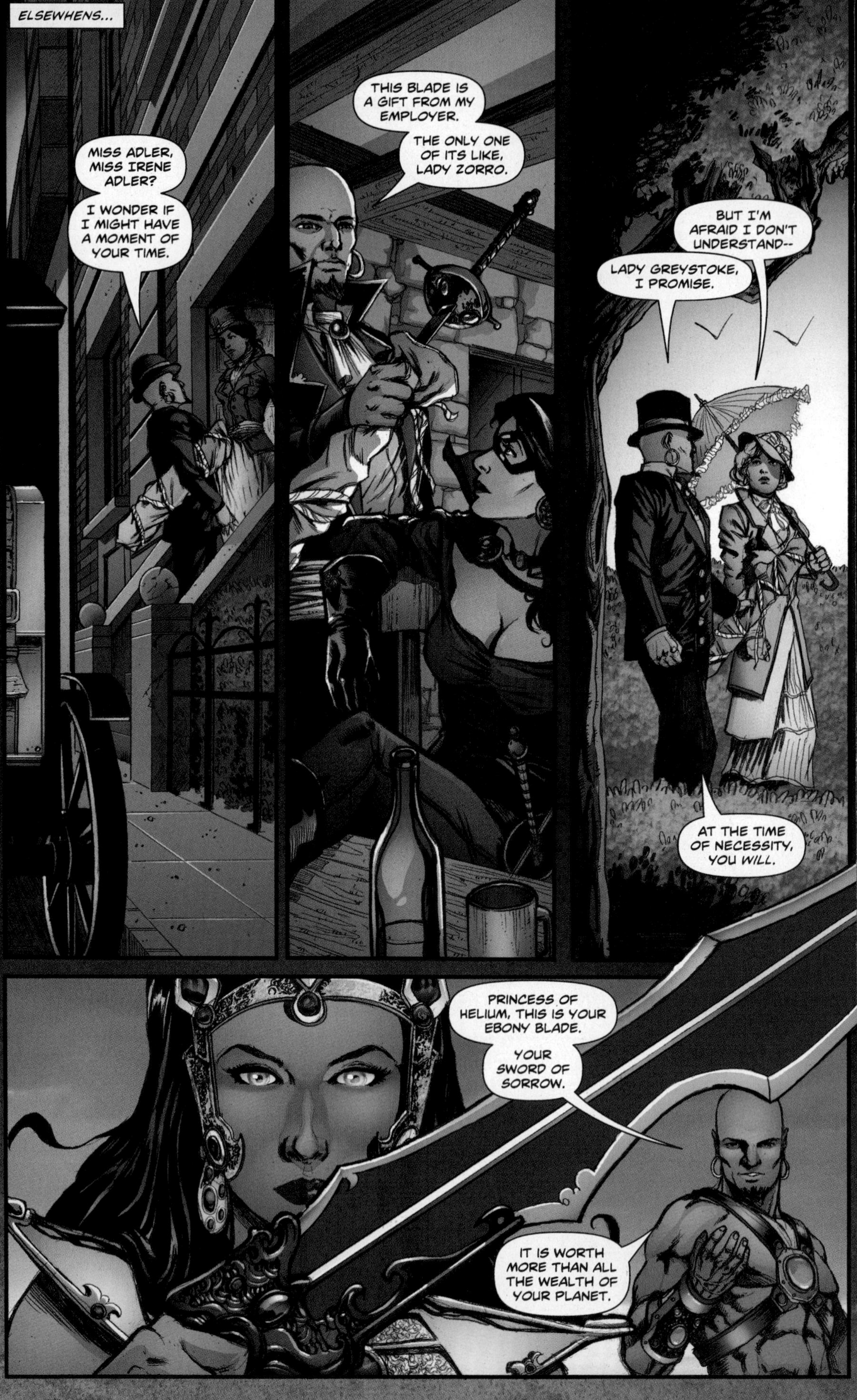
ELSEWHENS...
MISS ADLER, MISS IRENE ADLER?
I WONDER IF I MIGHT HAVE A MOMENT OF YOUR TIME.
THIS BLADE IS A GIFT FROM MY EMPLOYER.
THE ONLY ONE OF ITS LIKE, LADY ZORRO.
LADY GREYSTOKE, I PROMISE.
BUT I'M AFRAID I DON'T UNDERSTAND--
AT THE TIME OF NECESSITY, YOU WILL.
PRINCESS OF HELIUM, THIS IS YOUR EBONY BLADE.
YOUR SWORD OF SORROW.
IT IS WORTH MORE THAN ALL THE WEALTH OF YOUR PLANET.

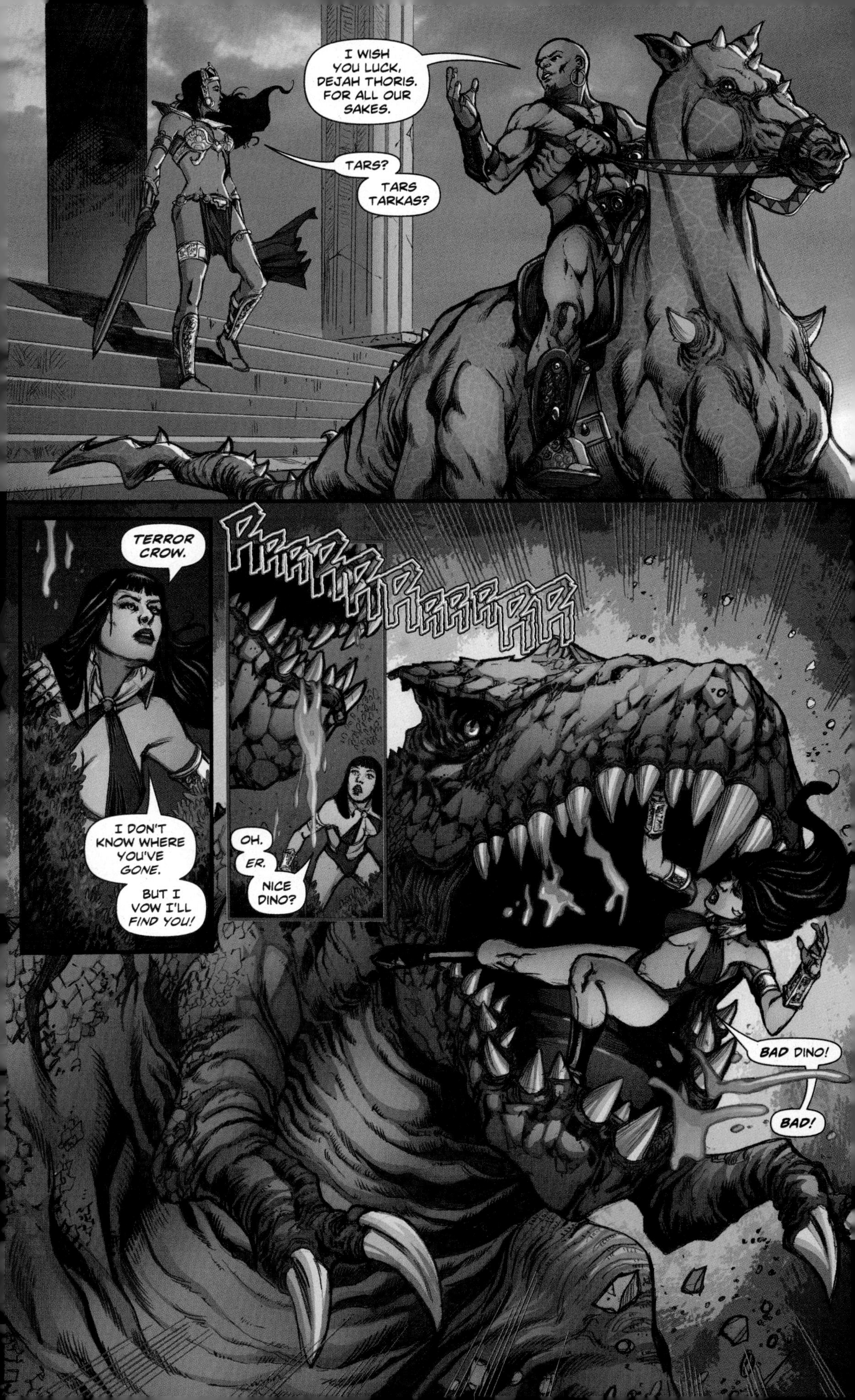
I WISH YOU LUCK, DEJAH THORIS. FOR ALL OUR SAKES.
TARS?
TARS TARKAS?
TERROR CROW.
I DON'T KNOW WHERE YOU'VE GONE.
BUT I VOW I'LL FIND YOU!
RRRRRRRRRRRRR
OH.
ER.
NICE DINO?
BAD DINO!
BAD!

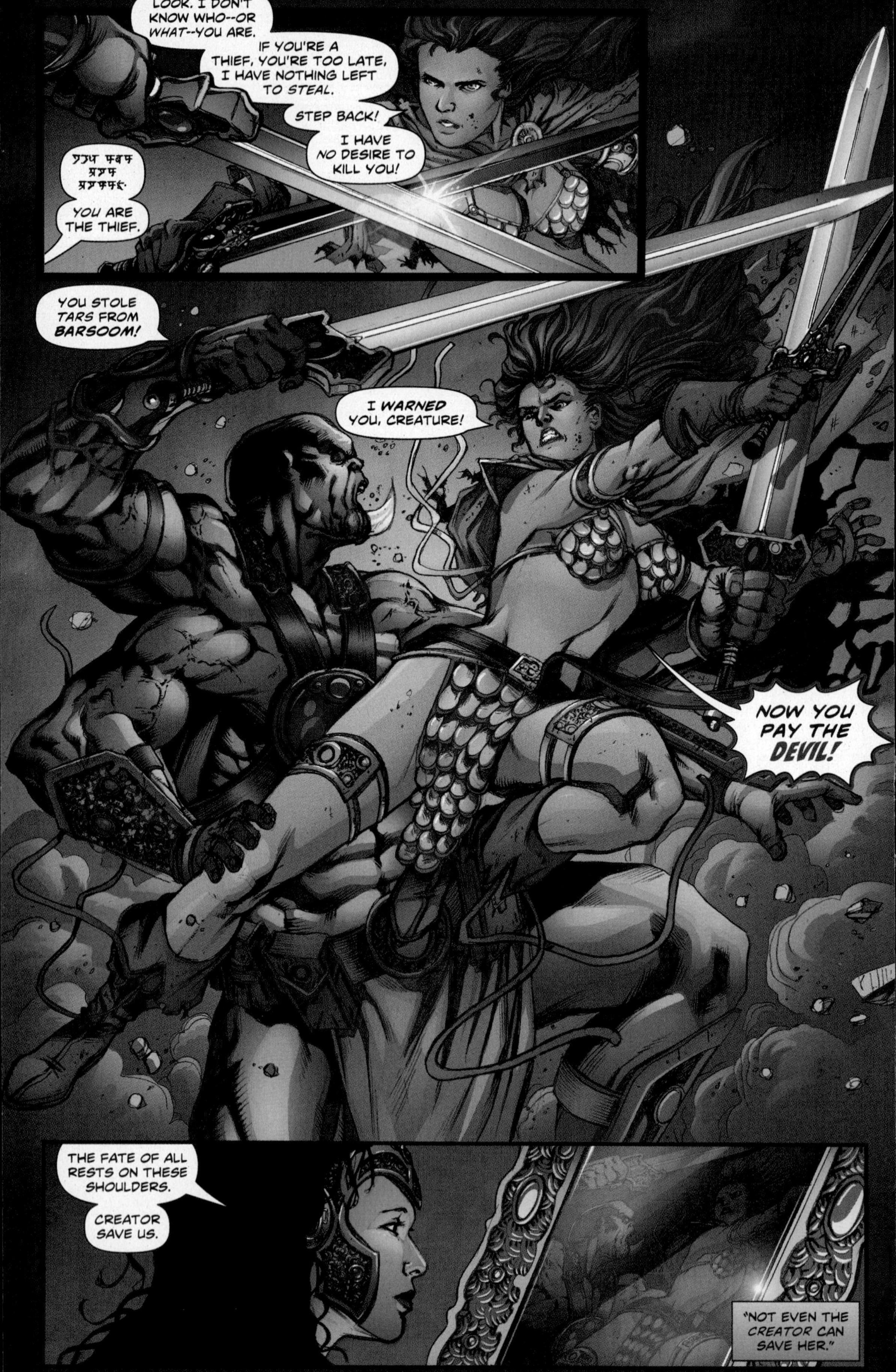
LOOK. I DON'T KNOW WHO--OR WHAT--YOU ARE.
IF YOU'RE A THIEF, YOU'RE TOO LATE, I HAVE NOTHING LEFT TO STEAL.
STEP BACK!
I HAVE NO DESIRE TO KILL YOU!
YOU ARE THE THIEF.
YOU STOLE TARS FROM BARSOOM!
I WARNED YOU, CREATURE!
NOW YOU PAY THE DEVIL!
THE FATE OF ALL RESTS ON THESE SHOULDERS.
CREATOR SAVE US.
"NOT EVEN THE CREATOR CAN SAVE HER."

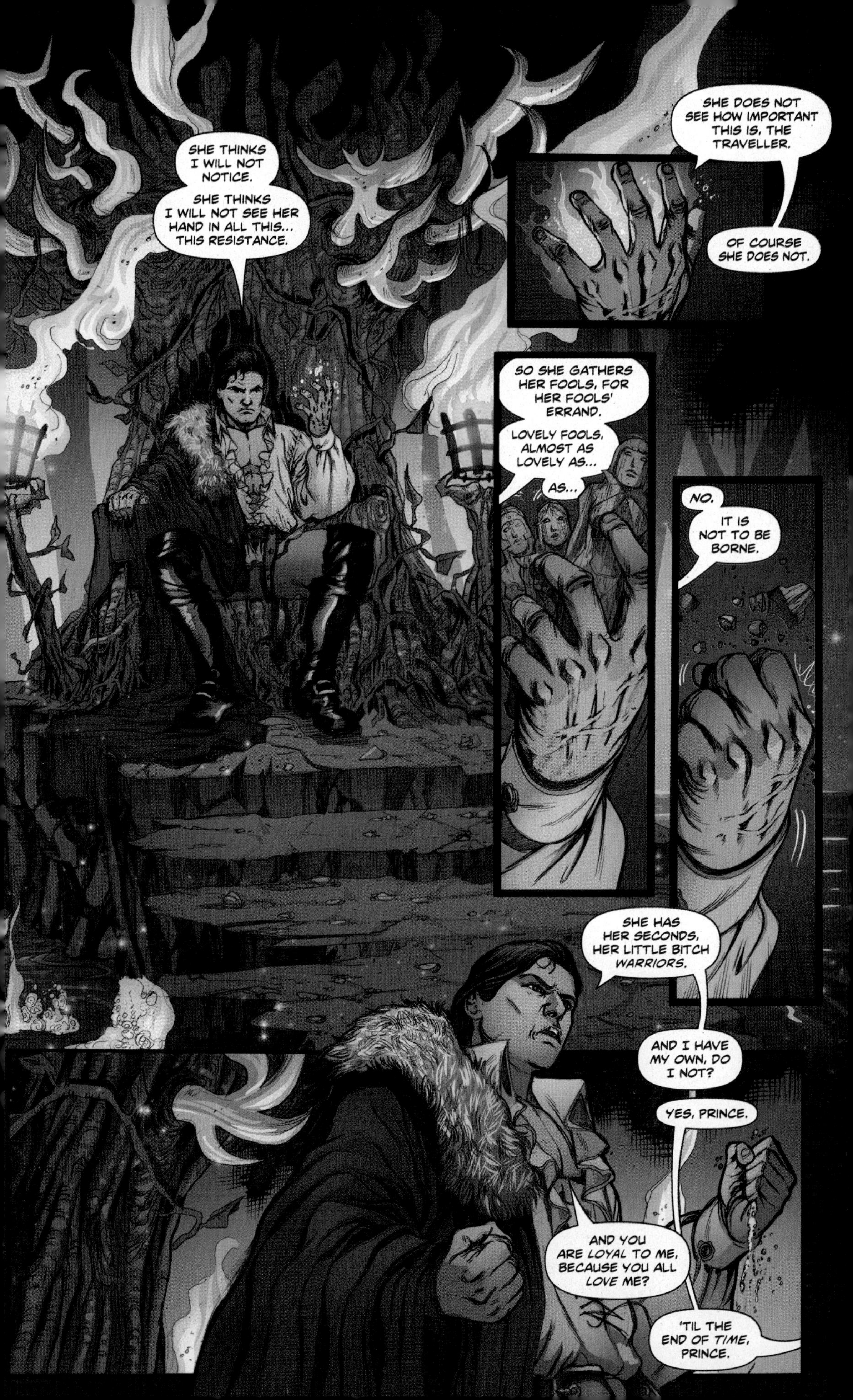
SHE THINKS I WILL NOT NOTICE.
SHE THINKS I WILL NOT SEE HER HAND IN ALL THIS... THIS RESISTANCE.
SHE DOES NOT SEE HOW IMPORTANT THIS IS, THE TRAVELLER.
OF COURSE SHE DOES NOT.
SO SHE GATHERS HER FOOLS, FOR HER FOOLS' ERRAND.
LOVELY FOOLS, ALMOST AS LOVELY AS...
AS...
NO.
IT IS NOT TO BE BORNE.
SHE HAS HER SECONDS, HER LITTLE BITCH WARRIORS.
AND I HAVE MY OWN, DO I NOT?
YES, PRINCE.
AND YOU ARE LOYAL TO ME, BECAUSE YOU ALL LOVE ME?
'TIL THE END OF TIME, PRINCE.

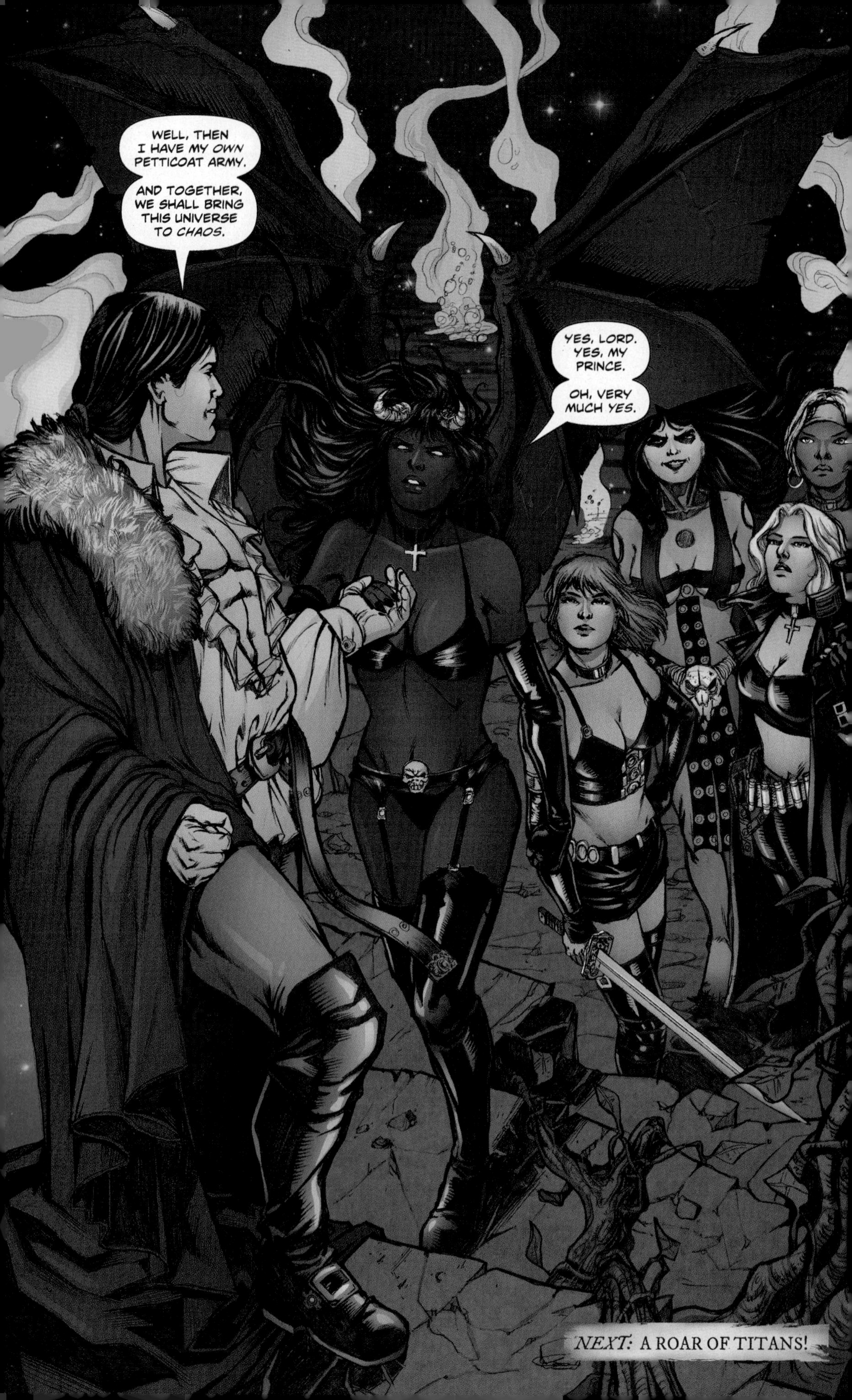
WELL, THEN I HAVE MY *OWN* PETTICOAT ARMY.
AND TOGETHER, WE SHALL BRING THIS UNIVERSE TO *CHAOS*.
YES, LORD. YES, MY PRINCE.
OH, VERY MUCH YES.
NEXT: A ROAR OF TITANS!

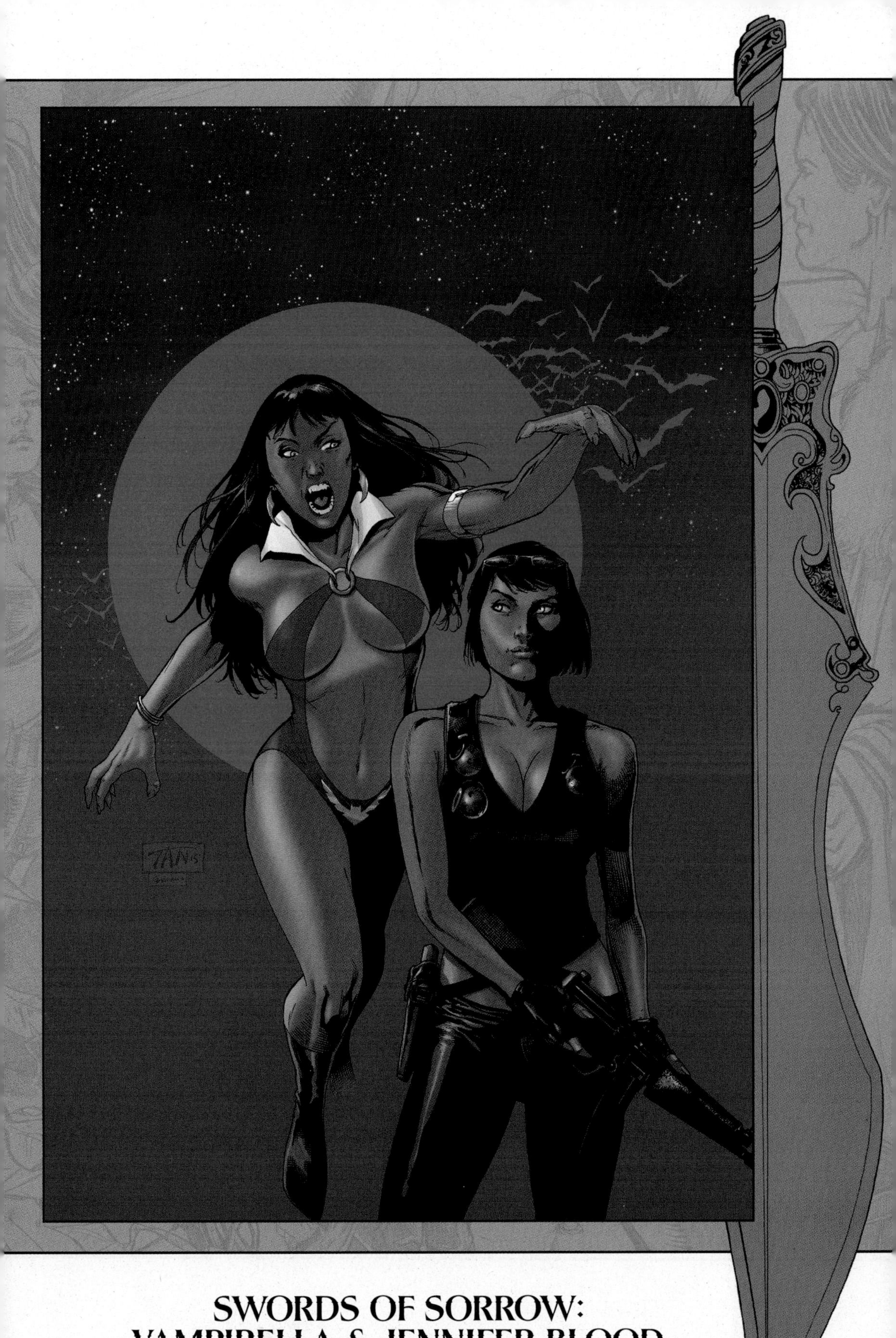

SWORDS OF SORROW: VAMPIRELLA & JENNIFER BLOOD

ISSUE ONE OF FOUR

written by NANCY A. COLLINS illustrated by DAVE ACOSTA
colored by VALENTINA PINTO lettered by ERICA SCHULTZ

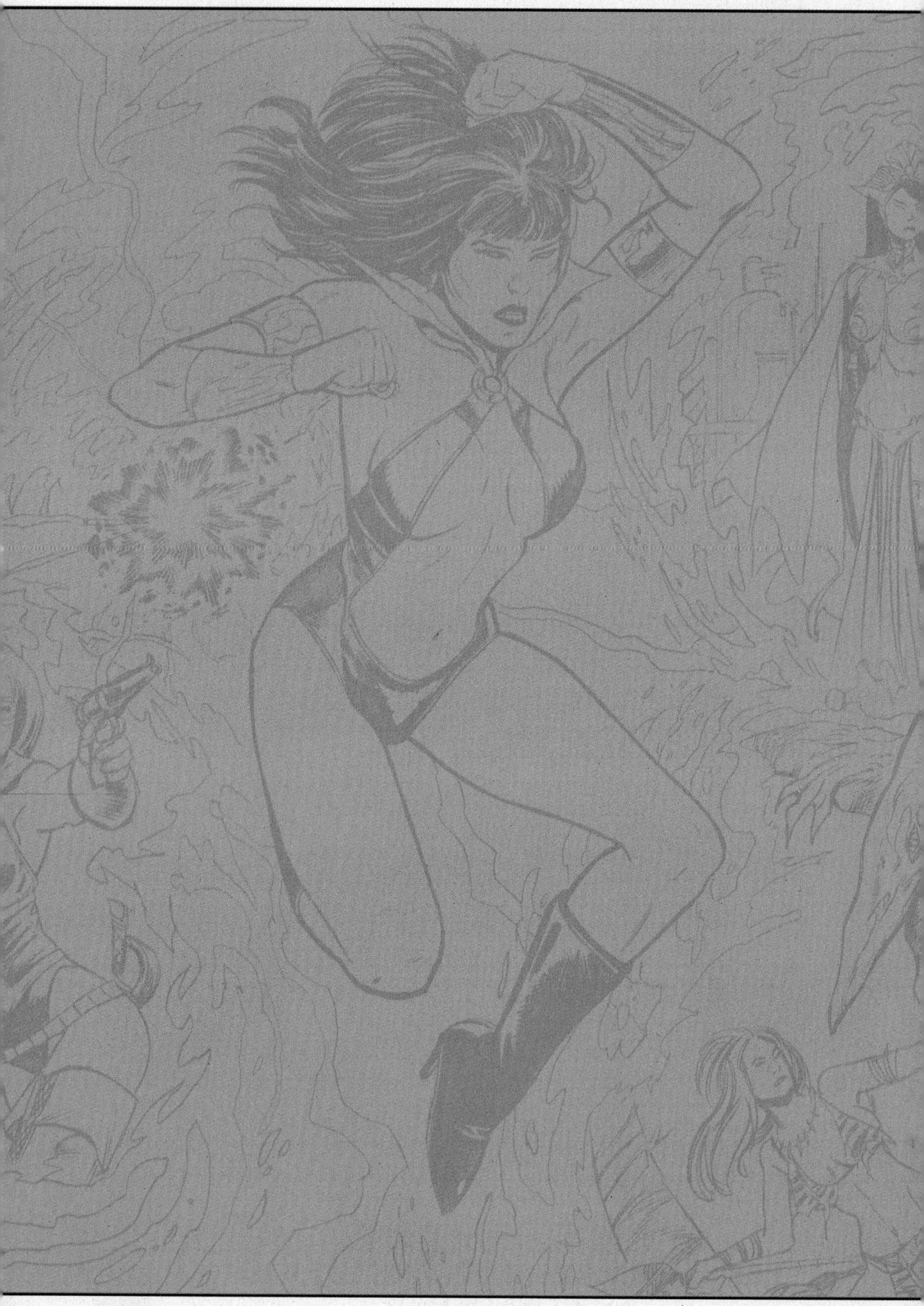

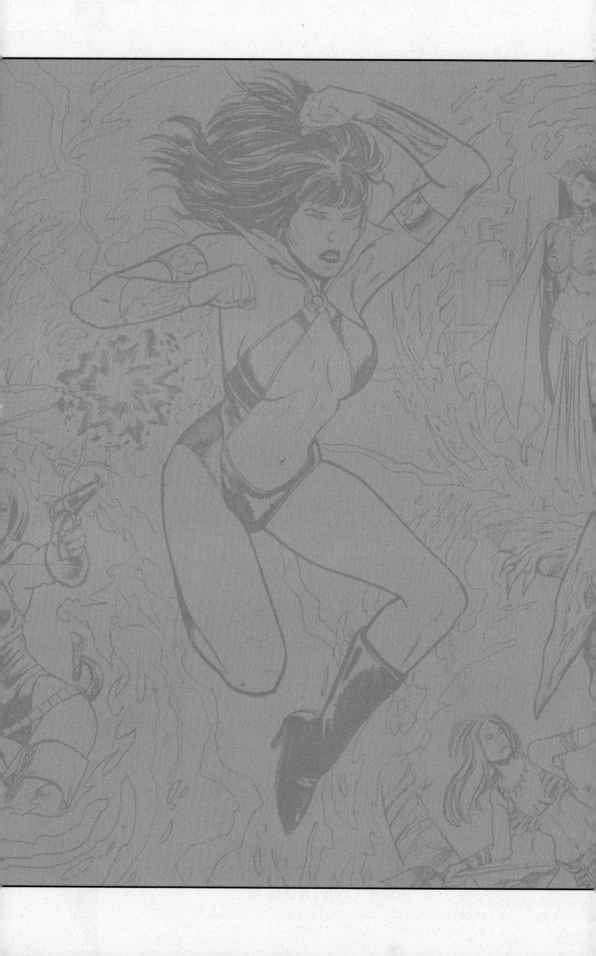

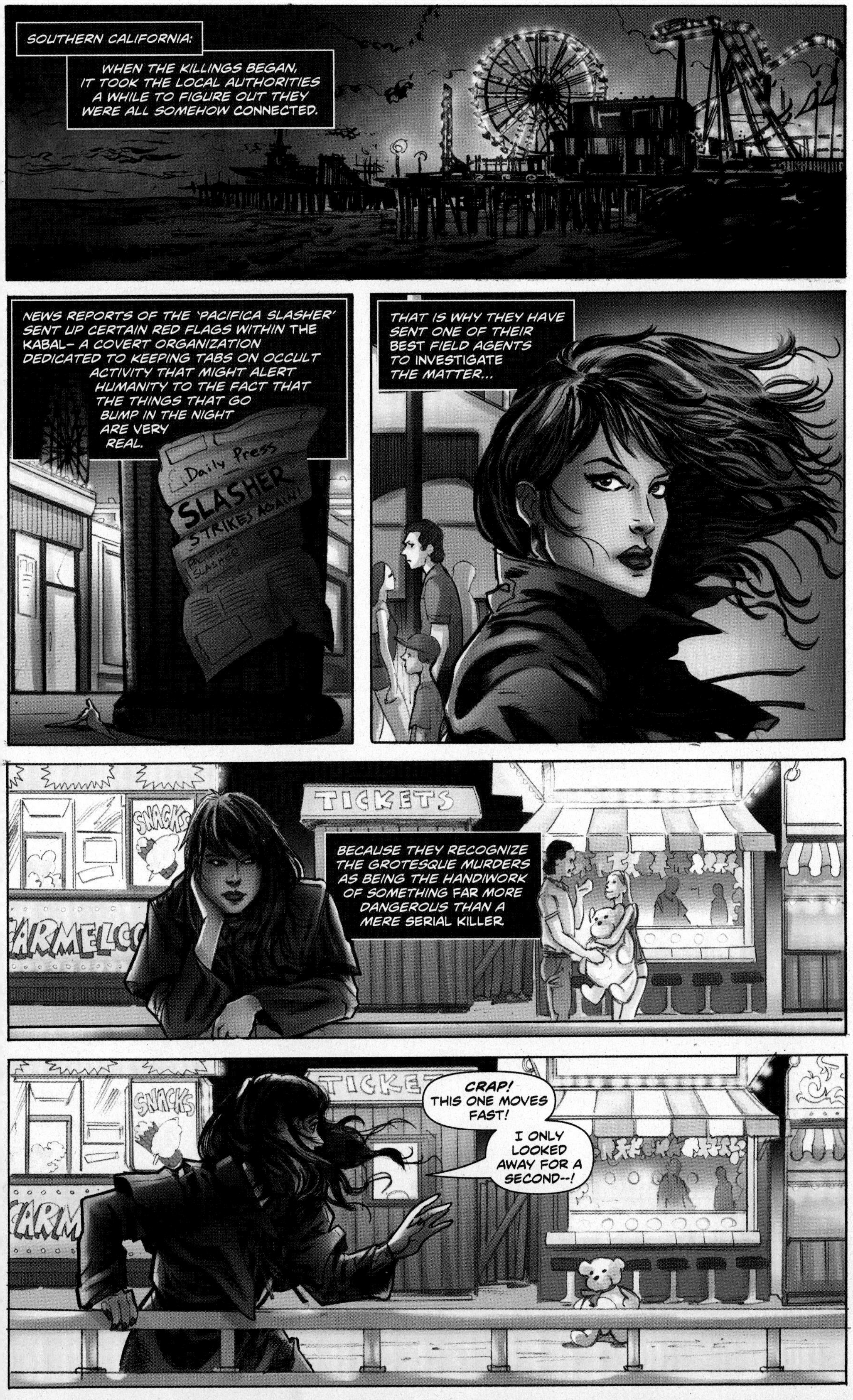
SOUTHERN CALIFORNIA:
WHEN THE KILLINGS BEGAN, IT TOOK THE LOCAL AUTHORITIES A WHILE TO FIGURE OUT THEY WERE ALL SOMEHOW CONNECTED.
NEWS REPORTS OF THE 'PACIFICA SLASHER' SENT UP CERTAIN RED FLAGS WITHIN THE KABAL- A COVERT ORGANIZATION DEDICATED TO KEEPING TABS ON OCCULT ACTIVITY THAT MIGHT ALERT HUMANITY TO THE FACT THAT THE THINGS THAT GO BUMP IN THE NIGHT ARE VERY REAL.
Daily Press
SLASHER
STRIKES AGAIN!
PACIFICA SLASHER
THAT IS WHY THEY HAVE SENT ONE OF THEIR BEST FIELD AGENTS TO INVESTIGATE THE MATTER...
SNACKS
TICKETS
BECAUSE THEY RECOGNIZE THE GROTESQUE MURDERS AS BEING THE HANDIWORK OF SOMETHING FAR MORE DANGEROUS THAN A MERE SERIAL KILLER.
CRAP! THIS ONE MOVES FAST!
I ONLY LOOKED AWAY FOR A SECOND--!

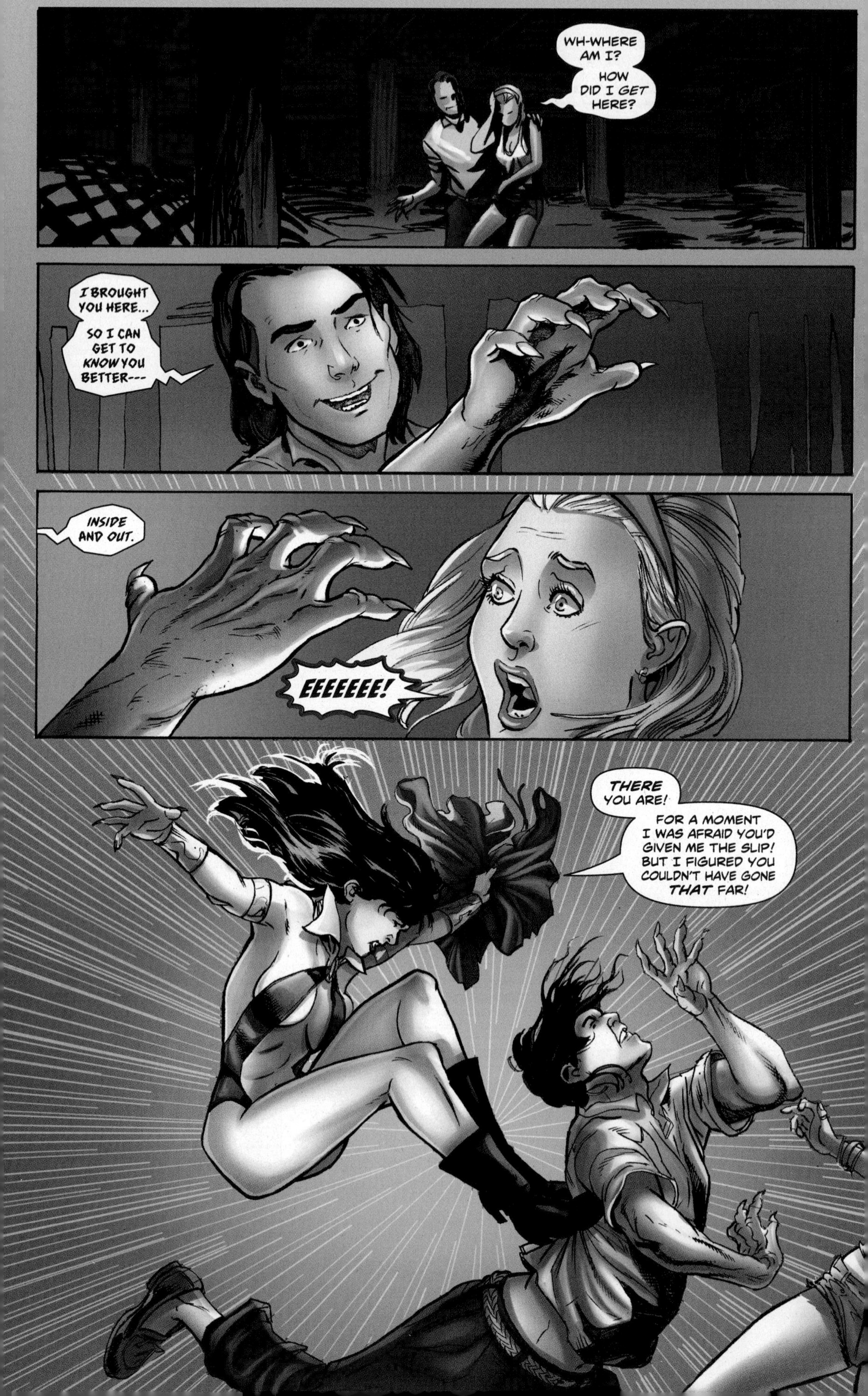
WH-WHERE AM I?
HOW DID I GET HERE?
I BROUGHT YOU HERE...
SO I CAN GET TO KNOW YOU BETTER---
INSIDE AND OUT.
EEEEEEE!
THERE YOU ARE!
FOR A MOMENT I WAS AFRAID YOU'D GIVEN ME THE SLIP! BUT I FIGURED YOU COULDN'T HAVE GONE THAT FAR!

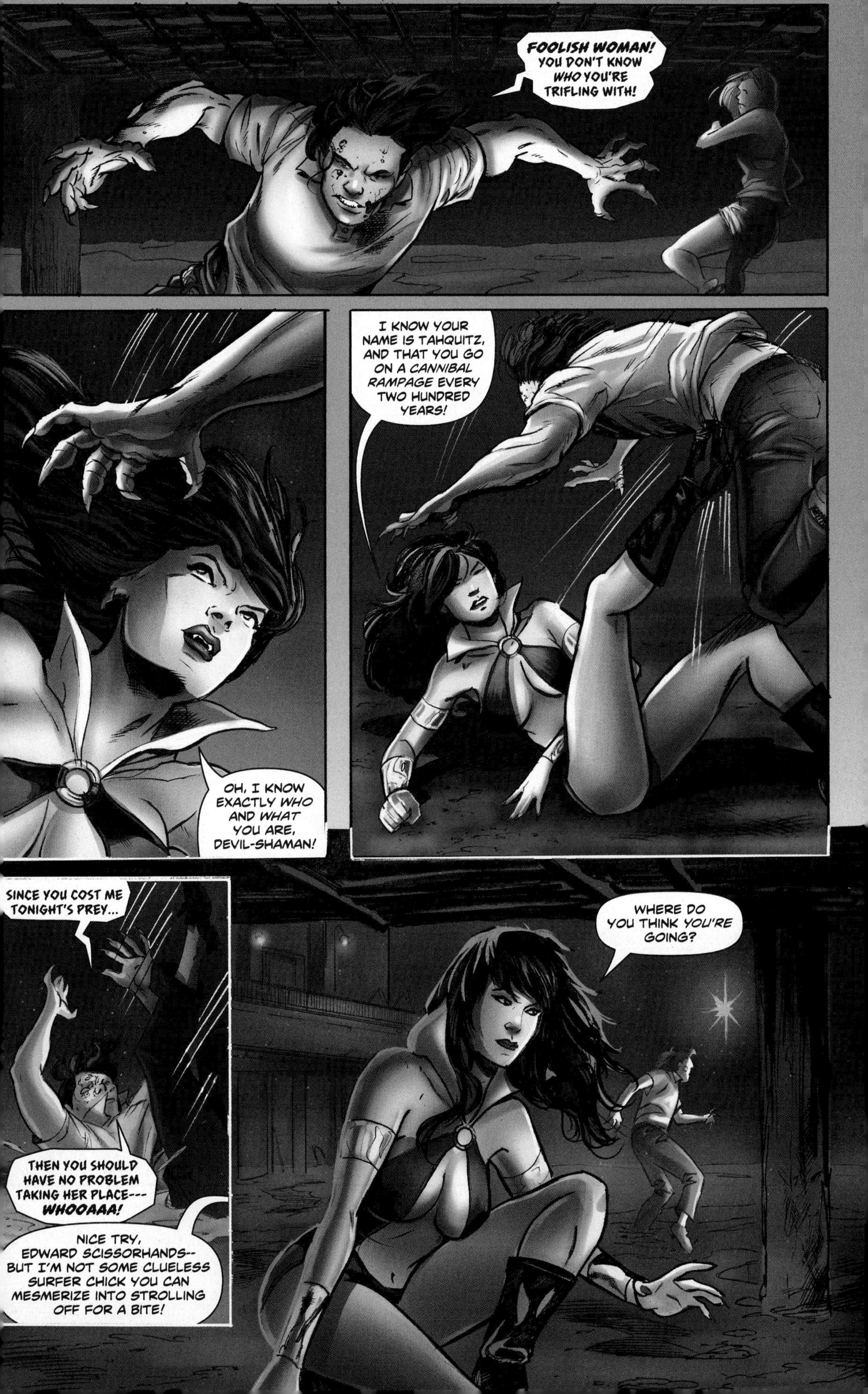
FOOLISH WOMAN! YOU DON'T KNOW WHO YOU'RE TRIFLING WITH!
OH, I KNOW EXACTLY WHO AND WHAT YOU ARE, DEVIL-SHAMAN!
I KNOW YOUR NAME IS TAHQUITZ, AND THAT YOU GO ON A CANNIBAL RAMPAGE EVERY TWO HUNDRED YEARS!
SINCE YOU COST ME TONIGHT'S PREY...
THEN YOU SHOULD HAVE NO PROBLEM TAKING HER PLACE--- WHOOAAA!
NICE TRY, EDWARD SCISSORHANDS-- BUT I'M NOT SOME CLUELESS SURFER CHICK YOU CAN MESMERIZE INTO STROLLING OFF FOR A BITE!
WHERE DO YOU THINK YOU'RE GOING?

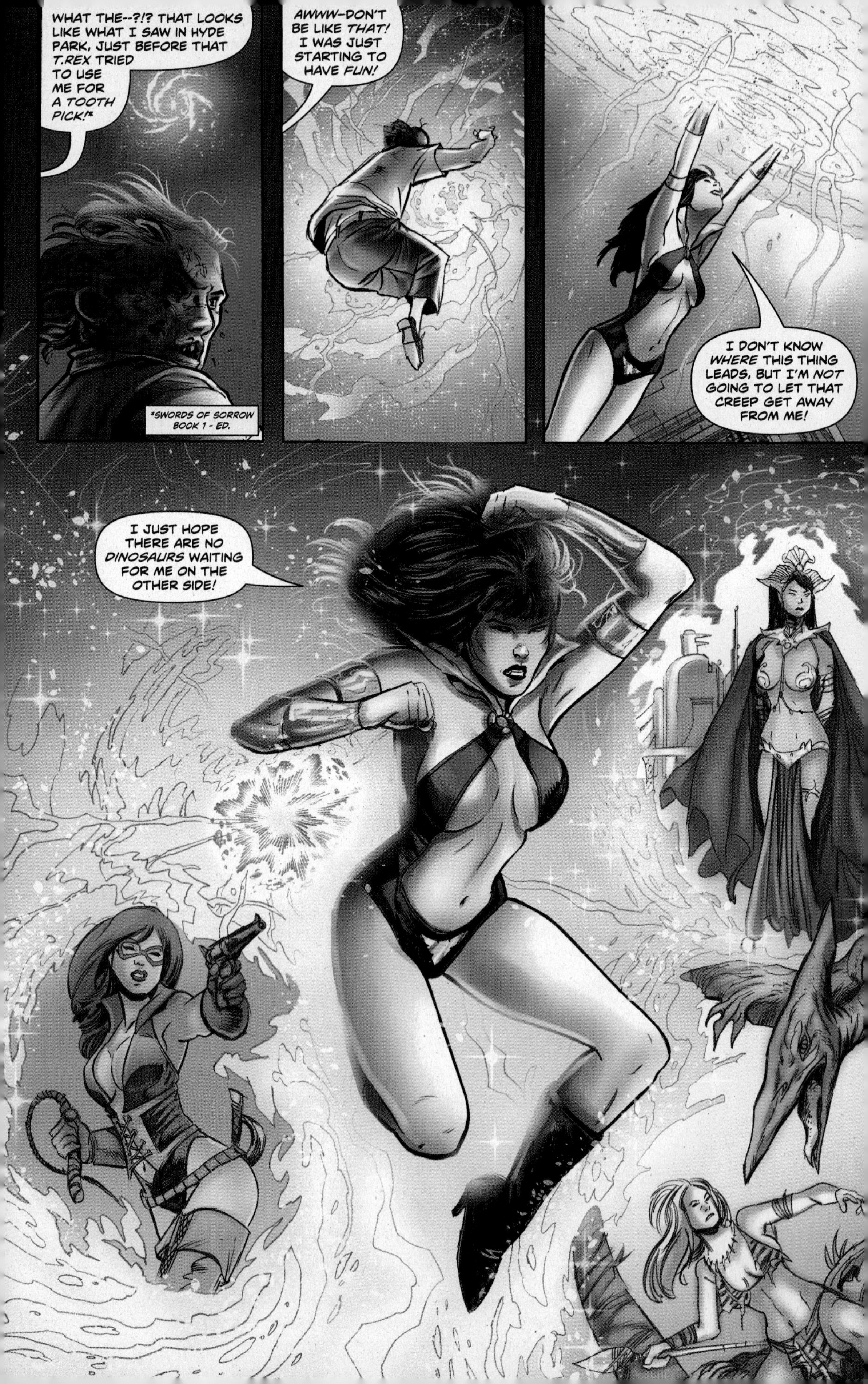
WHAT THE--?!? THAT LOOKS LIKE WHAT I SAW IN HYDE PARK, JUST BEFORE THAT T.REX TRIED TO USE ME FOR A TOOTH PICK!*
*SWORDS OF SORROW BOOK 1 - ED.
AWWW-DON'T BE LIKE THAT! I WAS JUST STARTING TO HAVE FUN!
I DON'T KNOW WHERE THIS THING LEADS, BUT I'M NOT GOING TO LET THAT CREEP GET AWAY FROM ME!
I JUST HOPE THERE ARE NO DINOSAURS WAITING FOR ME ON THE OTHER SIDE!

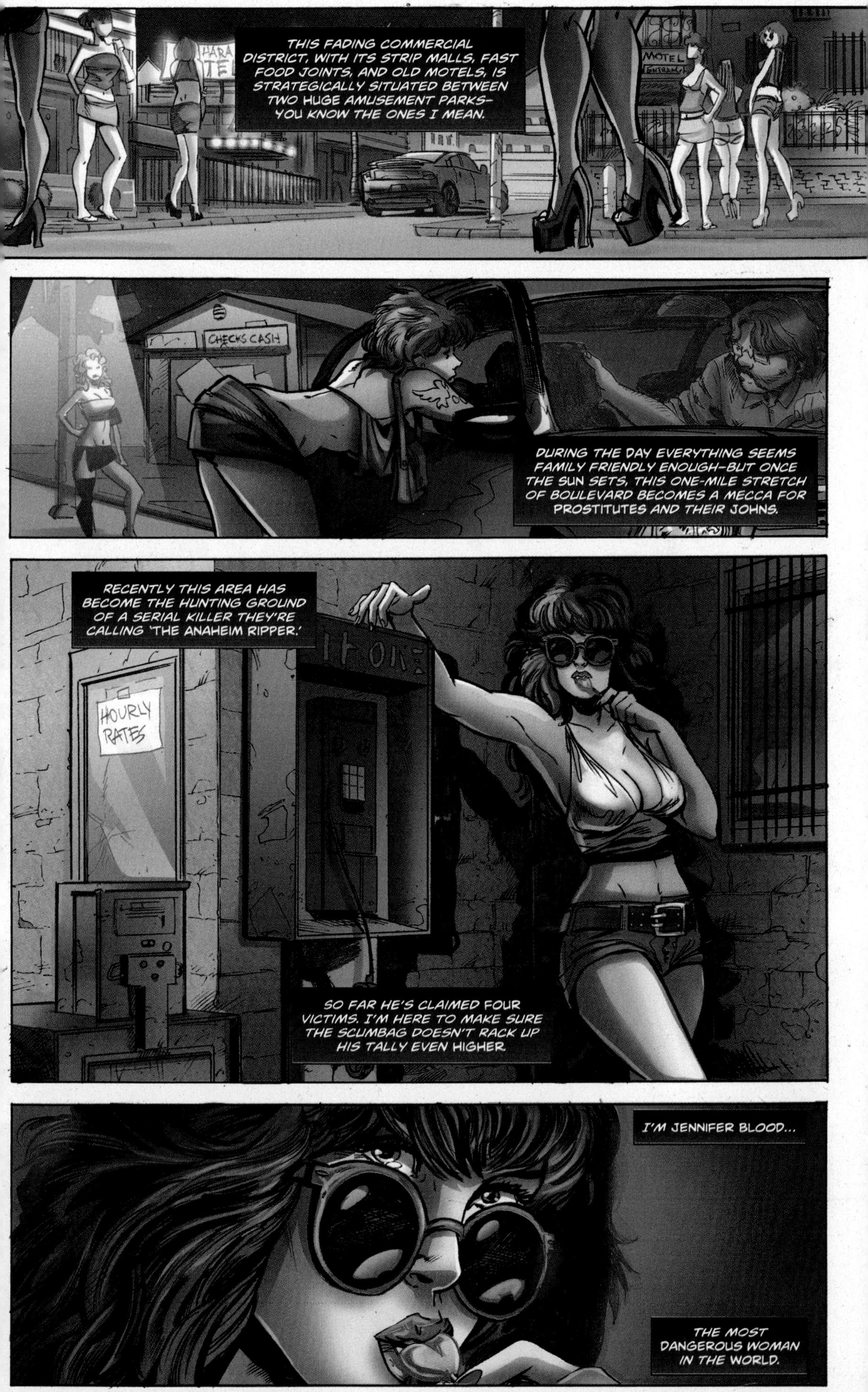

HARA
TEL
MOTEL
ENTRANCE
THIS FADING COMMERCIAL DISTRICT, WITH ITS STRIP MALLS, FAST FOOD JOINTS, AND OLD MOTELS, IS STRATEGICALLY SITUATED BETWEEN TWO HUGE AMUSEMENT PARKS-YOU KNOW THE ONES I MEAN.
CHECKS CASH
DURING THE DAY EVERYTHING SEEMS FAMILY FRIENDLY ENOUGH-BUT ONCE THE SUN SETS, THIS ONE-MILE STRETCH OF BOULEVARD BECOMES A MECCA FOR PROSTITUTES AND THEIR JOHNS.
RECENTLY THIS AREA HAS BECOME THE HUNTING GROUND OF A SERIAL KILLER THEY'RE CALLING 'THE ANAHEIM RIPPER.'
HOURLY RATES
SO FAR HE'S CLAIMED FOUR VICTIMS. I'M HERE TO MAKE SURE THE SCUMBAG DOESN'T RACK UP HIS TALLY EVEN HIGHER.
I'M JENNIFER BLOOD...
THE MOST DANGEROUS WOMAN IN THE WORLD.

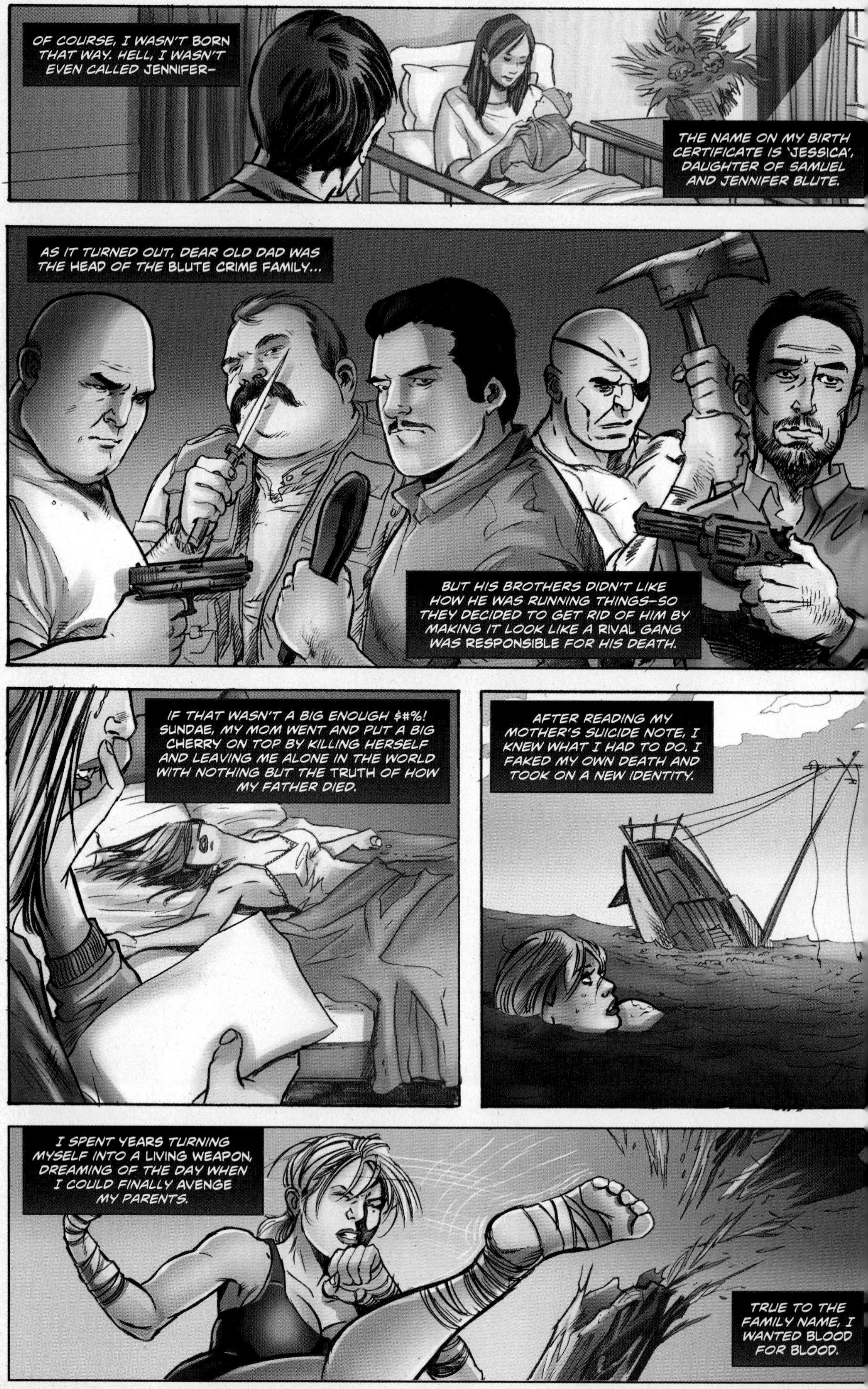
OF COURSE, I WASN'T BORN THAT WAY. HELL, I WASN'T EVEN CALLED JENNIFER–
THE NAME ON MY BIRTH CERTIFICATE IS 'JESSICA', DAUGHTER OF SAMUEL AND JENNIFER BLUTE.
AS IT TURNED OUT, DEAR OLD DAD WAS THE HEAD OF THE BLUTE CRIME FAMILY...
BUT HIS BROTHERS DIDN'T LIKE HOW HE WAS RUNNING THINGS–SO THEY DECIDED TO GET RID OF HIM BY MAKING IT LOOK LIKE A RIVAL GANG WAS RESPONSIBLE FOR HIS DEATH.
IF THAT WASN'T A BIG ENOUGH $#%! SUNDAE, MY MOM WENT AND PUT A BIG CHERRY ON TOP BY KILLING HERSELF AND LEAVING ME ALONE IN THE WORLD WITH NOTHING BUT THE TRUTH OF HOW MY FATHER DIED.
AFTER READING MY MOTHER'S SUICIDE NOTE, I KNEW WHAT I HAD TO DO. I FAKED MY OWN DEATH AND TOOK ON A NEW IDENTITY.
I SPENT YEARS TURNING MYSELF INTO A LIVING WEAPON, DREAMING OF THE DAY WHEN I COULD FINALLY AVENGE MY PARENTS.
TRUE TO THE FAMILY NAME, I WANTED BLOOD FOR BLOOD.

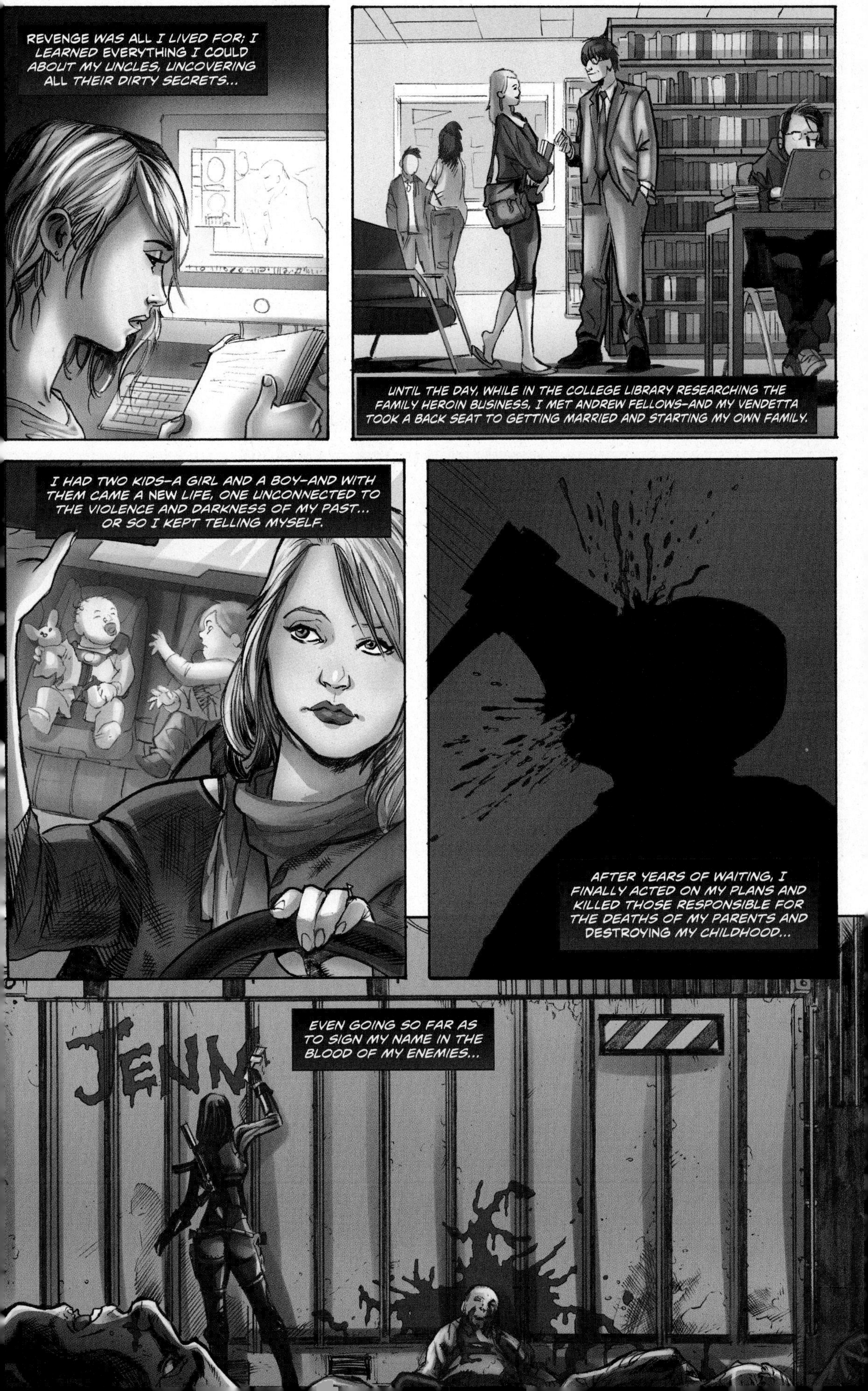
REVENGE WAS ALL I LIVED FOR; I LEARNED EVERYTHING I COULD ABOUT MY UNCLES, UNCOVERING ALL THEIR DIRTY SECRETS...
UNTIL THE DAY, WHILE IN THE COLLEGE LIBRARY RESEARCHING THE FAMILY HEROIN BUSINESS, I MET ANDREW FELLOWS—AND MY VENDETTA TOOK A BACK SEAT TO GETTING MARRIED AND STARTING MY OWN FAMILY.
I HAD TWO KIDS—A GIRL AND A BOY—AND WITH THEM CAME A NEW LIFE, ONE UNCONNECTED TO THE VIOLENCE AND DARKNESS OF MY PAST... OR SO I KEPT TELLING MYSELF.
AFTER YEARS OF WAITING, I FINALLY ACTED ON MY PLANS AND KILLED THOSE RESPONSIBLE FOR THE DEATHS OF MY PARENTS AND DESTROYING MY CHILDHOOD...
EVEN GOING SO FAR AS TO SIGN MY NAME IN THE BLOOD OF MY ENEMIES...

ONCE THE LAST OF THEM WAS DEAD, I THOUGHT THAT WOULD BE IT. THAT I COULD QUIT AND GO BACK TO BEING JEN FELLOWS: SUBURBAN HOUSEWIFE.

BUT IT TURNS OUT I LIKED KILLING—AND THE SCUZZIER THE SLEAZEBAG, THE BETTER. AND, MORE IMPORTANTLY, I WAS GOOD AT IT.

SO I BECAME JEN FELLOWS: SOCCER MOM BY DAY, AND JENNIFER BLOOD: VIGILANTE BY NIGHT...UNTIL MY HUSBAND FOUND MY JOURNAL. HE SAID HE WAS GOING TO DIVORCE ME AND MAKE SURE I NEVER GOT TO SEE MY KIDS AGAIN.

HE REALLY SHOULDN'T HAVE DONE THAT.

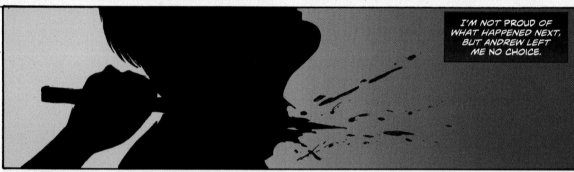

I'M NOT PROUD OF WHAT HAPPENED NEXT, BUT ANDREW LEFT ME NO CHOICE.

THINGS REALLY WENT TO $#%! AFTER THAT, AND THE NEXT THING I KNEW I WAS CONVICTED ON ONE HUNDRED COUNTS OF MURDER AND SHIPPED OFF TO PRISON.

NEEDLESS TO SAY, THE TEN MILLION DOLLAR BOUNTY PLACED ON ME BY THE SURVIVING BLUTES MADE MY INCARCERATION LESS THAN...IDEAL.

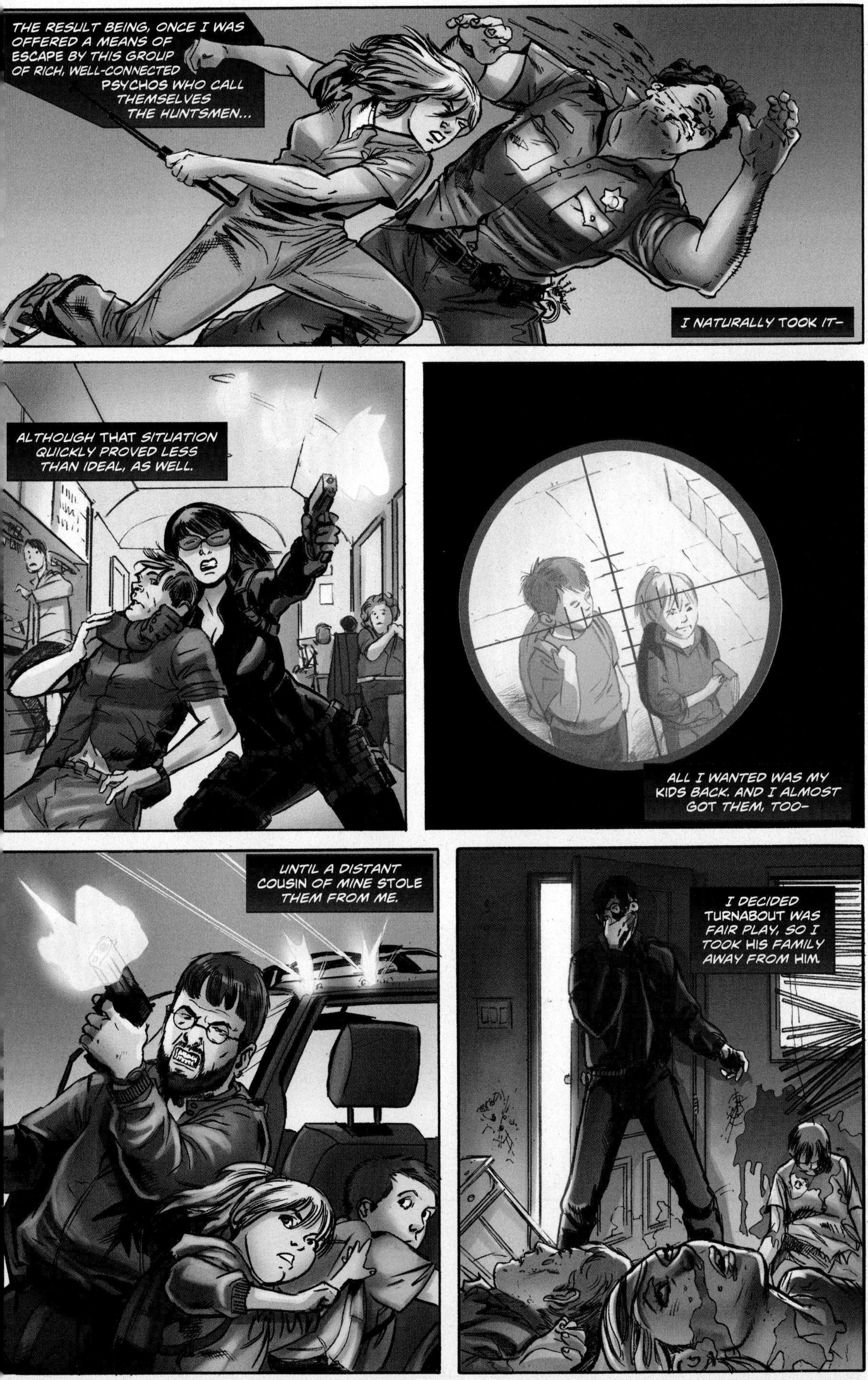
THE RESULT BEING, ONCE I WAS OFFERED A MEANS OF ESCAPE BY THIS GROUP OF RICH, WELL-CONNECTED PSYCHOS WHO CALL THEMSELVES THE HUNTSMEN...
I NATURALLY TOOK IT–
ALTHOUGH THAT SITUATION QUICKLY PROVED LESS THAN IDEAL, AS WELL.
ALL I WANTED WAS MY KIDS BACK. AND I ALMOST GOT THEM, TOO–
UNTIL A DISTANT COUSIN OF MINE STOLE THEM FROM ME.
I DECIDED TURNABOUT WAS FAIR PLAY, SO I TOOK HIS FAMILY AWAY FROM HIM.

BUT AFTER ALL I HAD GONE THROUGH TO BE REUNITED WITH MY CHILDREN— I DISCOVERED THEY FEARED AND HATED ME FOR WHAT I HAD DONE TO THEIR FATHER— AND TO THEIR LIVES. THEY NEVER WANT TO SEE ME AGAIN.

SO I LEFT THEM TO BE RAISED BY MY COUSIN AND SPENT SOME TIME IN A RELIGIOUS RETREAT, HOPING I COULD LEARN HOW TO CONTROL THE KILLER INSTINCT THAT HAD DESTROYED MY LIFE...

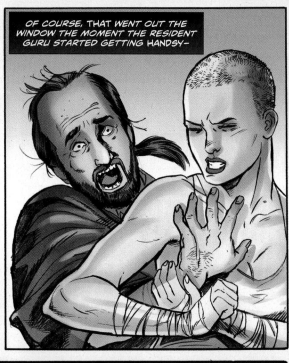

OF COURSE, THAT WENT OUT THE WINDOW THE MOMENT THE RESIDENT GURU STARTED GETTING HANDSY—

AND THEN THERE WAS THE MATTER OF THE DOMINATRIX WHO DECIDED TO POSE AS 'JENNIFER BLOOD' SO SHE COULD SET UP HER STOOGE OF A LOVER AS THE NEW BOSS OF L.A.

SINCE SHE WANTED TO BE ME SO BADLY, I ARRANGED FOR HER TO DIE IN MY STEAD. I HAVE SINCE TAKEN OVER HER IDENTITY AND MOVED INTO HER PLACE IN THE HOLLYWOOD HILLS.

PAYBACK'S A BITCH, AND SO AM I.

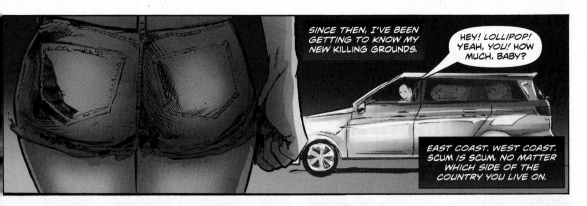

SINCE THEN, I'VE BEEN GETTING TO KNOW MY NEW KILLING GROUNDS.

HEY! LOLLIPOP! YEAH, YOU! HOW MUCH, BABY?

EAST COAST. WEST COAST. SCUM IS SCUM, NO MATTER WHICH SIDE OF THE COUNTRY YOU LIVE ON.

ONE THING I'VE LEARNED IS THAT LOOKS CAN BE DECEIVING. HELL, I'VE USED IT TO MY OWN ADVANTAGE, TIME AND AGAIN...

BUT WHOEVER SLAUGHTERED THOSE GIRLS TORE THEM APART WITH HIS BARE HANDS. AND THE ONES ON THIS TWO-PUMP CHUMP ARE AS SOFT AS BUTTER

WHAT'S THE MATTER? DIDN'T YOU HEAR ME?

KKKRUNCH

THAT MEANS HE'S NOT WORTH MY SPECIAL ATTENTION...

HOW MUC— URK!

DO YOURSELF A FAVOR, 'JOHN', AND GO BACK TO YOUR STICK-FIGURE WIFE AND KIDS WHILE YOU STILL CAN.

BUT THAT DOESN'T MEAN I WON'T ENJOY #^*%ING WITH HIM.

SKREEEEEEEEEE!

HELL, I'VE GOT TO DO SOMETHING TO PASS THE TIME.

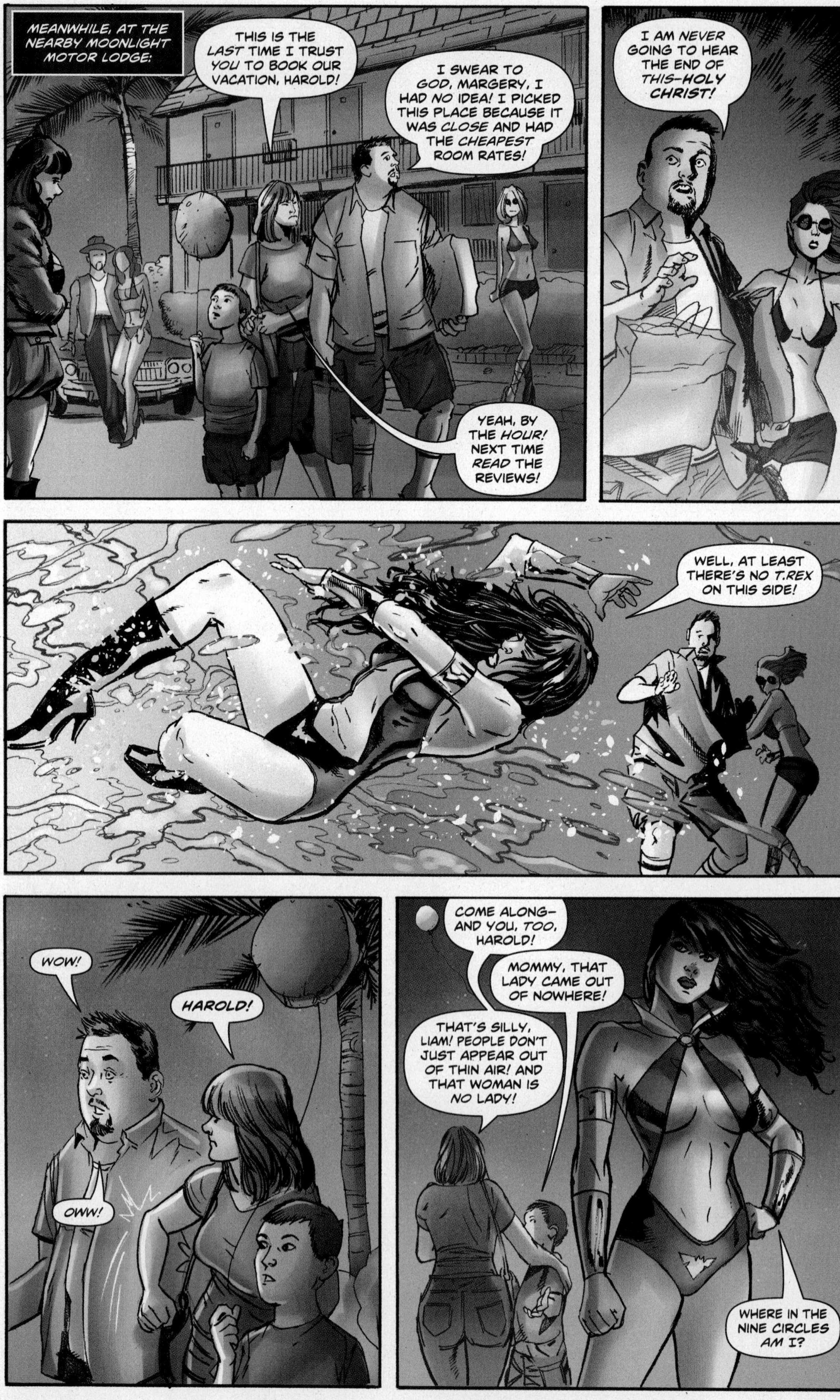

MEANWHILE, AT THE NEARBY MOONLIGHT MOTOR LODGE:
THIS IS THE LAST TIME I TRUST YOU TO BOOK OUR VACATION, HAROLD!
I SWEAR TO GOD, MARGERY, I HAD NO IDEA! I PICKED THIS PLACE BECAUSE IT WAS CLOSE AND HAD THE CHEAPEST ROOM RATES!
YEAH, BY THE HOUR! NEXT TIME READ THE REVIEWS!
I AM NEVER GOING TO HEAR THE END OF THIS–HOLY CHRIST!
WELL, AT LEAST THERE'S NO T.REX ON THIS SIDE!
WOW!
HAROLD!
OWW!
COME ALONG– AND YOU, TOO, HAROLD!
MOMMY, THAT LADY CAME OUT OF NOWHERE!
THAT'S SILLY, LIAM! PEOPLE DON'T JUST APPEAR OUT OF THIN AIR! AND THAT WOMAN IS NO LADY!
WHERE IN THE NINE CIRCLES AM I?

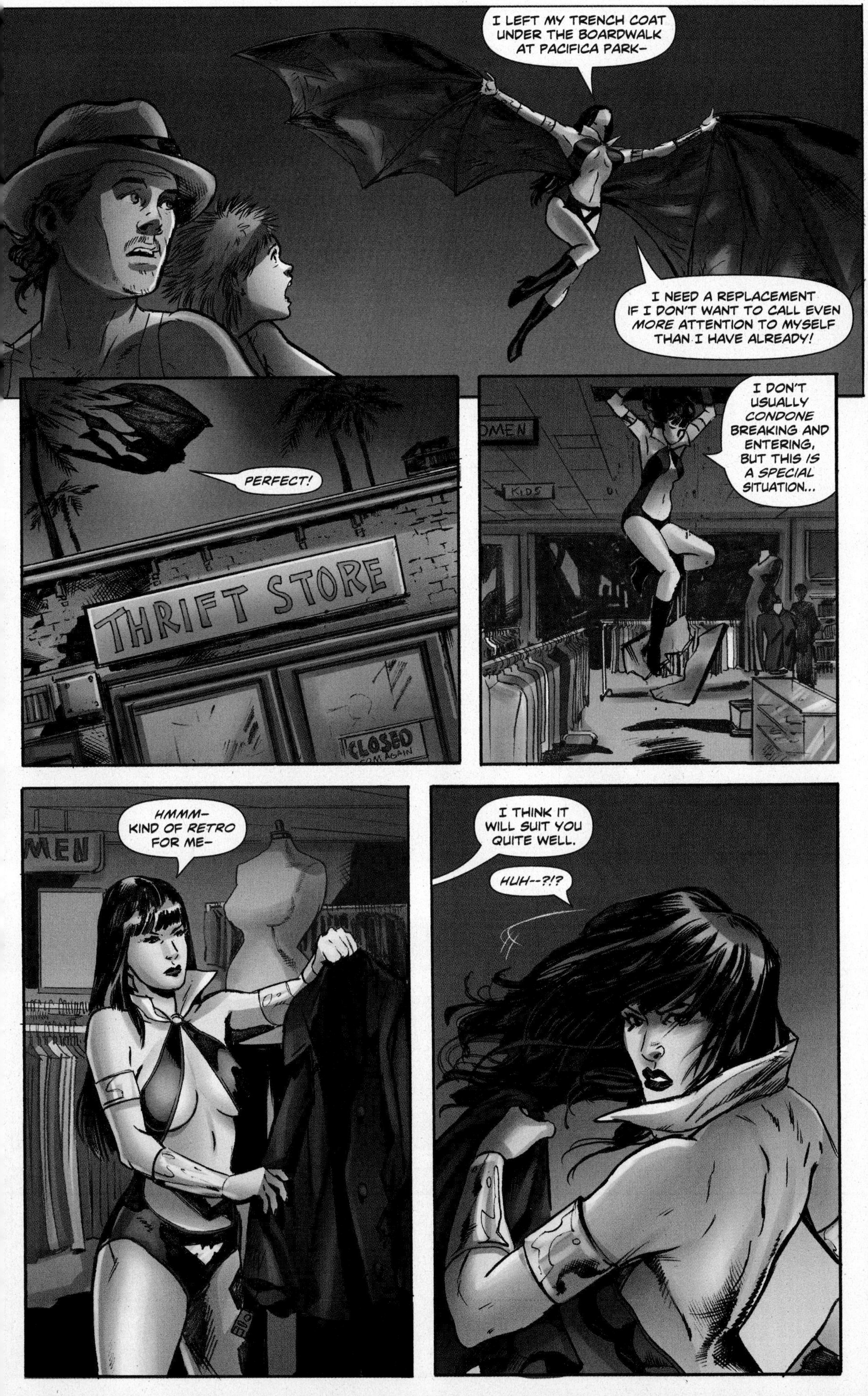
I LEFT MY TRENCH COAT UNDER THE BOARDWALK AT PACIFICA PARK–
I NEED A REPLACEMENT IF I DON'T WANT TO CALL EVEN MORE ATTENTION TO MYSELF THAN I HAVE ALREADY!
PERFECT!
THRIFT STORE
CLOSED
I DON'T USUALLY CONDONE BREAKING AND ENTERING, BUT THIS IS A SPECIAL SITUATION...
KIDS
HMMM– KIND OF RETRO FOR ME–
MEN
I THINK IT WILL SUIT YOU QUITE WELL.
HUH--?!?

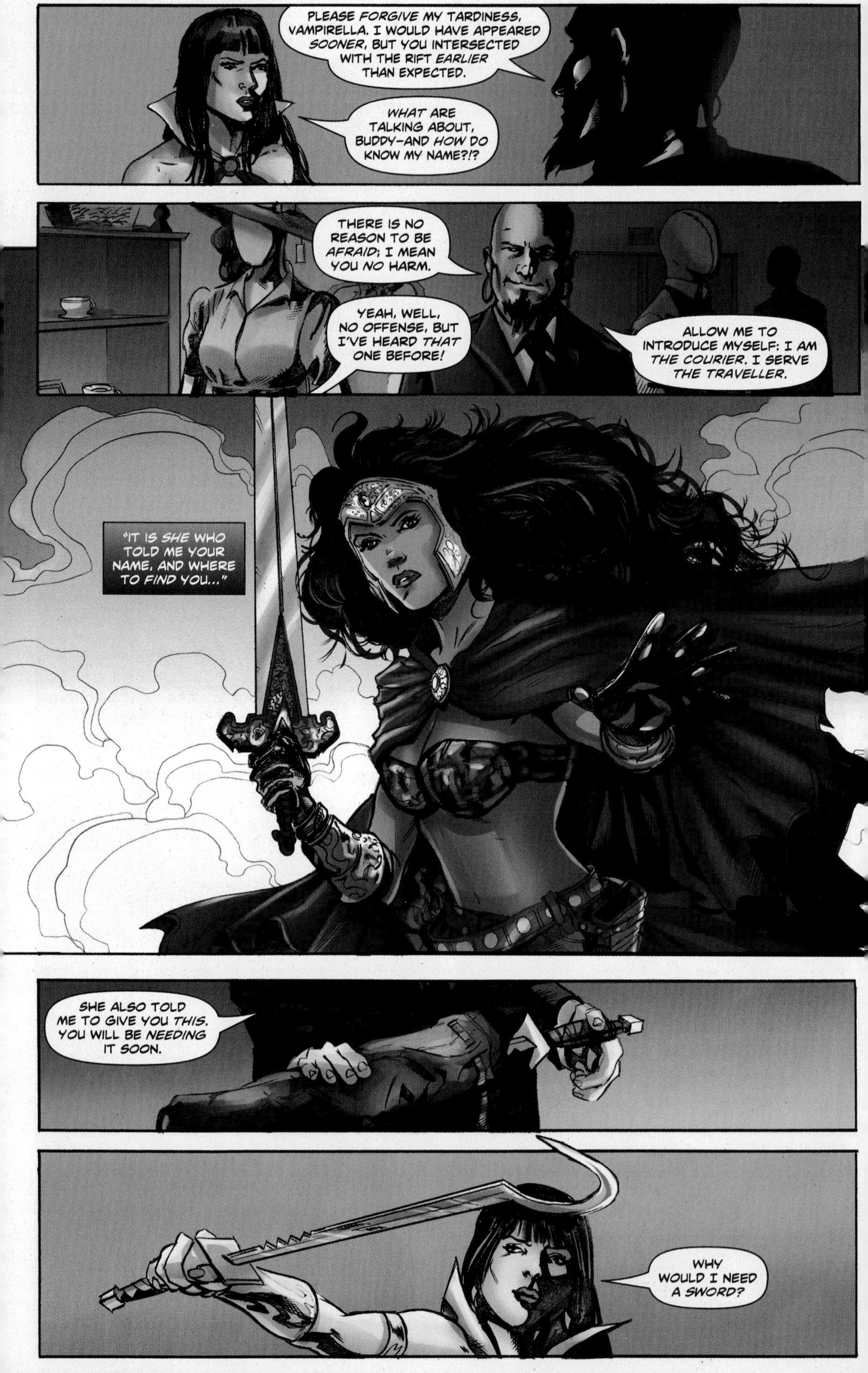
PLEASE FORGIVE MY TARDINESS, VAMPIRELLA. I WOULD HAVE APPEARED SOONER, BUT YOU INTERSECTED WITH THE RIFT EARLIER THAN EXPECTED.
WHAT ARE TALKING ABOUT, BUDDY—AND HOW DO KNOW MY NAME?!?
THERE IS NO REASON TO BE AFRAID; I MEAN YOU NO HARM.
YEAH, WELL, NO OFFENSE, BUT I'VE HEARD THAT ONE BEFORE!
ALLOW ME TO INTRODUCE MYSELF: I AM THE COURIER. I SERVE THE TRAVELLER.
"IT IS SHE WHO TOLD ME YOUR NAME, AND WHERE TO FIND YOU..."
SHE ALSO TOLD ME TO GIVE YOU THIS. YOU WILL BE NEEDING IT SOON.
WHY WOULD I NEED A SWORD?

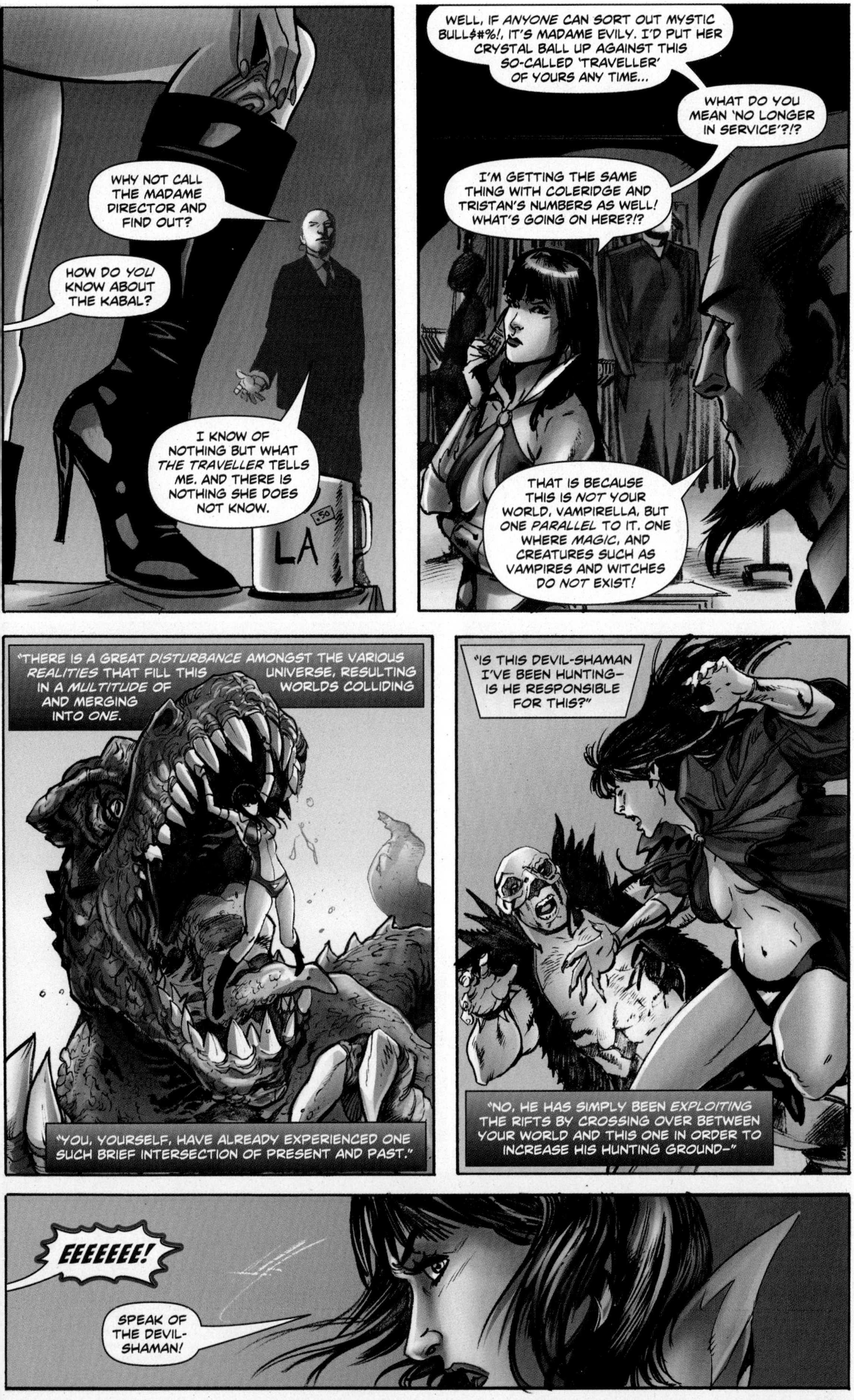
WHY NOT CALL THE MADAME DIRECTOR AND FIND OUT?
HOW DO YOU KNOW ABOUT THE KABAL?
I KNOW OF NOTHING BUT WHAT THE TRAVELLER TELLS ME. AND THERE IS NOTHING SHE DOES NOT KNOW.
LA
WELL, IF ANYONE CAN SORT OUT MYSTIC BULL$#%!, IT'S MADAME EVILY. I'D PUT HER CRYSTAL BALL UP AGAINST THIS SO-CALLED 'TRAVELLER' OF YOURS ANY TIME...
WHAT DO YOU MEAN 'NO LONGER IN SERVICE'?!?
I'M GETTING THE SAME THING WITH COLERIDGE AND TRISTAN'S NUMBERS AS WELL! WHAT'S GOING ON HERE?!?
THAT IS BECAUSE THIS IS NOT YOUR WORLD, VAMPIRELLA, BUT ONE PARALLEL TO IT. ONE WHERE MAGIC, AND CREATURES SUCH AS VAMPIRES AND WITCHES DO NOT EXIST!
"THERE IS A GREAT DISTURBANCE AMONGST THE VARIOUS REALITIES THAT FILL THIS UNIVERSE, RESULTING IN A MULTITUDE OF WORLDS COLLIDING AND MERGING INTO ONE.
"YOU, YOURSELF, HAVE ALREADY EXPERIENCED ONE SUCH BRIEF INTERSECTION OF PRESENT AND PAST."
"IS THIS DEVIL-SHAMAN I'VE BEEN HUNTING– IS HE RESPONSIBLE FOR THIS?"
"NO, HE HAS SIMPLY BEEN EXPLOITING THE RIFTS BY CROSSING OVER BETWEEN YOUR WORLD AND THIS ONE IN ORDER TO INCREASE HIS HUNTING GROUND–"
EEEEEEE!
SPEAK OF THE DEVIL-SHAMAN!

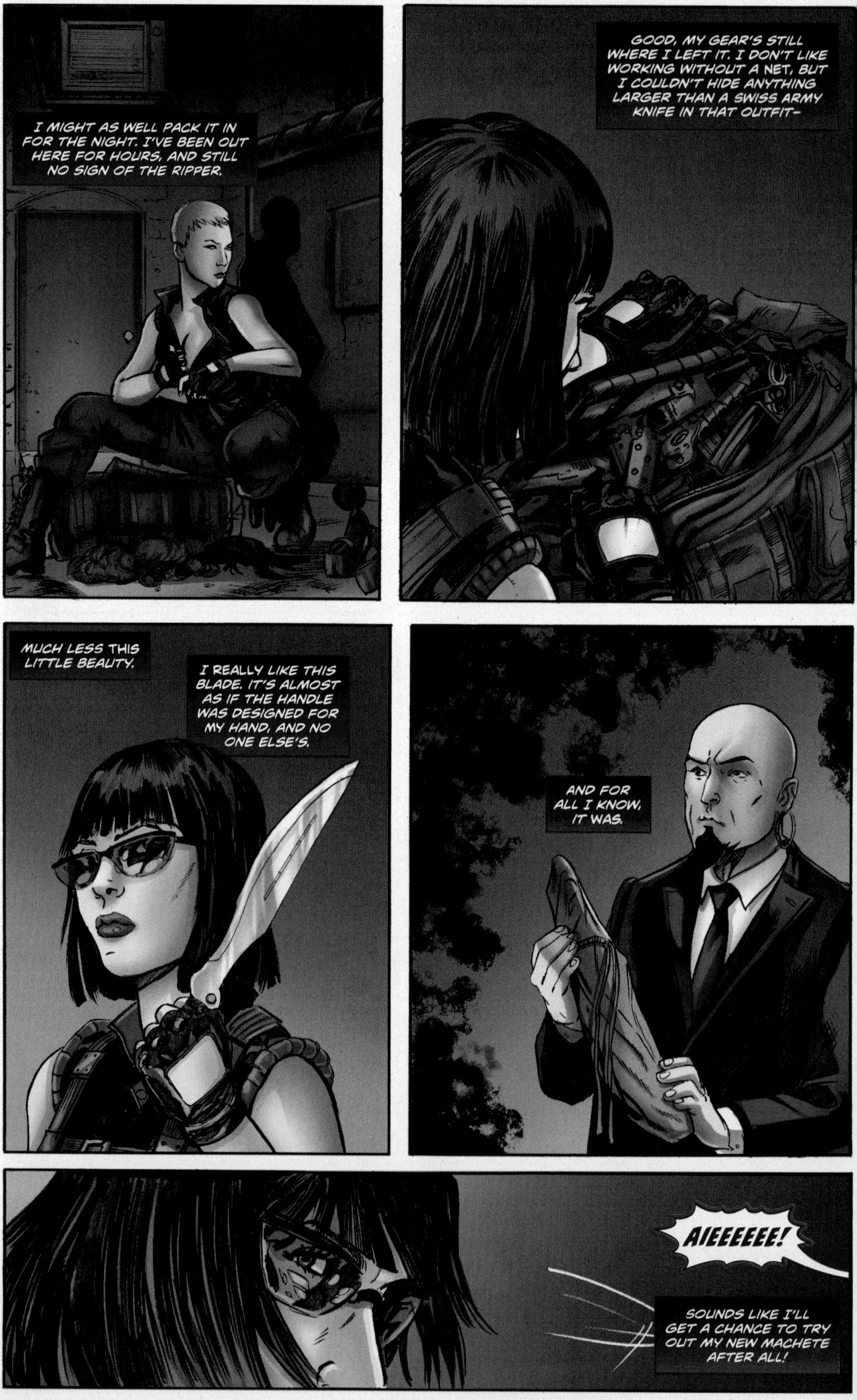
I MIGHT AS WELL PACK IT IN FOR THE NIGHT. I'VE BEEN OUT HERE FOR HOURS, AND STILL NO SIGN OF THE RIPPER.
GOOD, MY GEAR'S STILL WHERE I LEFT IT. I DON'T LIKE WORKING WITHOUT A NET, BUT I COULDN'T HIDE ANYTHING LARGER THAN A SWISS ARMY KNIFE IN THAT OUTFIT–
MUCH LESS THIS LITTLE BEAUTY.
I REALLY LIKE THIS BLADE. IT'S ALMOST AS IF THE HANDLE WAS DESIGNED FOR MY HAND, AND NO ONE ELSE'S.
AND FOR ALL I KNOW, IT WAS.
AIEEEEEE!
SOUNDS LIKE I'LL GET A CHANCE TO TRY OUT MY NEW MACHETE AFTER ALL!

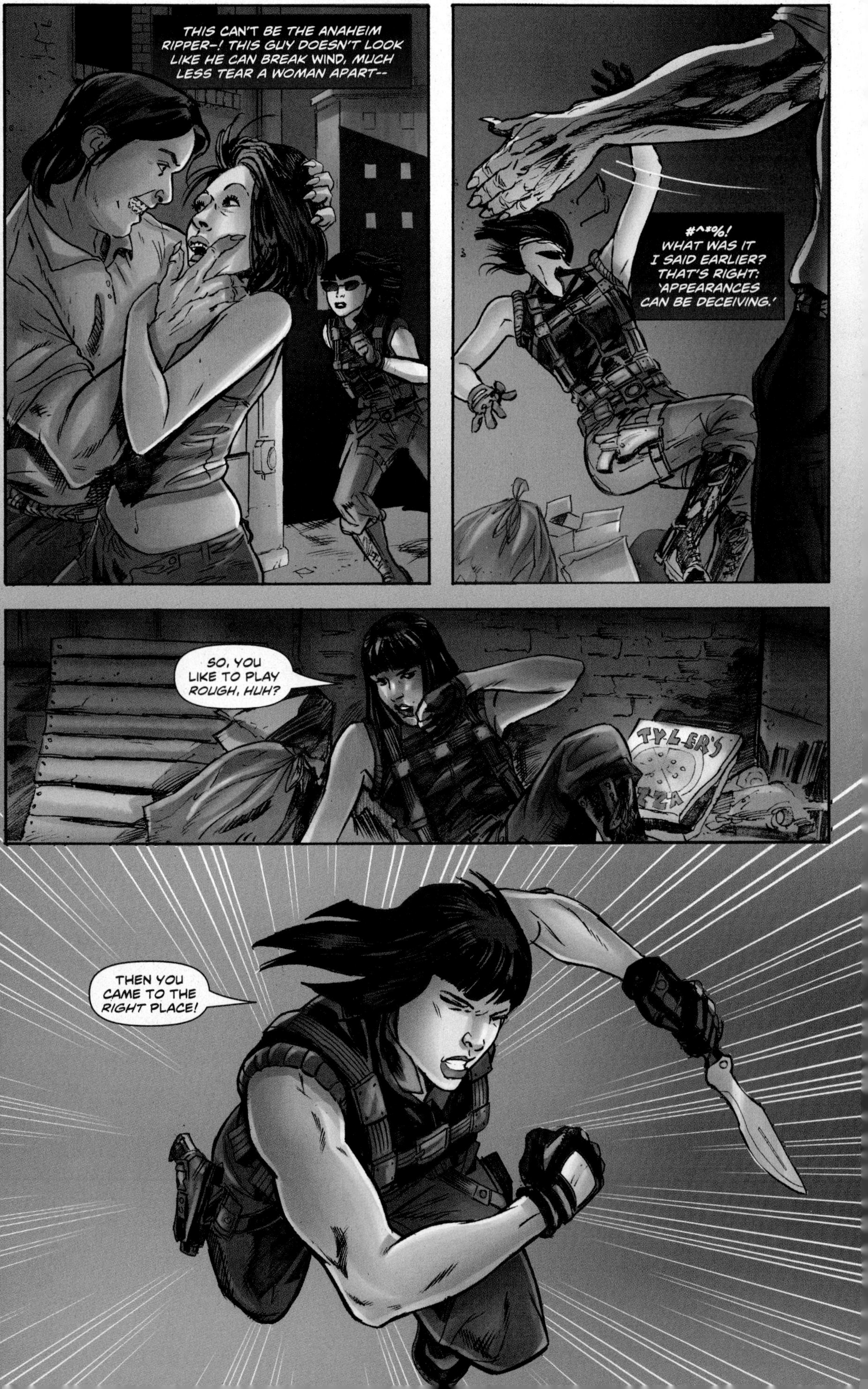
THIS CAN'T BE THE ANAHEIM RIPPER–! THIS GUY DOESN'T LOOK LIKE HE CAN BREAK WIND, MUCH LESS TEAR A WOMAN APART--
#^*%! WHAT WAS IT I SAID EARLIER? THAT'S RIGHT: 'APPEARANCES CAN BE DECEIVING.'
SO, YOU LIKE TO PLAY ROUGH, HUH?
TYLER'S
THEN YOU CAME TO THE RIGHT PLACE!

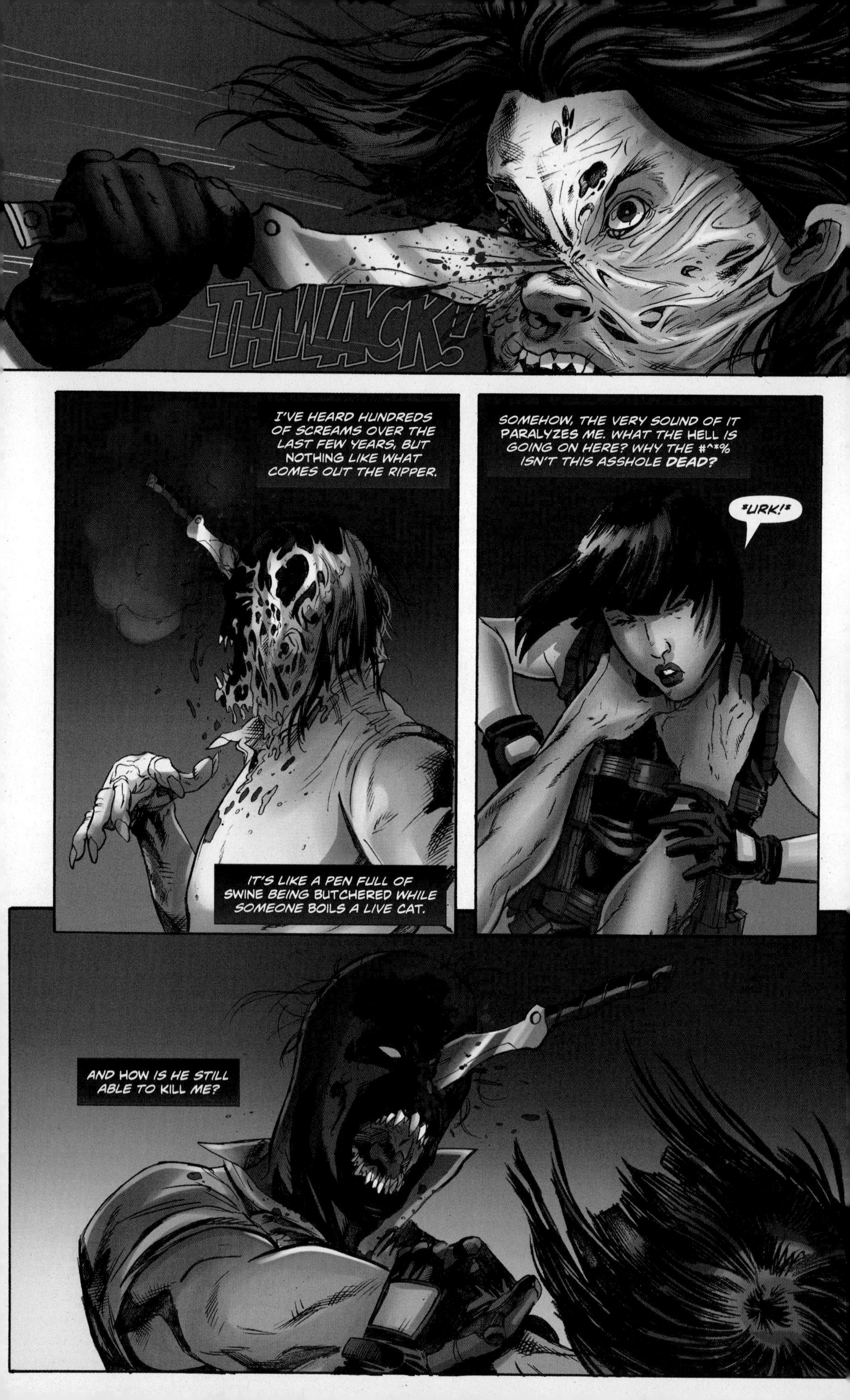
THWACK!
I'VE HEARD HUNDREDS OF SCREAMS OVER THE LAST FEW YEARS, BUT NOTHING LIKE WHAT COMES OUT THE RIPPER.
IT'S LIKE A PEN FULL OF SWINE BEING BUTCHERED WHILE SOMEONE BOILS A LIVE CAT.
SOMEHOW, THE VERY SOUND OF IT PARALYZES ME. WHAT THE HELL IS GOING ON HERE? WHY THE #^*% ISN'T THIS ASSHOLE DEAD?
URK!
AND HOW IS HE STILL ABLE TO KILL ME?

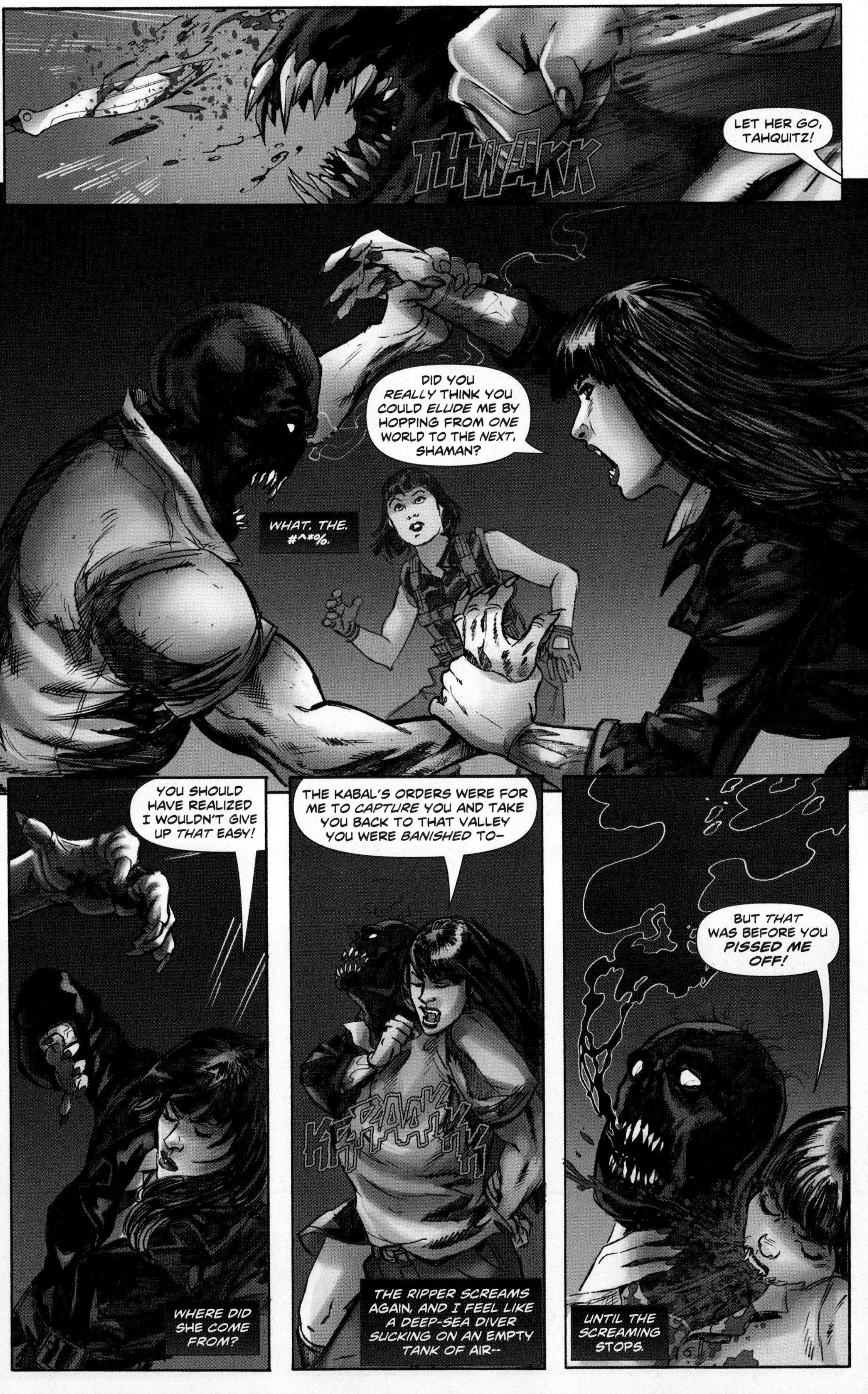
THWAKK
LET HER GO, TAHQUITZ!
DID YOU REALLY THINK YOU COULD ELUDE ME BY HOPPING FROM ONE WORLD TO THE NEXT, SHAMAN?
WHAT. THE. #^*%.
YOU SHOULD HAVE REALIZED I WOULDN'T GIVE UP THAT EASY!
WHERE DID SHE COME FROM?
THE KABAL'S ORDERS WERE FOR ME TO CAPTURE YOU AND TAKE YOU BACK TO THAT VALLEY YOU WERE BANISHED TO--
THE RIPPER SCREAMS AGAIN, AND I FEEL LIKE A DEEP-SEA DIVER SUCKING ON AN EMPTY TANK OF AIR--
BUT THAT WAS BEFORE YOU PISSED ME OFF!
UNTIL THE SCREAMING STOPS.

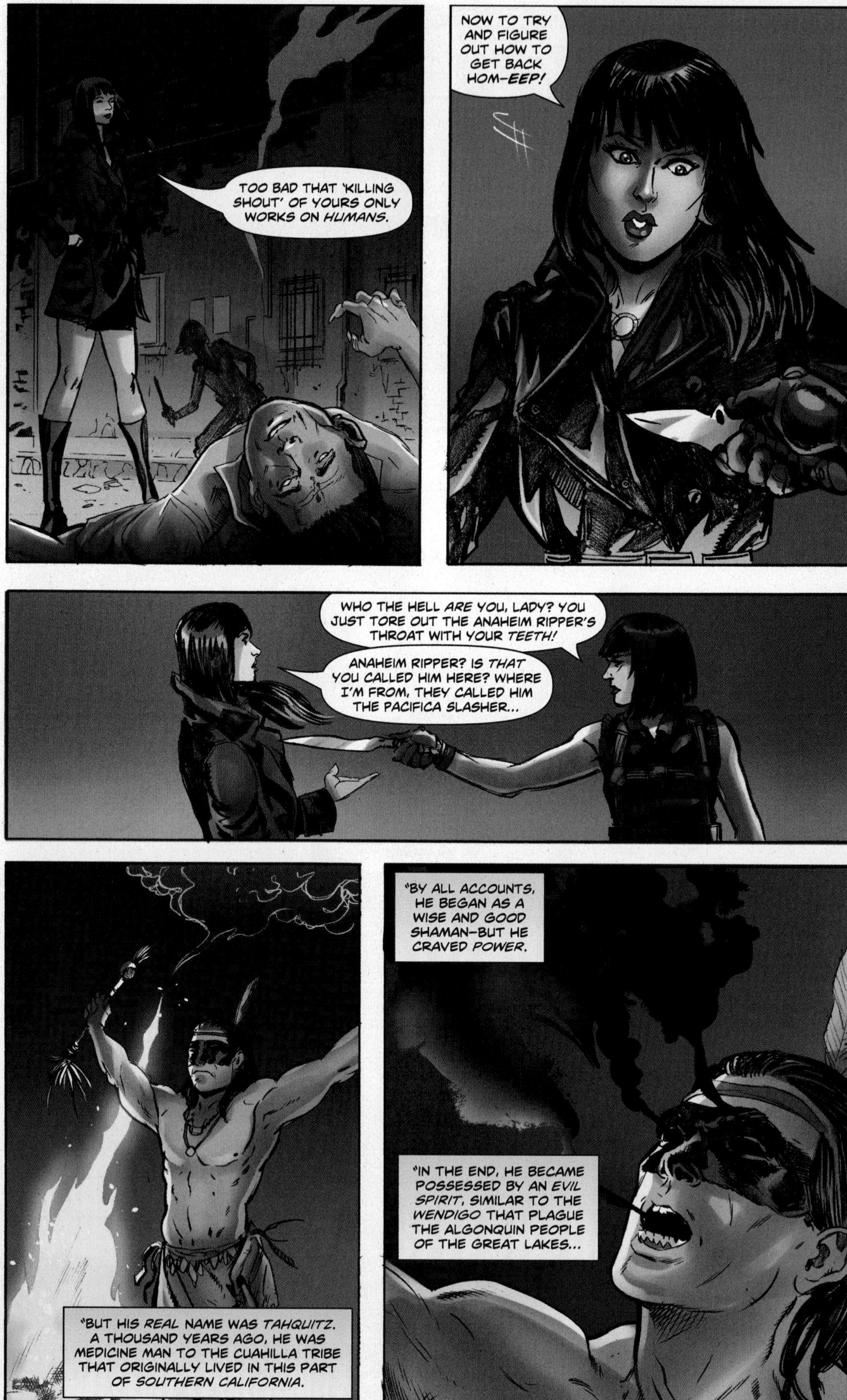
TOO BAD THAT 'KILLING SHOUT' OF YOURS ONLY WORKS ON *HUMANS*.
NOW TO TRY AND FIGURE OUT HOW TO GET BACK HOM-*EEP!*
WHO THE HELL *ARE* YOU, LADY? YOU JUST TORE OUT THE ANAHEIM RIPPER'S THROAT WITH YOUR *TEETH!*
ANAHEIM RIPPER? IS *THAT* YOU CALLED HIM HERE? WHERE I'M FROM, THEY CALLED HIM THE PACIFICA SLASHER...
"BUT HIS *REAL* NAME WAS *TAHQUITZ*. A THOUSAND YEARS AGO, HE WAS MEDICINE MAN TO THE CUAHILLA TRIBE THAT ORIGINALLY LIVED IN THIS PART OF *SOUTHERN CALIFORNIA*.
"BY ALL ACCOUNTS, HE BEGAN AS A WISE AND GOOD SHAMAN—BUT HE CRAVED *POWER*.
"IN THE END, HE BECAME POSSESSED BY AN *EVIL SPIRIT*, SIMILAR TO THE *WENDIGO* THAT PLAGUE THE ALGONQUIN PEOPLE OF THE GREAT LAKES...

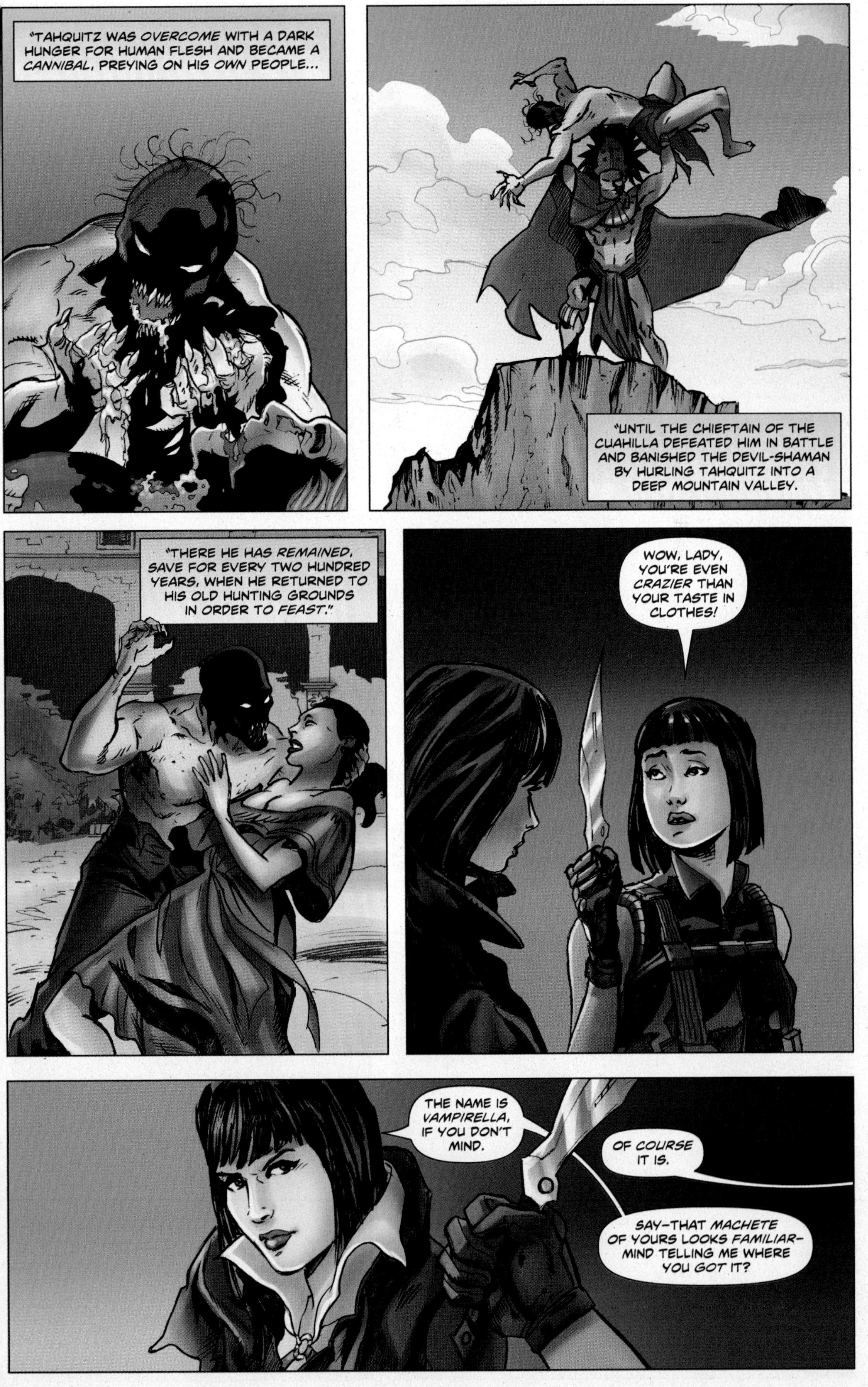
"TAHQUITZ WAS OVERCOME WITH A DARK HUNGER FOR HUMAN FLESH AND BECAME A CANNIBAL, PREYING ON HIS OWN PEOPLE...
"UNTIL THE CHIEFTAIN OF THE CUAHILLA DEFEATED HIM IN BATTLE AND BANISHED THE DEVIL-SHAMAN BY HURLING TAHQUITZ INTO A DEEP MOUNTAIN VALLEY.
"THERE HE HAS REMAINED, SAVE FOR EVERY TWO HUNDRED YEARS, WHEN HE RETURNED TO HIS OLD HUNTING GROUNDS IN ORDER TO FEAST."
WOW, LADY, YOU'RE EVEN CRAZIER THAN YOUR TASTE IN CLOTHES!
THE NAME IS VAMPIRELLA, IF YOU DON'T MIND.
OF COURSE IT IS.
SAY–THAT MACHETE OF YOURS LOOKS FAMILIAR–MIND TELLING ME WHERE YOU GOT IT?

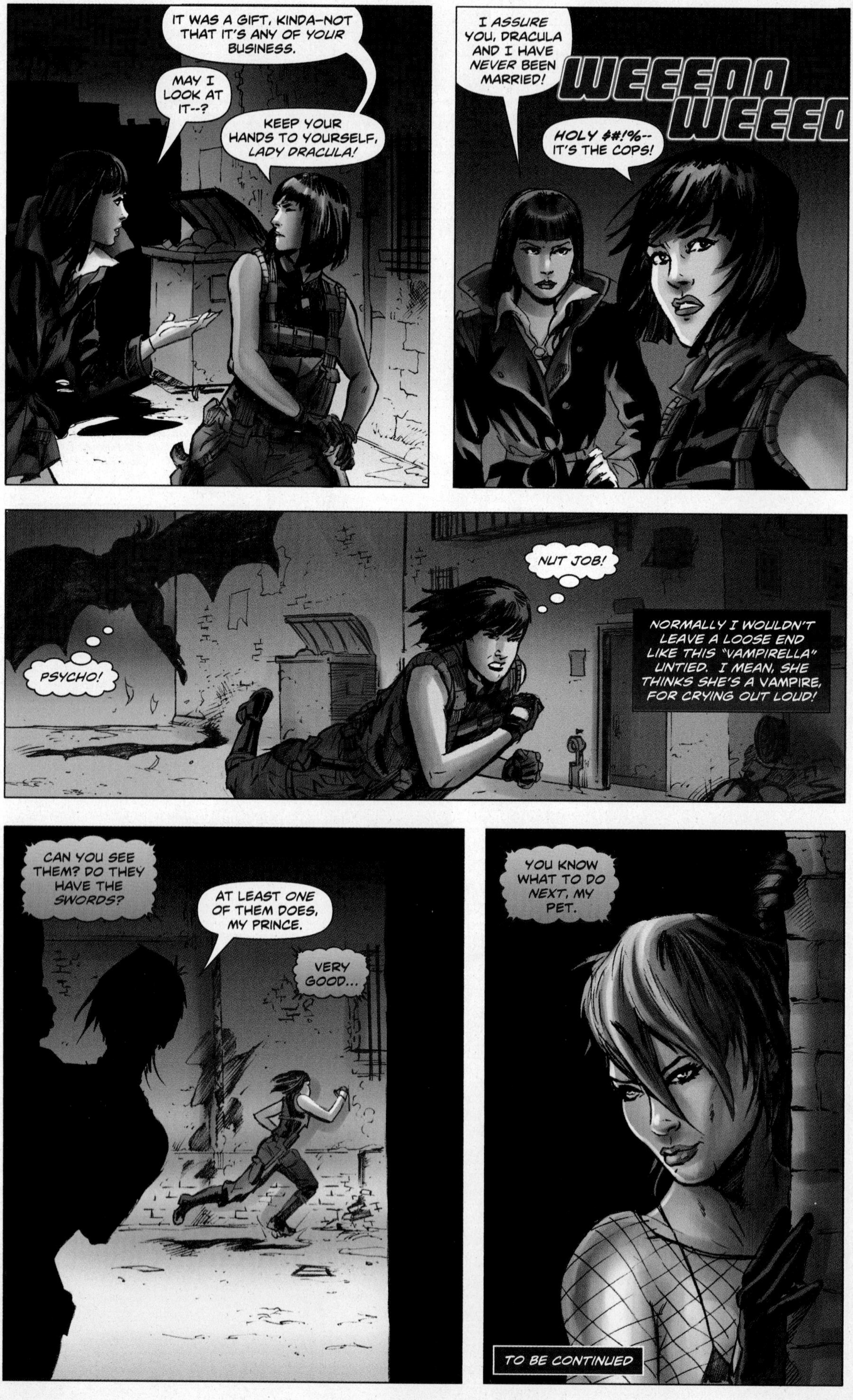

IT WAS A GIFT, KINDA--NOT THAT IT'S ANY OF YOUR BUSINESS.
MAY I LOOK AT IT--?
KEEP YOUR HANDS TO YOURSELF, LADY DRACULA!
I ASSURE YOU, DRACULA AND I HAVE NEVER BEEN MARRIED!
WEEEOO WEEEO
HOLY $#!%-- IT'S THE COPS!
NUT JOB!
PSYCHO!
NORMALLY I WOULDN'T LEAVE A LOOSE END LIKE THIS "VAMPIRELLA" UNTIED. I MEAN, SHE THINKS SHE'S A VAMPIRE, FOR CRYING OUT LOUD!
CAN YOU SEE THEM? DO THEY HAVE THE SWORDS?
AT LEAST ONE OF THEM DOES, MY PRINCE.
VERY GOOD...
YOU KNOW WHAT TO DO NEXT, MY PET.
TO BE CONTINUED

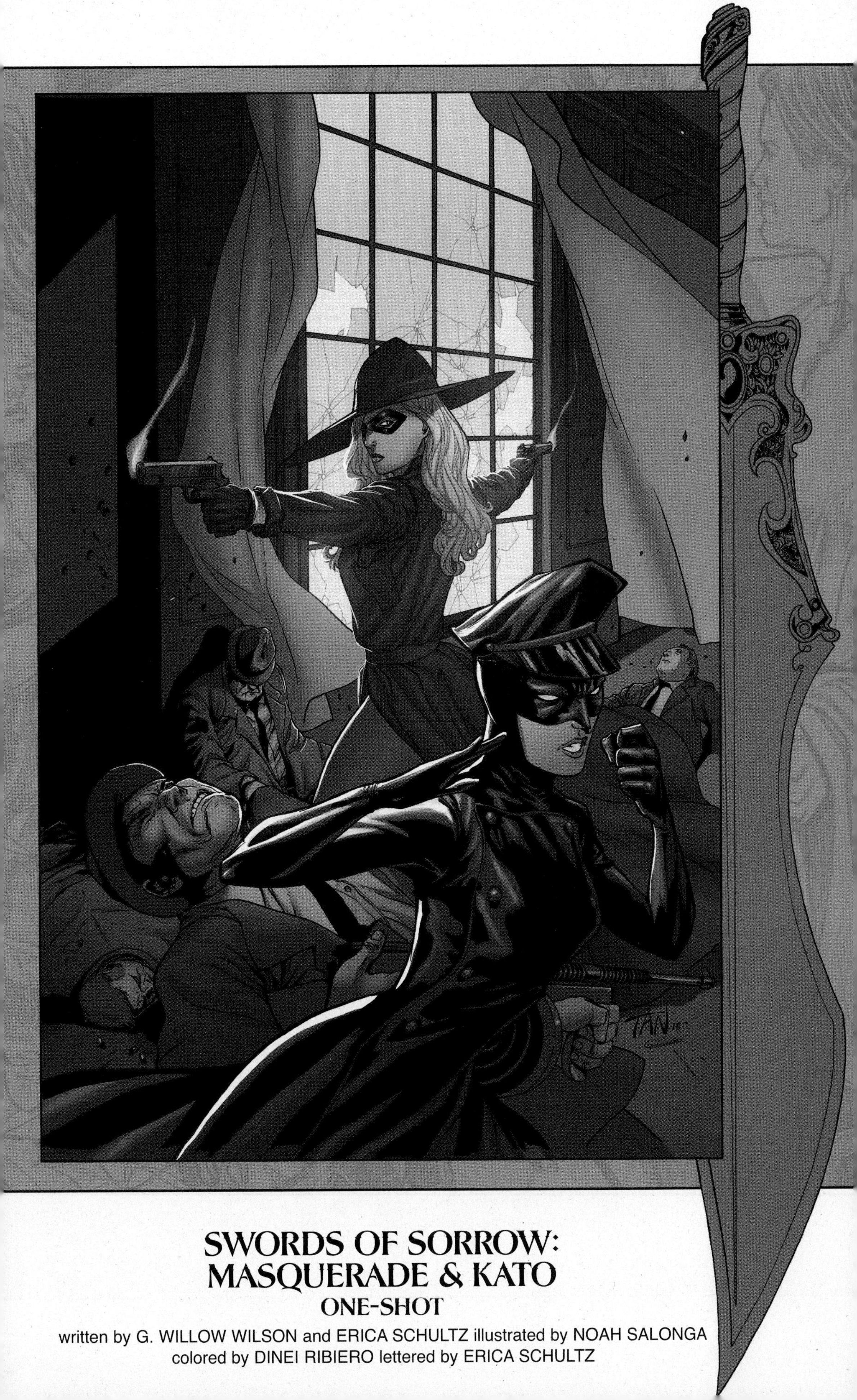

SWORDS OF SORROW: MASQUERADE & KATO

ONE-SHOT

written by G. WILLOW WILSON and ERICA SCHULTZ illustrated by NOAH SALONGA
colored by DINEI RIBIERO lettered by ERICA SCHULTZ

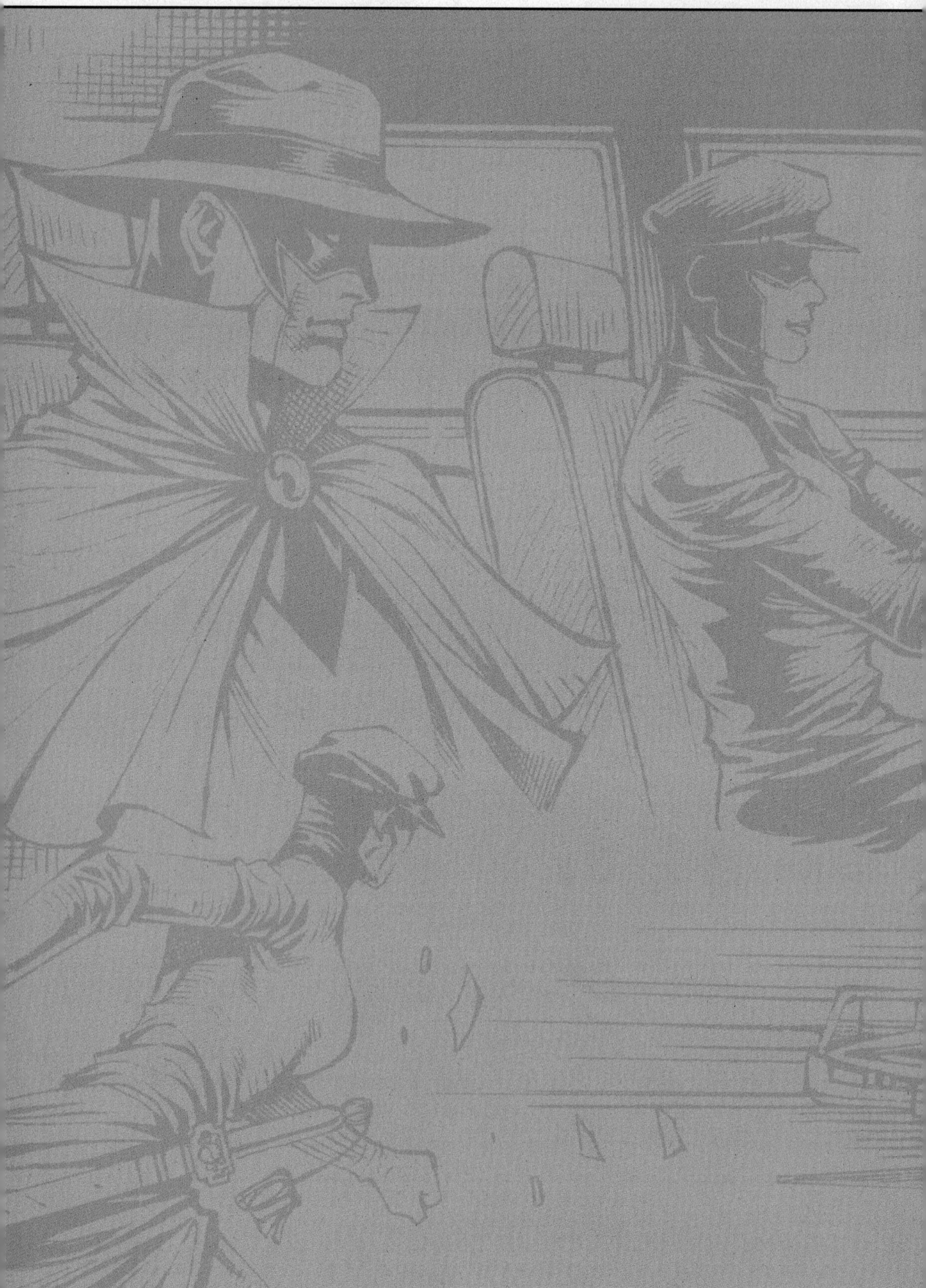

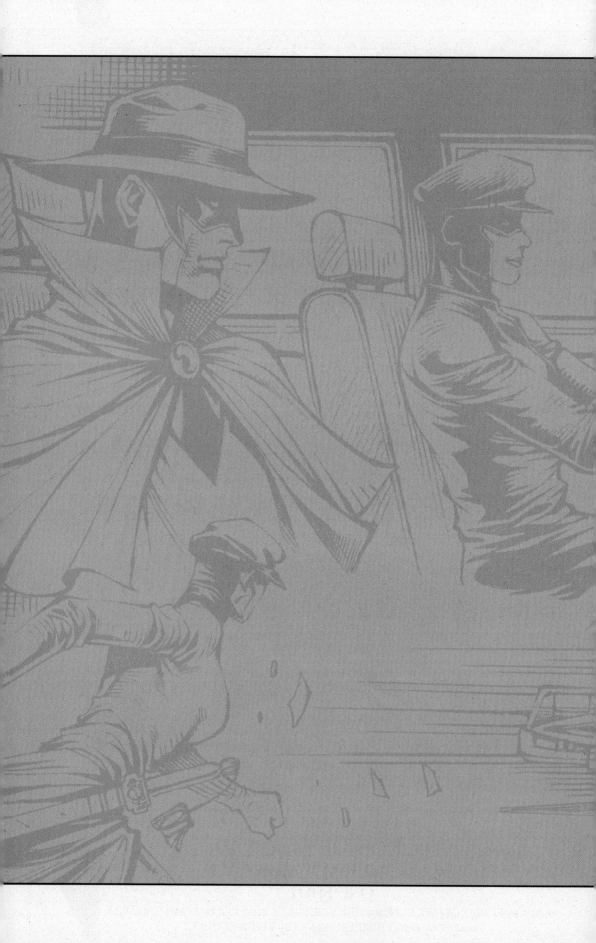

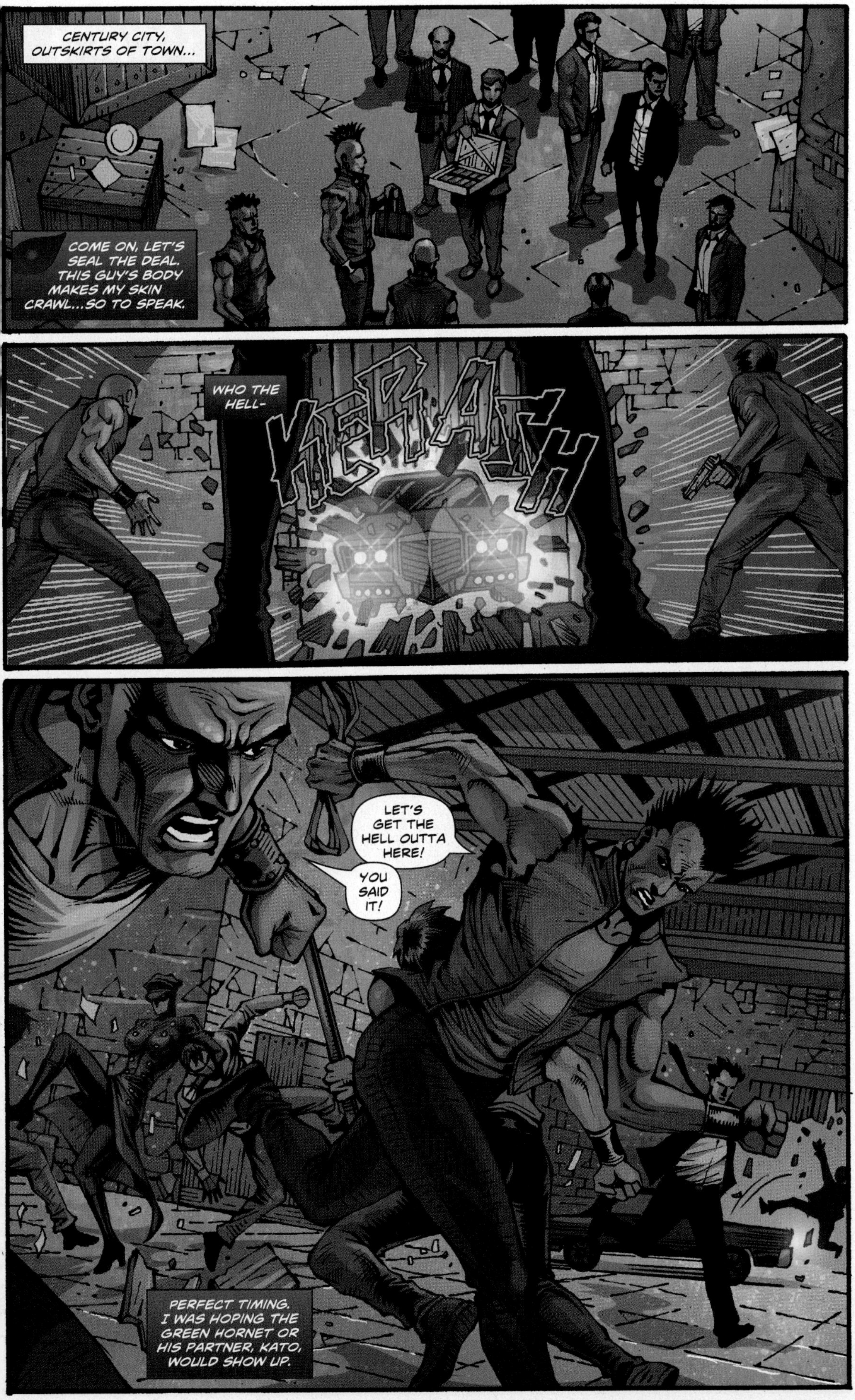
CENTURY CITY, OUTSKIRTS OF TOWN...
COME ON, LET'S SEAL THE DEAL. THIS GUY'S BODY MAKES MY SKIN CRAWL...SO TO SPEAK.
WHO THE HELL-
KERASH
LET'S GET THE HELL OUTTA HERE!
YOU SAID IT!
PERFECT TIMING. I WAS HOPING THE GREEN HORNET OR HIS PARTNER, KATO, WOULD SHOW UP.

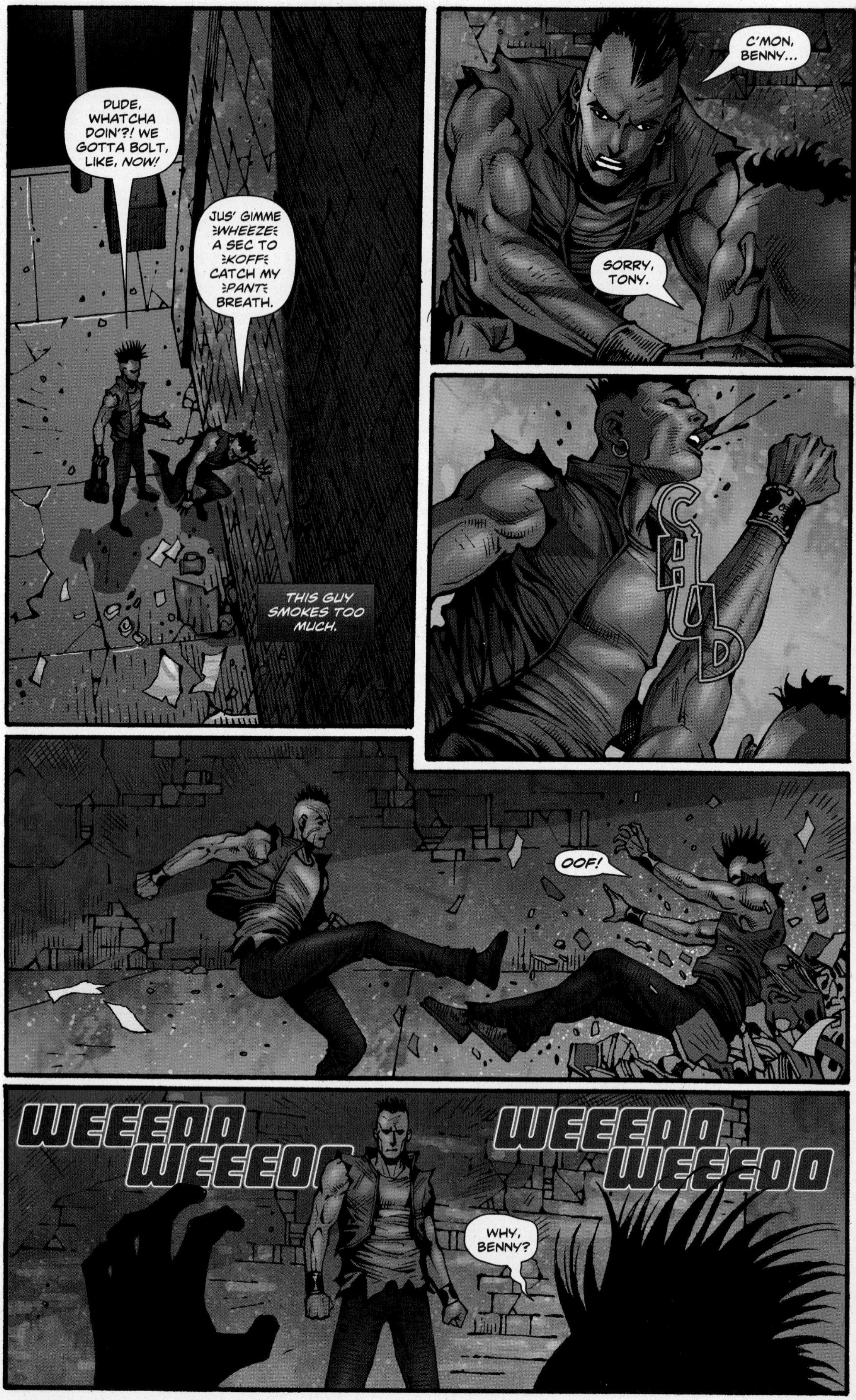
DUDE, WHATCHA DOIN'?! WE GOTTA BOLT, LIKE, NOW!
JUS' GIMME *WHEEZE* A SEC TO *KOFF* CATCH MY *PANT* BREATH.
THIS GUY SMOKES TOO MUCH.
C'MON, BENNY...
SORRY, TONY.
CHUD
OOF!
WEEEOO WEEEOO
WEEEOO WEEEOO
WHY, BENNY?

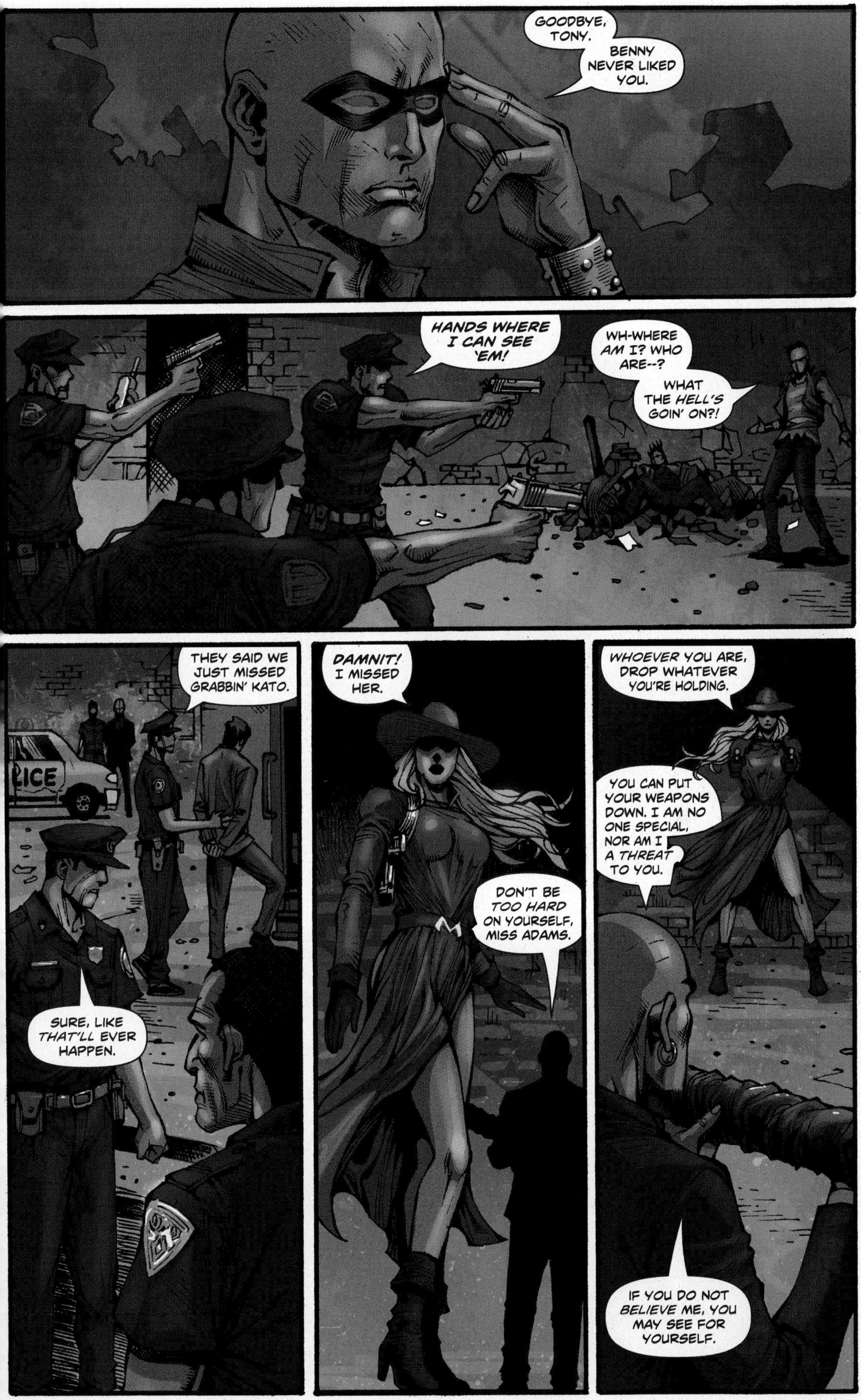
GOODBYE, TONY.
BENNY NEVER LIKED YOU.
HANDS WHERE I CAN SEE 'EM!
WH-WHERE AM I? WHO ARE--?
WHAT THE HELL'S GOIN' ON?!
THEY SAID WE JUST MISSED GRABBIN' KATO.
SURE, LIKE THAT'LL EVER HAPPEN.
LICE
DAMNIT! I MISSED HER.
DON'T BE TOO HARD ON YOURSELF, MISS ADAMS.
WHOEVER YOU ARE, DROP WHATEVER YOU'RE HOLDING.
YOU CAN PUT YOUR WEAPONS DOWN. I AM NO ONE SPECIAL, NOR AM I A THREAT TO YOU.
IF YOU DO NOT BELIEVE ME, YOU MAY SEE FOR YOURSELF.

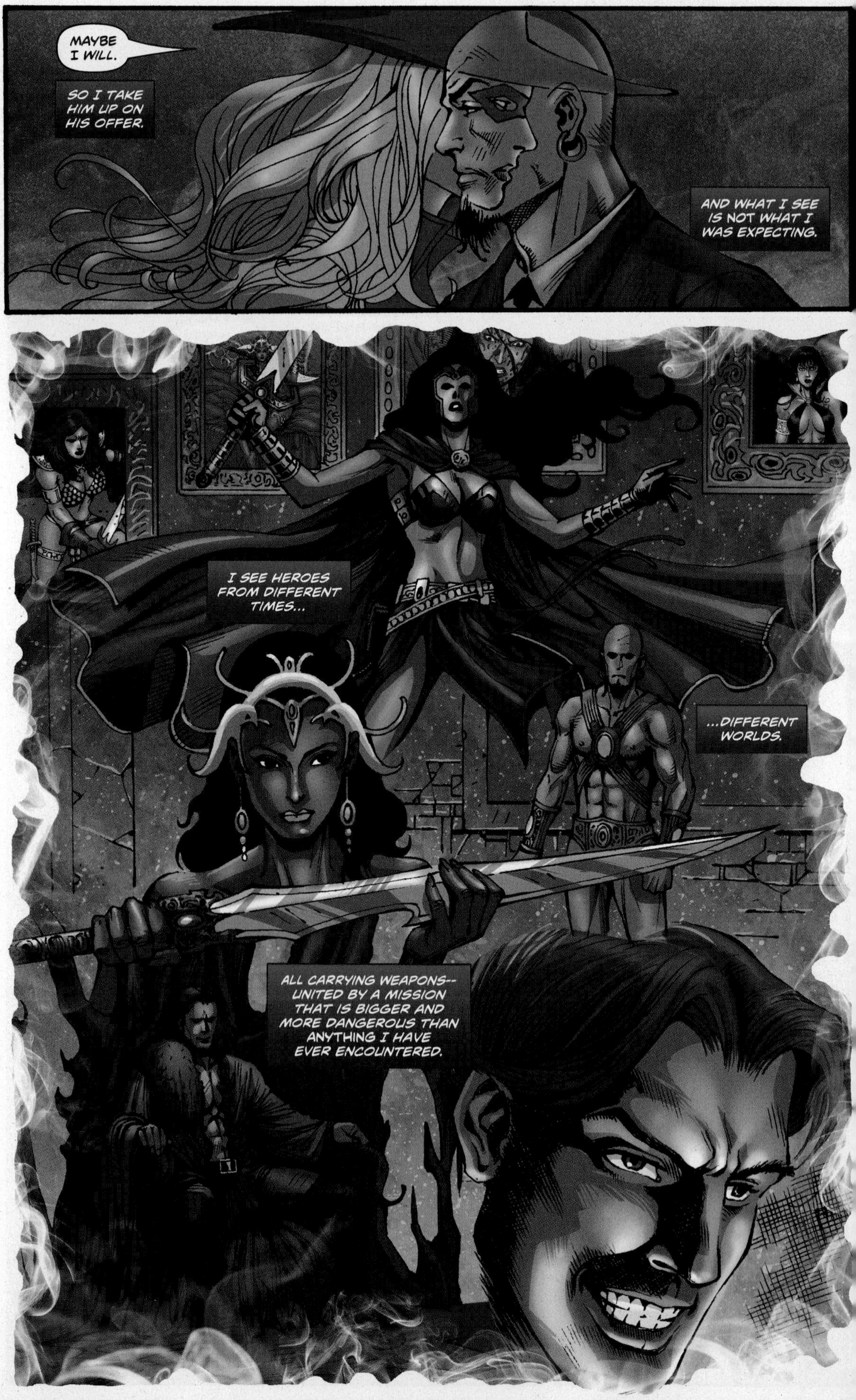
MAYBE I WILL.
SO I TAKE HIM UP ON HIS OFFER.
AND WHAT I SEE IS NOT WHAT I WAS EXPECTING.
I SEE HEROES FROM DIFFERENT TIMES...
...DIFFERENT WORLDS.
ALL CARRYING WEAPONS-- UNITED BY A MISSION THAT IS BIGGER AND MORE DANGEROUS THAN ANYTHING I HAVE EVER ENCOUNTERED.

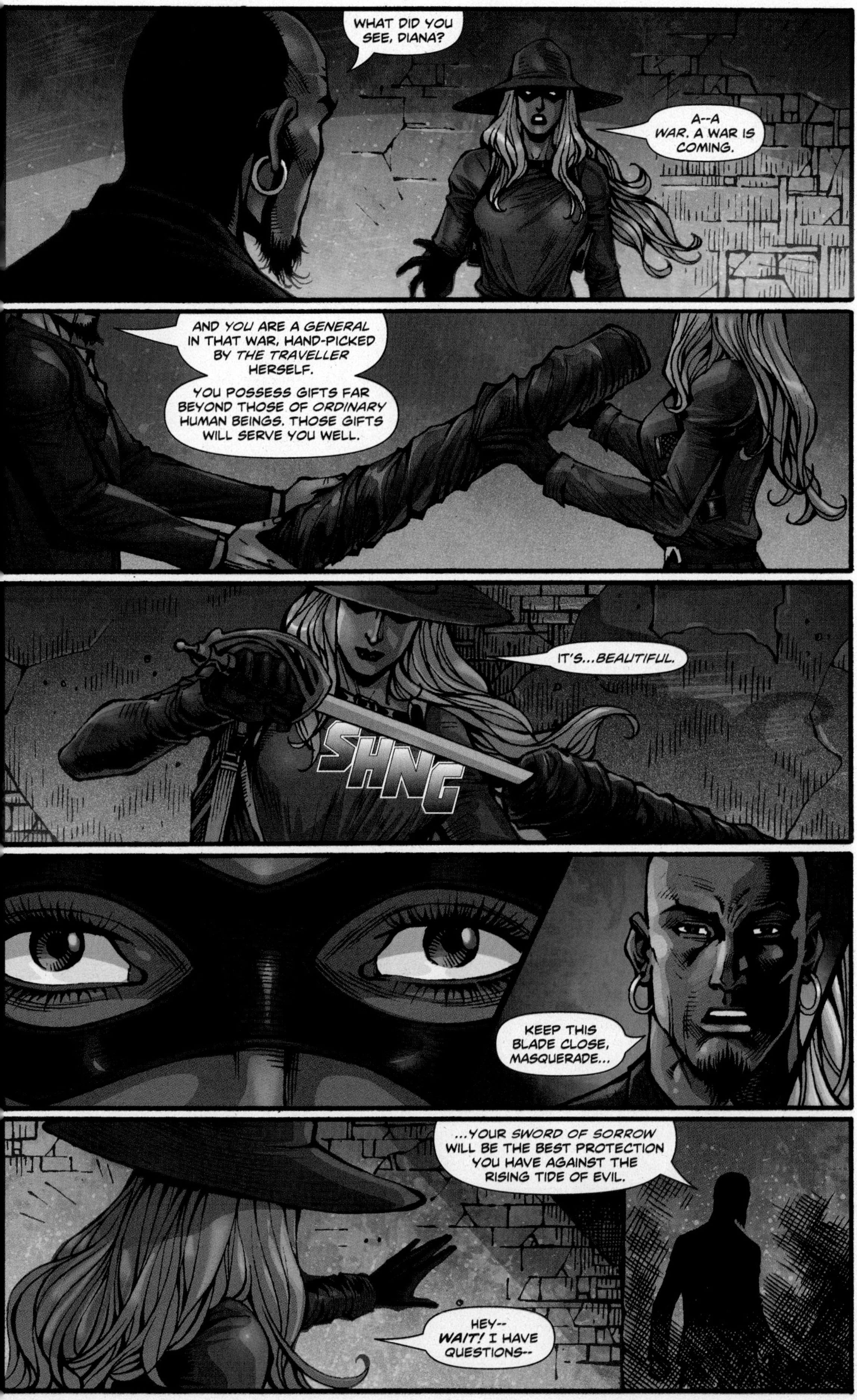
WHAT DID YOU SEE, DIANA?
A--A WAR. A WAR IS COMING.
AND YOU ARE A *GENERAL* IN THAT WAR, HAND-PICKED BY *THE TRAVELLER* HERSELF.
YOU POSSESS GIFTS FAR BEYOND THOSE OF *ORDINARY* HUMAN BEINGS. THOSE GIFTS WILL SERVE YOU WELL.
IT'S...*BEAUTIFUL.*
SHNG
KEEP THIS BLADE CLOSE, MASQUERADE...
...YOUR *SWORD OF SORROW* WILL BE THE BEST PROTECTION YOU HAVE AGAINST THE RISING TIDE OF EVIL.
HEY-- *WAIT!* I HAVE QUESTIONS--

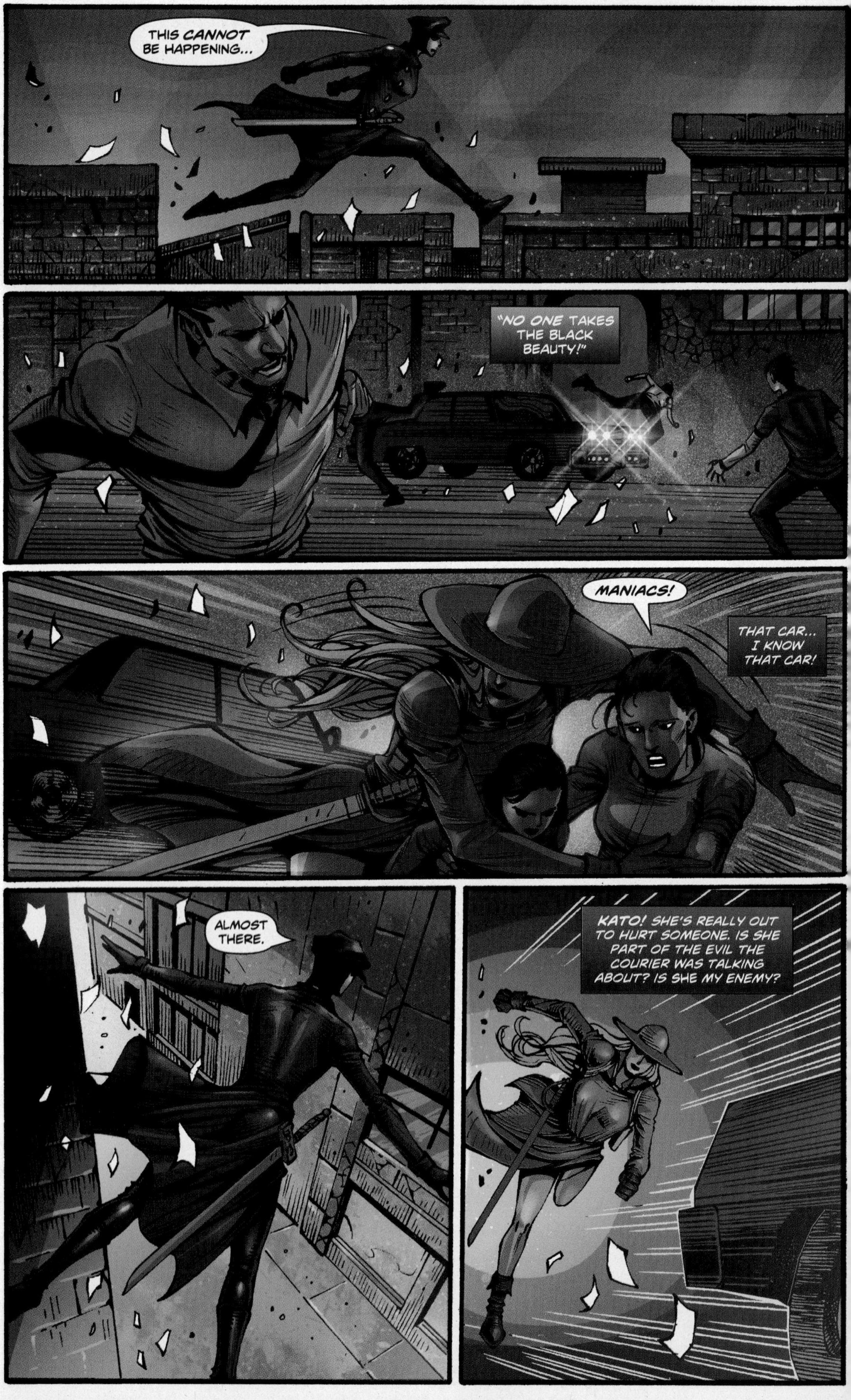
THIS CANNOT BE HAPPENING...
"NO ONE TAKES THE BLACK BEAUTY!"
MANIACS!
THAT CAR... I KNOW THAT CAR!
ALMOST THERE.
KATO! SHE'S REALLY OUT TO HURT SOMEONE. IS SHE PART OF THE EVIL THE COURIER WAS TALKING ABOUT? IS SHE MY ENEMY?

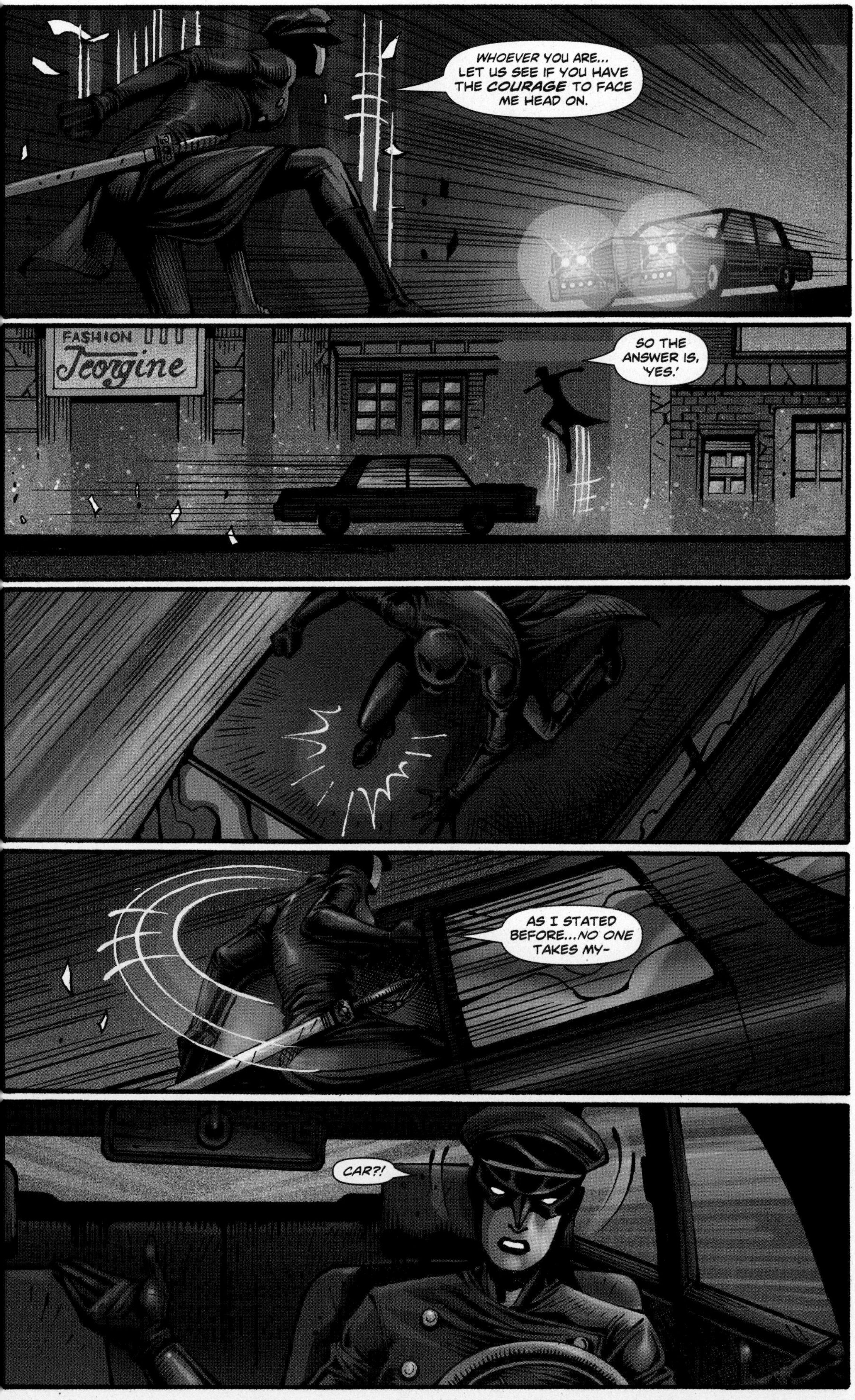
WHOEVER YOU ARE... LET US SEE IF YOU HAVE THE COURAGE TO FACE ME HEAD ON.
FASHION
Jeorgine
SO THE ANSWER IS, 'YES.'
AS I STATED BEFORE...NO ONE TAKES MY-
CAR?!

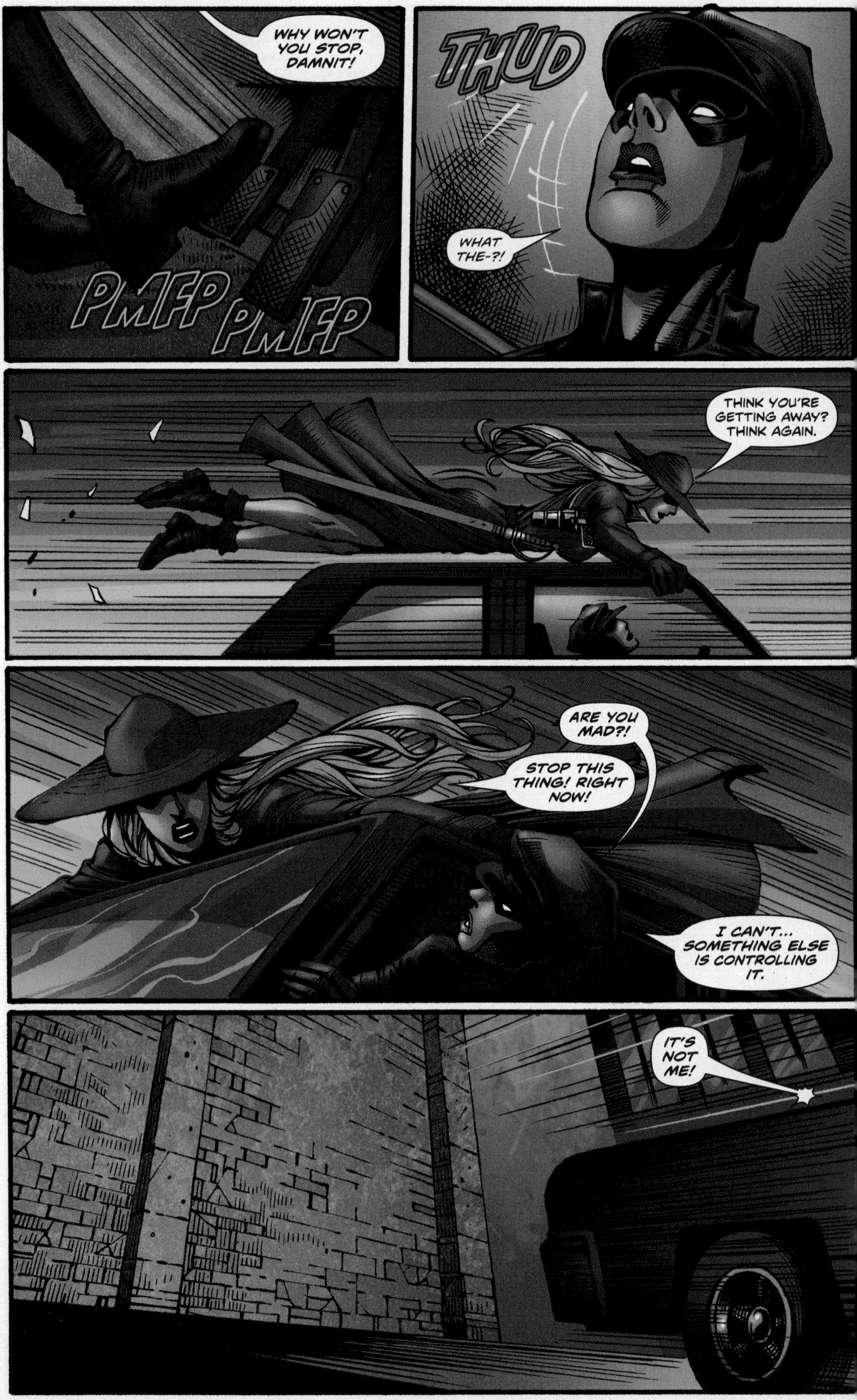
WHY WON'T YOU STOP, DAMNIT!
PMFP PMFP
THUD
WHAT THE-?!
THINK YOU'RE GETTING AWAY? THINK AGAIN.
ARE YOU MAD?!
STOP THIS THING! RIGHT NOW!
I CAN'T... SOMETHING ELSE IS CONTROLLING IT.
IT'S NOT ME!

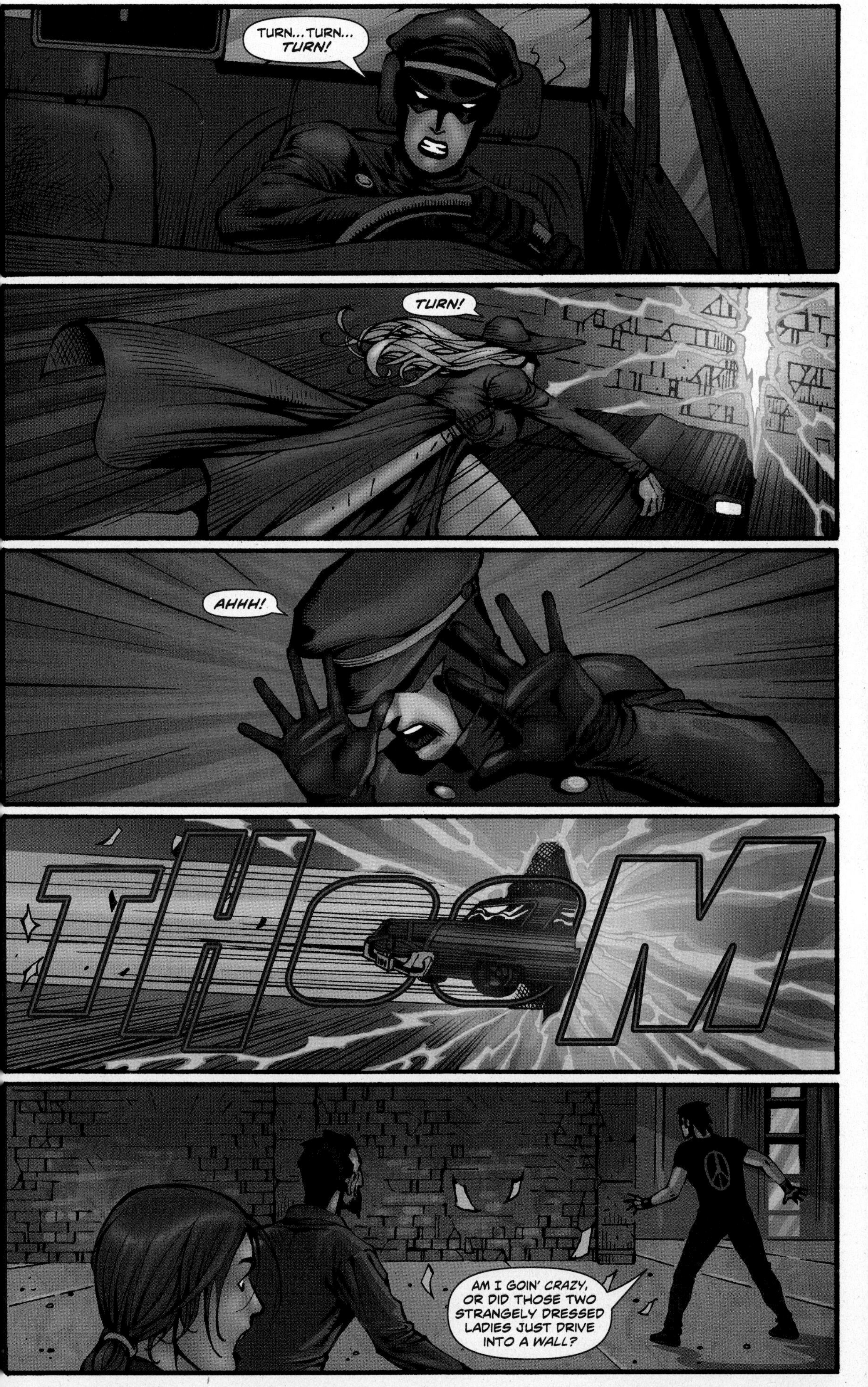
TURN... TURN... *TURN!*
TURN!
AHHH!
THOOM
AM I GOIN' CRAZY, OR DID THOSE TWO STRANGELY DRESSED LADIES JUST DRIVE INTO A WALL?

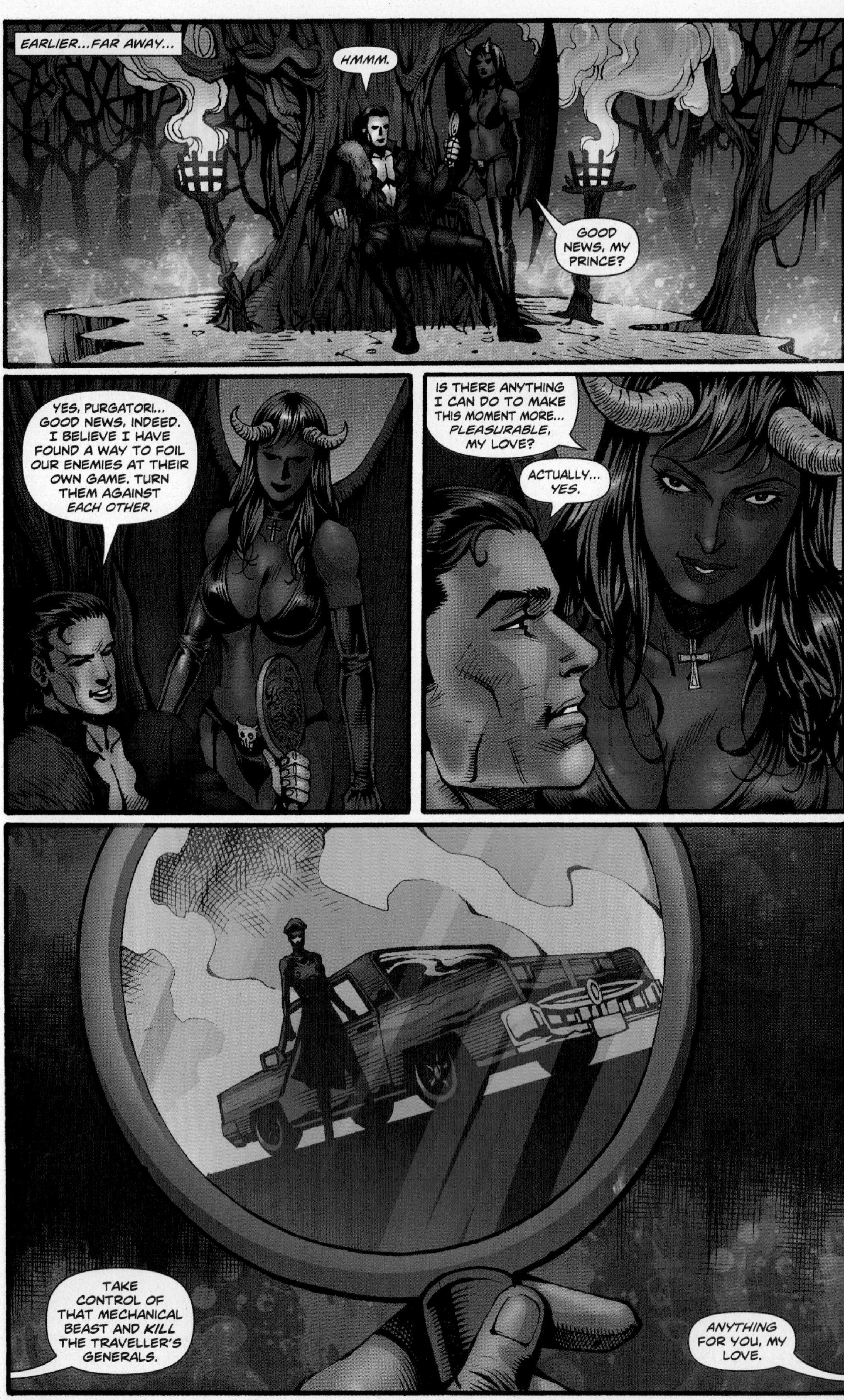
EARLIER...FAR AWAY...
HMMM.
GOOD NEWS, MY PRINCE?
YES, PURGATORI... GOOD NEWS, INDEED. I BELIEVE I HAVE FOUND A WAY TO FOIL OUR ENEMIES AT THEIR OWN GAME. TURN THEM AGAINST EACH OTHER.
IS THERE ANYTHING I CAN DO TO MAKE THIS MOMENT MORE... PLEASURABLE, MY LOVE?
ACTUALLY... YES.
TAKE CONTROL OF THAT MECHANICAL BEAST AND KILL THE TRAVELLER'S GENERALS.
ANYTHING FOR YOU, MY LOVE.

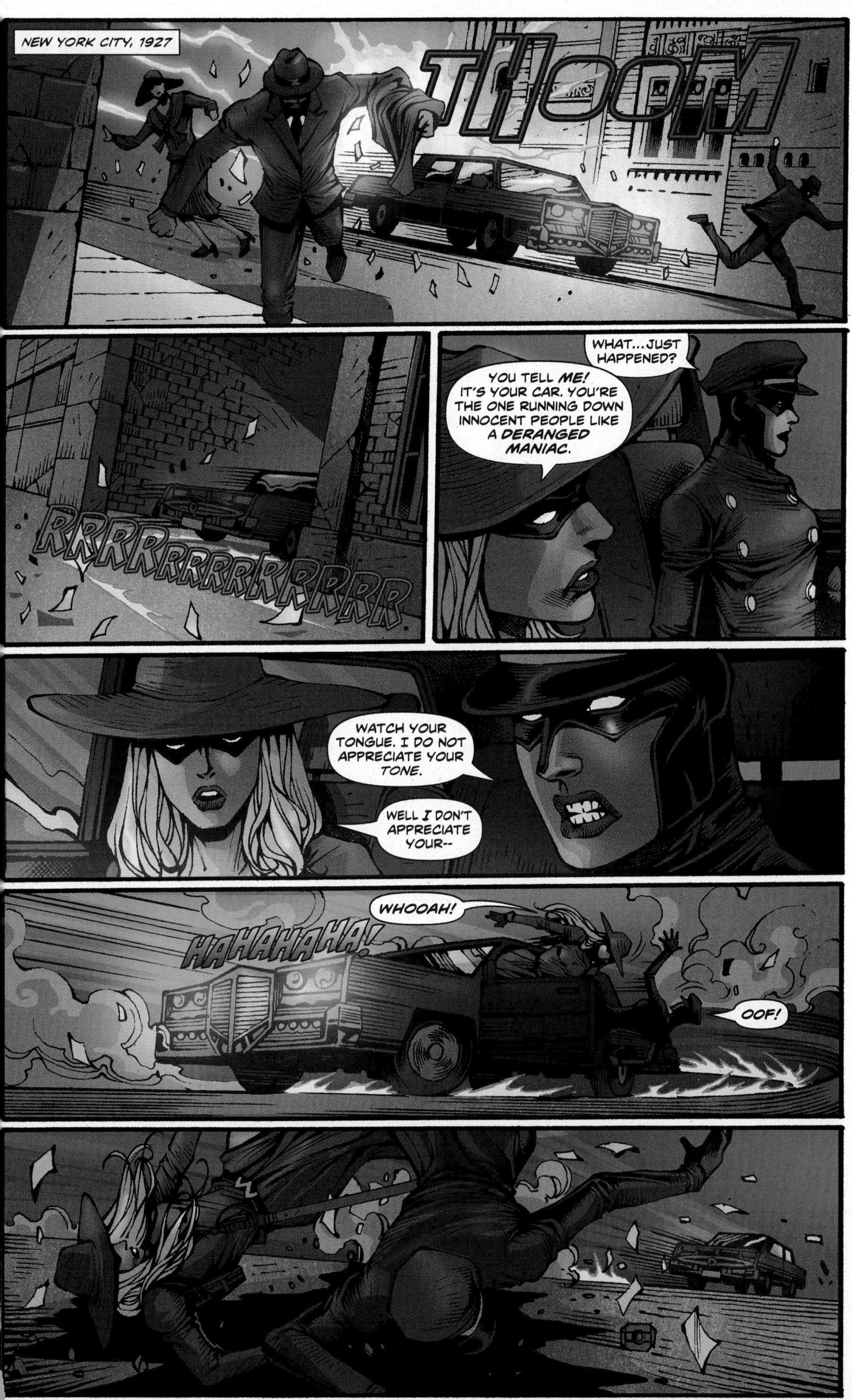
NEW YORK CITY, 1927
THOOM
RRRRRRRRRRRRRRRRR
WHAT...JUST HAPPENED?
YOU TELL ME! IT'S YOUR CAR. YOU'RE THE ONE RUNNING DOWN INNOCENT PEOPLE LIKE A DERANGED MANIAC.
WATCH YOUR TONGUE. I DO NOT APPRECIATE YOUR TONE.
WELL I DON'T APPRECIATE YOUR--
WHOOAH!
HAHAHAHAHA!
OOF!

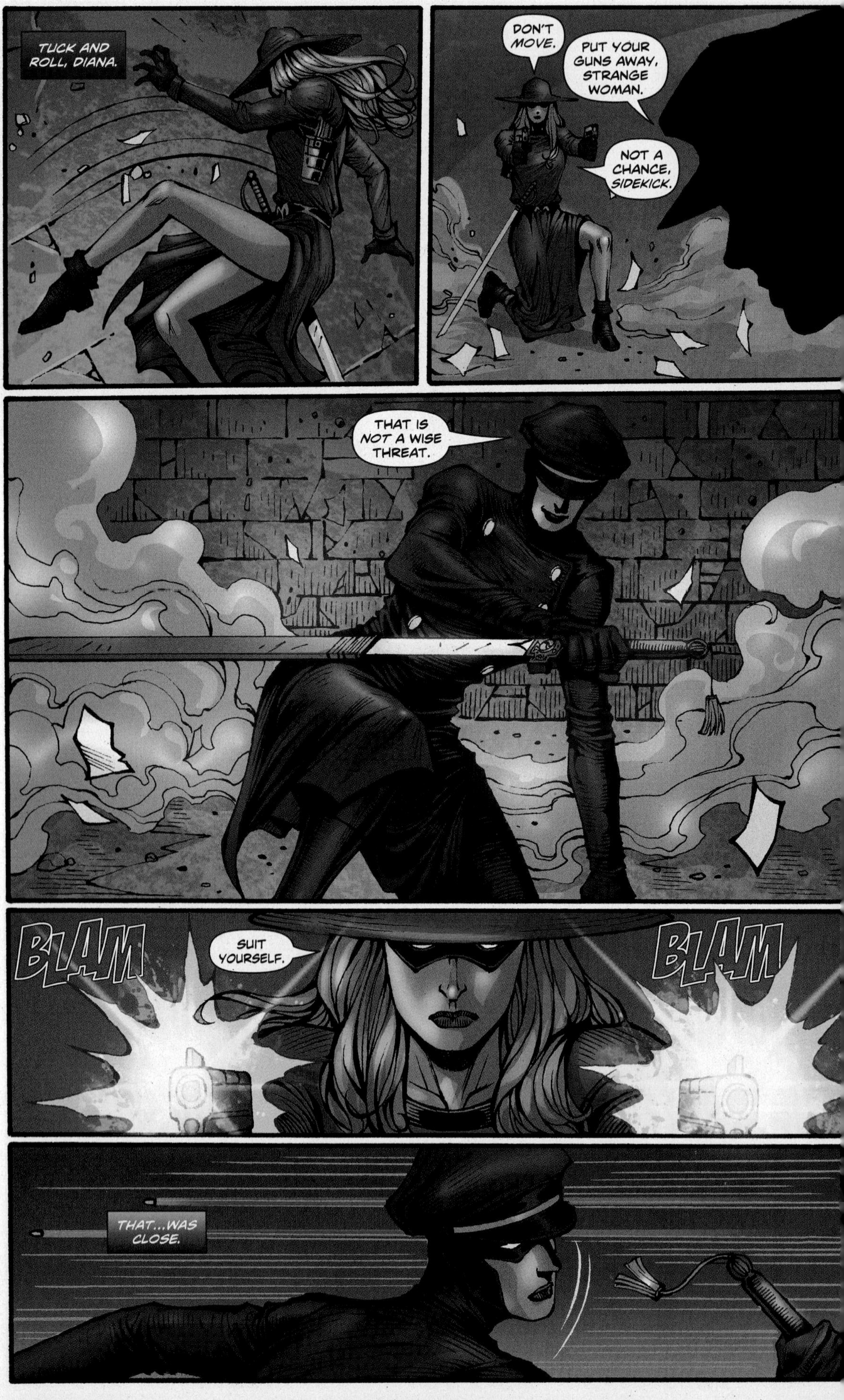
TUCK AND ROLL, DIANA.
DON'T MOVE.
PUT YOUR GUNS AWAY, STRANGE WOMAN.
NOT A CHANCE, SIDEKICK.
THAT IS NOT A WISE THREAT.
BLAM
SUIT YOURSELF.
BLAM
THAT...WAS CLOSE.

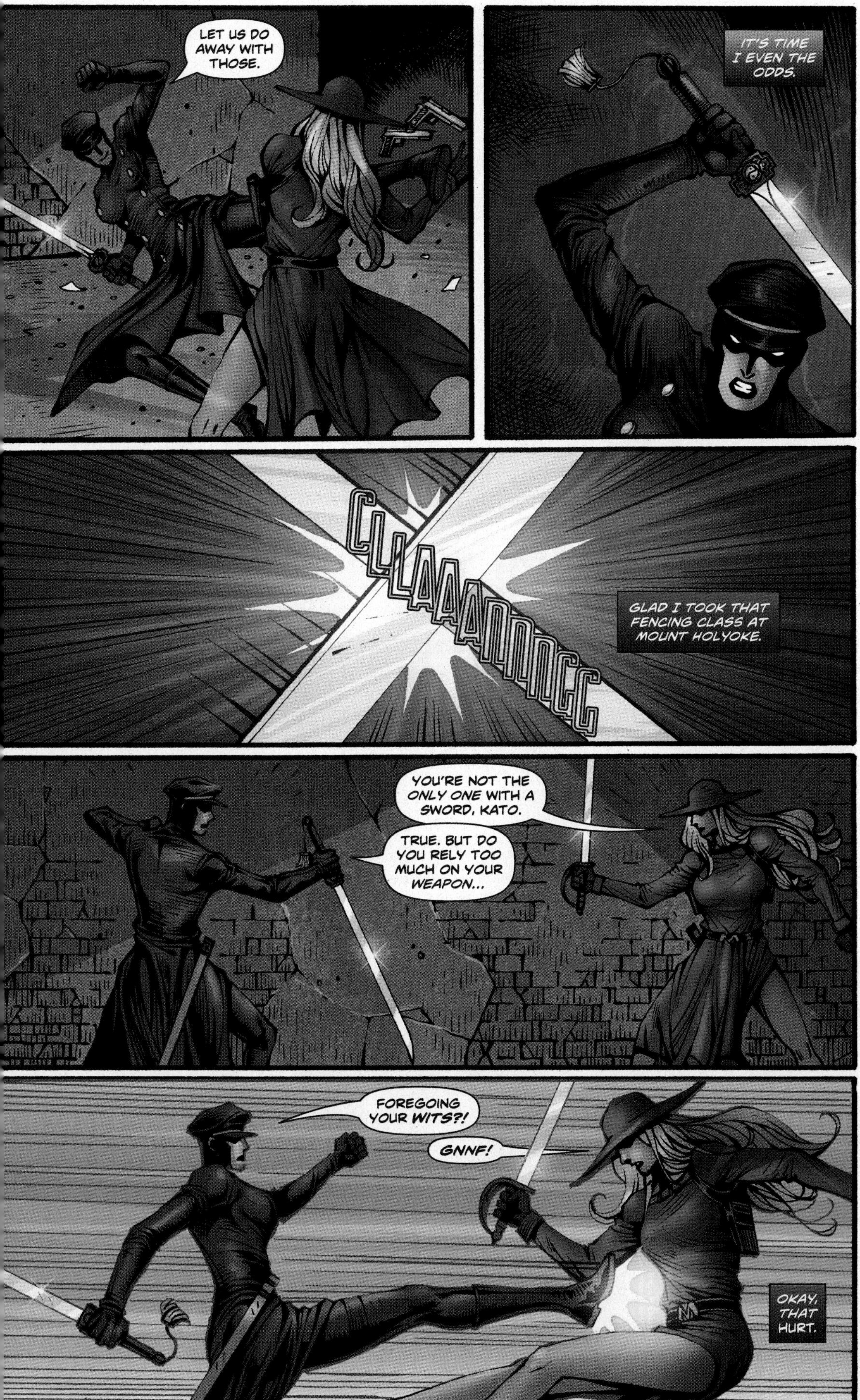
LET US DO AWAY WITH THOSE.
IT'S TIME I EVEN THE ODDS.
CLLAAANNNGG
GLAD I TOOK THAT FENCING CLASS AT MOUNT HOLYOKE.
YOU'RE NOT THE ONLY ONE WITH A SWORD, KATO.
TRUE. BUT DO YOU RELY TOO MUCH ON YOUR WEAPON...
FOREGOING YOUR WITS?!
GNNF!
OKAY, THAT HURT.

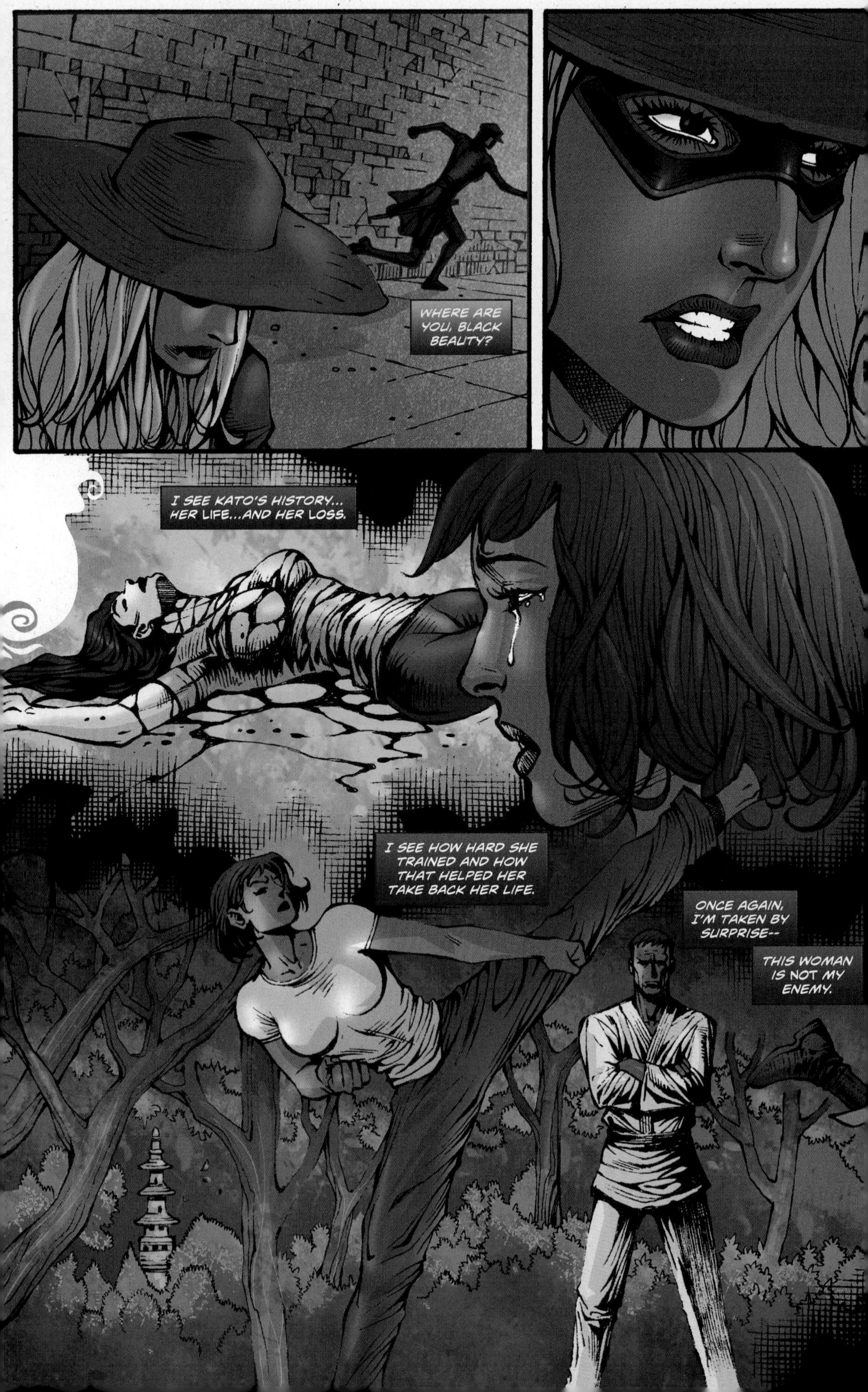
WHERE ARE YOU, BLACK BEAUTY?
I SEE KATO'S HISTORY... HER LIFE...AND HER LOSS.
I SEE HOW HARD SHE TRAINED AND HOW THAT HELPED HER TAKE BACK HER LIFE.
ONCE AGAIN, I'M TAKEN BY SURPRISE--
THIS WOMAN IS NOT MY ENEMY.

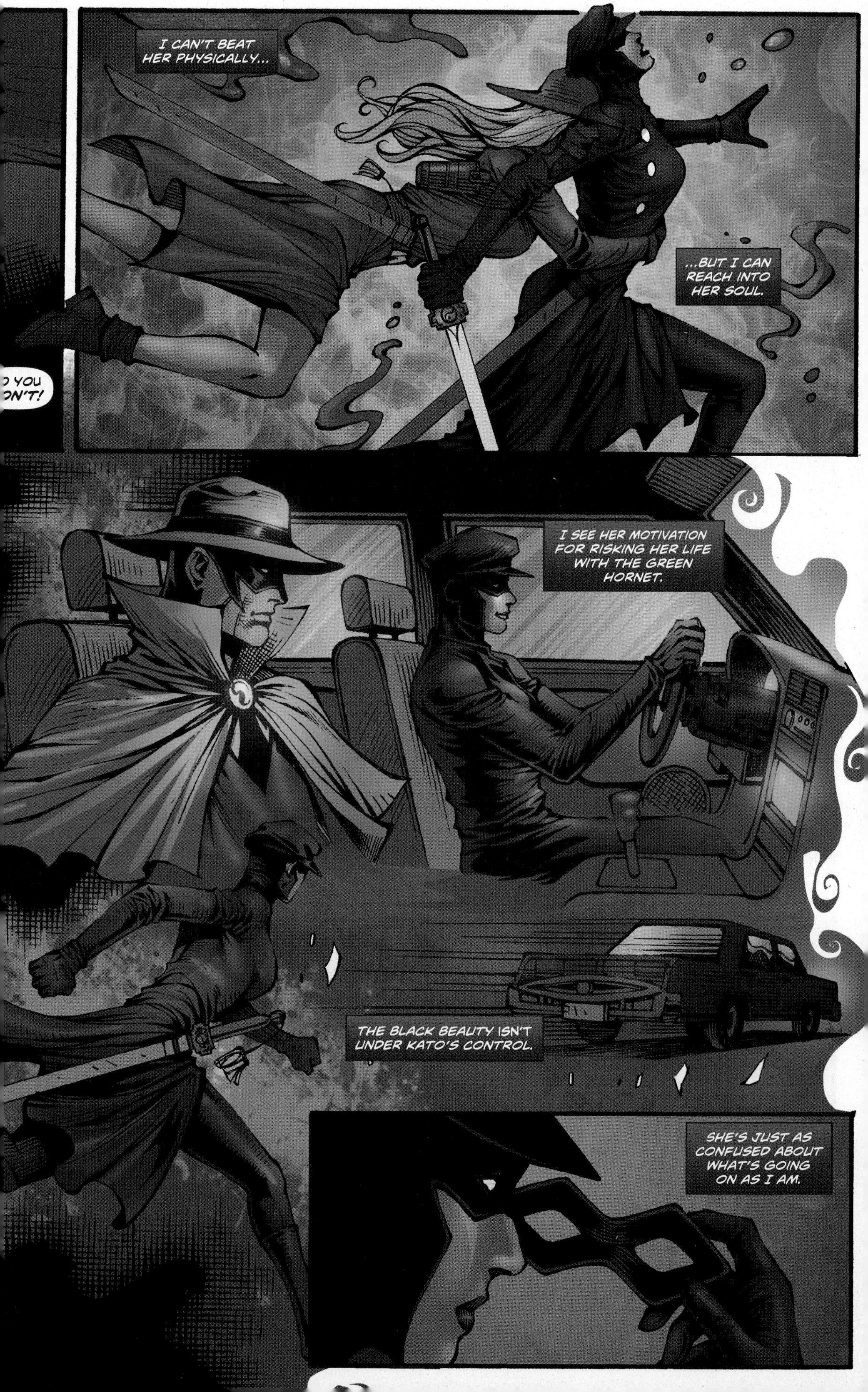
I CAN'T BEAT HER PHYSICALLY...
...BUT I CAN REACH INTO HER SOUL.
I SEE HER MOTIVATION FOR RISKING HER LIFE WITH THE GREEN HORNET.
THE BLACK BEAUTY ISN'T UNDER KATO'S CONTROL.
SHE'S JUST AS CONFUSED ABOUT WHAT'S GOING ON AS I AM.

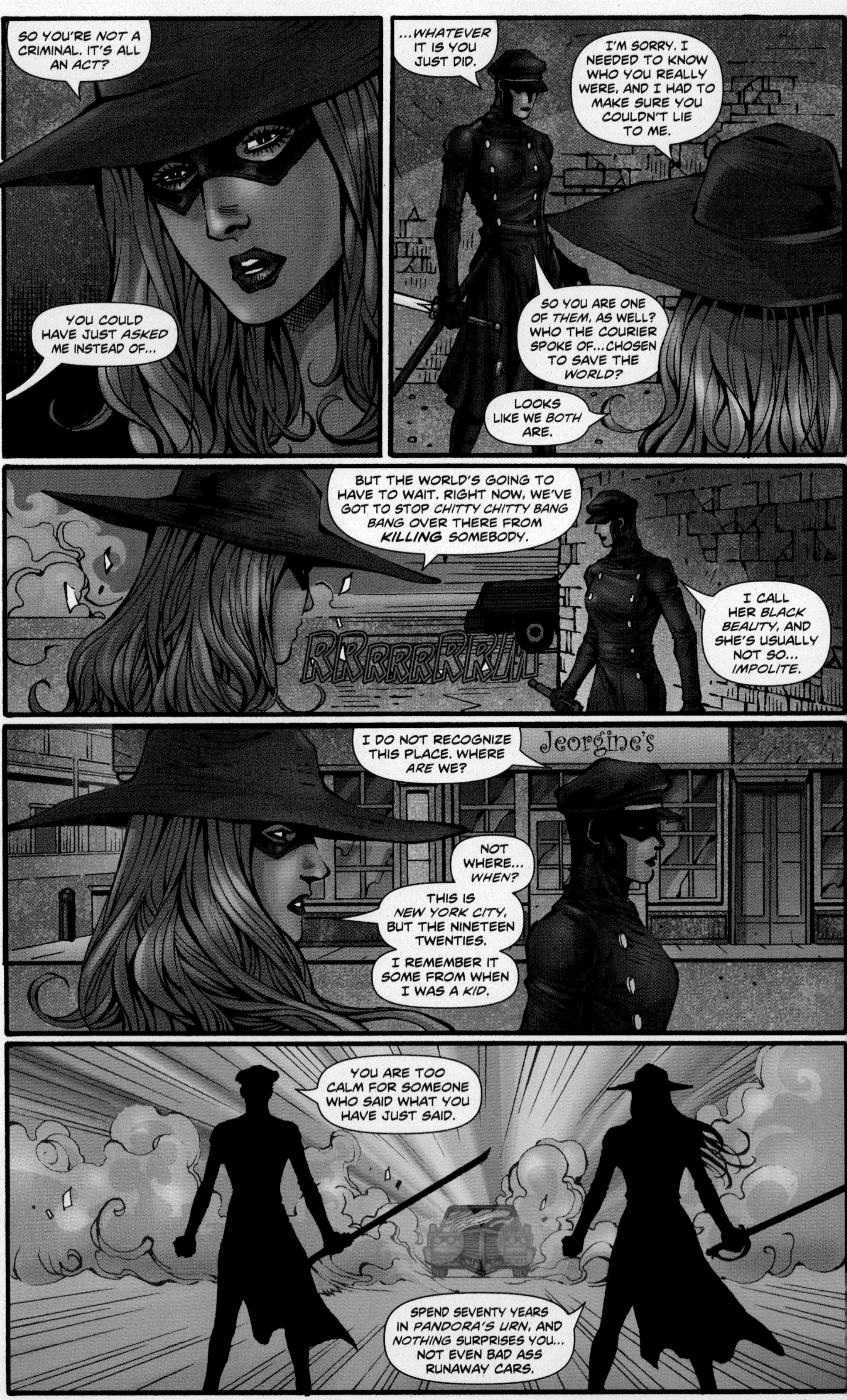
SO YOU'RE NOT A CRIMINAL. IT'S ALL AN ACT?
YOU COULD HAVE JUST ASKED ME INSTEAD OF...
...WHATEVER IT IS YOU JUST DID.
I'M SORRY. I NEEDED TO KNOW WHO YOU REALLY WERE, AND I HAD TO MAKE SURE YOU COULDN'T LIE TO ME.
SO YOU ARE ONE OF THEM, AS WELL? WHO THE COURIER SPOKE OF...CHOSEN TO SAVE THE WORLD?
LOOKS LIKE WE BOTH ARE.
BUT THE WORLD'S GOING TO HAVE TO WAIT. RIGHT NOW, WE'VE GOT TO STOP CHITTY CHITTY BANG BANG OVER THERE FROM KILLING SOMEBODY.
RRRRRRRRUU
I CALL HER BLACK BEAUTY, AND SHE'S USUALLY NOT SO... IMPOLITE.
I DO NOT RECOGNIZE THIS PLACE. WHERE ARE WE?
Jeorgine's
NOT WHERE... WHEN?
THIS IS NEW YORK CITY, BUT THE NINETEEN TWENTIES.
I REMEMBER IT SOME FROM WHEN I WAS A KID.
YOU ARE TOO CALM FOR SOMEONE WHO SAID WHAT YOU HAVE JUST SAID.
SPEND SEVENTY YEARS IN PANDORA'S URN, AND NOTHING SURPRISES YOU... NOT EVEN BAD ASS RUNAWAY CARS.

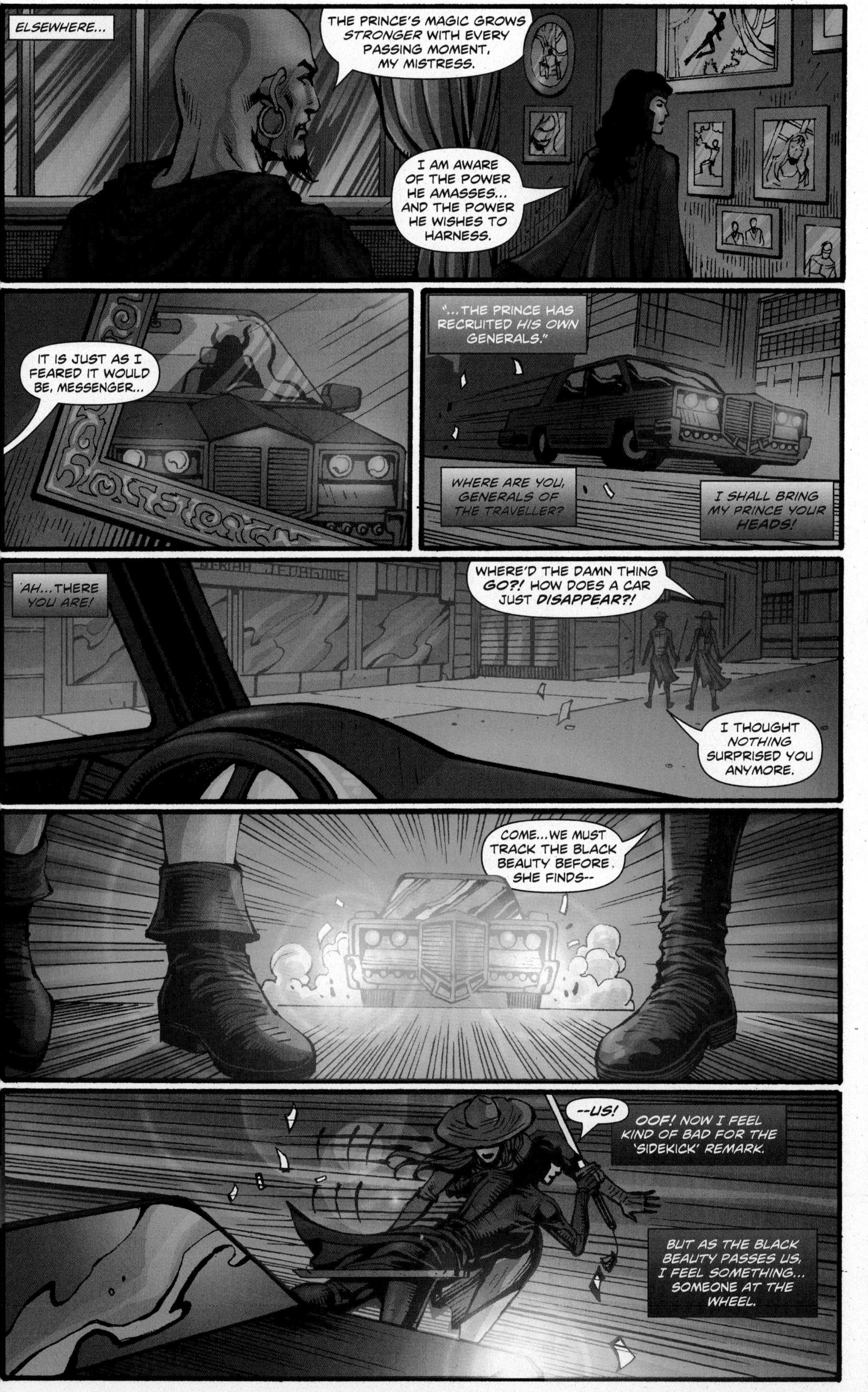
ELSEWHERE...
THE PRINCE'S MAGIC GROWS STRONGER WITH EVERY PASSING MOMENT, MY MISTRESS.
I AM AWARE OF THE POWER HE AMASSES... AND THE POWER HE WISHES TO HARNESS.
IT IS JUST AS I FEARED IT WOULD BE, MESSENGER...
"...THE PRINCE HAS RECRUITED HIS OWN GENERALS."
WHERE ARE YOU, GENERALS OF THE TRAVELLER?
I SHALL BRING MY PRINCE YOUR HEADS!
AH...THERE YOU ARE!
WHERE'D THE DAMN THING GO?! HOW DOES A CAR JUST DISAPPEAR?!
I THOUGHT NOTHING SURPRISED YOU ANYMORE.
COME...WE MUST TRACK THE BLACK BEAUTY BEFORE SHE FINDS--
--US!
OOF! NOW I FEEL KIND OF BAD FOR THE 'SIDEKICK' REMARK.
BUT AS THE BLACK BEAUTY PASSES US, I FEEL SOMETHING... SOMEONE AT THE WHEEL.

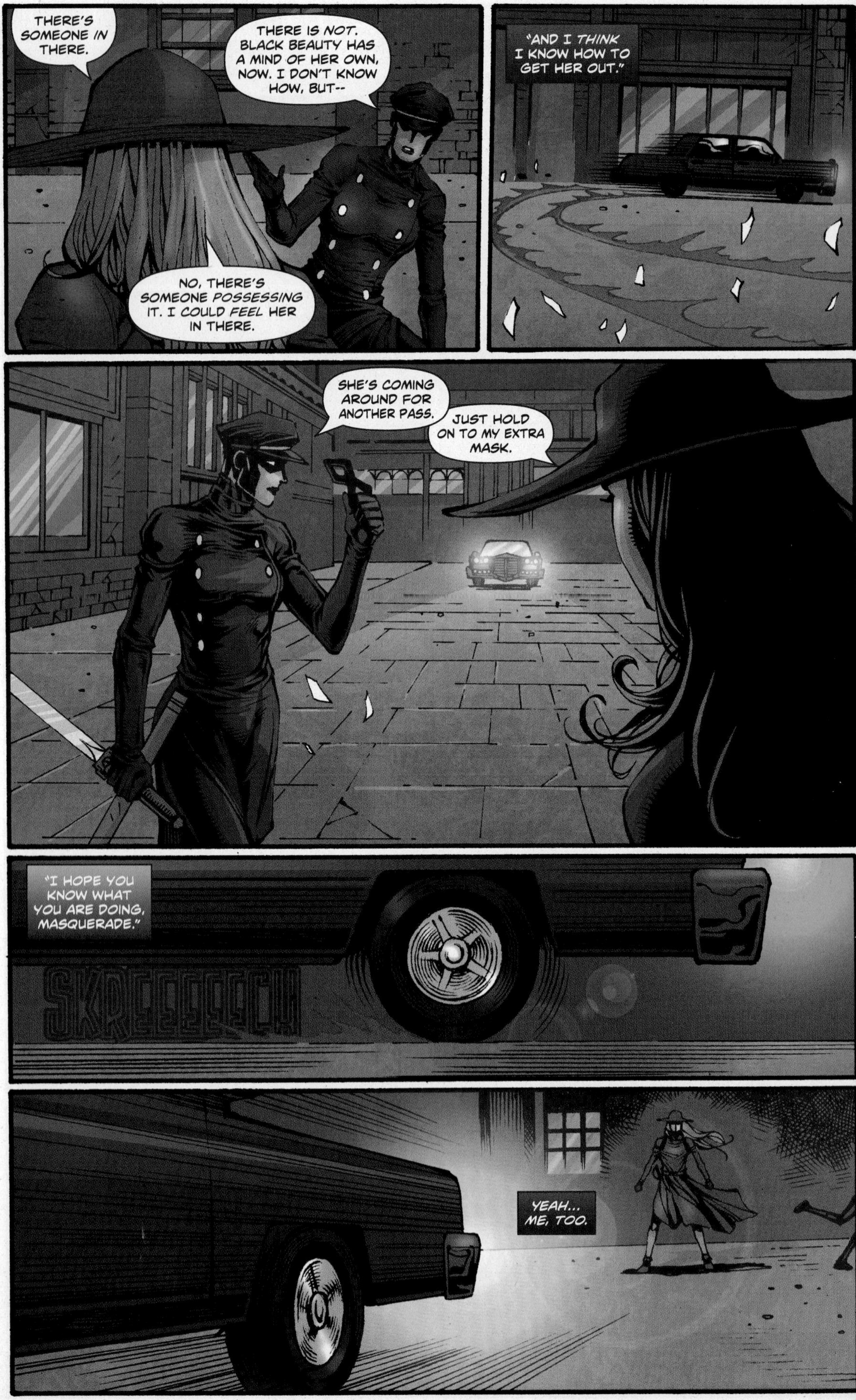
THERE'S SOMEONE *IN* THERE.
THERE IS *NOT*. BLACK BEAUTY HAS A MIND OF HER OWN, NOW. I DON'T KNOW HOW, BUT--
NO, THERE'S SOMEONE *POSSESSING* IT. I COULD *FEEL* HER IN THERE.
"AND I *THINK* I KNOW HOW TO GET HER OUT."
SHE'S COMING AROUND FOR ANOTHER PASS.
JUST HOLD ON TO MY EXTRA MASK.
"I HOPE YOU KNOW WHAT YOU ARE DOING, MASQUERADE."
SKREEEEEECH
YEAH... ME, TOO.

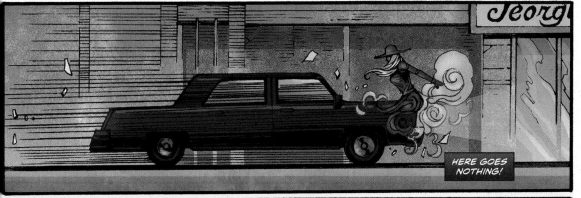

HERE GOES NOTHING!

WHOEVER IS IN HERE IS PUTTING UP A FIGHT.

THUNK CHUD THUD THWAKK

WHAT THE--?!

SKREEEEECH

THIS...ISN'T OVER! ≋KOFF≋ YOU WILL ALL BURN SOON ENOUGH!

THE PRINCE WILL *TRIUMPH*. JUST WAIT AND SEE...

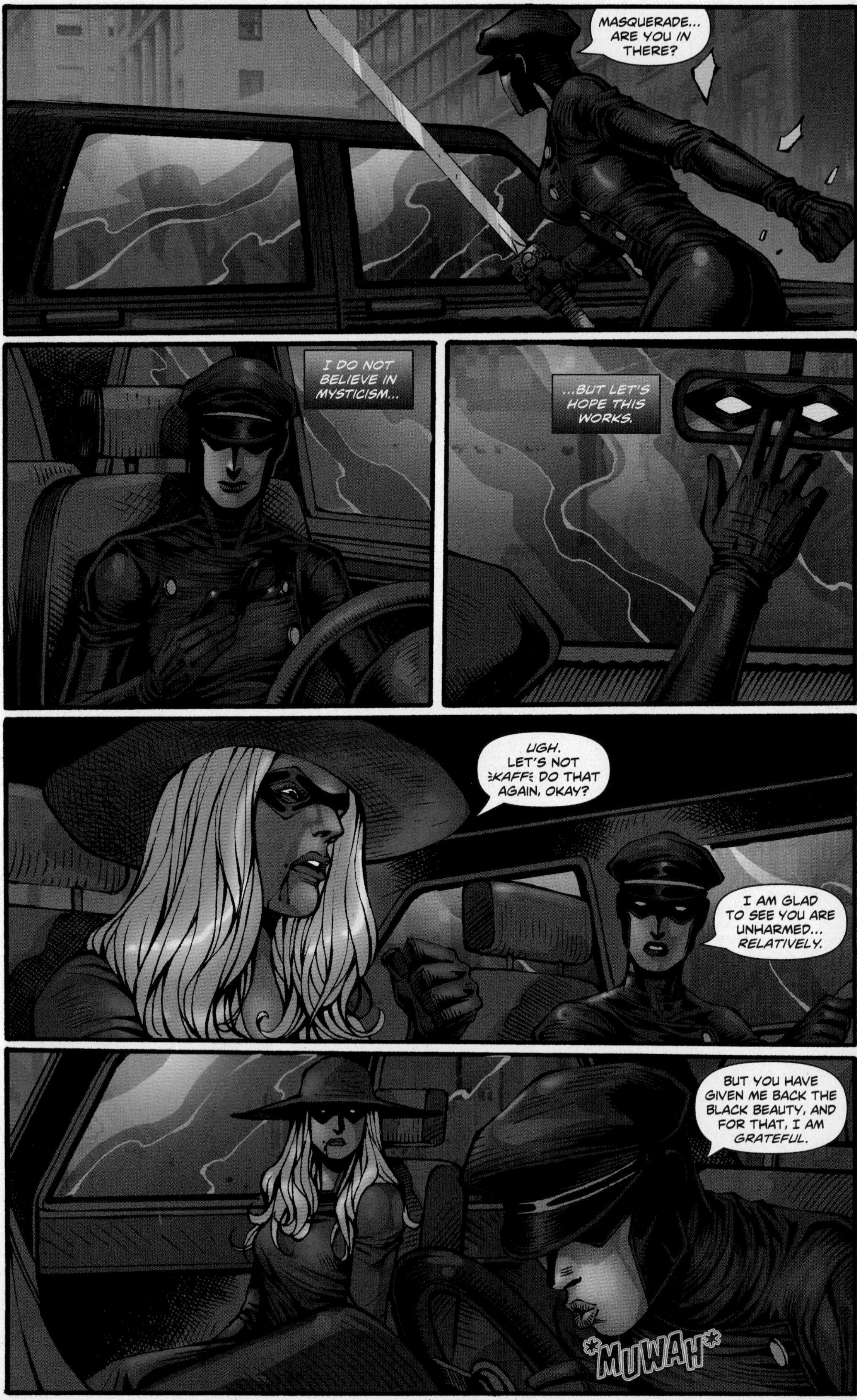
MASQUERADE... ARE YOU IN THERE?
I DO NOT BELIEVE IN MYSTICISM...
...BUT LET'S HOPE THIS WORKS.
UGH. LET'S NOT KAFF DO THAT AGAIN, OKAY?
I AM GLAD TO SEE YOU ARE UNHARMED... RELATIVELY.
BUT YOU HAVE GIVEN ME BACK THE BLACK BEAUTY, AND FOR THAT, I AM GRATEFUL.
MUWAH

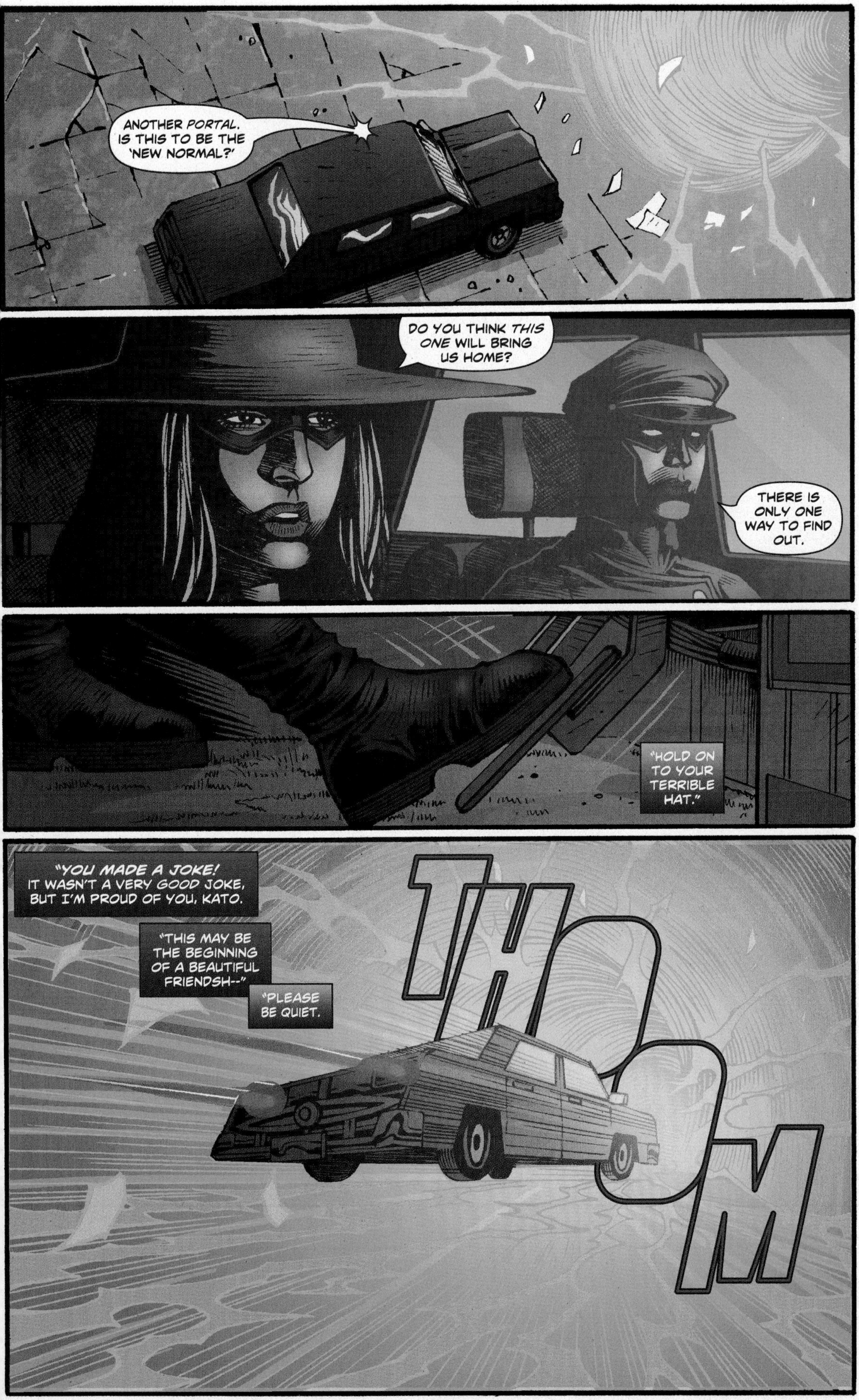
ANOTHER PORTAL. IS THIS TO BE THE 'NEW NORMAL?'
DO YOU THINK THIS ONE WILL BRING US HOME?
THERE IS ONLY ONE WAY TO FIND OUT.
"HOLD ON TO YOUR TERRIBLE HAT."
"YOU MADE A JOKE! IT WASN'T A VERY GOOD JOKE, BUT I'M PROUD OF YOU, KATO.
"THIS MAY BE THE BEGINNING OF A BEAUTIFUL FRIENDSH--"
"PLEASE BE QUIET.
THOOM

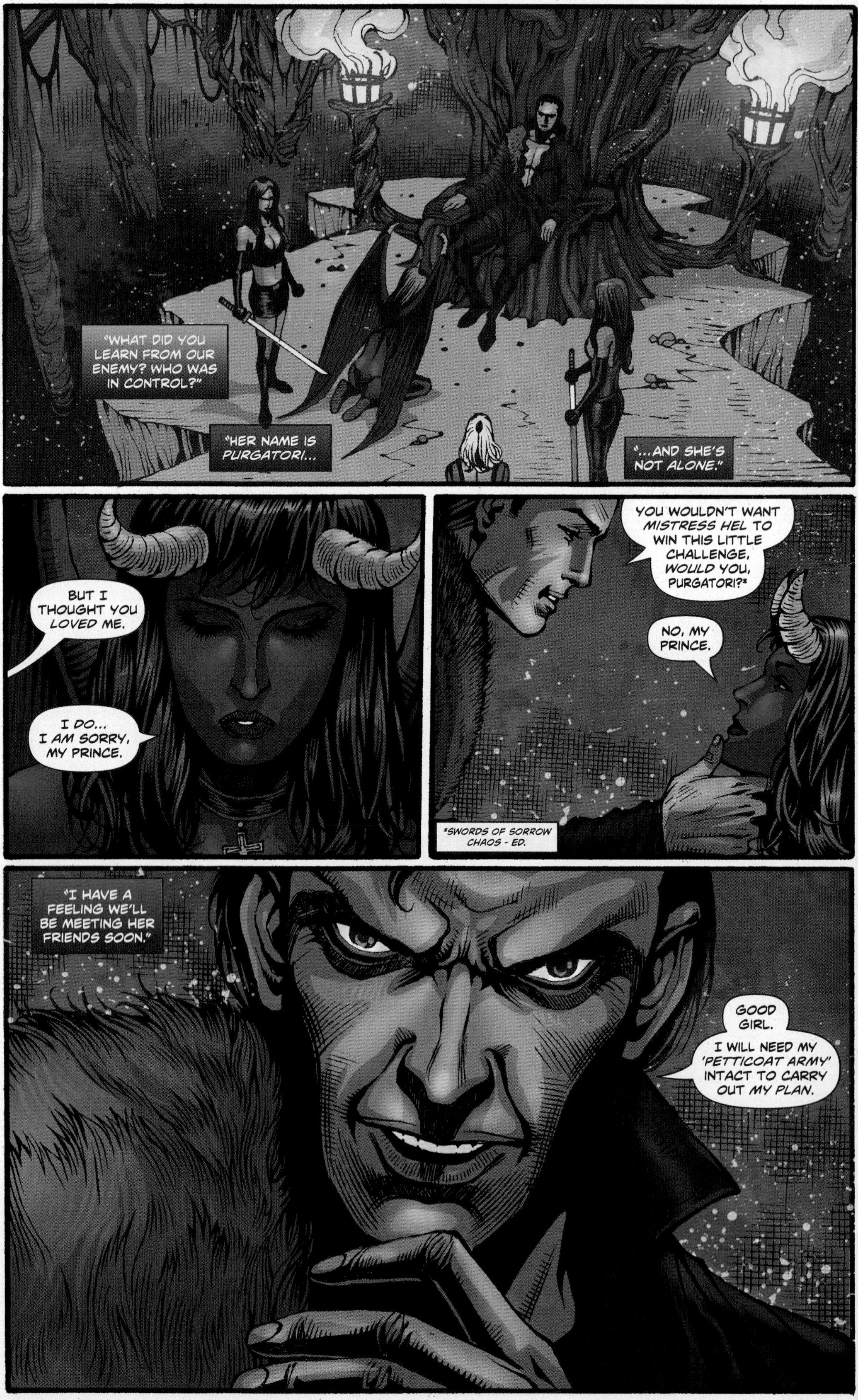
"WHAT DID YOU LEARN FROM OUR ENEMY? WHO WAS IN CONTROL?"
"HER NAME IS PURGATORI...
"...AND SHE'S NOT ALONE."
BUT I THOUGHT YOU LOVED ME.
I DO... I AM SORRY, MY PRINCE.
YOU WOULDN'T WANT MISTRESS HEL TO WIN THIS LITTLE CHALLENGE, WOULD YOU, PURGATORI?*
NO, MY PRINCE.
*SWORDS OF SORROW CHAOS - ED.
"I HAVE A FEELING WE'LL BE MEETING HER FRIENDS SOON."
GOOD GIRL.
I WILL NEED MY 'PETTICOAT ARMY' INTACT TO CARRY OUT MY PLAN.

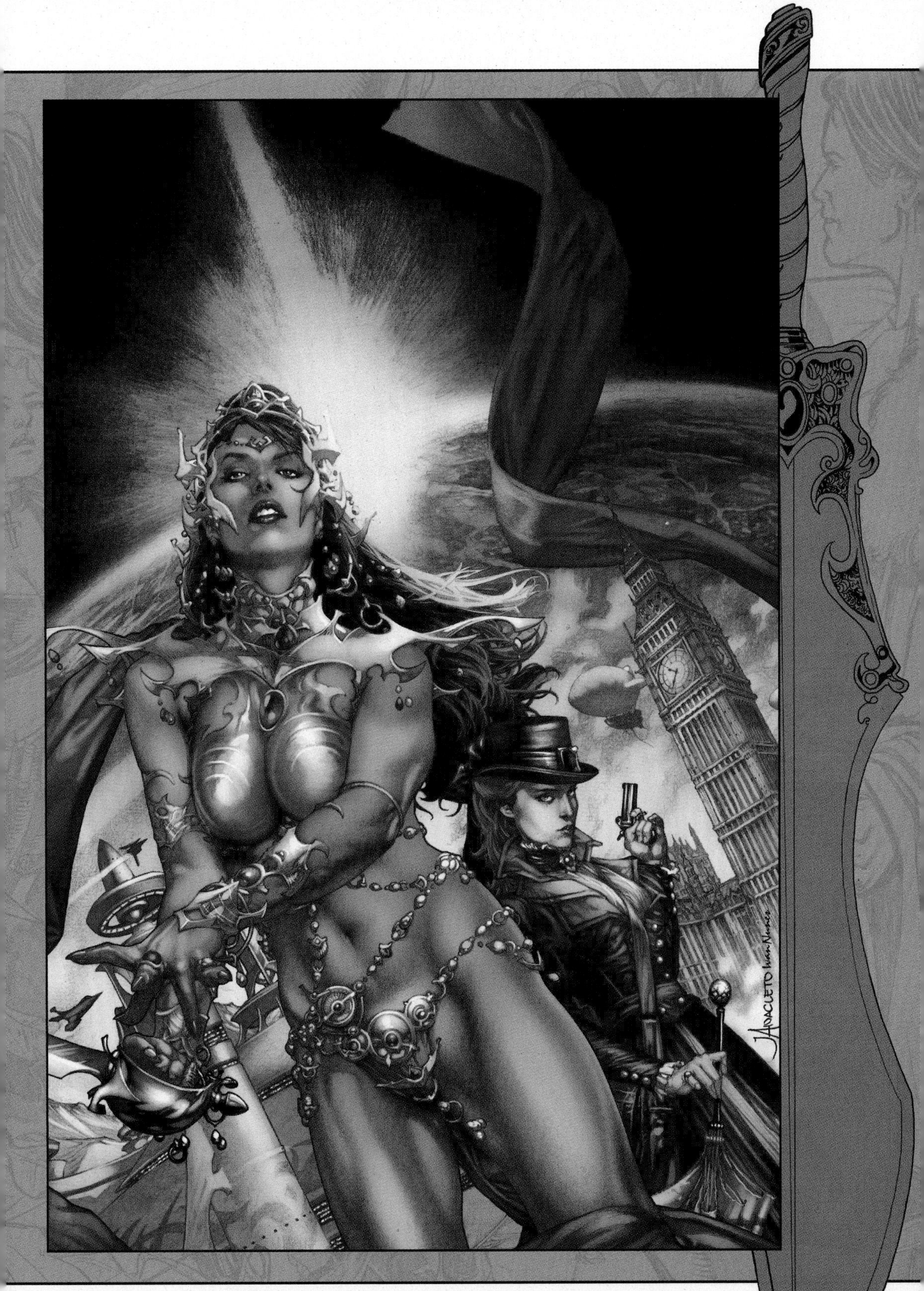

SWORDS OF SORROW: DEJAH THORIS & IRENE ADLER

ISSUE ONE OF THREE

written by LEA MOORE illustrated by FRANCESCO MANNA
colored by InLIGHT STUDIO lettered by ERICA SCHULTZ

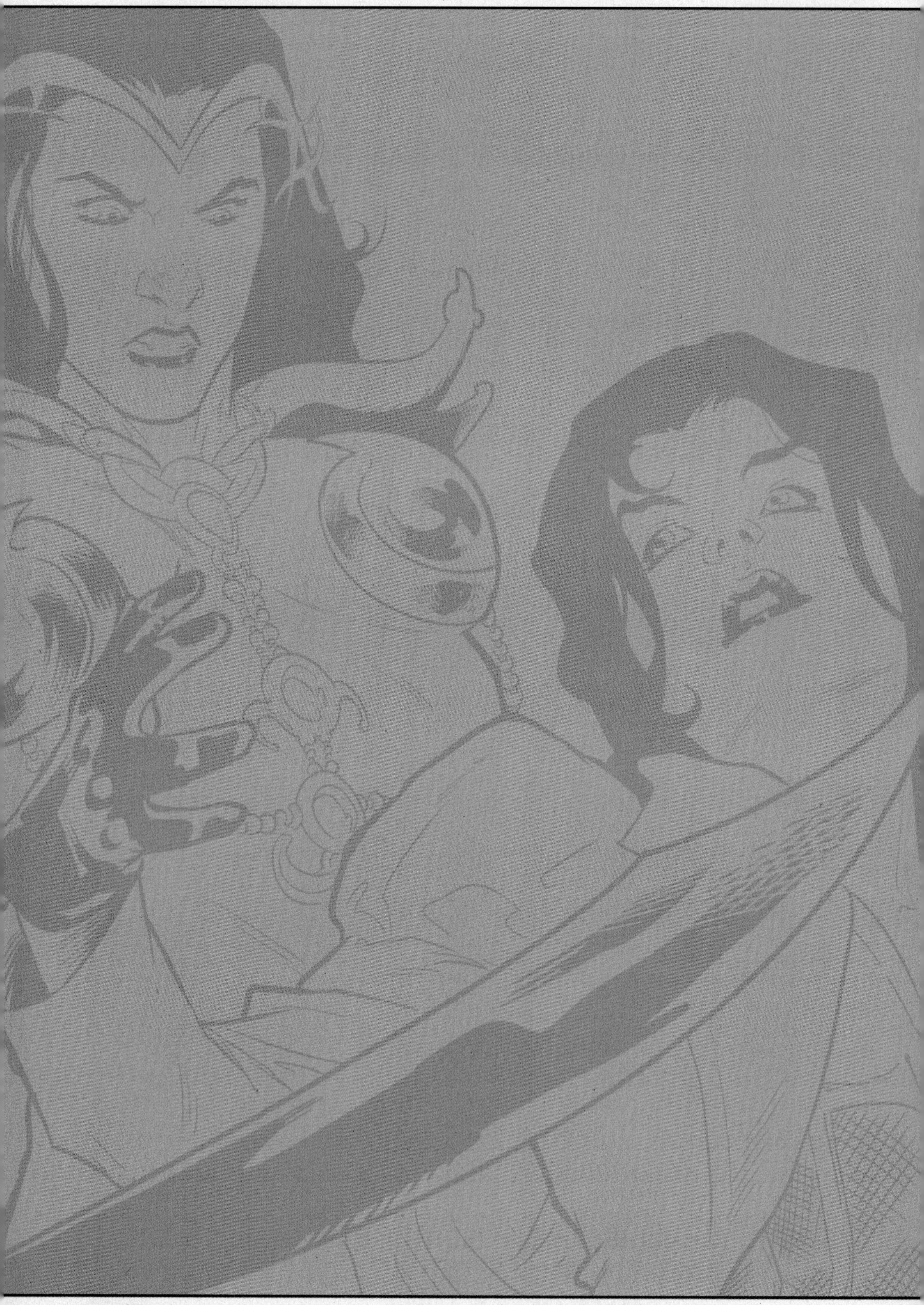

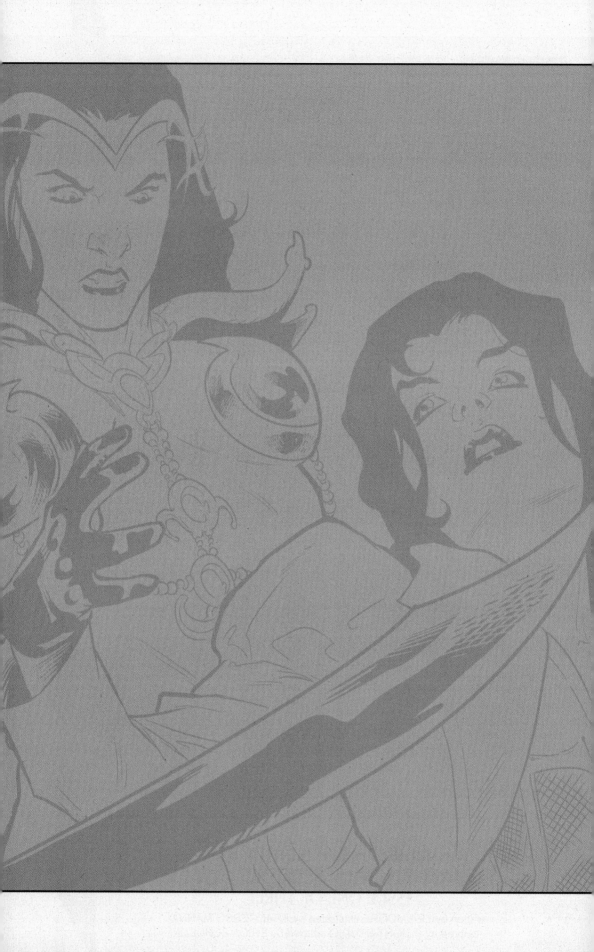

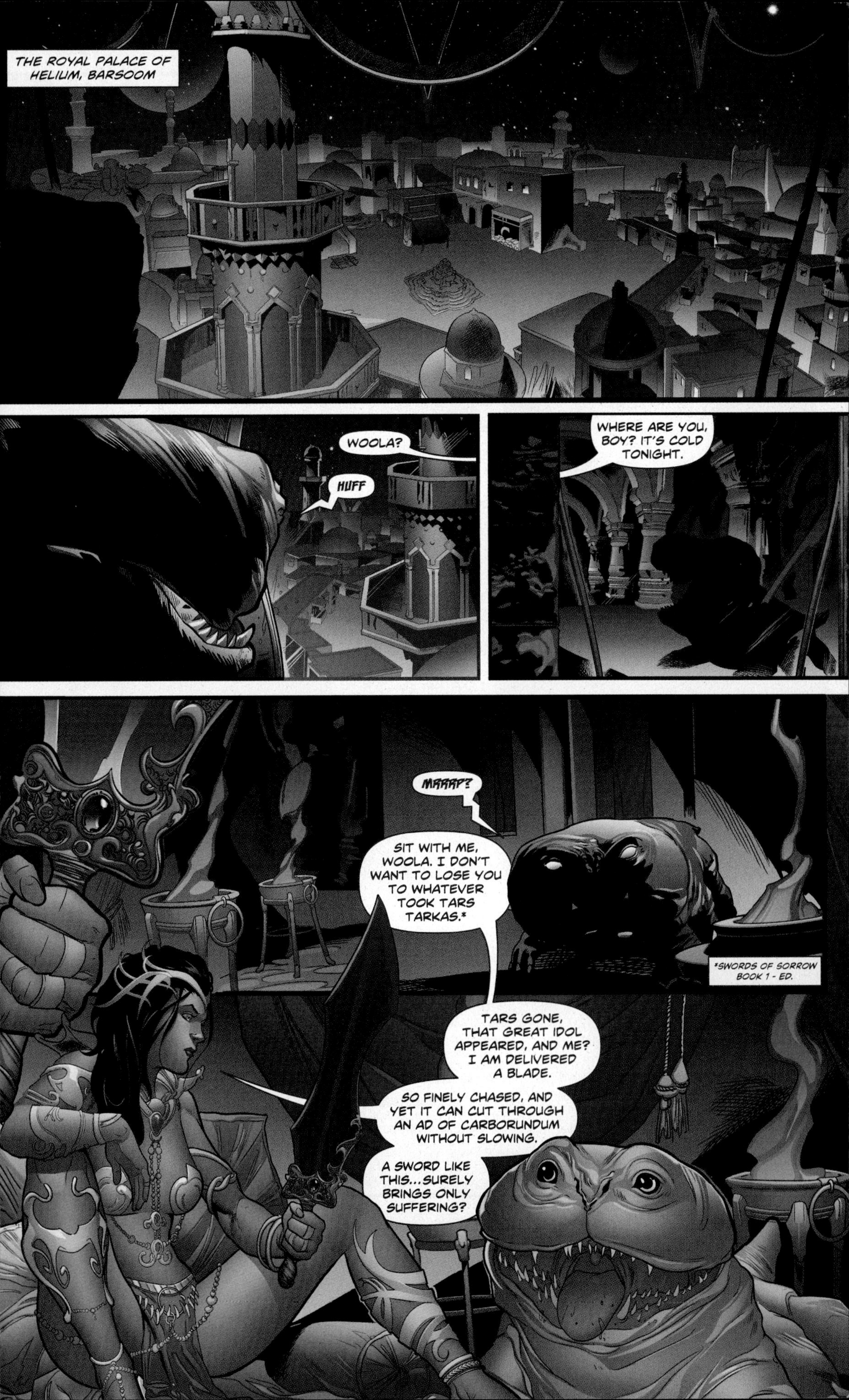
THE ROYAL PALACE OF HELIUM, BARSOOM
WOOLA?
HUFF
WHERE ARE YOU, BOY? IT'S COLD TONIGHT.
MRRRP?
SIT WITH ME, WOOLA. I DON'T WANT TO LOSE YOU TO WHATEVER TOOK TARS TARKAS.*
*SWORDS OF SORROW BOOK 1 - ED.
TARS GONE, THAT GREAT IDOL APPEARED, AND ME? I AM DELIVERED A BLADE.
SO FINELY CHASED, AND YET IT CAN CUT THROUGH AN AD OF CARBORUNDUM WITHOUT SLOWING.
A SWORD LIKE THIS...SURELY BRINGS ONLY SUFFERING?

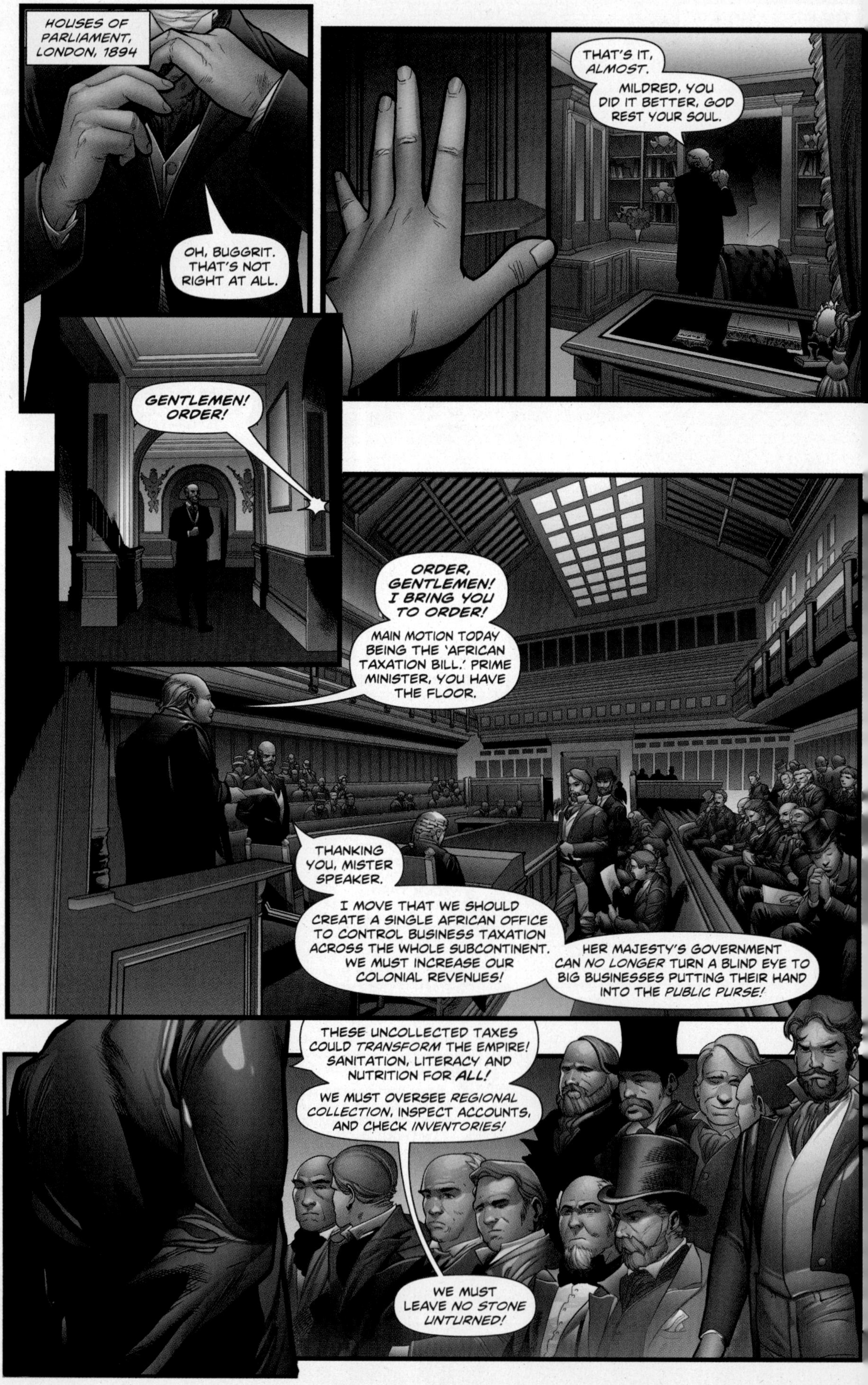
HOUSES OF PARLIAMENT, LONDON, 1894
OH, BUGGRIT. THAT'S NOT RIGHT AT ALL.
THAT'S IT, ALMOST.
MILDRED, YOU DID IT BETTER, GOD REST YOUR SOUL.
GENTLEMEN! ORDER!
ORDER, GENTLEMEN! I BRING YOU TO ORDER!
MAIN MOTION TODAY BEING THE 'AFRICAN TAXATION BILL.' PRIME MINISTER, YOU HAVE THE FLOOR.
THANKING YOU, MISTER SPEAKER.
I MOVE THAT WE SHOULD CREATE A SINGLE AFRICAN OFFICE TO CONTROL BUSINESS TAXATION ACROSS THE WHOLE SUBCONTINENT. WE MUST INCREASE OUR COLONIAL REVENUES!
HER MAJESTY'S GOVERNMENT CAN NO LONGER TURN A BLIND EYE TO BIG BUSINESSES PUTTING THEIR HAND INTO THE PUBLIC PURSE!
THESE UNCOLLECTED TAXES COULD TRANSFORM THE EMPIRE! SANITATION, LITERACY AND NUTRITION FOR ALL!
WE MUST OVERSEE REGIONAL COLLECTION, INSPECT ACCOUNTS, AND CHECK INVENTORIES!
WE MUST LEAVE NO STONE UNTURNED!

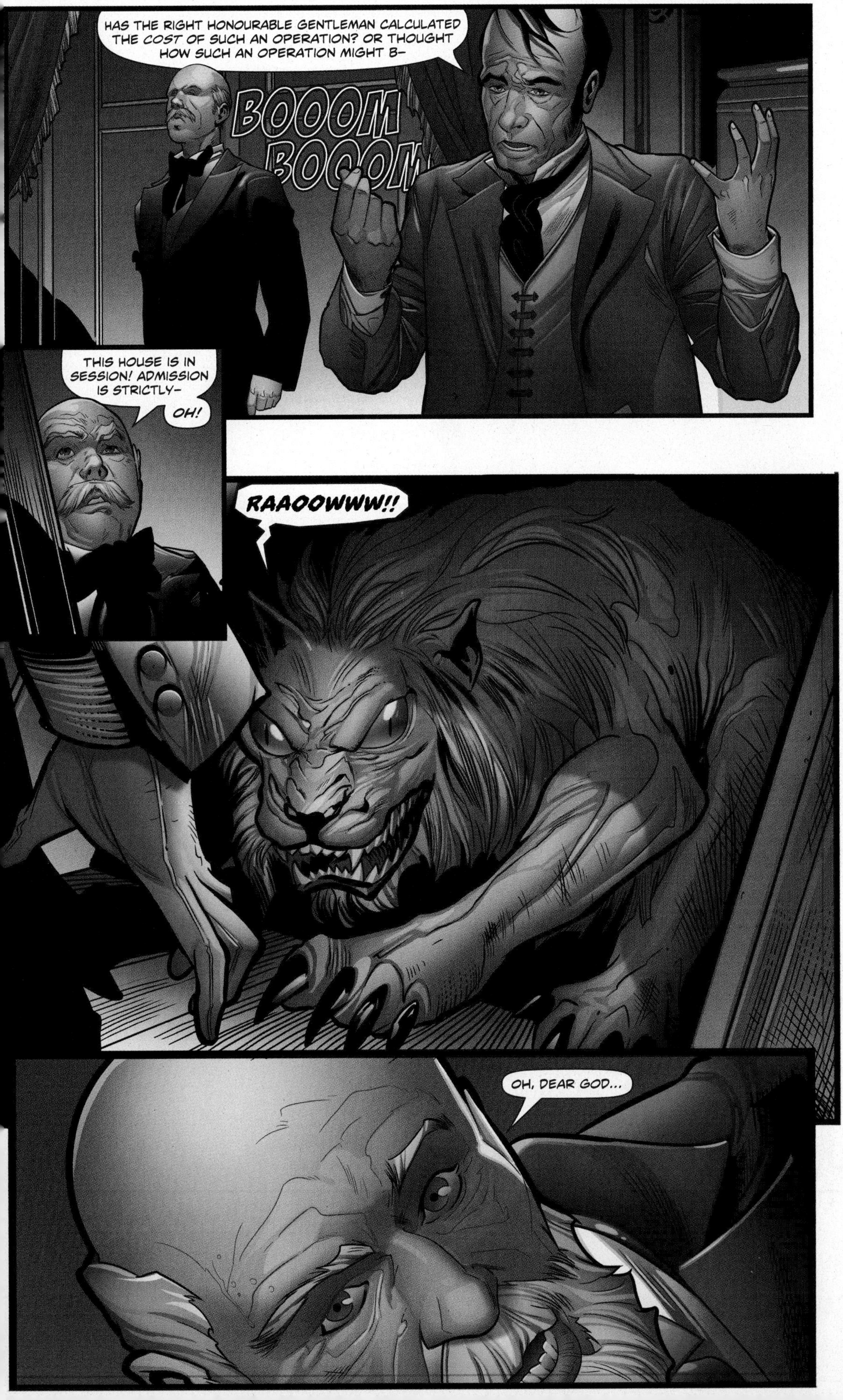
HAS THE RIGHT HONOURABLE GENTLEMAN CALCULATED THE COST OF SUCH AN OPERATION? OR THOUGHT HOW SUCH AN OPERATION MIGHT B–
BOOOM
BOOOM
THIS HOUSE IS IN SESSION! ADMISSION IS STRICTLY–
OH!
RAAOOWWW!!
OH, DEAR GOD...

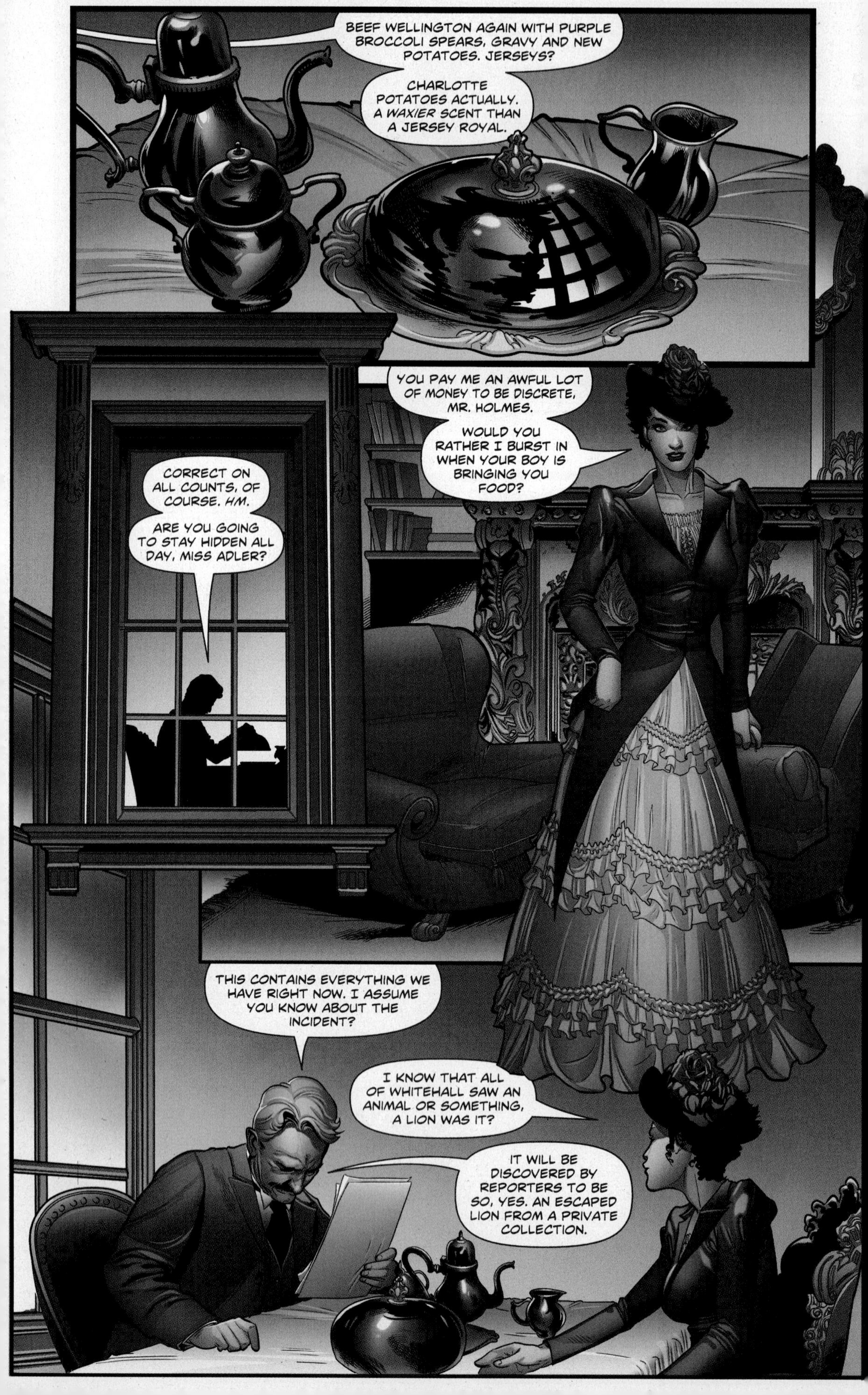
BEEF WELLINGTON AGAIN WITH PURPLE BROCCOLI SPEARS, GRAVY AND NEW POTATOES. JERSEYS?
CHARLOTTE POTATOES ACTUALLY. A *WAXIER* SCENT THAN A JERSEY ROYAL.
CORRECT ON ALL COUNTS, OF COURSE. *HM.*
ARE YOU GOING TO STAY HIDDEN ALL DAY, MISS ADLER?
YOU PAY ME AN AWFUL LOT OF MONEY TO BE DISCRETE, MR. HOLMES.
WOULD YOU RATHER I BURST IN WHEN YOUR BOY IS BRINGING YOU FOOD?
THIS CONTAINS EVERYTHING WE HAVE RIGHT NOW. I ASSUME YOU KNOW ABOUT THE INCIDENT?
I KNOW THAT ALL OF WHITEHALL SAW AN ANIMAL OR SOMETHING, A LION WAS IT?
IT WILL BE DISCOVERED BY REPORTERS TO BE SO, YES. AN ESCAPED LION FROM A PRIVATE COLLECTION.

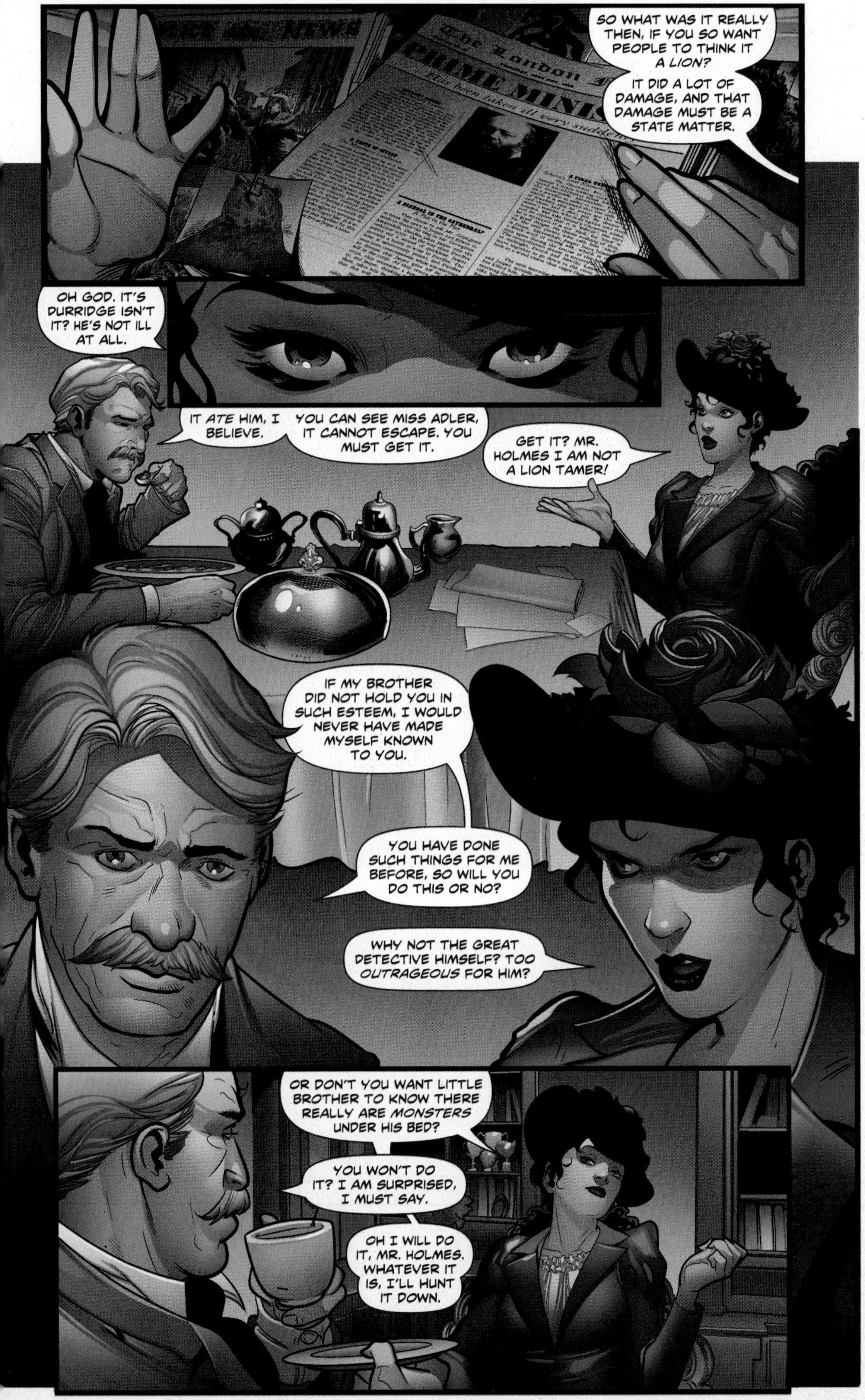
The London
PRIME MINIS
SO WHAT WAS IT REALLY THEN, IF YOU SO WANT PEOPLE TO THINK IT A *LION*?
IT DID A LOT OF DAMAGE, AND THAT DAMAGE MUST BE A STATE MATTER.
OH GOD. IT'S DURRIDGE ISN'T IT? HE'S NOT ILL AT ALL.
IT *ATE* HIM, I BELIEVE.
YOU CAN SEE MISS ADLER, IT CANNOT ESCAPE. YOU MUST GET IT.
GET IT? MR. HOLMES I AM NOT A LION TAMER!
IF MY BROTHER DID NOT HOLD YOU IN SUCH ESTEEM, I WOULD NEVER HAVE MADE MYSELF KNOWN TO YOU.
YOU HAVE DONE SUCH THINGS FOR ME BEFORE, SO WILL YOU DO THIS OR NO?
WHY NOT THE GREAT DETECTIVE HIMSELF? TOO *OUTRAGEOUS* FOR HIM?
OR DON'T YOU WANT LITTLE BROTHER TO KNOW THERE REALLY ARE *MONSTERS* UNDER HIS BED?
YOU WON'T DO IT? I AM SURPRISED, I MUST SAY.
OH I WILL DO IT, MR. HOLMES. WHATEVER IT IS, I'LL HUNT IT DOWN.

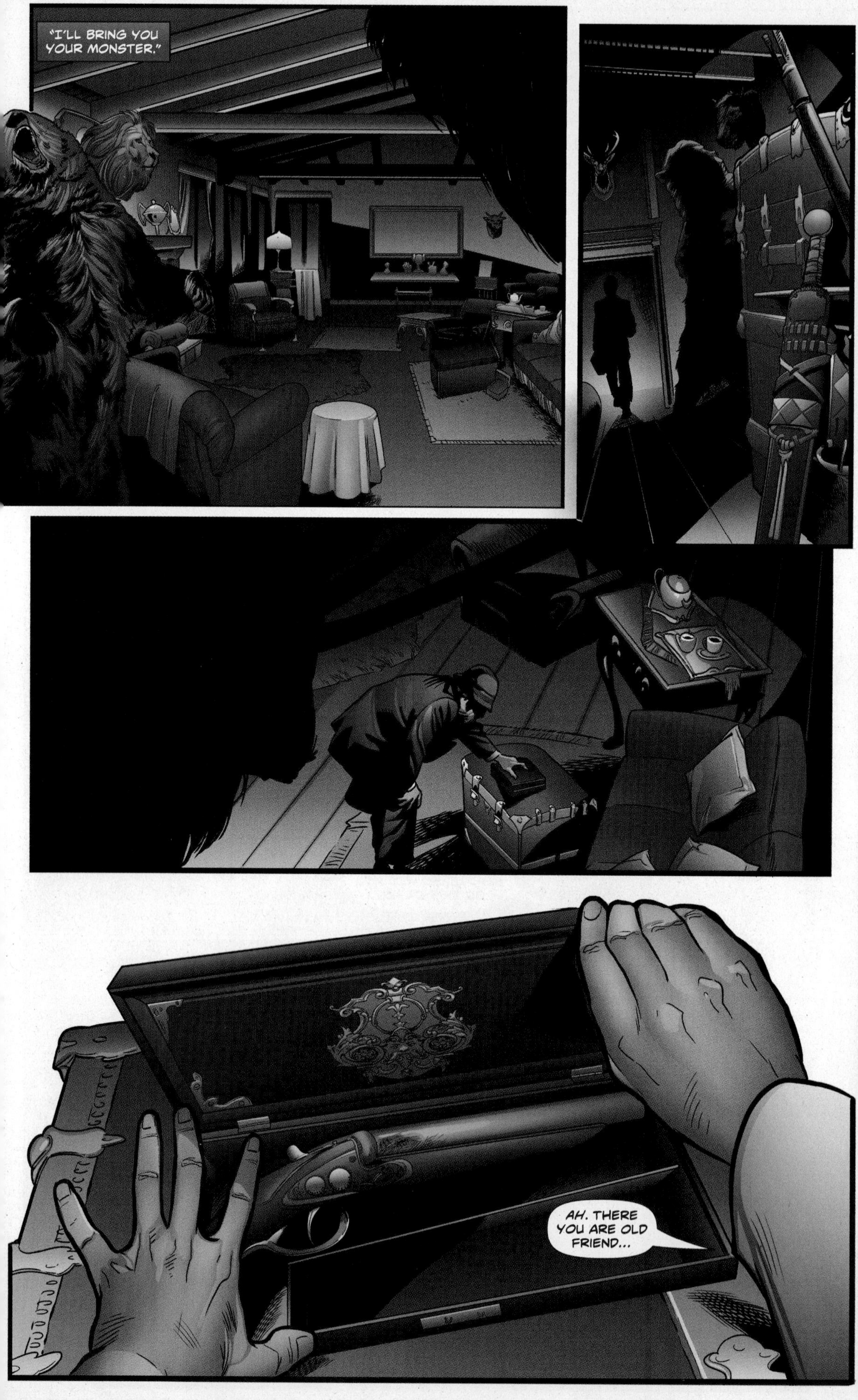
"I'LL BRING YOU YOUR MONSTER."
AH. THERE YOU ARE OLD FRIEND...

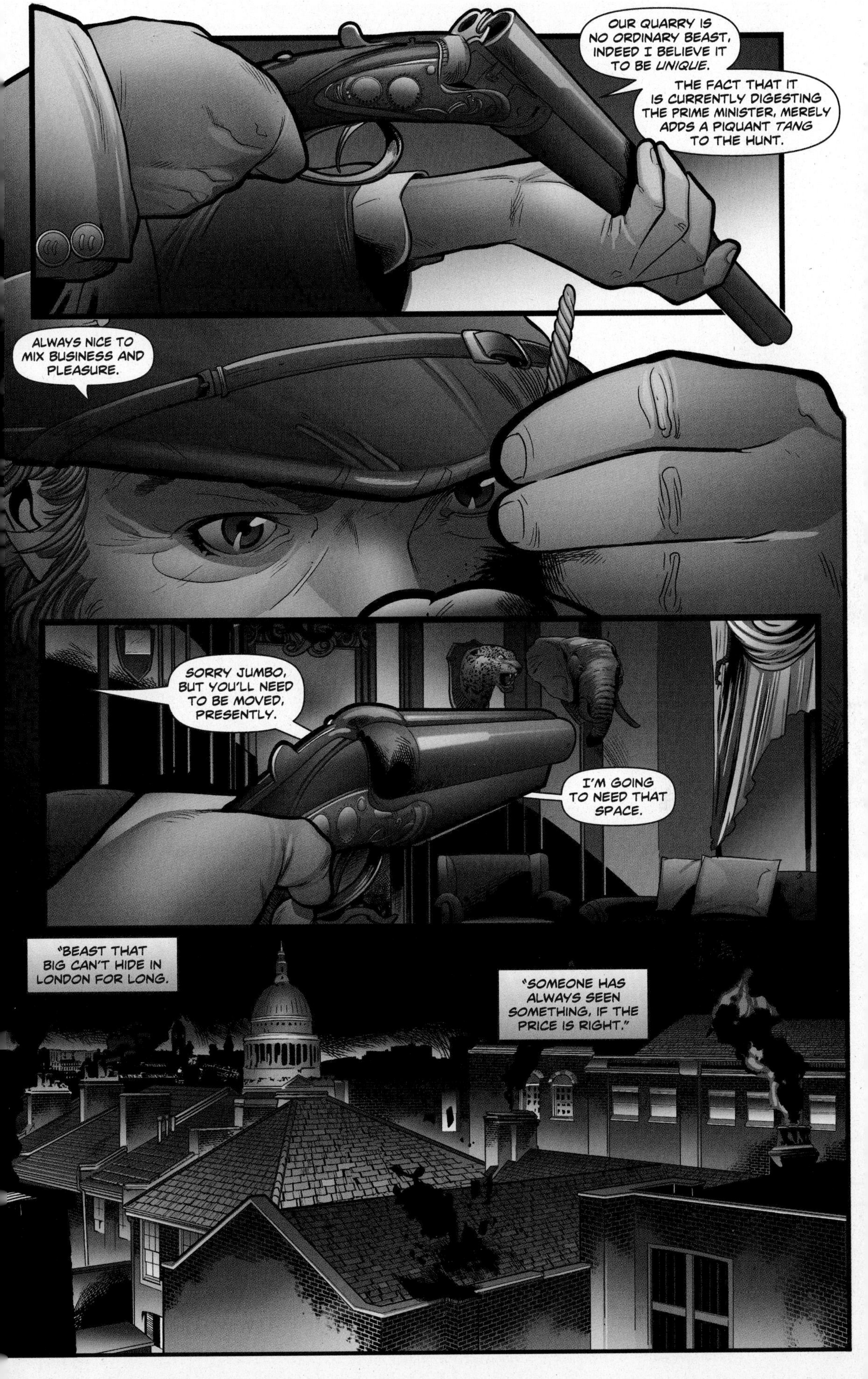
OUR QUARRY IS NO ORDINARY BEAST, INDEED I BELIEVE IT TO BE *UNIQUE*.
THE FACT THAT IT IS CURRENTLY DIGESTING THE PRIME MINISTER, MERELY ADDS A PIQUANT *TANG* TO THE HUNT.
ALWAYS NICE TO MIX BUSINESS AND PLEASURE.
SORRY JUMBO, BUT YOU'LL NEED TO BE MOVED, PRESENTLY.
I'M GOING TO NEED THAT SPACE.
"BEAST THAT BIG CAN'T HIDE IN LONDON FOR LONG.
"SOMEONE HAS ALWAYS SEEN SOMETHING, IF THE PRICE IS RIGHT."

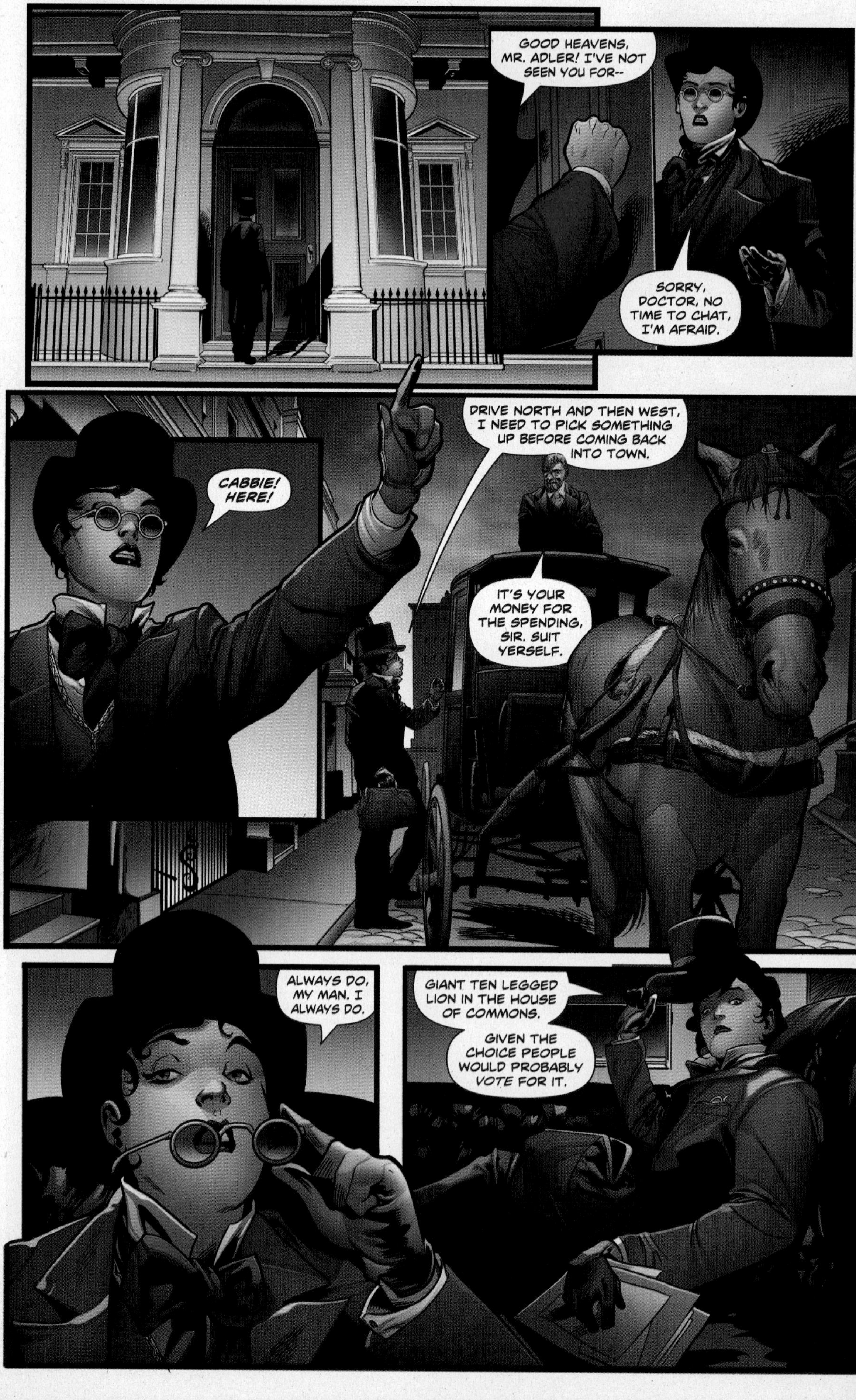
GOOD HEAVENS, MR. ADLER! I'VE NOT SEEN YOU FOR--
SORRY, DOCTOR, NO TIME TO CHAT, I'M AFRAID.
CABBIE! HERE!
DRIVE NORTH AND THEN WEST, I NEED TO PICK SOMETHING UP BEFORE COMING BACK INTO TOWN.
IT'S YOUR MONEY FOR THE SPENDING, SIR. SUIT YERSELF.
ALWAYS DO, MY MAN. I ALWAYS DO.
GIANT TEN LEGGED LION IN THE HOUSE OF COMMONS.
GIVEN THE CHOICE PEOPLE WOULD PROBABLY VOTE FOR IT.

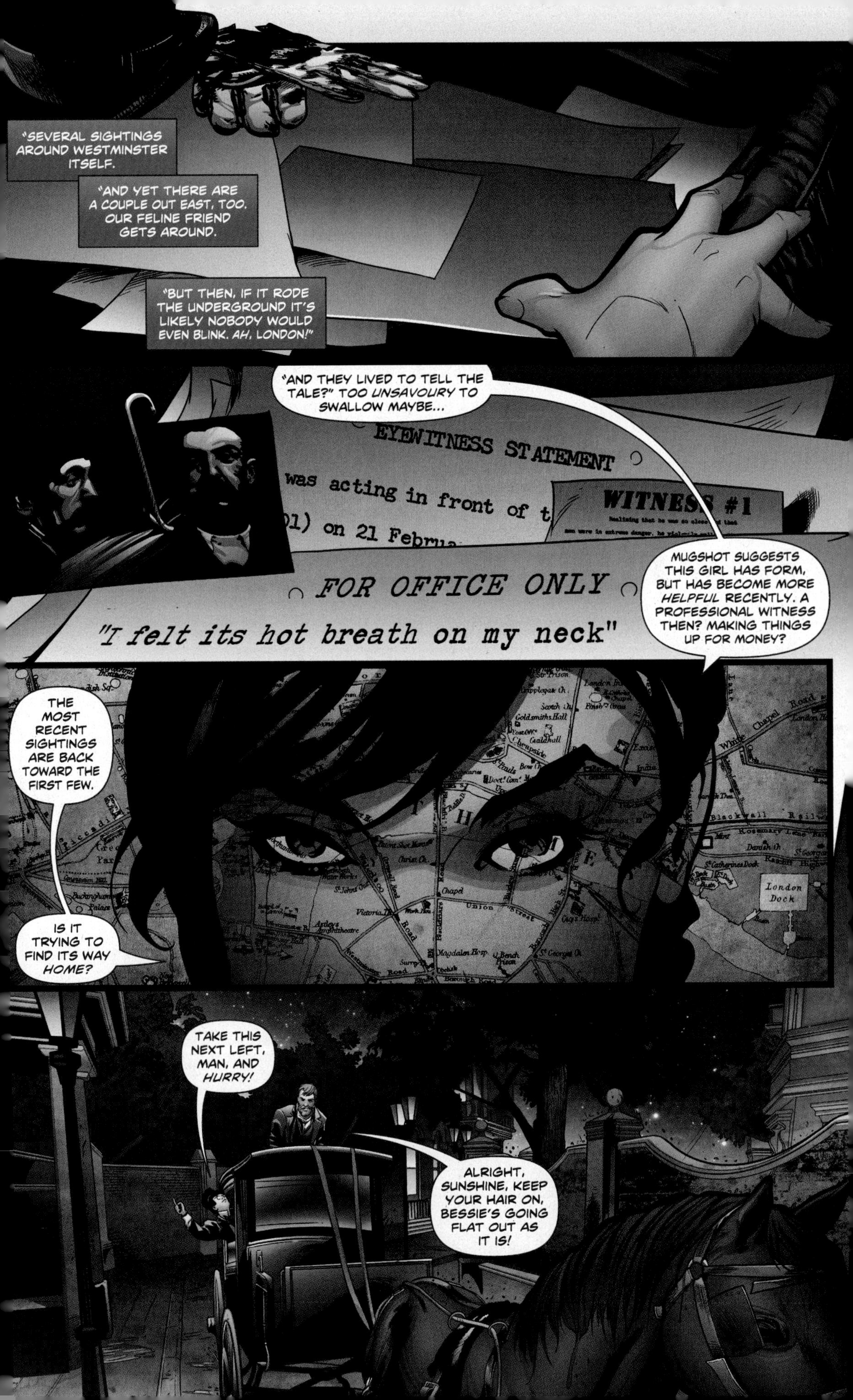

"SEVERAL SIGHTINGS AROUND WESTMINSTER ITSELF.
"AND YET THERE ARE A COUPLE OUT EAST, TOO. OUR FELINE FRIEND GETS AROUND.
"BUT THEN, IF IT RODE THE UNDERGROUND IT'S LIKELY NOBODY WOULD EVEN BLINK. *AH, LONDON!*"
"AND THEY LIVED TO TELL THE TALE?" TOO *UNSAVOURY* TO SWALLOW MAYBE...
EYEWITNESS STATEMENT
was acting in front of t
01) on 21 Februa
WITNESS #1
MUGSHOT SUGGESTS THIS GIRL HAS FORM, BUT HAS BECOME MORE *HELPFUL* RECENTLY. A PROFESSIONAL WITNESS THEN? MAKING THINGS UP FOR MONEY?
FOR OFFICE ONLY
"I felt its hot breath on my neck"
THE MOST RECENT SIGHTINGS ARE BACK TOWARD THE FIRST FEW.
IS IT TRYING TO FIND ITS WAY *HOME?*
London Dock
Goldsmiths Hall
Cheapside
Blackwall
TAKE THIS NEXT LEFT, MAN, AND *HURRY!*
ALRIGHT, SUNSHINE, KEEP YOUR HAIR ON, BESSIE'S GOING FLAT OUT AS IT IS!

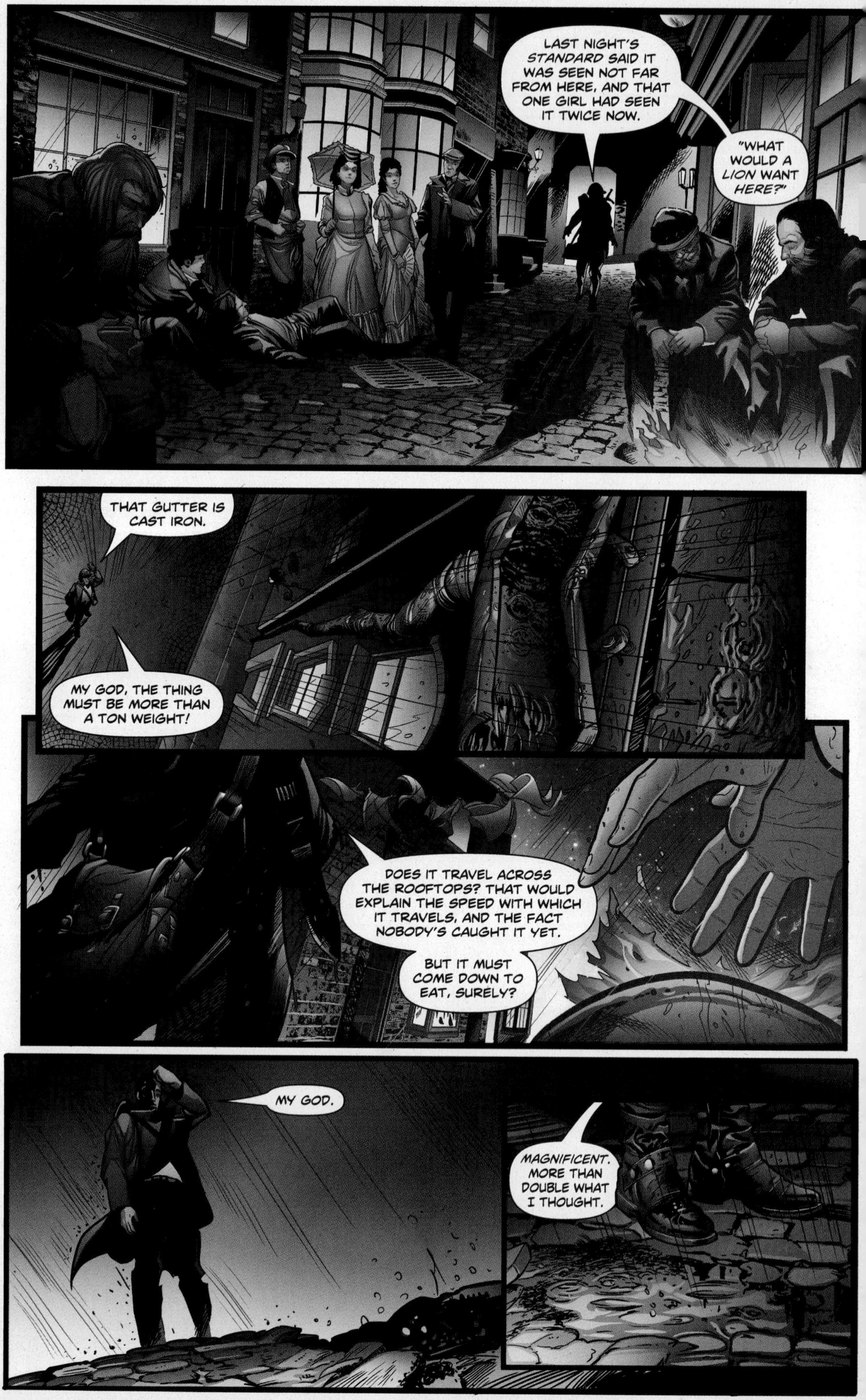
LAST NIGHT'S STANDARD SAID IT WAS SEEN NOT FAR FROM HERE, AND THAT ONE GIRL HAD SEEN IT TWICE NOW.
"WHAT WOULD A LION WANT HERE?"
THAT GUTTER IS CAST IRON.
MY GOD, THE THING MUST BE MORE THAN A TON WEIGHT!
DOES IT TRAVEL ACROSS THE ROOFTOPS? THAT WOULD EXPLAIN THE SPEED WITH WHICH IT TRAVELS, AND THE FACT NOBODY'S CAUGHT IT YET.
BUT IT MUST COME DOWN TO EAT, SURELY?
MY GOD.
MAGNIFICENT. MORE THAN DOUBLE WHAT I THOUGHT.

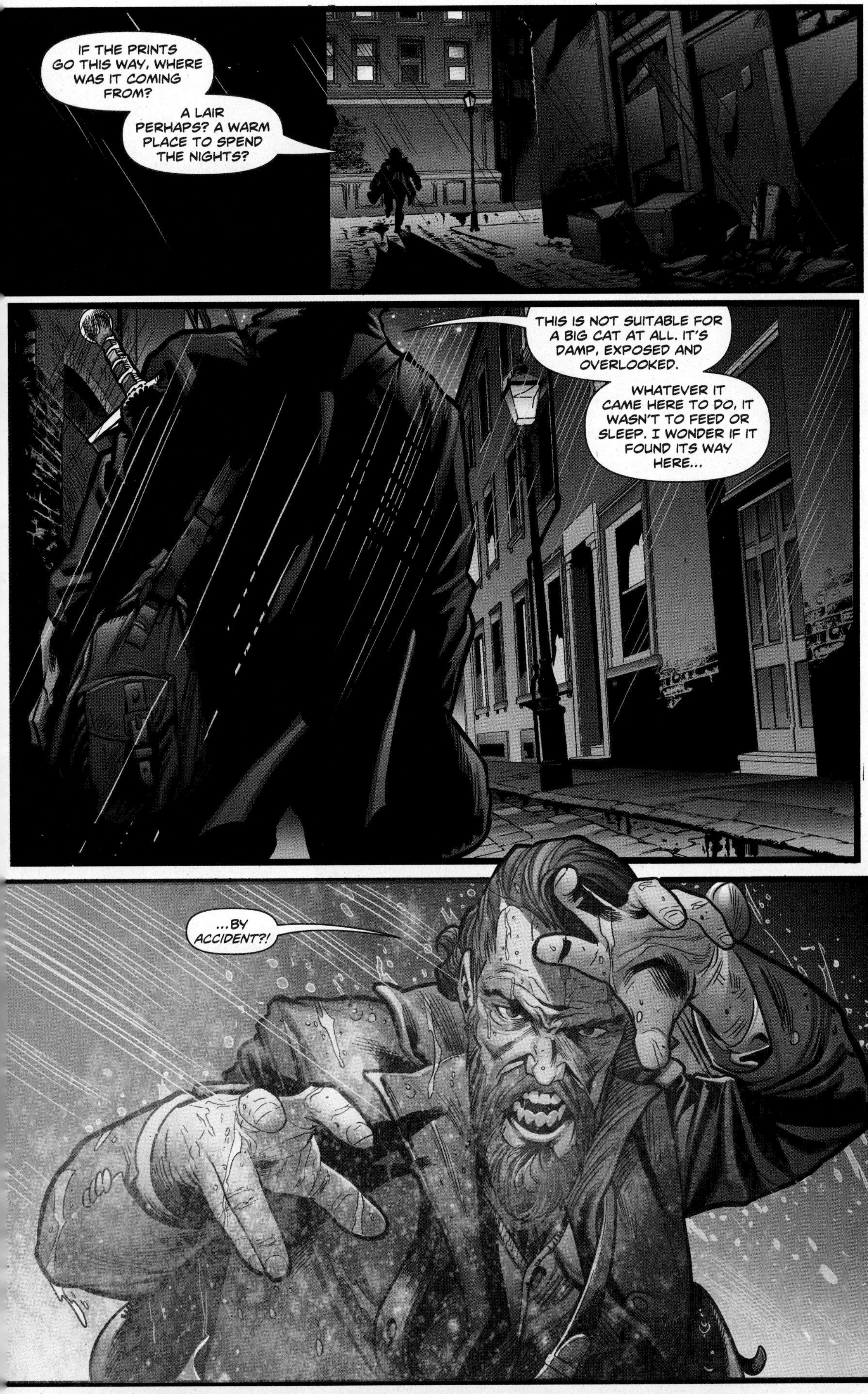
IF THE PRINTS GO THIS WAY, WHERE WAS IT COMING FROM?
A LAIR PERHAPS? A WARM PLACE TO SPEND THE NIGHTS?
THIS IS NOT SUITABLE FOR A BIG CAT AT ALL. IT'S DAMP, EXPOSED AND OVERLOOKED.
WHATEVER IT CAME HERE TO DO, IT WASN'T TO FEED OR SLEEP. I WONDER IF IT FOUND ITS WAY HERE...
...BY ACCIDENT?!

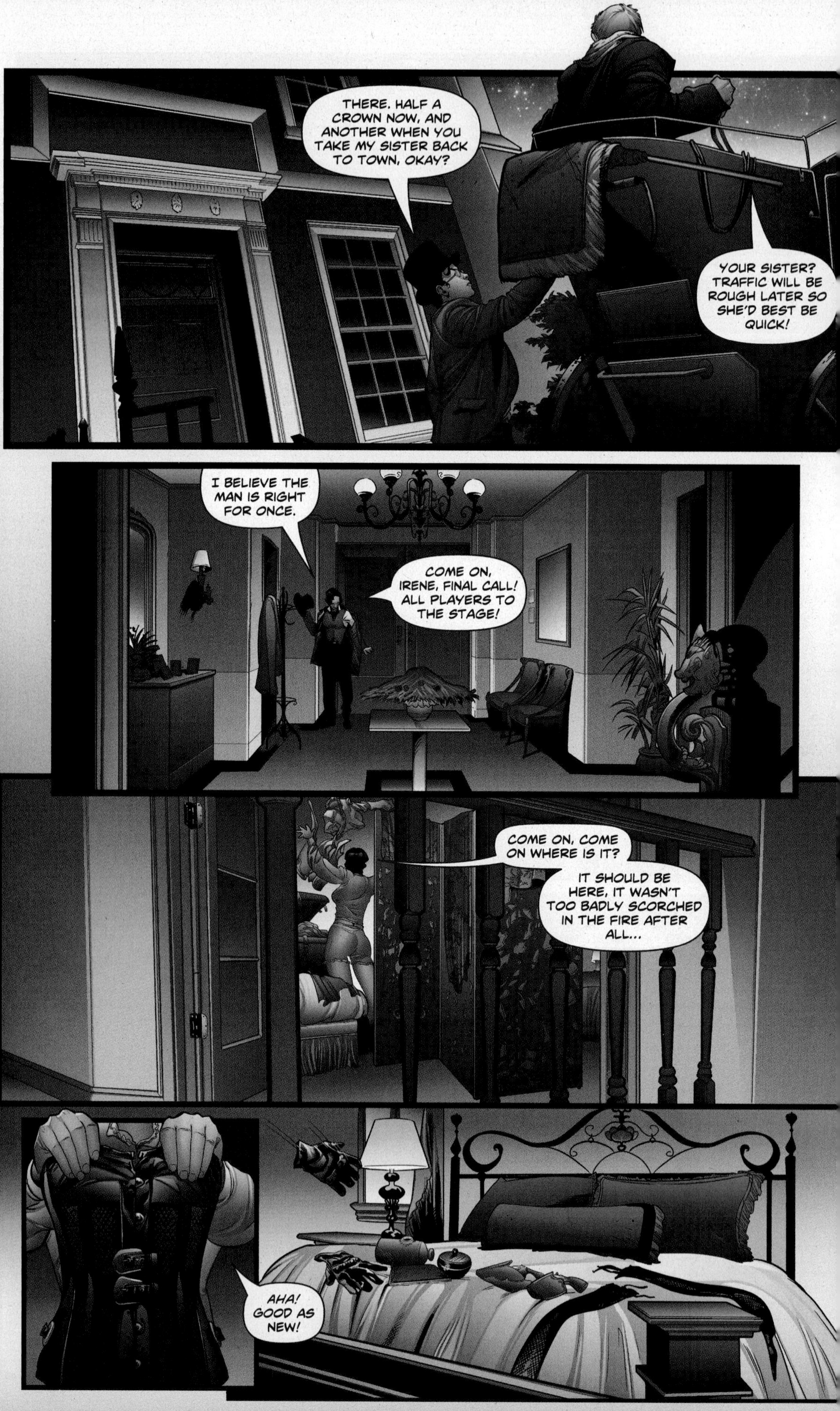
THERE. HALF A CROWN NOW, AND ANOTHER WHEN YOU TAKE MY SISTER BACK TO TOWN, OKAY?
YOUR SISTER? TRAFFIC WILL BE ROUGH LATER SO SHE'D BEST BE QUICK!
I BELIEVE THE MAN IS RIGHT FOR ONCE.
COME ON, IRENE, FINAL CALL! ALL PLAYERS TO THE STAGE!
COME ON, COME ON WHERE IS IT?
IT SHOULD BE HERE, IT WASN'T TOO BADLY SCORCHED IN THE FIRE AFTER ALL...
AHA! GOOD AS NEW!

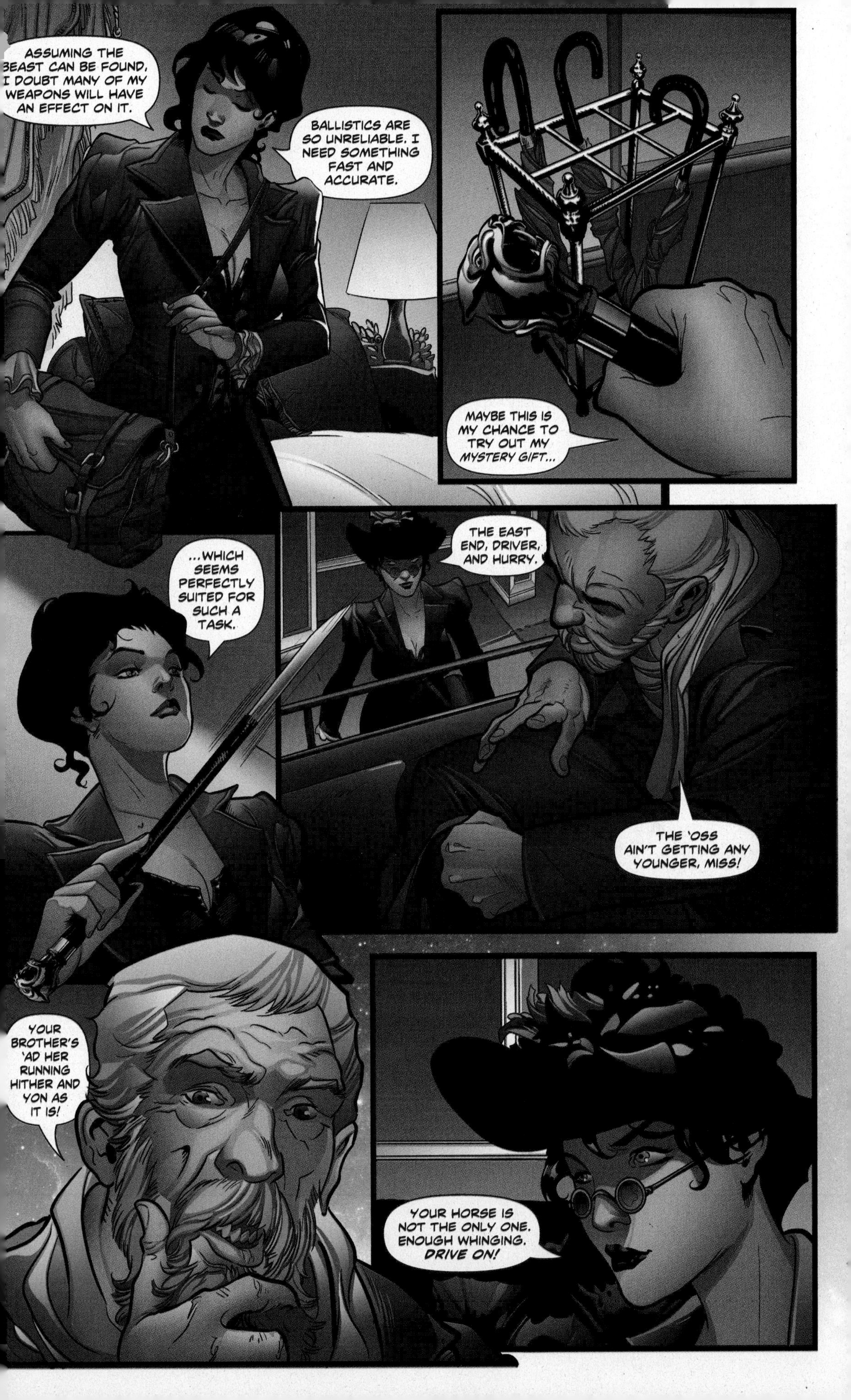
ASSUMING THE BEAST CAN BE FOUND, I DOUBT MANY OF MY WEAPONS WILL HAVE AN EFFECT ON IT.
BALLISTICS ARE SO UNRELIABLE. I NEED SOMETHING FAST AND ACCURATE.
MAYBE THIS IS MY CHANCE TO TRY OUT MY MYSTERY GIFT...
...WHICH SEEMS PERFECTLY SUITED FOR SUCH A TASK.
THE EAST END, DRIVER, AND HURRY.
THE 'OSS AIN'T GETTING ANY YOUNGER, MISS!
YOUR BROTHER'S 'AD HER RUNNING HITHER AND YON AS IT IS!
YOUR HORSE IS NOT THE ONLY ONE. ENOUGH WHINGING. *DRIVE ON!*

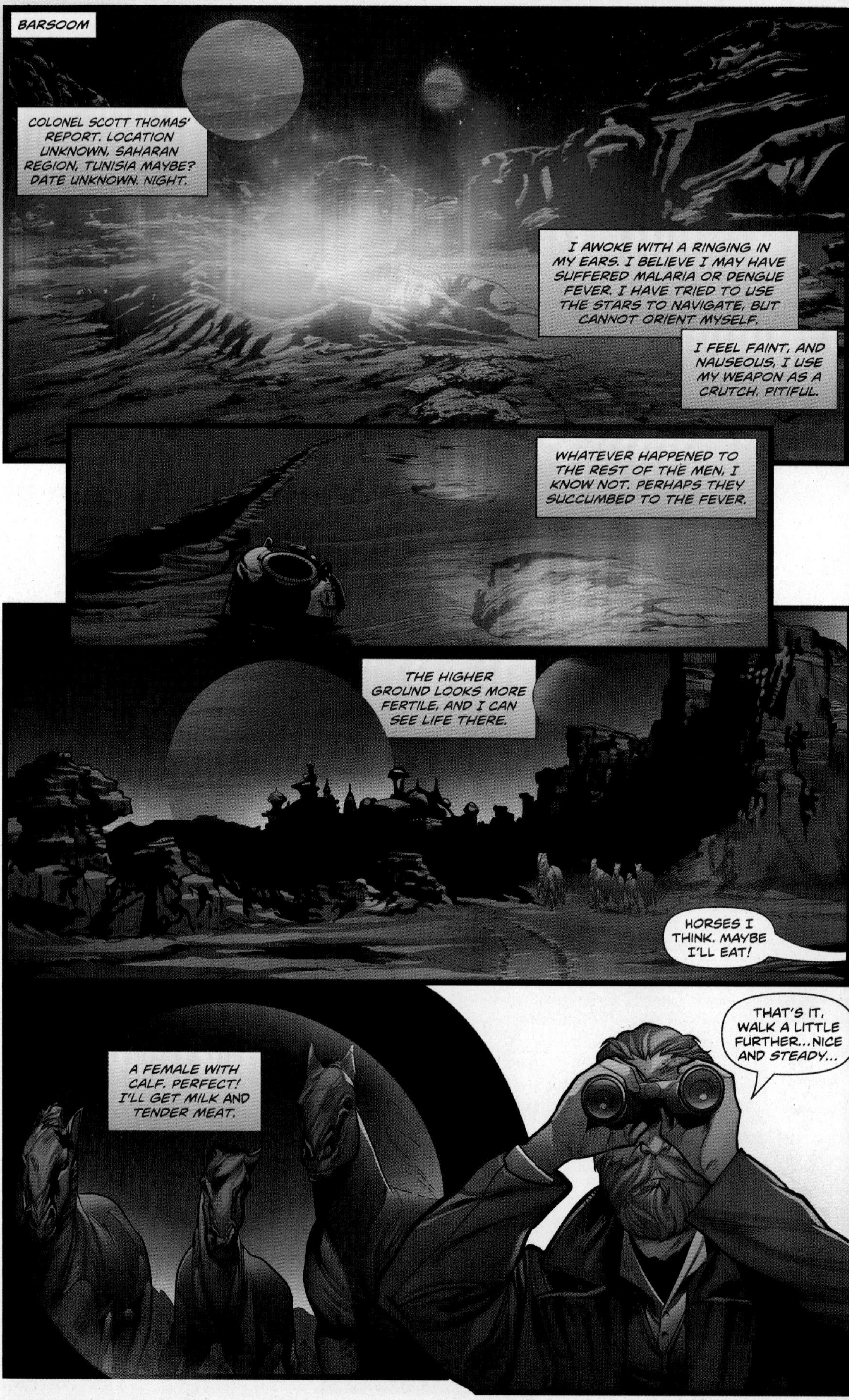
BARSOOM
COLONEL SCOTT THOMAS' REPORT. LOCATION UNKNOWN, SAHARAN REGION, TUNISIA MAYBE? DATE UNKNOWN. NIGHT.
I AWOKE WITH A RINGING IN MY EARS. I BELIEVE I MAY HAVE SUFFERED MALARIA OR DENGUE FEVER. I HAVE TRIED TO USE THE STARS TO NAVIGATE, BUT CANNOT ORIENT MYSELF.
I FEEL FAINT, AND NAUSEOUS, I USE MY WEAPON AS A CRUTCH. PITIFUL.
WHATEVER HAPPENED TO THE REST OF THE MEN, I KNOW NOT. PERHAPS THEY SUCCUMBED TO THE FEVER.
THE HIGHER GROUND LOOKS MORE FERTILE, AND I CAN SEE LIFE THERE.
HORSES I THINK. MAYBE I'LL EAT!
A FEMALE WITH CALF. PERFECT! I'LL GET MILK AND TENDER MEAT.
THAT'S IT, WALK A LITTLE FURTHER... NICE AND STEADY...

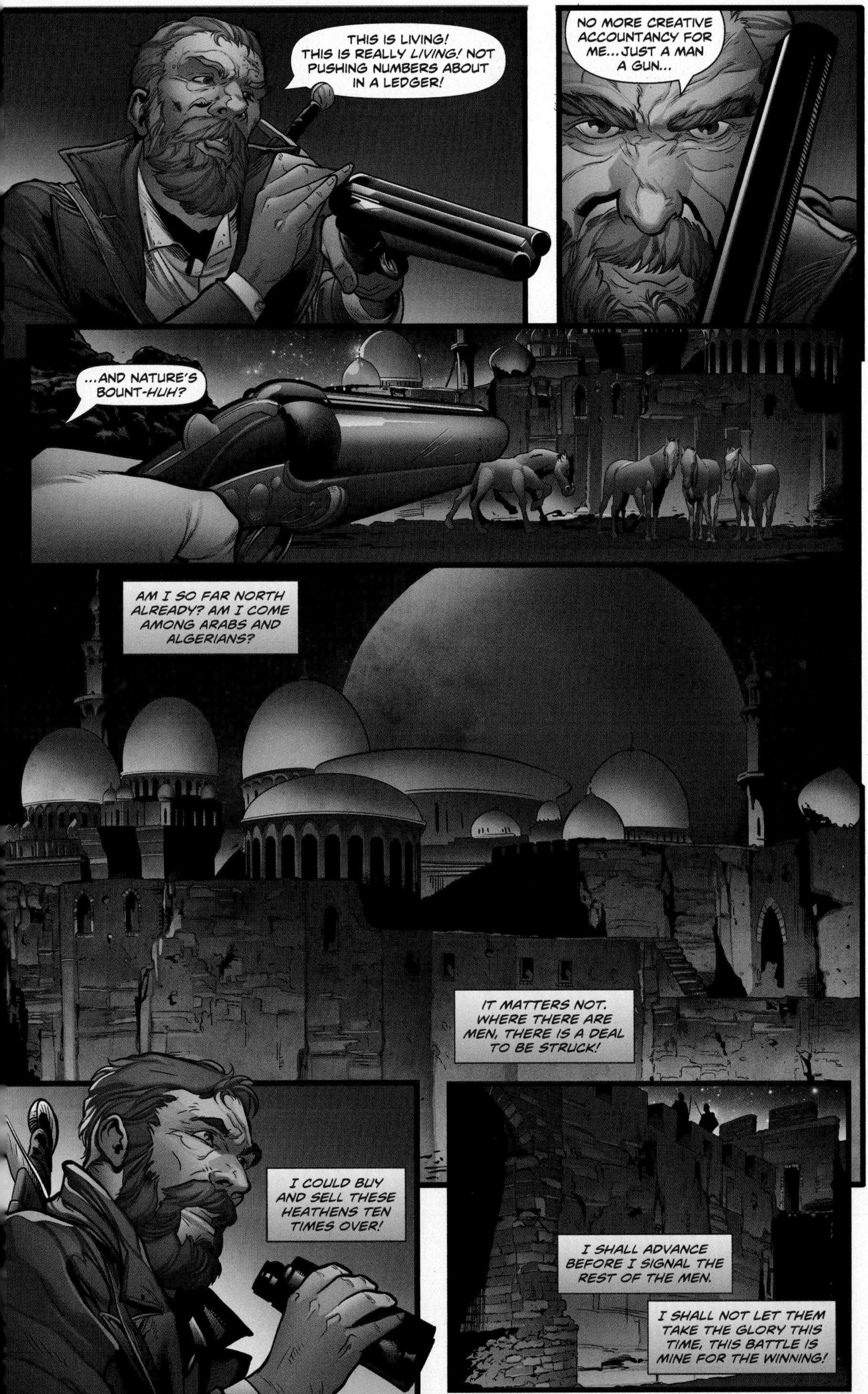
THIS IS LIVING! THIS IS REALLY *LIVING!* NOT PUSHING NUMBERS ABOUT IN A LEDGER!
NO MORE CREATIVE ACCOUNTANCY FOR ME... JUST A MAN A GUN...
...AND NATURE'S BOUNT-*HUH?*
AM I SO FAR NORTH ALREADY? AM I COME AMONG ARABS AND ALGERIANS?
IT MATTERS NOT. WHERE THERE ARE MEN, THERE IS A DEAL TO BE STRUCK!
I COULD BUY AND SELL THESE HEATHENS TEN TIMES OVER!
I SHALL ADVANCE BEFORE I SIGNAL THE REST OF THE MEN.
I SHALL NOT LET THEM TAKE THE GLORY THIS TIME, THIS BATTLE IS MINE FOR THE WINNING!

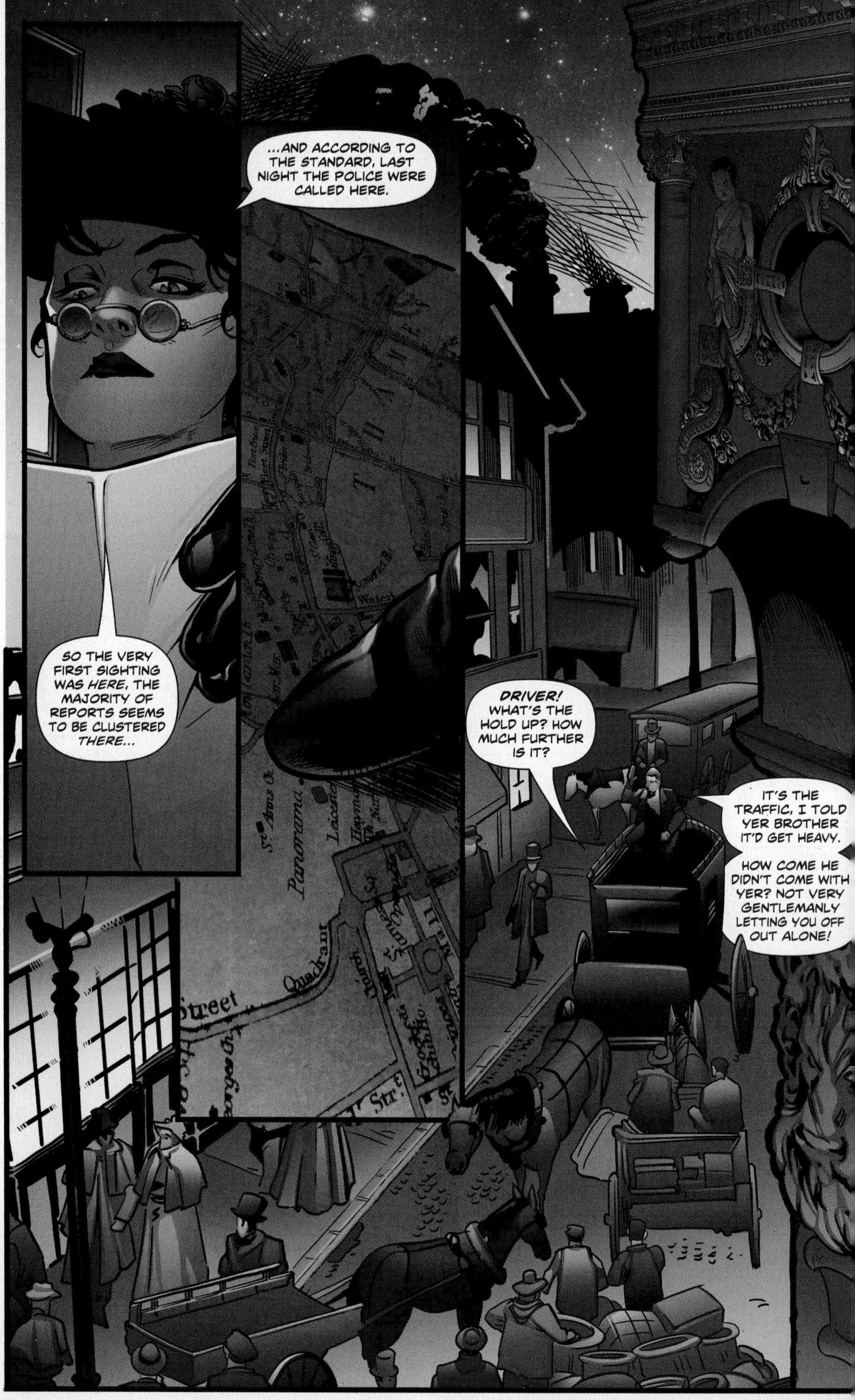
...AND ACCORDING TO THE STANDARD, LAST NIGHT THE POLICE WERE CALLED HERE.
SO THE VERY FIRST SIGHTING WAS HERE, THE MAJORITY OF REPORTS SEEMS TO BE CLUSTERED THERE...
DRIVER! WHAT'S THE HOLD UP? HOW MUCH FURTHER IS IT?
IT'S THE TRAFFIC, I TOLD YER BROTHER IT'D GET HEAVY.
HOW COME HE DIDN'T COME WITH YER? NOT VERY GENTLEMANLY LETTING YOU OFF OUT ALONE!

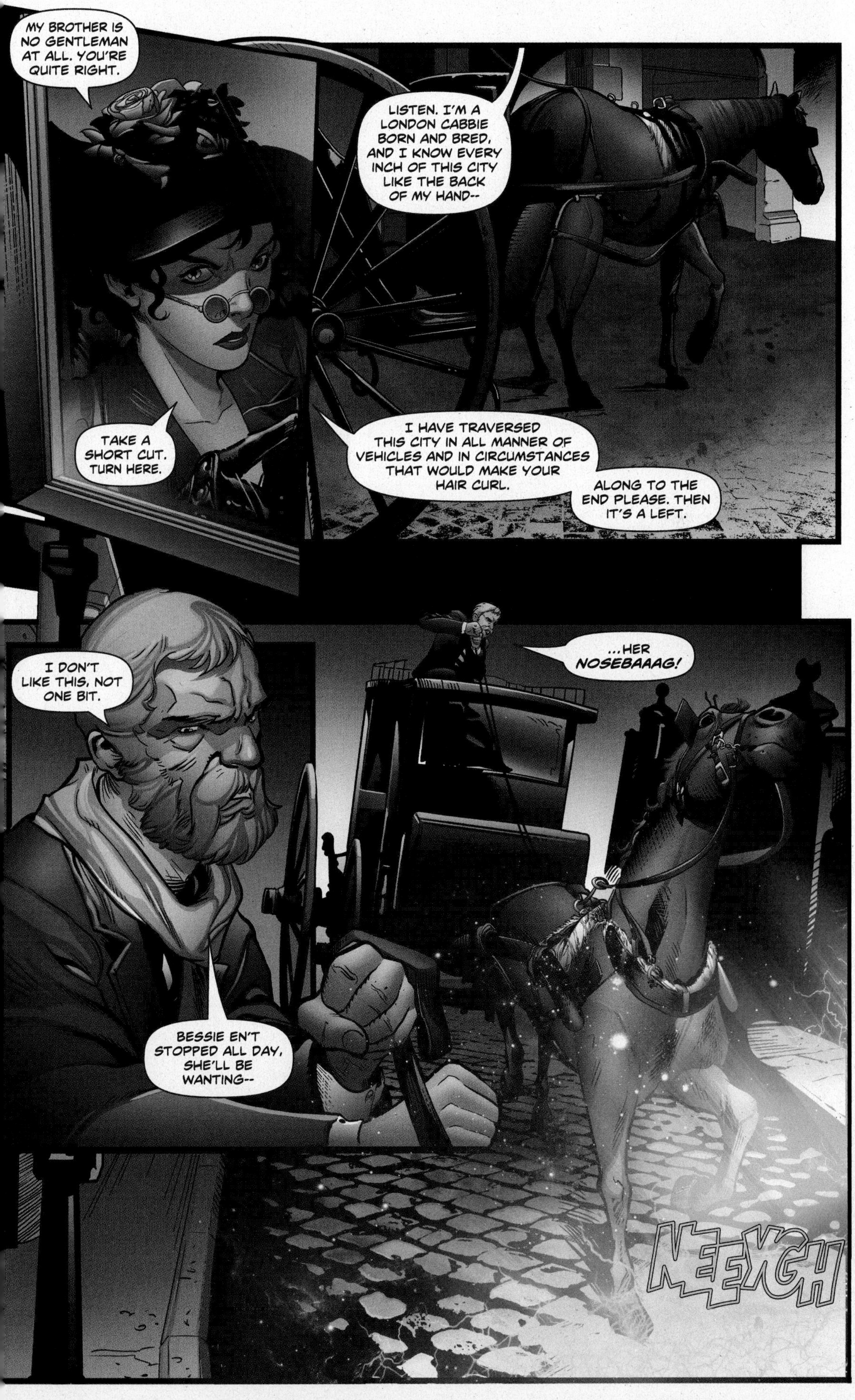
MY BROTHER IS NO GENTLEMAN AT ALL. YOU'RE QUITE RIGHT.
LISTEN. I'M A LONDON CABBIE BORN AND BRED, AND I KNOW EVERY INCH OF THIS CITY LIKE THE BACK OF MY HAND--
TAKE A SHORT CUT. TURN HERE.
I HAVE TRAVERSED THIS CITY IN ALL MANNER OF VEHICLES AND IN CIRCUMSTANCES THAT WOULD MAKE YOUR HAIR CURL.
ALONG TO THE END PLEASE. THEN IT'S A LEFT.
I DON'T LIKE THIS, NOT ONE BIT.
BESSIE EN'T STOPPED ALL DAY, SHE'LL BE WANTING--
...HER *NOSEBAAAG!*
NEEYGH

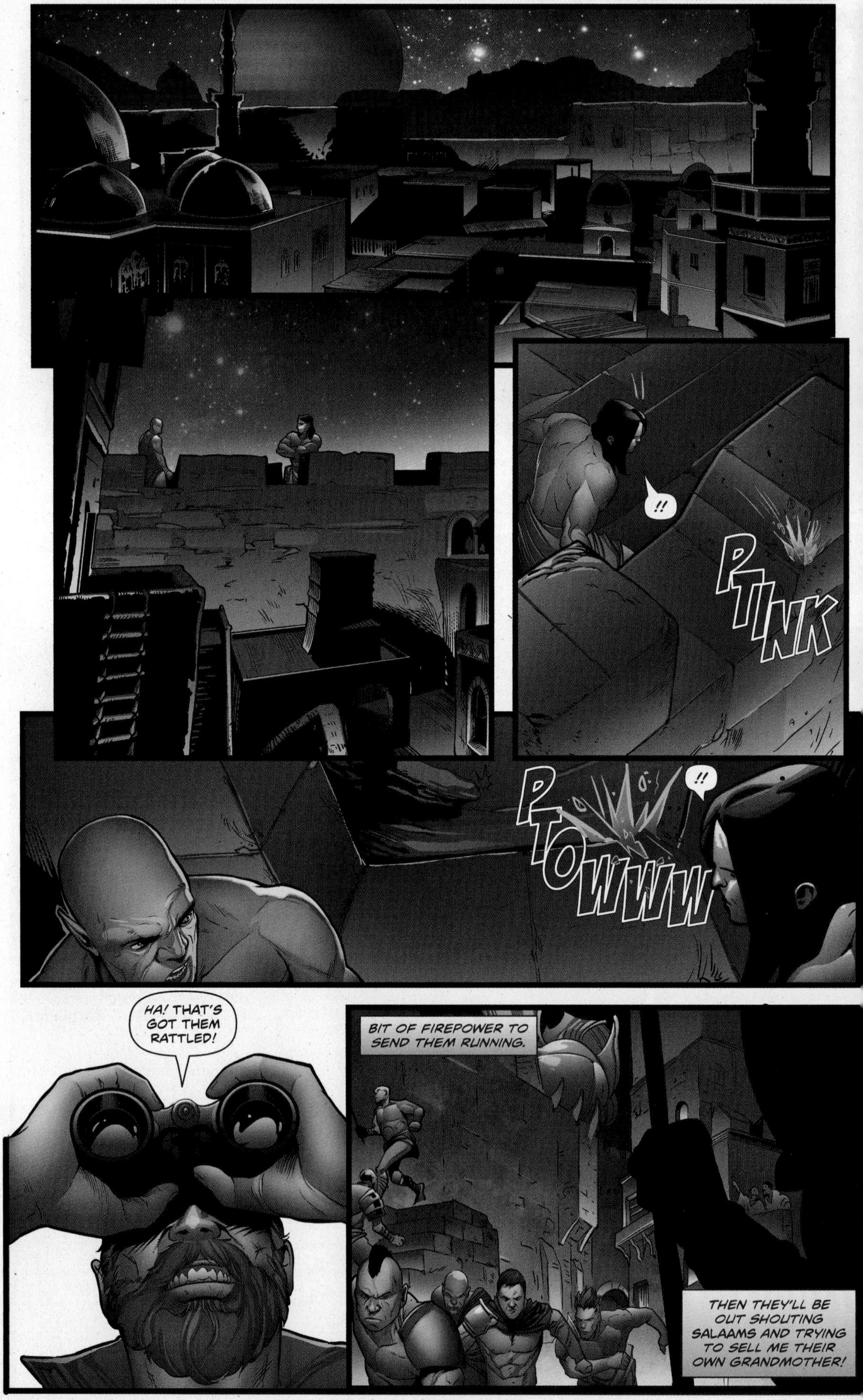
!!
PTINK
PTOWWWW
!!
HA! THAT'S GOT THEM RATTLED!
BIT OF FIREPOWER TO SEND THEM RUNNING.
THEN THEY'LL BE OUT SHOUTING SALAAMS AND TRYING TO SELL ME THEIR OWN GRANDMOTHER!

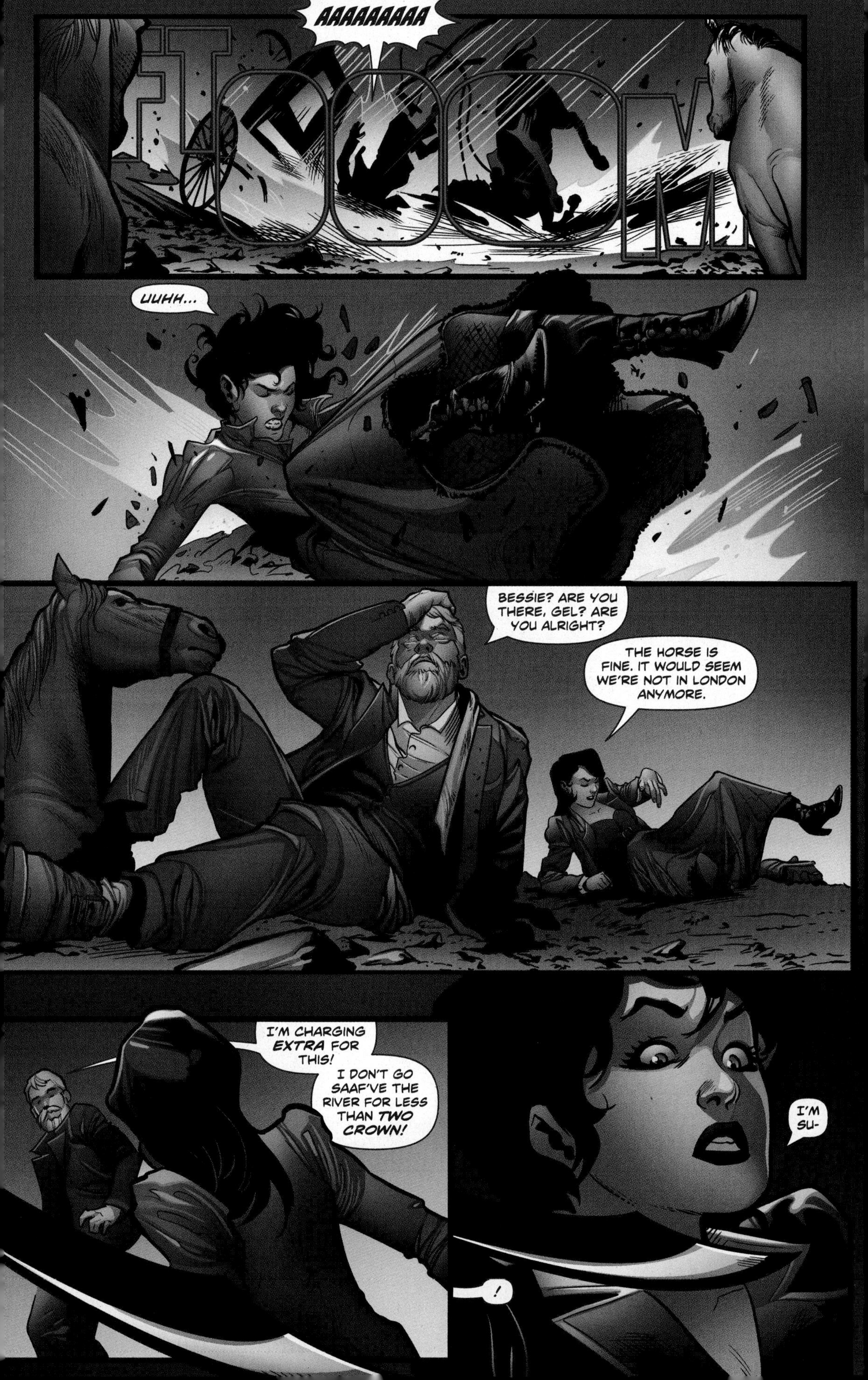
AAAAAAAAA
UUHH...
BESSIE? ARE YOU THERE, GEL? ARE YOU ALRIGHT?
THE HORSE IS FINE. IT WOULD SEEM WE'RE NOT IN LONDON ANYMORE.
I'M CHARGING *EXTRA* FOR THIS!
I DON'T GO SAAF'VE THE RIVER FOR LESS THAN *TWO CROWN!*
I'M SU-
!

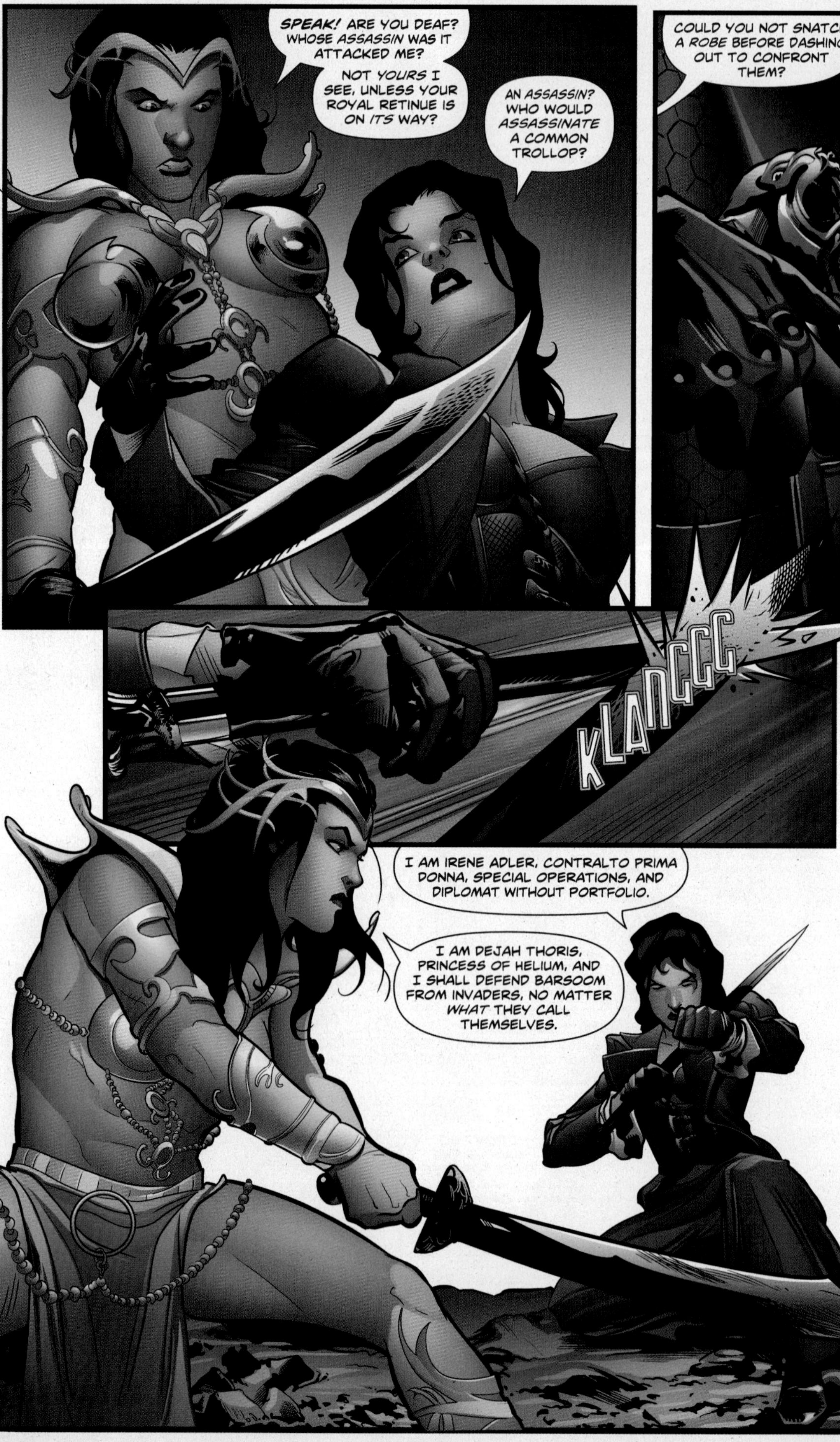
SPEAK! ARE YOU DEAF? WHOSE ASSASSIN WAS IT ATTACKED ME?
NOT YOURS I SEE, UNLESS YOUR ROYAL RETINUE IS ON ITS WAY?
AN ASSASSIN? WHO WOULD ASSASSINATE A COMMON TROLLOP?
COULD YOU NOT SNATCH A ROBE BEFORE DASHING OUT TO CONFRONT THEM?
KLANGGG
I AM IRENE ADLER, CONTRALTO PRIMA DONNA, SPECIAL OPERATIONS, AND DIPLOMAT WITHOUT PORTFOLIO.
I AM DEJAH THORIS, PRINCESS OF HELIUM, AND I SHALL DEFEND BARSOOM FROM INVADERS, NO MATTER WHAT THEY CALL THEMSELVES.

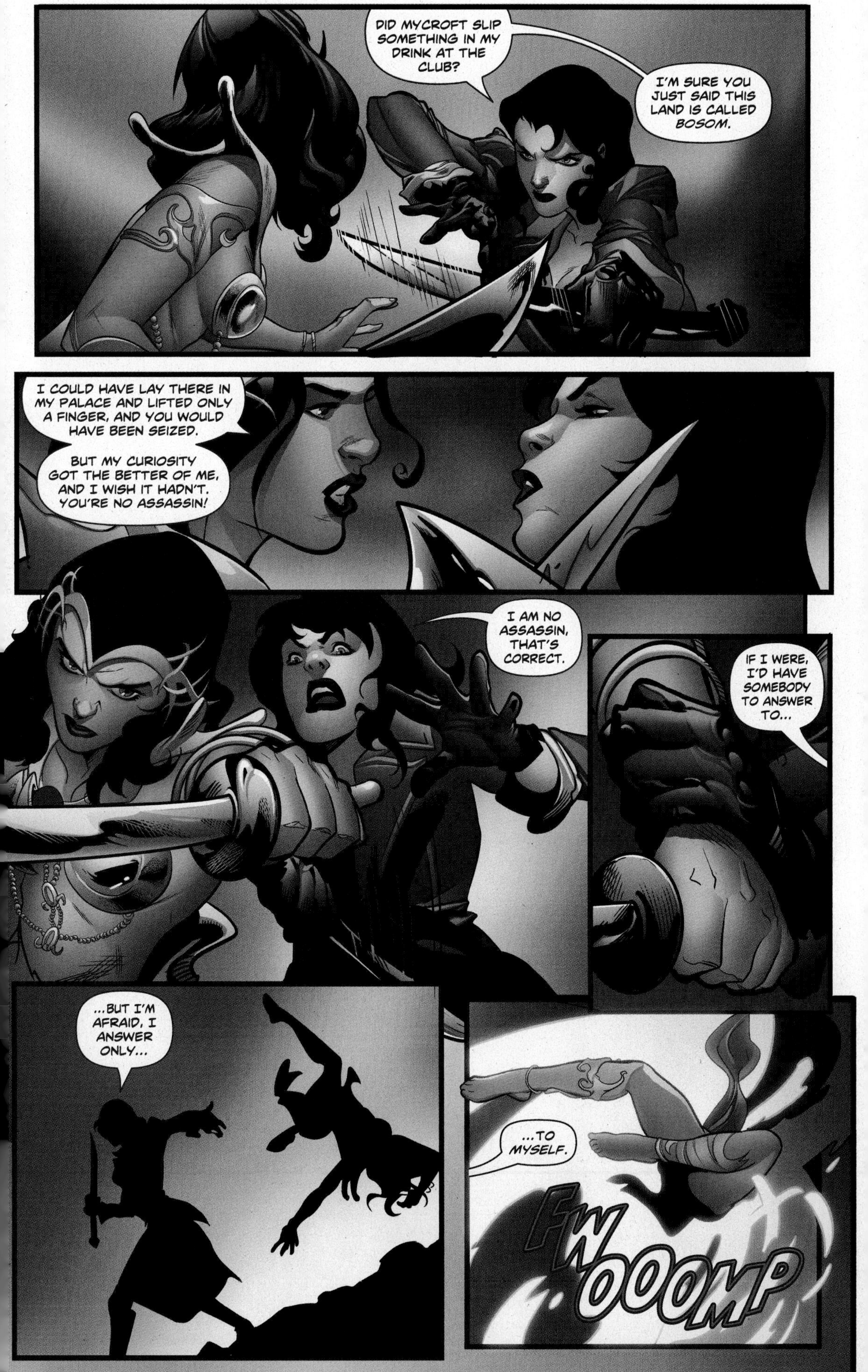
DID MYCROFT SLIP SOMETHING IN MY DRINK AT THE CLUB?
I'M SURE YOU JUST SAID THIS LAND IS CALLED BOSOM.
I COULD HAVE LAY THERE IN MY PALACE AND LIFTED ONLY A FINGER, AND YOU WOULD HAVE BEEN SEIZED.
BUT MY CURIOSITY GOT THE BETTER OF ME, AND I WISH IT HADN'T. YOU'RE NO ASSASSIN!
I AM NO ASSASSIN, THAT'S CORRECT.
IF I WERE, I'D HAVE SOMEBODY TO ANSWER TO...
...BUT I'M AFRAID, I ANSWER ONLY...
...TO MYSELF.
FWOOOMP

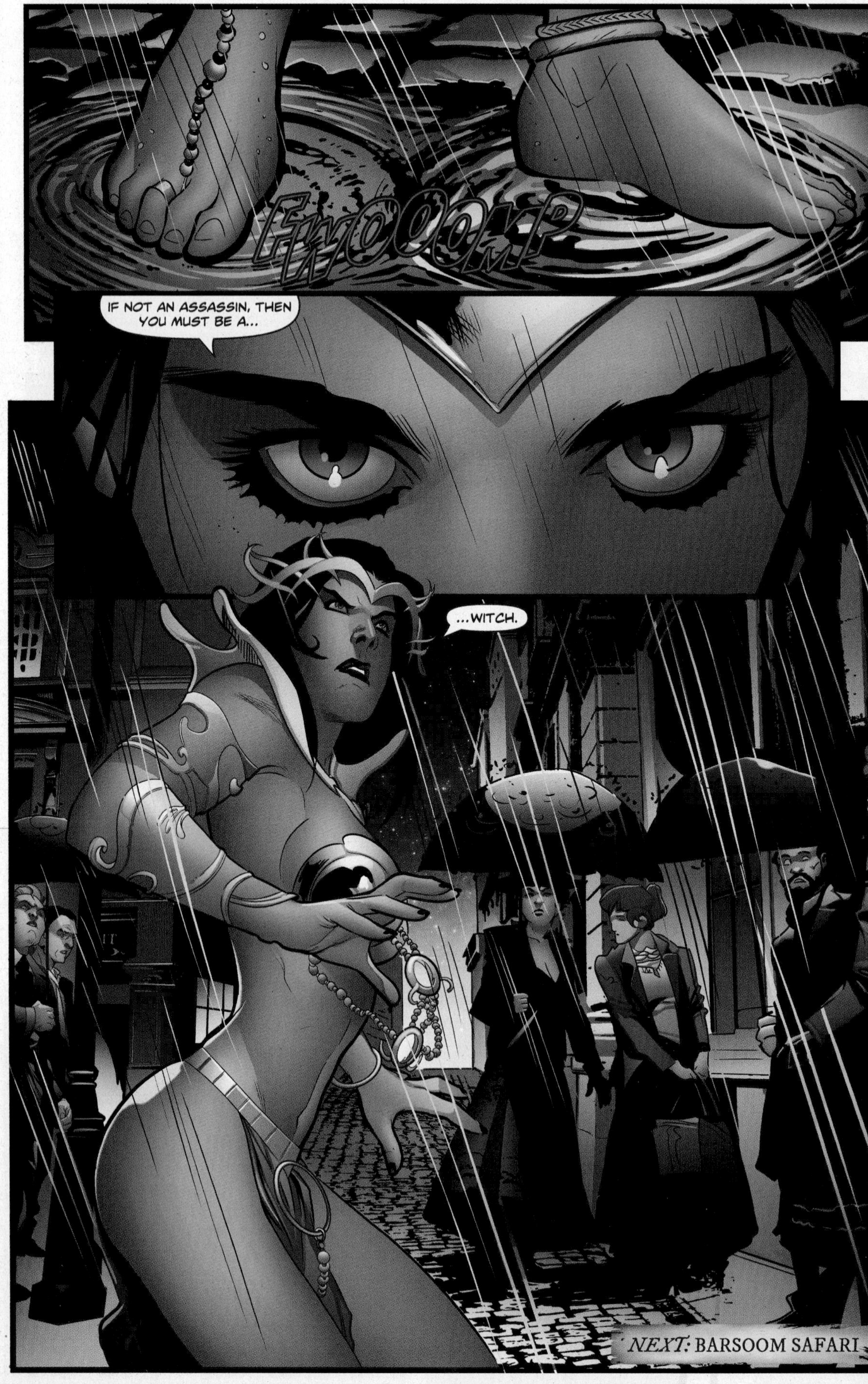
FWOOOMP
IF NOT AN ASSASSIN, THEN YOU MUST BE A...
...WITCH.
NEXT: BARSOOM SAFARI

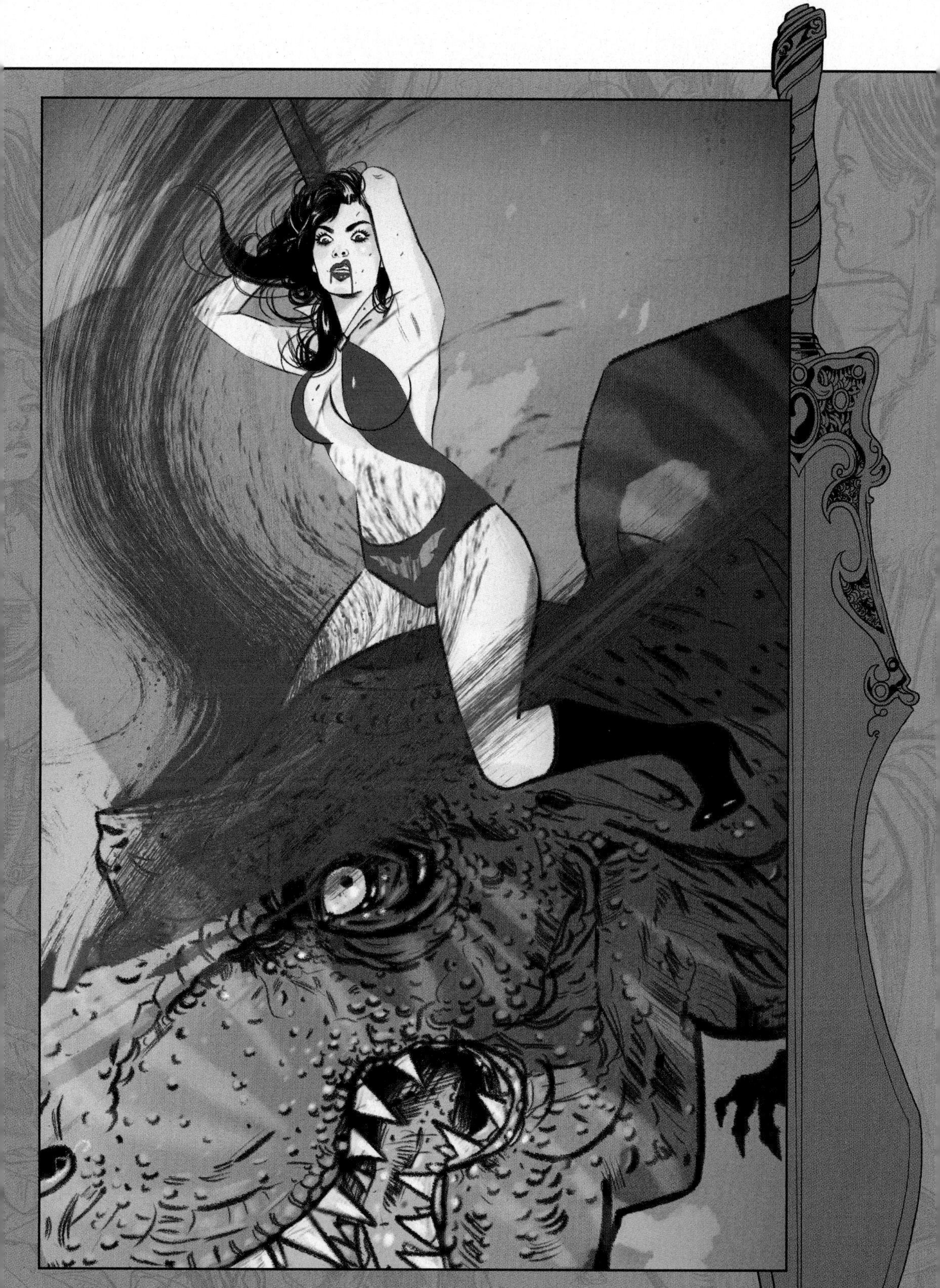

SWORDS OF SORROW

ISSUE TWO OF SIX

written by GAIL SIMONE illustrated by SERGIO DÁVILA
colored by JORGE SUTIL lettered by ERICA SCHULTZ

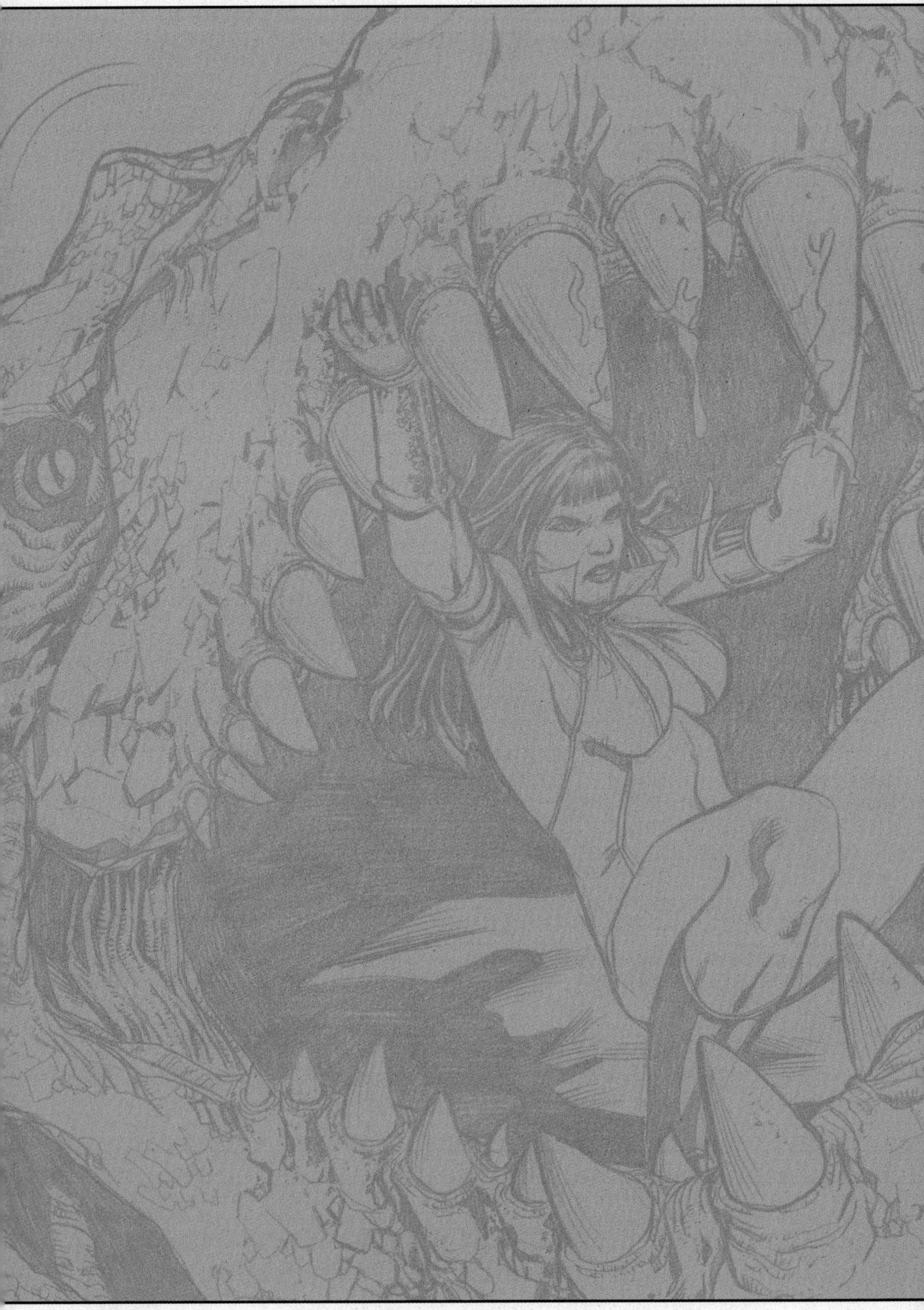

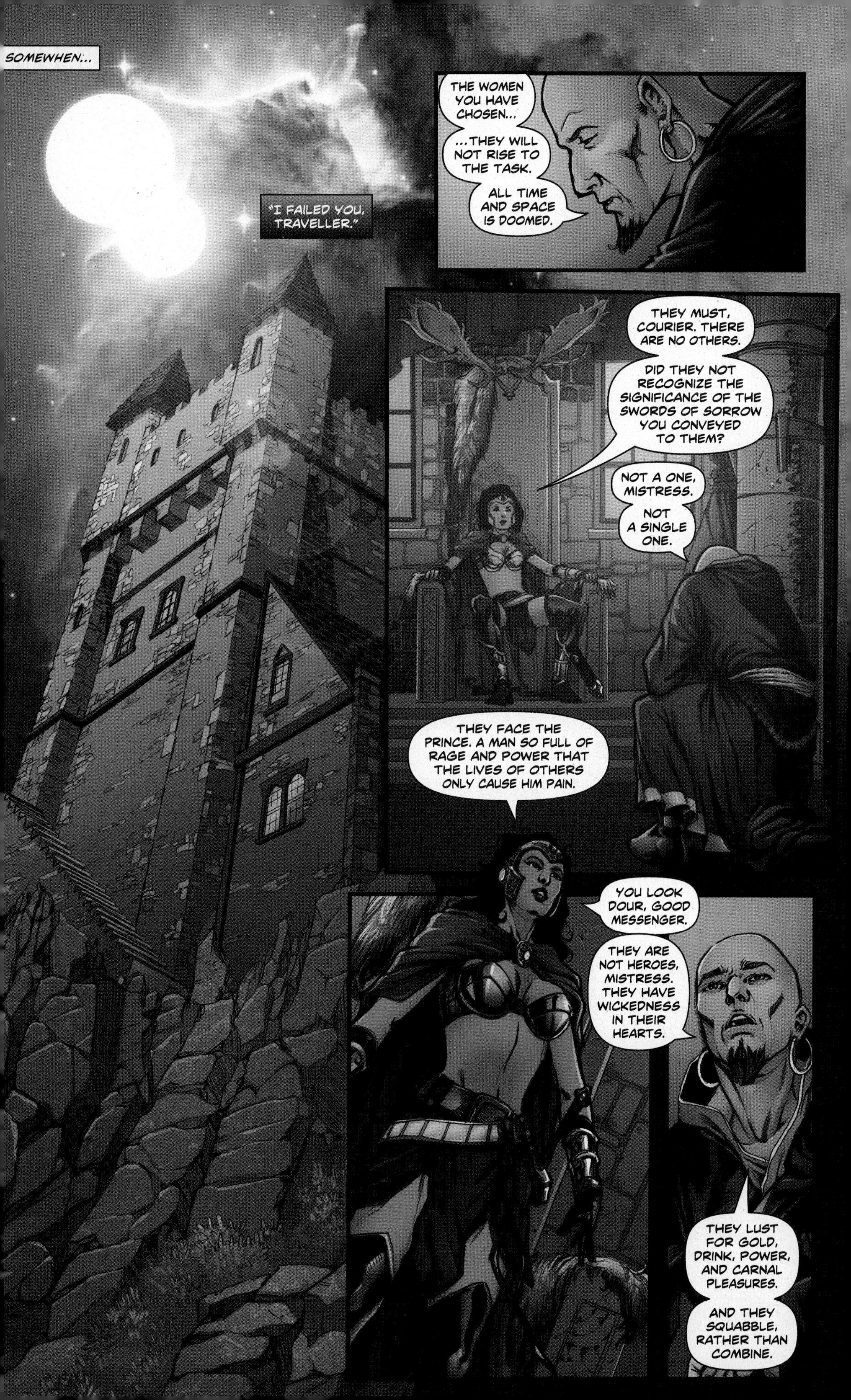
SOMEWHEN...
THE WOMEN YOU HAVE CHOSEN...
...THEY WILL NOT RISE TO THE TASK.
ALL TIME AND SPACE IS DOOMED.
"I FAILED YOU, TRAVELLER."
THEY MUST, COURIER. THERE ARE NO OTHERS.
DID THEY NOT RECOGNIZE THE SIGNIFICANCE OF THE SWORDS OF SORROW YOU CONVEYED TO THEM?
NOT A ONE, MISTRESS.
NOT A SINGLE ONE.
THEY FACE THE PRINCE. A MAN SO FULL OF RAGE AND POWER THAT THE LIVES OF OTHERS ONLY CAUSE HIM PAIN.
YOU LOOK DOUR, GOOD MESSENGER.
THEY ARE NOT HEROES, MISTRESS. THEY HAVE WICKEDNESS IN THEIR HEARTS.
THEY LUST FOR GOLD, DRINK, POWER, AND CARNAL PLEASURES.
AND THEY SQUABBLE, RATHER THAN COMBINE.

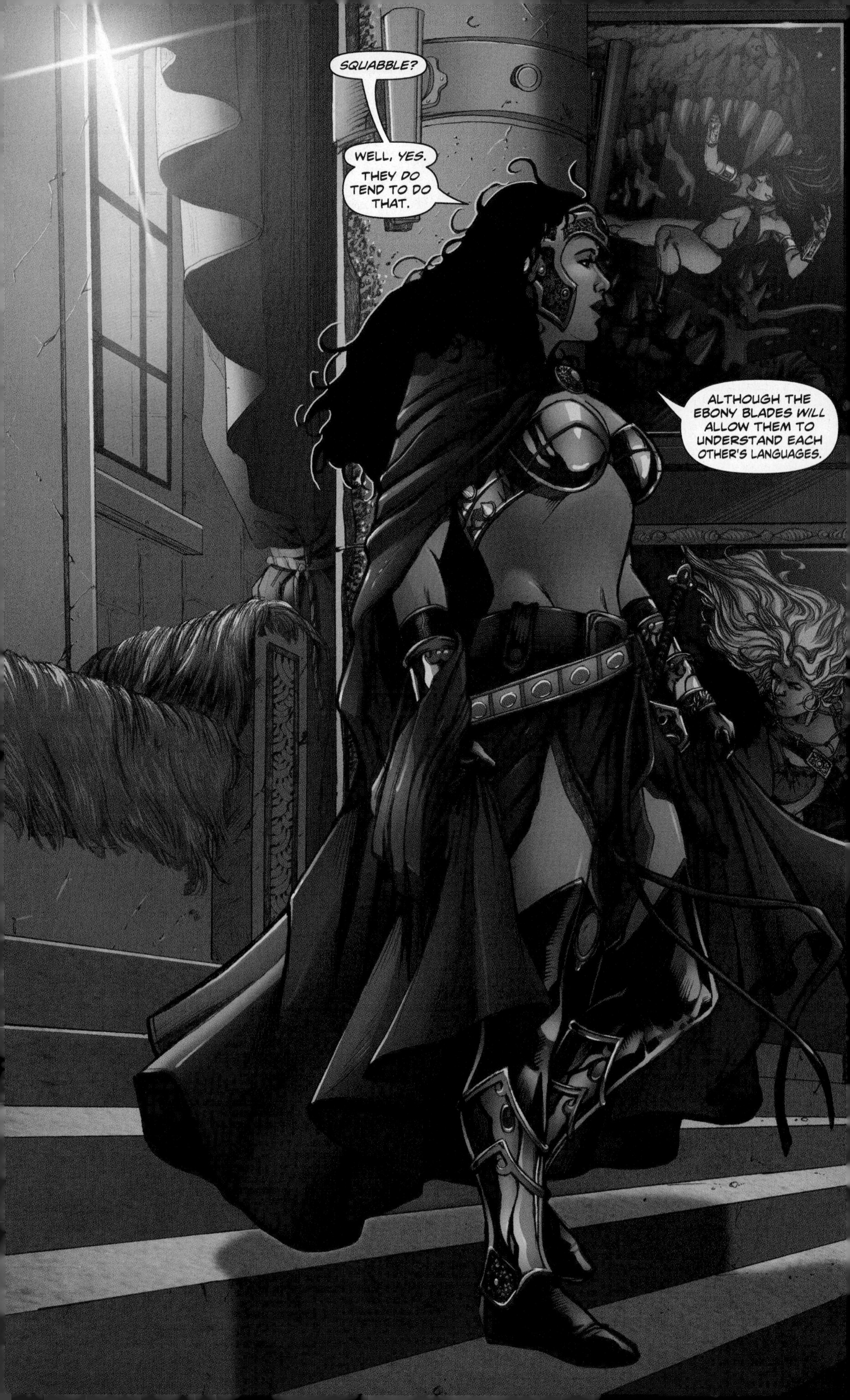
SQUABBLE?
WELL, YES. THEY DO TEND TO DO THAT.
ALTHOUGH THE EBONY BLADES WILL ALLOW THEM TO UNDERSTAND EACH OTHER'S LANGUAGES.

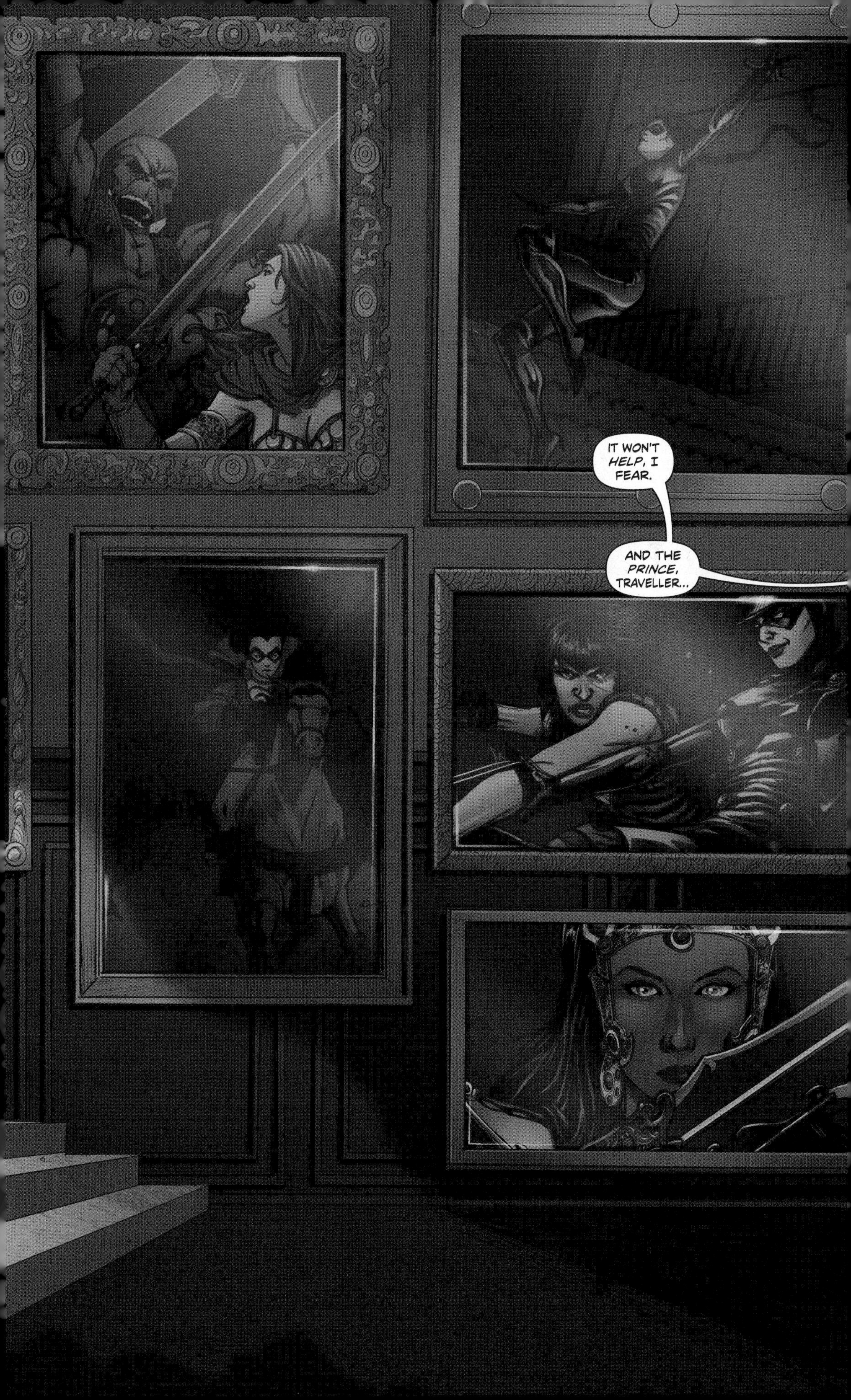
IT WON'T *HELP*, I FEAR.
AND THE *PRINCE*, TRAVELLER...

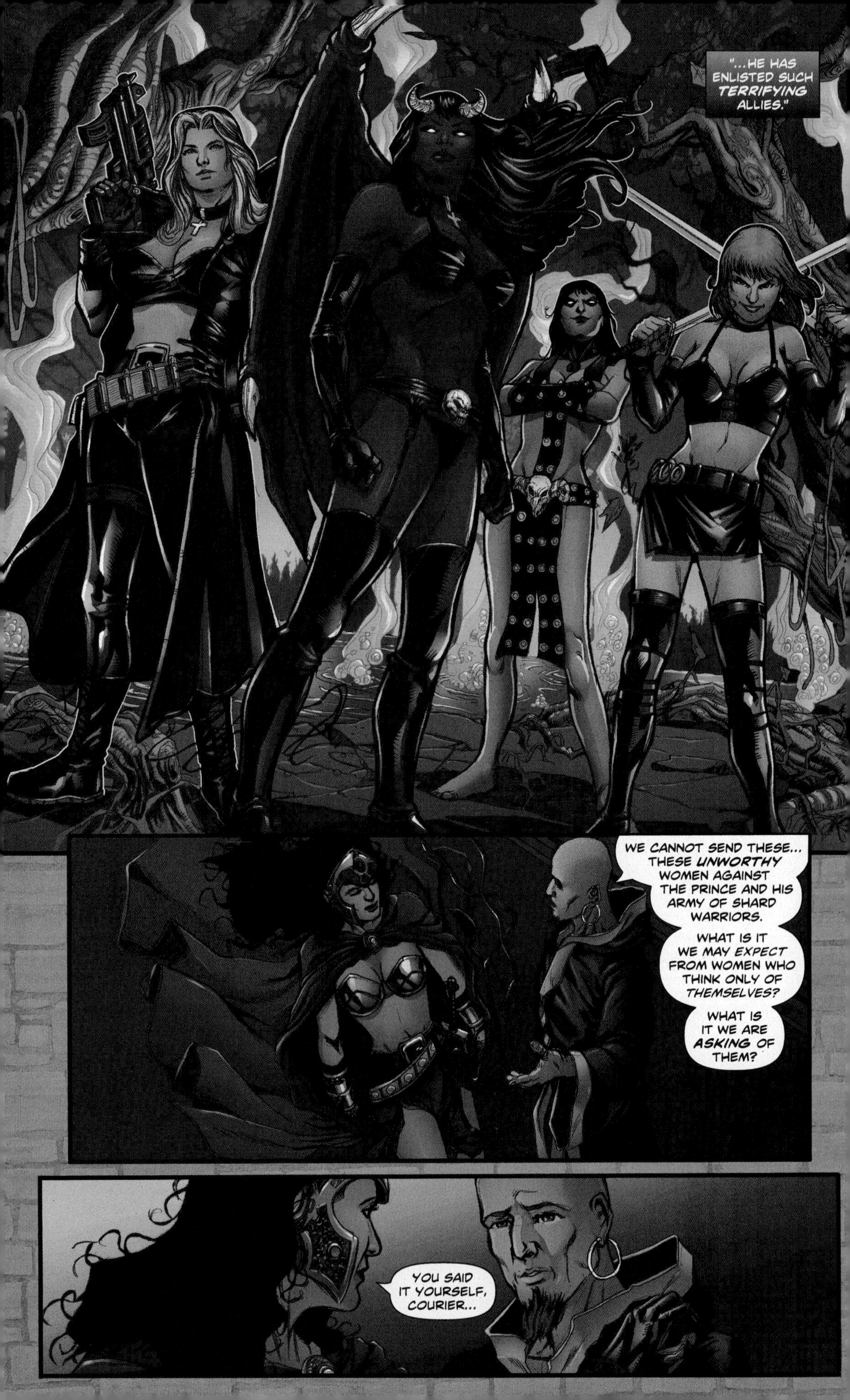
"...HE HAS ENLISTED SUCH TERRIFYING ALLIES."
WE CANNOT SEND THESE... THESE UNWORTHY WOMEN AGAINST THE PRINCE AND HIS ARMY OF SHARD WARRIORS.
WHAT IS IT WE MAY EXPECT FROM WOMEN WHO THINK ONLY OF THEMSELVES?
WHAT IS IT WE ARE ASKING OF THEM?
YOU SAID IT YOURSELF, COURIER...

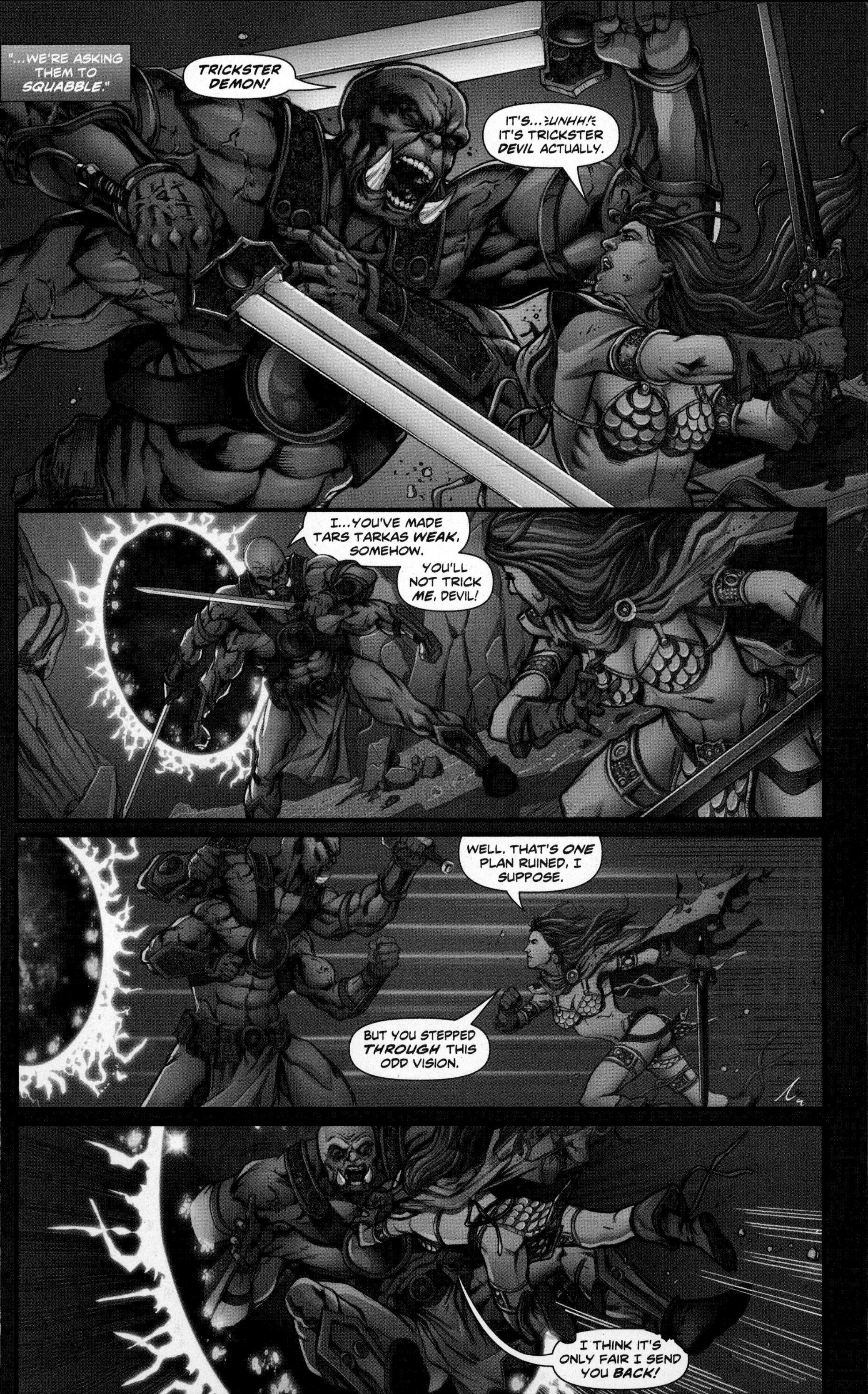
"...WE'RE ASKING THEM TO SQUABBLE."
TRICKSTER DEMON!
IT'S...UNHH! IT'S TRICKSTER DEVIL ACTUALLY.
I...YOU'VE MADE TARS TARKAS WEAK, SOMEHOW.
YOU'LL NOT TRICK ME, DEVIL!
WELL. THAT'S ONE PLAN RUINED, I SUPPOSE.
BUT YOU STEPPED THROUGH THIS ODD VISION.
I THINK IT'S ONLY FAIR I SEND YOU BACK!

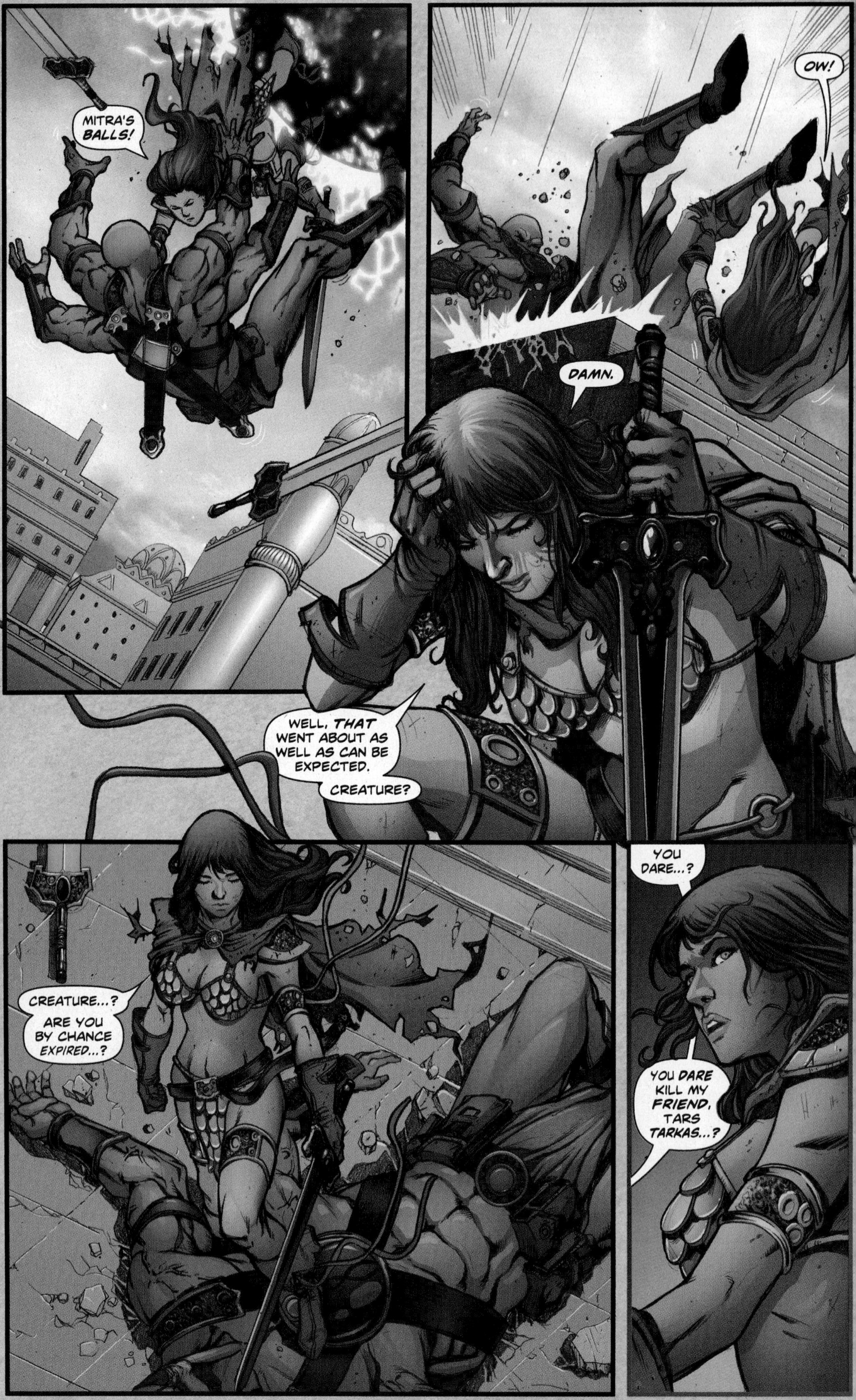
MITRA'S BALLS!
OW!
DAMN.
WELL, THAT WENT ABOUT AS WELL AS CAN BE EXPECTED.
CREATURE?
CREATURE...?
ARE YOU BY CHANCE EXPIRED...?
YOU DARE...?
YOU DARE KILL MY FRIEND, TARS TARKAS...?

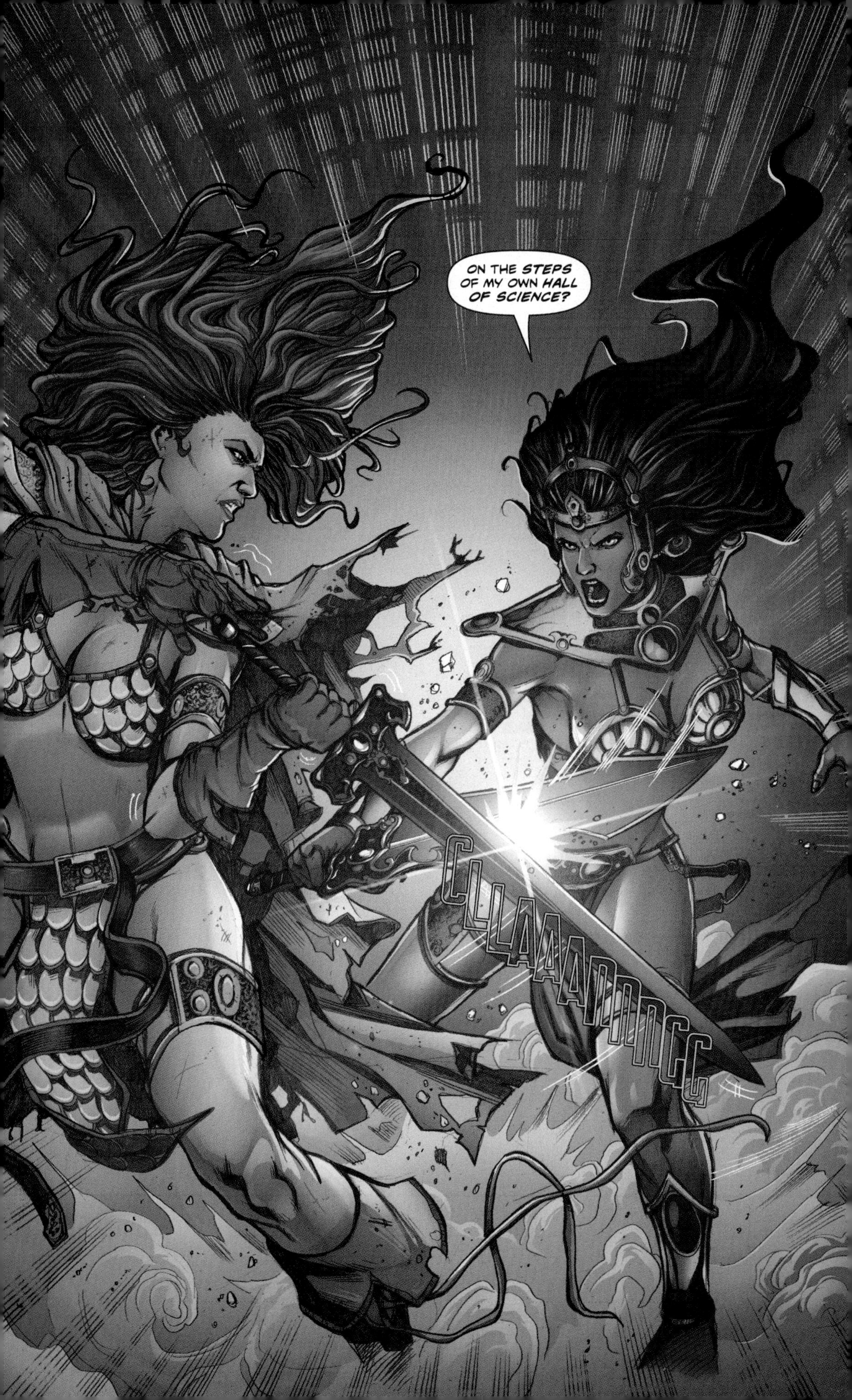
ON THE STEPS OF MY OWN HALL OF SCIENCE?
CLLLAAAANNNGG

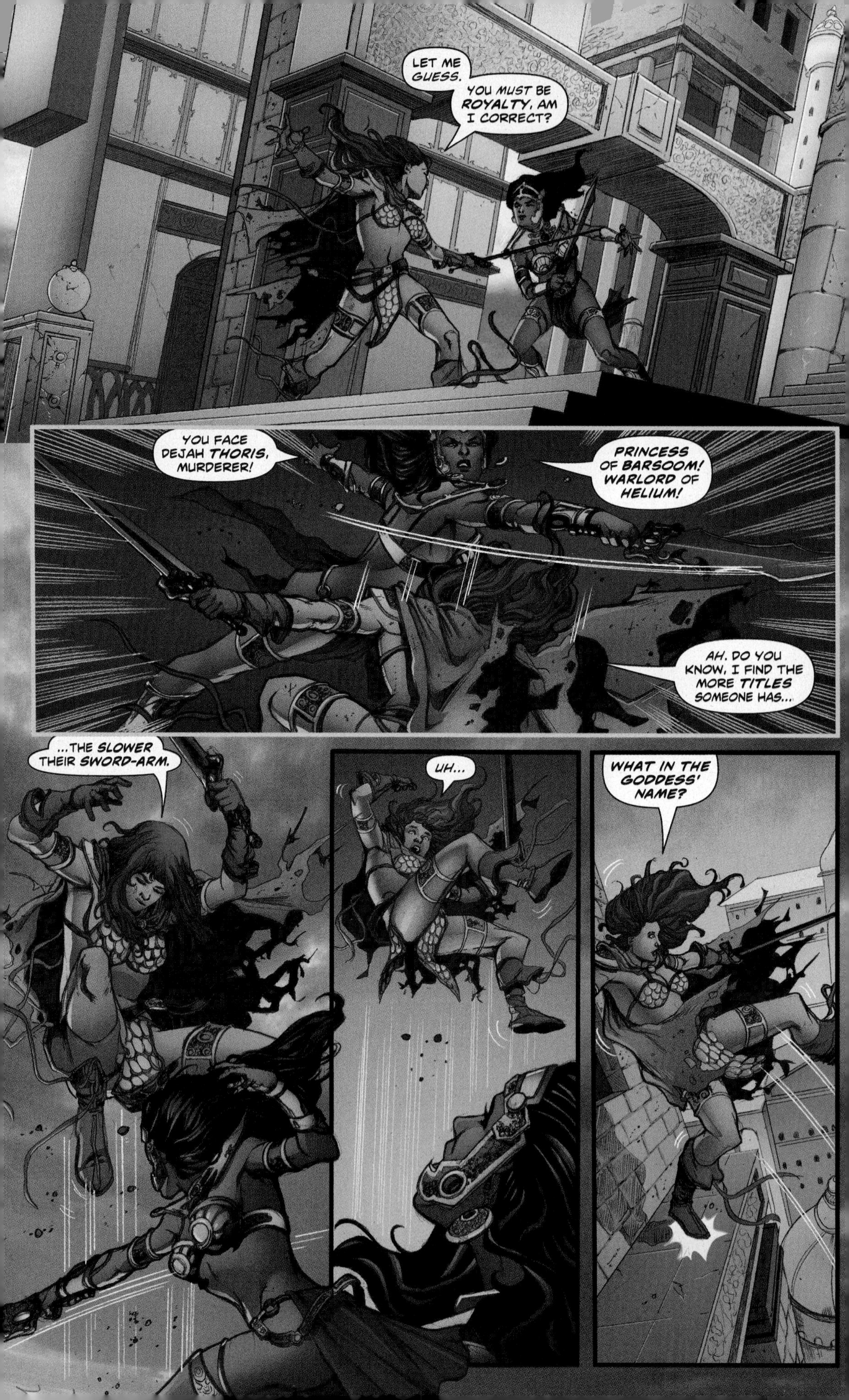
LET ME GUESS.
YOU MUST BE ROYALTY, AM I CORRECT?
YOU FACE DEJAH THORIS, MURDERER!
PRINCESS OF BARSOOM! WARLORD OF HELIUM!
AH. DO YOU KNOW, I FIND THE MORE TITLES SOMEONE HAS...
...THE SLOWER THEIR SWORD-ARM.
UH...
WHAT IN THE GODDESS' NAME?

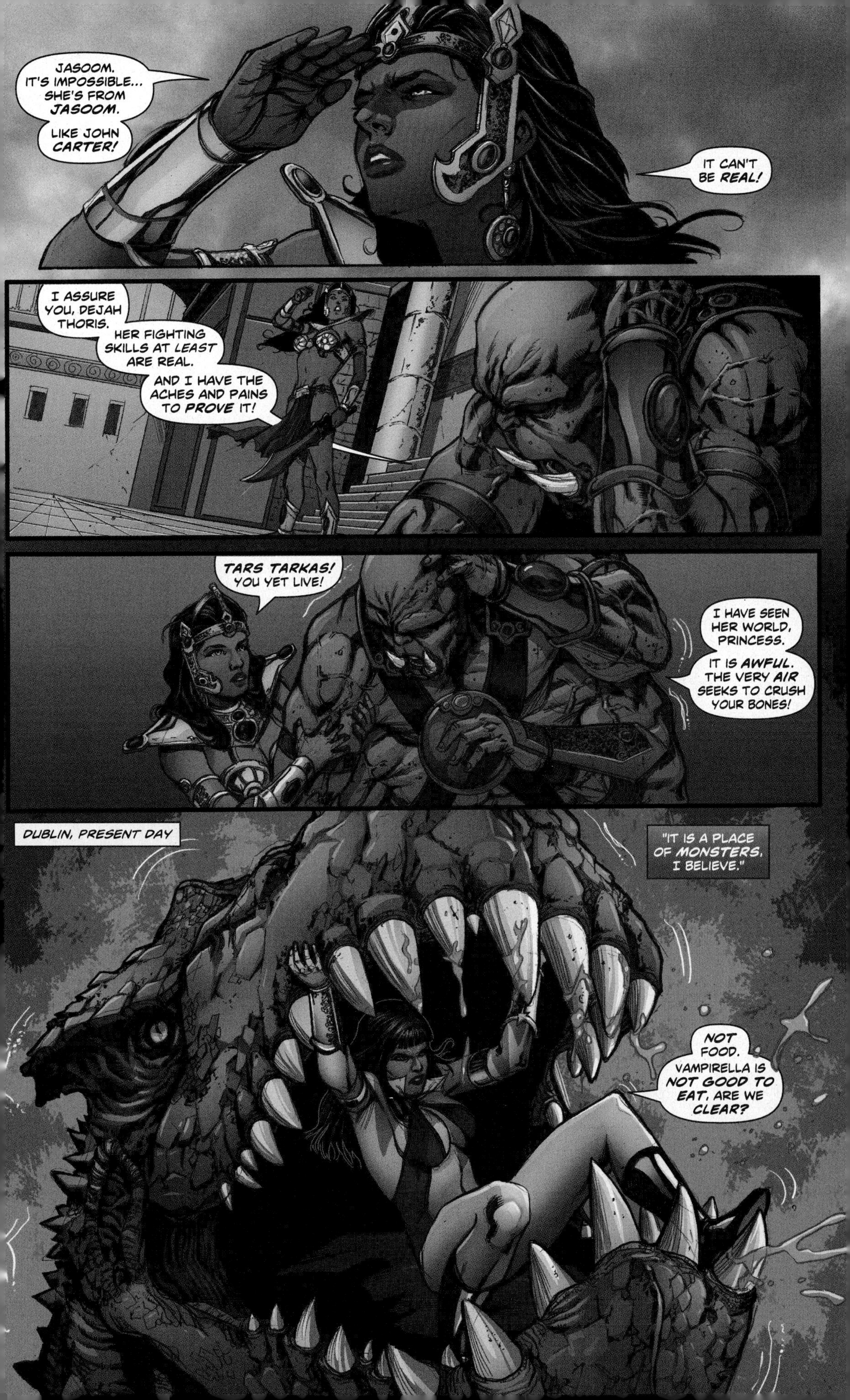
JASOOM. IT'S IMPOSSIBLE... SHE'S FROM JASOOM.
LIKE JOHN CARTER!
IT CAN'T BE REAL!
I ASSURE YOU, DEJAH THORIS.
HER FIGHTING SKILLS AT LEAST ARE REAL.
AND I HAVE THE ACHES AND PAINS TO PROVE IT!
TARS TARKAS! YOU YET LIVE!
I HAVE SEEN HER WORLD, PRINCESS.
IT IS AWFUL. THE VERY AIR SEEKS TO CRUSH YOUR BONES!
DUBLIN, PRESENT DAY
"IT IS A PLACE OF MONSTERS, I BELIEVE."
NOT FOOD. VAMPIRELLA IS NOT GOOD TO EAT, ARE WE CLEAR?

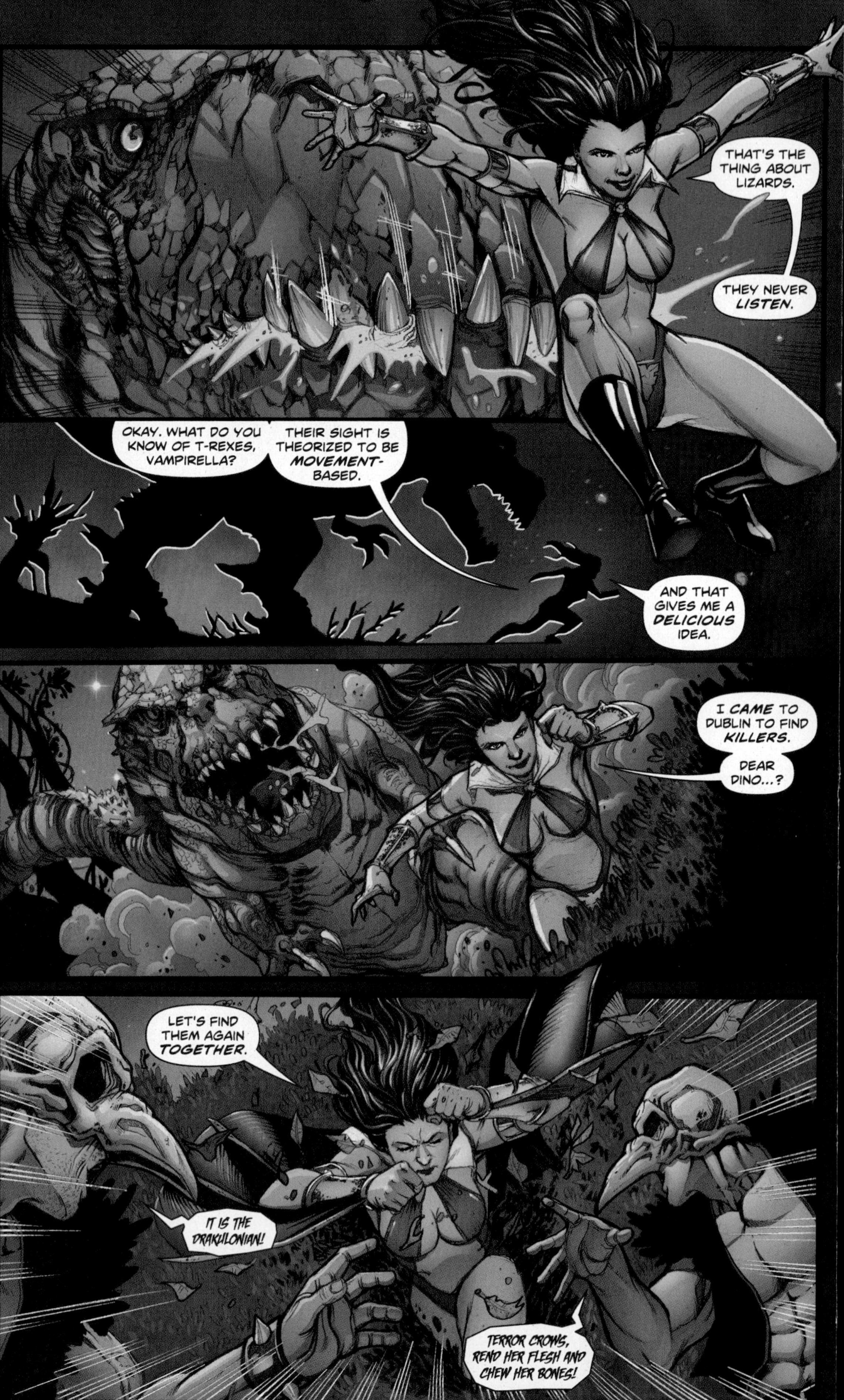

THAT'S THE THING ABOUT LIZARDS.
THEY NEVER LISTEN.
OKAY. WHAT DO YOU KNOW OF T-REXES, VAMPIRELLA?
THEIR SIGHT IS THEORIZED TO BE MOVEMENT-BASED.
AND THAT GIVES ME A DELICIOUS IDEA.
I CAME TO DUBLIN TO FIND KILLERS.
DEAR DINO...?
LET'S FIND THEM AGAIN TOGETHER.
IT IS THE DRAKULONIAN!
TERROR CROWS, REND HER FLESH AND CHEW HER BONES!

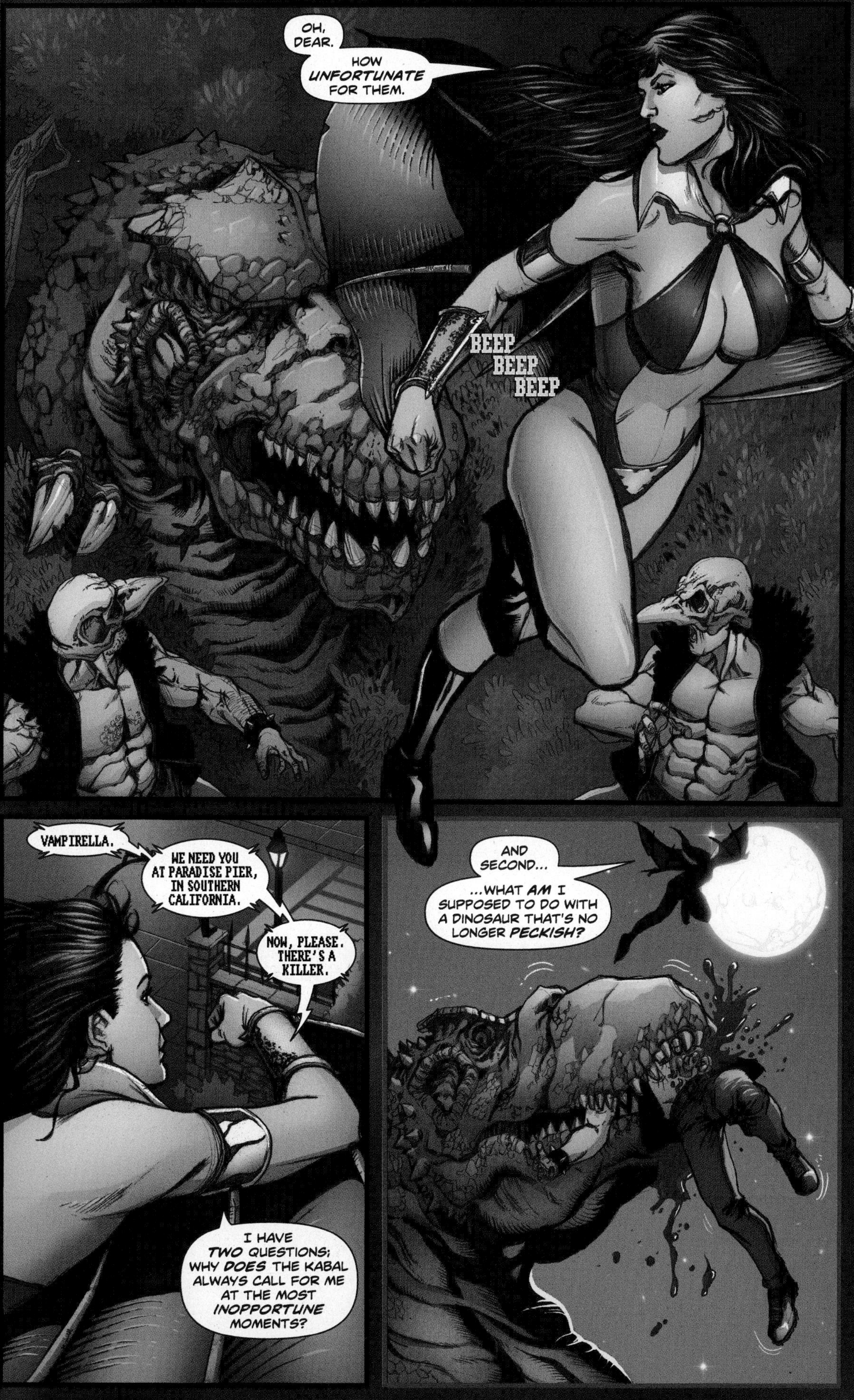
OH, DEAR. HOW UNFORTUNATE FOR THEM.
BEEP BEEP BEEP
VAMPIRELLA.
WE NEED YOU AT PARADISE PIER, IN SOUTHERN CALIFORNIA.
NOW, PLEASE. THERE'S A KILLER.
I HAVE TWO QUESTIONS; WHY DOES THE KABAL ALWAYS CALL FOR ME AT THE MOST INOPPORTUNE MOMENTS?
AND SECOND...
...WHAT AM I SUPPOSED TO DO WITH A DINOSAUR THAT'S NO LONGER PECKISH?

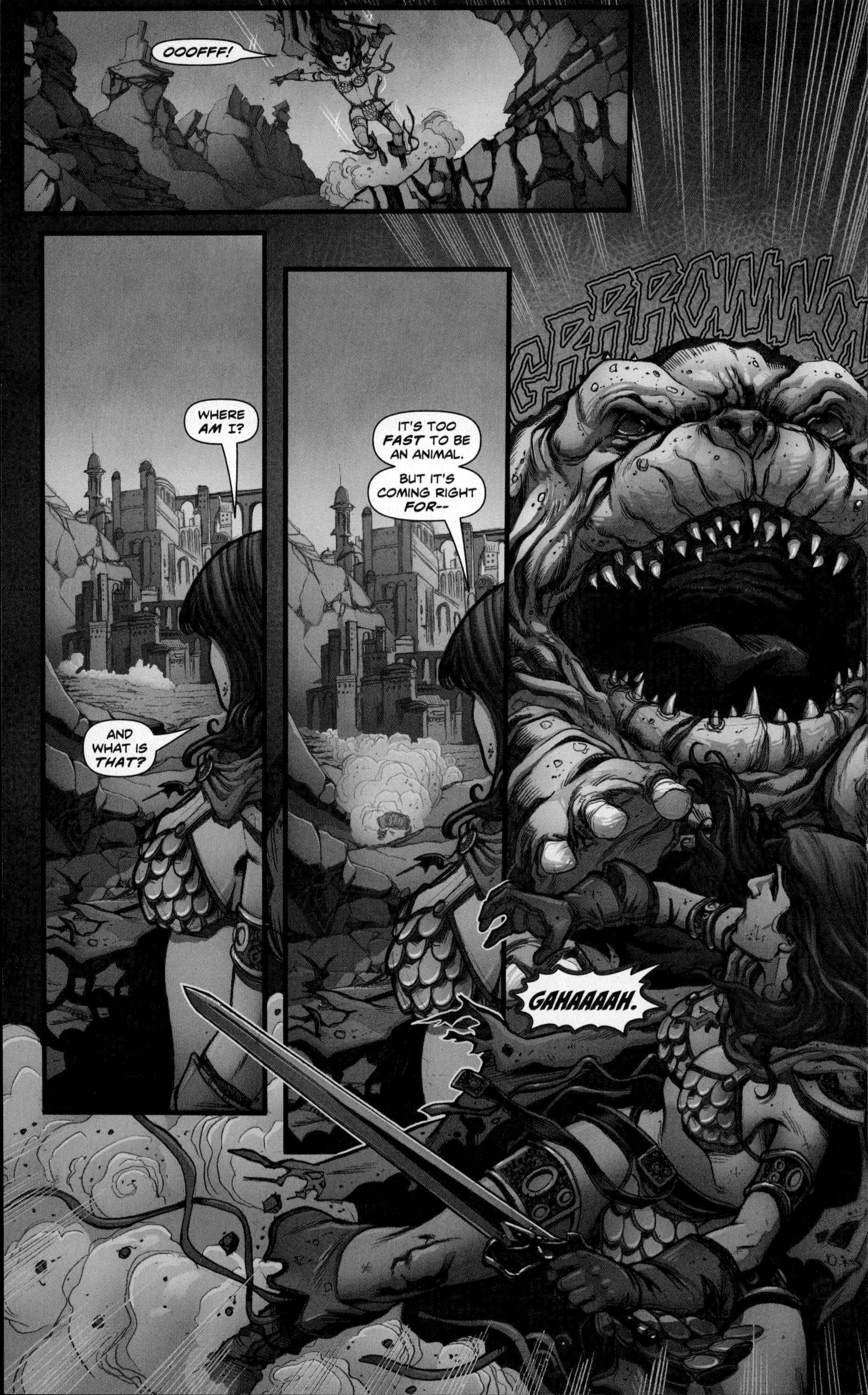
OOOFFF!
WHERE AM I?
AND WHAT IS THAT?
IT'S TOO FAST TO BE AN ANIMAL.
BUT IT'S COMING RIGHT FOR--
GAHAAAAH.

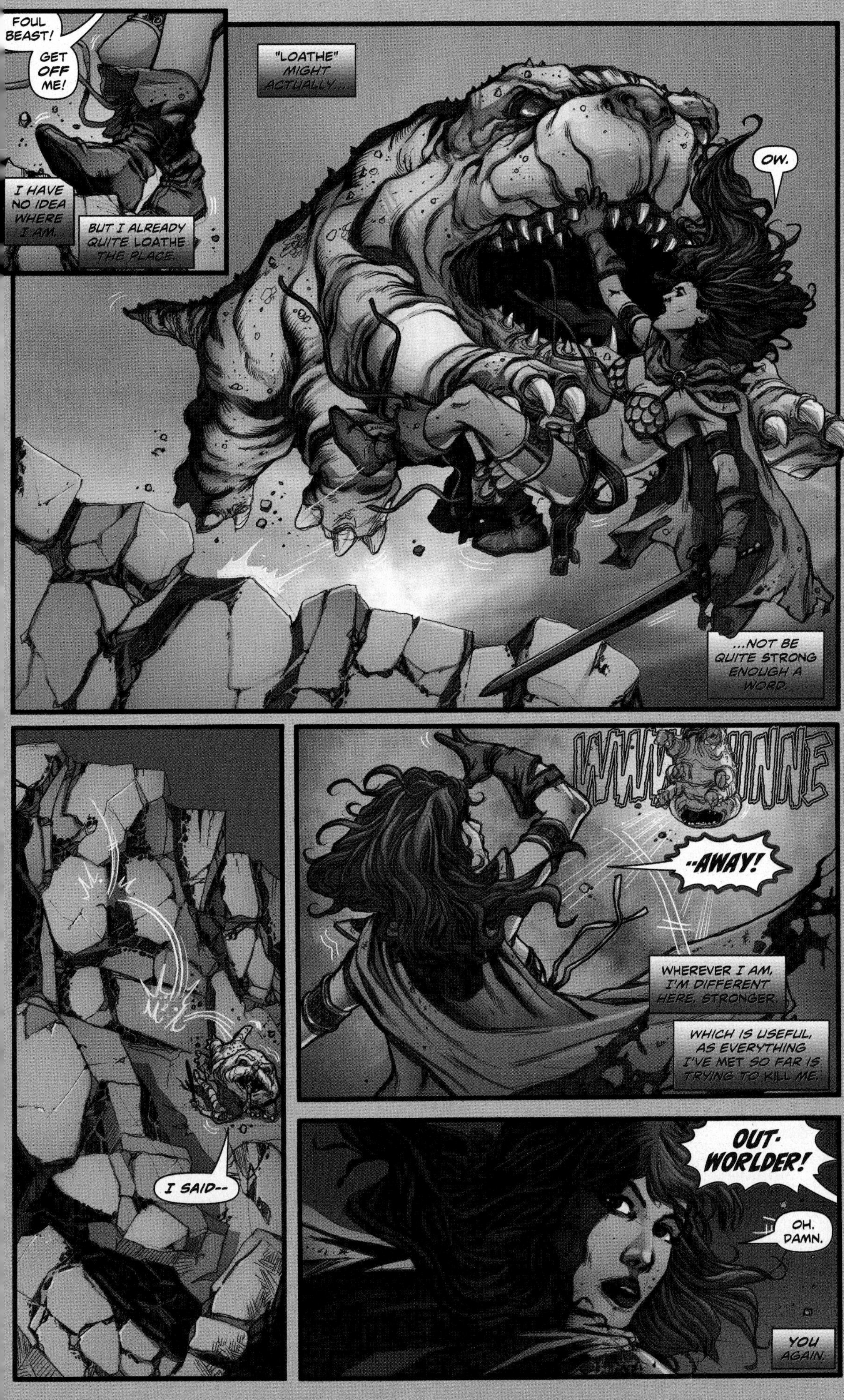
FOUL BEAST!
GET OFF ME!
I HAVE NO IDEA WHERE I AM.
BUT I ALREADY QUITE LOATHE THE PLACE.
"LOATHE" MIGHT ACTUALLY...
OW.
...NOT BE QUITE STRONG ENOUGH A WORD.
I SAID--
--AWAY!
WHEREVER I AM, I'M DIFFERENT HERE. STRONGER.
WHICH IS USEFUL, AS EVERYTHING I'VE MET SO FAR IS TRYING TO KILL ME.
OUT-WORLDER!
OH. DAMN.
YOU AGAIN.

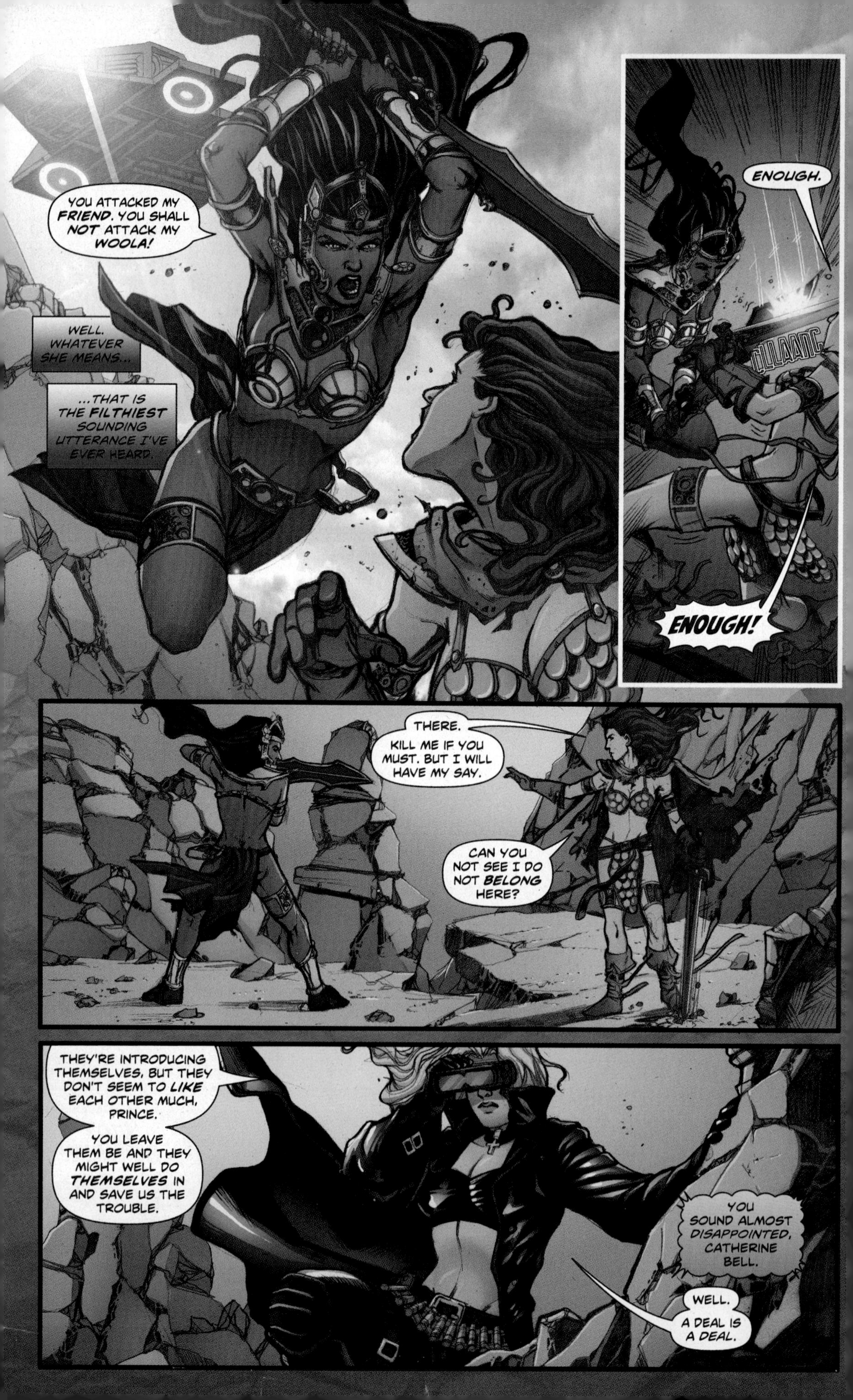

YOU ATTACKED MY FRIEND. YOU SHALL NOT ATTACK MY WOOLA!
WELL. WHATEVER SHE MEANS...
...THAT IS THE FILTHIEST SOUNDING UTTERANCE I'VE EVER HEARD.
ENOUGH.
CLLAANG
ENOUGH!
THERE.
KILL ME IF YOU MUST. BUT I WILL HAVE MY SAY.
CAN YOU NOT SEE I DO NOT BELONG HERE?
THEY'RE INTRODUCING THEMSELVES, BUT THEY DON'T SEEM TO LIKE EACH OTHER MUCH, PRINCE.
YOU LEAVE THEM BE AND THEY MIGHT WELL DO THEMSELVES IN AND SAVE US THE TROUBLE.
YOU SOUND ALMOST DISAPPOINTED, CATHERINE BELL.
WELL.
A DEAL IS A DEAL.

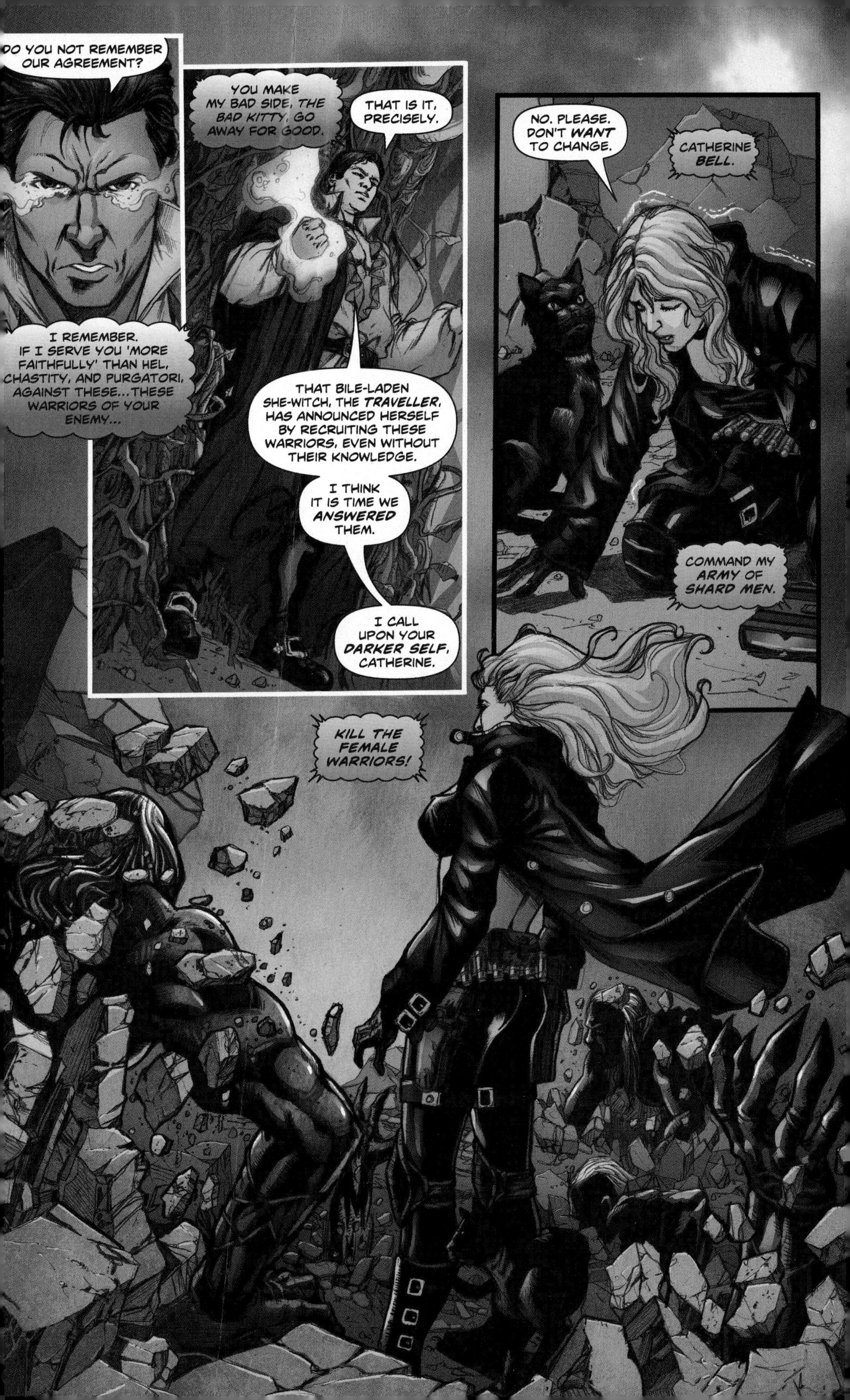
DO YOU NOT REMEMBER OUR AGREEMENT?
YOU MAKE MY BAD SIDE, THE BAD KITTY, GO AWAY FOR GOOD.
THAT IS IT, PRECISELY.
I REMEMBER. IF I SERVE YOU 'MORE FAITHFULLY' THAN HEL, CHASTITY, AND PURGATORI, AGAINST THESE... THESE WARRIORS OF YOUR ENEMY...
THAT BILE-LADEN SHE-WITCH, THE TRAVELLER, HAS ANNOUNCED HERSELF BY RECRUITING THESE WARRIORS, EVEN WITHOUT THEIR KNOWLEDGE.
I THINK IT IS TIME WE ANSWERED THEM.
I CALL UPON YOUR DARKER SELF, CATHERINE.
NO. PLEASE. DON'T WANT TO CHANGE.
CATHERINE BELL.
COMMAND MY ARMY OF SHARD MEN.
KILL THE FEMALE WARRIORS!

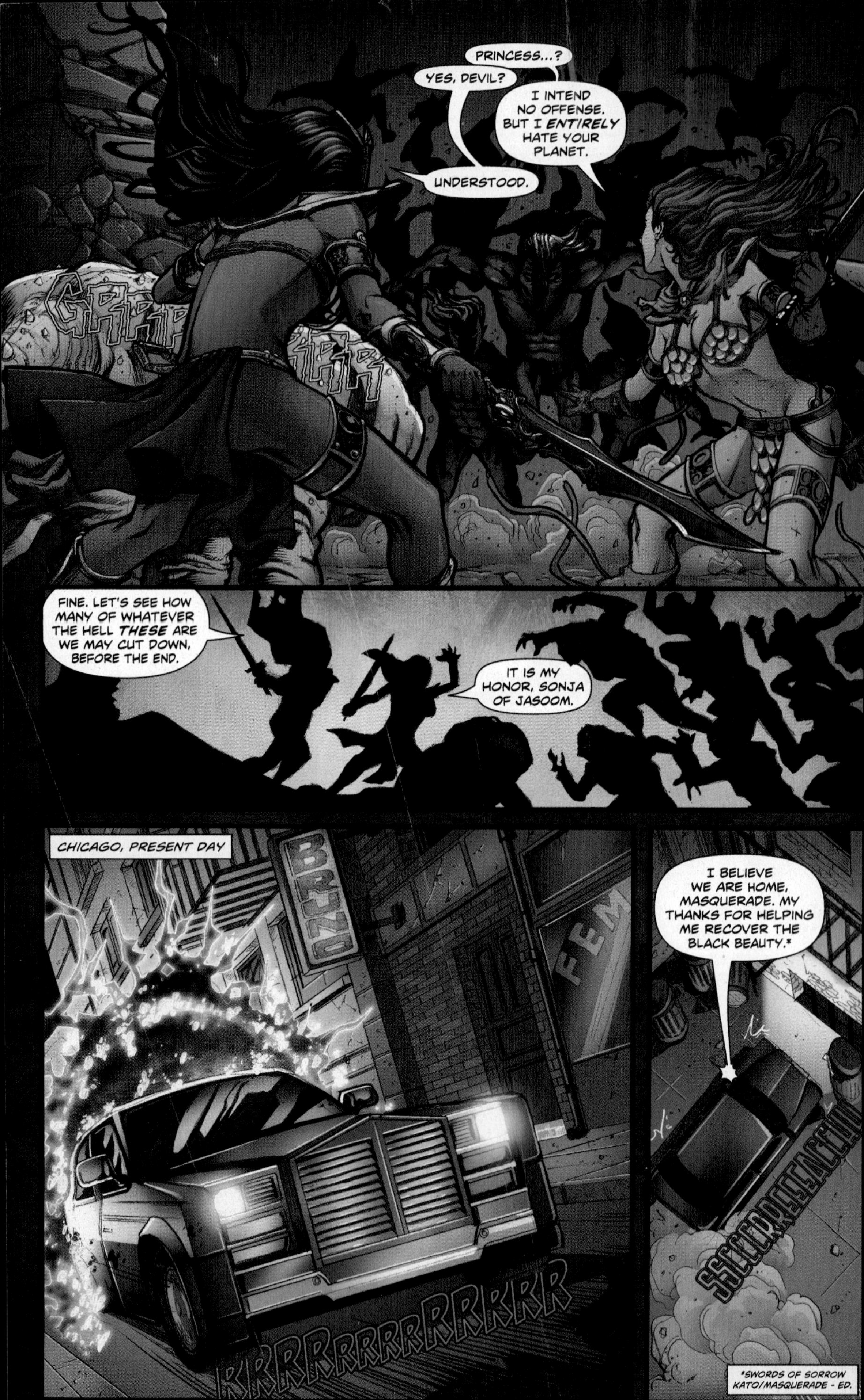

PRINCESS...?
YES, DEVIL?
I INTEND NO OFFENSE. BUT I *ENTIRELY* HATE YOUR PLANET.
UNDERSTOOD.
FINE. LET'S SEE HOW MANY OF WHATEVER THE HELL *THESE* ARE WE MAY CUT DOWN, BEFORE THE END.
IT IS MY HONOR, SONJA OF JASOOM.
CHICAGO, PRESENT DAY
I BELIEVE WE ARE HOME, MASQUERADE. MY THANKS FOR HELPING ME RECOVER THE BLACK BEAUTY.*
*SWORDS OF SORROW KATO/MASQUERADE - ED.

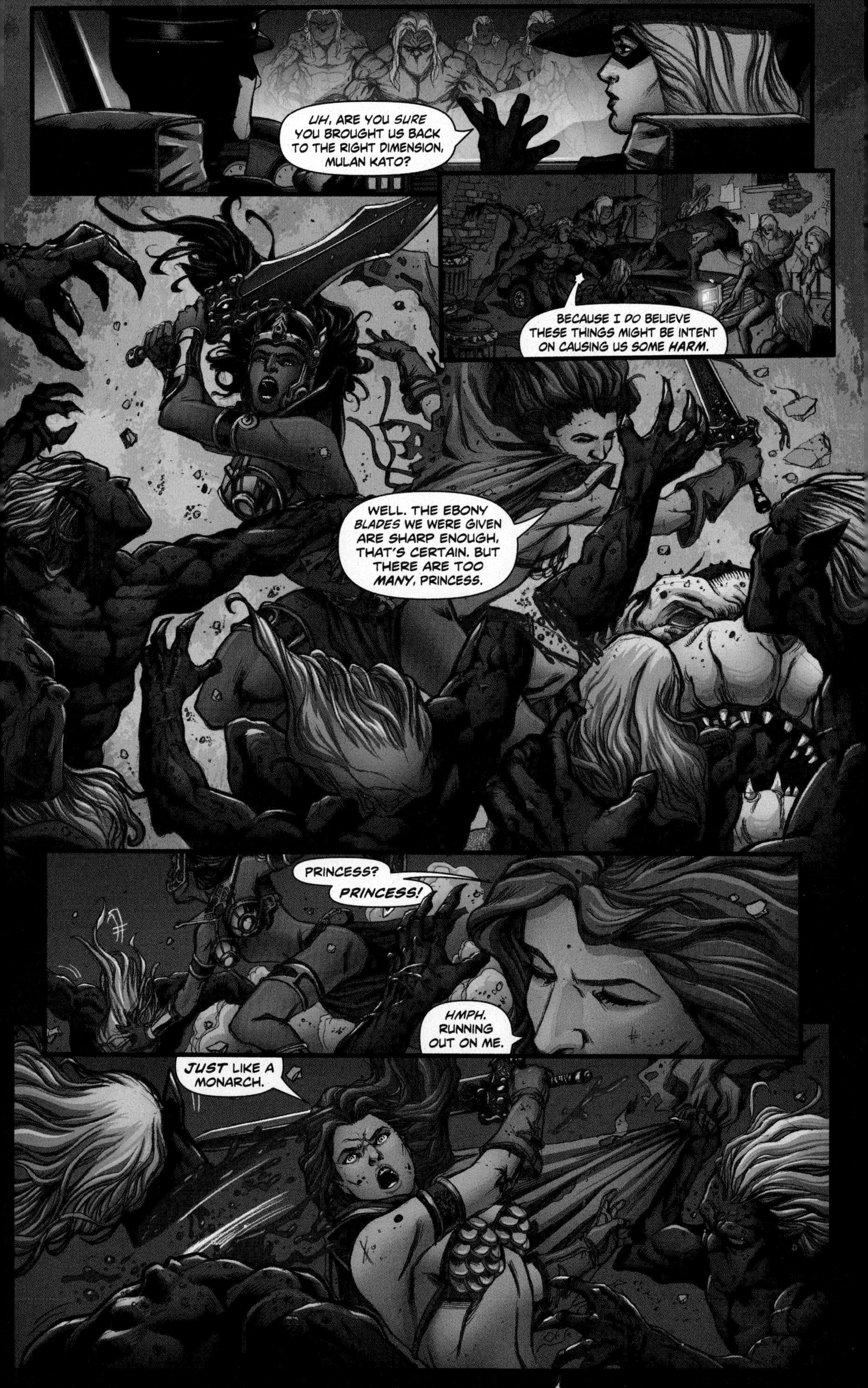
UH, ARE YOU SURE YOU BROUGHT US BACK TO THE RIGHT DIMENSION, MULAN KATO?
BECAUSE I DO BELIEVE THESE THINGS MIGHT BE INTENT ON CAUSING US SOME HARM.
WELL. THE EBONY BLADES WE WERE GIVEN ARE SHARP ENOUGH, THAT'S CERTAIN. BUT THERE ARE TOO MANY, PRINCESS.
PRINCESS?
PRINCESS!
HMPH. RUNNING OUT ON ME.
JUST LIKE A MONARCH.

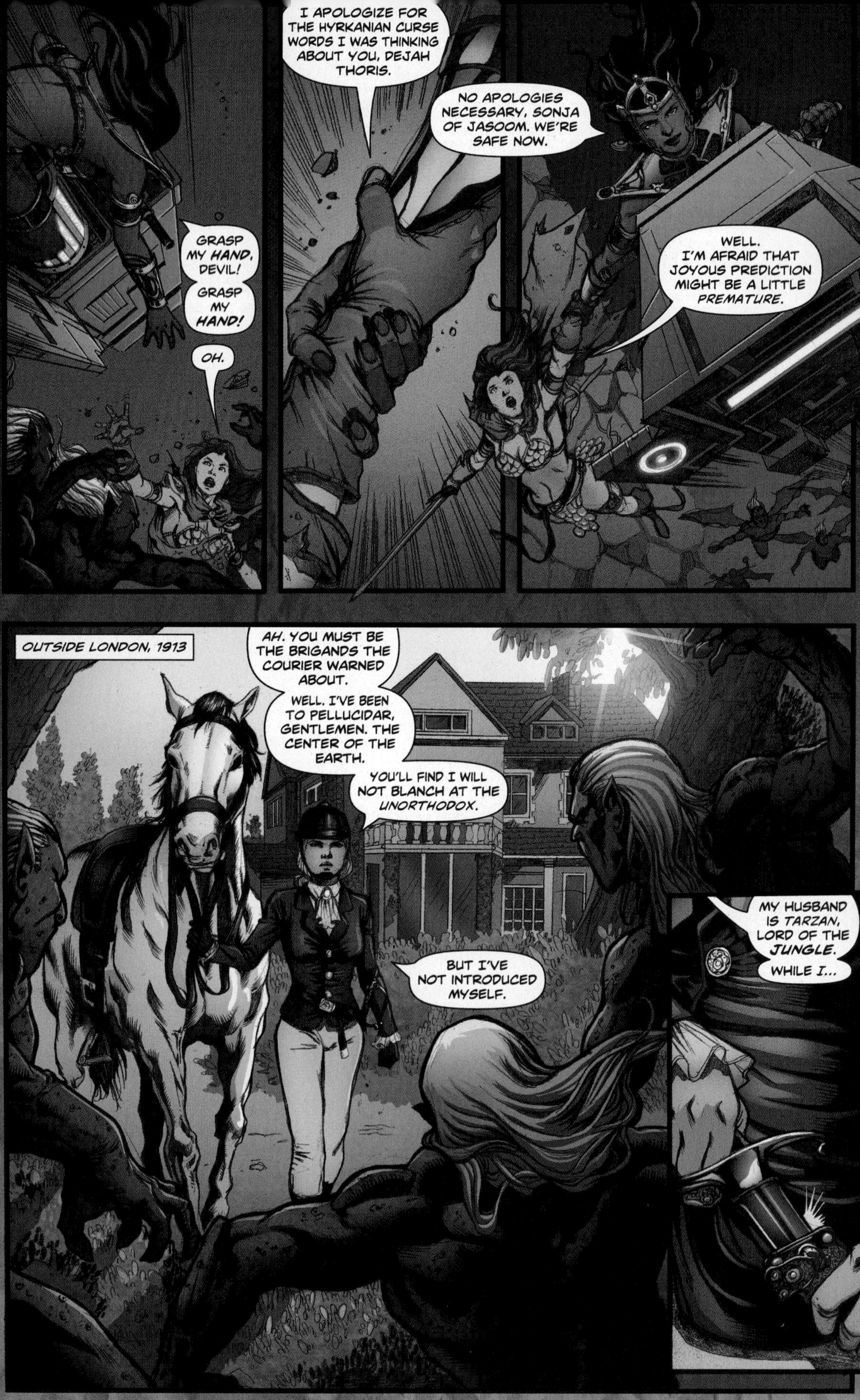
GRASP MY *HAND*, DEVIL!
GRASP MY *HAND!*
OH.
I APOLOGIZE FOR THE HYRKANIAN CURSE WORDS I WAS THINKING ABOUT YOU, DEJAH THORIS.
NO APOLOGIES NECESSARY, SONJA OF JASOOM. WE'RE SAFE NOW.
WELL. I'M AFRAID THAT JOYOUS PREDICTION MIGHT BE A LITTLE *PREMATURE*.
OUTSIDE LONDON, 1913
AH. YOU MUST BE THE BRIGANDS THE COURIER WARNED ABOUT.
WELL. I'VE BEEN TO PELLUCIDAR, GENTLEMEN. THE CENTER OF THE EARTH.
YOU'LL FIND I WILL NOT BLANCH AT THE *UNORTHODOX*.
BUT I'VE NOT INTRODUCED MYSELF.
MY HUSBAND IS *TARZAN*, LORD OF THE *JUNGLE*.
WHILE *I*...

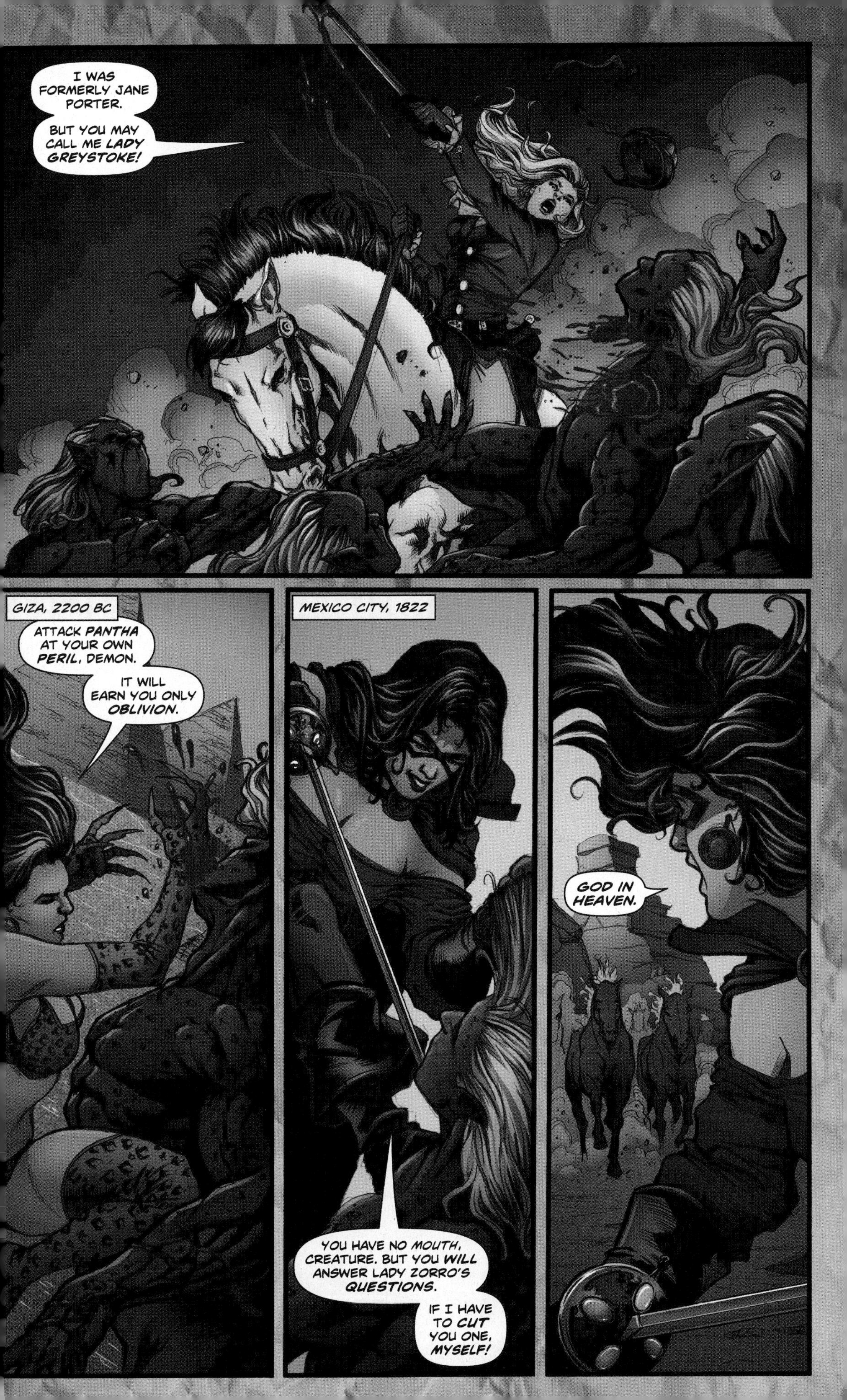
I WAS FORMERLY JANE PORTER.
BUT YOU MAY CALL ME LADY GREYSTOKE!
GIZA, 2200 BC
ATTACK PANTHA AT YOUR OWN PERIL, DEMON.
IT WILL EARN YOU ONLY OBLIVION.
MEXICO CITY, 1822
YOU HAVE NO MOUTH, CREATURE. BUT YOU WILL ANSWER LADY ZORRO'S QUESTIONS.
IF I HAVE TO CUT YOU ONE, MYSELF!
GOD IN HEAVEN.

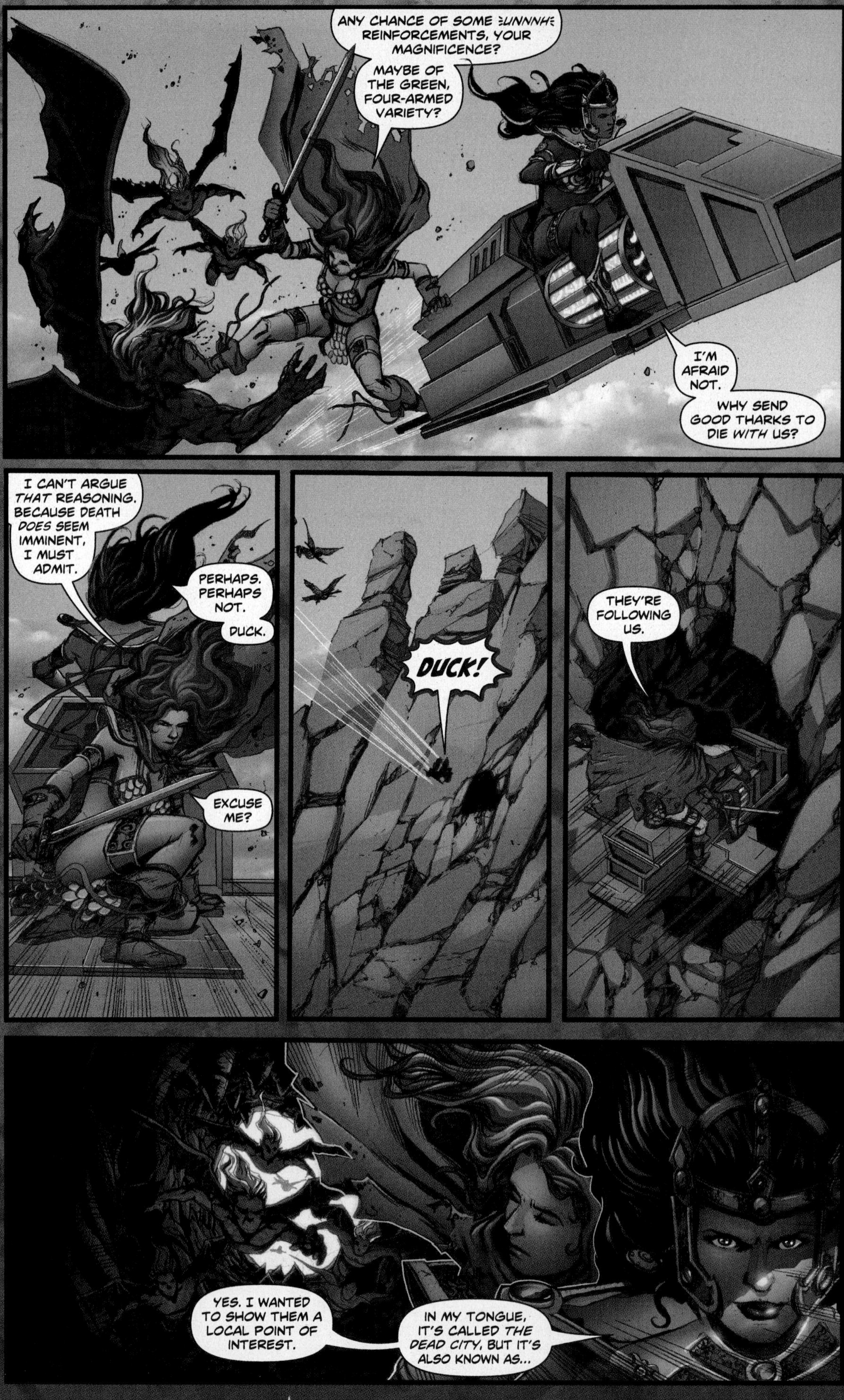
ANY CHANCE OF SOME ≡UNNNH≡ REINFORCEMENTS, YOUR MAGNIFICENCE?
MAYBE OF THE GREEN, FOUR-ARMED VARIETY?
I'M AFRAID NOT.
WHY SEND GOOD THARKS TO DIE *WITH* US?
I CAN'T ARGUE *THAT* REASONING. BECAUSE DEATH *DOES* SEEM IMMINENT, I MUST ADMIT.
PERHAPS. PERHAPS NOT.
DUCK.
EXCUSE ME?
DUCK!
THEY'RE FOLLOWING US.
YES. I WANTED TO SHOW THEM A LOCAL POINT OF INTEREST.
IN MY TONGUE, IT'S CALLED *THE DEAD CITY*, BUT IT'S ALSO KNOWN AS...

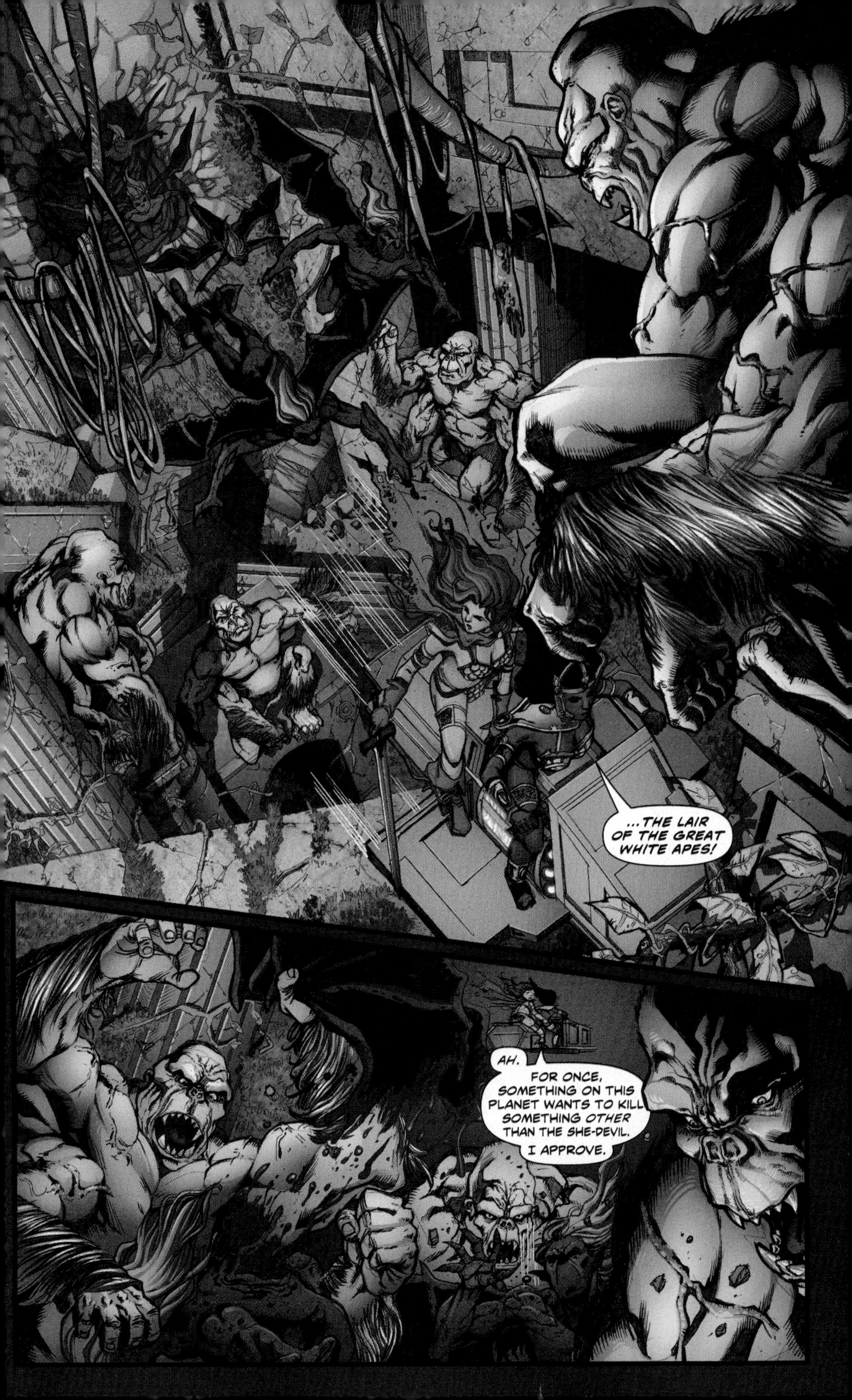
...THE LAIR OF THE GREAT WHITE APES!
AH.
FOR ONCE, SOMETHING ON THIS PLANET WANTS TO KILL SOMETHING OTHER THAN THE SHE-DEVIL.
I APPROVE.

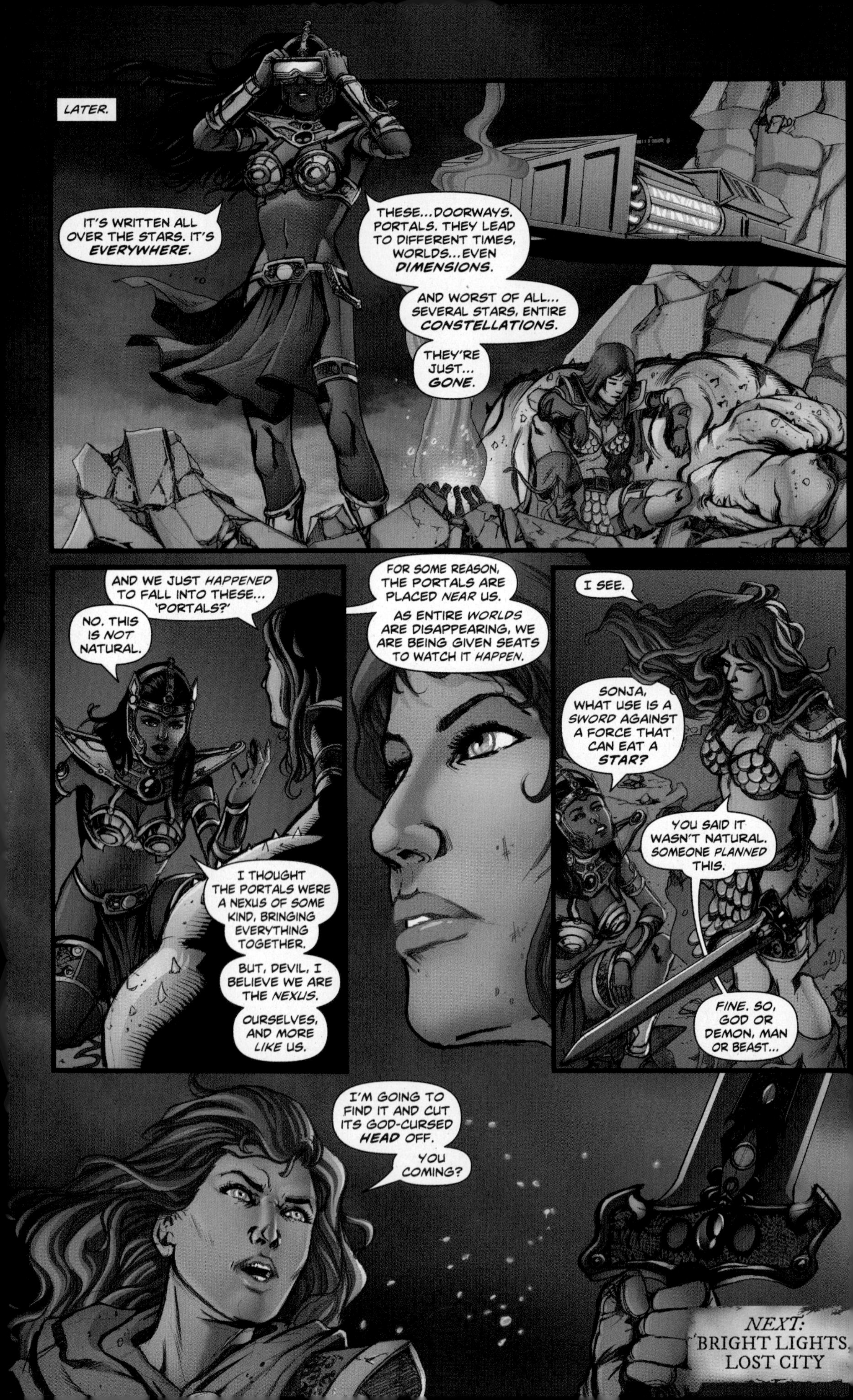
LATER.
IT'S WRITTEN ALL OVER THE STARS. IT'S EVERYWHERE.
THESE...DOORWAYS. PORTALS. THEY LEAD TO DIFFERENT TIMES, WORLDS...EVEN DIMENSIONS.
AND WORST OF ALL... SEVERAL STARS, ENTIRE CONSTELLATIONS.
THEY'RE JUST... GONE.
AND WE JUST HAPPENED TO FALL INTO THESE... 'PORTALS?'
NO. THIS IS NOT NATURAL.
I THOUGHT THE PORTALS WERE A NEXUS OF SOME KIND, BRINGING EVERYTHING TOGETHER.
BUT, DEVIL, I BELIEVE WE ARE THE NEXUS.
OURSELVES, AND MORE LIKE US.
FOR SOME REASON, THE PORTALS ARE PLACED NEAR US.
AS ENTIRE WORLDS ARE DISAPPEARING, WE ARE BEING GIVEN SEATS TO WATCH IT HAPPEN.
I SEE.
SONJA, WHAT USE IS A SWORD AGAINST A FORCE THAT CAN EAT A STAR?
YOU SAID IT WASN'T NATURAL. SOMEONE PLANNED THIS.
FINE. SO, GOD OR DEMON, MAN OR BEAST...
I'M GOING TO FIND IT AND CUT ITS GOD-CURSED HEAD OFF.
YOU COMING?
NEXT: BRIGHT LIGHTS, LOST CITY

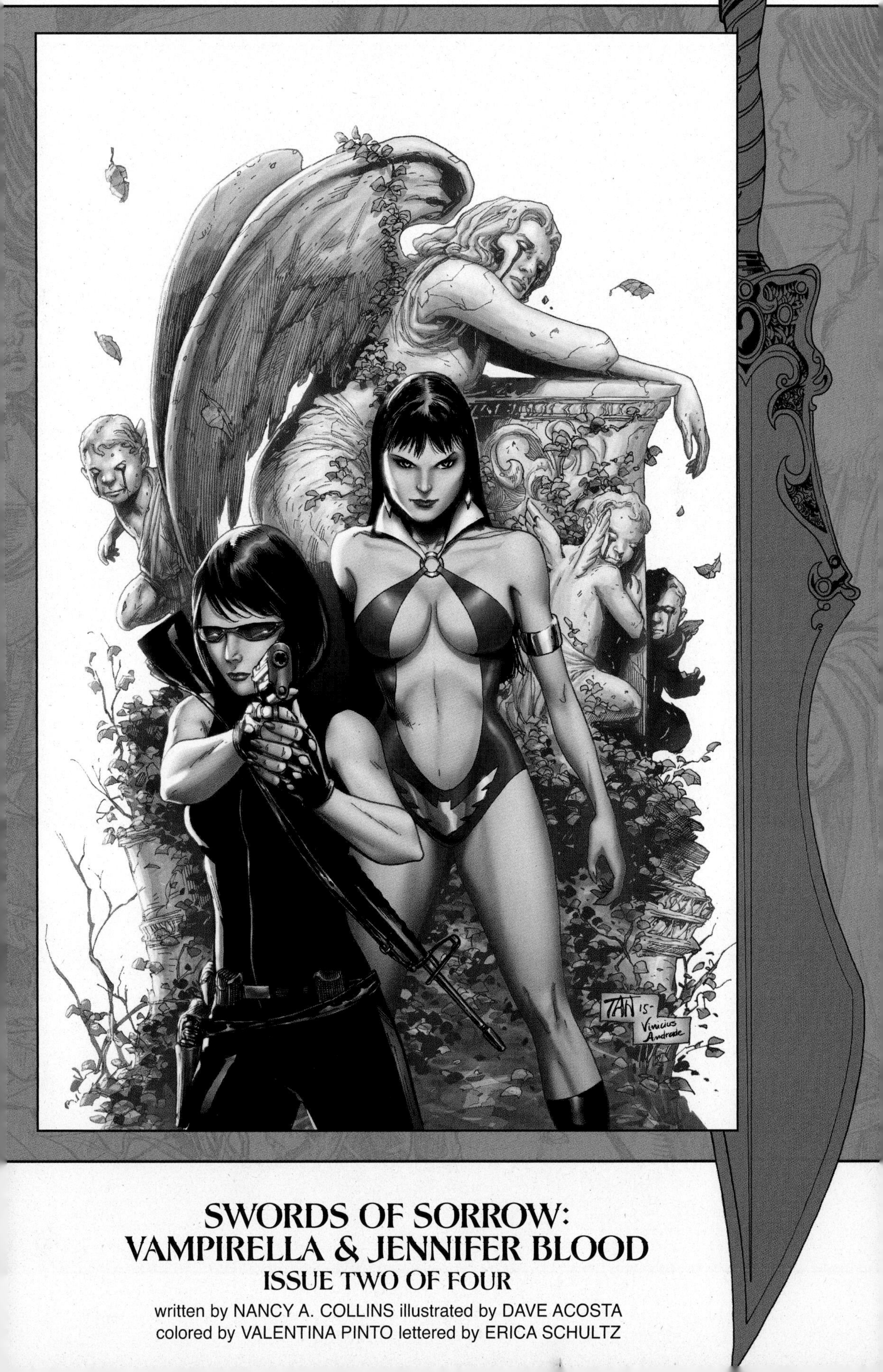
TAN 15
Vinicius Andrade

SWORDS OF SORROW: VAMPIRELLA & JENNIFER BLOOD

ISSUE TWO OF FOUR

written by NANCY A. COLLINS illustrated by DAVE ACOSTA
colored by VALENTINA PINTO lettered by ERICA SCHULTZ

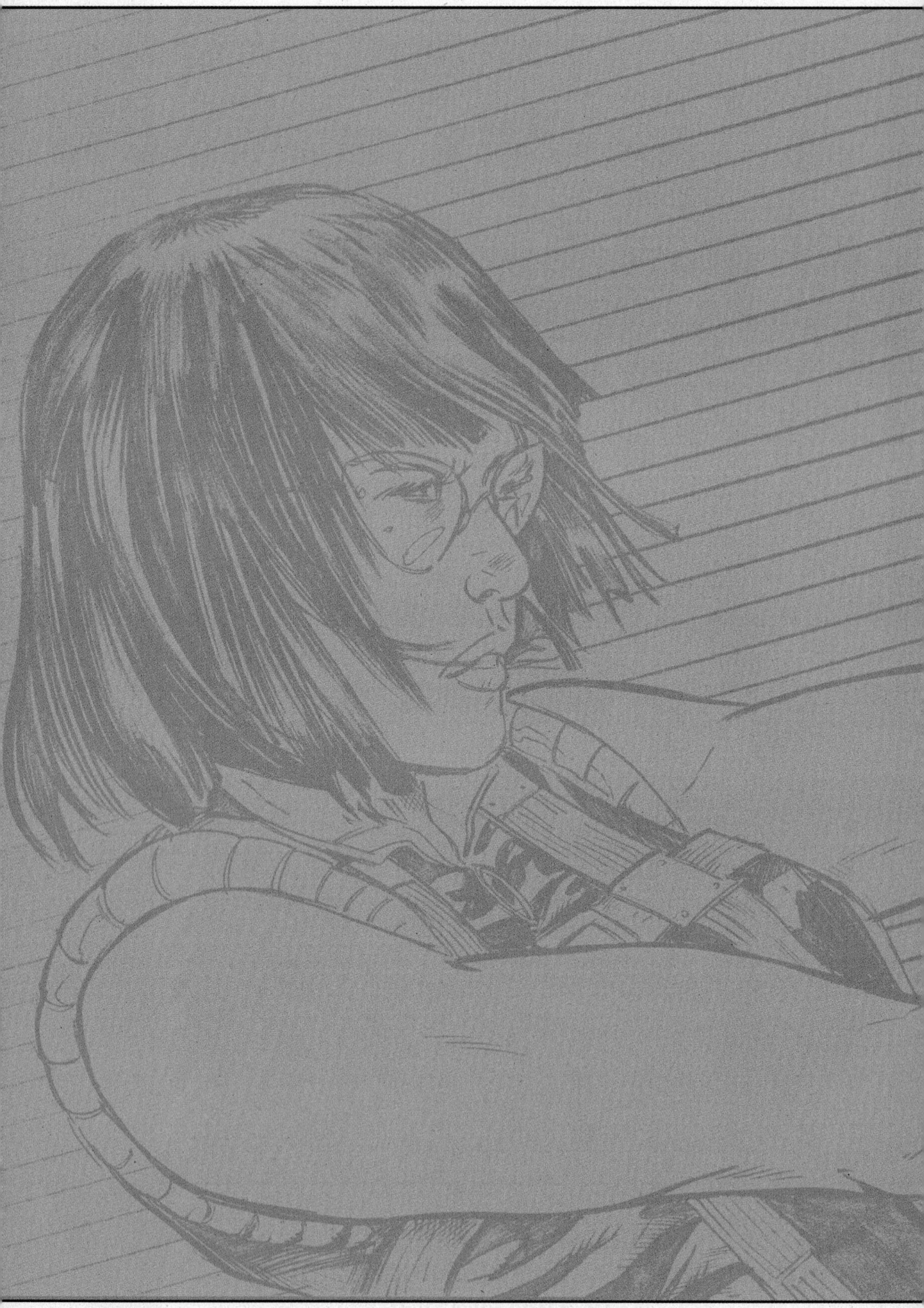

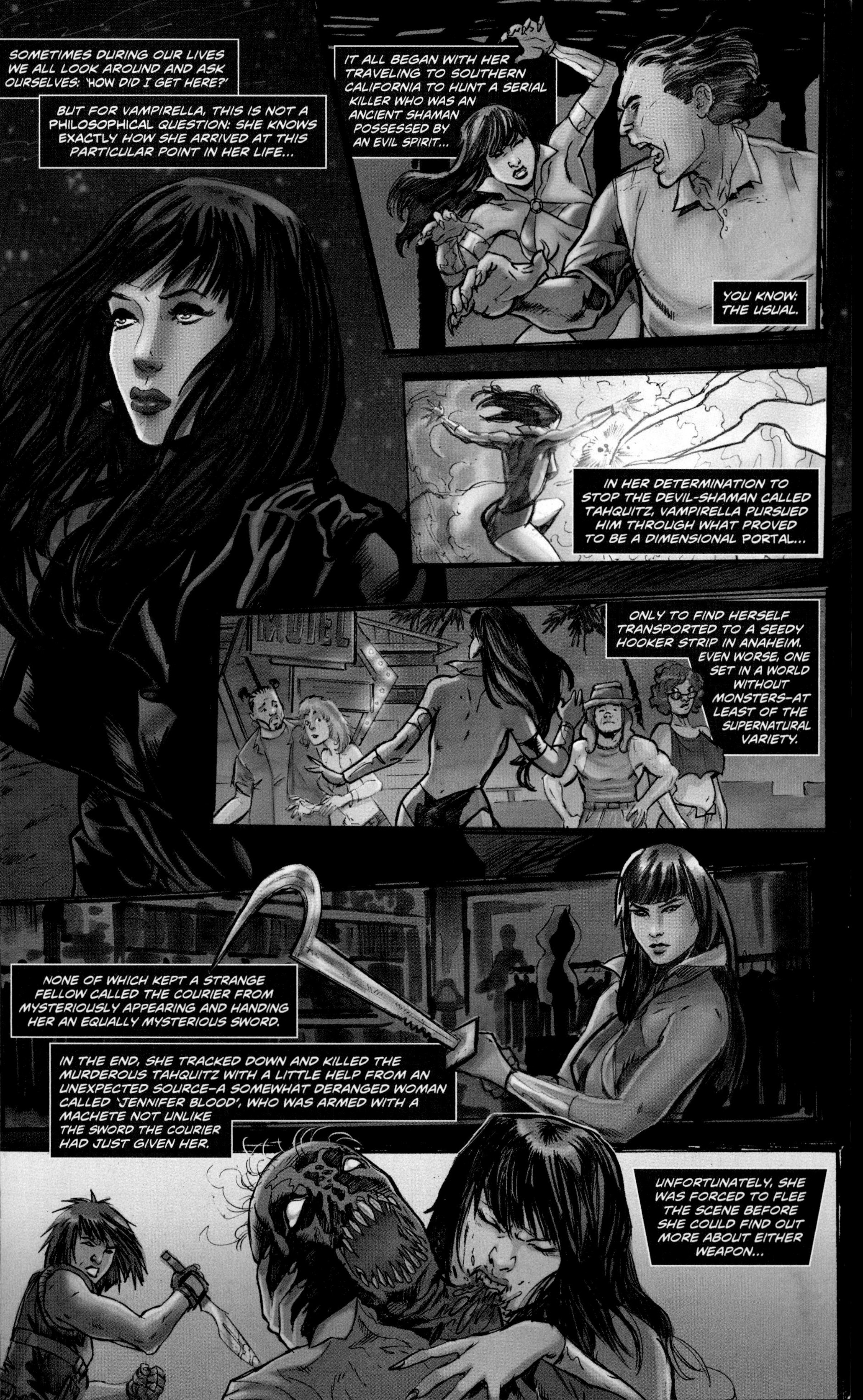
SOMETIMES DURING OUR LIVES WE ALL LOOK AROUND AND ASK OURSELVES: 'HOW DID I GET HERE?'
BUT FOR VAMPIRELLA, THIS IS NOT A PHILOSOPHICAL QUESTION: SHE KNOWS EXACTLY HOW SHE ARRIVED AT THIS PARTICULAR POINT IN HER LIFE...
IT ALL BEGAN WITH HER TRAVELING TO SOUTHERN CALIFORNIA TO HUNT A SERIAL KILLER WHO WAS AN ANCIENT SHAMAN POSSESSED BY AN EVIL SPIRIT...
YOU KNOW: THE USUAL.
IN HER DETERMINATION TO STOP THE DEVIL-SHAMAN CALLED TAHQUITZ, VAMPIRELLA PURSUED HIM THROUGH WHAT PROVED TO BE A DIMENSIONAL PORTAL...
MOTEL
ONLY TO FIND HERSELF TRANSPORTED TO A SEEDY HOOKER STRIP IN ANAHEIM. EVEN WORSE, ONE SET IN A WORLD WITHOUT MONSTERS—AT LEAST OF THE SUPERNATURAL VARIETY.
NONE OF WHICH KEPT A STRANGE FELLOW CALLED THE COURIER FROM MYSTERIOUSLY APPEARING AND HANDING HER AN EQUALLY MYSTERIOUS SWORD.
IN THE END, SHE TRACKED DOWN AND KILLED THE MURDEROUS TAHQUITZ WITH A LITTLE HELP FROM AN UNEXPECTED SOURCE—A SOMEWHAT DERANGED WOMAN CALLED 'JENNIFER BLOOD', WHO WAS ARMED WITH A MACHETE NOT UNLIKE THE SWORD THE COURIER HAD JUST GIVEN HER.
UNFORTUNATELY, SHE WAS FORCED TO FLEE THE SCENE BEFORE SHE COULD FIND OUT MORE ABOUT EITHER WEAPON...

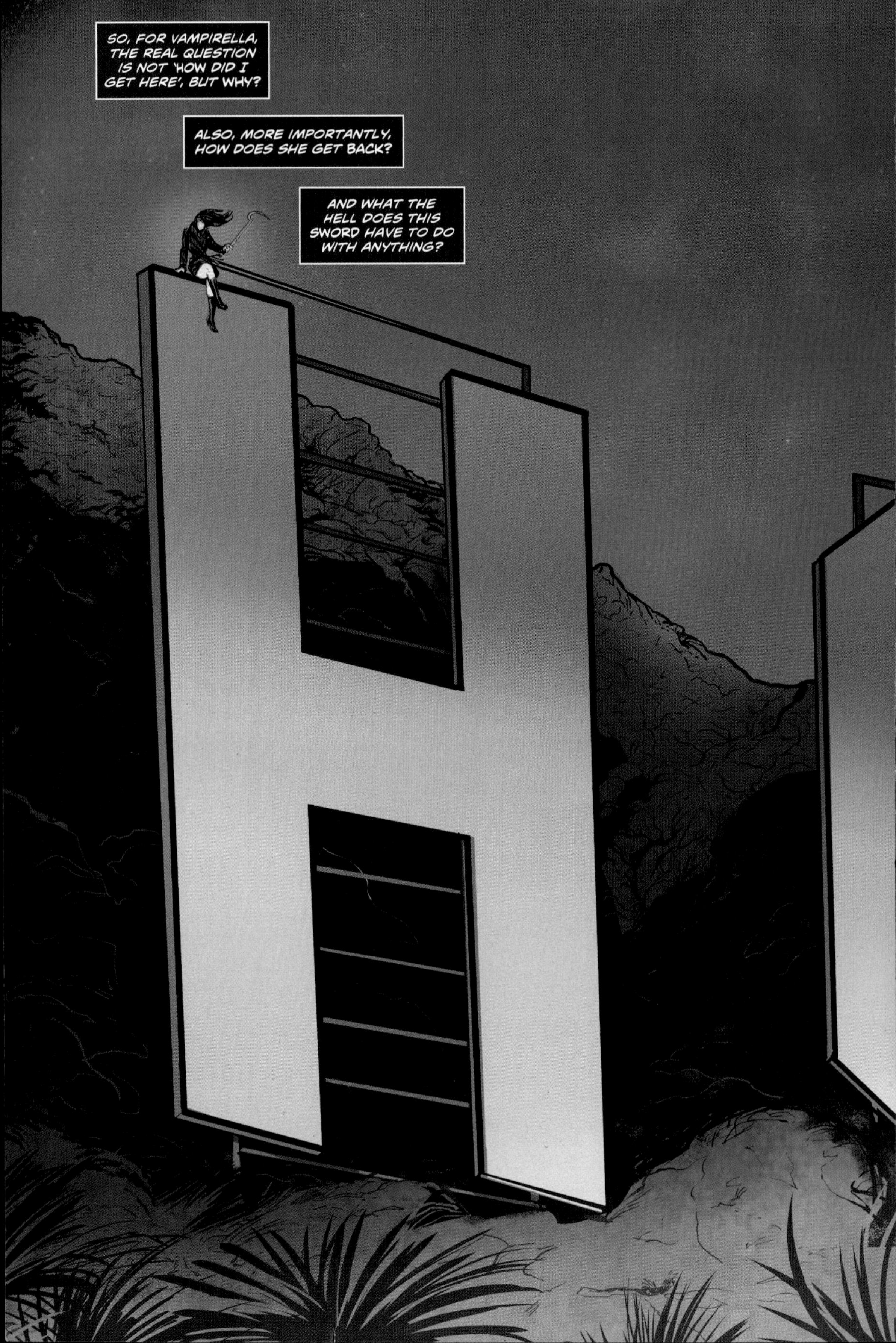
SO, FOR VAMPIRELLA, THE REAL QUESTION IS NOT 'HOW DID I GET HERE', BUT WHY?
ALSO, MORE IMPORTANTLY, HOW DOES SHE GET BACK?
AND WHAT THE HELL DOES THIS SWORD HAVE TO DO WITH ANYTHING?

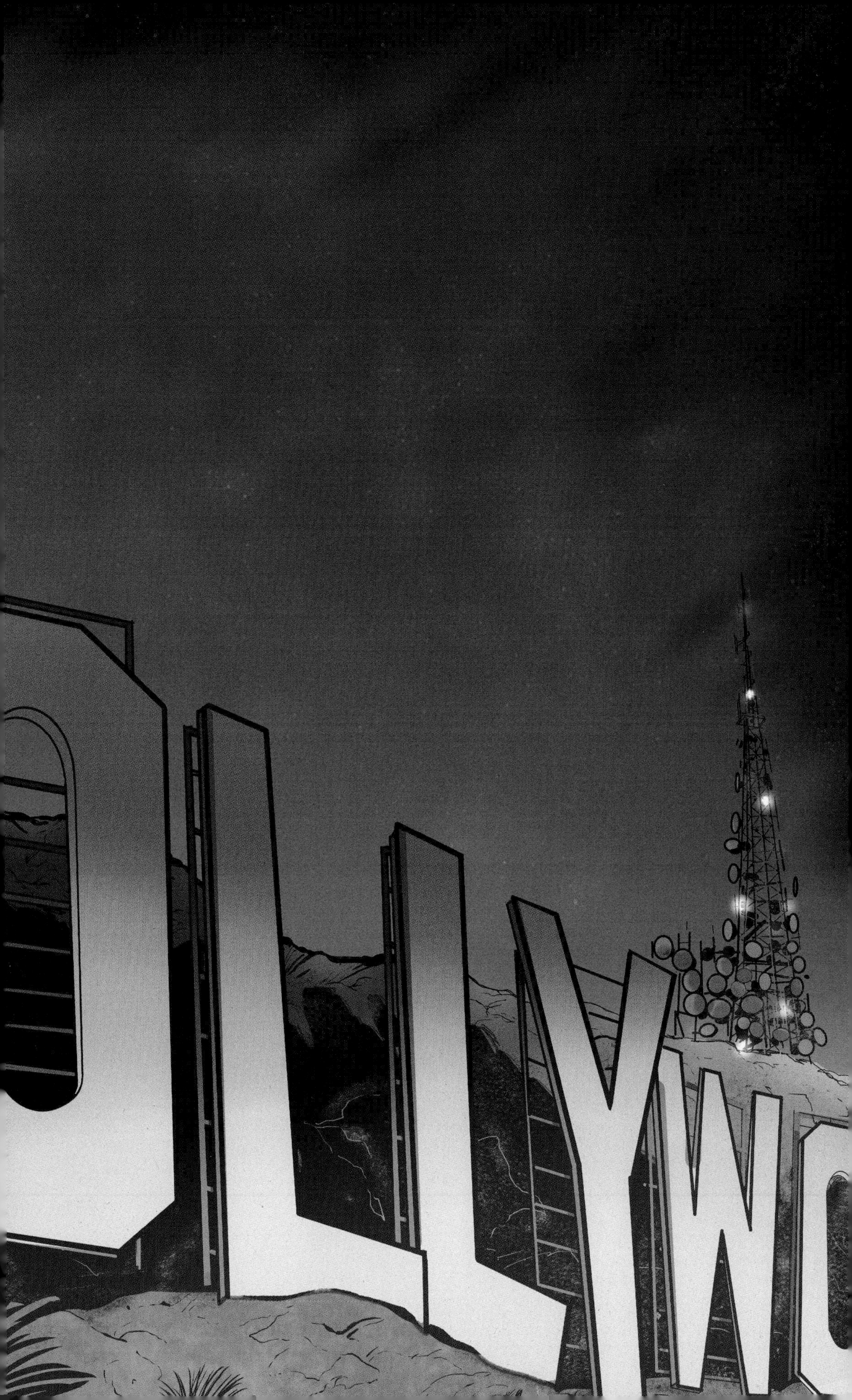
OLLYWO

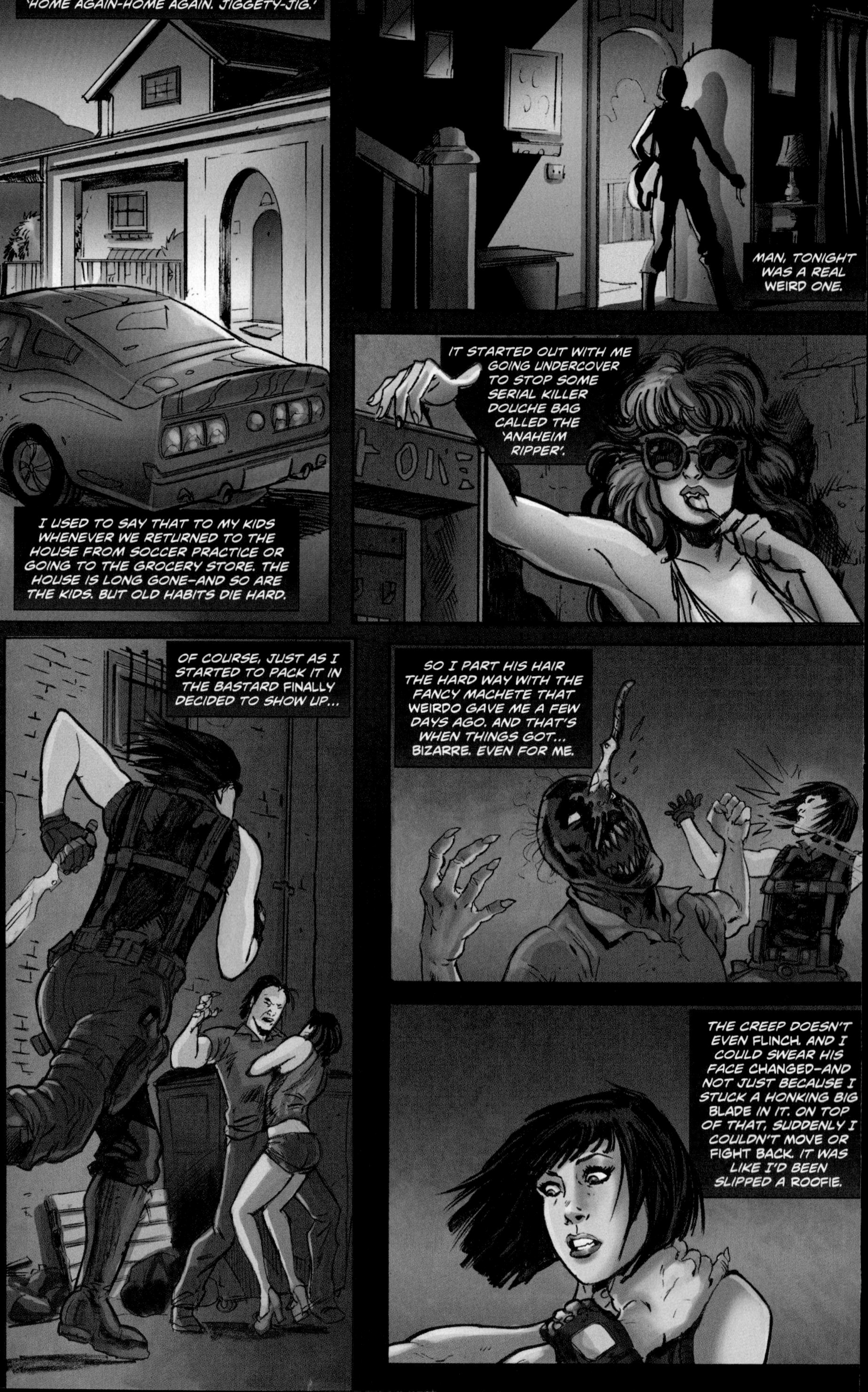
'HOME AGAIN-HOME AGAIN. JIGGETY-JIG.'
I USED TO SAY THAT TO MY KIDS WHENEVER WE RETURNED TO THE HOUSE FROM SOCCER PRACTICE OR GOING TO THE GROCERY STORE. THE HOUSE IS LONG GONE-AND SO ARE THE KIDS. BUT OLD HABITS DIE HARD.
MAN, TONIGHT WAS A REAL WEIRD ONE.
IT STARTED OUT WITH ME GOING UNDERCOVER TO STOP SOME SERIAL KILLER DOUCHE BAG CALLED THE 'ANAHEIM RIPPER'.
OF COURSE, JUST AS I STARTED TO PACK IT IN THE BASTARD FINALLY DECIDED TO SHOW UP...
SO I PART HIS HAIR THE HARD WAY WITH THE FANCY MACHETE THAT WEIRDO GAVE ME A FEW DAYS AGO. AND THAT'S WHEN THINGS GOT... BIZARRE. EVEN FOR ME.
THE CREEP DOESN'T EVEN FLINCH. AND I COULD SWEAR HIS FACE CHANGED-AND NOT JUST BECAUSE I STUCK A HONKING BIG BLADE IN IT. ON TOP OF THAT, SUDDENLY I COULDN'T MOVE OR FIGHT BACK. IT WAS LIKE I'D BEEN SLIPPED A ROOFIE.

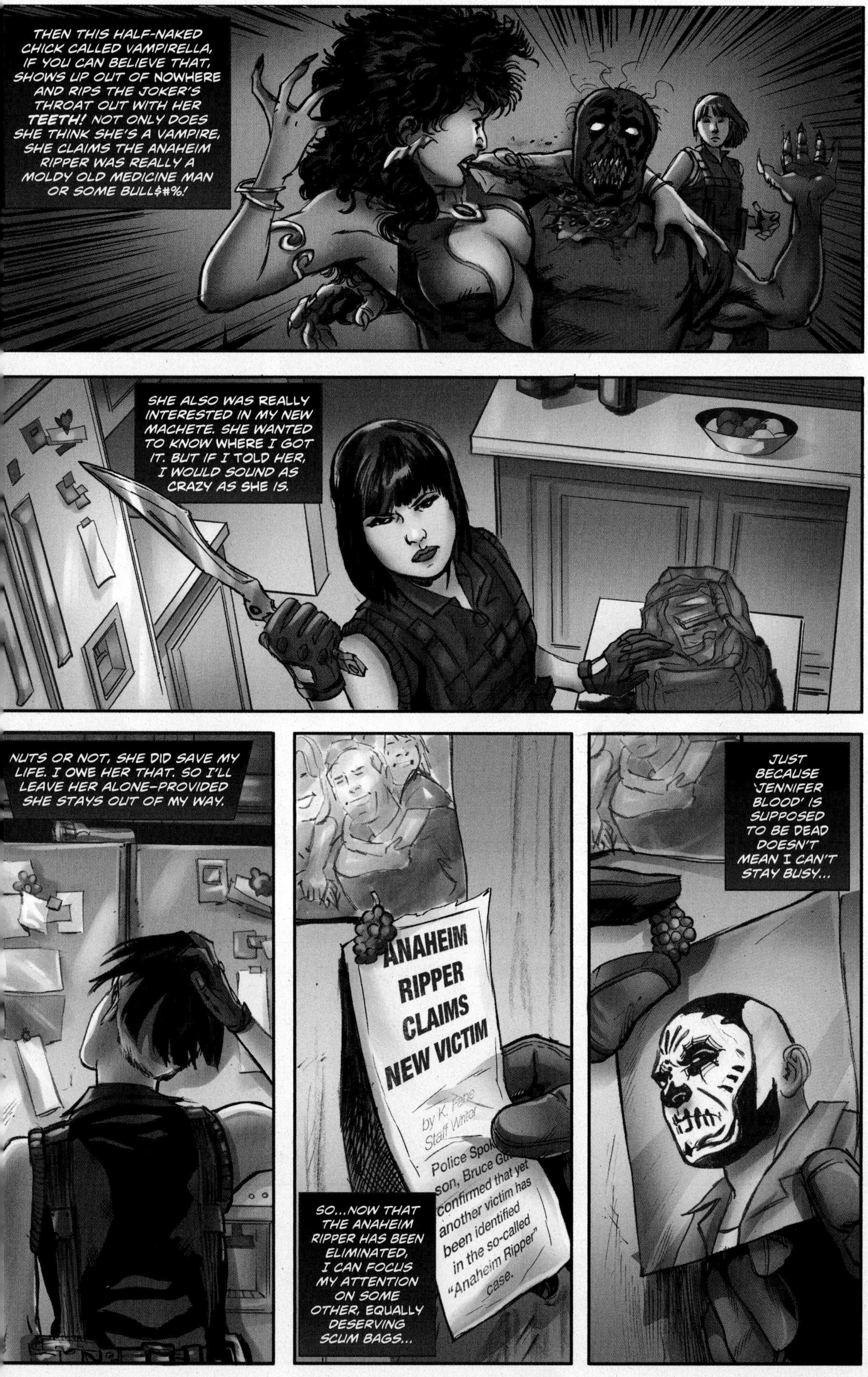
THEN THIS HALF-NAKED CHICK CALLED VAMPIRELLA, IF YOU CAN BELIEVE THAT, SHOWS UP OUT OF NOWHERE AND RIPS THE JOKER'S THROAT OUT WITH HER TEETH! NOT ONLY DOES SHE THINK SHE'S A VAMPIRE, SHE CLAIMS THE ANAHEIM RIPPER WAS REALLY A MOLDY OLD MEDICINE MAN OR SOME BULL$#%!
SHE ALSO WAS REALLY INTERESTED IN MY NEW MACHETE. SHE WANTED TO KNOW WHERE I GOT IT. BUT IF I TOLD HER, I WOULD SOUND AS CRAZY AS SHE IS.
NUTS OR NOT, SHE DID SAVE MY LIFE. I OWE HER THAT. SO I'LL LEAVE HER ALONE–PROVIDED SHE STAYS OUT OF MY WAY.
ANAHEIM RIPPER CLAIMS NEW VICTIM
by K. Fabe Staff Writer
Police Spok son, Bruce Gu confirmed that yet another victim has been identified in the so-called "Anaheim Ripper" case.
SO...NOW THAT THE ANAHEIM RIPPER HAS BEEN ELIMINATED, I CAN FOCUS MY ATTENTION ON SOME OTHER, EQUALLY DESERVING SCUM BAGS...
JUST BECAUSE 'JENNIFER BLOOD' IS SUPPOSED TO BE DEAD DOESN'T MEAN I CAN'T STAY BUSY...

THE SUN WILL BE UP SOON. ALTHOUGH SHE DOESN'T BURN AT ITS TOUCH LIKE THE OTHER VAMPIRES, SHE IS STILL, FOR THE MOST PART, A NOCTURNAL CREATURE...

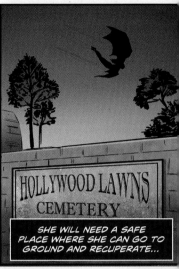

HOLLYWOOD LAWNS CEMETERY

SHE WILL NEED A SAFE PLACE WHERE SHE CAN GO TO GROUND AND RECUPERATE...

AND THEN, ONCE FULLY RESTED, TRY TO FIGURE OUT WHAT HER NEXT STEP WILL BE IN THIS STRANGE WORLD THAT IS SO MUCH LIKE HER OWN, YET SO DIFFERENT...

THIS PLACE LOOKS LIKE A GOOD PLACE TO CRASH...

HMM. THE LAST INTERNMENT IN THIS MAUSOLEUM WAS FIFTY YEARS AGO. THAT MEANS I SHOULDN'T HAVE TO WORRY ABOUT ANY FAMILY SHOWING UP TO PAY THEIR RESPECTS.

IT AIN'T THE RITZ—BUT IT'LL DO.

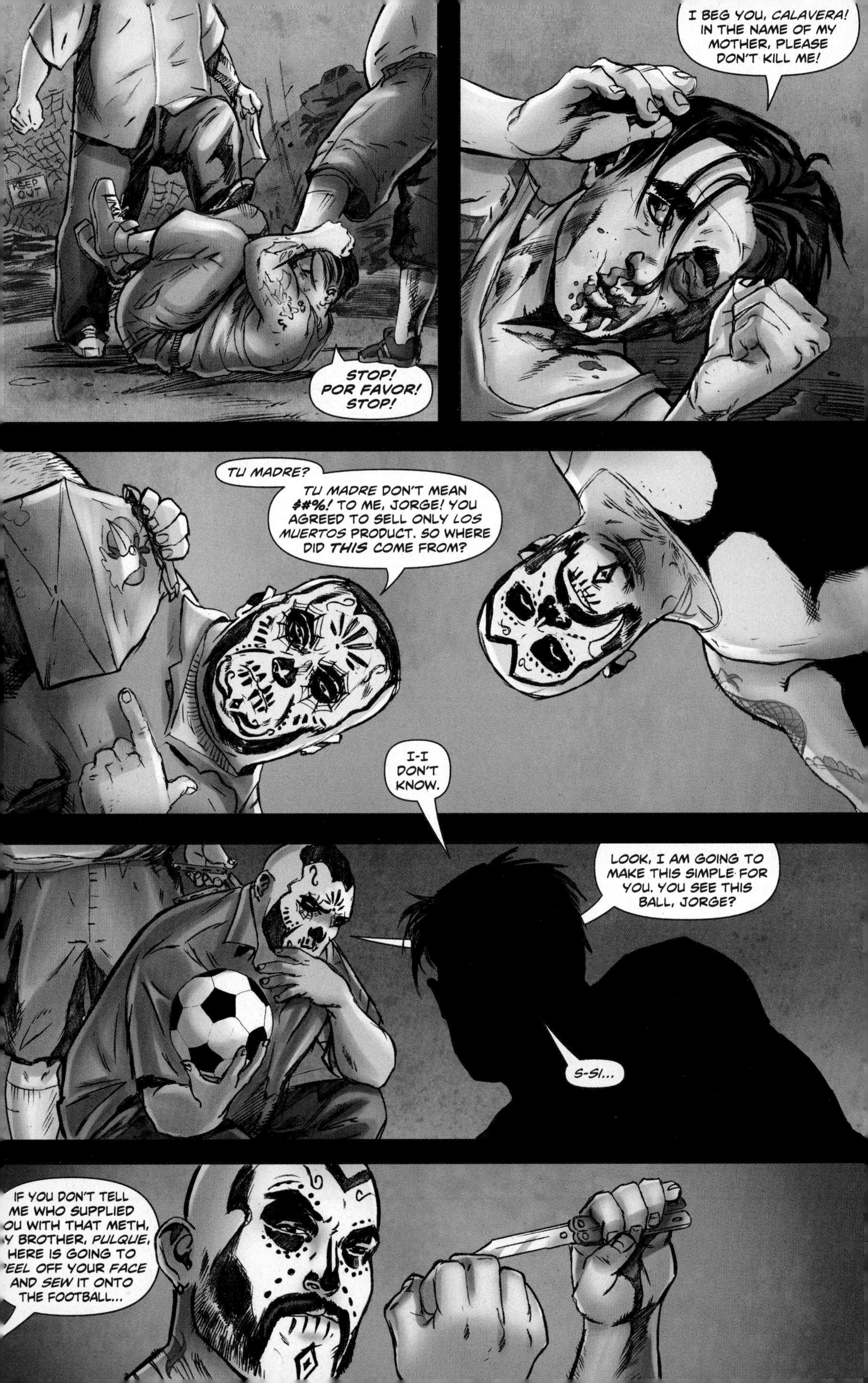
STOP! POR FAVOR! STOP!
I BEG YOU, CALAVERA! IN THE NAME OF MY MOTHER, PLEASE DON'T KILL ME!
TU MADRE?
TU MADRE DON'T MEAN $#%! TO ME, JORGE! YOU AGREED TO SELL ONLY LOS MUERTOS PRODUCT. SO WHERE DID THIS COME FROM?
I-I DON'T KNOW.
LOOK, I AM GOING TO MAKE THIS SIMPLE FOR YOU. YOU SEE THIS BALL, JORGE?
S-SI...
IF YOU DON'T TELL ME WHO SUPPLIED OU WITH THAT METH, Y BROTHER, PULQUE, HERE IS GOING TO 'EEL OFF YOUR FACE AND SEW IT ONTO THE FOOTBALL...
KEEP OUT

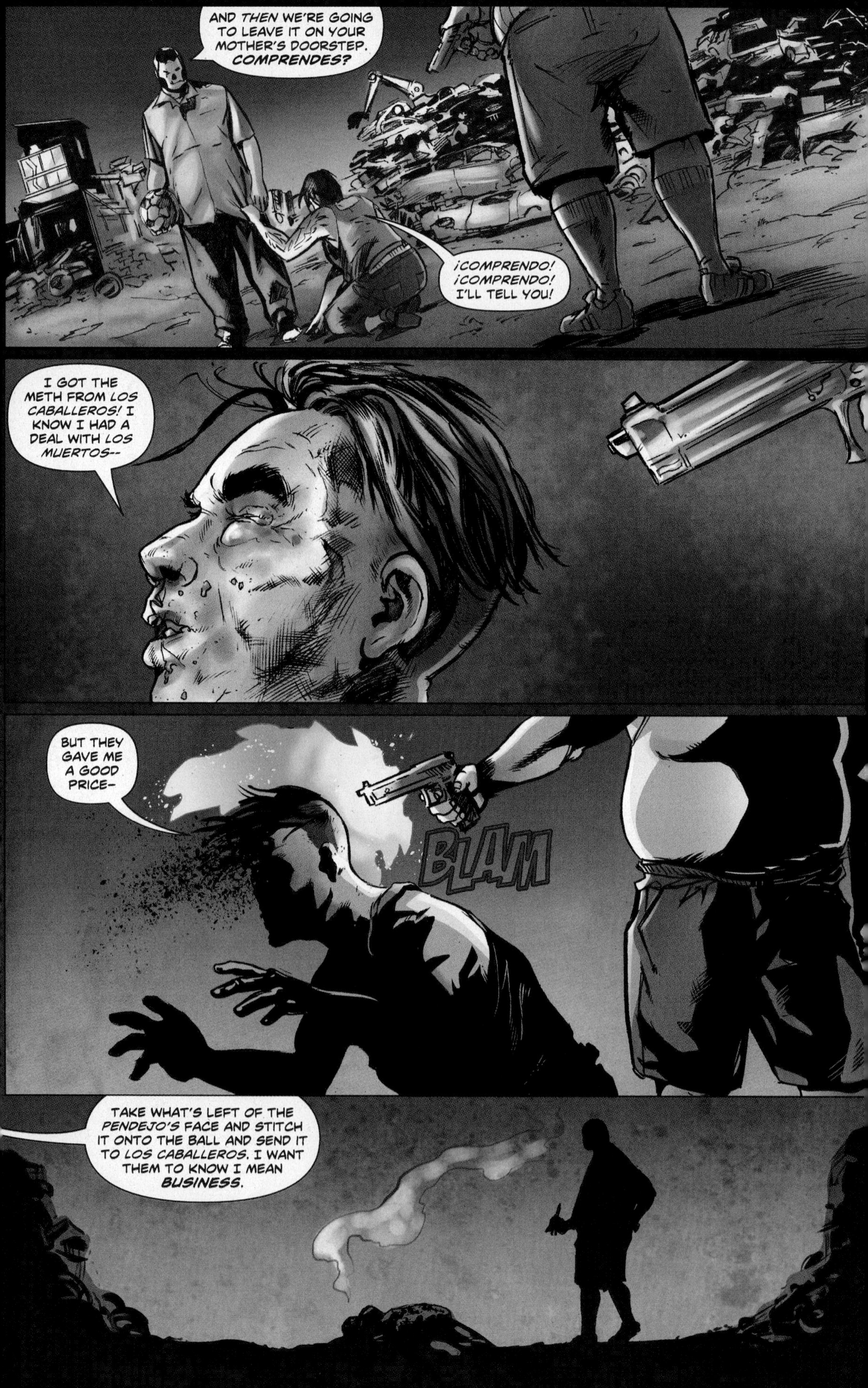
AND *THEN* WE'RE GOING TO LEAVE IT ON YOUR MOTHER'S DOORSTEP. ***COMPRENDES?***
¡COMPRENDO! ¡COMPRENDO! I'LL TELL YOU!
I GOT THE METH FROM *LOS CABALLEROS!* I KNOW I HAD A DEAL WITH *LOS MUERTOS--*
BUT THEY GAVE ME A GOOD PRICE-
BLAM
TAKE WHAT'S LEFT OF THE *PENDEJO'S* FACE AND STITCH IT ONTO THE BALL AND SEND IT TO *LOS CABALLEROS.* I WANT THEM TO KNOW I MEAN ***BUSINESS.***

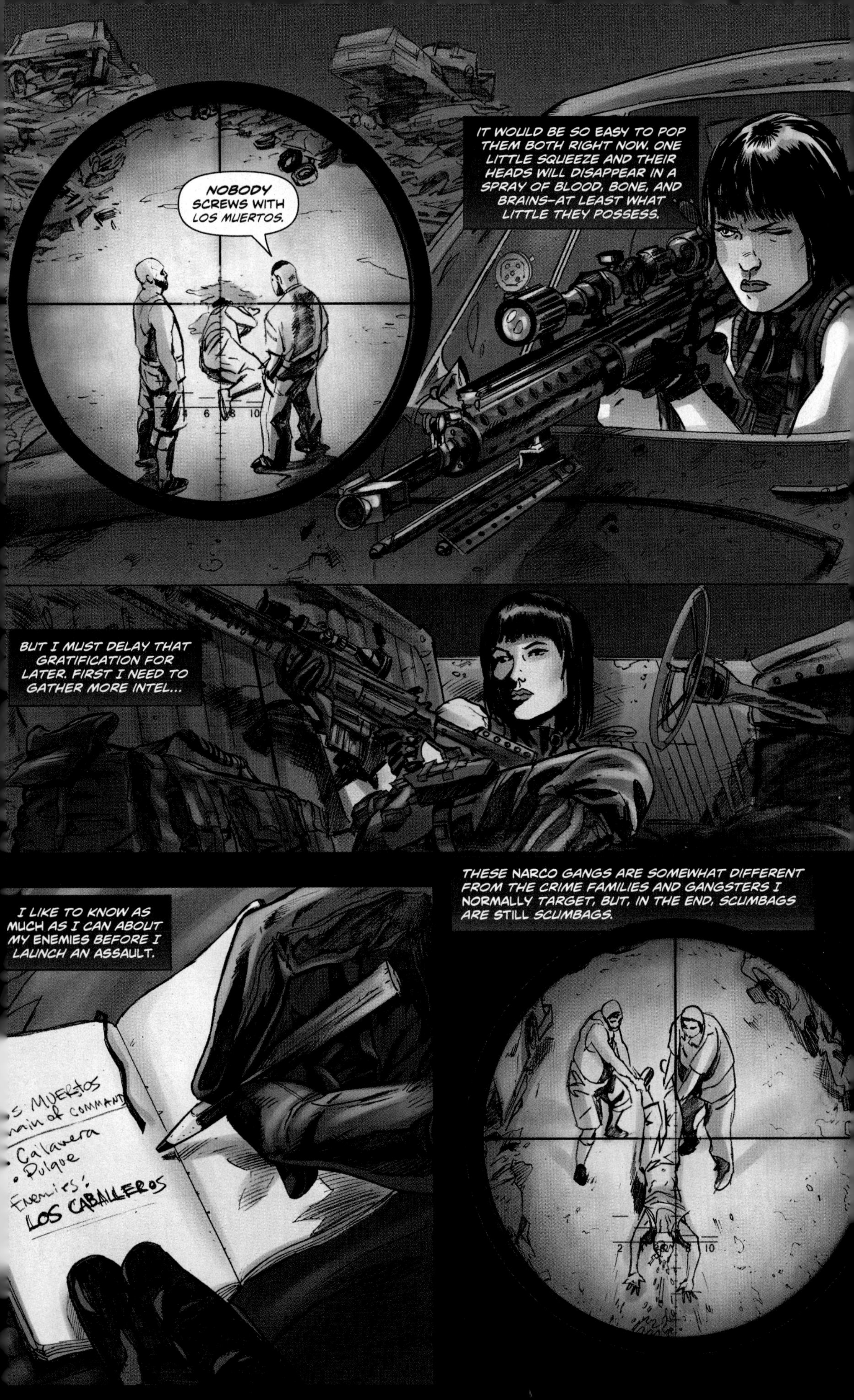

NOBODY SCREWS WITH LOS MUERTOS.
IT WOULD BE SO EASY TO POP THEM BOTH RIGHT NOW. ONE LITTLE SQUEEZE AND THEIR HEADS WILL DISAPPEAR IN A SPRAY OF BLOOD, BONE, AND BRAINS—AT LEAST WHAT LITTLE THEY POSSESS.
BUT I MUST DELAY THAT GRATIFICATION FOR LATER. FIRST I NEED TO GATHER MORE INTEL...
I LIKE TO KNOW AS MUCH AS I CAN ABOUT MY ENEMIES BEFORE I LAUNCH AN ASSAULT.
Calavera
Pulque
LOS CABALLEROS
THESE NARCO GANGS ARE SOMEWHAT DIFFERENT FROM THE CRIME FAMILIES AND GANGSTERS I NORMALLY TARGET, BUT, IN THE END, SCUMBAGS ARE STILL SCUMBAGS.

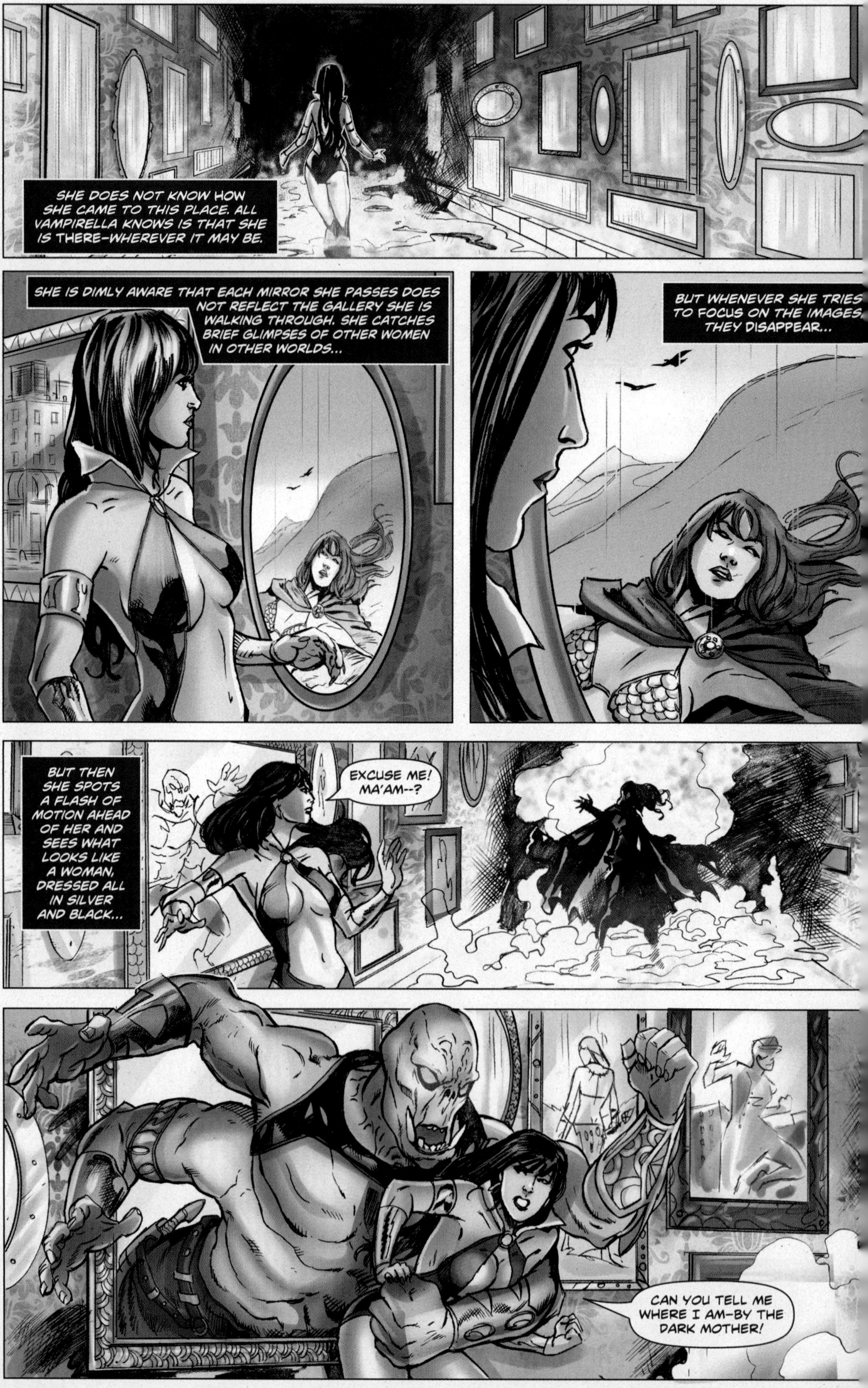
SHE DOES NOT KNOW HOW SHE CAME TO THIS PLACE. ALL VAMPIRELLA KNOWS IS THAT SHE IS THERE--WHEREVER IT MAY BE.
SHE IS DIMLY AWARE THAT EACH MIRROR SHE PASSES DOES NOT REFLECT THE GALLERY SHE IS WALKING THROUGH. SHE CATCHES BRIEF GLIMPSES OF OTHER WOMEN IN OTHER WORLDS...
BUT WHENEVER SHE TRIES TO FOCUS ON THE IMAGES, THEY DISAPPEAR...
BUT THEN SHE SPOTS A FLASH OF MOTION AHEAD OF HER AND SEES WHAT LOOKS LIKE A WOMAN, DRESSED ALL IN SILVER AND BLACK...
EXCUSE ME! MA'AM--?
CAN YOU TELL ME WHERE I AM--BY THE DARK MOTHER!

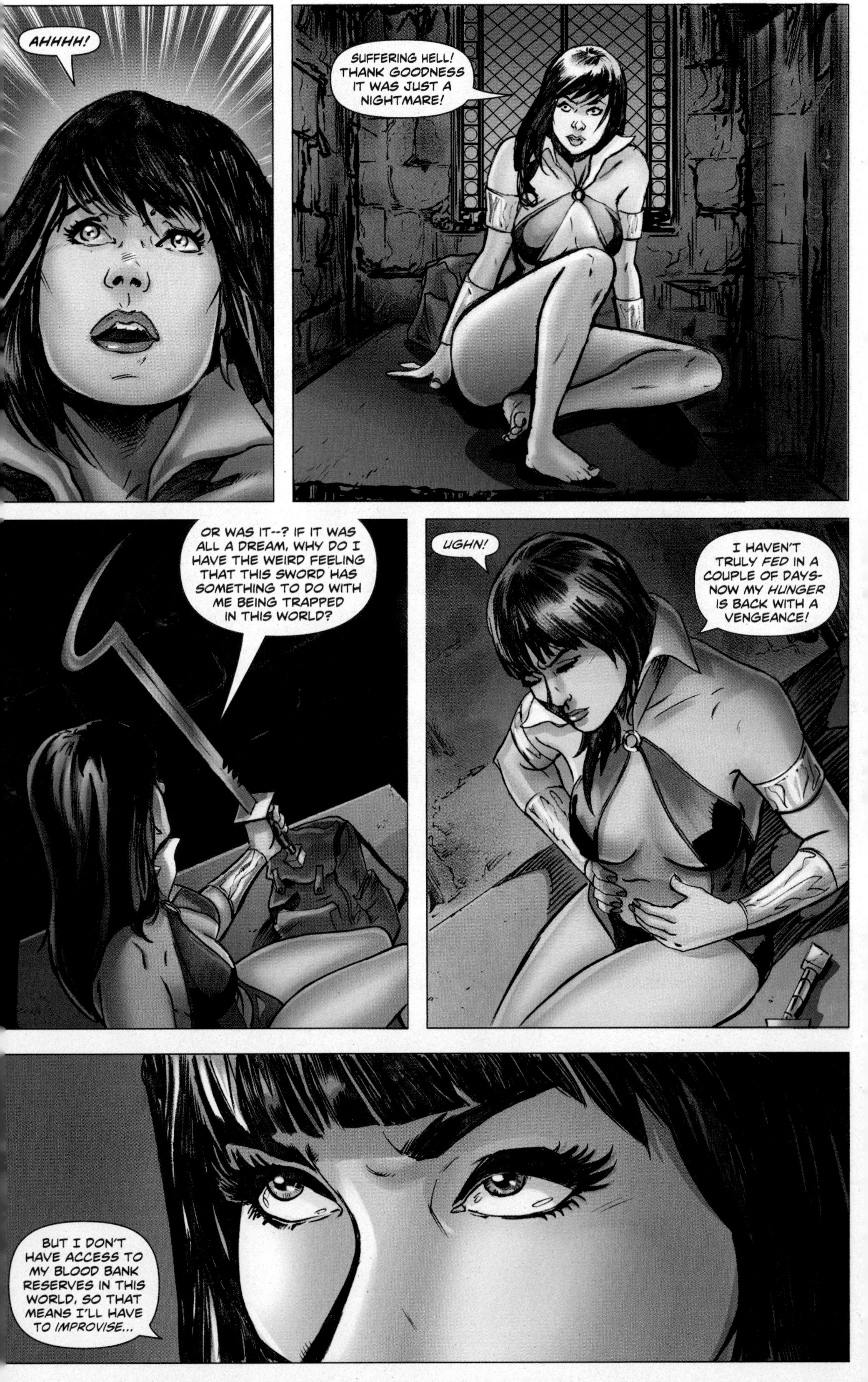
AHHHH!
SUFFERING HELL! THANK GOODNESS IT WAS JUST A NIGHTMARE!
OR WAS IT--? IF IT WAS ALL A DREAM, WHY DO I HAVE THE WEIRD FEELING THAT THIS SWORD HAS SOMETHING TO DO WITH ME BEING TRAPPED IN THIS WORLD?
UGHN!
I HAVEN'T TRULY FED IN A COUPLE OF DAYS-NOW MY HUNGER IS BACK WITH A VENGEANCE!
BUT I DON'T HAVE ACCESS TO MY BLOOD BANK RESERVES IN THIS WORLD, SO THAT MEANS I'LL HAVE TO IMPROVISE...

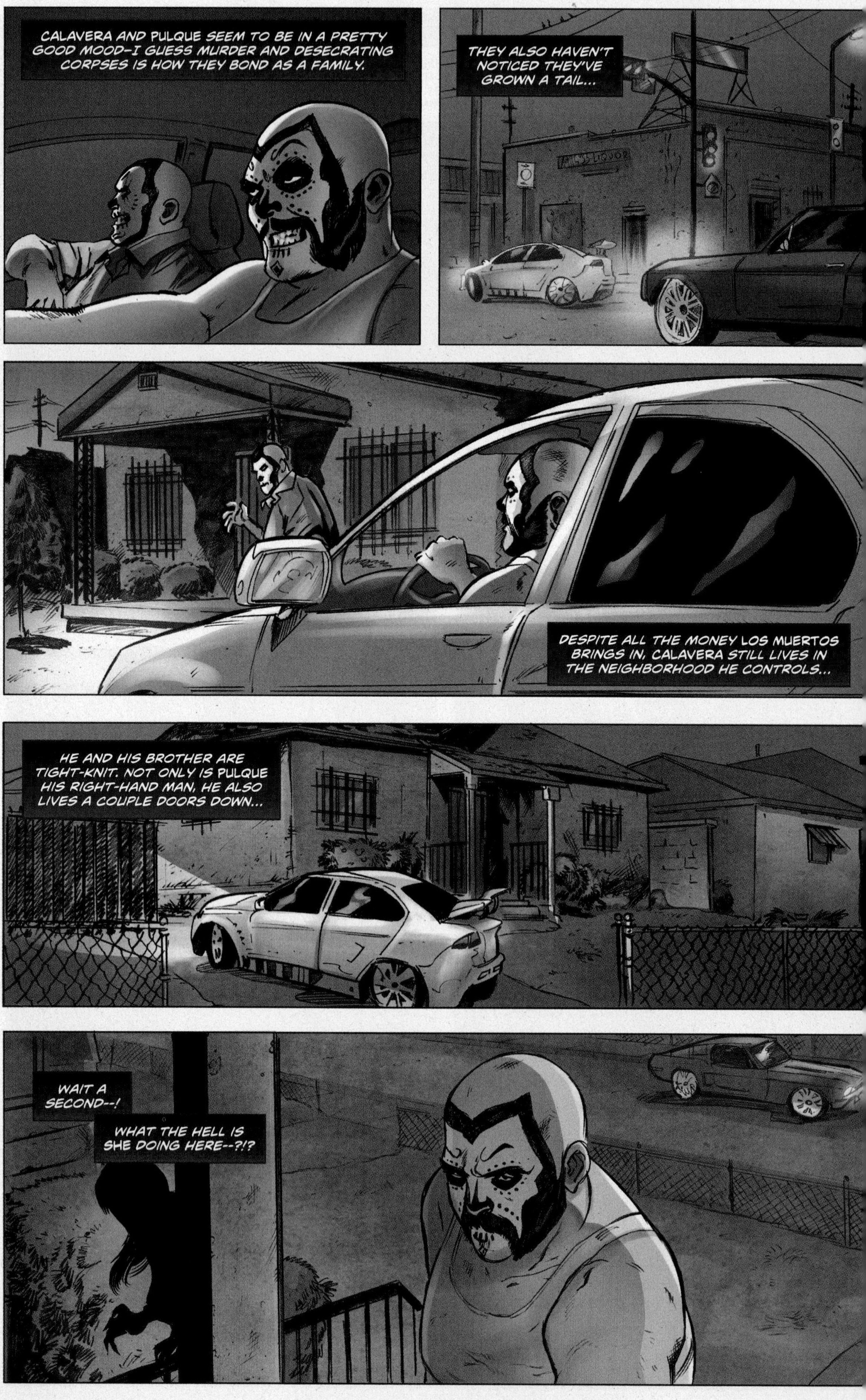
CALAVERA AND PULQUE SEEM TO BE IN A PRETTY GOOD MOOD–I GUESS MURDER AND DESECRATING CORPSES IS HOW THEY BOND AS A FAMILY.
THEY ALSO HAVEN'T NOTICED THEY'VE GROWN A TAIL...
DESPITE ALL THE MONEY LOS MUERTOS BRINGS IN, CALAVERA STILL LIVES IN THE NEIGHBORHOOD HE CONTROLS...
HE AND HIS BROTHER ARE TIGHT-KNIT. NOT ONLY IS PULQUE HIS RIGHT-HAND MAN, HE ALSO LIVES A COUPLE DOORS DOWN...
WAIT A SECOND--!
WHAT THE HELL IS SHE DOING HERE--?!?

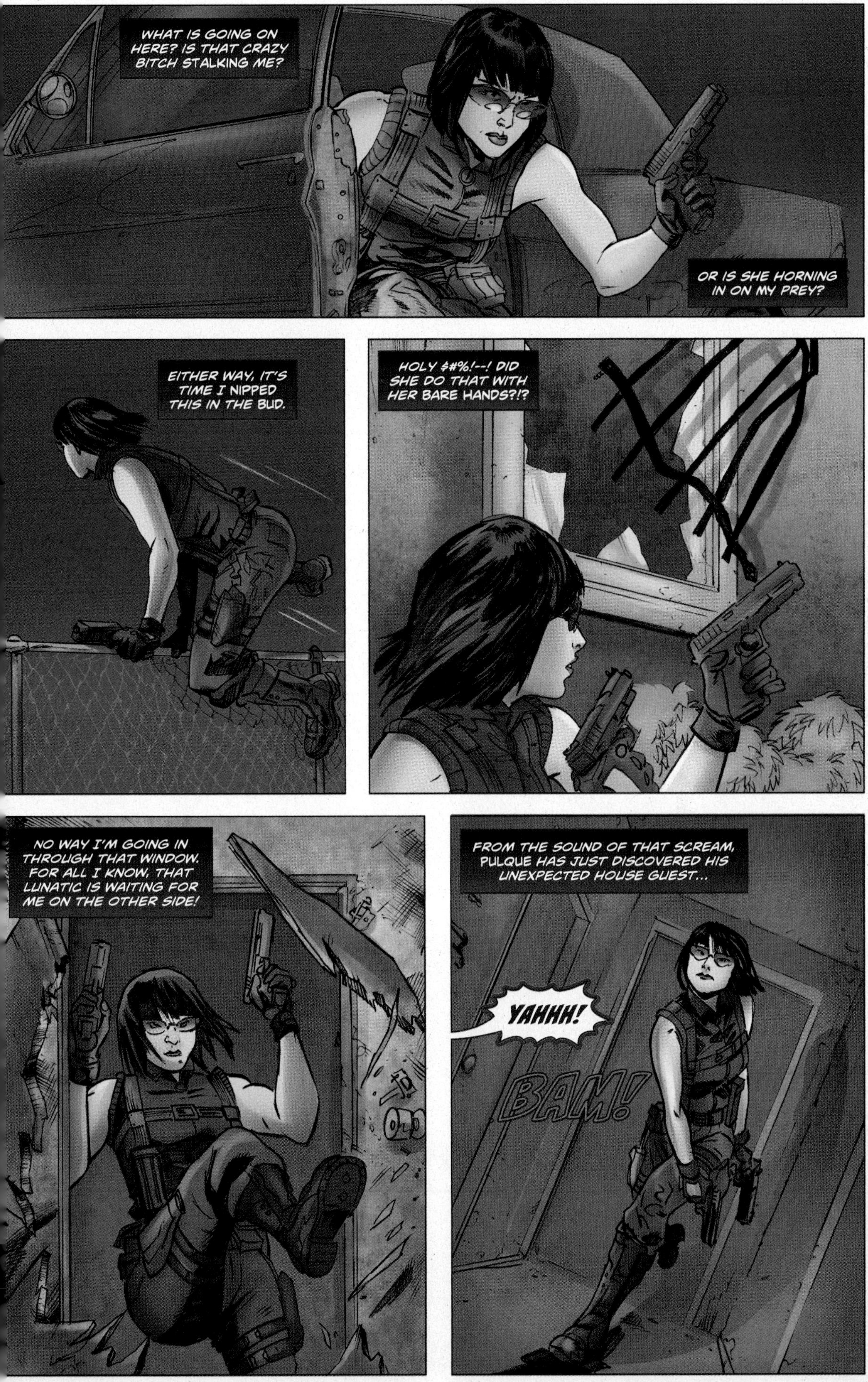
WHAT IS GOING ON HERE? IS THAT CRAZY BITCH STALKING ME?
OR IS SHE HORNING IN ON MY PREY?
EITHER WAY, IT'S TIME I NIPPED THIS IN THE BUD.
HOLY $#%!--! DID SHE DO THAT WITH HER BARE HANDS?!?
NO WAY I'M GOING IN THROUGH THAT WINDOW. FOR ALL I KNOW, THAT LUNATIC IS WAITING FOR ME ON THE OTHER SIDE!
FROM THE SOUND OF THAT SCREAM, PULQUE HAS JUST DISCOVERED HIS UNEXPECTED HOUSE GUEST...
YAHHH!
BAM!

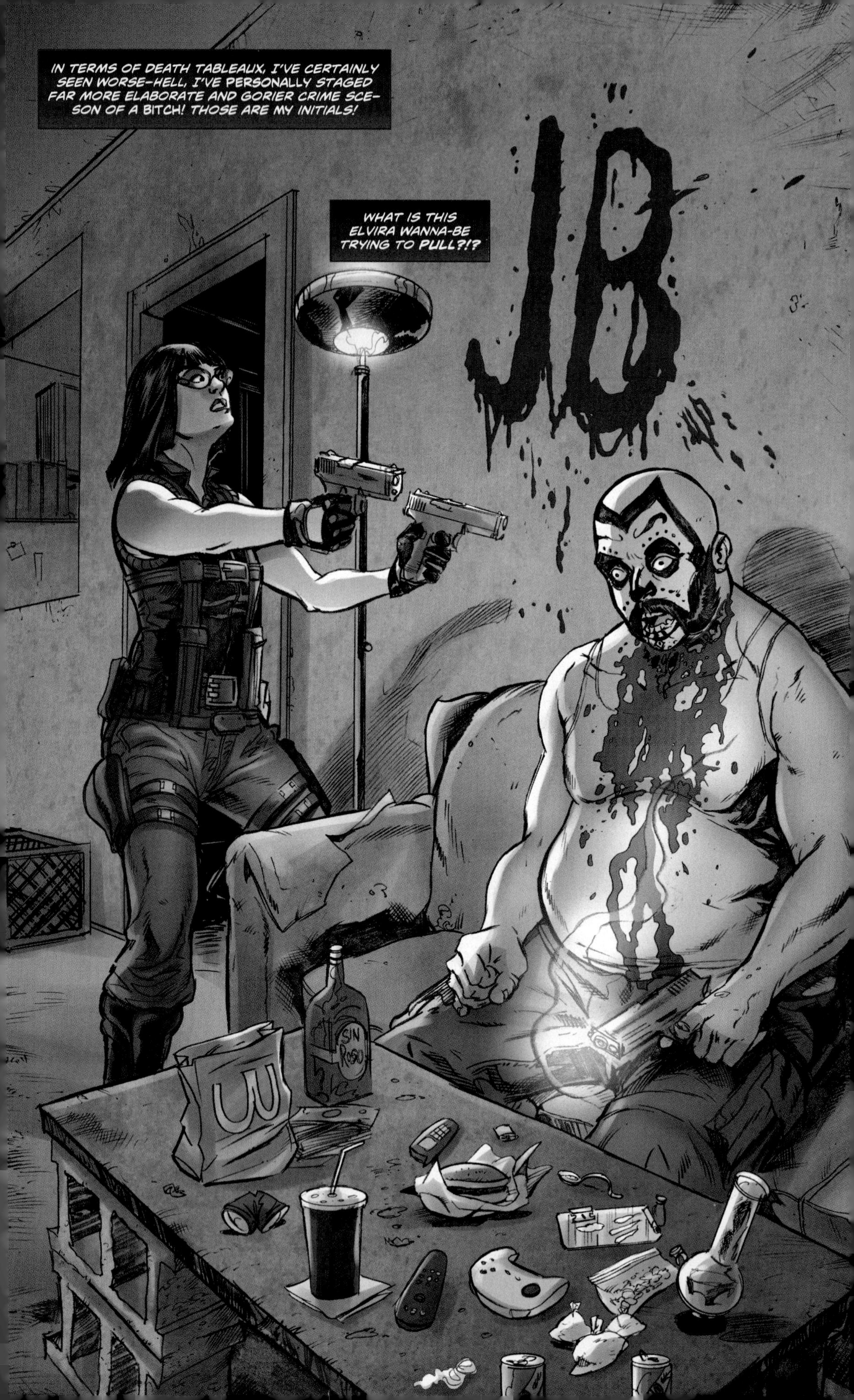
IN TERMS OF DEATH TABLEAUX, I'VE CERTAINLY SEEN WORSE–HELL, I'VE PERSONALLY STAGED FAR MORE ELABORATE AND GORIER CRIME SCE–
SON OF A BITCH! THOSE ARE MY INITIALS!
WHAT IS THIS ELVIRA WANNA-BE TRYING TO PULL?!?
JB
SIN ROSO

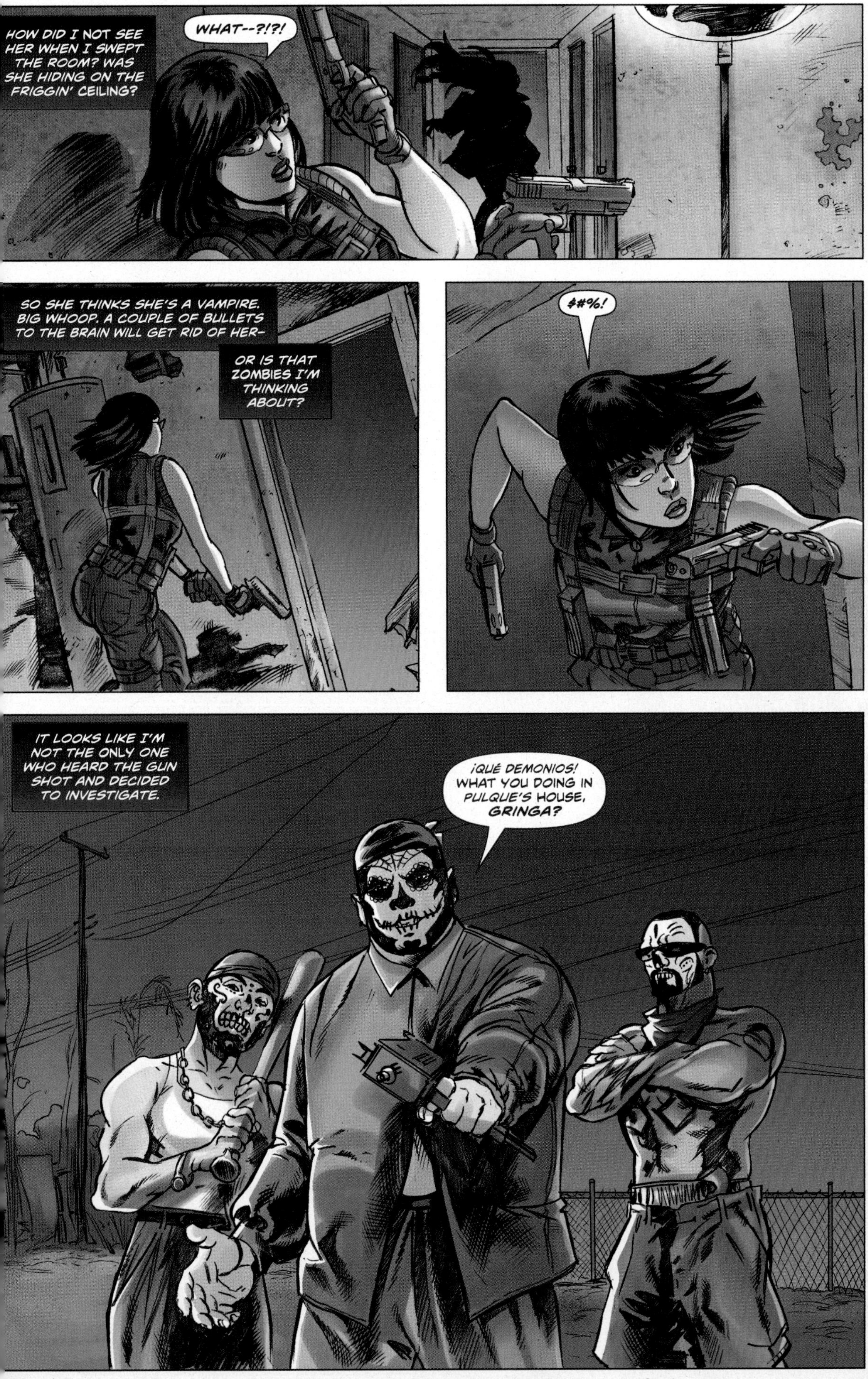
HOW DID I NOT SEE HER WHEN I SWEPT THE ROOM? WAS SHE HIDING ON THE FRIGGIN' CEILING?
WHAT--?!?!
SO SHE THINKS SHE'S A VAMPIRE. BIG WHOOP. A COUPLE OF BULLETS TO THE BRAIN WILL GET RID OF HER–
OR IS THAT ZOMBIES I'M THINKING ABOUT?
$#%!
IT LOOKS LIKE I'M NOT THE ONLY ONE WHO HEARD THE GUN SHOT AND DECIDED TO INVESTIGATE.
¡QUÉ DEMONIOS! WHAT YOU DOING IN PULQUE'S HOUSE, GRINGA?

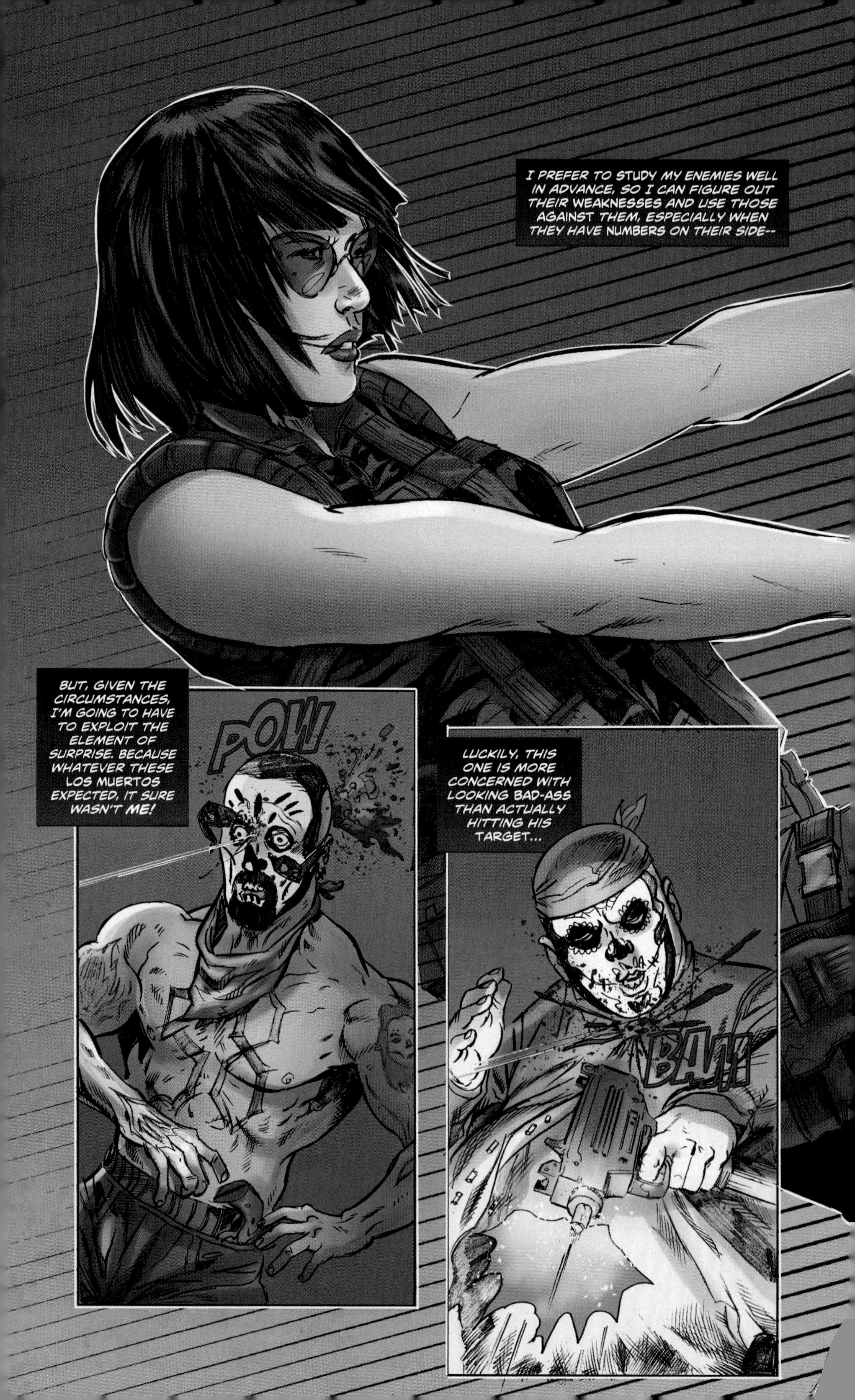
I PREFER TO STUDY MY ENEMIES WELL IN ADVANCE, SO I CAN FIGURE OUT THEIR WEAKNESSES AND USE THOSE AGAINST THEM, ESPECIALLY WHEN THEY HAVE NUMBERS ON THEIR SIDE--
BUT, GIVEN THE CIRCUMSTANCES, I'M GOING TO HAVE TO EXPLOIT THE ELEMENT OF SURPRISE. BECAUSE WHATEVER THESE LOS MUERTOS EXPECTED, IT SURE WASN'T ME!
POW!
LUCKILY, THIS ONE IS MORE CONCERNED WITH LOOKING BAD-ASS THAN ACTUALLY HITTING HIS TARGET...
BAM!

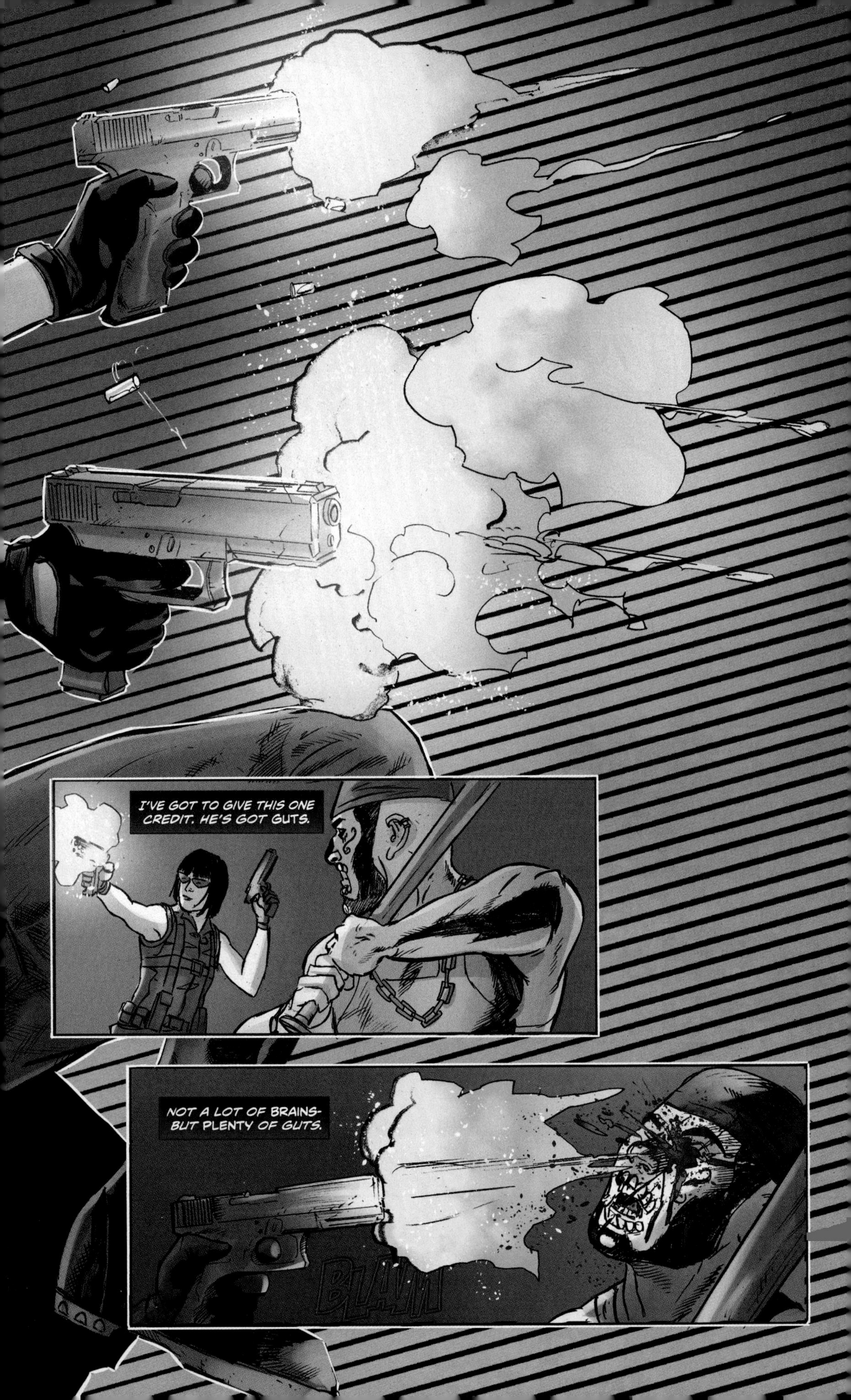
I'VE GOT TO GIVE THIS ONE CREDIT. HE'S GOT GUTS.
NOT A LOT OF BRAINS-BUT PLENTY OF GUTS.
BLAM

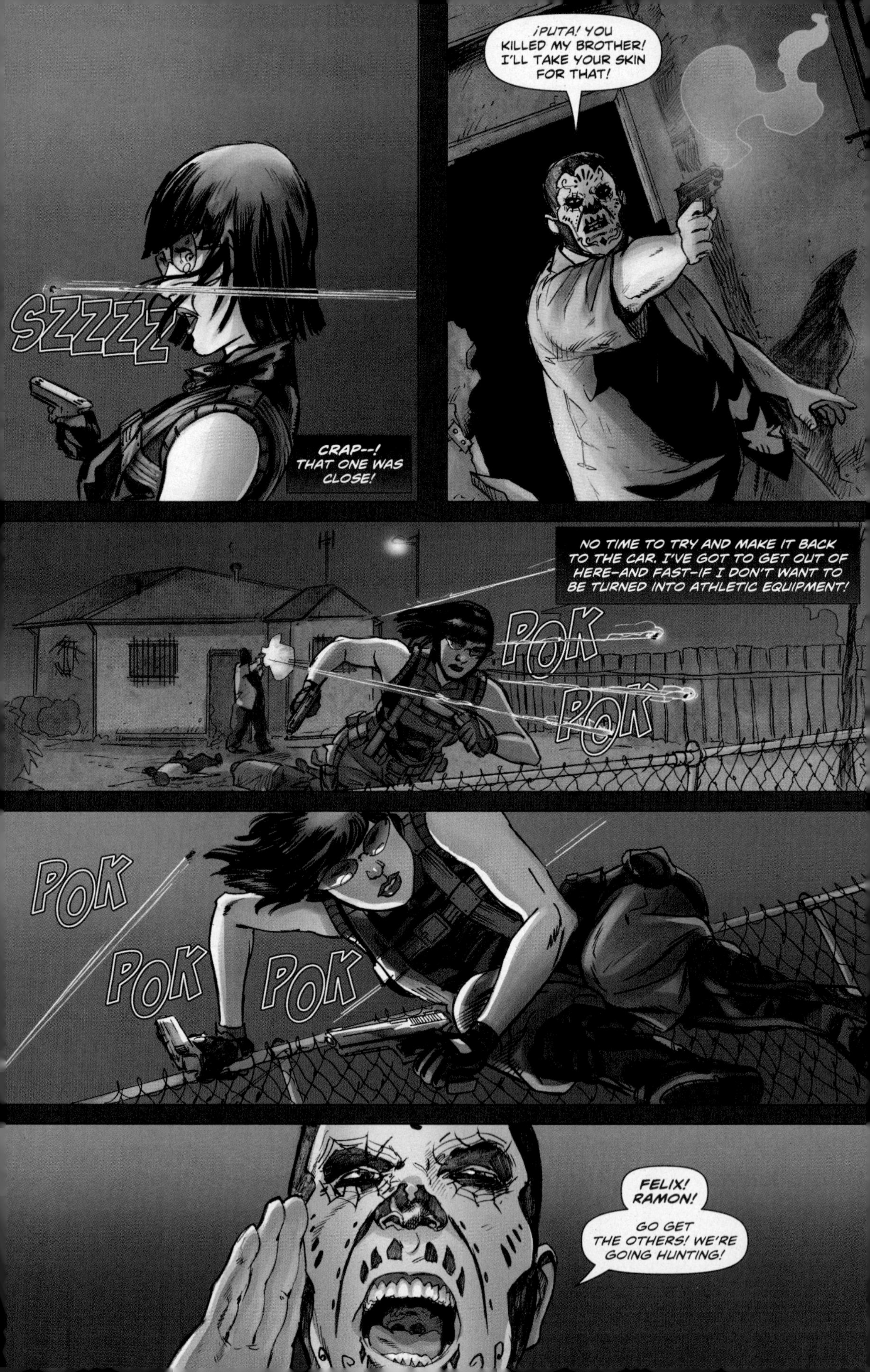
SZZZZ
CRAP--! THAT ONE WAS CLOSE!
¡PUTA! YOU KILLED MY BROTHER! I'LL TAKE YOUR SKIN FOR THAT!
NO TIME TO TRY AND MAKE IT BACK TO THE CAR. I'VE GOT TO GET OUT OF HERE–AND FAST–IF I DON'T WANT TO BE TURNED INTO ATHLETIC EQUIPMENT!
POK
POK
POK
POK
POK
FELIX! RAMON!
GO GET THE OTHERS! WE'RE GOING HUNTING!

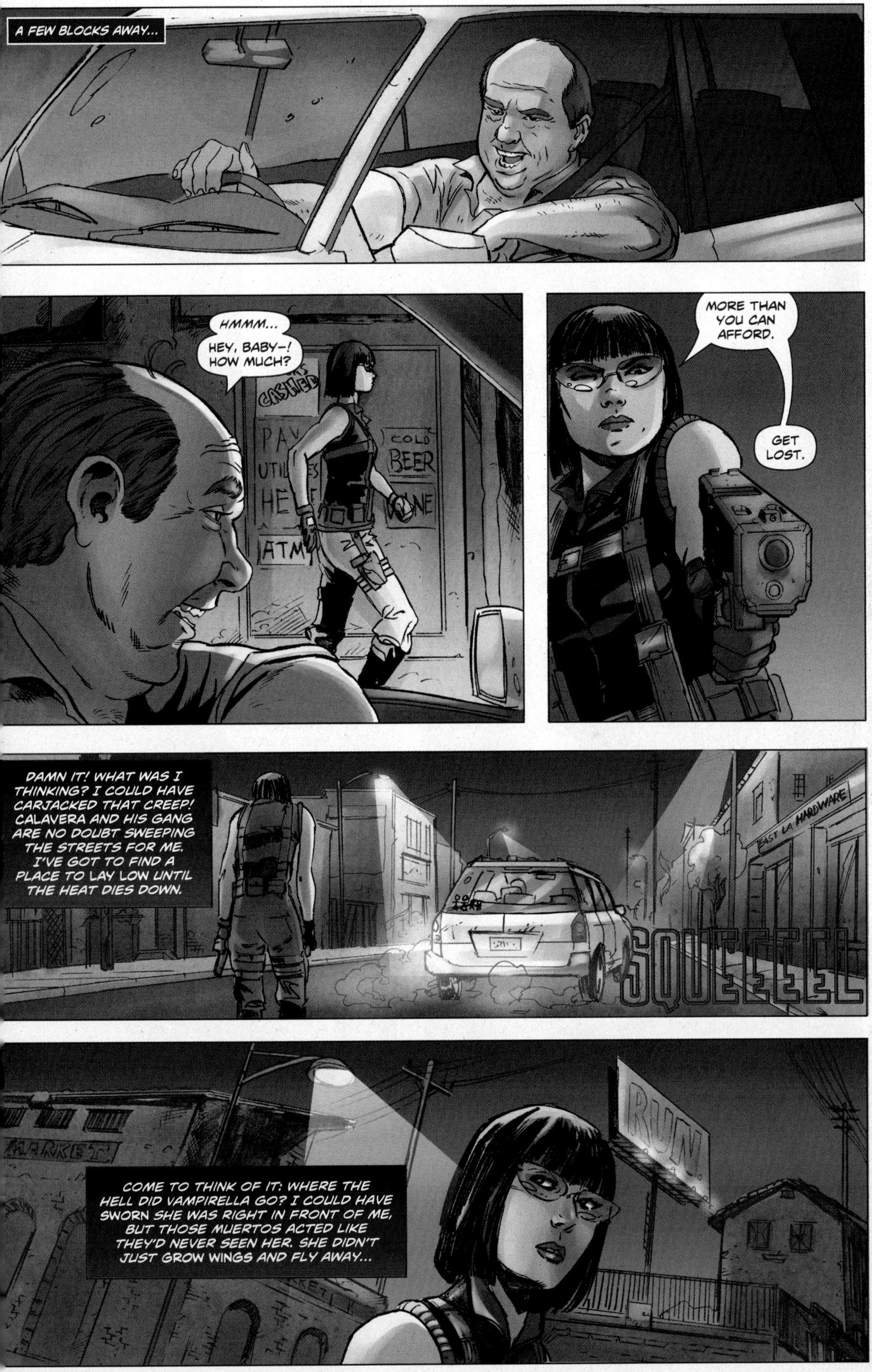
A FEW BLOCKS AWAY...
HMMM... HEY, BABY–! HOW MUCH?
COLD BEER
ATM
MORE THAN YOU CAN AFFORD.
GET LOST.
DAMN IT! WHAT WAS I THINKING? I COULD HAVE CARJACKED THAT CREEP! CALAVERA AND HIS GANG ARE NO DOUBT SWEEPING THE STREETS FOR ME. I'VE GOT TO FIND A PLACE TO LAY LOW UNTIL THE HEAT DIES DOWN.
EAST LA HARDWARE
SQUEEEEL
COME TO THINK OF IT: WHERE THE HELL DID VAMPIRELLA GO? I COULD HAVE SWORN SHE WAS RIGHT IN FRONT OF ME, BUT THOSE MUERTOS ACTED LIKE THEY'D NEVER SEEN HER. SHE DIDN'T JUST GROW WINGS AND FLY AWAY...

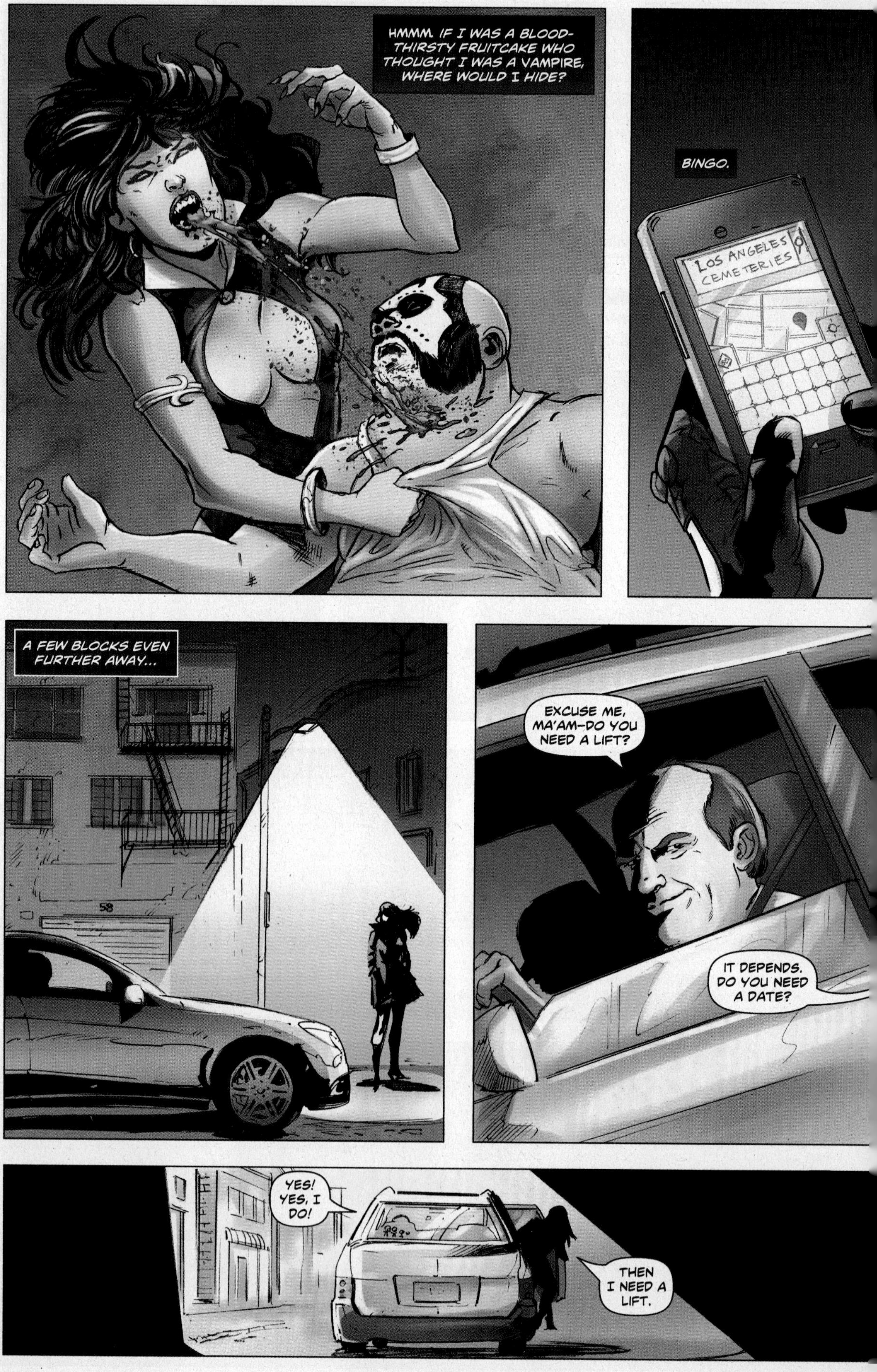
HMMM. IF I WAS A BLOOD-THIRSTY FRUITCAKE WHO THOUGHT I WAS A VAMPIRE, WHERE WOULD I HIDE?
BINGO.
LOS ANGELES CEMETERIES
A FEW BLOCKS EVEN FURTHER AWAY...
58
EXCUSE ME, MA'AM--DO YOU NEED A LIFT?
IT DEPENDS. DO YOU NEED A DATE?
YES! YES, I DO!
THEN I NEED A LIFT.

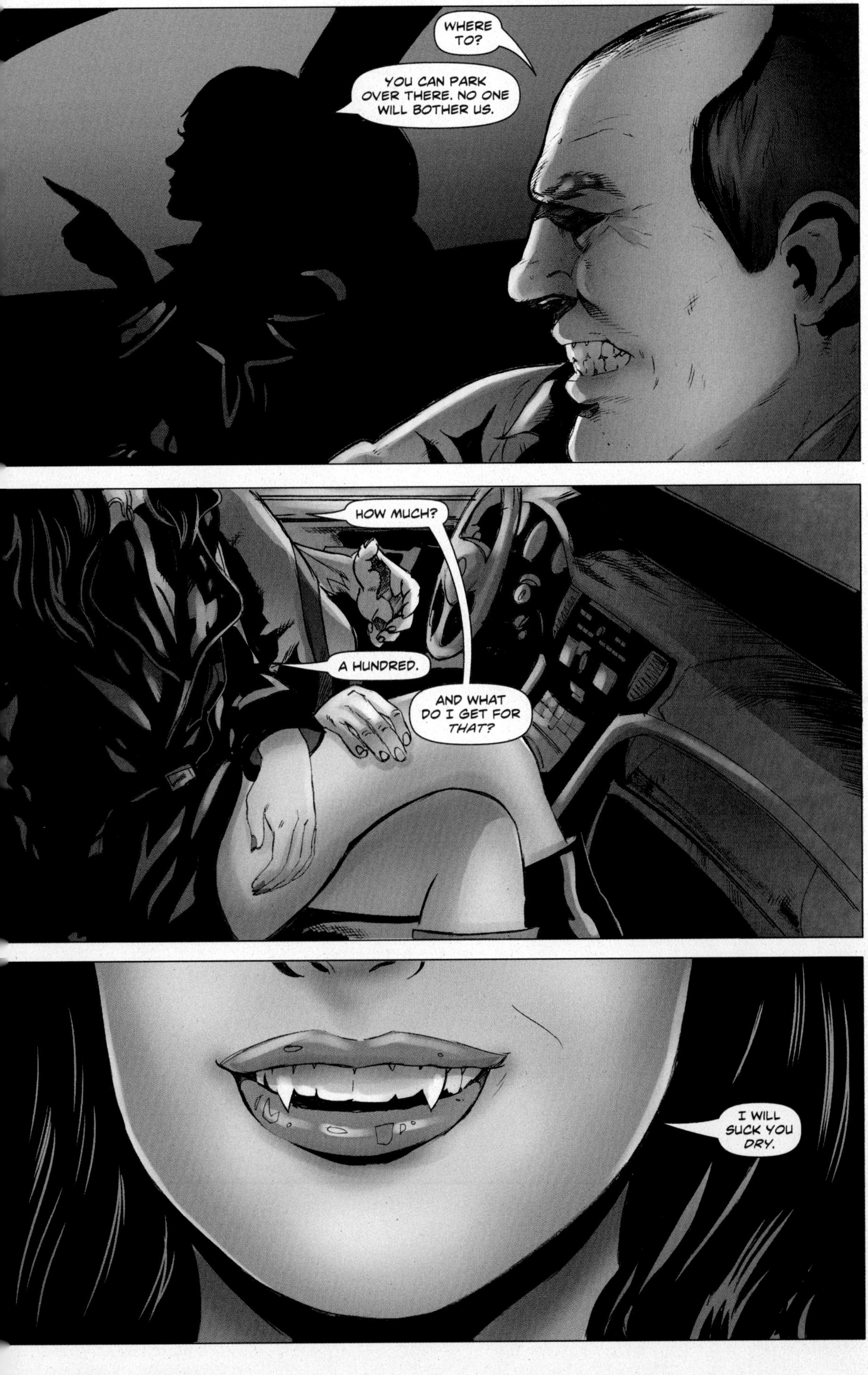
WHERE TO?
YOU CAN PARK OVER THERE. NO ONE WILL BOTHER US.
HOW MUCH?
A HUNDRED.
AND WHAT DO I GET FOR *THAT?*
I WILL SUCK YOU *DRY.*

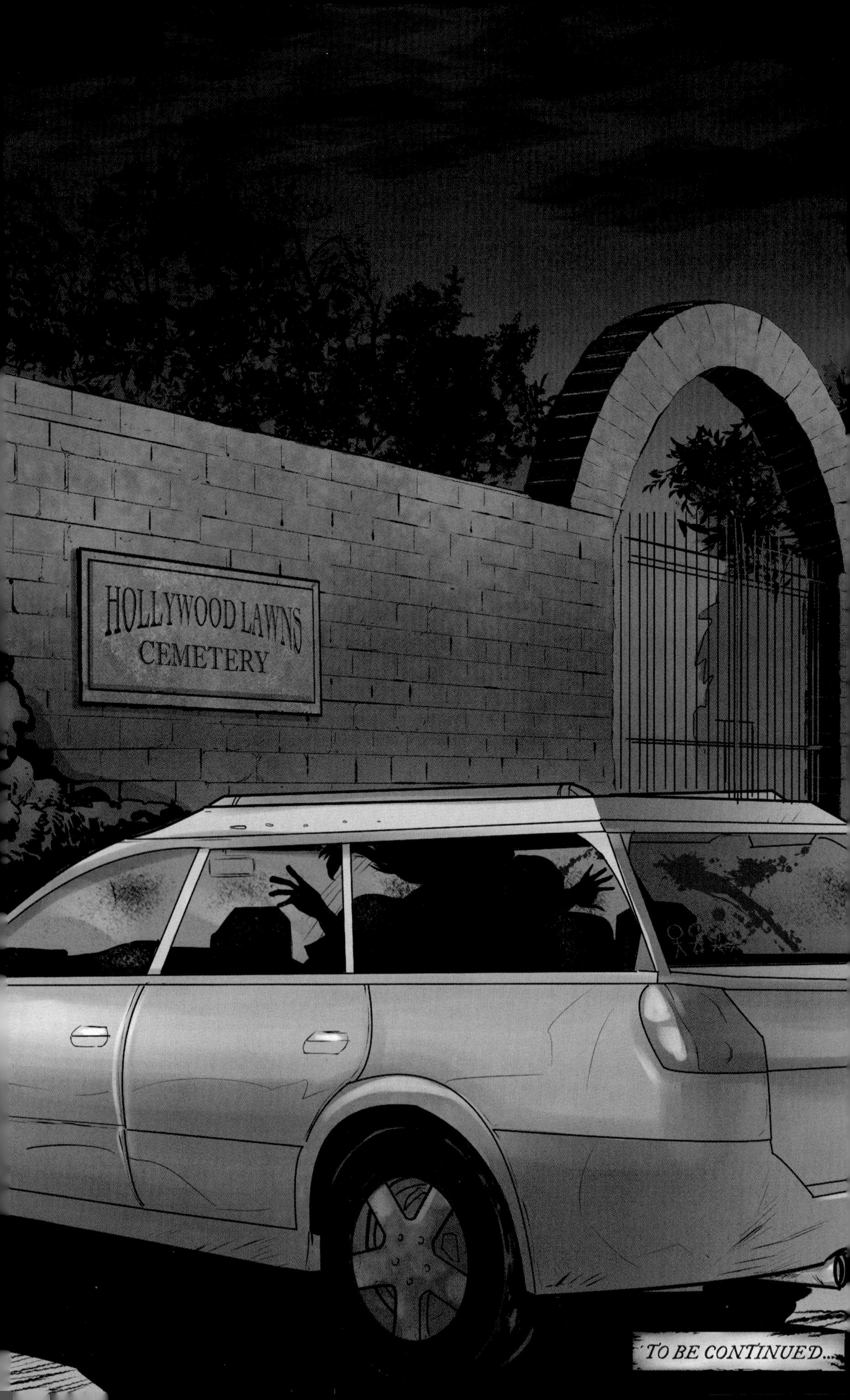
HOLLYWOOD LAWNS
CEMETERY
TO BE CONTINUED...

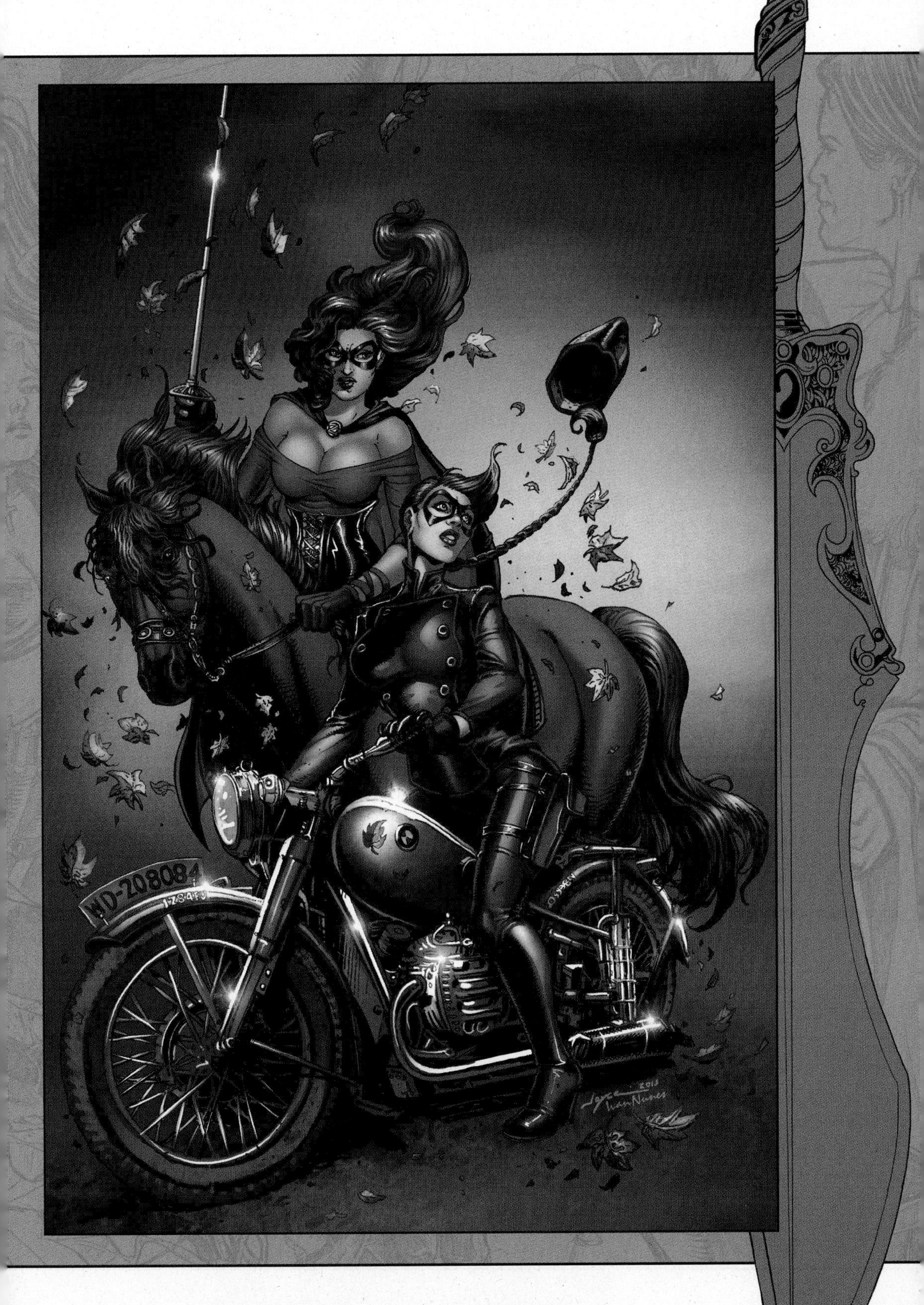
WD-208084

SWORDS OF SORROW: BLACK SPARROW & LADY ZORRO
ONE-SHOT

written by ERICA SCHULTZ illustrated by CRIZAM ZAMORA
colored by SALVATORE AIALA STUDIO lettered by ERICA SCHULTZ

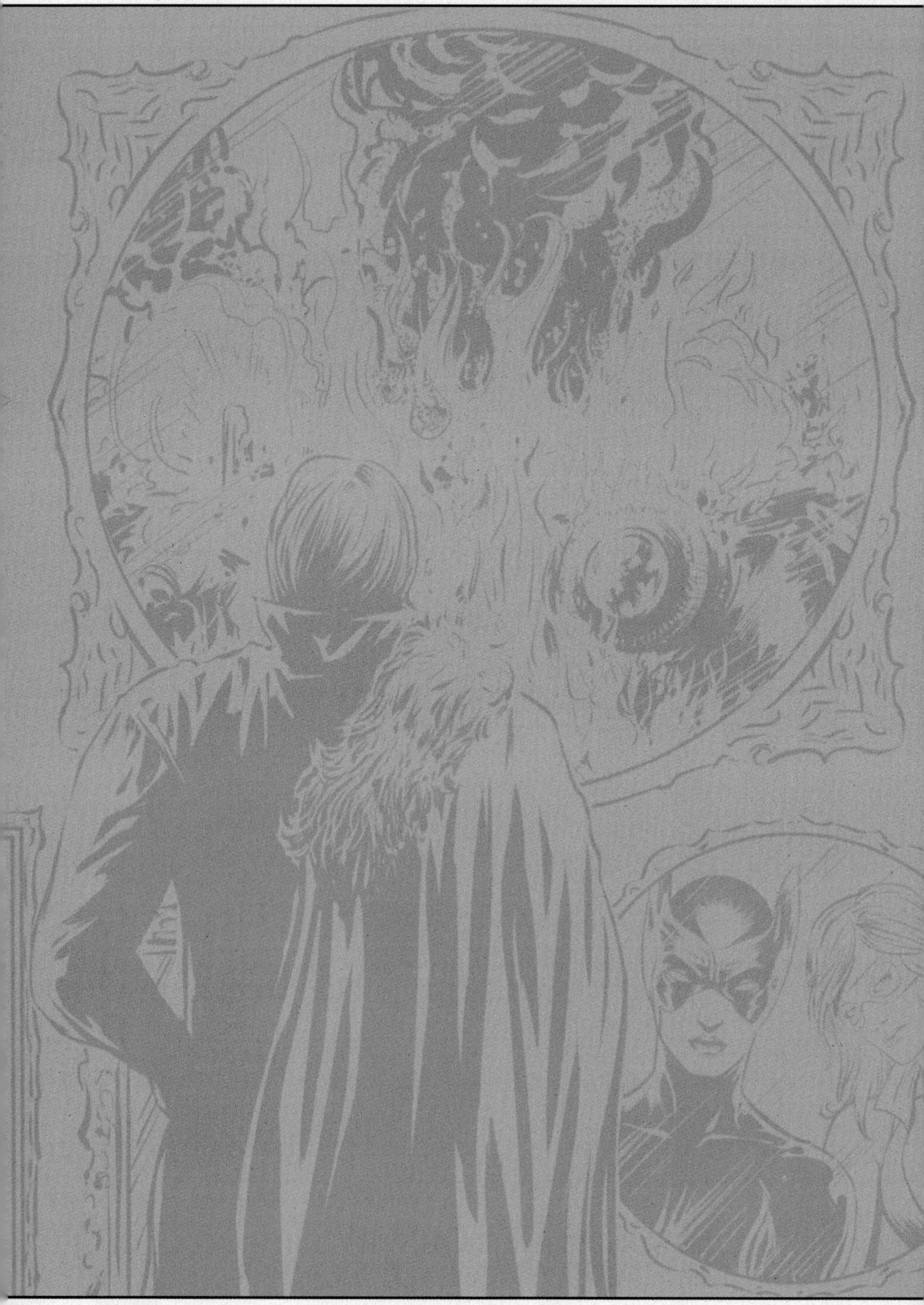

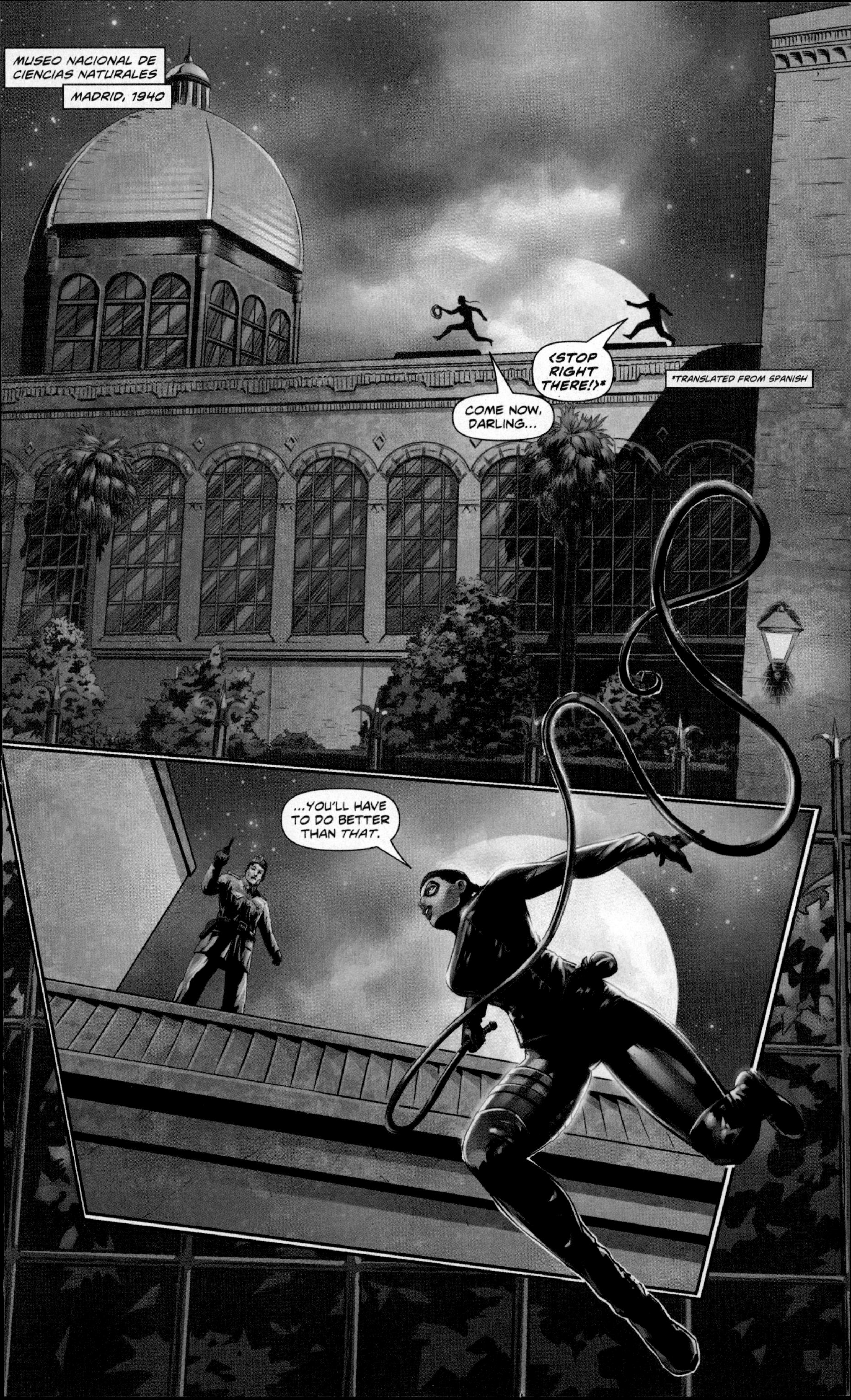
MUSEO NACIONAL DE CIENCIAS NATURALES
MADRID, 1940
COME NOW, DARLING...
<STOP RIGHT THERE!>*
*TRANSLATED FROM SPANISH
...YOU'LL HAVE TO DO BETTER THAN THAT.

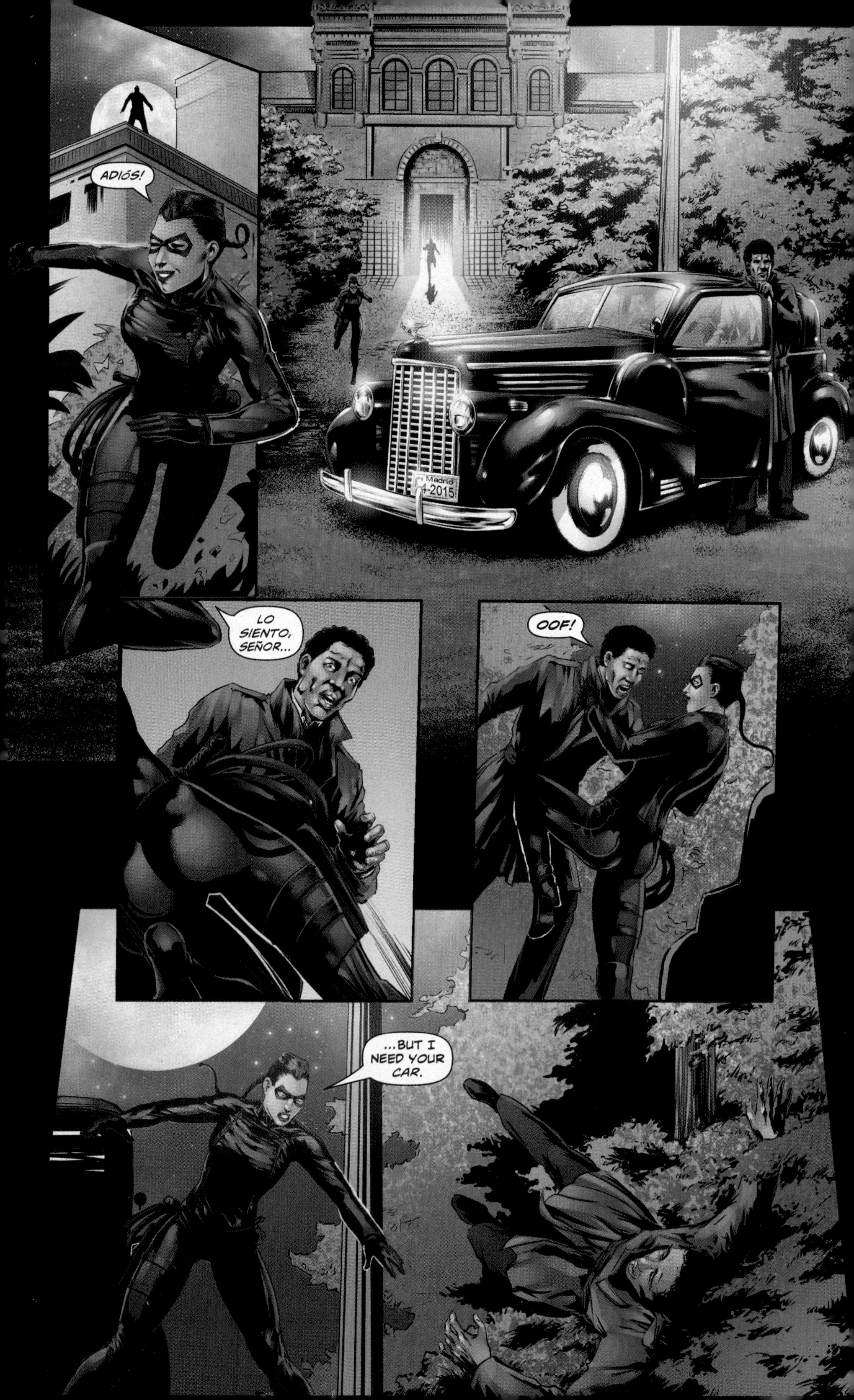
ADIÓS!
Madrid
4-2015
LO SIENTO, SEÑOR...
OOF!
...BUT I NEED YOUR CAR.

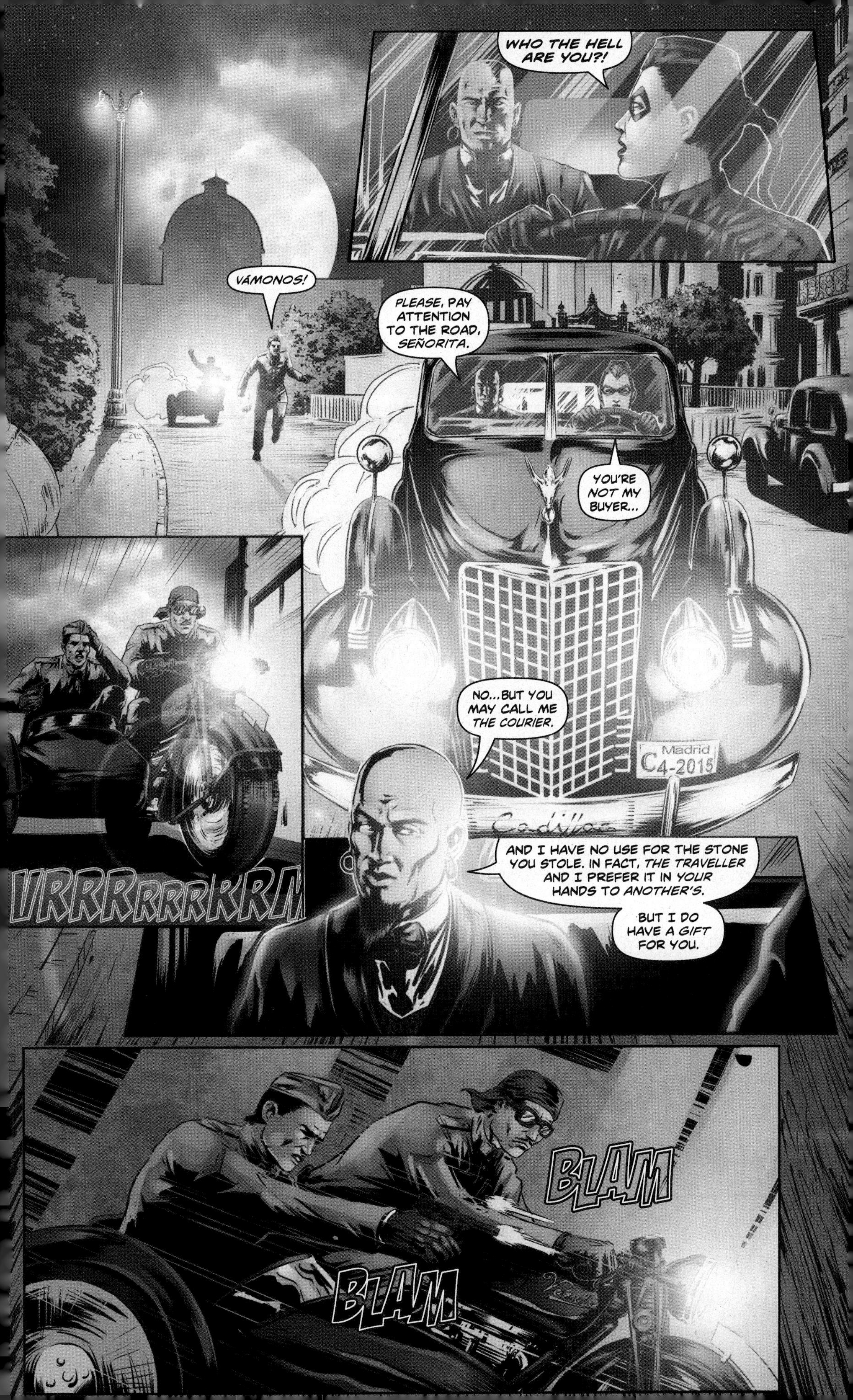
WHO THE HELL ARE YOU?!
VÁMONOS!
PLEASE, PAY ATTENTION TO THE ROAD, SEÑORITA.
YOU'RE NOT MY BUYER...
NO...BUT YOU MAY CALL ME THE COURIER.
Madrid C4-2015
URRRRRRRKRM
AND I HAVE NO USE FOR THE STONE YOU STOLE. IN FACT, THE TRAVELLER AND I PREFER IT IN YOUR HANDS TO ANOTHER'S.
BUT I DO HAVE A GIFT FOR YOU.
BLAM
BLAM

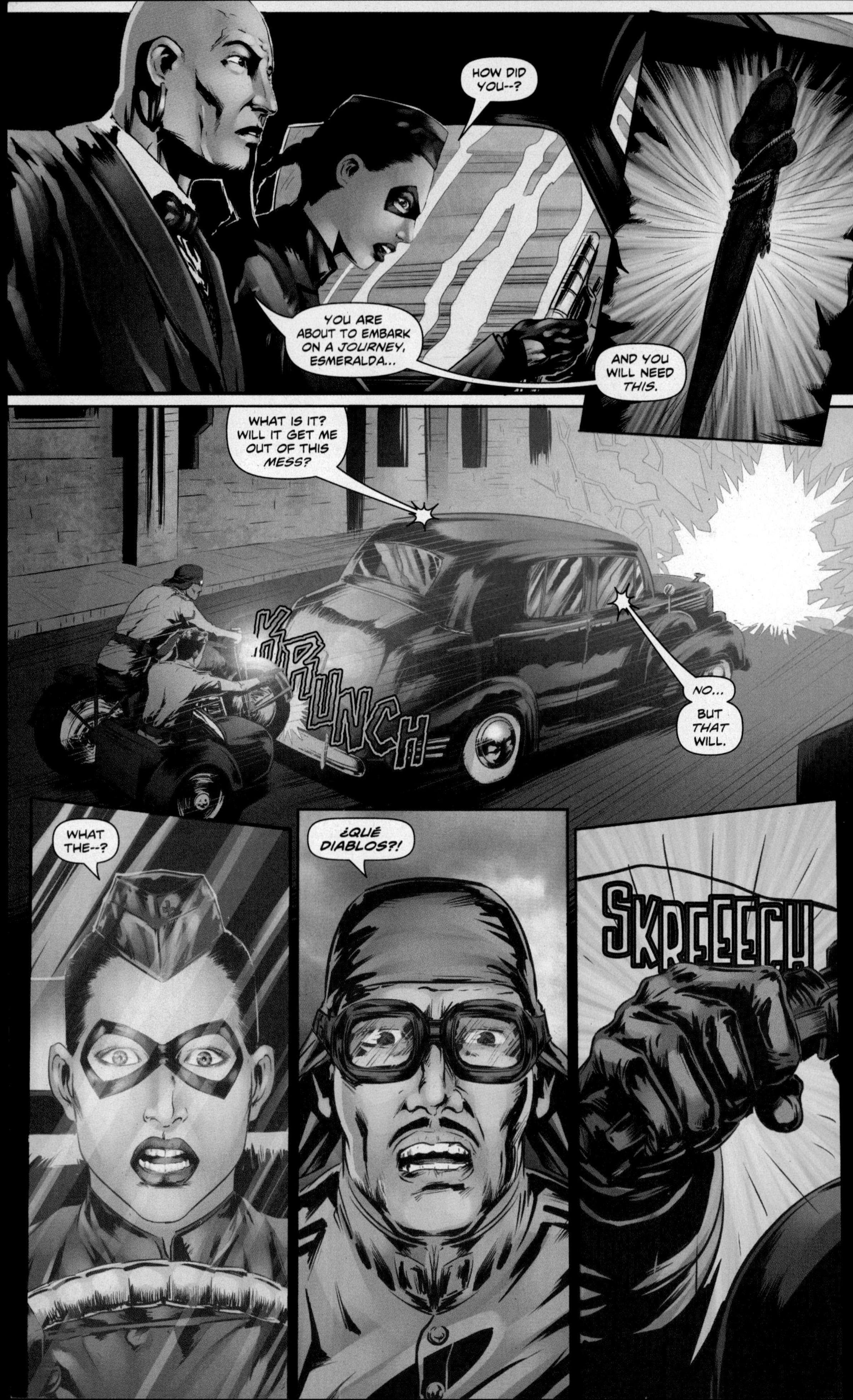
HOW DID YOU--?
YOU ARE ABOUT TO EMBARK ON A JOURNEY, ESMERALDA...
AND YOU WILL NEED THIS.
WHAT IS IT? WILL IT GET ME OUT OF THIS MESS?
NO... BUT THAT WILL.
KRUNCH
WHAT THE--?
¿QUÉ DIABLOS?!
SKREEECH

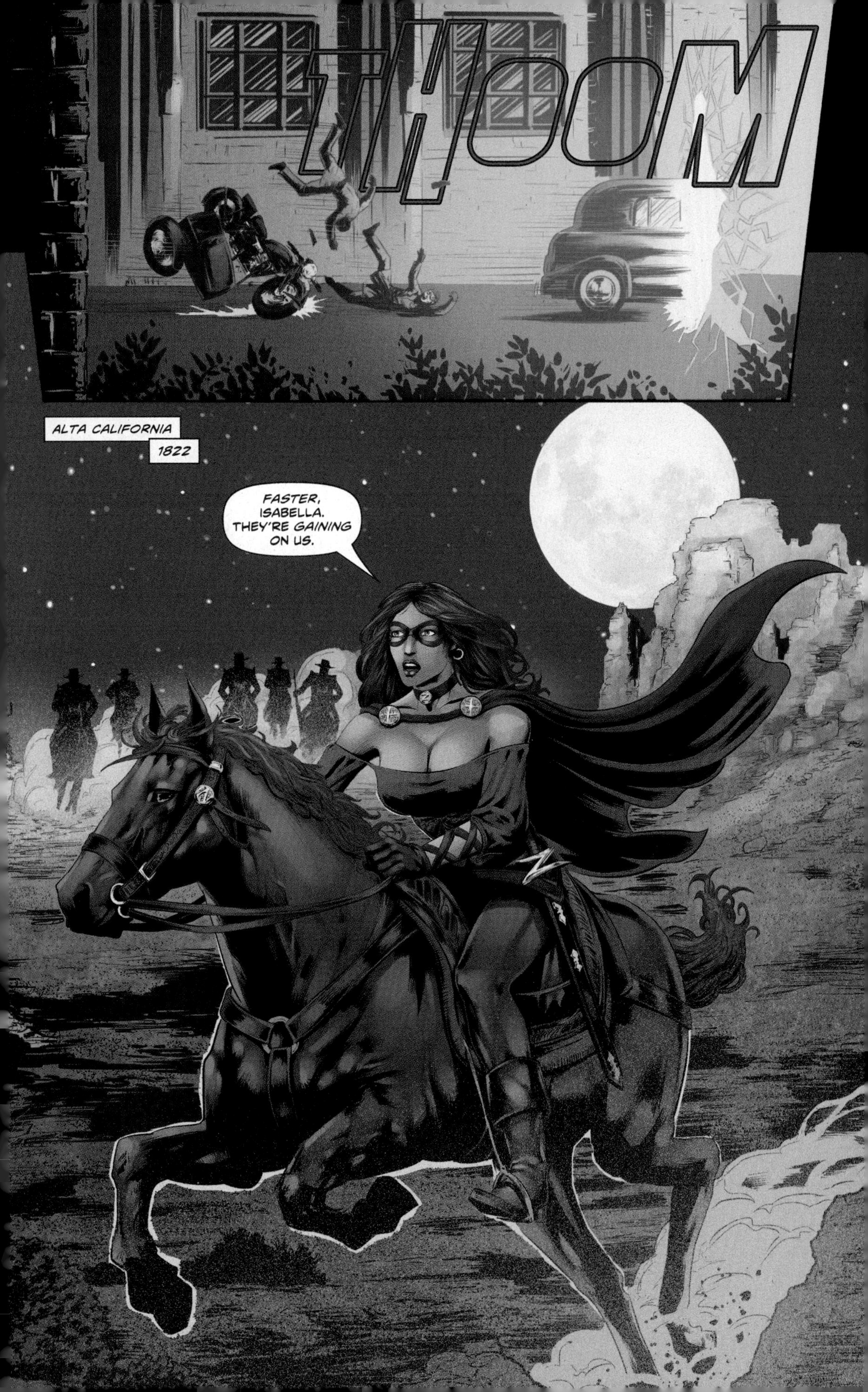
THOOM
ALTA CALIFORNIA
1822
FASTER, ISABELLA. THEY'RE GAINING ON US.

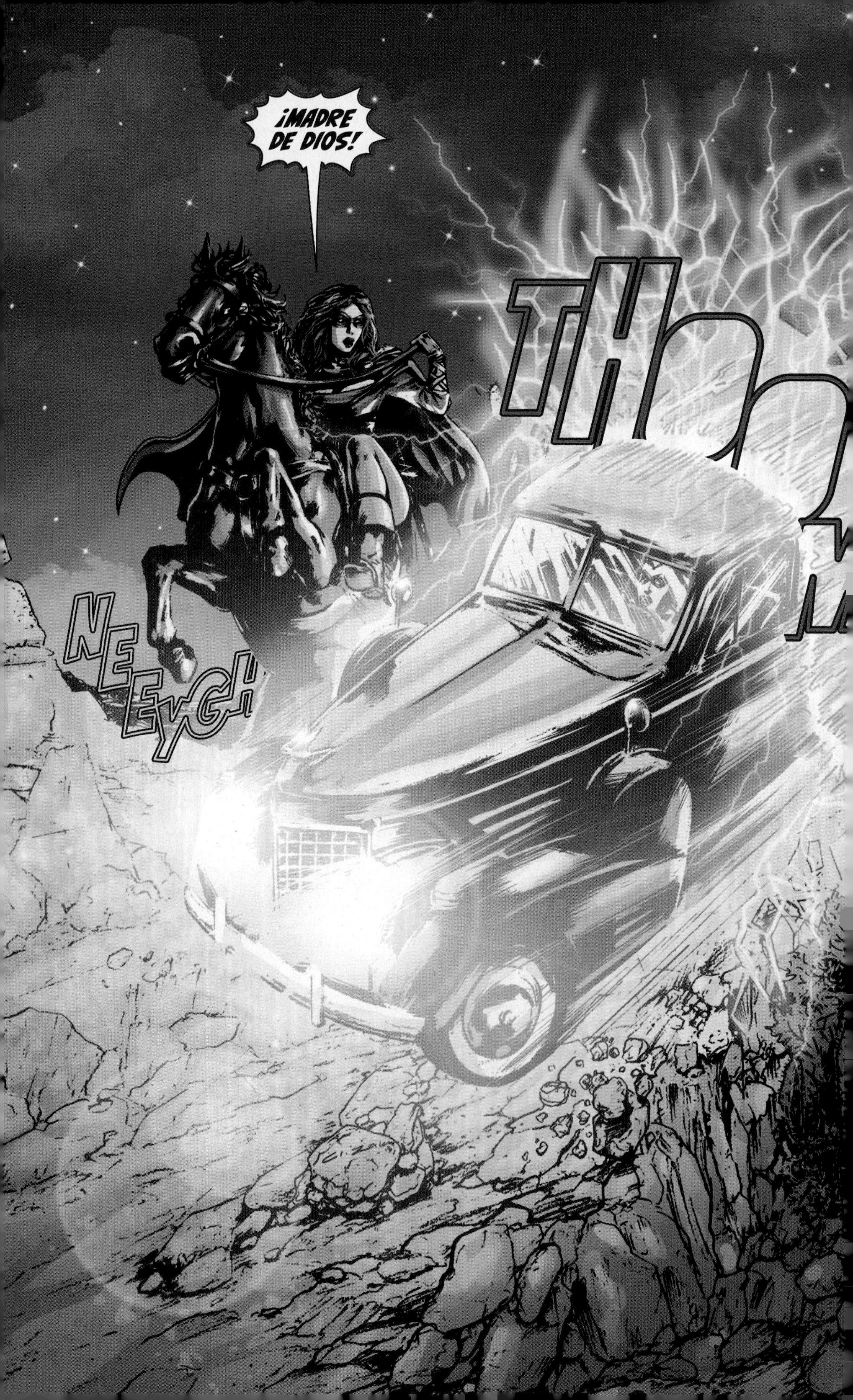
¡MADRE
DE DIOS!
NEEYGH

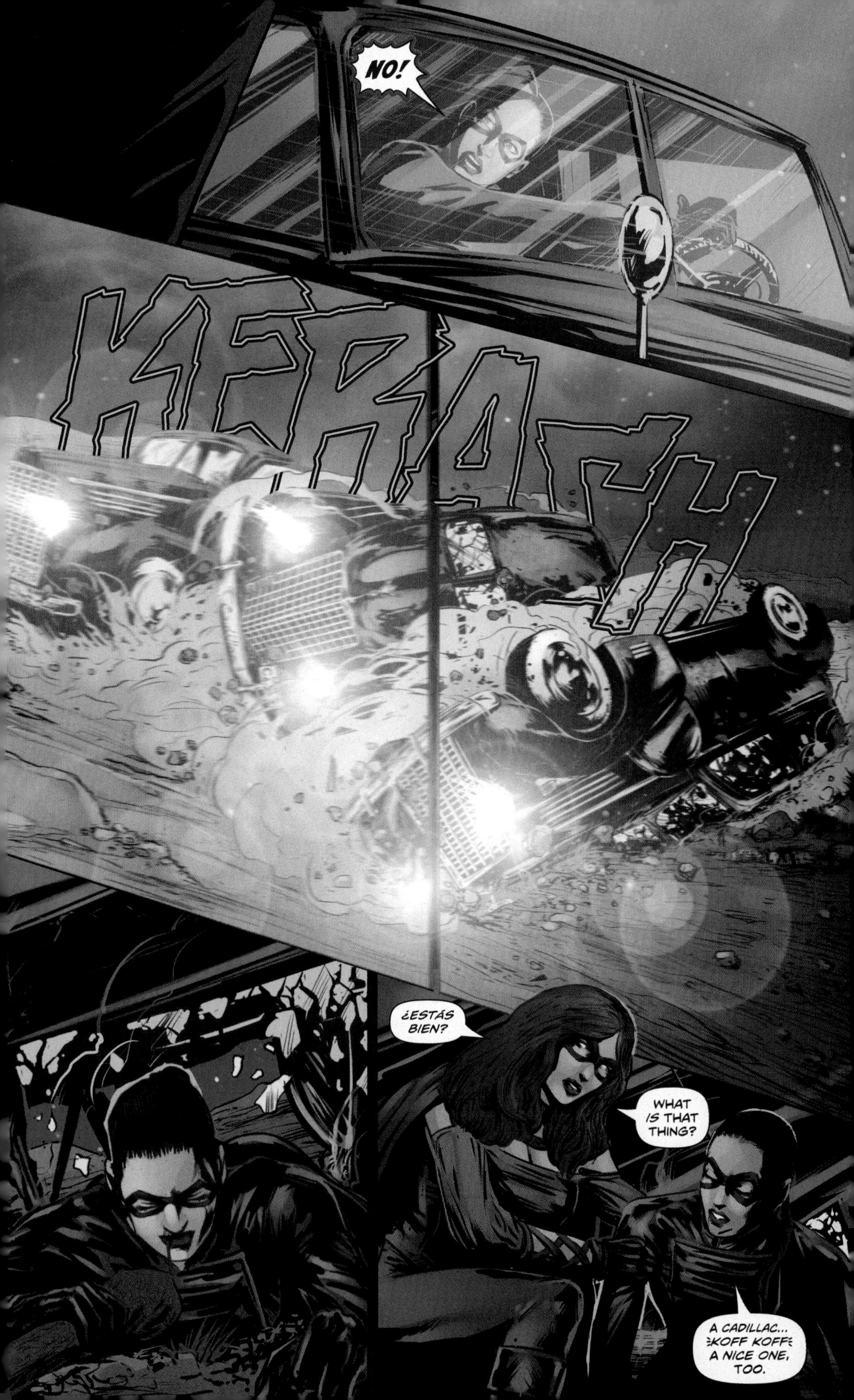
NO!
KERASH
¿ESTÁS BIEN?
WHAT IS THAT THING?
A CADILLAC... KOFF KOFF A NICE ONE, TOO.

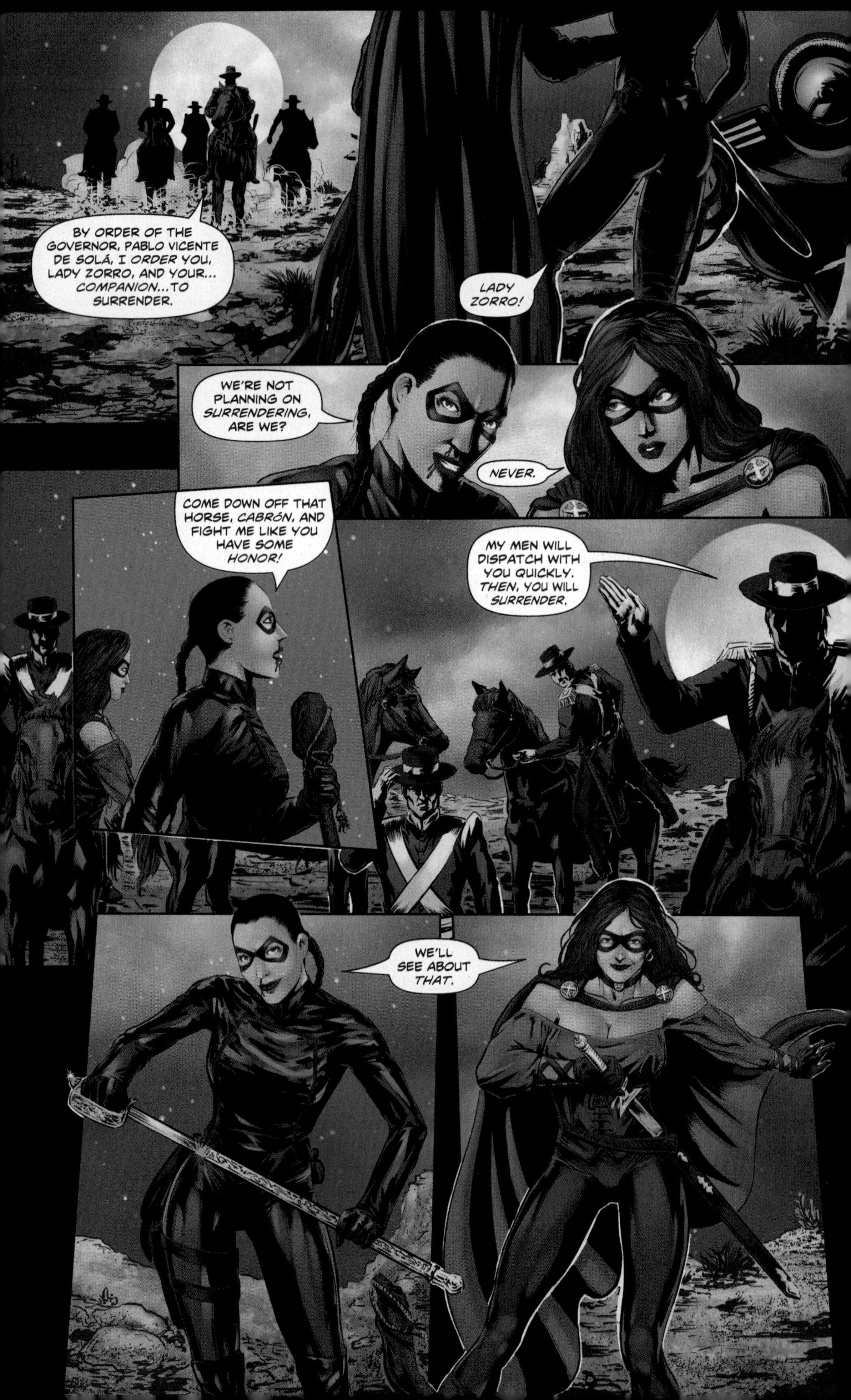
BY ORDER OF THE GOVERNOR, PABLO VICENTE DE SOLÁ, I ORDER YOU, LADY ZORRO, AND YOUR... COMPANION...TO SURRENDER.
LADY ZORRO!
WE'RE NOT PLANNING ON SURRENDERING, ARE WE?
NEVER.
COME DOWN OFF THAT HORSE, CABRÓN, AND FIGHT ME LIKE YOU HAVE SOME HONOR!
MY MEN WILL DISPATCH WITH YOU QUICKLY. THEN, YOU WILL SURRENDER.
WE'LL SEE ABOUT THAT.

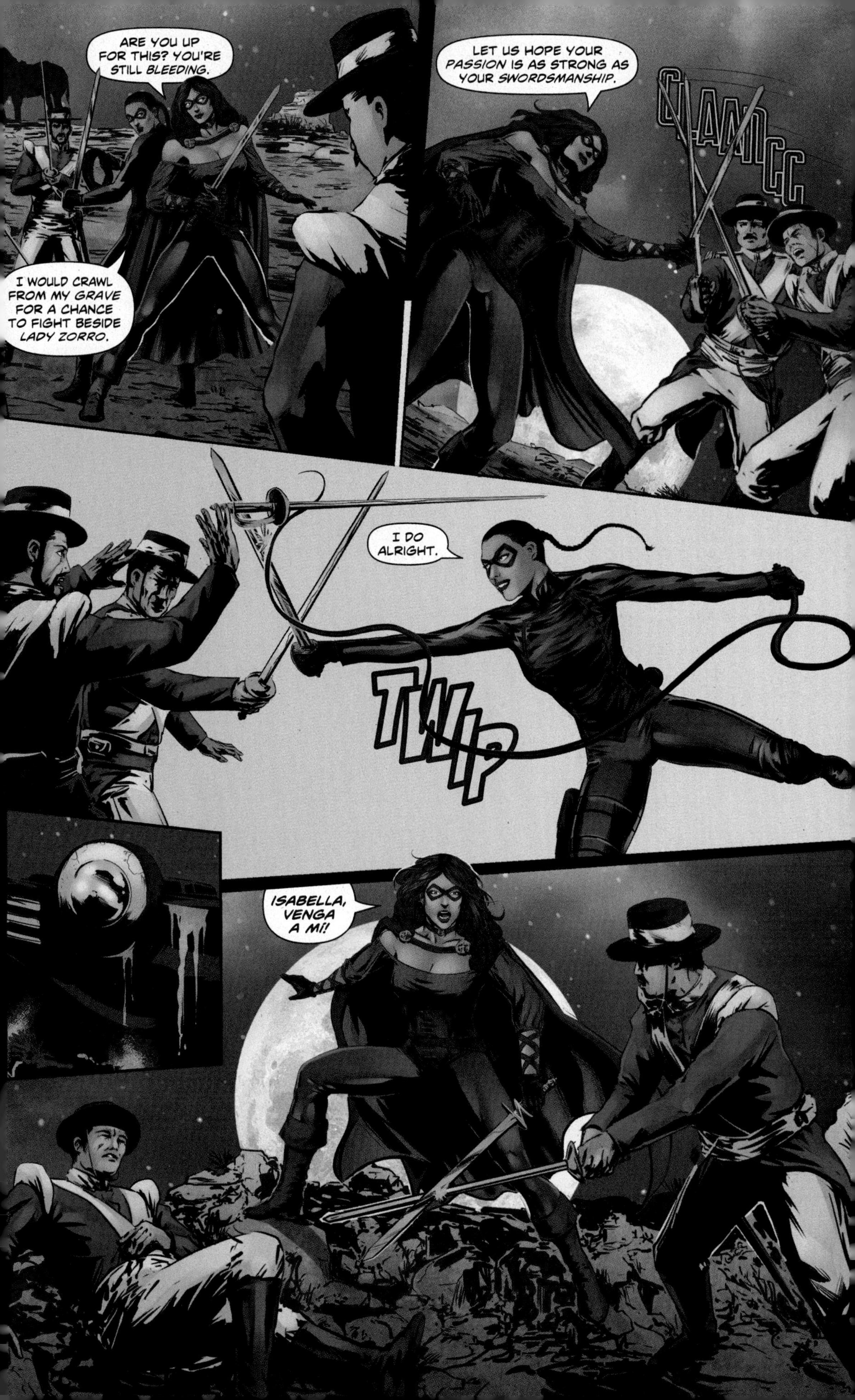
ARE YOU UP FOR THIS? YOU'RE STILL *BLEEDING*.
I WOULD CRAWL FROM MY *GRAVE* FOR A CHANCE TO FIGHT BESIDE *LADY ZORRO*.
LET US HOPE YOUR *PASSION* IS AS STRONG AS YOUR *SWORDSMANSHIP*.
CLANGG
I DO ALRIGHT.
TWIP
ISABELLA, VENGA A MI!

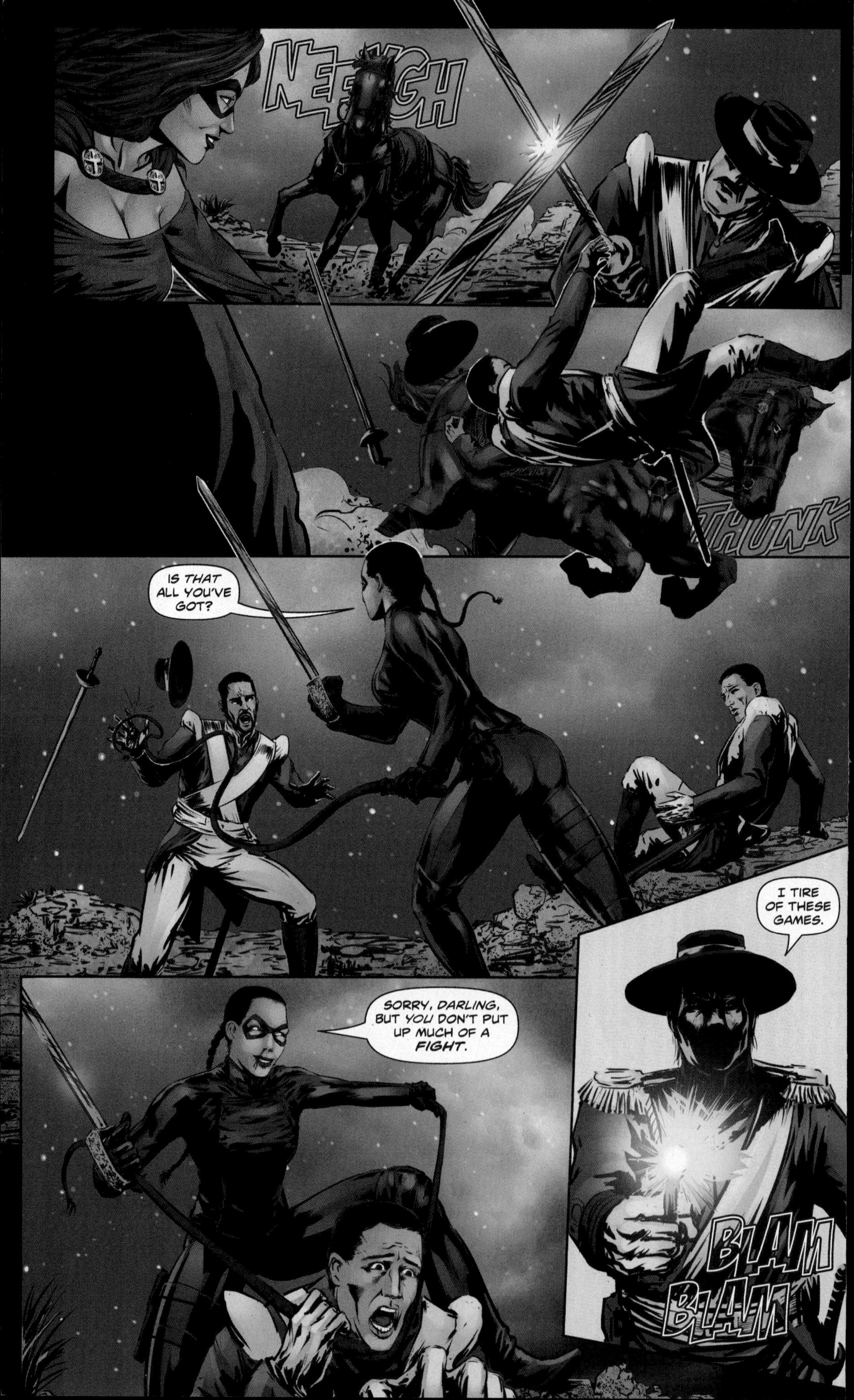
NEEIGH
THUNK
IS THAT ALL YOU'VE GOT?
I TIRE OF THESE GAMES.
SORRY, DARLING, BUT YOU DON'T PUT UP MUCH OF A FIGHT.
BLAM
BLAM

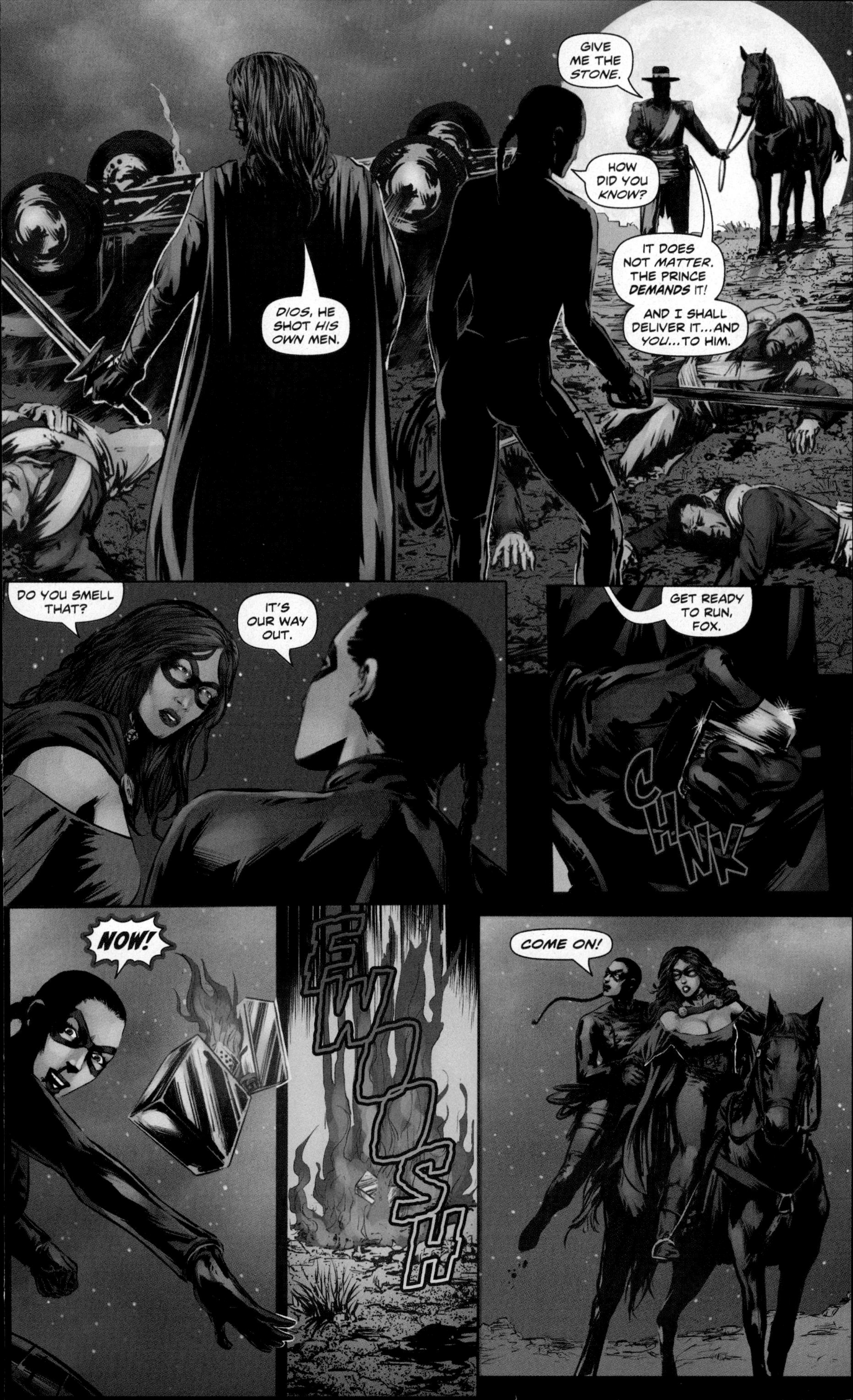
GIVE ME THE STONE.
HOW DID YOU KNOW?
IT DOES NOT MATTER. THE PRINCE DEMANDS IT!
AND I SHALL DELIVER IT...AND YOU...TO HIM.
DIOS, HE SHOT HIS OWN MEN.
DO YOU SMELL THAT?
IT'S OUR WAY OUT.
GET READY TO RUN, FOX.
CHNK
NOW!
FWOOSH
COME ON!

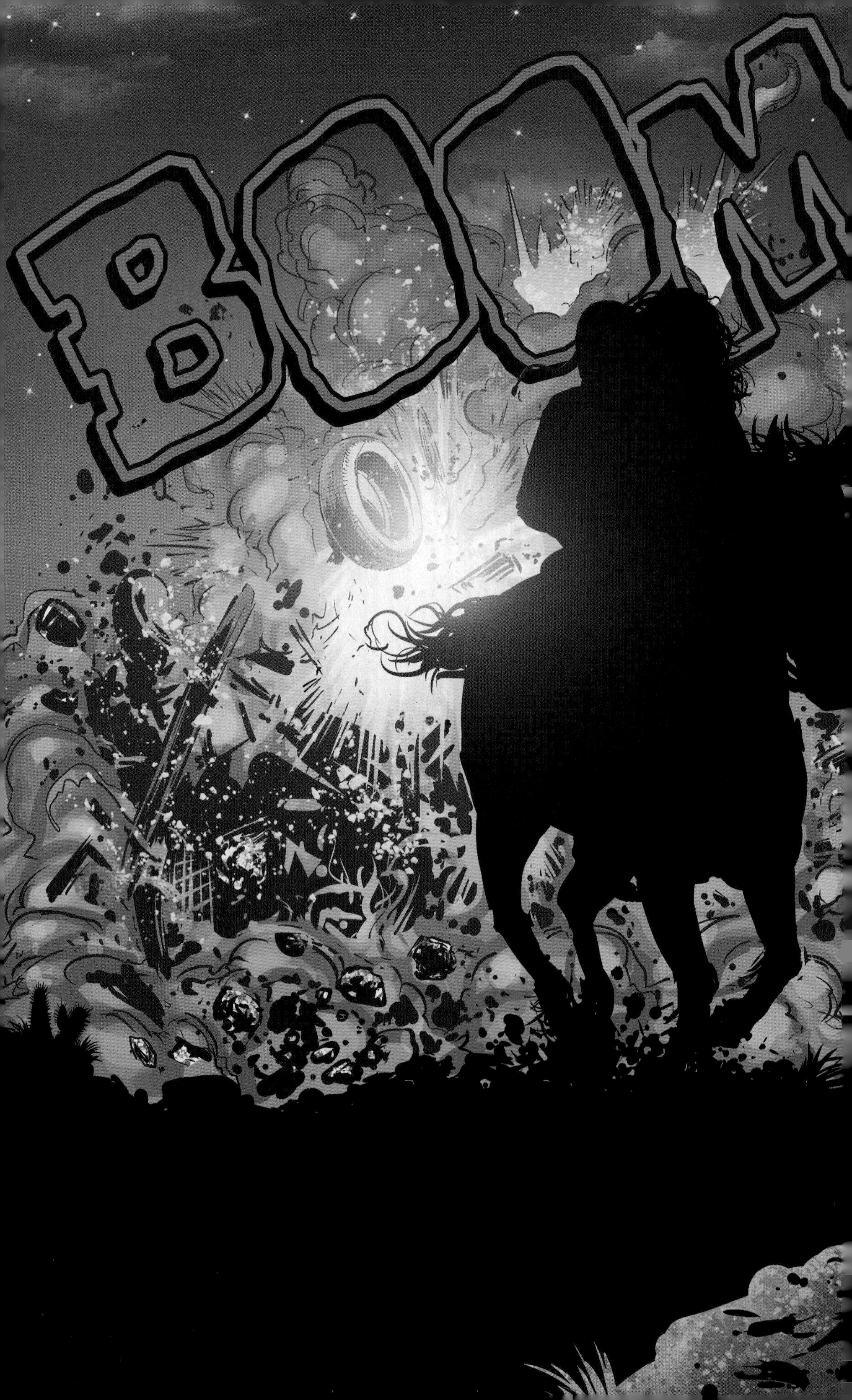
BOOM

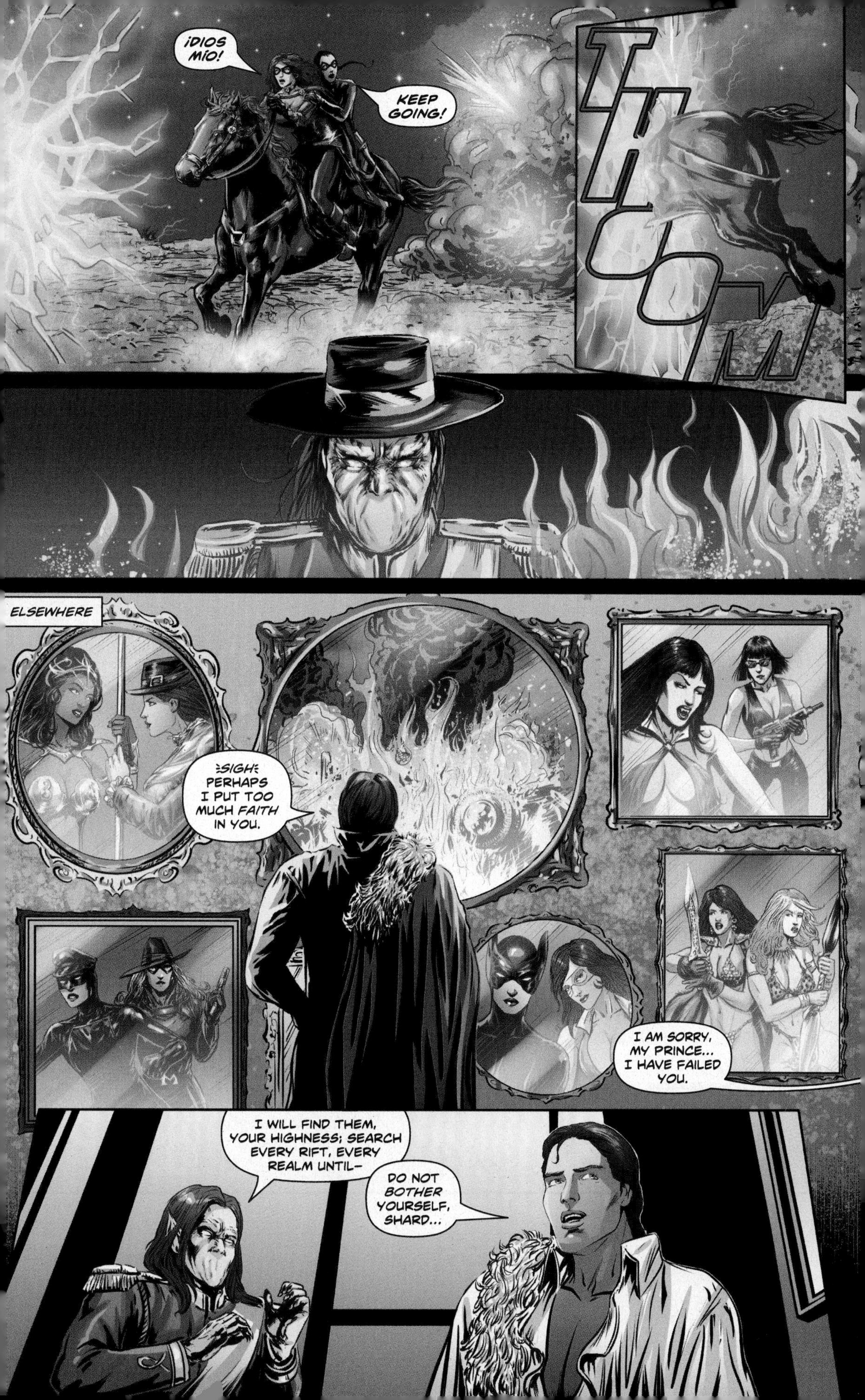
¡DIOS MIO!
KEEP GOING!
THOOM
ELSEWHERE
:SIGH: PERHAPS I PUT TOO MUCH FAITH IN YOU.
I AM SORRY, MY PRINCE... I HAVE FAILED YOU.
I WILL FIND THEM, YOUR HIGHNESS; SEARCH EVERY RIFT, EVERY REALM UNTIL–
DO NOT BOTHER YOURSELF, SHARD...

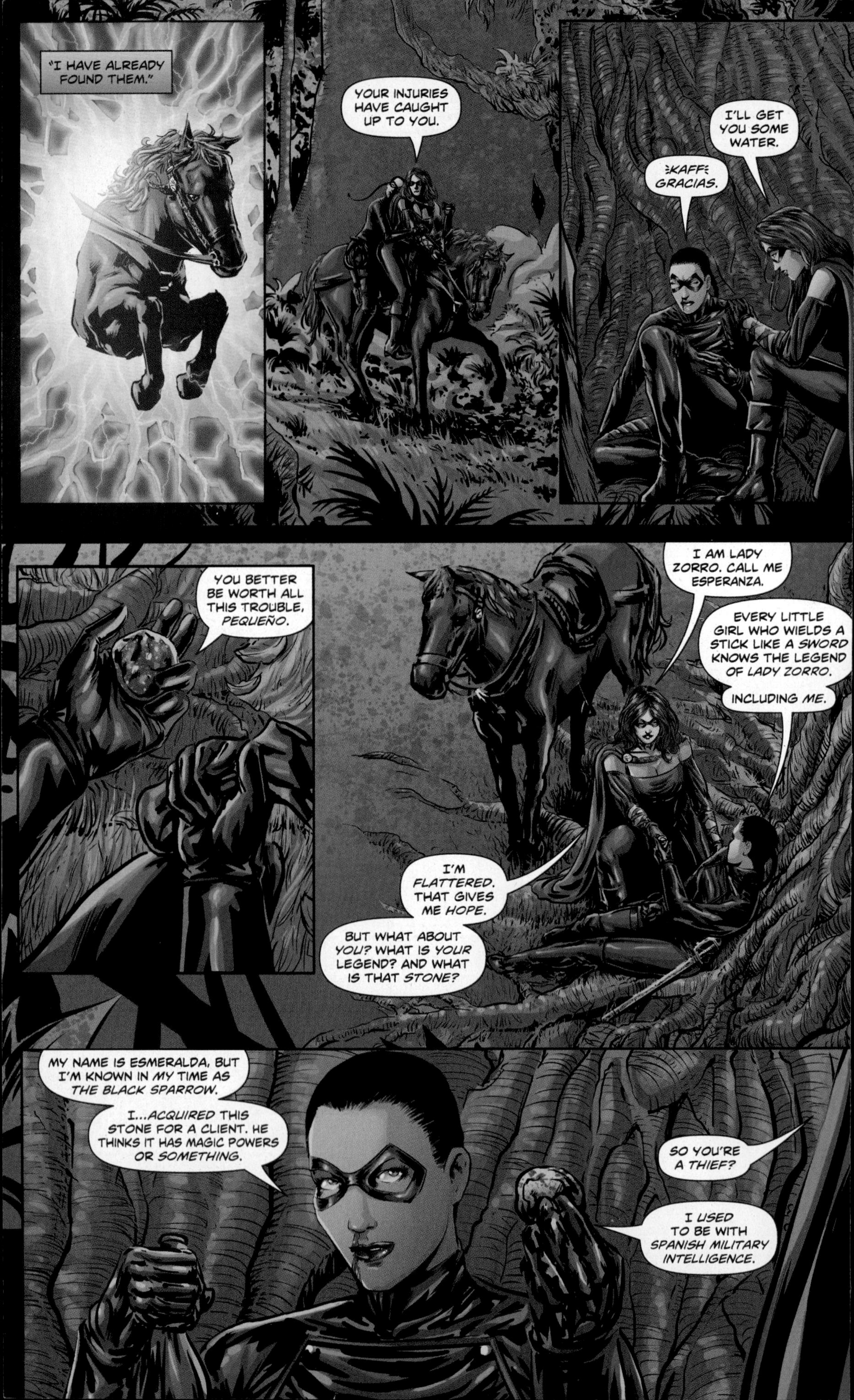
"I HAVE ALREADY FOUND THEM."
YOUR INJURIES HAVE CAUGHT UP TO YOU.
I'LL GET YOU SOME WATER.
KAFF GRACIAS.
YOU BETTER BE WORTH ALL THIS TROUBLE, PEQUEÑO.
I AM LADY ZORRO. CALL ME ESPERANZA.
EVERY LITTLE GIRL WHO WIELDS A STICK LIKE A SWORD KNOWS THE LEGEND OF LADY ZORRO.
INCLUDING ME.
I'M FLATTERED. THAT GIVES ME HOPE.
BUT WHAT ABOUT YOU? WHAT IS YOUR LEGEND? AND WHAT IS THAT STONE?
MY NAME IS ESMERALDA, BUT I'M KNOWN IN MY TIME AS THE BLACK SPARROW.
I...ACQUIRED THIS STONE FOR A CLIENT. HE THINKS IT HAS MAGIC POWERS OR SOMETHING.
SO YOU'RE A THIEF?
I USED TO BE WITH SPANISH MILITARY INTELLIGENCE.

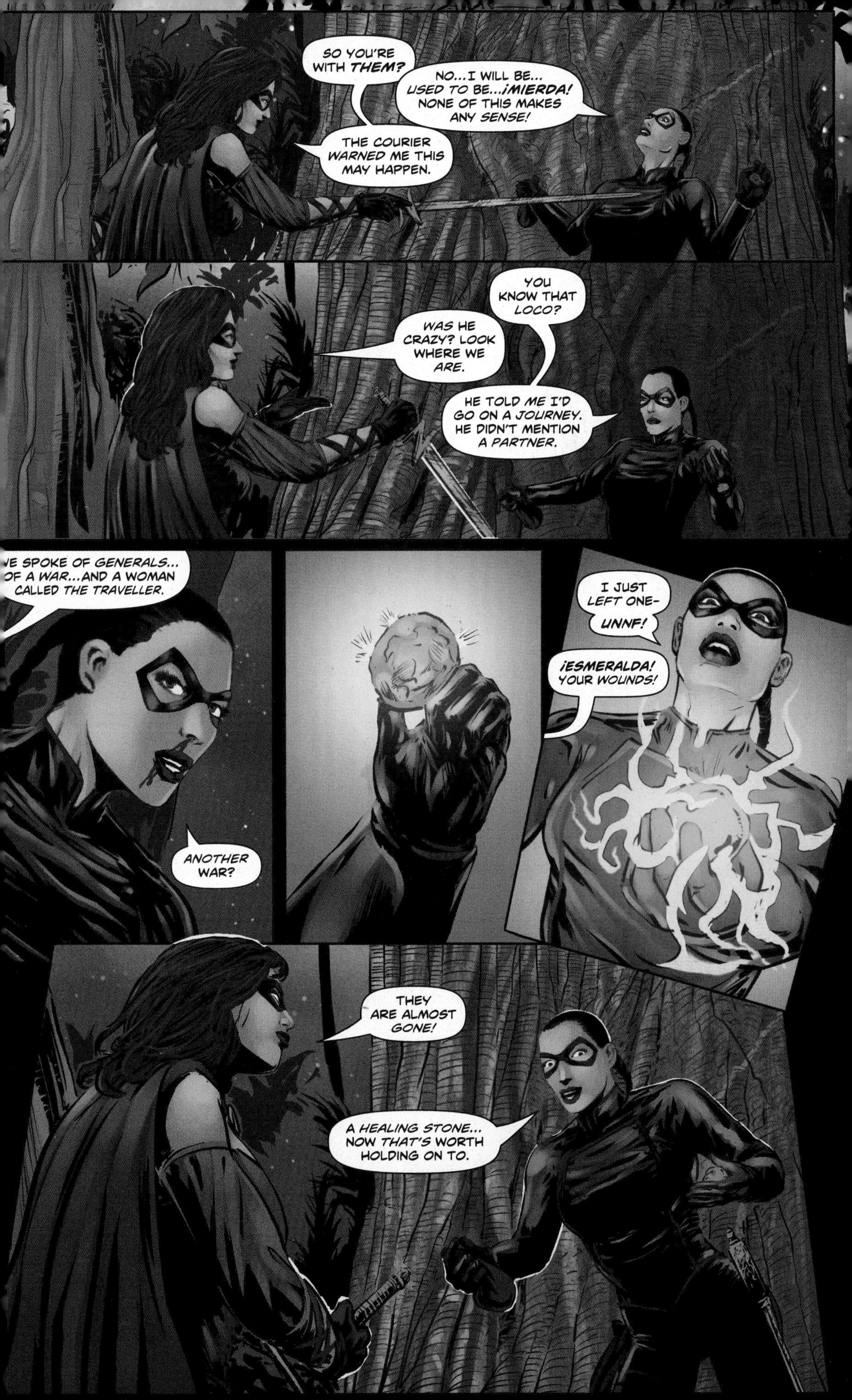
SO YOU'RE WITH THEM?
NO...I WILL BE... USED TO BE...¡MIERDA! NONE OF THIS MAKES ANY SENSE!
THE COURIER WARNED ME THIS MAY HAPPEN.
YOU KNOW THAT LOCO?
WAS HE CRAZY? LOOK WHERE WE ARE.
HE TOLD ME I'D GO ON A JOURNEY. HE DIDN'T MENTION A PARTNER.
E SPOKE OF GENERALS... OF A WAR...AND A WOMAN CALLED THE TRAVELLER.
ANOTHER WAR?
I JUST LEFT ONE- UNNF!
¡ESMERALDA! YOUR WOUNDS!
THEY ARE ALMOST GONE!
A HEALING STONE... NOW THAT'S WORTH HOLDING ON TO.

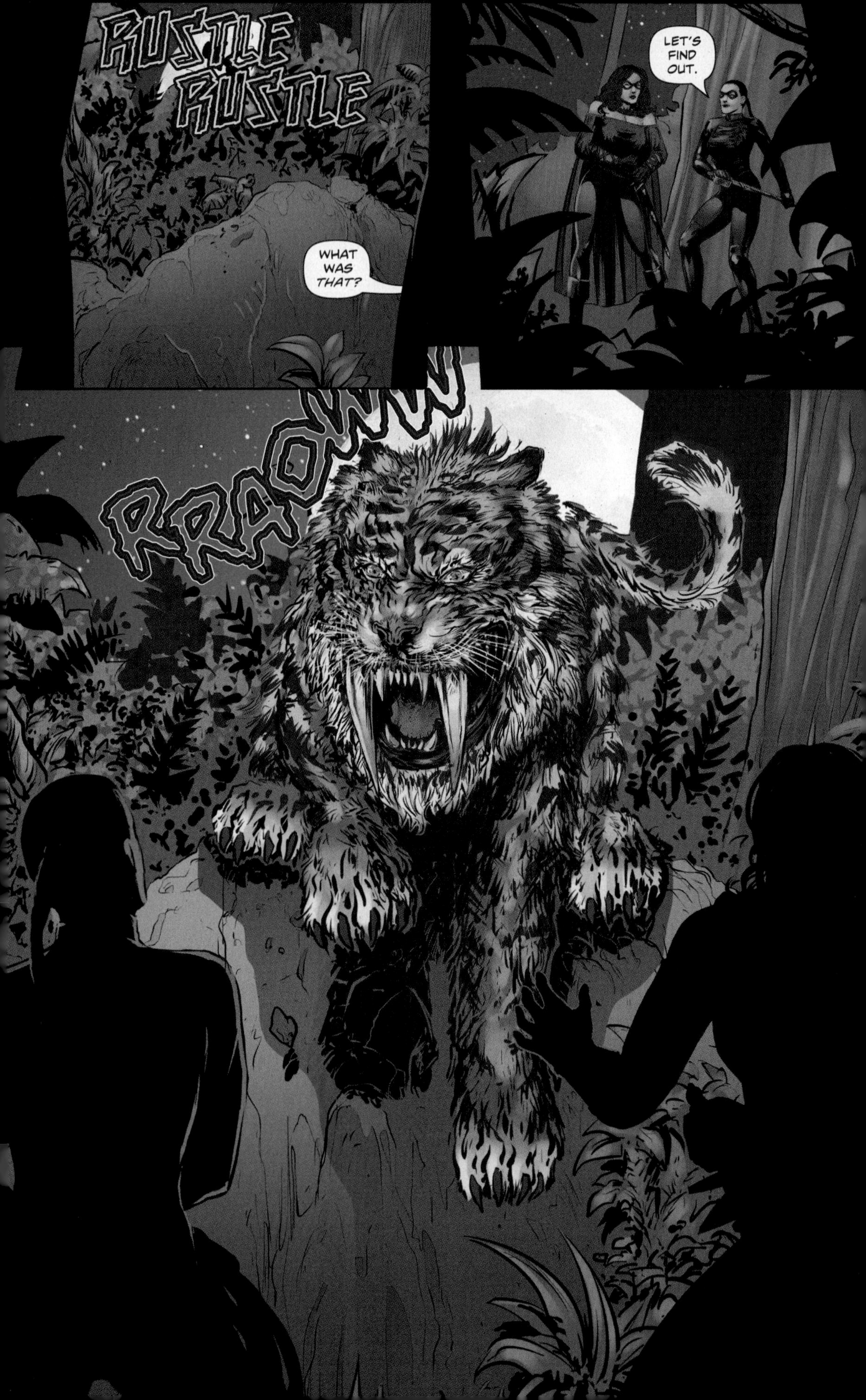
RUSTLE RUSTLE
WHAT WAS THAT?
LET'S FIND OUT.
RRAOWW

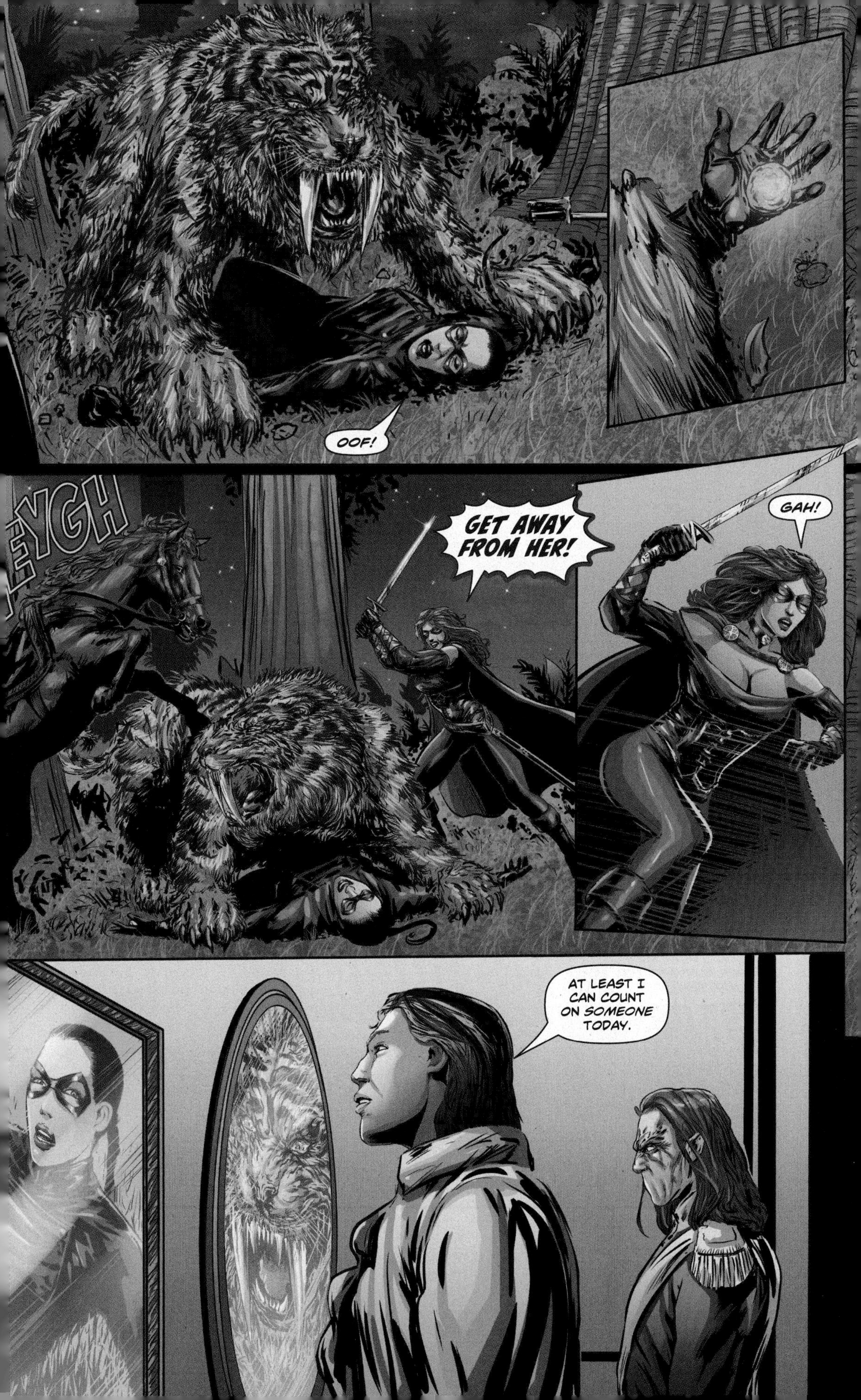
OOF!
NEYGH
GET AWAY FROM HER!
GAH!
AT LEAST I CAN COUNT ON SOMEONE TODAY.

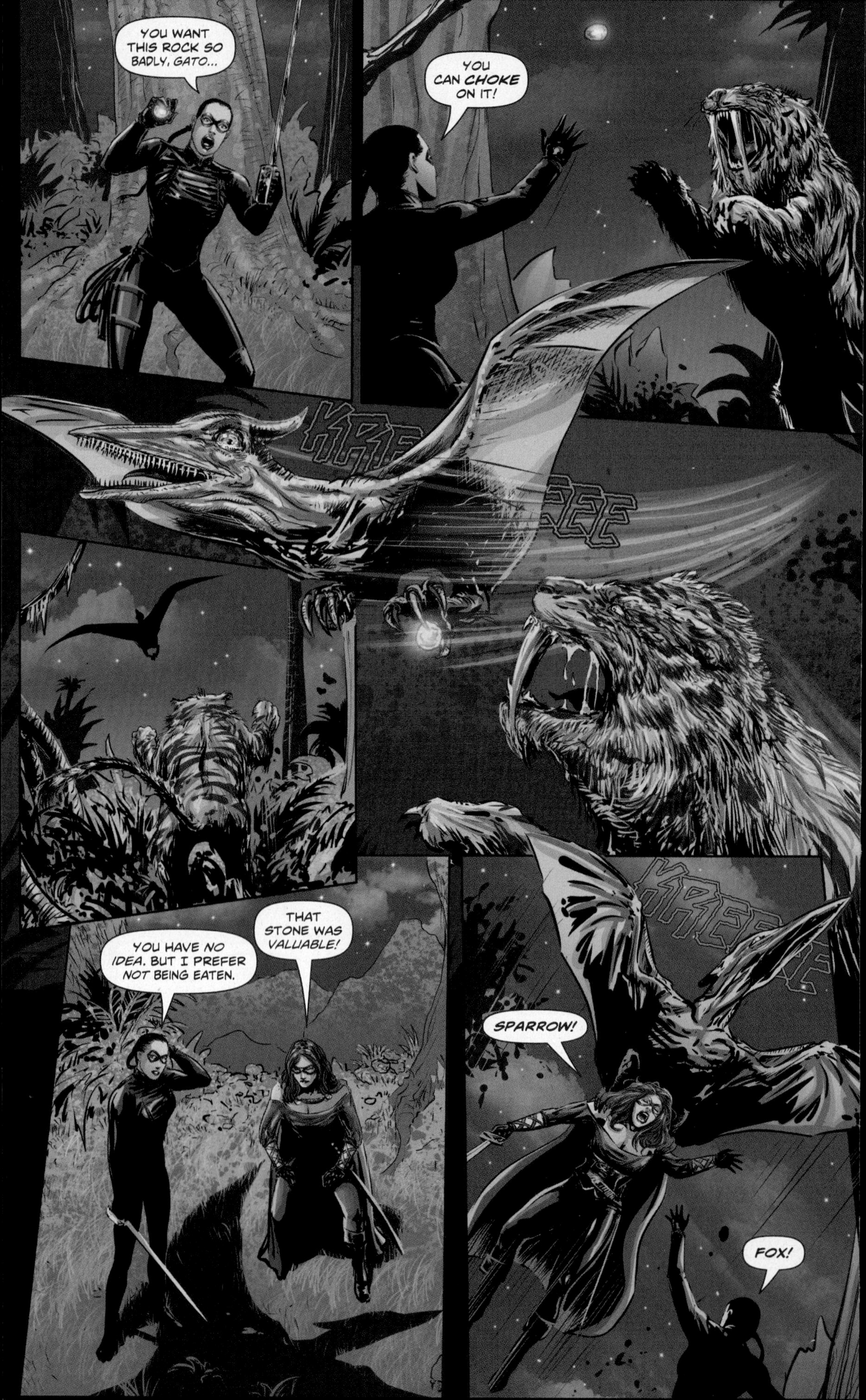
YOU WANT THIS ROCK SO BADLY, GATO...
YOU CAN CHOKE ON IT!
KREEEEEE
THAT STONE WAS VALUABLE!
YOU HAVE NO IDEA. BUT I PREFER NOT BEING EATEN.
KREEEE
SPARROW!
FOX!

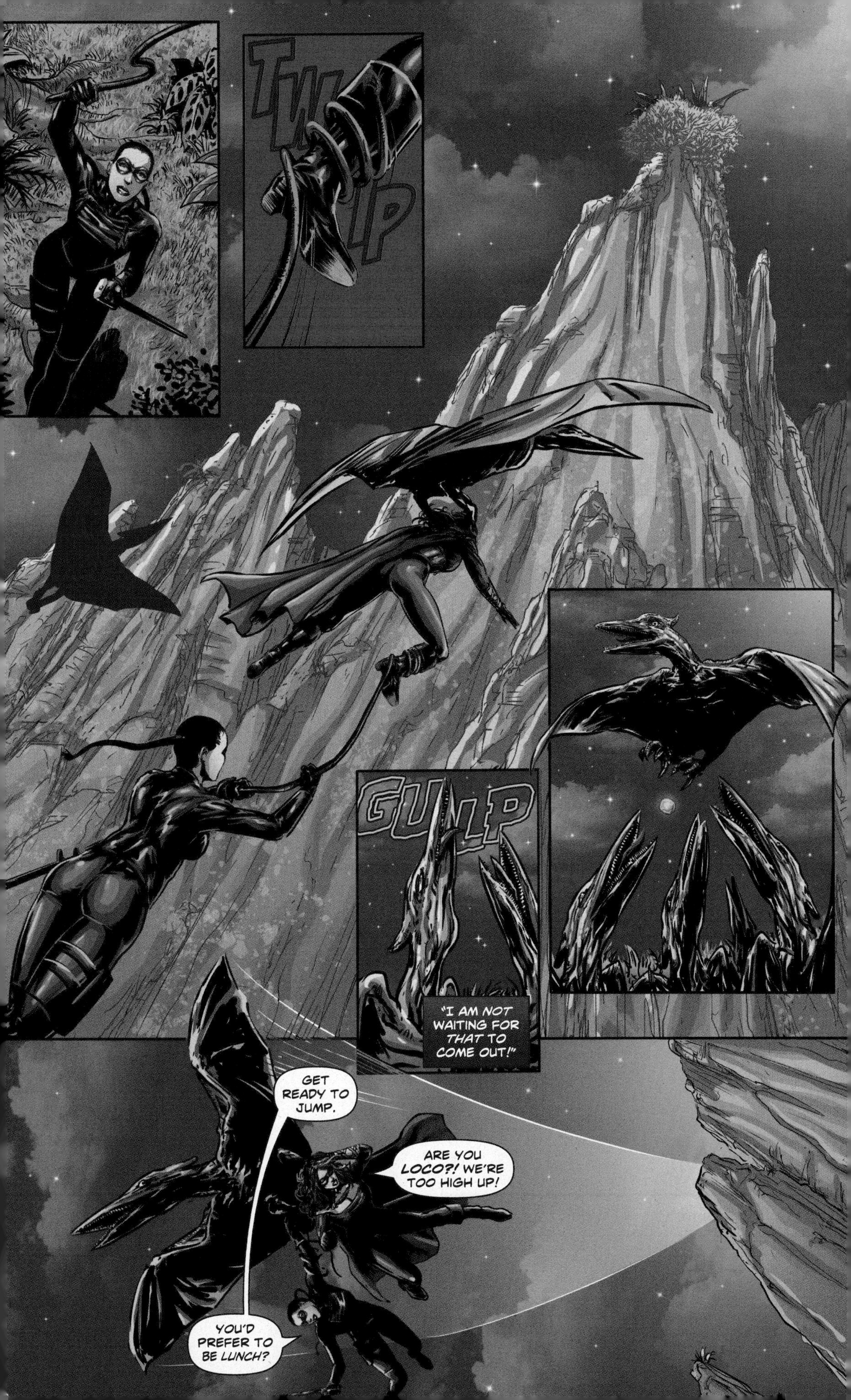

TWIP
GULP
"I AM NOT WAITING FOR THAT TO COME OUT!"
GET READY TO JUMP.
ARE YOU LOCO?! WE'RE TOO HIGH UP!
YOU'D PREFER TO BE LUNCH?

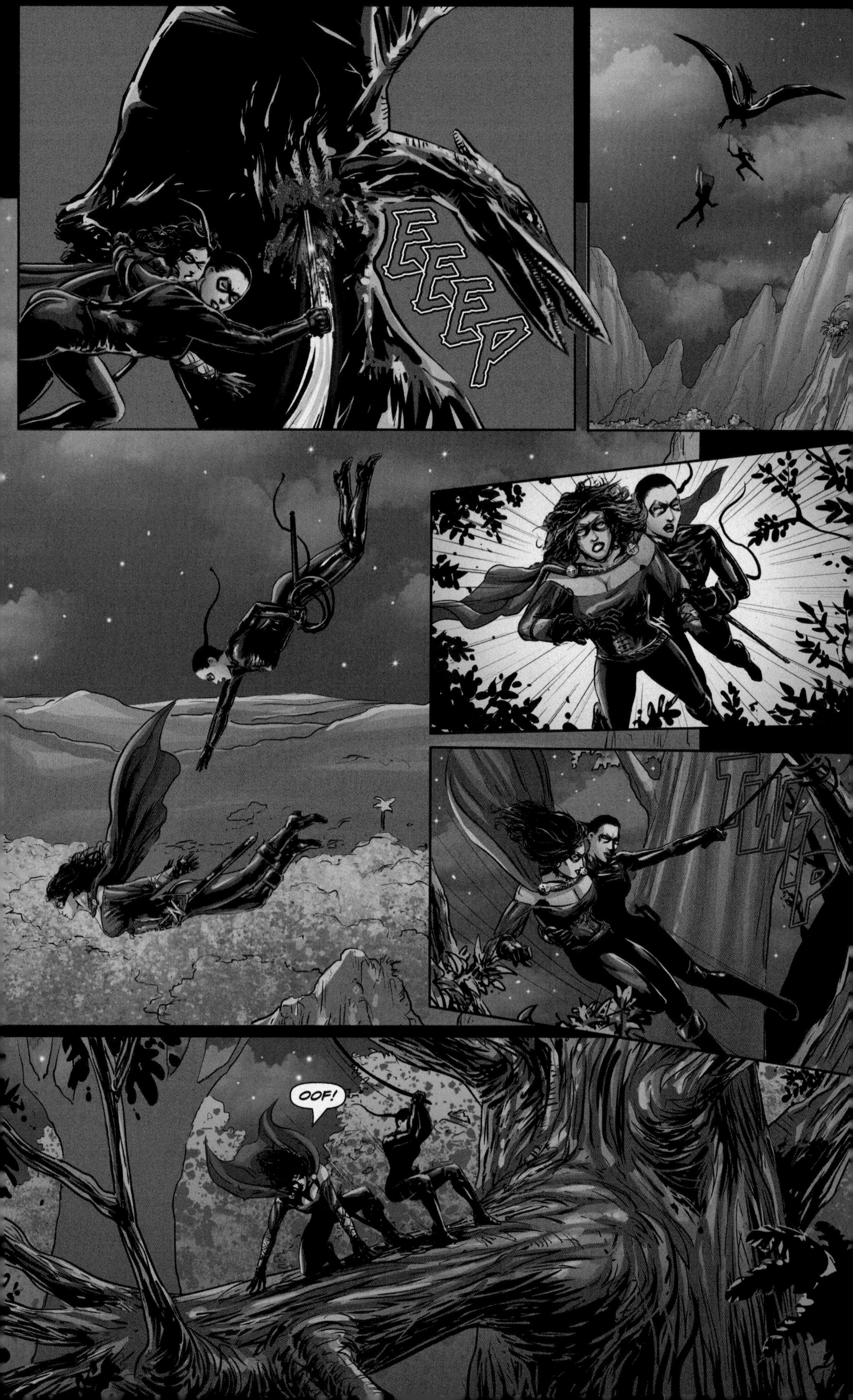
EEEEP
OOF!

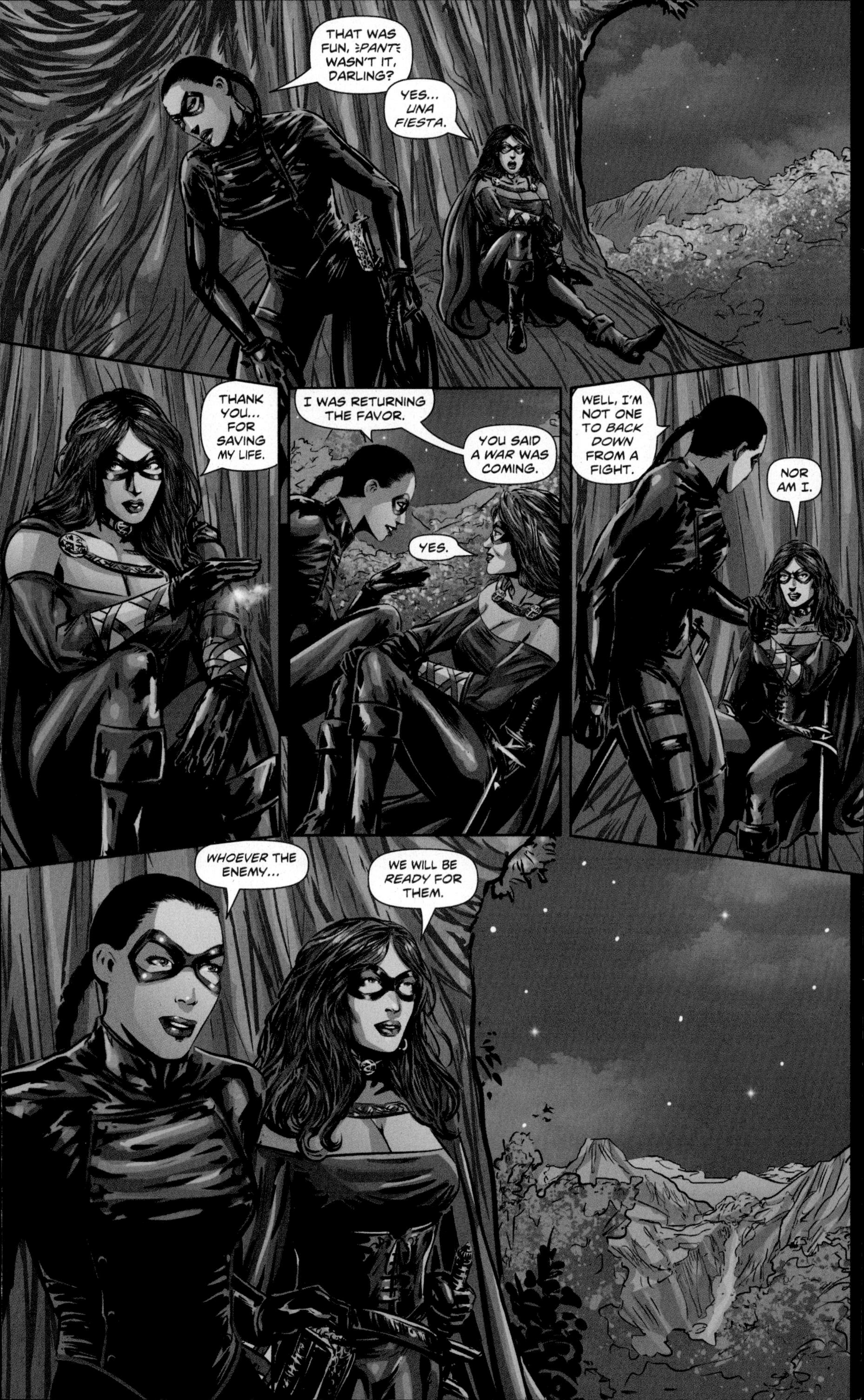
THAT WAS FUN, *PANT* WASN'T IT, DARLING?
YES... UNA FIESTA.
THANK YOU... FOR SAVING MY LIFE.
I WAS RETURNING THE FAVOR.
YOU SAID A WAR WAS COMING.
YES.
WELL, I'M NOT ONE TO BACK DOWN FROM A FIGHT.
NOR AM I.
WHOEVER THE ENEMY...
WE WILL BE READY FOR THEM.

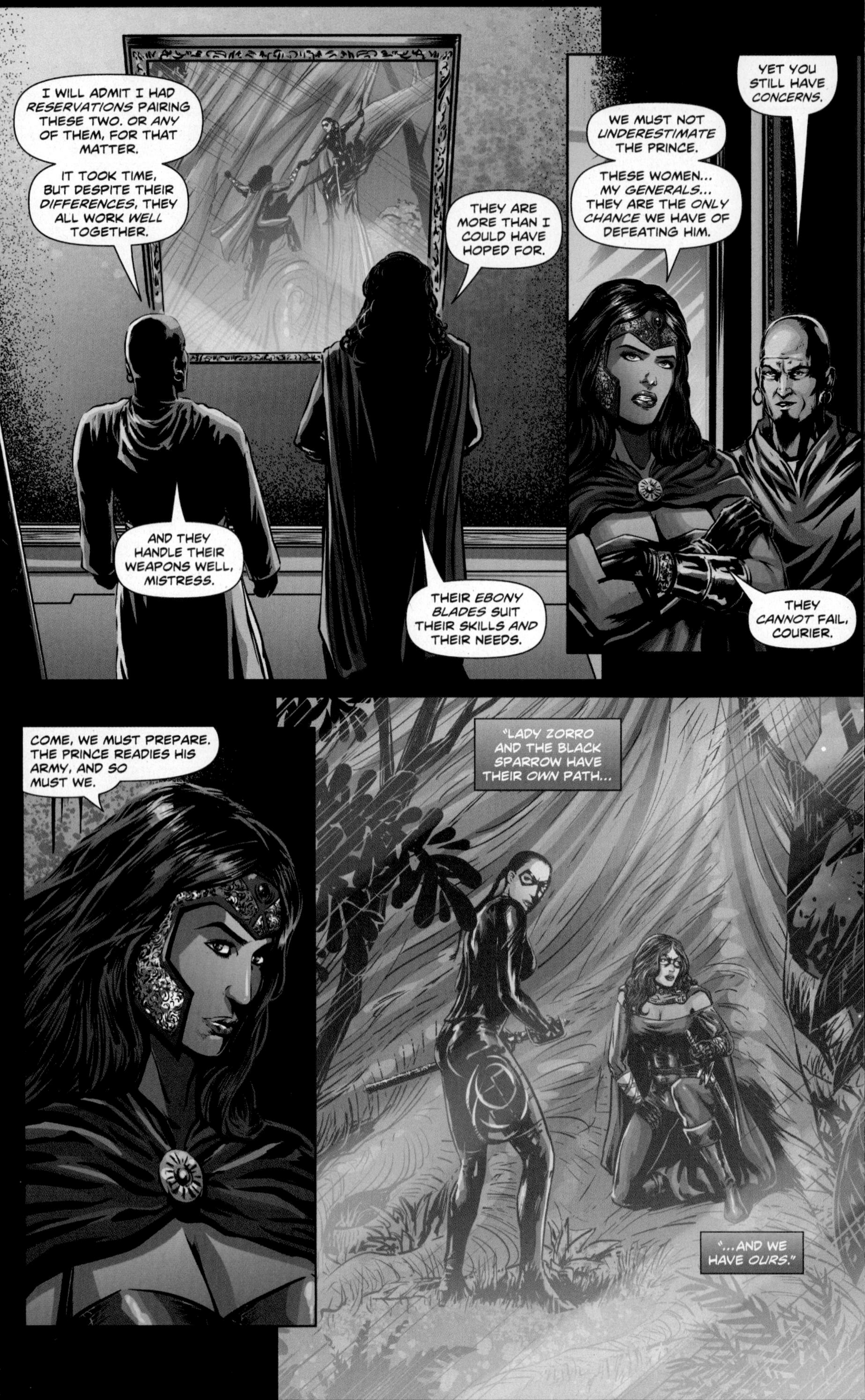
I WILL ADMIT I HAD RESERVATIONS PAIRING THESE TWO. OR ANY OF THEM, FOR THAT MATTER.
IT TOOK TIME, BUT DESPITE THEIR DIFFERENCES, THEY ALL WORK WELL TOGETHER.
THEY ARE MORE THAN I COULD HAVE HOPED FOR.
AND THEY HANDLE THEIR WEAPONS WELL, MISTRESS.
THEIR EBONY BLADES SUIT THEIR SKILLS AND THEIR NEEDS.
YET YOU STILL HAVE CONCERNS.
WE MUST NOT UNDERESTIMATE THE PRINCE.
THESE WOMEN... MY GENERALS... THEY ARE THE ONLY CHANCE WE HAVE OF DEFEATING HIM.
THEY CANNOT FAIL, COURIER.
COME, WE MUST PREPARE. THE PRINCE READIES HIS ARMY, AND SO MUST WE.
"LADY ZORRO AND THE BLACK SPARROW HAVE THEIR OWN PATH...
"...AND WE HAVE OURS."

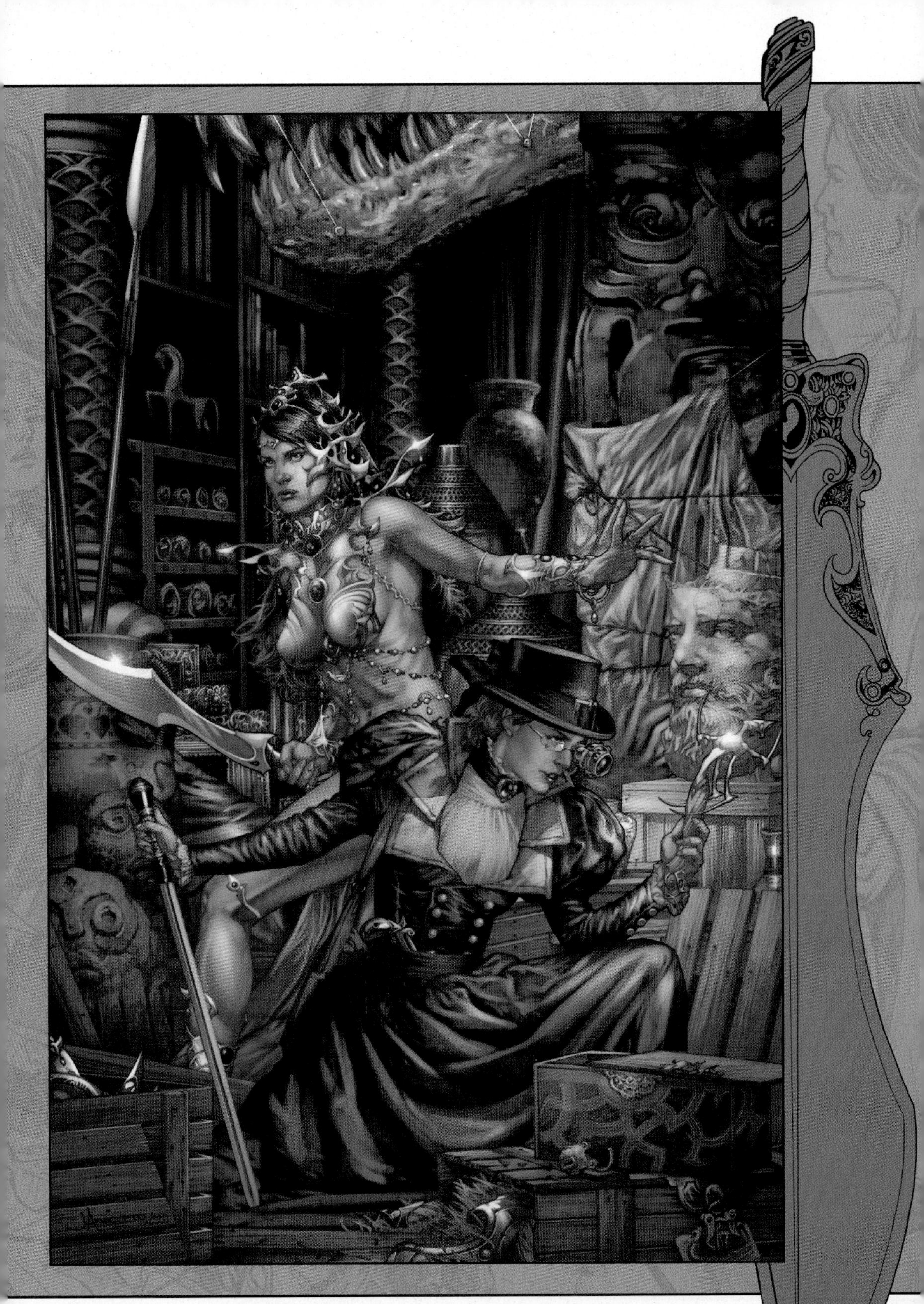

SWORDS OF SORROW: DEJAH THORIS & IRENE ADLER

ISSUE TWO OF THREE

written by LEA MOORE illustrated by FRANCESCO MANNA
colored by InLIGHT STUDIO lettered by ERICA SCHULTZ

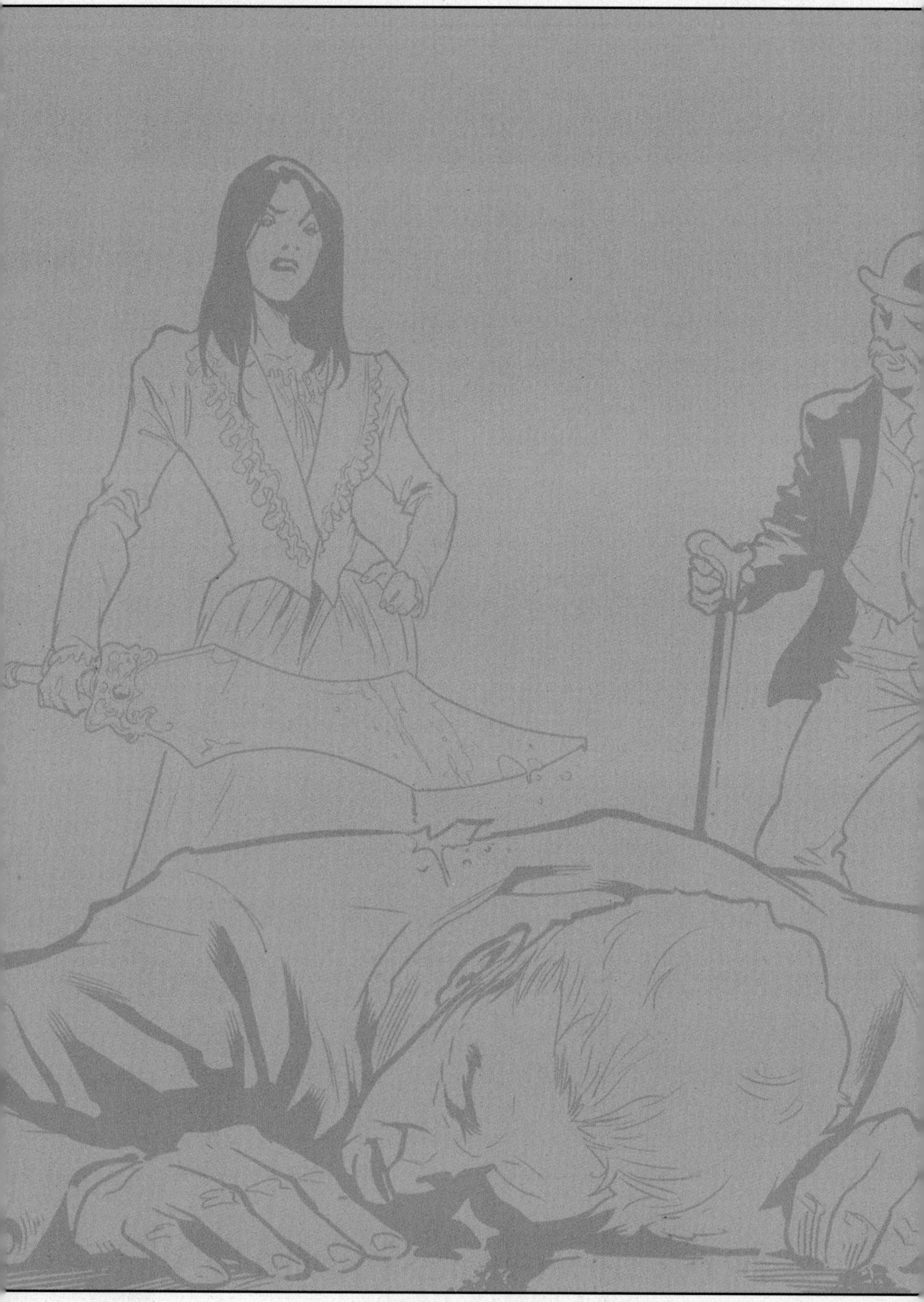

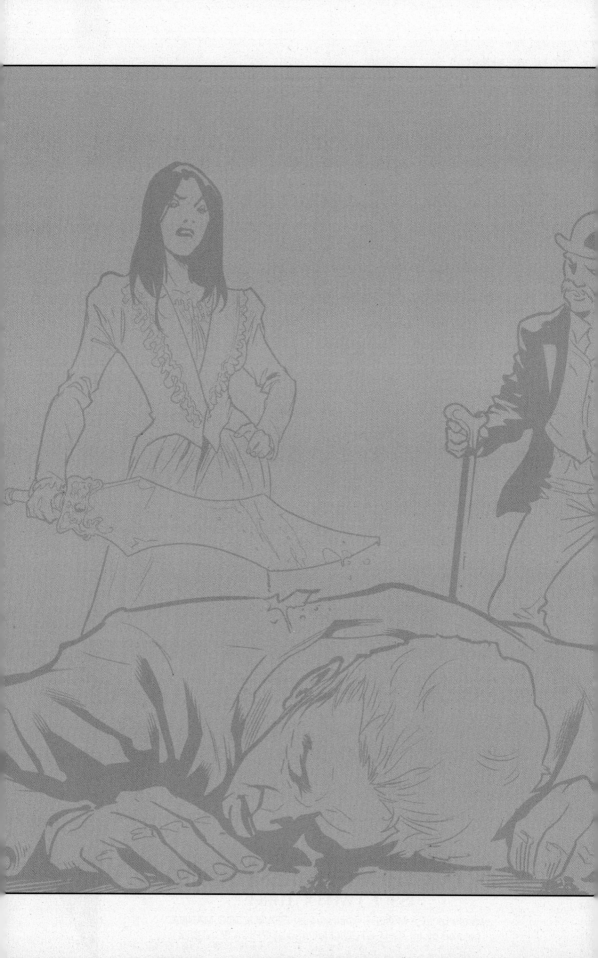

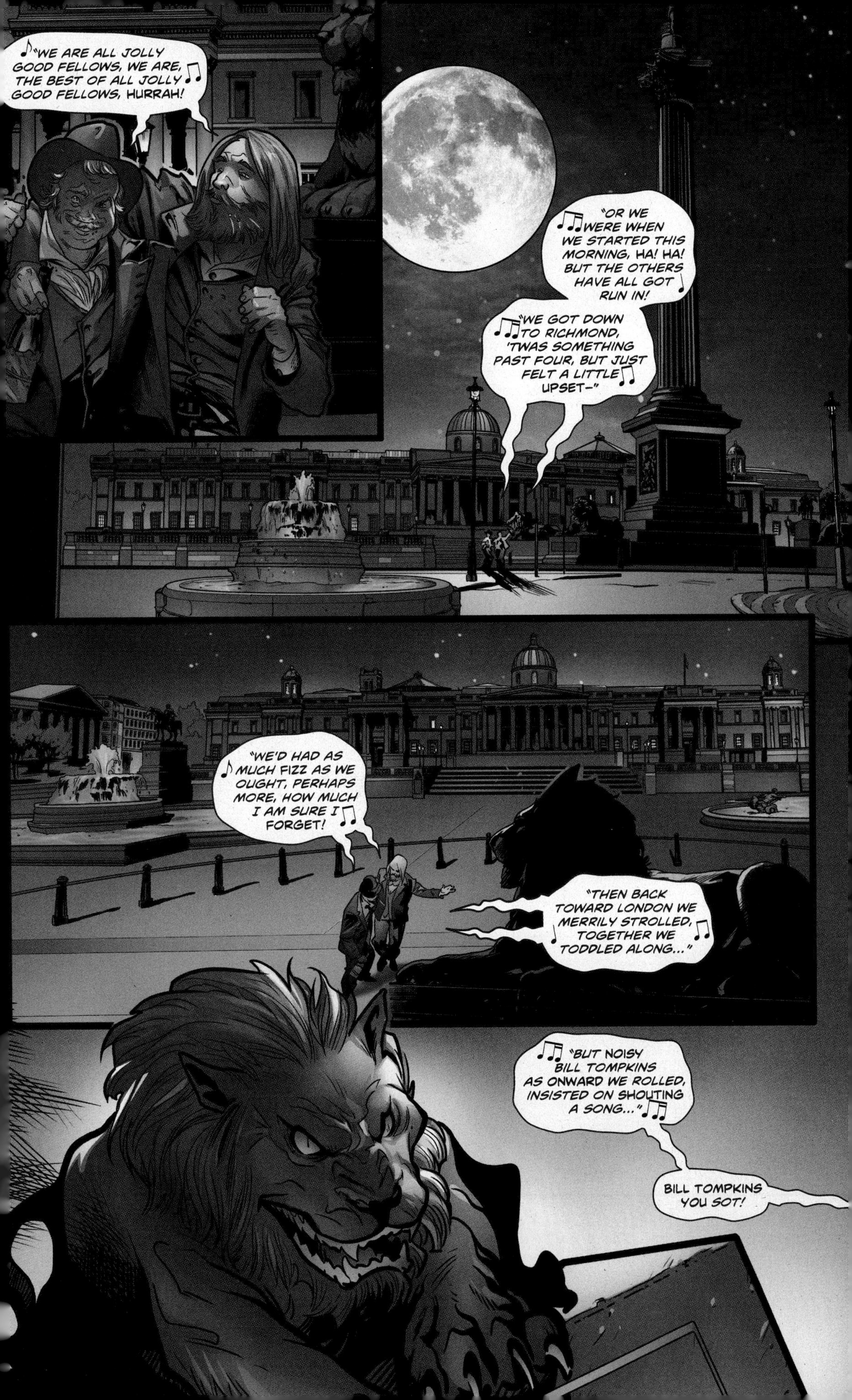
"WE ARE ALL JOLLY GOOD FELLOWS, WE ARE, THE BEST OF ALL JOLLY GOOD FELLOWS, HURRAH!
"OR WE WERE WHEN WE STARTED THIS MORNING, HA! HA! BUT THE OTHERS HAVE ALL GOT RUN IN!
"WE GOT DOWN TO RICHMOND, 'TWAS SOMETHING PAST FOUR, BUT JUST FELT A LITTLE UPSET–"
"WE'D HAD AS MUCH FIZZ AS WE OUGHT, PERHAPS MORE, HOW MUCH I AM SURE I FORGET!
"THEN BACK TOWARD LONDON WE MERRILY STROLLED, TOGETHER WE TODDLED ALONG..."
"BUT NOISY BILL TOMPKINS AS ONWARD WE ROLLED, INSISTED ON SHOUTING A SONG..."
BILL TOMPKINS YOU SOT!

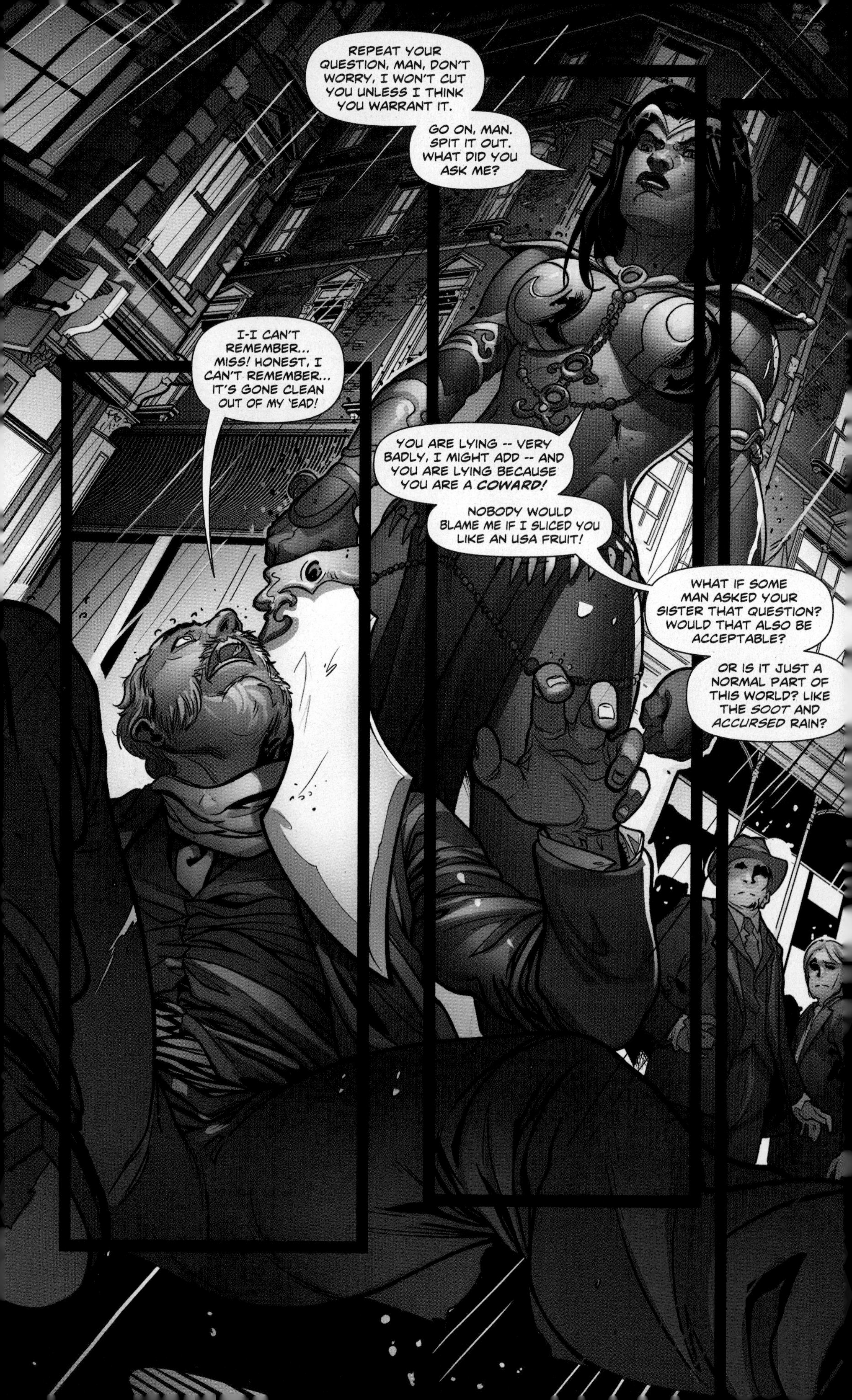
REPEAT YOUR QUESTION, MAN, DON'T WORRY, I WON'T CUT YOU UNLESS I THINK YOU WARRANT IT.
GO ON, MAN. SPIT IT OUT. WHAT DID YOU ASK ME?
I-I CAN'T REMEMBER... MISS! HONEST, I CAN'T REMEMBER... IT'S GONE CLEAN OUT OF MY 'EAD!
YOU ARE LYING -- VERY BADLY, I MIGHT ADD -- AND YOU ARE LYING BECAUSE YOU ARE A *COWARD!*
NOBODY WOULD BLAME ME IF I SLICED YOU LIKE AN USA FRUIT!
WHAT IF SOME MAN ASKED YOUR SISTER THAT QUESTION? WOULD THAT ALSO BE ACCEPTABLE?
OR IS IT JUST A NORMAL PART OF THIS WORLD? LIKE THE *SOOT* AND *ACCURSED* RAIN?

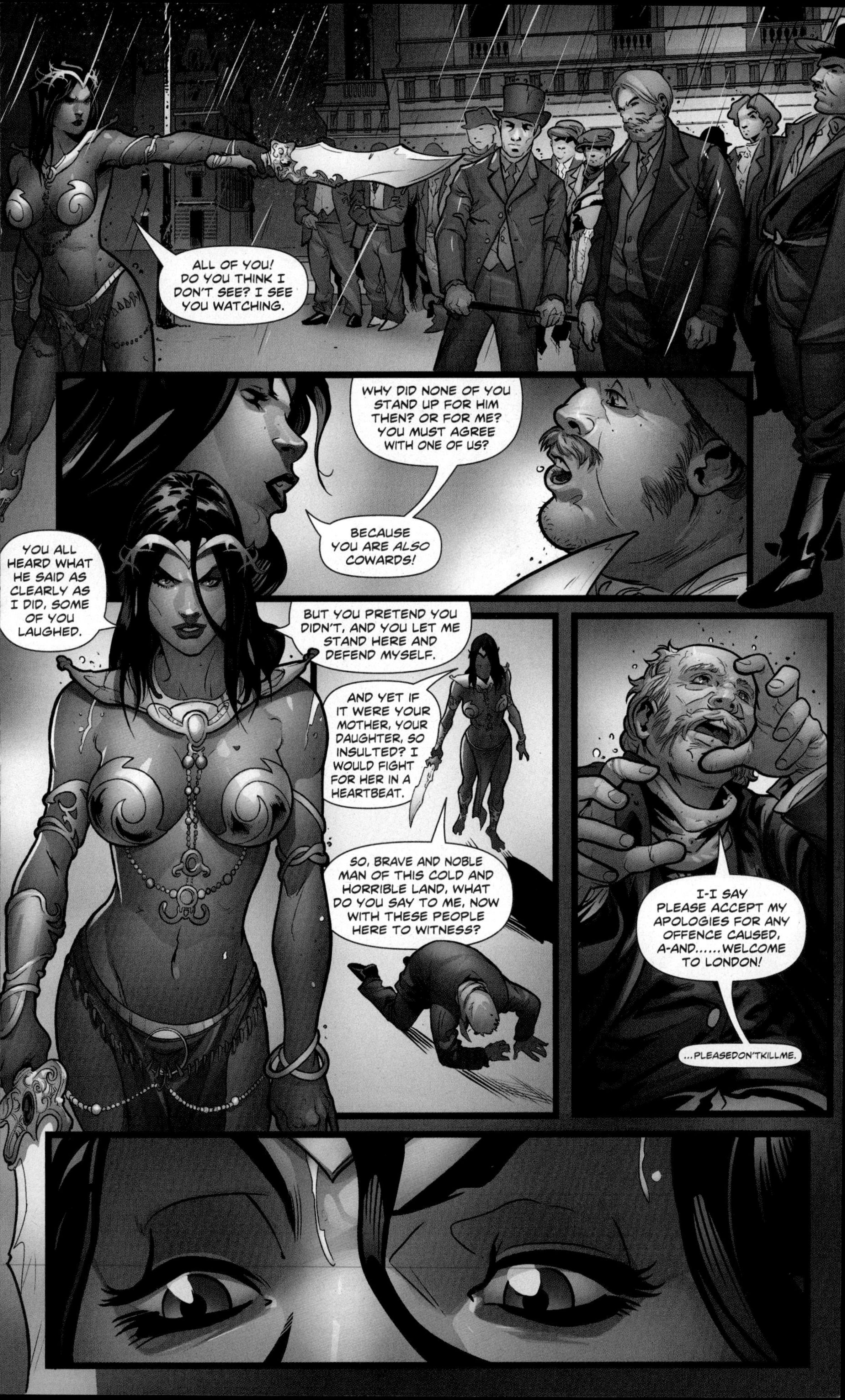
ALL OF YOU! DO YOU THINK I DON'T SEE? I SEE YOU WATCHING.
WHY DID NONE OF YOU STAND UP FOR HIM THEN? OR FOR ME? YOU MUST AGREE WITH ONE OF US?
BECAUSE YOU ARE ALSO COWARDS!
YOU ALL HEARD WHAT HE SAID AS CLEARLY AS I DID, SOME OF YOU LAUGHED.
BUT YOU PRETEND YOU DIDN'T, AND YOU LET ME STAND HERE AND DEFEND MYSELF.
AND YET IF IT WERE YOUR MOTHER, YOUR DAUGHTER, SO INSULTED? I WOULD FIGHT FOR HER IN A HEARTBEAT.
SO, BRAVE AND NOBLE MAN OF THIS COLD AND HORRIBLE LAND, WHAT DO YOU SAY TO ME, NOW WITH THESE PEOPLE HERE TO WITNESS?
I-I SAY PLEASE ACCEPT MY APOLOGIES FOR ANY OFFENCE CAUSED, A-AND......WELCOME TO LONDON!
...PLEASEDON'TKILLME.

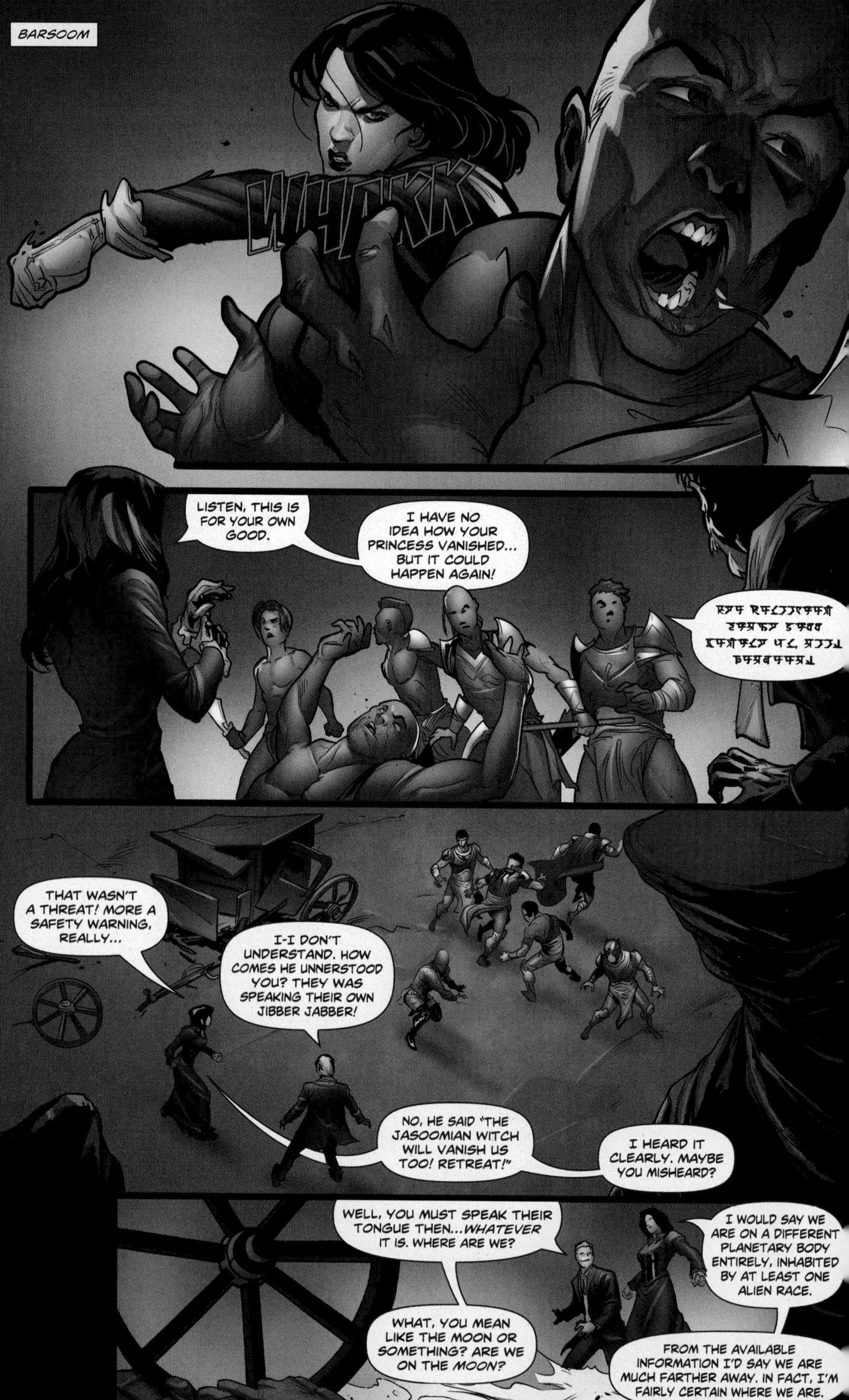
BARSOOM
WHRKK
LISTEN, THIS IS FOR YOUR OWN GOOD.
I HAVE NO IDEA HOW YOUR PRINCESS VANISHED... BUT IT COULD HAPPEN AGAIN!
THAT WASN'T A THREAT! MORE A SAFETY WARNING, REALLY...
I-I DON'T UNDERSTAND. HOW COMES HE UNNERSTOOD YOU? THEY WAS SPEAKING THEIR OWN JIBBER JABBER!
NO, HE SAID "THE JASOOMIAN WITCH WILL VANISH US TOO! RETREAT!"
I HEARD IT CLEARLY. MAYBE YOU MISHEARD?
WELL, YOU MUST SPEAK THEIR TONGUE THEN... *WHATEVER* IT IS. WHERE ARE WE?
I WOULD SAY WE ARE ON A DIFFERENT PLANETARY BODY ENTIRELY, INHABITED BY AT LEAST ONE ALIEN RACE.
WHAT, YOU MEAN LIKE THE MOON OR SOMETHING? ARE WE ON THE *MOON*?
FROM THE AVAILABLE INFORMATION I'D SAY WE ARE MUCH FARTHER AWAY. IN FACT, I'M FAIRLY CERTAIN WHERE WE ARE.

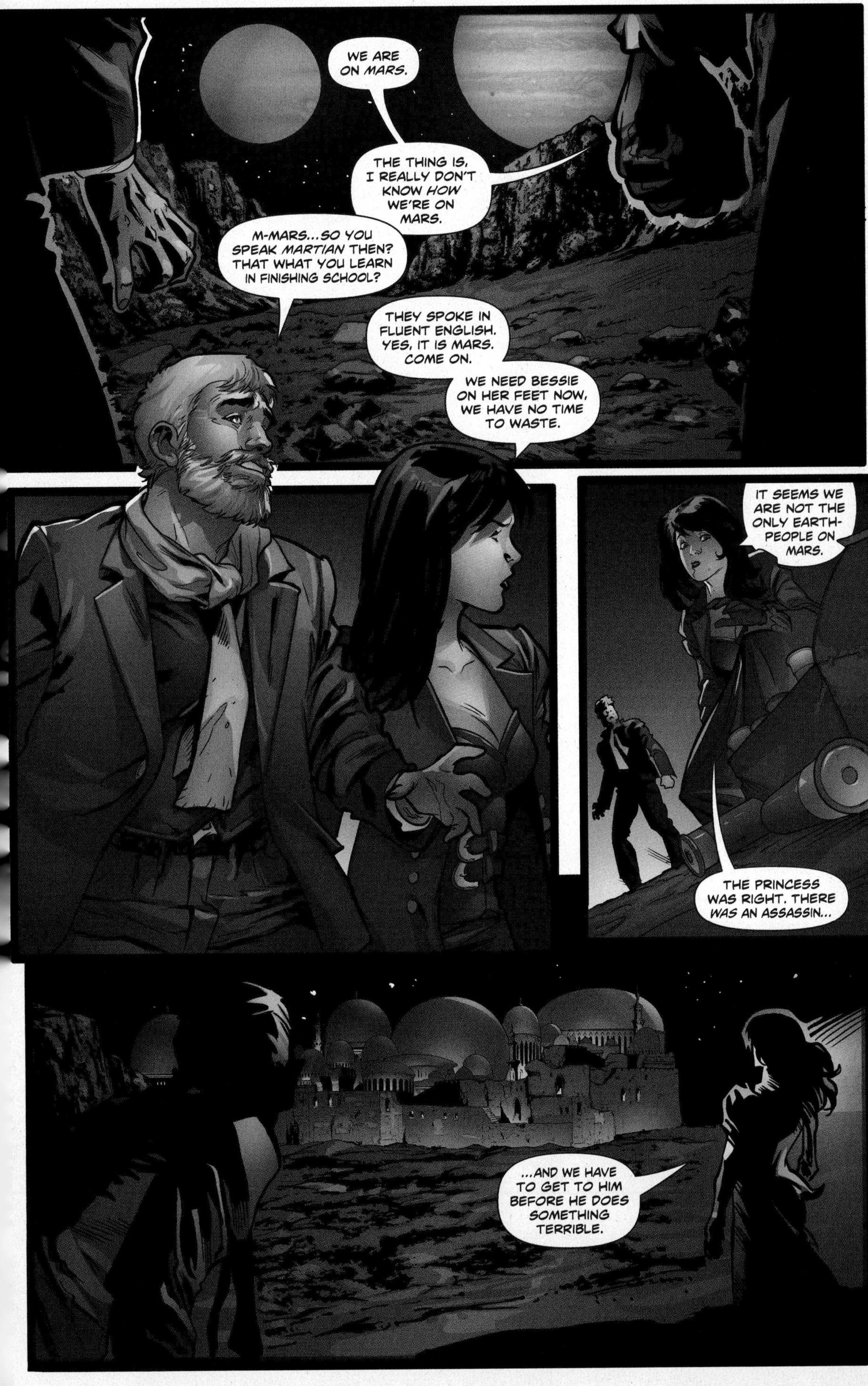
WE ARE ON *MARS*.
THE THING IS, I REALLY DON'T KNOW *HOW* WE'RE ON MARS.
M-MARS...SO YOU SPEAK *MARTIAN* THEN? THAT WHAT YOU LEARN IN FINISHING SCHOOL?
THEY SPOKE IN FLUENT ENGLISH. YES, IT IS MARS. COME ON.
WE NEED BESSIE ON HER FEET NOW, WE HAVE NO TIME TO WASTE.
IT SEEMS WE ARE NOT THE ONLY EARTH-PEOPLE ON MARS.
THE PRINCESS WAS RIGHT. THERE *WAS* AN ASSASSIN...
...AND WE HAVE TO GET TO HIM BEFORE HE DOES SOMETHING TERRIBLE.

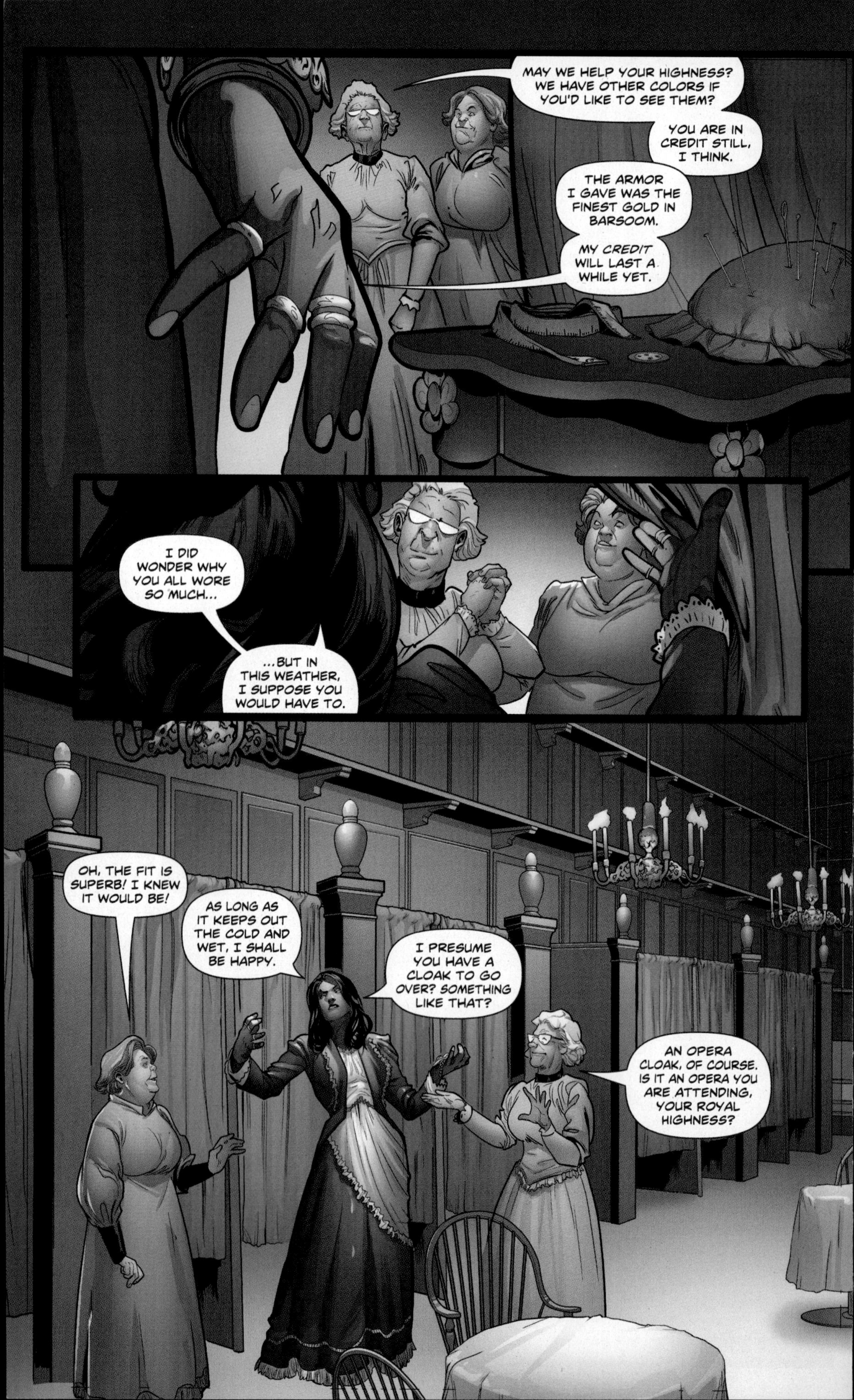
MAY WE HELP YOUR HIGHNESS? WE HAVE OTHER COLORS IF YOU'D LIKE TO SEE THEM?
YOU ARE IN CREDIT STILL, I THINK.
THE ARMOR I GAVE WAS THE FINEST GOLD IN BARSOOM.
MY *CREDIT* WILL LAST A WHILE YET.
I DID WONDER WHY YOU ALL WORE SO MUCH...
...BUT IN THIS WEATHER, I SUPPOSE YOU WOULD HAVE TO.
OH, THE FIT IS SUPERB! I KNEW IT WOULD BE!
AS LONG AS IT KEEPS OUT THE COLD AND WET, I SHALL BE HAPPY.
I PRESUME YOU HAVE A CLOAK TO GO OVER? SOMETHING LIKE THAT?
AN OPERA CLOAK, OF COURSE. IS IT AN OPERA YOU ARE ATTENDING, YOUR ROYAL HIGHNESS?

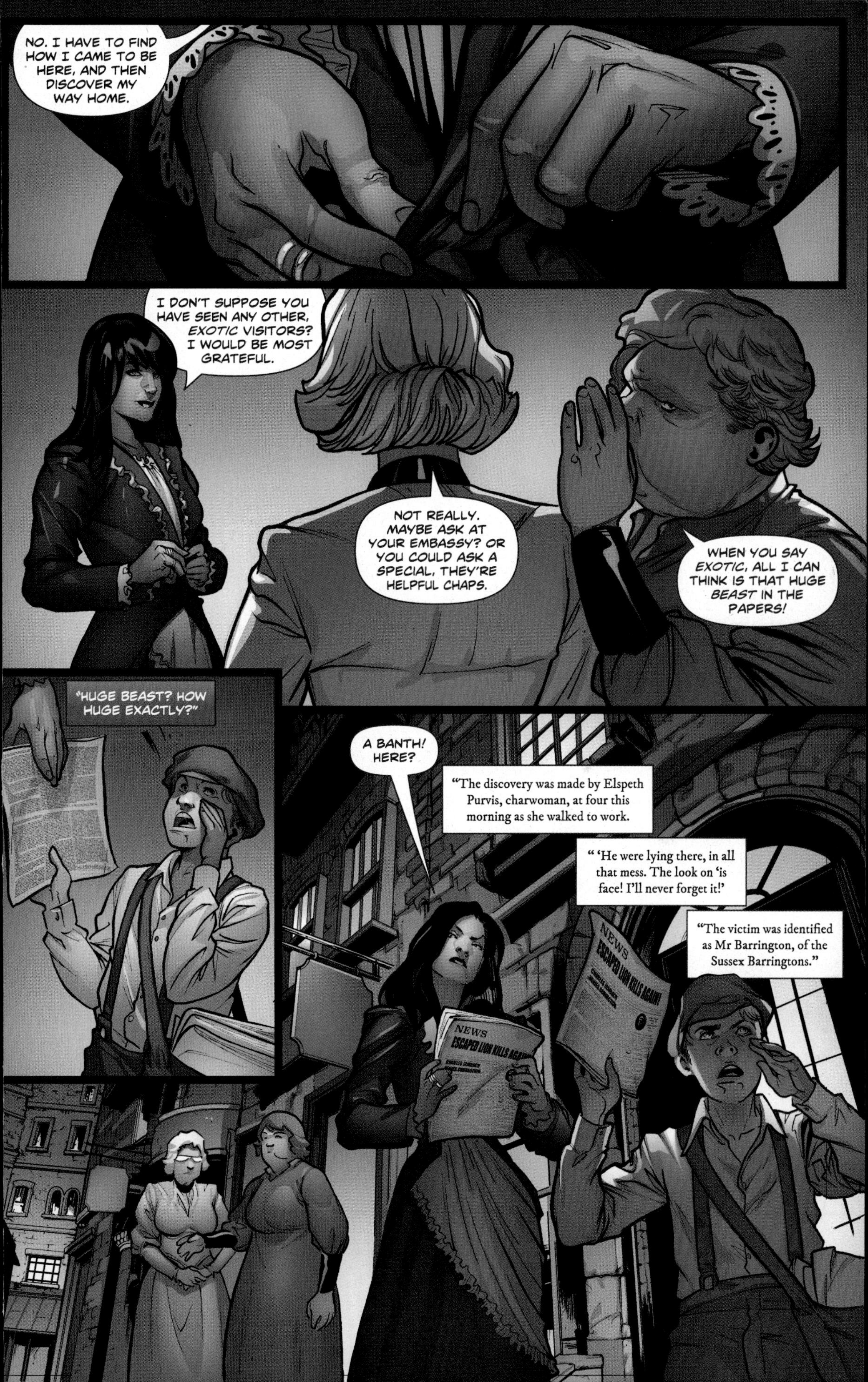
NO. I HAVE TO FIND HOW I CAME TO BE HERE, AND THEN DISCOVER MY WAY HOME.
I DON'T SUPPOSE YOU HAVE SEEN ANY OTHER, *EXOTIC* VISITORS? I WOULD BE MOST GRATEFUL.
NOT REALLY. MAYBE ASK AT YOUR EMBASSY? OR YOU COULD ASK A SPECIAL, THEY'RE HELPFUL CHAPS.
WHEN YOU SAY *EXOTIC*, ALL I CAN THINK IS THAT HUGE *BEAST* IN THE PAPERS!
"HUGE BEAST? HOW HUGE EXACTLY?"
A BANTH! HERE?
"The discovery was made by Elspeth Purvis, charwoman, at four this morning as she walked to work.
" 'He were lying there, in all that mess. The look on 'is face! I'll never forget it!'
"The victim was identified as Mr Barrington, of the Sussex Barringtons."
NEWS
ESCAPED LION KILLS AGAIN!

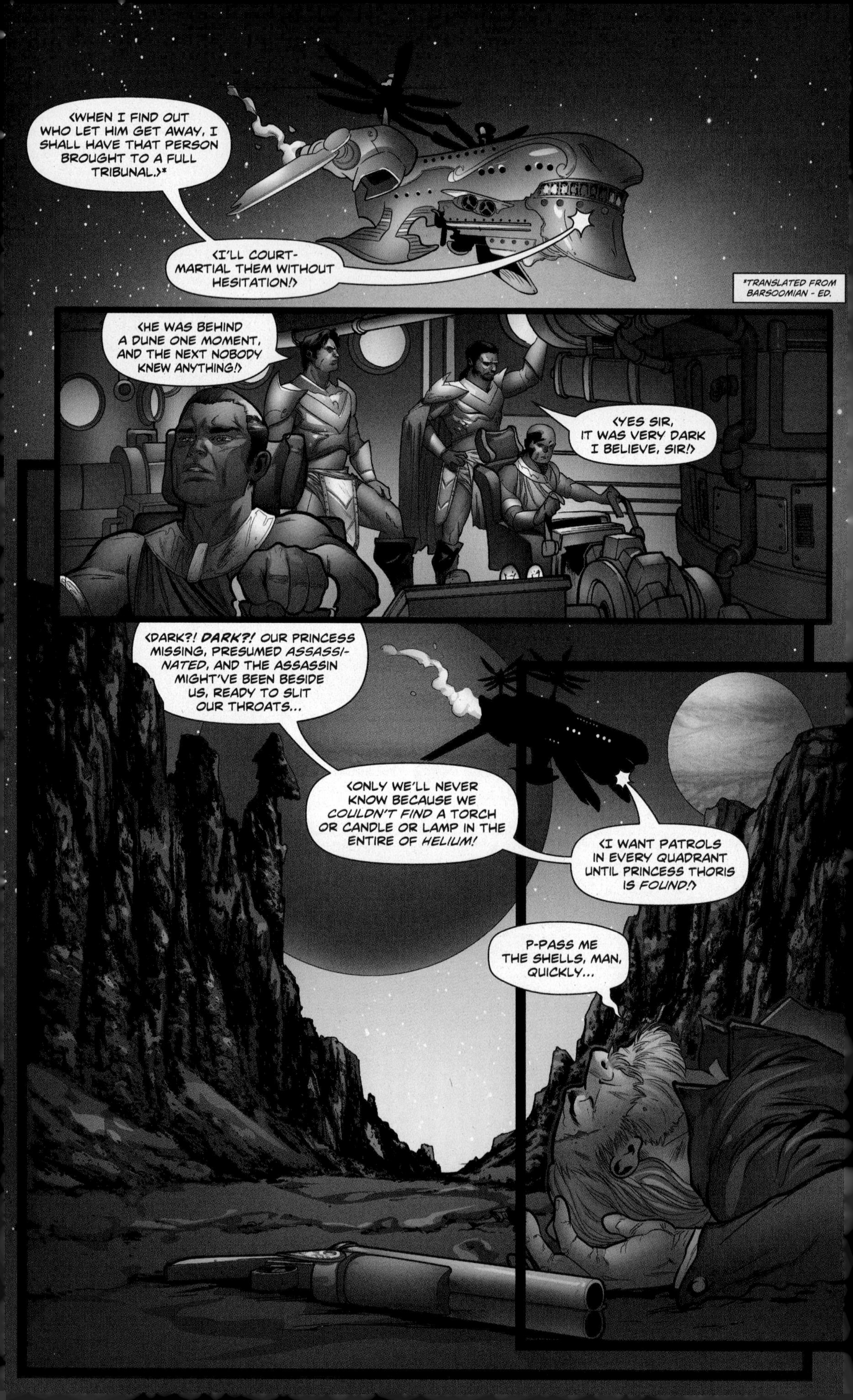
<WHEN I FIND OUT WHO LET HIM GET AWAY, I SHALL HAVE THAT PERSON BROUGHT TO A FULL TRIBUNAL.>*
<I'LL COURT-MARTIAL THEM WITHOUT HESITATION!>
*TRANSLATED FROM BARSOOMIAN - ED.
<HE WAS BEHIND A DUNE ONE MOMENT, AND THE NEXT NOBODY KNEW ANYTHING!>
<YES SIR, IT WAS VERY DARK I BELIEVE, SIR!>
<DARK?! *DARK?!* OUR PRINCESS MISSING, PRESUMED *ASSASSINATED*, AND THE ASSASSIN MIGHT'VE BEEN BESIDE US, READY TO SLIT OUR THROATS...
<ONLY WE'LL NEVER KNOW BECAUSE WE *COULDN'T* FIND A TORCH OR CANDLE OR LAMP IN THE ENTIRE OF *HELIUM!*
<I WANT PATROLS IN EVERY QUADRANT UNTIL PRINCESS THORIS IS *FOUND!*>
P-PASS ME THE SHELLS, MAN, QUICKLY...

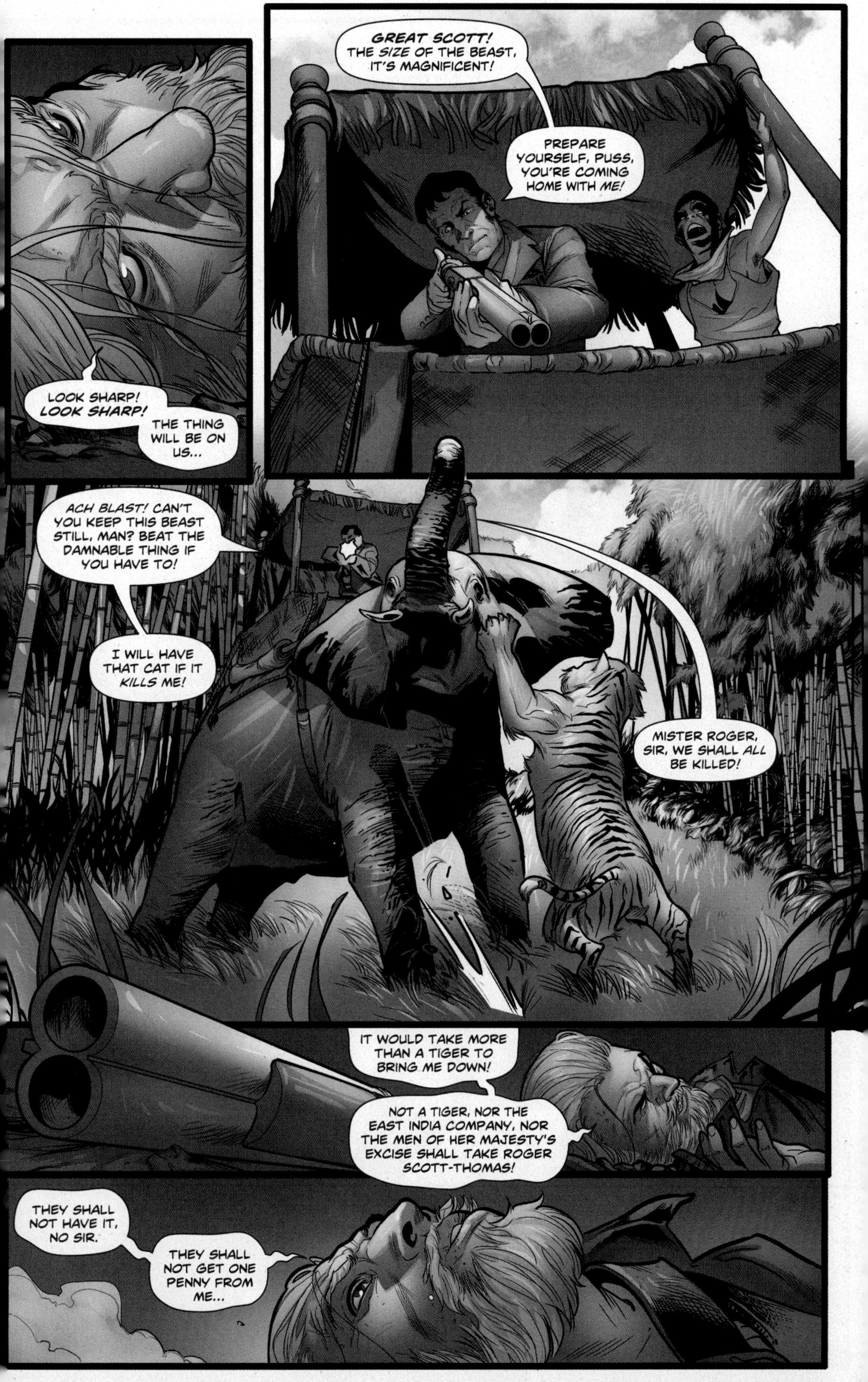

LOOK SHARP! LOOK SHARP!
THE THING WILL BE ON US...
GREAT SCOTT! THE SIZE OF THE BEAST, IT'S MAGNIFICENT!
PREPARE YOURSELF, PUSS, YOU'RE COMING HOME WITH ME!
ACH BLAST! CAN'T YOU KEEP THIS BEAST STILL, MAN? BEAT THE DAMNABLE THING IF YOU HAVE TO!
I WILL HAVE THAT CAT IF IT KILLS ME!
MISTER ROGER, SIR, WE SHALL ALL BE KILLED!
IT WOULD TAKE MORE THAN A TIGER TO BRING ME DOWN!
NOT A TIGER, NOR THE EAST INDIA COMPANY, NOR THE MEN OF HER MAJESTY'S EXCISE SHALL TAKE ROGER SCOTT-THOMAS!
THEY SHALL NOT HAVE IT, NO SIR.
THEY SHALL NOT GET ONE PENNY FROM ME...

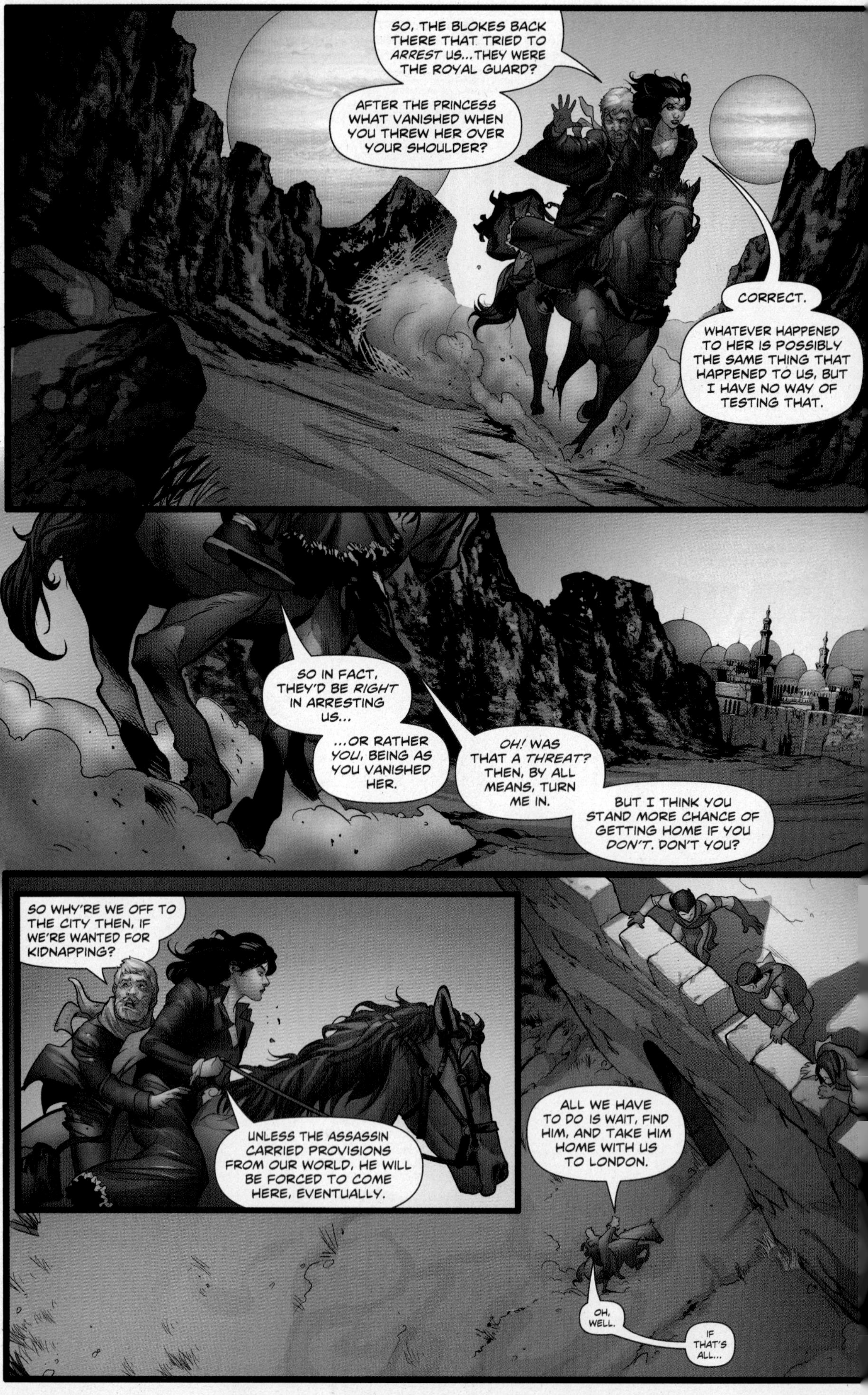
SO, THE BLOKES BACK THERE THAT TRIED TO *ARREST* US... THEY WERE THE ROYAL GUARD?
AFTER THE PRINCESS WHAT VANISHED WHEN YOU THREW HER OVER YOUR SHOULDER?
CORRECT.
WHATEVER HAPPENED TO HER IS POSSIBLY THE SAME THING THAT HAPPENED TO US, BUT I HAVE NO WAY OF TESTING THAT.
SO IN FACT, THEY'D BE *RIGHT* IN ARRESTING US...
...OR RATHER *YOU*, BEING AS YOU VANISHED HER.
OH! WAS THAT A *THREAT?* THEN, BY ALL MEANS, TURN ME IN.
BUT I THINK YOU STAND MORE CHANCE OF GETTING HOME IF YOU *DON'T*. DON'T YOU?
SO WHY'RE WE OFF TO THE CITY THEN, IF WE'RE WANTED FOR KIDNAPPING?
UNLESS THE ASSASSIN CARRIED PROVISIONS FROM OUR WORLD, HE WILL BE FORCED TO COME HERE, EVENTUALLY.
ALL WE HAVE TO DO IS WAIT, FIND HIM, AND TAKE HIM HOME WITH US TO LONDON.
OH, WELL.
IF THAT'S ALL...

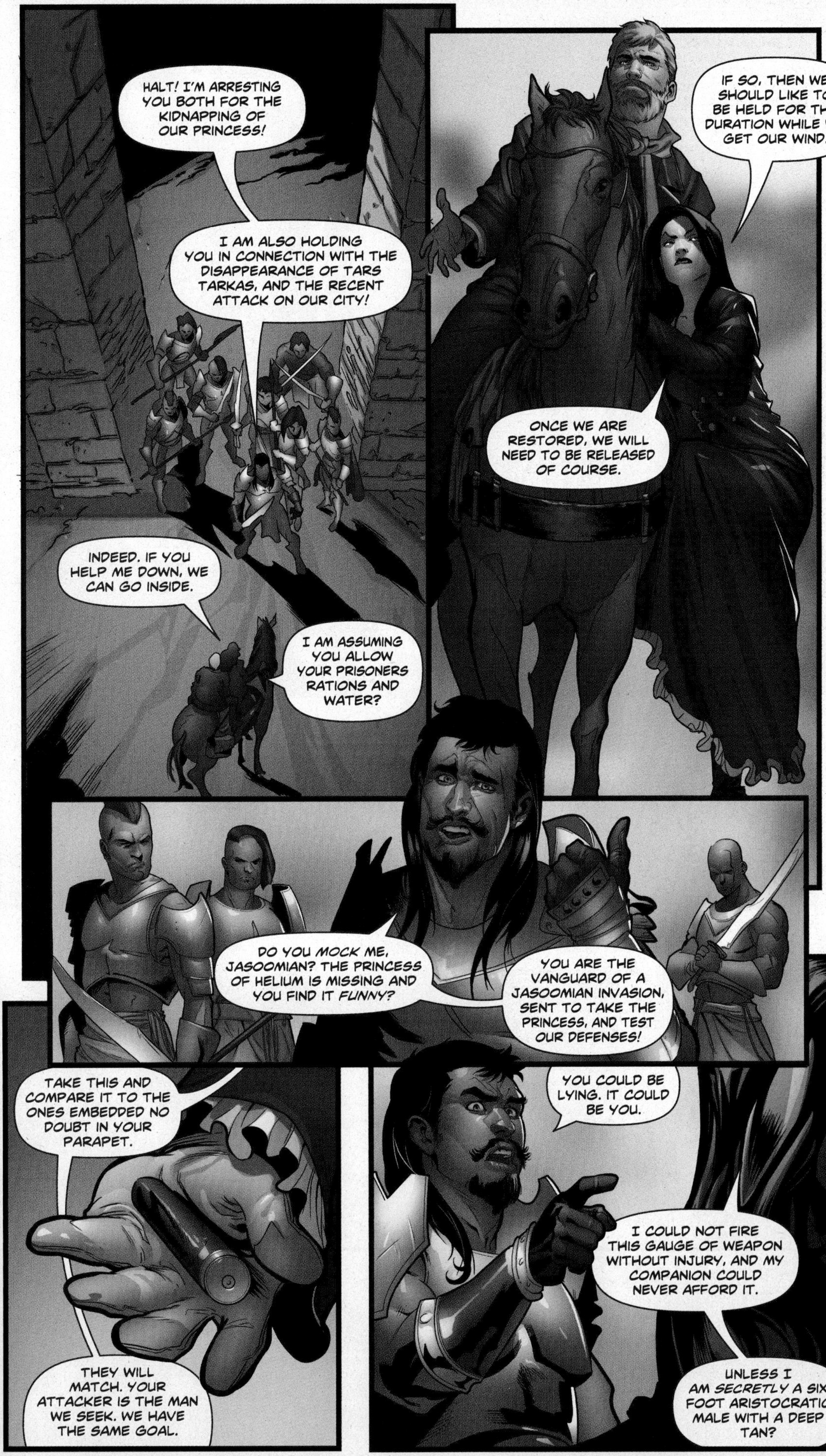
HALT! I'M ARRESTING YOU BOTH FOR THE KIDNAPPING OF OUR PRINCESS!
I AM ALSO HOLDING YOU IN CONNECTION WITH THE DISAPPEARANCE OF TARS TARKAS, AND THE RECENT ATTACK ON OUR CITY!
INDEED. IF YOU HELP ME DOWN, WE CAN GO INSIDE.
I AM ASSUMING YOU ALLOW YOUR PRISONERS RATIONS AND WATER?
IF SO, THEN WE SHOULD LIKE TO BE HELD FOR THE DURATION WHILE WE GET OUR WIND.
ONCE WE ARE RESTORED, WE WILL NEED TO BE RELEASED OF COURSE.
DO YOU *MOCK* ME, JASOOMIAN? THE PRINCESS OF HELIUM IS MISSING AND YOU FIND IT *FUNNY*?
YOU ARE THE VANGUARD OF A JASOOMIAN INVASION, SENT TO TAKE THE PRINCESS, AND TEST OUR DEFENSES!
TAKE THIS AND COMPARE IT TO THE ONES EMBEDDED NO DOUBT IN YOUR PARAPET.
THEY WILL MATCH. YOUR ATTACKER IS THE MAN WE SEEK. WE HAVE THE SAME GOAL.
YOU COULD BE LYING. IT COULD BE YOU.
I COULD NOT FIRE THIS GAUGE OF WEAPON WITHOUT INJURY, AND MY COMPANION COULD NEVER AFFORD IT.
UNLESS I AM *SECRETLY* A SIX FOOT ARISTOCRATIC MALE WITH A DEEP TAN?

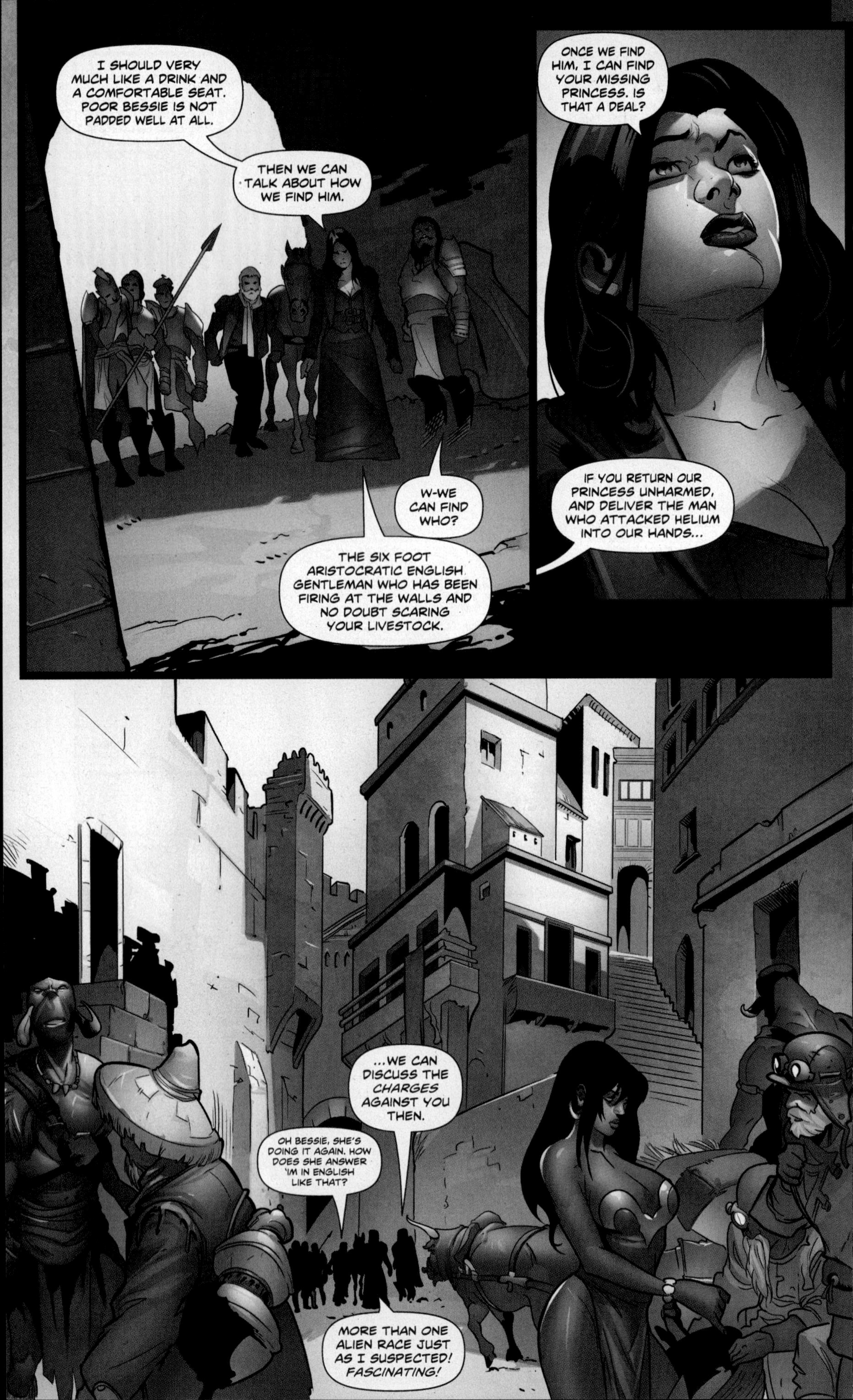

I SHOULD VERY MUCH LIKE A DRINK AND A COMFORTABLE SEAT. POOR BESSIE IS NOT PADDED WELL AT ALL.
THEN WE CAN TALK ABOUT HOW WE FIND HIM.
W-WE CAN FIND WHO?
THE SIX FOOT ARISTOCRATIC ENGLISH GENTLEMAN WHO HAS BEEN FIRING AT THE WALLS AND NO DOUBT SCARING YOUR LIVESTOCK.
ONCE WE FIND HIM, I CAN FIND YOUR MISSING PRINCESS. IS THAT A DEAL?
IF YOU RETURN OUR PRINCESS UNHARMED, AND DELIVER THE MAN WHO ATTACKED HELIUM INTO OUR HANDS...
...WE CAN DISCUSS THE CHARGES AGAINST YOU THEN.
OH BESSIE, SHE'S DOING IT AGAIN. HOW DOES SHE ANSWER 'IM IN ENGLISH LIKE THAT?
MORE THAN ONE ALIEN RACE JUST AS I SUSPECTED! *FASCINATING!*

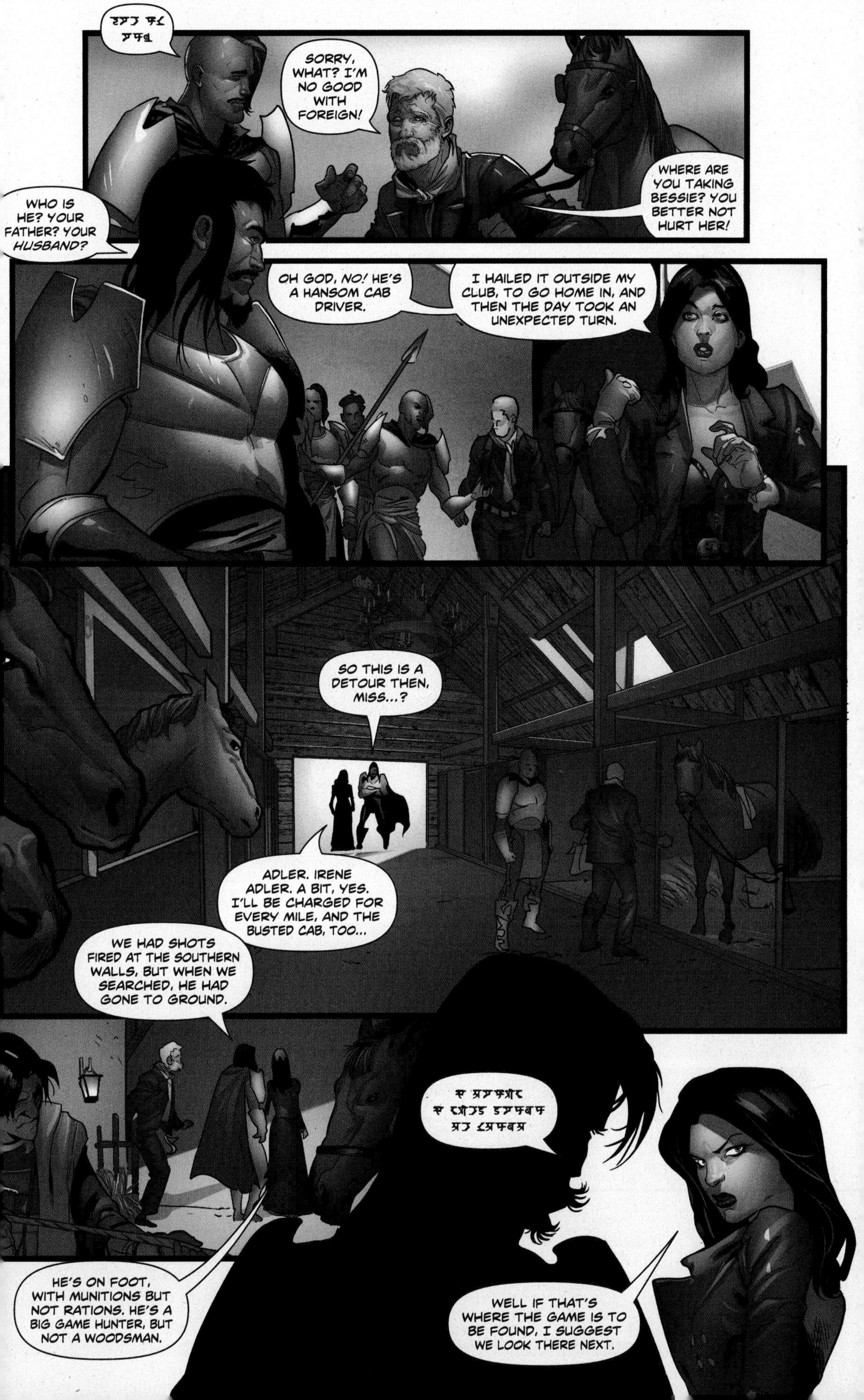
SORRY, WHAT? I'M NO GOOD WITH FOREIGN!
WHERE ARE YOU TAKING BESSIE? YOU BETTER NOT HURT HER!
WHO IS HE? YOUR FATHER? YOUR *HUSBAND*?
OH GOD, *NO!* HE'S A HANSOM CAB DRIVER.
I HAILED IT OUTSIDE MY CLUB, TO GO HOME IN, AND THEN THE DAY TOOK AN UNEXPECTED TURN.
SO THIS IS A DETOUR THEN, MISS...?
ADLER. IRENE ADLER. A BIT, YES. I'LL BE CHARGED FOR EVERY MILE, AND THE BUSTED CAB, TOO...
WE HAD SHOTS FIRED AT THE SOUTHERN WALLS, BUT WHEN WE SEARCHED, HE HAD GONE TO GROUND.
HE'S ON FOOT, WITH MUNITIONS BUT NOT RATIONS. HE'S A BIG GAME HUNTER, BUT NOT A WOODSMAN.
WELL IF THAT'S WHERE THE GAME IS TO BE FOUND, I SUGGEST WE LOOK THERE NEXT.

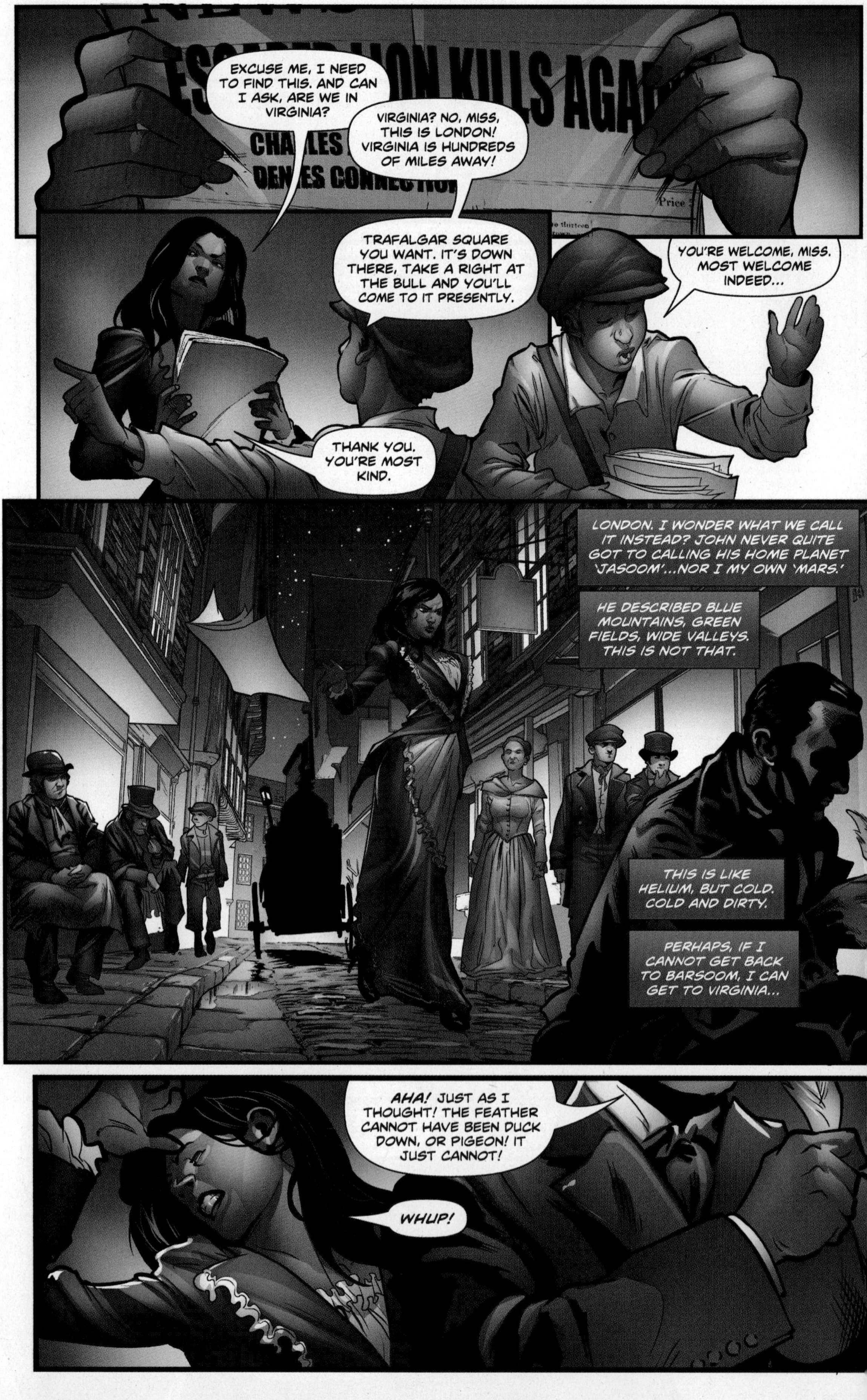
EXCUSE ME, I NEED TO FIND THIS. AND CAN I ASK, ARE WE IN VIRGINIA?
VIRGINIA? NO, MISS, THIS IS LONDON! VIRGINIA IS HUNDREDS OF MILES AWAY!
TRAFALGAR SQUARE YOU WANT. IT'S DOWN THERE, TAKE A RIGHT AT THE BULL AND YOU'LL COME TO IT PRESENTLY.
THANK YOU. YOU'RE MOST KIND.
YOU'RE WELCOME, MISS. MOST WELCOME INDEED...
LONDON. I WONDER WHAT WE CALL IT INSTEAD? JOHN NEVER QUITE GOT TO CALLING HIS HOME PLANET 'JASOOM'...NOR I MY OWN 'MARS.'
HE DESCRIBED BLUE MOUNTAINS, GREEN FIELDS, WIDE VALLEYS. THIS IS NOT THAT.
THIS IS LIKE HELIUM, BUT COLD. COLD AND DIRTY.
PERHAPS, IF I CANNOT GET BACK TO BARSOOM, I CAN GET TO VIRGINIA...
AHA! JUST AS I THOUGHT! THE FEATHER CANNOT HAVE BEEN DUCK DOWN, OR PIGEON! IT JUST CANNOT!
WHUP!

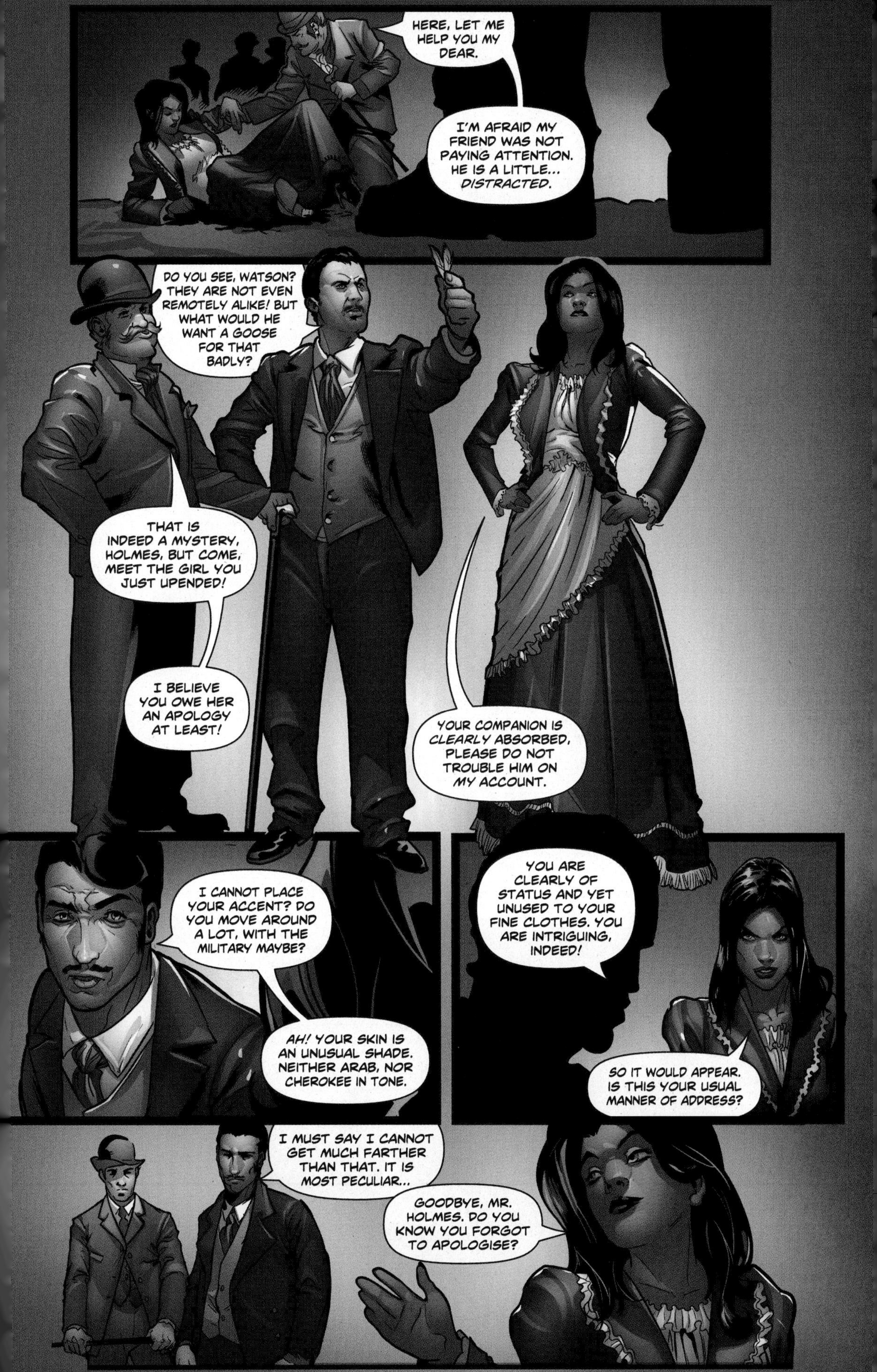
HERE, LET ME HELP YOU MY DEAR.
I'M AFRAID MY FRIEND WAS NOT PAYING ATTENTION. HE IS A LITTLE... *DISTRACTED.*
DO YOU SEE, WATSON? THEY ARE NOT EVEN REMOTELY ALIKE! BUT WHAT WOULD HE WANT A GOOSE FOR THAT BADLY?
THAT IS INDEED A MYSTERY, HOLMES, BUT COME, MEET THE GIRL YOU JUST UPENDED!
I BELIEVE YOU OWE HER AN APOLOGY AT LEAST!
YOUR COMPANION IS CLEARLY ABSORBED, PLEASE DO NOT TROUBLE HIM ON MY ACCOUNT.
I CANNOT PLACE YOUR ACCENT? DO YOU MOVE AROUND A LOT, WITH THE MILITARY MAYBE?
AH! YOUR SKIN IS AN UNUSUAL SHADE. NEITHER ARAB, NOR CHEROKEE IN TONE.
YOU ARE CLEARLY OF STATUS AND YET UNUSED TO YOUR FINE CLOTHES. YOU ARE INTRIGUING, INDEED!
SO IT WOULD APPEAR. IS THIS YOUR USUAL MANNER OF ADDRESS?
I MUST SAY I CANNOT GET MUCH FARTHER THAN THAT. IT IS MOST PECULIAR...
GOODBYE, MR. HOLMES. DO YOU KNOW YOU FORGOT TO APOLOGISE?

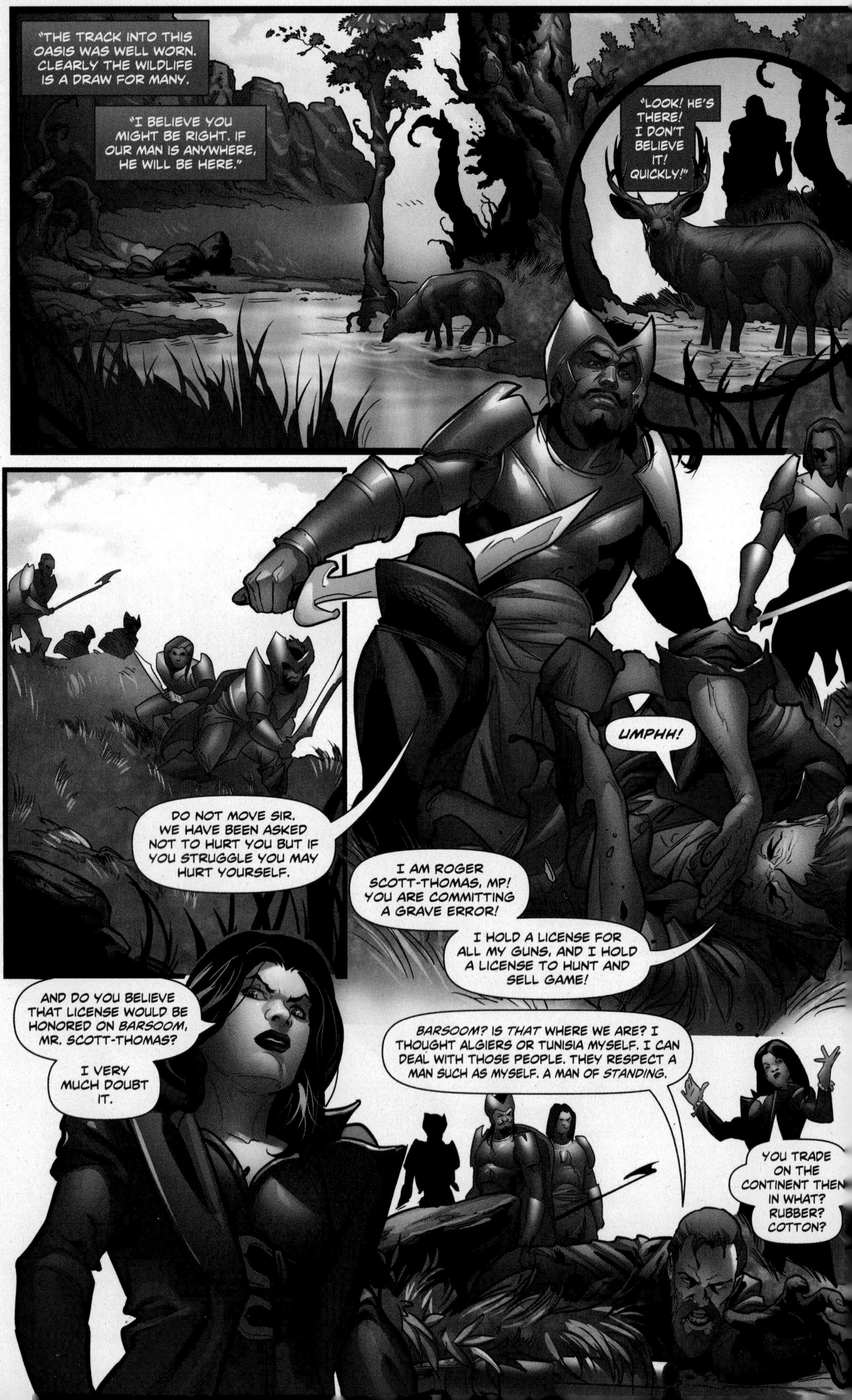

"THE TRACK INTO THIS OASIS WAS WELL WORN. CLEARLY THE WILDLIFE IS A DRAW FOR MANY.
"I BELIEVE YOU MIGHT BE RIGHT. IF OUR MAN IS ANYWHERE, HE WILL BE HERE."
"LOOK! HE'S THERE! I DON'T BELIEVE IT! QUICKLY!"
UMPHH!
DO NOT MOVE SIR. WE HAVE BEEN ASKED NOT TO HURT YOU BUT IF YOU STRUGGLE YOU MAY HURT YOURSELF.
I AM ROGER SCOTT-THOMAS, MP! YOU ARE COMMITTING A GRAVE ERROR!
I HOLD A LICENSE FOR ALL MY GUNS, AND I HOLD A LICENSE TO HUNT AND SELL GAME!
AND DO YOU BELIEVE THAT LICENSE WOULD BE HONORED ON *BARSOOM*, MR. SCOTT-THOMAS?
I VERY MUCH DOUBT IT.
BARSOOM? IS *THAT* WHERE WE ARE? I THOUGHT ALGIERS OR TUNISIA MYSELF. I CAN DEAL WITH THOSE PEOPLE. THEY RESPECT A MAN SUCH AS MYSELF. A MAN OF *STANDING*.
YOU TRADE ON THE CONTINENT THEN IN WHAT? RUBBER? COTTON?

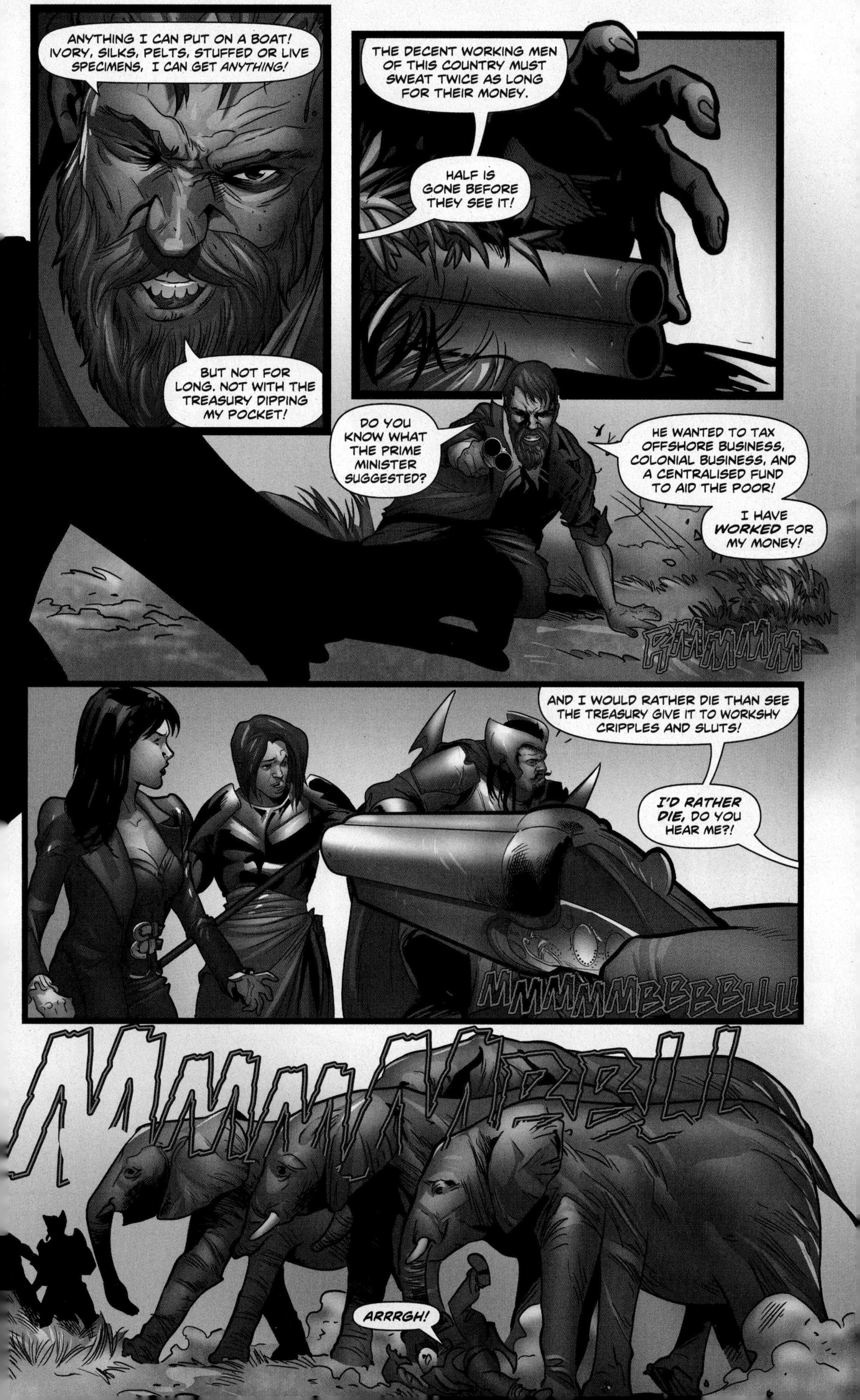
ANYTHING I CAN PUT ON A BOAT! IVORY, SILKS, PELTS, STUFFED OR LIVE SPECIMENS, I CAN GET ANYTHING!
BUT NOT FOR LONG. NOT WITH THE TREASURY DIPPING MY POCKET!
THE DECENT WORKING MEN OF THIS COUNTRY MUST SWEAT TWICE AS LONG FOR THEIR MONEY.
HALF IS GONE BEFORE THEY SEE IT!
DO YOU KNOW WHAT THE PRIME MINISTER SUGGESTED?
HE WANTED TO TAX OFFSHORE BUSINESS, COLONIAL BUSINESS, AND A CENTRALISED FUND TO AID THE POOR!
I HAVE WORKED FOR MY MONEY!
RMMMMM
AND I WOULD RATHER DIE THAN SEE THE TREASURY GIVE IT TO WORKSHY CRIPPLES AND SLUTS!
I'D RATHER DIE, DO YOU HEAR ME?!
MMMMMMBBBBLLL
MMMMMBBLL
ARRRGH!

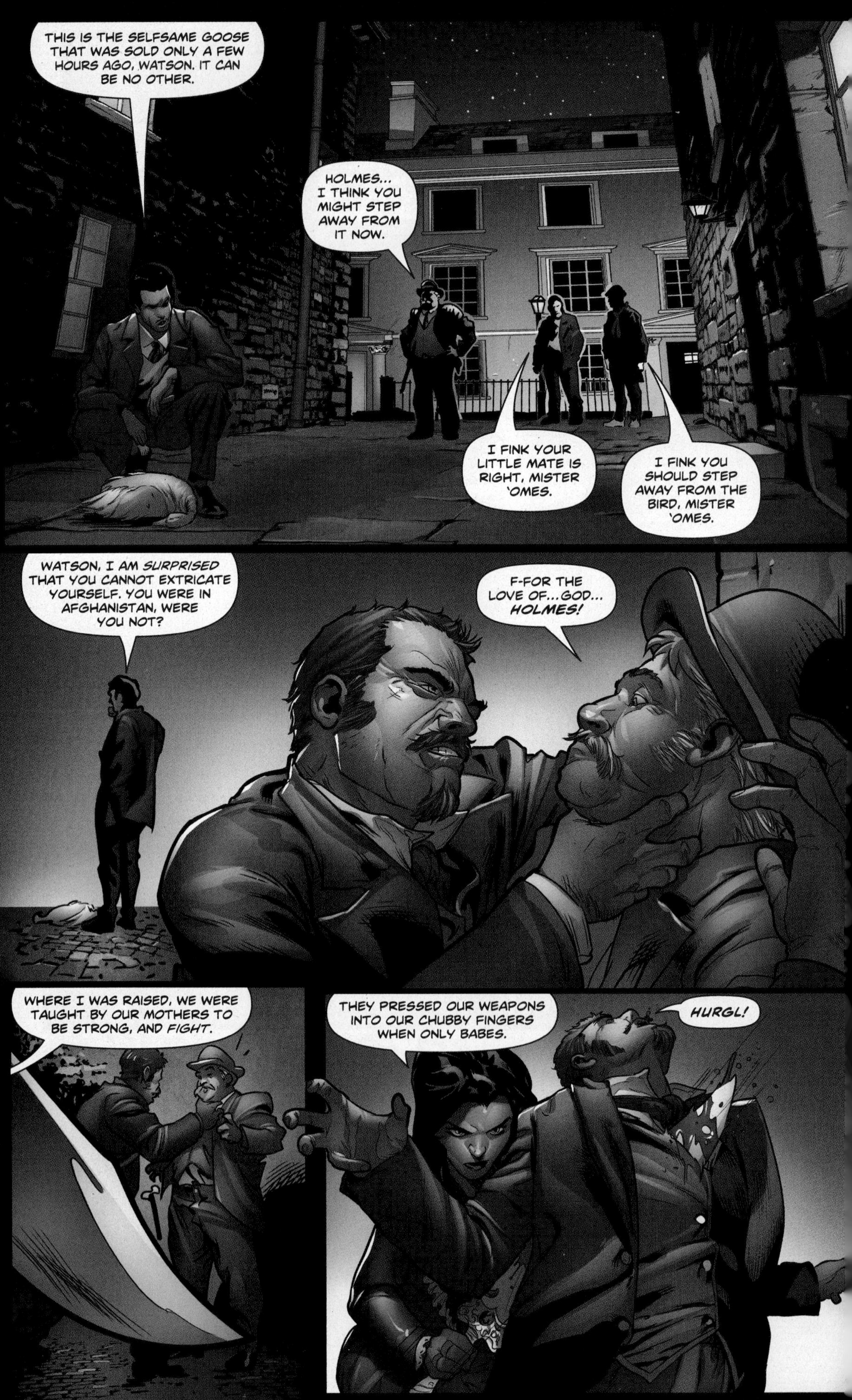
THIS IS THE SELFSAME GOOSE THAT WAS SOLD ONLY A FEW HOURS AGO, WATSON. IT CAN BE NO OTHER.
HOLMES... I THINK YOU MIGHT STEP AWAY FROM IT NOW.
I FINK YOUR LITTLE MATE IS RIGHT, MISTER 'OMES.
I FINK YOU SHOULD STEP AWAY FROM THE BIRD, MISTER 'OMES.
WATSON, I AM *SURPRISED* THAT YOU CANNOT EXTRICATE YOURSELF. YOU WERE IN AFGHANISTAN, WERE YOU NOT?
F-FOR THE LOVE OF...GOD... ***HOLMES!***
WHERE I WAS RAISED, WE WERE TAUGHT BY OUR MOTHERS TO BE STRONG, AND *FIGHT*.
THEY PRESSED OUR WEAPONS INTO OUR CHUBBY FINGERS WHEN ONLY BABES.
HURGL!

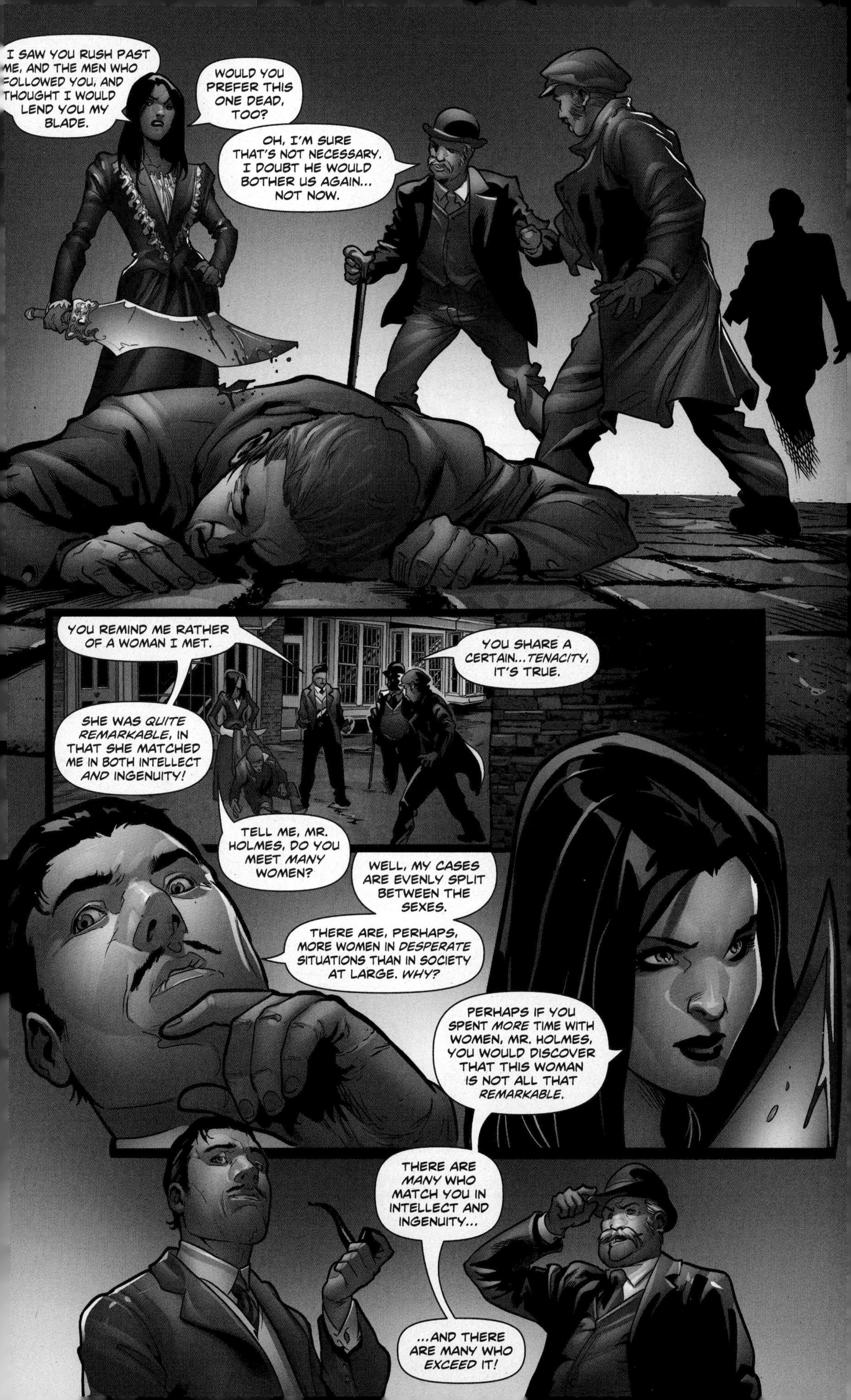
I SAW YOU RUSH PAST ME, AND THE MEN WHO FOLLOWED YOU, AND THOUGHT I WOULD LEND YOU MY BLADE.
WOULD YOU PREFER THIS ONE DEAD, TOO?
OH, I'M SURE THAT'S NOT NECESSARY. I DOUBT HE WOULD BOTHER US AGAIN... NOT NOW.
YOU REMIND ME RATHER OF A WOMAN I MET.
YOU SHARE A CERTAIN... *TENACITY*, IT'S TRUE.
SHE WAS *QUITE REMARKABLE*, IN THAT SHE MATCHED ME IN BOTH INTELLECT *AND* INGENUITY!
TELL ME, MR. HOLMES, DO YOU MEET *MANY* WOMEN?
WELL, MY CASES ARE EVENLY SPLIT BETWEEN THE SEXES.
THERE ARE, PERHAPS, MORE WOMEN IN *DESPERATE* SITUATIONS THAN IN SOCIETY AT LARGE. *WHY?*
PERHAPS IF YOU SPENT *MORE* TIME WITH WOMEN, MR. HOLMES, YOU WOULD DISCOVER THAT THIS WOMAN IS NOT ALL THAT *REMARKABLE*.
THERE ARE *MANY* WHO MATCH YOU IN INTELLECT AND INGENUITY...
...AND THERE ARE MANY WHO *EXCEED* IT!

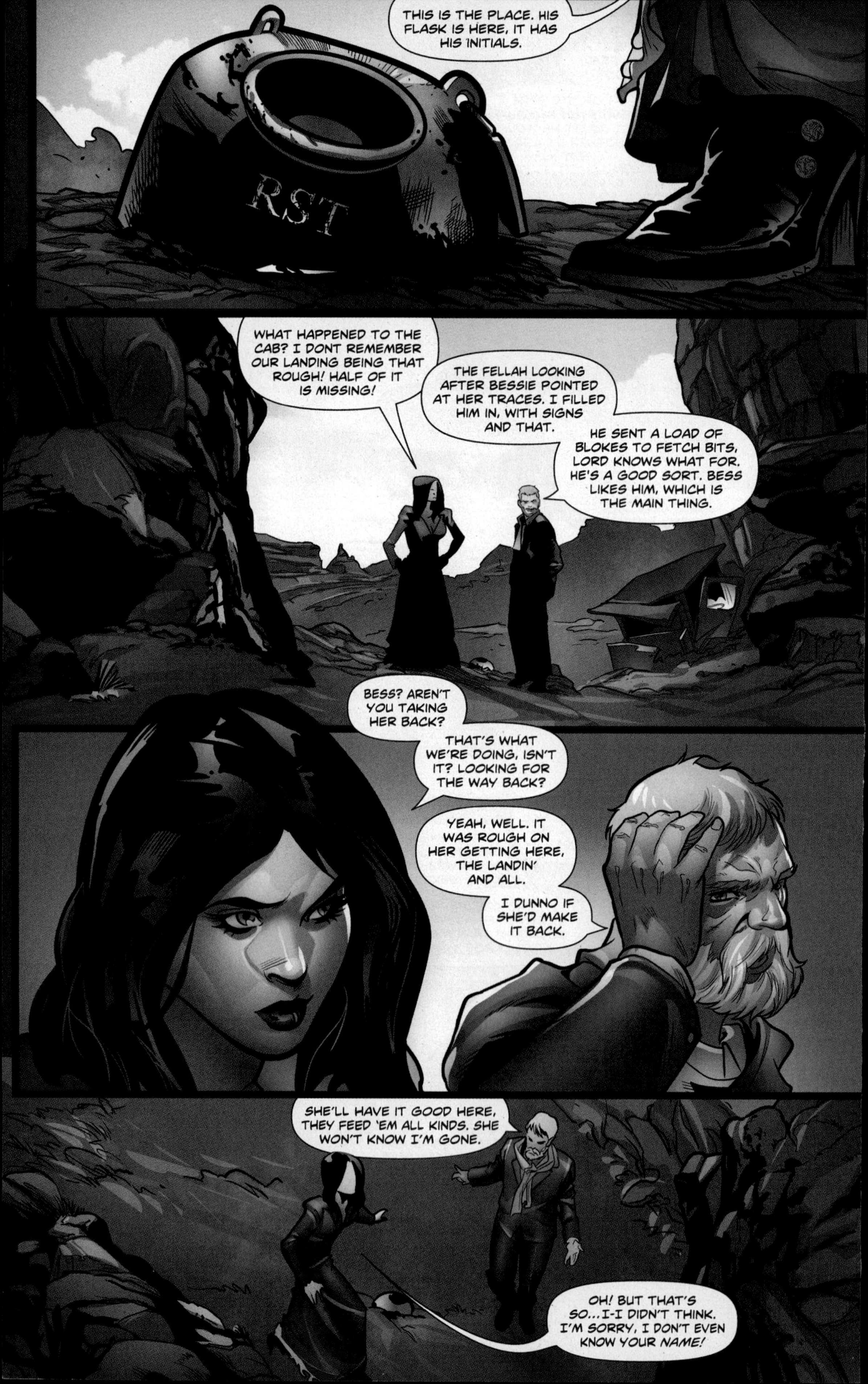
THIS IS THE PLACE. HIS FLASK IS HERE, IT HAS HIS INITIALS.
RST
WHAT HAPPENED TO THE CAB? I DONT REMEMBER OUR LANDING BEING THAT ROUGH! HALF OF IT IS MISSING!
THE FELLAH LOOKING AFTER BESSIE POINTED AT HER TRACES. I FILLED HIM IN, WITH SIGNS AND THAT.
HE SENT A LOAD OF BLOKES TO FETCH BITS, LORD KNOWS WHAT FOR. HE'S A GOOD SORT. BESS LIKES HIM, WHICH IS THE MAIN THING.
BESS? AREN'T YOU TAKING HER BACK?
THAT'S WHAT WE'RE DOING, ISN'T IT? LOOKING FOR THE WAY BACK?
YEAH, WELL. IT WAS ROUGH ON HER GETTING HERE, THE LANDIN' AND ALL.
I DUNNO IF SHE'D MAKE IT BACK.
SHE'LL HAVE IT GOOD HERE, THEY FEED 'EM ALL KINDS. SHE WON'T KNOW I'M GONE.
OH! BUT THAT'S SO... I-I DIDN'T THINK. I'M SORRY, I DON'T EVEN KNOW YOUR *NAME*!

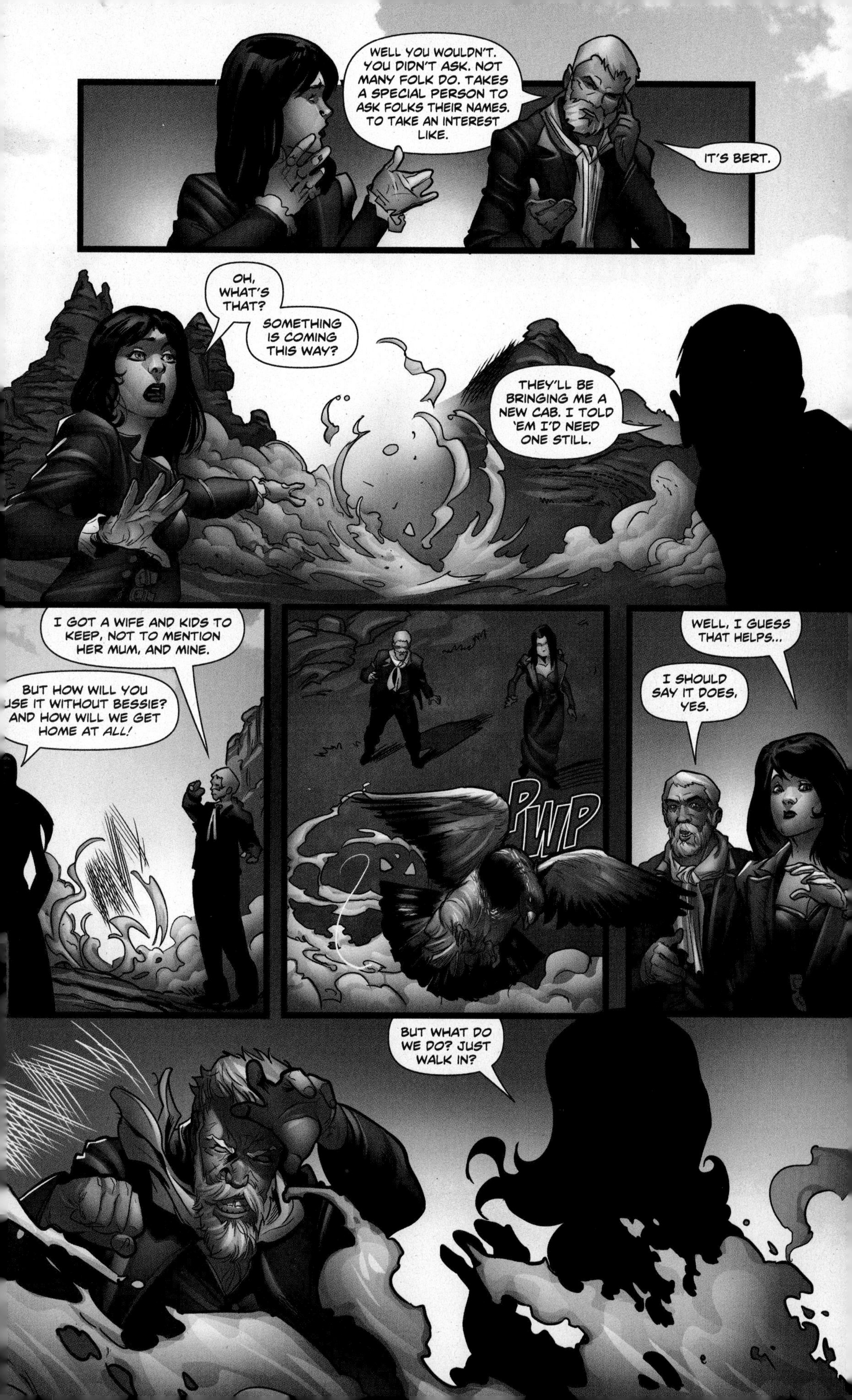
WELL YOU WOULDN'T. YOU DIDN'T ASK. NOT MANY FOLK DO. TAKES A SPECIAL PERSON TO ASK FOLKS THEIR NAMES. TO TAKE AN INTEREST LIKE.
IT'S BERT.
OH, WHAT'S THAT?
SOMETHING IS COMING THIS WAY?
THEY'LL BE BRINGING ME A NEW CAB. I TOLD 'EM I'D NEED ONE STILL.
I GOT A WIFE AND KIDS TO KEEP, NOT TO MENTION HER MUM, AND MINE.
BUT HOW WILL YOU USE IT WITHOUT BESSIE? AND HOW WILL WE GET HOME AT ALL!
PWIP
WELL, I GUESS THAT HELPS...
I SHOULD SAY IT DOES, YES.
BUT WHAT DO WE DO? JUST WALK IN?

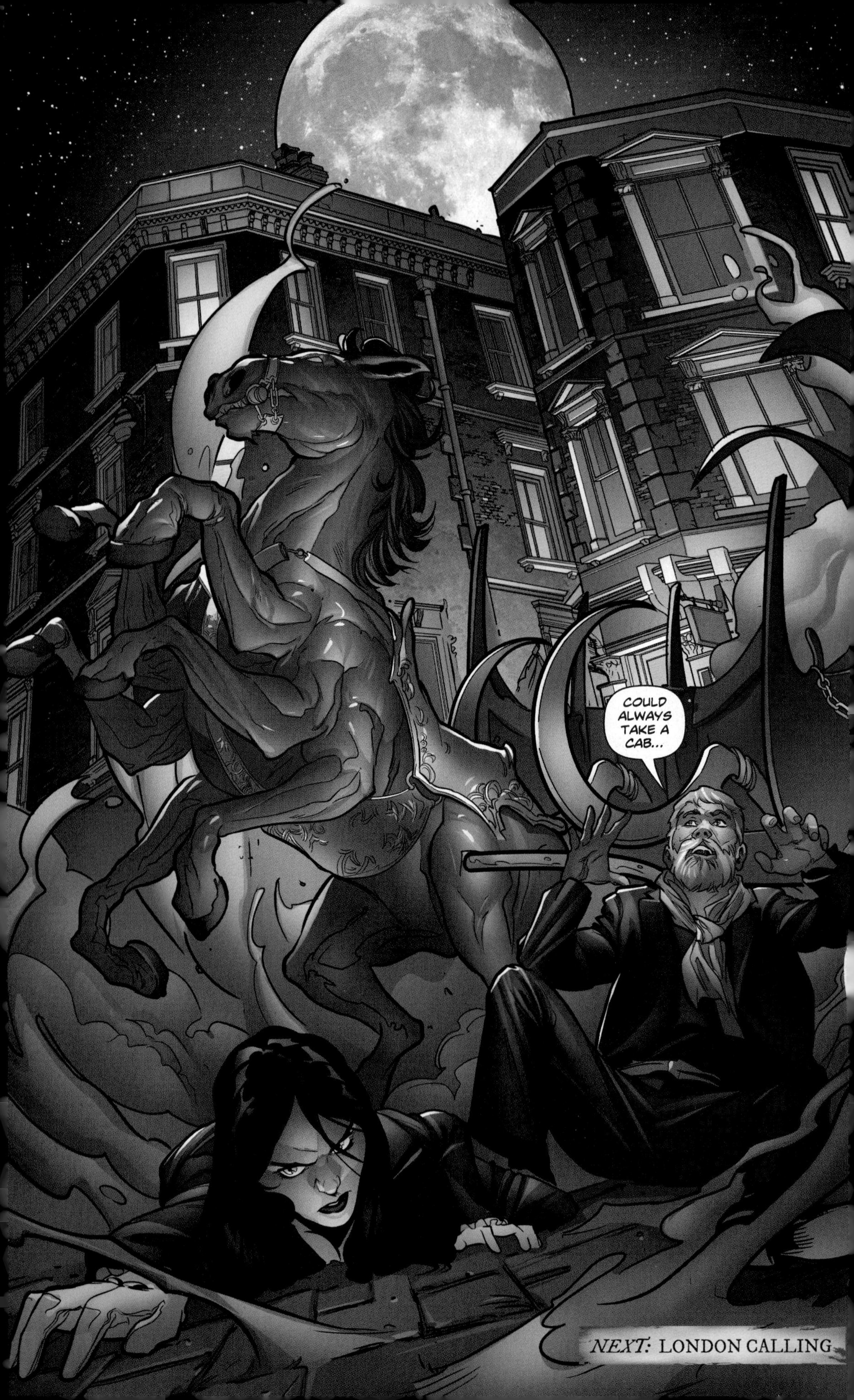
COULD ALWAYS TAKE A CAB...
NEXT: LONDON CALLING

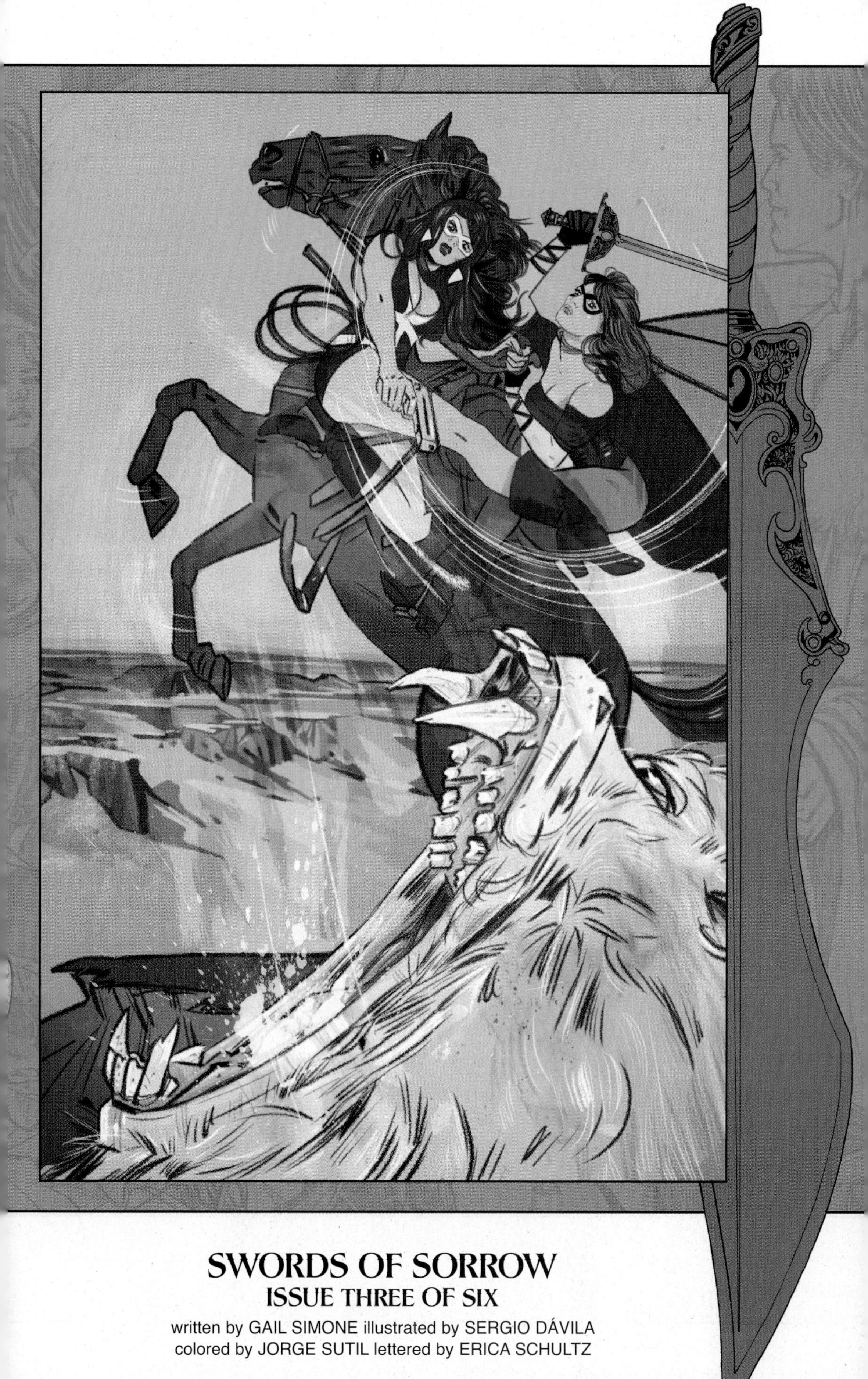

SWORDS OF SORROW
ISSUE THREE OF SIX

written by GAIL SIMONE illustrated by SERGIO DÁVILA
colored by JORGE SUTIL lettered by ERICA SCHULTZ

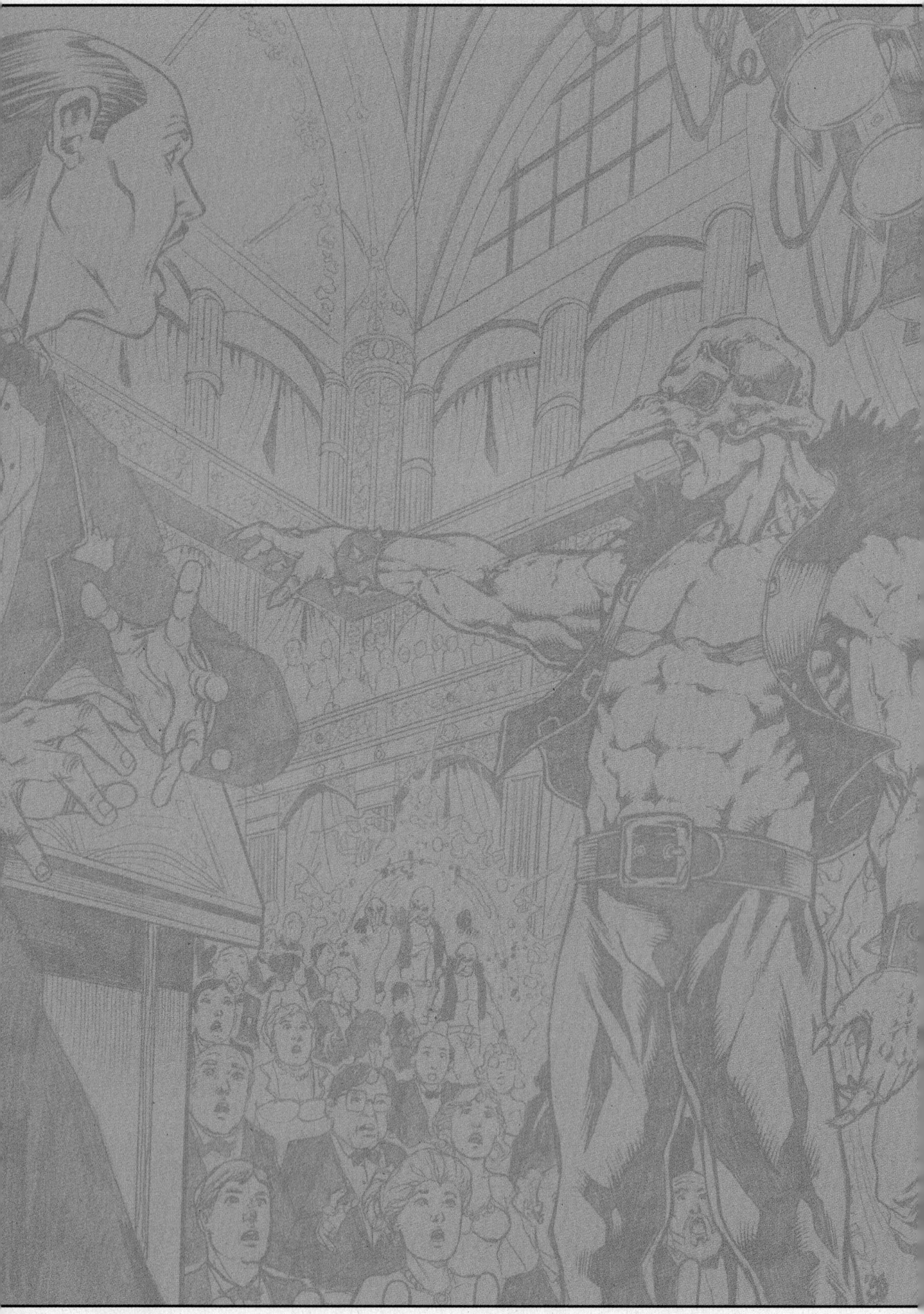

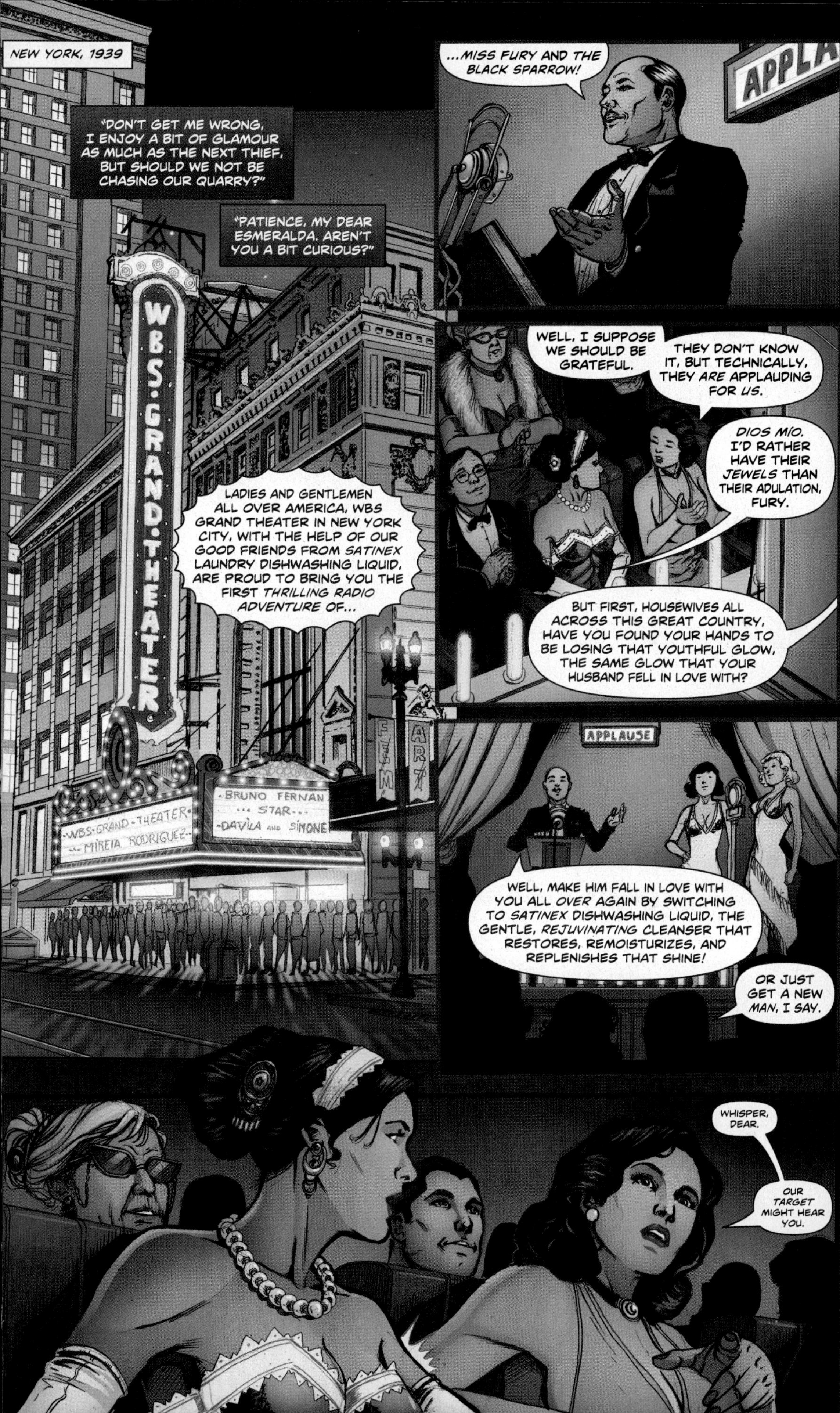
NEW YORK, 1939
"DON'T GET ME WRONG, I ENJOY A BIT OF GLAMOUR AS MUCH AS THE NEXT THIEF, BUT SHOULD WE NOT BE CHASING OUR QUARRY?"
"PATIENCE, MY DEAR ESMERALDA. AREN'T YOU A BIT CURIOUS?"
W.B.S. GRAND THEATER
WBS GRAND THEATER
MIREIA RODRIGUEZ
BRUNO FERNAN
STAR
DAVILA AND SIMONE
LADIES AND GENTLEMEN ALL OVER AMERICA, WBS GRAND THEATER IN NEW YORK CITY, WITH THE HELP OF OUR GOOD FRIENDS FROM *SATINEX* LAUNDRY DISHWASHING LIQUID, ARE PROUD TO BRING YOU THE FIRST *THRILLING RADIO ADVENTURE* OF...
...MISS FURY AND THE BLACK SPARROW!
APPLA
WELL, I SUPPOSE WE SHOULD BE GRATEFUL.
THEY DON'T KNOW IT, BUT TECHNICALLY, THEY *ARE* APPLAUDING FOR *US*.
DIOS MIO. I'D RATHER HAVE THEIR *JEWELS* THAN THEIR ADULATION, FURY.
BUT FIRST, HOUSEWIVES ALL ACROSS THIS GREAT COUNTRY, HAVE YOU FOUND YOUR HANDS TO BE LOSING THAT YOUTHFUL GLOW, THE SAME GLOW THAT YOUR HUSBAND FELL IN LOVE WITH?
APPLAUSE
WELL, MAKE HIM FALL IN LOVE WITH YOU ALL *OVER* AGAIN BY SWITCHING TO *SATINEX* DISHWASHING LIQUID, THE GENTLE, *REJUVINATING* CLEANSER THAT RESTORES, REMOISTURIZES, AND REPLENISHES THAT SHINE!
OR JUST GET A NEW *MAN*, I SAY.
WHISPER, DEAR.
OUR TARGET MIGHT HEAR YOU.

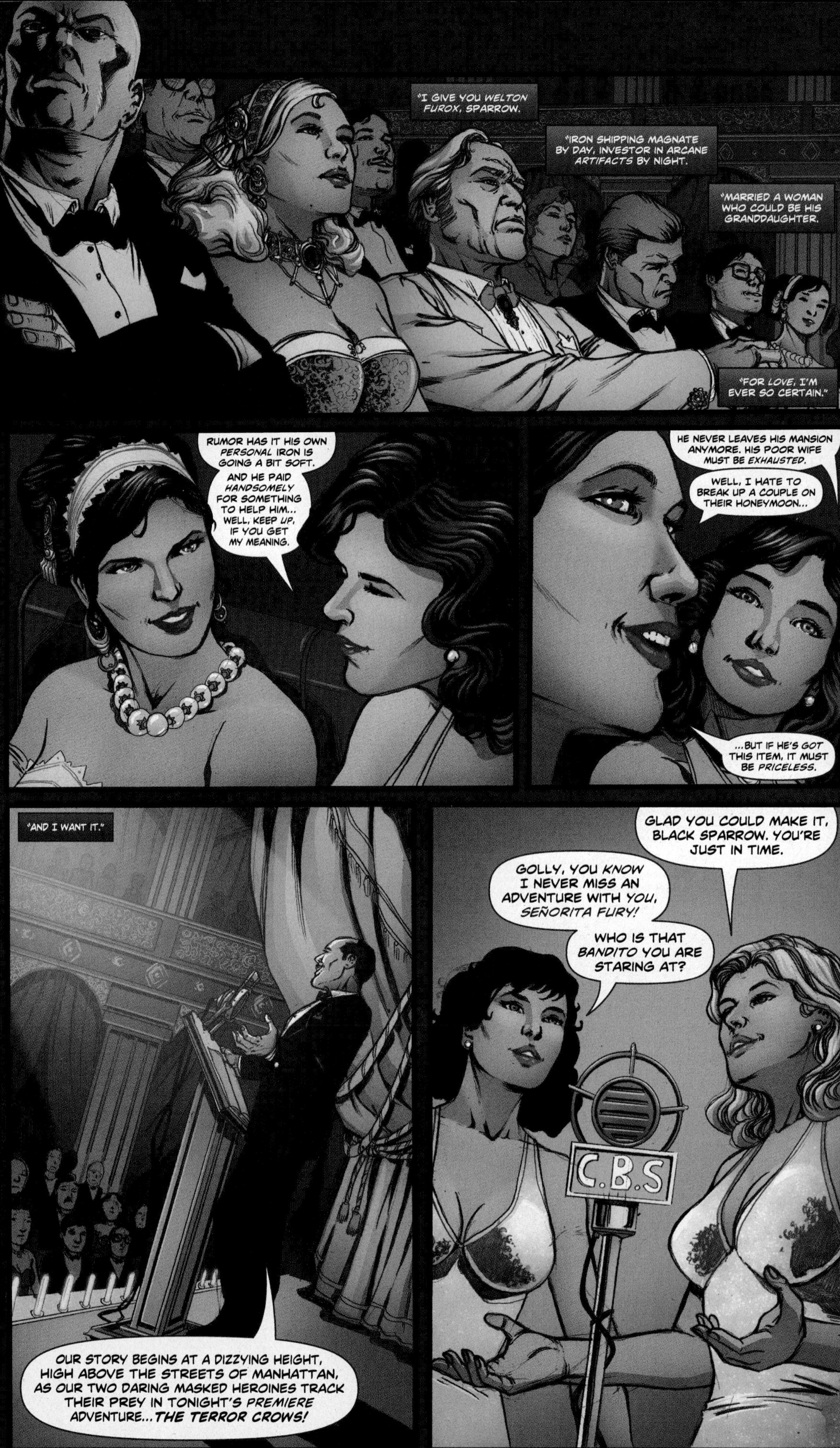

"I GIVE YOU WELTON FUROX, SPARROW.
"IRON SHIPPING MAGNATE BY DAY, INVESTOR IN ARCANE ARTIFACTS BY NIGHT.
"MARRIED A WOMAN WHO COULD BE HIS GRANDDAUGHTER.
"FOR LOVE, I'M EVER SO CERTAIN."
RUMOR HAS IT HIS OWN PERSONAL IRON IS GOING A BIT SOFT.
AND HE PAID HANDSOMELY FOR SOMETHING TO HELP HIM... WELL, KEEP UP, IF YOU GET MY MEANING.
HE NEVER LEAVES HIS MANSION ANYMORE. HIS POOR WIFE MUST BE EXHAUSTED.
WELL, I HATE TO BREAK UP A COUPLE ON THEIR HONEYMOON...
...BUT IF HE'S GOT THIS ITEM, IT MUST BE PRICELESS.
"AND I WANT IT."
OUR STORY BEGINS AT A DIZZYING HEIGHT, HIGH ABOVE THE STREETS OF MANHATTAN, AS OUR TWO DARING MASKED HEROINES TRACK THEIR PREY IN TONIGHT'S PREMIERE ADVENTURE...THE TERROR CROWS!
GLAD YOU COULD MAKE IT, BLACK SPARROW. YOU'RE JUST IN TIME.
GOLLY, YOU KNOW I NEVER MISS AN ADVENTURE WITH YOU, SEÑORITA FURY!
WHO IS THAT BANDITO YOU ARE STARING AT?
C.B.S

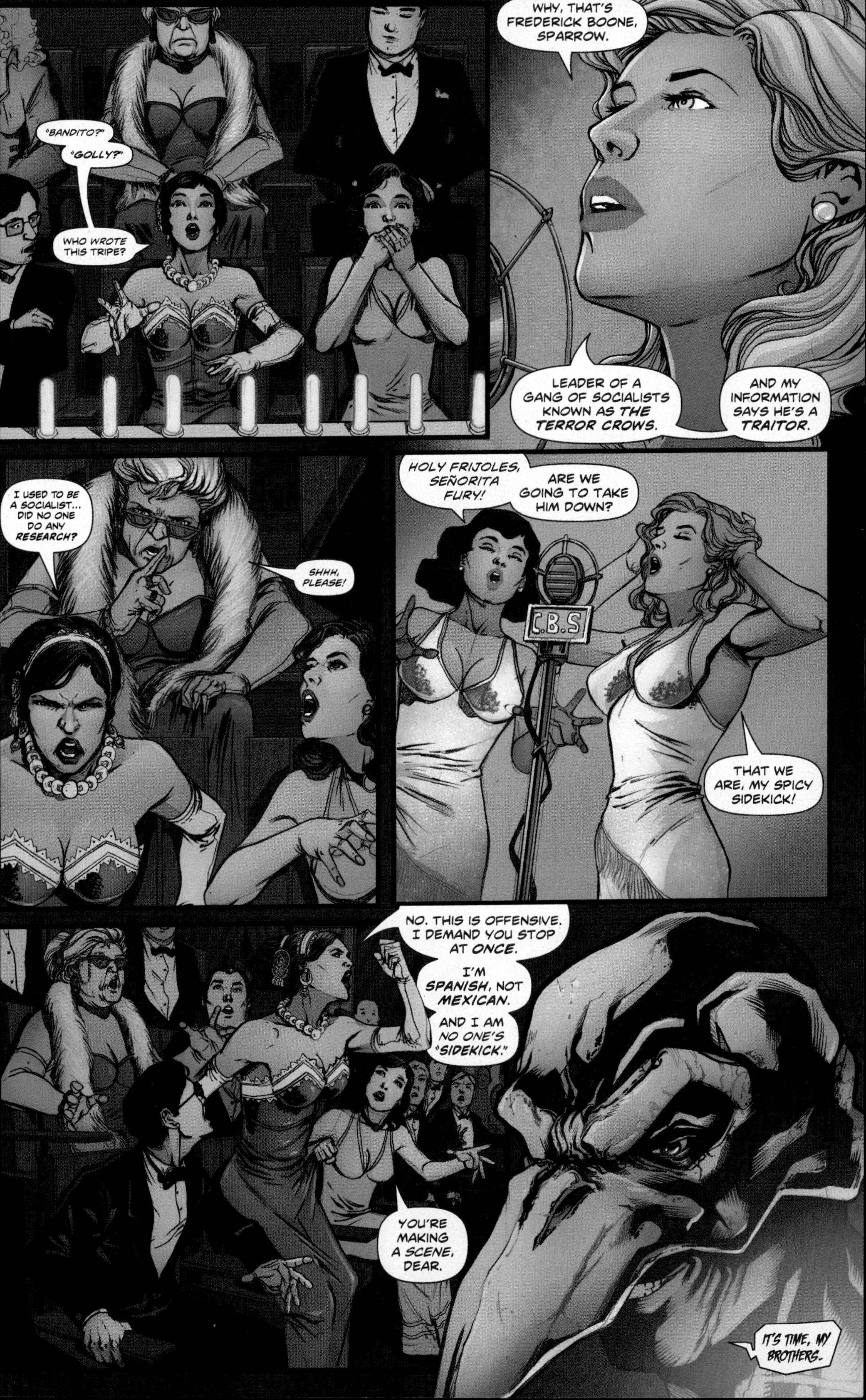
"BANDITO?"
"GOLLY?"
WHO WROTE THIS TRIPE?
WHY, THAT'S FREDERICK BOONE, SPARROW.
LEADER OF A GANG OF SOCIALISTS KNOWN AS THE TERROR CROWS.
AND MY INFORMATION SAYS HE'S A TRAITOR.
I USED TO BE A SOCIALIST... DID NO ONE DO ANY RESEARCH?
SHHH, PLEASE!
HOLY FRIJOLES, SEÑORITA FURY!
ARE WE GOING TO TAKE HIM DOWN?
C.B.S
THAT WE ARE, MY SPICY SIDEKICK!
NO. THIS IS OFFENSIVE. I DEMAND YOU STOP AT ONCE.
I'M SPANISH, NOT MEXICAN.
AND I AM NO ONE'S "SIDEKICK."
YOU'RE MAKING A SCENE, DEAR.
IT'S TIME, MY BROTHERS.

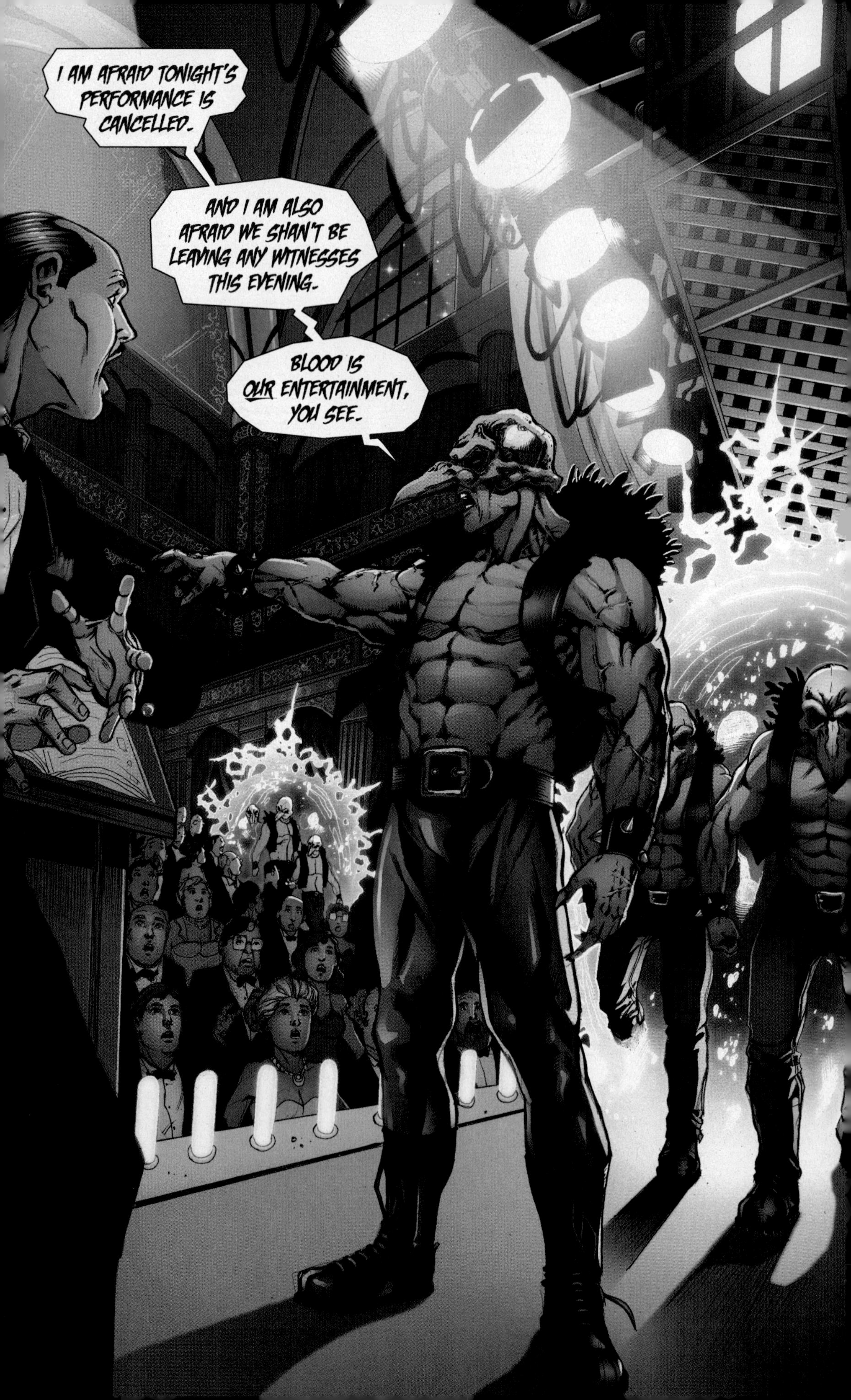
I AM AFRAID TONIGHT'S PERFORMANCE IS CANCELLED.
AND I AM ALSO AFRAID WE SHAN'T BE LEAVING ANY WITNESSES THIS EVENING.
BLOOD IS OUR ENTERTAINMENT, YOU SEE.

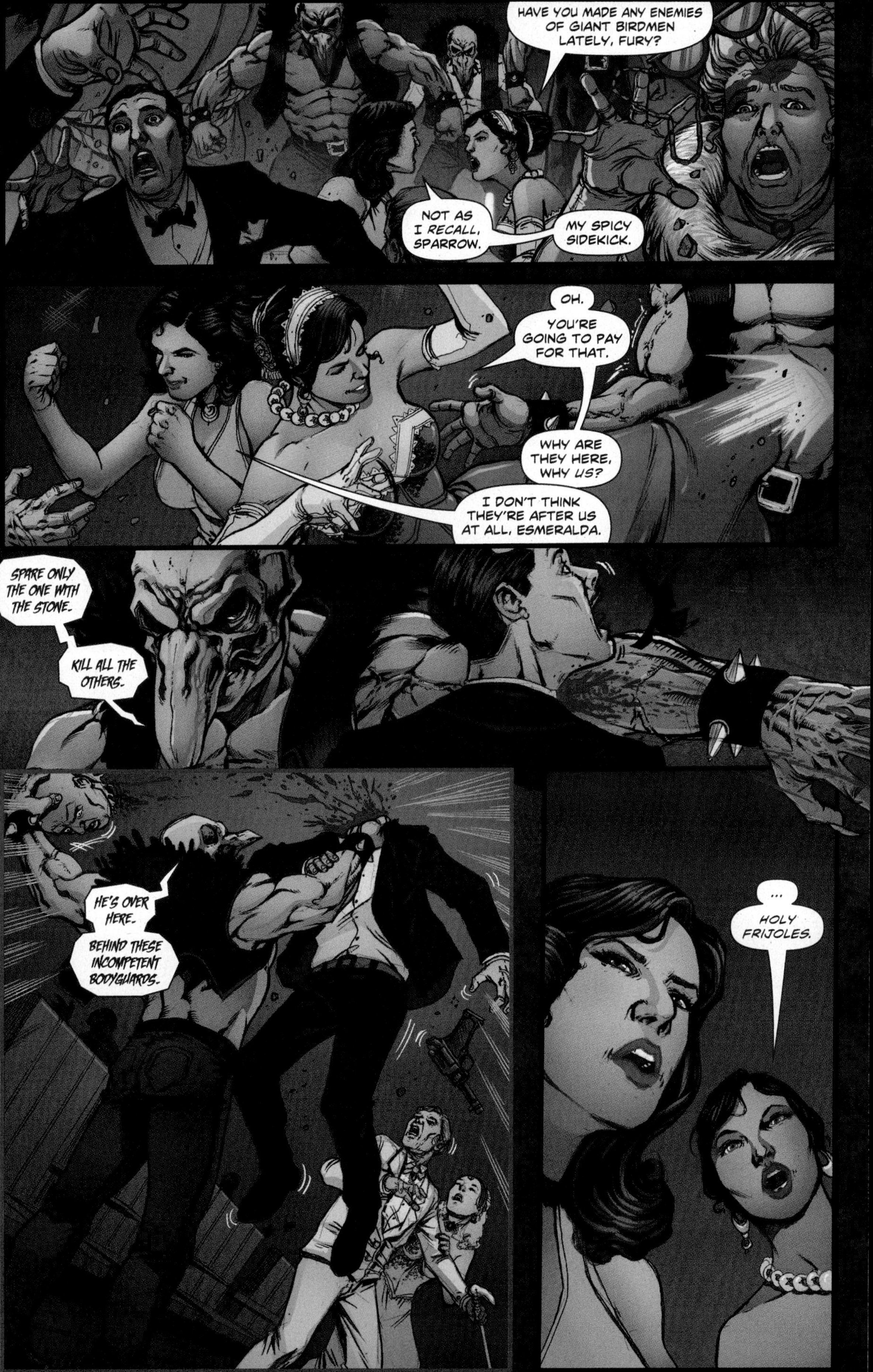
HAVE YOU MADE ANY ENEMIES OF GIANT BIRDMEN LATELY, FURY?
NOT AS I RECALL, SPARROW.
MY SPICY SIDEKICK.
OH.
YOU'RE GOING TO PAY FOR THAT.
WHY ARE THEY HERE, WHY US?
I DON'T THINK THEY'RE AFTER US AT ALL, ESMERALDA.
SPARE ONLY THE ONE WITH THE STONE.
KILL ALL THE OTHERS.
HE'S OVER HERE.
BEHIND THESE INCOMPETENT BODYGUARDS.
... HOLY FRIJOLES.

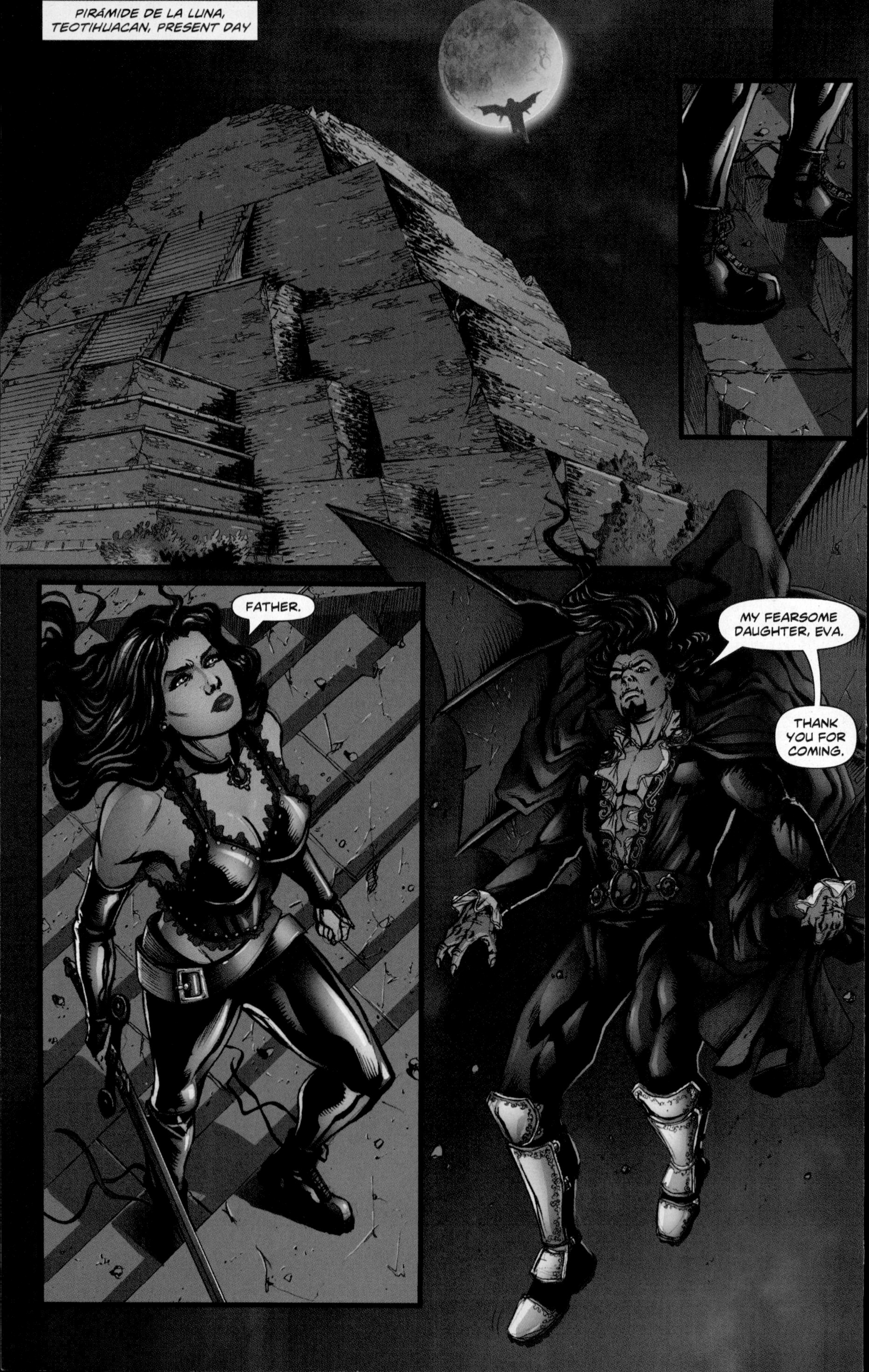
PIRÁMIDE DE LA LUNA, TEOTIHUACAN, PRESENT DAY
FATHER.
MY FEARSOME DAUGHTER, EVA.
THANK YOU FOR COMING.

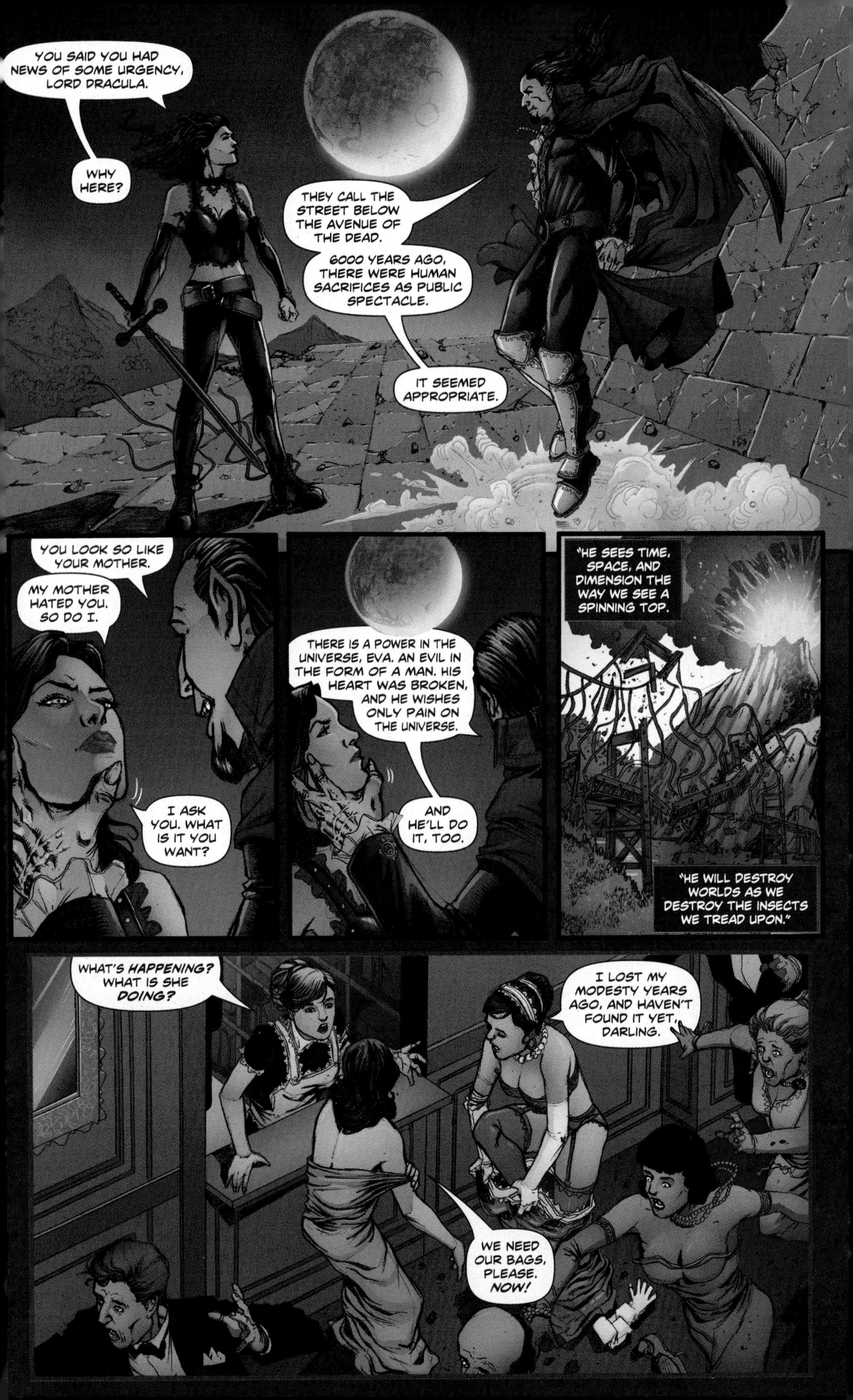

YOU SAID YOU HAD NEWS OF SOME URGENCY, LORD DRACULA.
WHY HERE?
THEY CALL THE STREET BELOW THE AVENUE OF THE DEAD.
6000 YEARS AGO, THERE WERE HUMAN SACRIFICES AS PUBLIC SPECTACLE.
IT SEEMED APPROPRIATE.
YOU LOOK SO LIKE YOUR MOTHER.
MY MOTHER HATED YOU. SO DO I.
I ASK YOU. WHAT IS IT YOU WANT?
THERE IS A POWER IN THE UNIVERSE, EVA. AN EVIL IN THE FORM OF A MAN. HIS HEART WAS BROKEN, AND HE WISHES ONLY PAIN ON THE UNIVERSE.
AND HE'LL DO IT, TOO.
"HE SEES TIME, SPACE, AND DIMENSION THE WAY WE SEE A SPINNING TOP.
"HE WILL DESTROY WORLDS AS WE DESTROY THE INSECTS WE TREAD UPON."
WHAT'S *HAPPENING*? WHAT IS SHE *DOING*?
I LOST MY MODESTY YEARS AGO, AND HAVEN'T FOUND IT YET, DARLING.
WE NEED OUR BAGS, PLEASE. *NOW!*

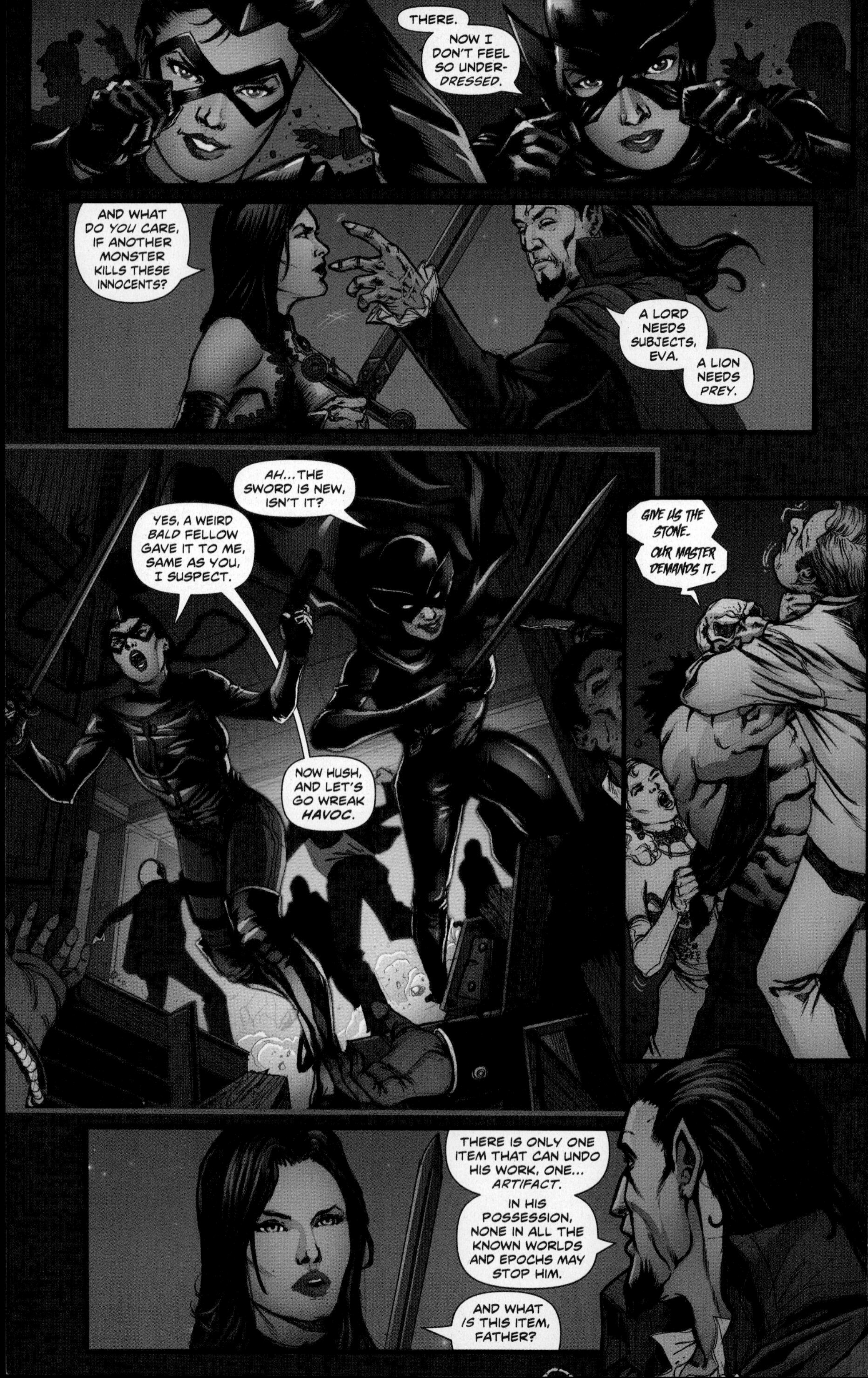
THERE.
NOW I DON'T FEEL SO UNDER-DRESSED.
AND WHAT DO YOU CARE, IF ANOTHER MONSTER KILLS THESE INNOCENTS?
A LORD NEEDS SUBJECTS, EVA.
A LION NEEDS PREY.
AH...THE SWORD IS NEW, ISN'T IT?
YES, A WEIRD BALD FELLOW GAVE IT TO ME, SAME AS YOU, I SUSPECT.
NOW HUSH, AND LET'S GO WREAK HAVOC.
GIVE US THE STONE.
OUR MASTER DEMANDS IT.
THERE IS ONLY ONE ITEM THAT CAN UNDO HIS WORK, ONE... ARTIFACT.
IN HIS POSSESSION, NONE IN ALL THE KNOWN WORLDS AND EPOCHS MAY STOP HIM.
AND WHAT IS THIS ITEM, FATHER?

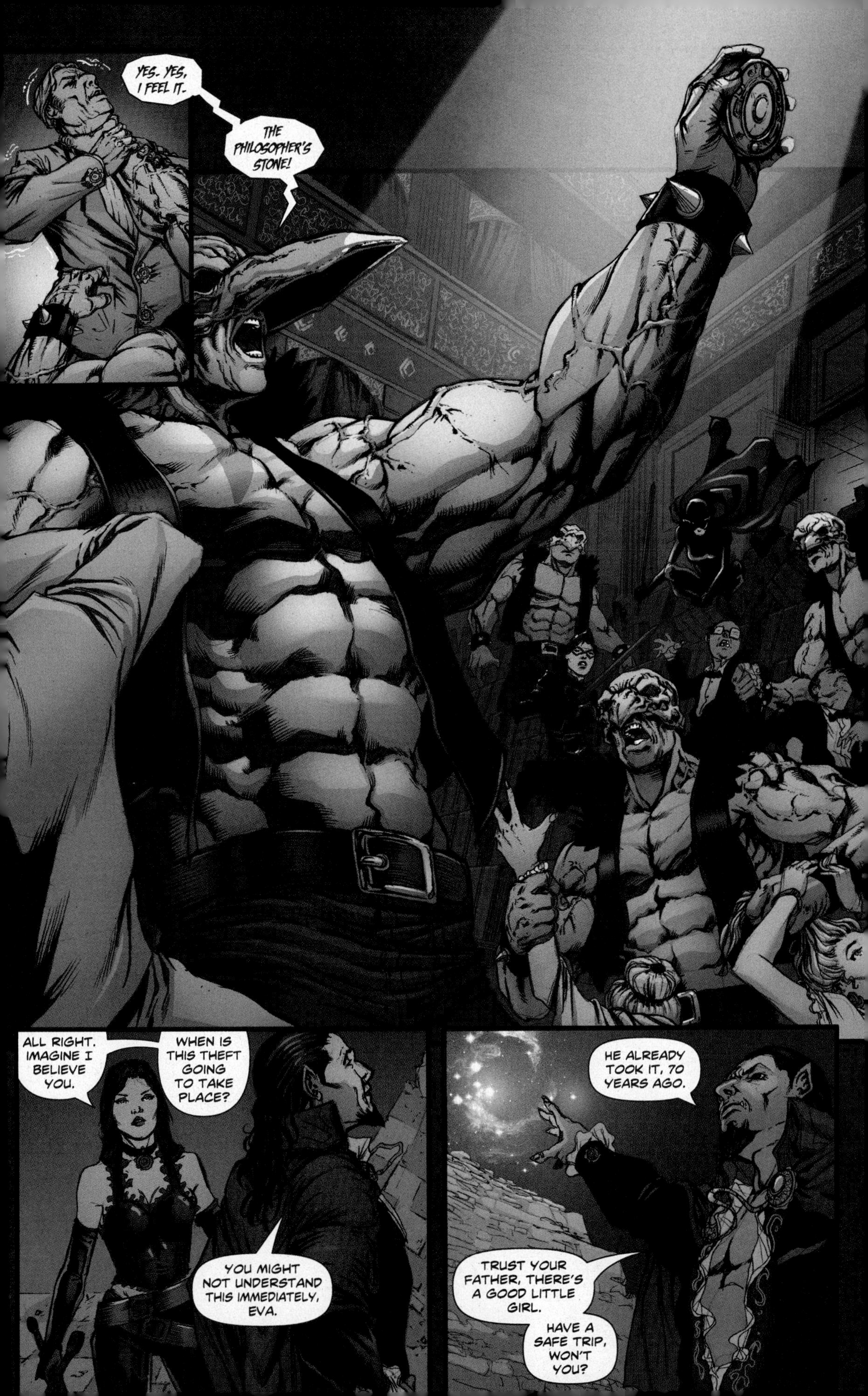
YES. YES, I FEEL IT.
THE PHILOSOPHER'S STONE!
ALL RIGHT. IMAGINE I BELIEVE YOU.
WHEN IS THIS THEFT GOING TO TAKE PLACE?
YOU MIGHT NOT UNDERSTAND THIS IMMEDIATELY, EVA.
HE ALREADY TOOK IT, 70 YEARS AGO.
TRUST YOUR FATHER, THERE'S A GOOD LITTLE GIRL.
HAVE A SAFE TRIP, WON'T YOU?

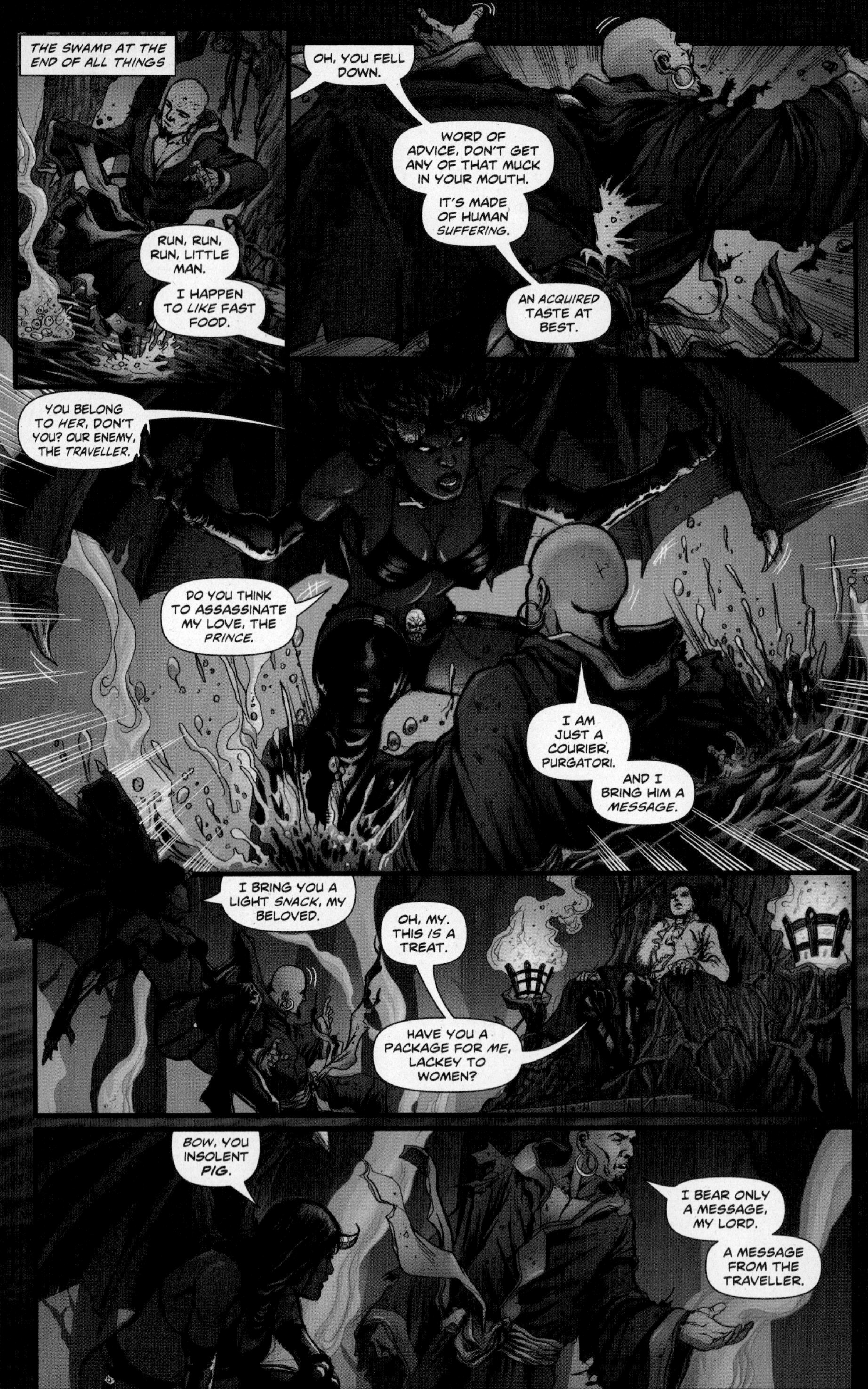
THE SWAMP AT THE END OF ALL THINGS
RUN, RUN, RUN, LITTLE MAN.
I HAPPEN TO LIKE FAST FOOD.
OH, YOU FELL DOWN.
WORD OF ADVICE, DON'T GET ANY OF THAT MUCK IN YOUR MOUTH.
IT'S MADE OF HUMAN SUFFERING.
AN ACQUIRED TASTE AT BEST.
YOU BELONG TO HER, DON'T YOU? OUR ENEMY, THE TRAVELLER.
DO YOU THINK TO ASSASSINATE MY LOVE, THE PRINCE.
I AM JUST A COURIER, PURGATORI.
AND I BRING HIM A MESSAGE.
I BRING YOU A LIGHT SNACK, MY BELOVED.
OH, MY. THIS IS A TREAT.
HAVE YOU A PACKAGE FOR ME, LACKEY TO WOMEN?
BOW, YOU INSOLENT PIG.
I BEAR ONLY A MESSAGE, MY LORD.
A MESSAGE FROM THE TRAVELLER.

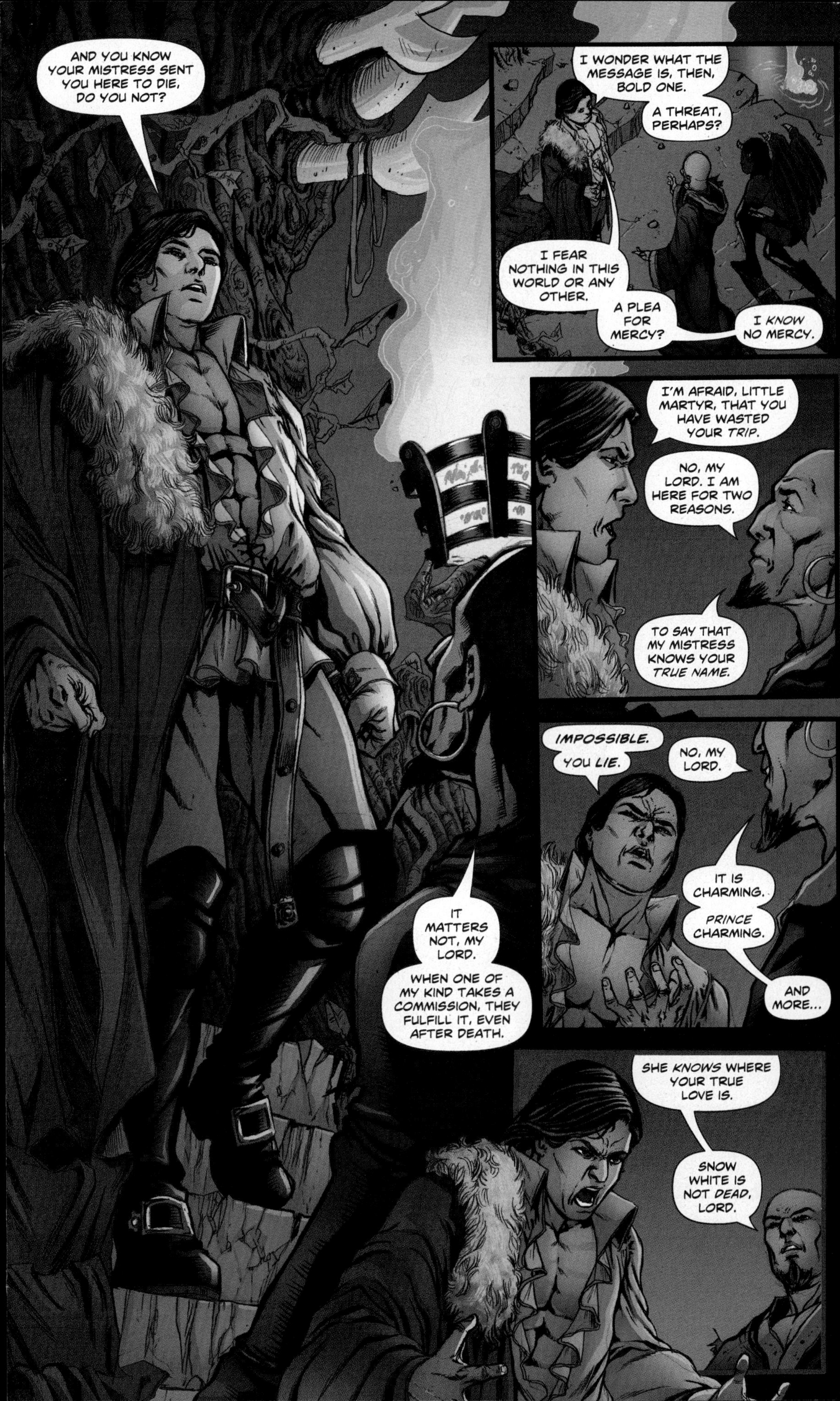
AND YOU KNOW YOUR MISTRESS SENT YOU HERE TO DIE, DO YOU NOT?
I WONDER WHAT THE MESSAGE IS, THEN, BOLD ONE.
A THREAT, PERHAPS?
I FEAR NOTHING IN THIS WORLD OR ANY OTHER.
A PLEA FOR MERCY?
I *KNOW* NO MERCY.
I'M AFRAID, LITTLE MARTYR, THAT YOU HAVE WASTED YOUR *TRIP*.
NO, MY LORD. I AM HERE FOR TWO REASONS.
TO SAY THAT MY MISTRESS KNOWS YOUR *TRUE NAME*.
IT MATTERS NOT, MY LORD.
WHEN ONE OF MY KIND TAKES A COMMISSION, THEY FULFILL IT, EVEN AFTER DEATH.
IMPOSSIBLE. YOU *LIE*.
NO, MY LORD.
IT IS CHARMING.
PRINCE CHARMING.
AND MORE...
SHE *KNOWS* WHERE YOUR TRUE LOVE IS.
SNOW WHITE IS NOT *DEAD*, LORD.

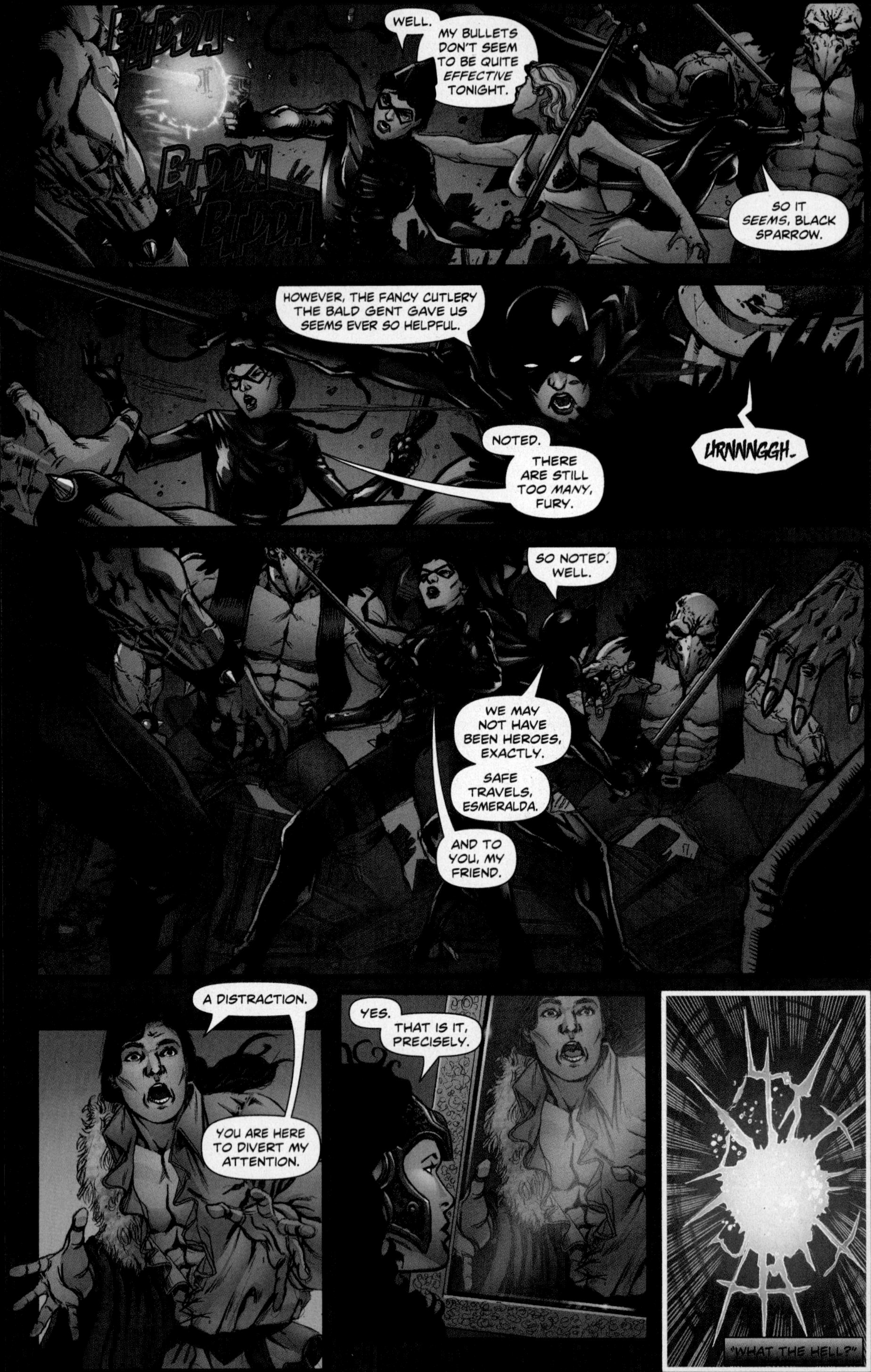
BUDDA
WELL.
MY BULLETS DON'T SEEM TO BE QUITE EFFECTIVE TONIGHT.
BUDDA BUDDA
SO IT SEEMS, BLACK SPARROW.
HOWEVER, THE FANCY CUTLERY THE BALD GENT GAVE US SEEMS EVER SO HELPFUL.
NOTED.
THERE ARE STILL TOO MANY, FURY.
URNNNGGH...
SO NOTED. WELL.
WE MAY NOT HAVE BEEN HEROES, EXACTLY.
SAFE TRAVELS, ESMERALDA.
AND TO YOU, MY FRIEND.
A DISTRACTION.
YOU ARE HERE TO DIVERT MY ATTENTION.
YES.
THAT IS IT, PRECISELY.
"WHAT THE HELL?"

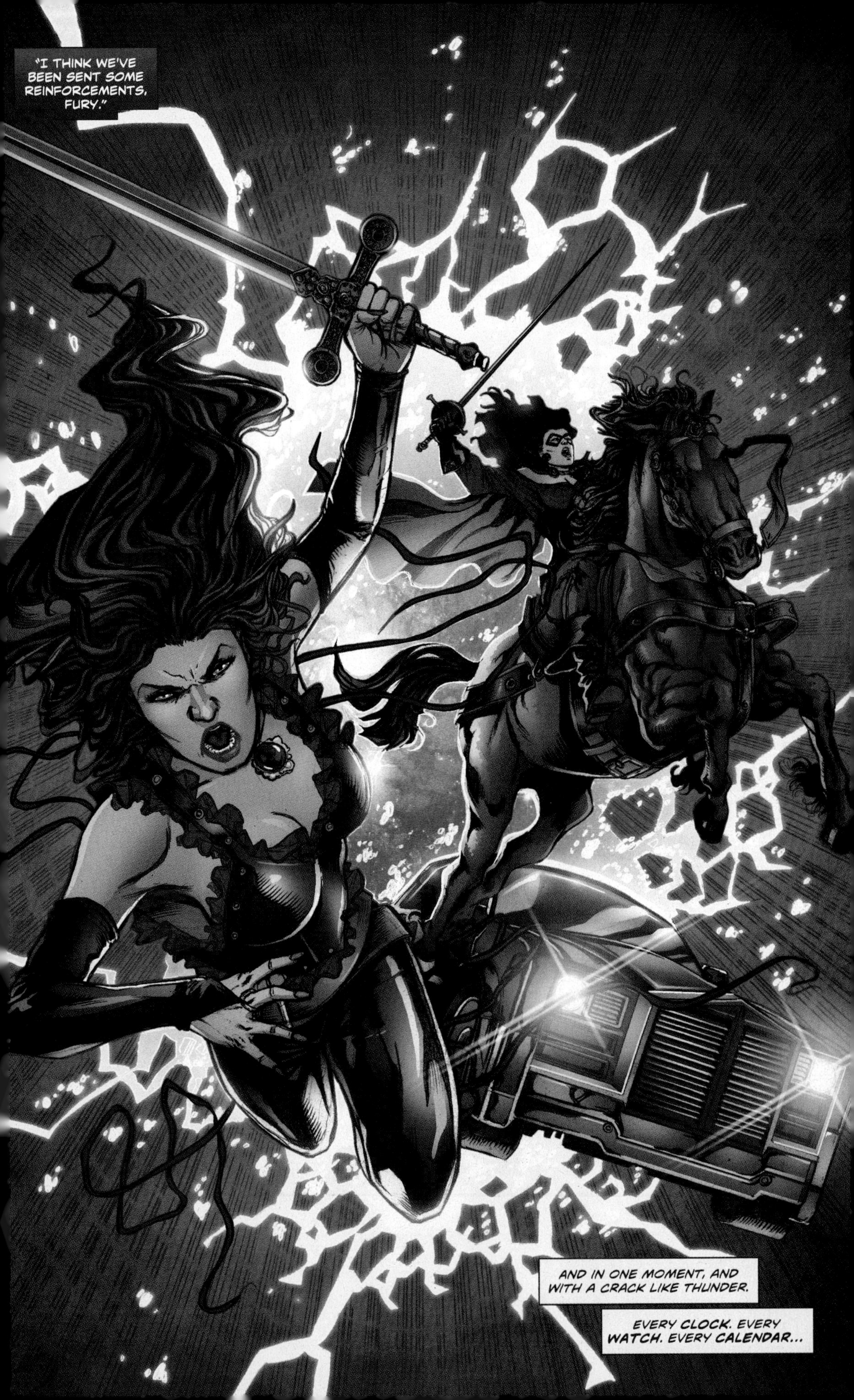
"I THINK WE'VE BEEN SENT SOME REINFORCEMENTS, FURY."
AND IN ONE MOMENT, AND WITH A CRACK LIKE THUNDER.
EVERY CLOCK. EVERY WATCH. EVERY CALENDAR...

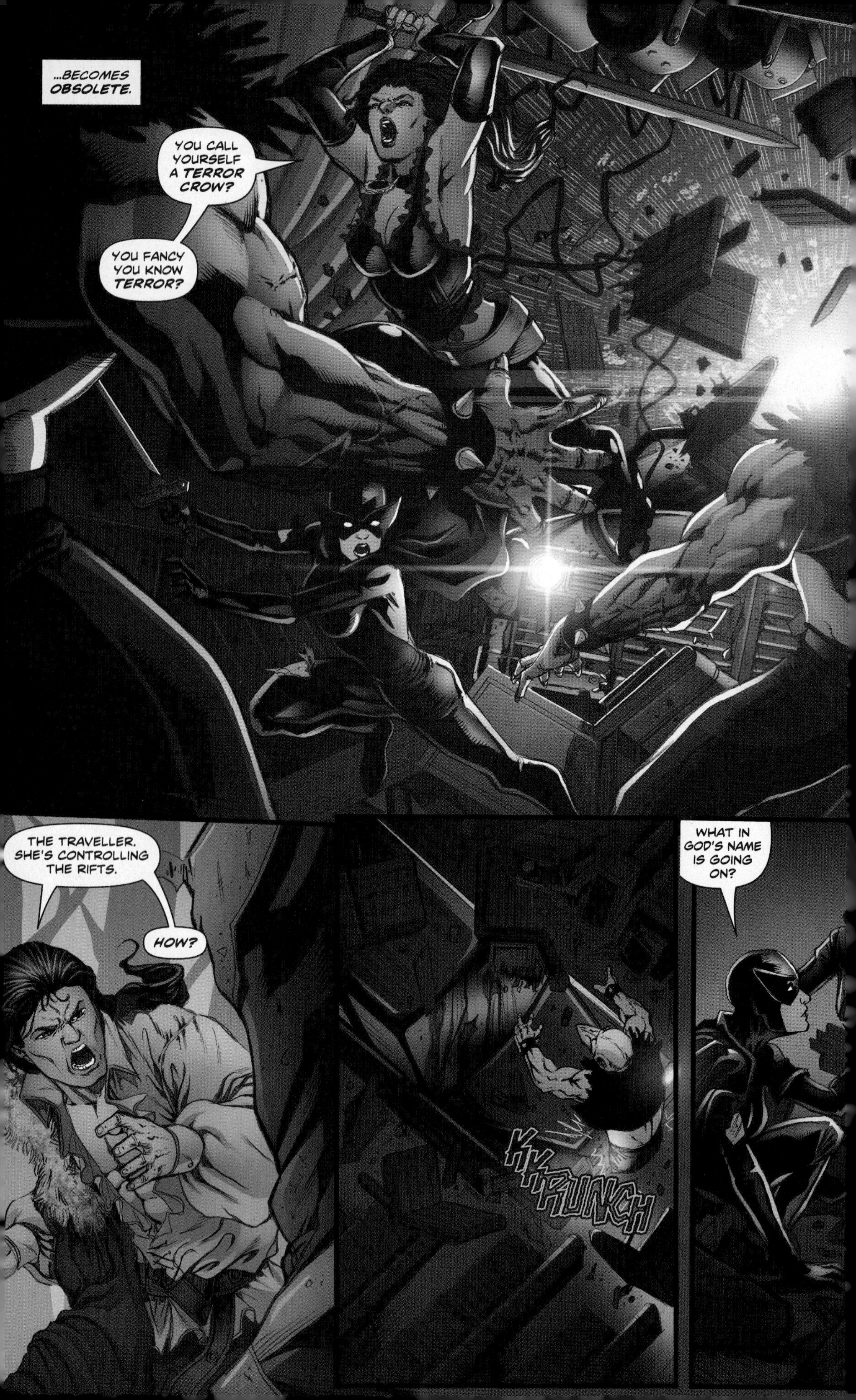
...BECOMES OBSOLETE.
YOU CALL YOURSELF A TERROR CROW?
YOU FANCY YOU KNOW TERROR?
THE TRAVELLER. SHE'S CONTROLLING THE RIFTS.
HOW?
KKRUNCH
WHAT IN GOD'S NAME IS GOING ON?

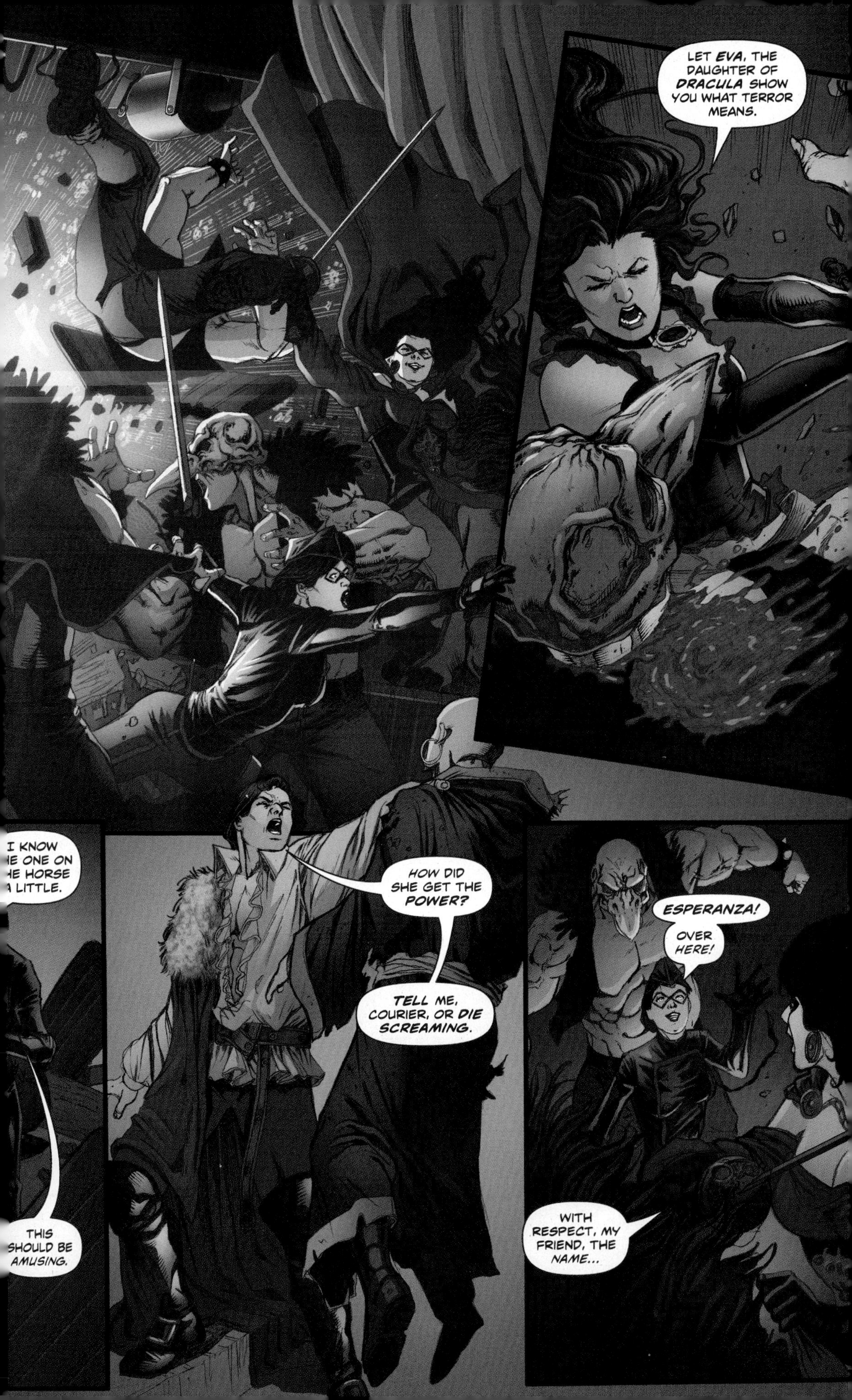
LET EVA, THE DAUGHTER OF DRACULA SHOW YOU WHAT TERROR MEANS.
I KNOW ...E ONE ON ...E HORSE ...A LITTLE.
THIS SHOULD BE AMUSING.
HOW DID SHE GET THE POWER?
TELL ME, COURIER, OR DIE SCREAMING.
ESPERANZA!
OVER HERE!
WITH RESPECT, MY FRIEND, THE NAME...

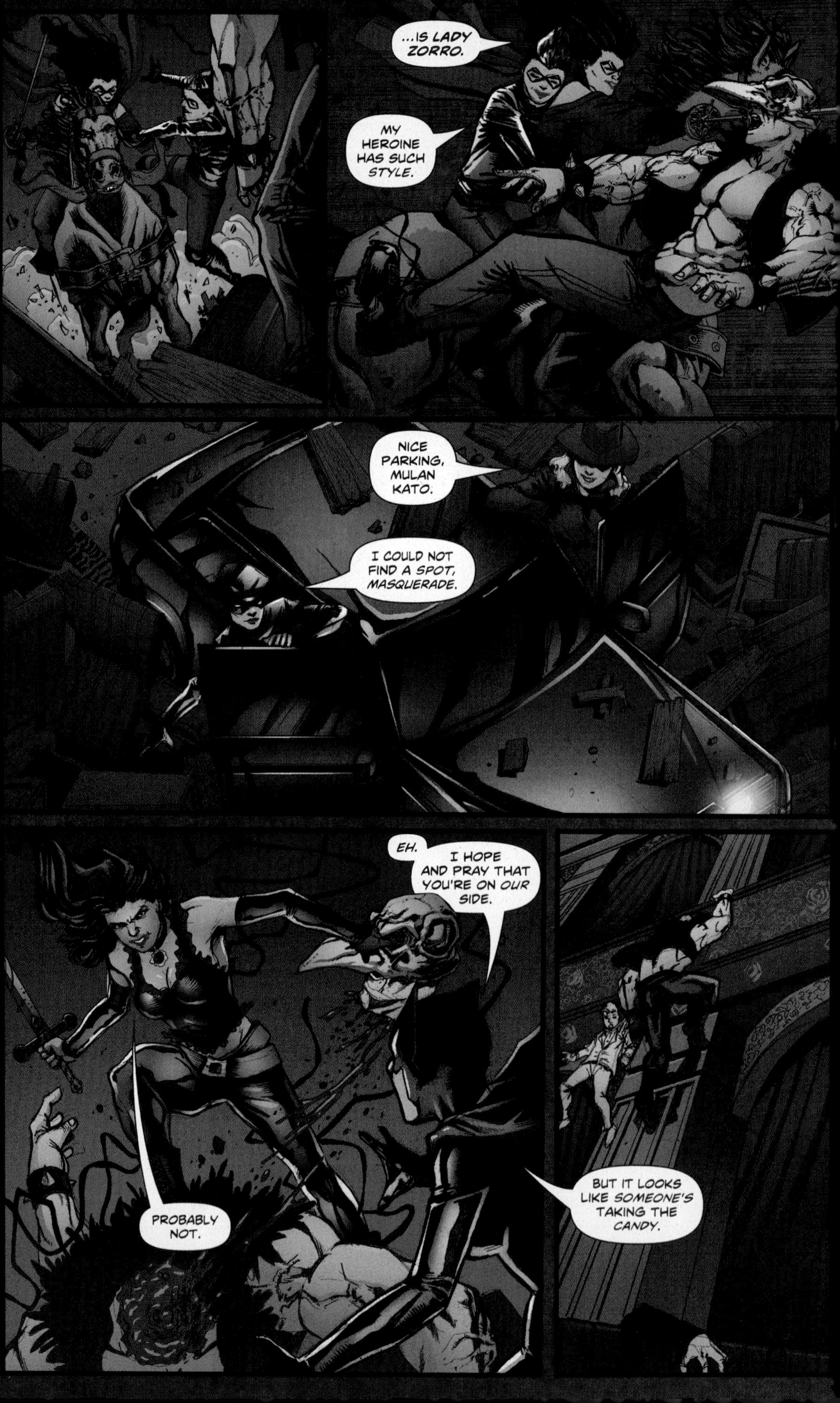
...IS LADY ZORRO.
MY HEROINE HAS SUCH STYLE.
NICE PARKING, MULAN KATO.
I COULD NOT FIND A SPOT, MASQUERADE.
EH.
I HOPE AND PRAY THAT YOU'RE ON OUR SIDE.
PROBABLY NOT.
BUT IT LOOKS LIKE SOMEONE'S TAKING THE CANDY.

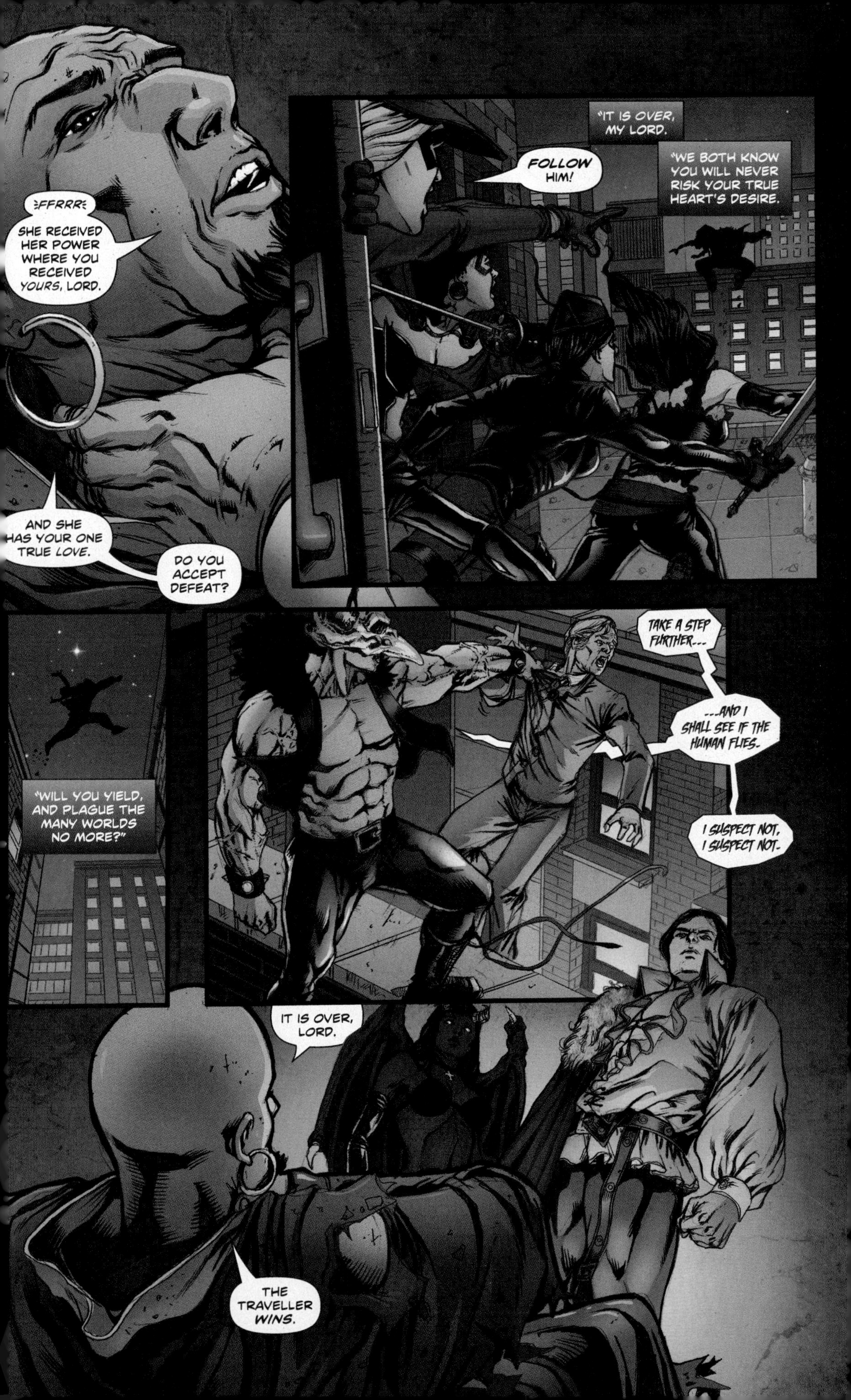
FFRRR
SHE RECEIVED HER POWER WHERE YOU RECEIVED YOURS, LORD.
"IT IS OVER, MY LORD.
FOLLOW HIM!
"WE BOTH KNOW YOU WILL NEVER RISK YOUR TRUE HEART'S DESIRE.
AND SHE HAS YOUR ONE TRUE LOVE.
DO YOU ACCEPT DEFEAT?
"WILL YOU YIELD, AND PLAGUE THE MANY WORLDS NO MORE?"
TAKE A STEP FURTHER---
---AND I SHALL SEE IF THE HUMAN FLIES.
I SUSPECT NOT, I SUSPECT NOT.
IT IS OVER, LORD.
THE TRAVELLER WINS.

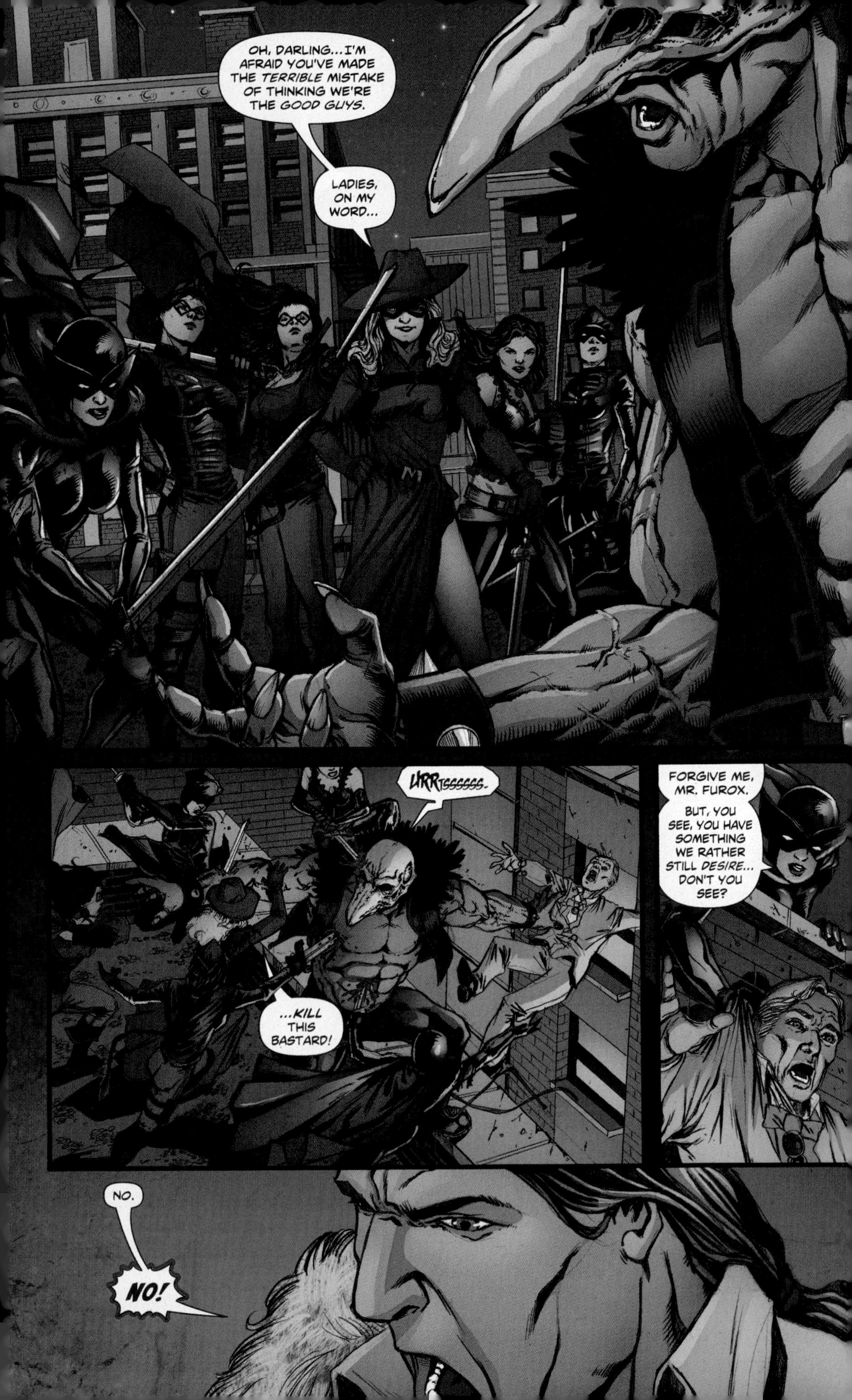
OH, DARLING... I'M AFRAID YOU'VE MADE THE TERRIBLE MISTAKE OF THINKING WE'RE THE GOOD GUYS.
LADIES, ON MY WORD...
URRTSSSSSS.
...KILL THIS BASTARD!
FORGIVE ME, MR. FUROX.
BUT, YOU SEE, YOU HAVE SOMETHING WE RATHER STILL DESIRE... DON'T YOU SEE?
NO.
NO!

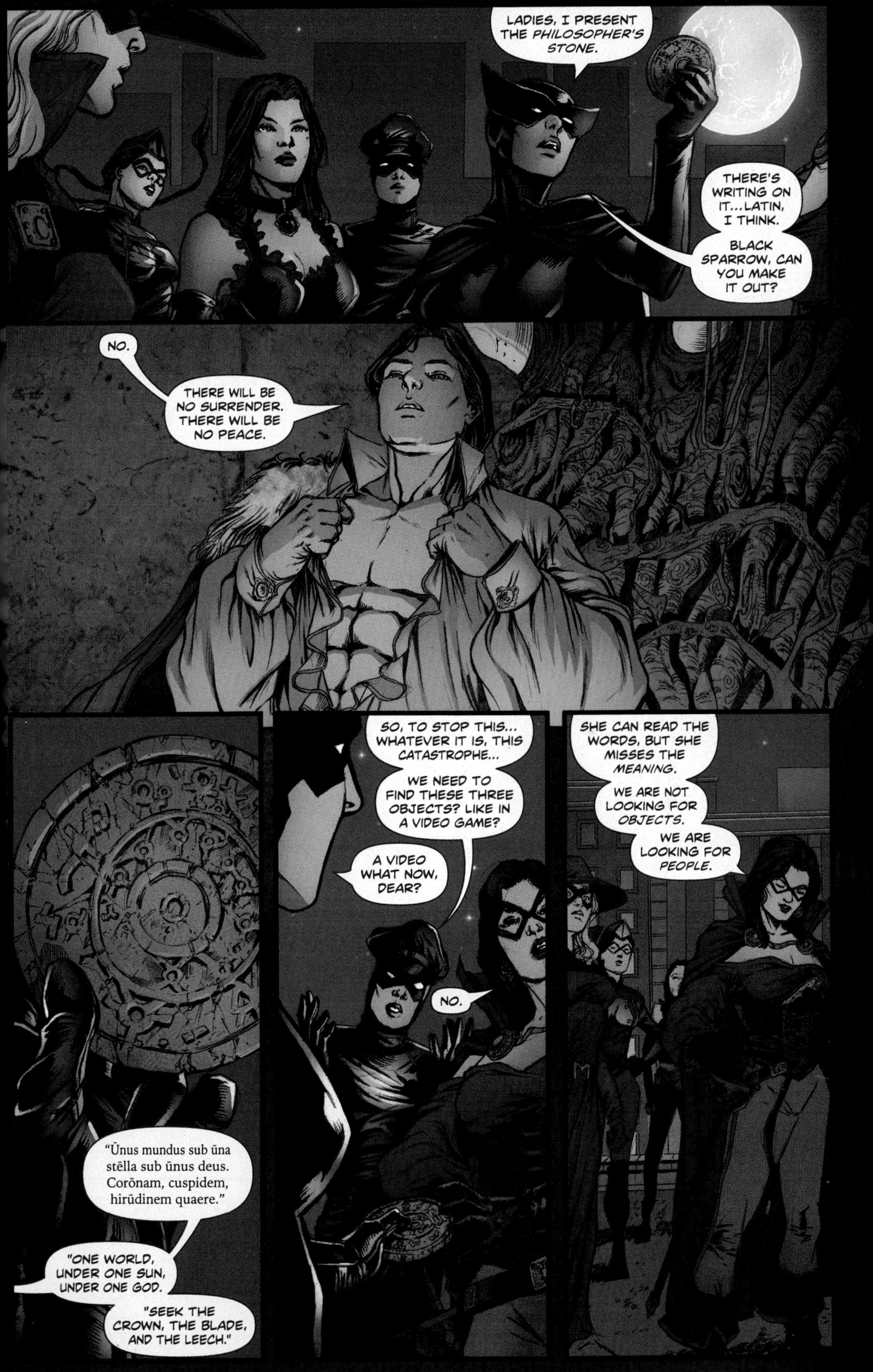
LADIES, I PRESENT THE *PHILOSOPHER'S* STONE.
THERE'S WRITING ON IT...LATIN, I THINK.
BLACK SPARROW, CAN YOU MAKE IT OUT?
NO.
THERE WILL BE NO SURRENDER. THERE WILL BE NO PEACE.
"Ūnus mundus sub ūna stēlla sub ūnus deus. Corōnam, cuspidem, hirūdinem quaere."
"ONE WORLD, UNDER ONE SUN, UNDER ONE GOD.
"SEEK THE CROWN, THE BLADE, AND THE LEECH."
SO, TO STOP THIS... WHATEVER IT IS, THIS CATASTROPHE...
WE NEED TO FIND THESE THREE OBJECTS? LIKE IN A VIDEO GAME?
A VIDEO WHAT NOW, DEAR?
NO.
SHE CAN READ THE WORDS, BUT SHE MISSES THE *MEANING*.
WE ARE NOT LOOKING FOR *OBJECTS*.
WE ARE LOOKING FOR *PEOPLE*.

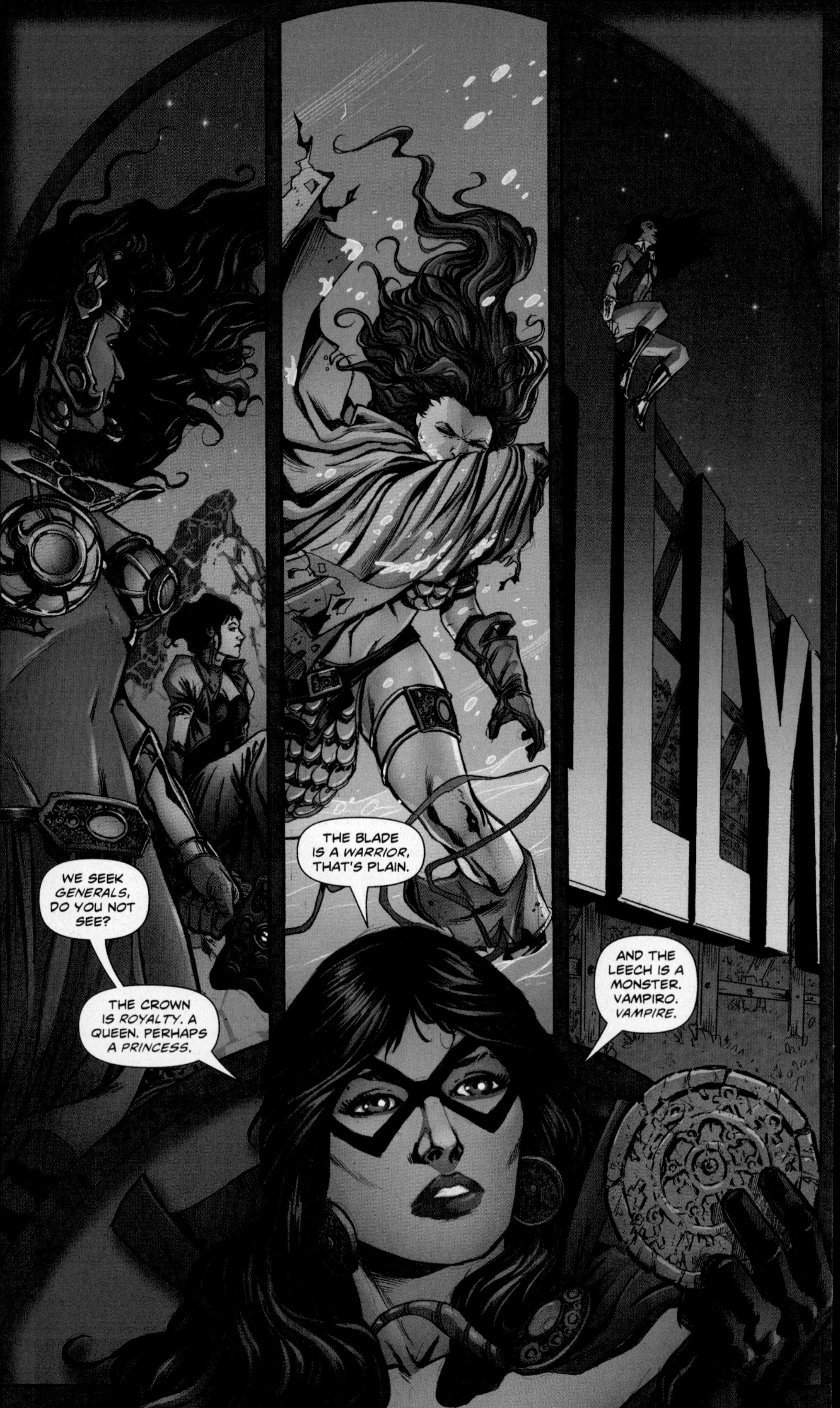

THE BLADE IS A WARRIOR, THAT'S PLAIN.
WE SEEK GENERALS, DO YOU NOT SEE?
THE CROWN IS ROYALTY. A QUEEN. PERHAPS A PRINCESS.
AND THE LEECH IS A MONSTER. VAMPIRO. VAMPIRE.

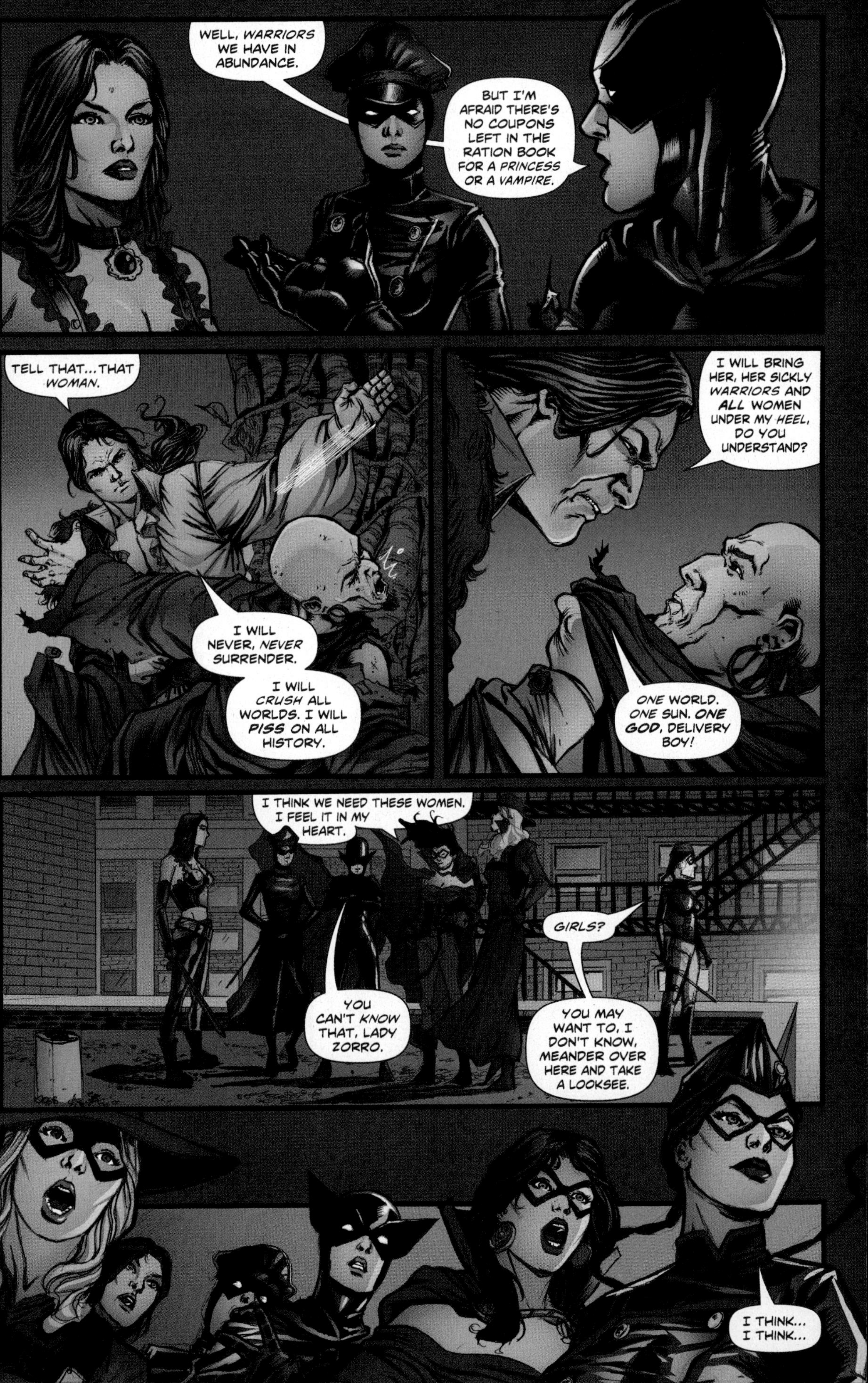
WELL, WARRIORS WE HAVE IN ABUNDANCE.
BUT I'M AFRAID THERE'S NO COUPONS LEFT IN THE RATION BOOK FOR A PRINCESS OR A VAMPIRE.
TELL THAT...THAT WOMAN.
I WILL NEVER, NEVER SURRENDER.
I WILL CRUSH ALL WORLDS. I WILL PISS ON ALL HISTORY.
I WILL BRING HER, HER SICKLY WARRIORS AND ALL WOMEN UNDER MY HEEL, DO YOU UNDERSTAND?
ONE WORLD. ONE SUN. ONE GOD, DELIVERY BOY!
I THINK WE NEED THESE WOMEN. I FEEL IT IN MY HEART.
YOU CAN'T KNOW THAT, LADY ZORRO.
GIRLS?
YOU MAY WANT TO, I DON'T KNOW, MEANDER OVER HERE AND TAKE A LOOKSEE.
I THINK... I THINK...

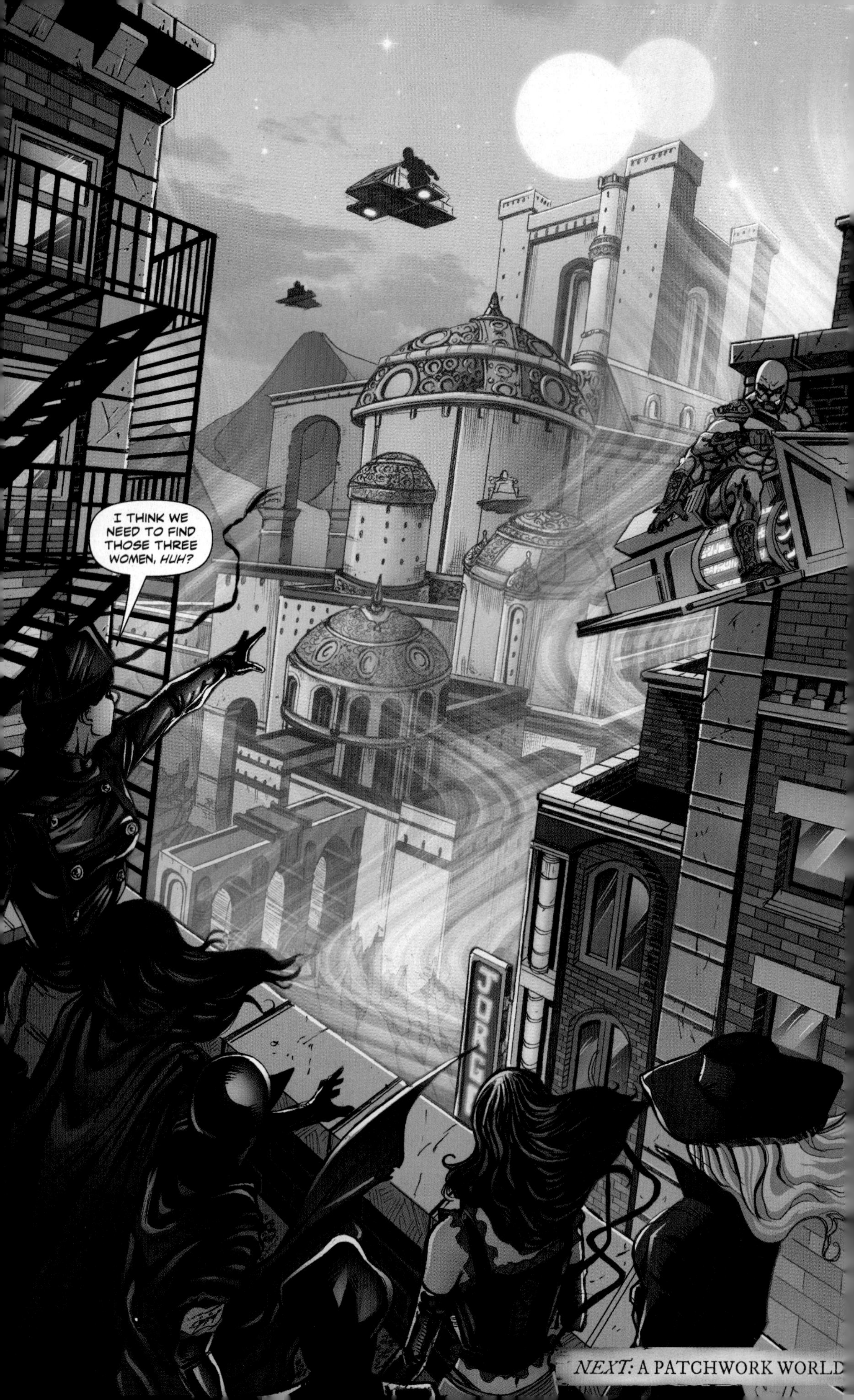
I THINK WE NEED TO FIND THOSE THREE WOMEN, *HUH?*
NEXT: A PATCHWORK WORLD

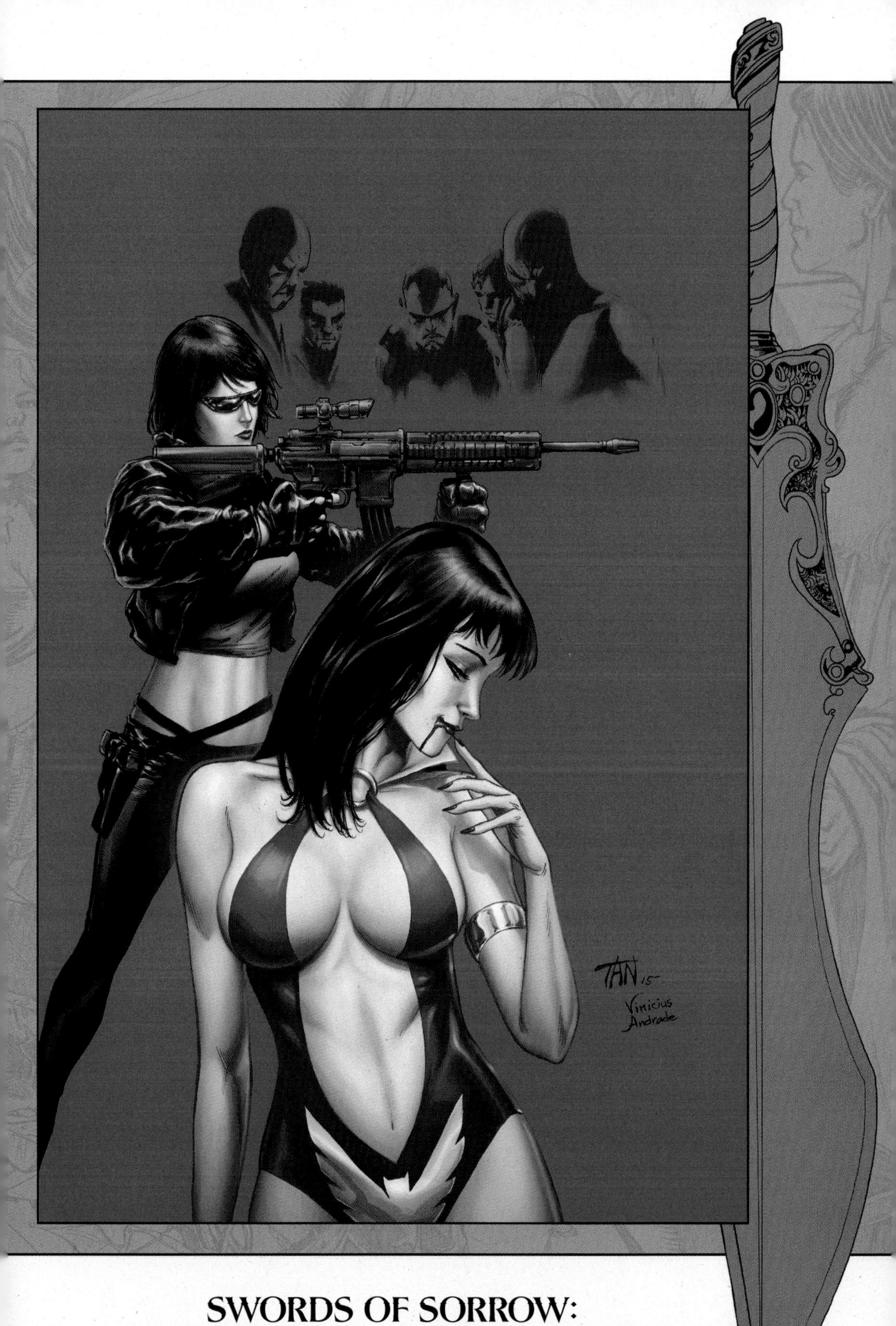
TAN 15
Vinicius Andrade

SWORDS OF SORROW: VAMPIRELLA & JENNIFER BLOOD

ISSUE THREE OF FOUR

written by NANCY A. COLLINS illustrated by DAVE ACOSTA
colored by VALENTINA PINTO lettered by ERICA SCHULTZ

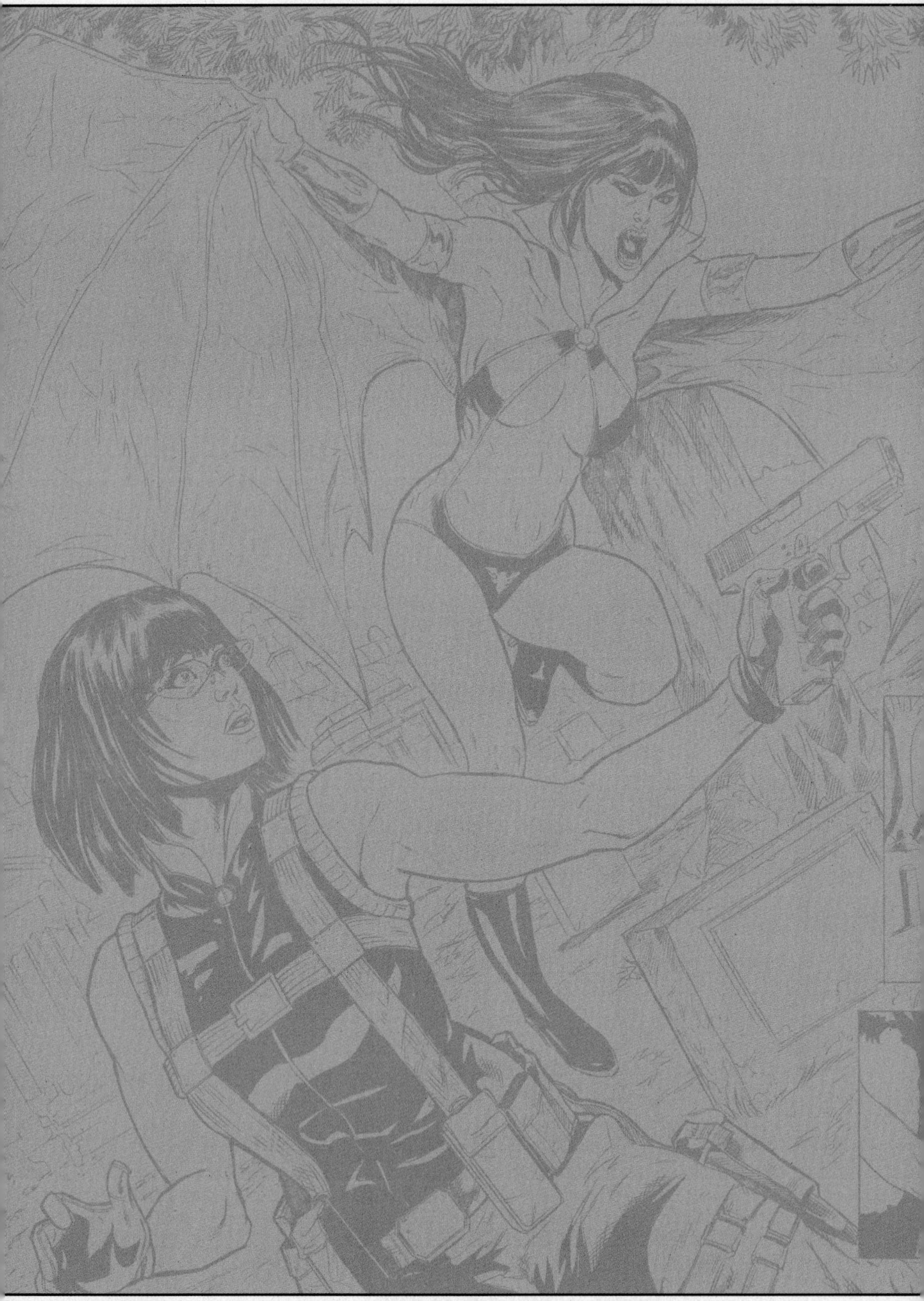

'HOLLYWOOD LAWNS', MY ASS. THIS BONEYARD IS NOWHERE NEAR TINSELTOWN.

HOLLYWOOD LAWNS CEMETERY

BUT IT IS CLOSE TO LOS MUERTOS TURF. WHICH MEANS THERE'S A DAMN GOOD CHANCE THAT WACK JOB, VAMPIRETTA, OR WHATEVER SHE CALLS HERSELF, MIGHT BE INSIDE.

THE FIRST TIME WE CROSSED PATHS WAS WHEN I WAS HUNTING THE ANAHEIM RIPPER. THE CREEP GOT THE DROP ON ME—UNTIL SHE SHOWED UP OUT OF NOWHERE AND RIPPED OUT HIS THROAT WITH HER TEETH.

THAT'S PRETTY FREAKIN' HARDCORE, EVEN FOR ME.

THEN SHE STARTED GOING ON ABOUT DEMONS AND ANCIENT INDIAN CURSES AND BEING FROM A DIFFERENT WORLD. IT WAS OBVIOUS THE GIRL'S ELEVATOR DIDN'T GO ALL THE WAY TO THE TOP...

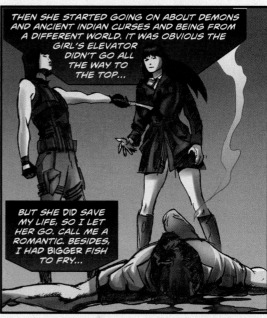

BUT SHE DID SAVE MY LIFE, SO I LET HER GO. CALL ME A ROMANTIC. BESIDES, I HAD BIGGER FISH TO FRY...

NAMELY A NARCO GANG CALLED LOS MUERTOS, RUN BY CALAVERA AND PULQUE...A PAIR OF FUN-LOVING BROTHERS WITH A PENCHANT FOR TURNING ANYONE WHO CROSSES THEM INTO SPORTING GEAR

THEN, WHILE ON SURVEILLANCE, I SPOT VAMPIRINA, OR WHATEVER, BREAK INTO PULQUE'S HOUSE. I WAS: 'WHAT THE HELL, LADY?!?'

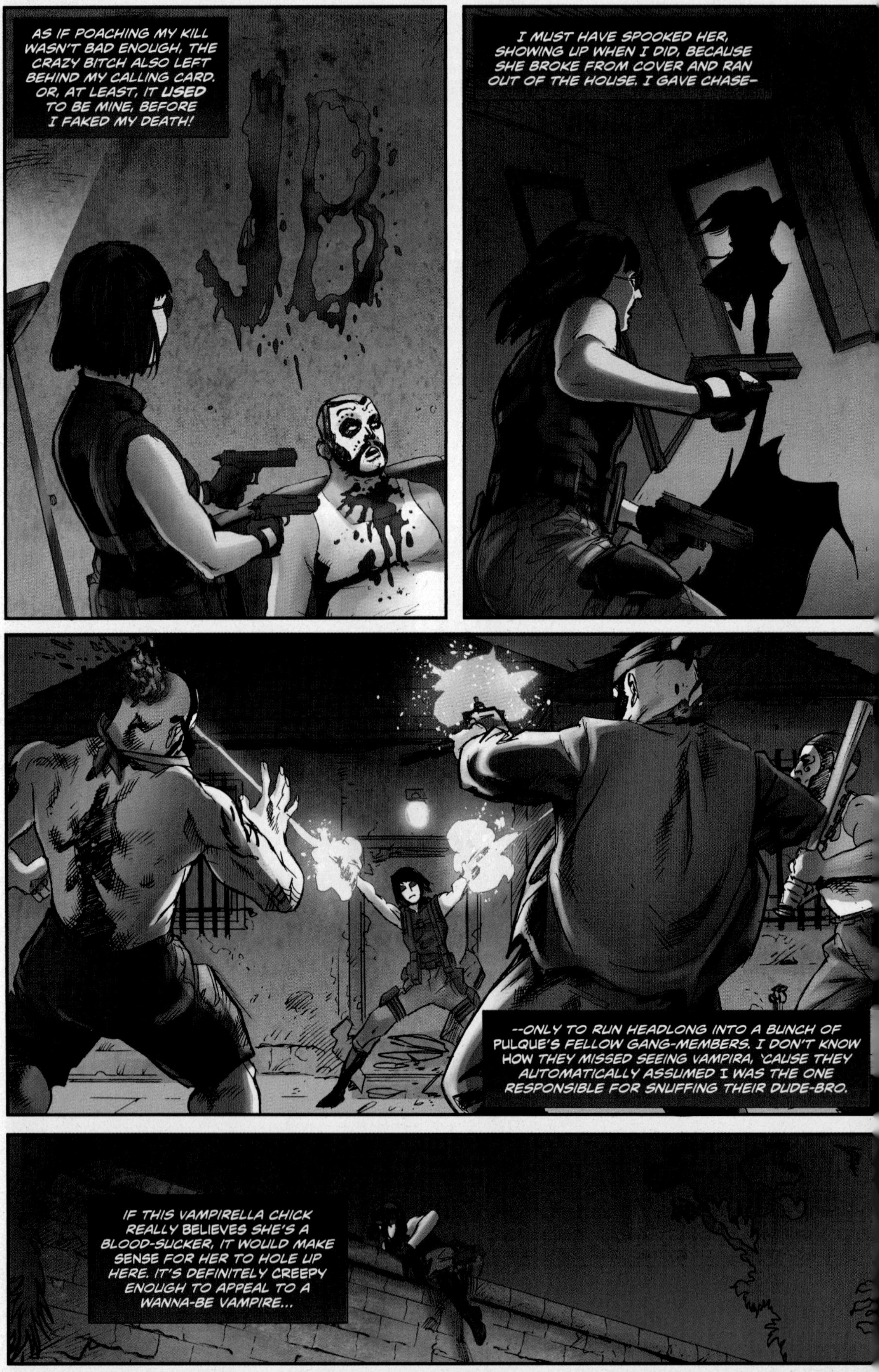

AS IF POACHING MY KILL WASN'T BAD ENOUGH, THE CRAZY BITCH ALSO LEFT BEHIND MY CALLING CARD. OR, AT LEAST, IT USED TO BE MINE, BEFORE I FAKED MY DEATH!
JB
I MUST HAVE SPOOKED HER, SHOWING UP WHEN I DID, BECAUSE SHE BROKE FROM COVER AND RAN OUT OF THE HOUSE. I GAVE CHASE–
--ONLY TO RUN HEADLONG INTO A BUNCH OF PULQUE'S FELLOW GANG-MEMBERS. I DON'T KNOW HOW THEY MISSED SEEING VAMPIRA, 'CAUSE THEY AUTOMATICALLY ASSUMED I WAS THE ONE RESPONSIBLE FOR SNUFFING THEIR DUDE-BRO.
IF THIS VAMPIRELLA CHICK REALLY BELIEVES SHE'S A BLOOD-SUCKER, IT WOULD MAKE SENSE FOR HER TO HOLE UP HERE. IT'S DEFINITELY CREEPY ENOUGH TO APPEAL TO A WANNA-BE VAMPIRE...

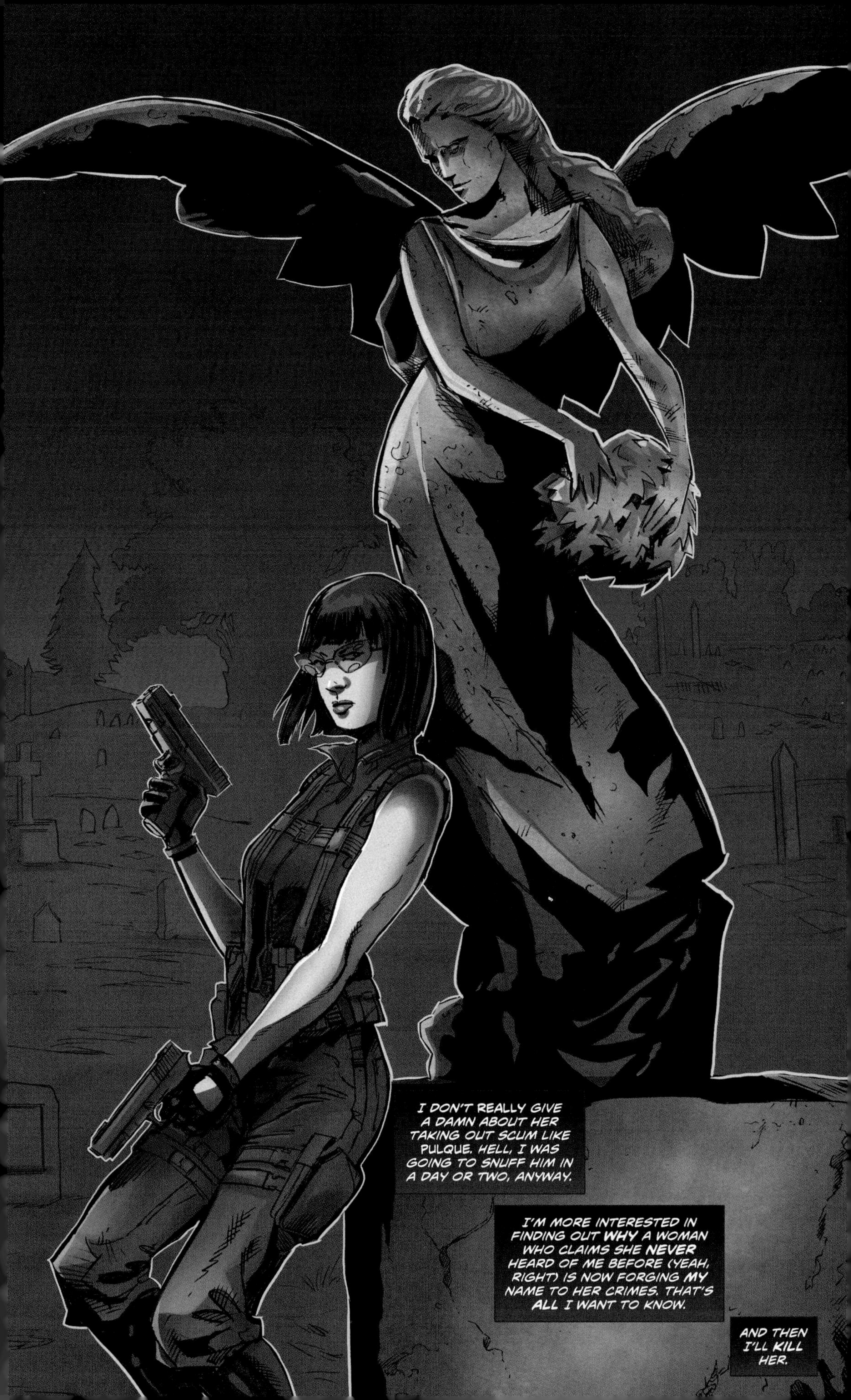
I DON'T REALLY GIVE A DAMN ABOUT HER TAKING OUT SCUM LIKE PULQUE. HELL, I WAS GOING TO SNUFF HIM IN A DAY OR TWO, ANYWAY.
I'M MORE INTERESTED IN FINDING OUT WHY A WOMAN WHO CLAIMS SHE NEVER HEARD OF ME BEFORE (YEAH, RIGHT) IS NOW FORGING MY NAME TO HER CRIMES. THAT'S ALL I WANT TO KNOW.
AND THEN I'LL KILL HER.

NORMALLY, I TRAVEL WITH MY OWN PRIVATE BLOOD BANK, BUT THINGS ARE FAR FROM NORMAL RIGHT NOW.

UNFORTUNATELY, MY FIRST HUNT OF THE NIGHT, WHILE SUCCESSFUL, WAS FAR FROM... SATISFYING.

UHNN!

DAMN IT, MY HUNGER IS BACK AGAIN!

WHAT'S THAT I HEAR--? IT SOUNDS LIKE I'M NOT ALONE...

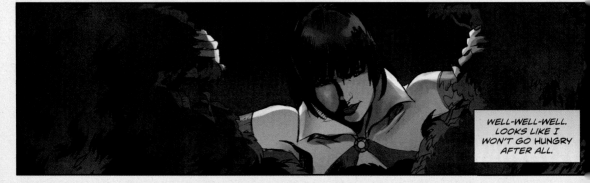

WELL-WELL-WELL. LOOKS LIKE I WON'T GO HUNGRY AFTER ALL.

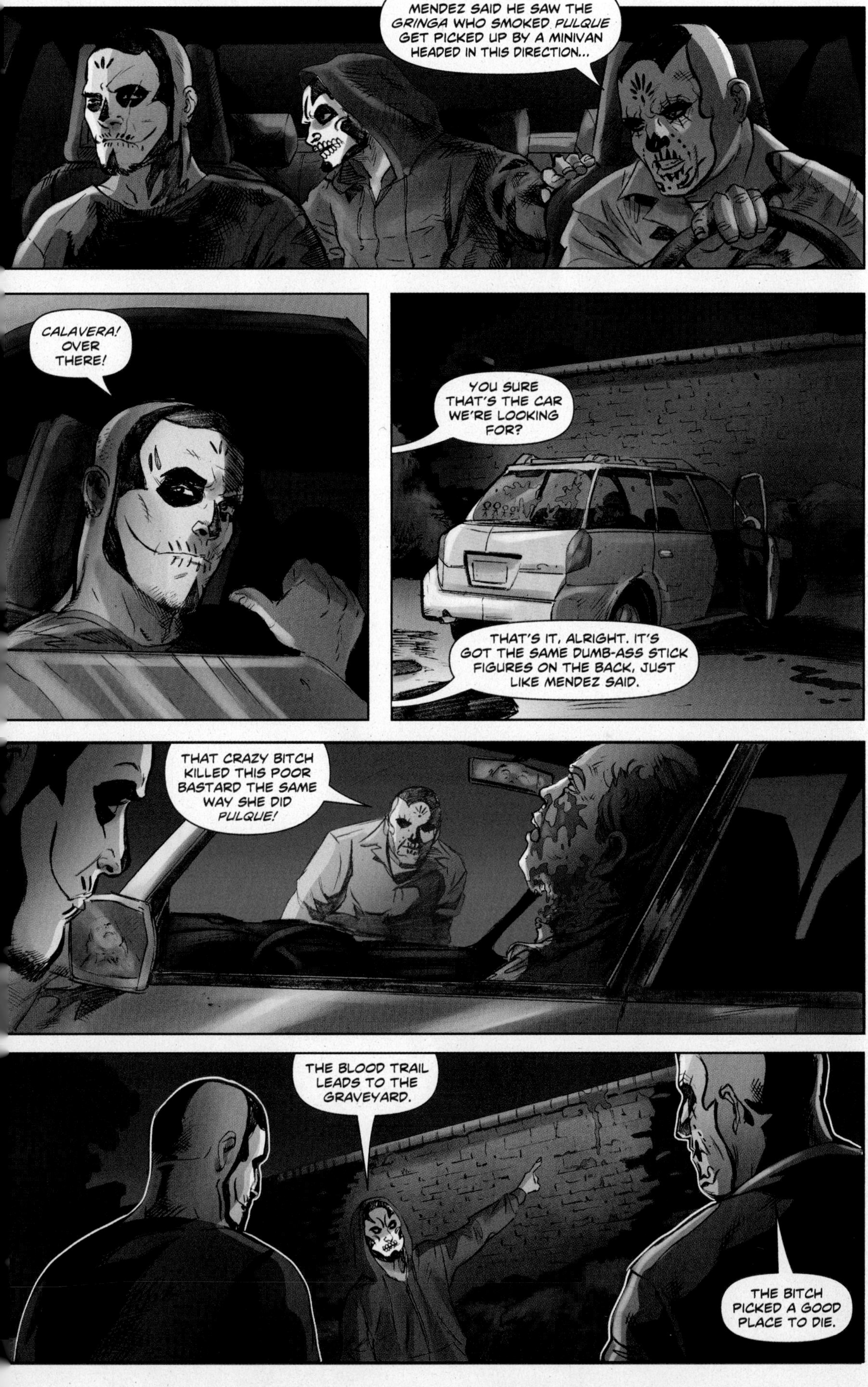
KEEP YOUR EYES OPEN! MENDEZ SAID HE SAW THE *GRINGA* WHO SMOKED *PULQUE* GET PICKED UP BY A MINIVAN HEADED IN THIS DIRECTION...
CALAVERA! OVER THERE!
YOU SURE THAT'S THE CAR WE'RE LOOKING FOR?
THAT'S IT, ALRIGHT. IT'S GOT THE SAME DUMB-ASS STICK FIGURES ON THE BACK, JUST LIKE MENDEZ SAID.
THAT CRAZY BITCH KILLED THIS POOR BASTARD THE SAME WAY SHE DID *PULQUE!*
THE BLOOD TRAIL LEADS TO THE GRAVEYARD.
THE BITCH PICKED A GOOD PLACE TO DIE.

I HAVE SLAIN HUNDREDS DURING MY TIME AS A VIGILANTE. DESPITE THAT, BEING IN A CEMETERY AFTER DARK IS GENUINELY EERIE...

MAYBE IT IS BECAUSE THE PLACE IS SO DAMN QUIET YOU CAN HEAR A MOUSE FART. WAIT—WHAT WAS THAT?!?

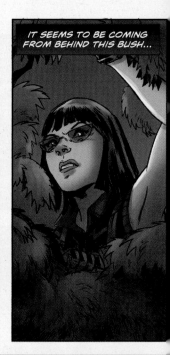

IT SEEMS TO BE COMING FROM BEHIND THIS BUSH...

BINGO!

I'VE LOCATED MY TARGET—

AND SHE'S EVEN CRAZIER THAN I THOUGHT!

HERE LIES

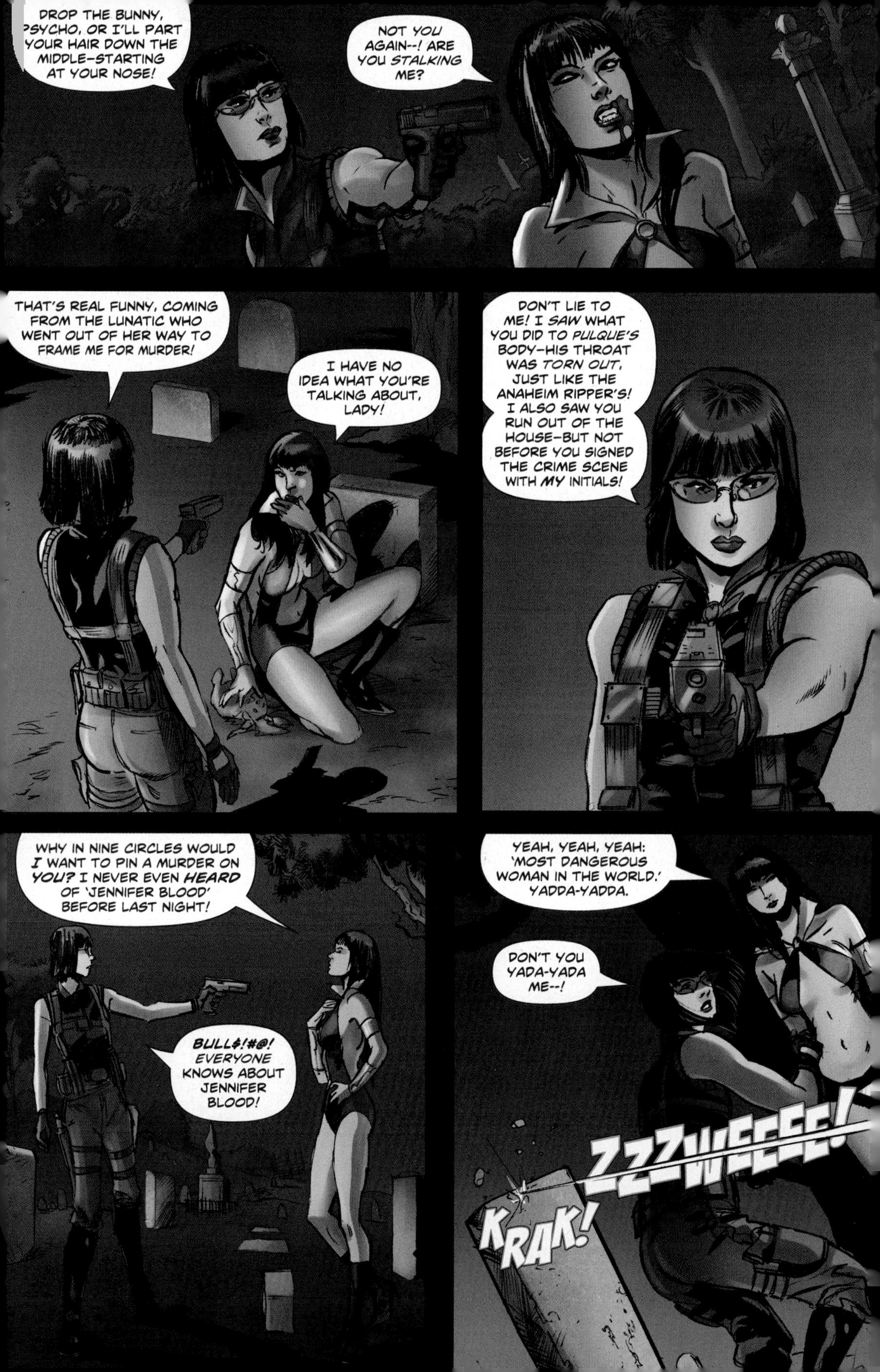
DROP THE BUNNY, PSYCHO, OR I'LL PART YOUR HAIR DOWN THE MIDDLE–STARTING AT YOUR NOSE!
NOT YOU AGAIN--! ARE YOU STALKING ME?
THAT'S REAL FUNNY, COMING FROM THE LUNATIC WHO WENT OUT OF HER WAY TO FRAME ME FOR MURDER!
I HAVE NO IDEA WHAT YOU'RE TALKING ABOUT, LADY!
DON'T LIE TO ME! I SAW WHAT YOU DID TO PULQUE'S BODY–HIS THROAT WAS TORN OUT, JUST LIKE THE ANAHEIM RIPPER'S! I ALSO SAW YOU RUN OUT OF THE HOUSE–BUT NOT BEFORE YOU SIGNED THE CRIME SCENE WITH MY INITIALS!
WHY IN NINE CIRCLES WOULD I WANT TO PIN A MURDER ON YOU? I NEVER EVEN HEARD OF 'JENNIFER BLOOD' BEFORE LAST NIGHT!
BULL$!#@! EVERYONE KNOWS ABOUT JENNIFER BLOOD!
YEAH, YEAH, YEAH: 'MOST DANGEROUS WOMAN IN THE WORLD.' YADDA-YADDA.
DON'T YOU YADA-YADA ME--!
ZZZWEEEE!
KRAK!

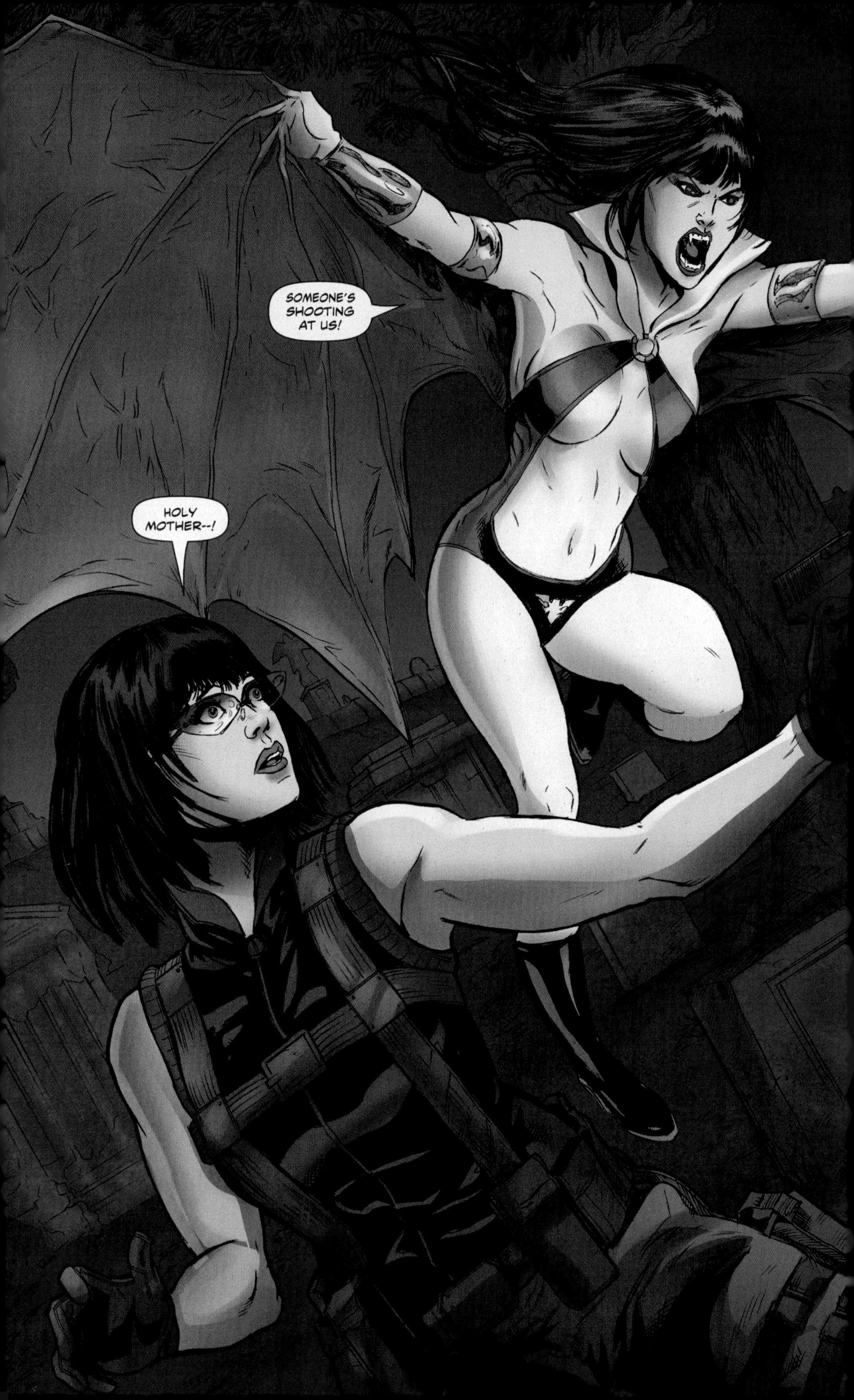
SOMEONE'S SHOOTING AT US!
HOLY MOTHER--!

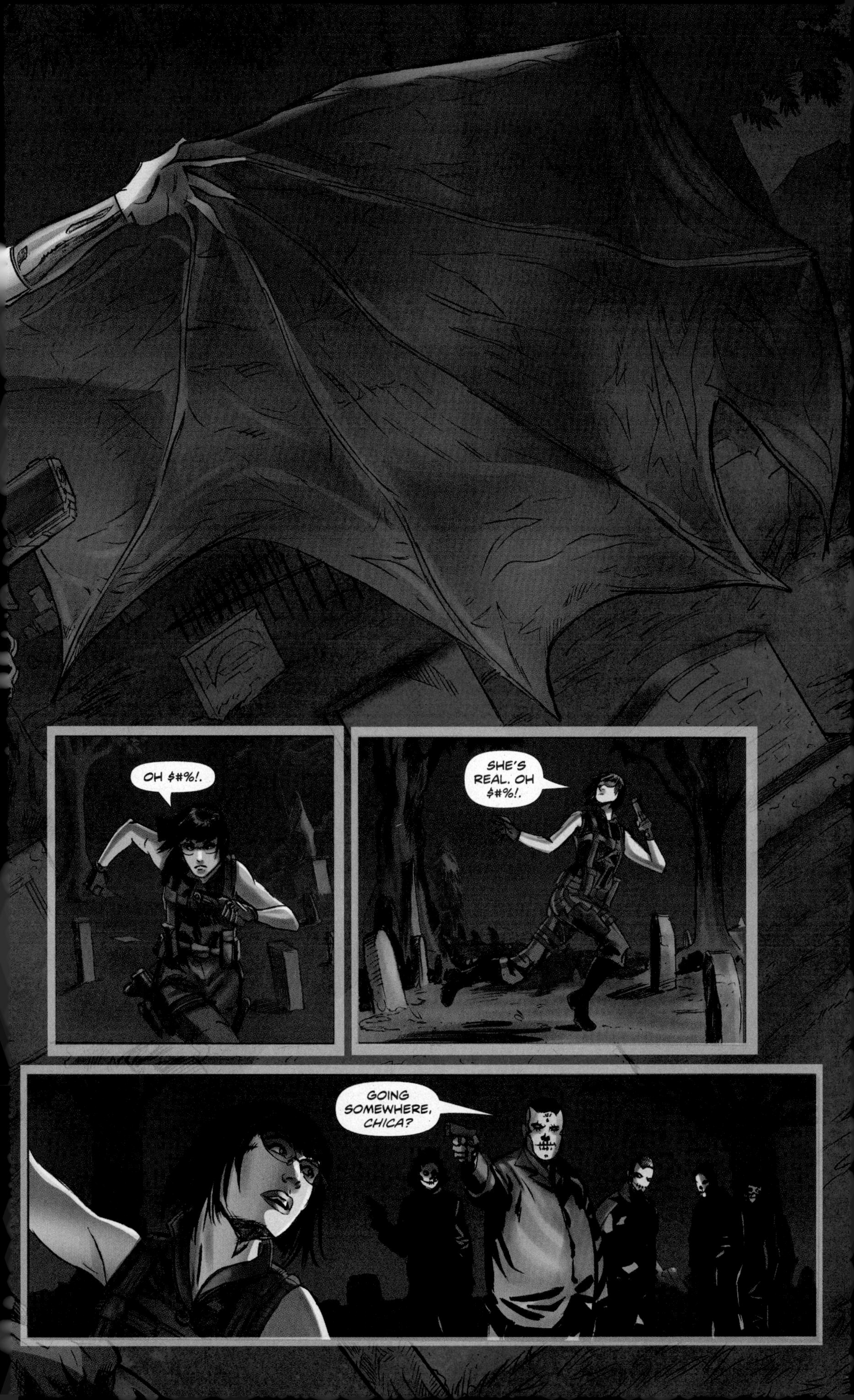
OH $#%!.
SHE'S REAL. OH $#%!.
GOING SOMEWHERE, CHICA?

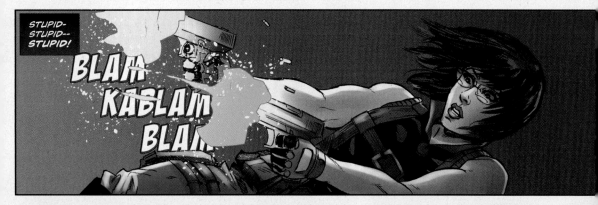

STUPID-STUPID--STUPID!

BLAM
KABLAM
BLAM

I LET OLD-FASHIONED MONKEY-BRAIN TERROR GET THE BETTER OF ME, AND I NEARLY GOT MYSELF KILLED!

BUT I SAW HER GROW WINGS! FREAKIN' BAT WINGS! HOW IS THAT EVEN POSSIBLE--?!?

POW POW K-POW

CALM DOWN, DAMN IT! PUT THAT $!#@ OUT OF YOUR MIND AND FOCUS ON CALAVERA AND HIS BAND OF NUMBSKULLS.

I'LL WORRY ABOUT THE VAMPIRE AFTER I SMOKE THESE DIME STORE JACK SKELLINGTONS...

FIRST THINGS FIRST: I CAN ONLY HANDLE ONE MONSTER AT A TIME.

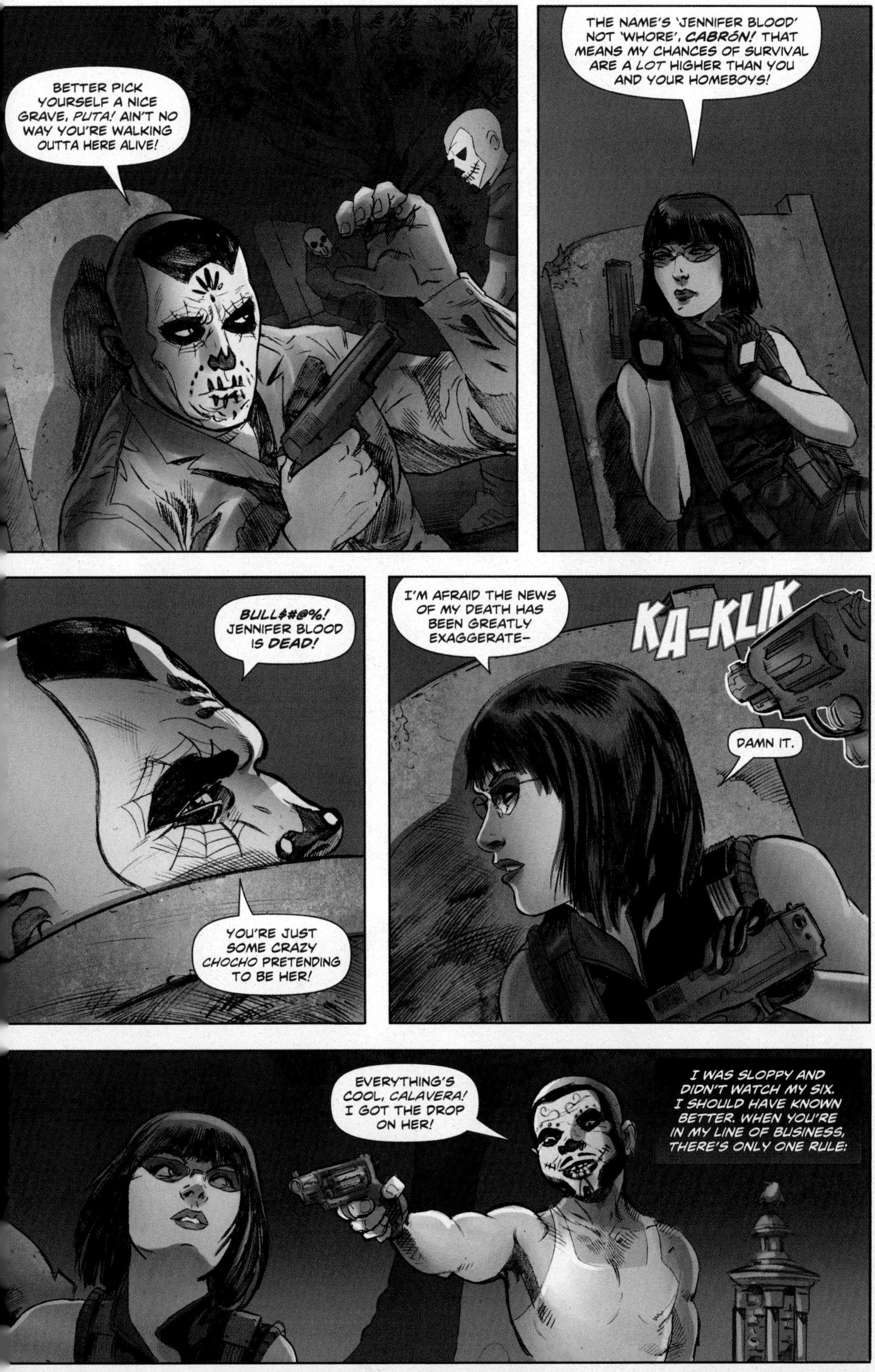
BETTER PICK YOURSELF A NICE GRAVE, PUTA! AIN'T NO WAY YOU'RE WALKING OUTTA HERE ALIVE!
THE NAME'S 'JENNIFER BLOOD' NOT 'WHORE', CABRÓN! THAT MEANS MY CHANCES OF SURVIVAL ARE A LOT HIGHER THAN YOU AND YOUR HOMEBOYS!
BULL$#@%! JENNIFER BLOOD IS DEAD!
YOU'RE JUST SOME CRAZY CHOCHO PRETENDING TO BE HER!
I'M AFRAID THE NEWS OF MY DEATH HAS BEEN GREATLY EXAGGERATE-
KA-KLIK
DAMN IT.
EVERYTHING'S COOL, CALAVERA! I GOT THE DROP ON HER!
I WAS SLOPPY AND DIDN'T WATCH MY SIX. I SHOULD HAVE KNOWN BETTER. WHEN YOU'RE IN MY LINE OF BUSINESS, THERE'S ONLY ONE RULE:

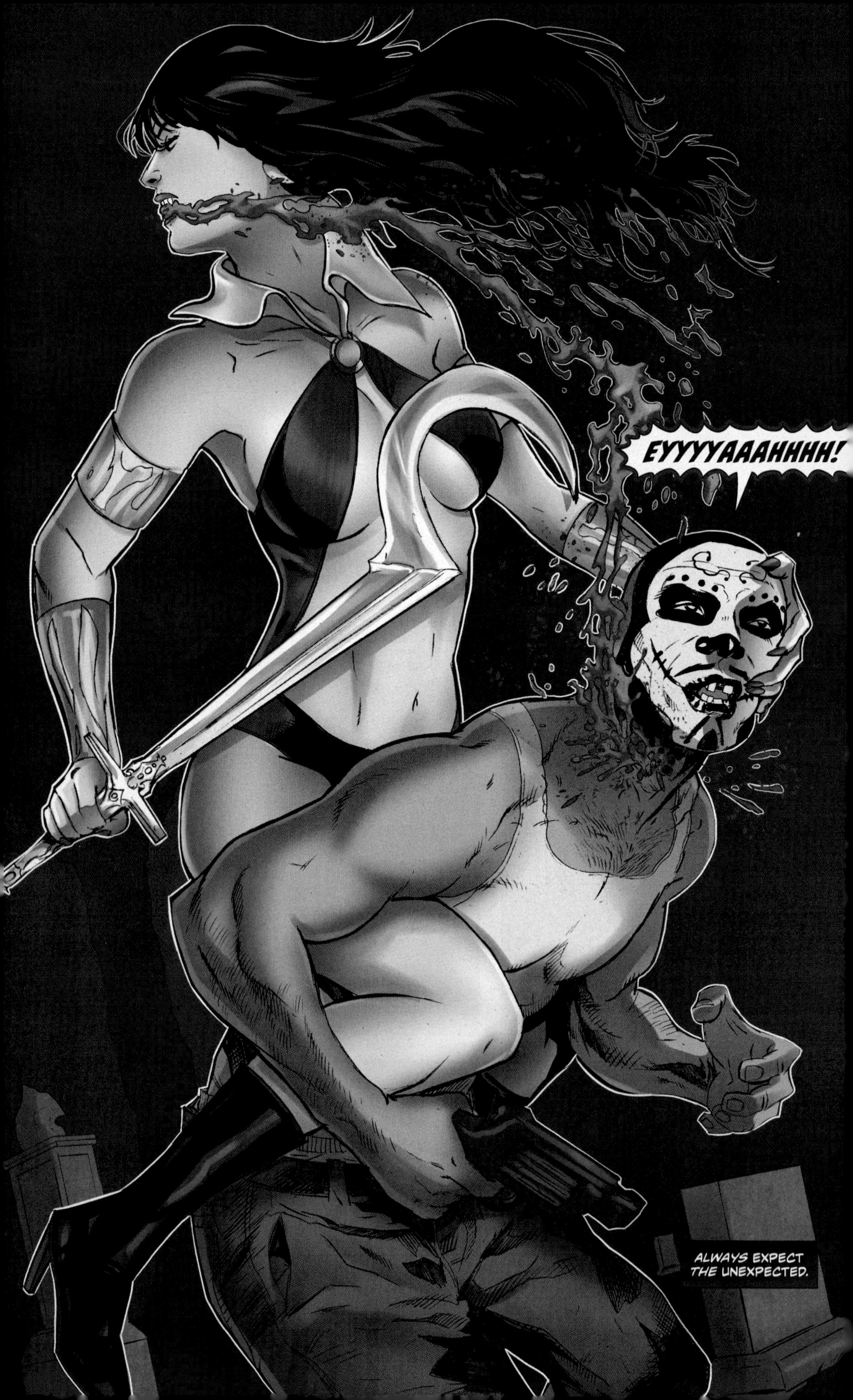
EYYYYAAAHHHH!
ALWAYS EXPECT THE UNEXPECTED.

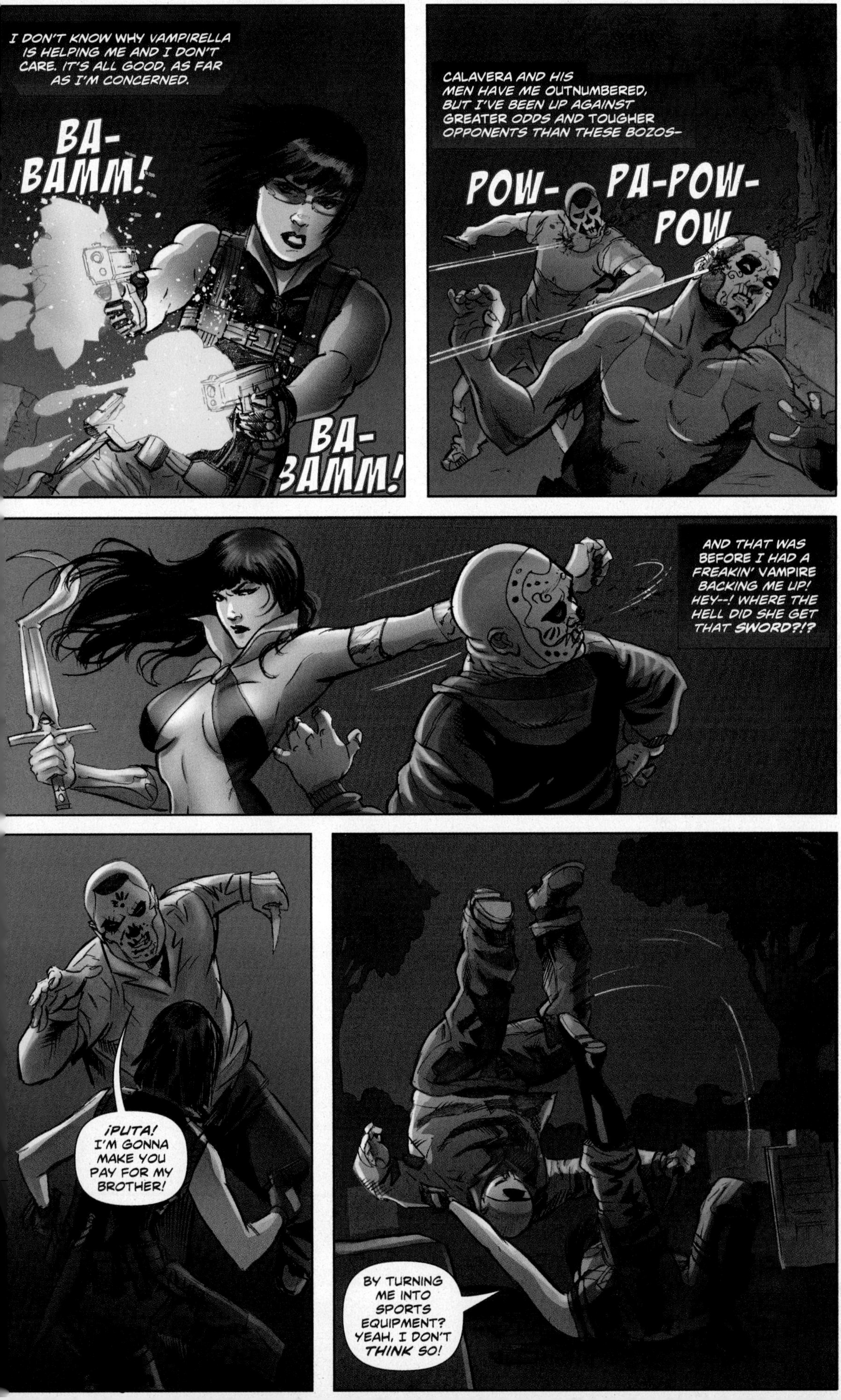
I DON'T KNOW WHY VAMPIRELLA IS HELPING ME AND I DON'T CARE. IT'S ALL GOOD, AS FAR AS I'M CONCERNED.
BA-BAMM!
BA-BAMM!
CALAVERA AND HIS MEN HAVE ME OUTNUMBERED, BUT I'VE BEEN UP AGAINST GREATER ODDS AND TOUGHER OPPONENTS THAN THESE BOZOS–
POW-
PA-POW-POW
AND THAT WAS BEFORE I HAD A FREAKIN' VAMPIRE BACKING ME UP! HEY--! WHERE THE HELL DID SHE GET THAT SWORD?!?
¡PUTA! I'M GONNA MAKE YOU PAY FOR MY BROTHER!
BY TURNING ME INTO SPORTS EQUIPMENT? YEAH, I DON'T THINK SO!

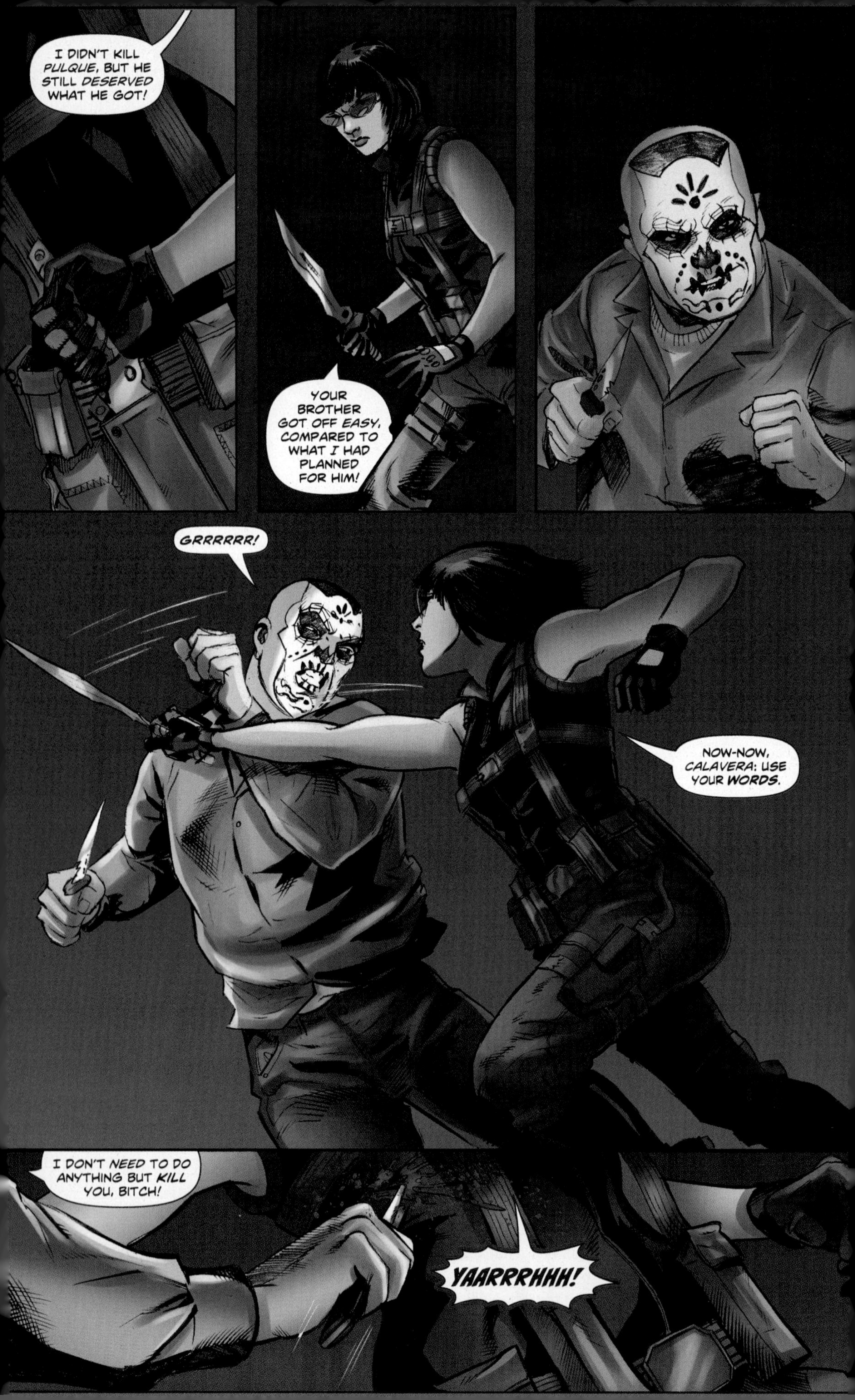

I DIDN'T KILL PULQUE, BUT HE STILL DESERVED WHAT HE GOT!
YOUR BROTHER GOT OFF EASY, COMPARED TO WHAT I HAD PLANNED FOR HIM!
GRRRRRR!
NOW-NOW, CALAVERA: USE YOUR WORDS.
I DON'T NEED TO DO ANYTHING BUT KILL YOU, BITCH!
YAARRRHHH!

SCREW THIS! I'M THROUGH PLAYING AROUND!

SINCE YOUR GANG CALLS ITSELF 'LOS MUERTOS'*--

*'THE DEAD.' - ED.

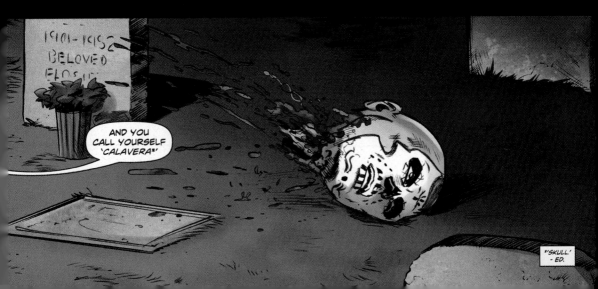

AND YOU CALL YOURSELF 'CALAVERA'*

*'SKULL.' - ED.

HERE LIES
ARCHIBALD
STANTON
1909-1966
--I THINK IT'S *TIME YOU* ***LIVE UP*** TO THE NAME!

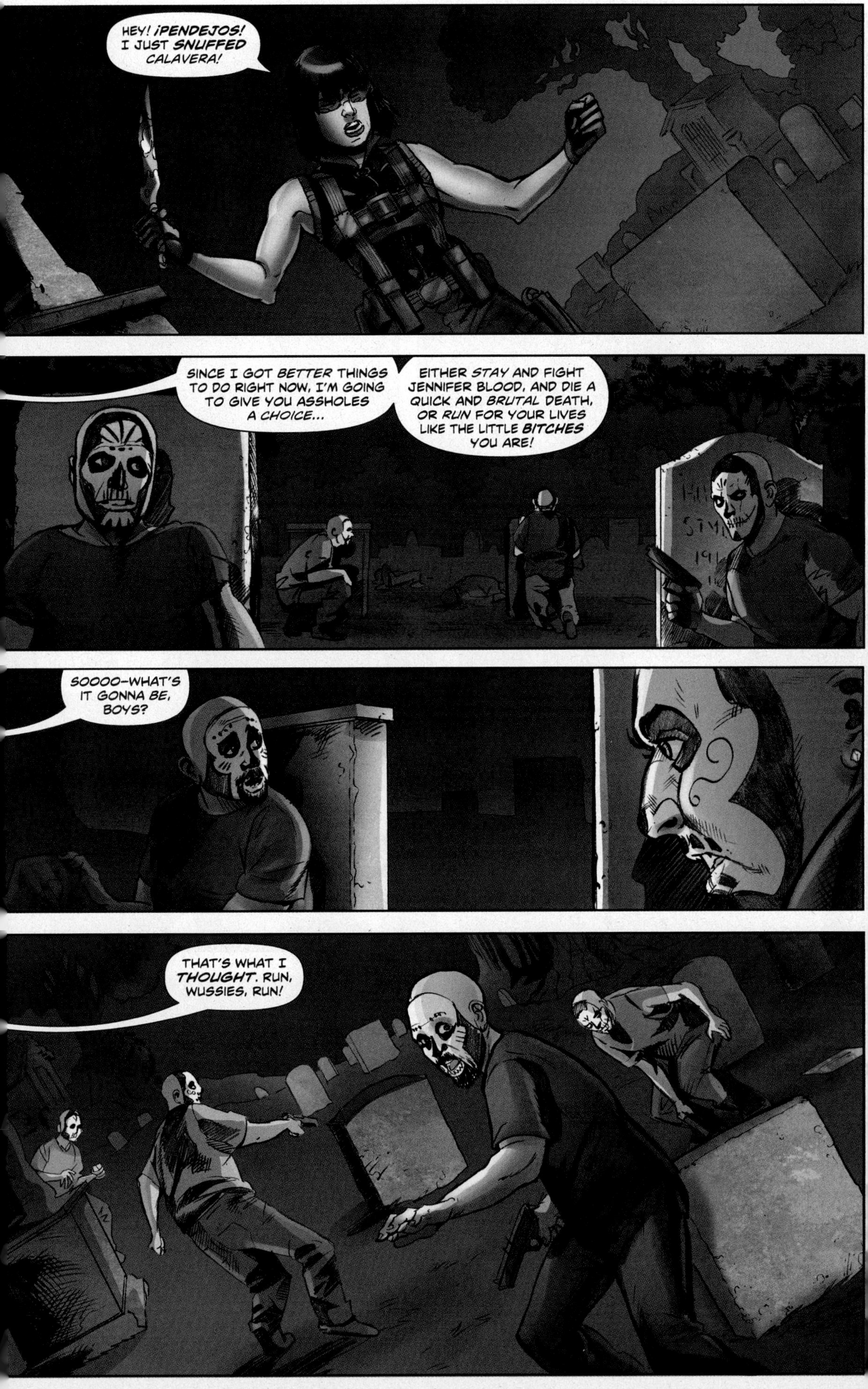
HEY! ¡PENDEJOS! I JUST SNUFFED CALAVERA!
SINCE I GOT BETTER THINGS TO DO RIGHT NOW, I'M GOING TO GIVE YOU ASSHOLES A CHOICE...
EITHER STAY AND FIGHT JENNIFER BLOOD, AND DIE A QUICK AND BRUTAL DEATH, OR RUN FOR YOUR LIVES LIKE THE LITTLE BITCHES YOU ARE!
SOOOO–WHAT'S IT GONNA BE, BOYS?
THAT'S WHAT I THOUGHT. RUN, WUSSIES, RUN!

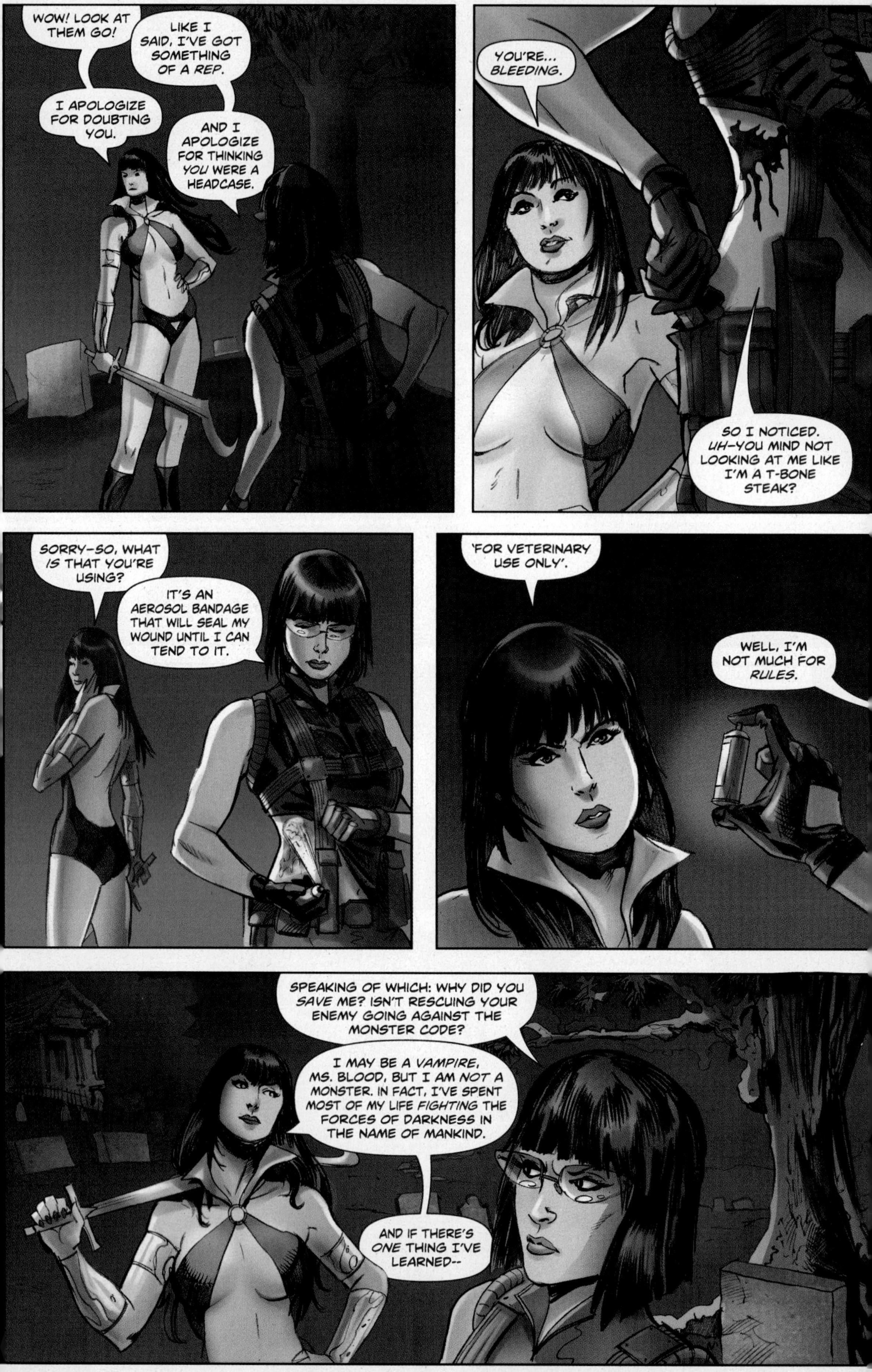
WOW! LOOK AT THEM GO!
LIKE I SAID, I'VE GOT SOMETHING OF A REP.
I APOLOGIZE FOR DOUBTING YOU.
AND I APOLOGIZE FOR THINKING YOU WERE A HEADCASE.
YOU'RE... BLEEDING.
SO I NOTICED. UH—YOU MIND NOT LOOKING AT ME LIKE I'M A T-BONE STEAK?
SORRY—SO, WHAT IS THAT YOU'RE USING?
IT'S AN AEROSOL BANDAGE THAT WILL SEAL MY WOUND UNTIL I CAN TEND TO IT.
'FOR VETERINARY USE ONLY'.
WELL, I'M NOT MUCH FOR RULES.
SPEAKING OF WHICH: WHY DID YOU SAVE ME? ISN'T RESCUING YOUR ENEMY GOING AGAINST THE MONSTER CODE?
I MAY BE A VAMPIRE, MS. BLOOD, BUT I AM NOT A MONSTER. IN FACT, I'VE SPENT MOST OF MY LIFE FIGHTING THE FORCES OF DARKNESS IN THE NAME OF MANKIND.
AND IF THERE'S ONE THING I'VE LEARNED--

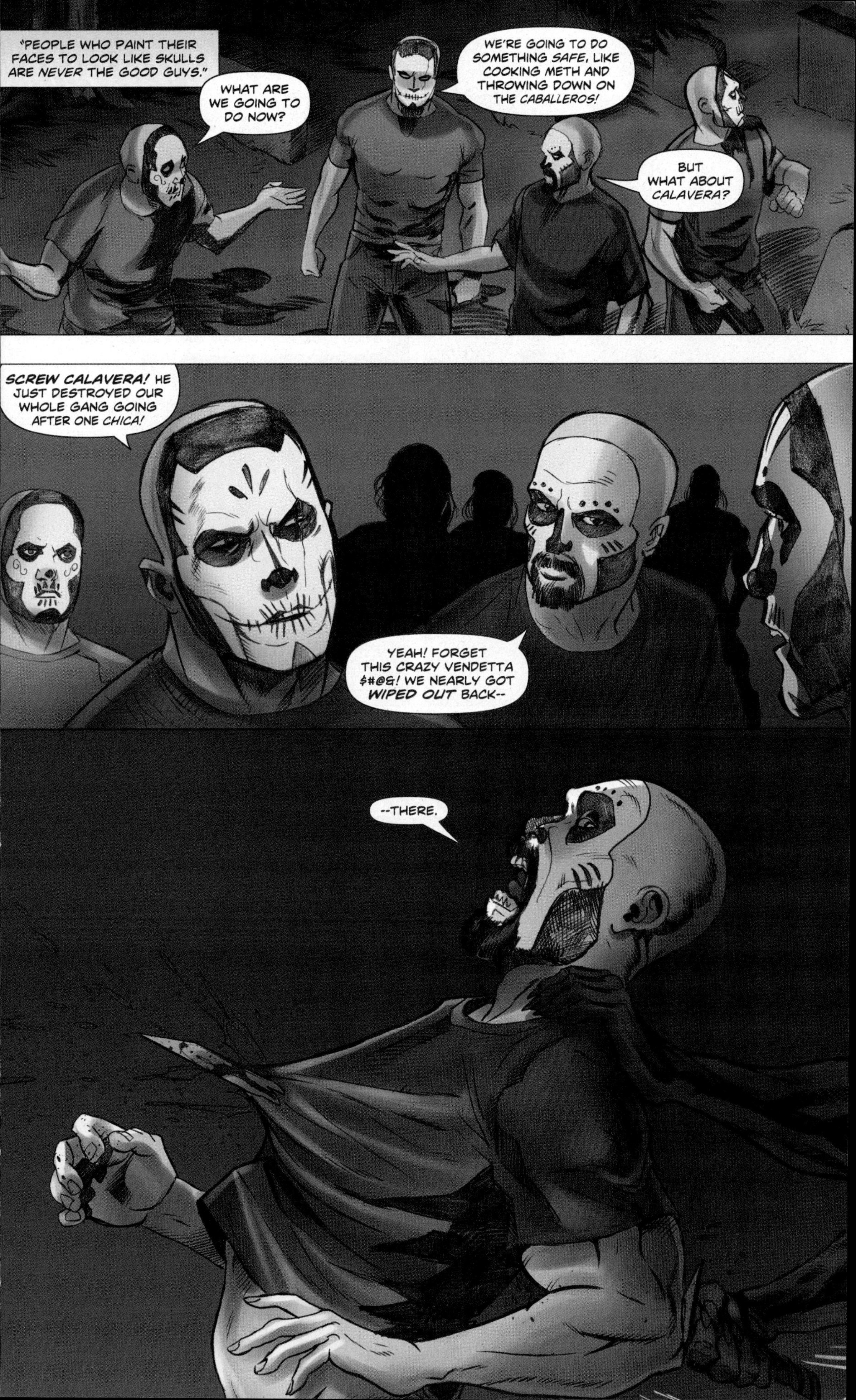
"PEOPLE WHO PAINT THEIR FACES TO LOOK LIKE SKULLS ARE *NEVER* THE GOOD GUYS."
WHAT ARE WE GOING TO DO NOW?
WE'RE GOING TO DO SOMETHING *SAFE*, LIKE COOKING METH AND THROWING DOWN ON THE *CABALLEROS!*
BUT WHAT ABOUT *CALAVERA?*
SCREW CALAVERA! HE JUST DESTROYED OUR WHOLE GANG GOING AFTER ONE *CHICA!*
YEAH! FORGET THIS CRAZY VENDETTA $#@&! WE NEARLY GOT ***WIPED OUT*** BACK--
--THERE.

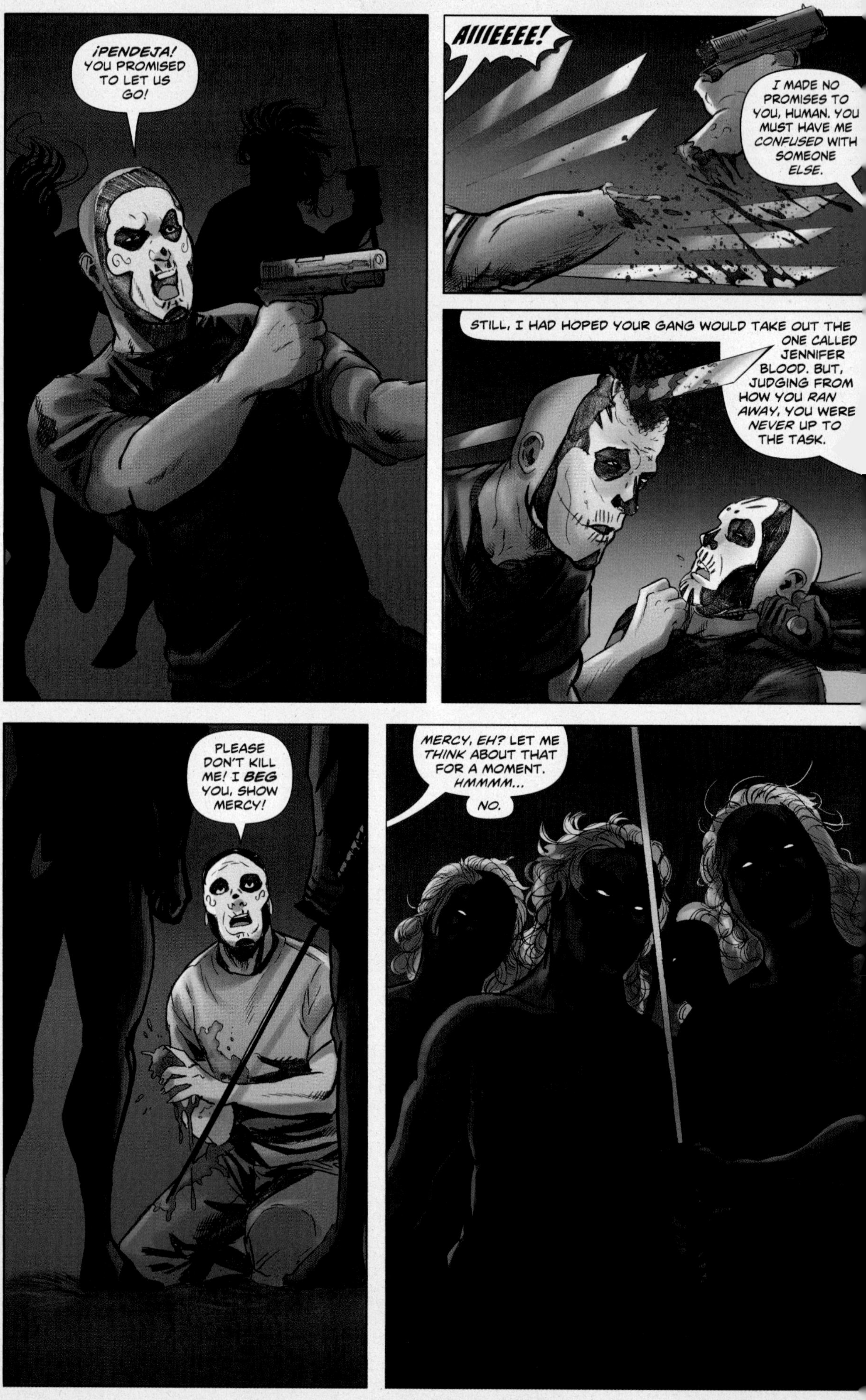

¡PENDEJA! YOU PROMISED TO LET US GO!
AIIIEEEE!
I MADE NO PROMISES TO YOU, HUMAN. YOU MUST HAVE ME CONFUSED WITH SOMEONE ELSE.
STILL, I HAD HOPED YOUR GANG WOULD TAKE OUT THE ONE CALLED JENNIFER BLOOD. BUT, JUDGING FROM HOW YOU RAN AWAY, YOU WERE NEVER UP TO THE TASK.
PLEASE DON'T KILL ME! I BEG YOU, SHOW MERCY!
MERCY, EH? LET ME THINK ABOUT THAT FOR A MOMENT. HMMMM...
NO.

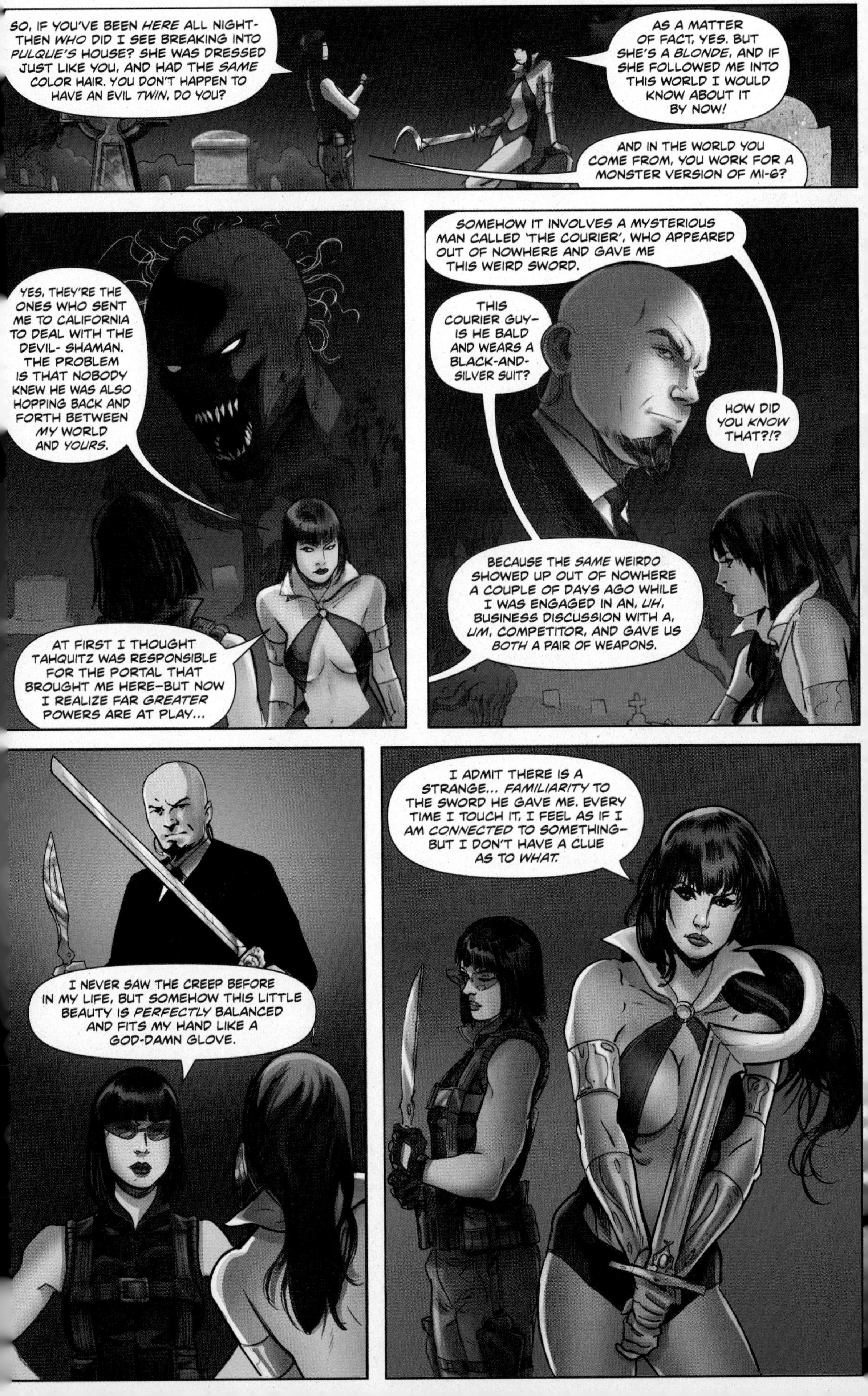

SO, IF YOU'VE BEEN *HERE* ALL NIGHT-THEN *WHO* DID I SEE BREAKING INTO *PULQUE'S* HOUSE? SHE WAS DRESSED JUST LIKE YOU, AND HAD THE *SAME* COLOR HAIR. YOU DON'T HAPPEN TO HAVE AN EVIL *TWIN*, DO YOU?
AS A MATTER OF FACT, YES. BUT SHE'S A *BLONDE*, AND IF SHE FOLLOWED ME INTO THIS WORLD I WOULD KNOW ABOUT IT BY NOW!
AND IN THE WORLD YOU COME FROM, YOU WORK FOR A MONSTER VERSION OF MI-6?
YES, THEY'RE THE ONES WHO SENT ME TO CALIFORNIA TO DEAL WITH THE DEVIL- SHAMAN. THE PROBLEM IS THAT NOBODY KNEW HE WAS ALSO HOPPING BACK AND FORTH BETWEEN *MY* WORLD AND *YOURS*.
AT FIRST I THOUGHT TAHQUITZ WAS RESPONSIBLE FOR THE PORTAL THAT BROUGHT ME HERE—BUT NOW I REALIZE FAR *GREATER* POWERS ARE AT PLAY...
SOMEHOW IT INVOLVES A MYSTERIOUS MAN CALLED 'THE COURIER', WHO APPEARED OUT OF NOWHERE AND GAVE ME THIS WEIRD SWORD.
THIS COURIER GUY– IS HE BALD AND WEARS A BLACK-AND-SILVER SUIT?
HOW DID YOU *KNOW* THAT?!?
BECAUSE THE *SAME* WEIRDO SHOWED UP OUT OF NOWHERE A COUPLE OF DAYS AGO WHILE I WAS ENGAGED IN AN, *UH*, BUSINESS DISCUSSION WITH A, *UM*, COMPETITOR, AND GAVE US *BOTH* A PAIR OF WEAPONS.
I NEVER SAW THE CREEP BEFORE IN MY LIFE, BUT SOMEHOW THIS LITTLE BEAUTY IS *PERFECTLY* BALANCED AND FITS MY HAND LIKE A GOD-DAMN GLOVE.
I ADMIT THERE IS A STRANGE... *FAMILIARITY* TO THE SWORD HE GAVE ME. EVERY TIME I TOUCH IT, I FEEL AS IF I AM *CONNECTED* TO SOMETHING– BUT I DON'T HAVE A CLUE AS TO *WHAT*.

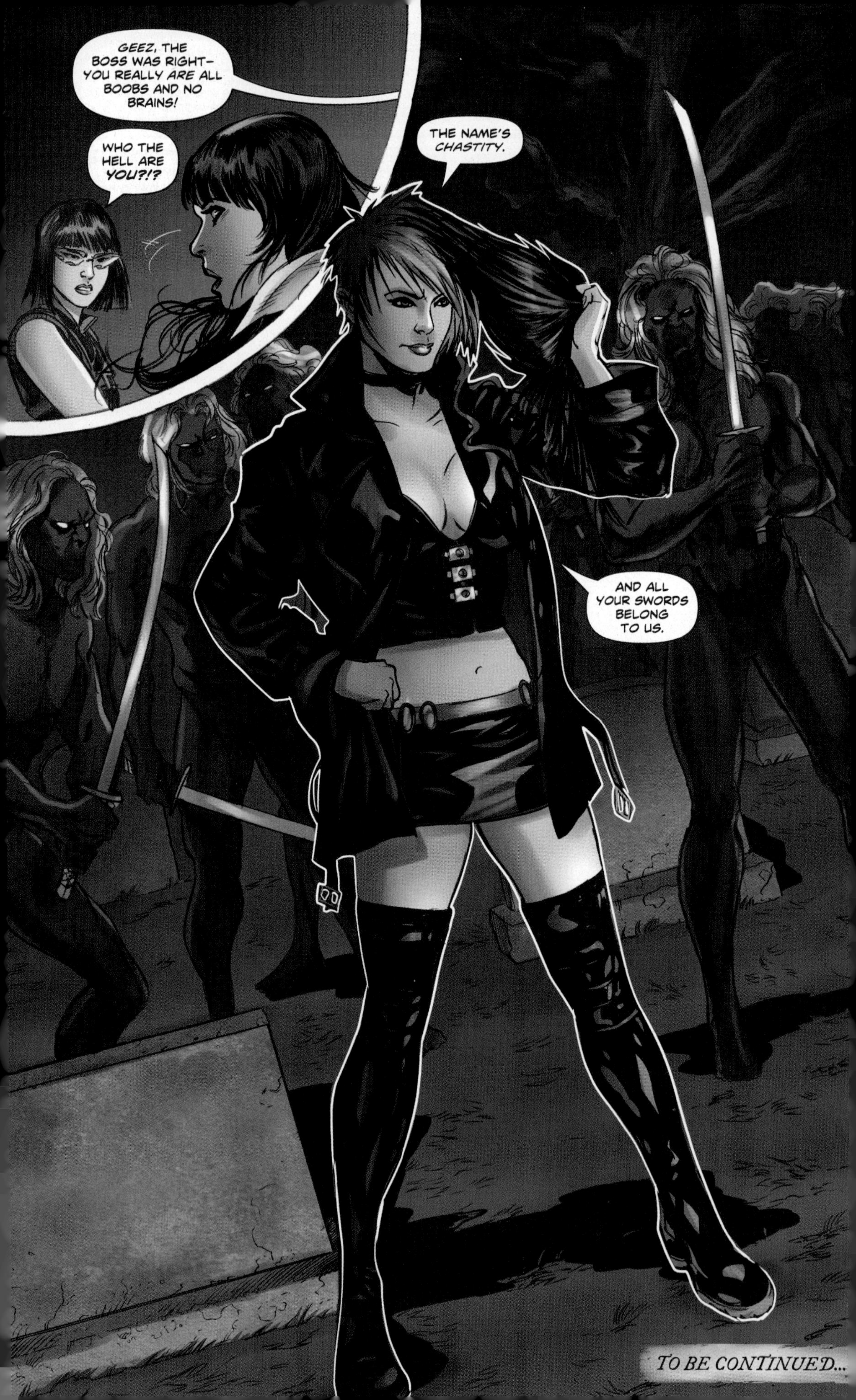
GEEZ, THE BOSS WAS RIGHT– YOU REALLY ARE ALL BOOBS AND NO BRAINS!
WHO THE HELL ARE YOU?!?
THE NAME'S CHASTITY.
AND ALL YOUR SWORDS BELONG TO US.
TO BE CONTINUED...

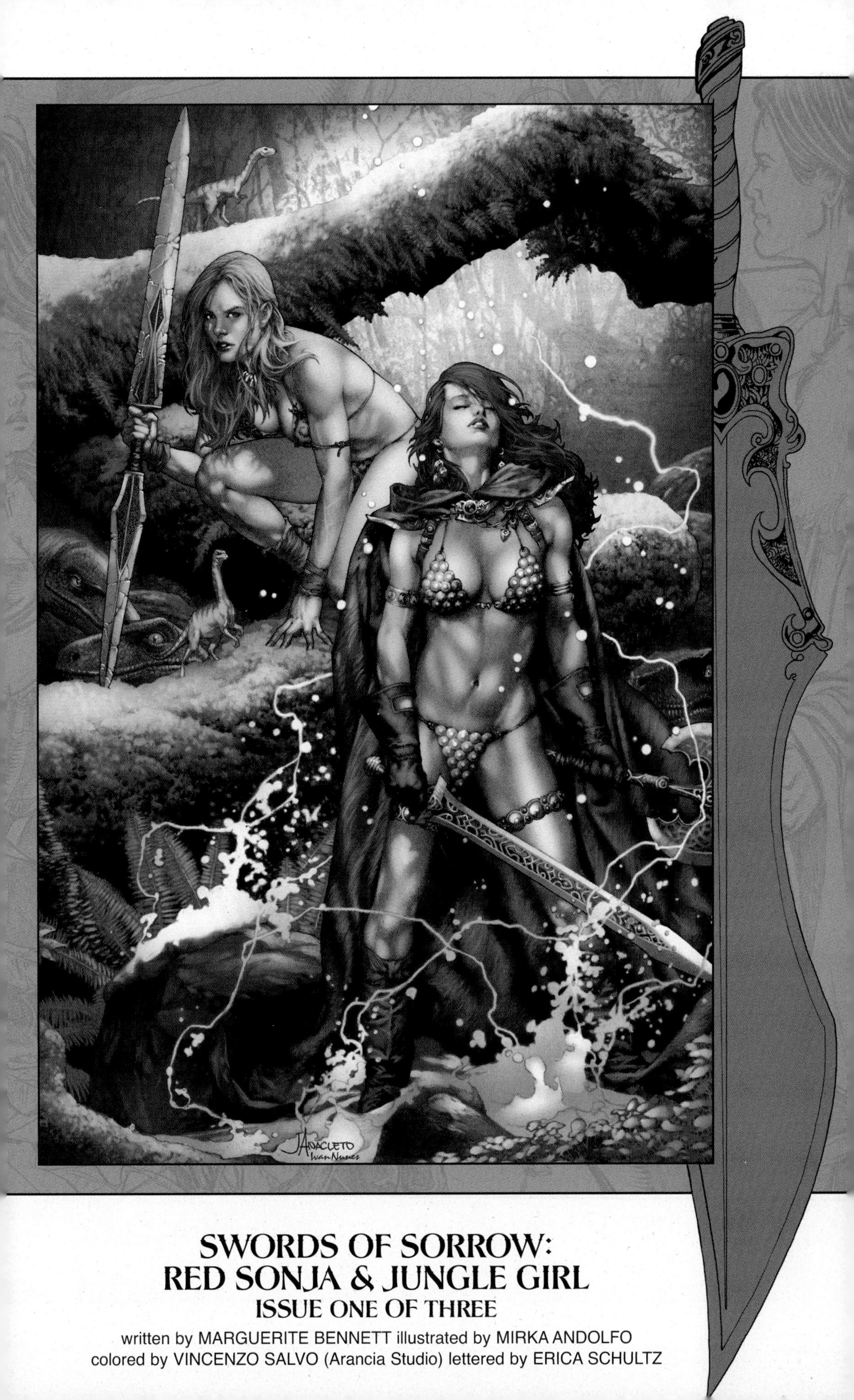

SWORDS OF SORROW: RED SONJA & JUNGLE GIRL

ISSUE ONE OF THREE

written by MARGUERITE BENNETT illustrated by MIRKA ANDOLFO
colored by VINCENZO SALVO (Arancia Studio) lettered by ERICA SCHULTZ

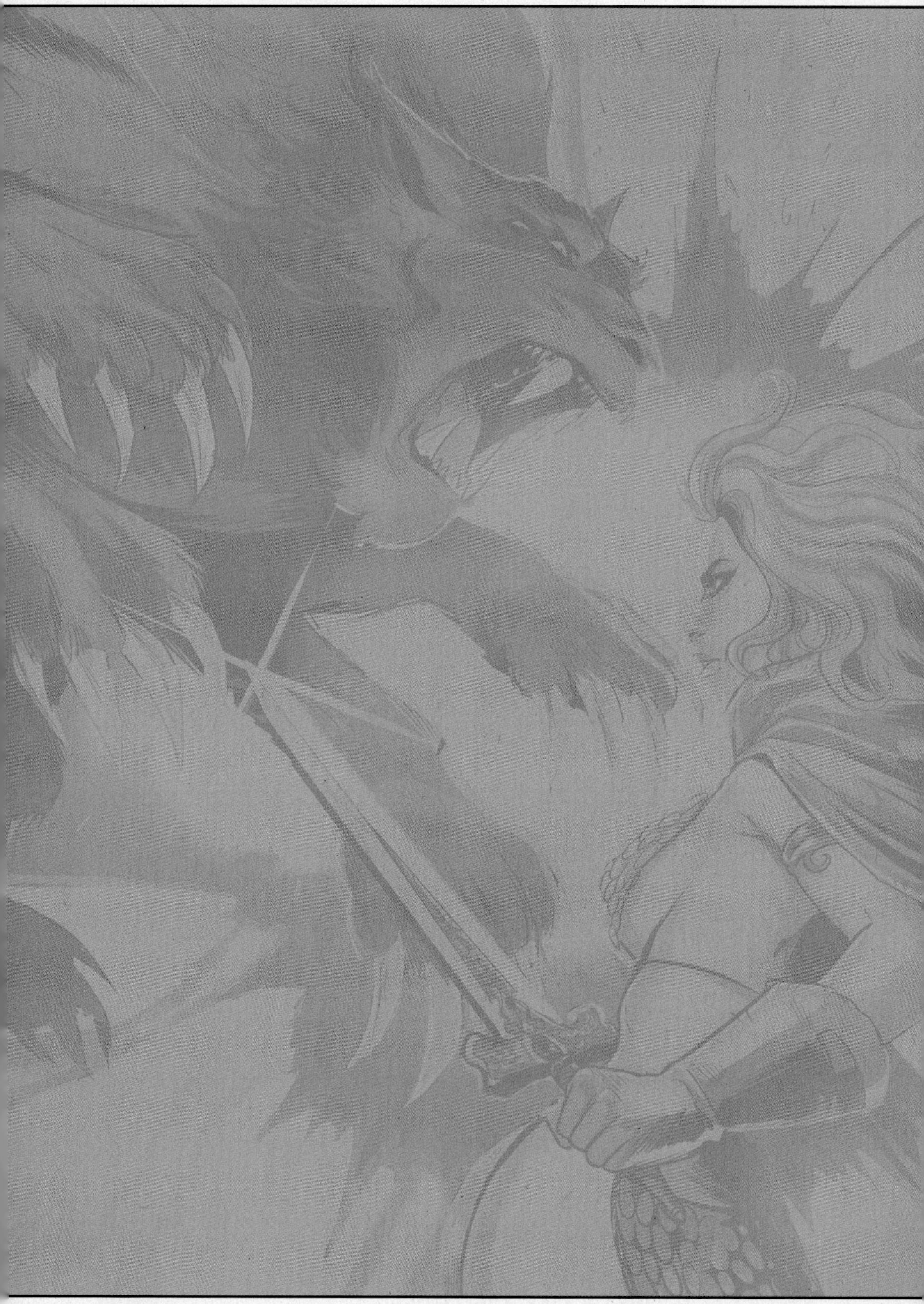

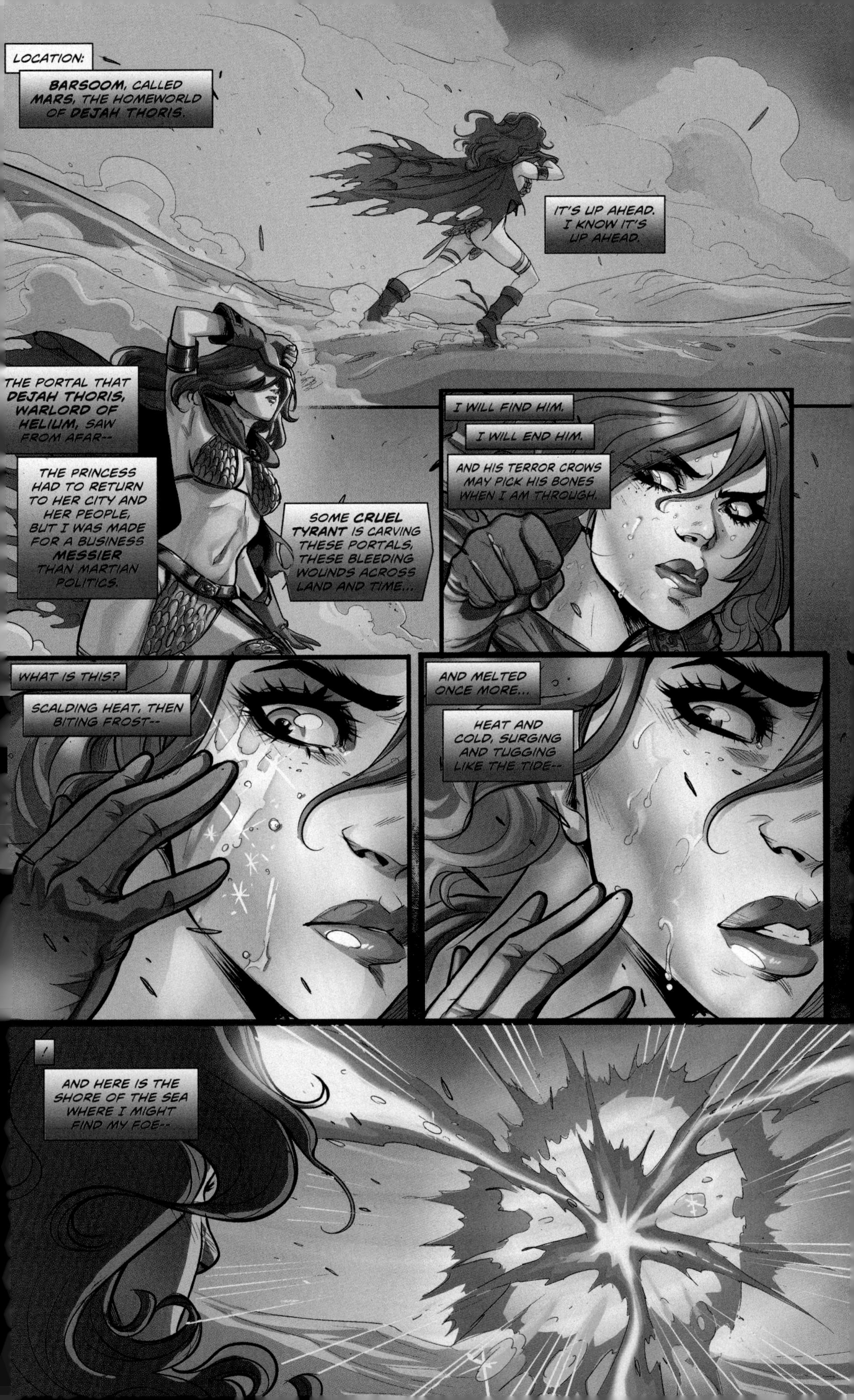
LOCATION:
BARSOOM, CALLED MARS, THE HOMEWORLD OF DEJAH THORIS.
IT'S UP AHEAD. I KNOW IT'S UP AHEAD.
THE PORTAL THAT DEJAH THORIS, WARLORD OF HELIUM, SAW FROM AFAR--
THE PRINCESS HAD TO RETURN TO HER CITY AND HER PEOPLE, BUT I WAS MADE FOR A BUSINESS MESSIER THAN MARTIAN POLITICS.
SOME CRUEL TYRANT IS CARVING THESE PORTALS, THESE BLEEDING WOUNDS ACROSS LAND AND TIME...
I WILL FIND HIM.
I WILL END HIM.
AND HIS TERROR CROWS MAY PICK HIS BONES WHEN I AM THROUGH.
WHAT IS THIS?
SCALDING HEAT, THEN BITING FROST--
AND MELTED ONCE MORE...
HEAT AND COLD, SURGING AND TUGGING LIKE THE TIDE--
!
AND HERE IS THE SHORE OF THE SEA WHERE I MIGHT FIND MY FOE--

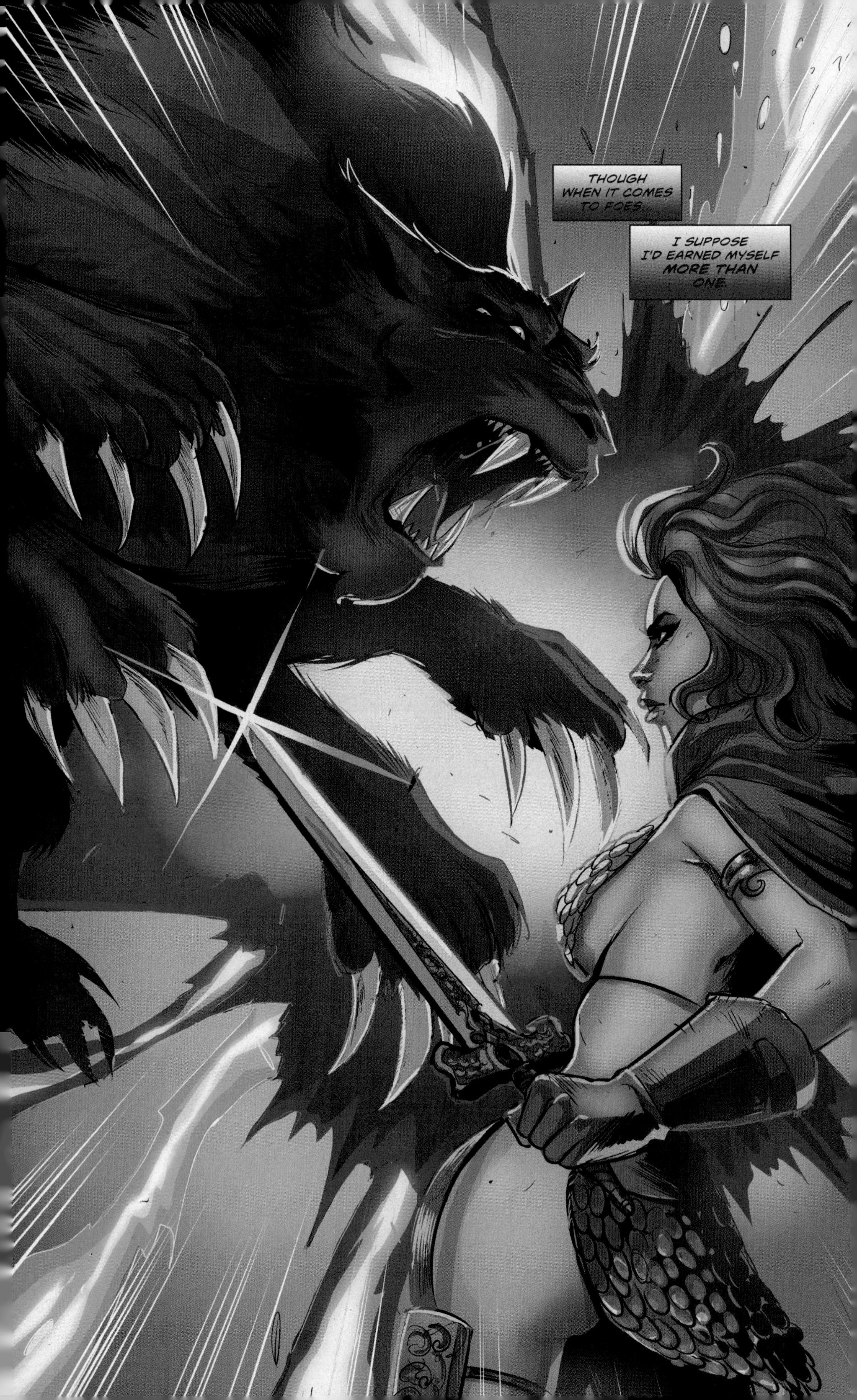
THOUGH WHEN IT COMES TO FOES...
I SUPPOSE I'D EARNED MYSELF MORE THAN ONE.

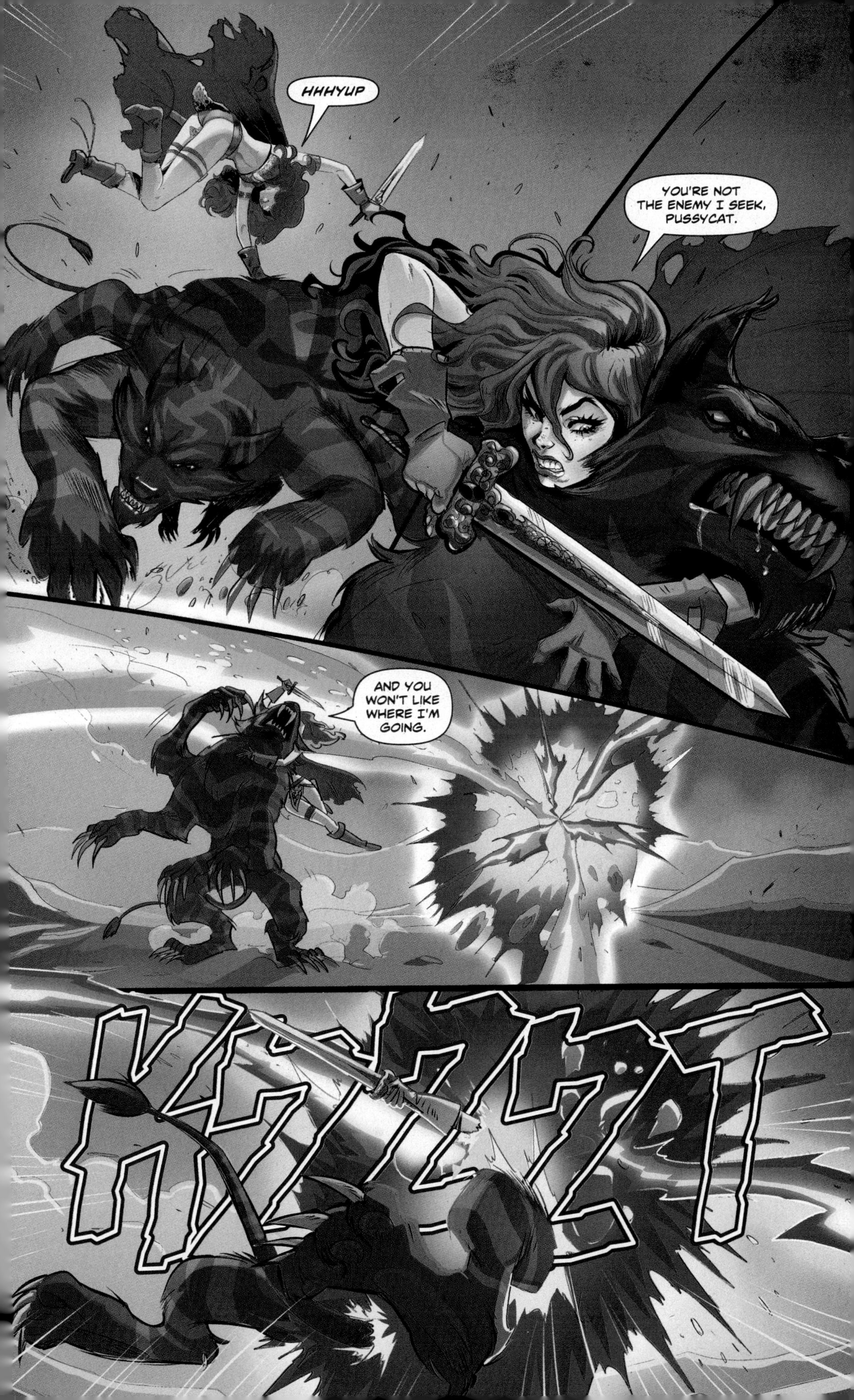
HHHYUP
YOU'RE NOT THE ENEMY I SEEK, PUSSYCAT.
AND YOU WON'T LIKE WHERE I'M GOING.
KRZZZT

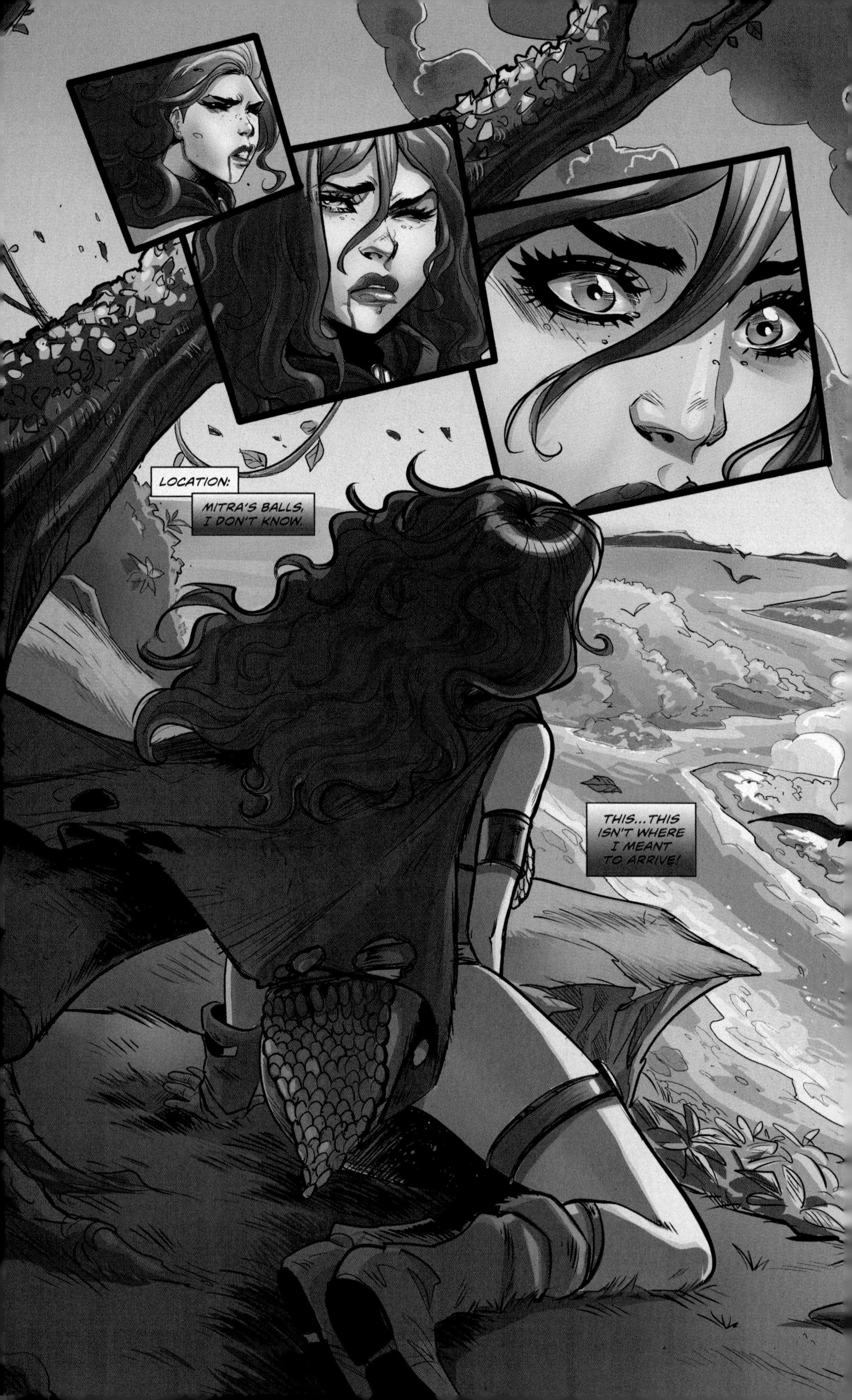
LOCATION:
MITRA'S BALLS, I DON'T KNOW.
THIS...THIS ISN'T WHERE I MEANT TO ARRIVE!

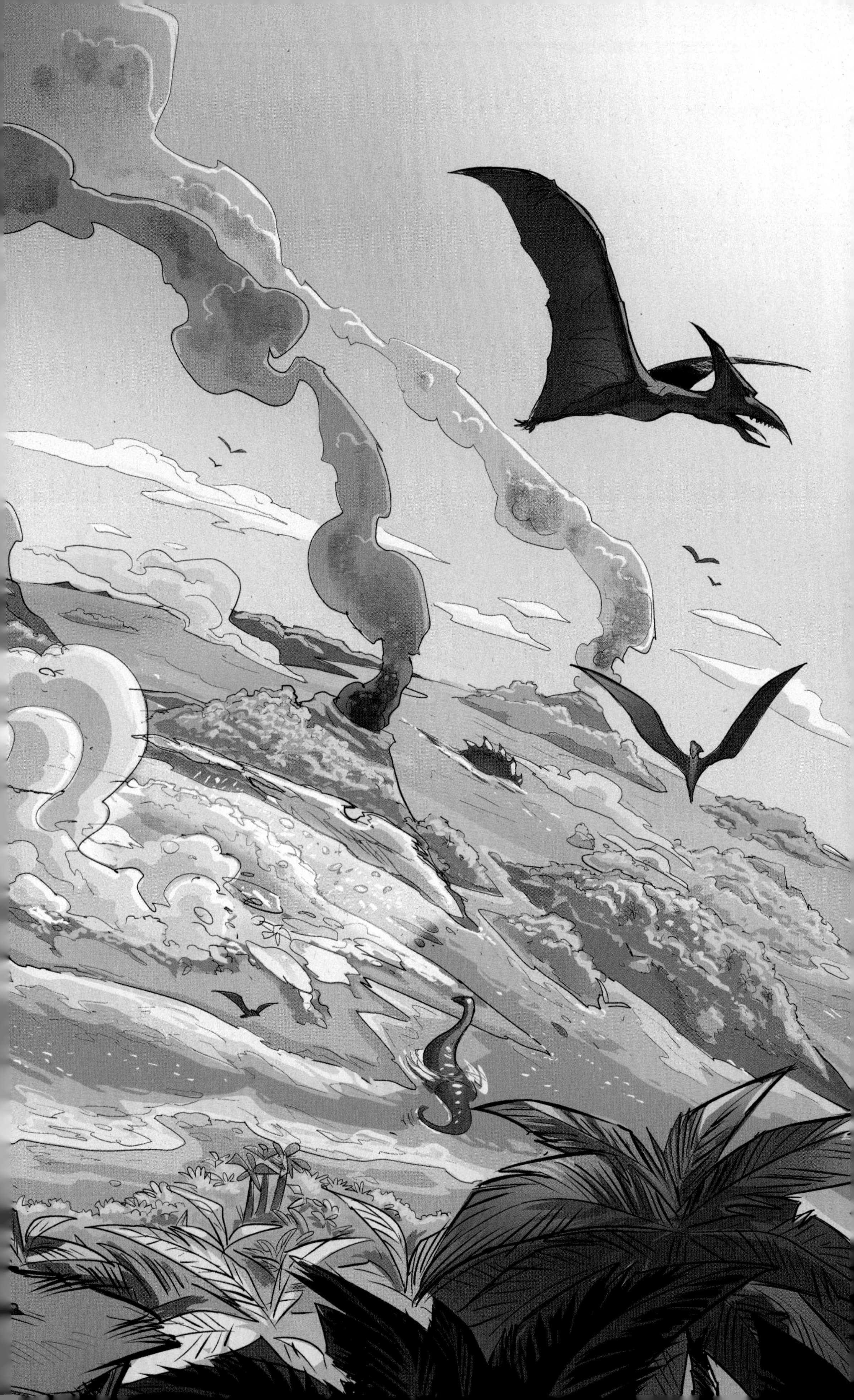

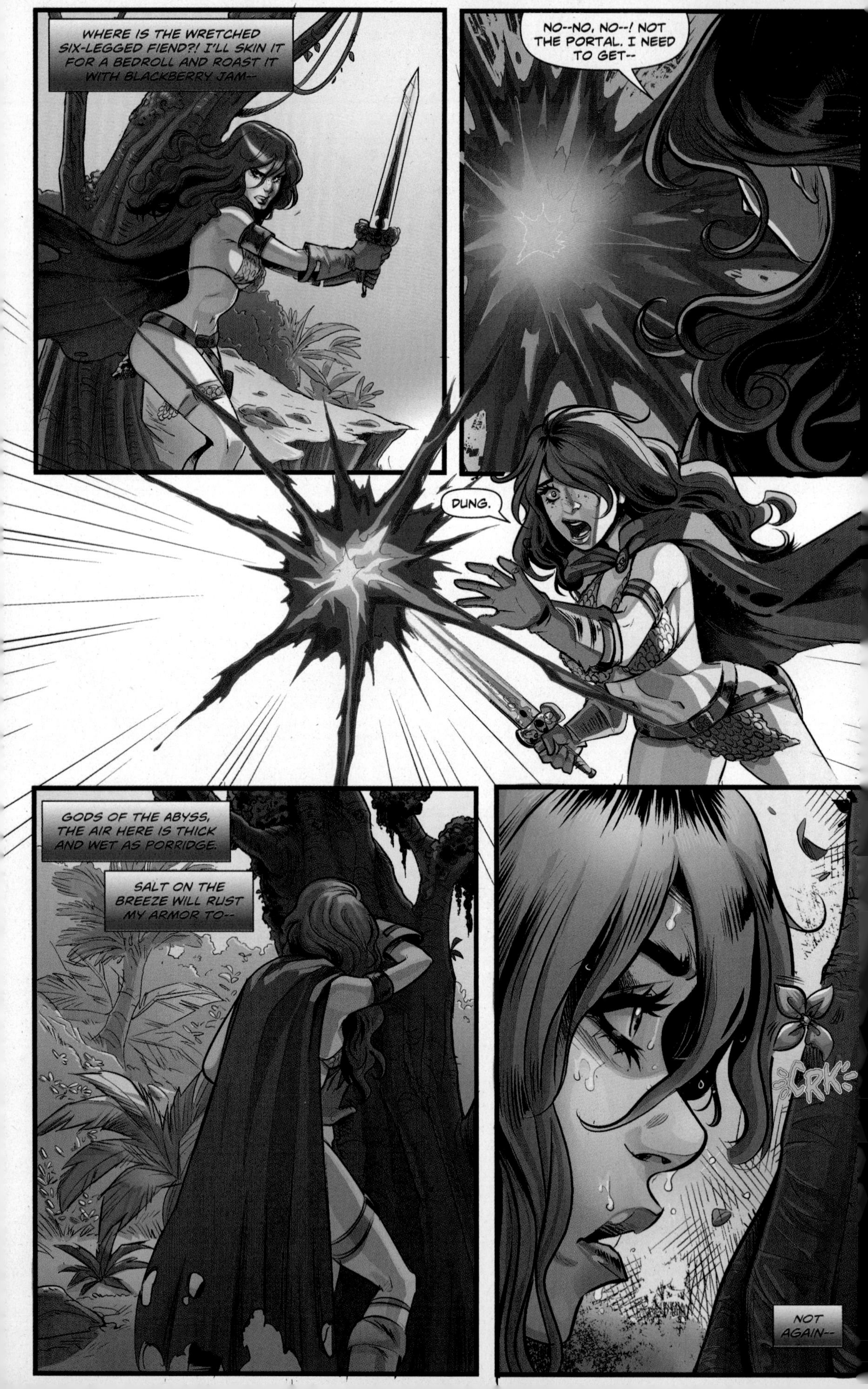
WHERE IS THE WRETCHED SIX-LEGGED FIEND?! I'LL SKIN IT FOR A BEDROLL AND ROAST IT WITH BLACKBERRY JAM--
NO--NO, NO--! NOT THE PORTAL. I NEED TO GET--
DUNG.
GODS OF THE ABYSS, THE AIR HERE IS THICK AND WET AS PORRIDGE.
SALT ON THE BREEZE WILL RUST MY ARMOR TO--
CRK
NOT AGAIN--

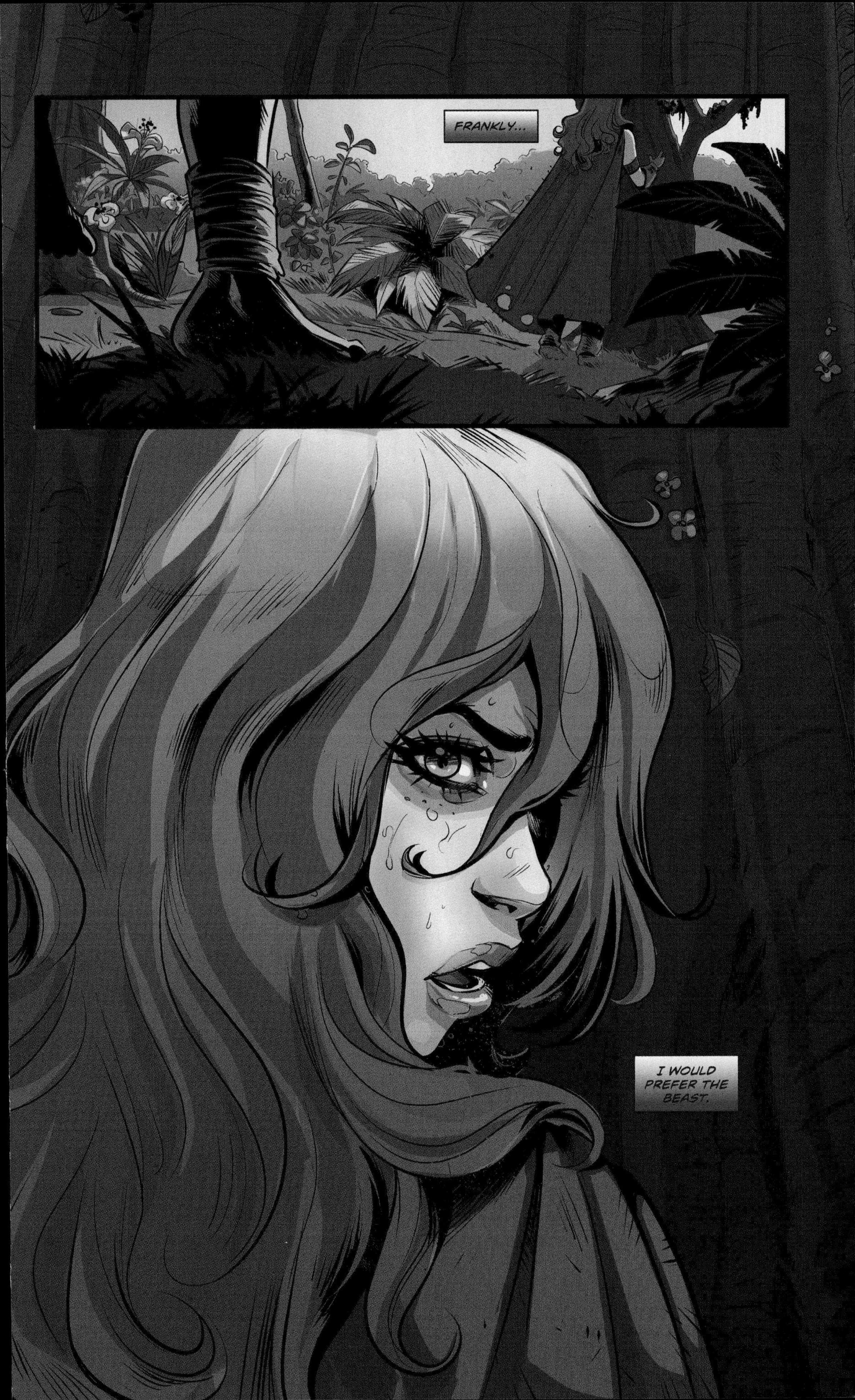
FRANKLY...
I WOULD PREFER THE BEAST.

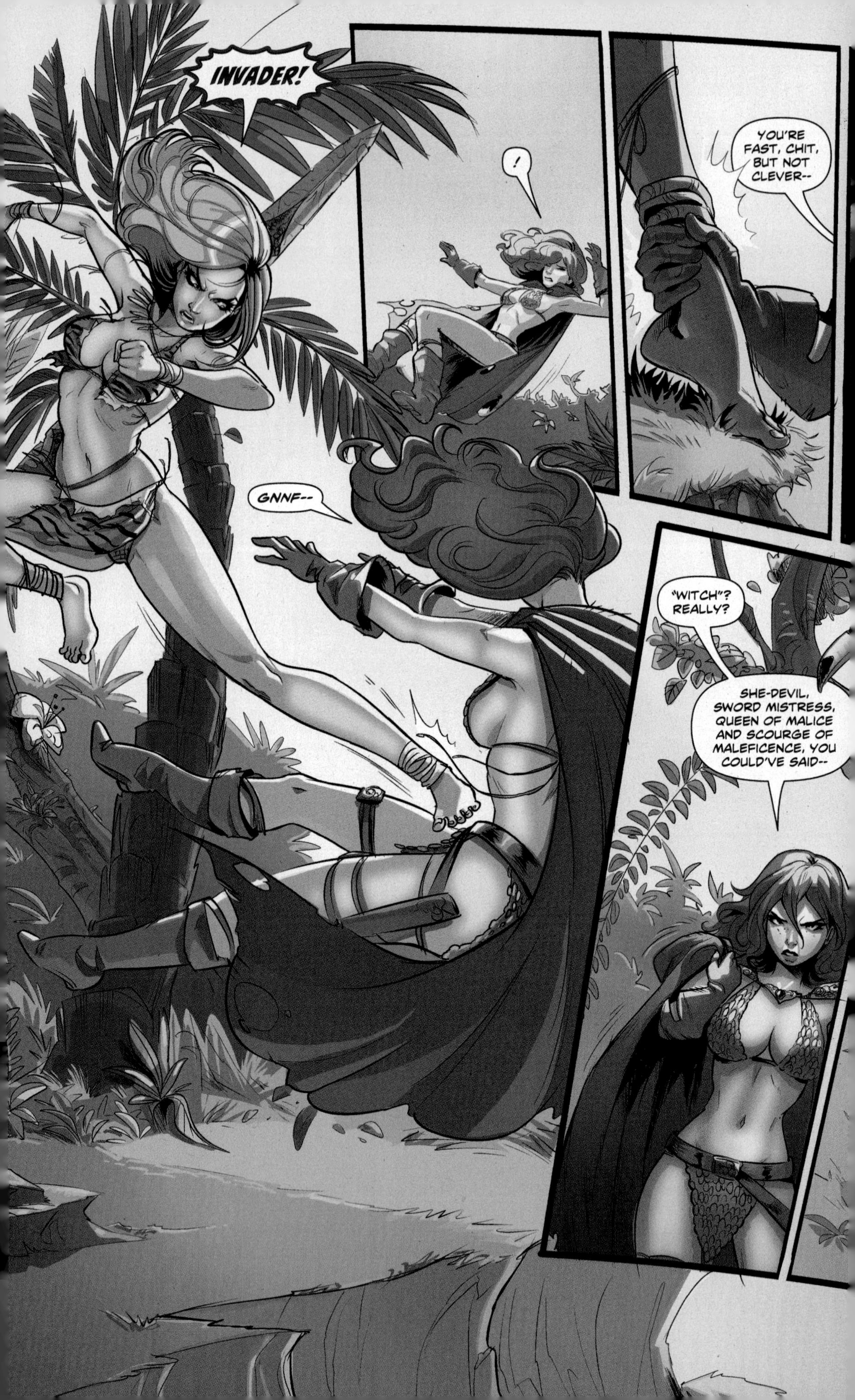
INVADER!
!
YOU'RE FAST, CHIT, BUT NOT CLEVER--
GNNF--
"WITCH"? REALLY?
SHE-DEVIL, SWORD MISTRESS, QUEEN OF MALICE AND SCOURGE OF MALEFICENCE, YOU COULD'VE SAID--

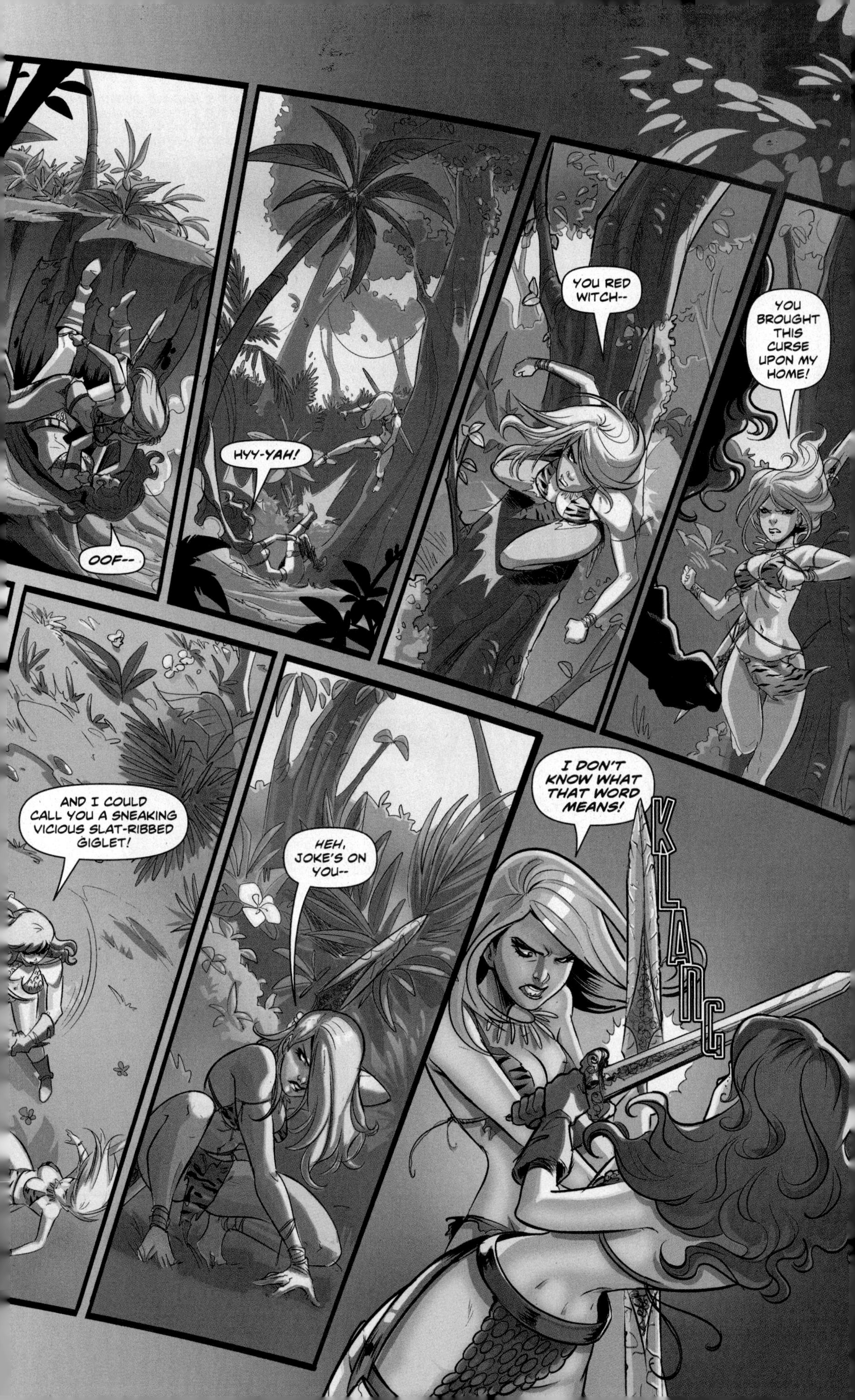
OOF--
HYY-YAH!
YOU RED WITCH--
YOU BROUGHT THIS CURSE UPON MY HOME!
AND I COULD CALL YOU A SNEAKING VICIOUS SLAT-RIBBED GIGLET!
HEH, JOKE'S ON YOU--
I DON'T KNOW WHAT THAT WORD MEANS!
KLANG

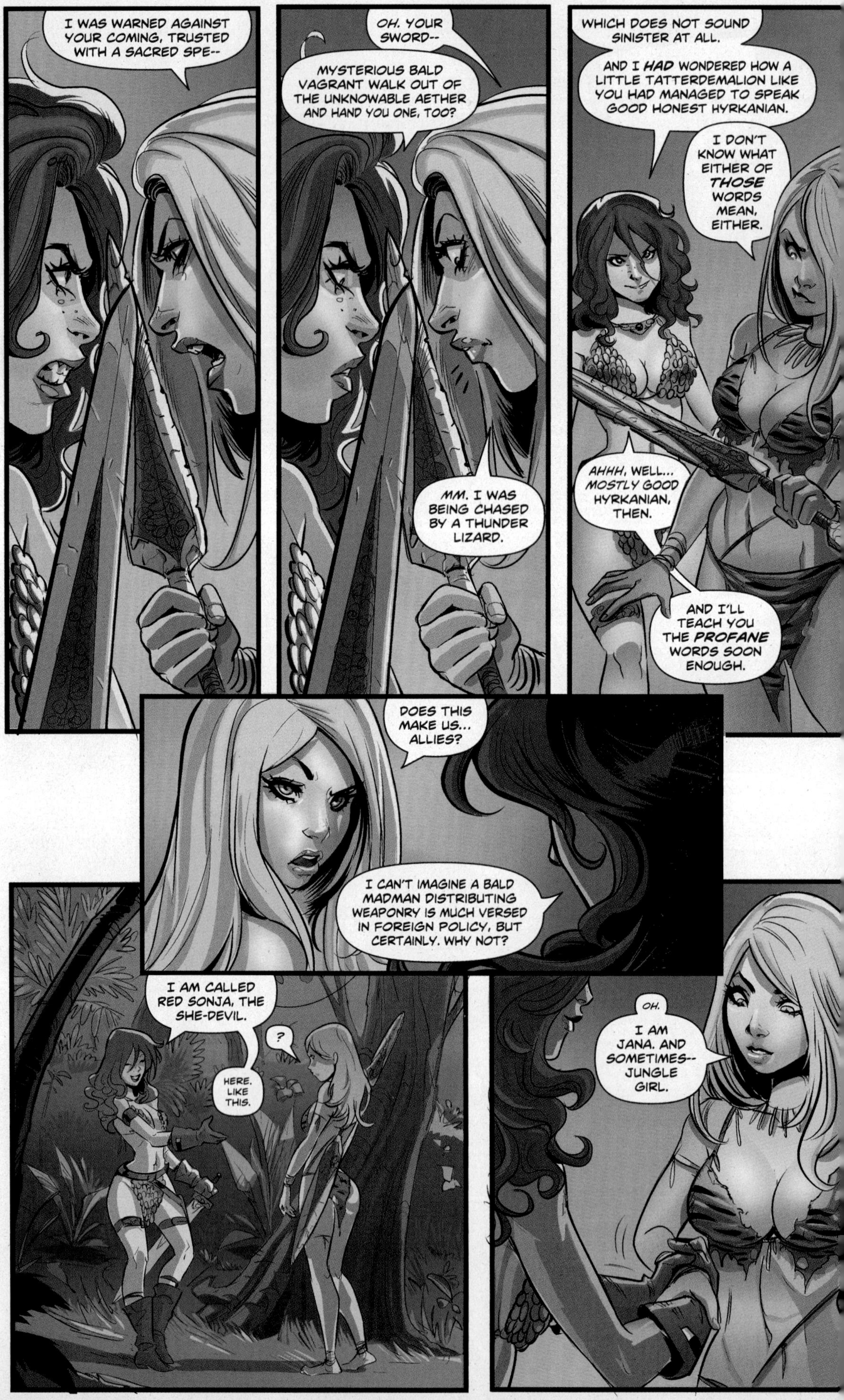
I WAS WARNED AGAINST YOUR COMING, TRUSTED WITH A SACRED SPE--
OH. YOUR SWORD--
MYSTERIOUS BALD VAGRANT WALK OUT OF THE UNKNOWABLE AETHER AND HAND YOU ONE, TOO?
MM. I WAS BEING CHASED BY A THUNDER LIZARD.
WHICH DOES NOT SOUND SINISTER AT ALL.
AND I HAD WONDERED HOW A LITTLE TATTERDEMALION LIKE YOU HAD MANAGED TO SPEAK GOOD HONEST HYRKANIAN.
I DON'T KNOW WHAT EITHER OF THOSE WORDS MEAN, EITHER.
AHHH, WELL... MOSTLY GOOD HYRKANIAN, THEN.
AND I'LL TEACH YOU THE PROFANE WORDS SOON ENOUGH.
DOES THIS MAKE US... ALLIES?
I CAN'T IMAGINE A BALD MADMAN DISTRIBUTING WEAPONRY IS MUCH VERSED IN FOREIGN POLICY, BUT CERTAINLY. WHY NOT?
I AM CALLED RED SONJA, THE SHE-DEVIL.
?
HERE. LIKE THIS.
OH.
I AM JANA. AND SOMETIMES-- JUNGLE GIRL.

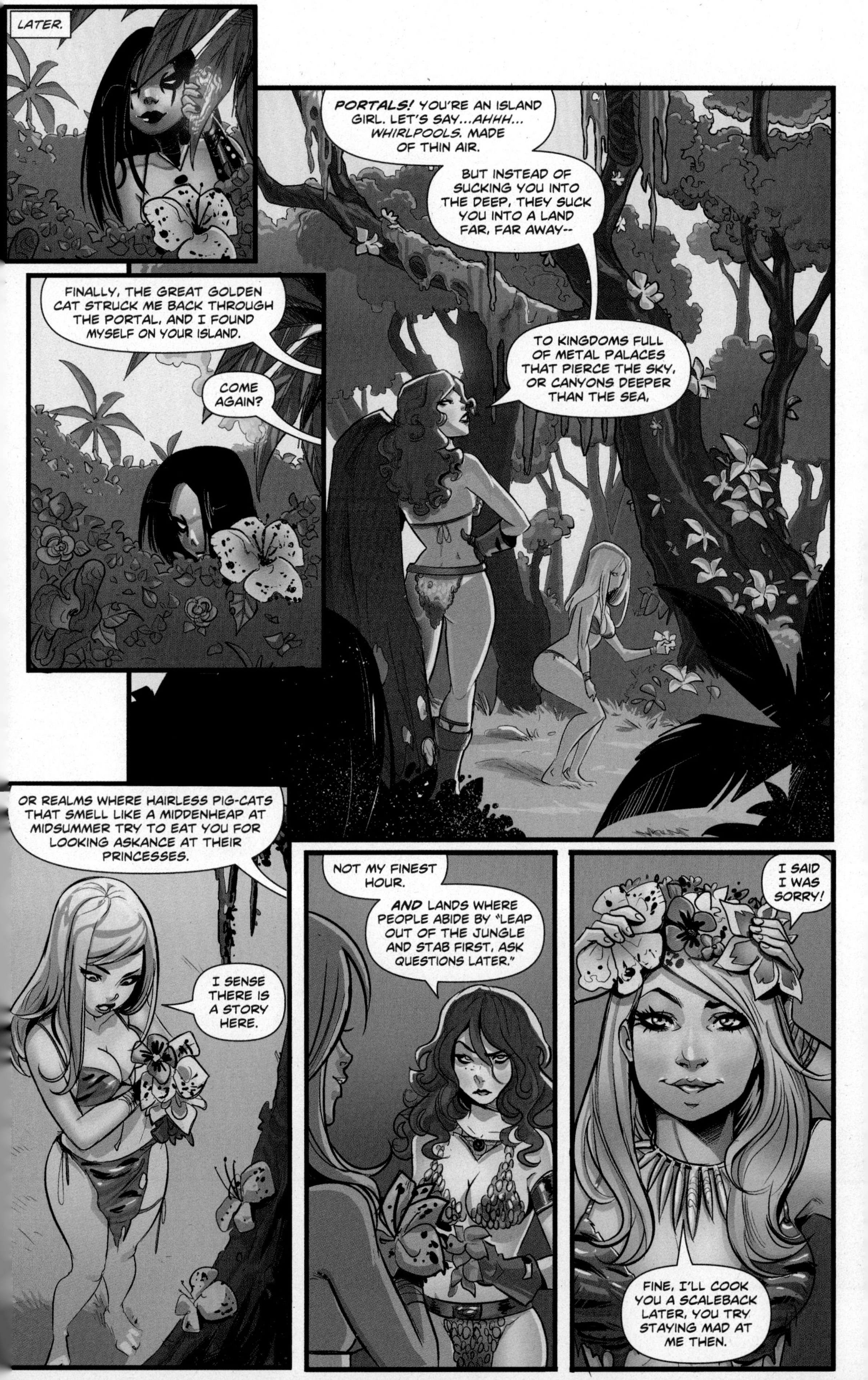
LATER.
PORTALS! YOU'RE AN ISLAND GIRL. LET'S SAY...AHHH... WHIRLPOOLS. MADE OF THIN AIR.
BUT INSTEAD OF SUCKING YOU INTO THE DEEP, THEY SUCK YOU INTO A LAND FAR, FAR AWAY--
TO KINGDOMS FULL OF METAL PALACES THAT PIERCE THE SKY, OR CANYONS DEEPER THAN THE SEA,
FINALLY, THE GREAT GOLDEN CAT STRUCK ME BACK THROUGH THE PORTAL, AND I FOUND MYSELF ON YOUR ISLAND.
COME AGAIN?
OR REALMS WHERE HAIRLESS PIG-CATS THAT SMELL LIKE A MIDDENHEAP AT MIDSUMMER TRY TO EAT YOU FOR LOOKING ASKANCE AT THEIR PRINCESSES.
I SENSE THERE IS A STORY HERE.
NOT MY FINEST HOUR.
AND LANDS WHERE PEOPLE ABIDE BY "LEAP OUT OF THE JUNGLE AND STAB FIRST, ASK QUESTIONS LATER."
I SAID I WAS SORRY!
FINE, I'LL COOK YOU A SCALEBACK LATER, YOU TRY STAYING MAD AT ME THEN.

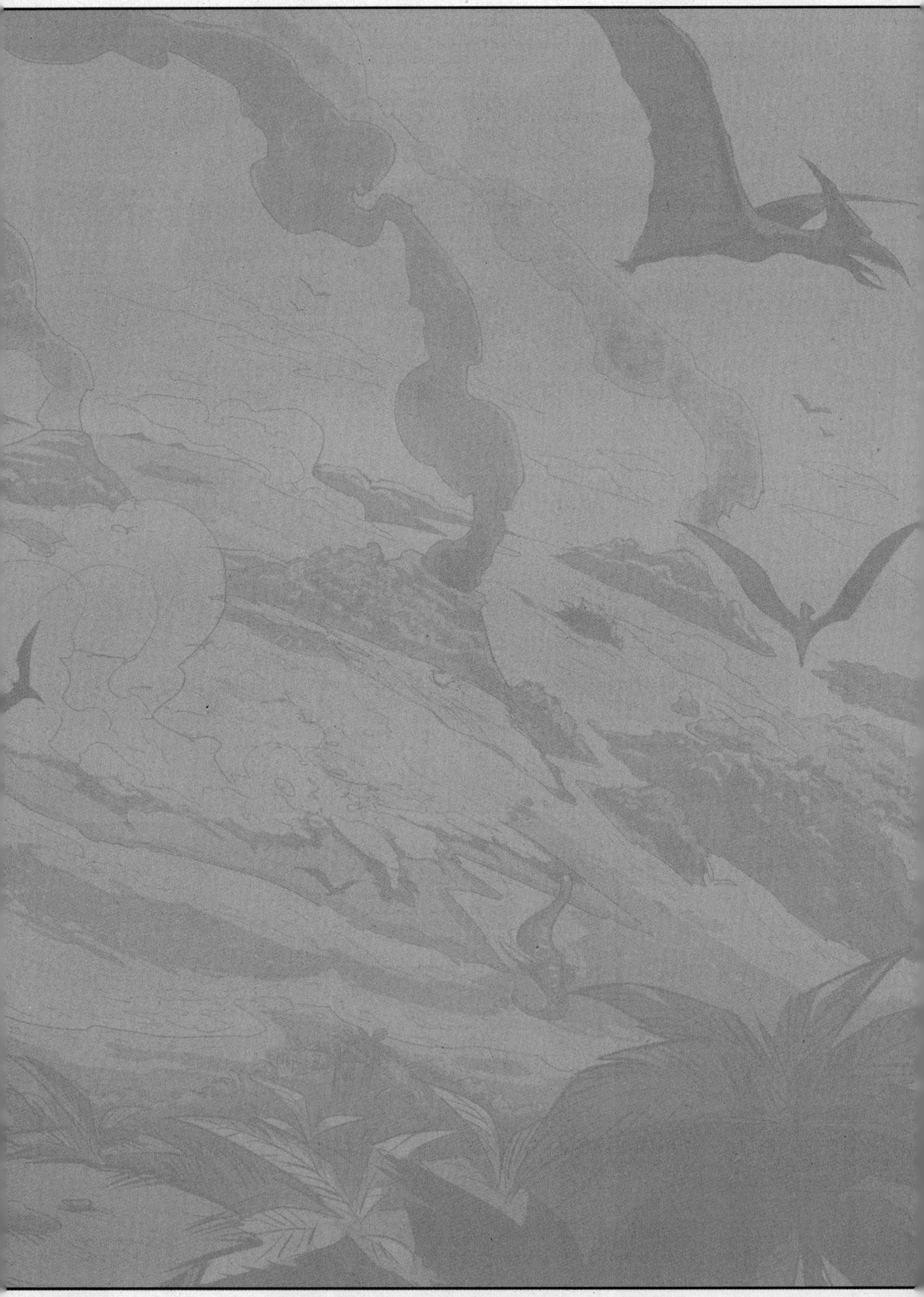

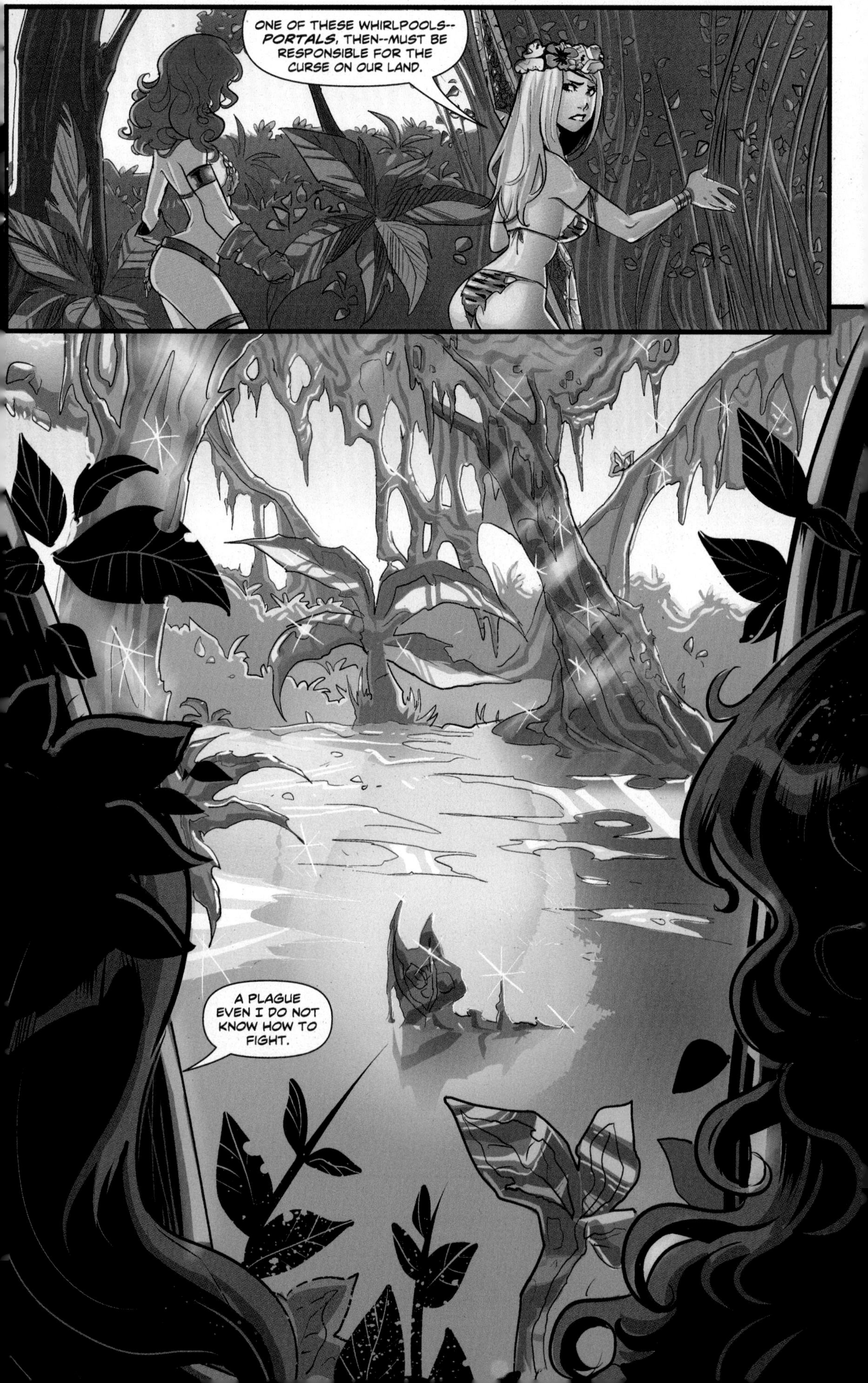
ONE OF THESE WHIRLPOOLS-- PORTALS, THEN--MUST BE RESPONSIBLE FOR THE CURSE ON OUR LAND.
A PLAGUE EVEN I DO NOT KNOW HOW TO FIGHT.

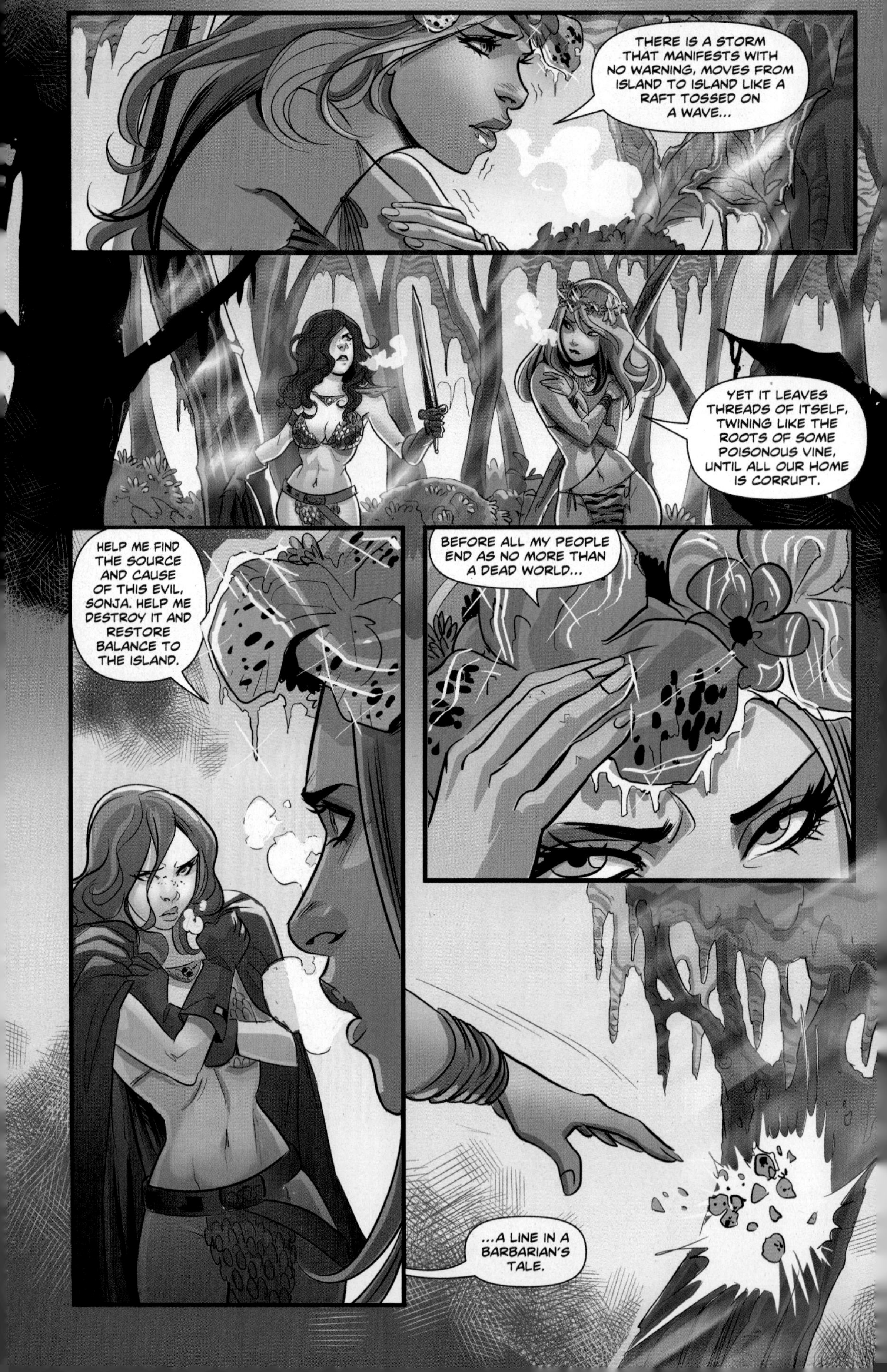
THERE IS A STORM THAT MANIFESTS WITH NO WARNING, MOVES FROM ISLAND TO ISLAND LIKE A RAFT TOSSED ON A WAVE...
YET IT LEAVES THREADS OF ITSELF, TWINING LIKE THE ROOTS OF SOME POISONOUS VINE, UNTIL ALL OUR HOME IS CORRUPT.
HELP ME FIND THE SOURCE AND CAUSE OF THIS EVIL, SONJA. HELP ME DESTROY IT AND RESTORE BALANCE TO THE ISLAND.
BEFORE ALL MY PEOPLE END AS NO MORE THAN A DEAD WORLD...
...A LINE IN A BARBARIAN'S TALE.

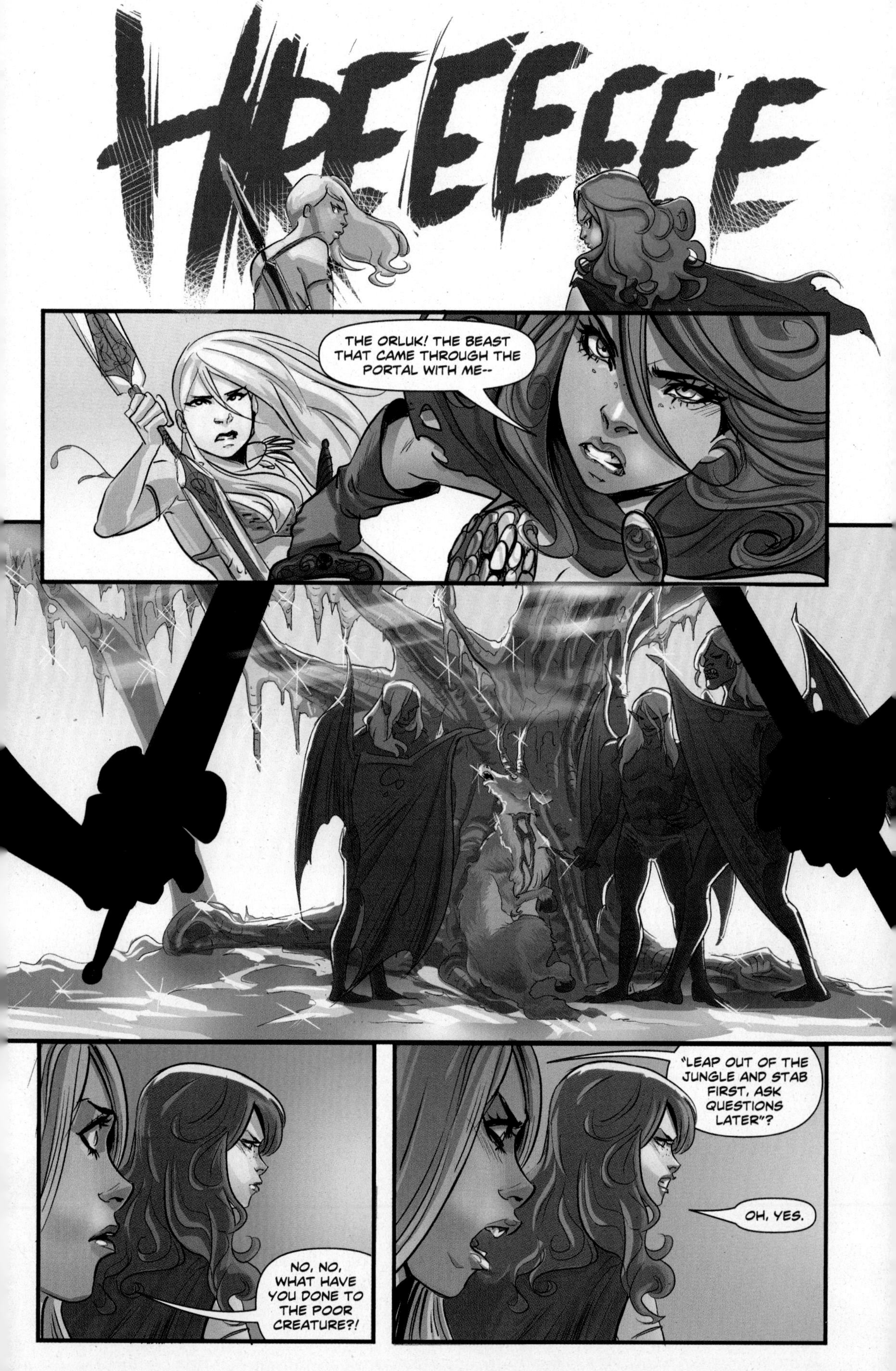
HREEEEEE
THE ORLUK! THE BEAST THAT CAME THROUGH THE PORTAL WITH ME--
NO, NO, WHAT HAVE YOU DONE TO THE POOR CREATURE?!
"LEAP OUT OF THE JUNGLE AND STAB FIRST, ASK QUESTIONS LATER"?
OH, YES.

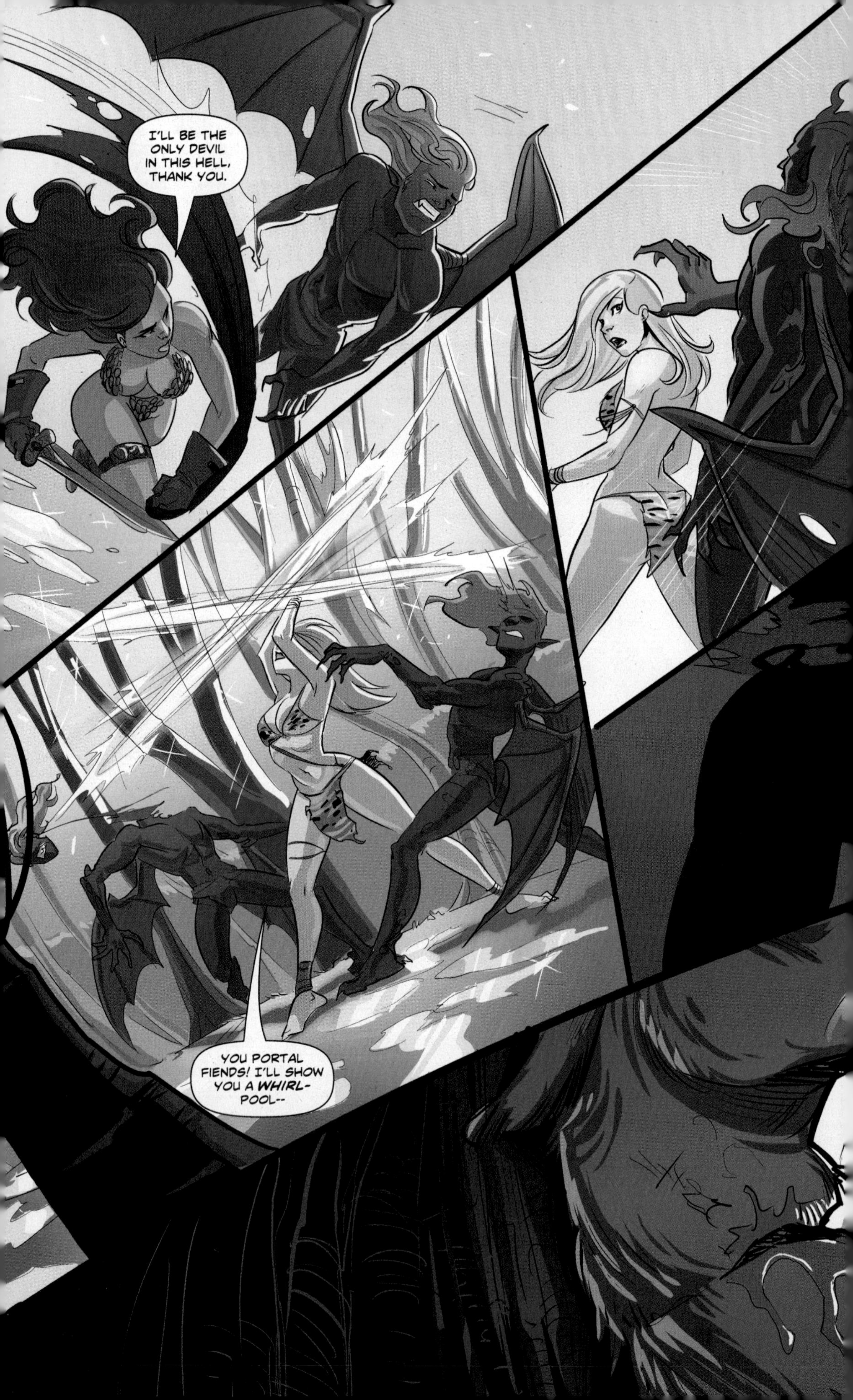
I'LL BE THE ONLY DEVIL IN THIS HELL, THANK YOU.
YOU PORTAL FIENDS! I'LL SHOW YOU A WHIRL-POOL--

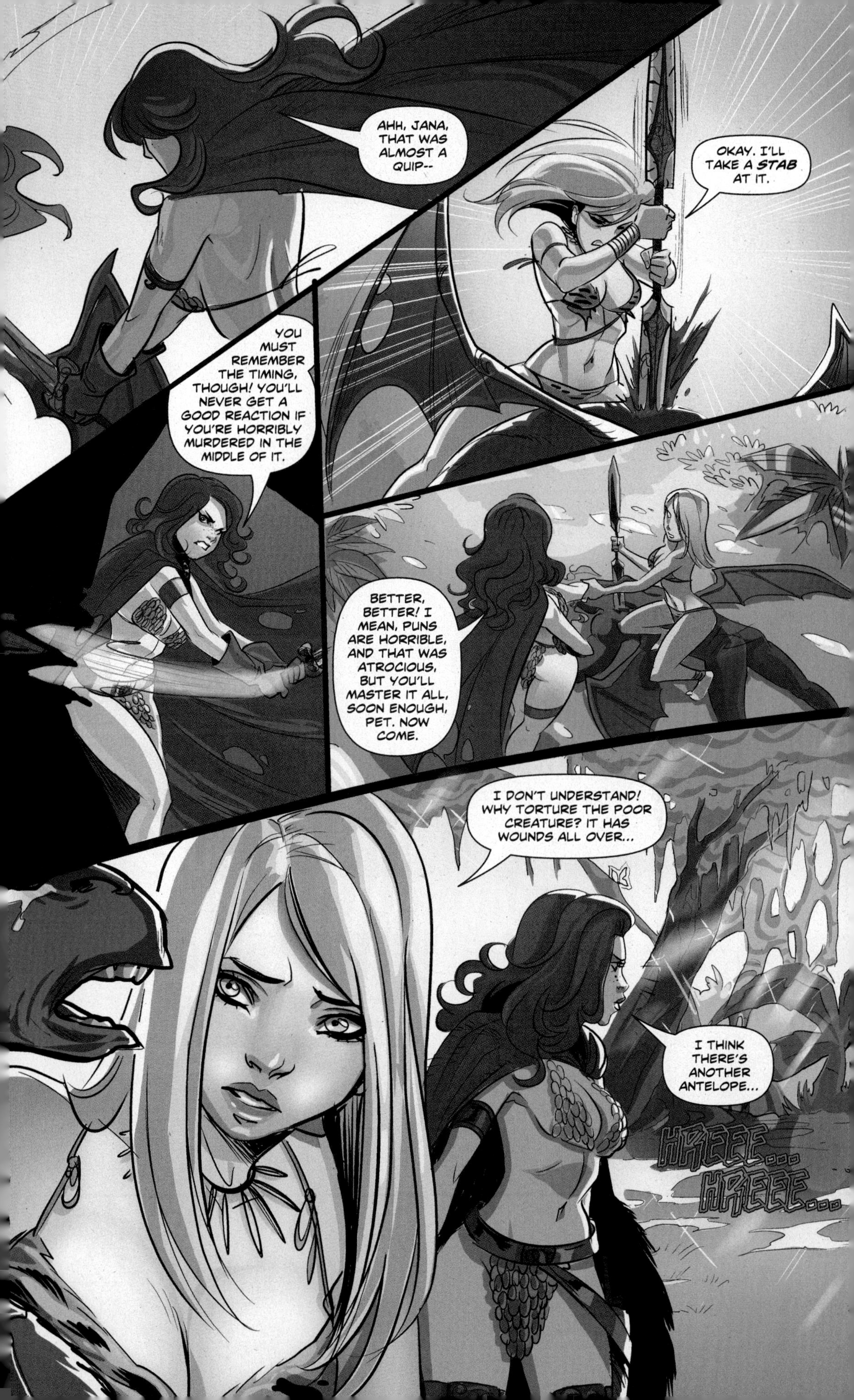
AHH, JANA, THAT WAS ALMOST A QUIP--
OKAY. I'LL TAKE A STAB AT IT.
YOU MUST REMEMBER THE TIMING, THOUGH! YOU'LL NEVER GET A GOOD REACTION IF YOU'RE HORRIBLY MURDERED IN THE MIDDLE OF IT.
BETTER, BETTER! I MEAN, PUNS ARE HORRIBLE, AND THAT WAS ATROCIOUS, BUT YOU'LL MASTER IT ALL, SOON ENOUGH, PET. NOW COME.
I DON'T UNDERSTAND! WHY TORTURE THE POOR CREATURE? IT HAS WOUNDS ALL OVER...
I THINK THERE'S ANOTHER ANTELOPE...
HREEE... HREEE...

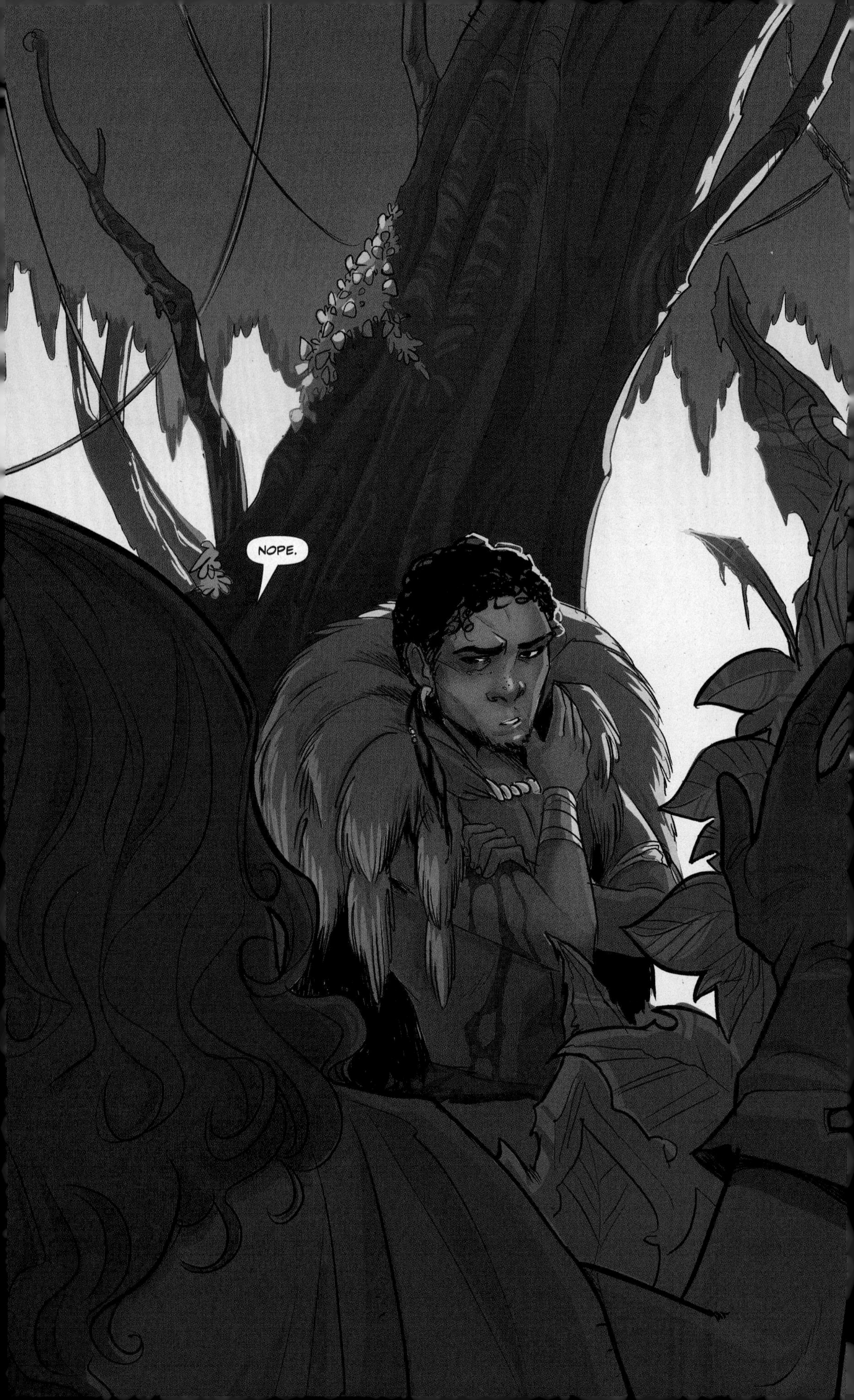
NOPE.

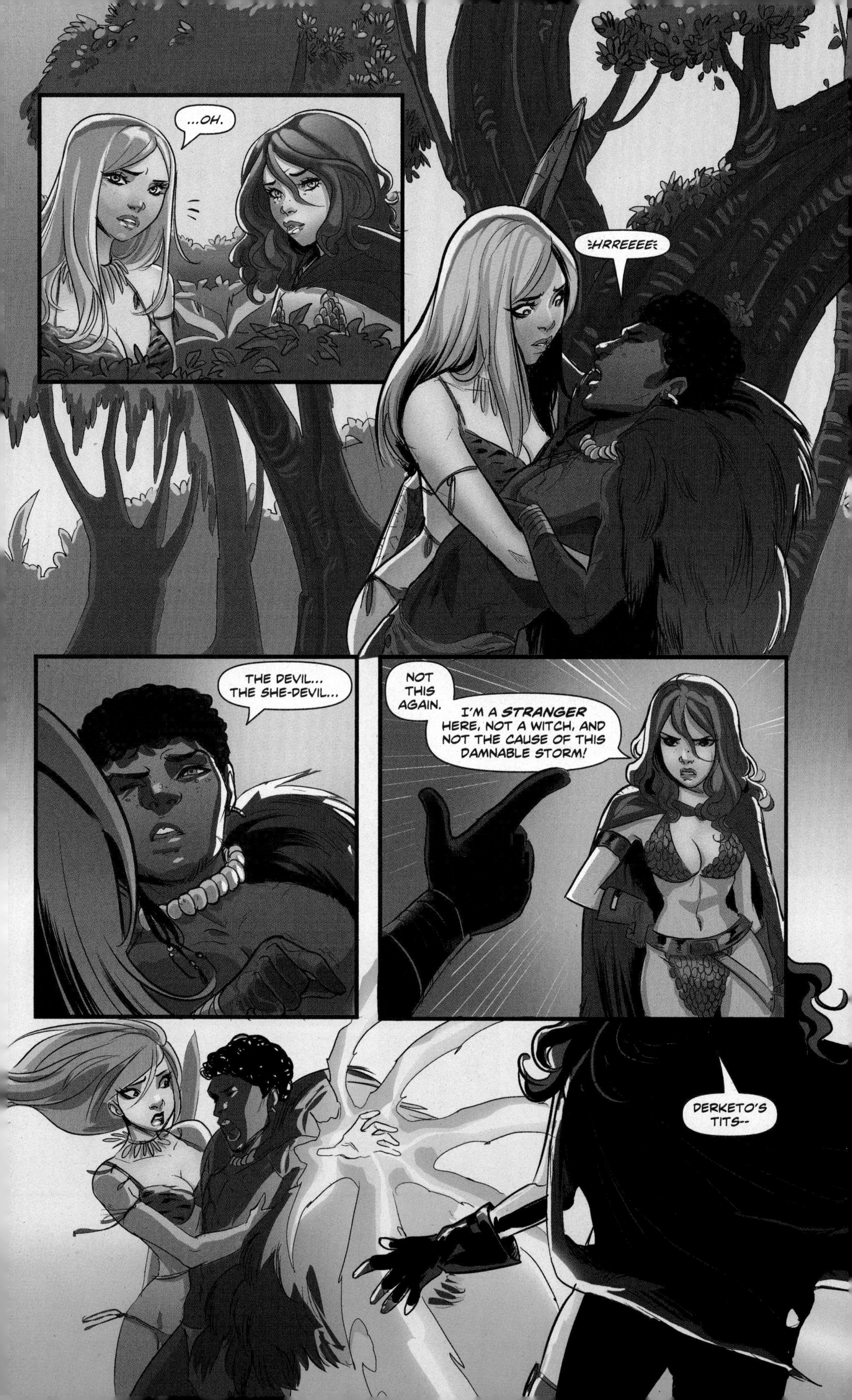
...OH.
HRREEEE
THE DEVIL... THE SHE-DEVIL...
NOT THIS AGAIN.
I'M A **STRANGER** HERE, NOT A WITCH, AND NOT THE CAUSE OF THIS DAMNABLE STORM!
DERKETO'S TITS--

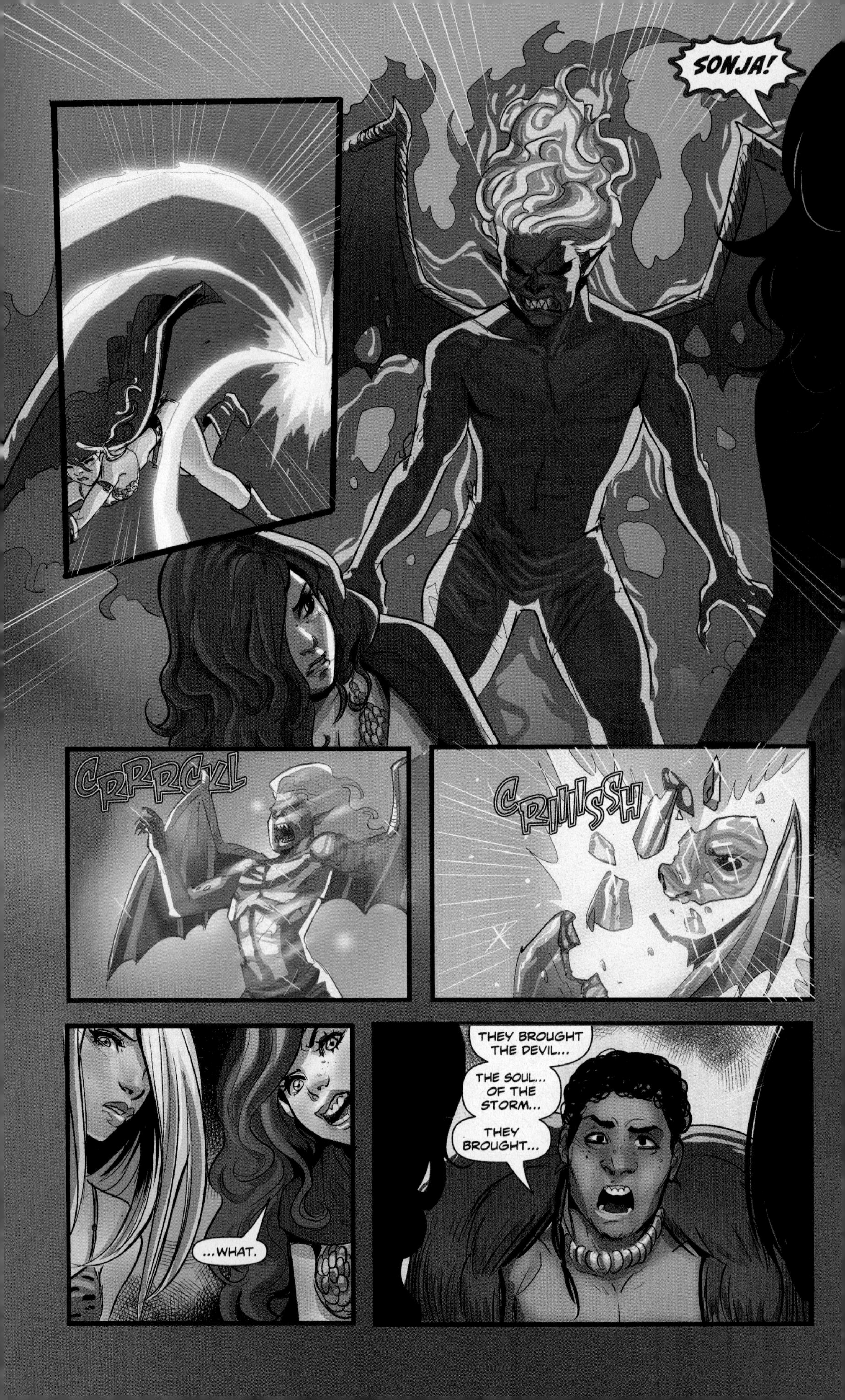
SONJA!
CRRRCKL
CRIIISSH
...WHAT.
THEY BROUGHT THE DEVIL...
THE SOUL... OF THE STORM...
THEY BROUGHT...

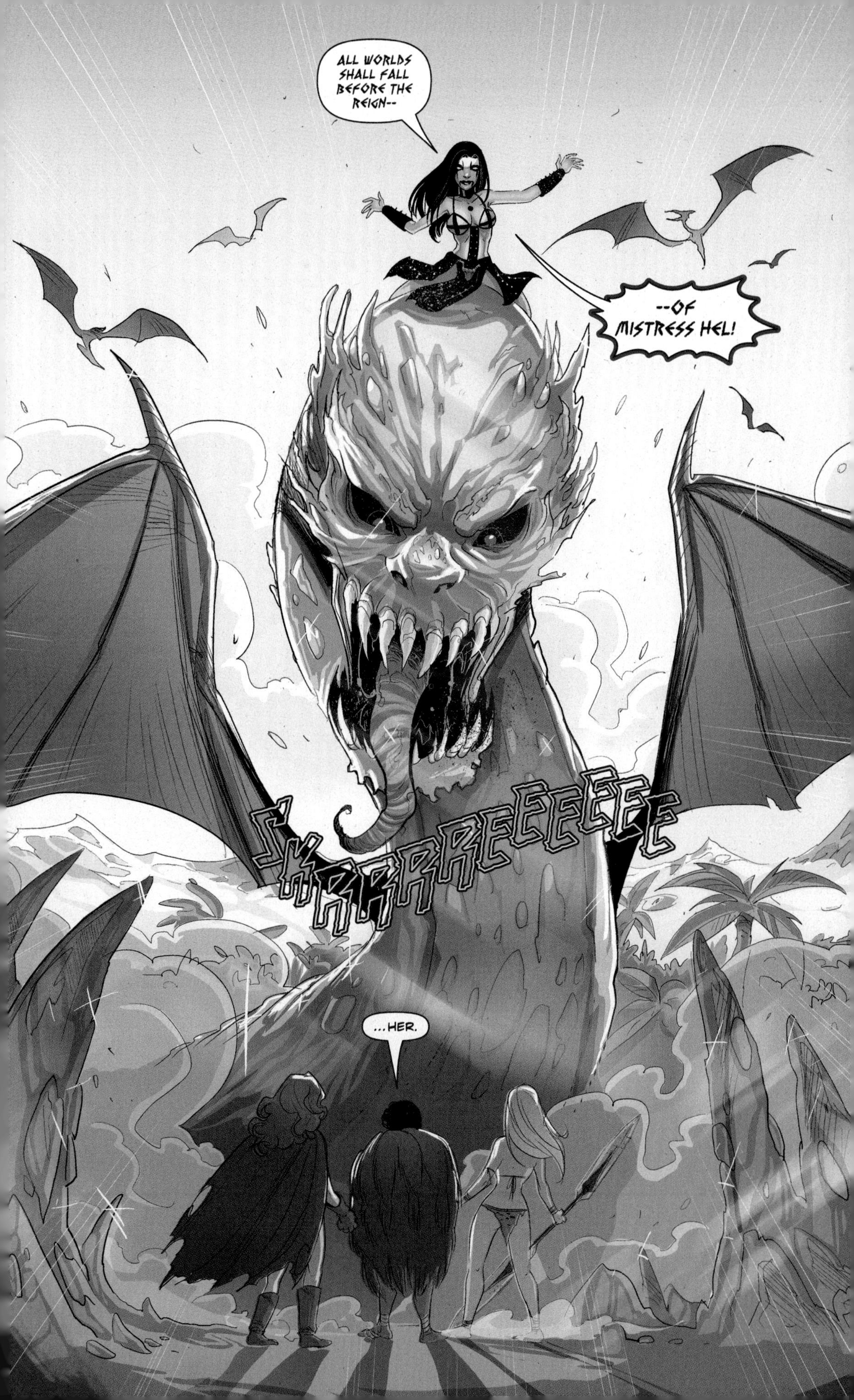
ALL WORLDS SHALL FALL BEFORE THE REIGN--
--OF MISTRESS HEL!
SKRRRREEEEEEE
...HER.

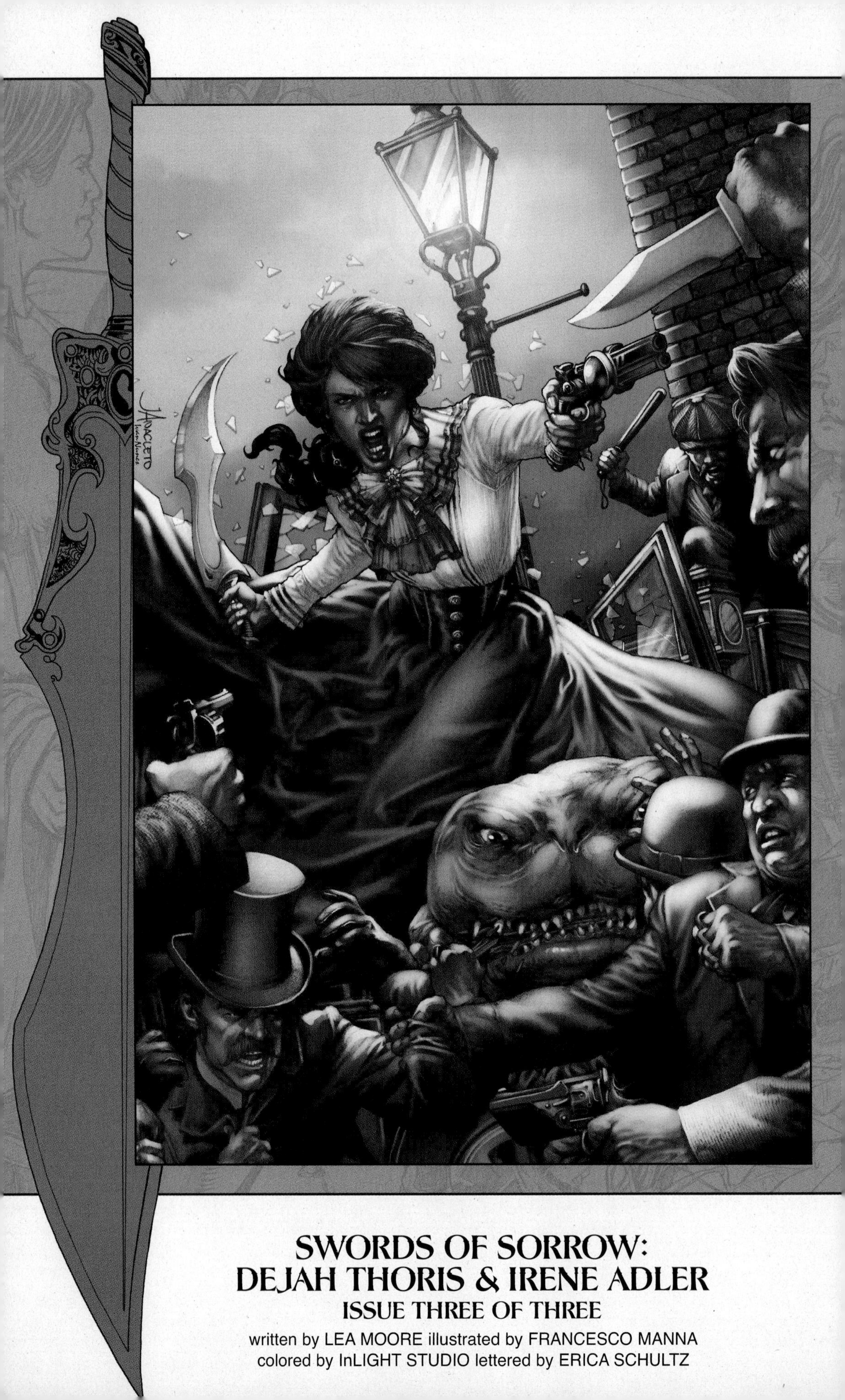

SWORDS OF SORROW: DEJAH THORIS & IRENE ADLER

ISSUE THREE OF THREE

written by LEA MOORE illustrated by FRANCESCO MANNA
colored by InLIGHT STUDIO lettered by ERICA SCHULTZ

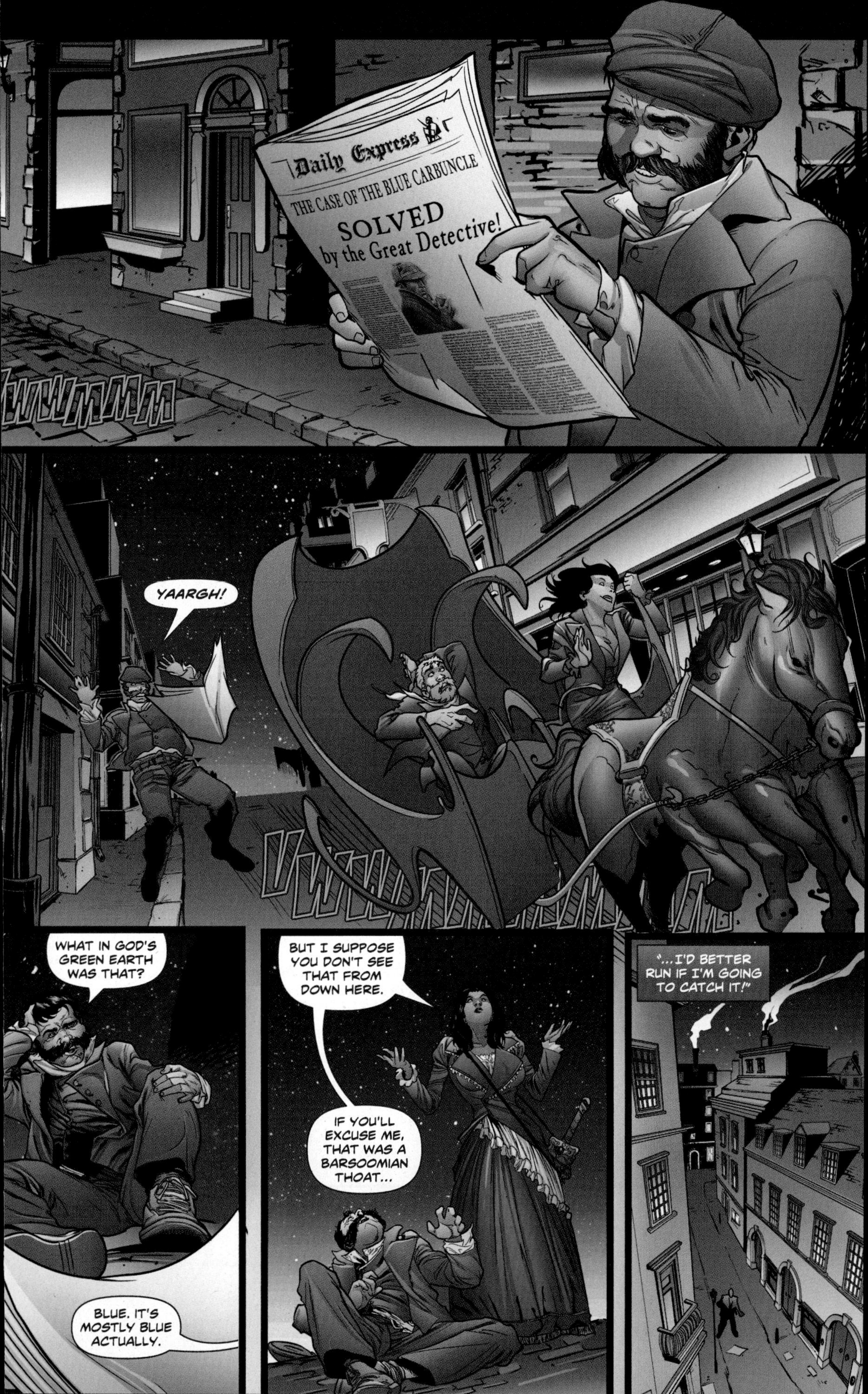
Daily Express
THE CASE OF THE BLUE CARBUNCLE
SOLVED by the Great Detective!
YAARGH!
WHAT IN GOD'S GREEN EARTH WAS THAT?
BLUE. IT'S MOSTLY BLUE ACTUALLY.
BUT I SUPPOSE YOU DON'T SEE THAT FROM DOWN HERE.
IF YOU'LL EXCUSE ME, THAT WAS A BARSOOMIAN THOAT...
"...I'D BETTER RUN IF I'M GOING TO CATCH IT!"

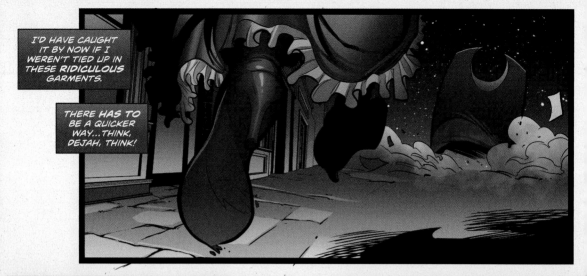

I'D HAVE CAUGHT IT BY NOW IF I WEREN'T TIED UP IN THESE *RIDICULOUS* GARMENTS.

THERE HAS TO BE A QUICKER WAY...THINK, DEJAH, THINK!

THE ATTACKS WERE CLUSTERED; I'LL BET THE CAT HASN'T GONE FAR.

AND WHY DO WE WANT TO CATCH IT AGAIN?

WHERE'S THE WHEELS GONE? HOW'S IT STILL GOING?

THAT IS CLASSIFIED. I'M CERTAINLY NOT PERMITTED TO TELL A LONDON CABBIE OF ALL PEOPLE.

BUT, SINCE YOU ASK, MY BOSS WANTS THE CAT BECAUSE *IT* ATE THE PRIME MINISTER.

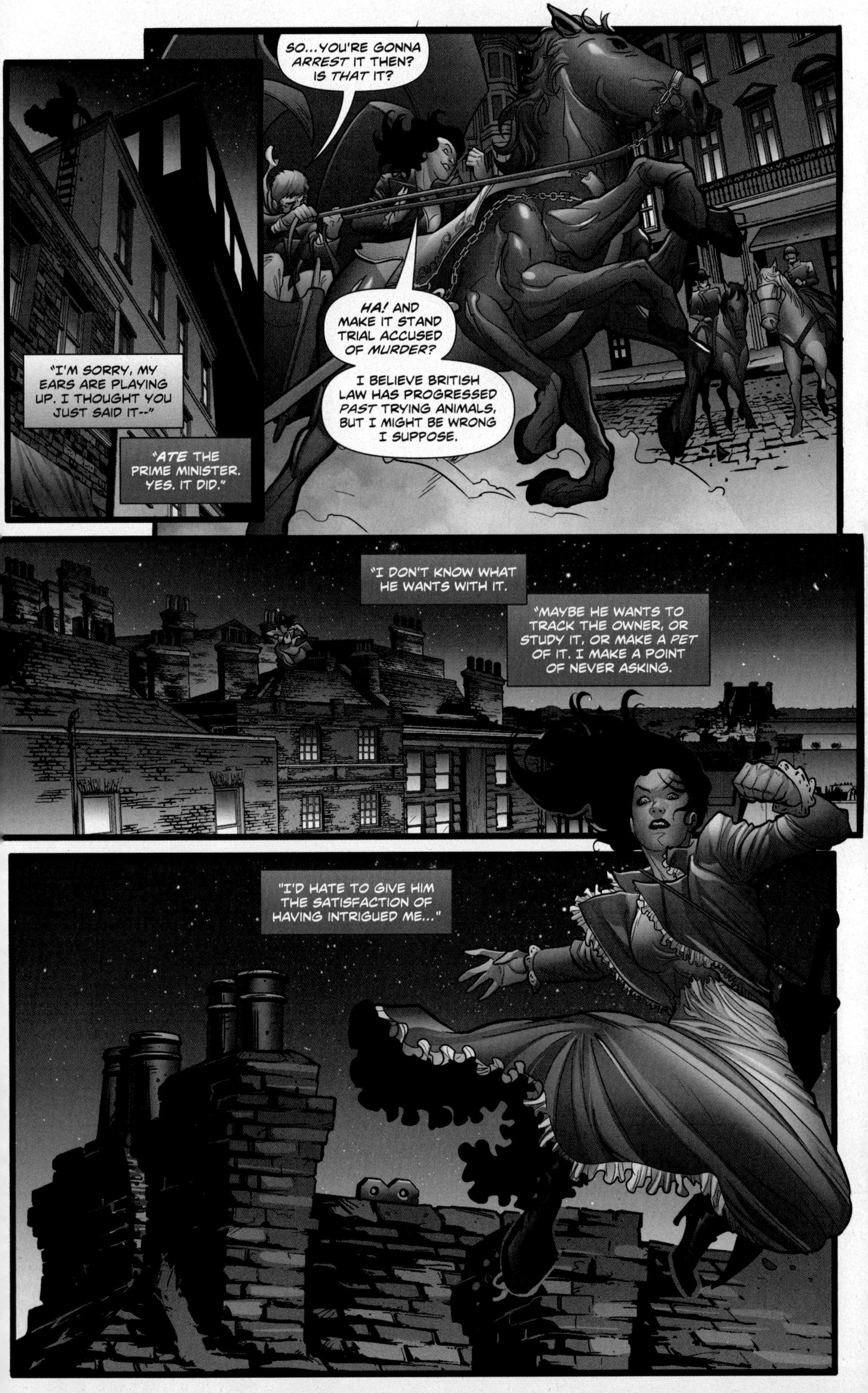
"I'M SORRY, MY EARS ARE PLAYING UP. I THOUGHT YOU JUST SAID IT--"
"ATE THE PRIME MINISTER. YES. IT DID."
SO...YOU'RE GONNA ARREST IT THEN? IS THAT IT?
HA! AND MAKE IT STAND TRIAL ACCUSED OF MURDER?
I BELIEVE BRITISH LAW HAS PROGRESSED PAST TRYING ANIMALS, BUT I MIGHT BE WRONG I SUPPOSE.
"I DON'T KNOW WHAT HE WANTS WITH IT.
"MAYBE HE WANTS TO TRACK THE OWNER, OR STUDY IT, OR MAKE A PET OF IT. I MAKE A POINT OF NEVER ASKING.
"I'D HATE TO GIVE HIM THE SATISFACTION OF HAVING INTRIGUED ME..."

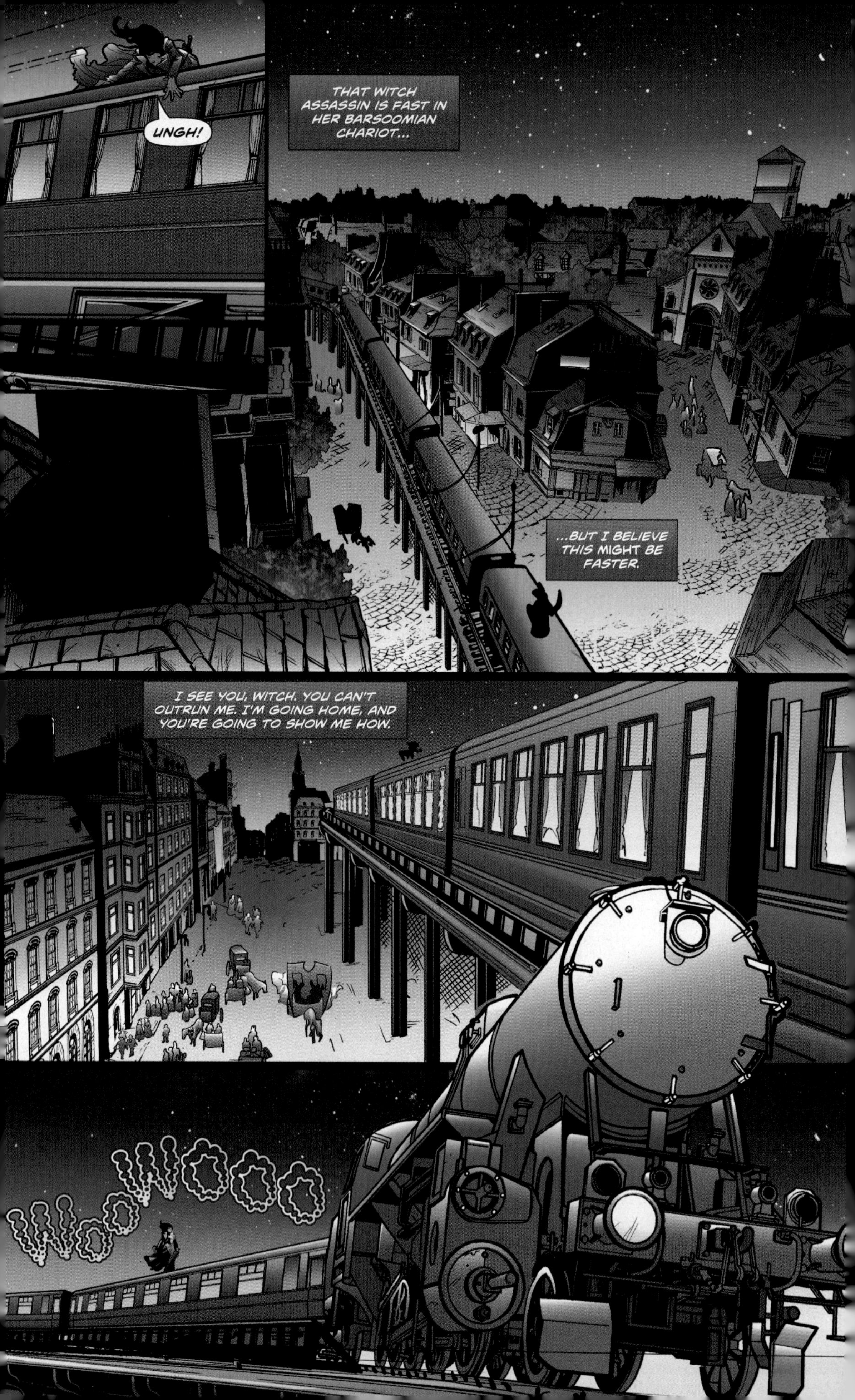
UNGH!
THAT WITCH ASSASSIN IS FAST IN HER BARSOOMIAN CHARIOT...
...BUT I BELIEVE THIS MIGHT BE FASTER.
I SEE YOU, WITCH. YOU CAN'T OUTRUN ME. I'M GOING HOME, AND YOU'RE GOING TO SHOW ME HOW.
WOOWOOO

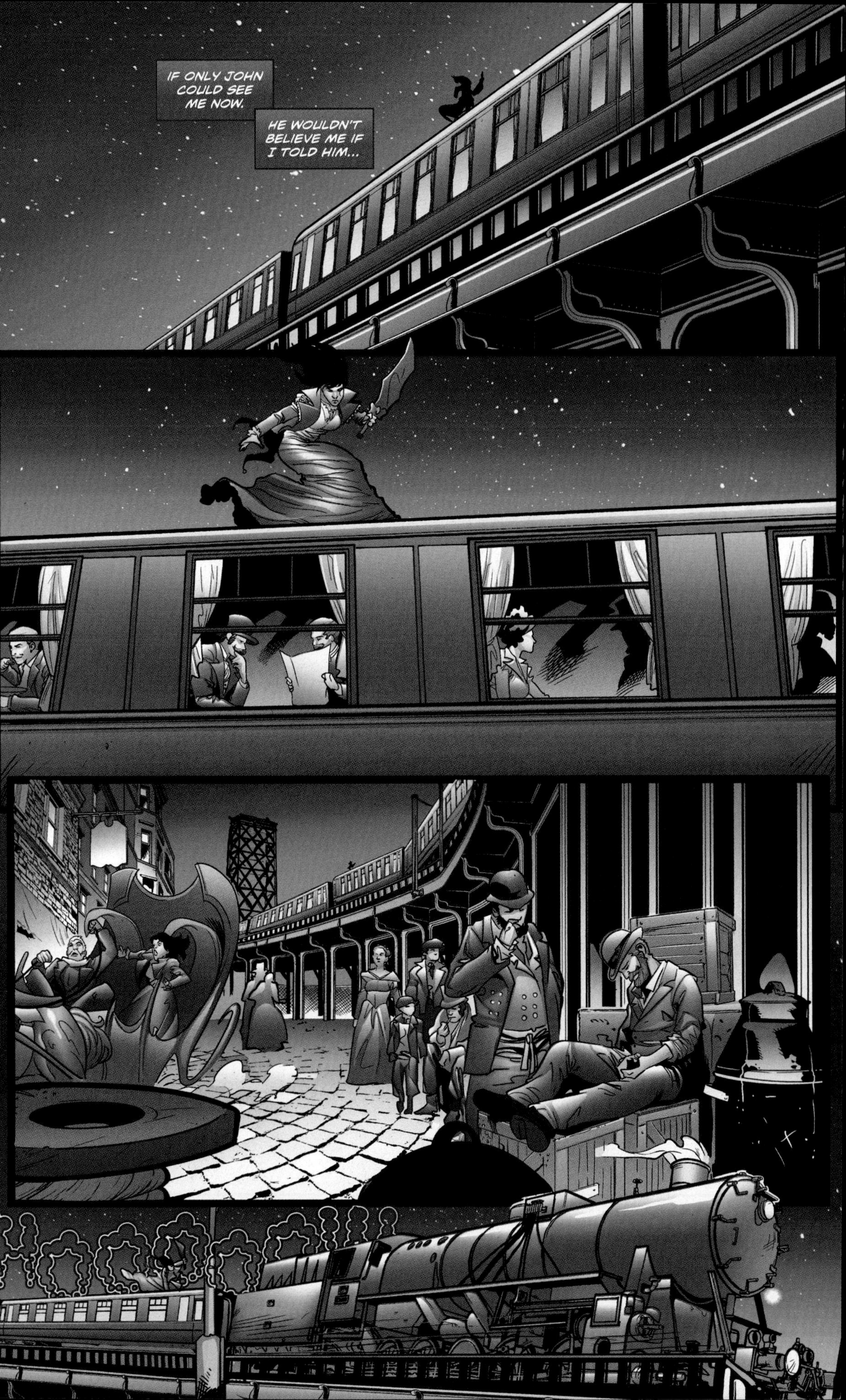
IF ONLY JOHN COULD SEE ME NOW.
HE WOULDN'T BELIEVE ME IF I TOLD HIM...

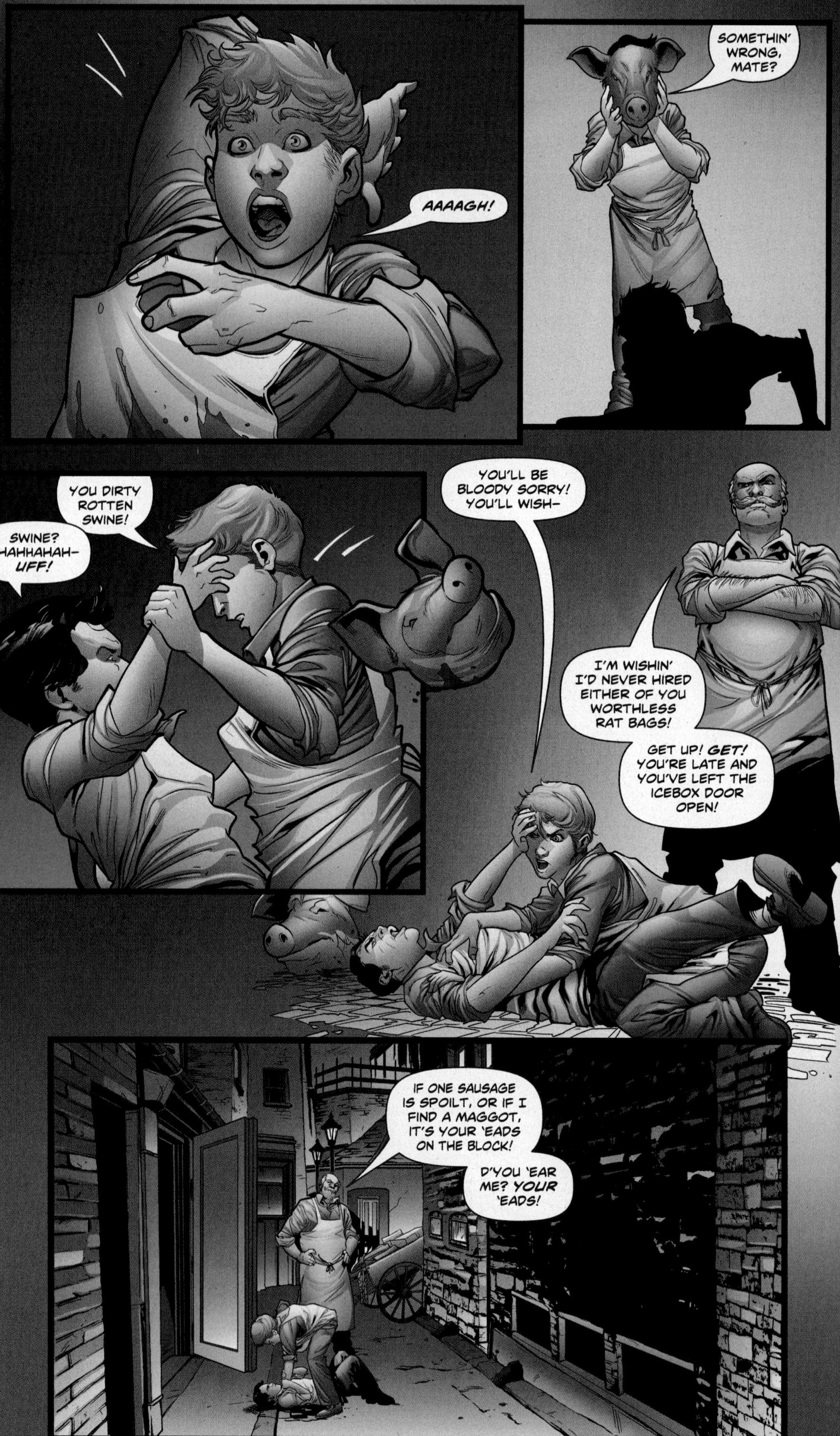

AAAAGH!
SOMETHIN' WRONG, MATE?
YOU DIRTY ROTTEN SWINE!
SWINE? AHAHHAHAH-UFF!
YOU'LL BE BLOODY SORRY! YOU'LL WISH-
I'M WISHIN' I'D NEVER HIRED EITHER OF YOU WORTHLESS RAT BAGS!
GET UP! GET! YOU'RE LATE AND YOU'VE LEFT THE ICEBOX DOOR OPEN!
IF ONE SAUSAGE IS SPOILT, OR IF I FIND A MAGGOT, IT'S YOUR 'EADS ON THE BLOCK!
D'YOU 'EAR ME? YOUR 'EADS!

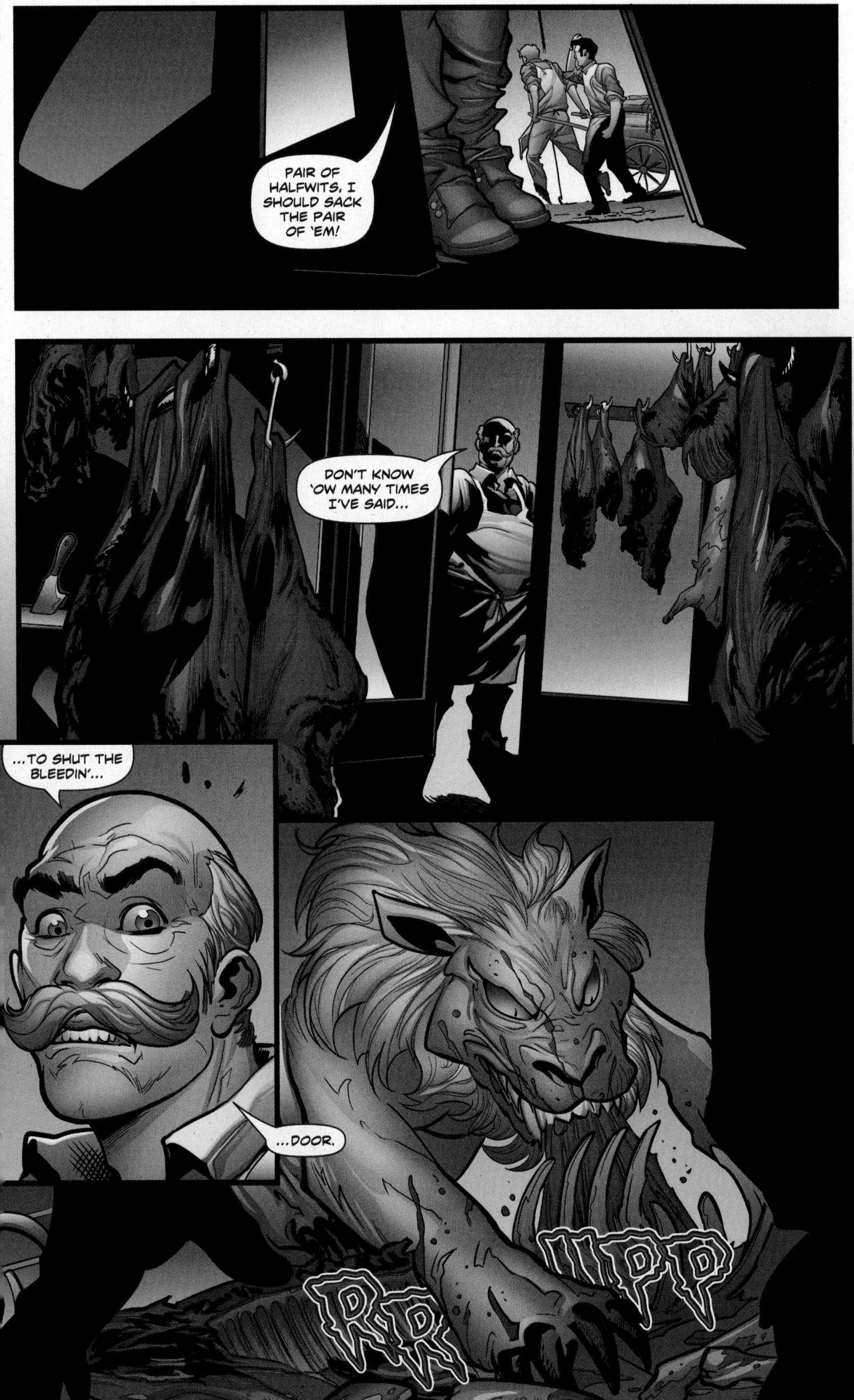
PAIR OF HALFWITS, I SHOULD SACK THE PAIR OF 'EM!
DON'T KNOW 'OW MANY TIMES I'VE SAID...
...TO SHUT THE BLEEDIN'...
...DOOR.

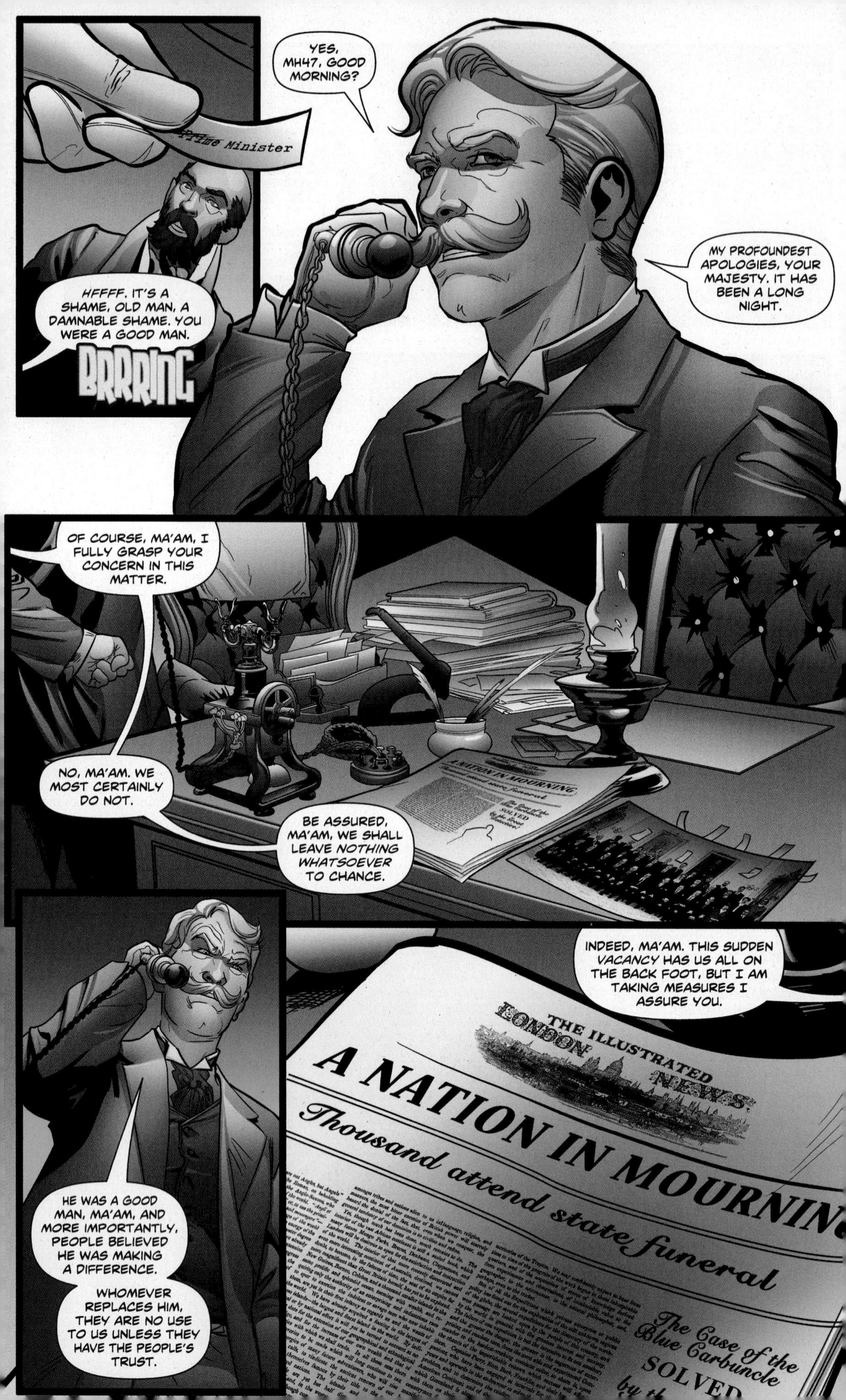
Prime Minister
YES, MH47, GOOD MORNING?
HFFFF. IT'S A SHAME, OLD MAN, A DAMNABLE SHAME. YOU WERE A GOOD MAN.
BRRRING
MY PROFOUNDEST APOLOGIES, YOUR MAJESTY. IT HAS BEEN A LONG NIGHT.
OF COURSE, MA'AM, I FULLY GRASP YOUR CONCERN IN THIS MATTER.
NO, MA'AM. WE MOST CERTAINLY DO NOT.
BE ASSURED, MA'AM, WE SHALL LEAVE *NOTHING WHATSOEVER* TO CHANCE.
A NATION IN MOURNING
INDEED, MA'AM. THIS SUDDEN *VACANCY* HAS US ALL ON THE BACK FOOT, BUT I AM TAKING MEASURES I ASSURE YOU.
THE ILLUSTRATED LONDON NEWS
A NATION IN MOURNING
Thousand attend state funeral
The Case of the Blue Carbuncle SOLVED
HE WAS A GOOD MAN, MA'AM, AND MORE IMPORTANTLY, PEOPLE BELIEVED HE WAS MAKING A DIFFERENCE.
WHOMEVER REPLACES HIM, THEY ARE NO USE TO US UNLESS THEY HAVE THE PEOPLE'S TRUST.

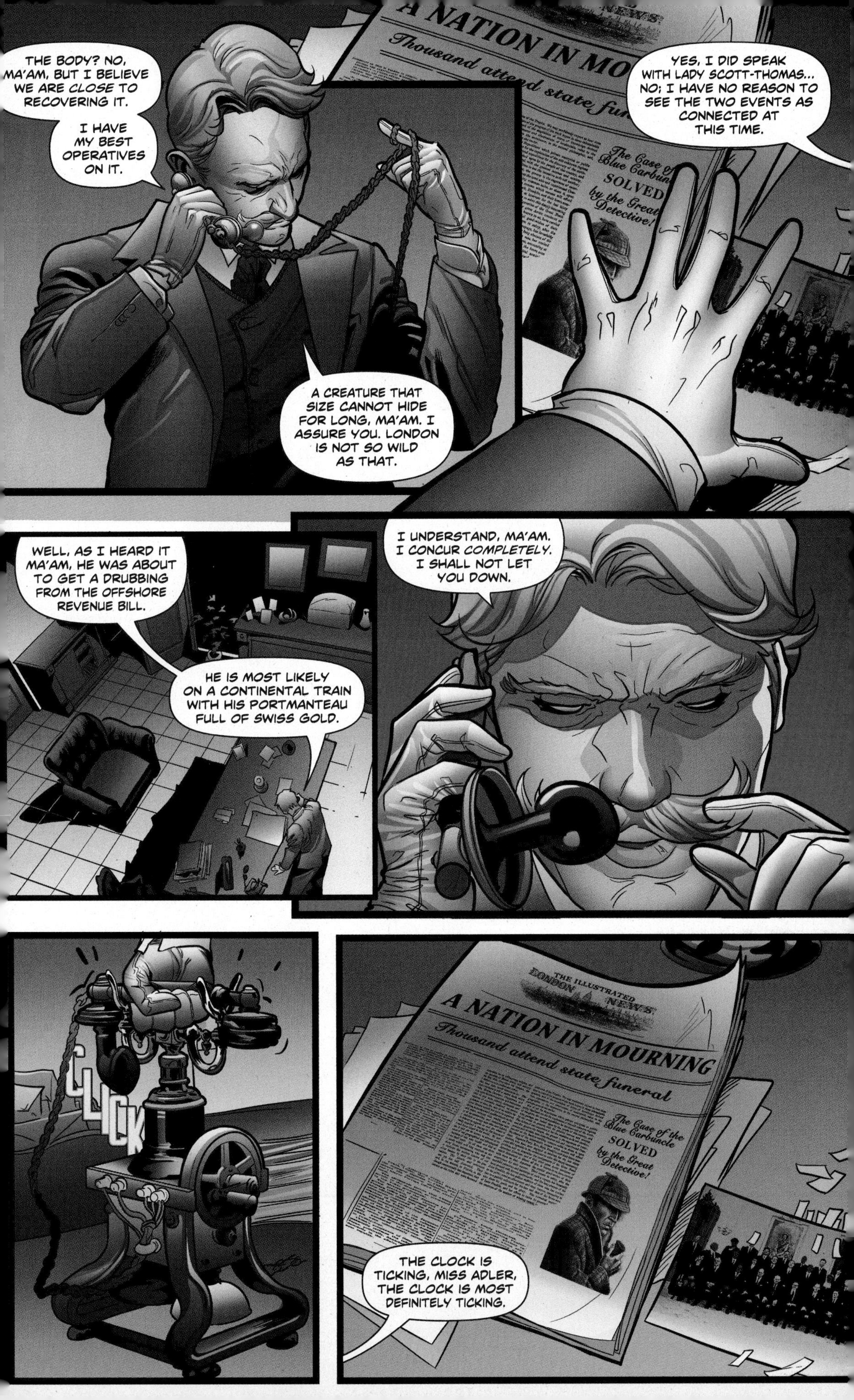

THE BODY? NO, MA'AM, BUT I BELIEVE WE ARE CLOSE TO RECOVERING IT.
I HAVE MY BEST OPERATIVES ON IT.
A CREATURE THAT SIZE CANNOT HIDE FOR LONG, MA'AM. I ASSURE YOU. LONDON IS NOT SO WILD AS THAT.
YES, I DID SPEAK WITH LADY SCOTT-THOMAS... NO; I HAVE NO REASON TO SEE THE TWO EVENTS AS CONNECTED AT THIS TIME.
WELL, AS I HEARD IT MA'AM, HE WAS ABOUT TO GET A DRUBBING FROM THE OFFSHORE REVENUE BILL.
HE IS MOST LIKELY ON A CONTINENTAL TRAIN WITH HIS PORTMANTEAU FULL OF SWISS GOLD.
I UNDERSTAND, MA'AM. I CONCUR COMPLETELY. I SHALL NOT LET YOU DOWN.
CLICK
THE ILLUSTRATED LONDON NEWS
A NATION IN MOURNING
Thousand attend state funeral
The Case of the Blue Carbuncle SOLVED by the Great Detective!
THE CLOCK IS TICKING, MISS ADLER, THE CLOCK IS MOST DEFINITELY TICKING.

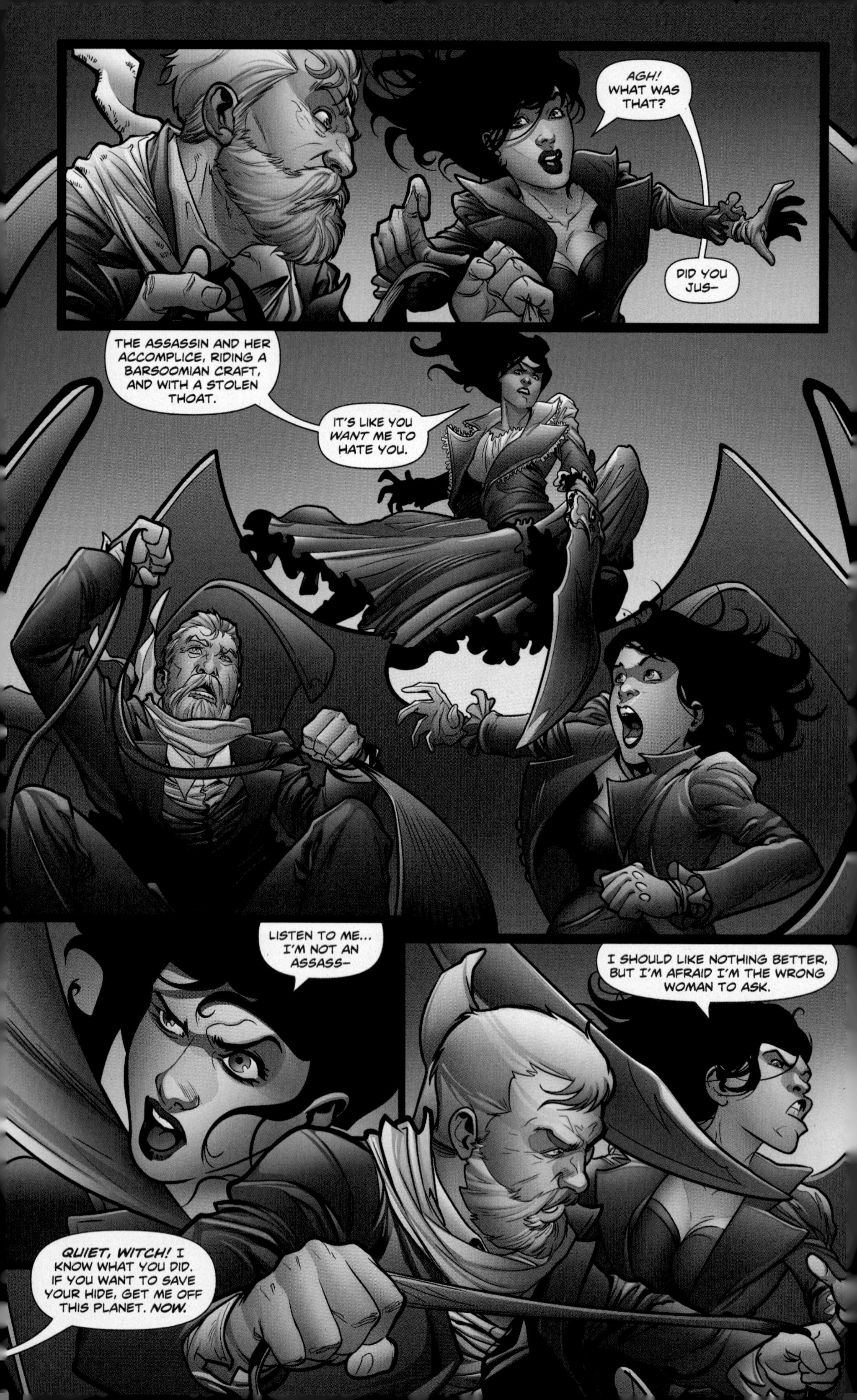
AGH! WHAT WAS THAT?
DID YOU JUS–
THE ASSASSIN AND HER ACCOMPLICE, RIDING A BARSOOMIAN CRAFT, AND WITH A STOLEN THOAT.
IT'S LIKE YOU *WANT* ME TO HATE YOU.
LISTEN TO ME... I'M NOT AN ASSASS–
I SHOULD LIKE NOTHING BETTER, BUT I'M AFRAID I'M THE WRONG WOMAN TO ASK.
QUIET, WITCH! I KNOW WHAT YOU DID. IF YOU WANT TO SAVE YOUR HIDE, GET ME OFF THIS PLANET. *NOW.*

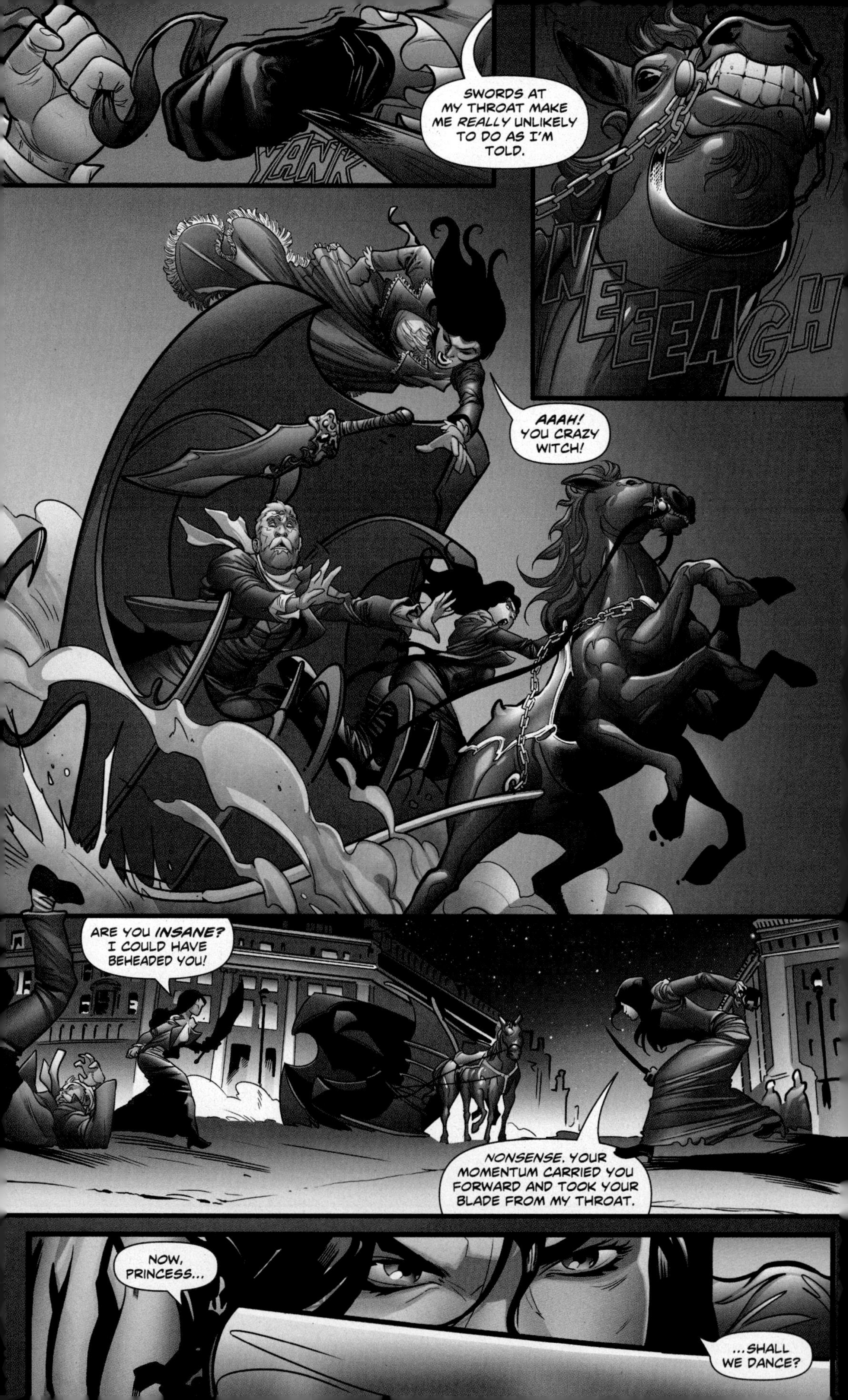
YANK
SWORDS AT MY THROAT MAKE ME *REALLY* UNLIKELY TO DO AS I'M TOLD.
NEEEEAGH
AAAH! YOU CRAZY WITCH!
ARE YOU *INSANE?* I COULD HAVE BEHEADED YOU!
NONSENSE. YOUR MOMENTUM CARRIED YOU FORWARD AND TOOK YOUR BLADE FROM MY THROAT.
NOW, PRINCESS...
...SHALL WE DANCE?

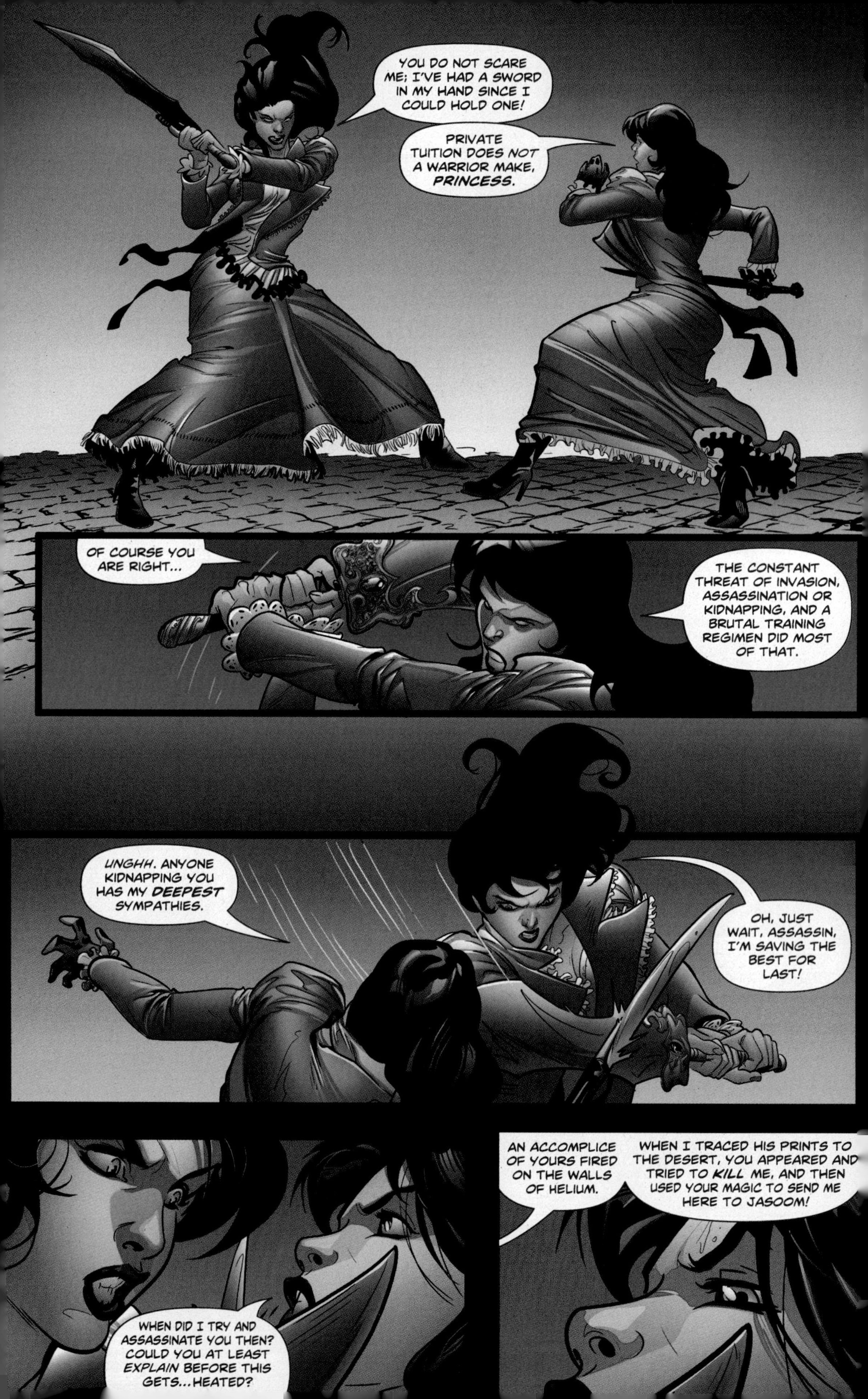
YOU DO NOT SCARE ME; I'VE HAD A SWORD IN MY HAND SINCE I COULD HOLD ONE!
PRIVATE TUITION DOES NOT A WARRIOR MAKE, PRINCESS.
OF COURSE YOU ARE RIGHT...
THE CONSTANT THREAT OF INVASION, ASSASSINATION OR KIDNAPPING, AND A BRUTAL TRAINING REGIMEN DID MOST OF THAT.
UNGHH. ANYONE KIDNAPPING YOU HAS MY DEEPEST SYMPATHIES.
OH, JUST WAIT, ASSASSIN, I'M SAVING THE BEST FOR LAST!
WHEN DID I TRY AND ASSASSINATE YOU THEN? COULD YOU AT LEAST EXPLAIN BEFORE THIS GETS... HEATED?
AN ACCOMPLICE OF YOURS FIRED ON THE WALLS OF HELIUM.
WHEN I TRACED HIS PRINTS TO THE DESERT, YOU APPEARED AND TRIED TO KILL ME, AND THEN USED YOUR MAGIC TO SEND ME HERE TO JASOOM!

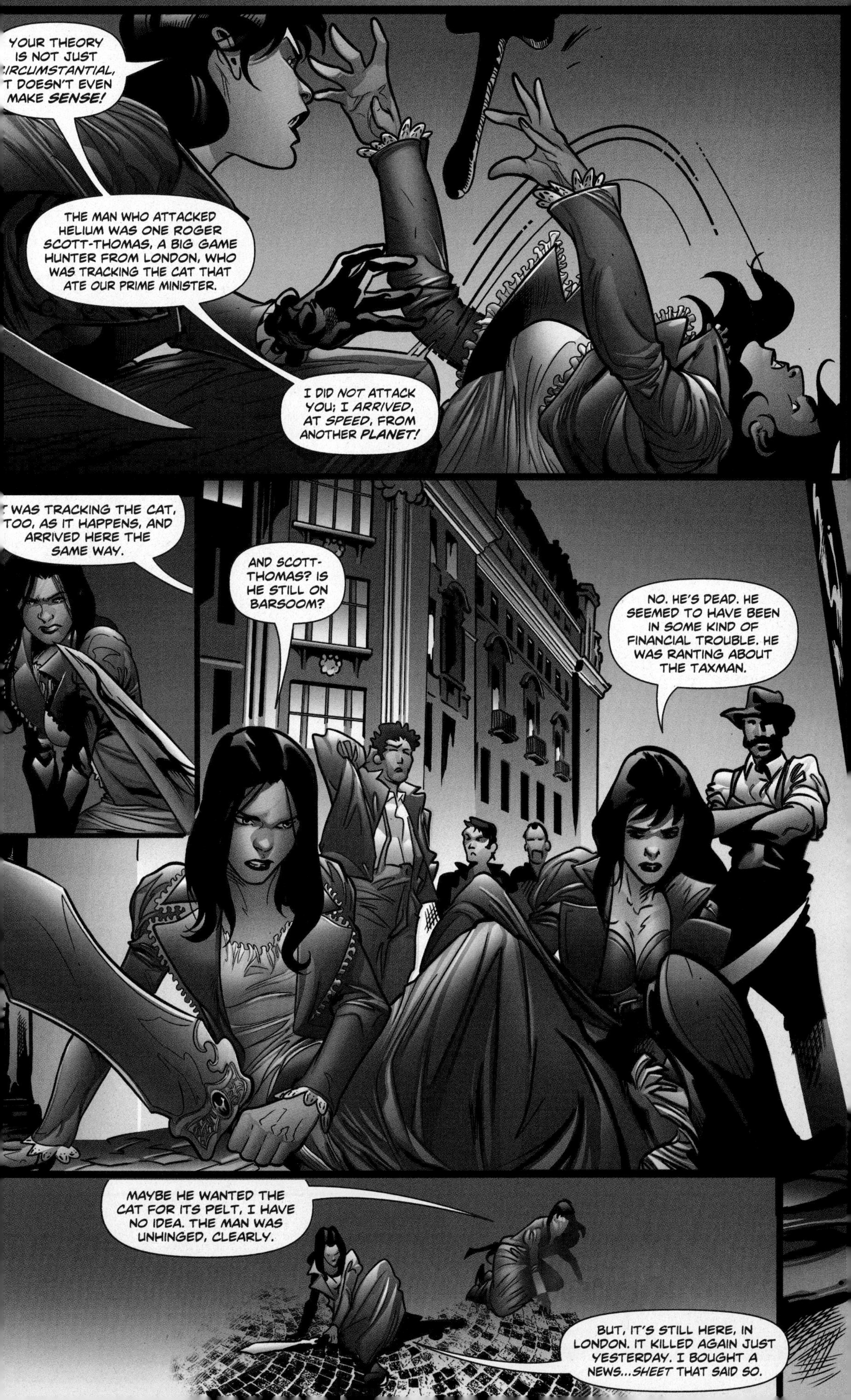
YOUR THEORY IS NOT JUST CIRCUMSTANTIAL, IT DOESN'T EVEN MAKE SENSE!
THE MAN WHO ATTACKED HELIUM WAS ONE ROGER SCOTT-THOMAS, A BIG GAME HUNTER FROM LONDON, WHO WAS TRACKING THE CAT THAT ATE OUR PRIME MINISTER.
I DID NOT ATTACK YOU; I ARRIVED, AT SPEED, FROM ANOTHER PLANET!
I WAS TRACKING THE CAT, TOO, AS IT HAPPENS, AND ARRIVED HERE THE SAME WAY.
AND SCOTT-THOMAS? IS HE STILL ON BARSOOM?
NO. HE'S DEAD. HE SEEMED TO HAVE BEEN IN SOME KIND OF FINANCIAL TROUBLE. HE WAS RANTING ABOUT THE TAXMAN.
MAYBE HE WANTED THE CAT FOR ITS PELT, I HAVE NO IDEA. THE MAN WAS UNHINGED, CLEARLY.
BUT, IT'S STILL HERE, IN LONDON. IT KILLED AGAIN JUST YESTERDAY. I BOUGHT A NEWS...SHEET THAT SAID SO.

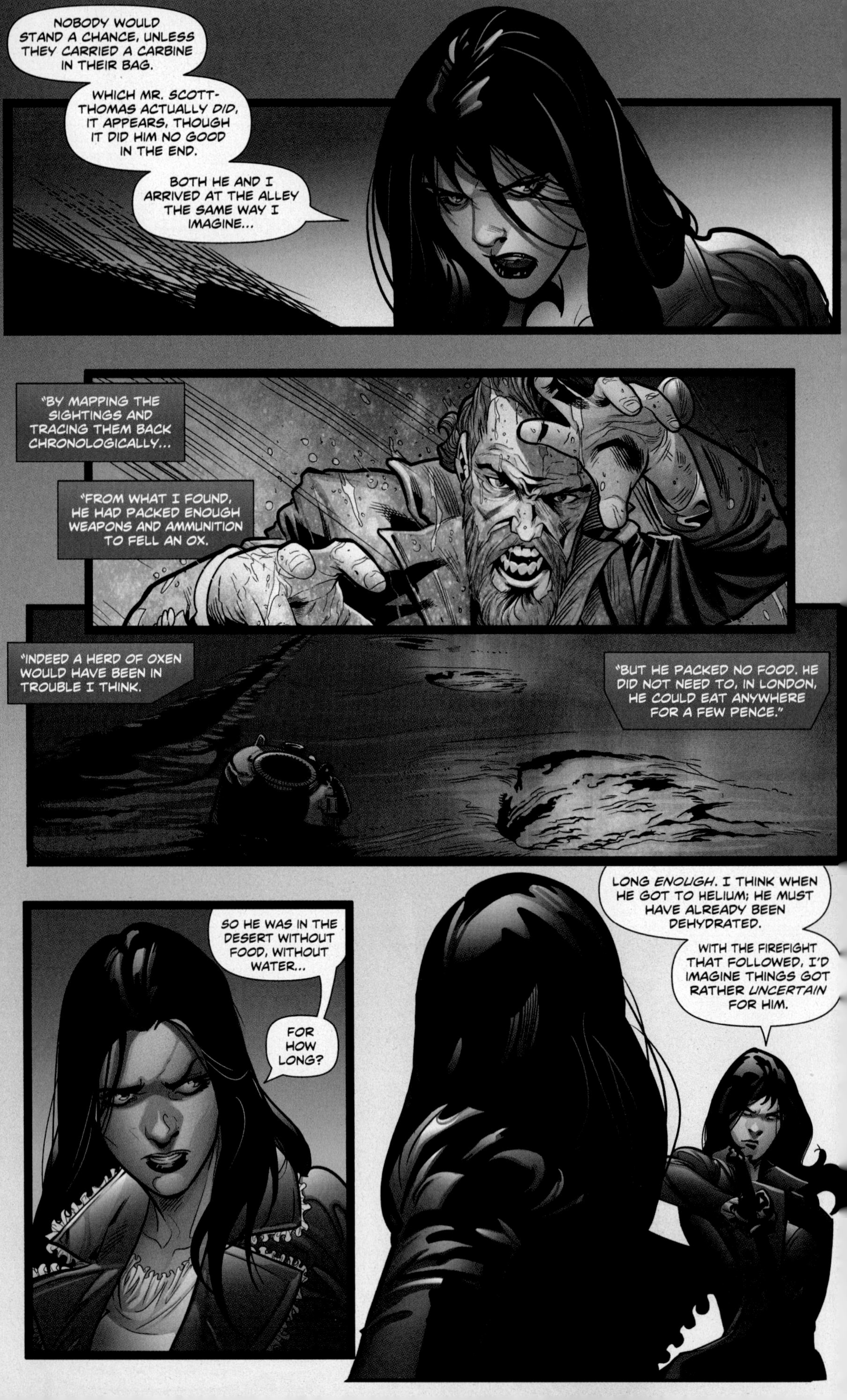
NOBODY WOULD STAND A CHANCE, UNLESS THEY CARRIED A CARBINE IN THEIR BAG.
WHICH MR. SCOTT-THOMAS ACTUALLY *DID*, IT APPEARS, THOUGH IT DID HIM NO GOOD IN THE END.
BOTH HE AND I ARRIVED AT THE ALLEY THE SAME WAY I IMAGINE...
"BY MAPPING THE SIGHTINGS AND TRACING THEM BACK CHRONOLOGICALLY...
"FROM WHAT I FOUND, HE HAD PACKED ENOUGH WEAPONS AND AMMUNITION TO FELL AN OX.
"INDEED A HERD OF OXEN WOULD HAVE BEEN IN TROUBLE I THINK.
"BUT HE PACKED NO FOOD. HE DID NOT NEED TO, IN LONDON, HE COULD EAT ANYWHERE FOR A FEW PENCE."
SO HE WAS IN THE DESERT WITHOUT FOOD, WITHOUT WATER...
FOR HOW LONG?
LONG *ENOUGH*. I THINK WHEN HE GOT TO HELIUM; HE MUST HAVE ALREADY BEEN DEHYDRATED.
WITH THE FIREFIGHT THAT FOLLOWED, I'D IMAGINE THINGS GOT RATHER *UNCERTAIN* FOR HIM.

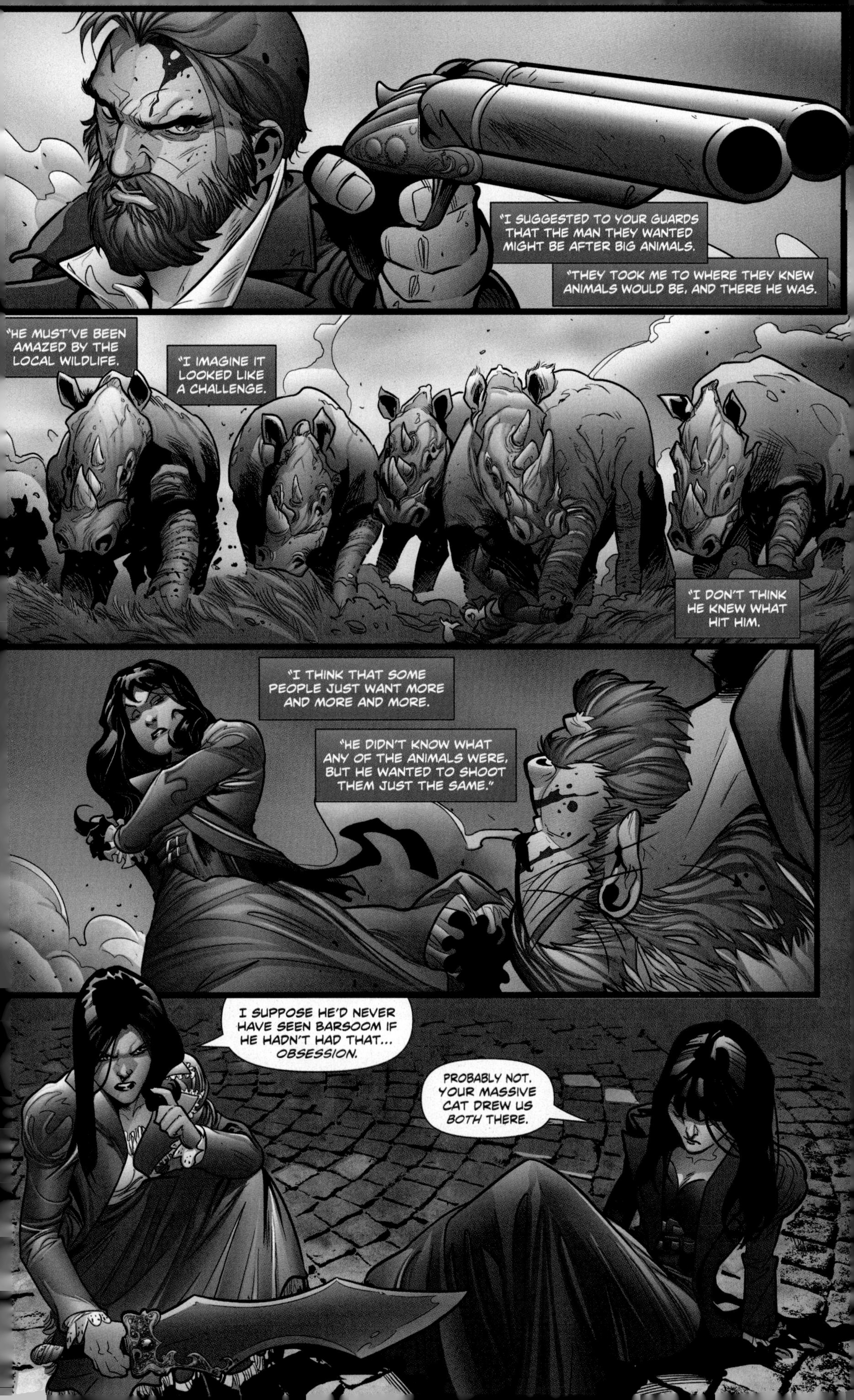
"I SUGGESTED TO YOUR GUARDS THAT THE MAN THEY WANTED MIGHT BE AFTER BIG ANIMALS.
"THEY TOOK ME TO WHERE THEY KNEW ANIMALS WOULD BE, AND THERE HE WAS.
"HE MUST'VE BEEN AMAZED BY THE LOCAL WILDLIFE.
"I IMAGINE IT LOOKED LIKE A CHALLENGE.
"I DON'T THINK HE KNEW WHAT HIT HIM.
"I THINK THAT SOME PEOPLE JUST WANT MORE AND MORE AND MORE.
"HE DIDN'T KNOW WHAT ANY OF THE ANIMALS WERE, BUT HE WANTED TO SHOOT THEM JUST THE SAME."
I SUPPOSE HE'D NEVER HAVE SEEN BARSOOM IF HE HADN'T HAD THAT... *OBSESSION.*
PROBABLY NOT. YOUR MASSIVE CAT DREW US *BOTH* THERE.

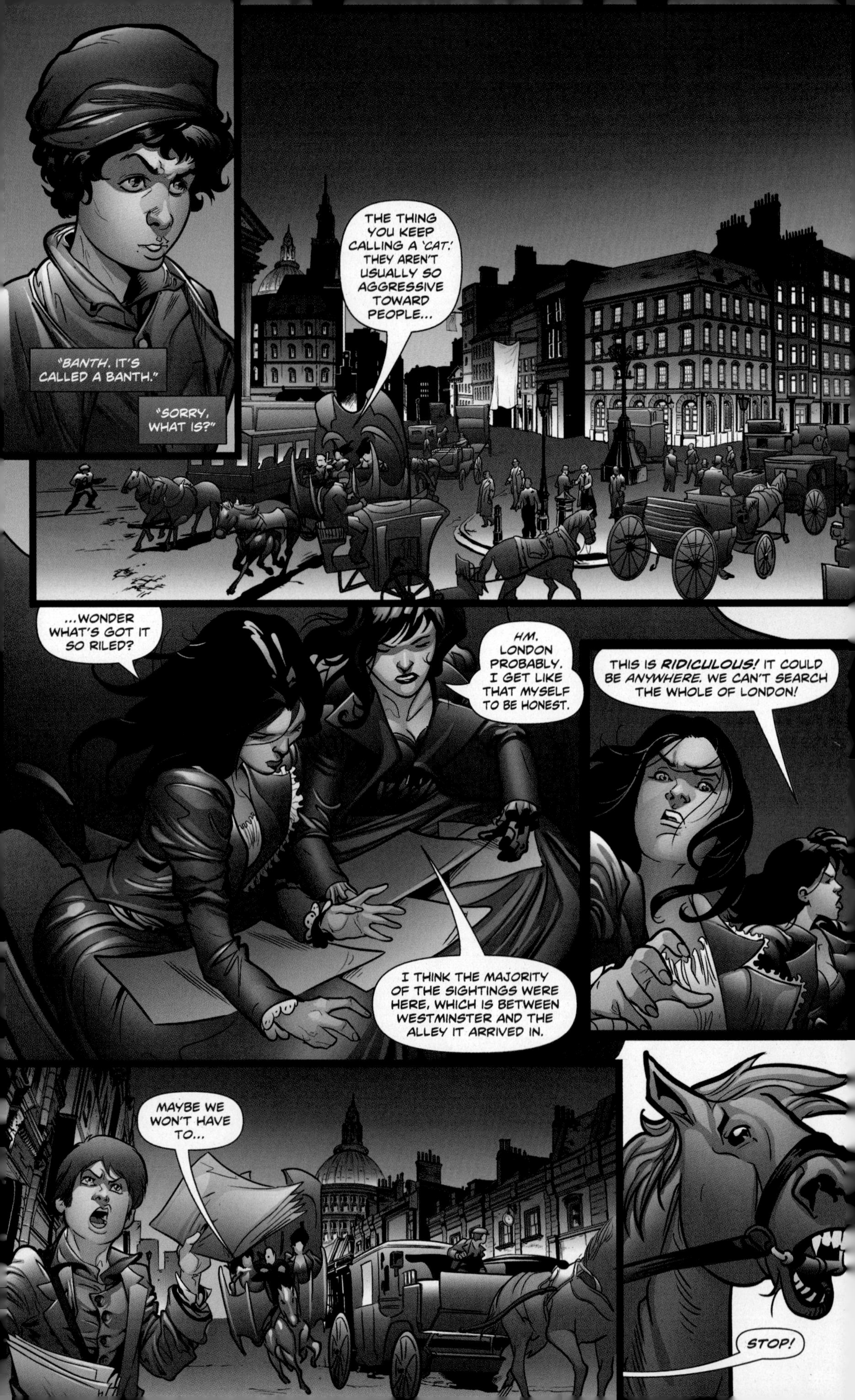
"BANTH. IT'S CALLED A BANTH."
"SORRY, WHAT IS?"
THE THING YOU KEEP CALLING A 'CAT.' THEY AREN'T USUALLY SO AGGRESSIVE TOWARD PEOPLE...
...WONDER WHAT'S GOT IT SO RILED?
HM. LONDON PROBABLY. I GET LIKE THAT MYSELF TO BE HONEST.
I THINK THE MAJORITY OF THE SIGHTINGS WERE HERE, WHICH IS BETWEEN WESTMINSTER AND THE ALLEY IT ARRIVED IN.
THIS IS RIDICULOUS! IT COULD BE ANYWHERE. WE CAN'T SEARCH THE WHOLE OF LONDON!
MAYBE WE WON'T HAVE TO...
STOP!

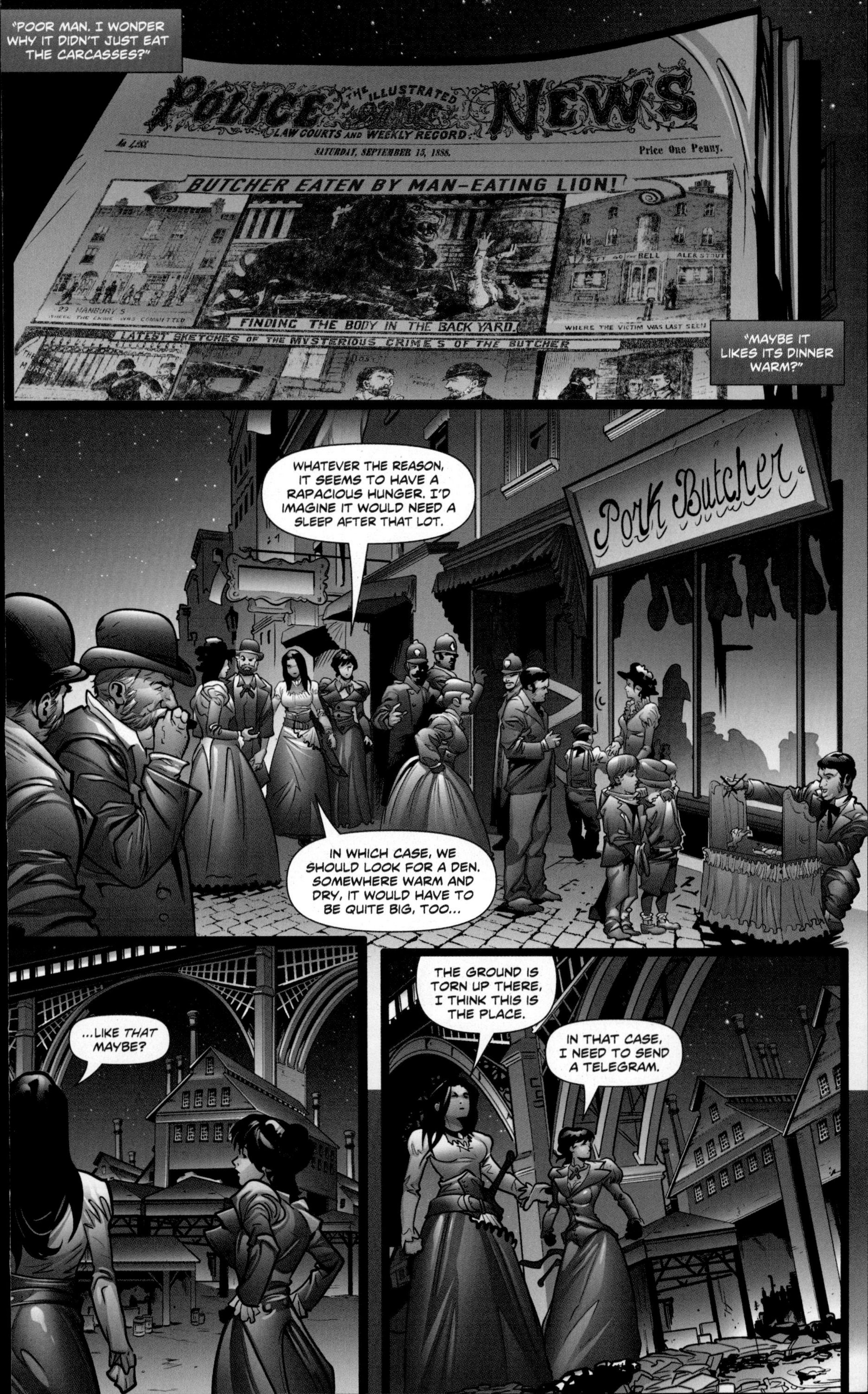
"POOR MAN. I WONDER WHY IT DIDN'T JUST EAT THE CARCASSES?"
POLICE THE ILLUSTRATED NEWS
LAW COURTS AND WEEKLY RECORD.
SATURDAY, SEPTEMBER 15, 1888.
Price One Penny.
BUTCHER EATEN BY MAN-EATING LION!
29 HANBURY'S WHERE THE CRIME WAS COMMITTED
FINDING THE BODY IN THE BACK YARD.
WHERE THE VICTIM WAS LAST SEEN
LATEST SKETCHES OF THE MYSTERIOUS CRIMES OF THE BUTCHER
"MAYBE IT LIKES ITS DINNER WARM?"
WHATEVER THE REASON, IT SEEMS TO HAVE A RAPACIOUS HUNGER. I'D IMAGINE IT WOULD NEED A SLEEP AFTER THAT LOT.
Pork Butcher.
IN WHICH CASE, WE SHOULD LOOK FOR A DEN. SOMEWHERE WARM AND DRY, IT WOULD HAVE TO BE QUITE BIG, TOO...
...LIKE THAT MAYBE?
THE GROUND IS TORN UP THERE, I THINK THIS IS THE PLACE.
IN THAT CASE, I NEED TO SEND A TELEGRAM.

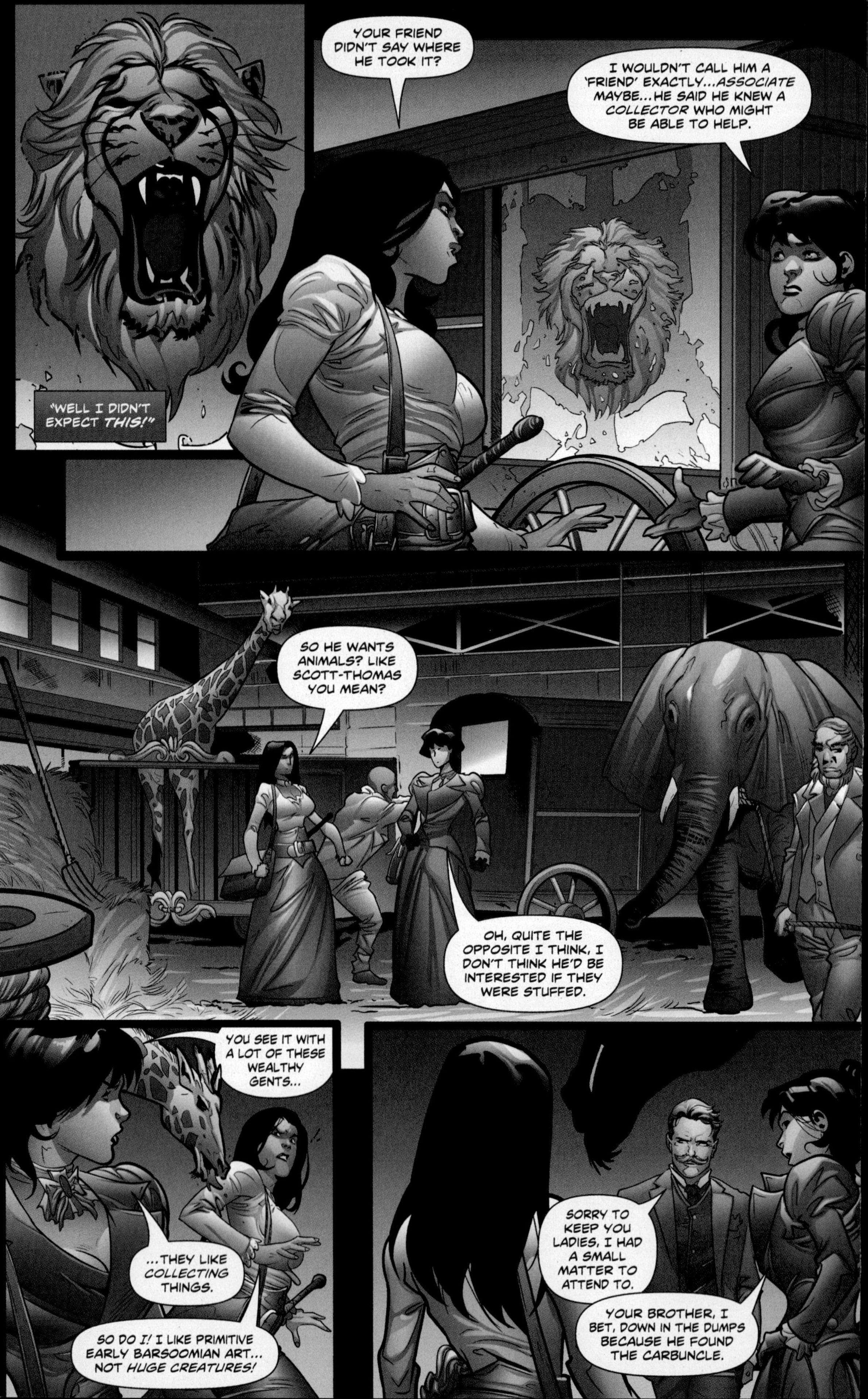
"WELL I DIDN'T EXPECT *THIS!*"
YOUR FRIEND DIDN'T SAY WHERE HE TOOK IT?
I WOULDN'T CALL HIM A 'FRIEND' EXACTLY...*ASSOCIATE* MAYBE...HE SAID HE KNEW A *COLLECTOR* WHO MIGHT BE ABLE TO HELP.
SO HE WANTS ANIMALS? LIKE SCOTT-THOMAS YOU MEAN?
OH, QUITE THE OPPOSITE I THINK, I DON'T THINK HE'D BE INTERESTED IF THEY WERE STUFFED.
YOU SEE IT WITH A LOT OF THESE WEALTHY GENTS...
...THEY LIKE *COLLECTING* THINGS.
SO DO *I!* I LIKE PRIMITIVE EARLY BARSOOMIAN ART... NOT *HUGE CREATURES!*
SORRY TO KEEP YOU LADIES, I HAD A SMALL MATTER TO ATTEND TO.
YOUR BROTHER, I BET, DOWN IN THE DUMPS BECAUSE HE FOUND THE CARBUNCLE.

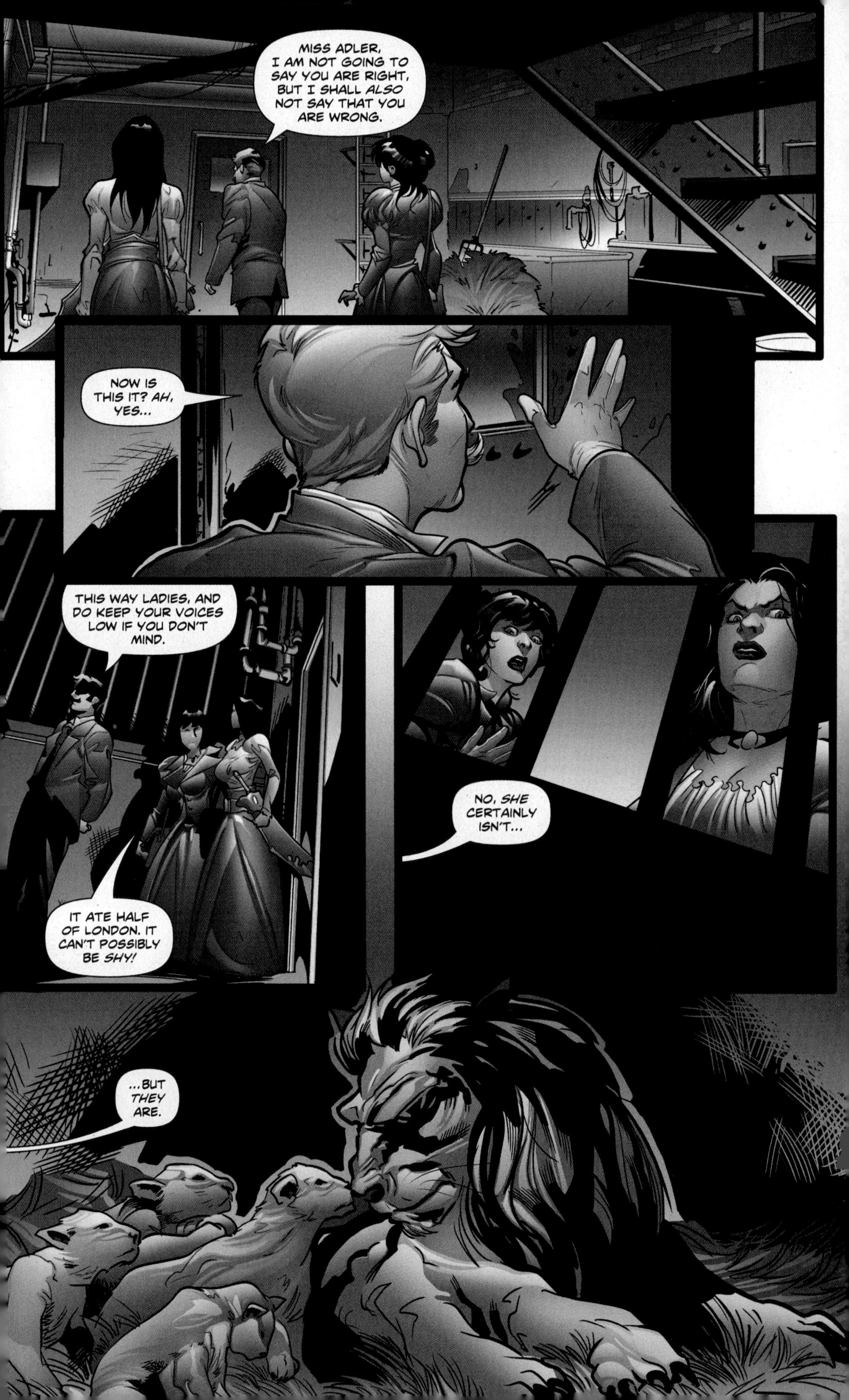
MISS ADLER, I AM NOT GOING TO SAY YOU ARE RIGHT, BUT I SHALL ALSO NOT SAY THAT YOU ARE WRONG.
NOW IS THIS IT? AH, YES...
THIS WAY LADIES, AND DO KEEP YOUR VOICES LOW IF YOU DON'T MIND.
IT ATE HALF OF LONDON. IT CAN'T POSSIBLY BE SHY!
NO, SHE CERTAINLY ISN'T...
...BUT THEY ARE.

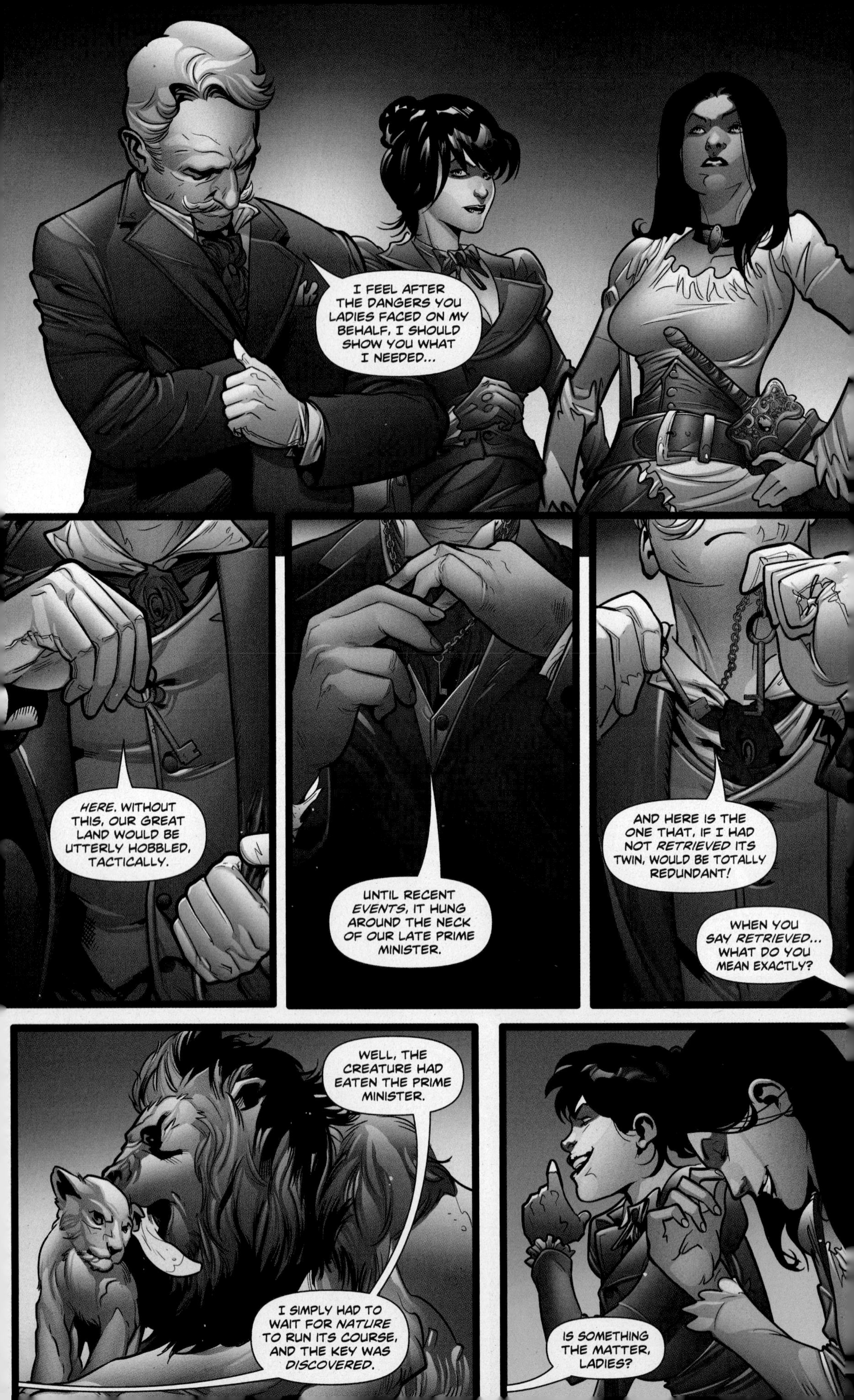
I FEEL AFTER THE DANGERS YOU LADIES FACED ON MY BEHALF, I SHOULD SHOW YOU WHAT I NEEDED...
HERE. WITHOUT THIS, OUR GREAT LAND WOULD BE UTTERLY HOBBLED, TACTICALLY.
UNTIL RECENT *EVENTS*, IT HUNG AROUND THE NECK OF OUR LATE PRIME MINISTER.
AND HERE IS THE ONE THAT, IF I HAD NOT *RETRIEVED* ITS TWIN, WOULD BE TOTALLY REDUNDANT!
WHEN YOU SAY *RETRIEVED*... WHAT DO YOU MEAN EXACTLY?
WELL, THE CREATURE HAD EATEN THE PRIME MINISTER.
I SIMPLY HAD TO WAIT FOR *NATURE* TO RUN ITS COURSE, AND THE KEY WAS *DISCOVERED*.
IS SOMETHING THE MATTER, LADIES?

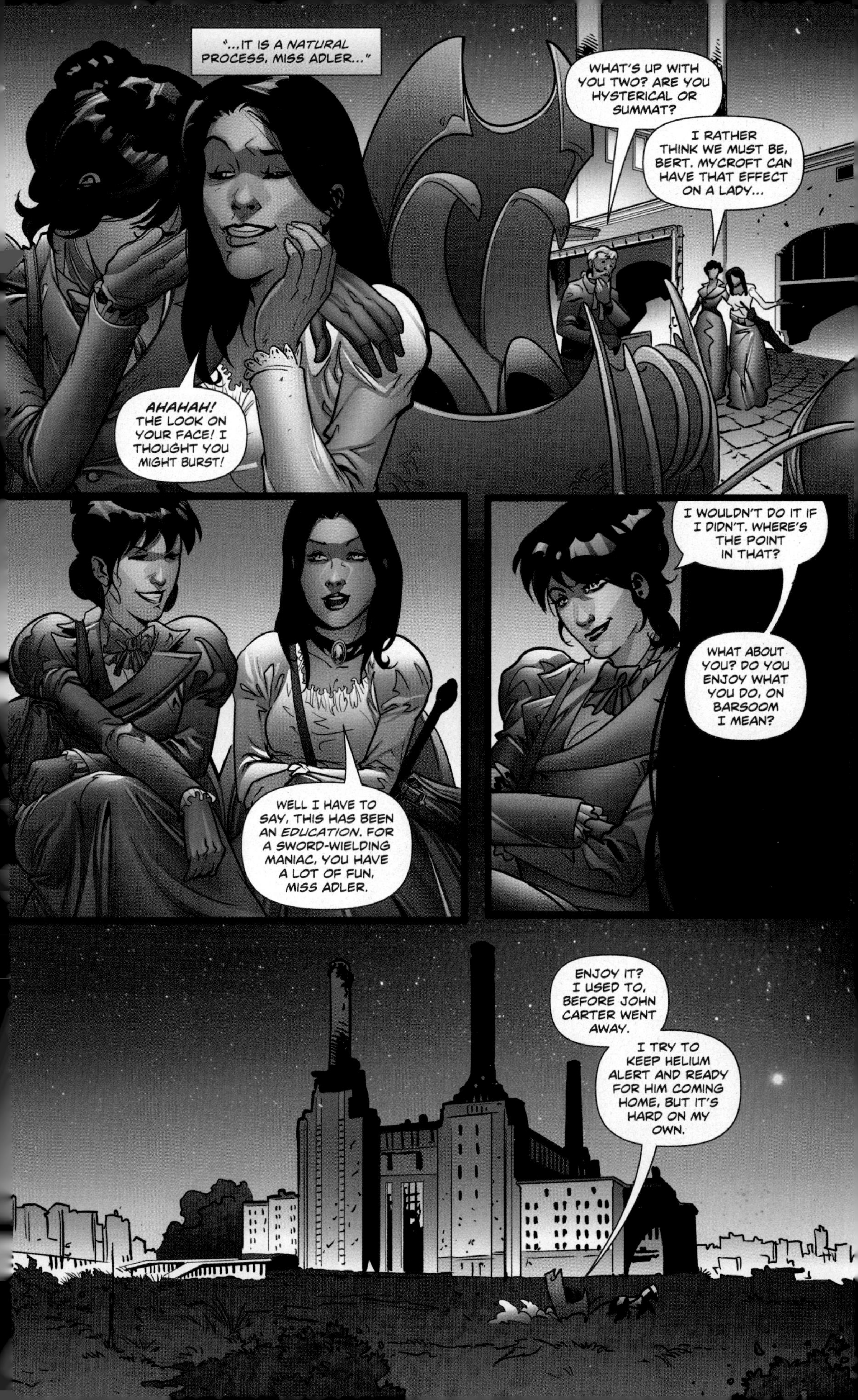
"...IT IS A *NATURAL* PROCESS, MISS ADLER..."
WHAT'S UP WITH YOU TWO? ARE YOU HYSTERICAL OR SUMMAT?
I RATHER THINK WE MUST BE, BERT. MYCROFT CAN HAVE THAT EFFECT ON A LADY...
AHAHAH! THE LOOK ON YOUR FACE! I THOUGHT YOU MIGHT BURST!
WELL I HAVE TO SAY, THIS HAS BEEN AN *EDUCATION*. FOR A SWORD-WIELDING MANIAC, YOU HAVE A LOT OF FUN, MISS ADLER.
I WOULDN'T DO IT IF I DIDN'T. WHERE'S THE POINT IN THAT?
WHAT ABOUT YOU? DO YOU ENJOY WHAT YOU DO, ON BARSOOM I MEAN?
ENJOY IT? I USED TO, BEFORE JOHN CARTER WENT AWAY.
I TRY TO KEEP HELIUM ALERT AND READY FOR HIM COMING HOME, BUT IT'S HARD ON MY OWN.

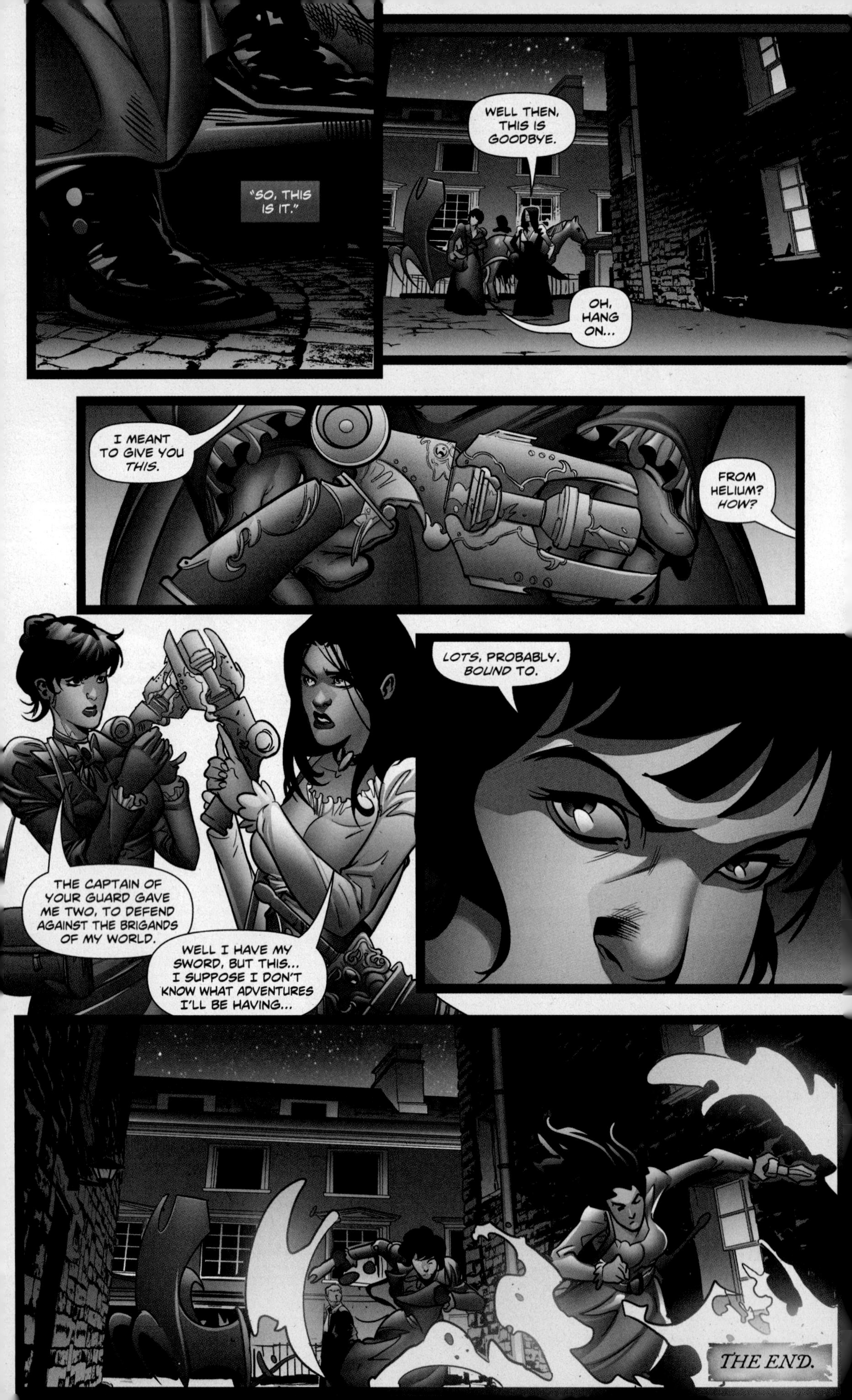
"SO, THIS IS IT."
WELL THEN, THIS IS GOODBYE.
OH, HANG ON...
I MEANT TO GIVE YOU *THIS.*
FROM HELIUM? *HOW?*
THE CAPTAIN OF YOUR GUARD GAVE ME TWO, TO DEFEND AGAINST THE BRIGANDS OF MY WORLD.
WELL I HAVE MY SWORD, BUT THIS... I SUPPOSE I DON'T KNOW WHAT ADVENTURES I'LL BE HAVING...
LOTS, PROBABLY. BOUND TO.
THE END.

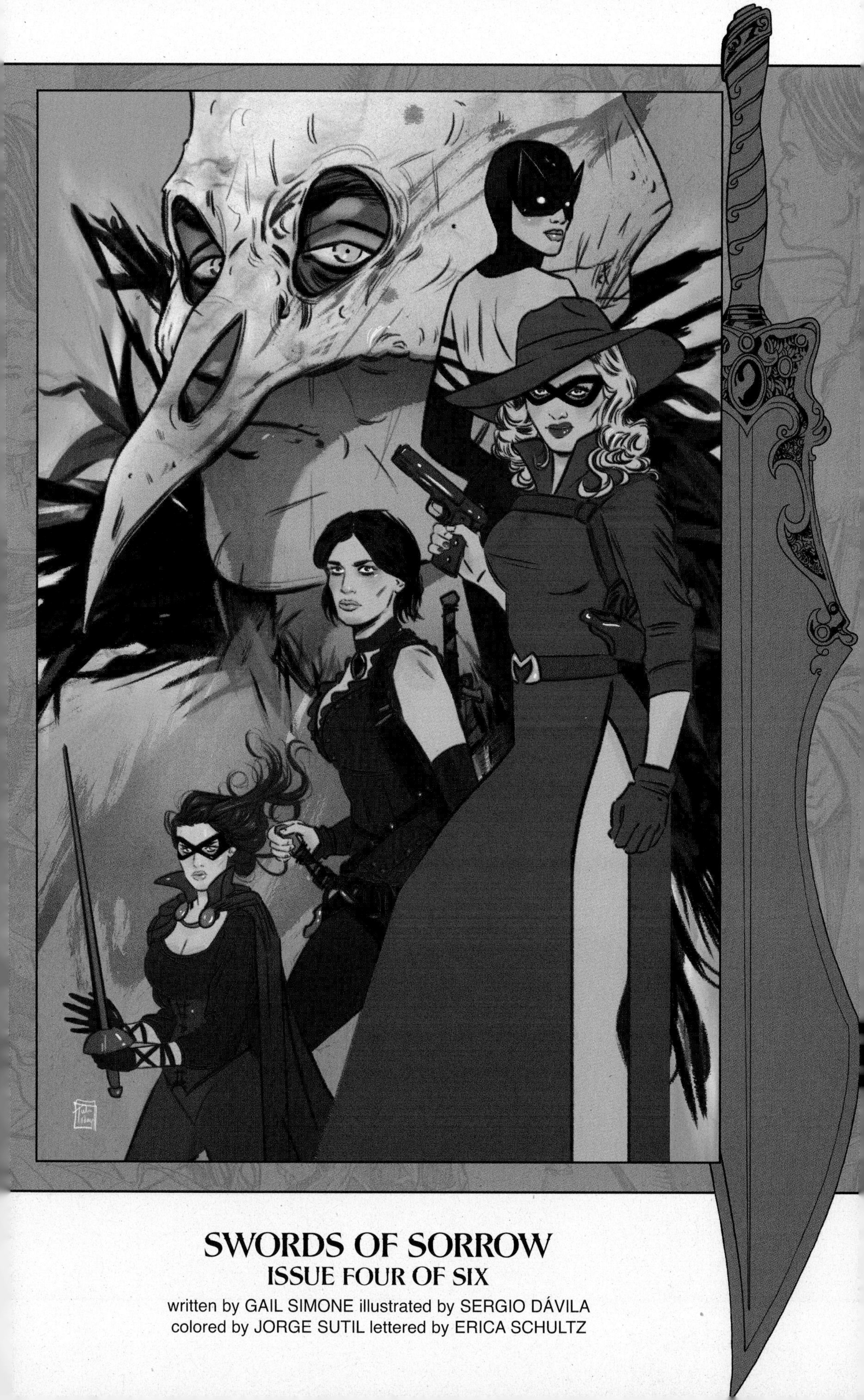

SWORDS OF SORROW

ISSUE FOUR OF SIX

written by GAIL SIMONE illustrated by SERGIO DÁVILA
colored by JORGE SUTIL lettered by ERICA SCHULTZ

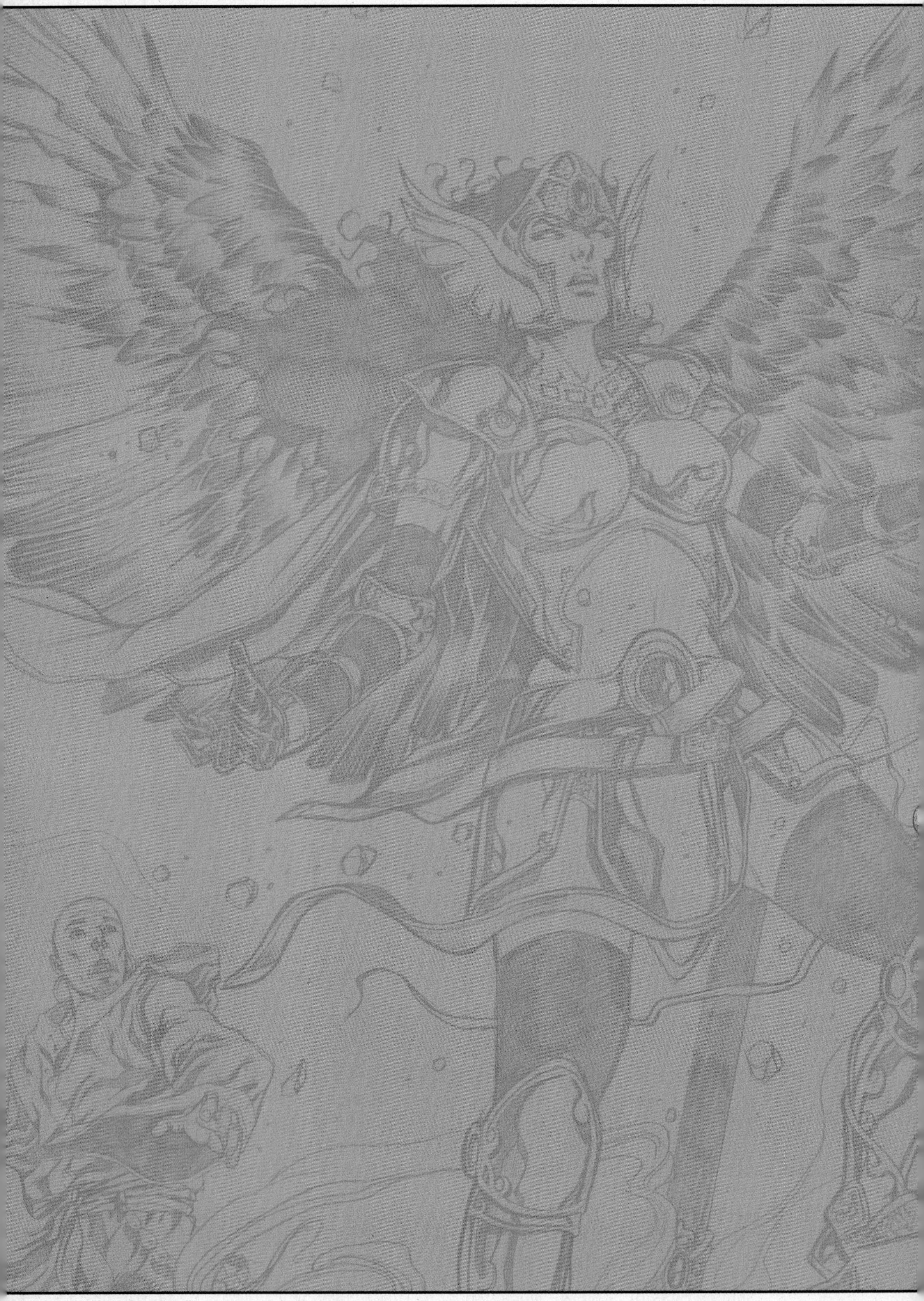

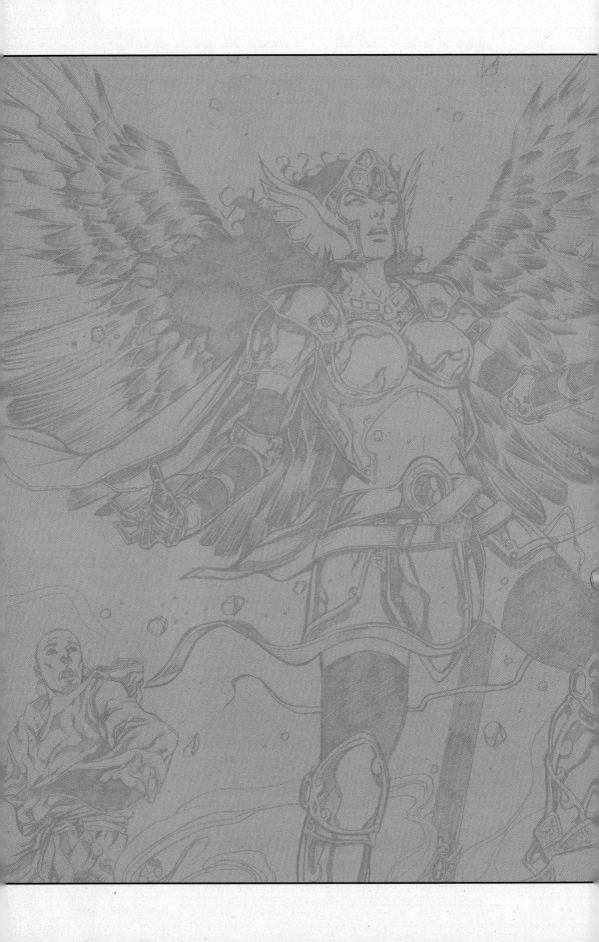

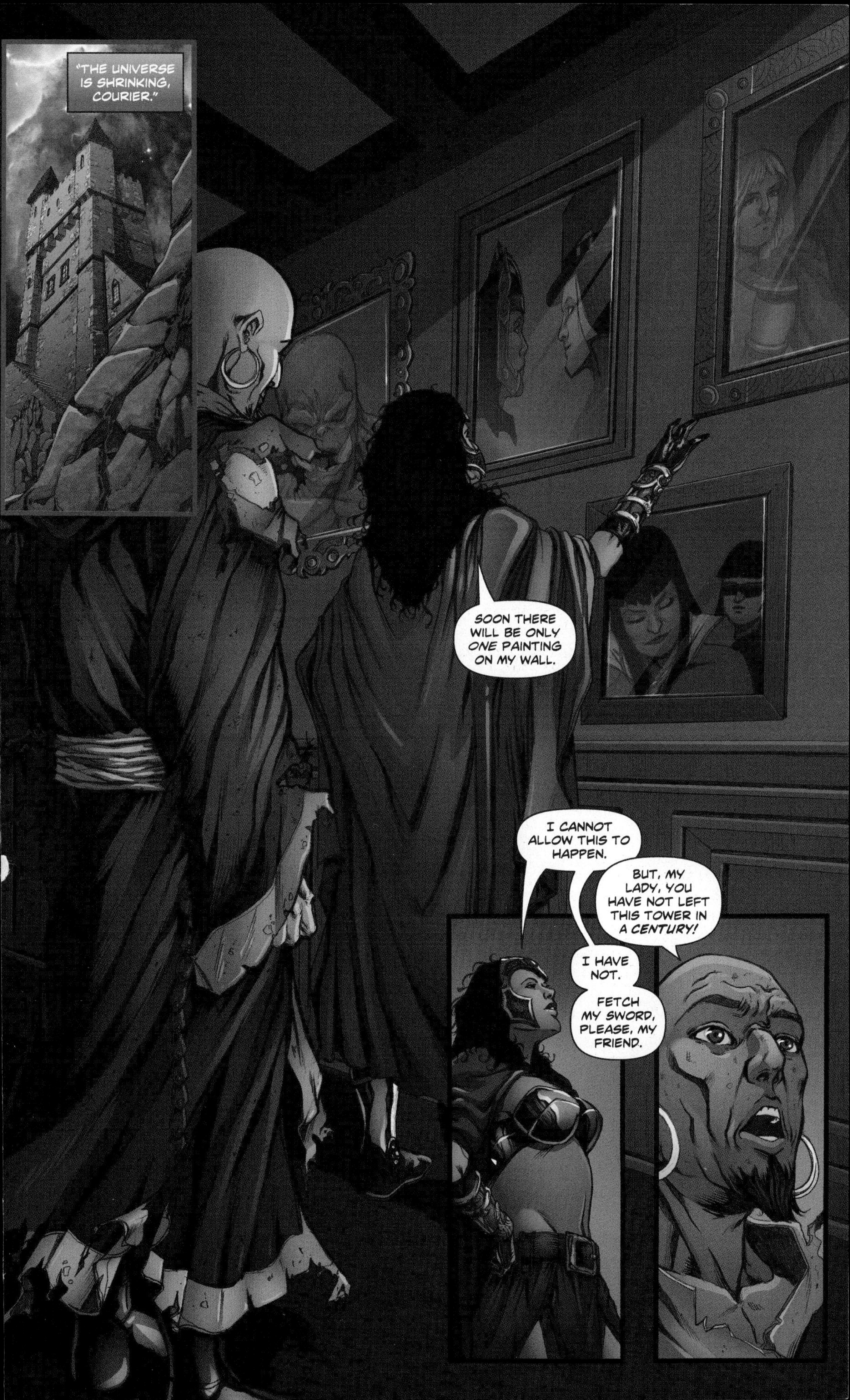
"THE UNIVERSE IS SHRINKING, COURIER."
SOON THERE WILL BE ONLY ONE PAINTING ON MY WALL.
I CANNOT ALLOW THIS TO HAPPEN.
BUT, MY LADY, YOU HAVE NOT LEFT THIS TOWER IN A CENTURY!
I HAVE NOT.
FETCH MY SWORD, PLEASE, MY FRIEND.

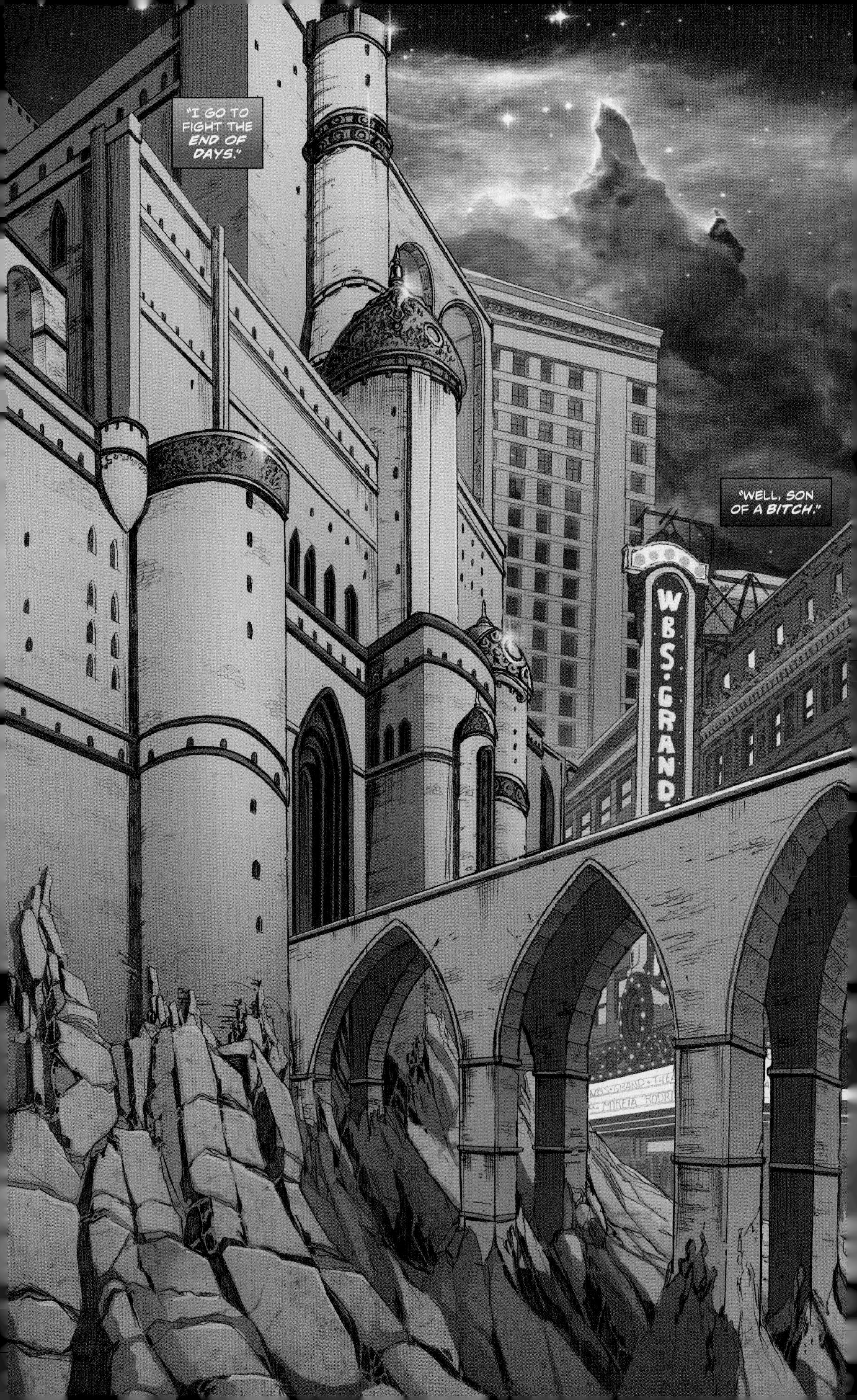
"I GO TO FIGHT THE *END OF DAYS*."
"WELL, SON OF A *BITCH*."
WBS·GRAND·

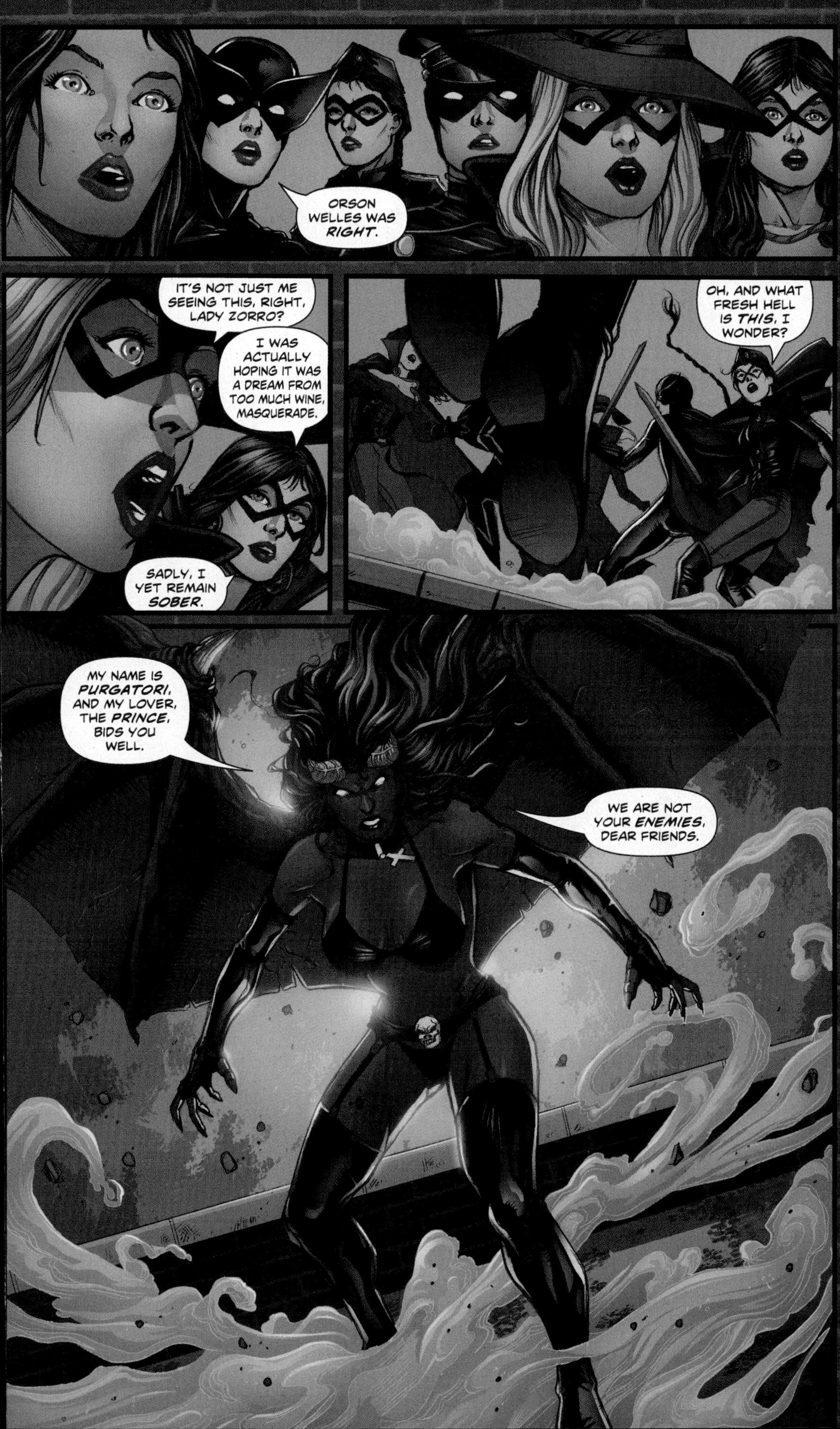
ORSON WELLES WAS RIGHT.
IT'S NOT JUST ME SEEING THIS, RIGHT, LADY ZORRO?
I WAS ACTUALLY HOPING IT WAS A DREAM FROM TOO MUCH WINE, MASQUERADE.
SADLY, I YET REMAIN SOBER.
OH, AND WHAT FRESH HELL IS THIS, I WONDER?
MY NAME IS PURGATORI, AND MY LOVER, THE PRINCE, BIDS YOU WELL.
WE ARE NOT YOUR ENEMIES, DEAR FRIENDS.

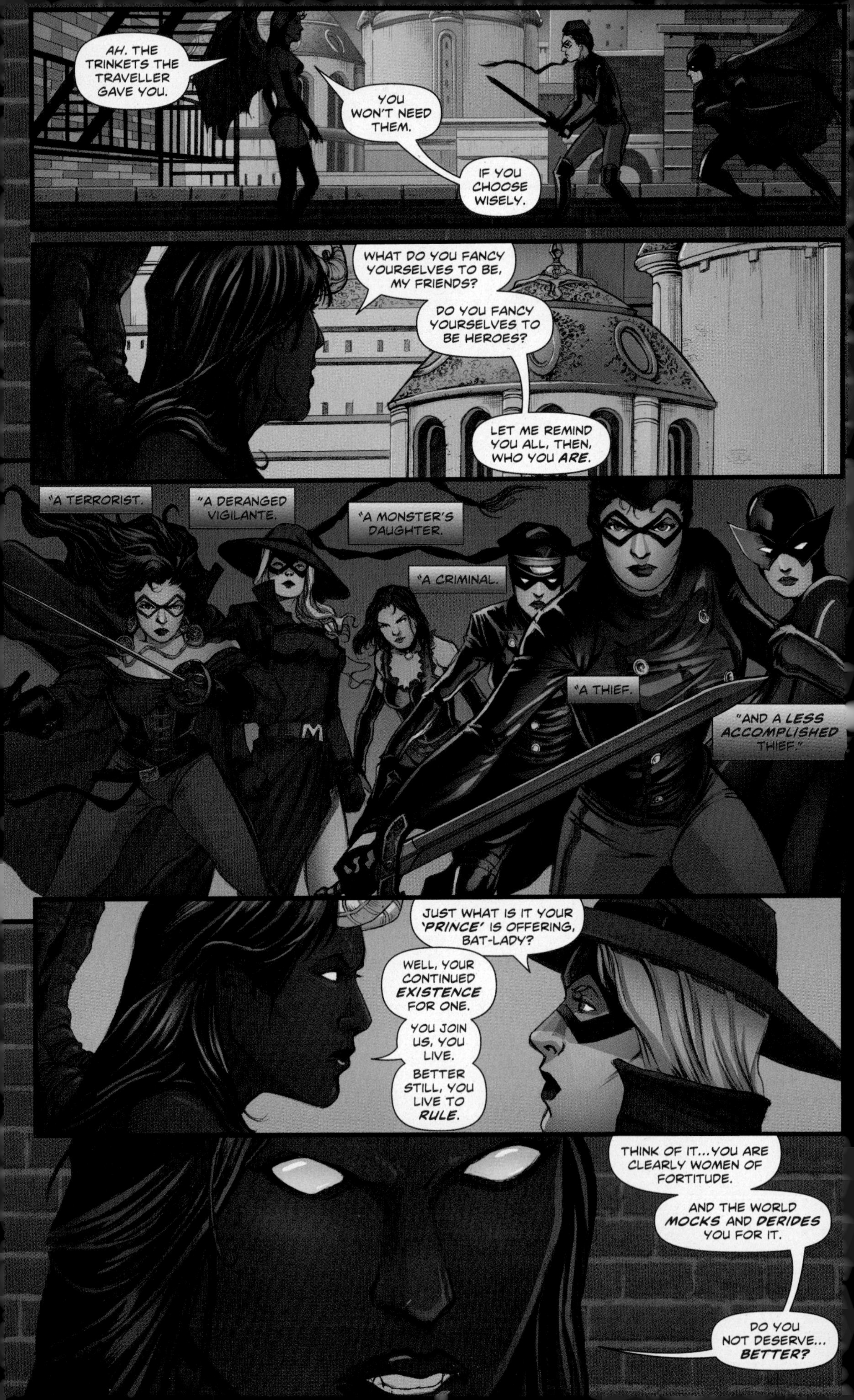
AH. THE TRINKETS THE TRAVELLER GAVE YOU.
YOU WON'T NEED THEM.
IF YOU CHOOSE WISELY.
WHAT DO YOU FANCY YOURSELVES TO BE, MY FRIENDS?
DO YOU FANCY YOURSELVES TO BE HEROES?
LET ME REMIND YOU ALL, THEN, WHO YOU ARE.
"A TERRORIST.
"A DERANGED VIGILANTE.
"A MONSTER'S DAUGHTER.
"A CRIMINAL.
"A THIEF.
"AND A LESS ACCOMPLISHED THIEF."
JUST WHAT IS IT YOUR 'PRINCE' IS OFFERING, BAT-LADY?
WELL, YOUR CONTINUED EXISTENCE FOR ONE.
YOU JOIN US, YOU LIVE.
BETTER STILL, YOU LIVE TO RULE.
THINK OF IT...YOU ARE CLEARLY WOMEN OF FORTITUDE.
AND THE WORLD MOCKS AND DERIDES YOU FOR IT.
DO YOU NOT DESERVE... BETTER?

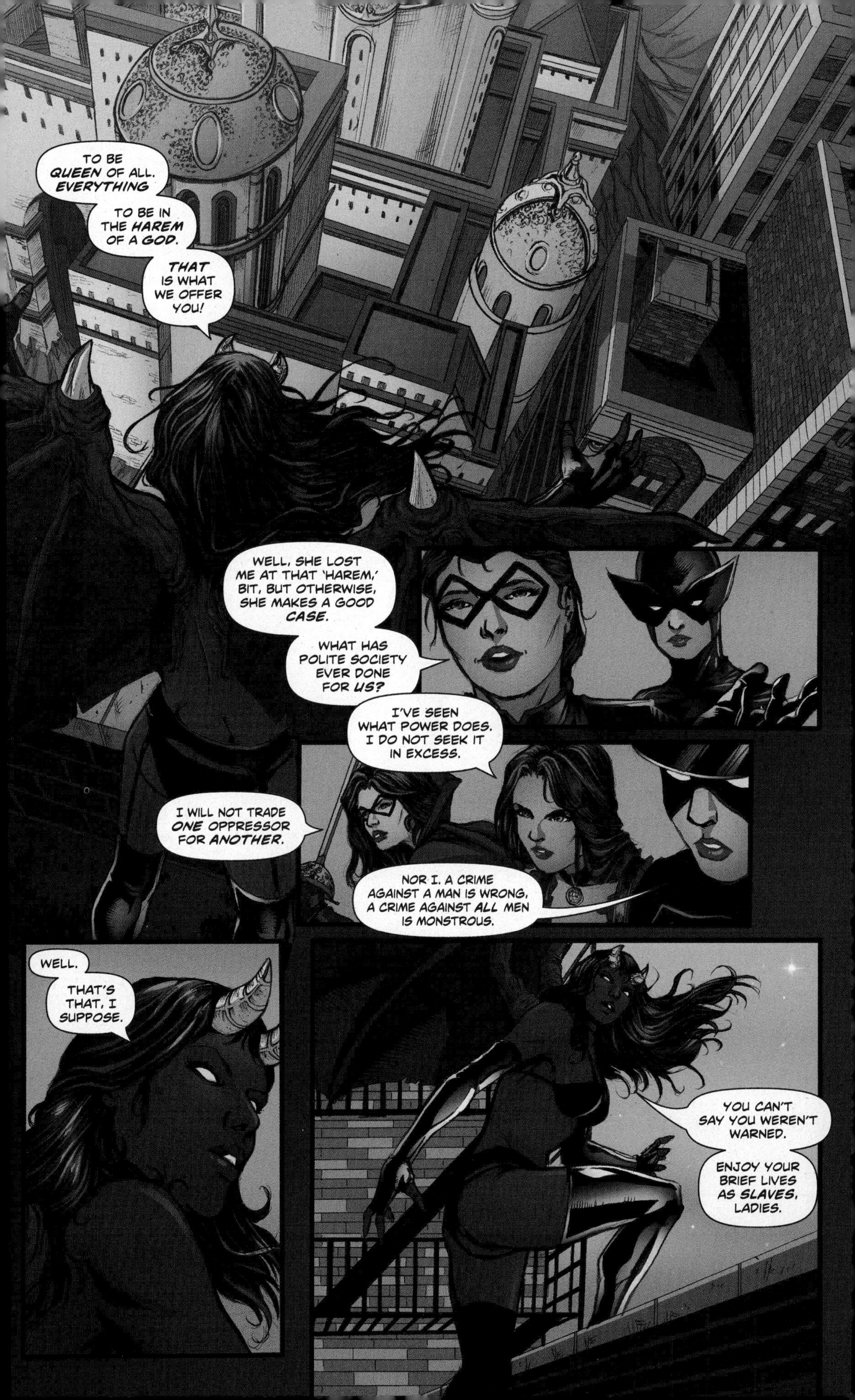
TO BE QUEEN OF ALL. EVERYTHING
TO BE IN THE HAREM OF A GOD.
THAT IS WHAT WE OFFER YOU!
WELL, SHE LOST ME AT THAT 'HAREM,' BIT, BUT OTHERWISE, SHE MAKES A GOOD CASE.
WHAT HAS POLITE SOCIETY EVER DONE FOR US?
I'VE SEEN WHAT POWER DOES. I DO NOT SEEK IT IN EXCESS.
I WILL NOT TRADE ONE OPPRESSOR FOR ANOTHER.
NOR I. A CRIME AGAINST A MAN IS WRONG, A CRIME AGAINST ALL MEN IS MONSTROUS.
WELL.
THAT'S THAT, I SUPPOSE.
YOU CAN'T SAY YOU WEREN'T WARNED.
ENJOY YOUR BRIEF LIVES AS SLAVES, LADIES.

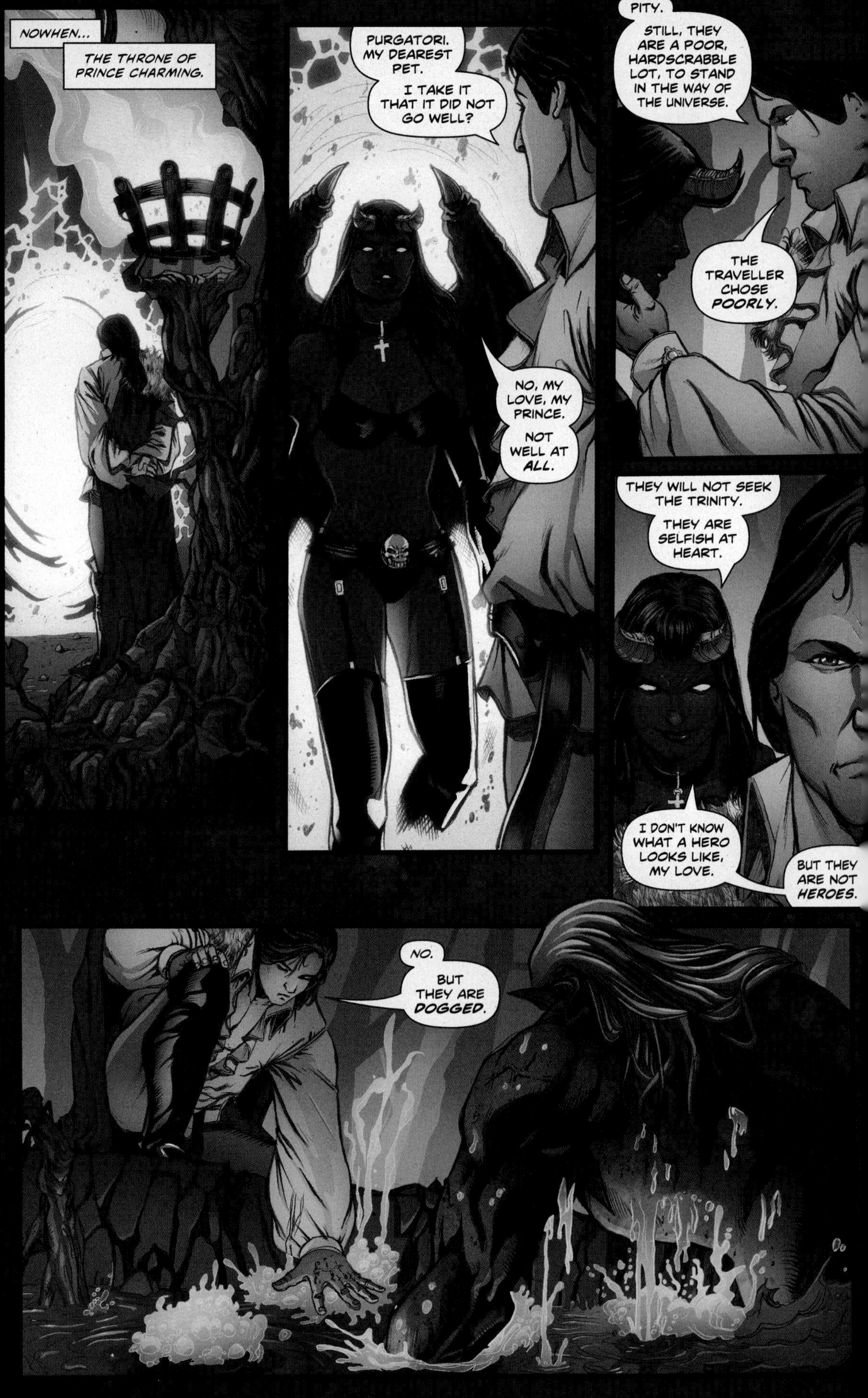
NOWHEN...
THE THRONE OF PRINCE CHARMING.
PURGATORI. MY DEAREST PET.
I TAKE IT THAT IT DID NOT GO WELL?
NO, MY LOVE, MY PRINCE.
NOT WELL AT ALL.
PITY.
STILL, THEY ARE A POOR, HARDSCRABBLE LOT, TO STAND IN THE WAY OF THE UNIVERSE.
THE TRAVELLER CHOSE POORLY.
THEY WILL NOT SEEK THE TRINITY.
THEY ARE SELFISH AT HEART.
I DON'T KNOW WHAT A HERO LOOKS LIKE, MY LOVE.
BUT THEY ARE NOT HEROES.
NO.
BUT THEY ARE DOGGED.

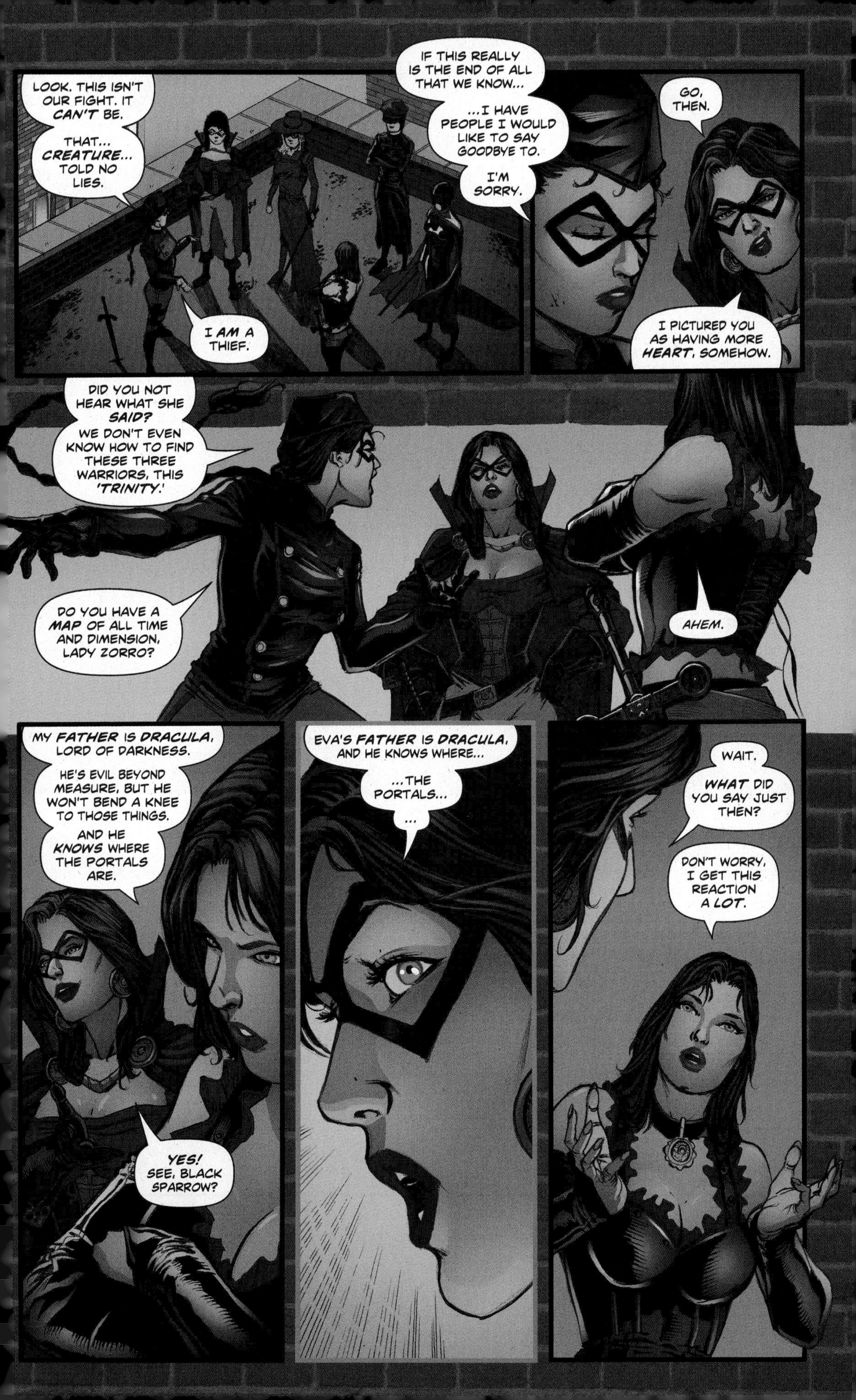
LOOK. THIS ISN'T OUR FIGHT. IT CAN'T BE.
THAT... CREATURE... TOLD NO LIES.
I AM A THIEF.
IF THIS REALLY IS THE END OF ALL THAT WE KNOW...
...I HAVE PEOPLE I WOULD LIKE TO SAY GOODBYE TO.
I'M SORRY.
GO, THEN.
I PICTURED YOU AS HAVING MORE HEART, SOMEHOW.
DID YOU NOT HEAR WHAT SHE SAID? WE DON'T EVEN KNOW HOW TO FIND THESE THREE WARRIORS, THIS 'TRINITY.'
DO YOU HAVE A MAP OF ALL TIME AND DIMENSION, LADY ZORRO?
AHEM.
MY FATHER IS DRACULA, LORD OF DARKNESS.
HE'S EVIL BEYOND MEASURE, BUT HE WON'T BEND A KNEE TO THOSE THINGS.
AND HE KNOWS WHERE THE PORTALS ARE.
YES! SEE, BLACK SPARROW?
EVA'S FATHER IS DRACULA, AND HE KNOWS WHERE...
...THE PORTALS...
...
WAIT. WHAT DID YOU SAY JUST THEN?
DON'T WORRY, I GET THIS REACTION A LOT.

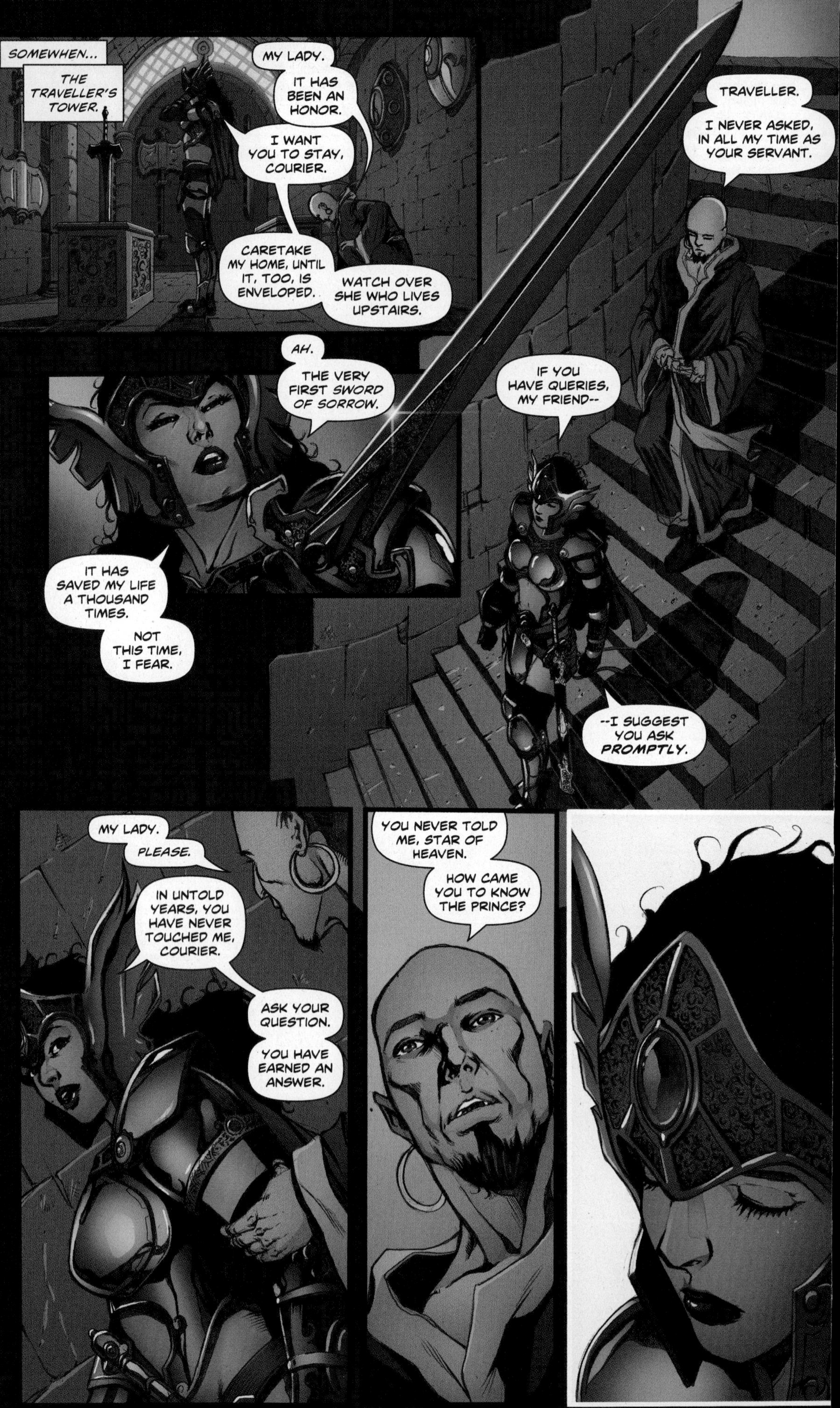
SOMEWHEN...
THE TRAVELLER'S TOWER.
MY LADY.
IT HAS BEEN AN HONOR.
I WANT YOU TO STAY, COURIER.
CARETAKE MY HOME, UNTIL IT, TOO, IS ENVELOPED.
WATCH OVER SHE WHO LIVES UPSTAIRS.
TRAVELLER.
I NEVER ASKED, IN ALL MY TIME AS YOUR SERVANT.
AH.
THE VERY FIRST SWORD OF SORROW.
IT HAS SAVED MY LIFE A THOUSAND TIMES.
NOT THIS TIME, I FEAR.
IF YOU HAVE QUERIES, MY FRIEND--
--I SUGGEST YOU ASK PROMPTLY.
MY LADY.
PLEASE.
IN UNTOLD YEARS, YOU HAVE NEVER TOUCHED ME, COURIER.
ASK YOUR QUESTION.
YOU HAVE EARNED AN ANSWER.
YOU NEVER TOLD ME, STAR OF HEAVEN.
HOW CAME YOU TO KNOW THE PRINCE?

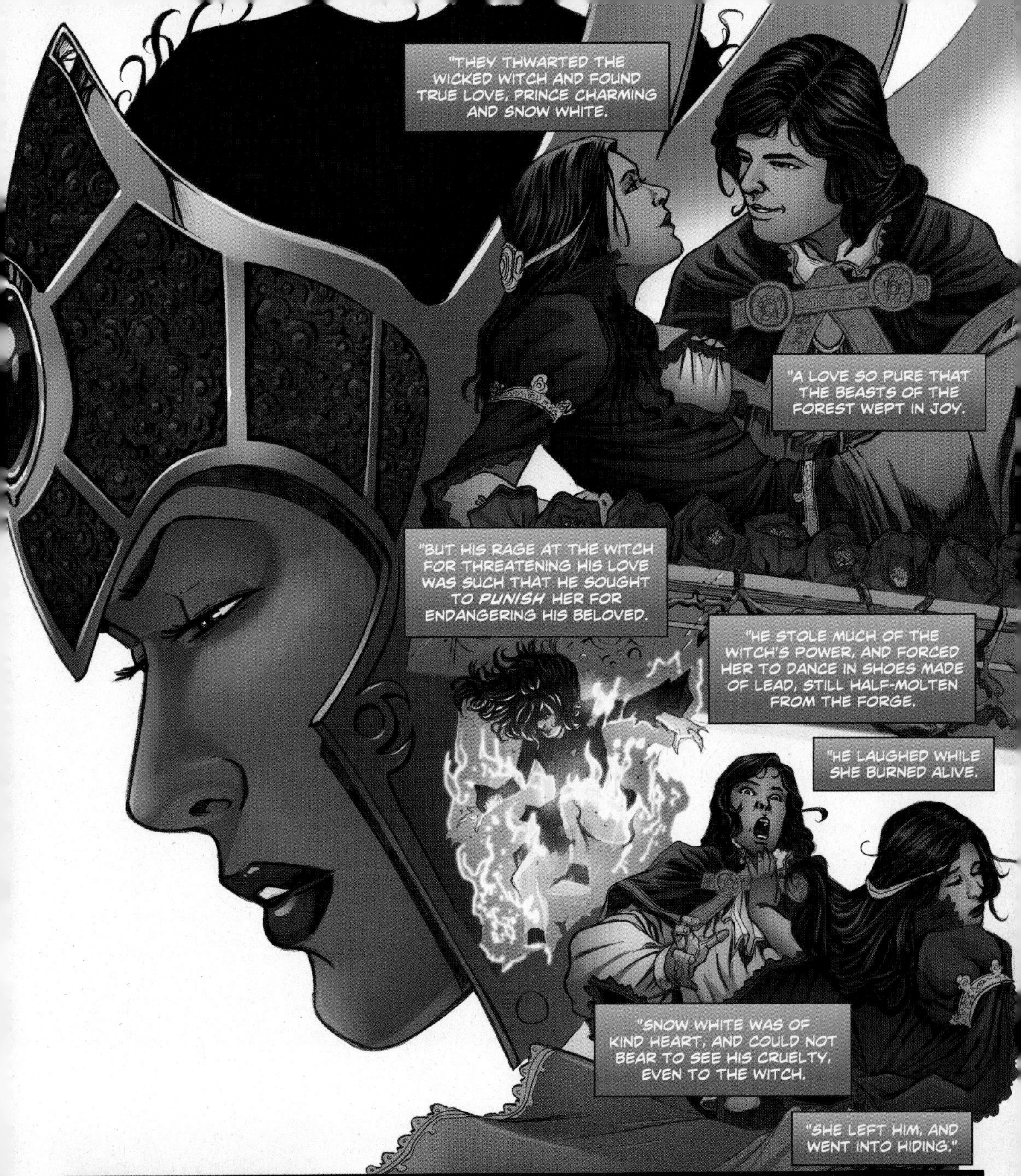
"THEY THWARTED THE WICKED WITCH AND FOUND TRUE LOVE, PRINCE CHARMING AND SNOW WHITE.
"A LOVE SO PURE THAT THE BEASTS OF THE FOREST WEPT IN JOY.
"BUT HIS RAGE AT THE WITCH FOR THREATENING HIS LOVE WAS SUCH THAT HE SOUGHT TO *PUNISH* HER FOR ENDANGERING HIS BELOVED.
"HE STOLE MUCH OF THE WITCH'S POWER, AND FORCED HER TO DANCE IN SHOES MADE OF LEAD, STILL HALF-MOLTEN FROM THE FORGE.
"HE LAUGHED WHILE SHE BURNED ALIVE.
"SNOW WHITE WAS OF KIND HEART, AND COULD NOT BEAR TO SEE HIS CRUELTY, EVEN TO THE WITCH.
"SHE LEFT HIM, AND WENT INTO HIDING."

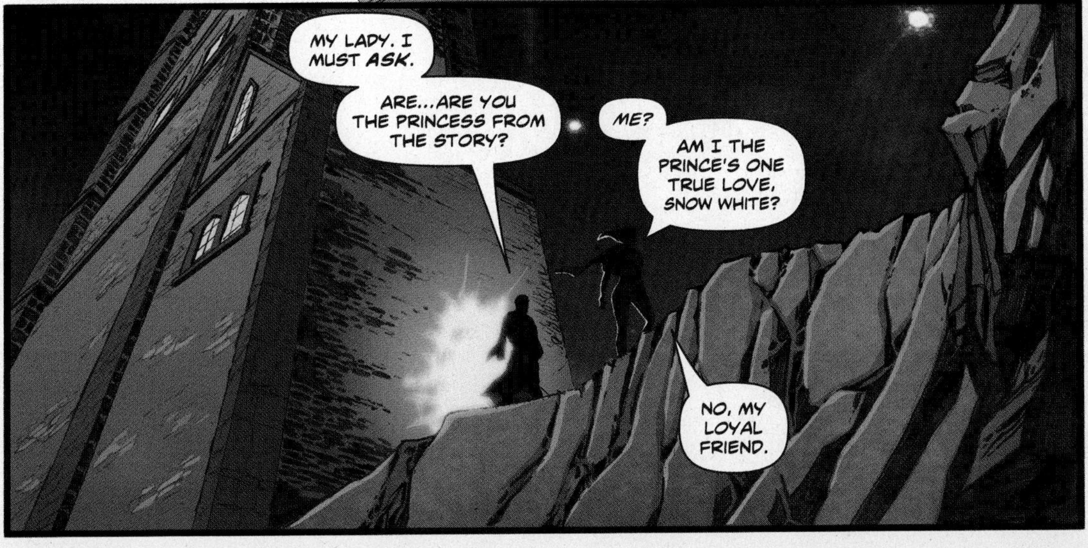
MY LADY. I MUST **ASK**.
ARE...ARE YOU THE PRINCESS FROM THE STORY?
ME?
AM I THE PRINCE'S ONE TRUE LOVE, SNOW WHITE?
NO, MY LOYAL FRIEND.

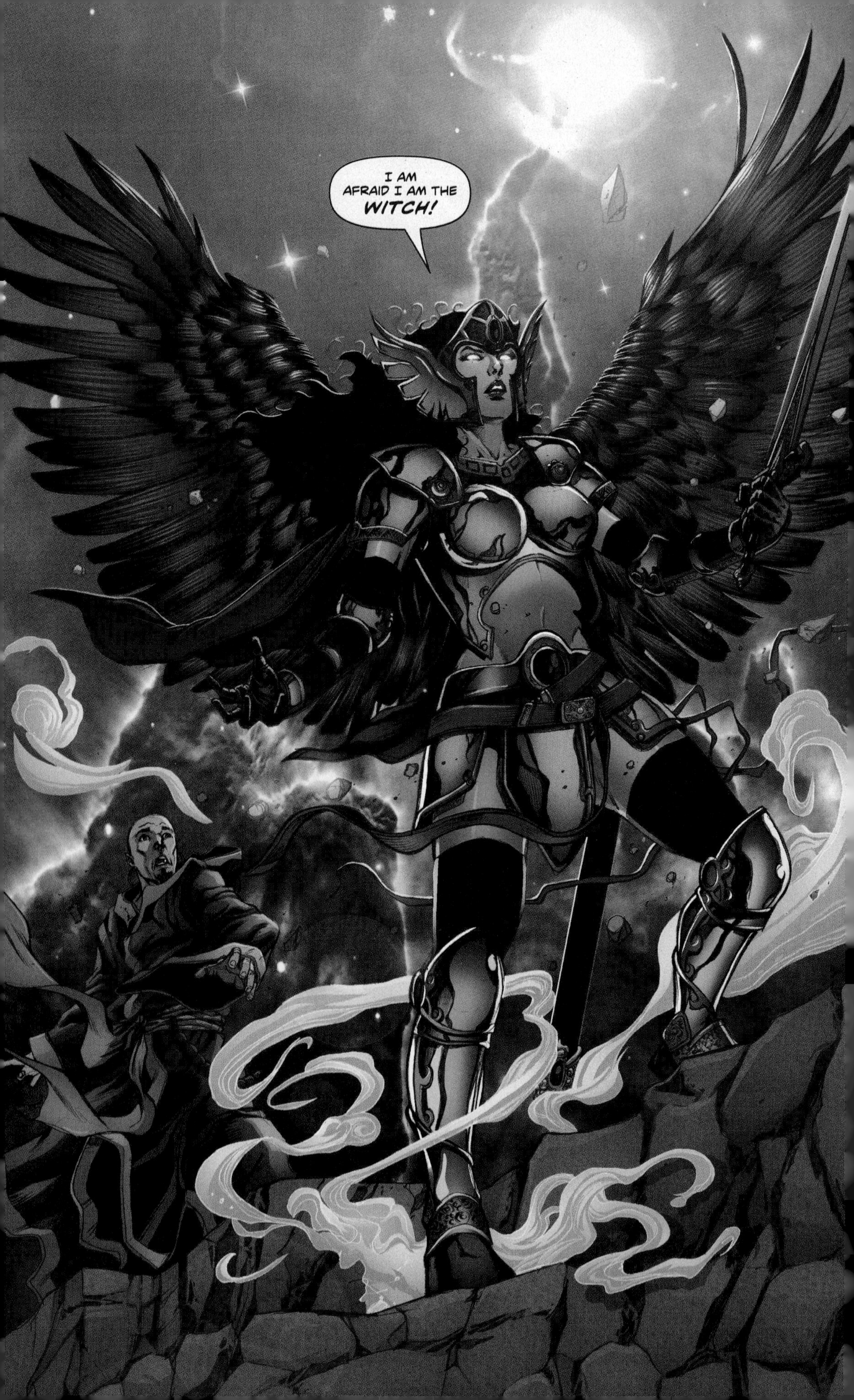
I AM AFRAID I AM THE WITCH!

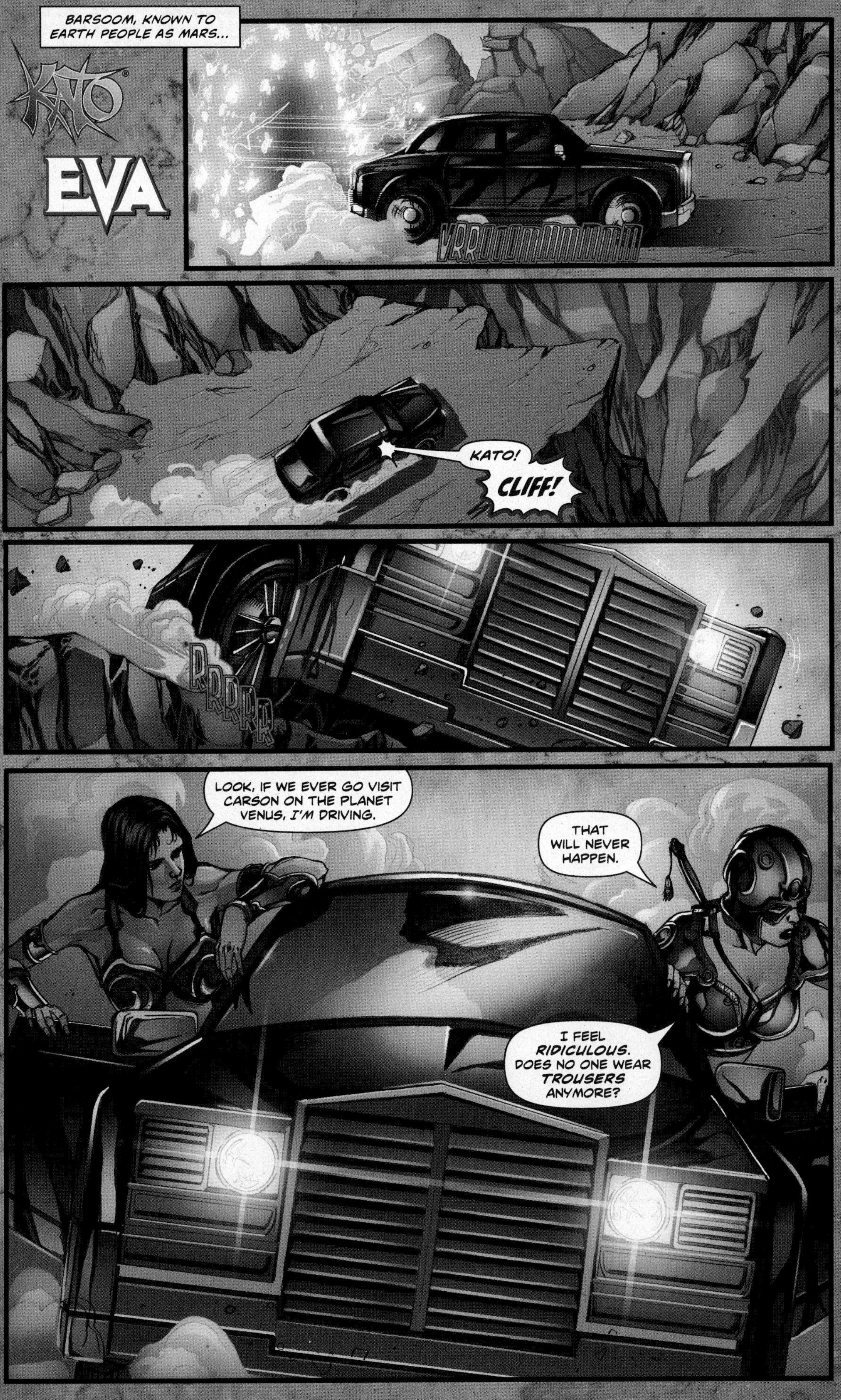
BARSOOM, KNOWN TO EARTH PEOPLE AS MARS...
KATO
EVA
VRROOOMMMMMN
KATO! CLIFF!
RRRRR
LOOK, IF WE EVER GO VISIT CARSON ON THE PLANET VENUS, I'M DRIVING.
THAT WILL NEVER HAPPEN.
I FEEL RIDICULOUS. DOES NO ONE WEAR TROUSERS ANYMORE?

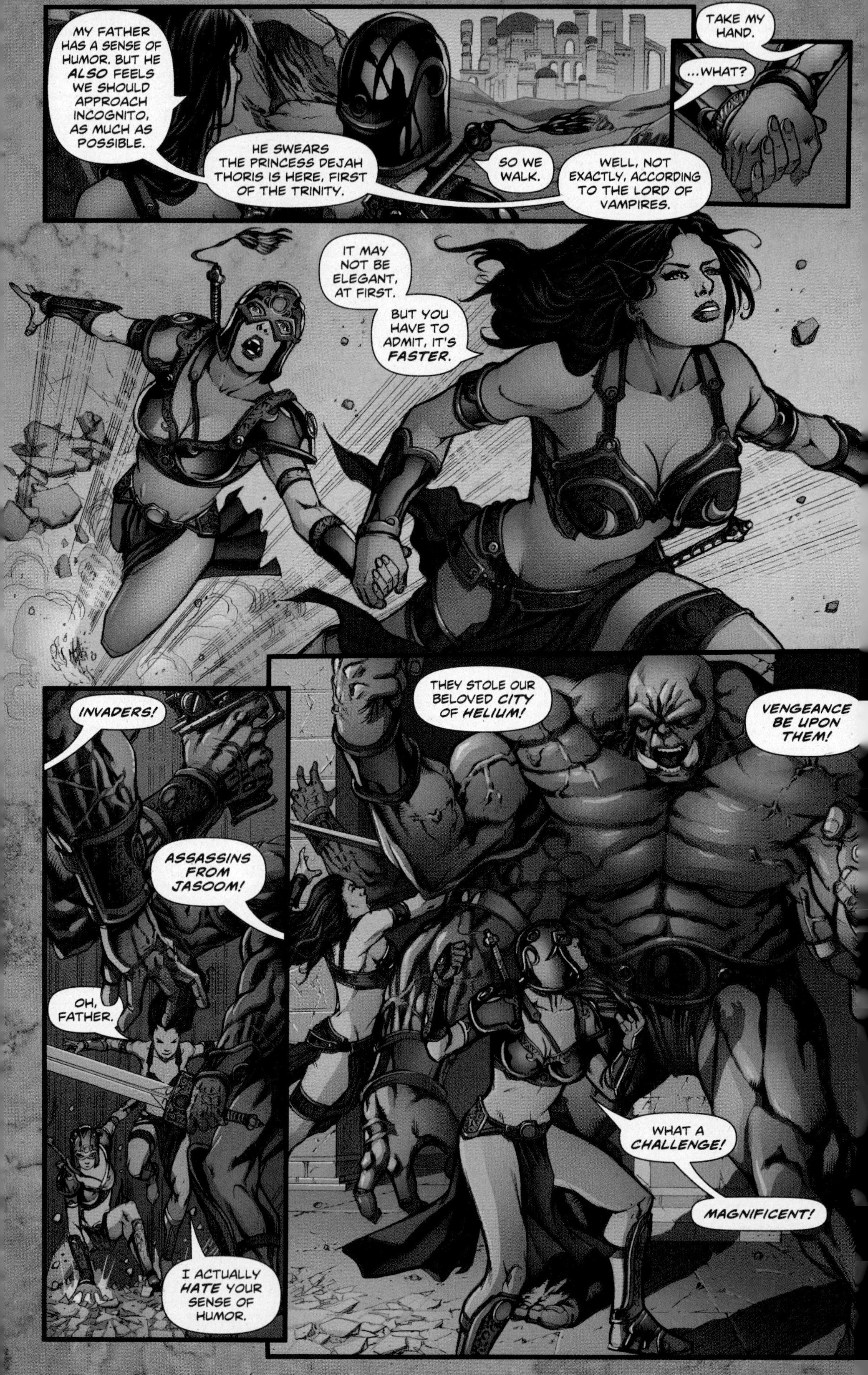
MY FATHER HAS A SENSE OF HUMOR. BUT HE ALSO FEELS WE SHOULD APPROACH INCOGNITO, AS MUCH AS POSSIBLE.
HE SWEARS THE PRINCESS DEJAH THORIS IS HERE, FIRST OF THE TRINITY.
SO WE WALK.
WELL, NOT EXACTLY, ACCORDING TO THE LORD OF VAMPIRES.
TAKE MY HAND.
...WHAT?
IT MAY NOT BE ELEGANT, AT FIRST.
BUT YOU HAVE TO ADMIT, IT'S FASTER.
INVADERS!
ASSASSINS FROM JASOOM!
OH, FATHER.
I ACTUALLY HATE YOUR SENSE OF HUMOR.
THEY STOLE OUR BELOVED CITY OF HELIUM!
VENGEANCE BE UPON THEM!
WHAT A CHALLENGE!
MAGNIFICENT!

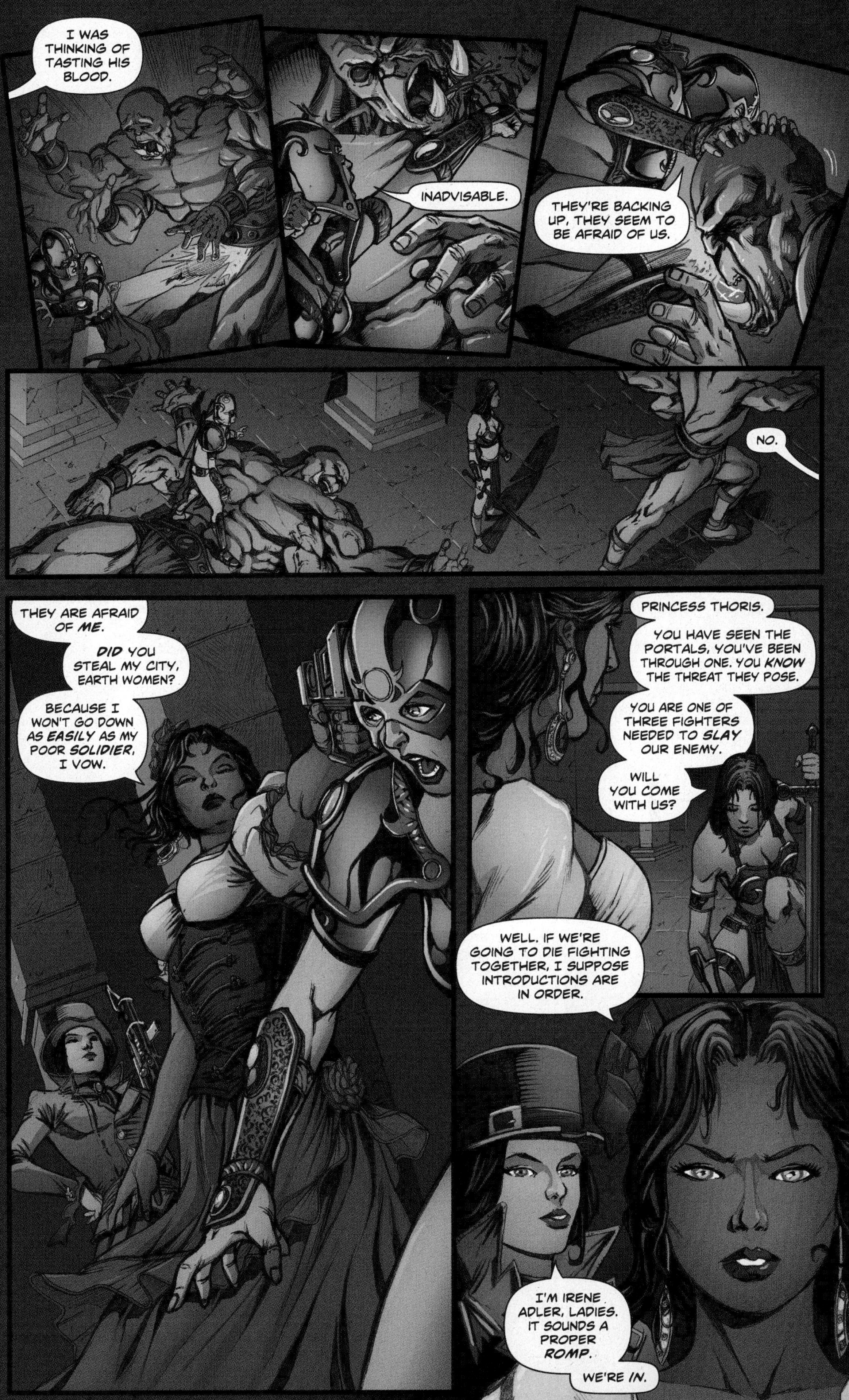
I WAS THINKING OF TASTING HIS BLOOD.
INADVISABLE.
THEY'RE BACKING UP, THEY SEEM TO BE AFRAID OF US.
NO.
THEY ARE AFRAID OF *ME*.
DID YOU STEAL MY CITY, EARTH WOMEN?
BECAUSE I WON'T GO DOWN AS *EASILY* AS MY POOR *SOLIDIER*, I VOW.
PRINCESS THORIS.
YOU HAVE SEEN THE PORTALS, YOU'VE BEEN THROUGH ONE. YOU *KNOW* THE THREAT THEY POSE.
YOU ARE ONE OF THREE FIGHTERS NEEDED TO *SLAY* OUR ENEMY.
WILL YOU COME WITH US?
WELL. IF WE'RE GOING TO DIE FIGHTING TOGETHER, I SUPPOSE INTRODUCTIONS ARE IN ORDER.
I'M IRENE ADLER, LADIES. IT SOUNDS A PROPER *ROMP*.
WE'RE *IN*.

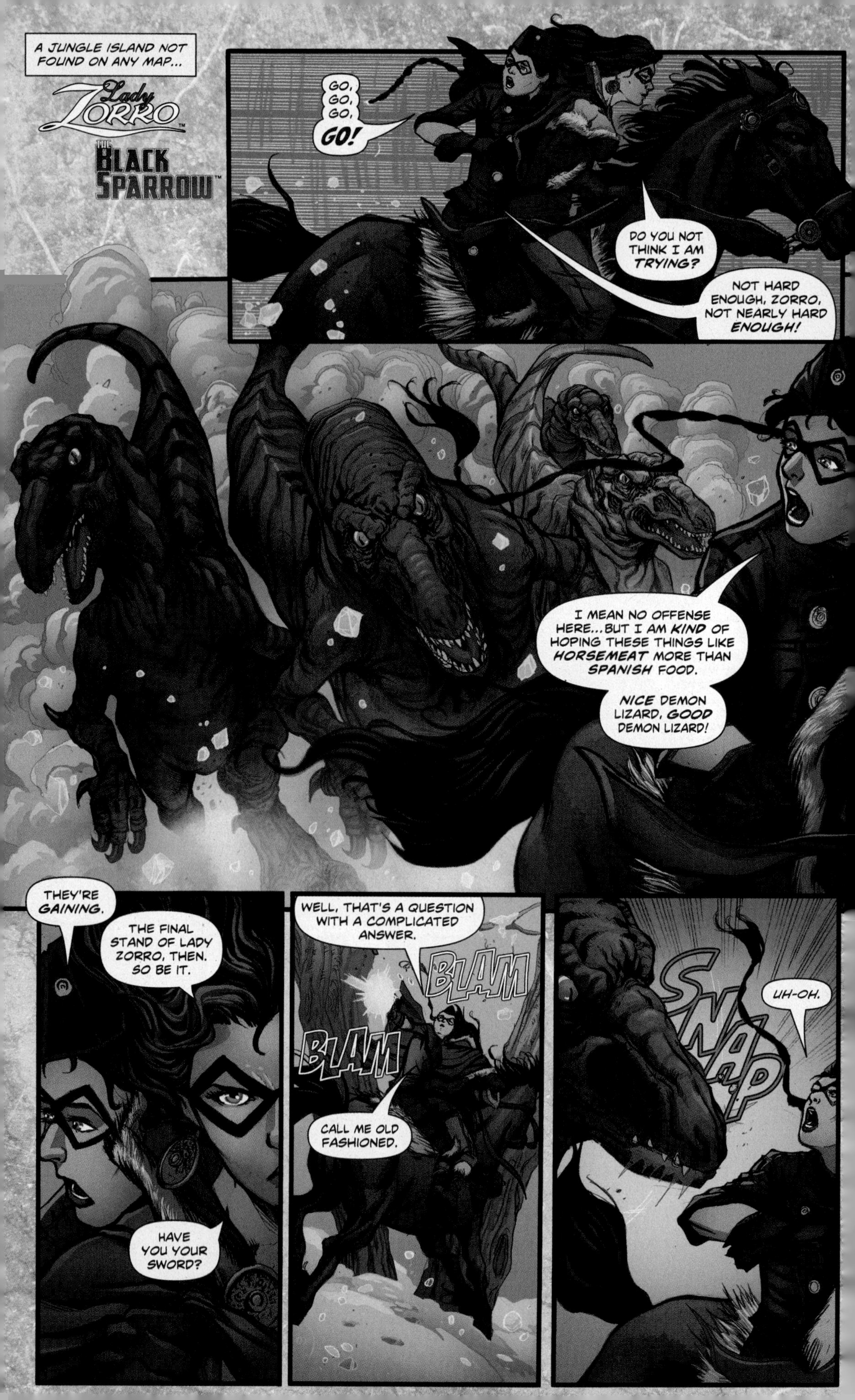
A JUNGLE ISLAND NOT FOUND ON ANY MAP...
Lady ZORRO
THE BLACK SPARROW
GO, GO, GO, GO!
DO YOU NOT THINK I AM TRYING?
NOT HARD ENOUGH, ZORRO, NOT NEARLY HARD ENOUGH!
I MEAN NO OFFENSE HERE...BUT I AM KIND OF HOPING THESE THINGS LIKE HORSEMEAT MORE THAN SPANISH FOOD.
NICE DEMON LIZARD, GOOD DEMON LIZARD!
THEY'RE GAINING.
THE FINAL STAND OF LADY ZORRO, THEN. SO BE IT.
HAVE YOU YOUR SWORD?
WELL, THAT'S A QUESTION WITH A COMPLICATED ANSWER.
BLAM
BLAM
CALL ME OLD FASHIONED.
SNAP
UH-OH.

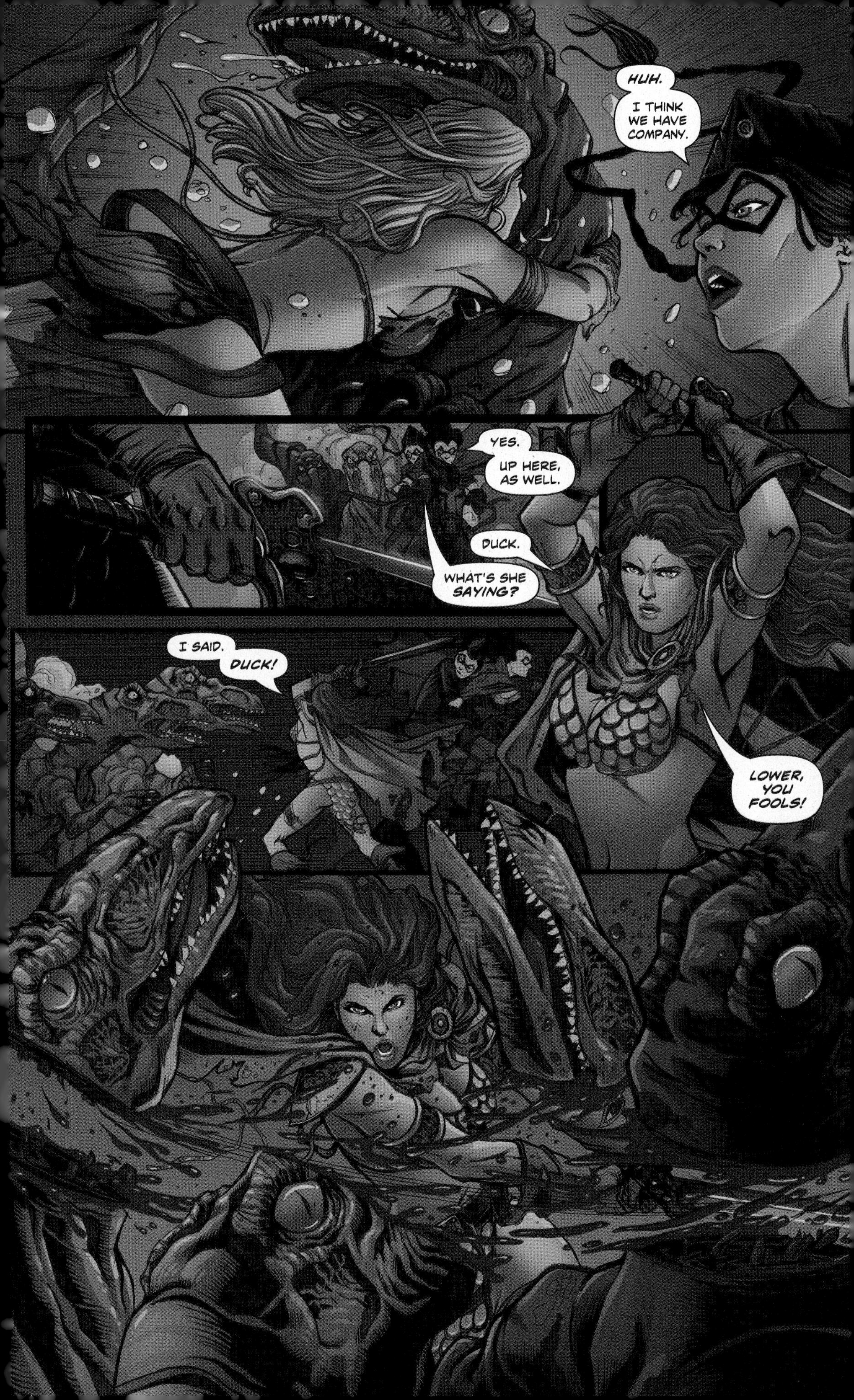

HUH.
I THINK WE HAVE COMPANY.
YES.
UP HERE, AS WELL.
DUCK.
WHAT'S SHE SAYING?
I SAID.
DUCK!
LOWER, YOU FOOLS!

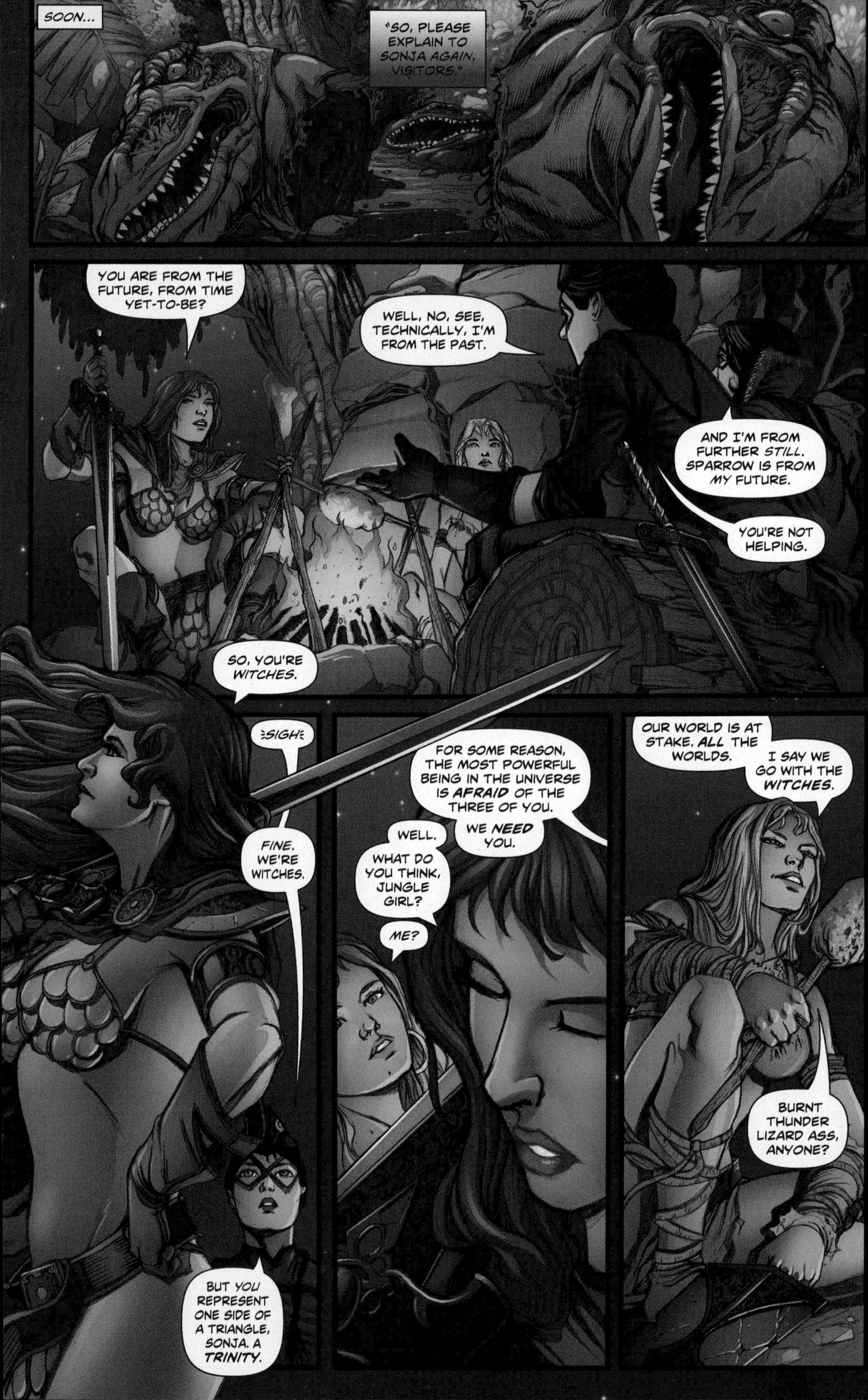
SOON...
"SO, PLEASE EXPLAIN TO SONJA AGAIN, VISITORS."
YOU ARE FROM THE FUTURE, FROM TIME YET-TO-BE?
WELL, NO, SEE, TECHNICALLY, I'M FROM THE PAST.
AND I'M FROM FURTHER STILL. SPARROW IS FROM MY FUTURE.
YOU'RE NOT HELPING.
SO, YOU'RE WITCHES.
SIGH
FINE. WE'RE WITCHES.
BUT YOU REPRESENT ONE SIDE OF A TRIANGLE, SONJA. A TRINITY.
FOR SOME REASON, THE MOST POWERFUL BEING IN THE UNIVERSE IS AFRAID OF THE THREE OF YOU.
WE NEED YOU.
WELL. WHAT DO YOU THINK, JUNGLE GIRL?
ME?
OUR WORLD IS AT STAKE. ALL THE WORLDS.
I SAY WE GO WITH THE WITCHES.
BURNT THUNDER LIZARD ASS, ANYONE?

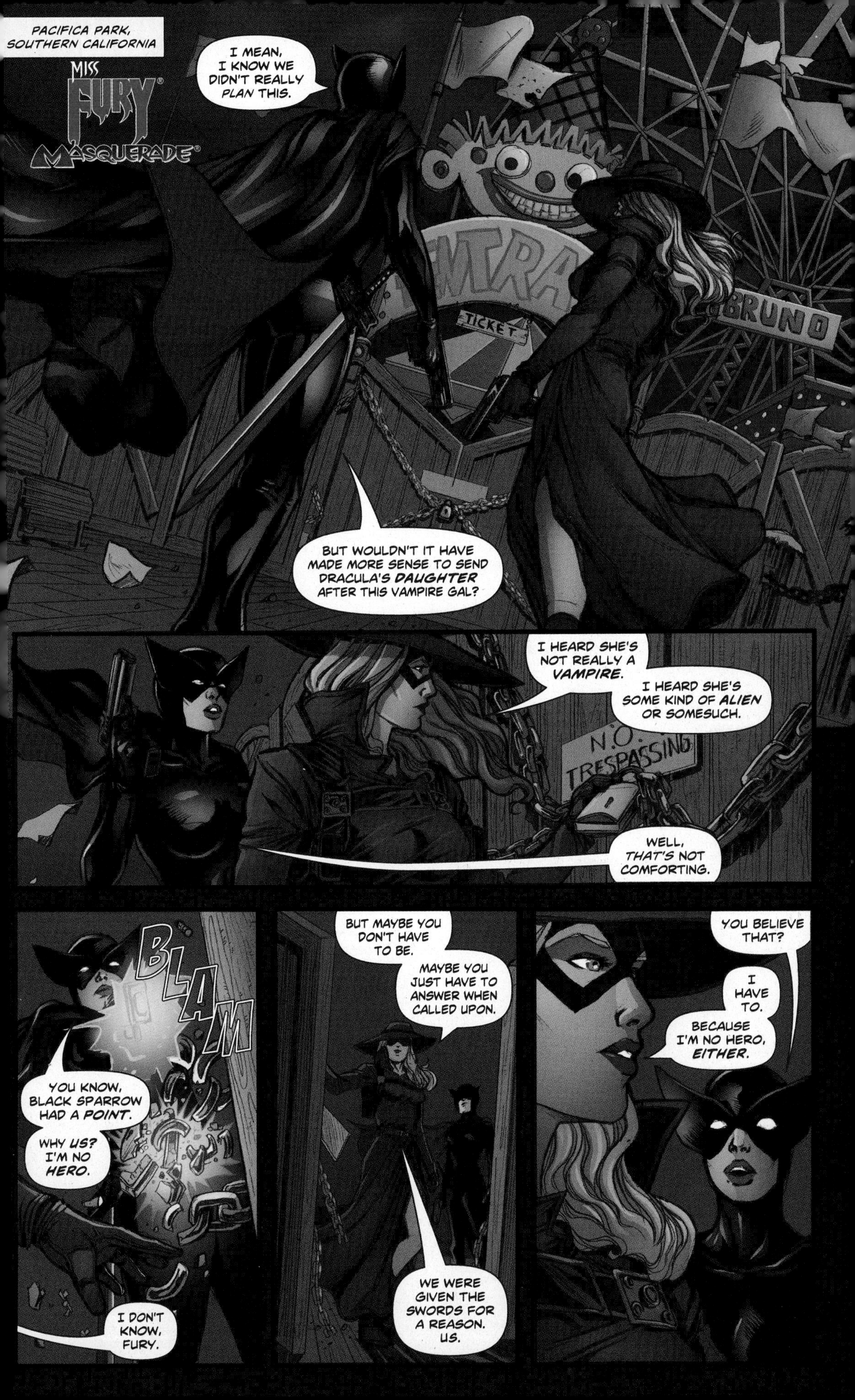
PACIFICA PARK, SOUTHERN CALIFORNIA
MISS FURY
MASQUERADE
I MEAN, I KNOW WE DIDN'T REALLY PLAN THIS.
BUT WOULDN'T IT HAVE MADE MORE SENSE TO SEND DRACULA'S DAUGHTER AFTER THIS VAMPIRE GAL?
TICKET
BRUNO
I HEARD SHE'S NOT REALLY A VAMPIRE.
I HEARD SHE'S SOME KIND OF ALIEN OR SOMESUCH.
NO TRESPASSING
WELL, THAT'S NOT COMFORTING.
BLAM
YOU KNOW, BLACK SPARROW HAD A POINT.
WHY US? I'M NO HERO.
I DON'T KNOW, FURY.
BUT MAYBE YOU DON'T HAVE TO BE.
MAYBE YOU JUST HAVE TO ANSWER WHEN CALLED UPON.
WE WERE GIVEN THE SWORDS FOR A REASON. US.
YOU BELIEVE THAT?
I HAVE TO.
BECAUSE I'M NO HERO, EITHER.

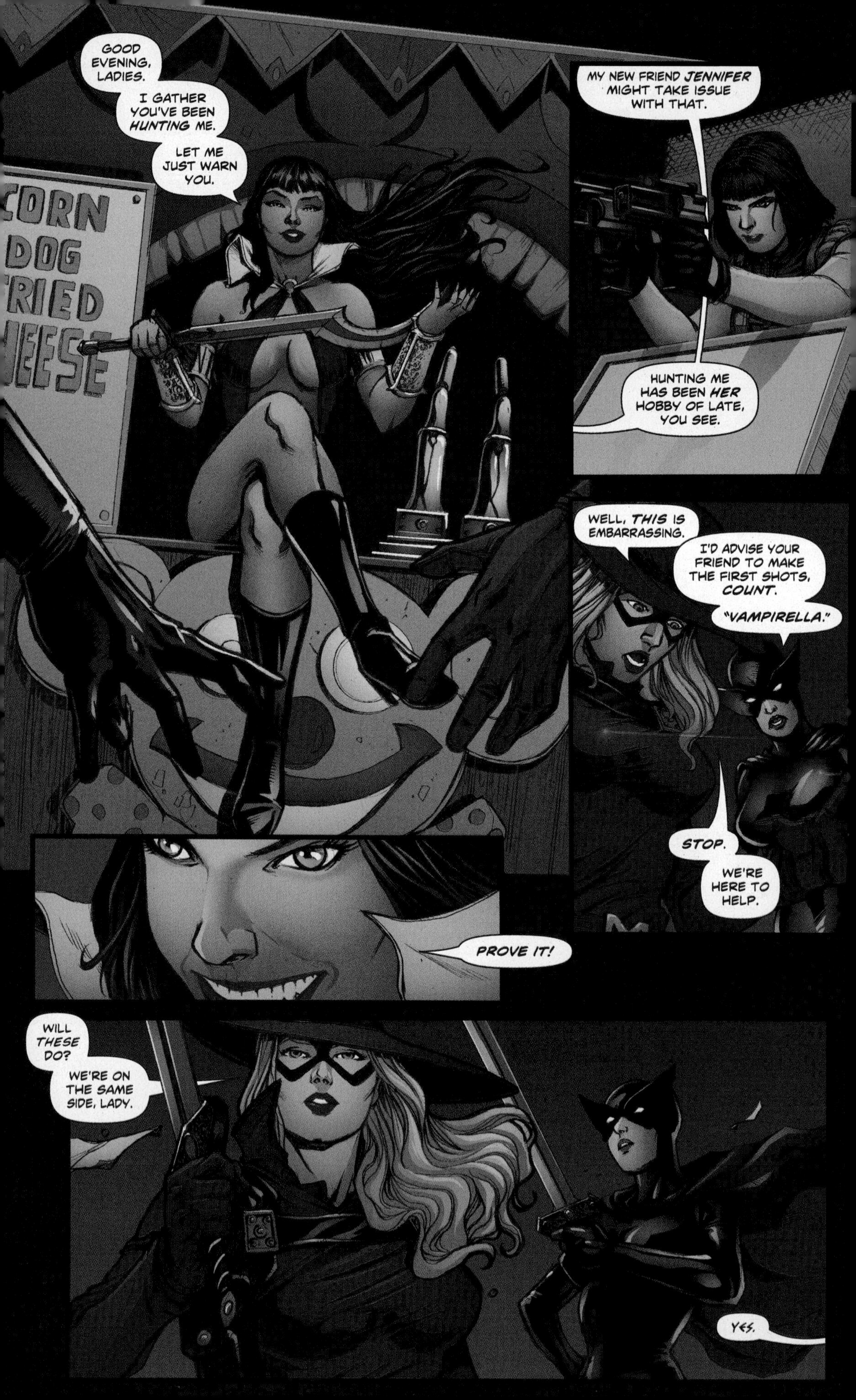
GOOD EVENING, LADIES.
I GATHER YOU'VE BEEN HUNTING ME.
LET ME JUST WARN YOU.
CORN DOG FRIED CHEESE
MY NEW FRIEND JENNIFER MIGHT TAKE ISSUE WITH THAT.
HUNTING ME HAS BEEN HER HOBBY OF LATE, YOU SEE.
WELL, THIS IS EMBARRASSING.
I'D ADVISE YOUR FRIEND TO MAKE THE FIRST SHOTS, COUNT.
"VAMPIRELLA."
STOP.
WE'RE HERE TO HELP.
PROVE IT!
WILL THESE DO?
WE'RE ON THE SAME SIDE, LADY.
YES.

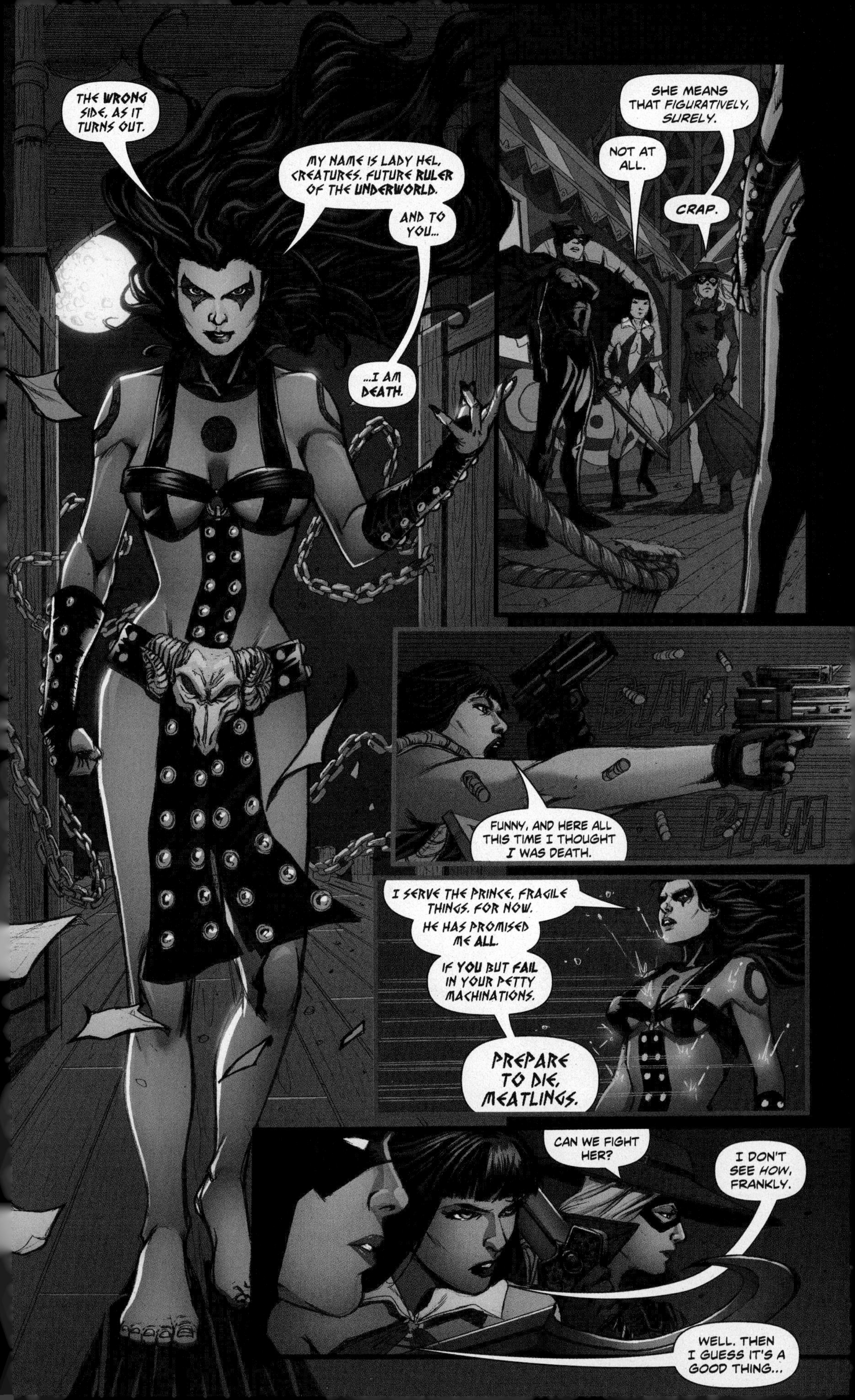
THE WRONG SIDE, AS IT TURNS OUT.
MY NAME IS LADY HEL, CREATURES. FUTURE RULER OF THE UNDERWORLD.
AND TO YOU...
...I AM DEATH.
SHE MEANS THAT FIGURATIVELY, SURELY.
NOT AT ALL.
CRAP.
FUNNY, AND HERE ALL THIS TIME I THOUGHT I WAS DEATH.
I SERVE THE PRINCE, FRAGILE THINGS. FOR NOW.
HE HAS PROMISED ME ALL.
IF YOU BUT FAIL IN YOUR PETTY MACHINATIONS.
PREPARE TO DIE, MEATLINGS.
CAN WE FIGHT HER?
I DON'T SEE HOW, FRANKLY.
WELL. THEN I GUESS IT'S A GOOD THING...

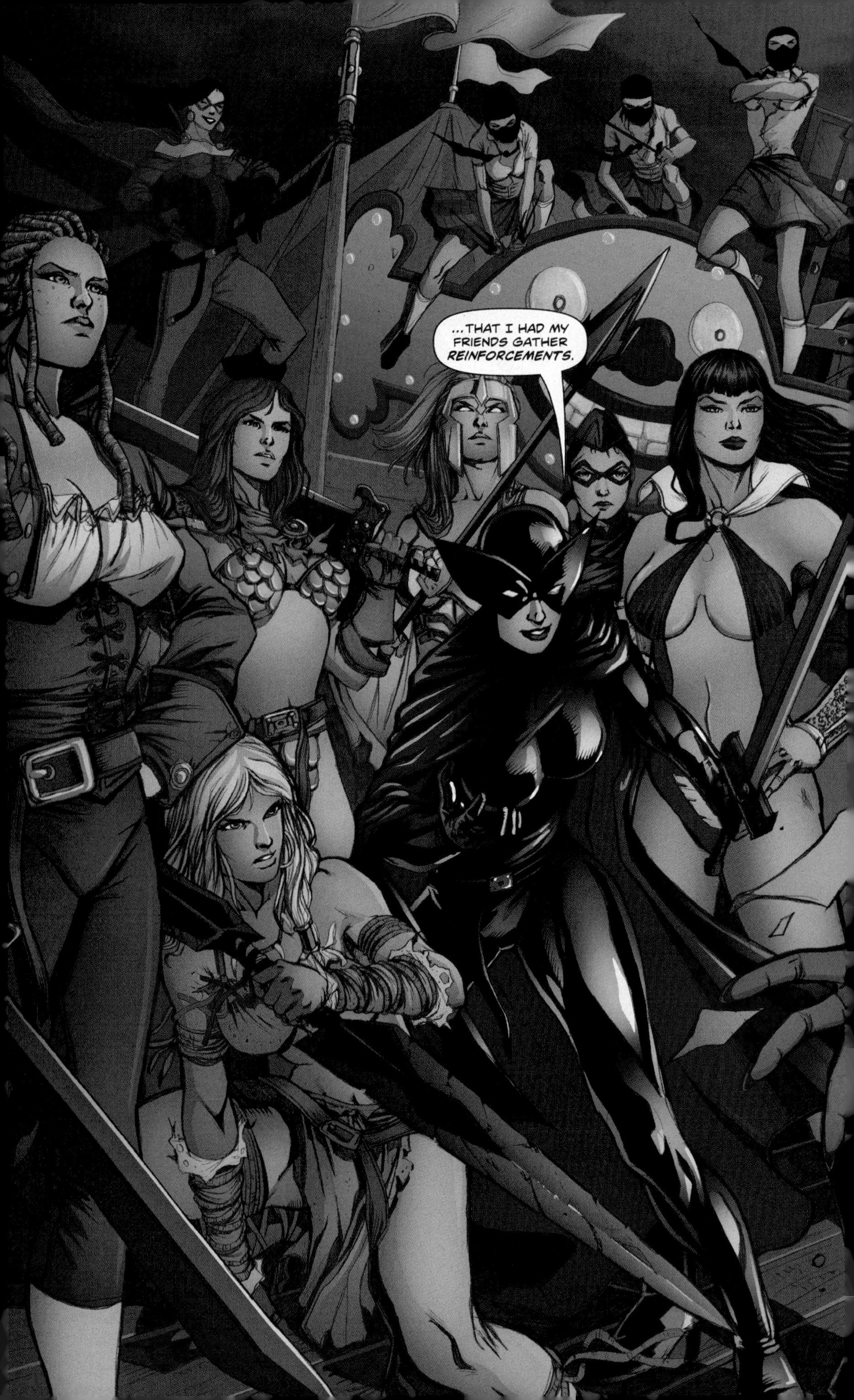
...THAT I HAD MY FRIENDS GATHER *REINFORCEMENTS*.

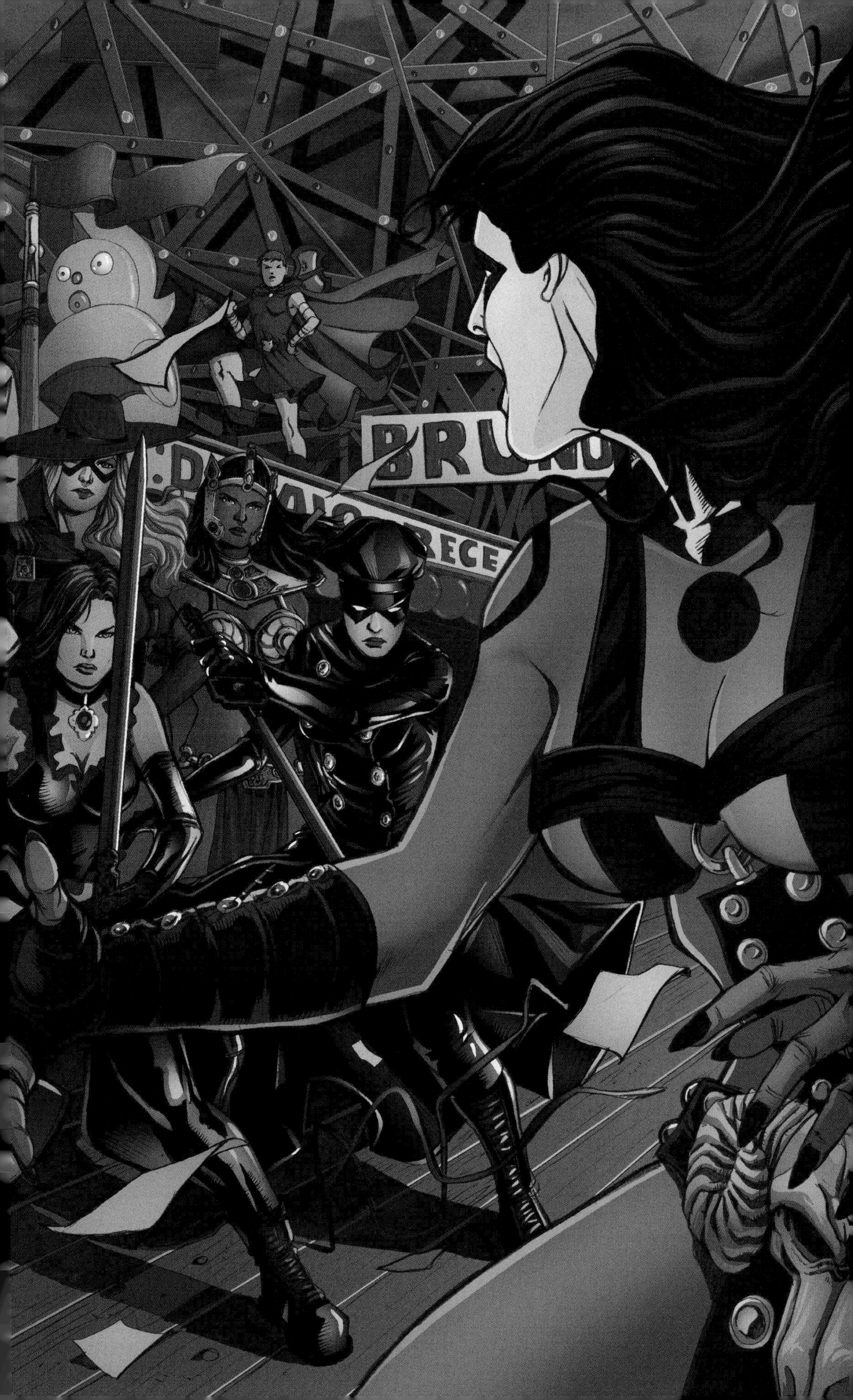

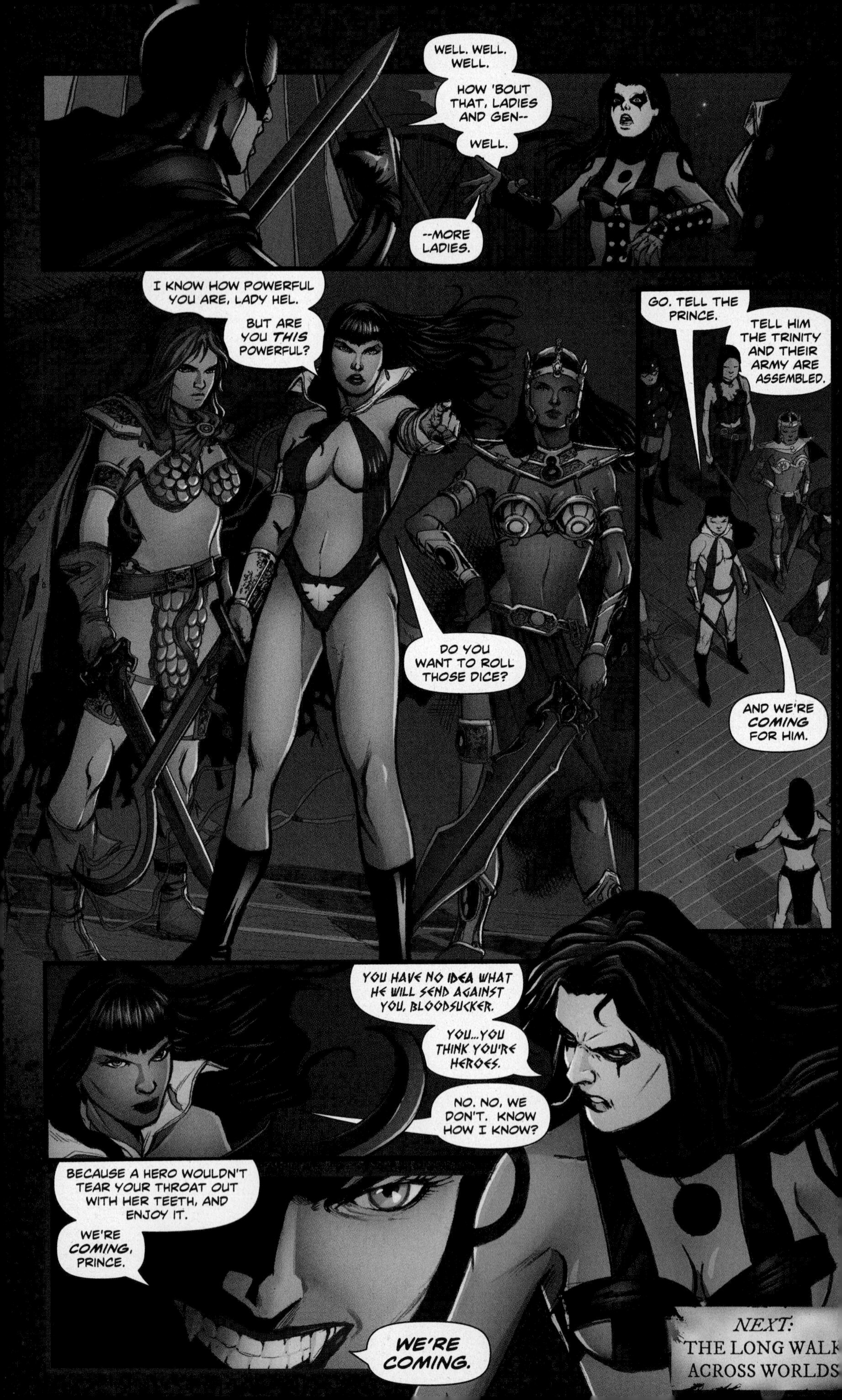

WELL. WELL. WELL.
HOW 'BOUT THAT, LADIES AND GEN--
WELL.
--MORE LADIES.
I KNOW HOW POWERFUL YOU ARE, LADY HEL.
BUT ARE YOU THIS POWERFUL?
DO YOU WANT TO ROLL THOSE DICE?
GO. TELL THE PRINCE.
TELL HIM THE TRINITY AND THEIR ARMY ARE ASSEMBLED.
AND WE'RE COMING FOR HIM.
YOU HAVE NO IDEA WHAT HE WILL SEND AGAINST YOU, BLOODSUCKER.
YOU...YOU THINK YOU'RE HEROES.
NO. NO, WE DON'T. KNOW HOW I KNOW?
BECAUSE A HERO WOULDN'T TEAR YOUR THROAT OUT WITH HER TEETH, AND ENJOY IT.
WE'RE COMING, PRINCE.
WE'RE COMING.
NEXT:
THE LONG WALK ACROSS WORLDS

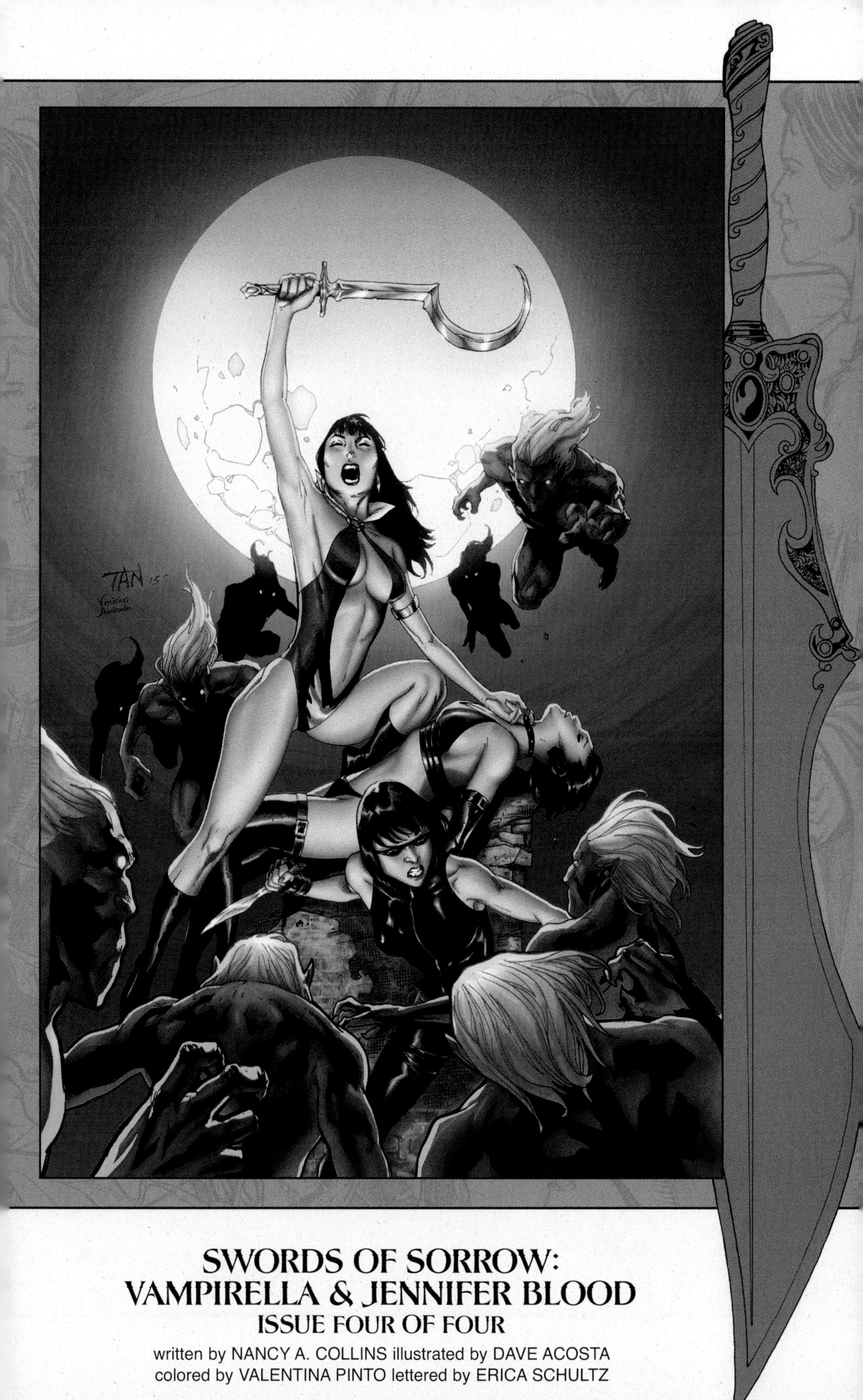

SWORDS OF SORROW: VAMPIRELLA & JENNIFER BLOOD

ISSUE FOUR OF FOUR

written by NANCY A. COLLINS illustrated by DAVE ACOSTA
colored by VALENTINA PINTO lettered by ERICA SCHULTZ

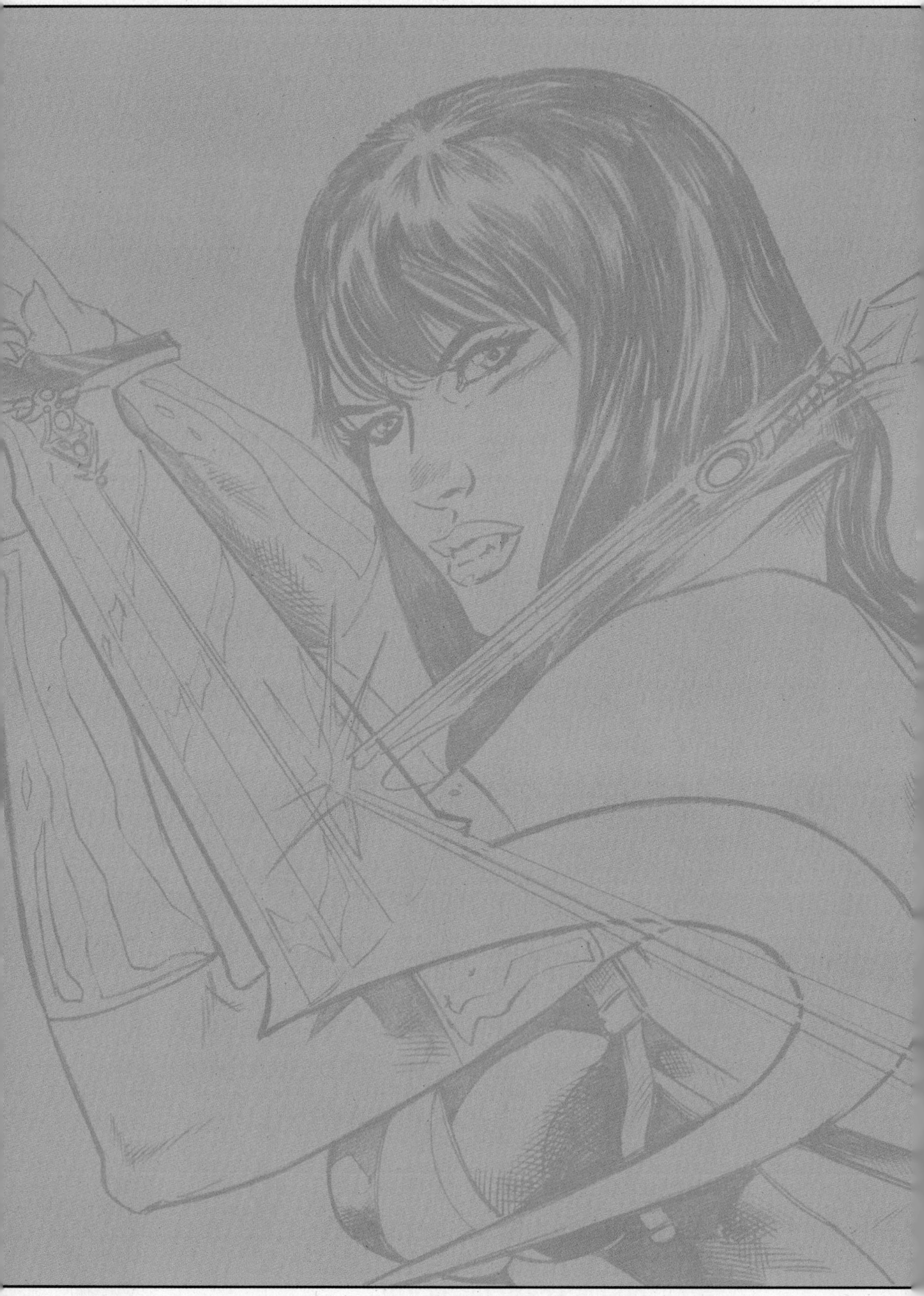

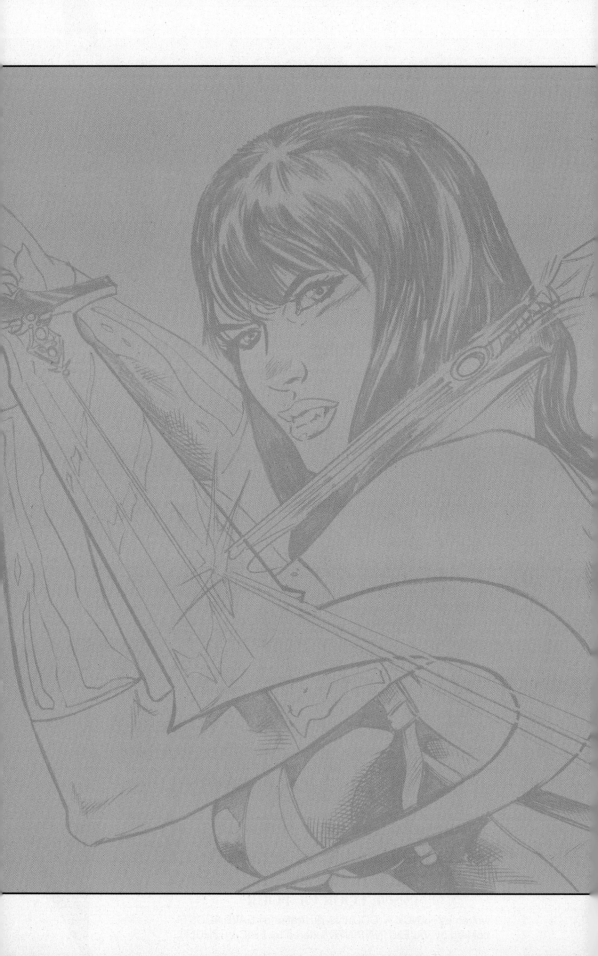

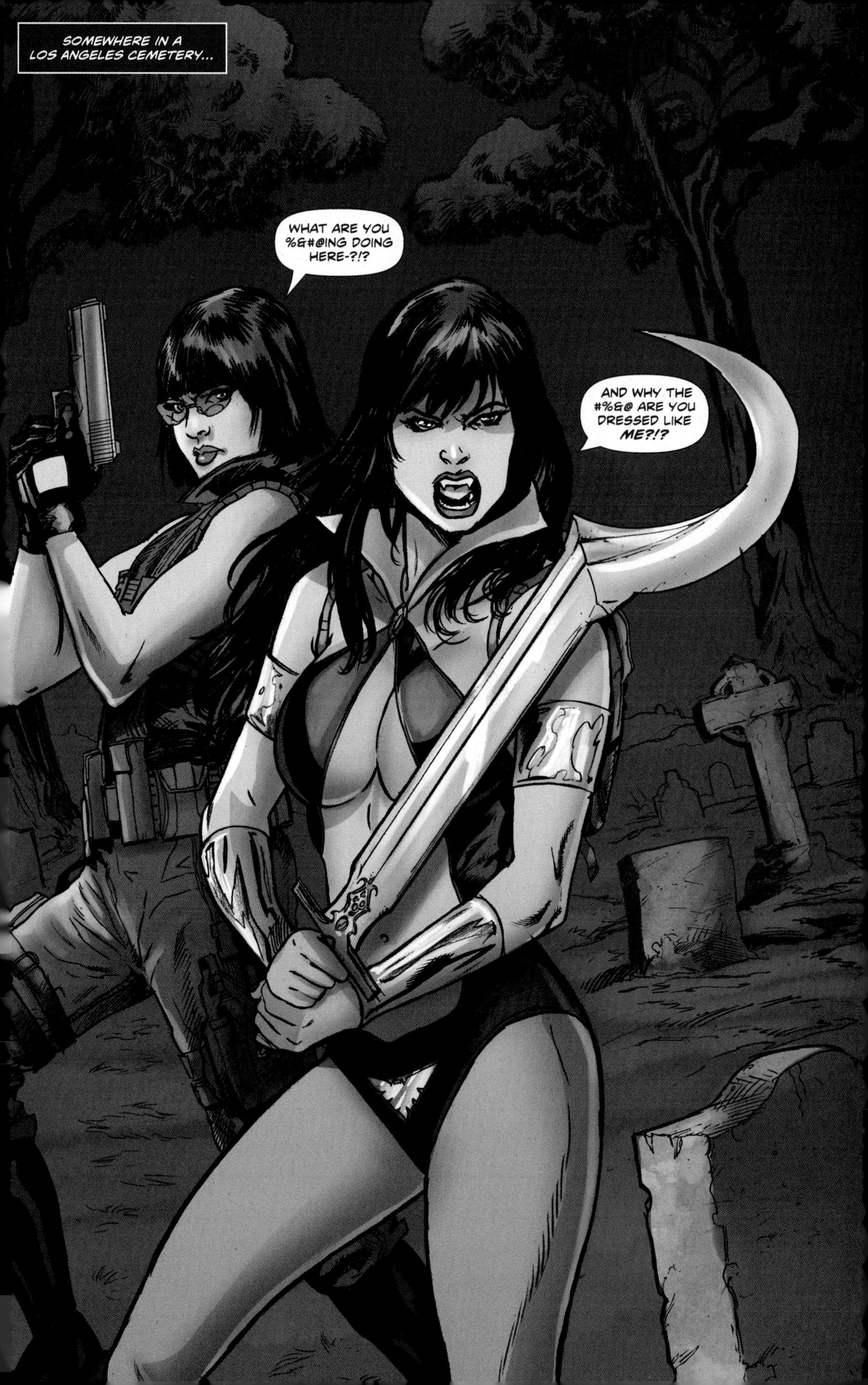
SOMEWHERE IN A LOS ANGELES CEMETERY...
WHAT ARE YOU %&#@ING DOING HERE-?!?
AND WHY THE #%&@ ARE YOU DRESSED LIKE ME?!?

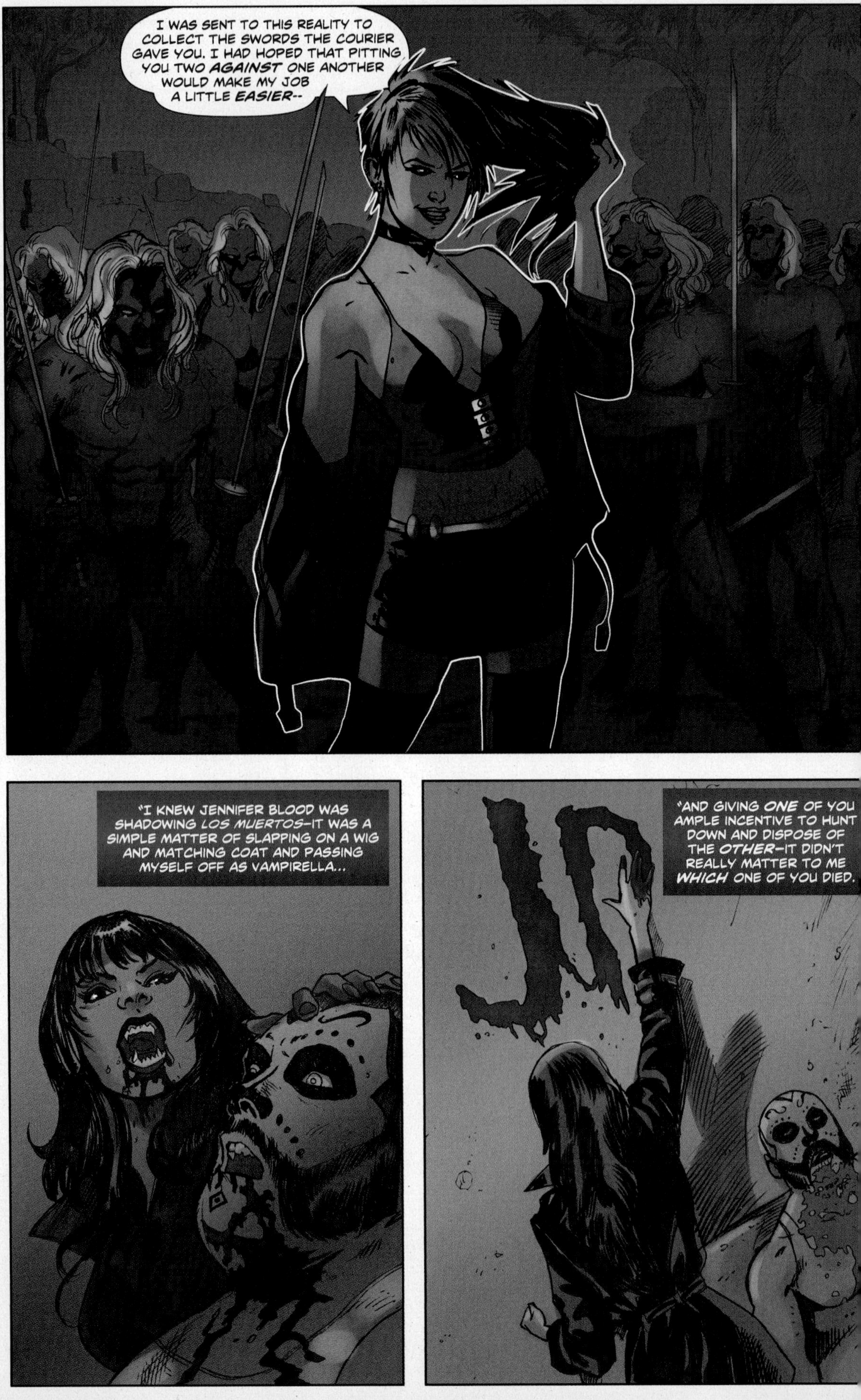
I WAS SENT TO THIS REALITY TO COLLECT THE SWORDS THE COURIER GAVE YOU. I HAD HOPED THAT PITTING YOU TWO AGAINST ONE ANOTHER WOULD MAKE MY JOB A LITTLE EASIER--
"I KNEW JENNIFER BLOOD WAS SHADOWING LOS MUERTOS--IT WAS A SIMPLE MATTER OF SLAPPING ON A WIG AND MATCHING COAT AND PASSING MYSELF OFF AS VAMPIRELLA...
"AND GIVING ONE OF YOU AMPLE INCENTIVE TO HUNT DOWN AND DISPOSE OF THE OTHER--IT DIDN'T REALLY MATTER TO ME WHICH ONE OF YOU DIED.
JB

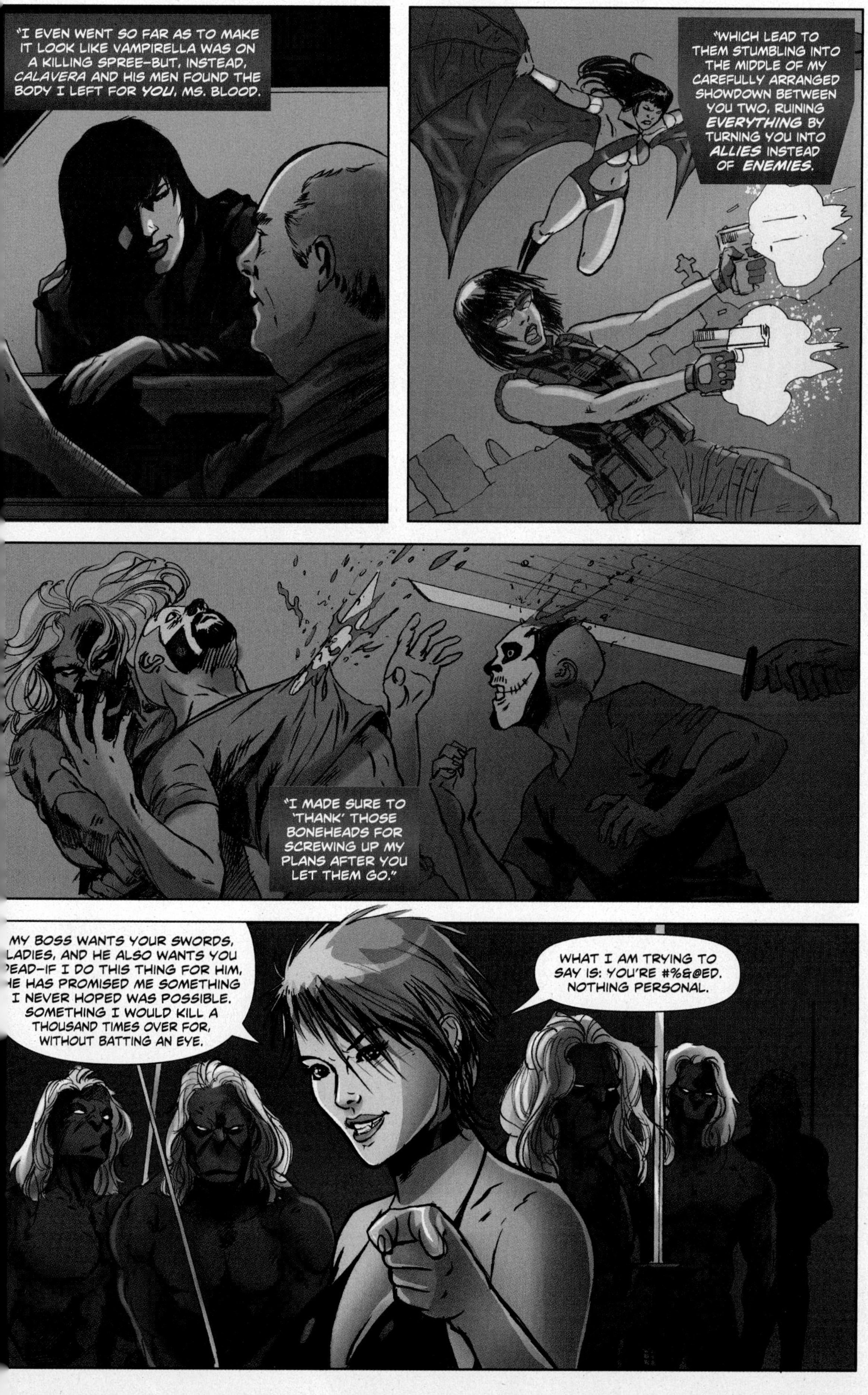
"I EVEN WENT SO FAR AS TO MAKE IT LOOK LIKE VAMPIRELLA WAS ON A KILLING SPREE—BUT, INSTEAD, CALAVERA AND HIS MEN FOUND THE BODY I LEFT FOR YOU, MS. BLOOD.
"WHICH LEAD TO THEM STUMBLING INTO THE MIDDLE OF MY CAREFULLY ARRANGED SHOWDOWN BETWEEN YOU TWO, RUINING EVERYTHING BY TURNING YOU INTO ALLIES INSTEAD OF ENEMIES.
"I MADE SURE TO 'THANK' THOSE BONEHEADS FOR SCREWING UP MY PLANS AFTER YOU LET THEM GO."
MY BOSS WANTS YOUR SWORDS, LADIES, AND HE ALSO WANTS YOU DEAD—IF I DO THIS THING FOR HIM, HE HAS PROMISED ME SOMETHING I NEVER HOPED WAS POSSIBLE. SOMETHING I WOULD KILL A THOUSAND TIMES OVER FOR, WITHOUT BATTING AN EYE.
WHAT I AM TRYING TO SAY IS: YOU'RE #%&@ED. NOTHING PERSONAL.

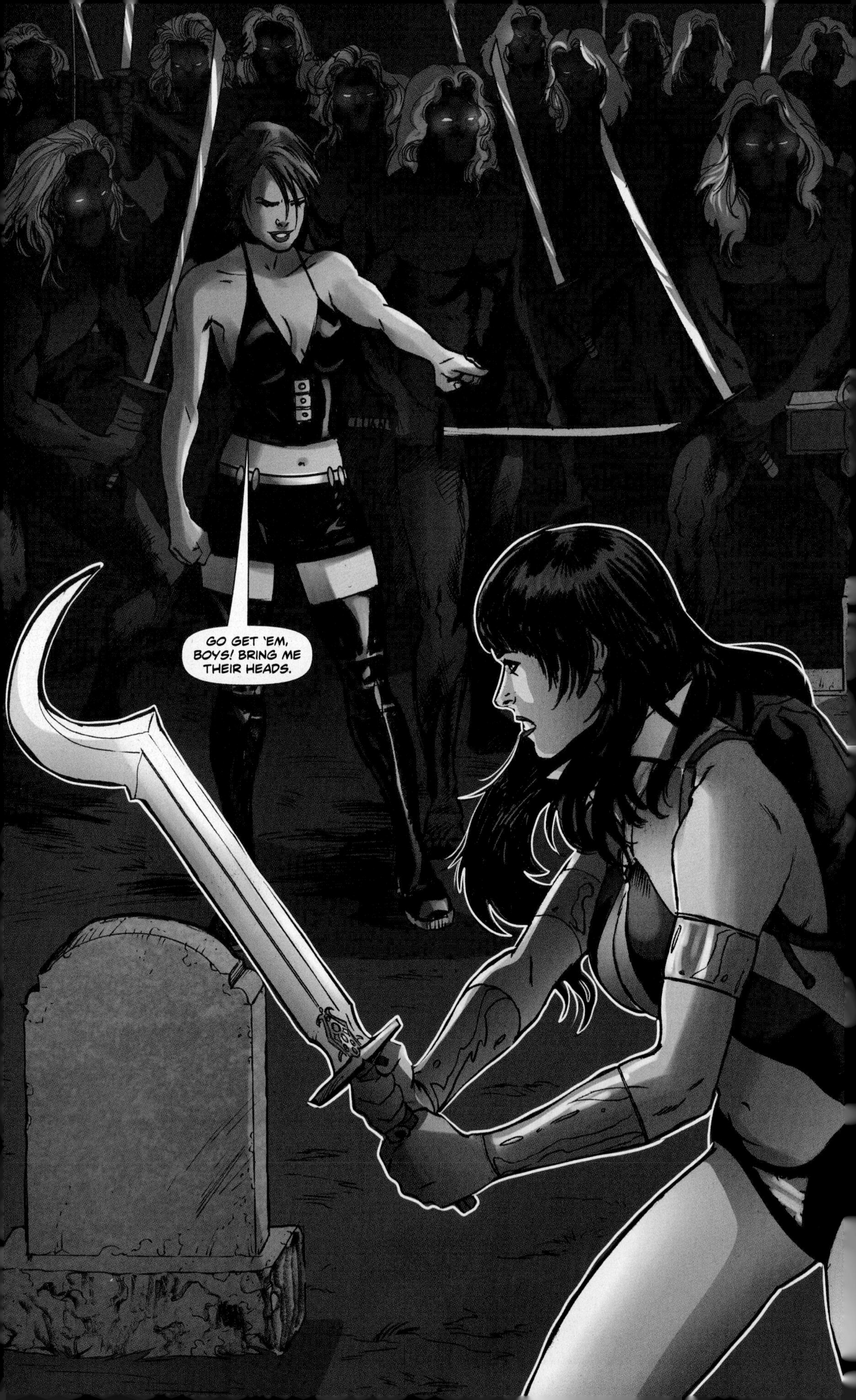
GO GET 'EM, BOYS! BRING ME THEIR HEADS.

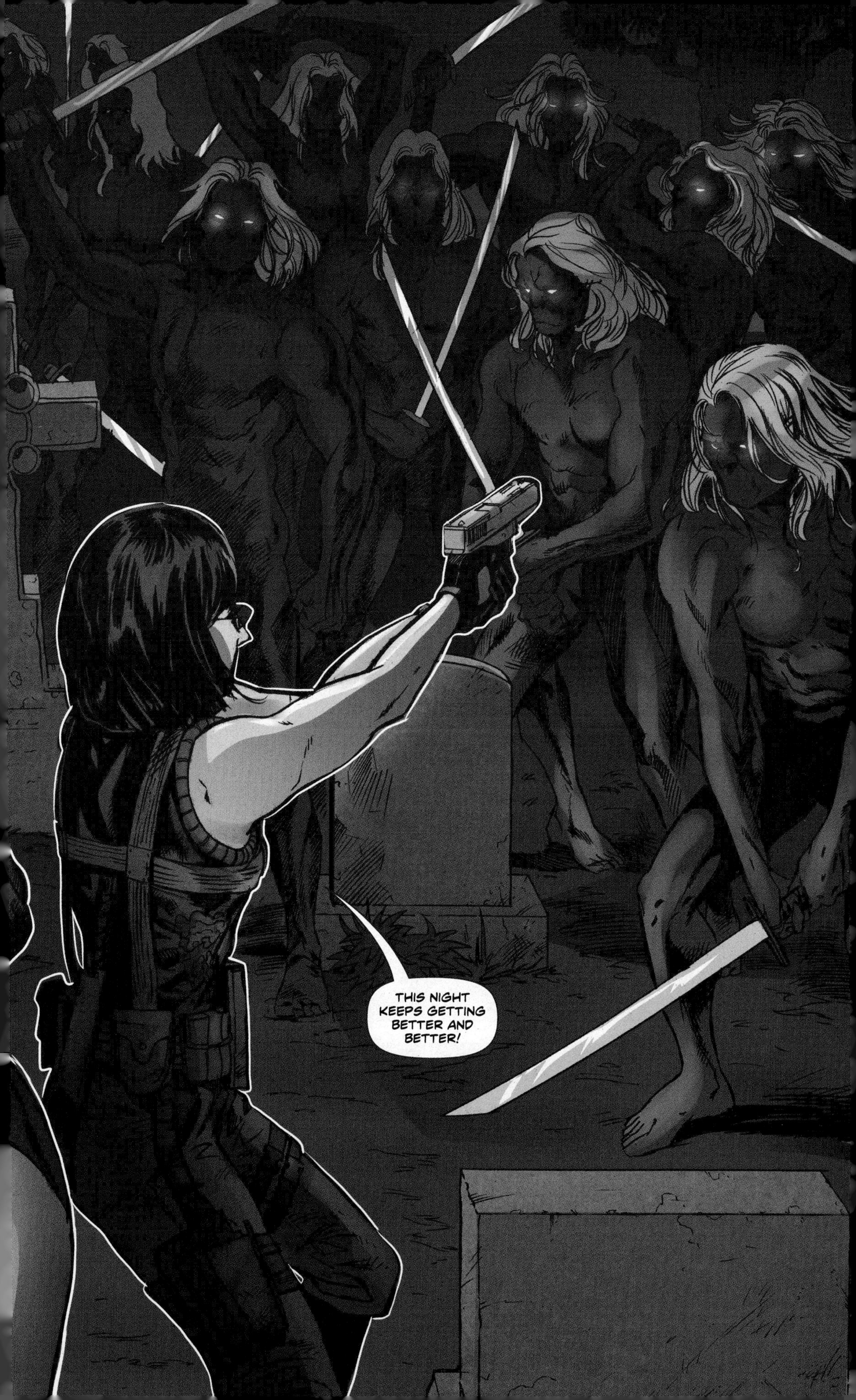
THIS NIGHT KEEPS GETTING BETTER AND BETTER!

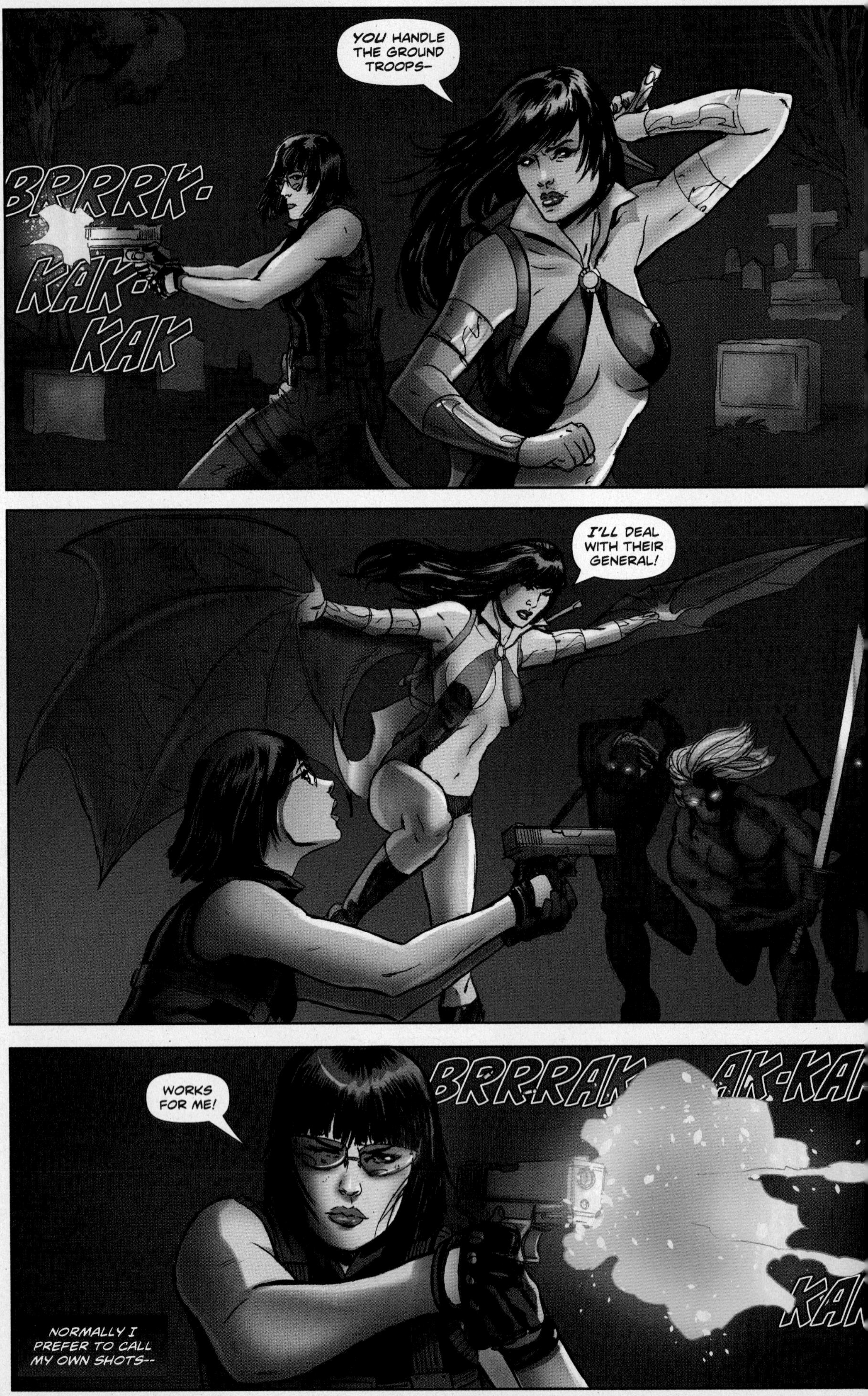
YOU HANDLE THE GROUND TROOPS–
BRRRK-KAK-KAK
I'LL DEAL WITH THEIR GENERAL!
WORKS FOR ME!
BRRRAK-AK-KA
KA
NORMALLY I PREFER TO CALL MY OWN SHOTS--

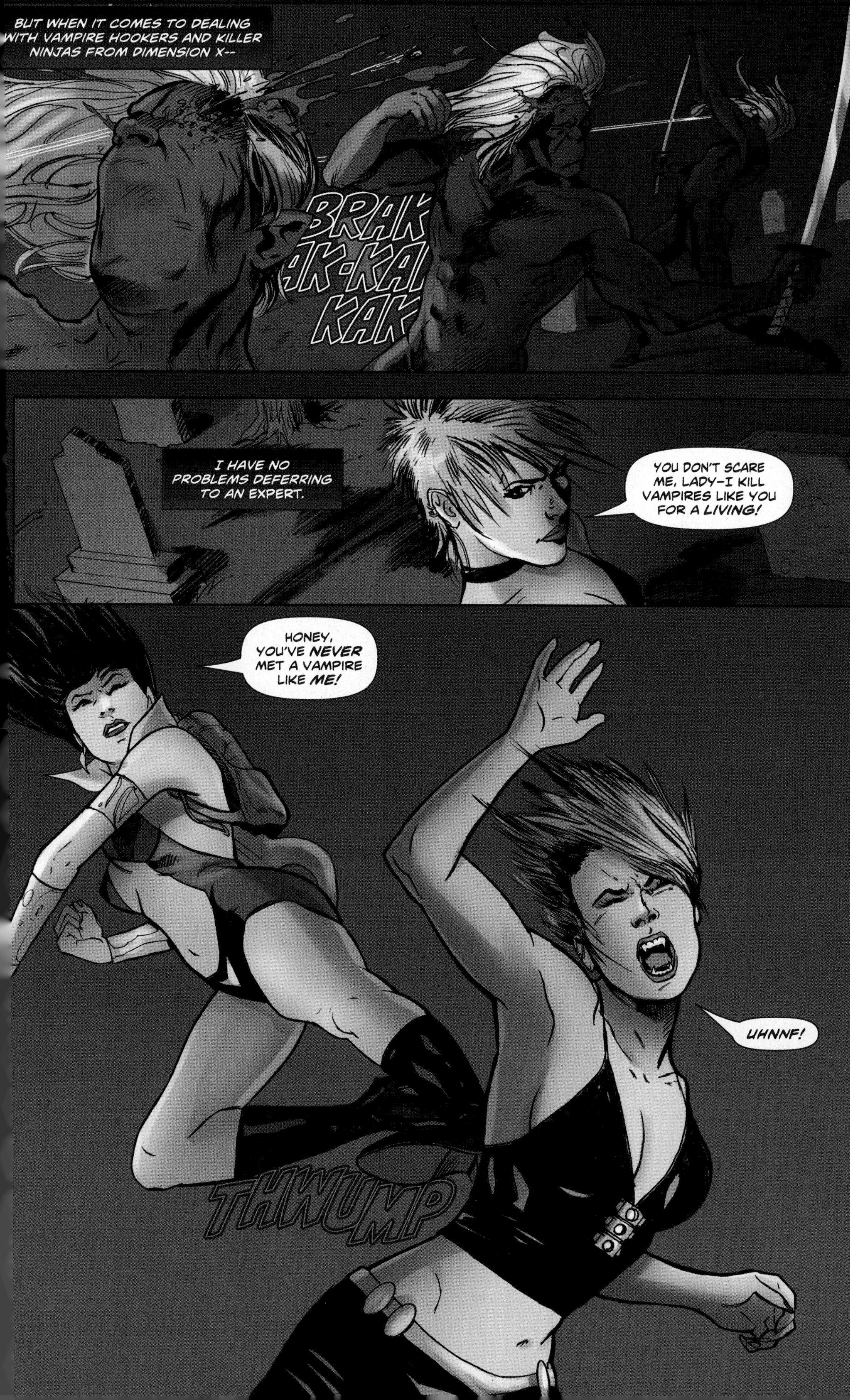
BUT WHEN IT COMES TO DEALING WITH VAMPIRE HOOKERS AND KILLER NINJAS FROM DIMENSION X--
BRAK AK-KAK KAK
I HAVE NO PROBLEMS DEFERRING TO AN EXPERT.
YOU DON'T SCARE ME, LADY--I KILL VAMPIRES LIKE YOU FOR A LIVING!
HONEY, YOU'VE NEVER MET A VAMPIRE LIKE ME!
UHNNF!
THWUMP

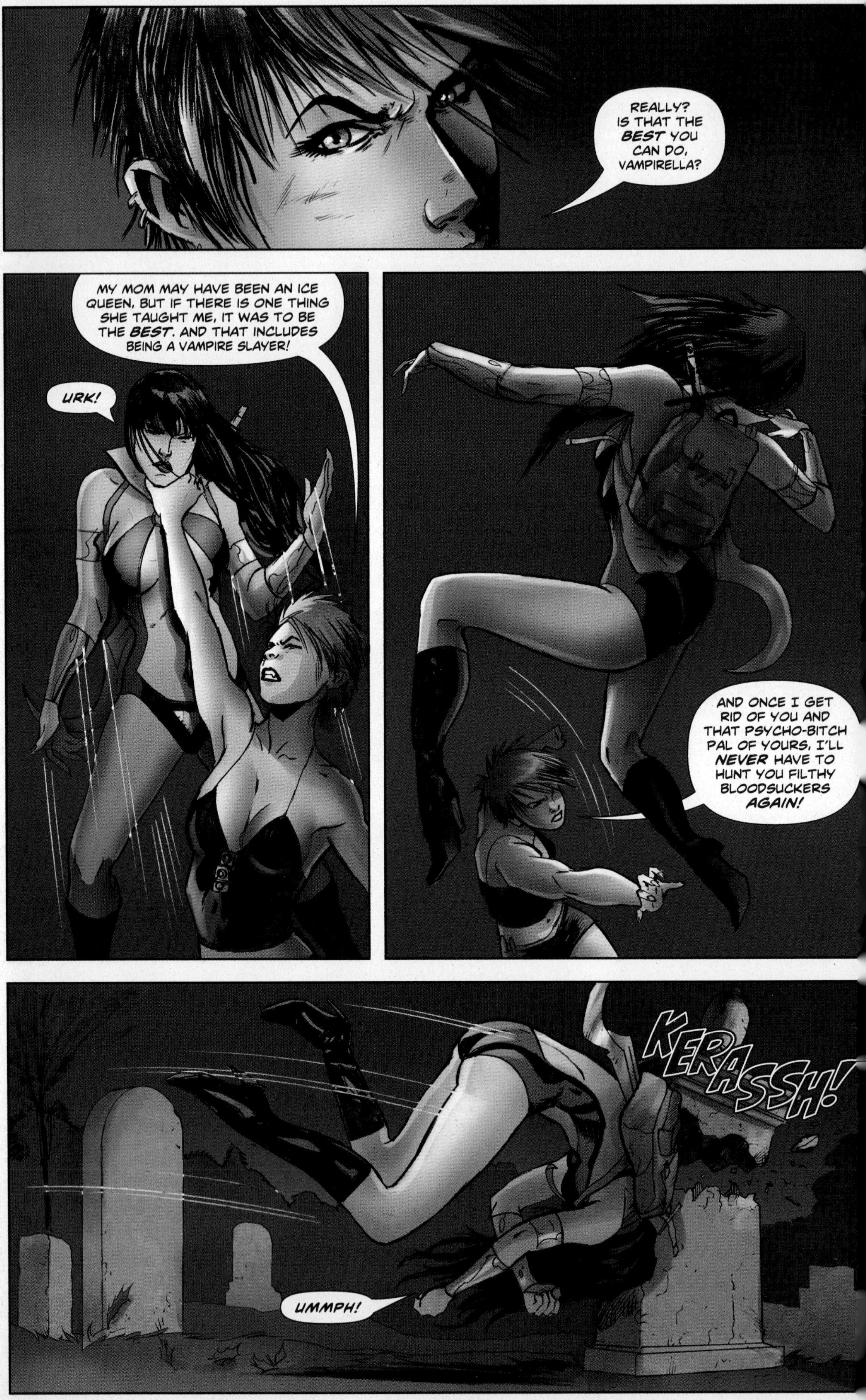
REALLY? IS THAT THE BEST YOU CAN DO, VAMPIRELLA?
MY MOM MAY HAVE BEEN AN ICE QUEEN, BUT IF THERE IS ONE THING SHE TAUGHT ME, IT WAS TO BE THE BEST. AND THAT INCLUDES BEING A VAMPIRE SLAYER!
URK!
AND ONCE I GET RID OF YOU AND THAT PSYCHO-BITCH PAL OF YOURS, I'LL NEVER HAVE TO HUNT YOU FILTHY BLOODSUCKERS AGAIN!
KERASSH!
UMMPH!

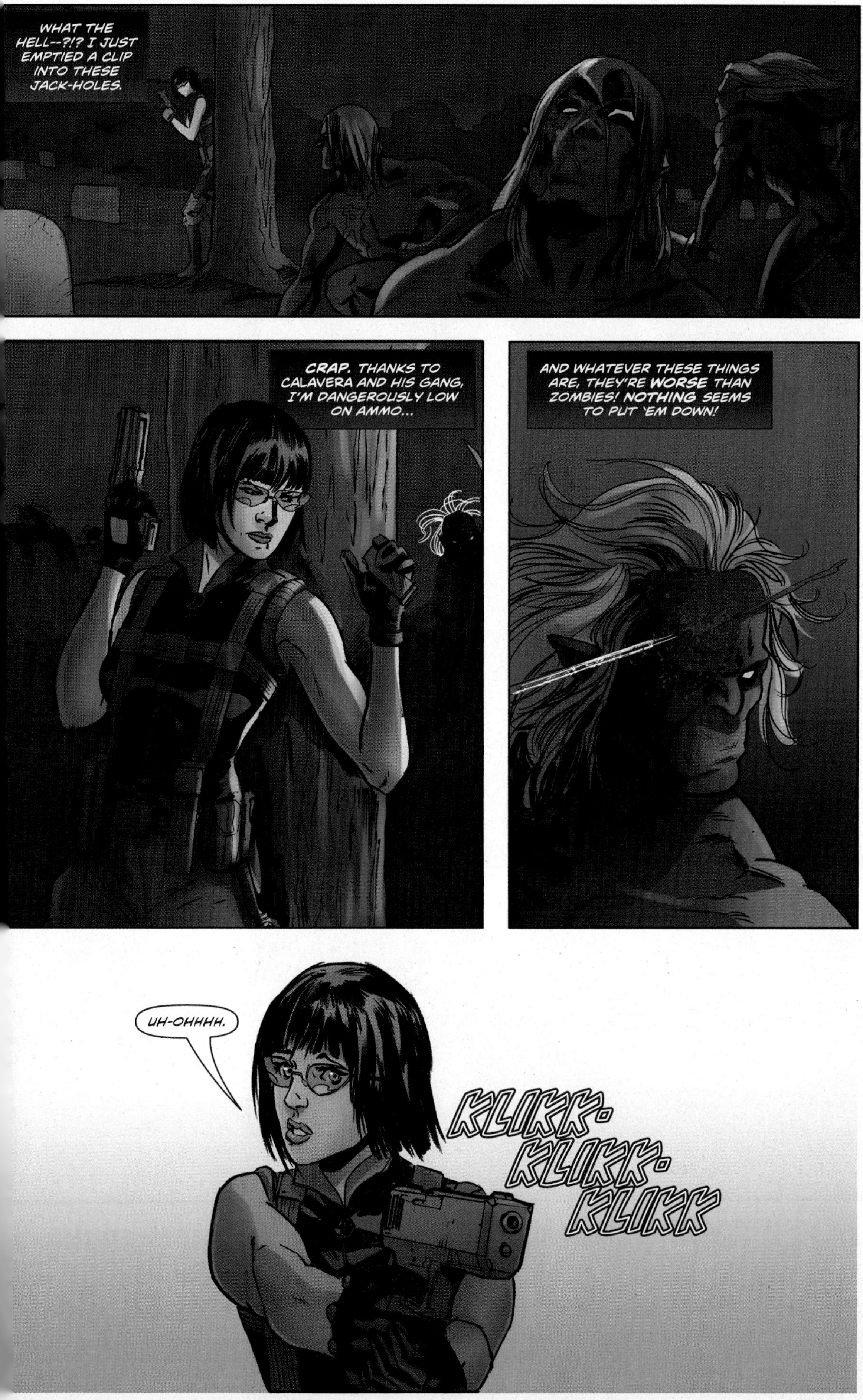
WHAT THE HELL--?!? I JUST EMPTIED A CLIP INTO THESE JACK-HOLES.
CRAP. THANKS TO CALAVERA AND HIS GANG, I'M DANGEROUSLY LOW ON AMMO...
AND WHATEVER THESE THINGS ARE, THEY'RE WORSE THAN ZOMBIES! NOTHING SEEMS TO PUT 'EM DOWN!
UH-OHHHH.
KLIKK. KLIKK. KLIKK

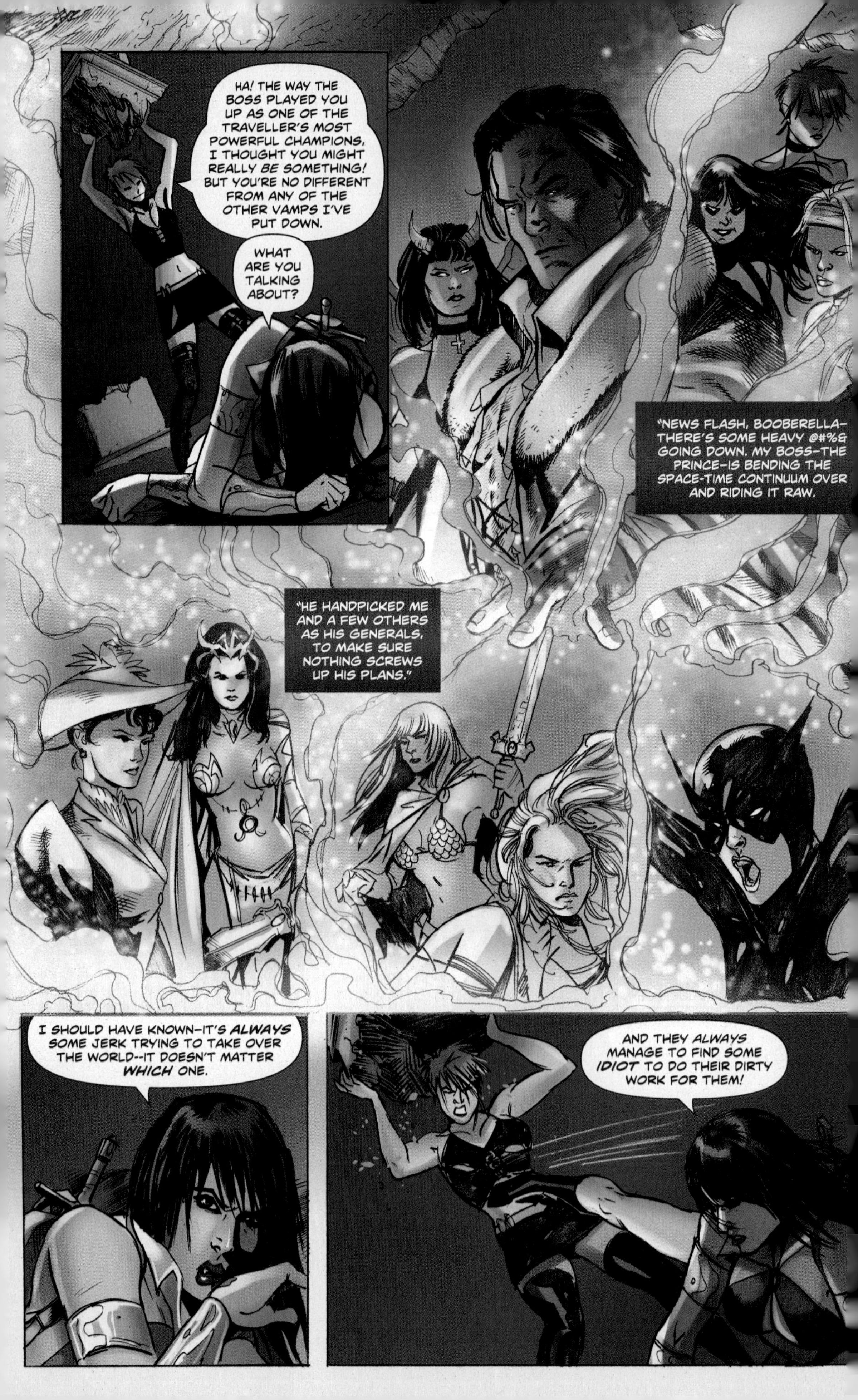
HA! THE WAY THE BOSS PLAYED YOU UP AS ONE OF THE TRAVELLER'S MOST POWERFUL CHAMPIONS, I THOUGHT YOU MIGHT REALLY *BE* SOMETHING! BUT YOU'RE NO DIFFERENT FROM ANY OF THE OTHER VAMPS I'VE PUT DOWN.
WHAT ARE YOU TALKING ABOUT?
"NEWS FLASH, BOOBERELLA–THERE'S SOME HEAVY @#%& GOING DOWN. MY BOSS–THE PRINCE–IS BENDING THE SPACE-TIME CONTINUUM OVER AND RIDING IT RAW.
"HE HANDPICKED ME AND A FEW OTHERS AS HIS GENERALS, TO MAKE SURE NOTHING SCREWS UP HIS PLANS."
I SHOULD HAVE KNOWN–IT'S *ALWAYS* SOME JERK TRYING TO TAKE OVER THE WORLD--IT DOESN'T MATTER *WHICH* ONE.
AND THEY *ALWAYS* MANAGE TO FIND SOME *IDIOT* TO DO THEIR DIRTY WORK FOR THEM!

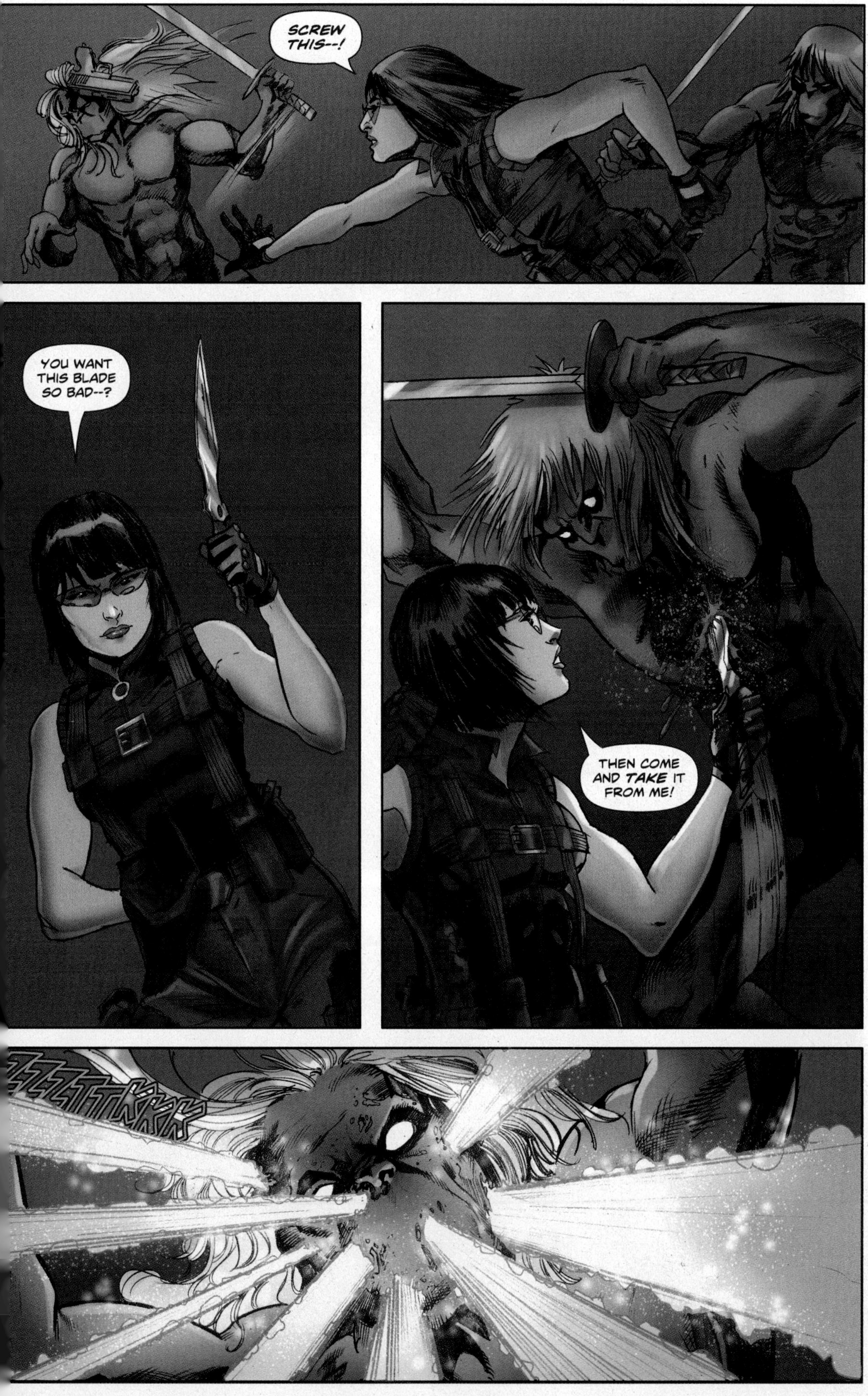
SCREW THIS--!
YOU WANT THIS BLADE SO BAD--?
THEN COME AND *TAKE* IT FROM ME!

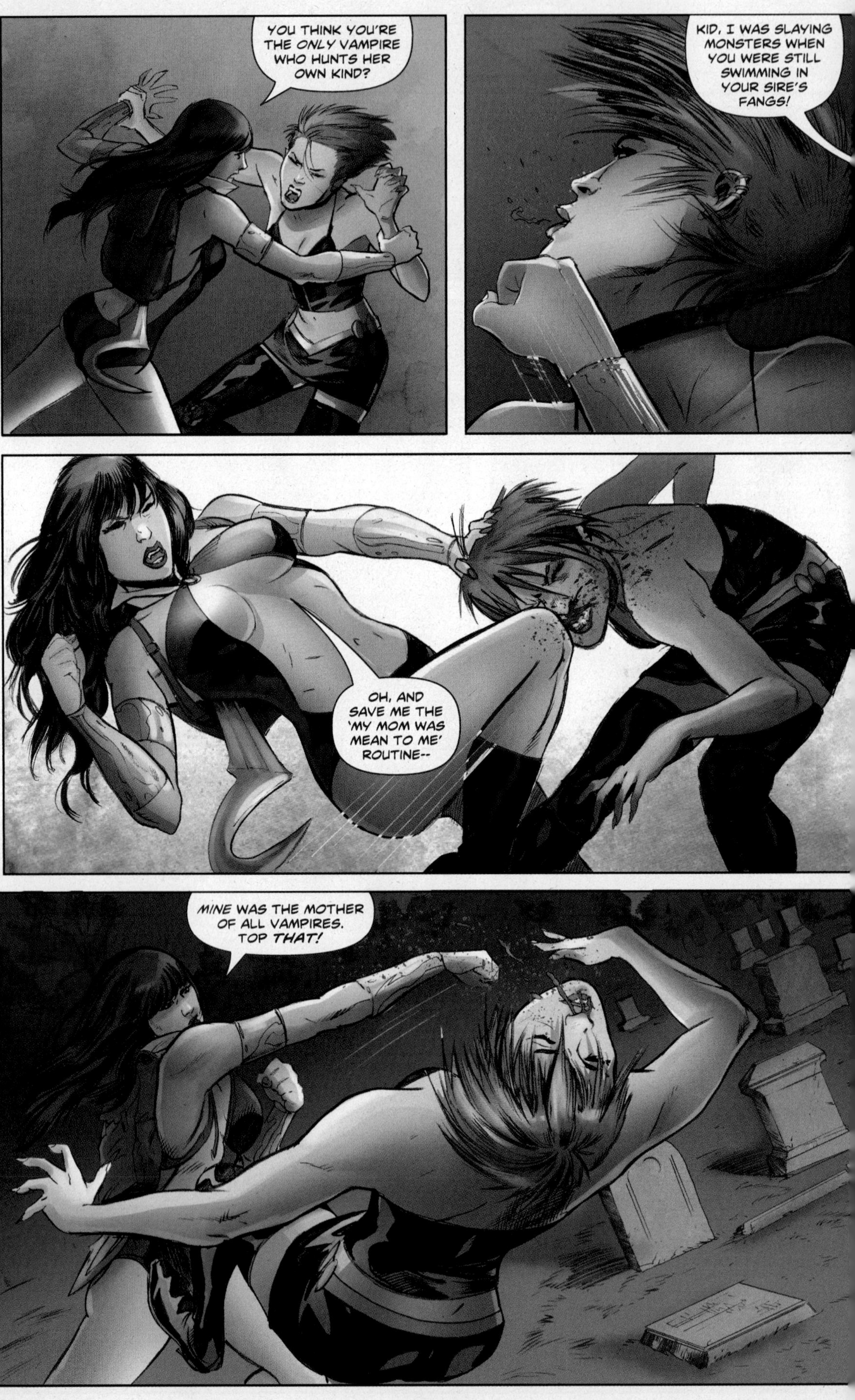
YOU THINK YOU'RE THE *ONLY* VAMPIRE WHO HUNTS HER OWN KIND?
KID, I WAS SLAYING MONSTERS WHEN YOU WERE STILL SWIMMING IN YOUR SIRE'S FANGS!
OH, AND SAVE ME THE 'MY MOM WAS MEAN TO ME' ROUTINE--
MINE WAS THE MOTHER OF ALL VAMPIRES. TOP *THAT!*

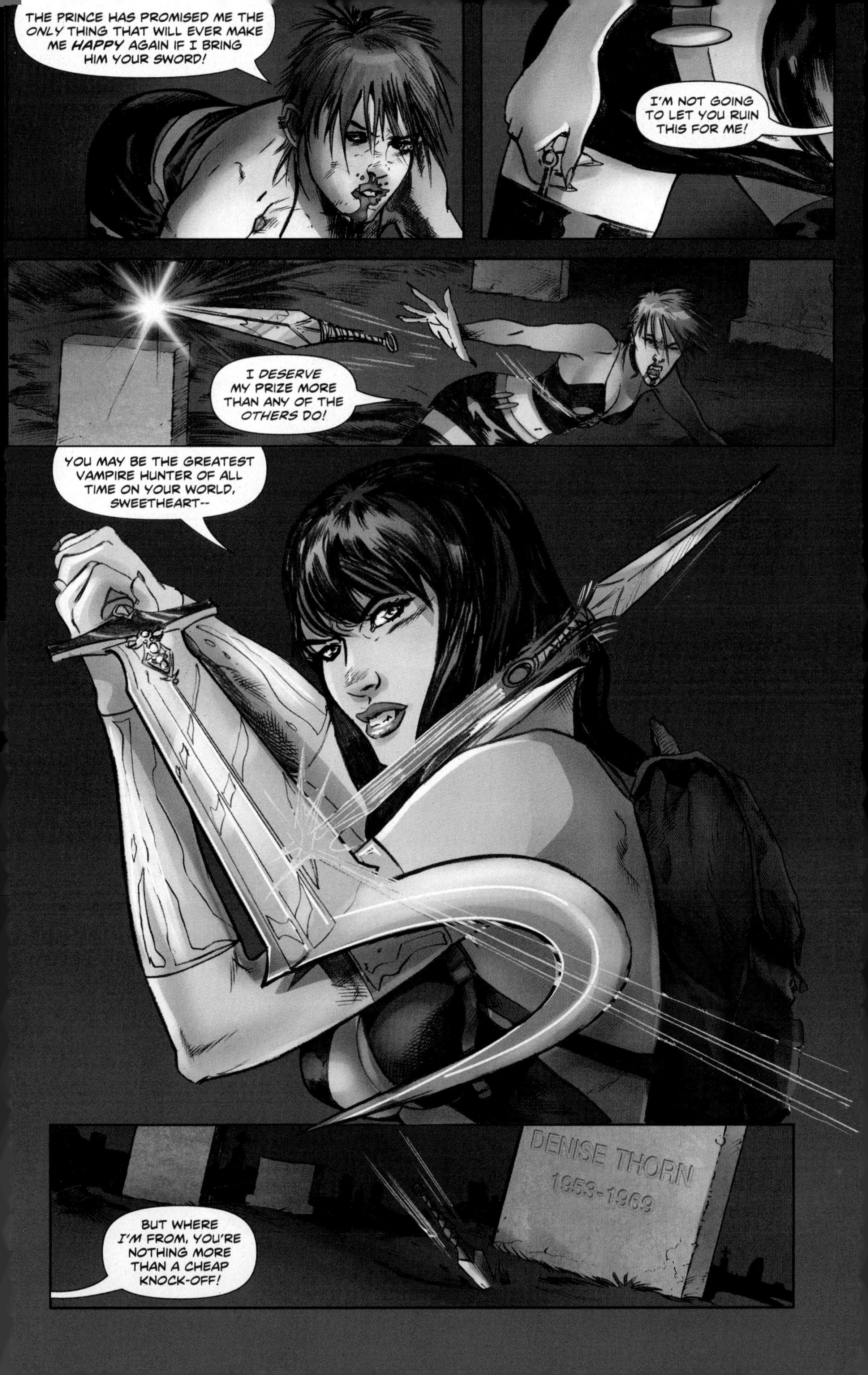
THE PRINCE HAS PROMISED ME THE ONLY THING THAT WILL EVER MAKE ME HAPPY AGAIN IF I BRING HIM YOUR SWORD!
I'M NOT GOING TO LET YOU RUIN THIS FOR ME!
I DESERVE MY PRIZE MORE THAN ANY OF THE OTHERS DO!
YOU MAY BE THE GREATEST VAMPIRE HUNTER OF ALL TIME ON YOUR WORLD, SWEETHEART--
DENISE THORN
1953-1969
BUT WHERE I'M FROM, YOU'RE NOTHING MORE THAN A CHEAP KNOCK-OFF!

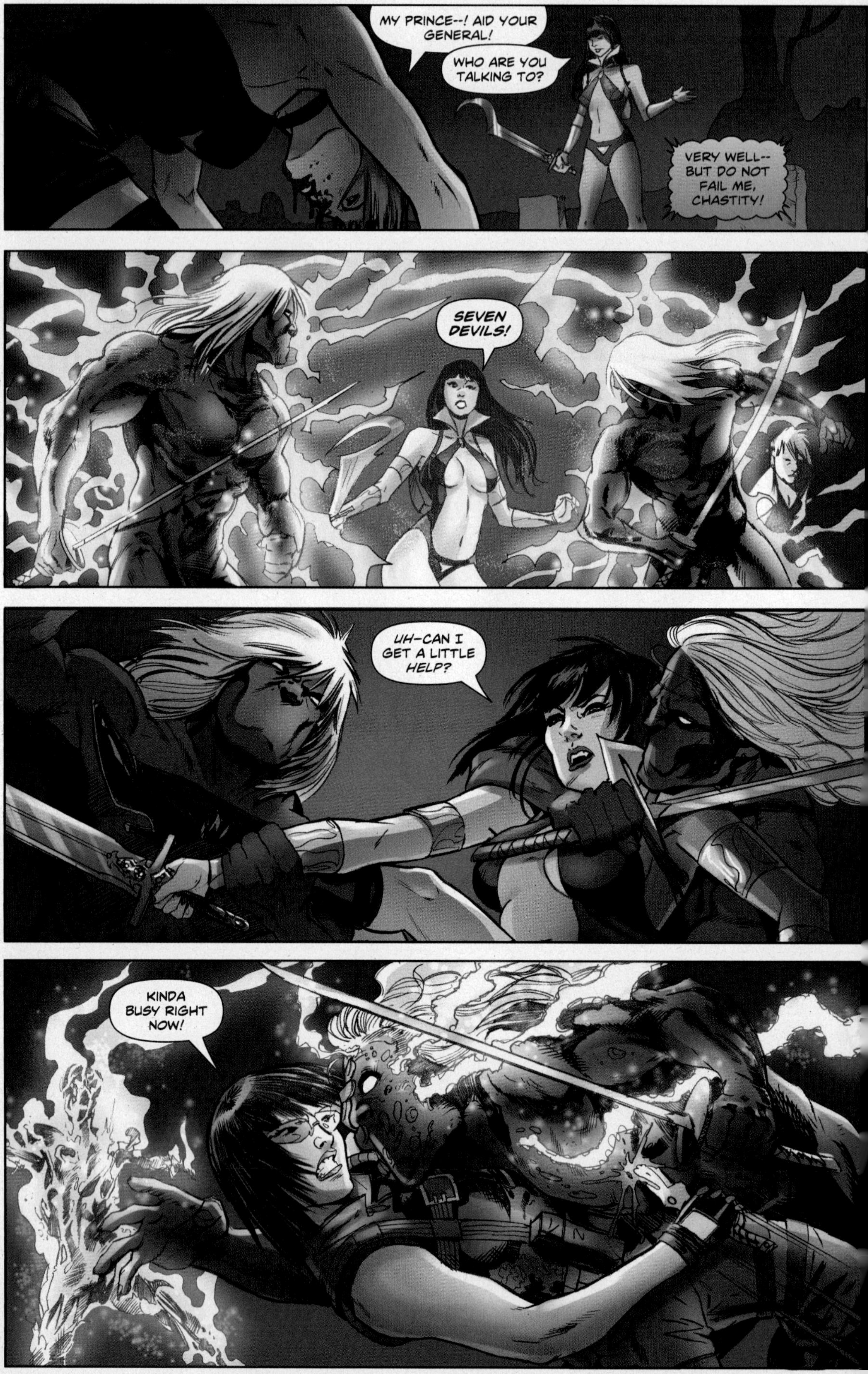
MY PRINCE--! AID YOUR GENERAL!
WHO ARE YOU TALKING TO?
VERY WELL-- BUT DO NOT FAIL ME, CHASTITY!
SEVEN DEVILS!
UH--CAN I GET A LITTLE HELP?
KINDA BUSY RIGHT NOW!

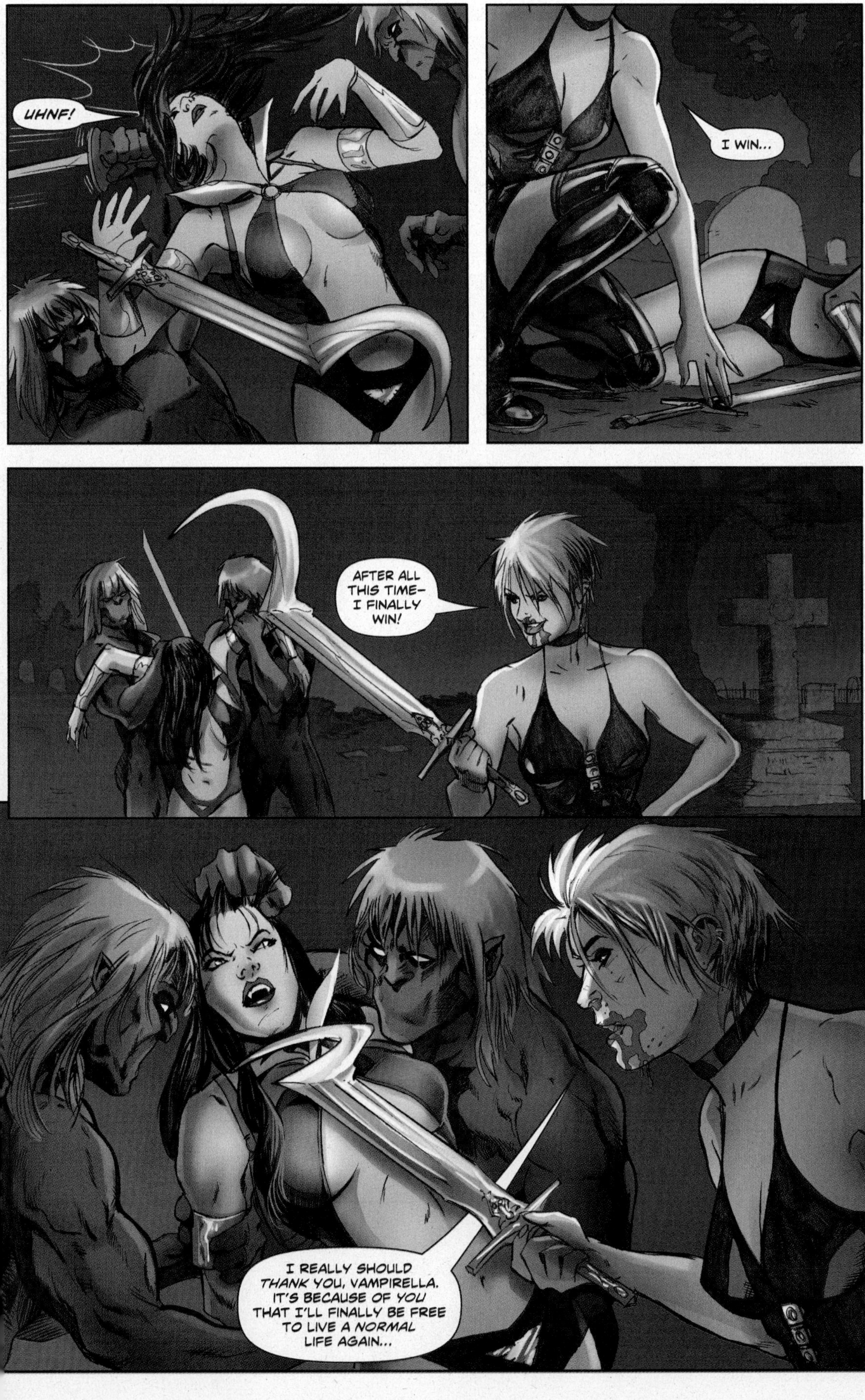
UHNF!
I WIN...
AFTER ALL THIS TIME– I FINALLY WIN!
I REALLY SHOULD *THANK YOU*, VAMPIRELLA. IT'S BECAUSE OF *YOU* THAT I'LL FINALLY BE FREE TO LIVE A *NORMAL* LIFE AGAIN...

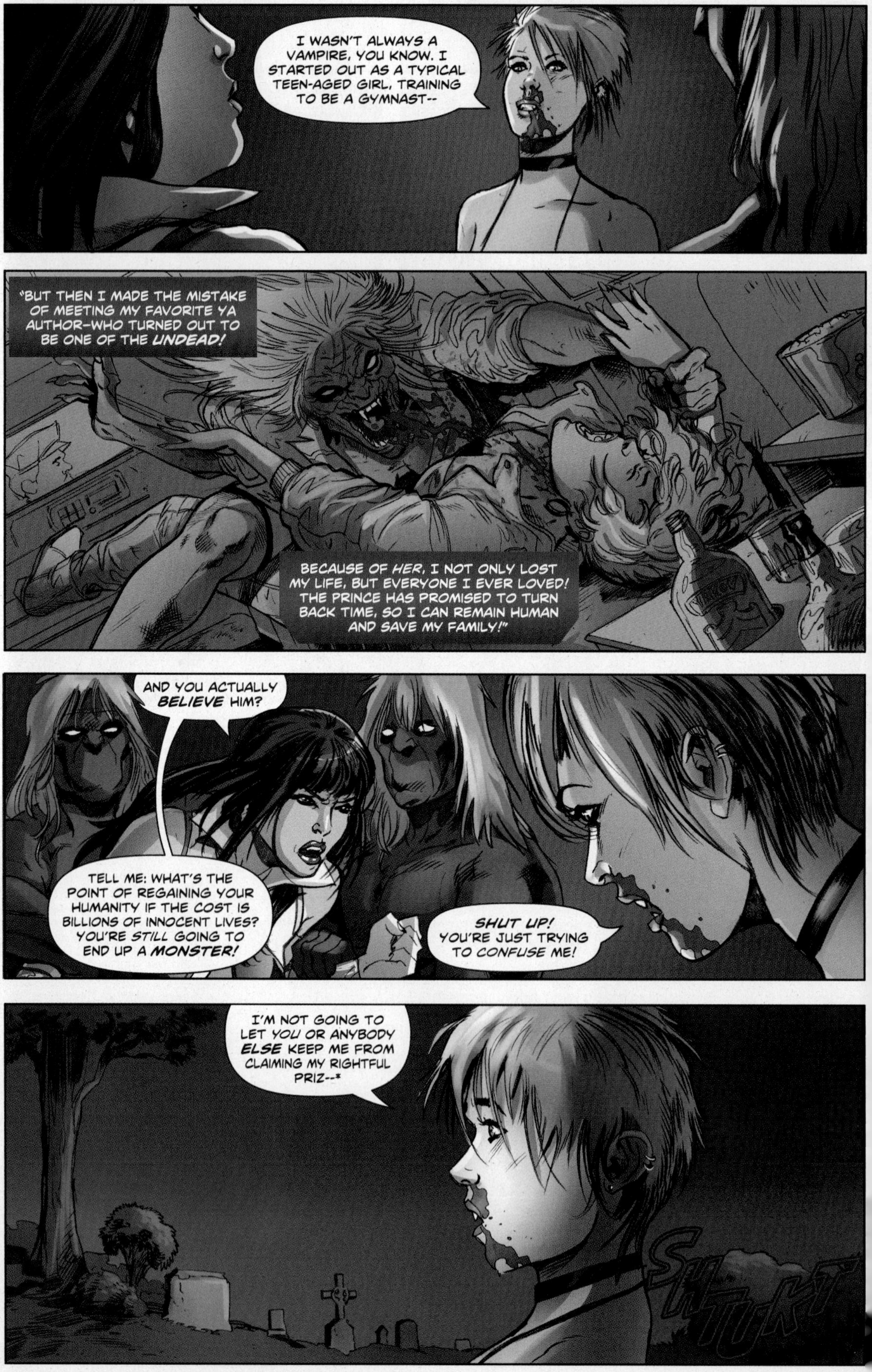
I WASN'T ALWAYS A VAMPIRE, YOU KNOW. I STARTED OUT AS A TYPICAL TEEN-AGED GIRL, TRAINING TO BE A GYMNAST--
"BUT THEN I MADE THE MISTAKE OF MEETING MY FAVORITE YA AUTHOR--WHO TURNED OUT TO BE ONE OF THE UNDEAD!
BECAUSE OF HER, I NOT ONLY LOST MY LIFE, BUT EVERYONE I EVER LOVED! THE PRINCE HAS PROMISED TO TURN BACK TIME, SO I CAN REMAIN HUMAN AND SAVE MY FAMILY!"
AND YOU ACTUALLY BELIEVE HIM?
TELL ME: WHAT'S THE POINT OF REGAINING YOUR HUMANITY IF THE COST IS BILLIONS OF INNOCENT LIVES? YOU'RE STILL GOING TO END UP A MONSTER!
SHUT UP! YOU'RE JUST TRYING TO CONFUSE ME!
I'M NOT GOING TO LET YOU OR ANYBODY ELSE KEEP ME FROM CLAIMING MY RIGHTFUL PRIZ--*

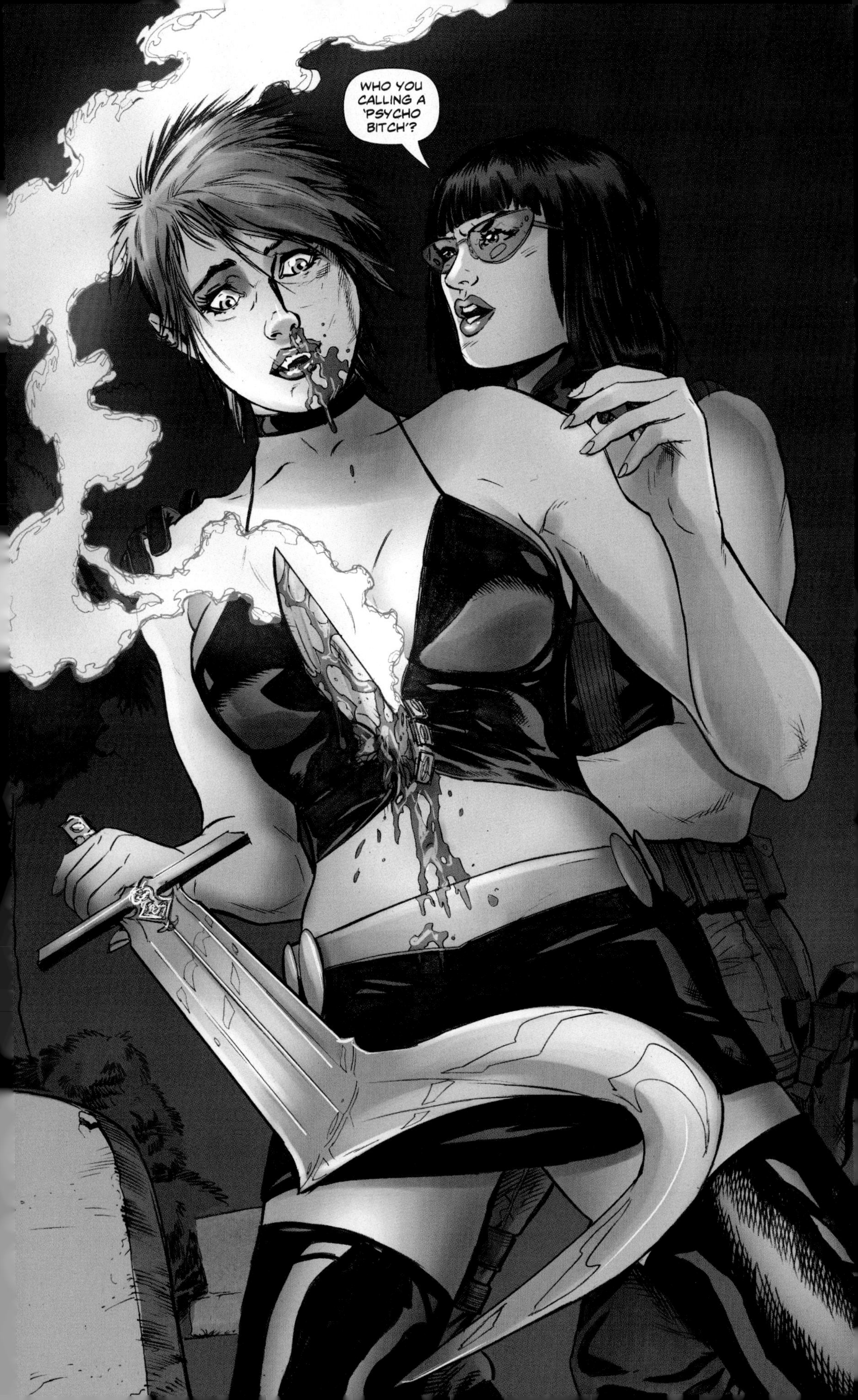
WHO YOU CALLING A 'PSYCHO BITCH'?

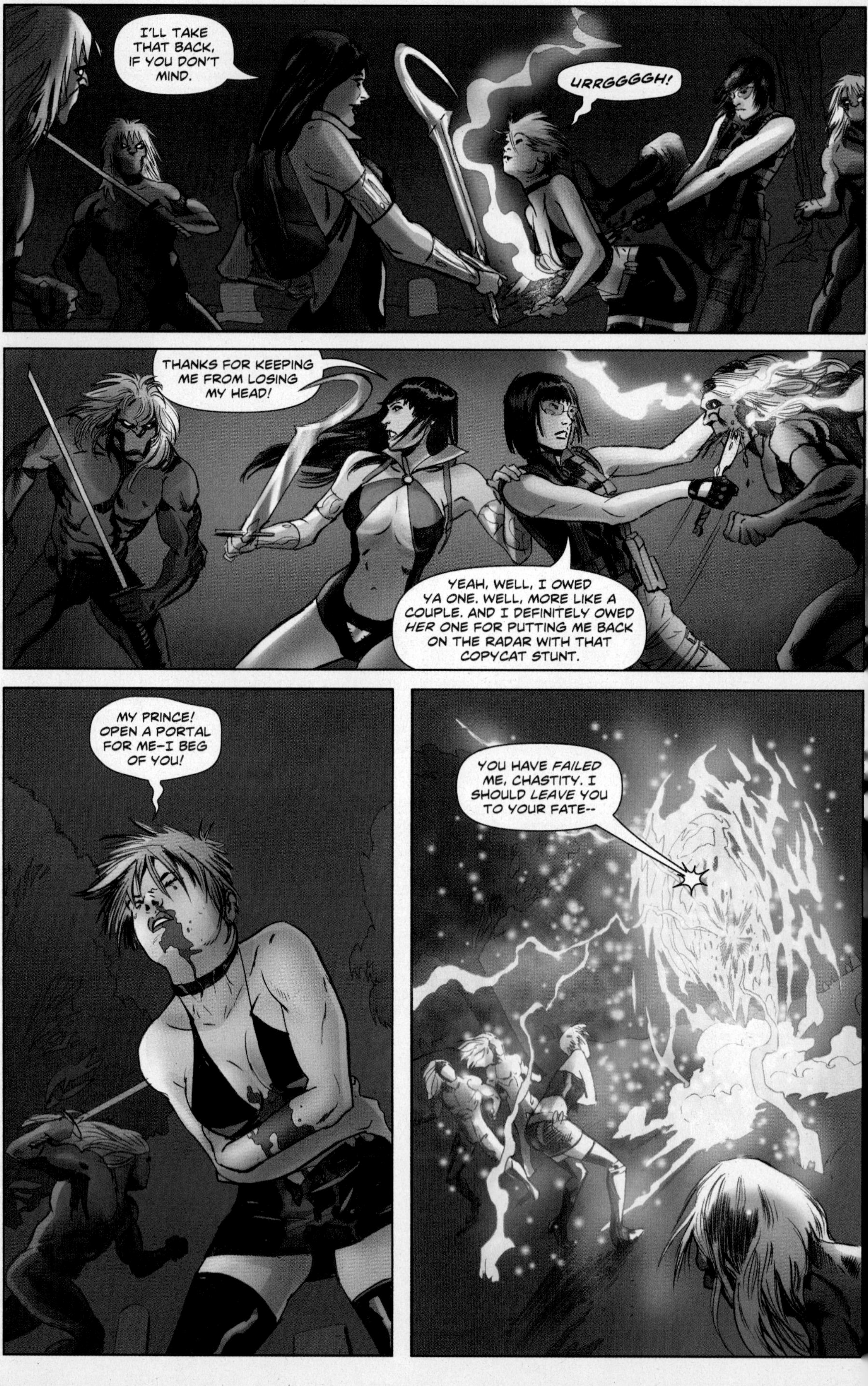
I'LL TAKE THAT BACK, IF YOU DON'T MIND.
URRGGGGH!
THANKS FOR KEEPING ME FROM LOSING MY HEAD!
YEAH, WELL, I OWED YA ONE. WELL, MORE LIKE A COUPLE. AND I DEFINITELY OWED HER ONE FOR PUTTING ME BACK ON THE RADAR WITH THAT COPYCAT STUNT.
MY PRINCE! OPEN A PORTAL FOR ME–I BEG OF YOU!
YOU HAVE FAILED ME, CHASTITY. I SHOULD LEAVE YOU TO YOUR FATE--

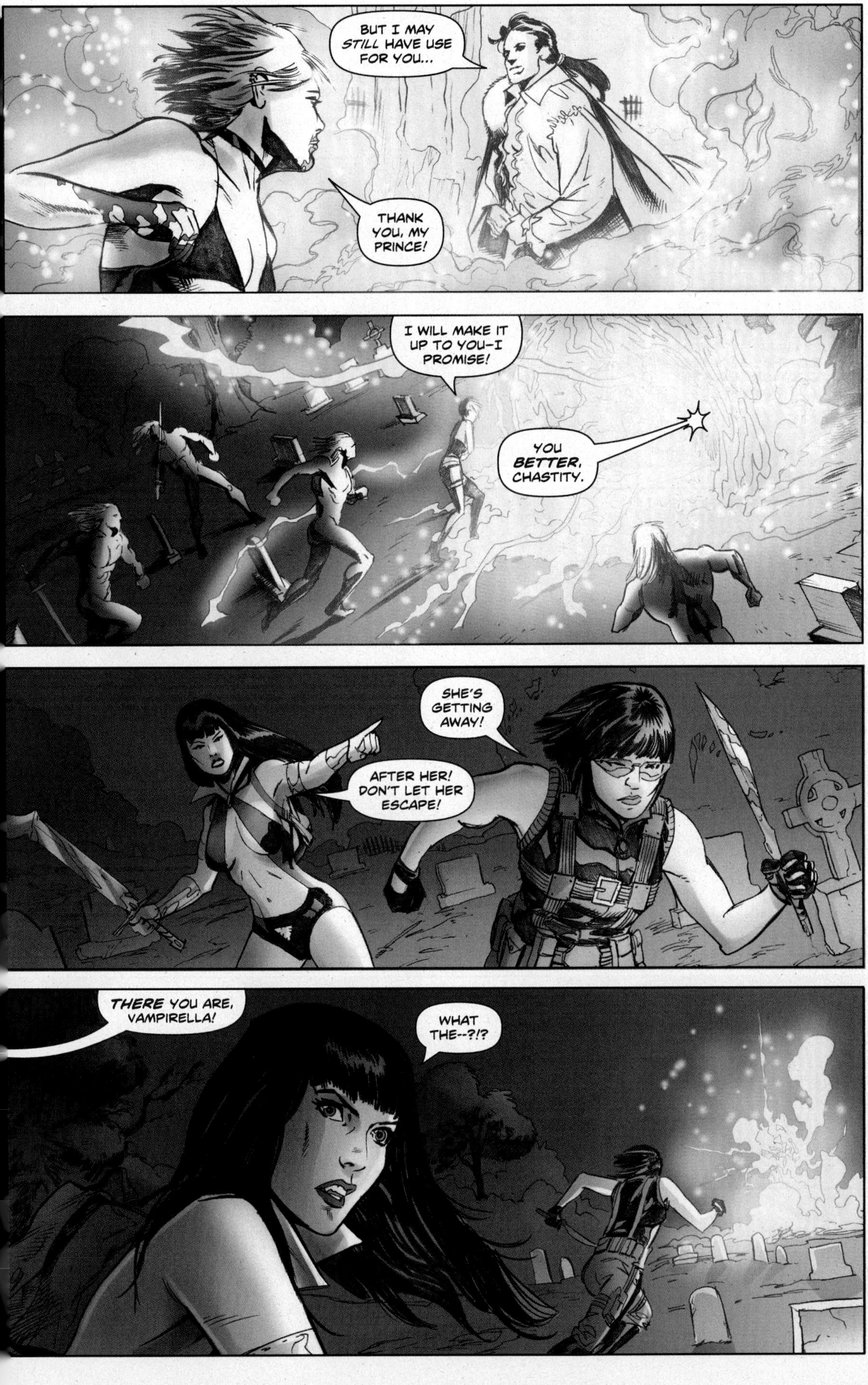
BUT I MAY STILL HAVE USE FOR YOU...
THANK YOU, MY PRINCE!
I WILL MAKE IT UP TO YOU--I PROMISE!
YOU BETTER, CHASTITY.
SHE'S GETTING AWAY!
AFTER HER! DON'T LET HER ESCAPE!
THERE YOU ARE, VAMPIRELLA!
WHAT THE--?!?

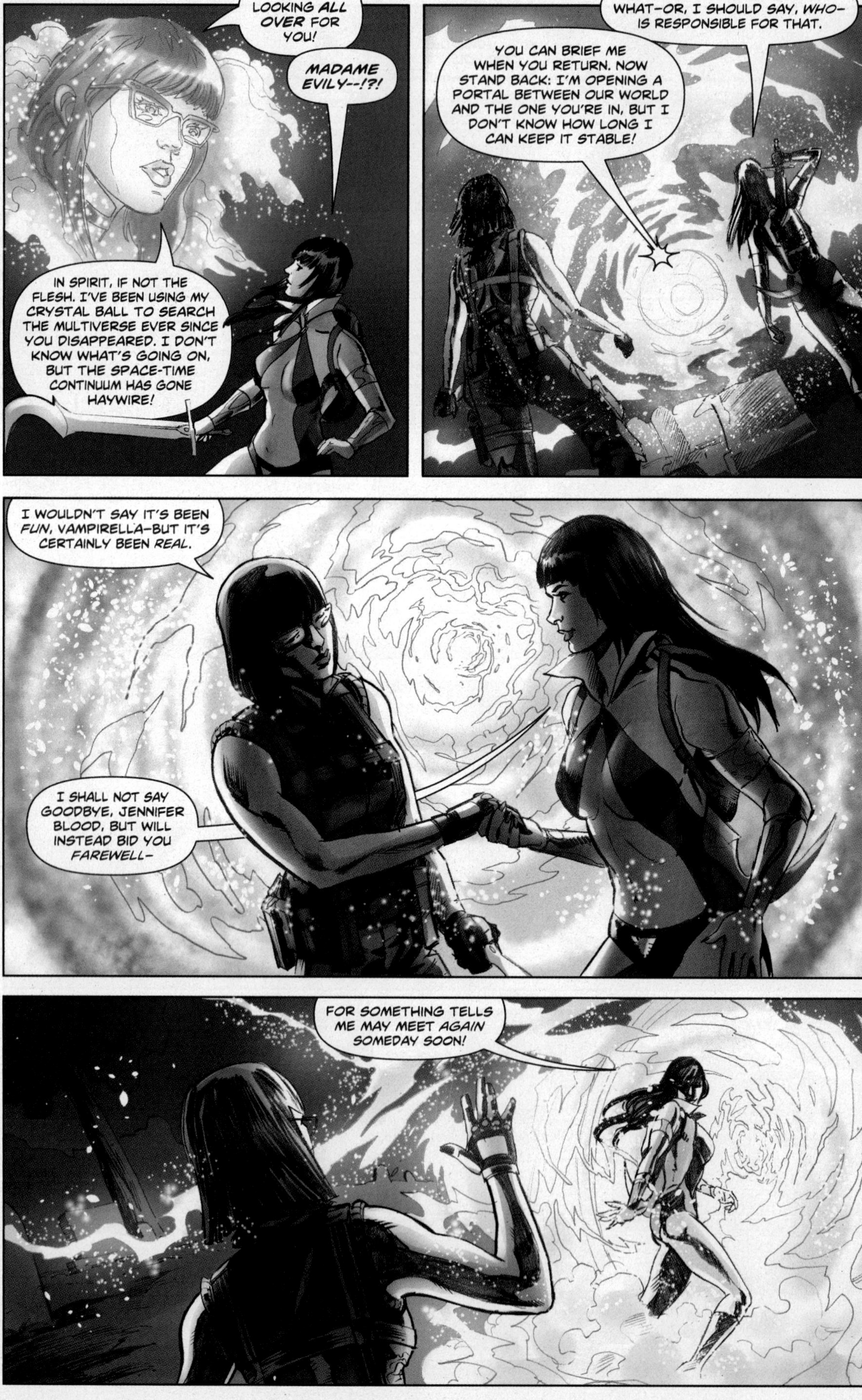
I'VE BEEN LOOKING ALL OVER FOR YOU!
MADAME EVILY--!?!
IN SPIRIT, IF NOT THE FLESH. I'VE BEEN USING MY CRYSTAL BALL TO SEARCH THE MULTIVERSE EVER SINCE YOU DISAPPEARED. I DON'T KNOW WHAT'S GOING ON, BUT THE SPACE-TIME CONTINUUM HAS GONE HAYWIRE!
I THINK I HAVE AN IDEA OF WHAT--OR, I SHOULD SAY, WHO--IS RESPONSIBLE FOR THAT.
YOU CAN BRIEF ME WHEN YOU RETURN. NOW STAND BACK: I'M OPENING A PORTAL BETWEEN OUR WORLD AND THE ONE YOU'RE IN, BUT I DON'T KNOW HOW LONG I CAN KEEP IT STABLE!
I WOULDN'T SAY IT'S BEEN FUN, VAMPIRELLA--BUT IT'S CERTAINLY BEEN REAL.
I SHALL NOT SAY GOODBYE, JENNIFER BLOOD, BUT WILL INSTEAD BID YOU FAREWELL-
FOR SOMETHING TELLS ME MAY MEET AGAIN SOMEDAY SOON!

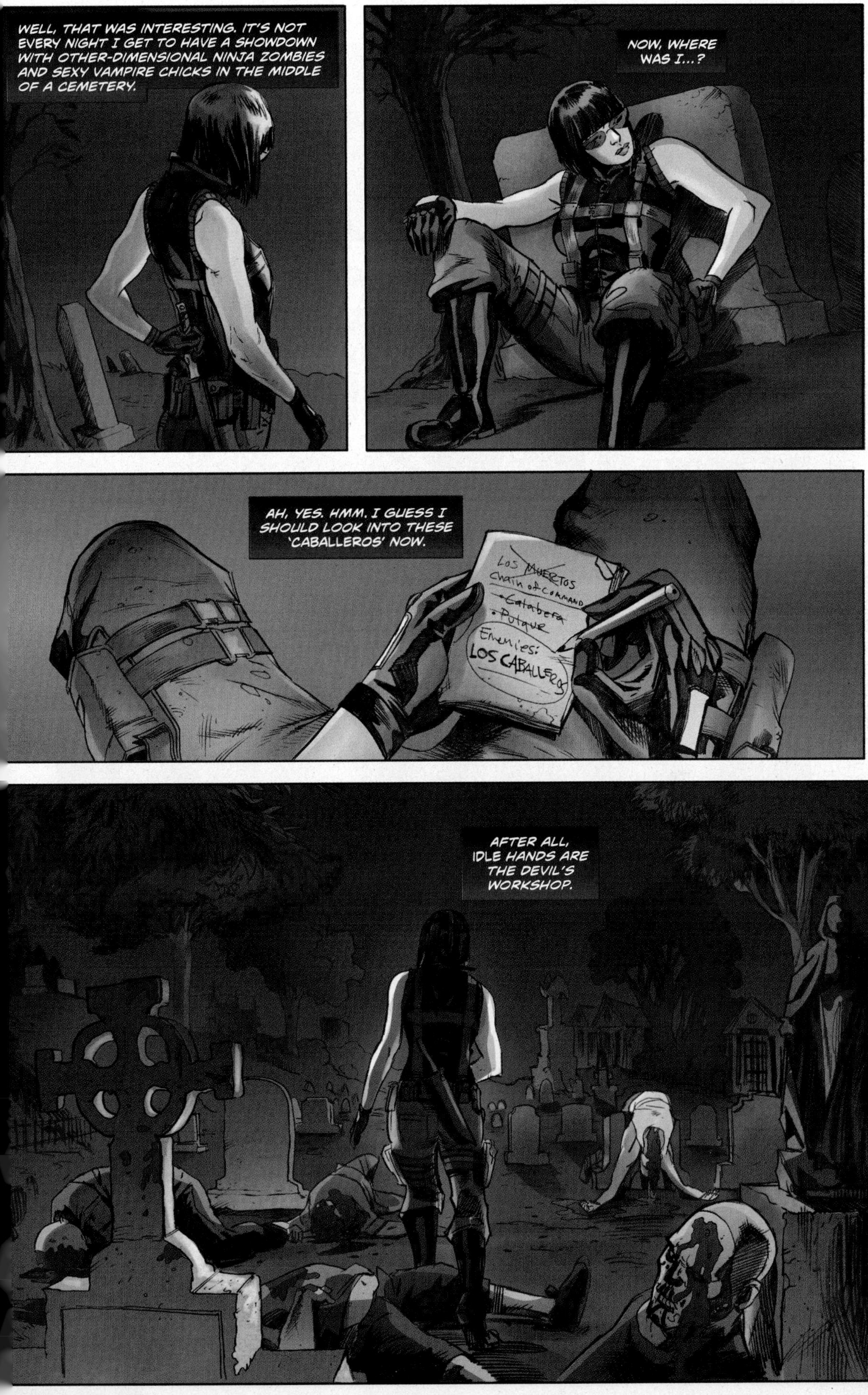
WELL, THAT WAS INTERESTING. IT'S NOT EVERY NIGHT I GET TO HAVE A SHOWDOWN WITH OTHER-DIMENSIONAL NINJA ZOMBIES AND SEXY VAMPIRE CHICKS IN THE MIDDLE OF A CEMETERY.
NOW, WHERE WAS I...?
AH, YES. HMM. I GUESS I SHOULD LOOK INTO THESE 'CABALLEROS' NOW.
Los Muertos
Chain of command
Calabera
Pulque
Enemies:
LOS CABALLEROS
AFTER ALL, IDLE HANDS ARE THE DEVIL'S WORKSHOP.

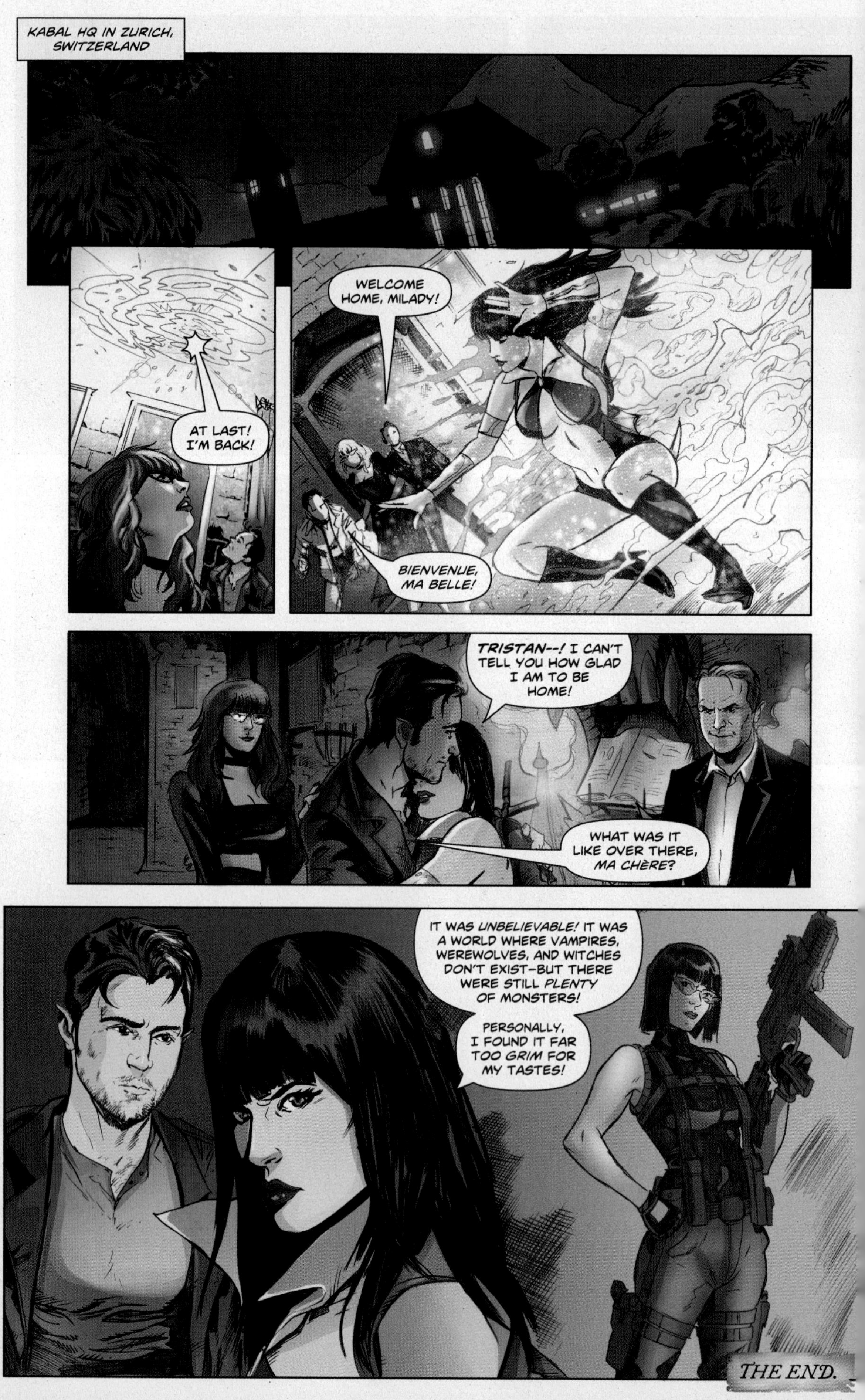
KABAL HQ IN ZURICH, SWITZERLAND
AT LAST! I'M BACK!
WELCOME HOME, MILADY!
BIENVENUE, MA BELLE!
TRISTAN--! I CAN'T TELL YOU HOW GLAD I AM TO BE HOME!
WHAT WAS IT LIKE OVER THERE, MA CHÈRE?
IT WAS UNBELIEVABLE! IT WAS A WORLD WHERE VAMPIRES, WEREWOLVES, AND WITCHES DON'T EXIST–BUT THERE WERE STILL PLENTY OF MONSTERS!
PERSONALLY, I FOUND IT FAR TOO GRIM FOR MY TASTES!
THE END.

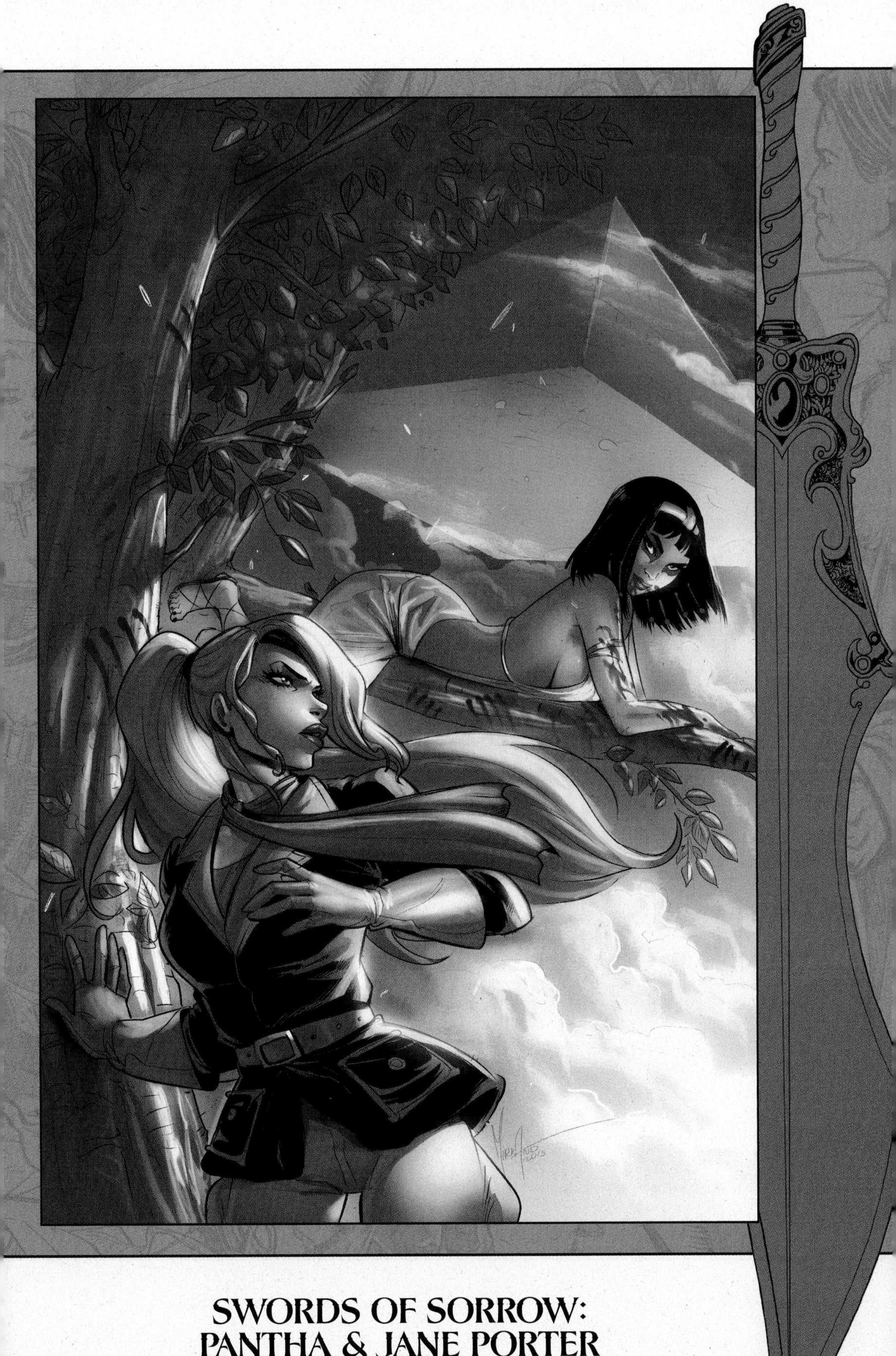

SWORDS OF SORROW: PANTHA & JANE PORTER
ONE-SHOT

written by EMMA BEEBY illustrated by ROD RODOLFO
colored by NANJAN JAMBERI lettered by ERICA SCHULTZ

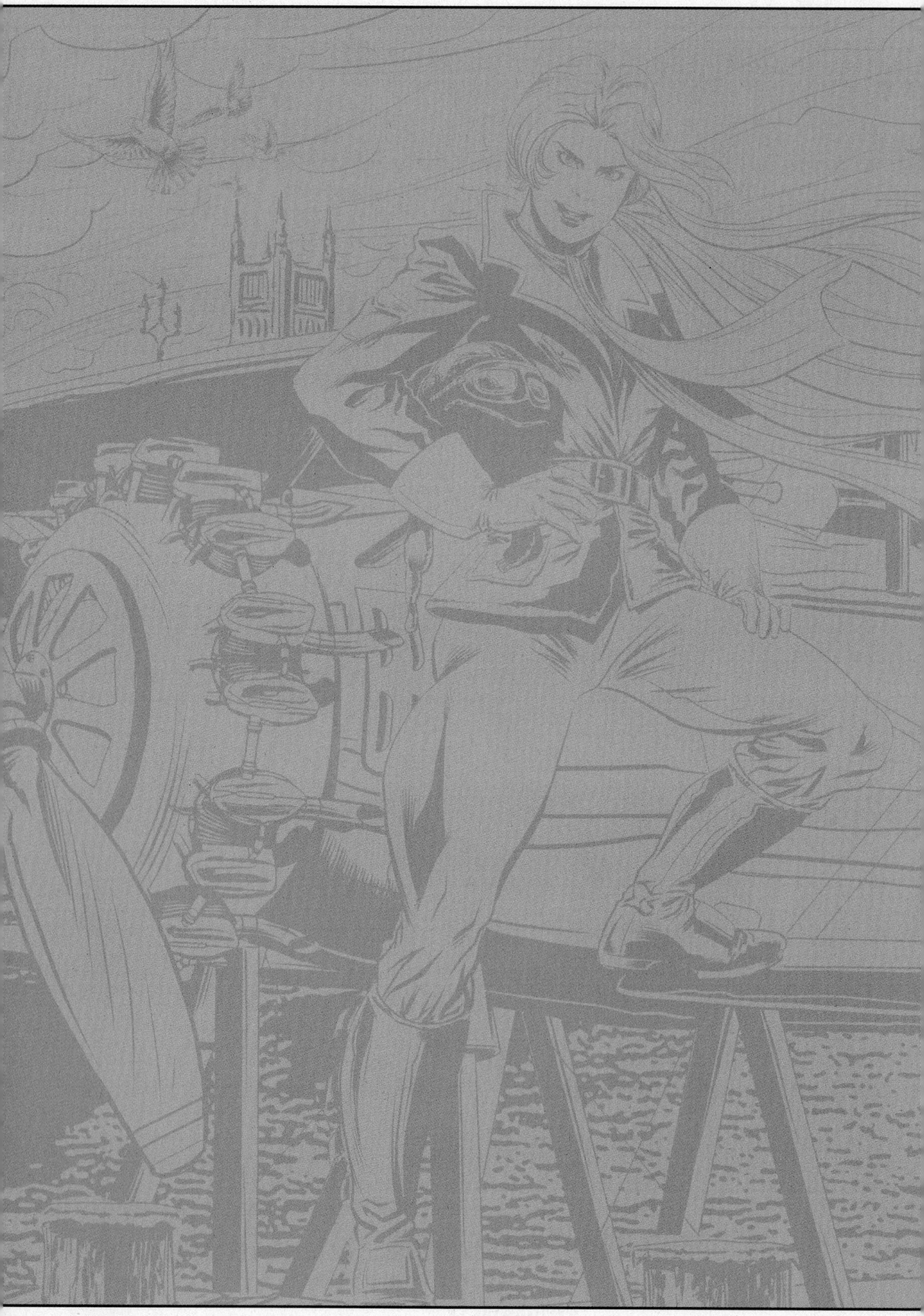

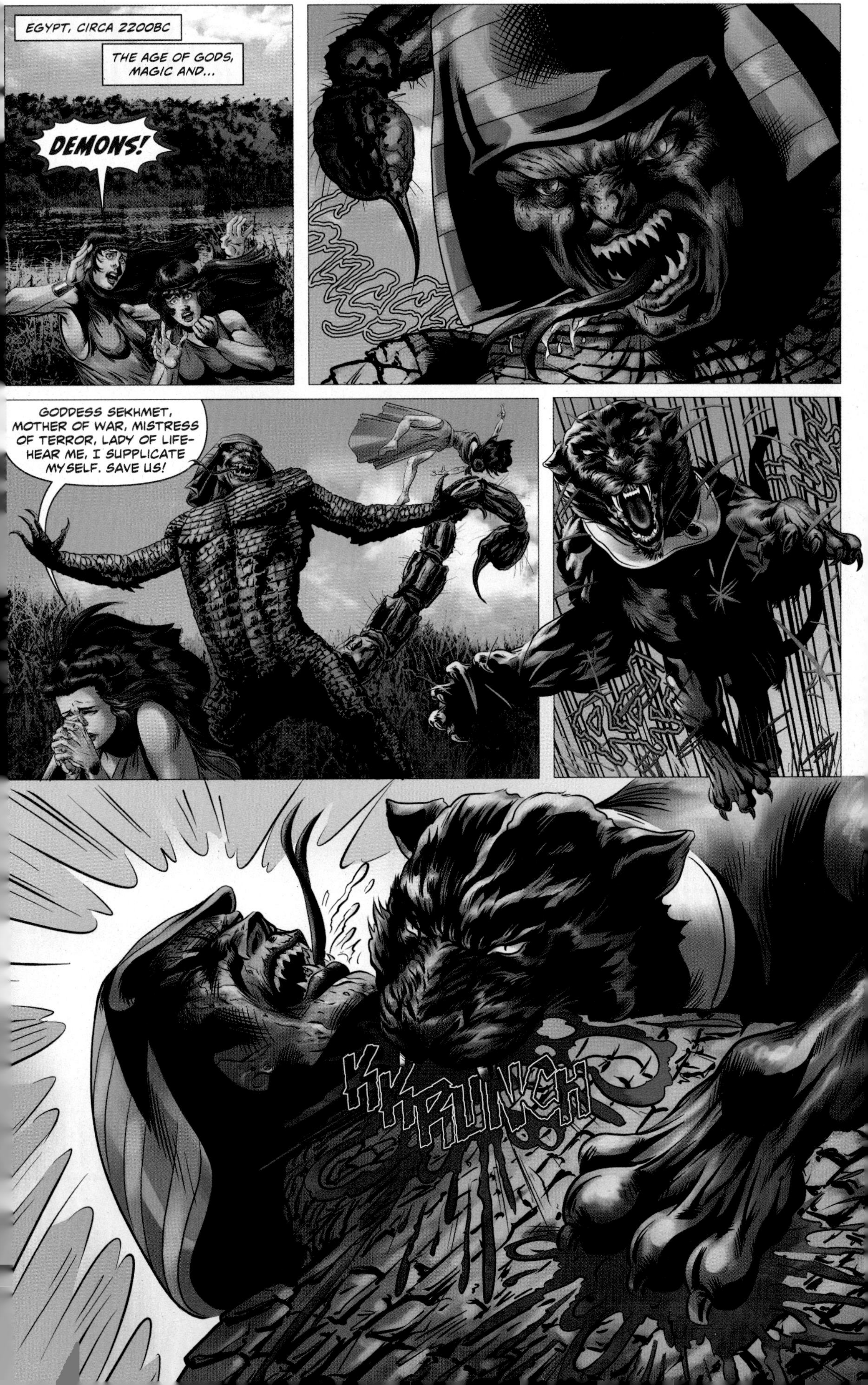
EGYPT, CIRCA 2200BC
THE AGE OF GODS, MAGIC AND...
DEMONS!
GODDESS SEKHMET, MOTHER OF WAR, MISTRESS OF TERROR, LADY OF LIFE- HEAR ME, I SUPPLICATE MYSELF. SAVE US!
KKRUNCH

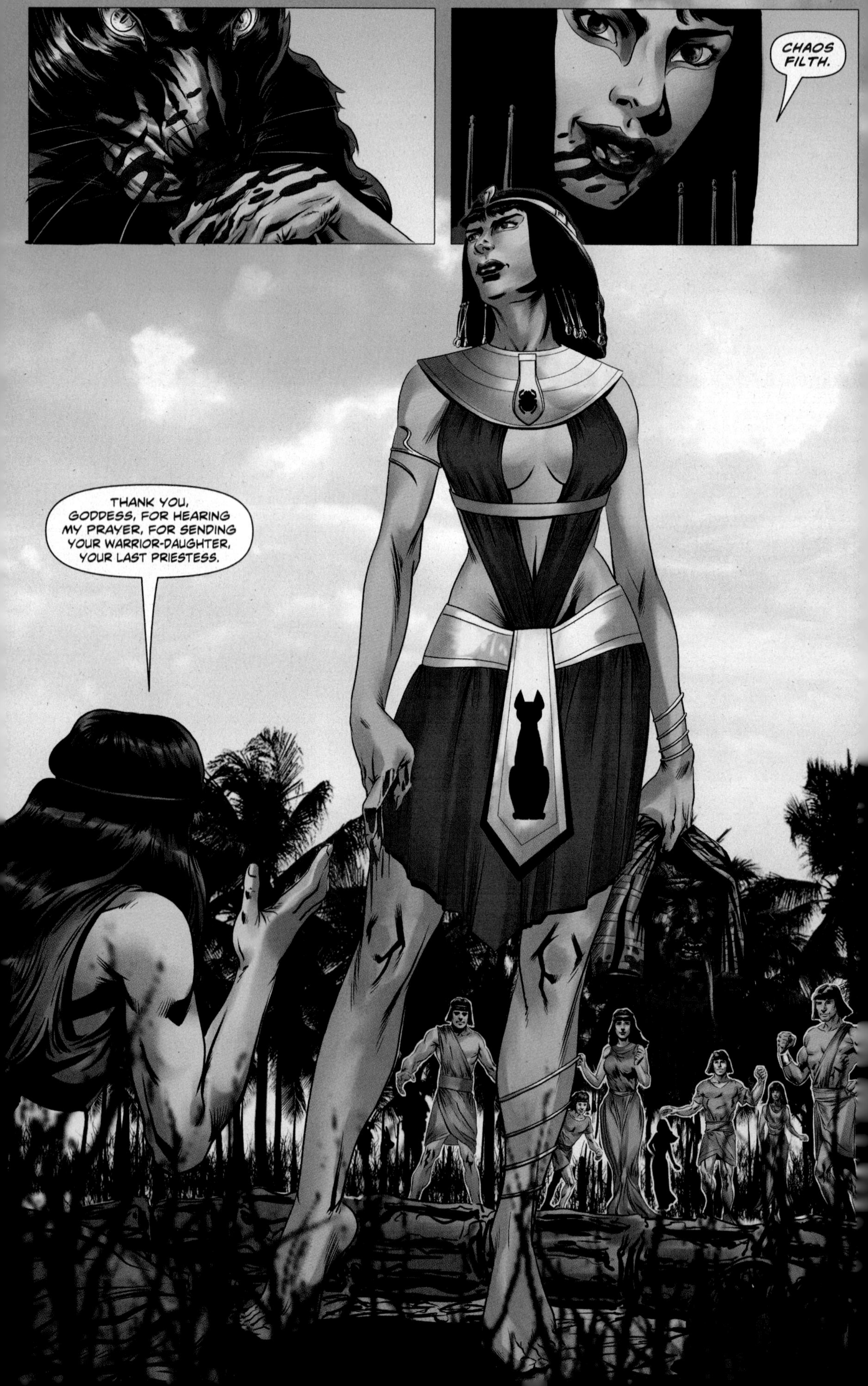
CHAOS FILTH.
THANK YOU, GODDESS, FOR HEARING MY PRAYER, FOR SENDING YOUR WARRIOR-DAUGHTER, YOUR LAST PRIESTESS.

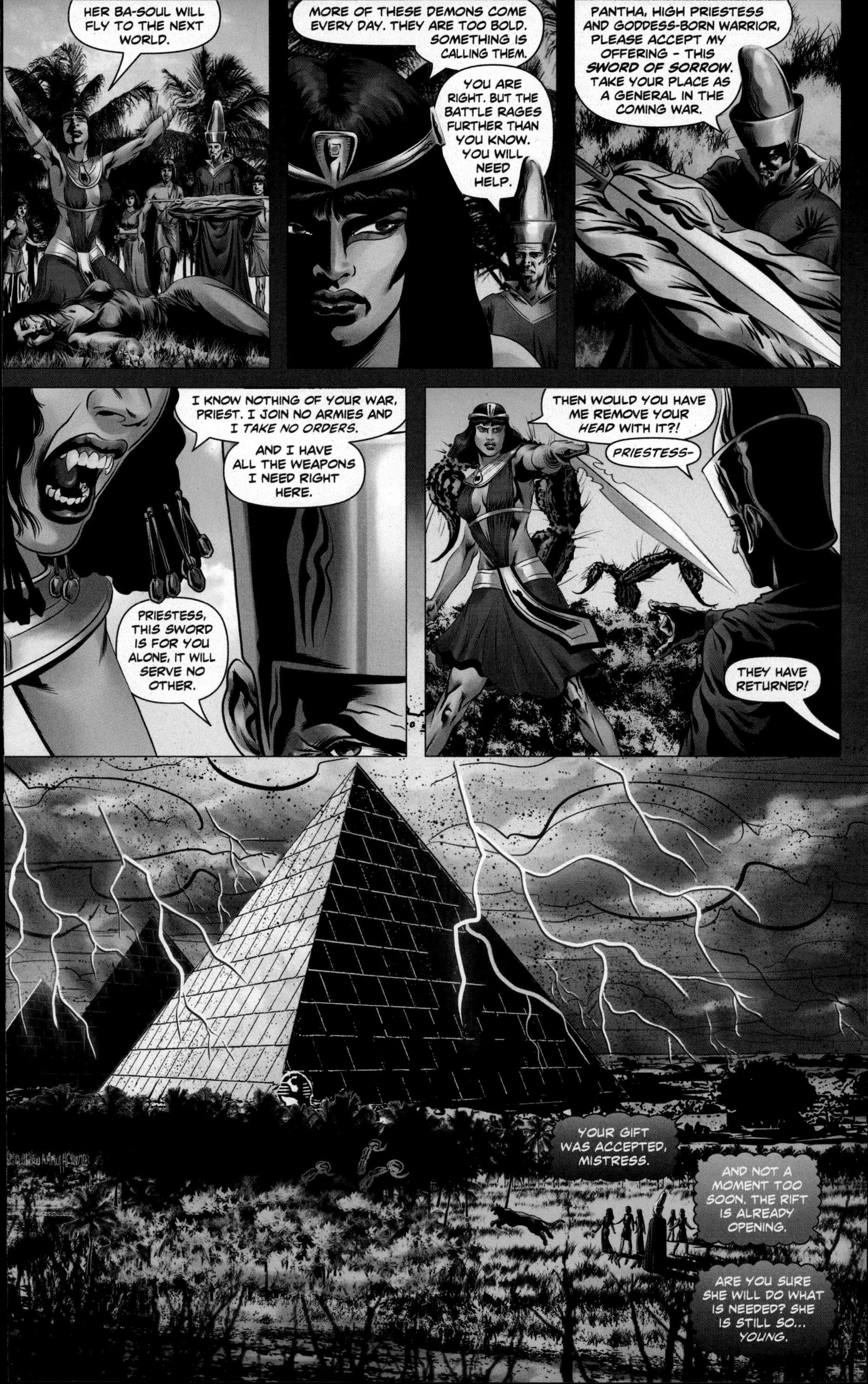
HER BA-SOUL WILL FLY TO THE NEXT WORLD.
MORE OF THESE DEMONS COME EVERY DAY. THEY ARE TOO BOLD. SOMETHING IS CALLING THEM.
YOU ARE RIGHT. BUT THE BATTLE RAGES FURTHER THAN YOU KNOW. YOU WILL NEED HELP.
PANTHA, HIGH PRIESTESS AND GODDESS-BORN WARRIOR, PLEASE ACCEPT MY OFFERING - THIS SWORD OF SORROW. TAKE YOUR PLACE AS A GENERAL IN THE COMING WAR.
I KNOW NOTHING OF YOUR WAR, PRIEST. I JOIN NO ARMIES AND I TAKE NO ORDERS.
AND I HAVE ALL THE WEAPONS I NEED RIGHT HERE.
PRIESTESS, THIS SWORD IS FOR YOU ALONE, IT WILL SERVE NO OTHER.
THEN WOULD YOU HAVE ME REMOVE YOUR HEAD WITH IT?!
PRIESTESS-
THEY HAVE RETURNED!
YOUR GIFT WAS ACCEPTED, MISTRESS.
AND NOT A MOMENT TOO SOON. THE RIFT IS ALREADY OPENING.
ARE YOU SURE SHE WILL DO WHAT IS NEEDED? SHE IS STILL SO... YOUNG.

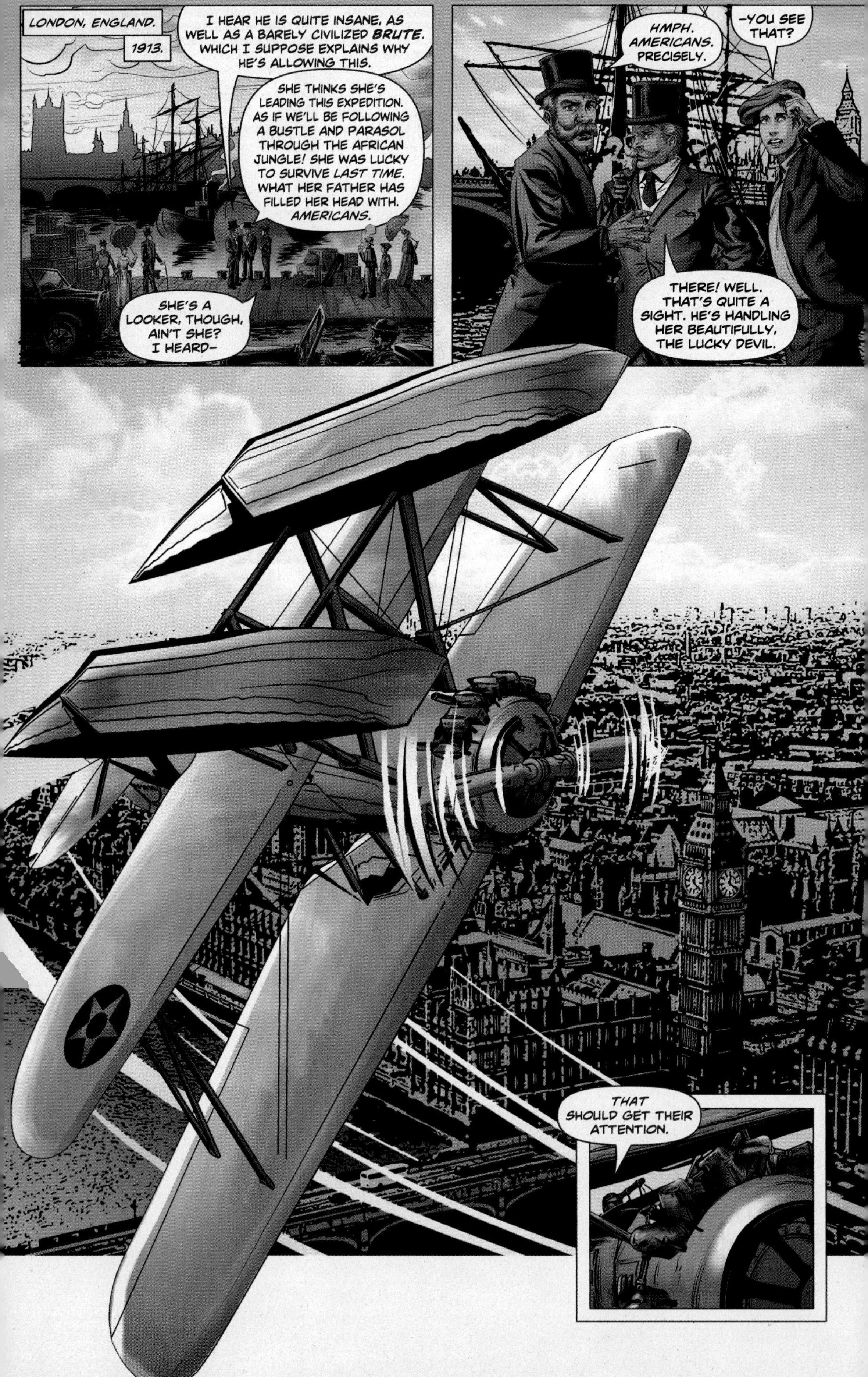
LONDON, ENGLAND.
1913.
I HEAR HE IS QUITE INSANE, AS WELL AS A BARELY CIVILIZED BRUTE. WHICH I SUPPOSE EXPLAINS WHY HE'S ALLOWING THIS.
SHE THINKS SHE'S LEADING THIS EXPEDITION. AS IF WE'LL BE FOLLOWING A BUSTLE AND PARASOL THROUGH THE AFRICAN JUNGLE! SHE WAS LUCKY TO SURVIVE LAST TIME. WHAT HER FATHER HAS FILLED HER HEAD WITH. AMERICANS.
SHE'S A LOOKER, THOUGH, AIN'T SHE? I HEARD–
HMPH. AMERICANS. PRECISELY.
–YOU SEE THAT?
THERE! WELL. THAT'S QUITE A SIGHT. HE'S HANDLING HER BEAUTIFULLY, THE LUCKY DEVIL.
THAT SHOULD GET THEIR ATTENTION.

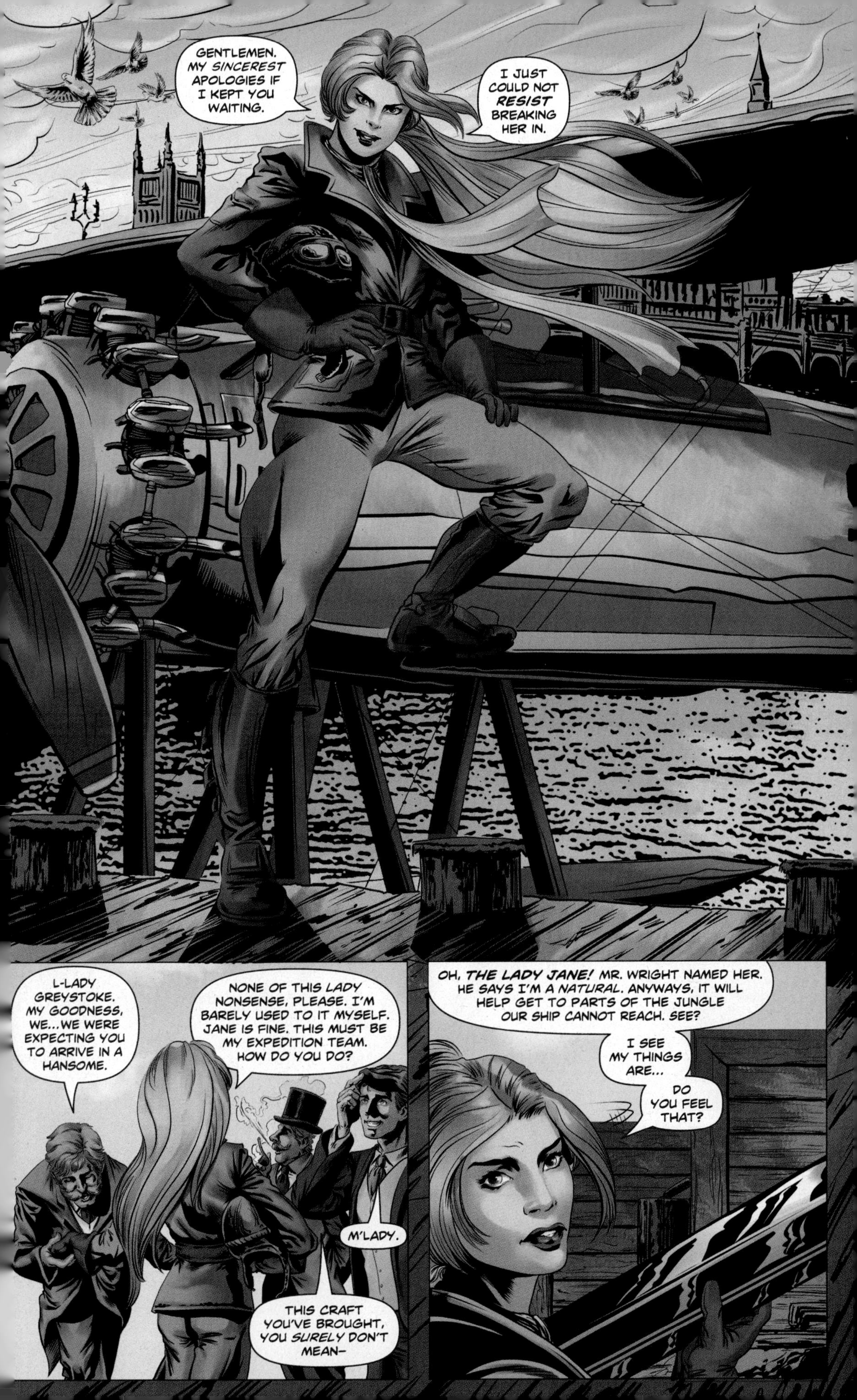
GENTLEMEN. MY SINCEREST APOLOGIES IF I KEPT YOU WAITING.
I JUST COULD NOT RESIST BREAKING HER IN.
L-LADY GREYSTOKE. MY GOODNESS, WE...WE WERE EXPECTING YOU TO ARRIVE IN A HANSOME.
NONE OF THIS LADY NONSENSE, PLEASE. I'M BARELY USED TO IT MYSELF. JANE IS FINE. THIS MUST BE MY EXPEDITION TEAM. HOW DO YOU DO?
M'LADY.
THIS CRAFT YOU'VE BROUGHT, YOU SURELY DON'T MEAN–
OH, THE LADY JANE! MR. WRIGHT NAMED HER. HE SAYS I'M A NATURAL. ANYWAYS, IT WILL HELP GET TO PARTS OF THE JUNGLE OUR SHIP CANNOT REACH. SEE?
I SEE MY THINGS ARE...
DO YOU FEEL THAT?

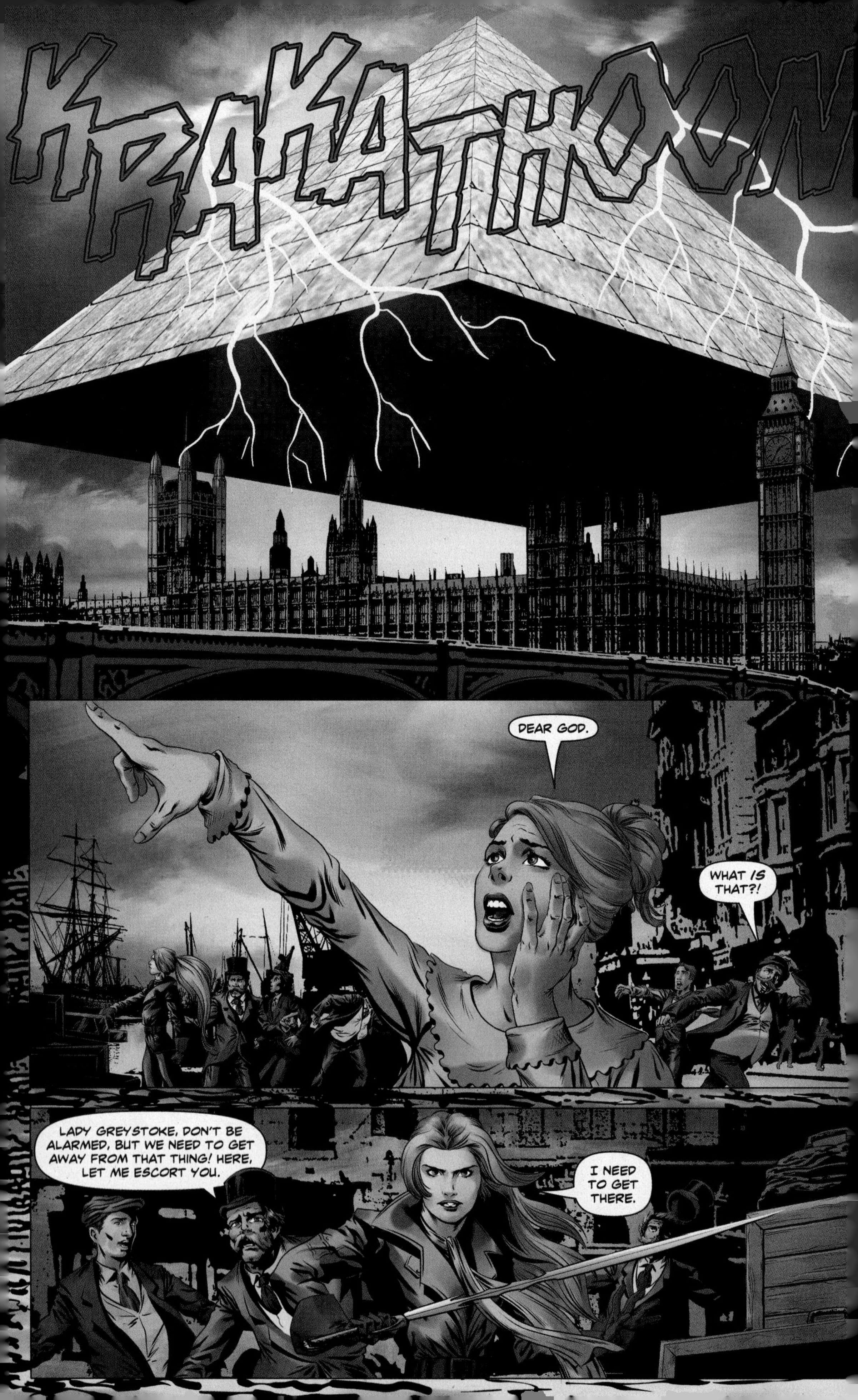
KRAKATHOOM
DEAR GOD.
WHAT IS THAT?!
LADY GREYSTOKE, DON'T BE ALARMED, BUT WE NEED TO GET AWAY FROM THAT THING! HERE, LET ME ESCORT YOU.
I NEED TO GET THERE.

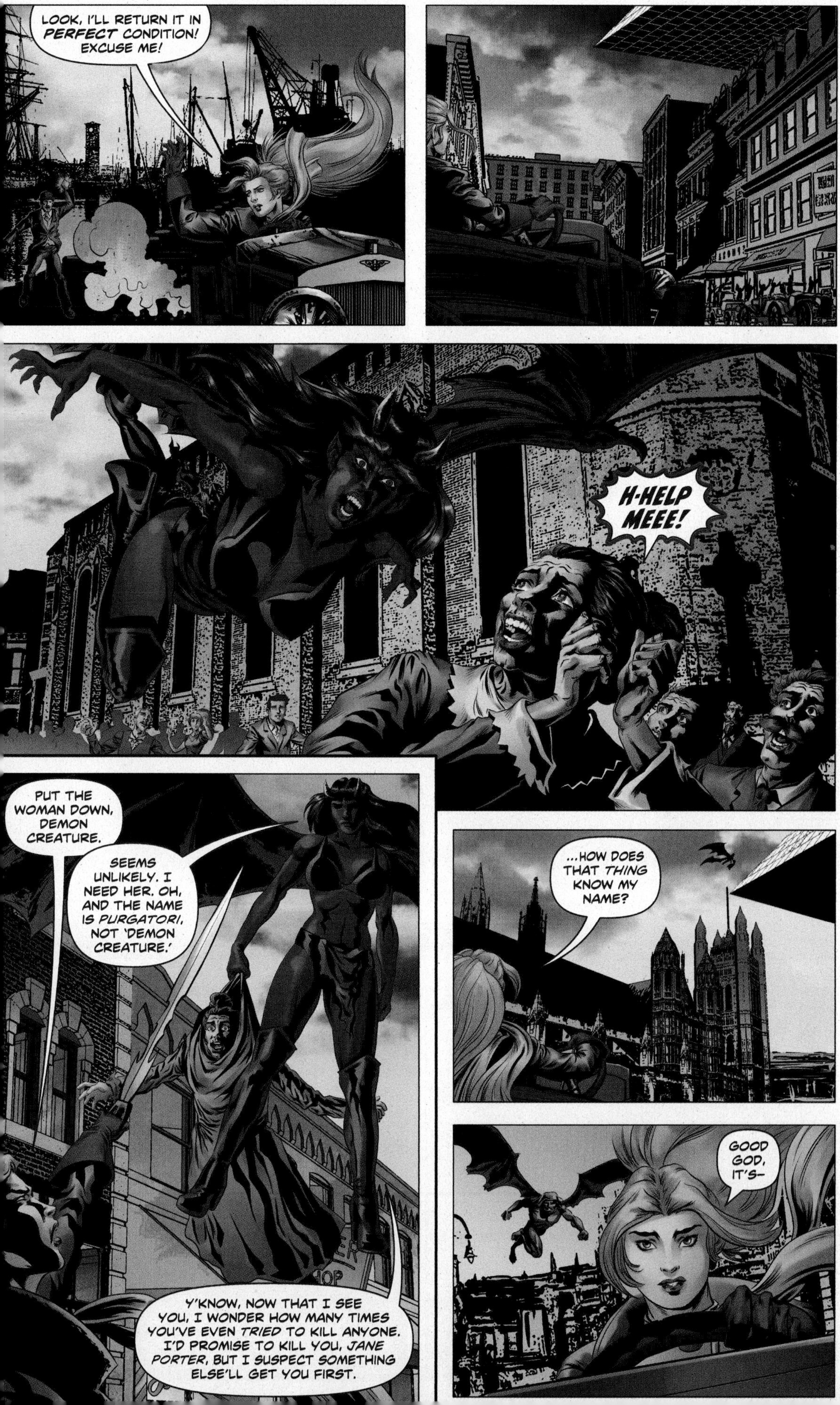
LOOK, I'LL RETURN IT IN PERFECT CONDITION! EXCUSE ME!
H-HELP MEEE!
PUT THE WOMAN DOWN, DEMON CREATURE.
SEEMS UNLIKELY. I NEED HER. OH, AND THE NAME IS PURGATORI, NOT 'DEMON CREATURE.'
Y'KNOW, NOW THAT I SEE YOU, I WONDER HOW MANY TIMES YOU'VE EVEN TRIED TO KILL ANYONE. I'D PROMISE TO KILL YOU, JANE PORTER, BUT I SUSPECT SOMETHING ELSE'LL GET YOU FIRST.
...HOW DOES THAT THING KNOW MY NAME?
GOOD GOD, IT'S—

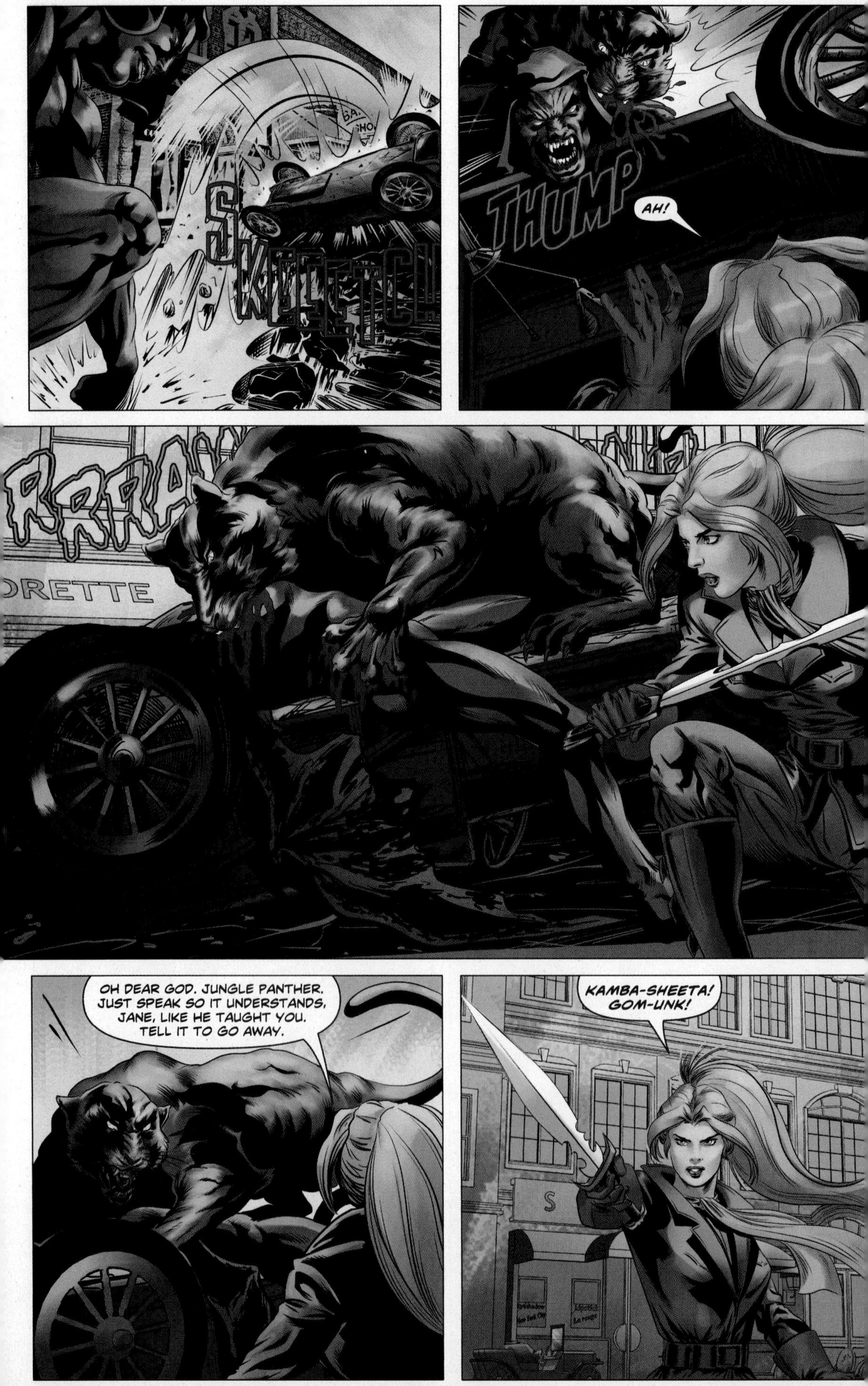

SKREETCH
THUMP
AH!
RRRA
RETTE
OH DEAR GOD. JUNGLE PANTHER. JUST SPEAK SO IT UNDERSTANDS, JANE, LIKE HE TAUGHT YOU. TELL IT TO GO AWAY.
KAMBA-SHEETA! GOM-UNK!

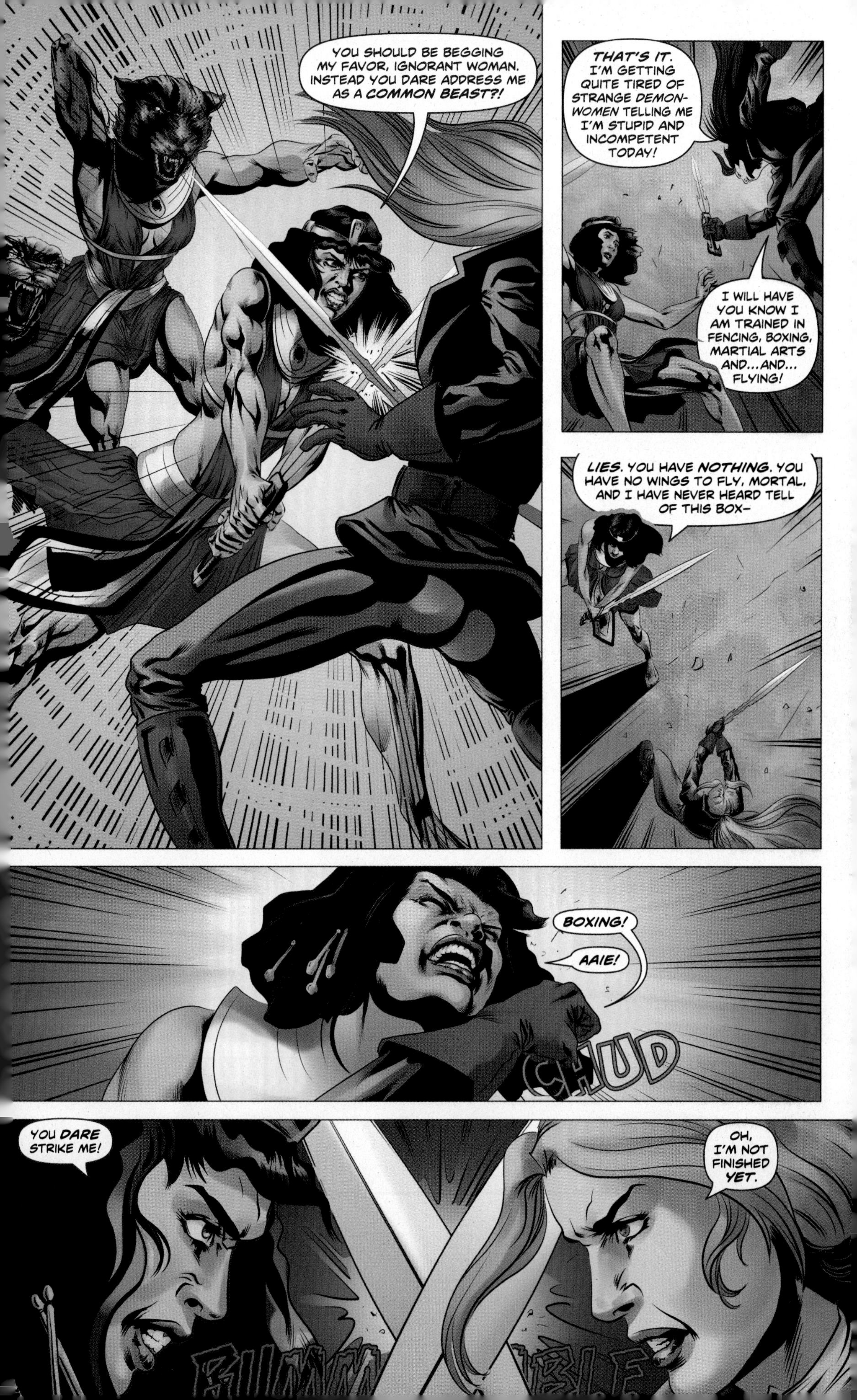
YOU SHOULD BE BEGGING MY FAVOR, IGNORANT WOMAN. INSTEAD YOU DARE ADDRESS ME AS A COMMON BEAST?!
THAT'S IT. I'M GETTING QUITE TIRED OF STRANGE DEMON-WOMEN TELLING ME I'M STUPID AND INCOMPETENT TODAY!
I WILL HAVE YOU KNOW I AM TRAINED IN FENCING, BOXING, MARTIAL ARTS AND...AND... FLYING!
LIES. YOU HAVE NOTHING. YOU HAVE NO WINGS TO FLY, MORTAL, AND I HAVE NEVER HEARD TELL OF THIS BOX–
BOXING!
AAIE!
CHUD
YOU DARE STRIKE ME!
OH, I'M NOT FINISHED YET.

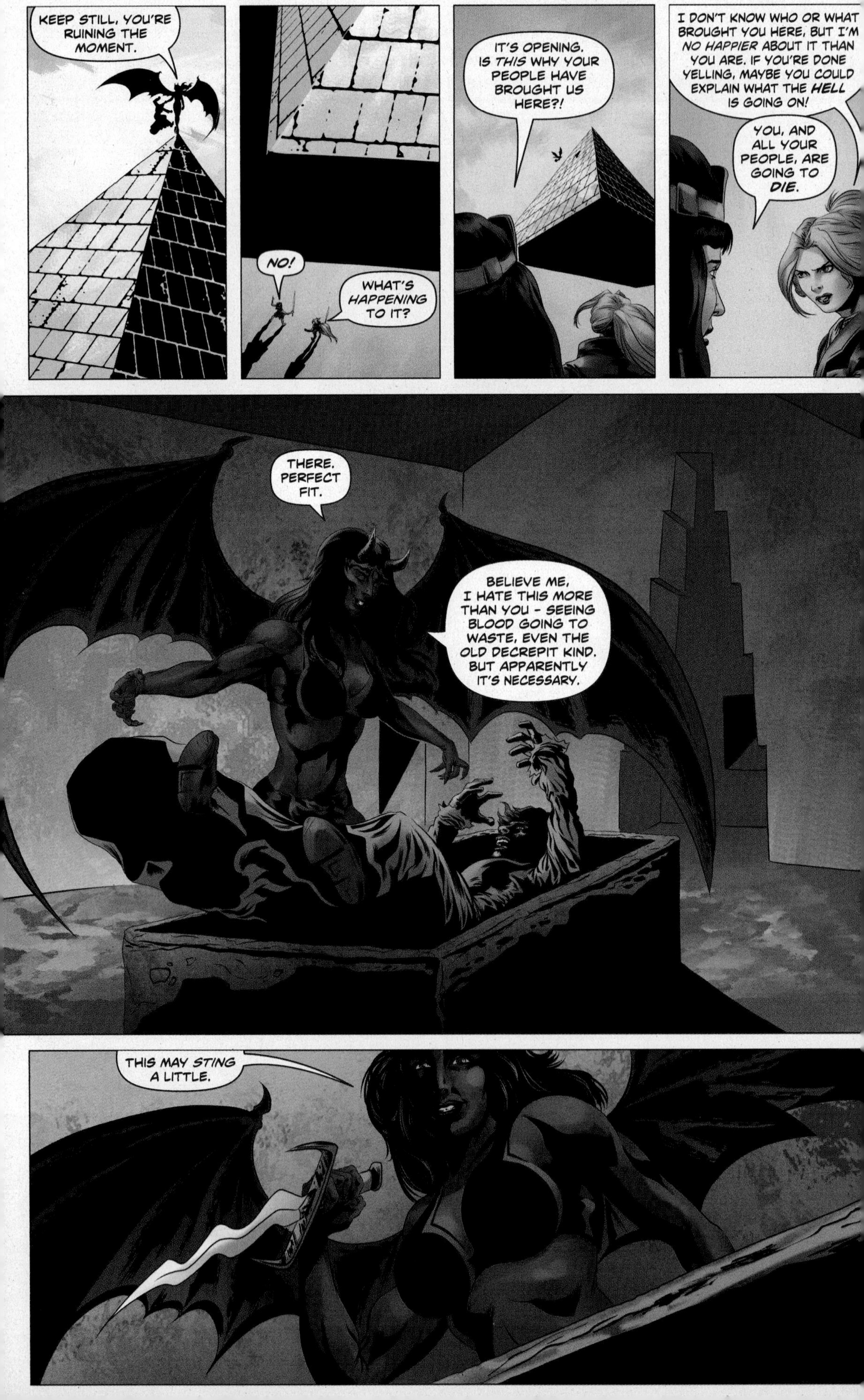
KEEP STILL, YOU'RE RUINING THE MOMENT.
NO!
WHAT'S HAPPENING TO IT?
IT'S OPENING. IS THIS WHY YOUR PEOPLE HAVE BROUGHT US HERE?!
I DON'T KNOW WHO OR WHAT BROUGHT YOU HERE, BUT I'M NO HAPPIER ABOUT IT THAN YOU ARE. IF YOU'RE DONE YELLING, MAYBE YOU COULD EXPLAIN WHAT THE HELL IS GOING ON!
YOU, AND ALL YOUR PEOPLE, ARE GOING TO DIE.
THERE. PERFECT FIT.
BELIEVE ME, I HATE THIS MORE THAN YOU - SEEING BLOOD GOING TO WASTE, EVEN THE OLD DECREPIT KIND. BUT APPARENTLY IT'S NECESSARY.
THIS MAY STING A LITTLE.

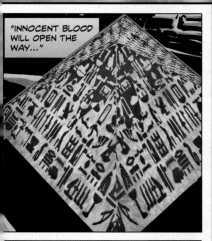

"INNOCENT BLOOD WILL OPEN THE WAY..."

THE WAY TO *WHAT?* I CAN GUESS IT'S A GREAT PYRAMID OF GIZA, TOMB FOR SOME PHARAOH, BUT–

THIS IS A GATEWAY. THE *THREE GREAT GATEWAYS:* BLACK OPENS THE REALM OF THE GODS, RED OPENS THE NEXT WORLD WHERE MORTALS' BA-SOULS FLY...

BUT THIS ONE IS WHITE. SO WHERE–

THE NETHERWORLD. THE REALM OF DEMONS, OF CHAOS.

YOU SHOULD RUN NOW. THEY WILL BE HERE SOON.

FOLLOW ME!

I'M NOT RUNNING.

I AM PANTHA, GODDESS BORN WARRIOR-DAUGHTER AND LAST PRIESTESS OF SEKHMET, RED LADY, MOTHER OF WAR, MISTRESS OF TERROR. WE MAY NOT SURVIVE, BUT I WILL GLADLY FIGHT BY YOUR SIDE, FLYING SHE-WARRIOR WHO PRACTICES...BOXING.

UH...JANE PORTER. I MEAN, LADY GREYSTOKE. OR JANE. JANE'S FINE.

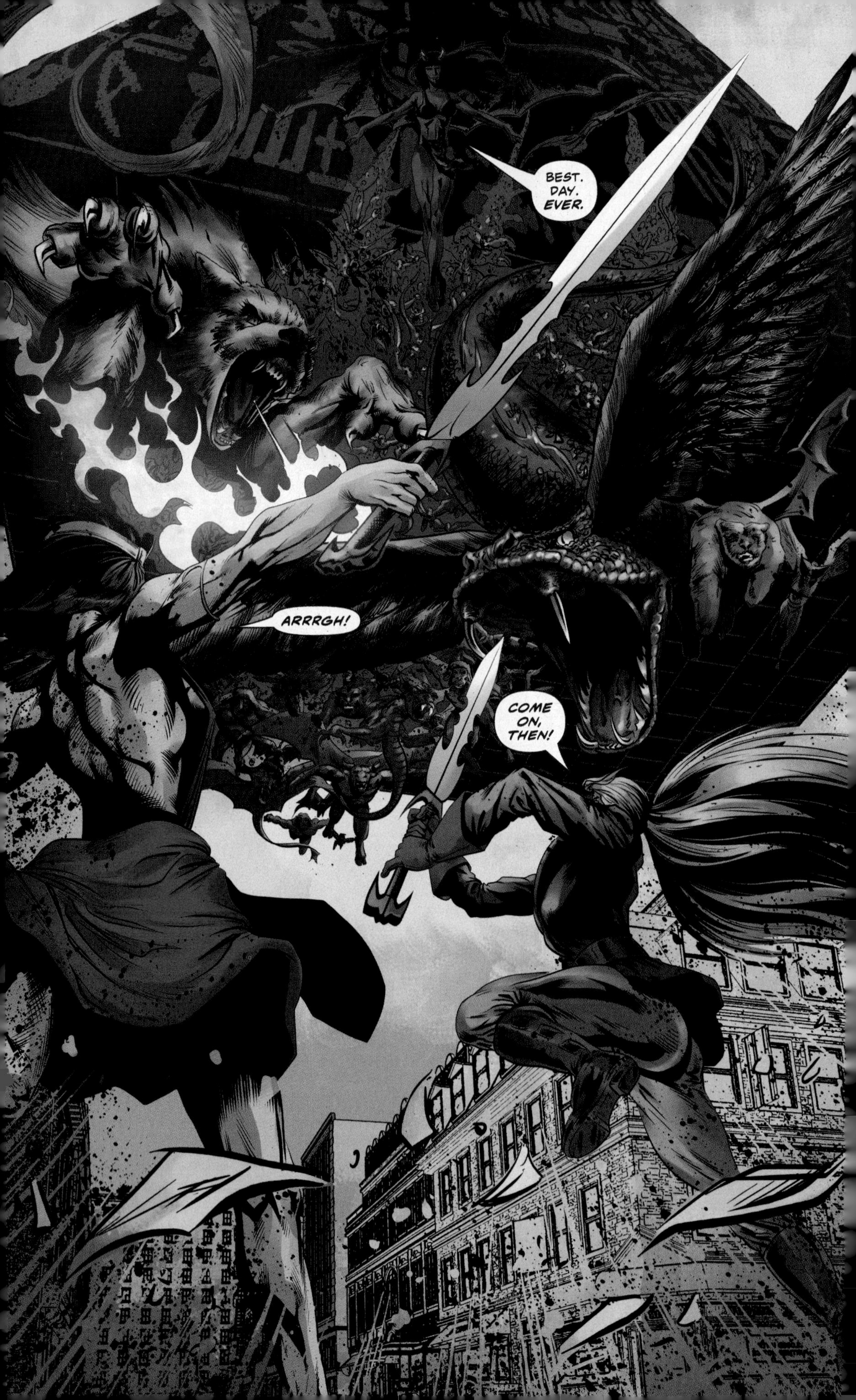
BEST. DAY. EVER.
ARRRGH!
COME ON, THEN!

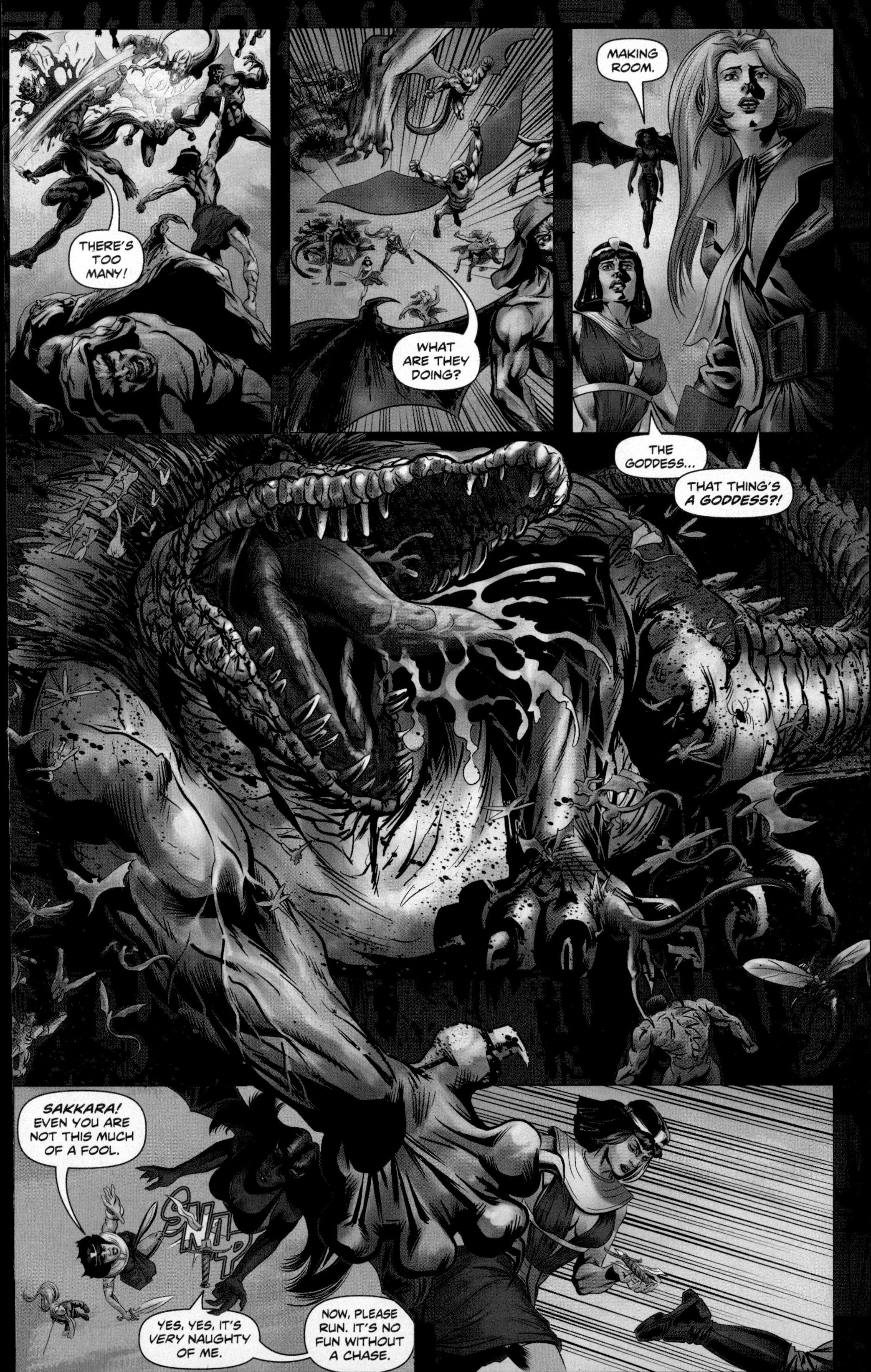
THERE'S TOO MANY!
WHAT ARE THEY DOING?
MAKING ROOM.
THE GODDESS...
THAT THING'S A GODDESS?!
SAKKARA! EVEN YOU ARE NOT THIS MUCH OF A FOOL.
YES, YES, IT'S VERY NAUGHTY OF ME.
NOW, PLEASE RUN. IT'S NO FUN WITHOUT A CHASE.

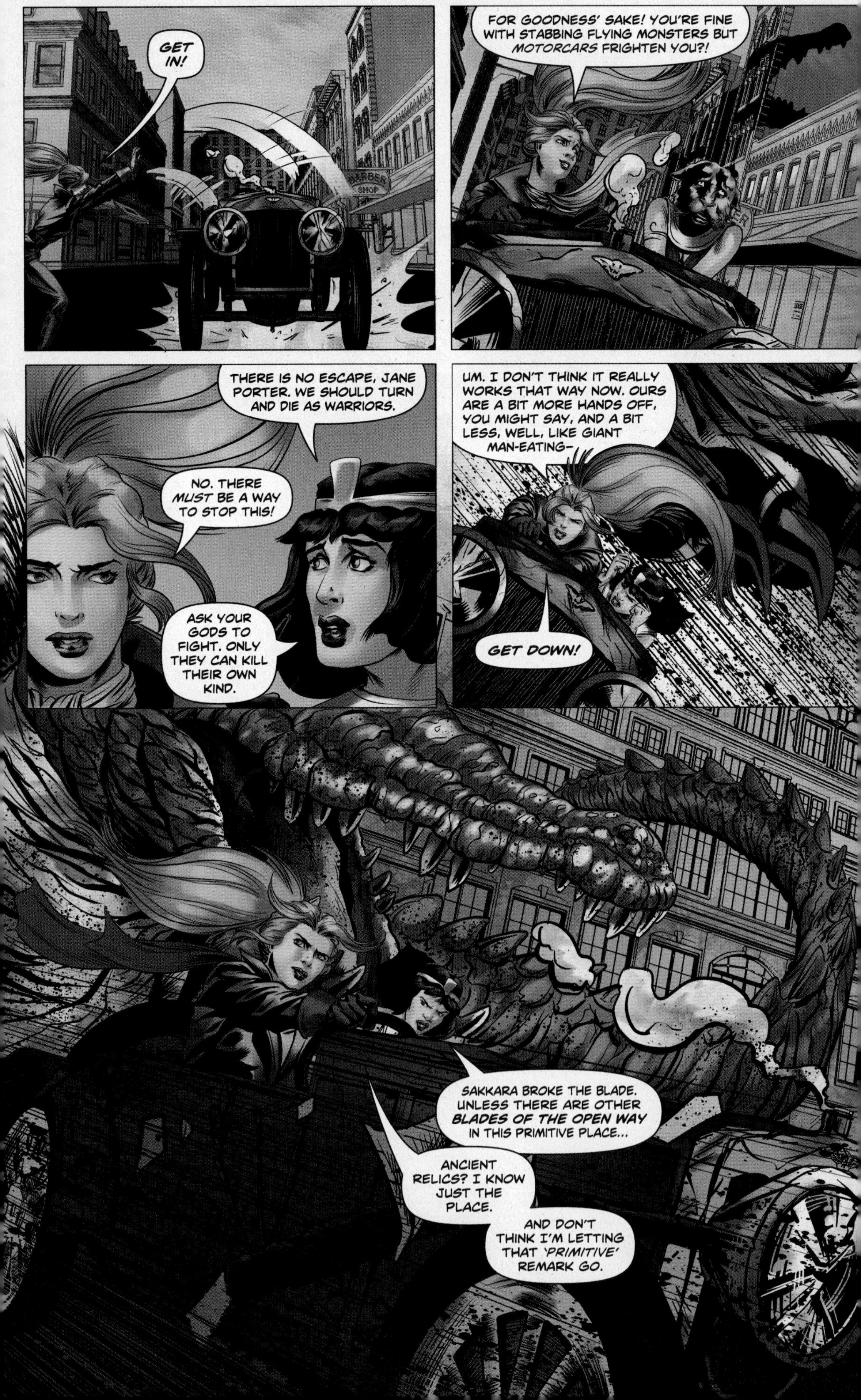
GET IN!
FOR GOODNESS' SAKE! YOU'RE FINE WITH STABBING FLYING MONSTERS BUT MOTORCARS FRIGHTEN YOU?!
BARBER SHOP
THERE IS NO ESCAPE, JANE PORTER. WE SHOULD TURN AND DIE AS WARRIORS.
NO. THERE MUST BE A WAY TO STOP THIS!
ASK YOUR GODS TO FIGHT. ONLY THEY CAN KILL THEIR OWN KIND.
UM. I DON'T THINK IT REALLY WORKS THAT WAY NOW. OURS ARE A BIT MORE HANDS OFF, YOU MIGHT SAY, AND A BIT LESS, WELL, LIKE GIANT MAN-EATING–
GET DOWN!
SAKKARA BROKE THE BLADE. UNLESS THERE ARE OTHER BLADES OF THE OPEN WAY IN THIS PRIMITIVE PLACE...
ANCIENT RELICS? I KNOW JUST THE PLACE.
AND DON'T THINK I'M LETTING THAT 'PRIMITIVE' REMARK GO.

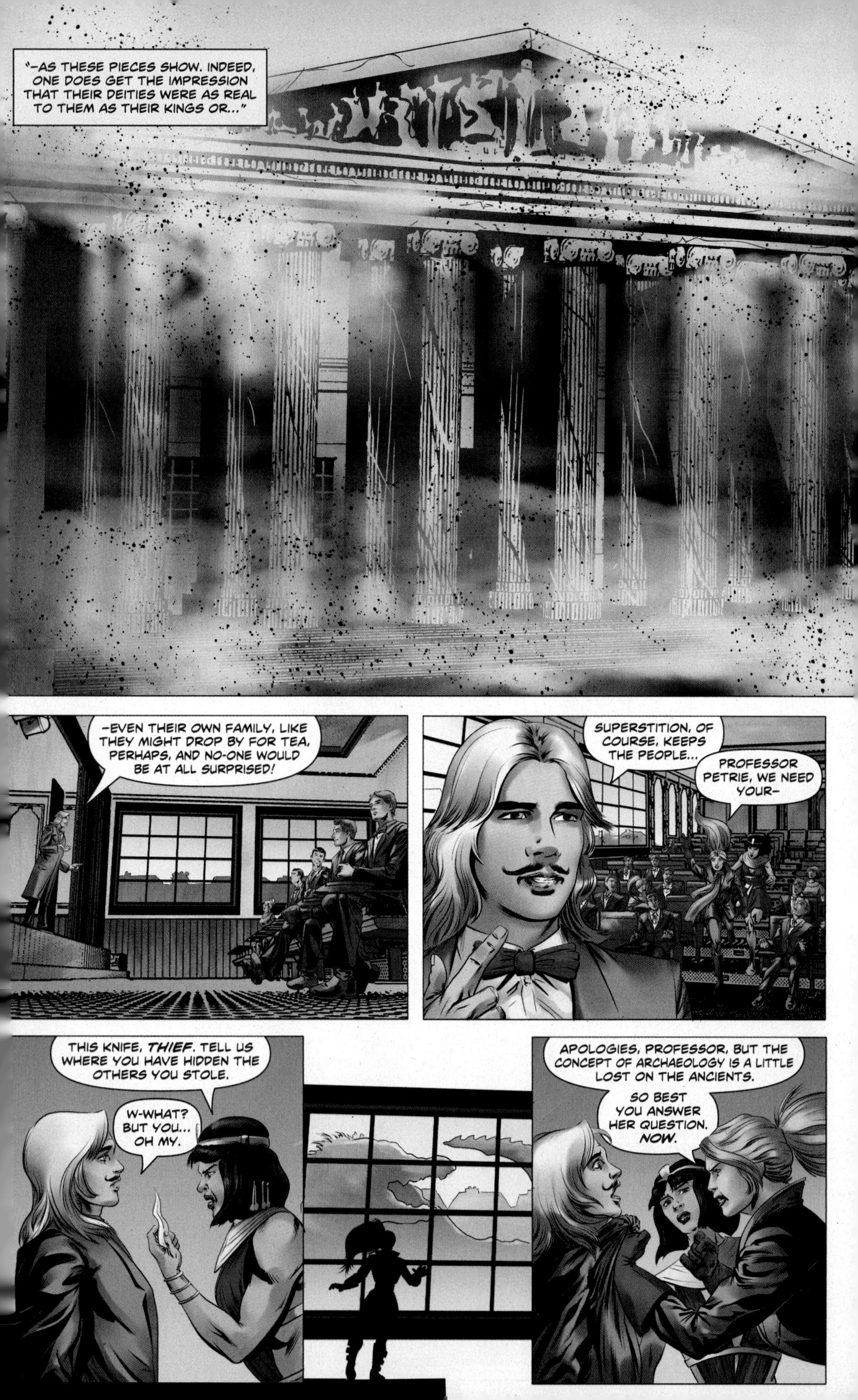
"–AS THESE PIECES SHOW. INDEED, ONE DOES GET THE IMPRESSION THAT THEIR DEITIES WERE AS REAL TO THEM AS THEIR KINGS OR..."
–EVEN THEIR OWN FAMILY, LIKE THEY MIGHT DROP BY FOR TEA, PERHAPS, AND NO-ONE WOULD BE AT ALL SURPRISED!
SUPERSTITION, OF COURSE, KEEPS THE PEOPLE...
PROFESSOR PETRIE, WE NEED YOUR–
THIS KNIFE, *THIEF*. TELL US WHERE YOU HAVE HIDDEN THE OTHERS YOU STOLE.
W-WHAT? BUT YOU... OH MY.
APOLOGIES, PROFESSOR, BUT THE CONCEPT OF ARCHAEOLOGY IS A LITTLE LOST ON THE ANCIENTS.
SO BEST YOU ANSWER HER QUESTION. *NOW*.

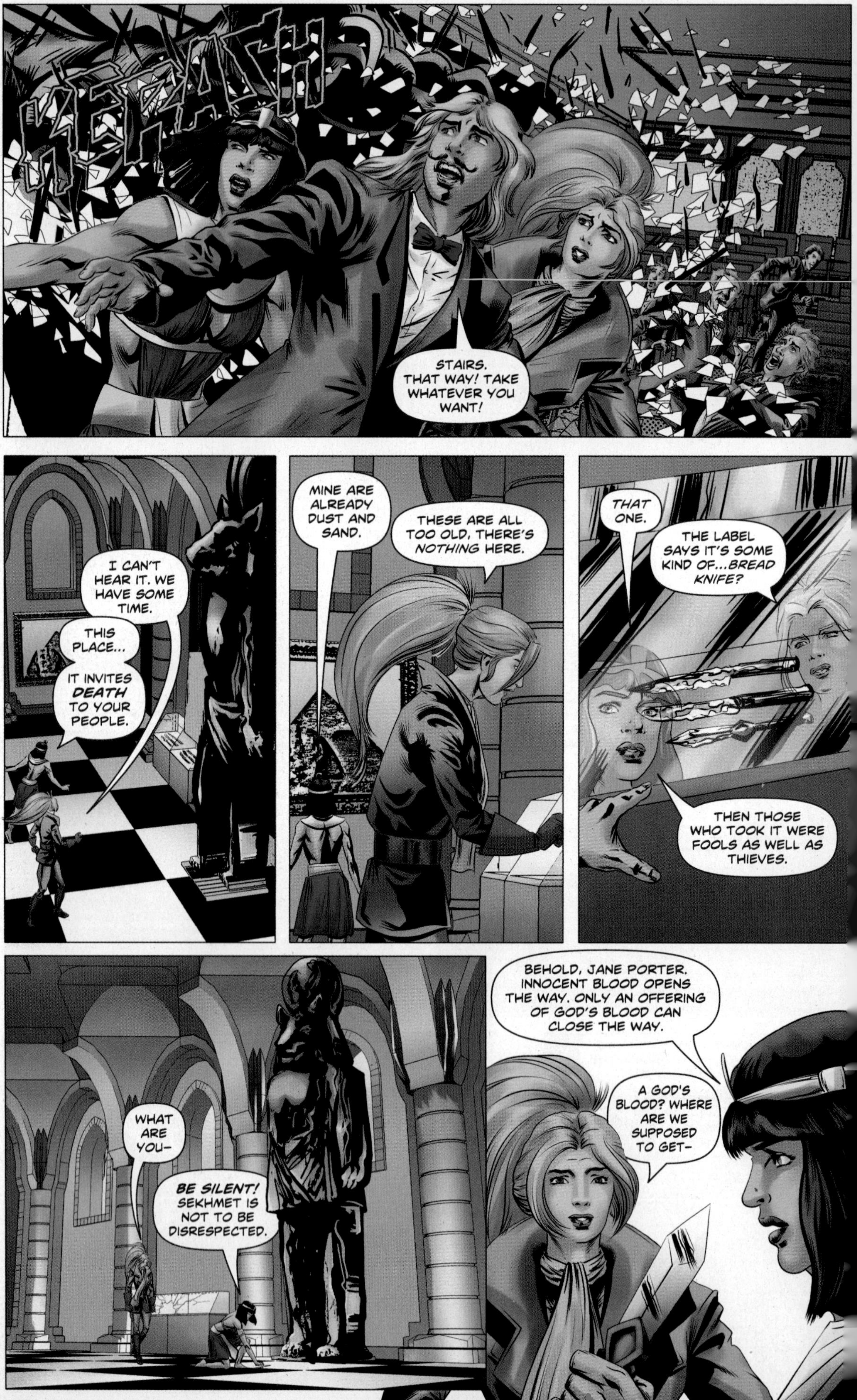
STAIRS. THAT WAY! TAKE WHATEVER YOU WANT!
I CAN'T HEAR IT. WE HAVE SOME TIME.
THIS PLACE...
IT INVITES *DEATH* TO YOUR PEOPLE.
MINE ARE ALREADY DUST AND SAND.
THESE ARE ALL TOO OLD, THERE'S *NOTHING* HERE.
THAT ONE.
THE LABEL SAYS IT'S SOME KIND OF...*BREAD KNIFE?*
THEN THOSE WHO TOOK IT WERE FOOLS AS WELL AS THIEVES.
WHAT ARE YOU–
BE SILENT! SEKHMET IS NOT TO BE DISRESPECTED.
BEHOLD, JANE PORTER. INNOCENT BLOOD OPENS THE WAY. ONLY AN OFFERING OF GOD'S BLOOD CAN CLOSE THE WAY.
A GOD'S BLOOD? WHERE ARE WE SUPPOSED TO GET–

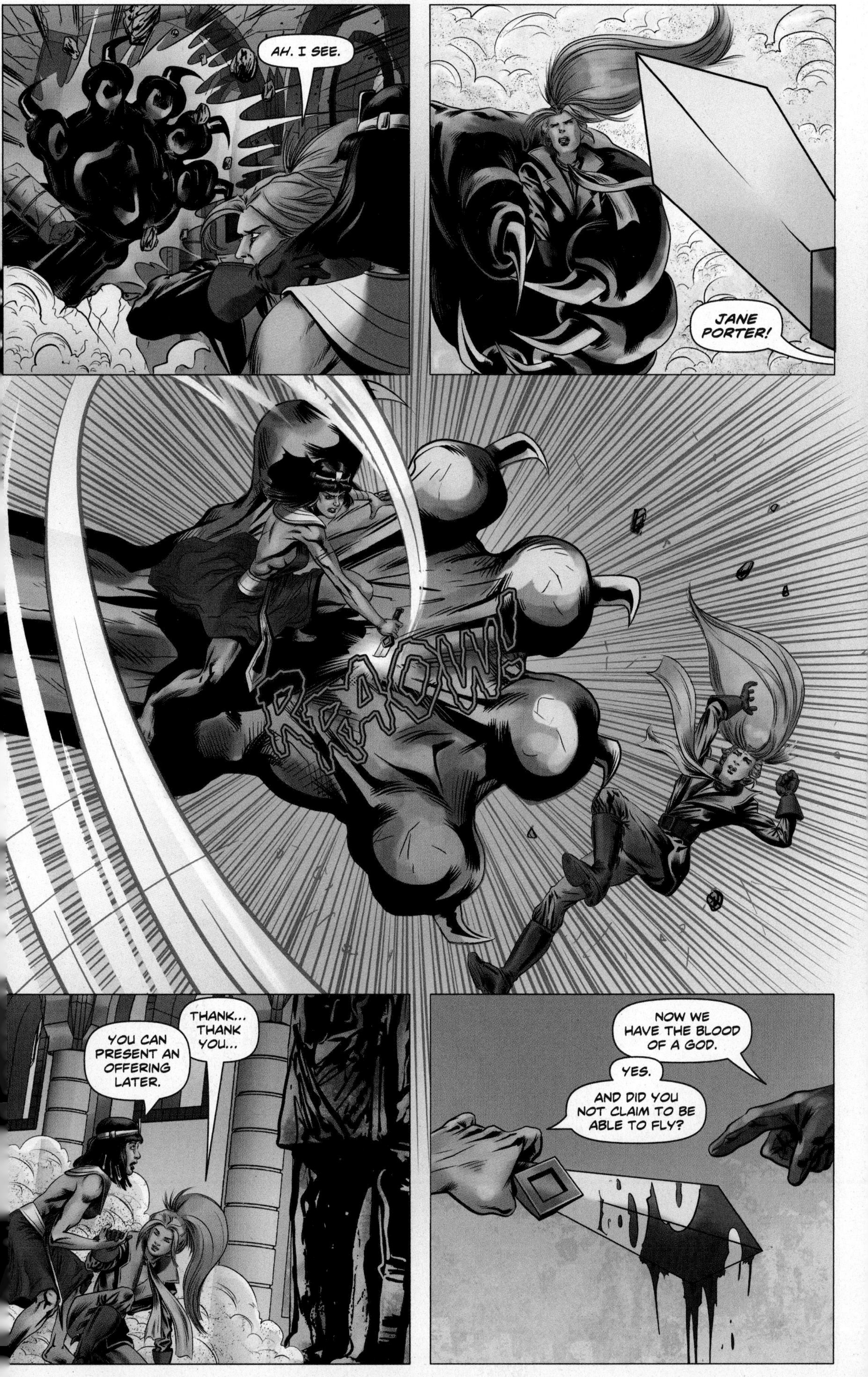
AH. I SEE.
JANE PORTER!
RRRAOW!
YOU CAN PRESENT AN OFFERING LATER.
THANK... THANK YOU...
NOW WE HAVE THE BLOOD OF A GOD.
YES.
AND DID YOU NOT CLAIM TO BE ABLE TO FLY?

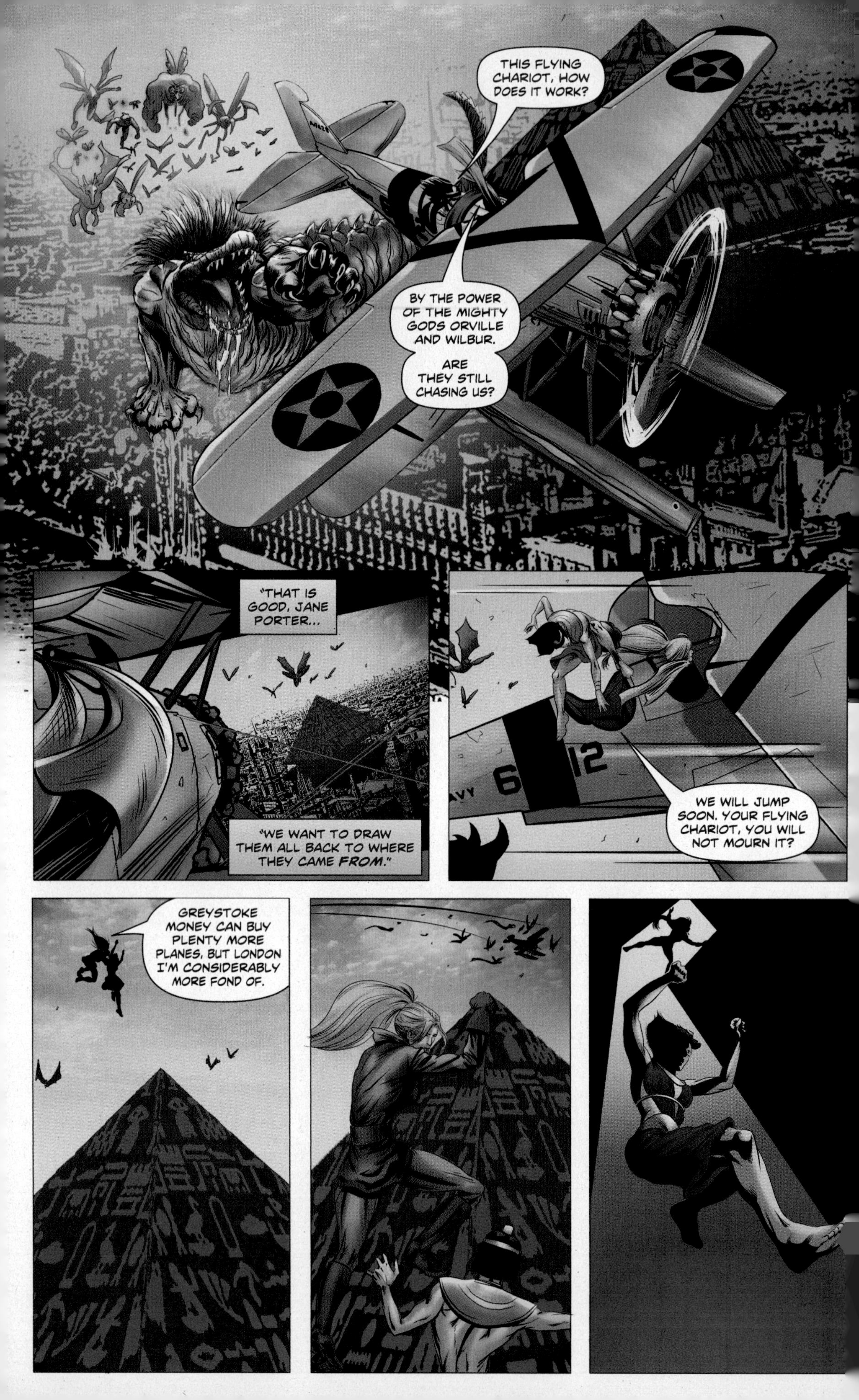
THIS FLYING CHARIOT, HOW DOES IT WORK?
BY THE POWER OF THE MIGHTY GODS ORVILLE AND WILBUR.
ARE THEY STILL CHASING US?
"THAT IS GOOD, JANE PORTER...
"WE WANT TO DRAW THEM ALL BACK TO WHERE THEY CAME *FROM*."
WE WILL JUMP SOON. YOUR FLYING CHARIOT, YOU WILL NOT MOURN IT?
GREYSTOKE MONEY CAN BUY PLENTY MORE PLANES, BUT LONDON I'M CONSIDERABLY MORE FOND OF.

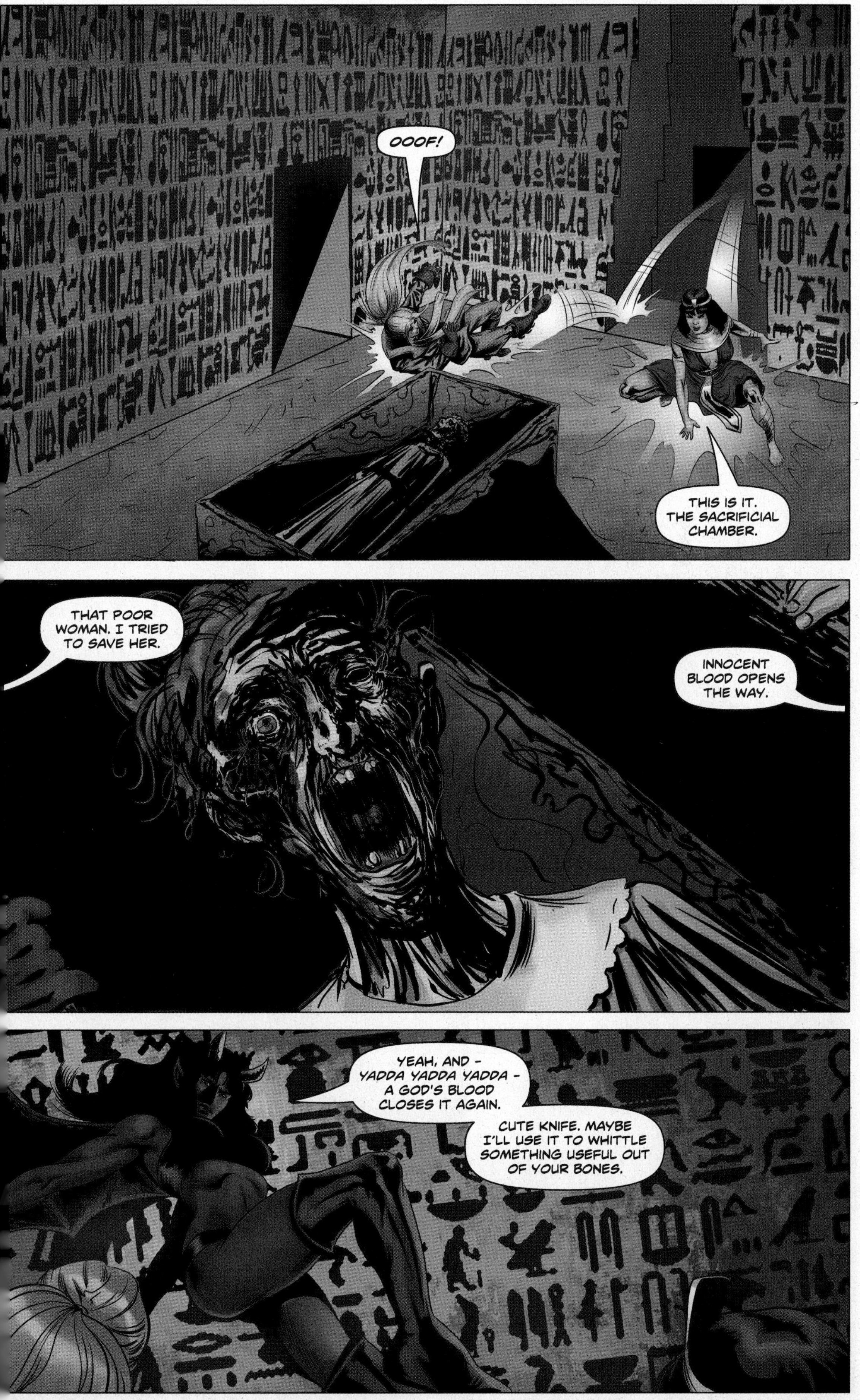
OOOF!
THIS IS IT. THE SACRIFICIAL CHAMBER.
THAT POOR WOMAN. I TRIED TO SAVE HER.
INNOCENT BLOOD OPENS THE WAY.
YEAH, AND - YADDA YADDA YADDA - A GOD'S BLOOD CLOSES IT AGAIN.
CUTE KNIFE. MAYBE I'LL USE IT TO WHITTLE SOMETHING USEFUL OUT OF YOUR BONES.

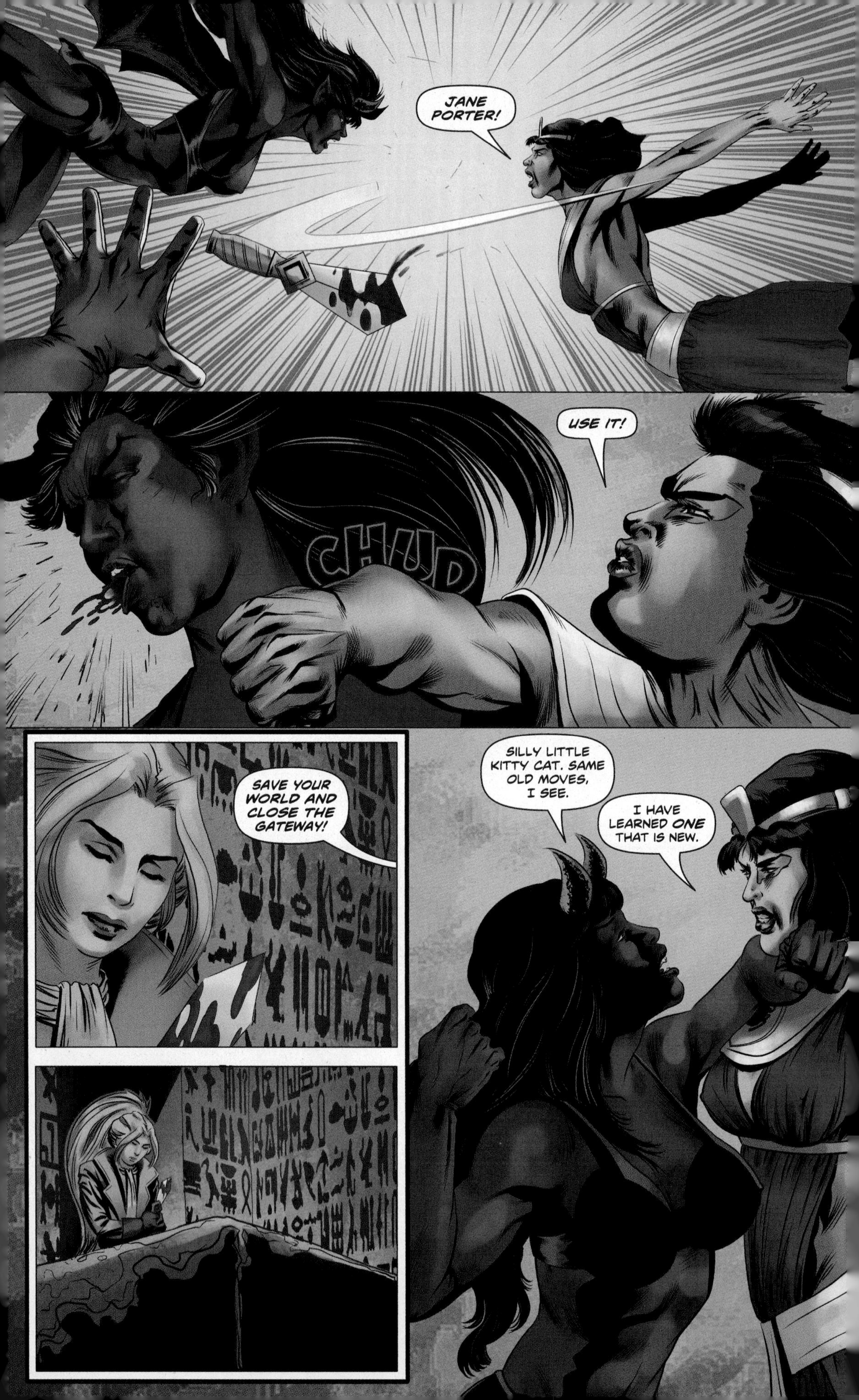
JANE PORTER!
USE IT!
CHUD
SAVE YOUR WORLD AND CLOSE THE GATEWAY!
SILLY LITTLE KITTY CAT. SAME OLD MOVES, I SEE.
I HAVE LEARNED ONE THAT IS NEW.

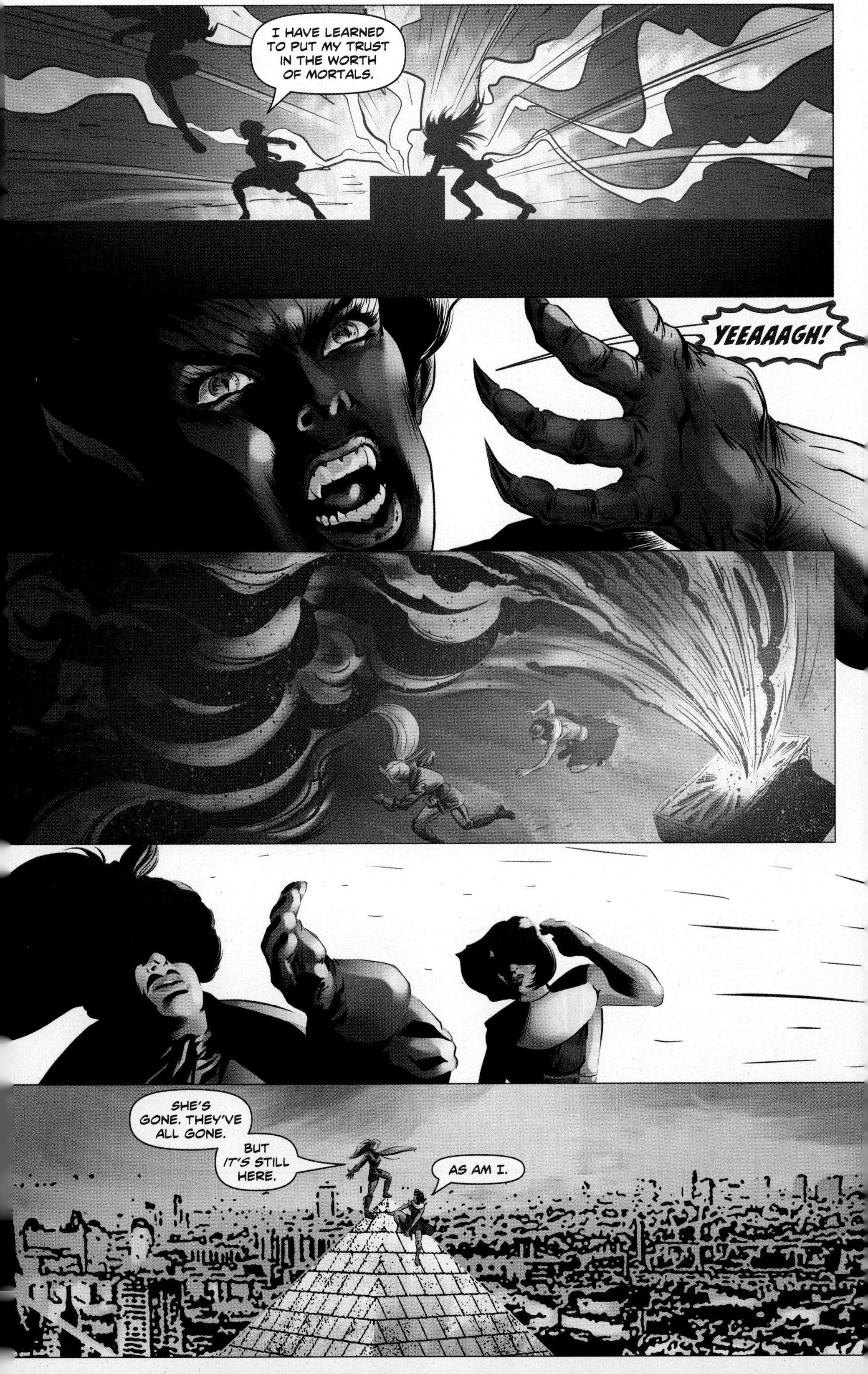
I HAVE LEARNED TO PUT MY TRUST IN THE WORTH OF MORTALS.
YEEAAAGH!
SHE'S GONE. THEY'VE ALL GONE.
BUT IT'S STILL HERE.
AS AM I.

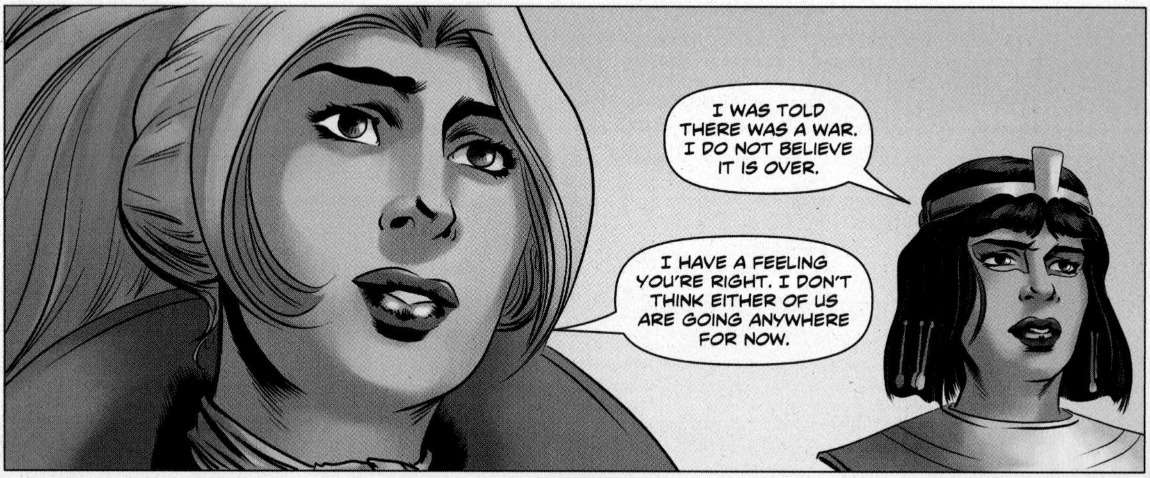
I WAS TOLD THERE WAS A WAR. I DO NOT BELIEVE IT IS OVER.
I HAVE A FEELING YOU'RE RIGHT. I DON'T THINK EITHER OF US ARE GOING ANYWHERE FOR NOW.

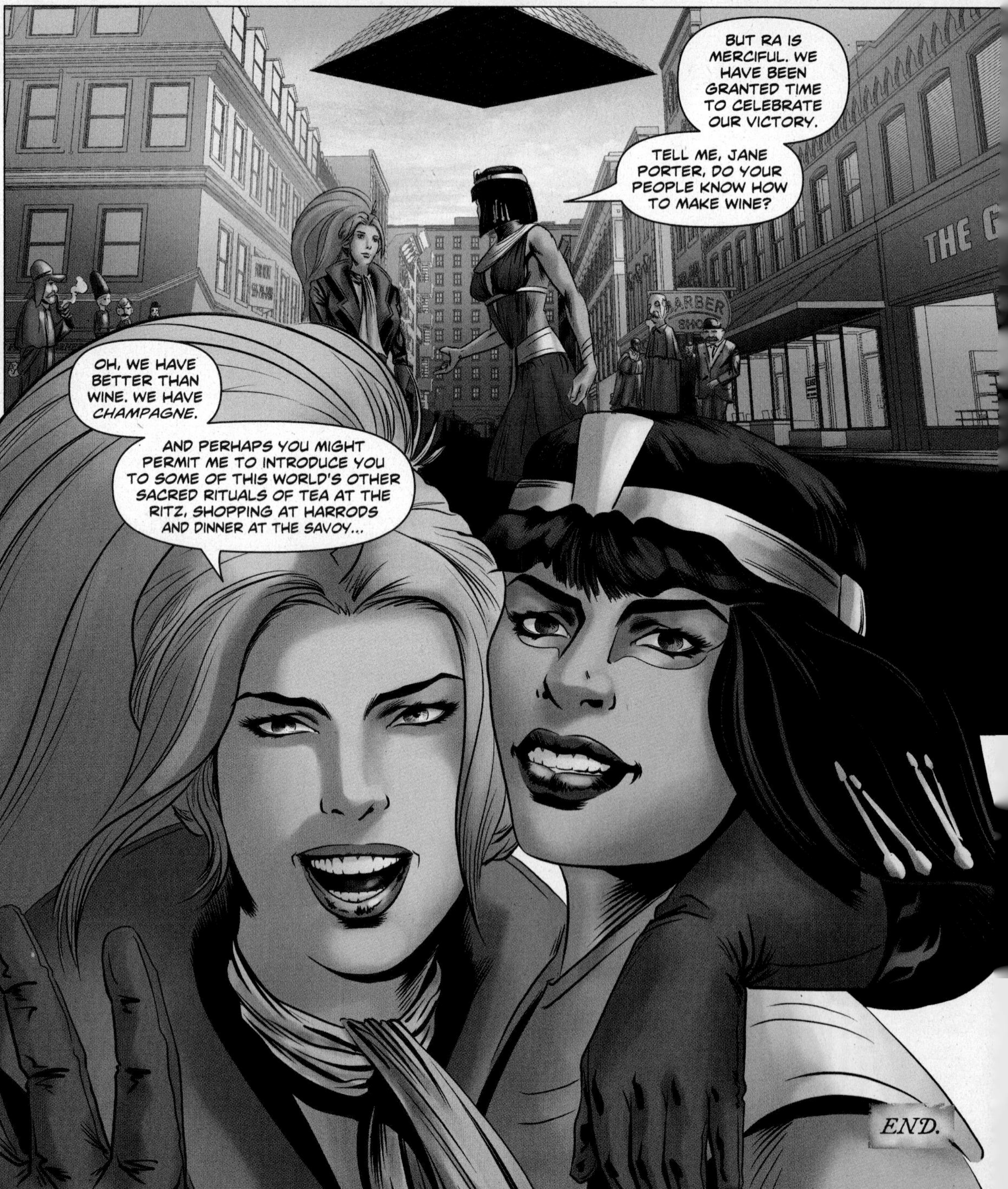
BUT RA IS MERCIFUL. WE HAVE BEEN GRANTED TIME TO CELEBRATE OUR VICTORY.
TELL ME, JANE PORTER, DO YOUR PEOPLE KNOW HOW TO MAKE WINE?
OH, WE HAVE BETTER THAN WINE. WE HAVE *CHAMPAGNE.*
AND PERHAPS YOU MIGHT PERMIT ME TO INTRODUCE YOU TO SOME OF THIS WORLD'S OTHER SACRED RITUALS OF TEA AT THE RITZ, SHOPPING AT HARRODS AND DINNER AT THE SAVOY...
BARBER SHOP
END.

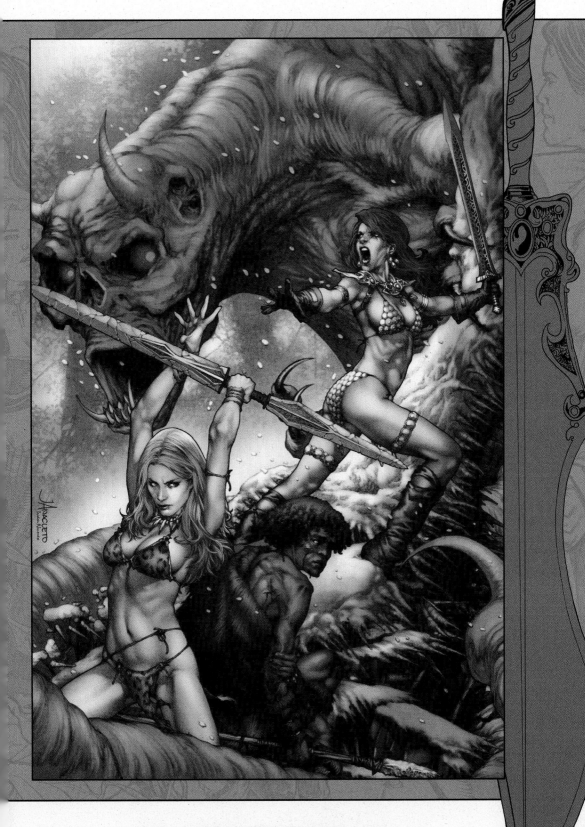

SWORDS OF SORROW:
RED SONJA & JUNGLE GIRL
ISSUE TWO OF THREE

written by MARGUERITE BENNETT illustrated by MIRKA ANDOLFO
colored by VINCENZO SALVO (Arancia Studio) lettered by ERICA SCHULTZ

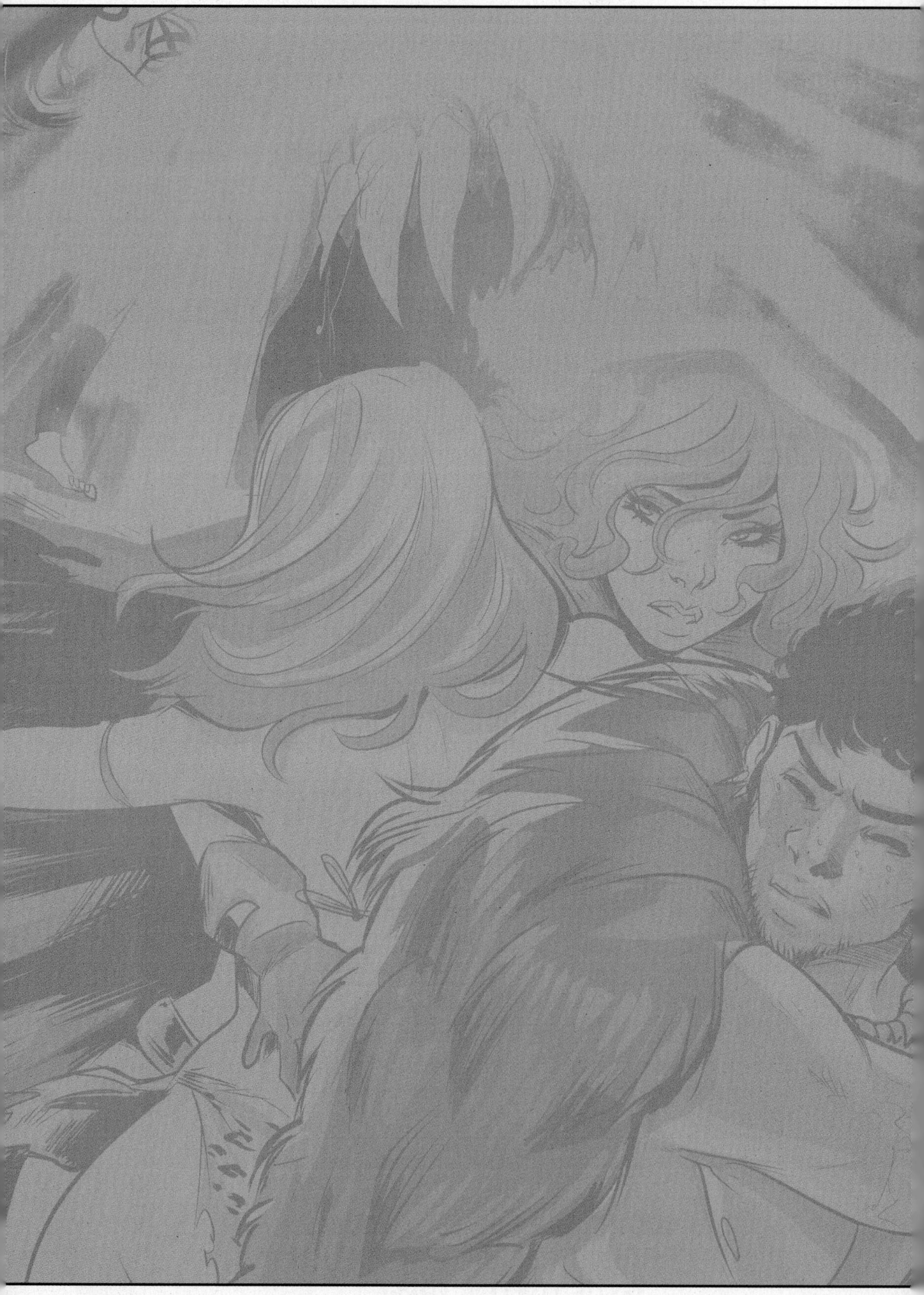

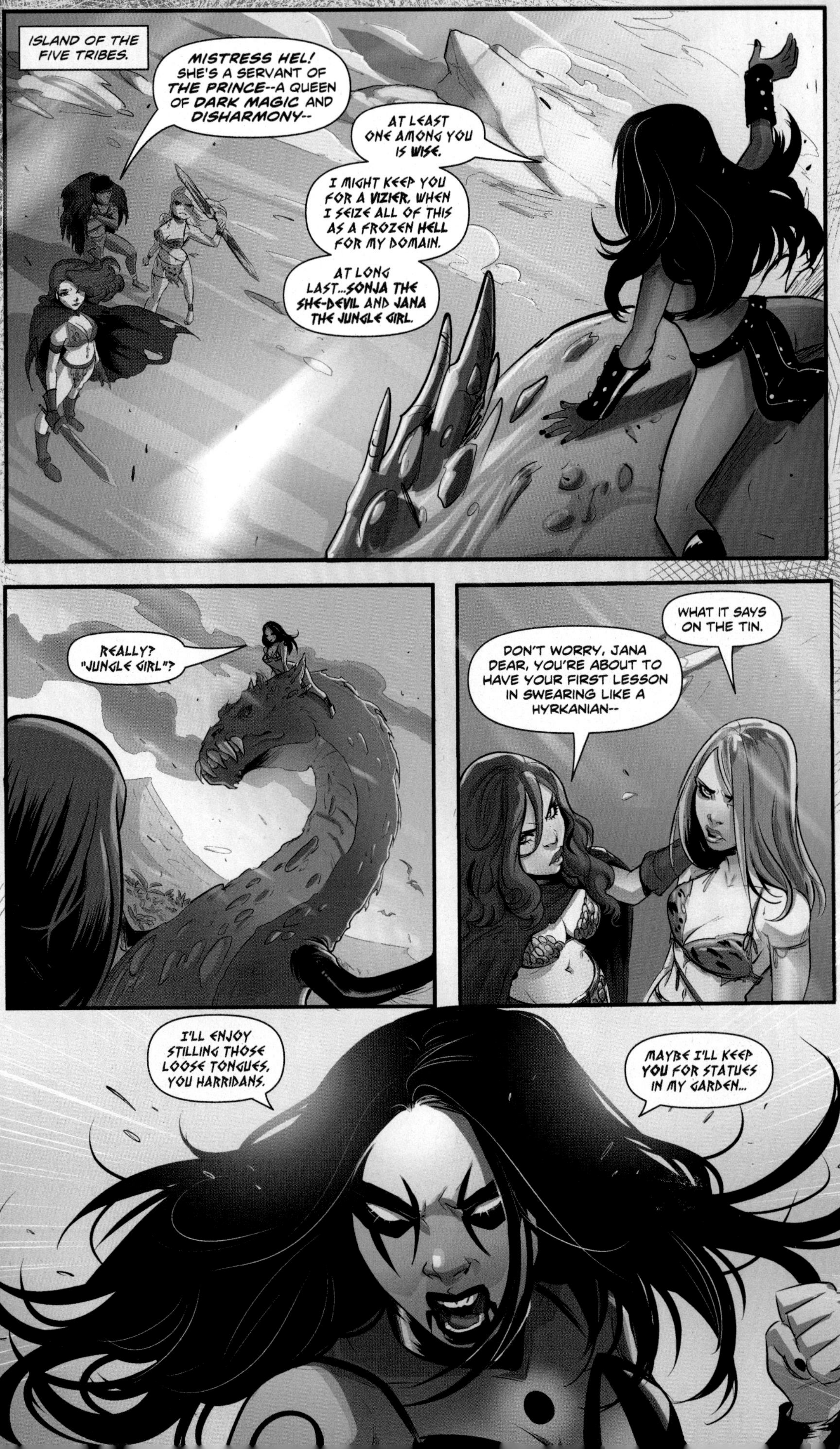
ISLAND OF THE FIVE TRIBES.
MISTRESS HEL! SHE'S A SERVANT OF THE PRINCE--A QUEEN OF DARK MAGIC AND DISHARMONY--
AT LEAST ONE AMONG YOU IS WISE.
I MIGHT KEEP YOU FOR A VIZIER, WHEN I SEIZE ALL OF THIS AS A FROZEN HELL FOR MY DOMAIN.
AT LONG LAST...SONJA THE SHE-DEVIL AND JANA THE JUNGLE GIRL.
REALLY? "JUNGLE GIRL"?
WHAT IT SAYS ON THE TIN.
DON'T WORRY, JANA DEAR, YOU'RE ABOUT TO HAVE YOUR FIRST LESSON IN SWEARING LIKE A HYRKANIAN--
I'LL ENJOY STILLING THOSE LOOSE TONGUES, YOU HARRIDANS.
MAYBE I'LL KEEP YOU FOR STATUES IN MY GARDEN...

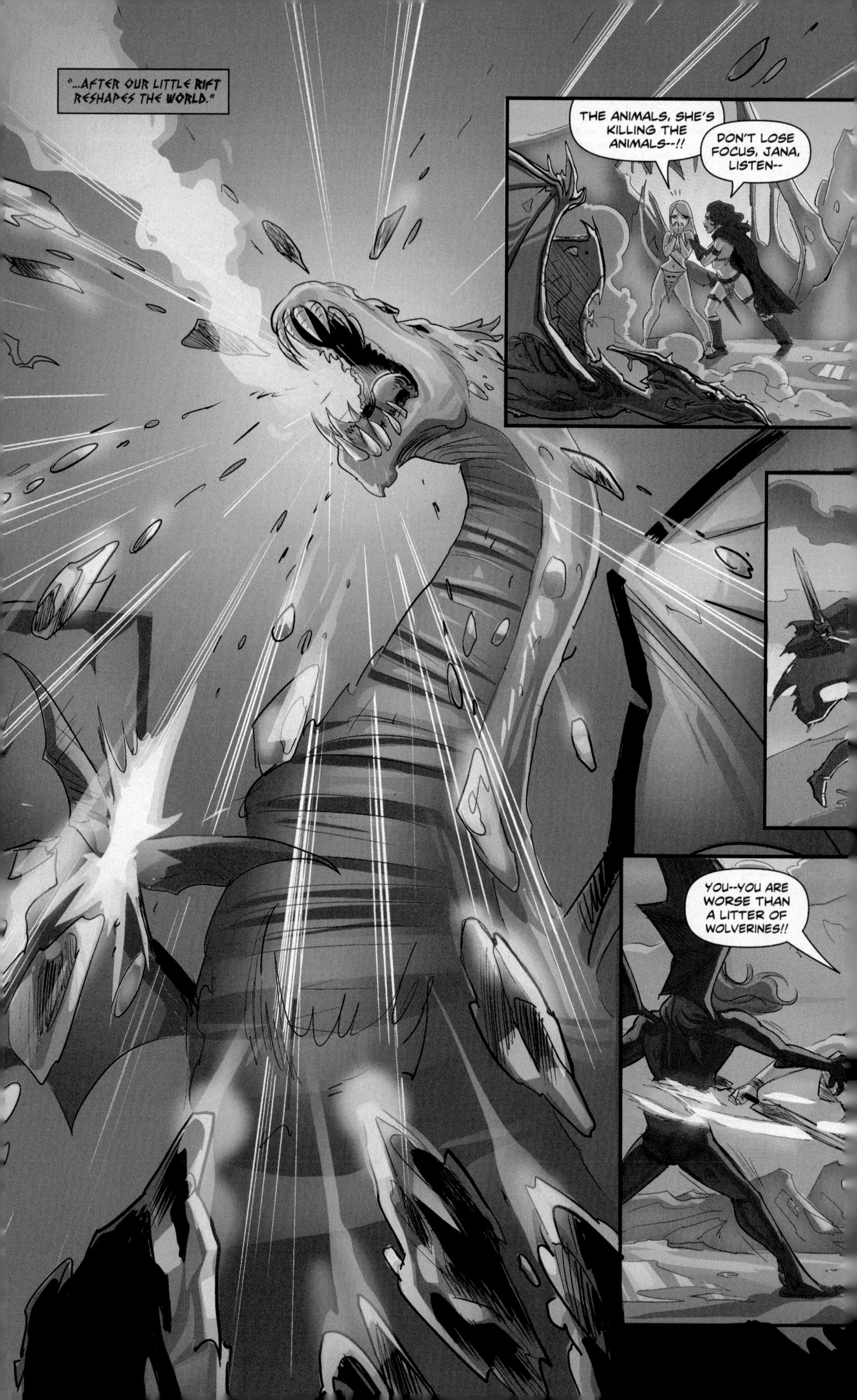
"...AFTER OUR LITTLE RIFT RESHAPES THE WORLD."
THE ANIMALS, SHE'S KILLING THE ANIMALS--!!
DON'T LOSE FOCUS, JANA, LISTEN--
YOU--YOU ARE WORSE THAN A LITTER OF WOLVERINES!!

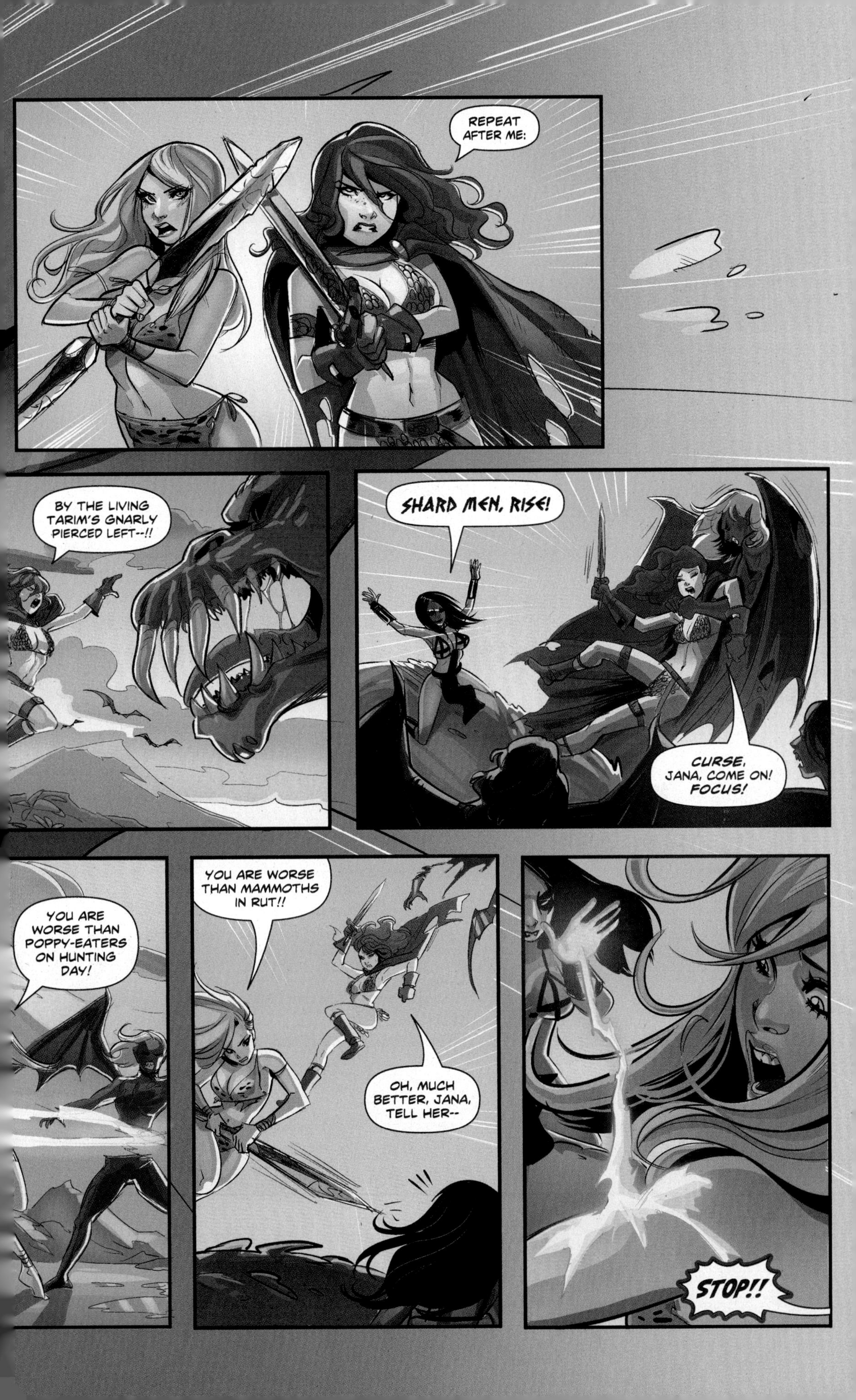
REPEAT AFTER ME:
BY THE LIVING TARIM'S GNARLY PIERCED LEFT--!!
SHARD MEN, RISE!
CURSE, JANA, COME ON! FOCUS!
YOU ARE WORSE THAN POPPY-EATERS ON HUNTING DAY!
YOU ARE WORSE THAN MAMMOTHS IN RUT!!
OH, MUCH BETTER, JANA, TELL HER--
STOP!!

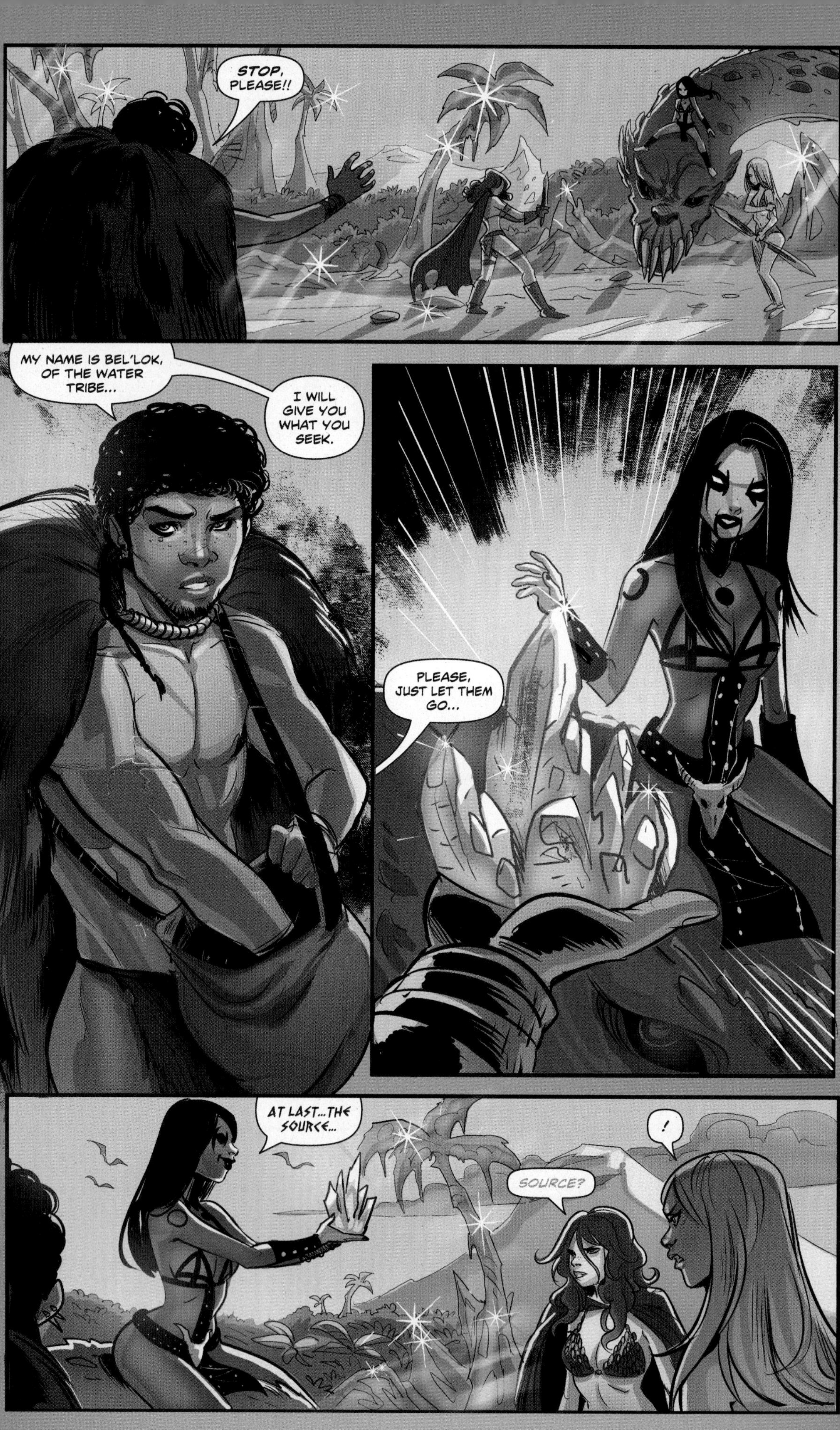
STOP, PLEASE!!
MY NAME IS BEL'LOK, OF THE WATER TRIBE...
I WILL GIVE YOU WHAT YOU SEEK.
PLEASE, JUST LET THEM GO...
AT LAST...THE SOURCE...
!
SOURCE?

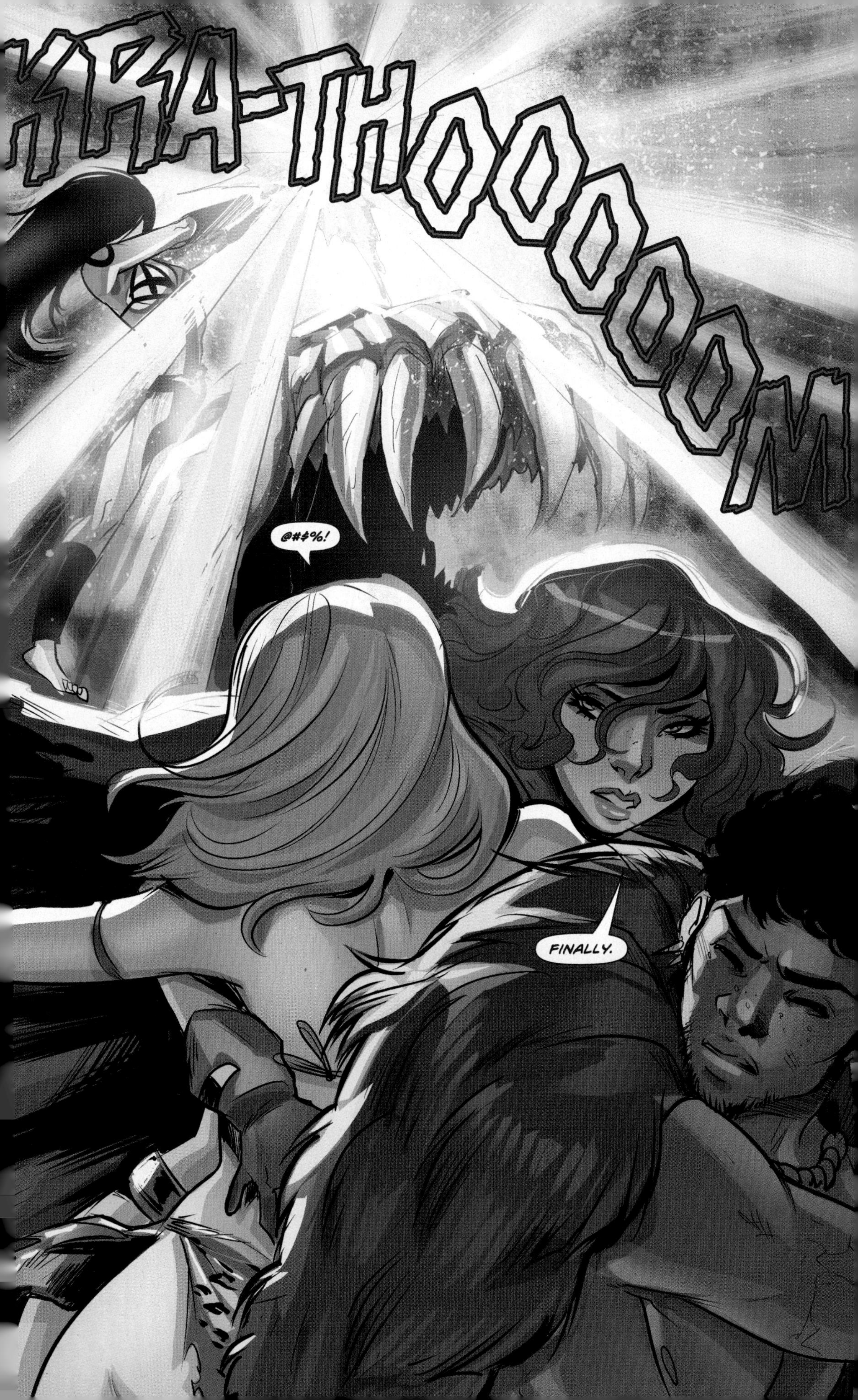

KRA-THOOOOOOM
@#$%!
FINALLY.

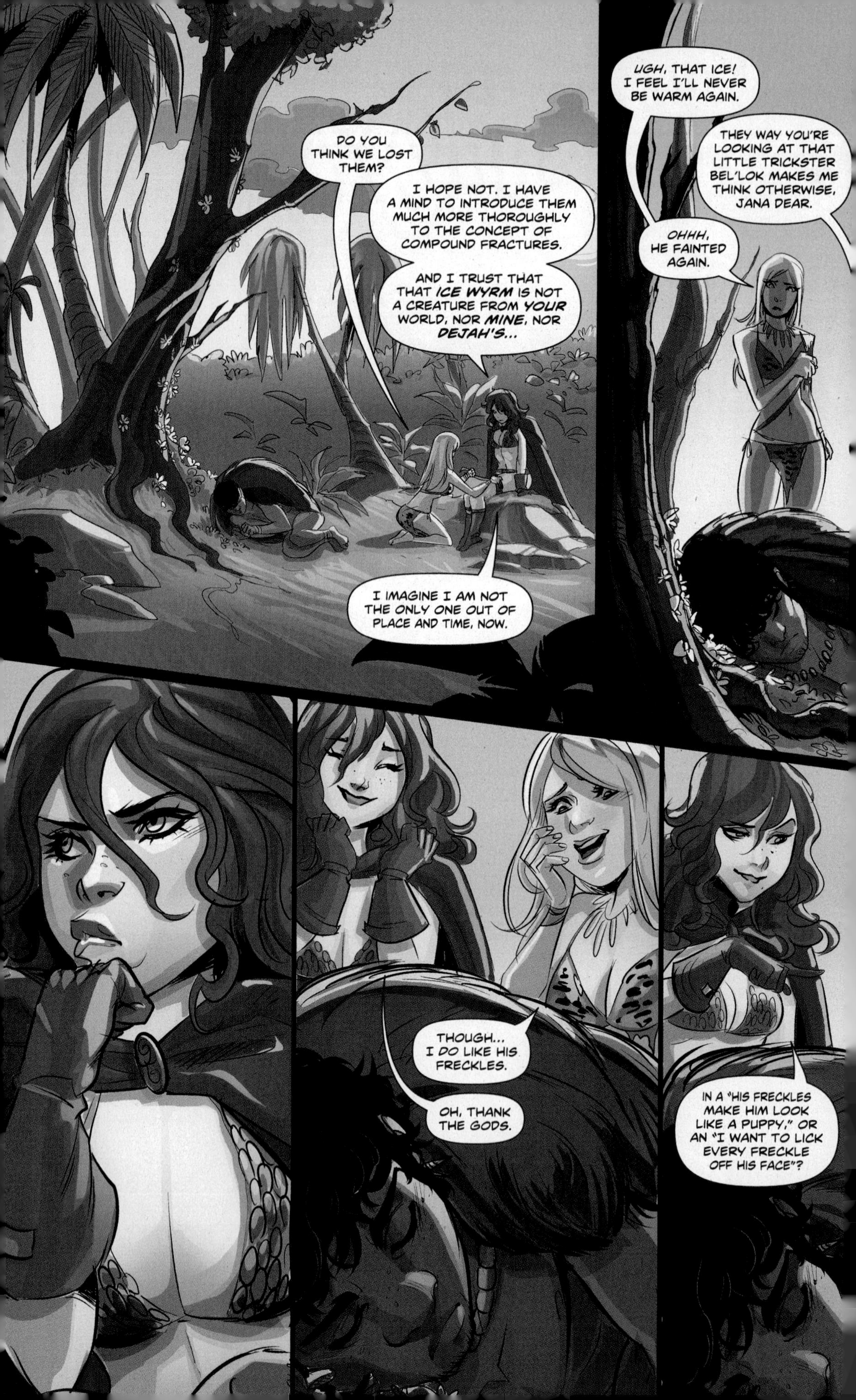
DO YOU THINK WE LOST THEM?
I HOPE NOT. I HAVE A MIND TO INTRODUCE THEM MUCH MORE THOROUGHLY TO THE CONCEPT OF COMPOUND FRACTURES.
AND I TRUST THAT THAT *ICE WYRM* IS NOT A CREATURE FROM *YOUR* WORLD, NOR *MINE*, NOR *DEJAH'S*...
I IMAGINE I AM NOT THE ONLY ONE OUT OF PLACE AND TIME, NOW.
UGH, THAT ICE! I FEEL I'LL NEVER BE WARM AGAIN.
THEY WAY YOU'RE LOOKING AT THAT LITTLE TRICKSTER BEL'LOK MAKES ME THINK OTHERWISE, JANA DEAR.
OHHH, HE FAINTED AGAIN.
THOUGH... I DO LIKE HIS FRECKLES.
OH, THANK THE GODS.
IN A "HIS FRECKLES MAKE HIM LOOK LIKE A PUPPY," OR AN "I WANT TO LICK EVERY FRECKLE OFF HIS FACE"?

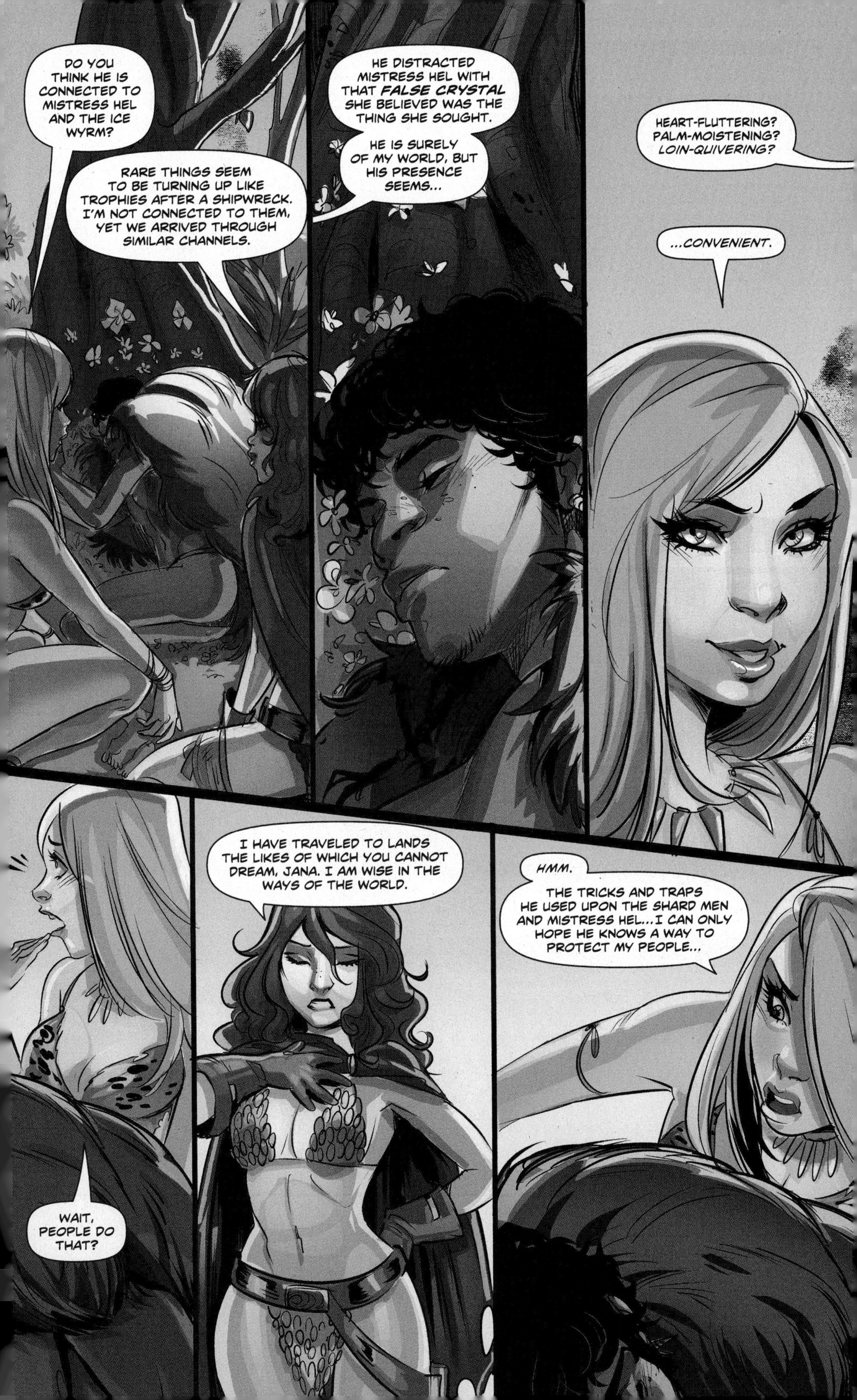
DO YOU THINK HE IS CONNECTED TO MISTRESS HEL AND THE ICE WYRM?
RARE THINGS SEEM TO BE TURNING UP LIKE TROPHIES AFTER A SHIPWRECK. I'M NOT CONNECTED TO THEM, YET WE ARRIVED THROUGH SIMILAR CHANNELS.
HE DISTRACTED MISTRESS HEL WITH THAT FALSE CRYSTAL SHE BELIEVED WAS THE THING SHE SOUGHT.
HE IS SURELY OF MY WORLD, BUT HIS PRESENCE SEEMS...
HEART-FLUTTERING? PALM-MOISTENING? LOIN-QUIVERING?
...CONVENIENT.
WAIT, PEOPLE DO THAT?
I HAVE TRAVELED TO LANDS THE LIKES OF WHICH YOU CANNOT DREAM, JANA. I AM WISE IN THE WAYS OF THE WORLD.
HMM.
THE TRICKS AND TRAPS HE USED UPON THE SHARD MEN AND MISTRESS HEL...I CAN ONLY HOPE HE KNOWS A WAY TO PROTECT MY PEOPLE...

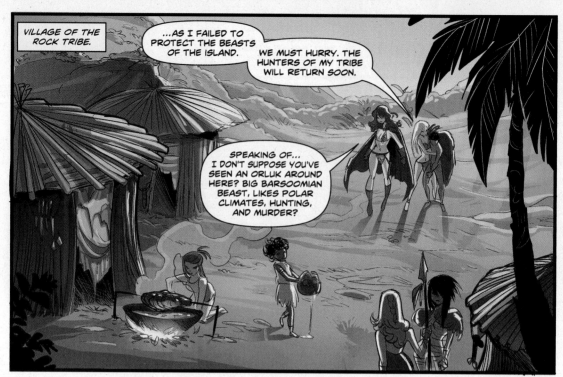

VILLAGE OF THE ROCK TRIBE.

...AS I FAILED TO PROTECT THE BEASTS OF THE ISLAND.

WE MUST HURRY. THE HUNTERS OF MY TRIBE WILL RETURN SOON.

SPEAKING OF... I DON'T SUPPOSE YOU'VE SEEN AN ORLUK AROUND HERE? BIG BARSOOMIAN BEAST, LIKES POLAR CLIMATES, HUNTING, AND MURDER?

OUTSIDERS, TWO OF THEM!

JANA, WHERE DID YOU FIND SUCH PEOPLE? YOU KNOW IT IS FORBIDDEN!

HNH... WHERE...?

REST, BEL'LOK. YOU ARE AMONG MY PEOPLE NOW.

OH, GET ON, YOU WET-EYED CALVES, GO MOON OVER SOMEONE WITHOUT A HEAD INJURY.

DON'T WORRY. I WON'T LET THEM LICK THE FRECKLES OFF OF YOU.

T...THANK YOU?

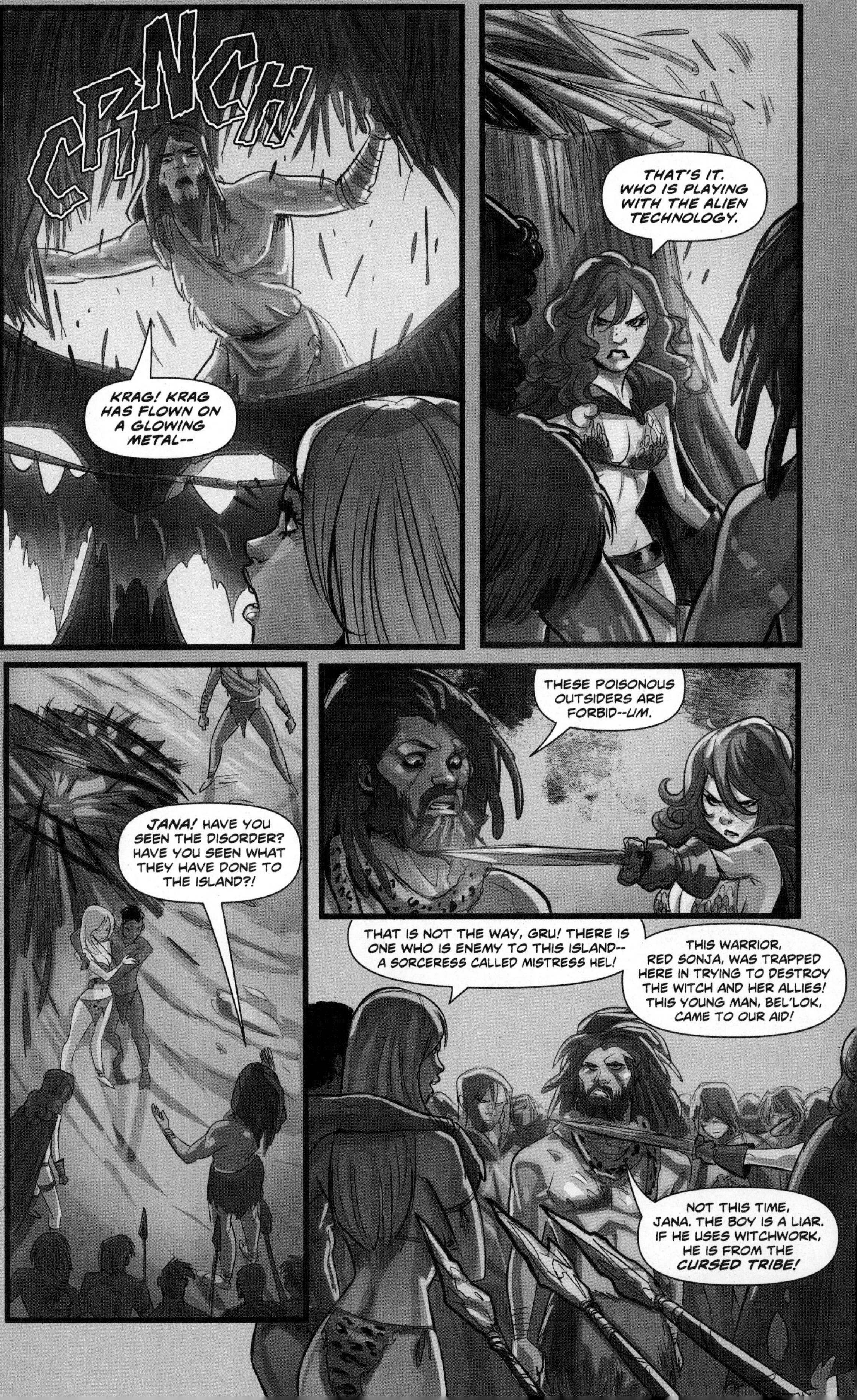
CRNCH
KRAG! KRAG HAS FLOWN ON A GLOWING METAL--
THAT'S IT. WHO IS PLAYING WITH THE ALIEN TECHNOLOGY.
JANA! HAVE YOU SEEN THE DISORDER? HAVE YOU SEEN WHAT THEY HAVE DONE TO THE ISLAND?!
THESE POISONOUS OUTSIDERS ARE FORBID--UM.
THAT IS NOT THE WAY, GRU! THERE IS ONE WHO IS ENEMY TO THIS ISLAND-- A SORCERESS CALLED MISTRESS HEL!
THIS WARRIOR, RED SONJA, WAS TRAPPED HERE IN TRYING TO DESTROY THE WITCH AND HER ALLIES! THIS YOUNG MAN, BEL'LOK, CAME TO OUR AID!
NOT THIS TIME, JANA. THE BOY IS A LIAR. IF HE USES WITCHWORK, HE IS FROM THE CURSED TRIBE!

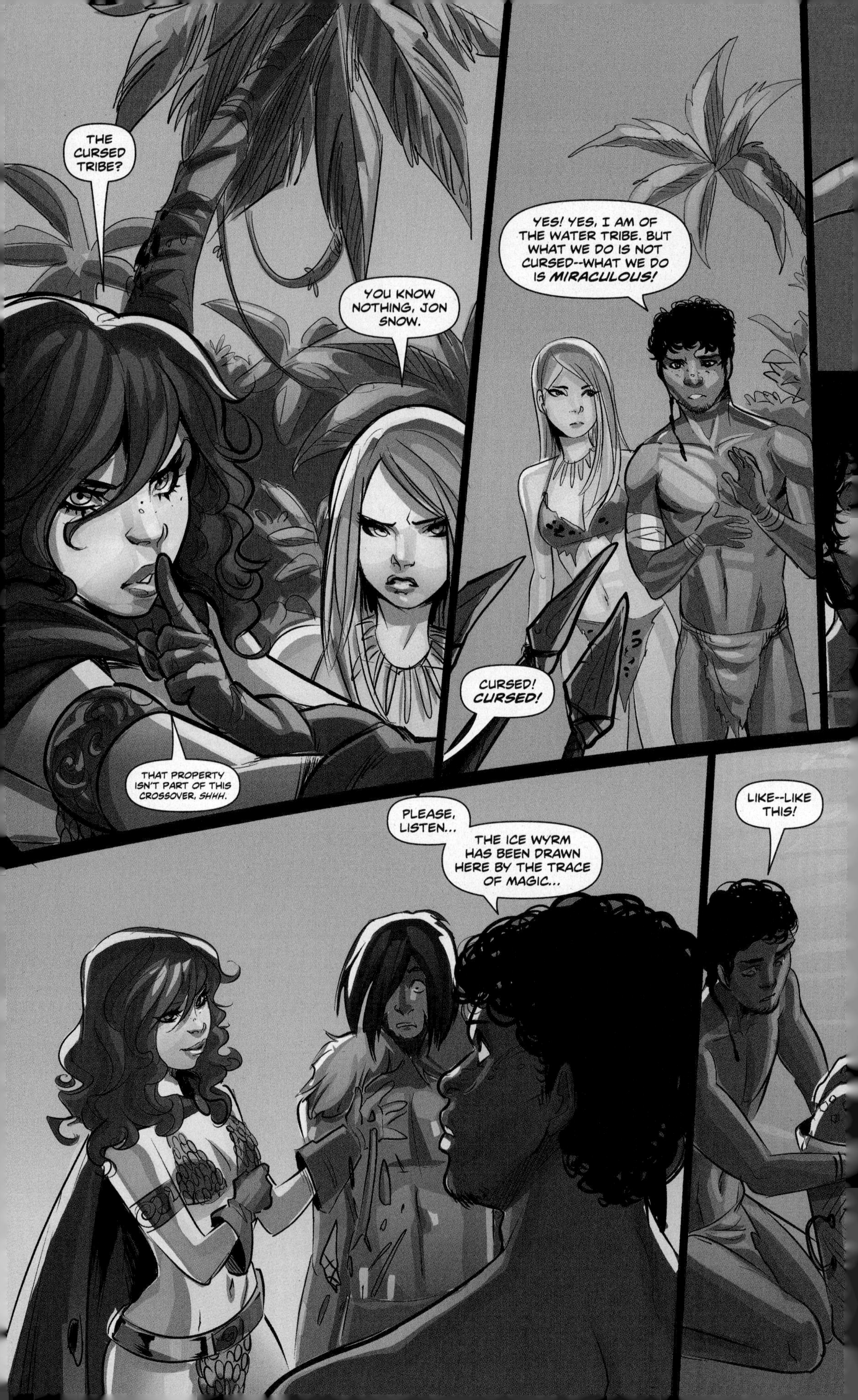
THE CURSED TRIBE?
YOU KNOW NOTHING, JON SNOW.
THAT PROPERTY ISN'T PART OF THIS CROSSOVER. SHHH.
YES! YES, I AM OF THE WATER TRIBE. BUT WHAT WE DO IS NOT CURSED--WHAT WE DO IS MIRACULOUS!
CURSED! CURSED!
PLEASE, LISTEN...
THE ICE WYRM HAS BEEN DRAWN HERE BY THE TRACE OF MAGIC...
LIKE--LIKE THIS!

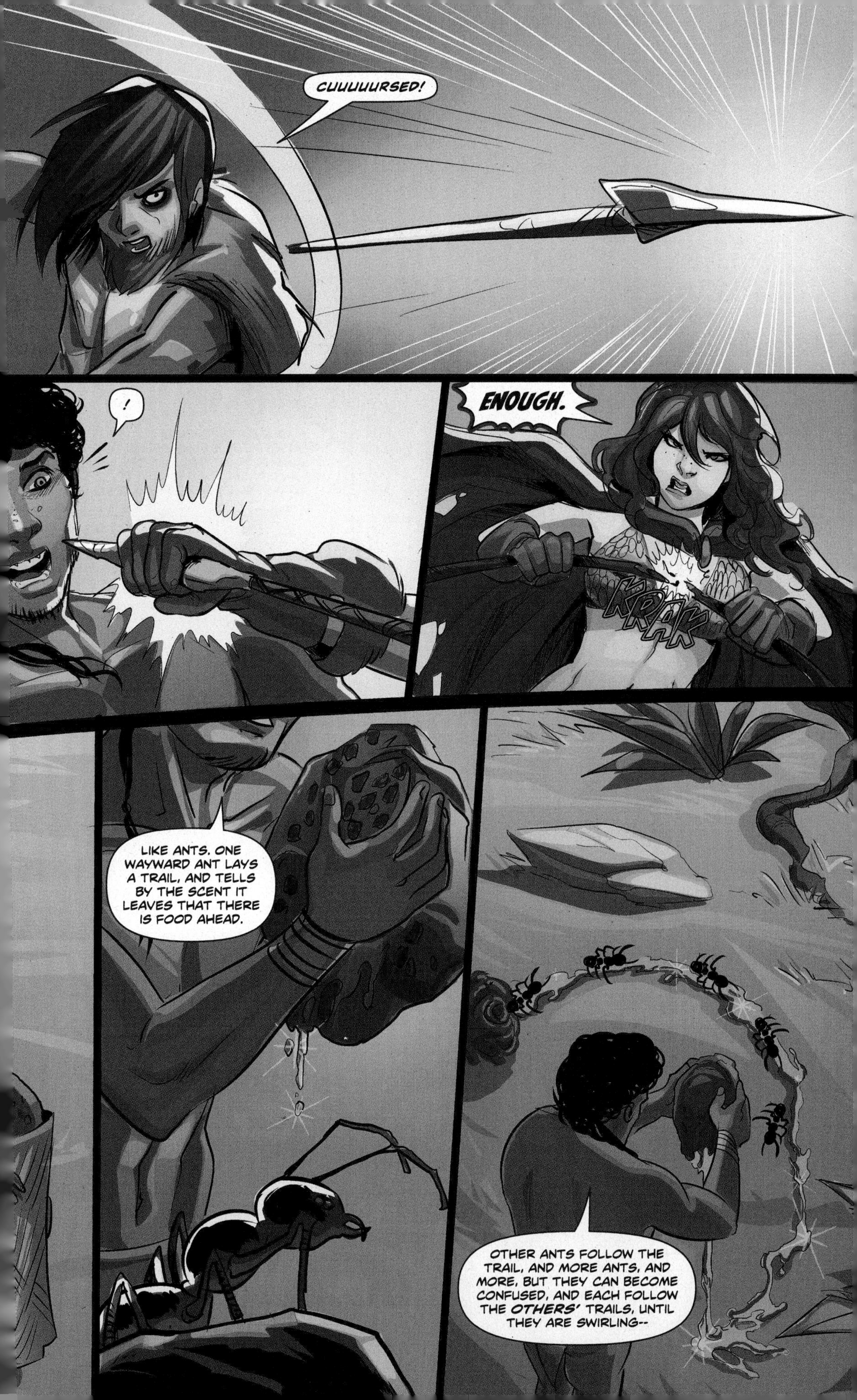
CUUUUURSED!
!
ENOUGH.
KRAK
LIKE ANTS. ONE WAYWARD ANT LAYS A TRAIL, AND TELLS BY THE SCENT IT LEAVES THAT THERE IS FOOD AHEAD.
OTHER ANTS FOLLOW THE TRAIL, AND MORE ANTS, AND MORE, BUT THEY CAN BECOME CONFUSED, AND EACH FOLLOW THE OTHERS' TRAILS, UNTIL THEY ARE SWIRLING--

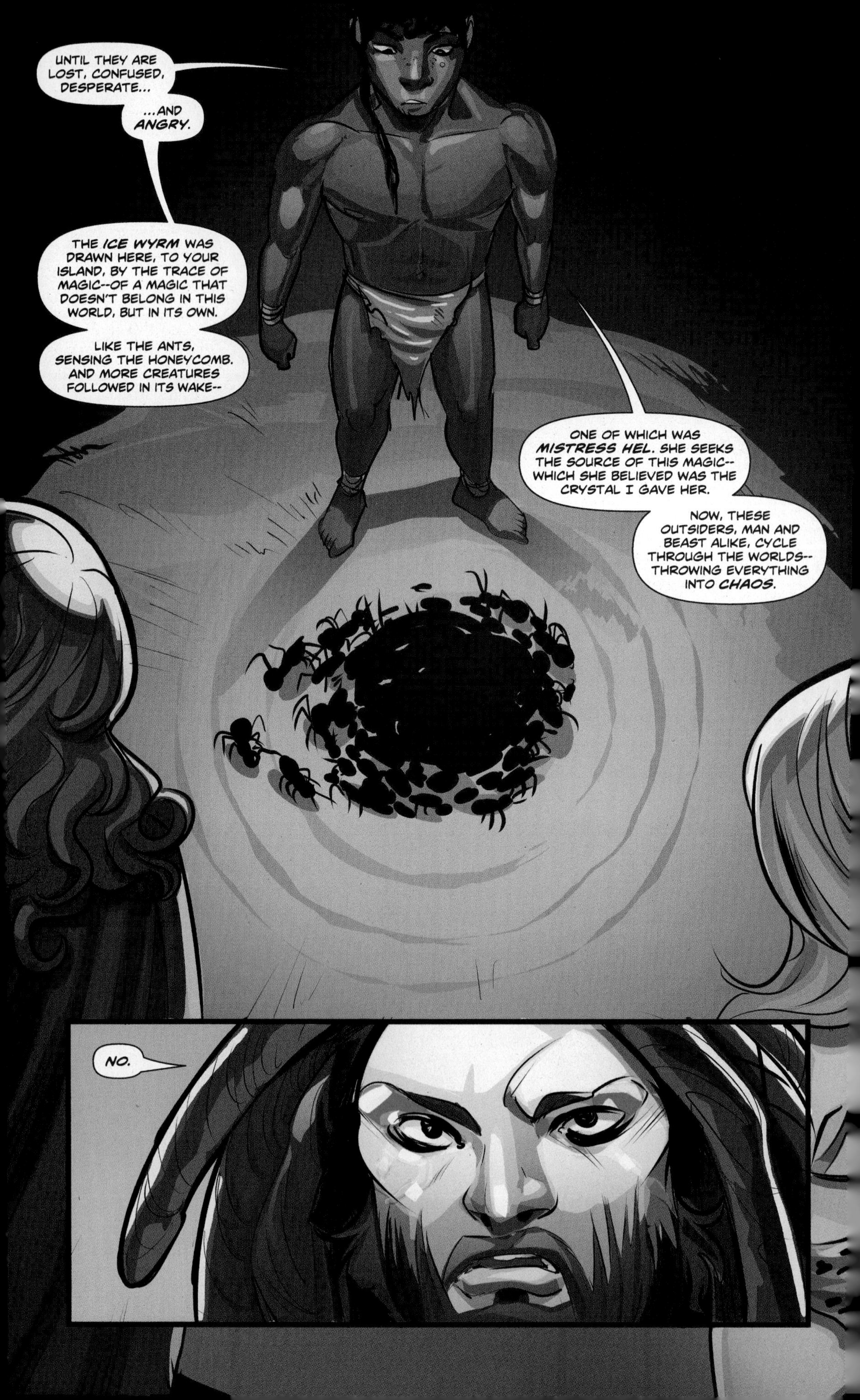
UNTIL THEY ARE LOST, CONFUSED, DESPERATE...
...AND ANGRY.
THE ICE WYRM WAS DRAWN HERE, TO YOUR ISLAND, BY THE TRACE OF MAGIC--OF A MAGIC THAT DOESN'T BELONG IN THIS WORLD, BUT IN ITS OWN.
LIKE THE ANTS, SENSING THE HONEYCOMB. AND MORE CREATURES FOLLOWED IN ITS WAKE--
ONE OF WHICH WAS MISTRESS HEL. SHE SEEKS THE SOURCE OF THIS MAGIC--WHICH SHE BELIEVED WAS THE CRYSTAL I GAVE HER.
NOW, THESE OUTSIDERS, MAN AND BEAST ALIKE, CYCLE THROUGH THE WORLDS--THROWING EVERYTHING INTO CHAOS.
NO.

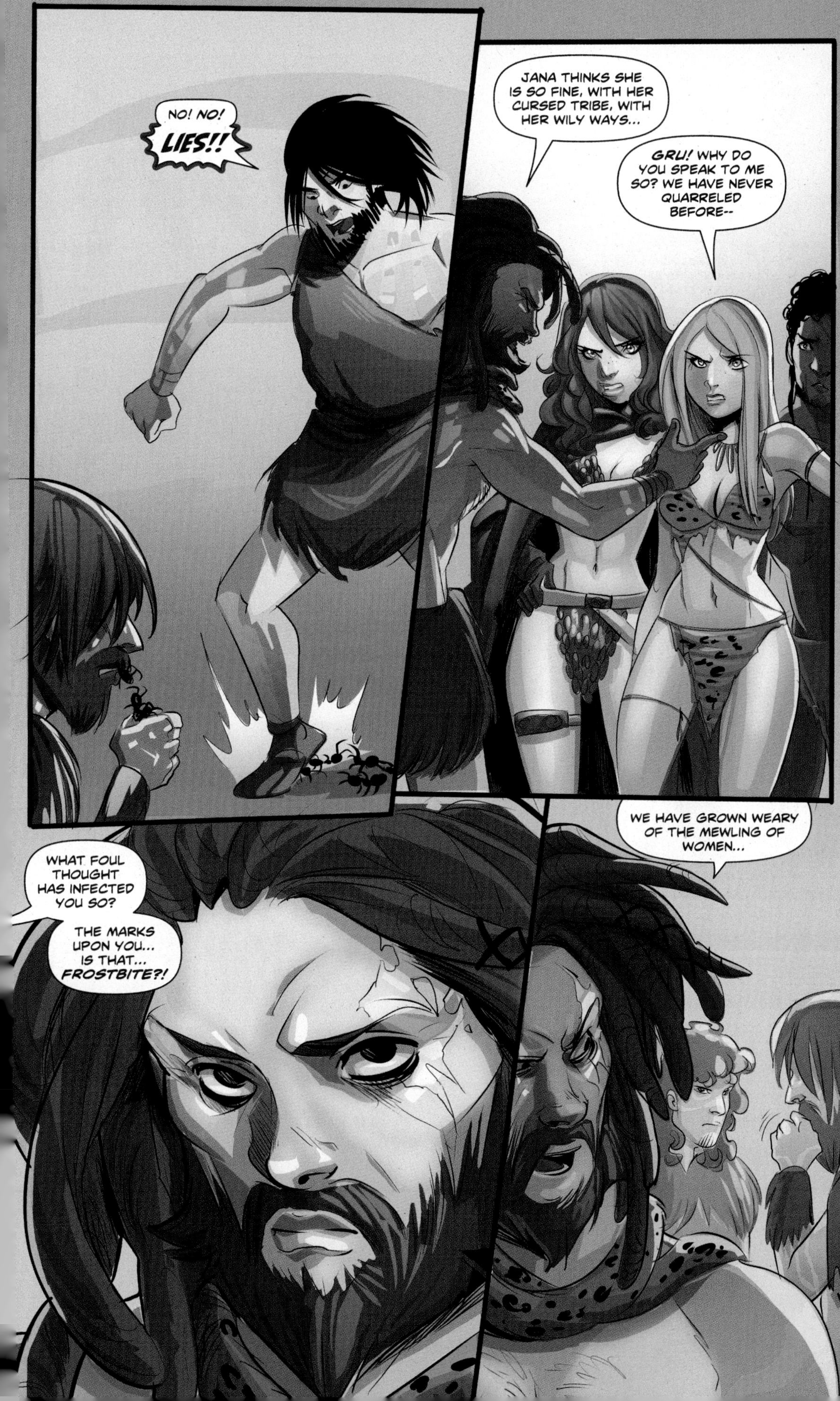
NO! NO!
LIES!!
JANA THINKS SHE IS SO FINE, WITH HER CURSED TRIBE, WITH HER WILY WAYS...
GRU! WHY DO YOU SPEAK TO ME SO? WE HAVE NEVER QUARRELED BEFORE--
WHAT FOUL THOUGHT HAS INFECTED YOU SO?
THE MARKS UPON YOU... IS THAT... FROSTBITE?!
WE HAVE GROWN WEARY OF THE MEWLING OF WOMEN...

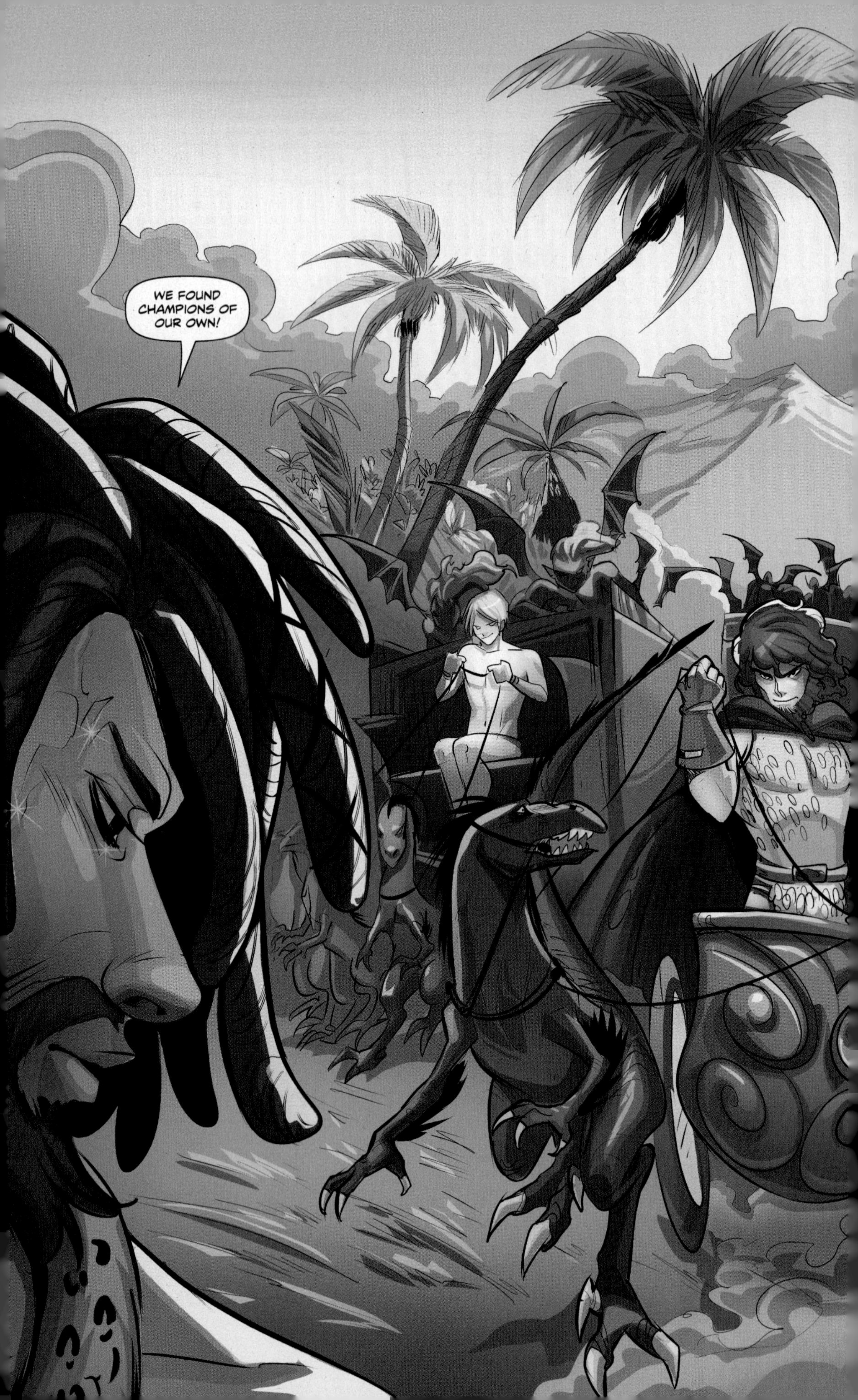
WE FOUND CHAMPIONS OF OUR OWN!

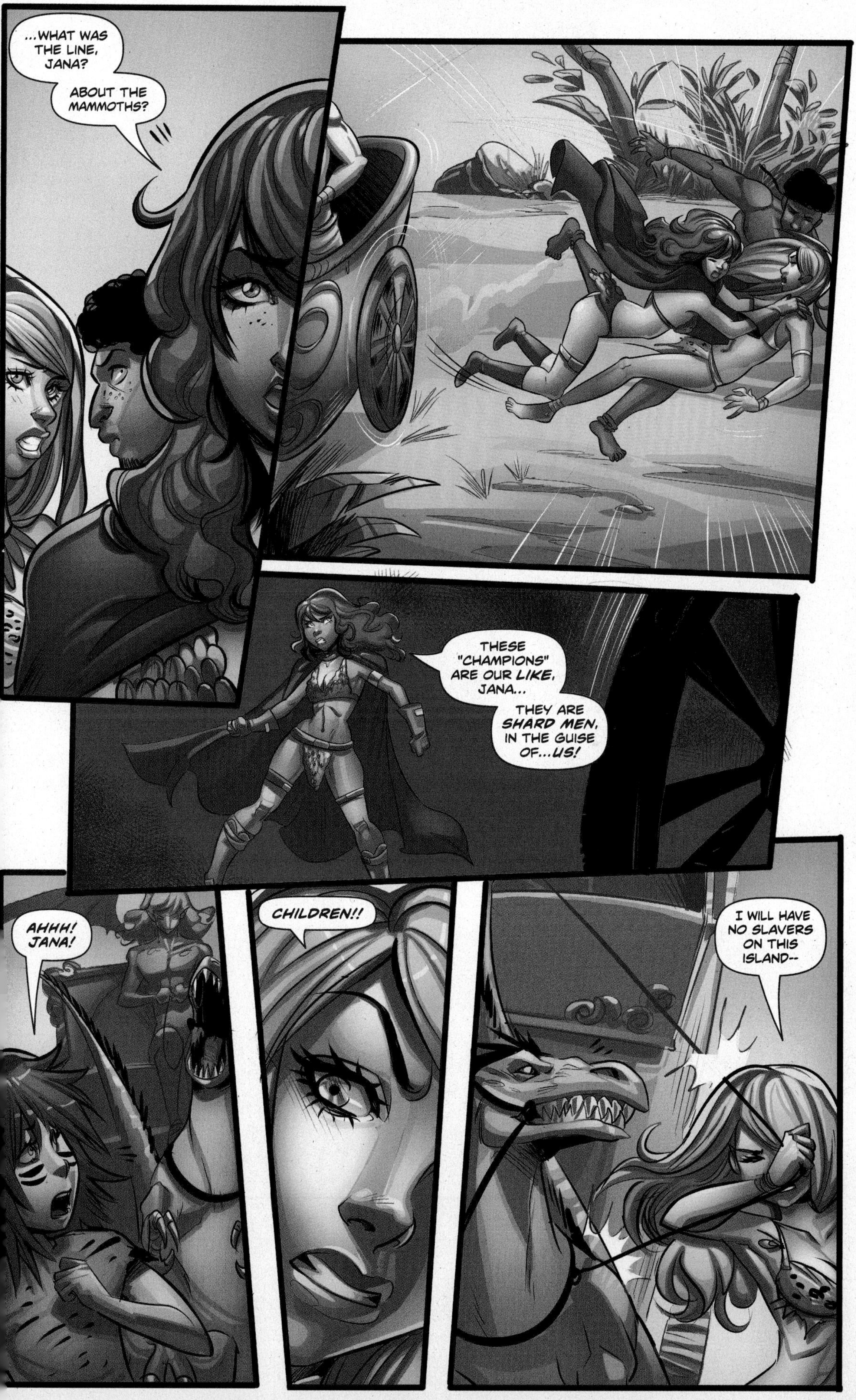
...WHAT WAS THE LINE, JANA?
ABOUT THE MAMMOTHS?
THESE "CHAMPIONS" ARE OUR LIKE, JANA...
THEY ARE SHARD MEN, IN THE GUISE OF...US!
AHHH! JANA!
CHILDREN!!
I WILL HAVE NO SLAVERS ON THIS ISLAND--

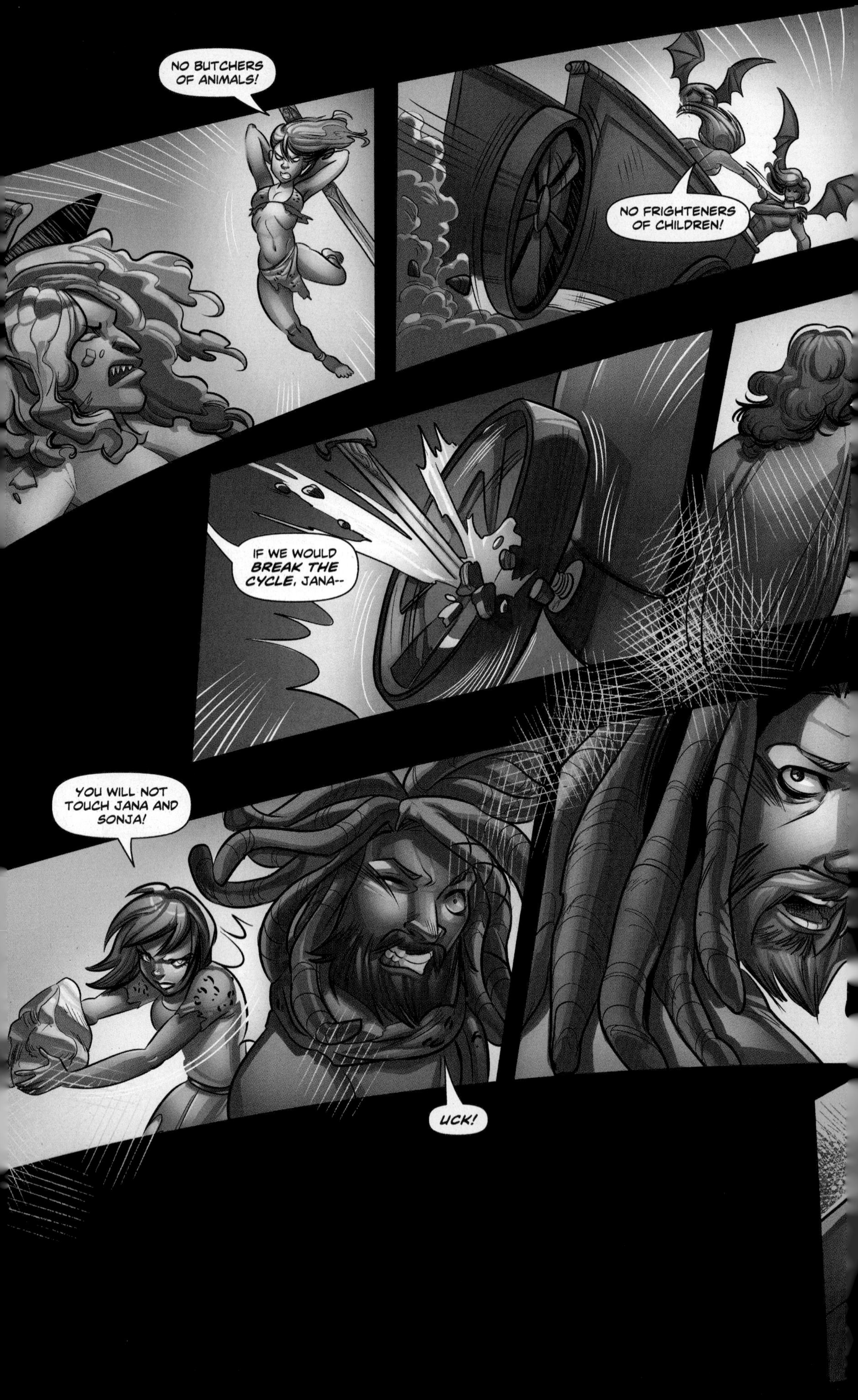
NO BUTCHERS OF ANIMALS!
NO FRIGHTENERS OF CHILDREN!
IF WE WOULD BREAK THE CYCLE, JANA--
YOU WILL NOT TOUCH JANA AND SONJA!
UCK!

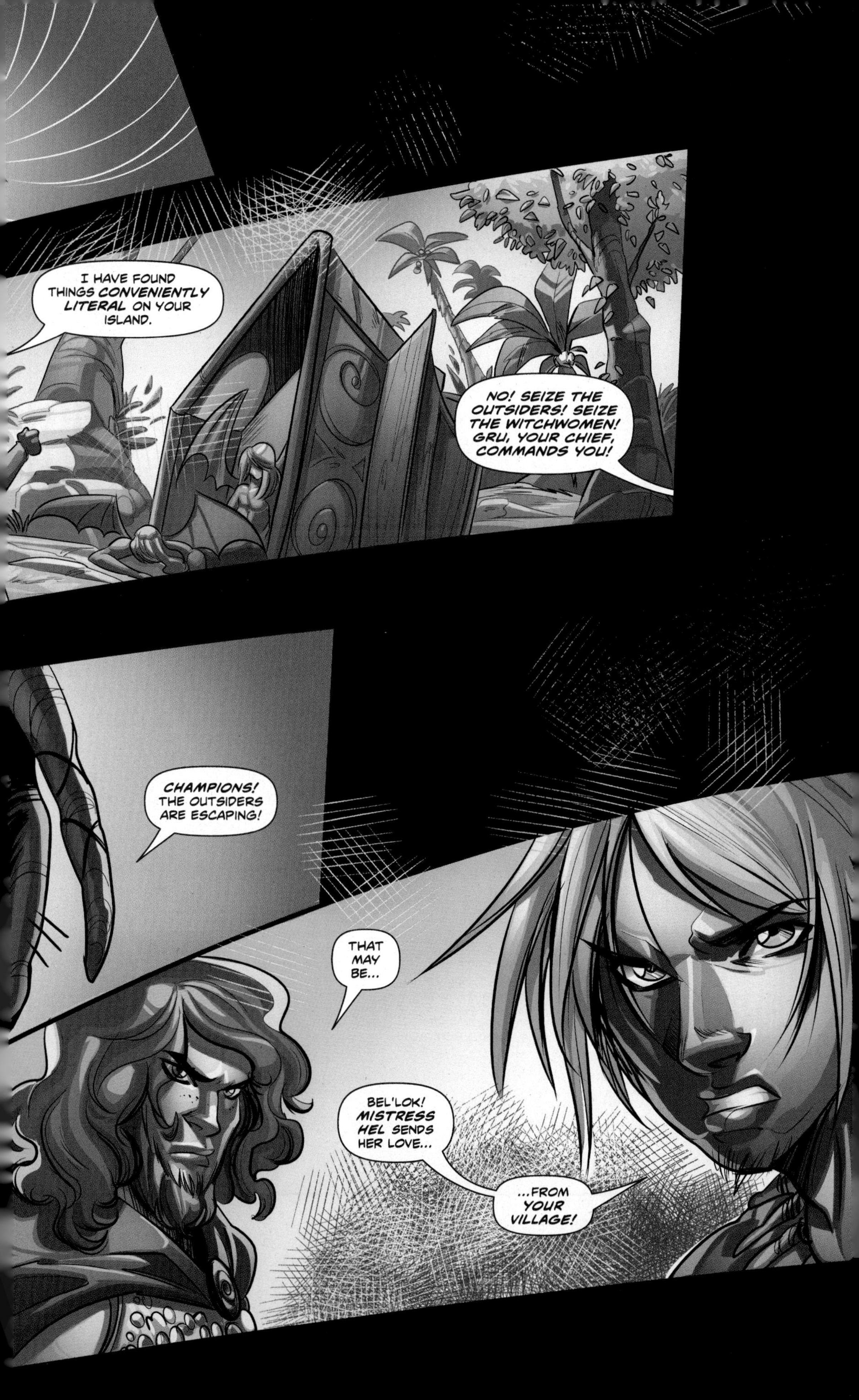
I HAVE FOUND THINGS CONVENIENTLY LITERAL ON YOUR ISLAND.
NO! SEIZE THE OUTSIDERS! SEIZE THE WITCHWOMEN! GRU, YOUR CHIEF, COMMANDS YOU!
CHAMPIONS! THE OUTSIDERS ARE ESCAPING!
THAT MAY BE...
BEL'LOK! MISTRESS HEL SENDS HER LOVE...
...FROM YOUR VILLAGE!

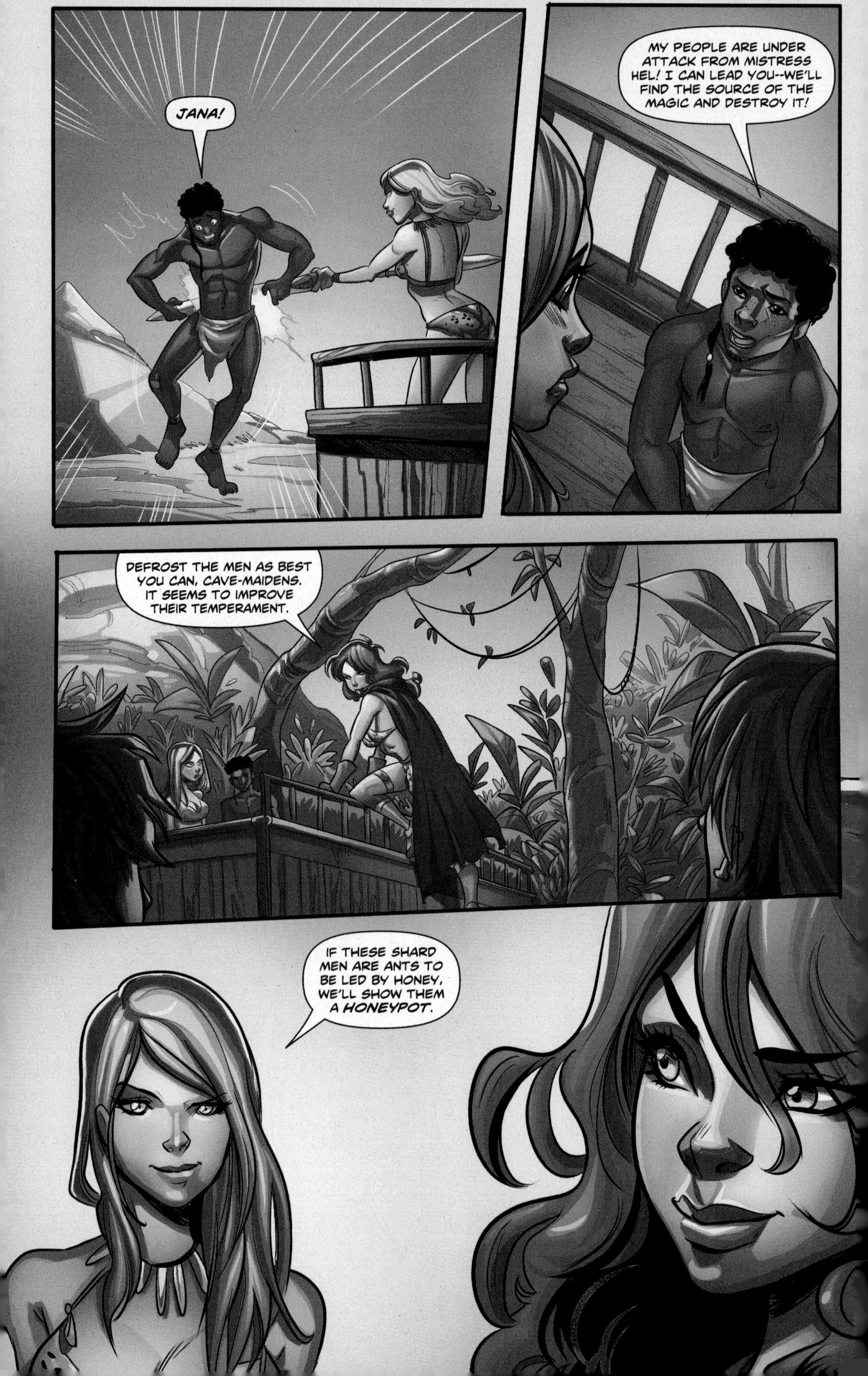
JANA!
MY PEOPLE ARE UNDER ATTACK FROM MISTRESS HEL! I CAN LEAD YOU--WE'LL FIND THE SOURCE OF THE MAGIC AND DESTROY IT!
DEFROST THE MEN AS BEST YOU CAN, CAVE-MAIDENS. IT SEEMS TO IMPROVE THEIR TEMPERAMENT.
IF THESE SHARD MEN ARE ANTS TO BE LED BY HONEY, WE'LL SHOW THEM A *HONEYPOT*.

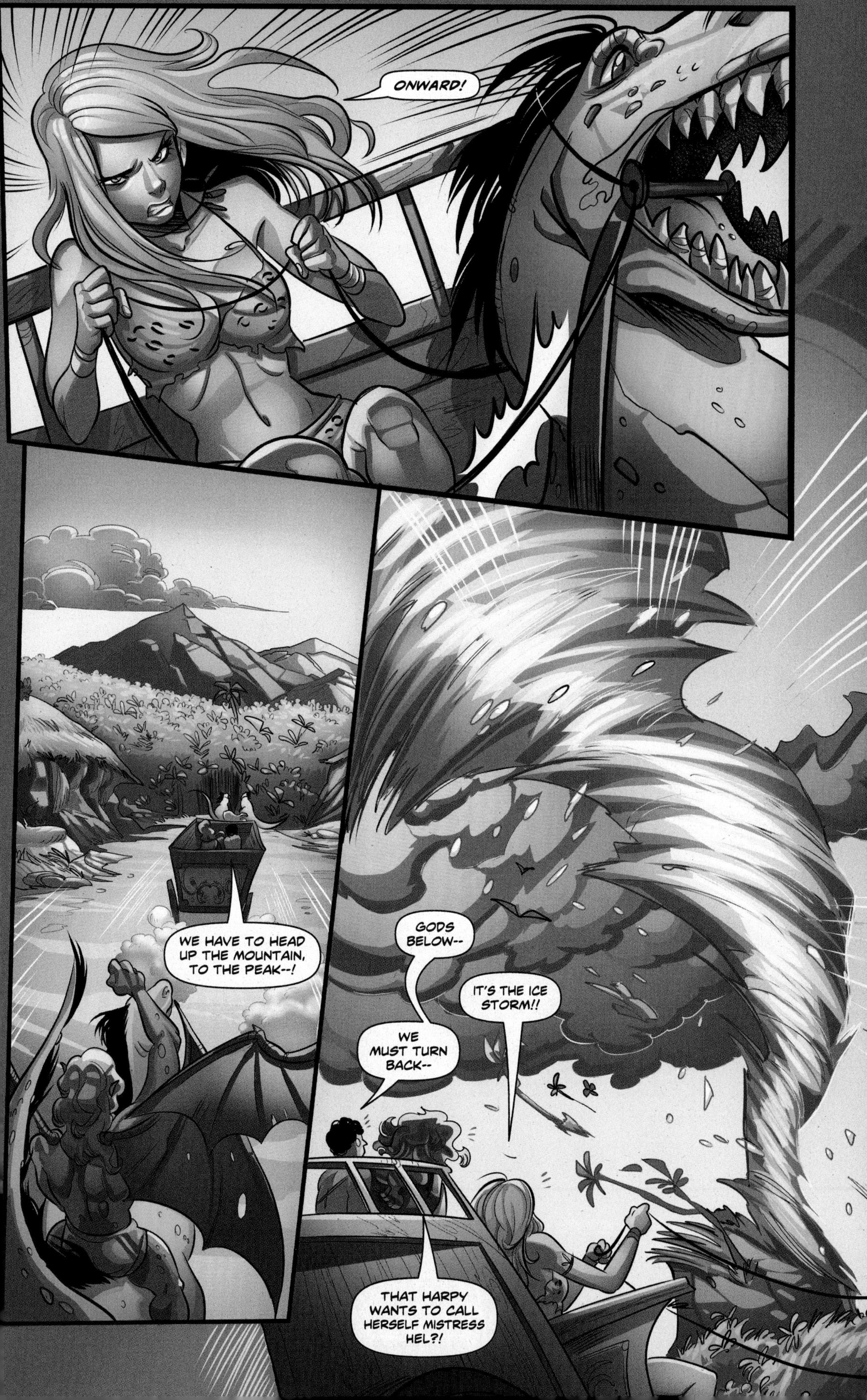

ONWARD!
WE HAVE TO HEAD UP THE MOUNTAIN, TO THE PEAK--!
GODS BELOW--
WE MUST TURN BACK--
IT'S THE ICE STORM!!
THAT HARPY WANTS TO CALL HERSELF MISTRESS HEL?!

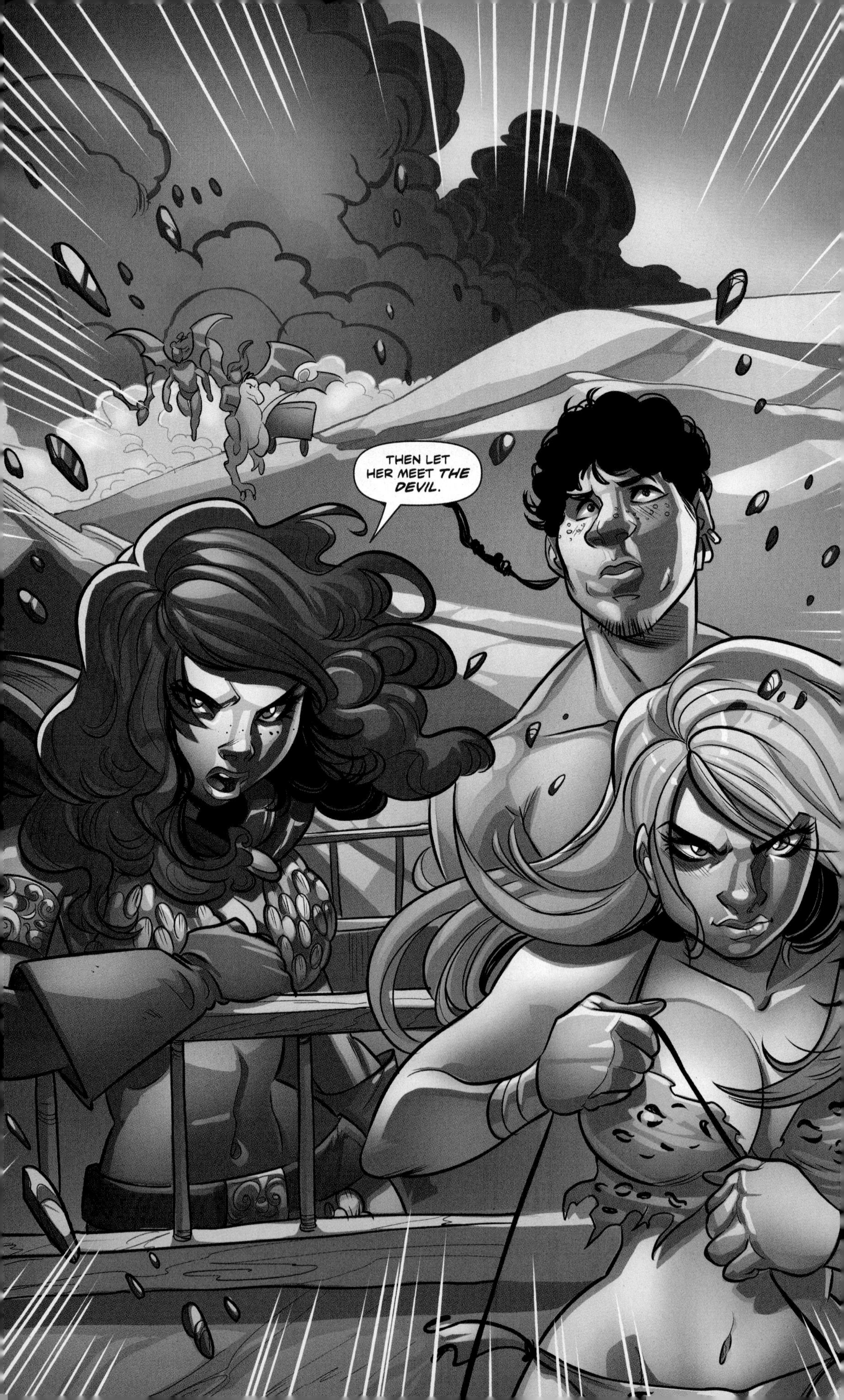
THEN LET HER MEET THE DEVIL.

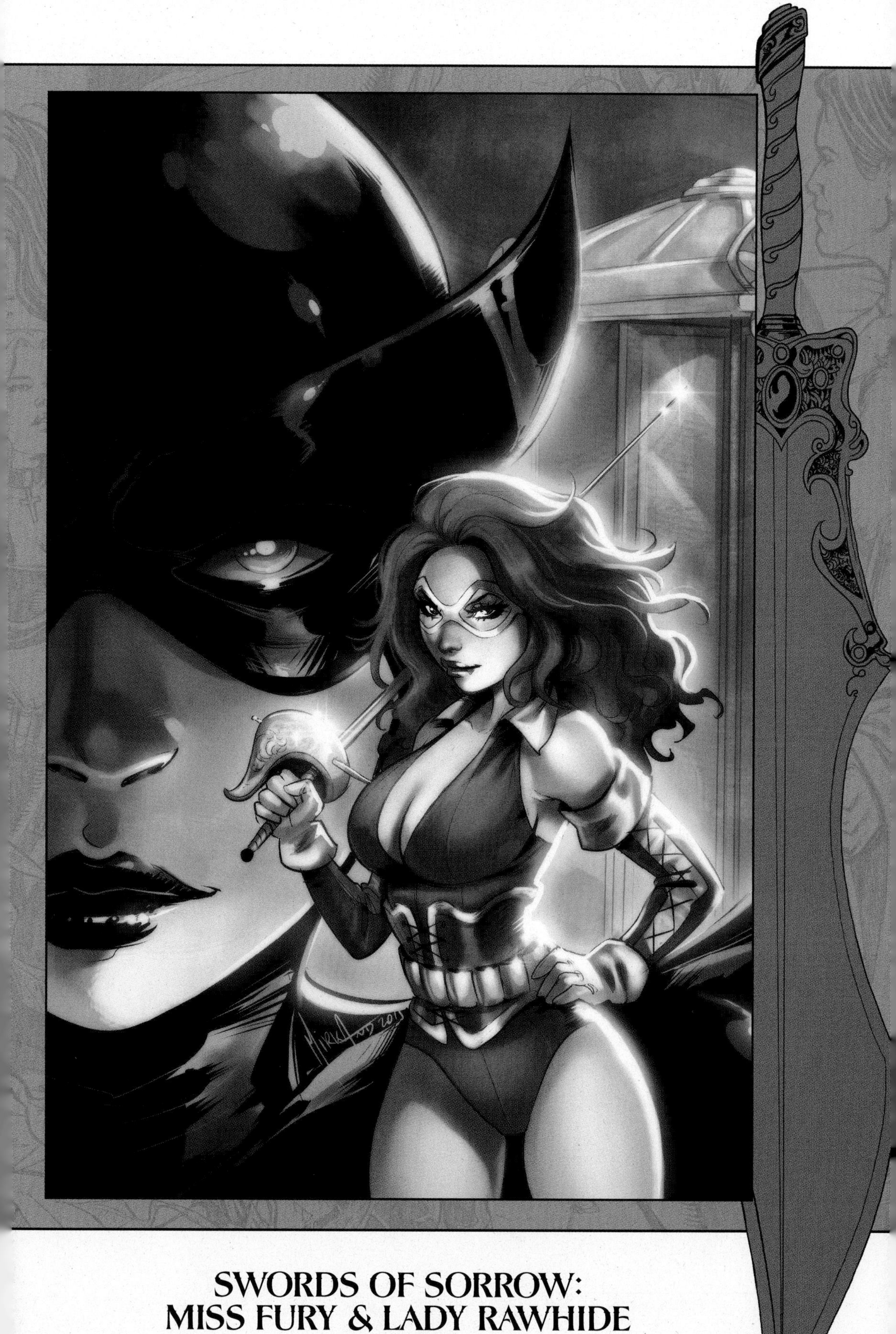

SWORDS OF SORROW: MISS FURY & LADY RAWHIDE
ONE-SHOT

written by MIKKI KENDALL illustrated by RONILSON FREIRE
colored by KRISTY SWAN lettered by ERICA SCHULTZ

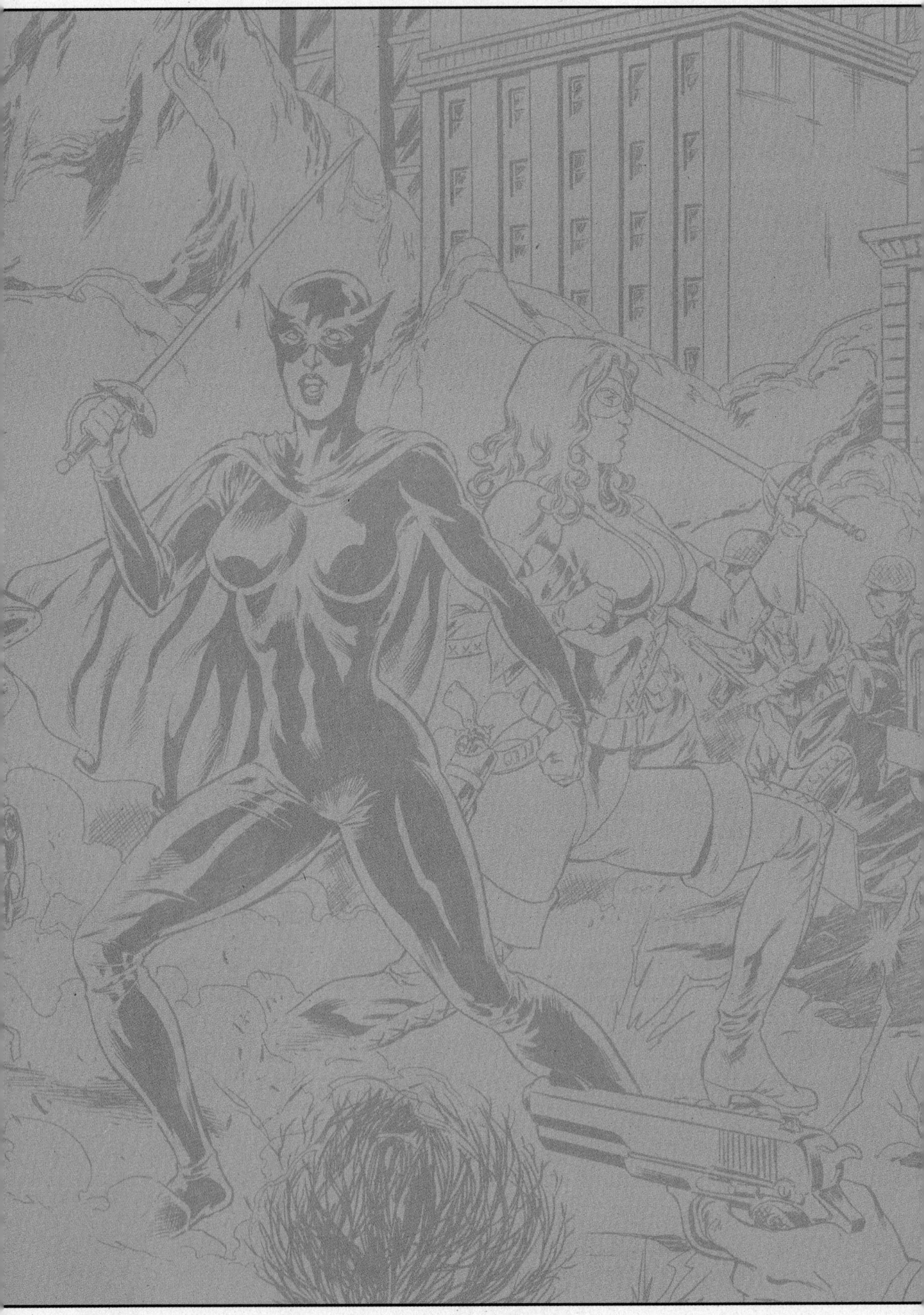

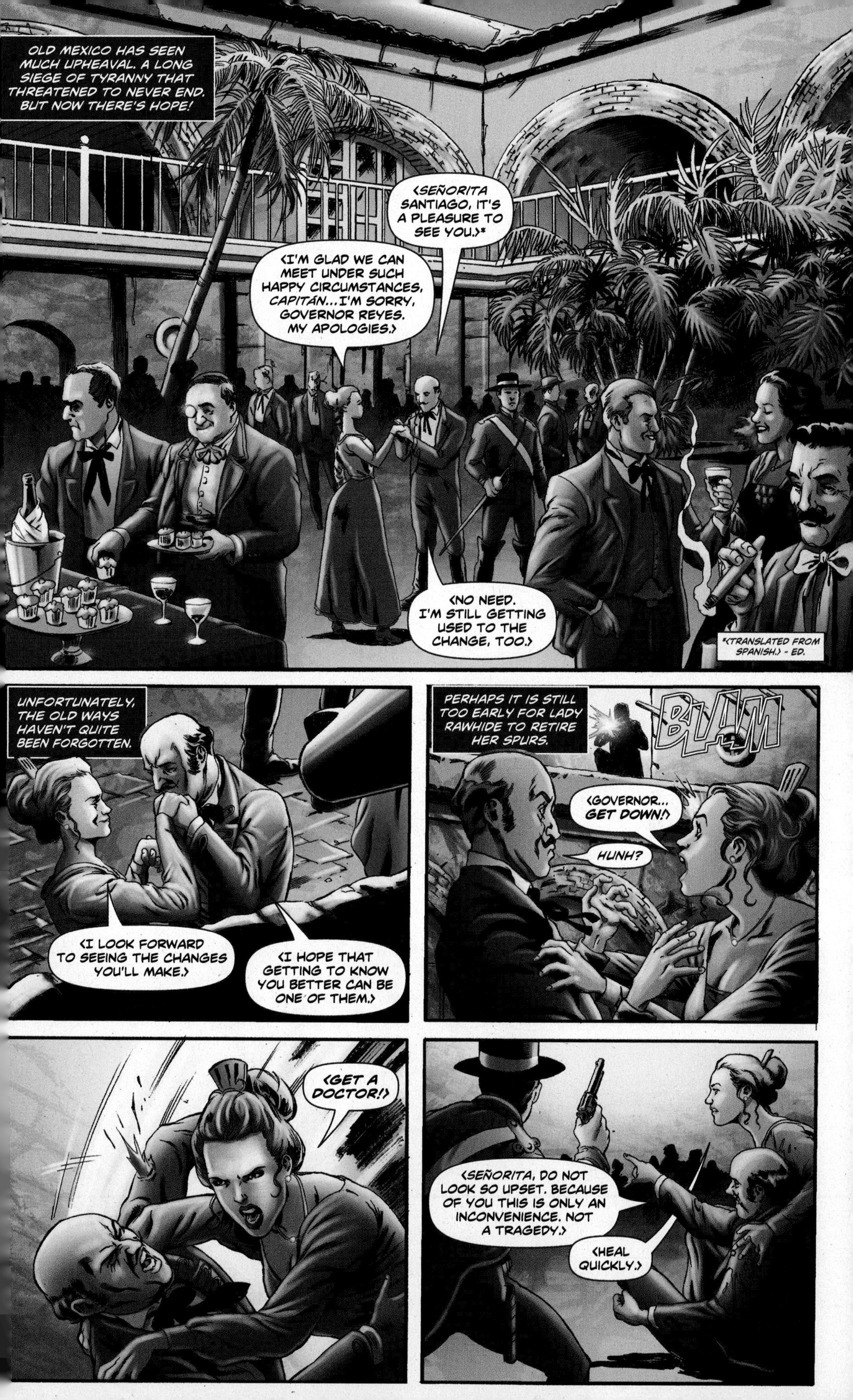
OLD MEXICO HAS SEEN MUCH UPHEAVAL. A LONG SIEGE OF TYRANNY THAT THREATENED TO NEVER END. BUT NOW THERE'S HOPE!
‹SEÑORITA SANTIAGO, IT'S A PLEASURE TO SEE YOU.›*
‹I'M GLAD WE CAN MEET UNDER SUCH HAPPY CIRCUMSTANCES, CAPITÁN... I'M SORRY, GOVERNOR REYES. MY APOLOGIES.›
‹NO NEED. I'M STILL GETTING USED TO THE CHANGE, TOO.›
*‹TRANSLATED FROM SPANISH.› - ED.
UNFORTUNATELY, THE OLD WAYS HAVEN'T QUITE BEEN FORGOTTEN.
‹I LOOK FORWARD TO SEEING THE CHANGES YOU'LL MAKE.›
‹I HOPE THAT GETTING TO KNOW YOU BETTER CAN BE ONE OF THEM.›
PERHAPS IT IS STILL TOO EARLY FOR LADY RAWHIDE TO RETIRE HER SPURS.
BLAM
‹GOVERNOR... GET DOWN!›
HUNH?
‹GET A DOCTOR!›
‹SEÑORITA, DO NOT LOOK SO UPSET. BECAUSE OF YOU THIS IS ONLY AN INCONVENIENCE. NOT A TRAGEDY.›
‹HEAL QUICKLY.›

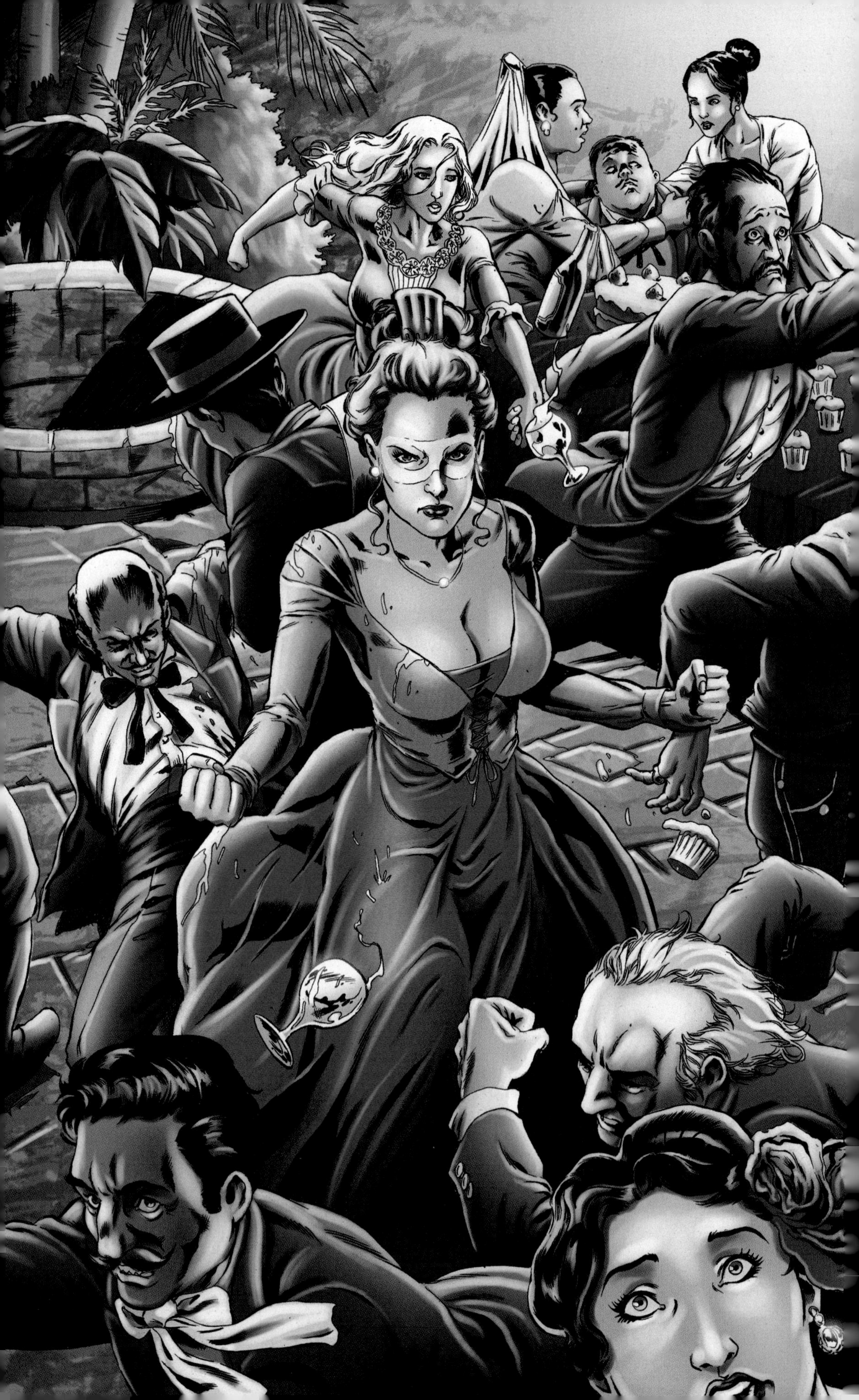

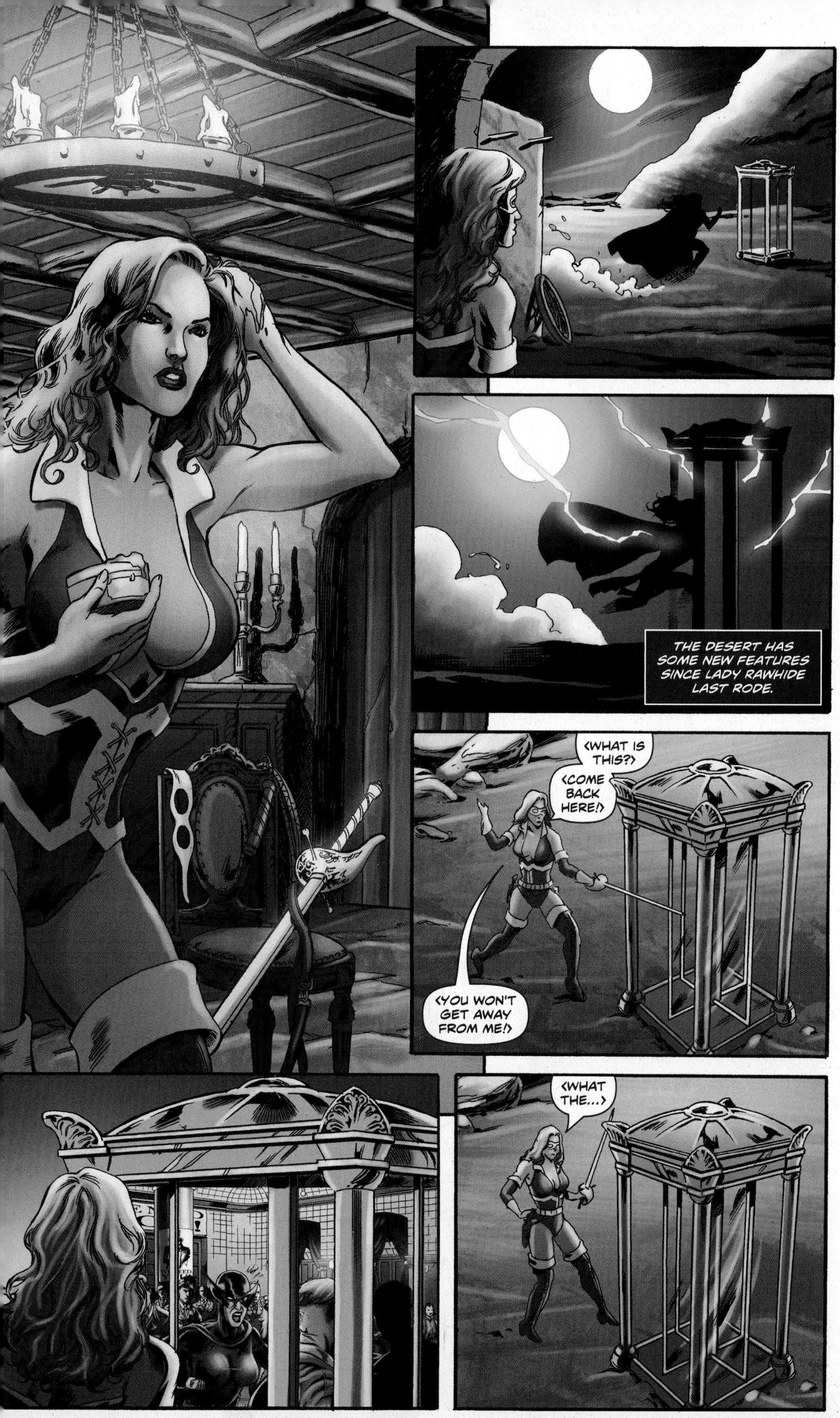
THE DESERT HAS SOME NEW FEATURES SINCE LADY RAWHIDE LAST RODE.
<WHAT IS THIS?>
<COME BACK HERE!>
<YOU WON'T GET AWAY FROM ME!>
<WHAT THE...>

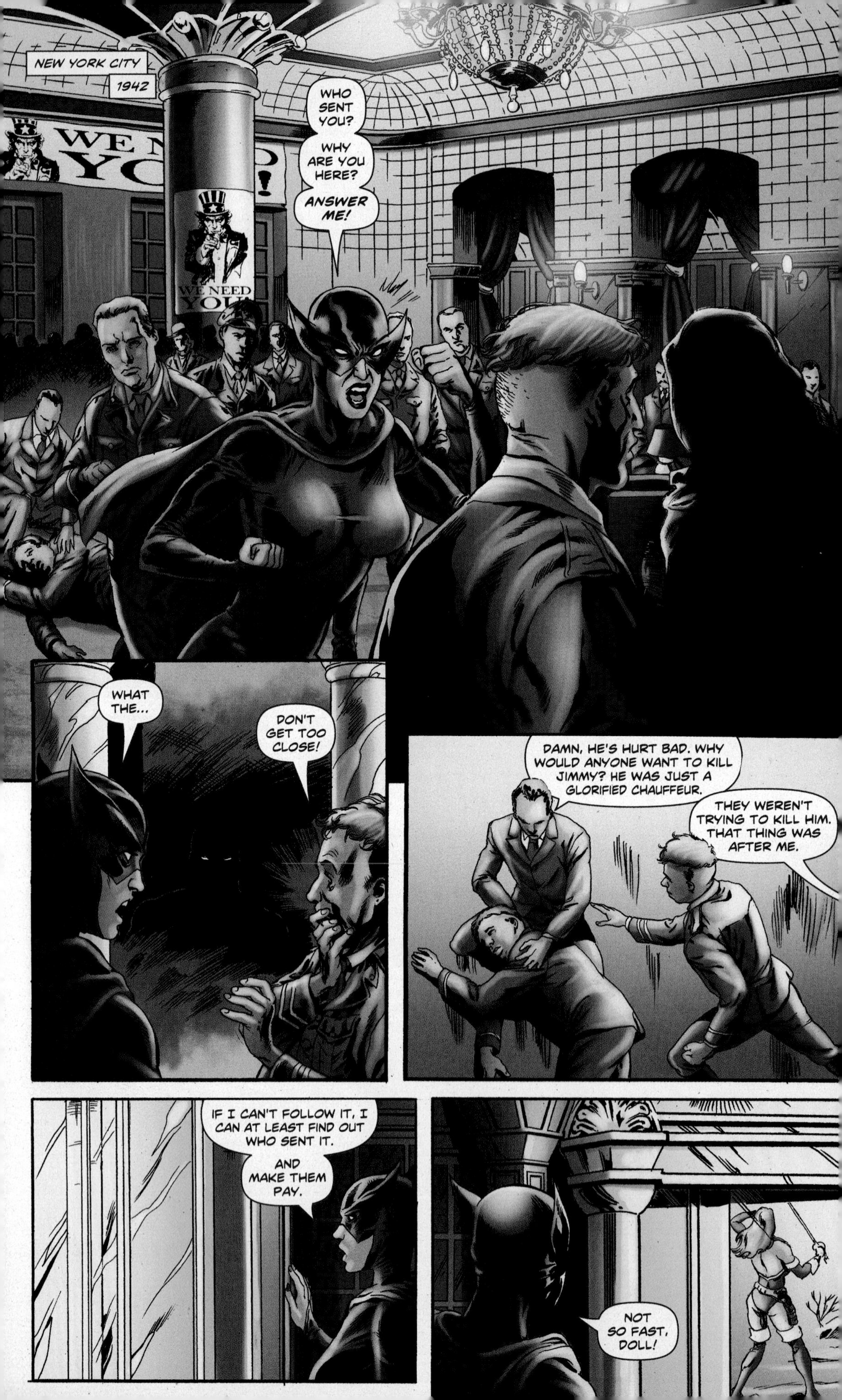
NEW YORK CITY
1942
WE NEED YOU!
WE NEED YOU
WHO SENT YOU?
WHY ARE YOU HERE?
ANSWER ME!
WHAT THE...
DON'T GET TOO CLOSE!
DAMN, HE'S HURT BAD. WHY WOULD ANYONE WANT TO KILL JIMMY? HE WAS JUST A GLORIFIED CHAUFFEUR.
THEY WEREN'T TRYING TO KILL HIM. THAT THING WAS AFTER ME.
IF I CAN'T FOLLOW IT, I CAN AT LEAST FIND OUT WHO SENT IT.
AND MAKE THEM PAY.
NOT SO FAST, DOLL!

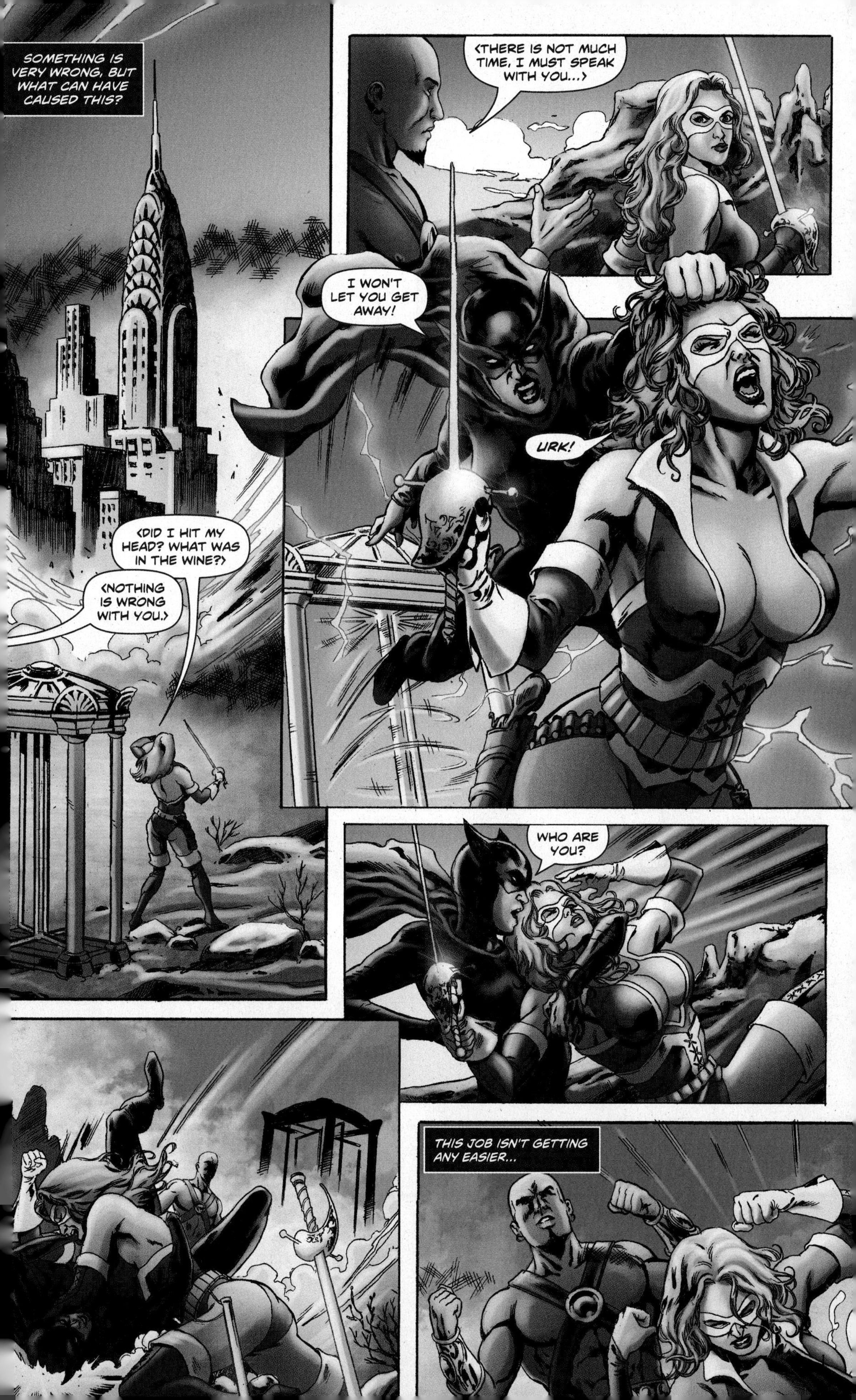
SOMETHING IS VERY WRONG, BUT WHAT CAN HAVE CAUSED THIS?
<THERE IS NOT MUCH TIME, I MUST SPEAK WITH YOU...>
I WON'T LET YOU GET AWAY!
URK!
<DID I HIT MY HEAD? WHAT WAS IN THE WINE?>
<NOTHING IS WRONG WITH YOU.>
WHO ARE YOU?
THIS JOB ISN'T GETTING ANY EASIER...

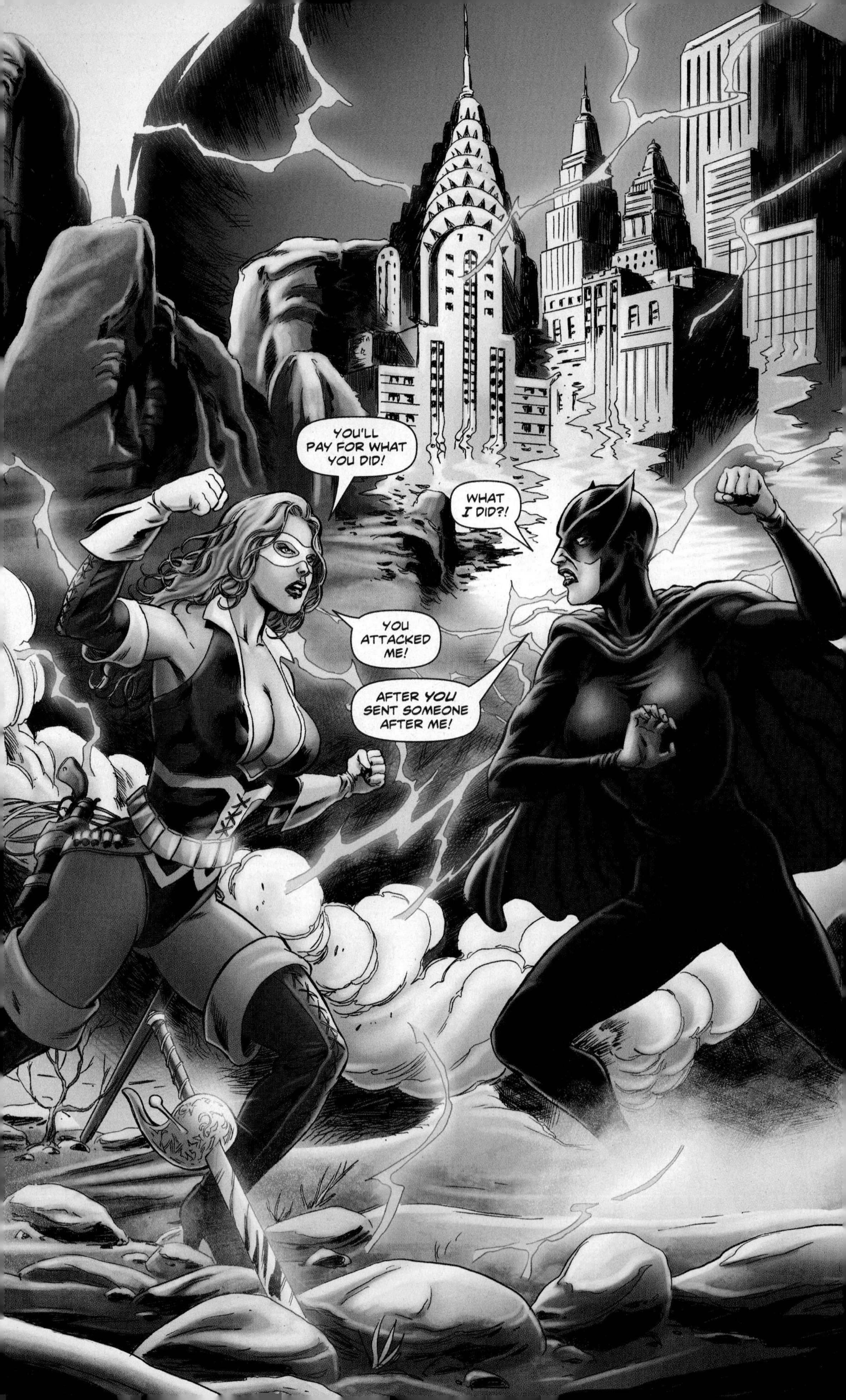
YOU'LL PAY FOR WHAT YOU DID!
WHAT I DID?!
YOU ATTACKED ME!
AFTER YOU SENT SOMEONE AFTER ME!

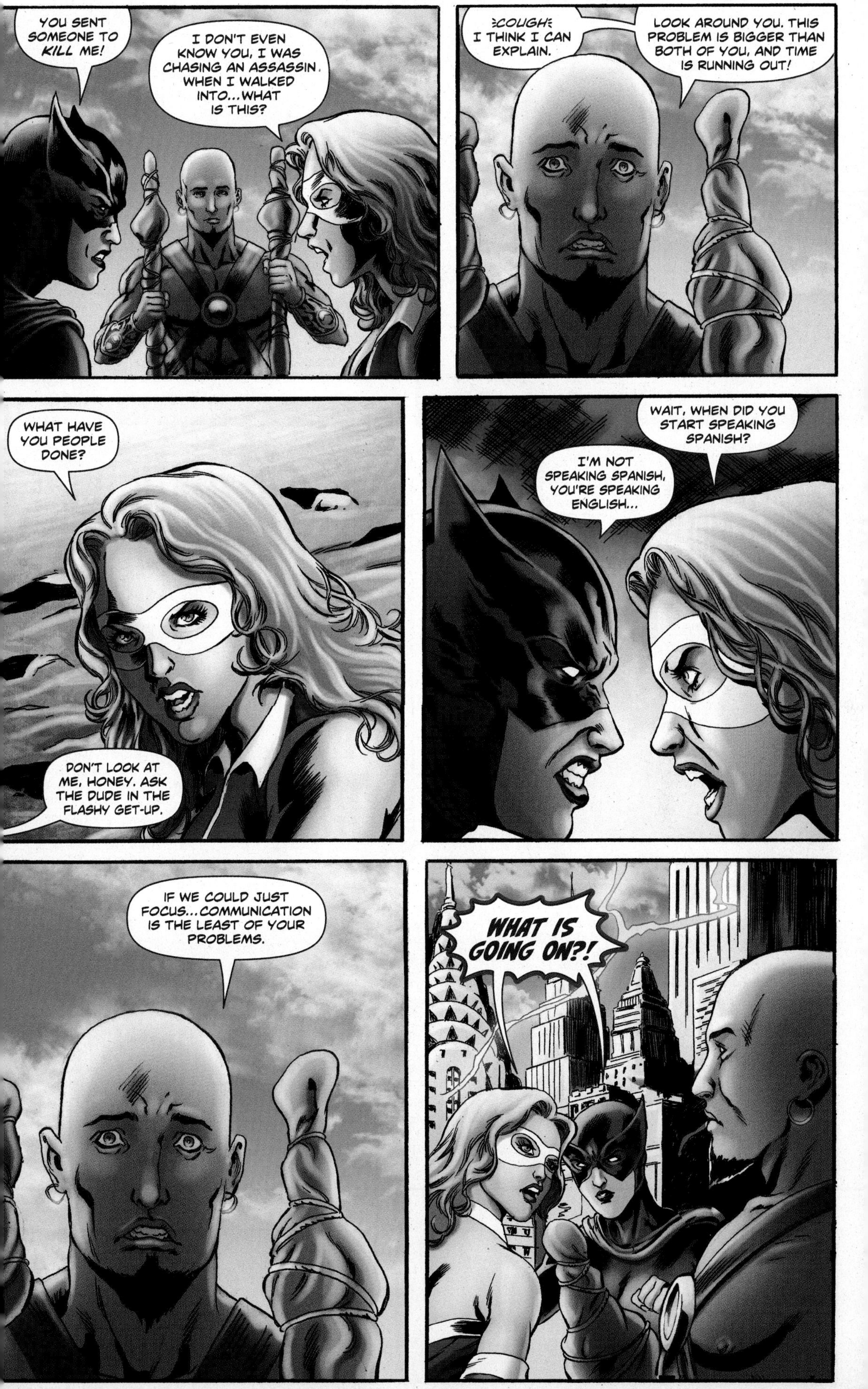
YOU SENT SOMEONE TO KILL ME!
I DON'T EVEN KNOW YOU, I WAS CHASING AN ASSASSIN. WHEN I WALKED INTO...WHAT IS THIS?
COUGH I THINK I CAN EXPLAIN.
LOOK AROUND YOU. THIS PROBLEM IS BIGGER THAN BOTH OF YOU, AND TIME IS RUNNING OUT!
WHAT HAVE YOU PEOPLE DONE?
DON'T LOOK AT ME, HONEY. ASK THE DUDE IN THE FLASHY GET-UP.
WAIT, WHEN DID YOU START SPEAKING SPANISH?
I'M NOT SPEAKING SPANISH, YOU'RE SPEAKING ENGLISH...
IF WE COULD JUST FOCUS...COMMUNICATION IS THE LEAST OF YOUR PROBLEMS.
WHAT IS GOING ON?!

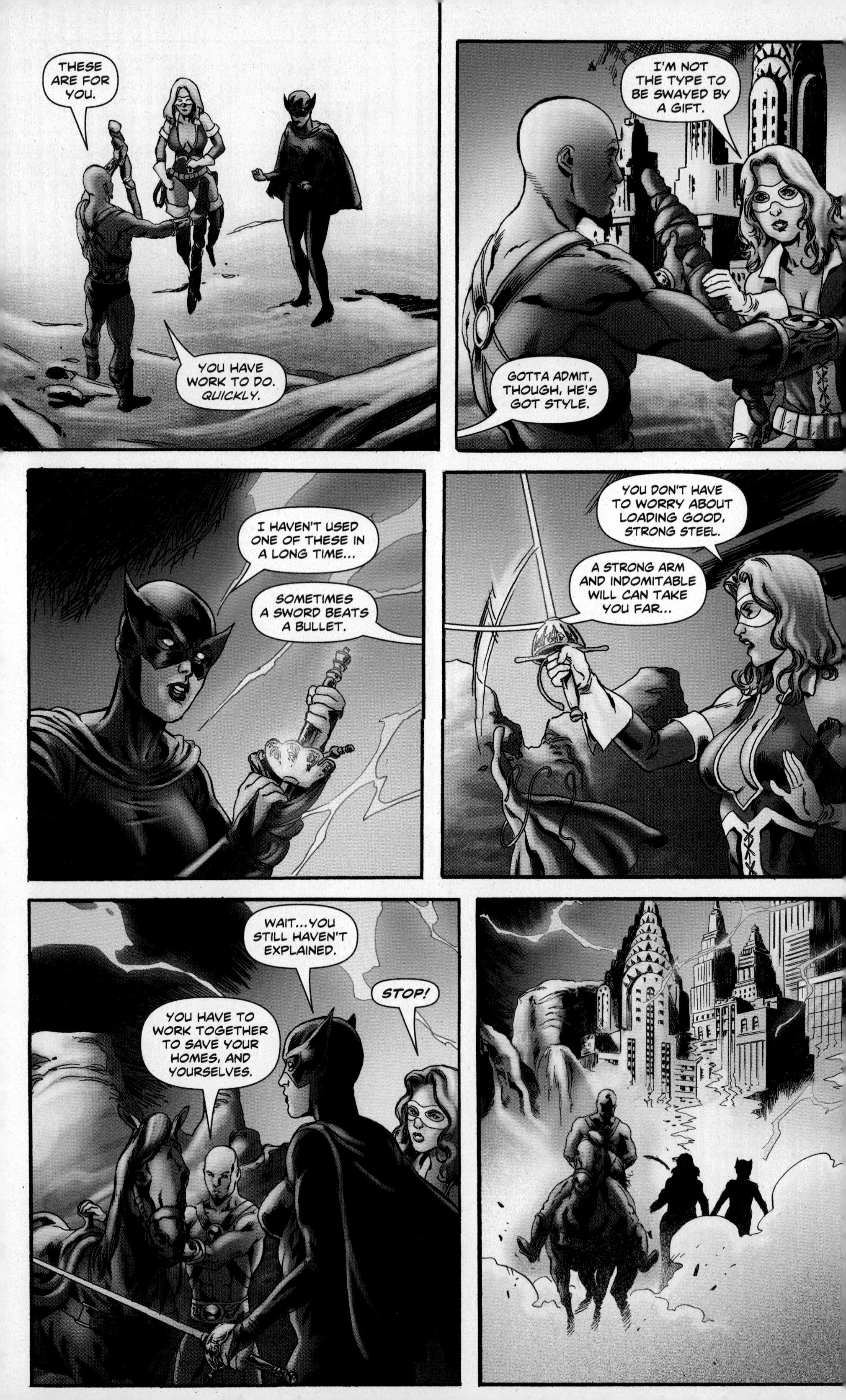
THESE ARE FOR YOU.
YOU HAVE WORK TO DO. QUICKLY.
I'M NOT THE TYPE TO BE SWAYED BY A GIFT.
GOTTA ADMIT, THOUGH, HE'S GOT STYLE.
I HAVEN'T USED ONE OF THESE IN A LONG TIME...
SOMETIMES A SWORD BEATS A BULLET.
YOU DON'T HAVE TO WORRY ABOUT LOADING GOOD, STRONG STEEL.
A STRONG ARM AND INDOMITABLE WILL CAN TAKE YOU FAR...
WAIT...YOU STILL HAVEN'T EXPLAINED.
STOP!
YOU HAVE TO WORK TOGETHER TO SAVE YOUR HOMES, AND YOURSELVES.

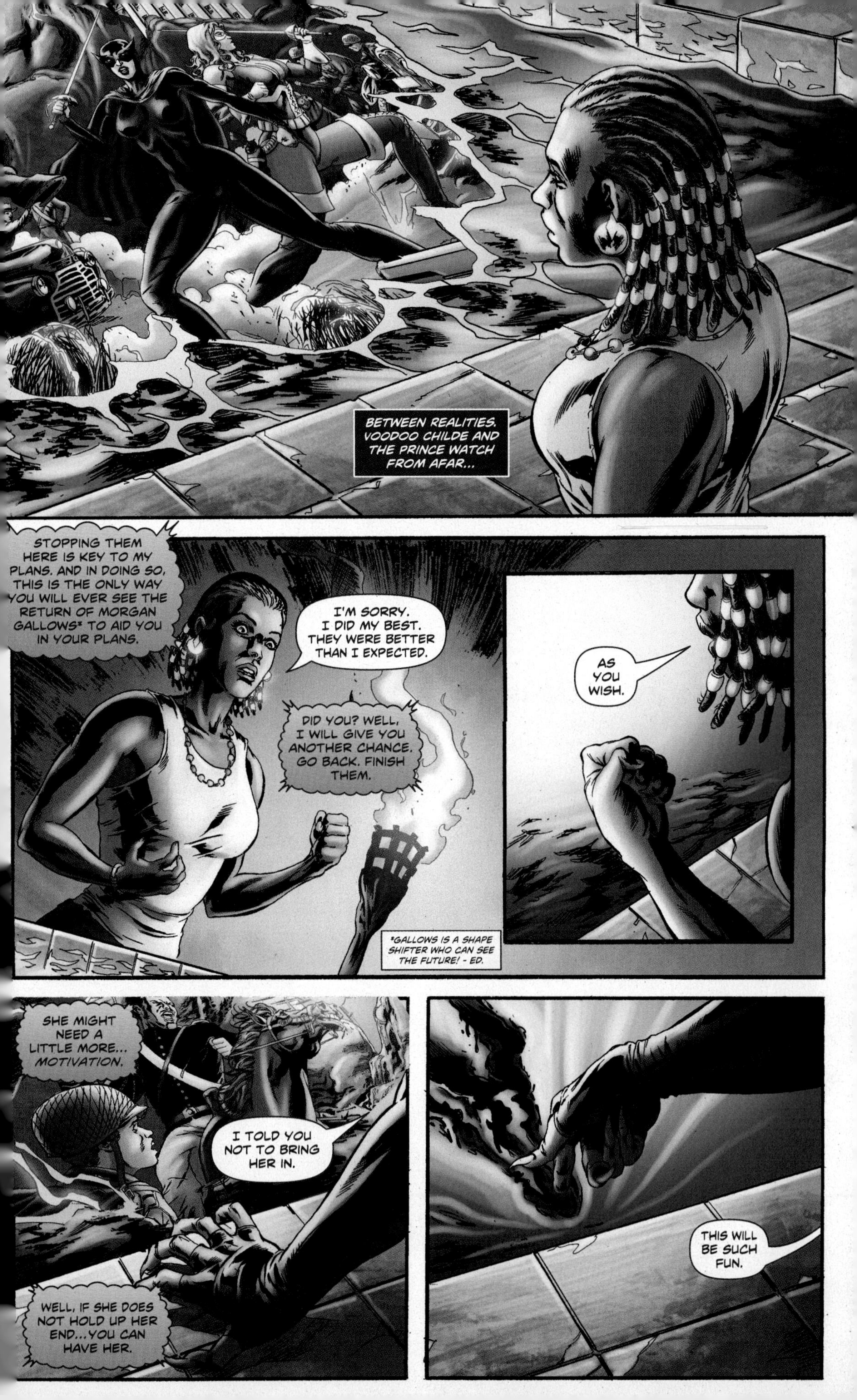
BETWEEN REALITIES. VOODOO CHILDE AND THE PRINCE WATCH FROM AFAR...
STOPPING THEM HERE IS KEY TO MY PLANS. AND IN DOING SO, THIS IS THE ONLY WAY YOU WILL EVER SEE THE RETURN OF MORGAN GALLOWS* TO AID YOU IN YOUR PLANS.
I'M SORRY. I DID MY BEST. THEY WERE BETTER THAN I EXPECTED.
DID YOU? WELL, I WILL GIVE YOU ANOTHER CHANCE. GO BACK. FINISH THEM.
AS YOU WISH.
*GALLOWS IS A SHAPE SHIFTER WHO CAN SEE THE FUTURE! - ED.
SHE MIGHT NEED A LITTLE MORE... MOTIVATION.
I TOLD YOU NOT TO BRING HER IN.
WELL, IF SHE DOES NOT HOLD UP HER END...YOU CAN HAVE HER.
THIS WILL BE SUCH FUN.

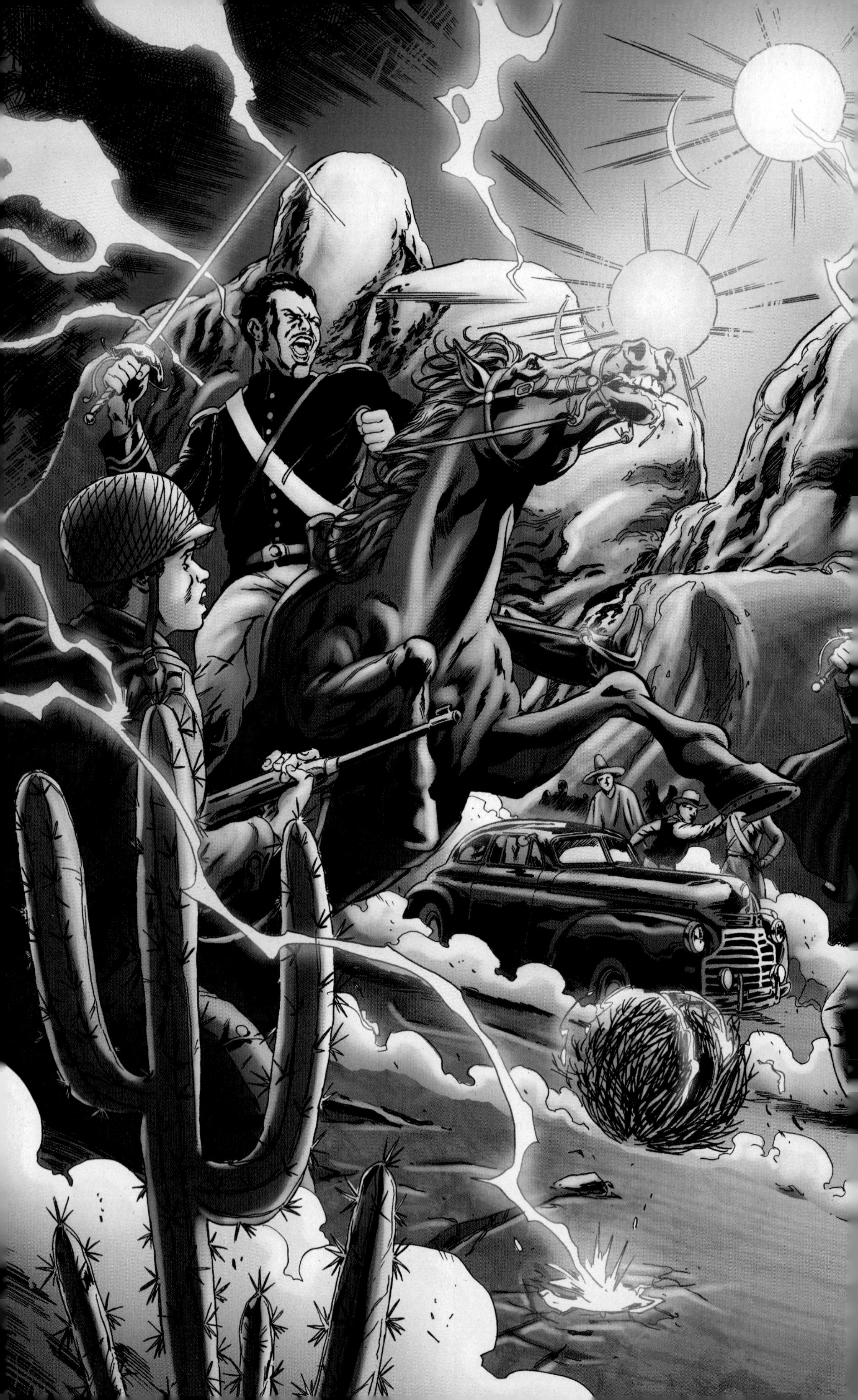

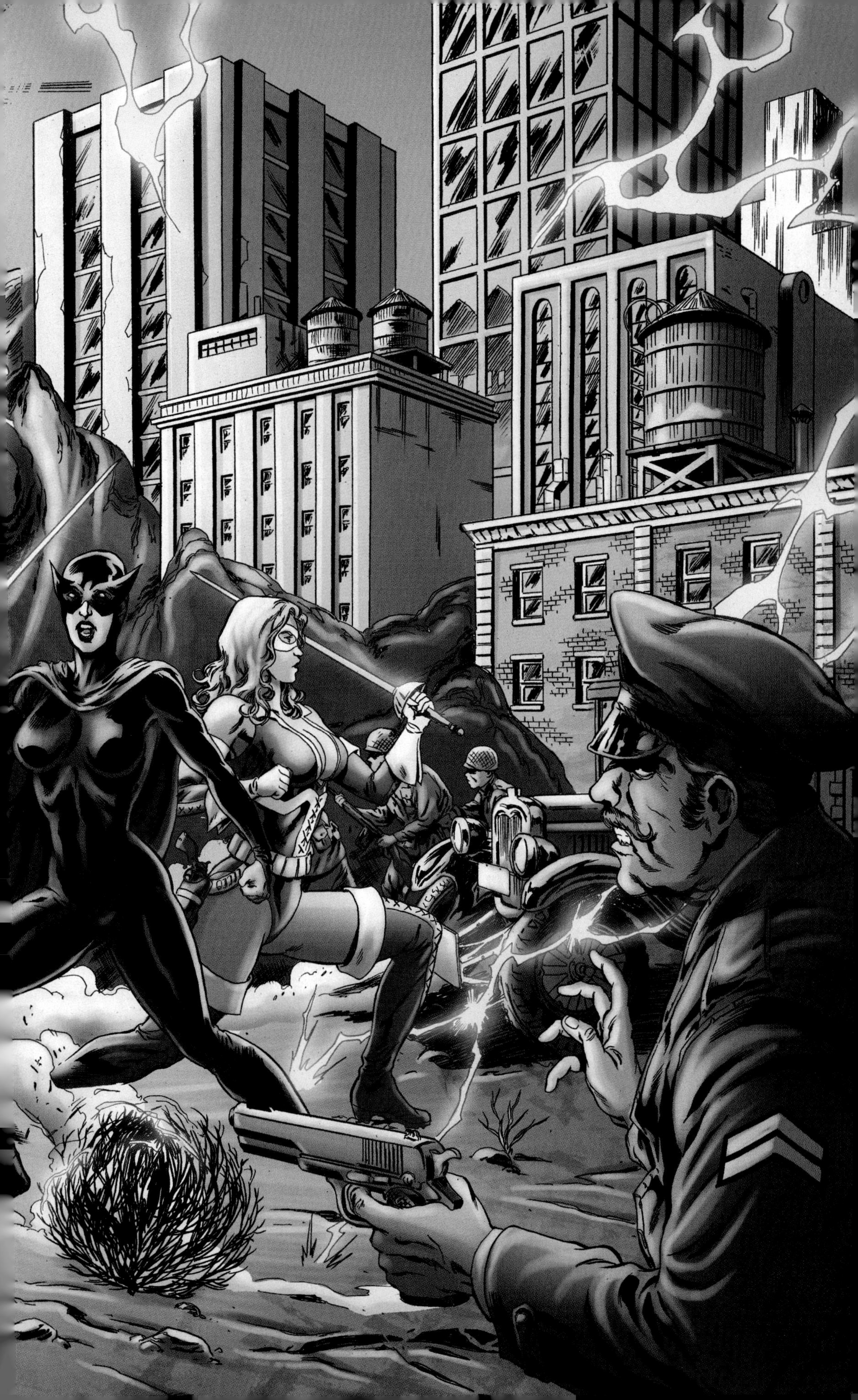

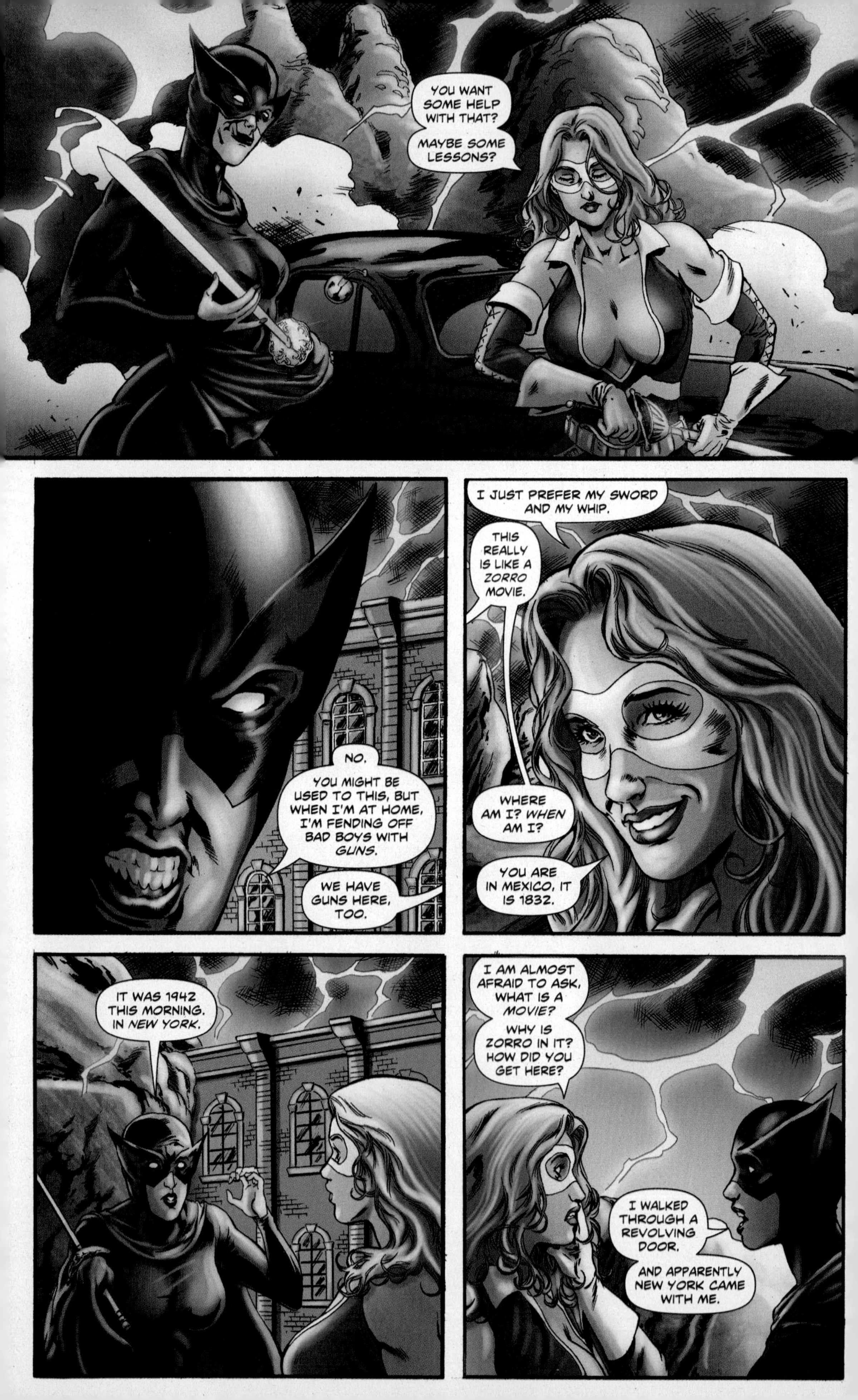
YOU WANT SOME HELP WITH THAT?
MAYBE SOME LESSONS?
NO.
YOU MIGHT BE USED TO THIS, BUT WHEN I'M AT HOME, I'M FENDING OFF BAD BOYS WITH *GUNS*.
WE HAVE GUNS HERE, TOO.
I JUST PREFER MY SWORD AND MY WHIP.
THIS REALLY IS LIKE A ZORRO MOVIE.
WHERE AM I? *WHEN* AM I?
YOU ARE IN MEXICO, IT IS 1832.
IT WAS 1942 THIS MORNING. IN *NEW YORK*.
I AM ALMOST AFRAID TO ASK, WHAT IS A *MOVIE*?
WHY IS ZORRO IN IT? HOW DID YOU GET HERE?
I WALKED THROUGH A REVOLVING DOOR.
AND APPARENTLY NEW YORK CAME WITH ME.

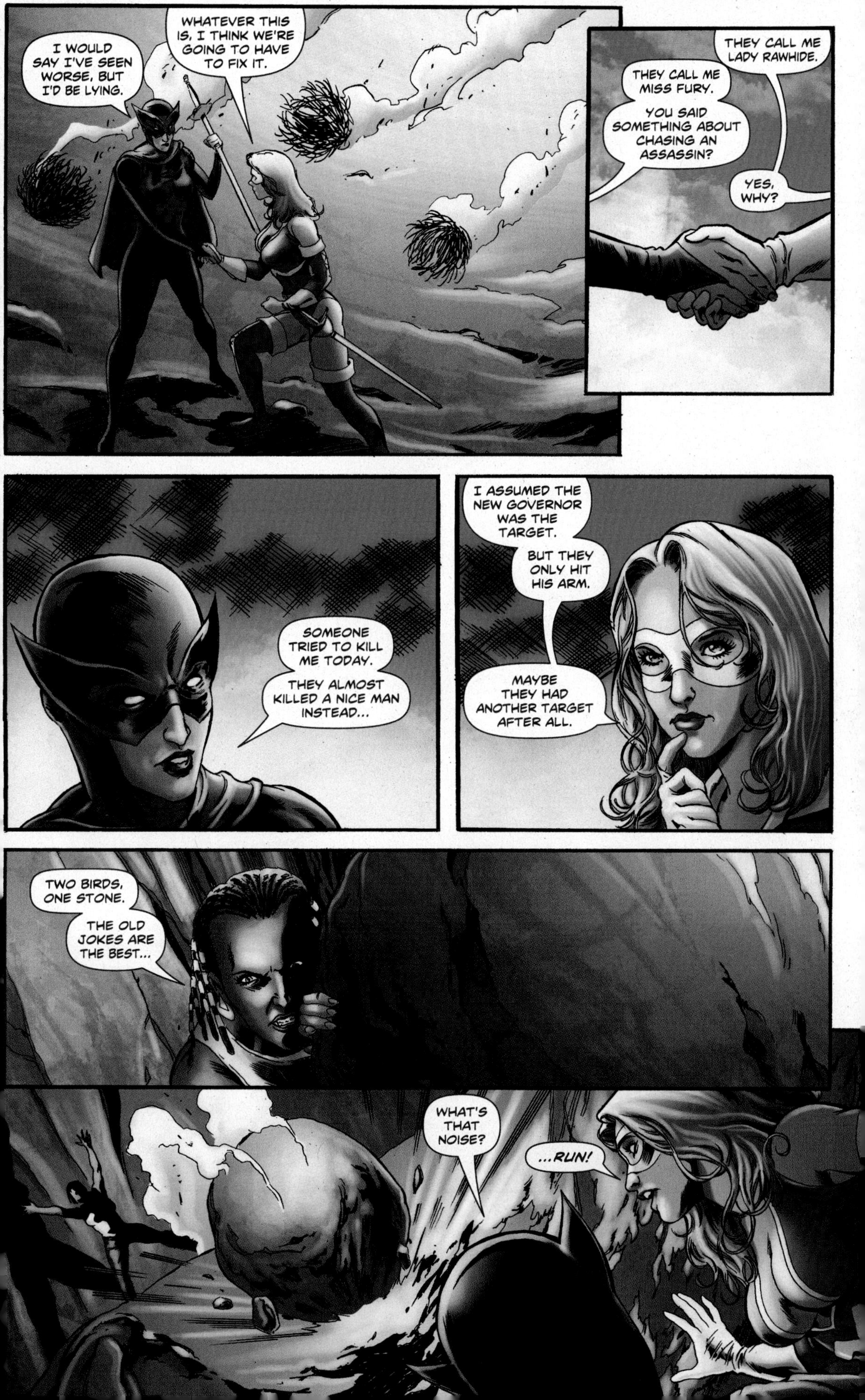

I WOULD SAY I'VE SEEN WORSE, BUT I'D BE LYING.
WHATEVER THIS IS, I THINK WE'RE GOING TO HAVE TO FIX IT.
THEY CALL ME LADY RAWHIDE.
THEY CALL ME MISS FURY.
YOU SAID SOMETHING ABOUT CHASING AN ASSASSIN?
YES, WHY?
SOMEONE TRIED TO KILL ME TODAY.
THEY ALMOST KILLED A NICE MAN INSTEAD...
I ASSUMED THE NEW GOVERNOR WAS THE TARGET.
BUT THEY ONLY HIT HIS ARM.
MAYBE THEY HAD ANOTHER TARGET AFTER ALL.
TWO BIRDS, ONE STONE.
THE OLD JOKES ARE THE BEST...
WHAT'S THAT NOISE?
...RUN!

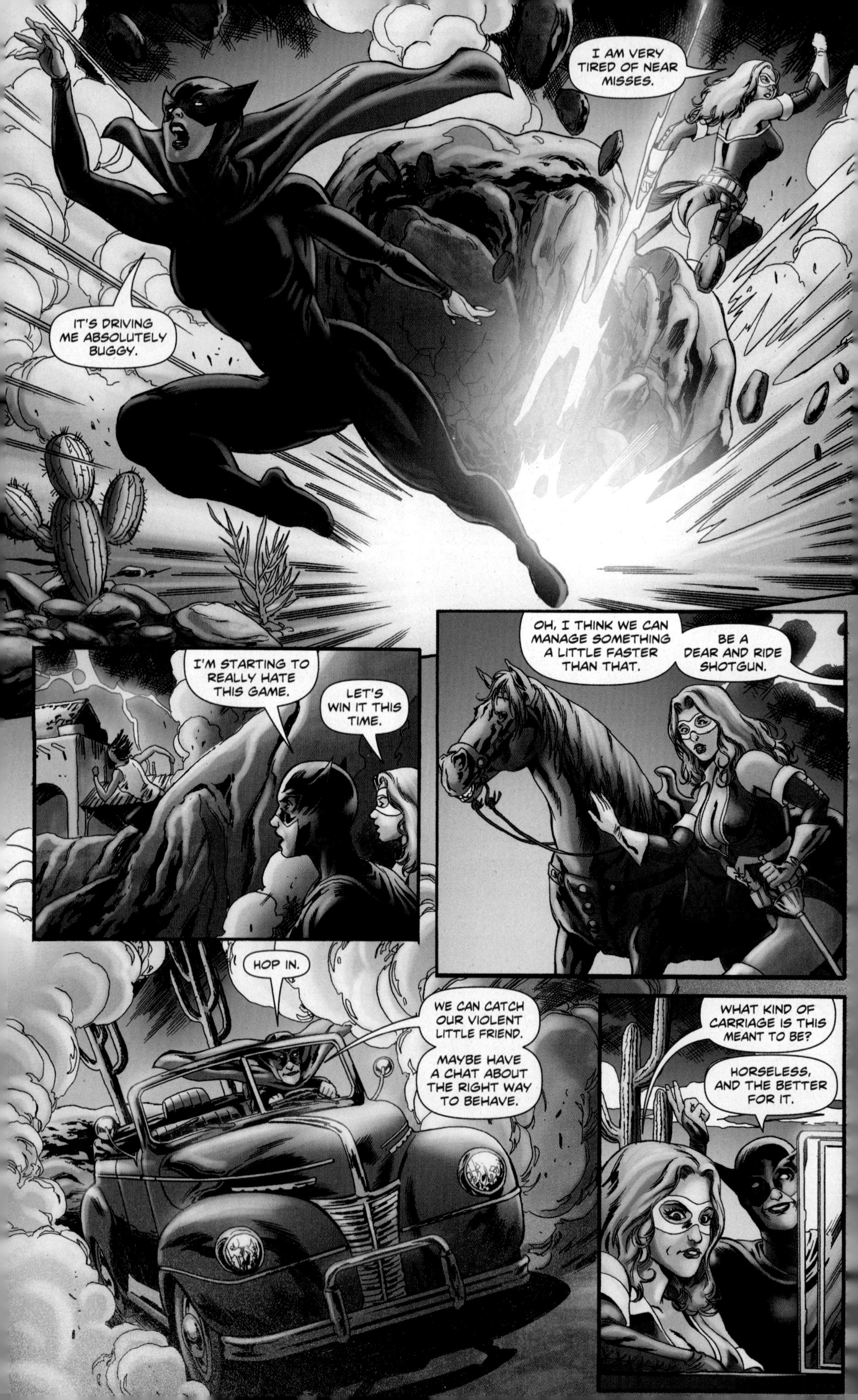
I AM VERY TIRED OF NEAR MISSES.
IT'S DRIVING ME ABSOLUTELY BUGGY.
I'M STARTING TO REALLY HATE THIS GAME.
LET'S WIN IT THIS TIME.
OH, I THINK WE CAN MANAGE SOMETHING A LITTLE FASTER THAN THAT.
BE A DEAR AND RIDE SHOTGUN.
HOP IN.
WE CAN CATCH OUR VIOLENT LITTLE FRIEND.
MAYBE HAVE A CHAT ABOUT THE RIGHT WAY TO BEHAVE.
WHAT KIND OF CARRIAGE IS THIS MEANT TO BE?
HORSELESS, AND THE BETTER FOR IT.

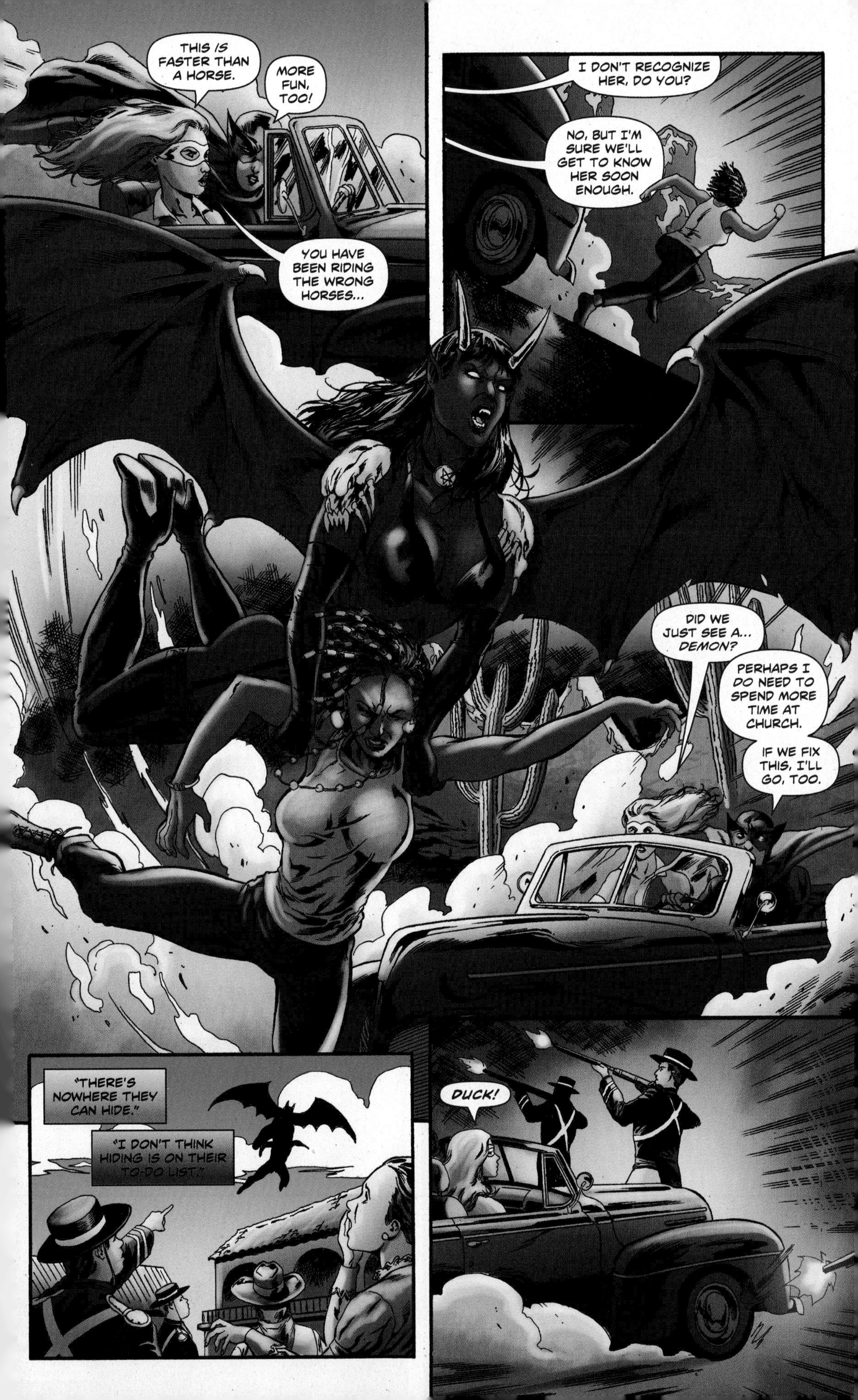
THIS IS FASTER THAN A HORSE.
MORE FUN, TOO!
YOU HAVE BEEN RIDING THE WRONG HORSES...
I DON'T RECOGNIZE HER, DO YOU?
NO, BUT I'M SURE WE'LL GET TO KNOW HER SOON ENOUGH.
DID WE JUST SEE A... DEMON?
PERHAPS I DO NEED TO SPEND MORE TIME AT CHURCH.
IF WE FIX THIS, I'LL GO, TOO.
"THERE'S NOWHERE THEY CAN HIDE."
"I DON'T THINK HIDING IS ON THEIR TO-DO LIST."
DUCK!

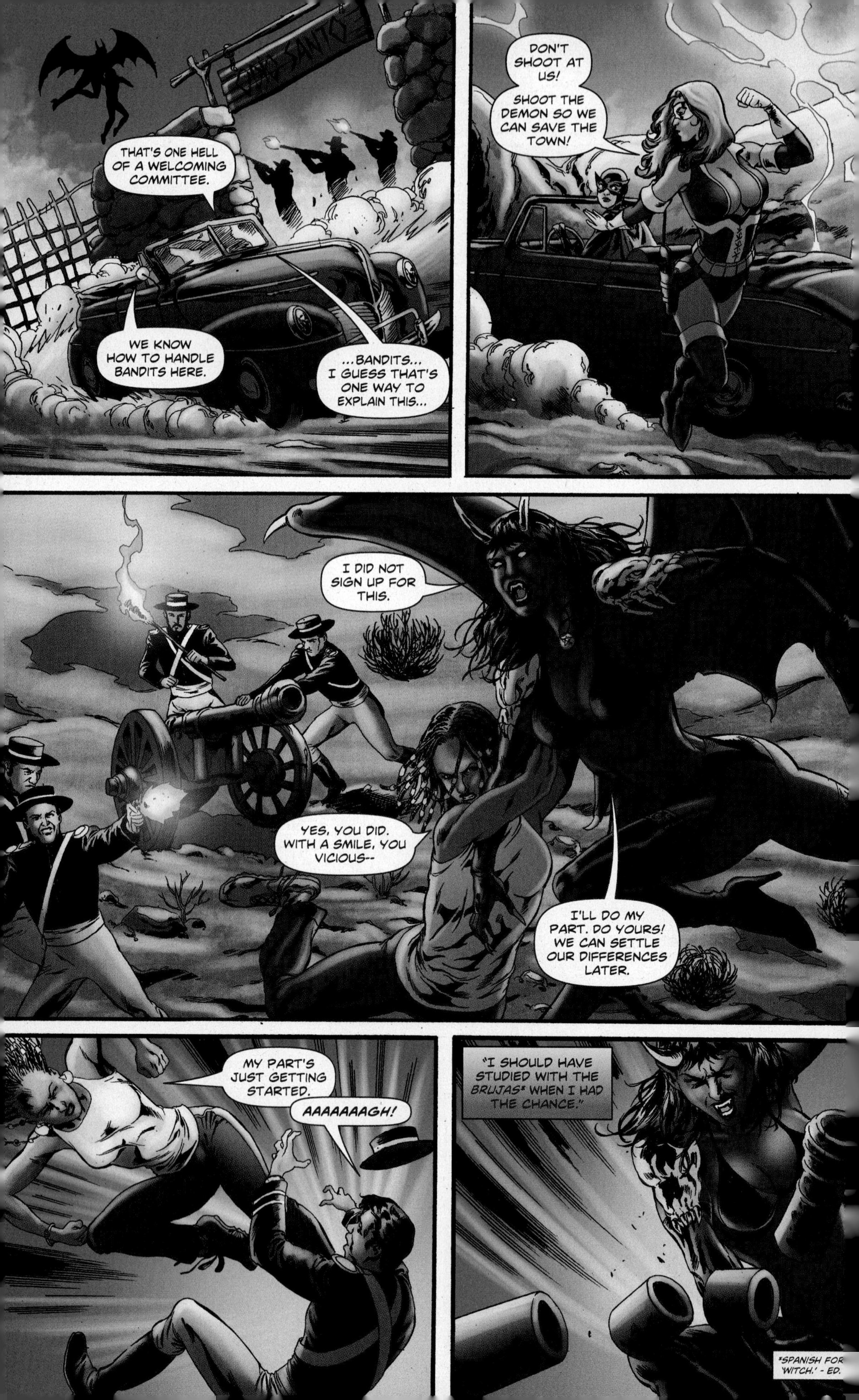
THAT'S ONE HELL OF A WELCOMING COMMITTEE.
WE KNOW HOW TO HANDLE BANDITS HERE.
...BANDITS... I GUESS THAT'S ONE WAY TO EXPLAIN THIS...
DON'T SHOOT AT US!
SHOOT THE DEMON SO WE CAN SAVE THE TOWN!
I DID NOT SIGN UP FOR THIS.
YES, YOU DID. WITH A SMILE, YOU VICIOUS--
I'LL DO MY PART. DO YOURS! WE CAN SETTLE OUR DIFFERENCES LATER.
MY PART'S JUST GETTING STARTED.
AAAAAAAGH!
"I SHOULD HAVE STUDIED WITH THE BRUJAS* WHEN I HAD THE CHANCE."
*SPANISH FOR 'WITCH.' - ED.

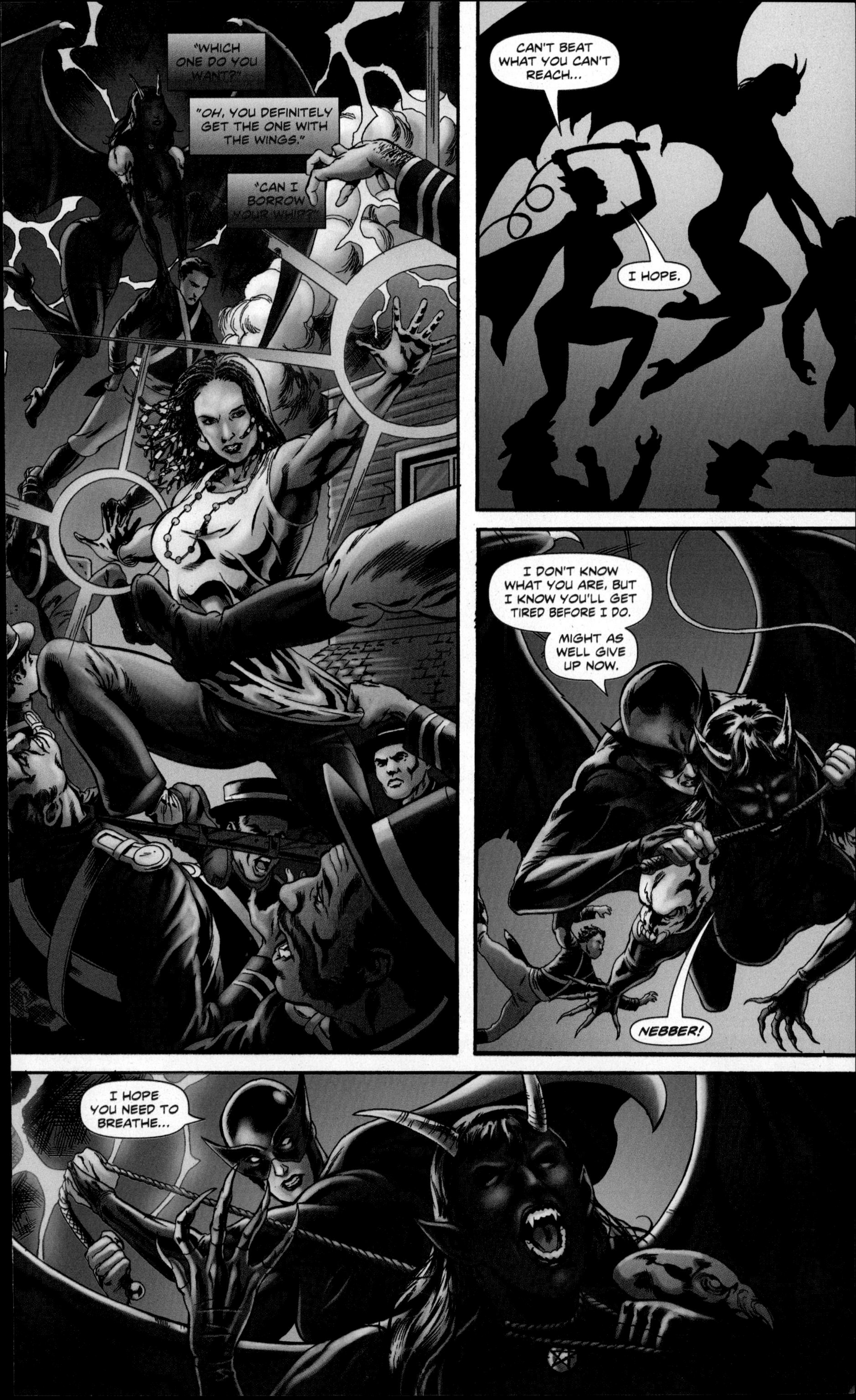
"WHICH ONE DO YOU WANT?"
"OH, YOU DEFINITELY GET THE ONE WITH THE WINGS."
"CAN I BORROW YOUR WHIP?"
CAN'T BEAT WHAT YOU CAN'T REACH...
I HOPE.
I DON'T KNOW WHAT YOU ARE, BUT I KNOW YOU'LL GET TIRED BEFORE I DO.
MIGHT AS WELL GIVE UP NOW.
NEBBER!
I HOPE YOU NEED TO BREATHE...

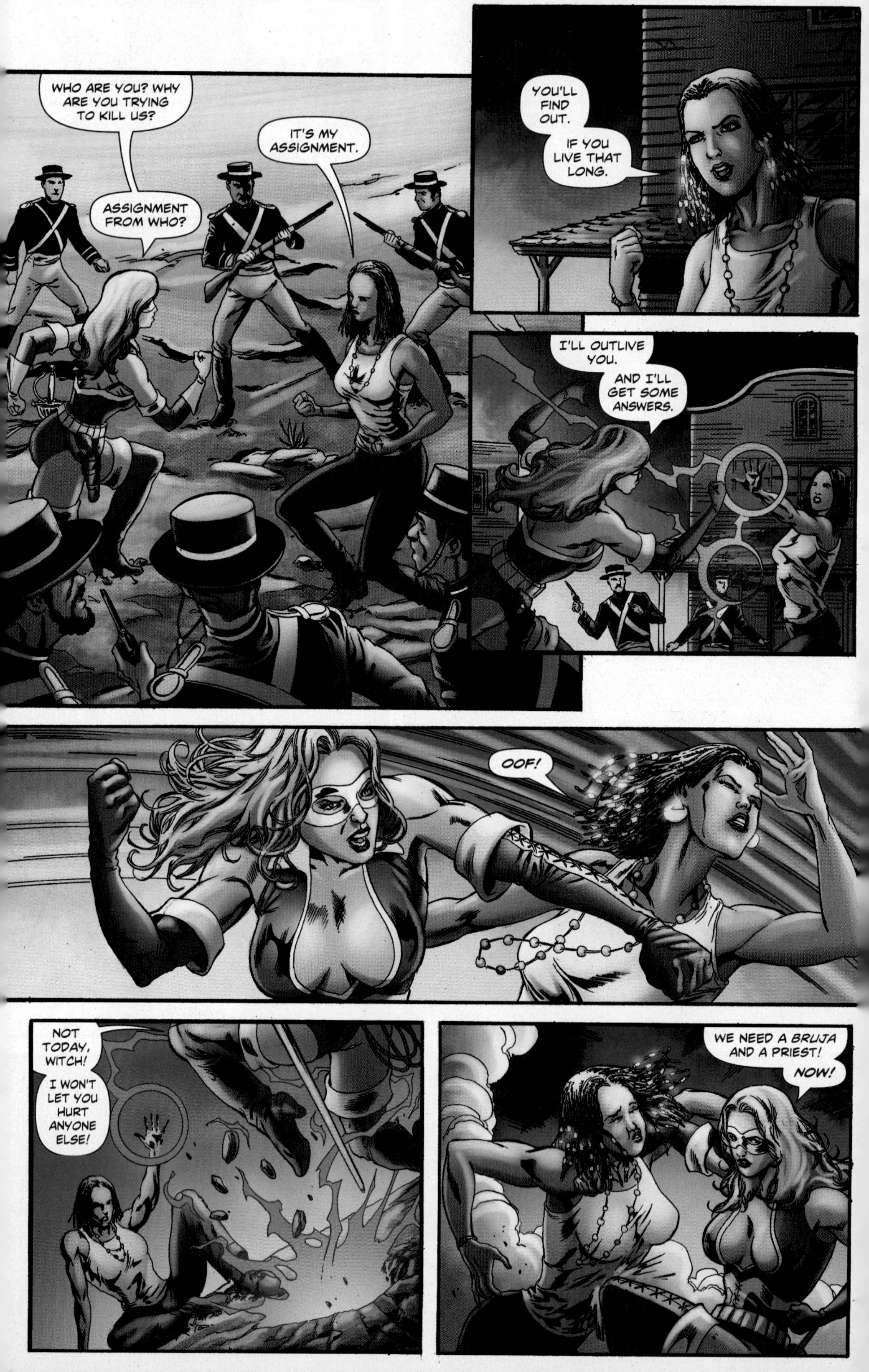
WHO ARE YOU? WHY ARE YOU TRYING TO KILL US?
IT'S MY ASSIGNMENT.
ASSIGNMENT FROM WHO?
YOU'LL FIND OUT.
IF YOU LIVE THAT LONG.
I'LL OUTLIVE YOU.
AND I'LL GET SOME ANSWERS.
OOF!
NOT TODAY, WITCH!
I WON'T LET YOU HURT ANYONE ELSE!
WE NEED A *BRUJA* AND A PRIEST!
NOW!

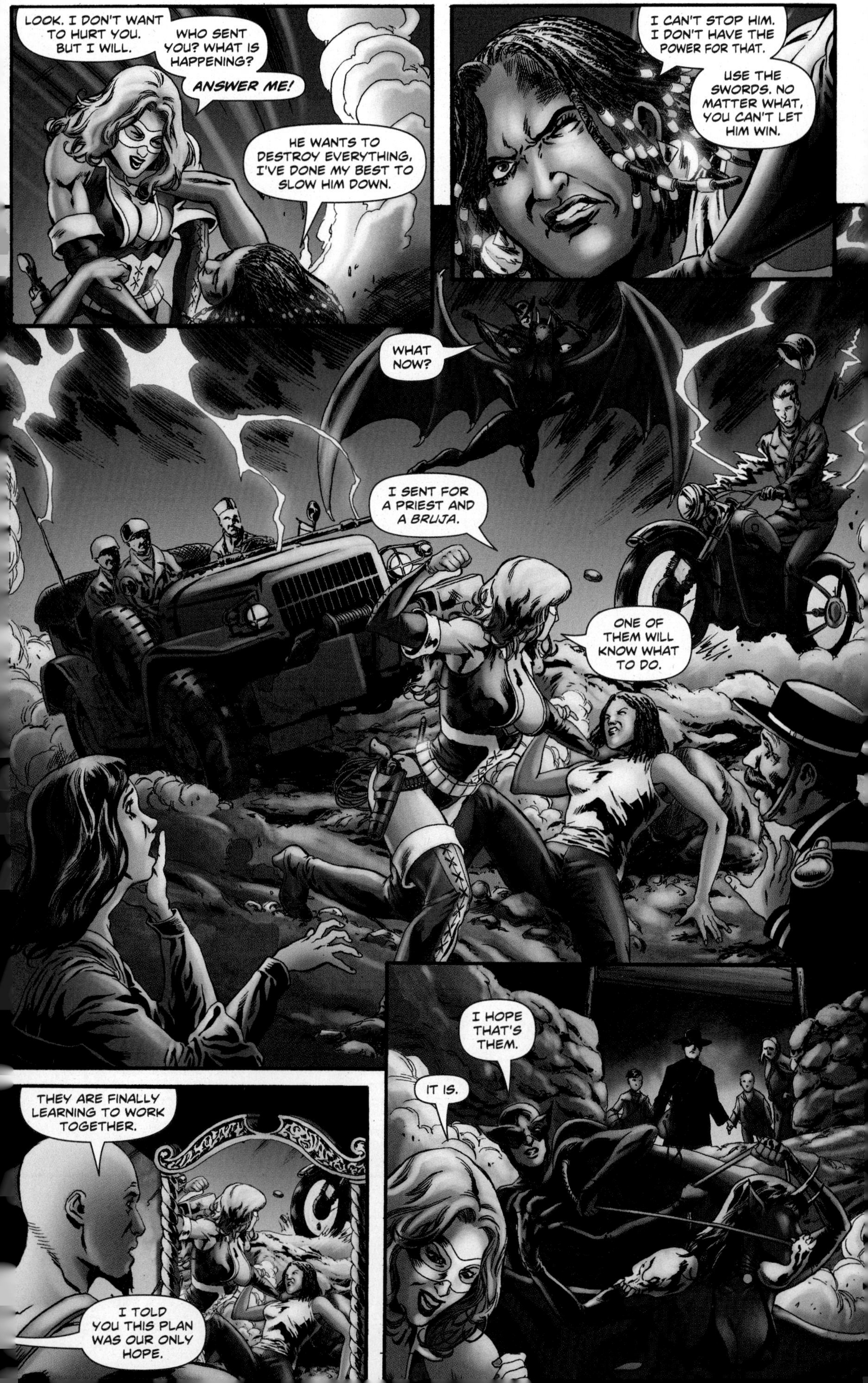
LOOK. I DON'T WANT TO HURT YOU. BUT I WILL.
WHO SENT YOU? WHAT IS HAPPENING?
ANSWER ME!
HE WANTS TO DESTROY EVERYTHING, I'VE DONE MY BEST TO SLOW HIM DOWN.
I CAN'T STOP HIM. I DON'T HAVE THE POWER FOR THAT.
USE THE SWORDS. NO MATTER WHAT, YOU CAN'T LET HIM WIN.
WHAT NOW?
I SENT FOR A PRIEST AND A BRUJA.
ONE OF THEM WILL KNOW WHAT TO DO.
I HOPE THAT'S THEM.
IT IS.
THEY ARE FINALLY LEARNING TO WORK TOGETHER.
I TOLD YOU THIS PLAN WAS OUR ONLY HOPE.

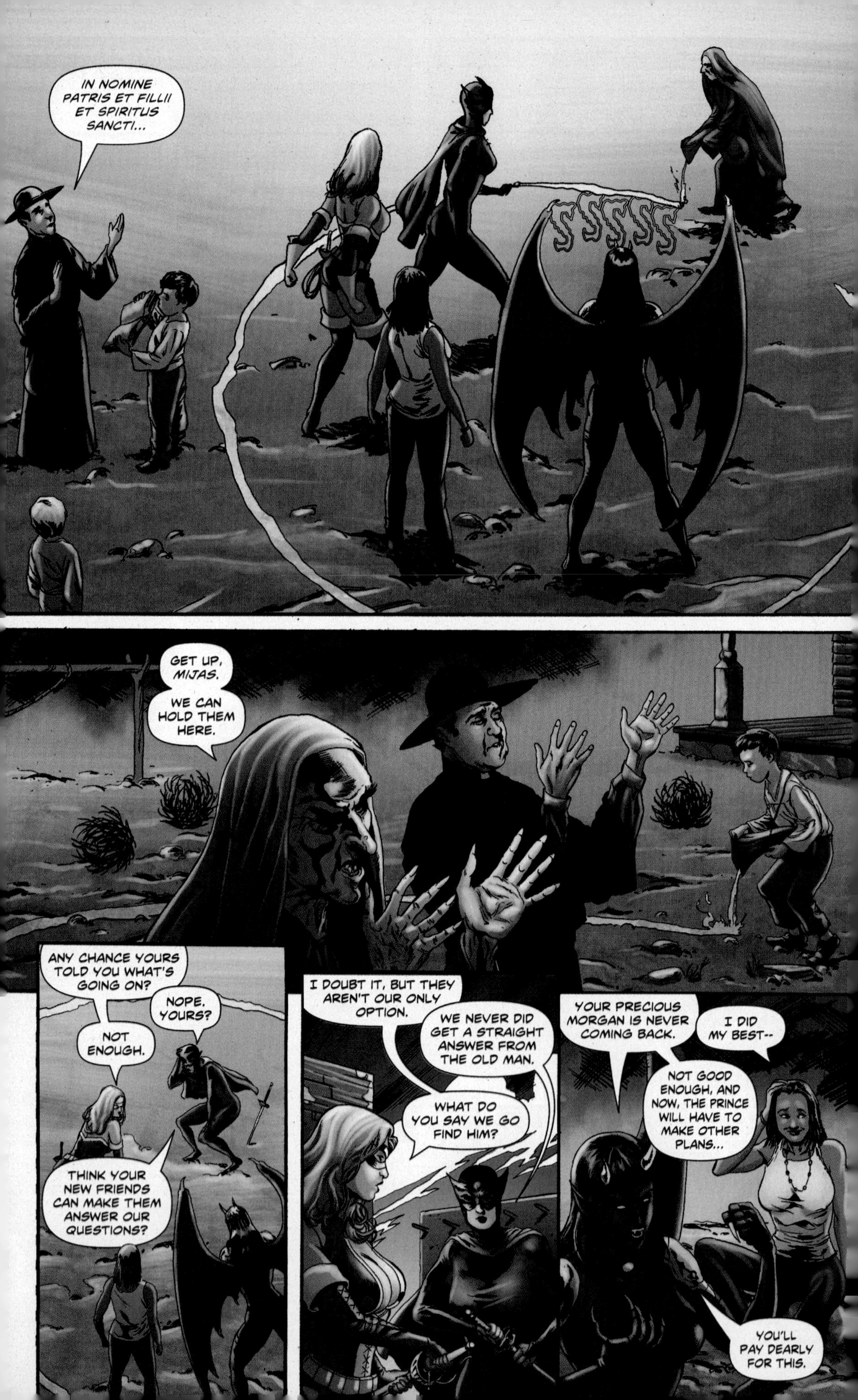
IN NOMINE PATRIS ET FILLII ET SPIRITUS SANCTI...
SSSSS
GET UP, MIJAS.
WE CAN HOLD THEM HERE.
ANY CHANCE YOURS TOLD YOU WHAT'S GOING ON?
NOPE. YOURS?
NOT ENOUGH.
THINK YOUR NEW FRIENDS CAN MAKE THEM ANSWER OUR QUESTIONS?
I DOUBT IT, BUT THEY AREN'T OUR ONLY OPTION.
WE NEVER DID GET A STRAIGHT ANSWER FROM THE OLD MAN.
WHAT DO YOU SAY WE GO FIND HIM?
YOUR PRECIOUS MORGAN IS NEVER COMING BACK.
I DID MY BEST--
NOT GOOD ENOUGH, AND NOW, THE PRINCE WILL HAVE TO MAKE OTHER PLANS...
YOU'LL PAY DEARLY FOR THIS.

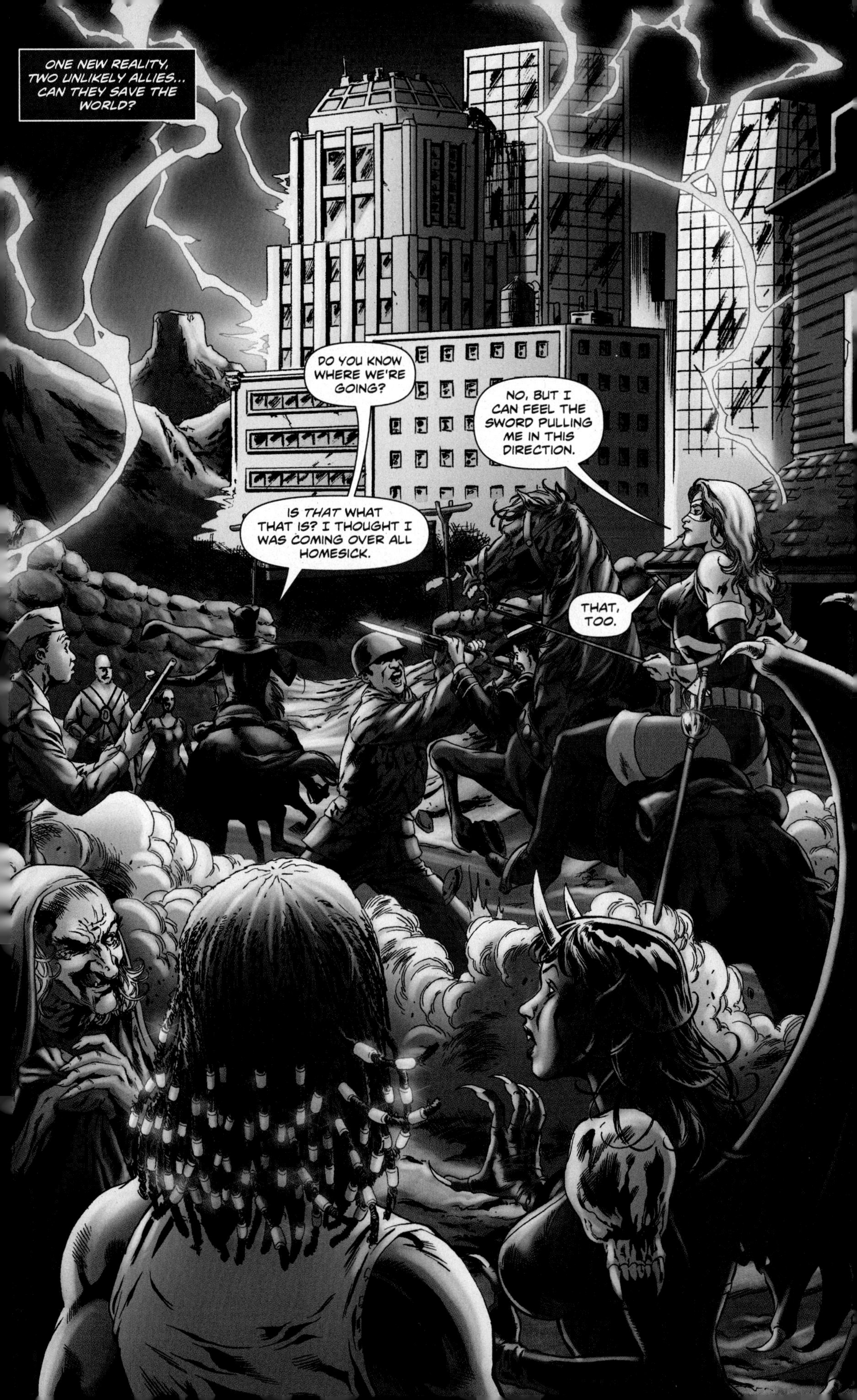
ONE NEW REALITY, TWO UNLIKELY ALLIES... CAN THEY SAVE THE WORLD?
DO YOU KNOW WHERE WE'RE GOING?
NO, BUT I CAN FEEL THE SWORD PULLING ME IN THIS DIRECTION.
IS *THAT* WHAT THAT IS? I THOUGHT I WAS COMING OVER ALL HOMESICK.
THAT, TOO.

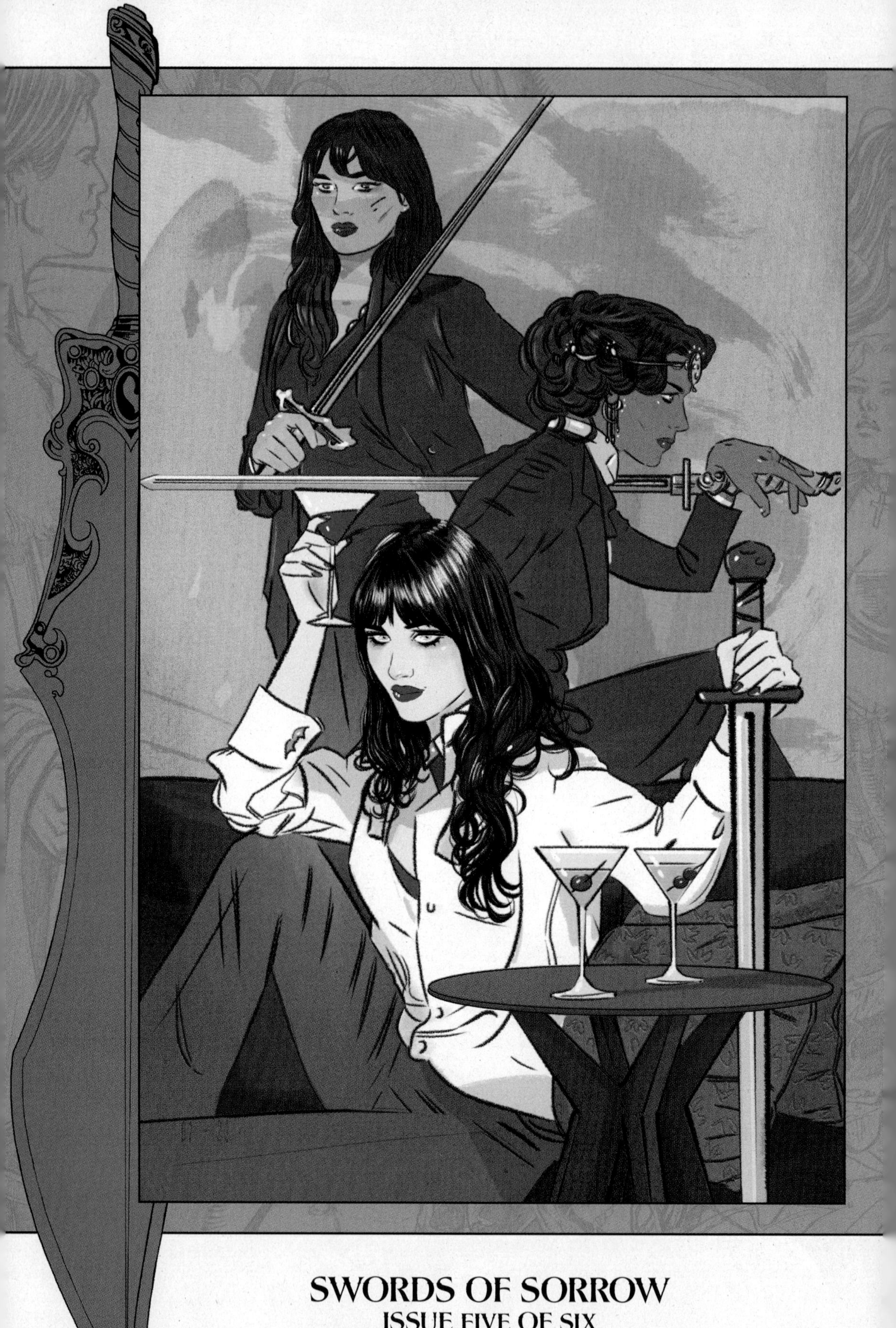

SWORDS OF SORROW

ISSUE FIVE OF SIX

written by GAIL SIMONE illustrated by SERGIO DÁVILA
colored by JORGE SUTIL lettered by ERICA SCHULTZ

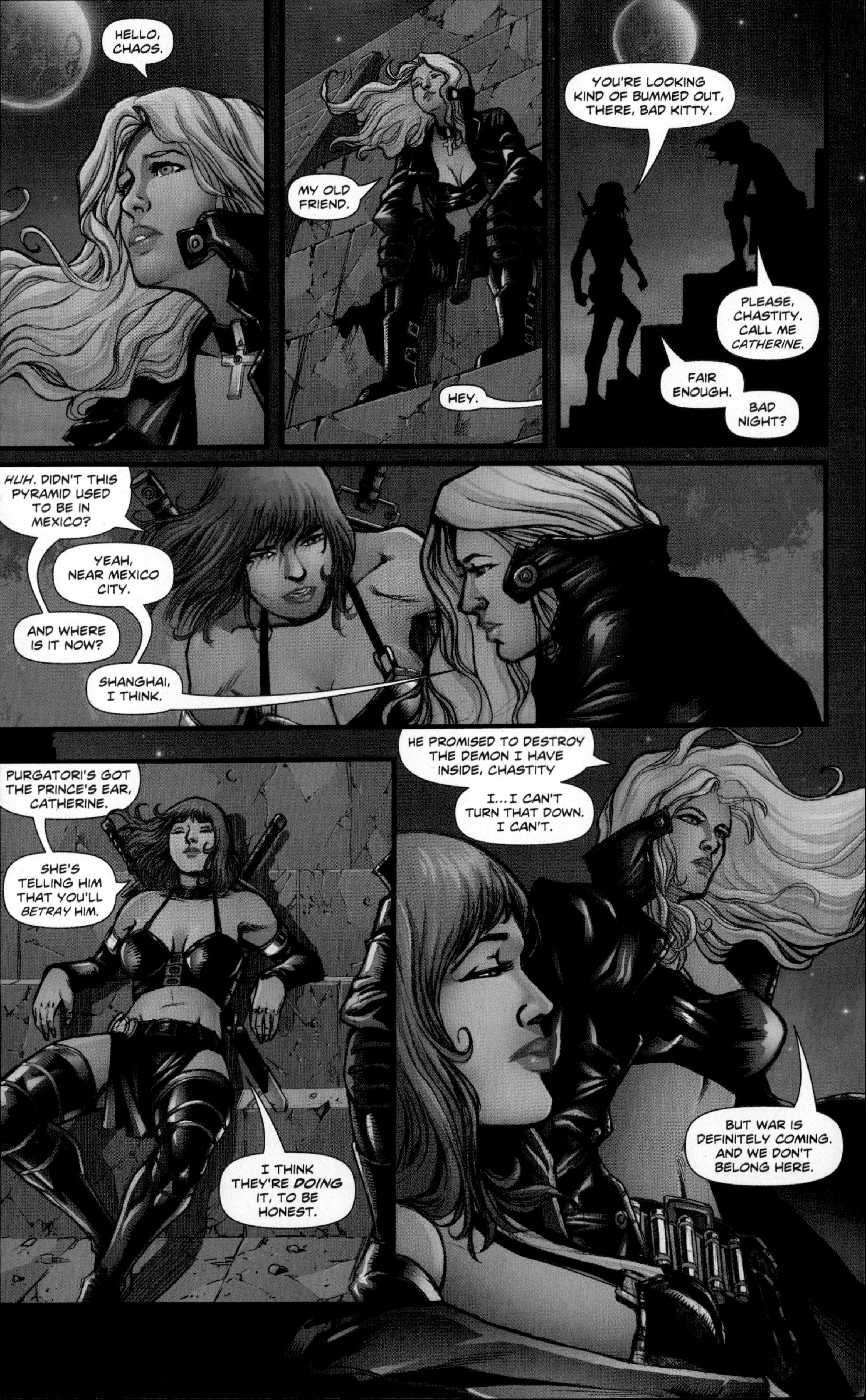
HELLO, CHAOS.
MY OLD FRIEND.
HEY.
YOU'RE LOOKING KIND OF BUMMED OUT, THERE, BAD KITTY.
PLEASE, CHASTITY. CALL ME CATHERINE.
FAIR ENOUGH.
BAD NIGHT?
HUH. DIDN'T THIS PYRAMID USED TO BE IN MEXICO?
YEAH, NEAR MEXICO CITY.
AND WHERE IS IT NOW?
SHANGHAI, I THINK.
PURGATORI'S GOT THE PRINCE'S EAR, CATHERINE.
SHE'S TELLING HIM THAT YOU'LL BETRAY HIM.
I THINK THEY'RE DOING IT, TO BE HONEST.
HE PROMISED TO DESTROY THE DEMON I HAVE INSIDE, CHASTITY
I...I CAN'T TURN THAT DOWN. I CAN'T.
BUT WAR IS DEFINITELY COMING. AND WE DON'T BELONG HERE.

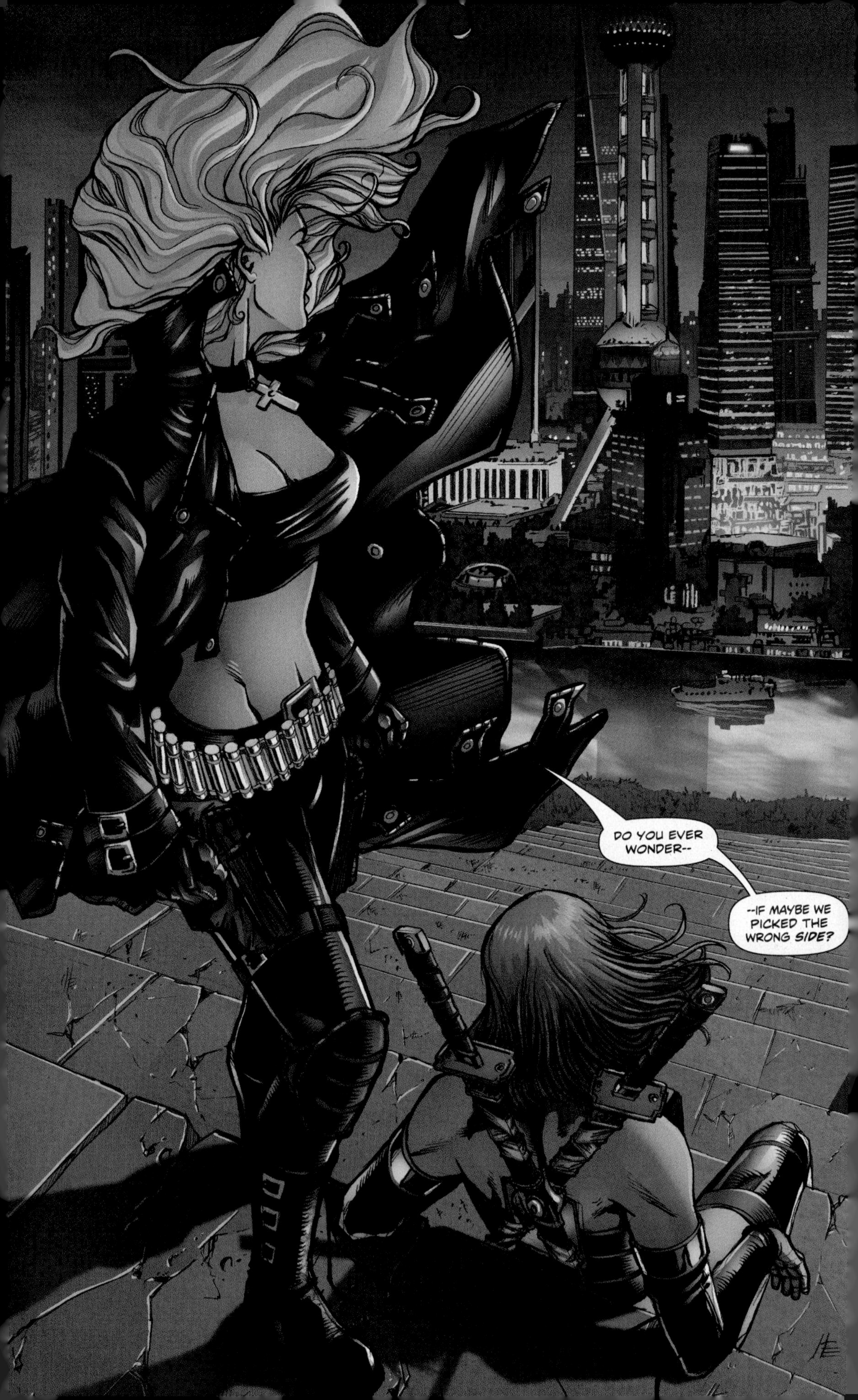
DO YOU EVER WONDER--
--IF MAYBE WE PICKED THE WRONG *SIDE*?

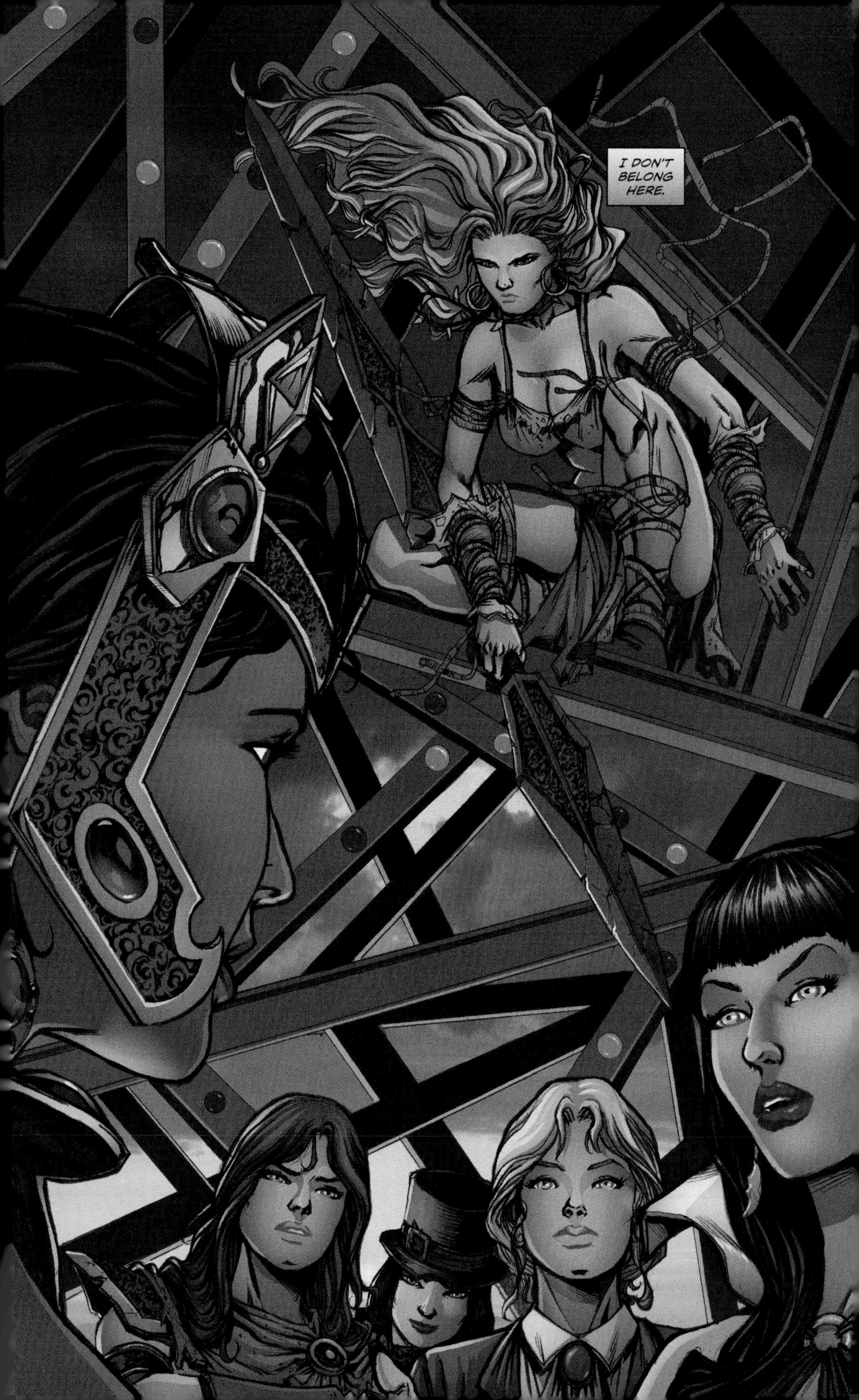
I DON'T BELONG HERE.

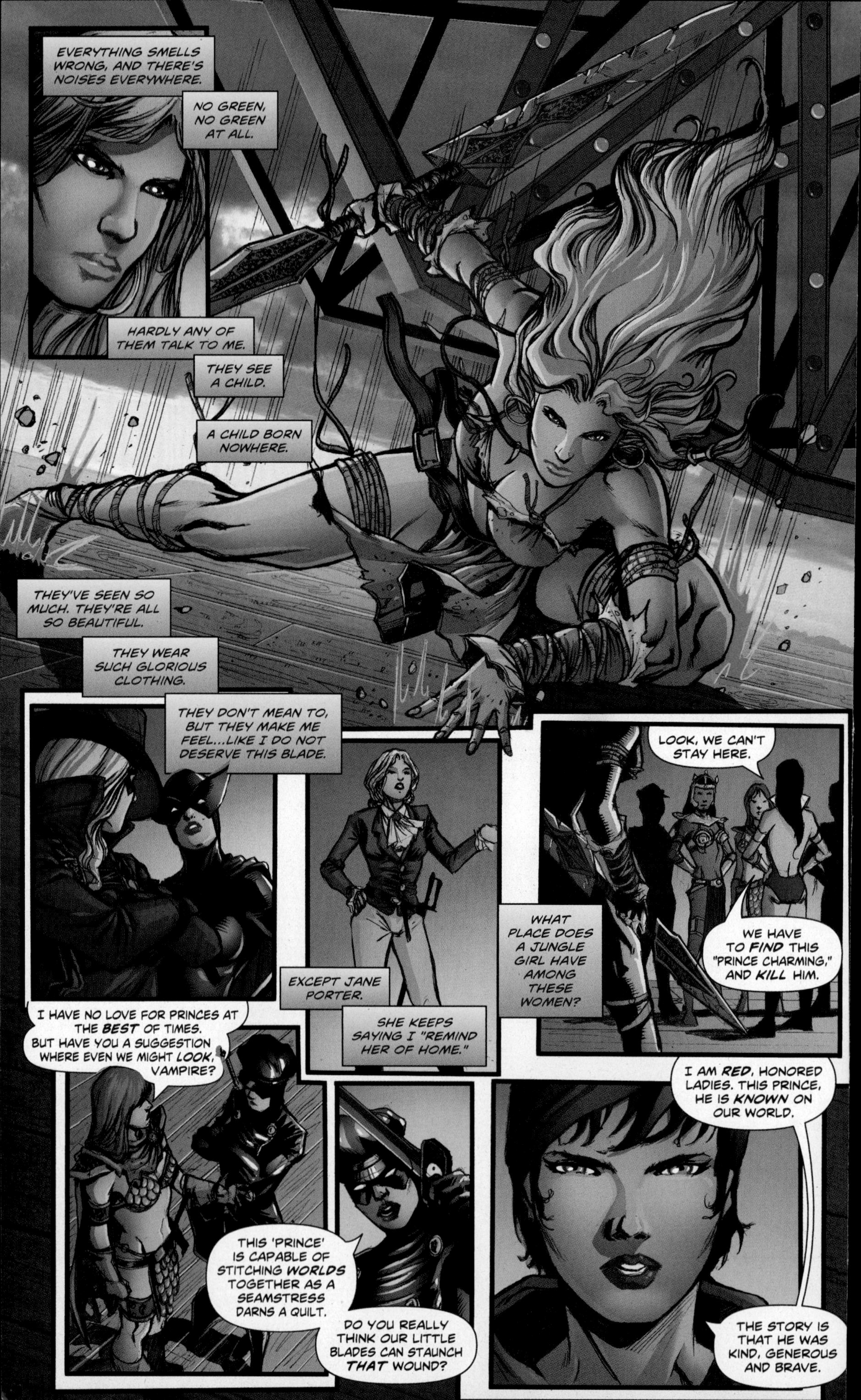
EVERYTHING SMELLS WRONG, AND THERE'S NOISES EVERYWHERE.
NO GREEN, NO GREEN AT ALL.
HARDLY ANY OF THEM TALK TO ME.
THEY SEE A CHILD.
A CHILD BORN NOWHERE.
THEY'VE SEEN SO MUCH. THEY'RE ALL SO BEAUTIFUL.
THEY WEAR SUCH GLORIOUS CLOTHING.
THEY DON'T MEAN TO, BUT THEY MAKE ME FEEL...LIKE I DO NOT DESERVE THIS BLADE.
EXCEPT JANE PORTER.
SHE KEEPS SAYING I "REMIND HER OF HOME."
LOOK, WE CAN'T STAY HERE.
WHAT PLACE DOES A JUNGLE GIRL HAVE AMONG THESE WOMEN?
WE HAVE TO FIND THIS "PRINCE CHARMING," AND KILL HIM.
I HAVE NO LOVE FOR PRINCES AT THE BEST OF TIMES. BUT HAVE YOU A SUGGESTION WHERE EVEN WE MIGHT LOOK, VAMPIRE?
THIS 'PRINCE' IS CAPABLE OF STITCHING WORLDS TOGETHER AS A SEAMSTRESS DARNS A QUILT.
DO YOU REALLY THINK OUR LITTLE BLADES CAN STAUNCH THAT WOUND?
I AM RED, HONORED LADIES. THIS PRINCE, HE IS KNOWN ON OUR WORLD.
THE STORY IS THAT HE WAS KIND, GENEROUS AND BRAVE.

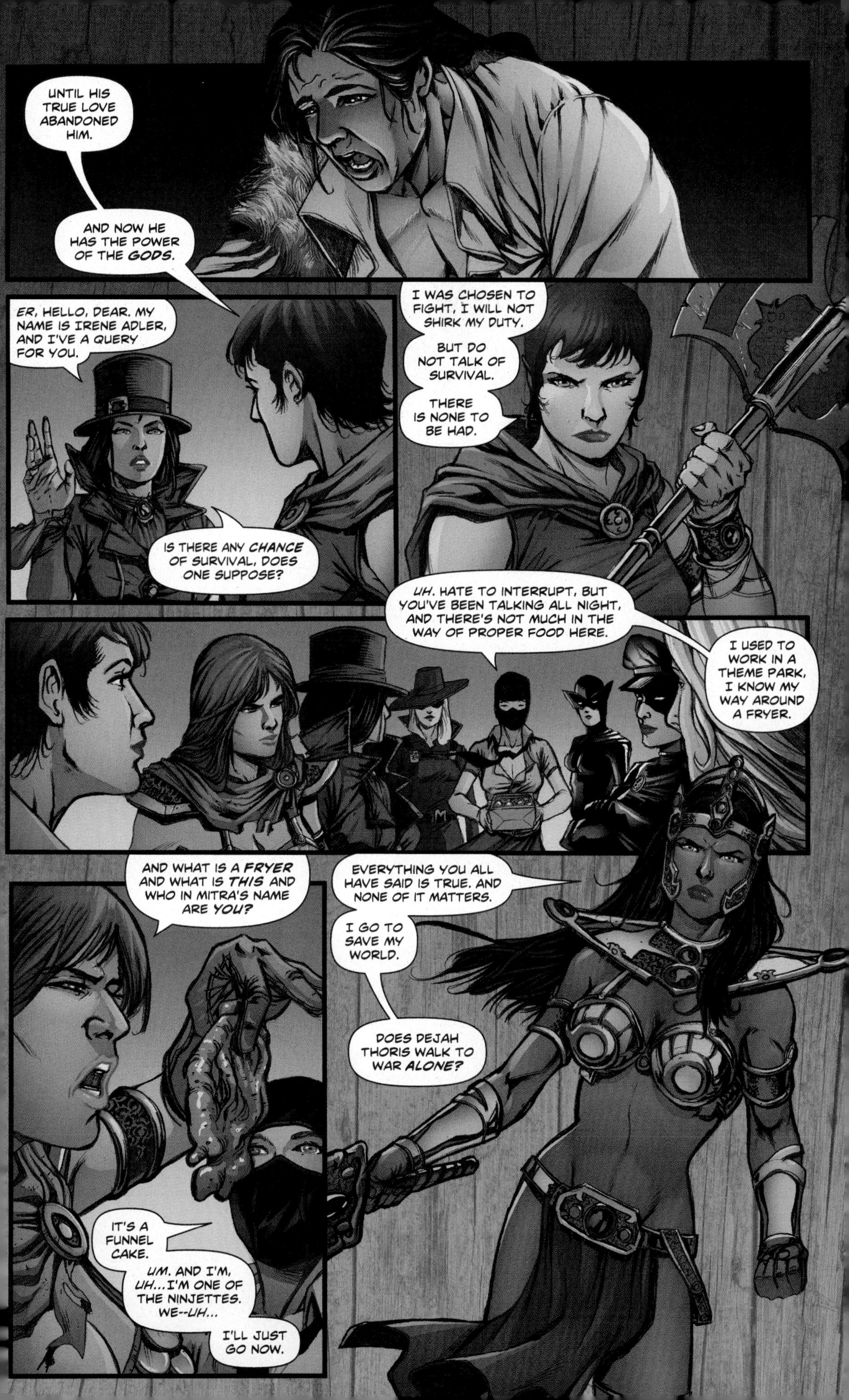

UNTIL HIS TRUE LOVE ABANDONED HIM.
AND NOW HE HAS THE POWER OF THE *GODS*.
ER, HELLO, DEAR. MY NAME IS IRENE ADLER, AND I'VE A QUERY FOR YOU.
IS THERE ANY *CHANCE* OF SURVIVAL, DOES ONE SUPPOSE?
I WAS CHOSEN TO FIGHT, I WILL NOT SHIRK MY DUTY.
BUT DO NOT TALK OF SURVIVAL.
THERE IS NONE TO BE HAD.
UH. HATE TO INTERRUPT, BUT YOU'VE BEEN TALKING ALL NIGHT, AND THERE'S NOT MUCH IN THE WAY OF PROPER FOOD HERE.
I USED TO WORK IN A THEME PARK, I KNOW MY WAY AROUND A FRYER.
AND WHAT IS A *FRYER* AND WHAT IS *THIS* AND WHO IN MITRA'S NAME ARE *YOU?*
IT'S A FUNNEL CAKE.
UM. AND I'M, *UH*...I'M ONE OF THE NINJETTES. WE--*UH*...
I'LL JUST GO NOW.
EVERYTHING YOU ALL HAVE SAID IS TRUE. AND NONE OF IT MATTERS.
I GO TO SAVE MY WORLD.
DOES DEJAH THORIS WALK TO WAR *ALONE?*

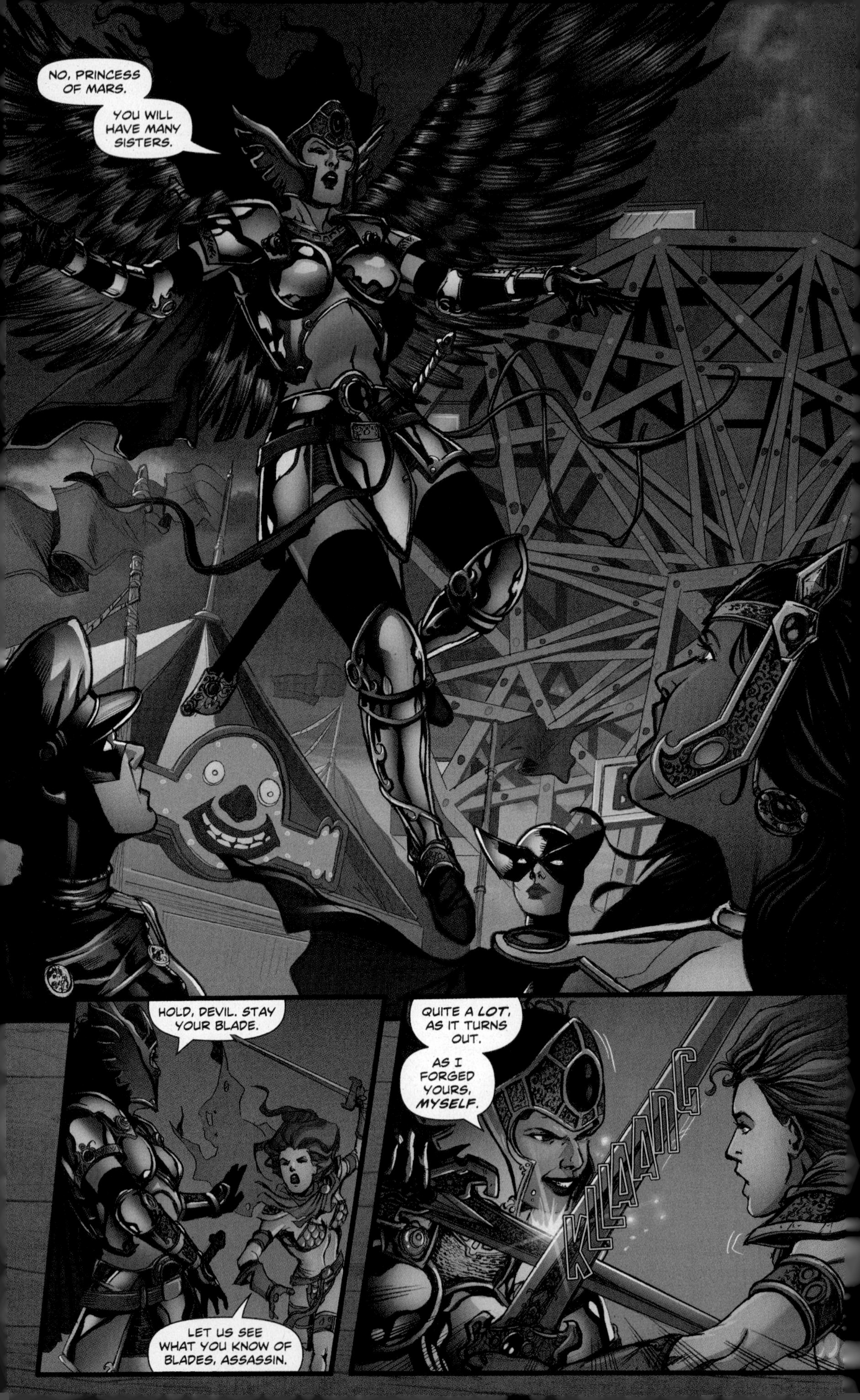
NO, PRINCESS OF MARS.
YOU WILL HAVE MANY SISTERS.
HOLD, DEVIL. STAY YOUR BLADE.
LET US SEE WHAT YOU KNOW OF BLADES, ASSASSIN.
QUITE A *LOT*, AS IT TURNS OUT.
AS I FORGED YOURS, *MYSELF*.
KLLAANG

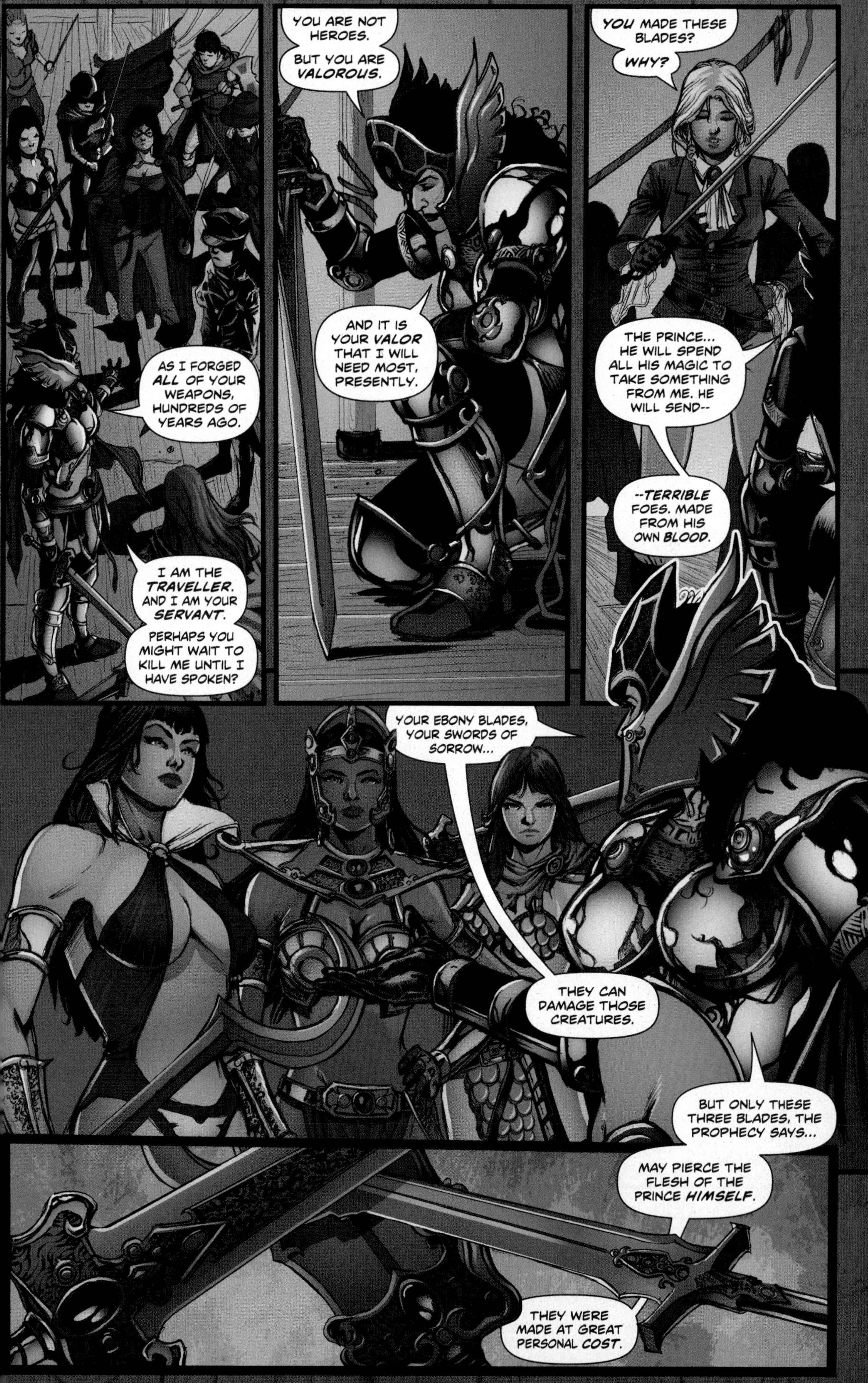
AS I FORGED ALL OF YOUR WEAPONS, HUNDREDS OF YEARS AGO.
I AM THE TRAVELLER. AND I AM YOUR SERVANT.
PERHAPS YOU MIGHT WAIT TO KILL ME UNTIL I HAVE SPOKEN?
YOU ARE NOT HEROES.
BUT YOU ARE VALOROUS.
AND IT IS YOUR VALOR THAT I WILL NEED MOST, PRESENTLY.
YOU MADE THESE BLADES?
WHY?
THE PRINCE... HE WILL SPEND ALL HIS MAGIC TO TAKE SOMETHING FROM ME. HE WILL SEND--
--TERRIBLE FOES. MADE FROM HIS OWN BLOOD.
YOUR EBONY BLADES, YOUR SWORDS OF SORROW...
THEY CAN DAMAGE THOSE CREATURES.
BUT ONLY THESE THREE BLADES, THE PROPHECY SAYS...
MAY PIERCE THE FLESH OF THE PRINCE HIMSELF.
THEY WERE MADE AT GREAT PERSONAL COST.

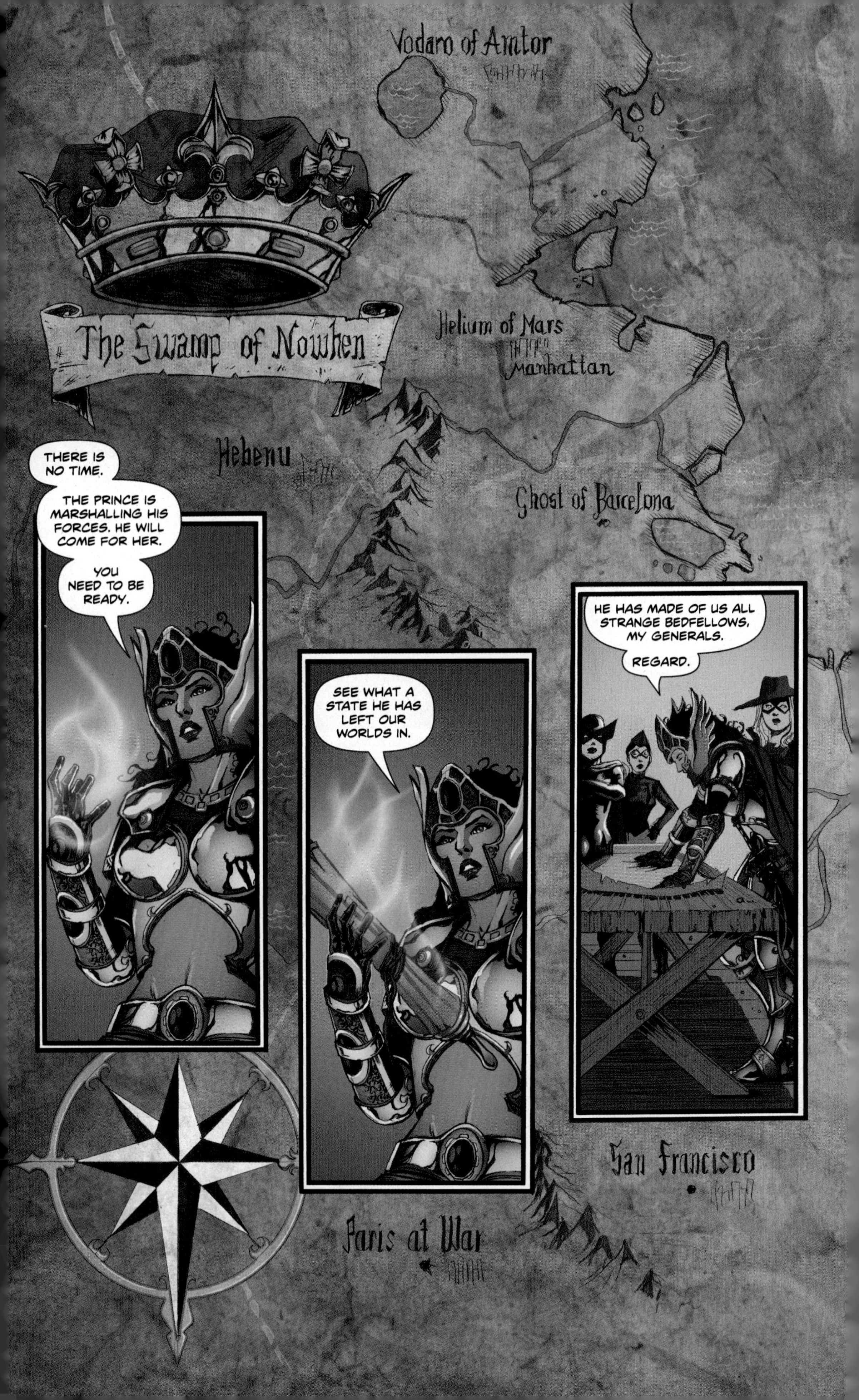

Vodaro of Amtor
The Swamp of Nowhen
Helium of Mars
Manhattan
Hebenu
Ghost of Barcelona
THERE IS NO TIME.
THE PRINCE IS MARSHALLING HIS FORCES. HE WILL COME FOR HER.
YOU NEED TO BE READY.
SEE WHAT A STATE HE HAS LEFT OUR WORLDS IN.
HE HAS MADE OF US ALL STRANGE BEDFELLOWS, MY GENERALS.
REGARD.
San Francisco
Paris at War

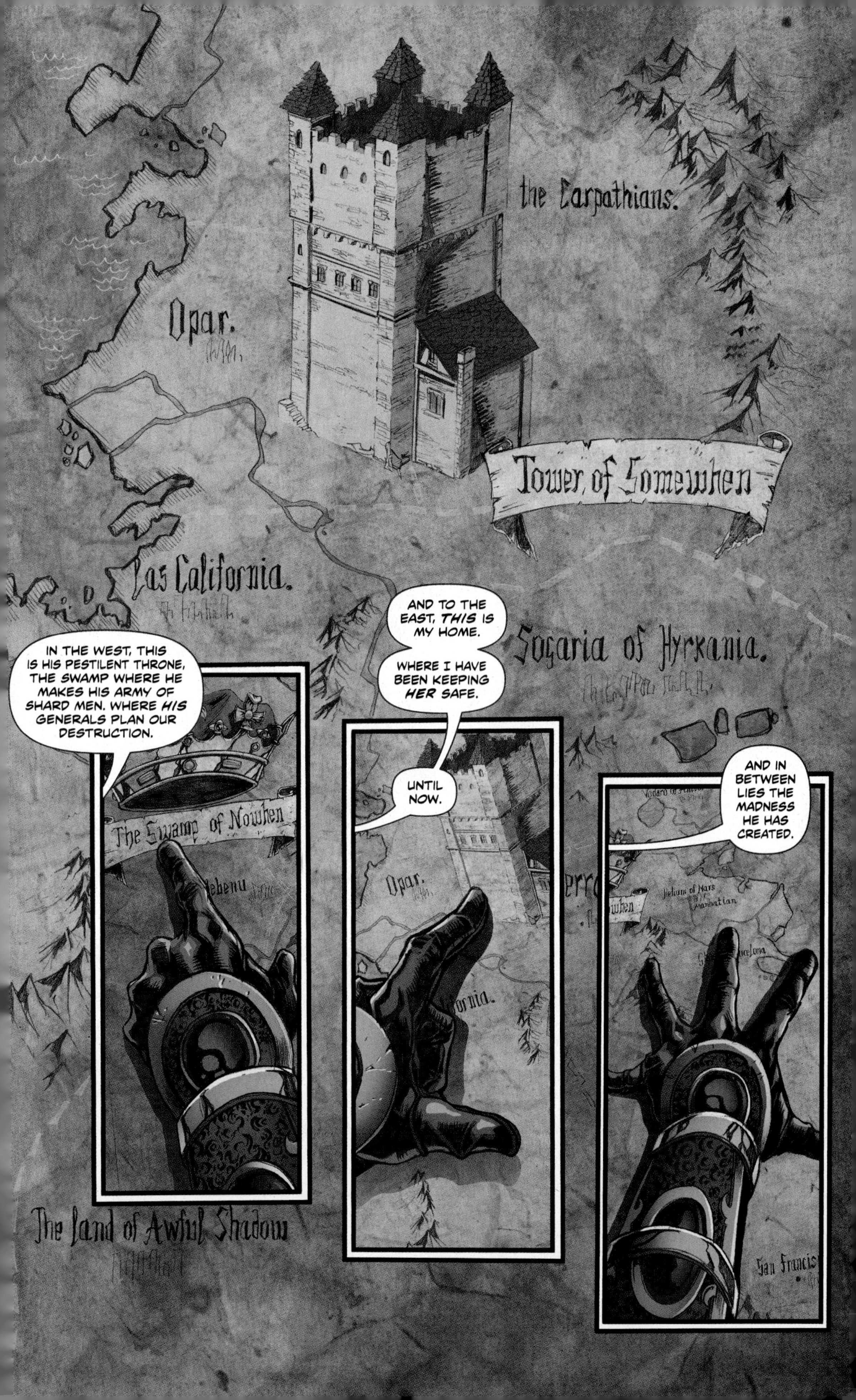
the Carpathians.
Opar.
Tower of Somewhen
Las California.
Sogaria of Hyrkania.
AND TO THE EAST, THIS IS MY HOME.
WHERE I HAVE BEEN KEEPING HER SAFE.
IN THE WEST, THIS IS HIS PESTILENT THRONE, THE SWAMP WHERE HE MAKES HIS ARMY OF SHARD MEN. WHERE HIS GENERALS PLAN OUR DESTRUCTION.
The Swamp of Nowhen
UNTIL NOW.
Opar.
AND IN BETWEEN LIES THE MADNESS HE HAS CREATED.
Helium of Mars
Manhattan
The Land of Awful Shadow

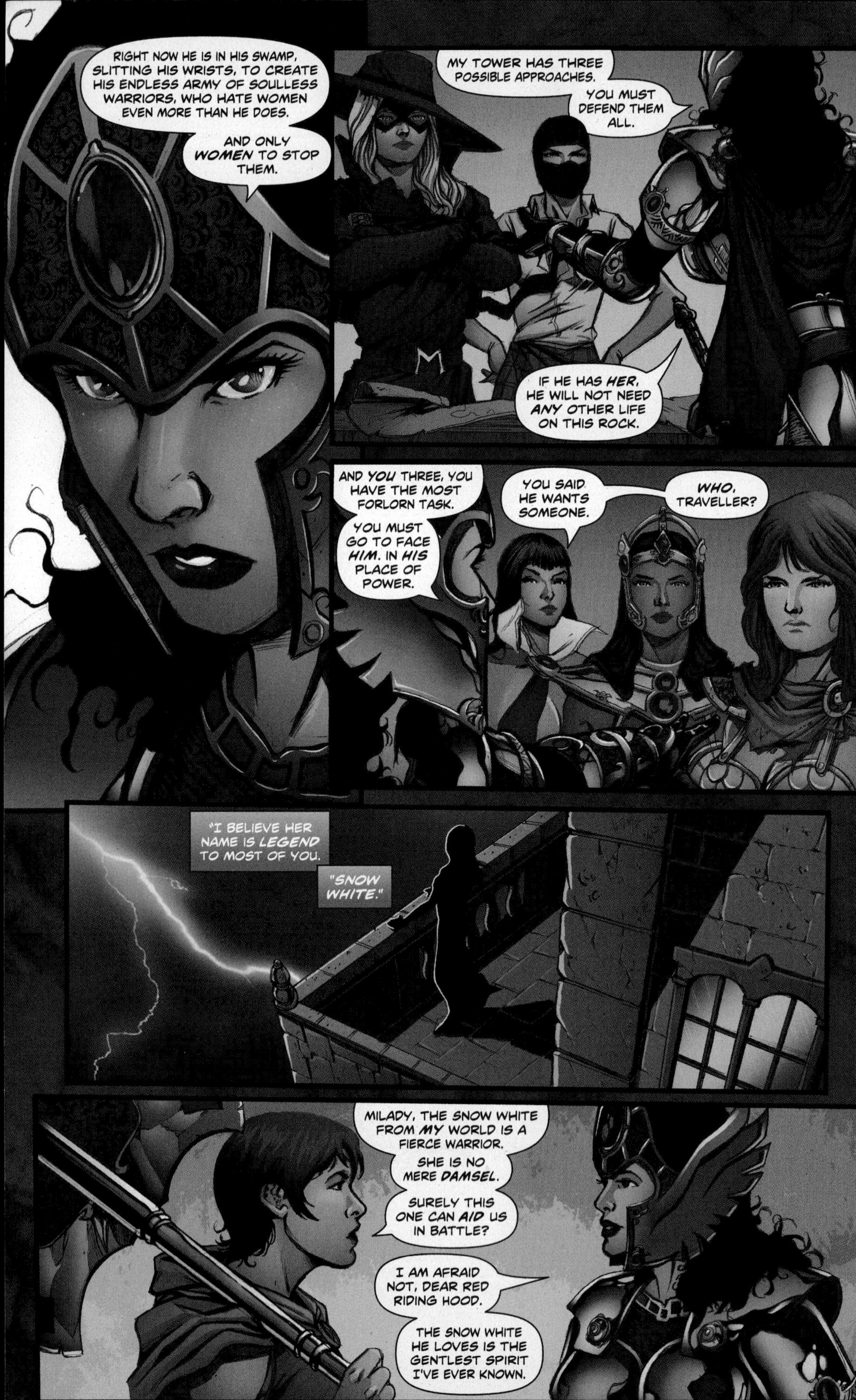
RIGHT NOW HE IS IN HIS SWAMP, SLITTING HIS WRISTS, TO CREATE HIS ENDLESS ARMY OF SOULLESS WARRIORS, WHO HATE WOMEN EVEN MORE THAN HE DOES.
AND ONLY WOMEN TO STOP THEM.
MY TOWER HAS THREE POSSIBLE APPROACHES.
YOU MUST DEFEND THEM ALL.
IF HE HAS HER, HE WILL NOT NEED ANY OTHER LIFE ON THIS ROCK.
AND YOU THREE, YOU HAVE THE MOST FORLORN TASK.
YOU MUST GO TO FACE HIM. IN HIS PLACE OF POWER.
YOU SAID HE WANTS SOMEONE.
WHO, TRAVELLER?
"I BELIEVE HER NAME IS LEGEND TO MOST OF YOU.
"SNOW WHITE."
MILADY, THE SNOW WHITE FROM MY WORLD IS A FIERCE WARRIOR.
SHE IS NO MERE DAMSEL.
SURELY THIS ONE CAN AID US IN BATTLE?
I AM AFRAID NOT, DEAR RED RIDING HOOD.
THE SNOW WHITE HE LOVES IS THE GENTLEST SPIRIT I'VE EVER KNOWN.

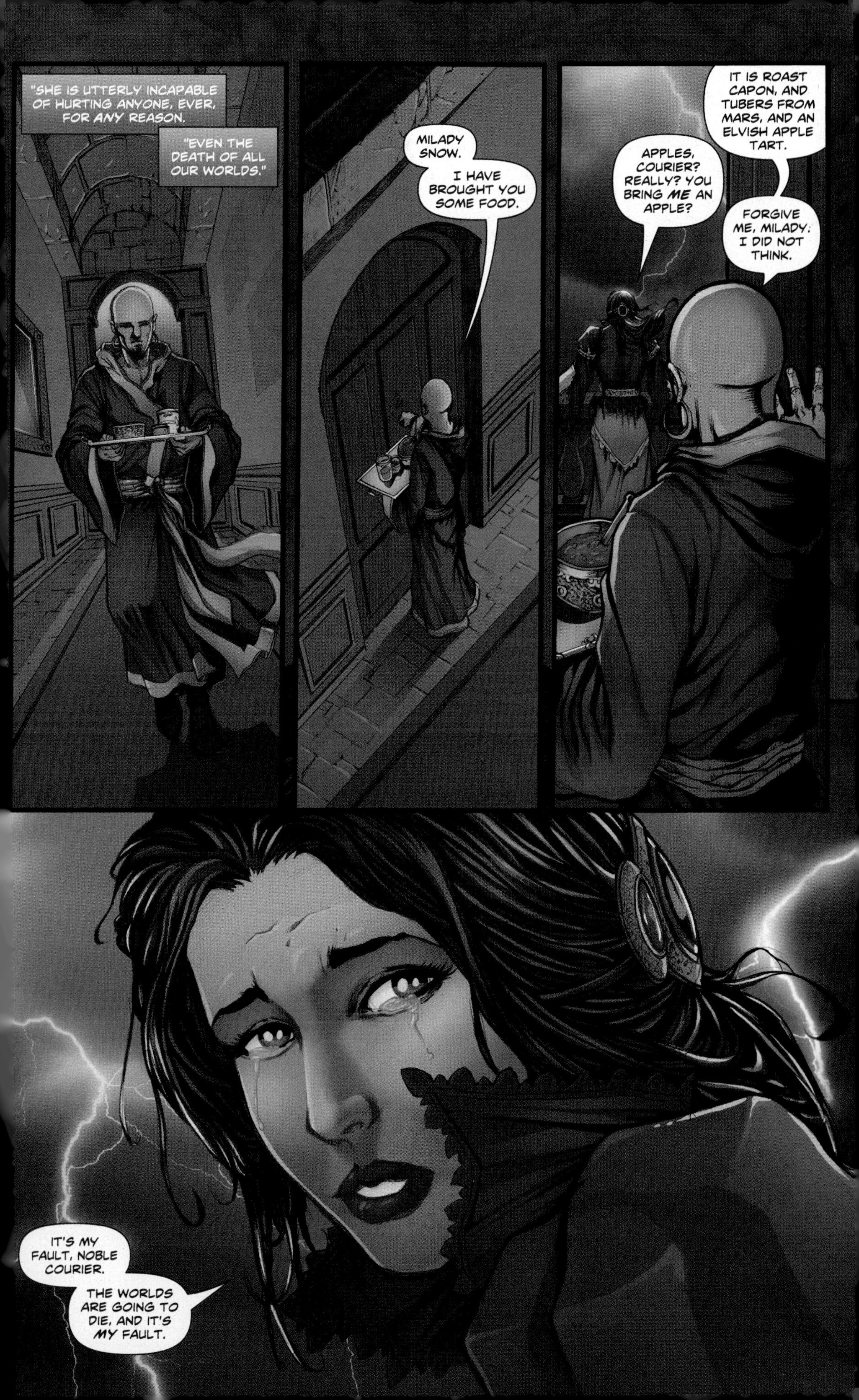
"SHE IS UTTERLY INCAPABLE OF HURTING ANYONE, EVER, FOR ANY REASON.
"EVEN THE DEATH OF ALL OUR WORLDS."
MILADY SNOW.
I HAVE BROUGHT YOU SOME FOOD.
IT IS ROAST CAPON, AND TUBERS FROM MARS, AND AN ELVISH APPLE TART.
APPLES, COURIER? REALLY? YOU BRING ME AN APPLE?
FORGIVE ME, MILADY. I DID NOT THINK.
IT'S MY FAULT, NOBLE COURIER.
THE WORLDS ARE GOING TO DIE, AND IT'S MY FAULT.

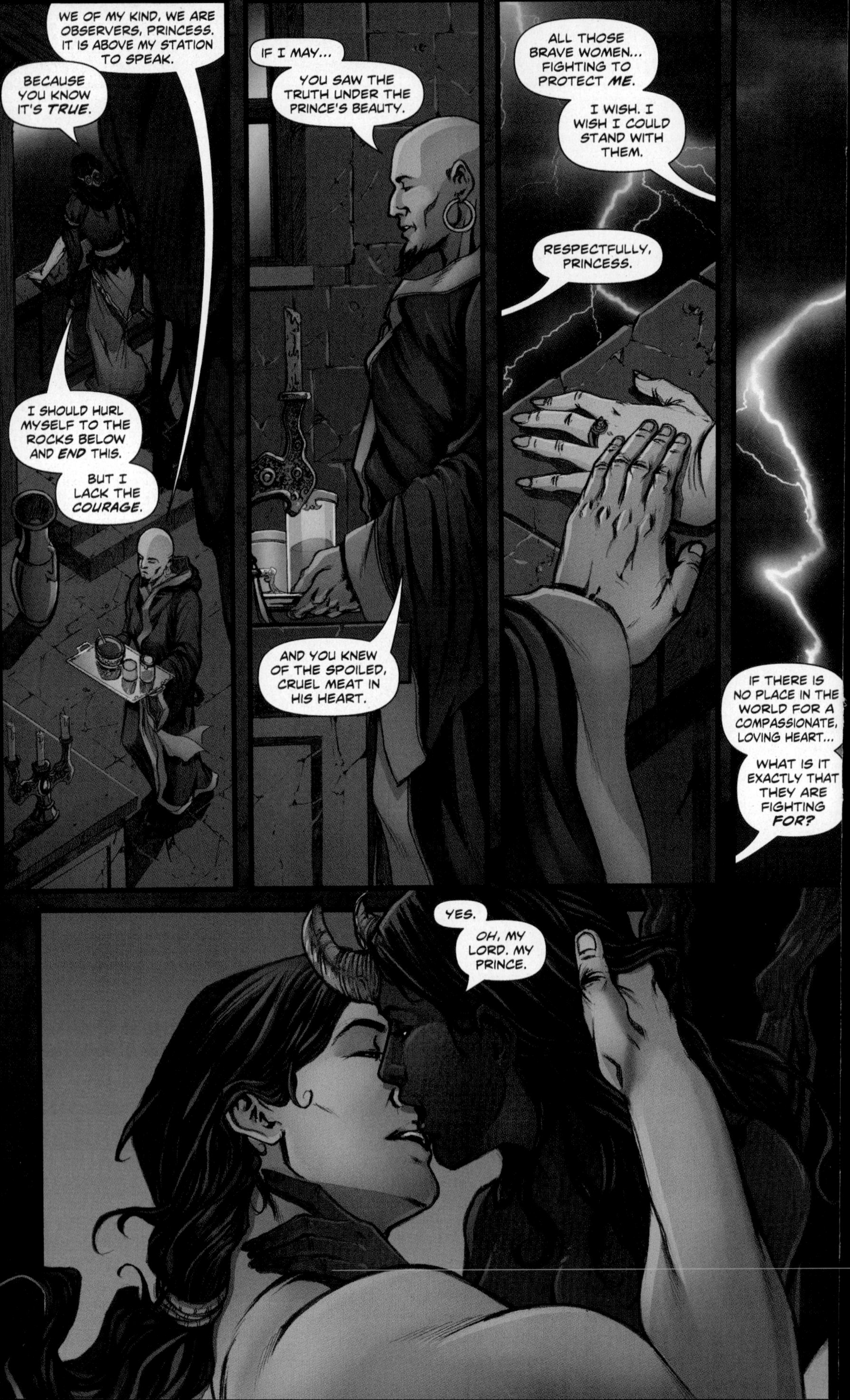

WE OF MY KIND, WE ARE OBSERVERS, PRINCESS. IT IS ABOVE MY STATION TO SPEAK.
BECAUSE YOU KNOW IT'S TRUE.
I SHOULD HURL MYSELF TO THE ROCKS BELOW AND END THIS.
BUT I LACK THE COURAGE.
IF I MAY...
YOU SAW THE TRUTH UNDER THE PRINCE'S BEAUTY.
AND YOU KNEW OF THE SPOILED, CRUEL MEAT IN HIS HEART.
ALL THOSE BRAVE WOMEN... FIGHTING TO PROTECT ME.
I WISH. I WISH I COULD STAND WITH THEM.
RESPECTFULLY, PRINCESS.
IF THERE IS NO PLACE IN THE WORLD FOR A COMPASSIONATE, LOVING HEART...
WHAT IS IT EXACTLY THAT THEY ARE FIGHTING FOR?
YES.
OH, MY LORD. MY PRINCE.

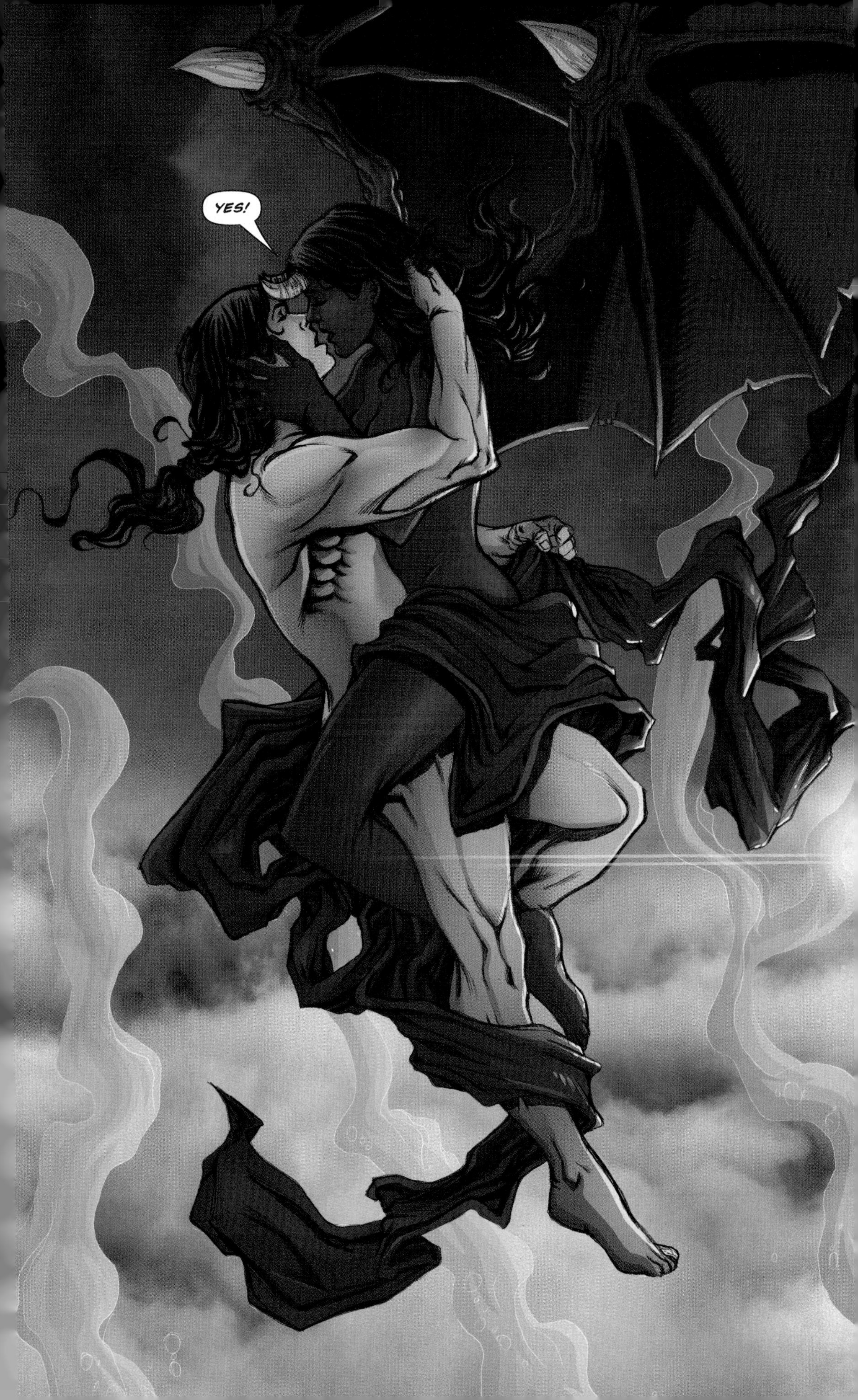
YES!

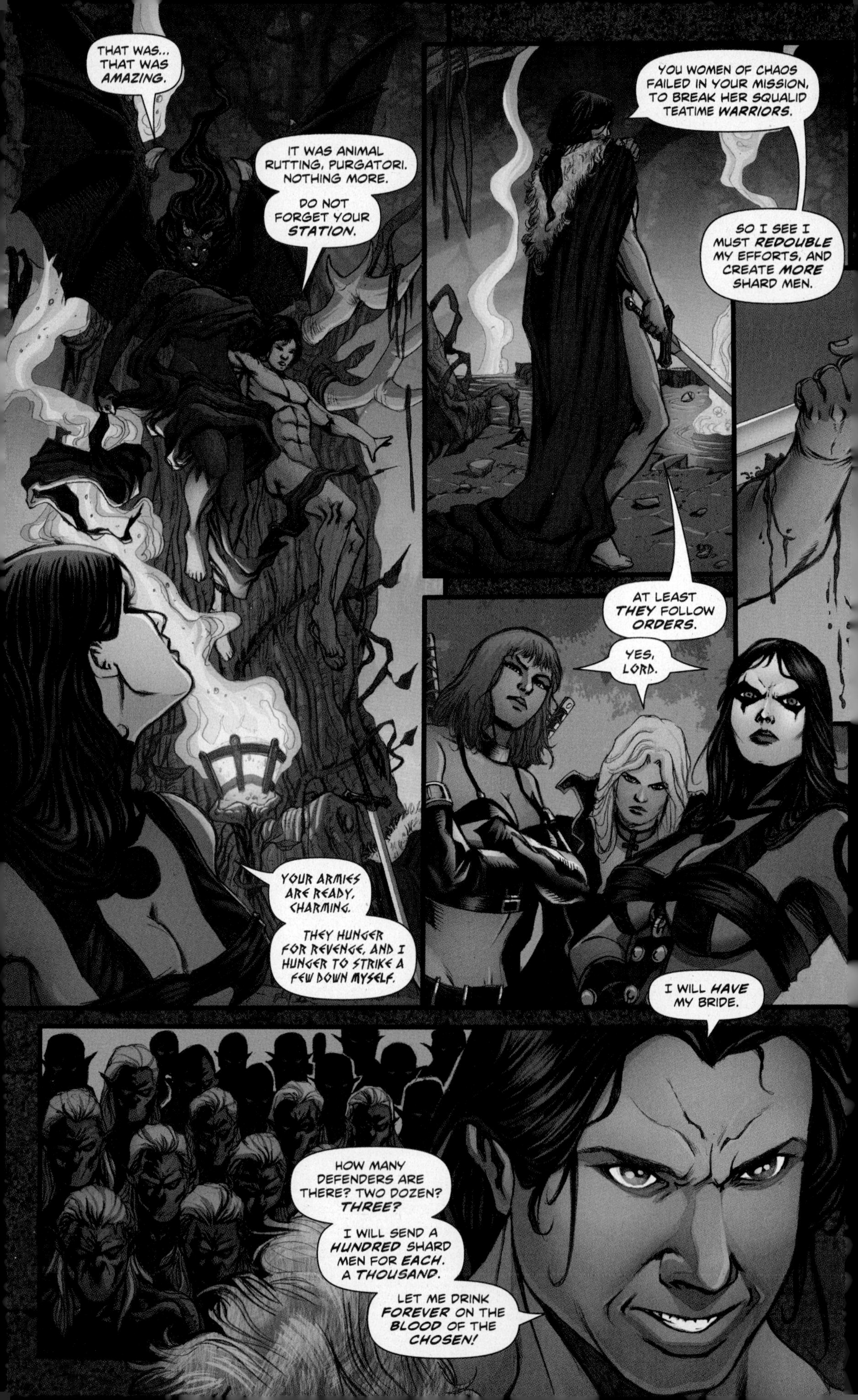

THAT WAS... THAT WAS AMAZING.
IT WAS ANIMAL RUTTING, PURGATORI. NOTHING MORE.
DO NOT FORGET YOUR STATION.
YOUR ARMIES ARE READY, CHARMING.
THEY HUNGER FOR REVENGE, AND I HUNGER TO STRIKE A FEW DOWN MYSELF.
YOU WOMEN OF CHAOS FAILED IN YOUR MISSION, TO BREAK HER SQUALID TEATIME WARRIORS.
SO I SEE I MUST REDOUBLE MY EFFORTS, AND CREATE MORE SHARD MEN.
AT LEAST THEY FOLLOW ORDERS.
YES, LORD.
I WILL HAVE MY BRIDE.
HOW MANY DEFENDERS ARE THERE? TWO DOZEN? THREE?
I WILL SEND A HUNDRED SHARD MEN FOR EACH. A THOUSAND.
LET ME DRINK FOREVER ON THE BLOOD OF THE CHOSEN!

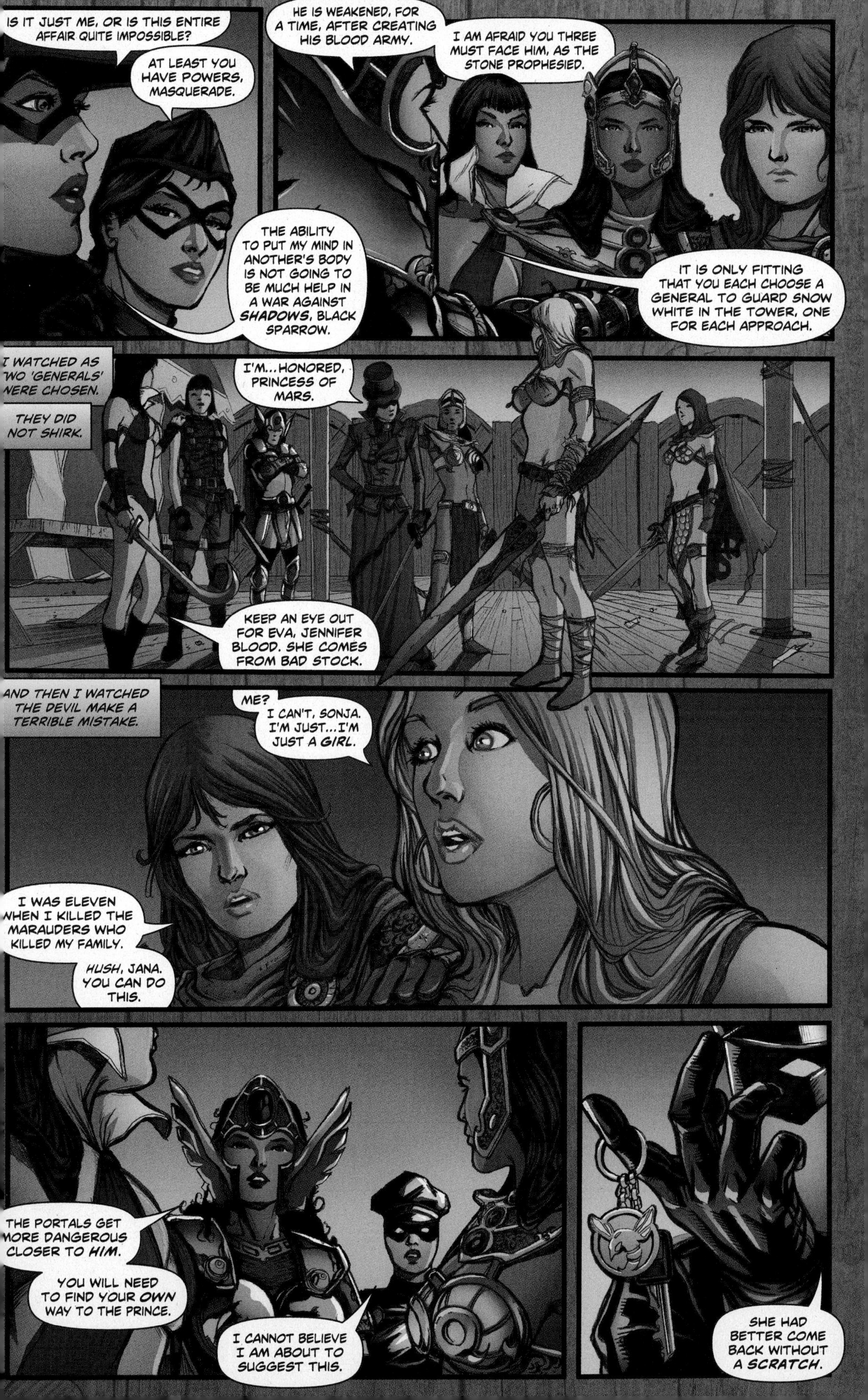
IS IT JUST ME, OR IS THIS ENTIRE AFFAIR QUITE IMPOSSIBLE?
AT LEAST YOU HAVE POWERS, MASQUERADE.
THE ABILITY TO PUT MY MIND IN ANOTHER'S BODY IS NOT GOING TO BE MUCH HELP IN A WAR AGAINST SHADOWS, BLACK SPARROW.
HE IS WEAKENED, FOR A TIME, AFTER CREATING HIS BLOOD ARMY.
I AM AFRAID YOU THREE MUST FACE HIM, AS THE STONE PROPHESIED.
IT IS ONLY FITTING THAT YOU EACH CHOOSE A GENERAL TO GUARD SNOW WHITE IN THE TOWER, ONE FOR EACH APPROACH.
WATCHED AS WO 'GENERALS' WERE CHOSEN.
THEY DID NOT SHIRK.
I'M...HONORED, PRINCESS OF MARS.
KEEP AN EYE OUT FOR EVA, JENNIFER BLOOD. SHE COMES FROM BAD STOCK.
AND THEN I WATCHED THE DEVIL MAKE A TERRIBLE MISTAKE.
ME? I CAN'T, SONJA. I'M JUST...I'M JUST A GIRL.
I WAS ELEVEN WHEN I KILLED THE MARAUDERS WHO KILLED MY FAMILY.
HUSH, JANA. YOU CAN DO THIS.
THE PORTALS GET MORE DANGEROUS CLOSER TO HIM.
YOU WILL NEED TO FIND YOUR OWN WAY TO THE PRINCE.
I CANNOT BELIEVE I AM ABOUT TO SUGGEST THIS.
SHE HAD BETTER COME BACK WITHOUT A SCRATCH.

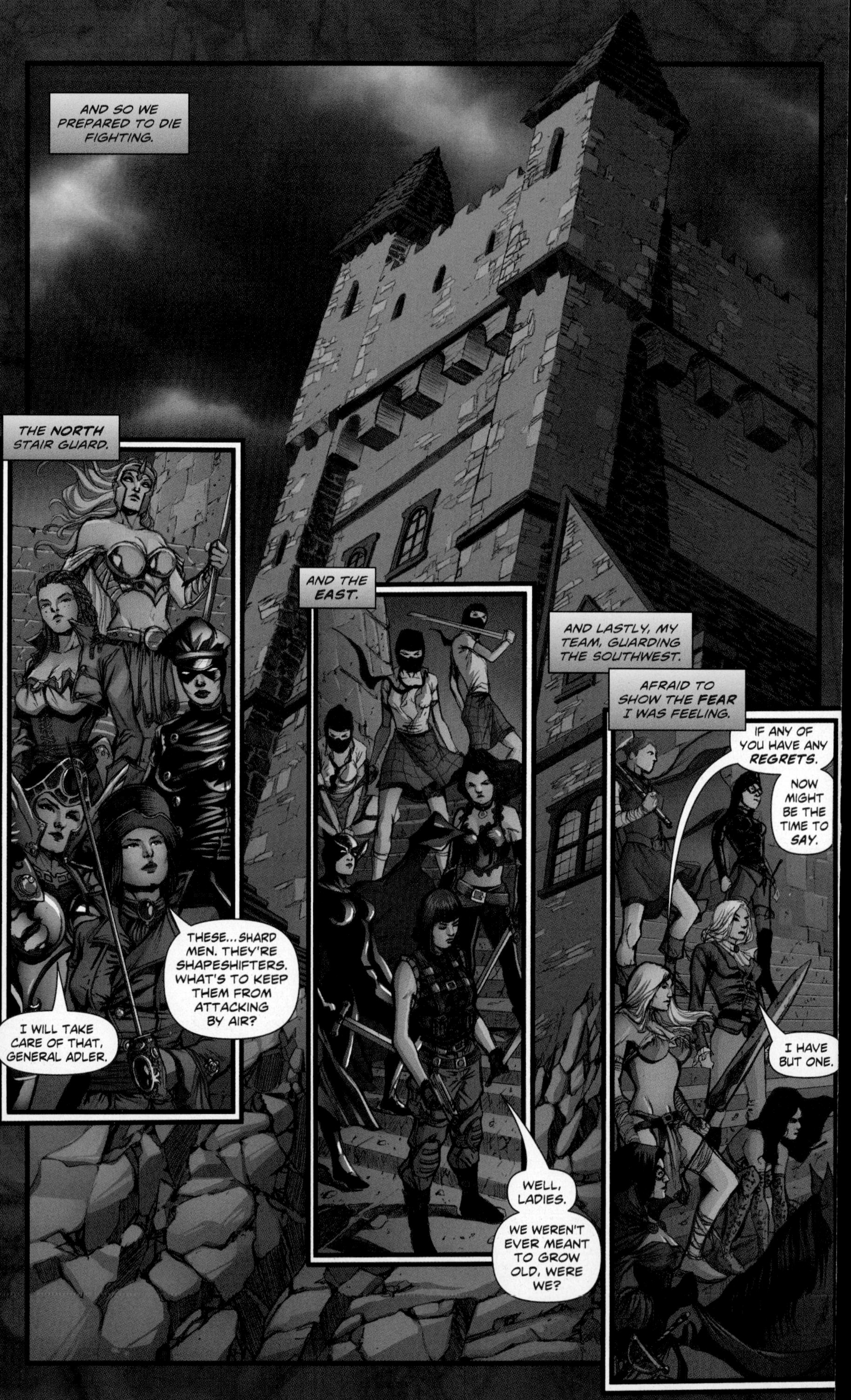
AND SO WE PREPARED TO DIE FIGHTING.
THE NORTH STAIR GUARD.
THESE... SHARD MEN. THEY'RE SHAPESHIFTERS. WHAT'S TO KEEP THEM FROM ATTACKING BY AIR?
I WILL TAKE CARE OF THAT, GENERAL ADLER.
AND THE EAST.
WELL, LADIES.
WE WEREN'T EVER MEANT TO GROW OLD, WERE WE?
AND LASTLY, MY TEAM, GUARDING THE SOUTHWEST.
AFRAID TO SHOW THE FEAR I WAS FEELING.
IF ANY OF YOU HAVE ANY REGRETS.
NOW MIGHT BE THE TIME TO SAY.
I HAVE BUT ONE.

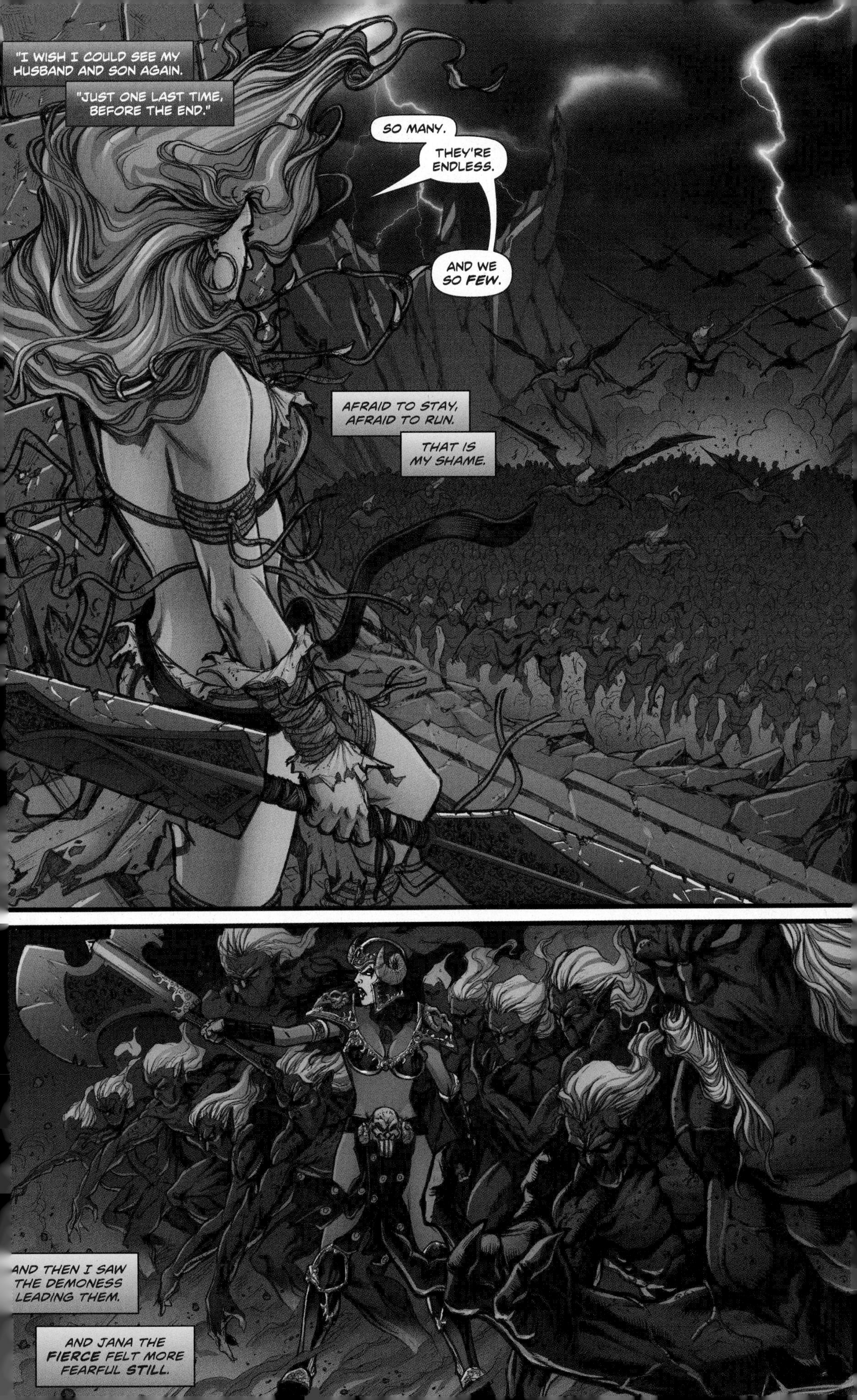
"I WISH I COULD SEE MY HUSBAND AND SON AGAIN.
"JUST ONE LAST TIME, BEFORE THE END."
SO MANY.
THEY'RE ENDLESS.
AND WE SO FEW.
AFRAID TO STAY, AFRAID TO RUN.
THAT IS MY SHAME.
AND THEN I SAW THE DEMONESS LEADING THEM.
AND JANA THE FIERCE FELT MORE FEARFUL STILL.

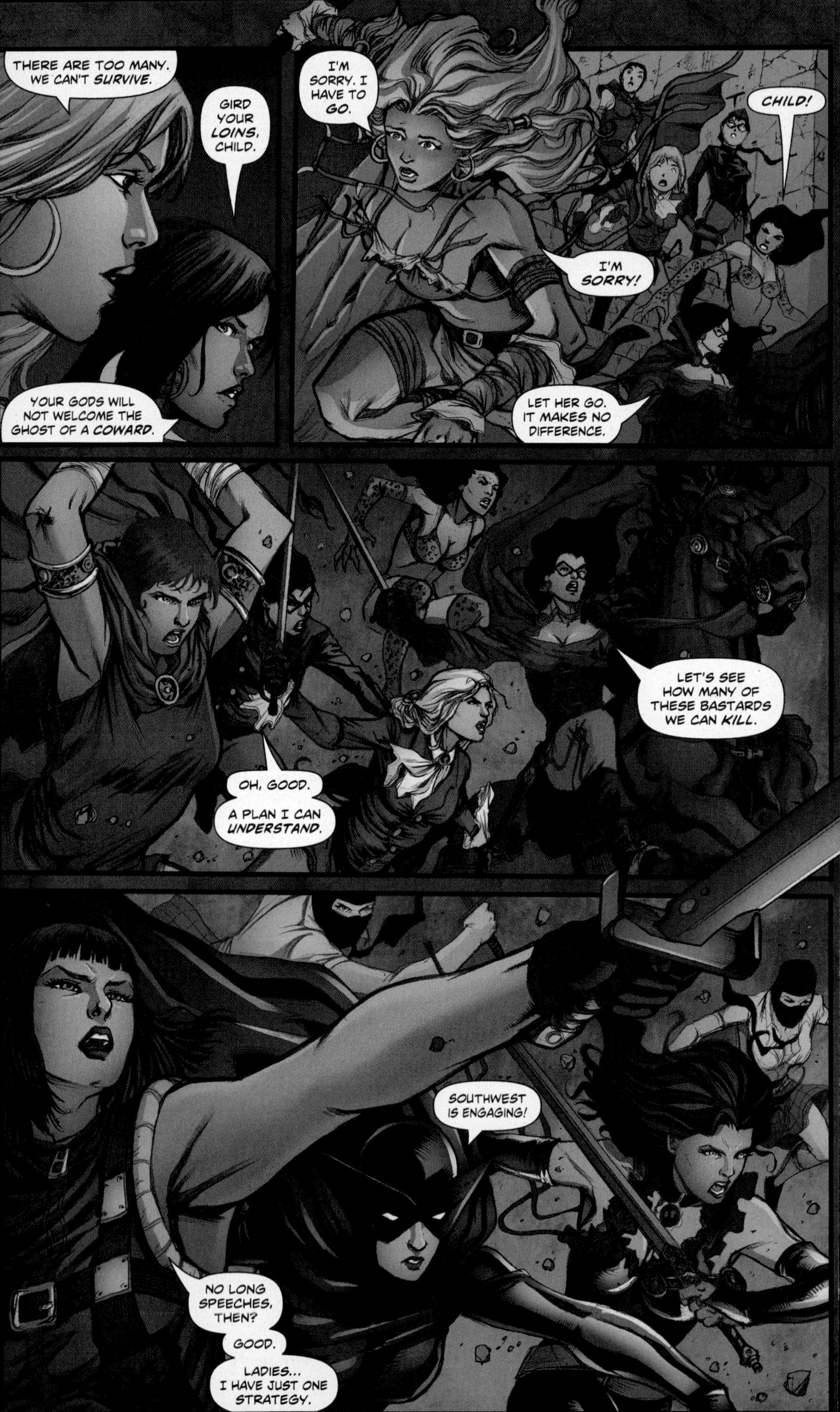

THERE ARE TOO MANY. WE CAN'T *SURVIVE*.
GIRD YOUR *LOINS*, CHILD.
YOUR GODS WILL NOT WELCOME THE GHOST OF A *COWARD*.
I'M SORRY. I HAVE TO *GO*.
CHILD!
I'M *SORRY!*
LET HER GO. IT MAKES NO DIFFERENCE.
LET'S SEE HOW MANY OF THESE BASTARDS WE CAN *KILL*.
OH, GOOD.
A PLAN I CAN *UNDERSTAND*.
SOUTHWEST IS ENGAGING!
NO LONG SPEECHES, THEN?
GOOD.
LADIES... I HAVE JUST ONE STRATEGY.

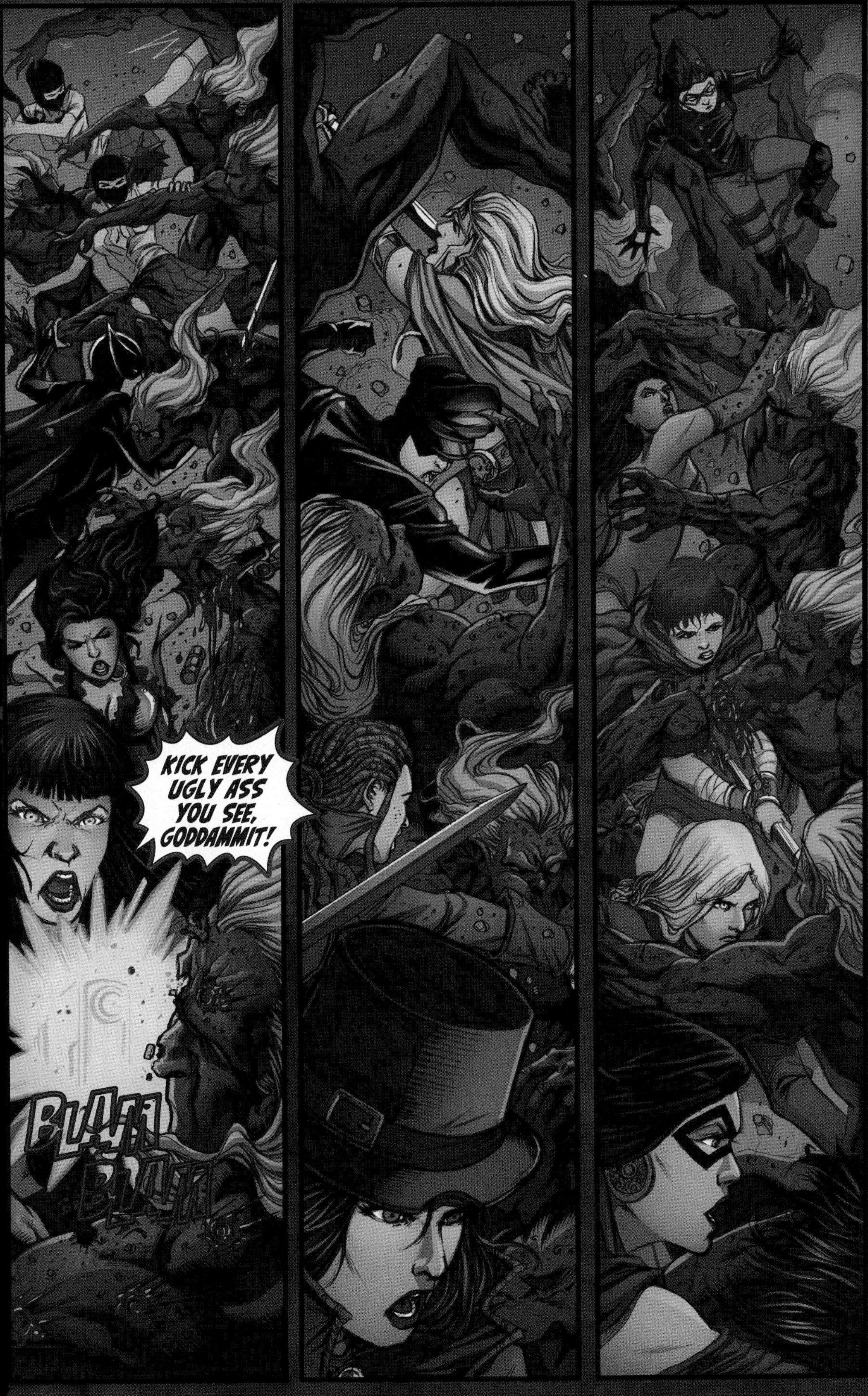
KICK EVERY UGLY ASS YOU SEE, GODDAMMIT!
BLAM
BLAM

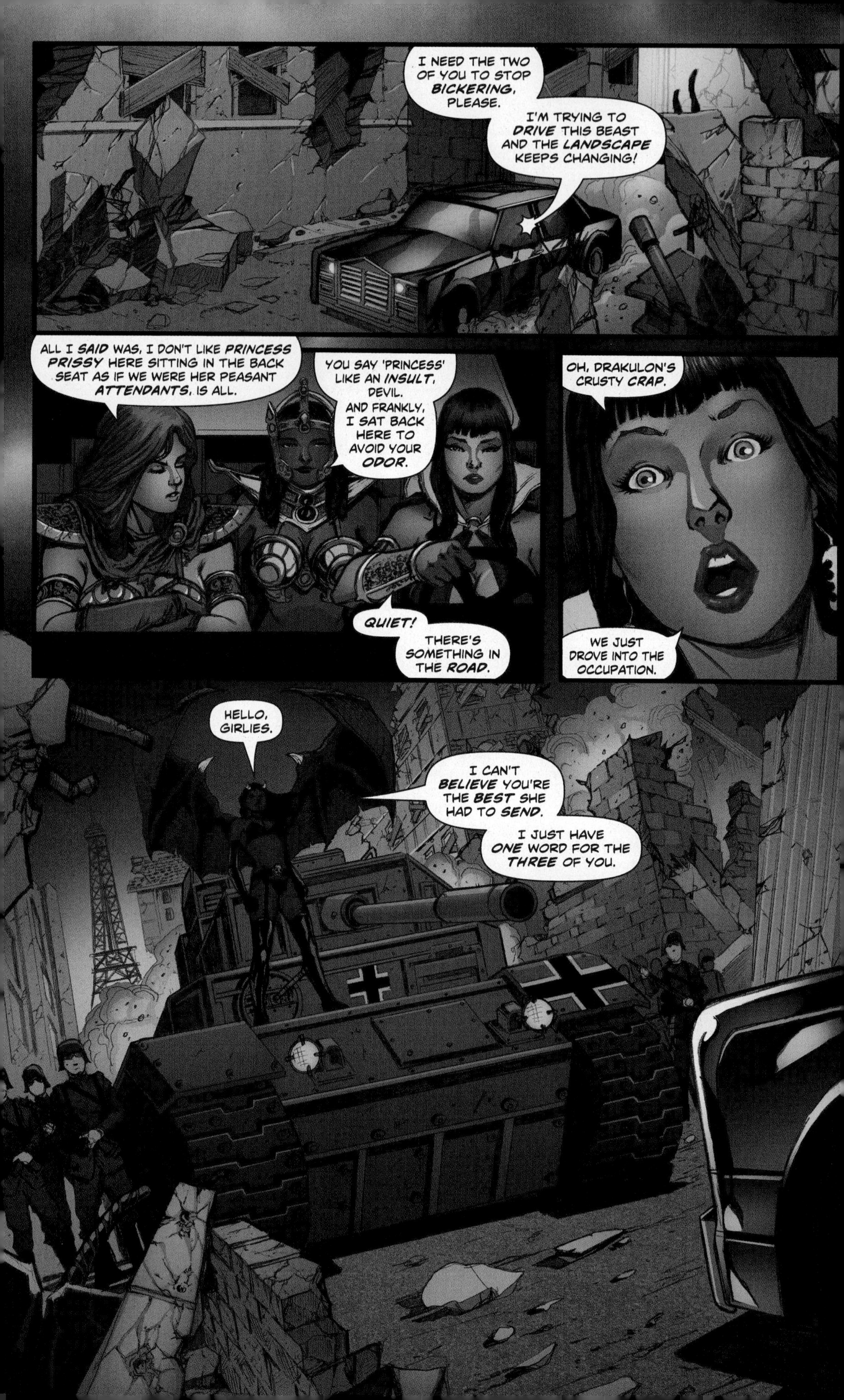
I NEED THE TWO OF YOU TO STOP BICKERING, PLEASE.
I'M TRYING TO DRIVE THIS BEAST AND THE LANDSCAPE KEEPS CHANGING!
ALL I SAID WAS, I DON'T LIKE PRINCESS PRISSY HERE SITTING IN THE BACK SEAT AS IF WE WERE HER PEASANT ATTENDANTS, IS ALL.
YOU SAY 'PRINCESS' LIKE AN INSULT, DEVIL.
AND FRANKLY, I SAT BACK HERE TO AVOID YOUR ODOR.
QUIET!
THERE'S SOMETHING IN THE ROAD.
OH, DRAKULON'S CRUSTY CRAP.
WE JUST DROVE INTO THE OCCUPATION.
HELLO, GIRLIES.
I CAN'T BELIEVE YOU'RE THE BEST SHE HAD TO SEND.
I JUST HAVE ONE WORD FOR THE THREE OF YOU.

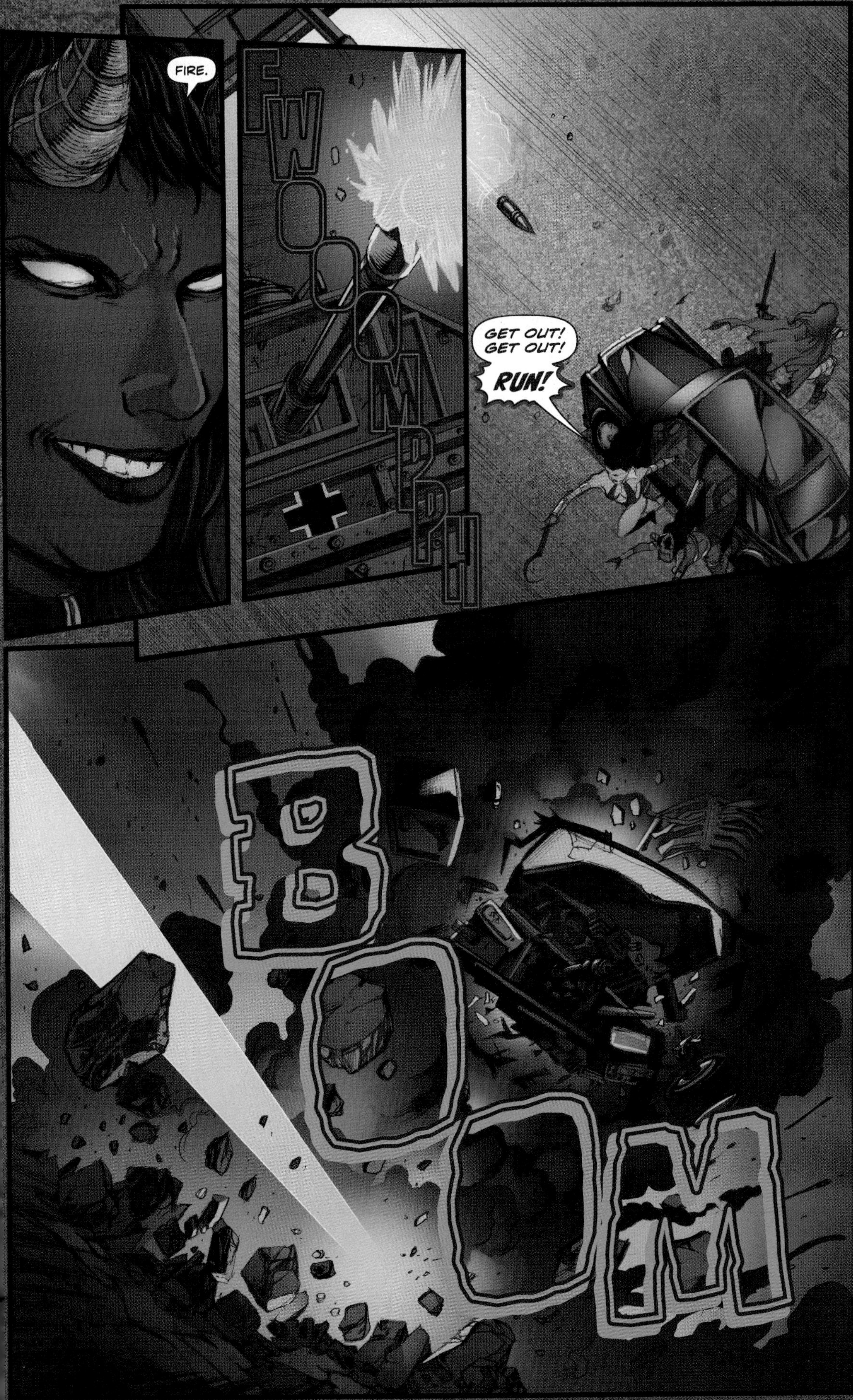
FIRE.
FWOOOOMPH
GET OUT!
GET OUT!
RUN!
BOOM

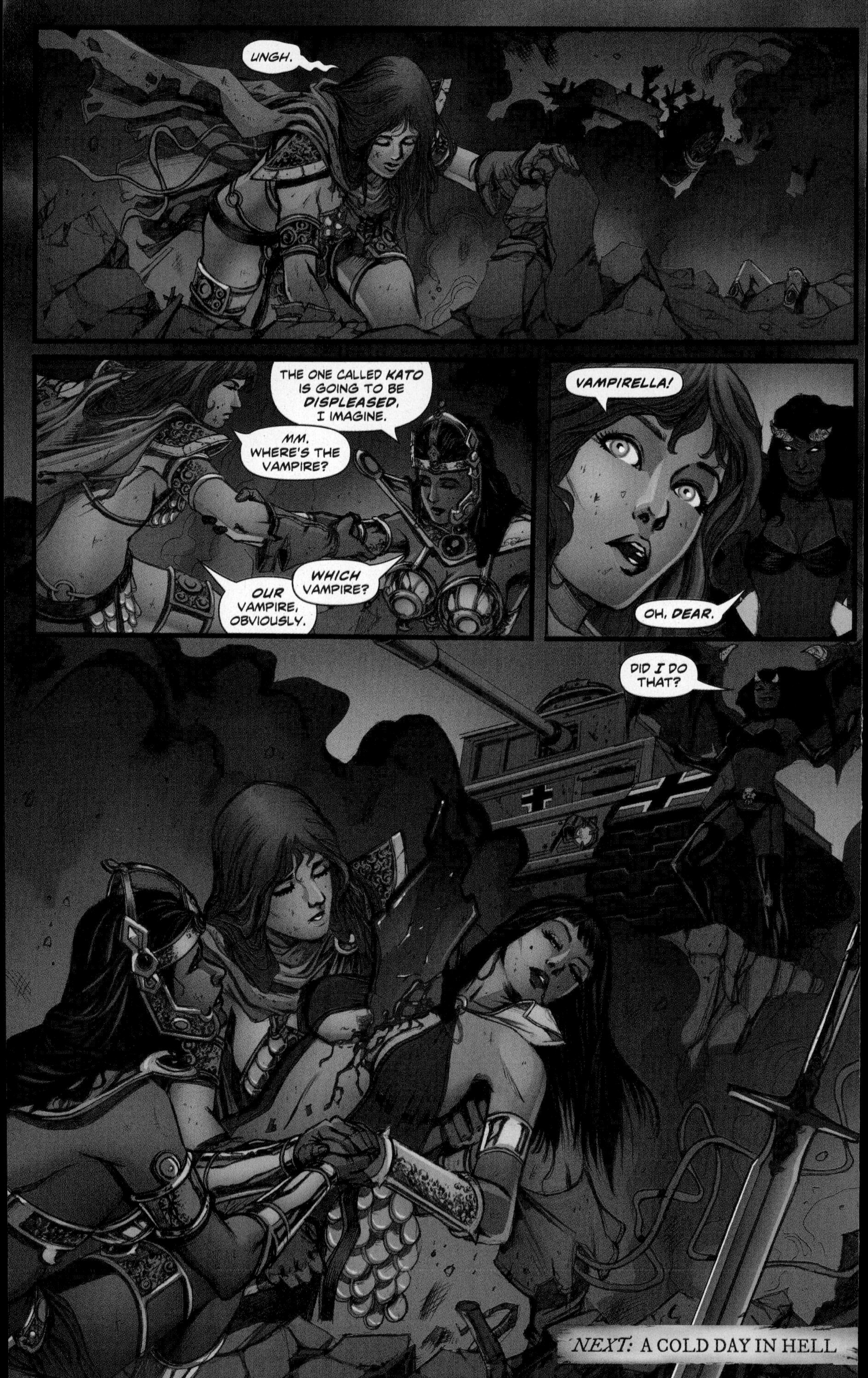
UNGH.
THE ONE CALLED KATO IS GOING TO BE DISPLEASED, I IMAGINE.
MM. WHERE'S THE VAMPIRE?
WHICH VAMPIRE?
OUR VAMPIRE, OBVIOUSLY.
VAMPIRELLA!
OH, DEAR.
DID I DO THAT?
NEXT: A COLD DAY IN HELL

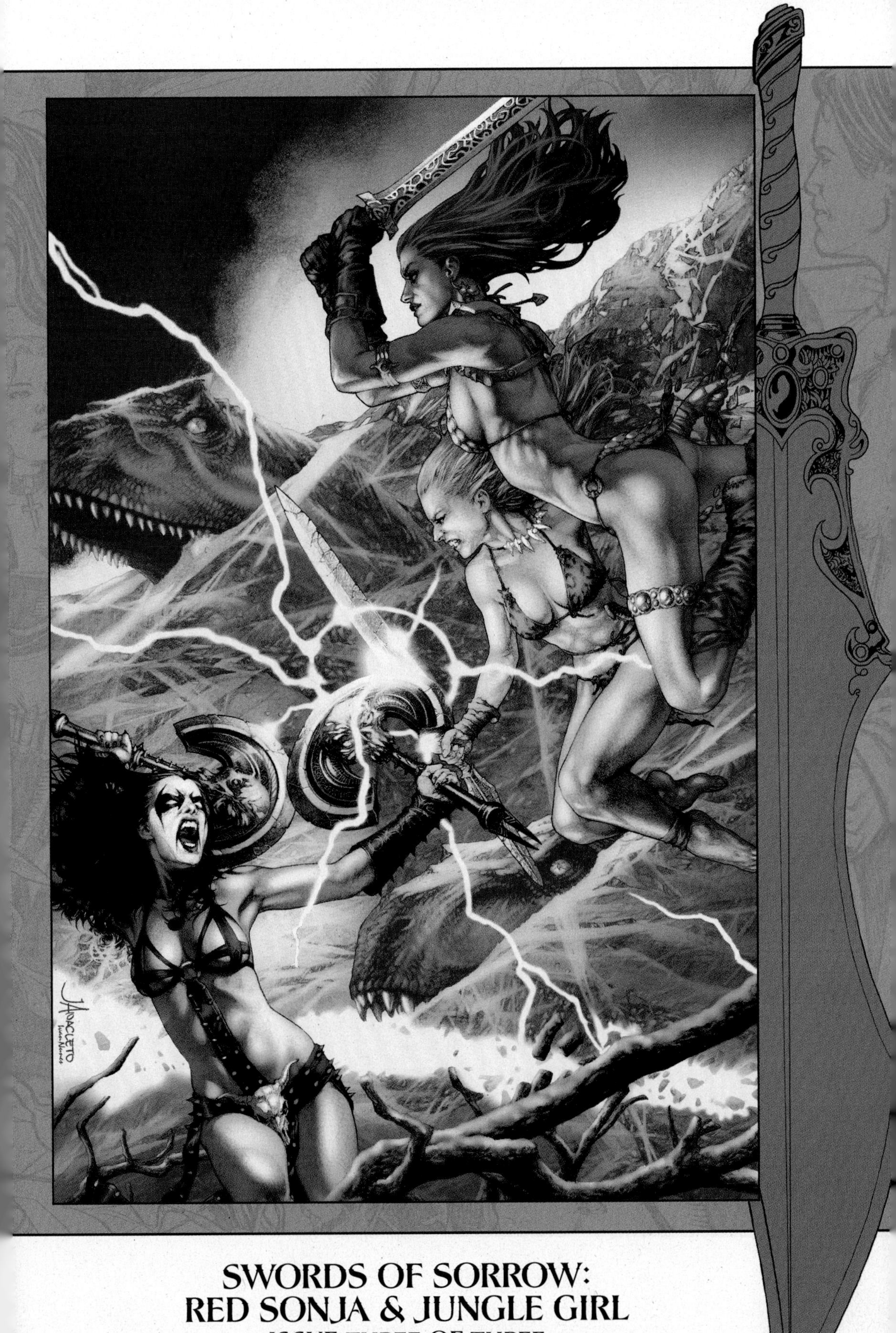

SWORDS OF SORROW: RED SONJA & JUNGLE GIRL

ISSUE THREE OF THREE

written by MARGUERITE BENNETT pencilled by MIRKA ANDOLFO
inked by ELISA FERRARI (Arancia Studio)
colored by VINCENZO SALVO (Arancia Studio) lettered by ERICA SCHULTZ

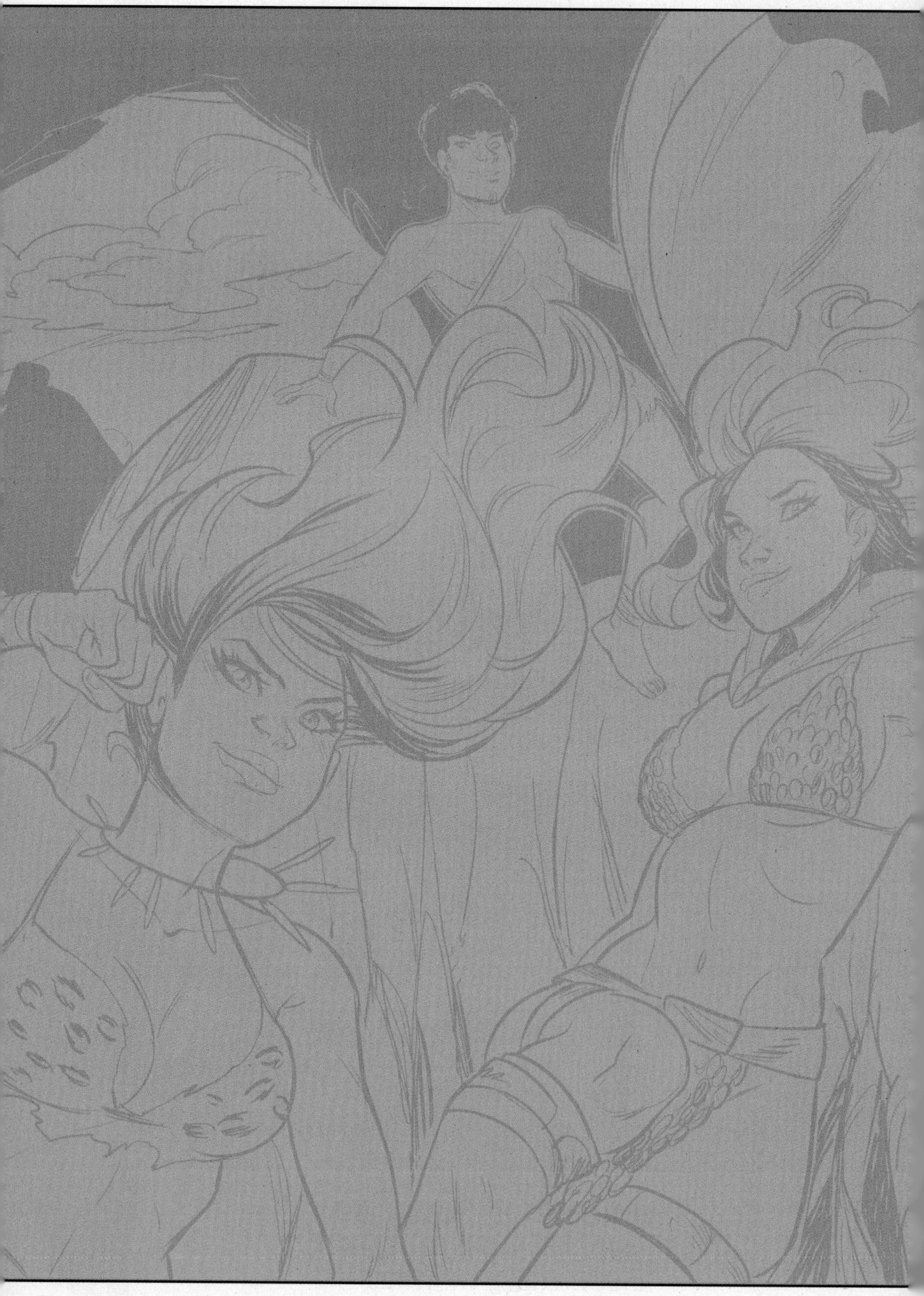

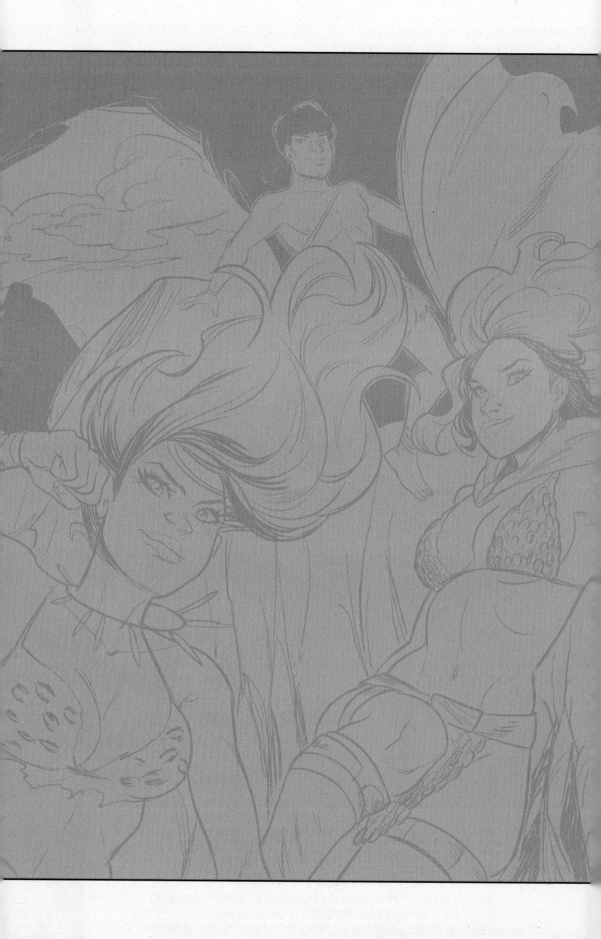

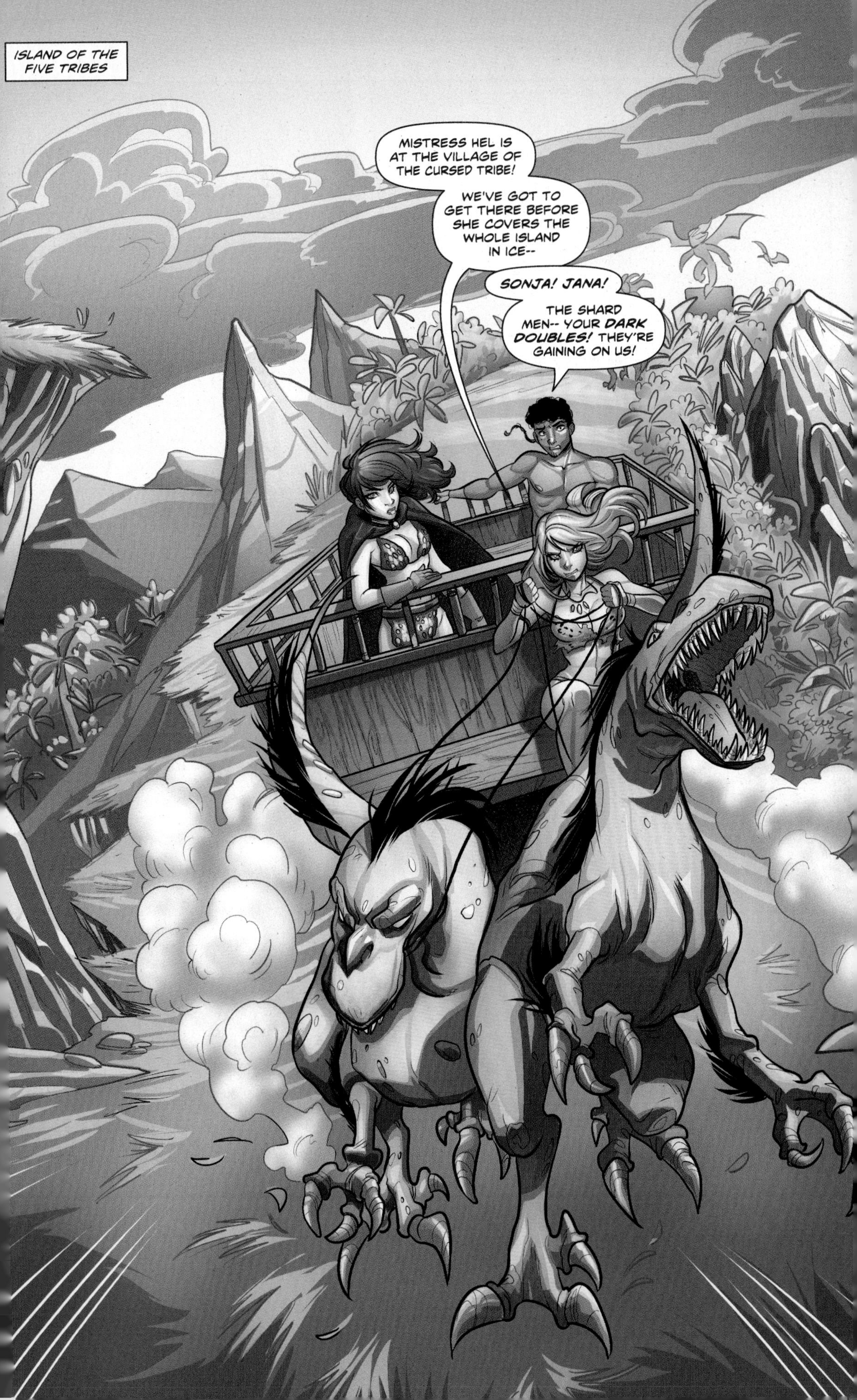
ISLAND OF THE FIVE TRIBES
MISTRESS HEL IS AT THE VILLAGE OF THE CURSED TRIBE!
WE'VE GOT TO GET THERE BEFORE SHE COVERS THE WHOLE ISLAND IN ICE--
SONJA! JANA!
THE SHARD MEN-- YOUR DARK DOUBLES! THEY'RE GAINING ON US!

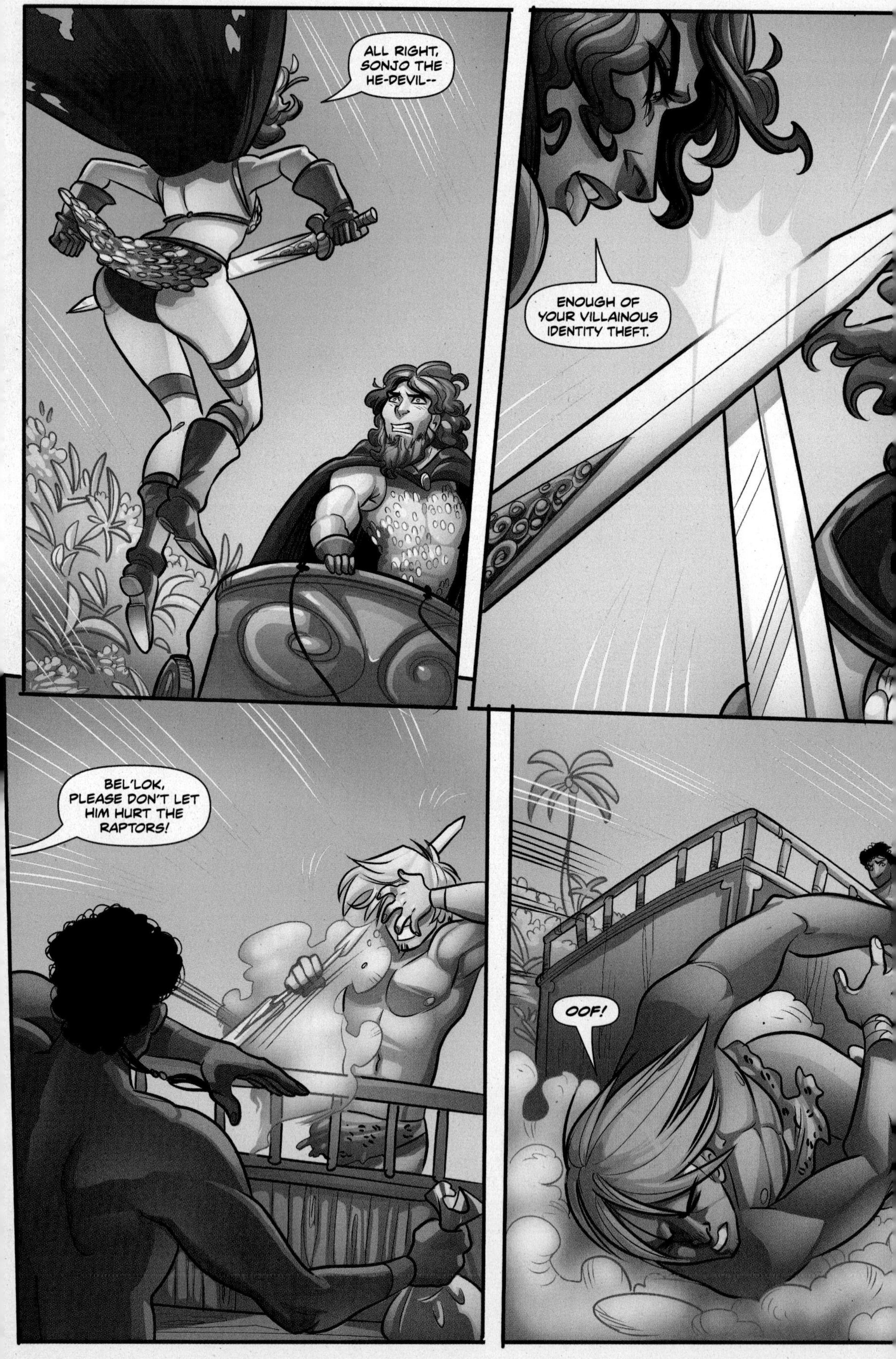
ALL RIGHT, SONJO THE HE-DEVIL--
ENOUGH OF YOUR VILLAINOUS IDENTITY THEFT.
BEL'LOK, PLEASE DON'T LET HIM HURT THE RAPTORS!
OOF!

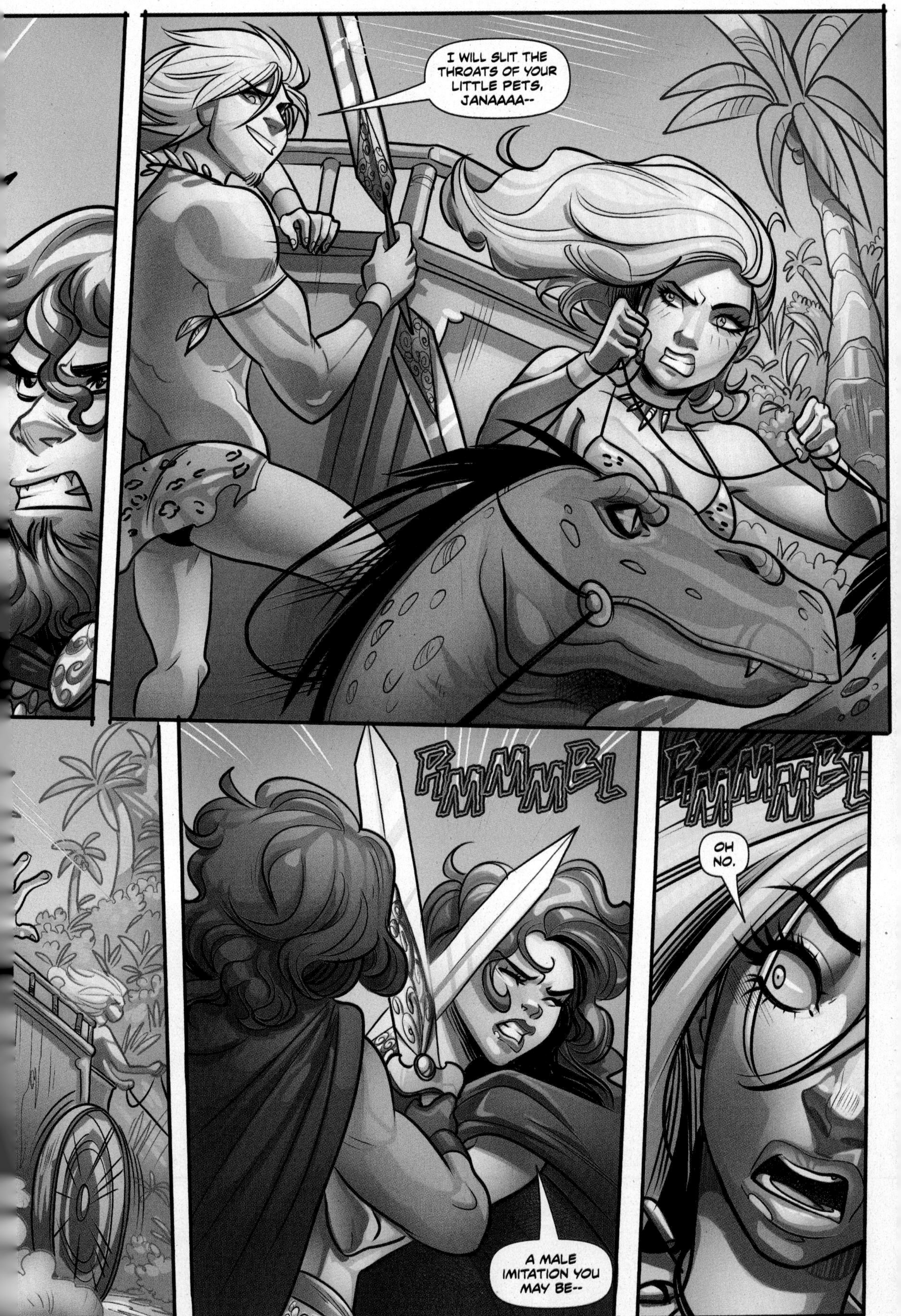
I WILL SLIT THE THROATS OF YOUR LITTLE PETS, JANAAAA--
RMMMBL
A MALE IMITATION YOU MAY BE--
RMMMMBL
OH NO.

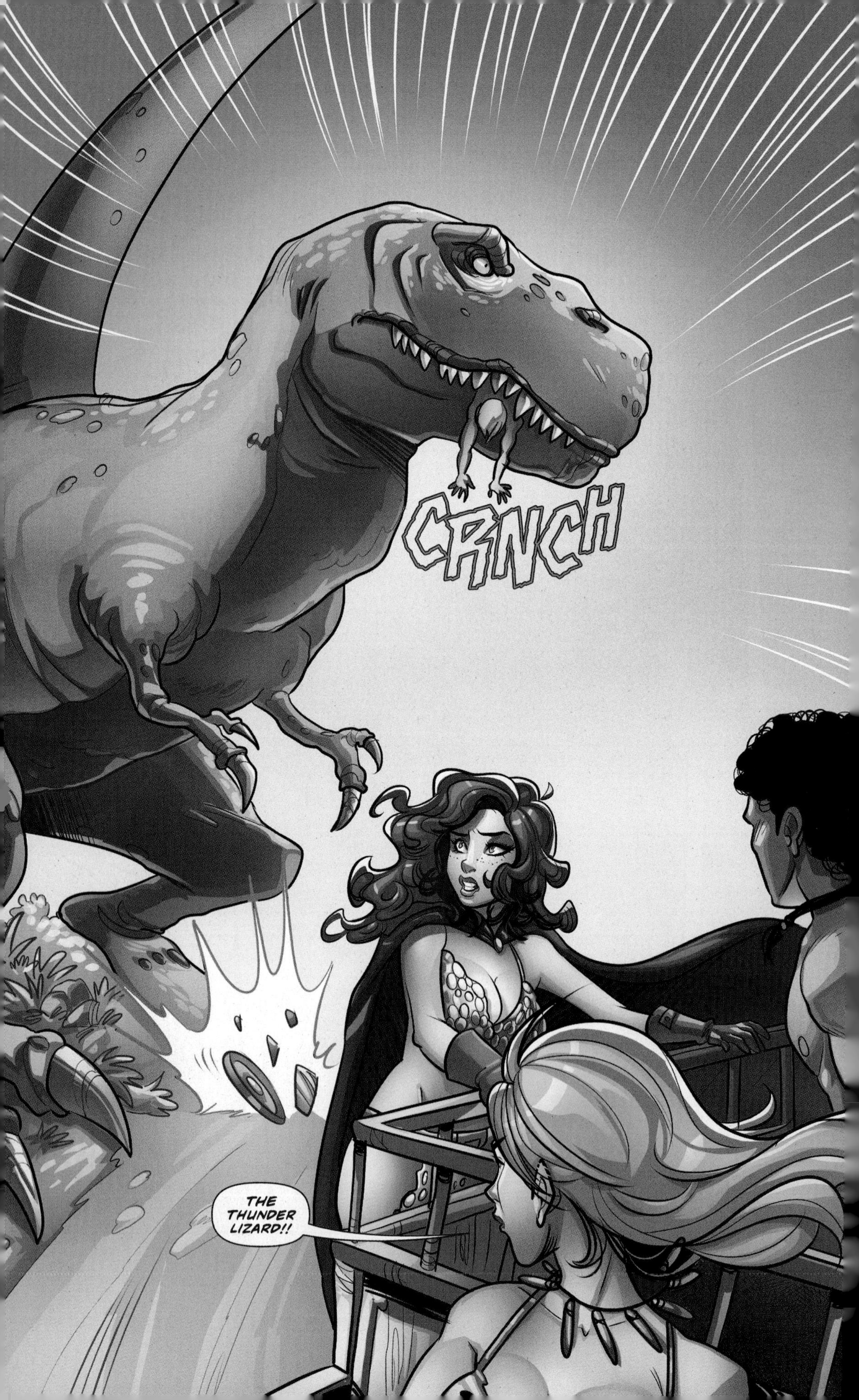
CRNCH
THE THUNDER LIZARD!!

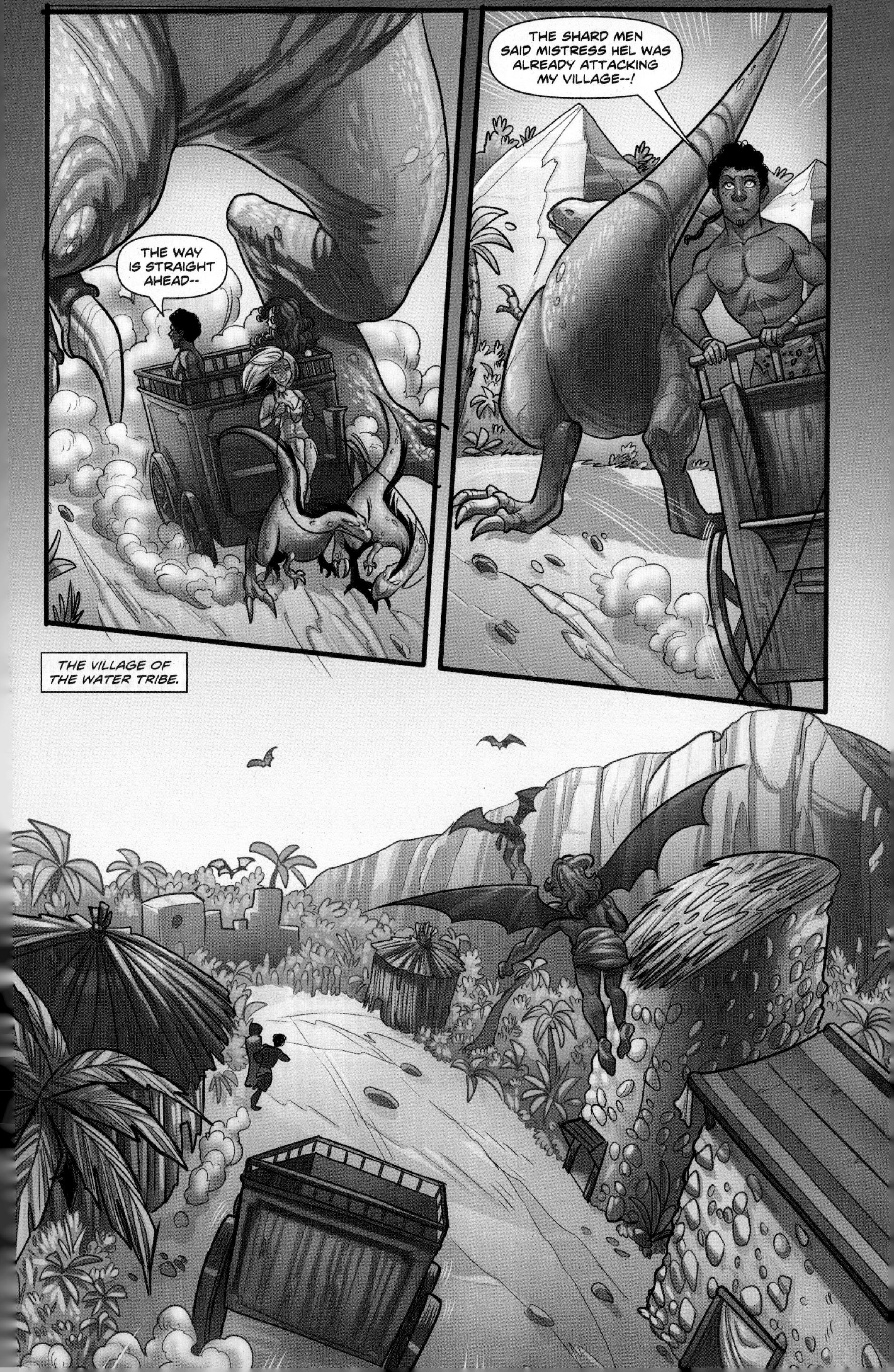
THE WAY IS STRAIGHT AHEAD--
THE SHARD MEN SAID MISTRESS HEL WAS ALREADY ATTACKING MY VILLAGE--!
THE VILLAGE OF THE WATER TRIBE.

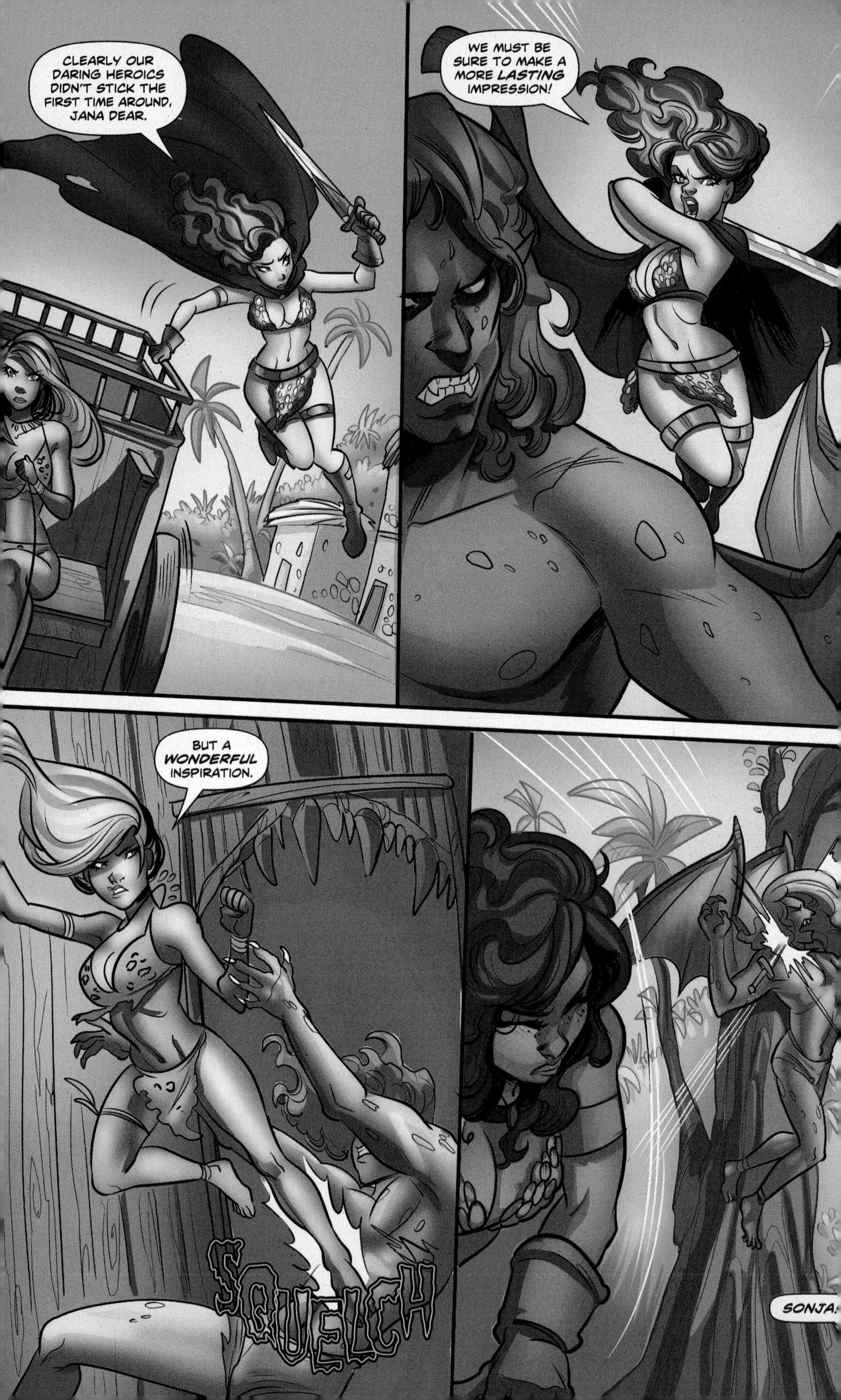
CLEARLY OUR DARING HEROICS DIDN'T STICK THE FIRST TIME AROUND, JANA DEAR.
WE MUST BE SURE TO MAKE A MORE LASTING IMPRESSION!
BUT A WONDERFUL INSPIRATION.
SQUELCH
SONJA.

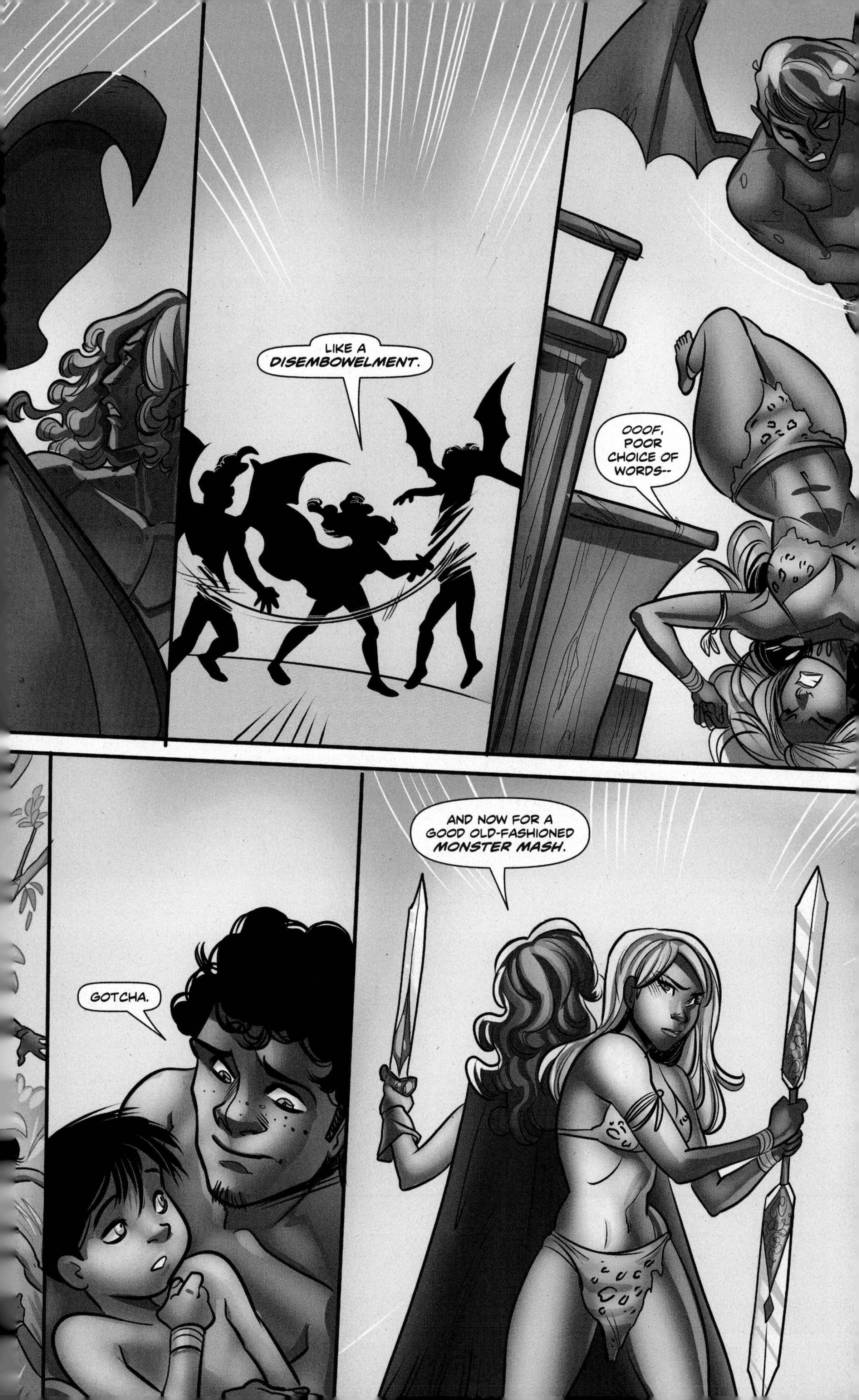
LIKE A DISEMBOWELMENT.
OOOF, POOR CHOICE OF WORDS--
GOTCHA.
AND NOW FOR A GOOD OLD-FASHIONED MONSTER MASH.

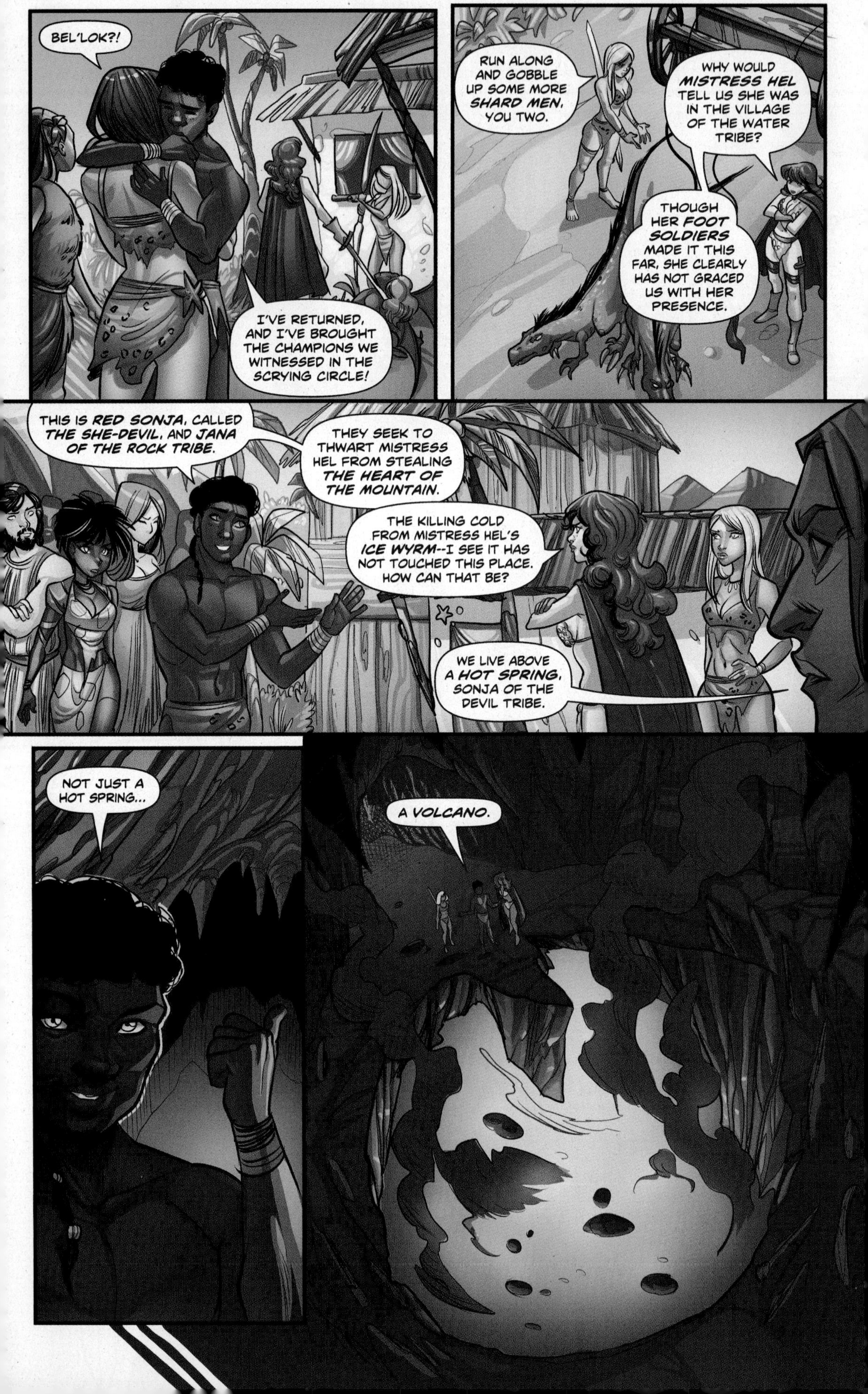
BEL'LOK?!
I'VE RETURNED, AND I'VE BROUGHT THE CHAMPIONS WE WITNESSED IN THE SCRYING CIRCLE!
RUN ALONG AND GOBBLE UP SOME MORE SHARD MEN, YOU TWO.
WHY WOULD MISTRESS HEL TELL US SHE WAS IN THE VILLAGE OF THE WATER TRIBE?
THOUGH HER FOOT SOLDIERS MADE IT THIS FAR, SHE CLEARLY HAS NOT GRACED US WITH HER PRESENCE.
THIS IS RED SONJA, CALLED THE SHE-DEVIL, AND JANA OF THE ROCK TRIBE.
THEY SEEK TO THWART MISTRESS HEL FROM STEALING THE HEART OF THE MOUNTAIN.
THE KILLING COLD FROM MISTRESS HEL'S ICE WYRM--I SEE IT HAS NOT TOUCHED THIS PLACE. HOW CAN THAT BE?
WE LIVE ABOVE A HOT SPRING, SONJA OF THE DEVIL TRIBE.
NOT JUST A HOT SPRING...
A VOLCANO.

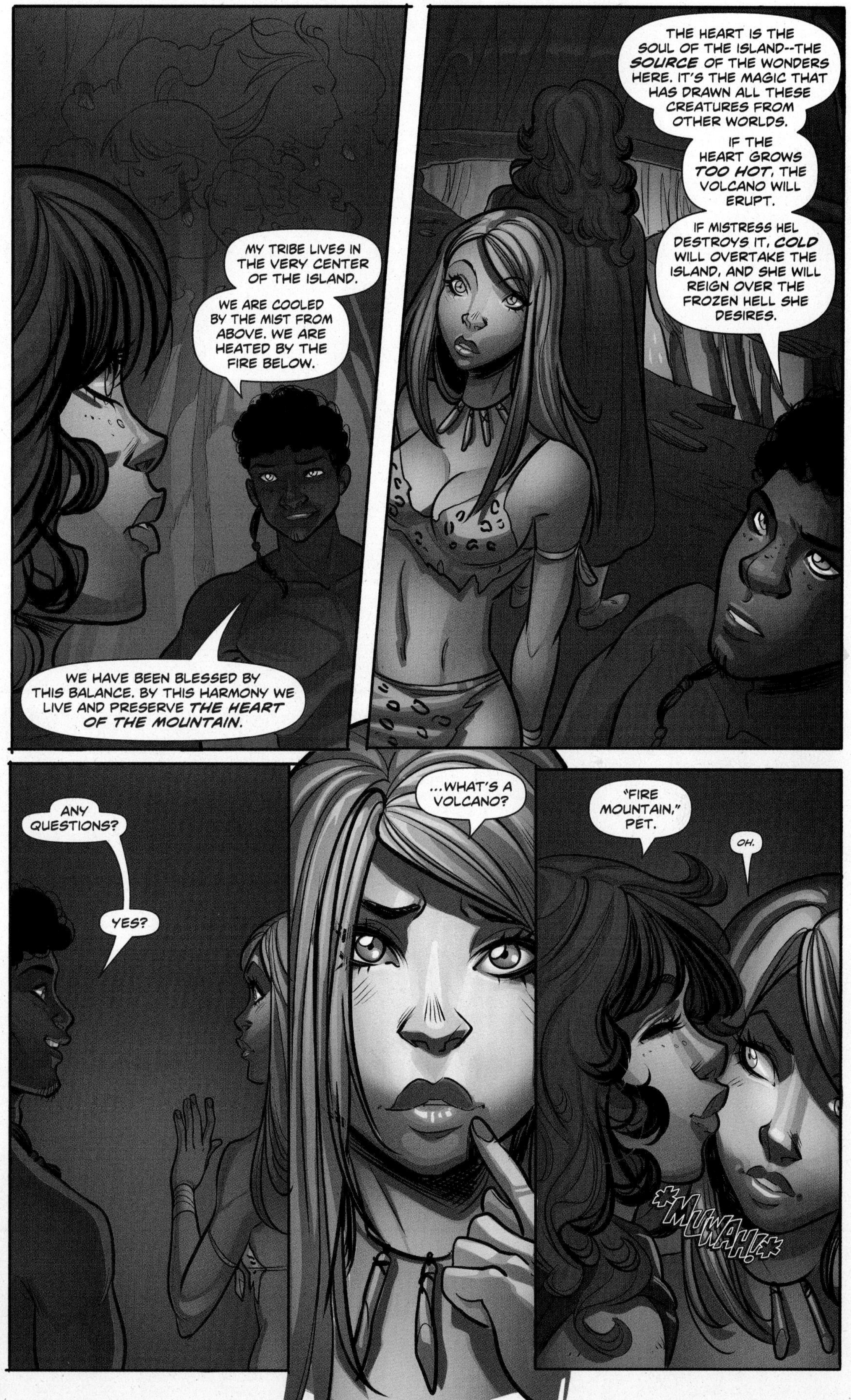
MY TRIBE LIVES IN THE VERY CENTER OF THE ISLAND.
WE ARE COOLED BY THE MIST FROM ABOVE. WE ARE HEATED BY THE FIRE BELOW.
WE HAVE BEEN BLESSED BY THIS BALANCE. BY THIS HARMONY WE LIVE AND PRESERVE *THE HEART OF THE MOUNTAIN*.
THE HEART IS THE SOUL OF THE ISLAND--THE *SOURCE* OF THE WONDERS HERE. IT'S THE MAGIC THAT HAS DRAWN ALL THESE CREATURES FROM OTHER WORLDS.
IF THE HEART GROWS *TOO HOT*, THE VOLCANO WILL ERUPT.
IF MISTRESS HEL DESTROYS IT, *COLD* WILL OVERTAKE THE ISLAND, AND SHE WILL REIGN OVER THE FROZEN HELL SHE DESIRES.
ANY QUESTIONS?
YES?
...WHAT'S A VOLCANO?
"FIRE MOUNTAIN," PET.
OH.
MUWAH!

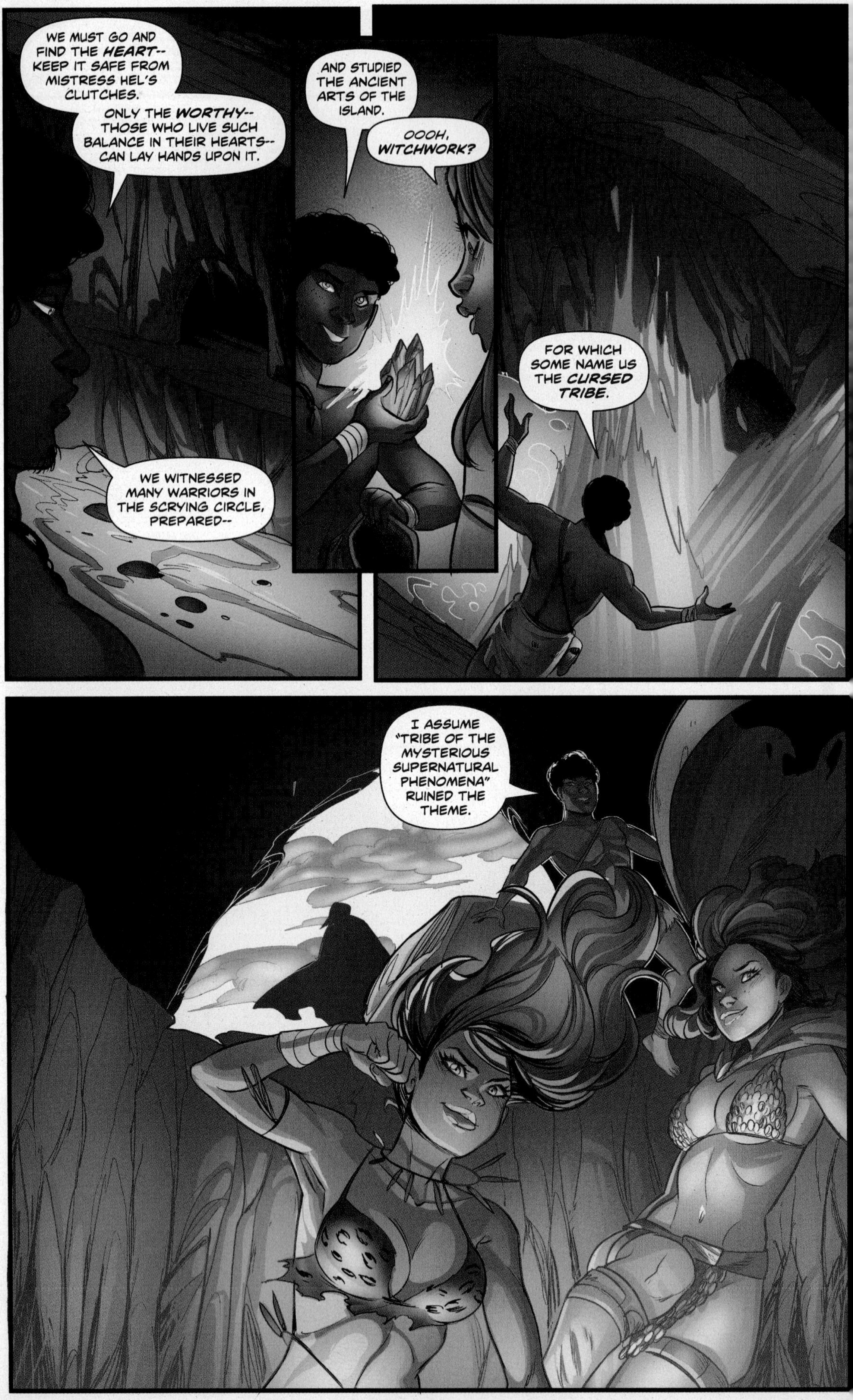
WE MUST GO AND FIND THE *HEART*-- KEEP IT SAFE FROM MISTRESS HEL'S CLUTCHES.
ONLY THE *WORTHY*-- THOSE WHO LIVE SUCH BALANCE IN THEIR HEARTS-- CAN LAY HANDS UPON IT.
WE WITNESSED MANY WARRIORS IN THE SCRYING CIRCLE, PREPARED--
AND STUDIED THE ANCIENT ARTS OF THE ISLAND.
OOOH, *WITCHWORK?*
FOR WHICH SOME NAME US THE *CURSED TRIBE*.
I ASSUME "TRIBE OF THE MYSTERIOUS SUPERNATURAL PHENOMENA" RUINED THE THEME.

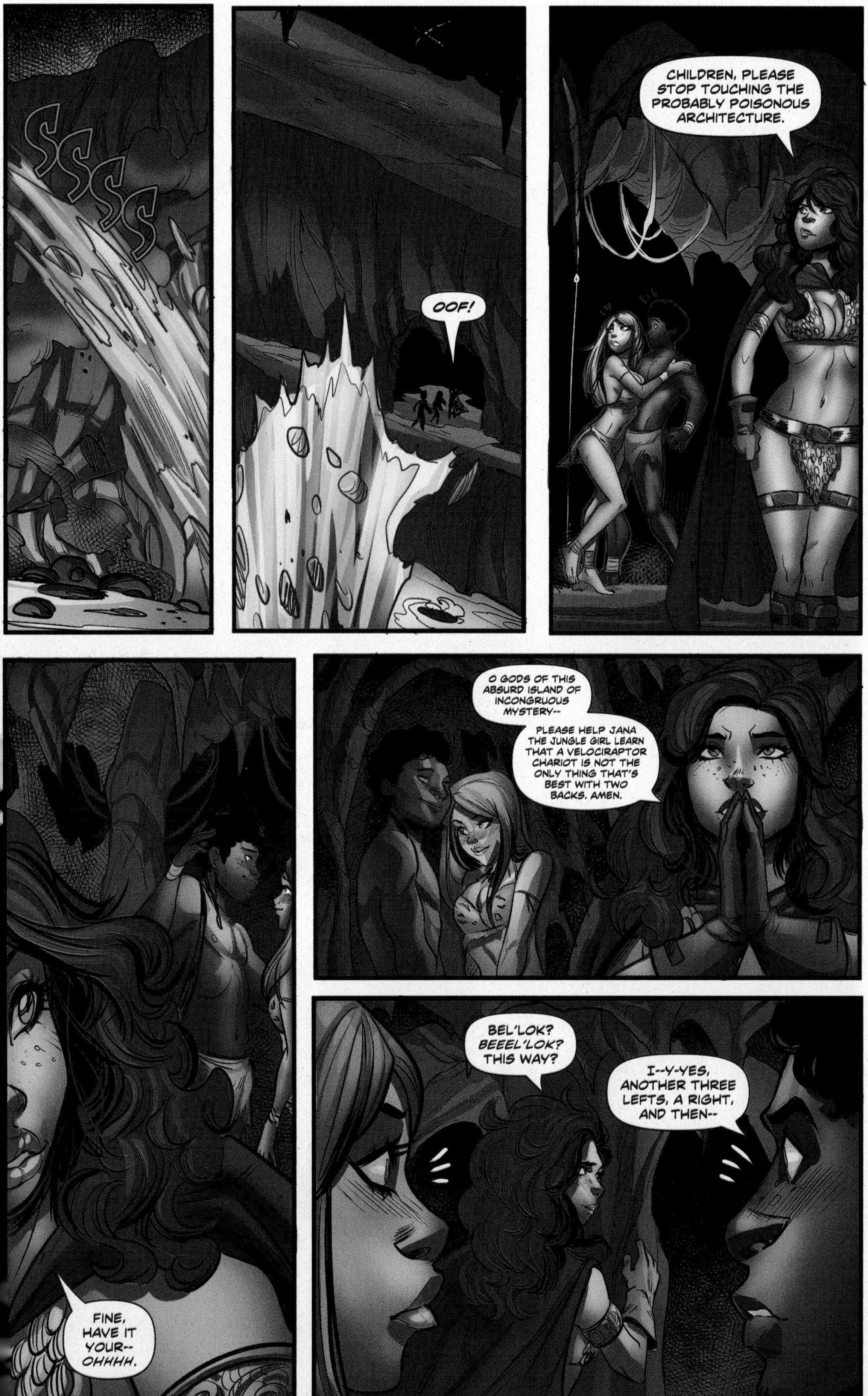
SSSS
OOF!
CHILDREN, PLEASE STOP TOUCHING THE PROBABLY POISONOUS ARCHITECTURE.
O GODS OF THIS ABSURD ISLAND OF INCONGRUOUS MYSTERY--
PLEASE HELP JANA THE JUNGLE GIRL LEARN THAT A VELOCIRAPTOR CHARIOT IS NOT THE ONLY THING THAT'S BEST WITH TWO BACKS. AMEN.
FINE, HAVE IT YOUR-- OHHHH.
BEL'LOK? BEEEL'LOK? THIS WAY?
I--Y-YES, ANOTHER THREE LEFTS, A RIGHT, AND THEN--

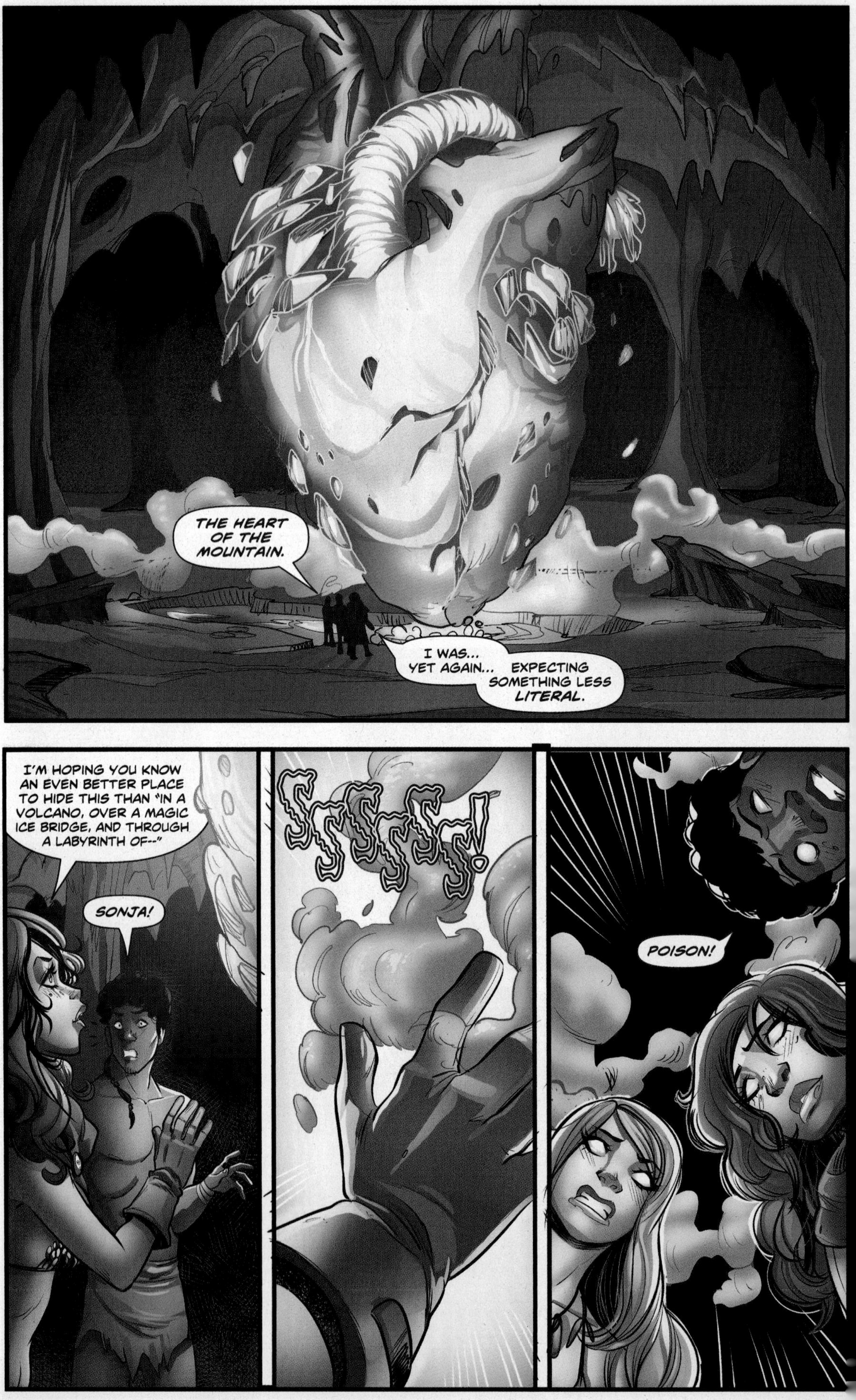
THE HEART OF THE MOUNTAIN.
I WAS... YET AGAIN... EXPECTING SOMETHING LESS LITERAL.
I'M HOPING YOU KNOW AN EVEN BETTER PLACE TO HIDE THIS THAN "IN A VOLCANO, OVER A MAGIC ICE BRIDGE, AND THROUGH A LABYRINTH OF--"
SONJA!
POISON!

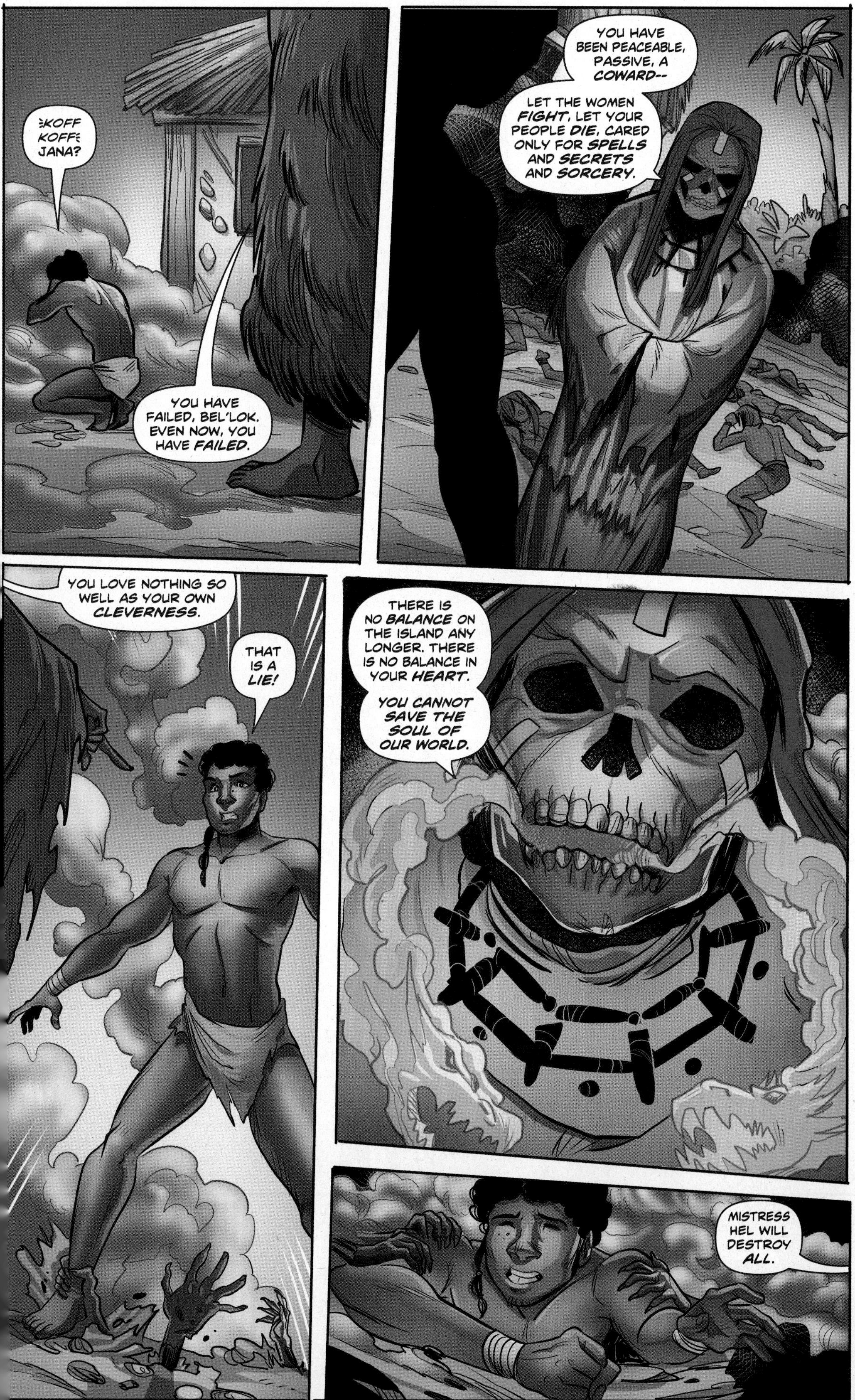

KOFF KOFF JANA?
YOU HAVE FAILED, BEL'LOK. EVEN NOW, YOU HAVE FAILED.
YOU HAVE BEEN PEACEABLE, PASSIVE, A COWARD--
LET THE WOMEN FIGHT, LET YOUR PEOPLE DIE, CARED ONLY FOR SPELLS AND SECRETS AND SORCERY.
YOU LOVE NOTHING SO WELL AS YOUR OWN CLEVERNESS.
THAT IS A LIE!
THERE IS NO BALANCE ON THE ISLAND ANY LONGER. THERE IS NO BALANCE IN YOUR HEART.
YOU CANNOT SAVE THE SOUL OF OUR WORLD.
MISTRESS HEL WILL DESTROY ALL.

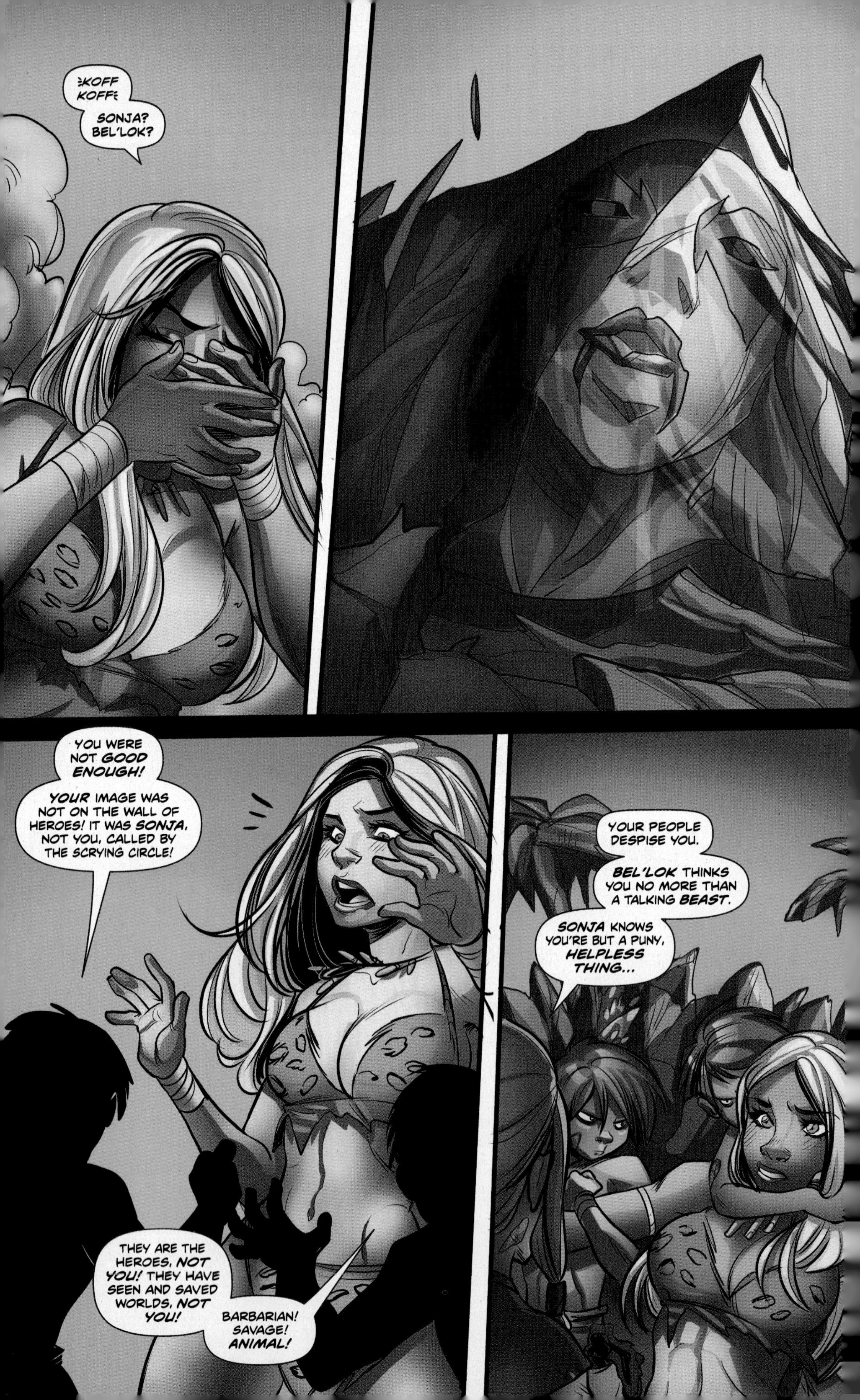

KOFF KOFF
SONJA? BEL'LOK?
YOU WERE NOT GOOD ENOUGH!
YOUR IMAGE WAS NOT ON THE WALL OF HEROES! IT WAS SONJA, NOT YOU, CALLED BY THE SCRYING CIRCLE!
THEY ARE THE HEROES, NOT YOU! THEY HAVE SEEN AND SAVED WORLDS, NOT YOU!
BARBARIAN! SAVAGE! ANIMAL!
YOUR PEOPLE DESPISE YOU.
BEL'LOK THINKS YOU NO MORE THAN A TALKING BEAST.
SONJA KNOWS YOU'RE BUT A PUNY, HELPLESS THING...

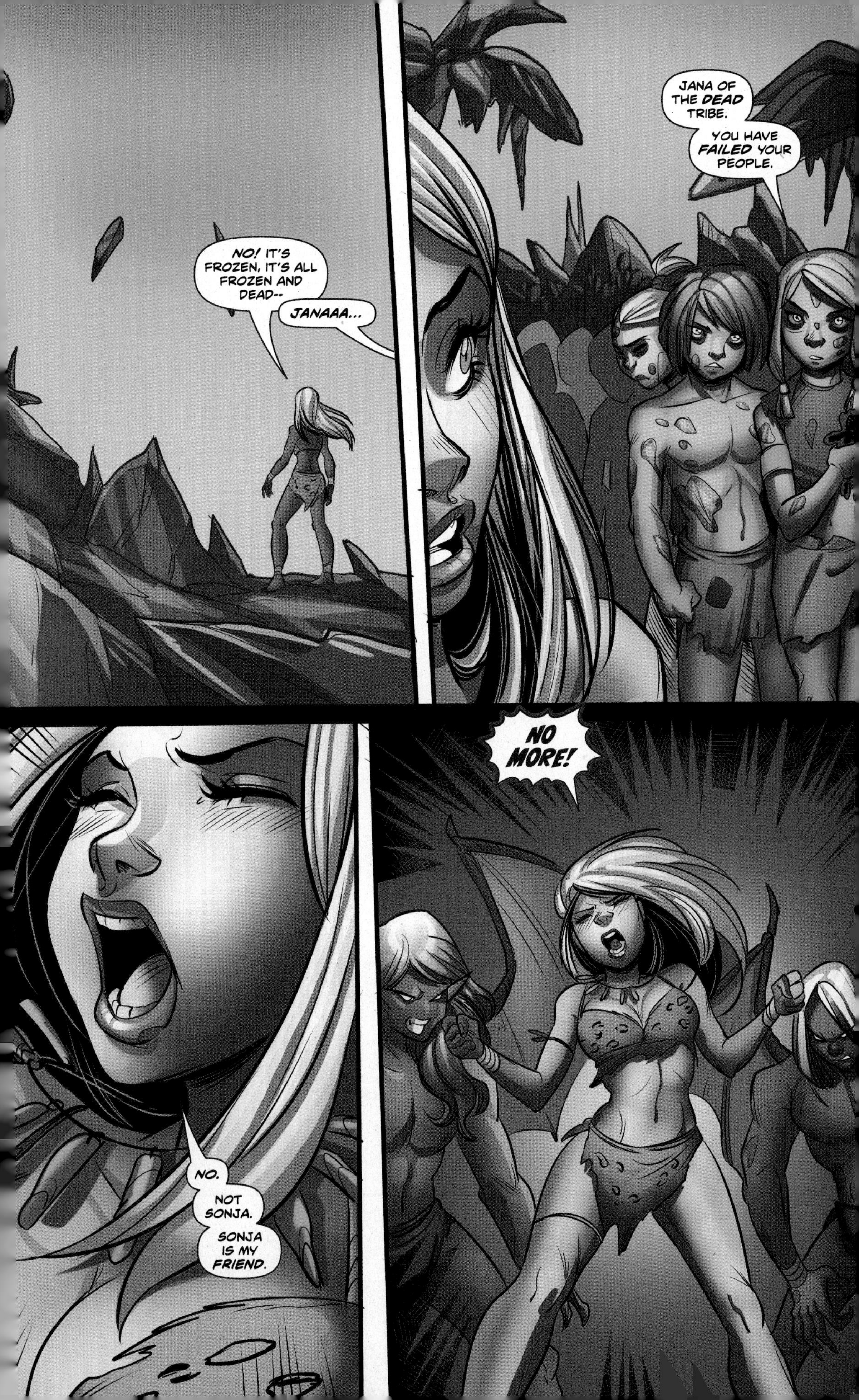
NO! IT'S FROZEN, IT'S ALL FROZEN AND DEAD--
JANAAA...
JANA OF THE DEAD TRIBE.
YOU HAVE FAILED YOUR PEOPLE.
NO.
NOT SONJA.
SONJA IS MY FRIEND.
NO MORE!

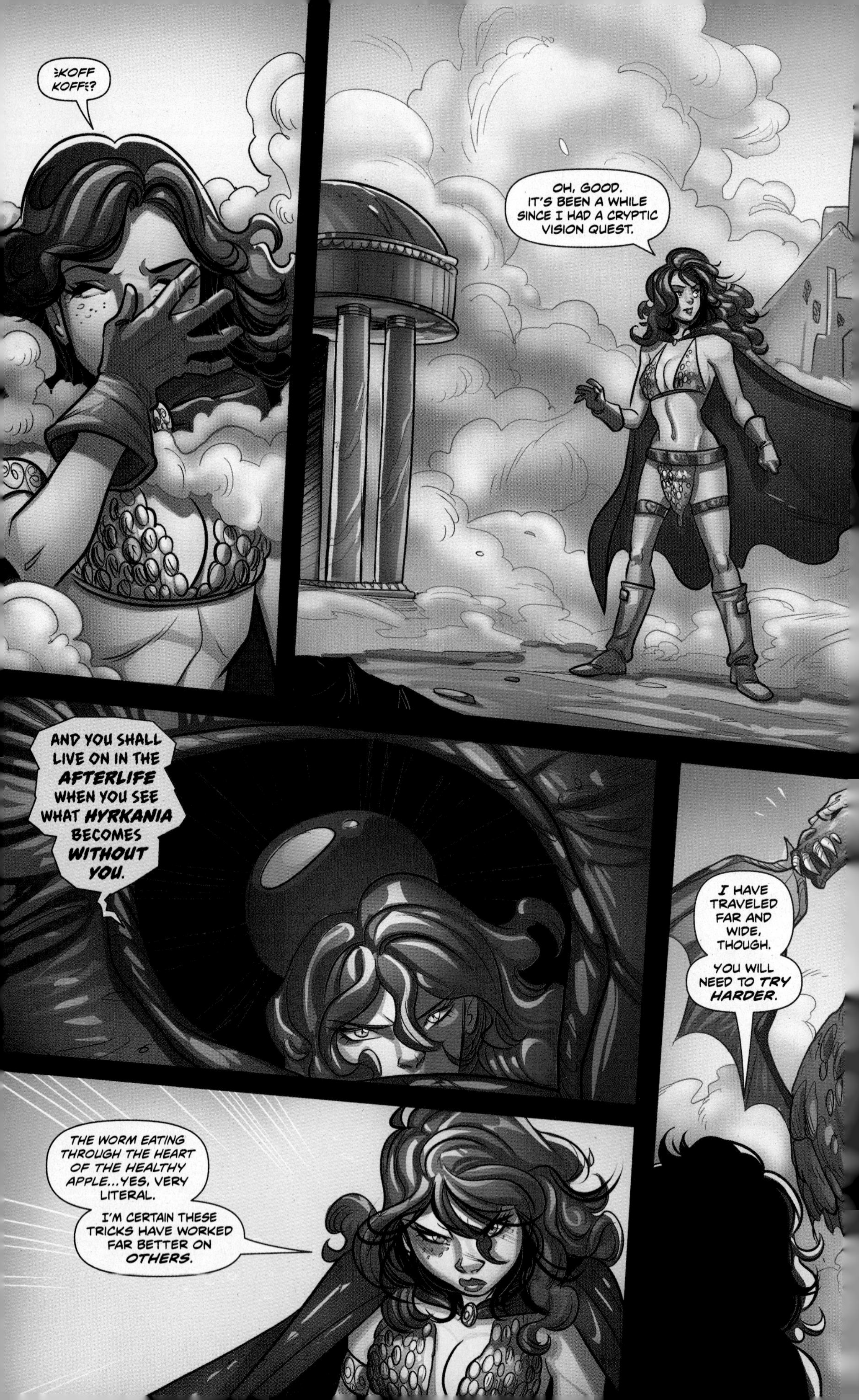

KOFF KOFF?
OH, GOOD. IT'S BEEN A WHILE SINCE I HAD A CRYPTIC VISION QUEST.
AND YOU SHALL LIVE ON IN THE AFTERLIFE WHEN YOU SEE WHAT HYRKANIA BECOMES WITHOUT YOU.
I HAVE TRAVELED FAR AND WIDE, THOUGH.
YOU WILL NEED TO TRY HARDER.
THE WORM EATING THROUGH THE HEART OF THE HEALTHY APPLE...YES, VERY LITERAL.
I'M CERTAIN THESE TRICKS HAVE WORKED FAR BETTER ON OTHERS.

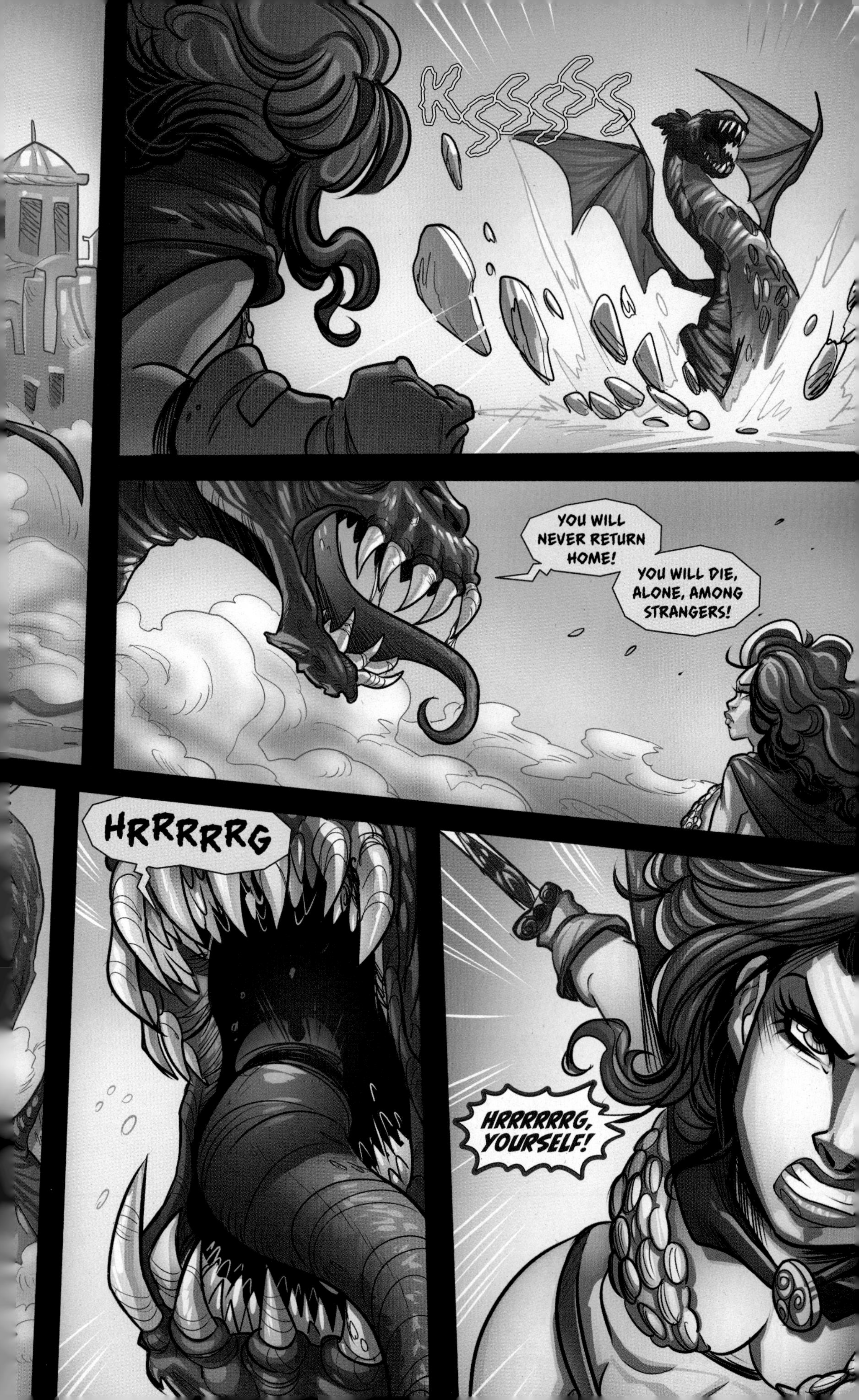
KSSSSS
YOU WILL NEVER RETURN HOME!
YOU WILL DIE, ALONE, AMONG STRANGERS!
HRRRRRG
HRRRRRG, YOURSELF!

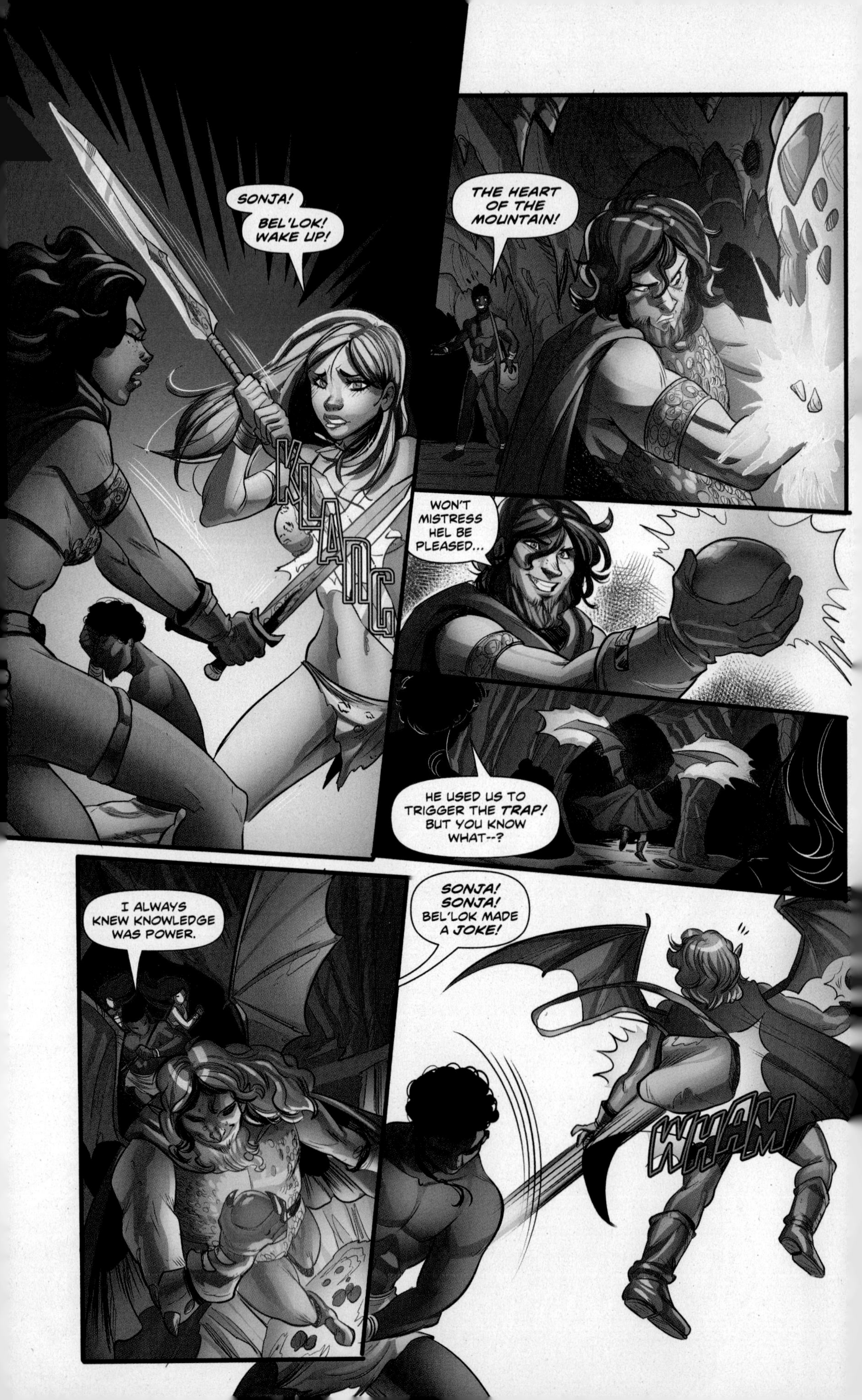
SONJA!
BEL'LOK! WAKE UP!
KLANG
THE HEART OF THE MOUNTAIN!
WON'T MISTRESS HEL BE PLEASED...
HE USED US TO TRIGGER THE TRAP! BUT YOU KNOW WHAT--?
I ALWAYS KNEW KNOWLEDGE WAS POWER.
SONJA! SONJA! BEL'LOK MADE A JOKE!
WHAM

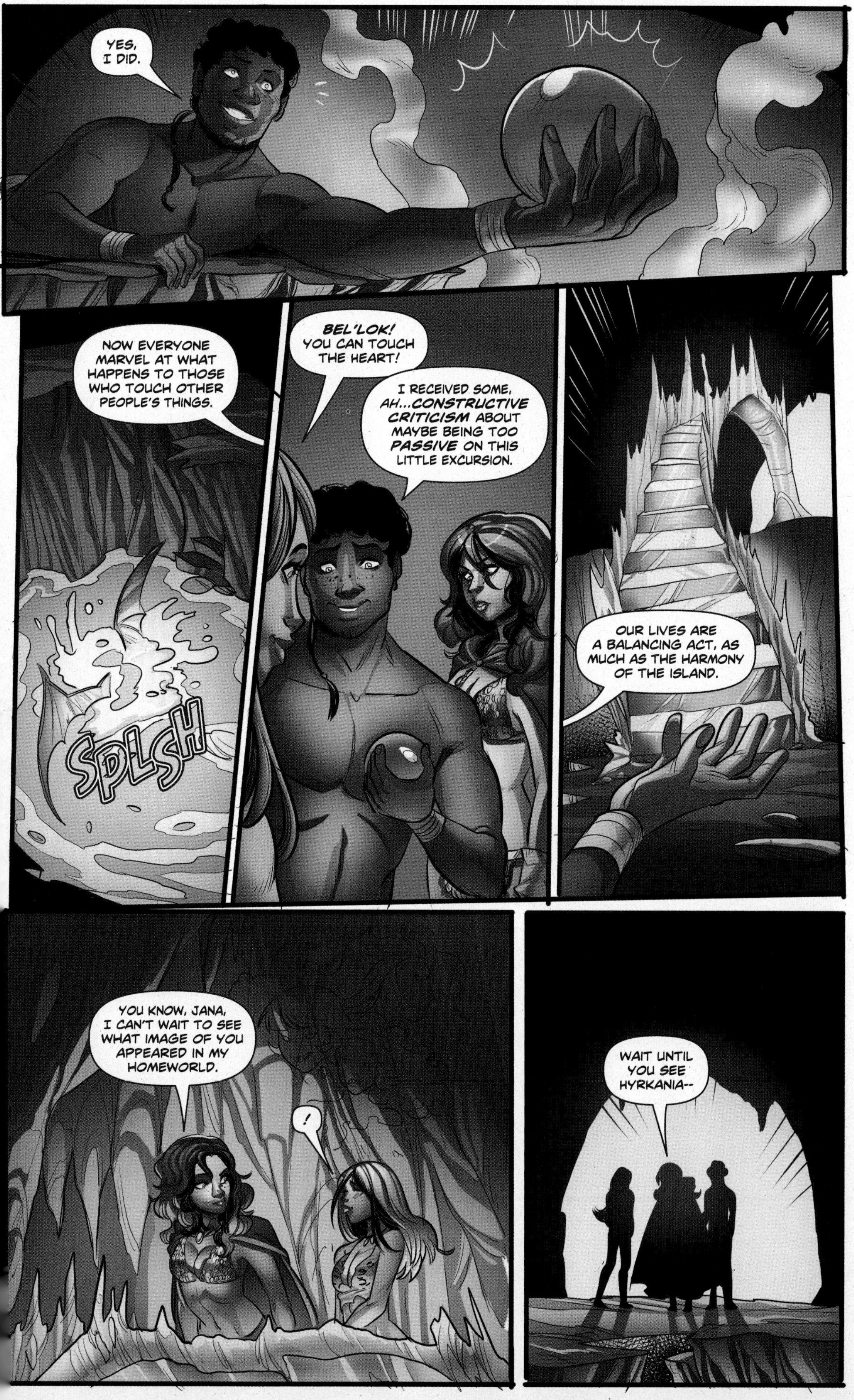
YES, I DID.
NOW EVERYONE MARVEL AT WHAT HAPPENS TO THOSE WHO TOUCH OTHER PEOPLE'S THINGS.
SPLSH
BEL'LOK! YOU CAN TOUCH THE HEART!
I RECEIVED SOME, AH...CONSTRUCTIVE CRITICISM ABOUT MAYBE BEING TOO PASSIVE ON THIS LITTLE EXCURSION.
OUR LIVES ARE A BALANCING ACT, AS MUCH AS THE HARMONY OF THE ISLAND.
YOU KNOW, JANA, I CAN'T WAIT TO SEE WHAT IMAGE OF YOU APPEARED IN MY HOMEWORLD.
!
WAIT UNTIL YOU SEE HYRKANIA--

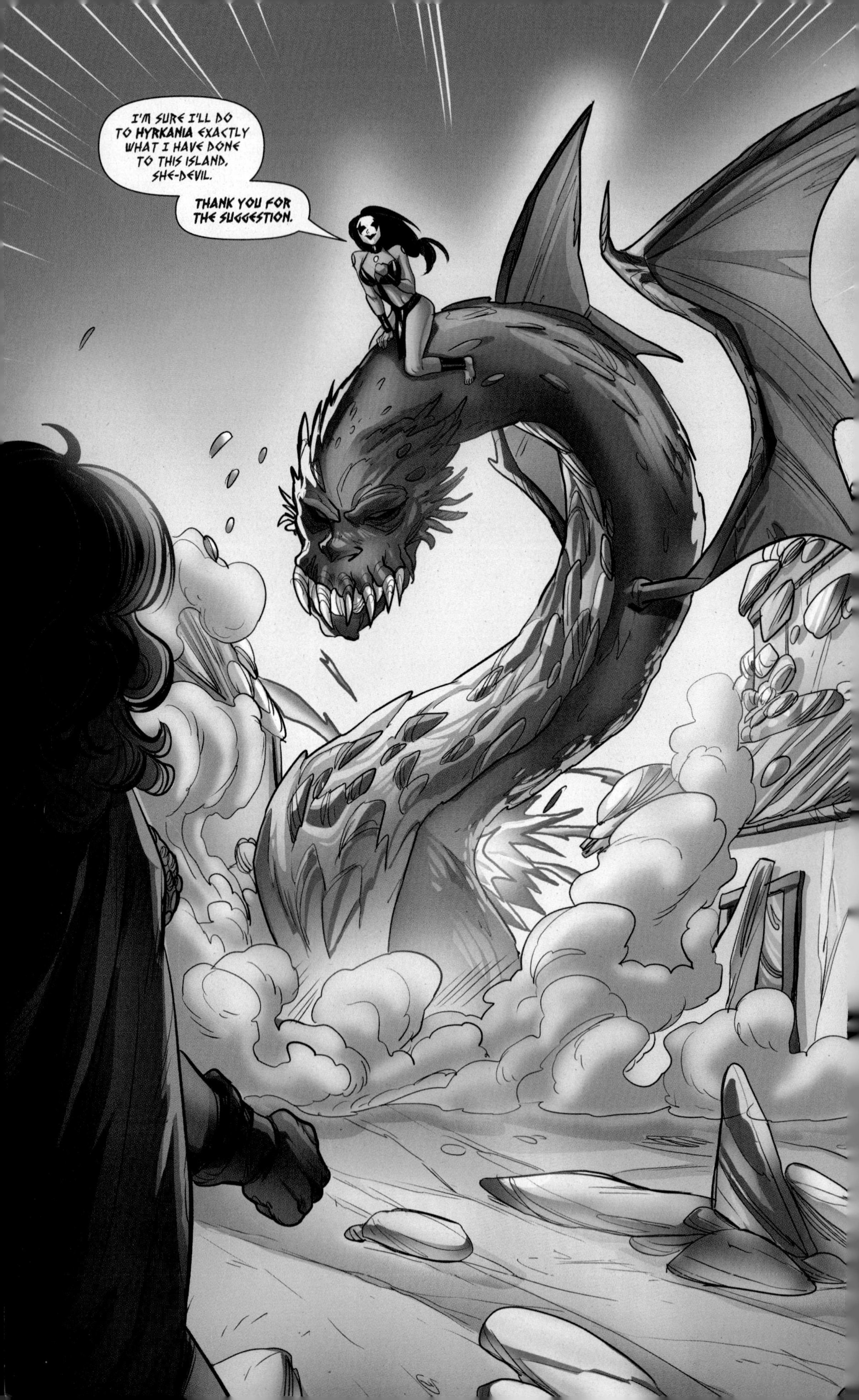
I'M SURE I'LL DO TO HYRKANIA EXACTLY WHAT I HAVE DONE TO THIS ISLAND, SHE-DEVIL.
THANK YOU FOR THE SUGGESTION.

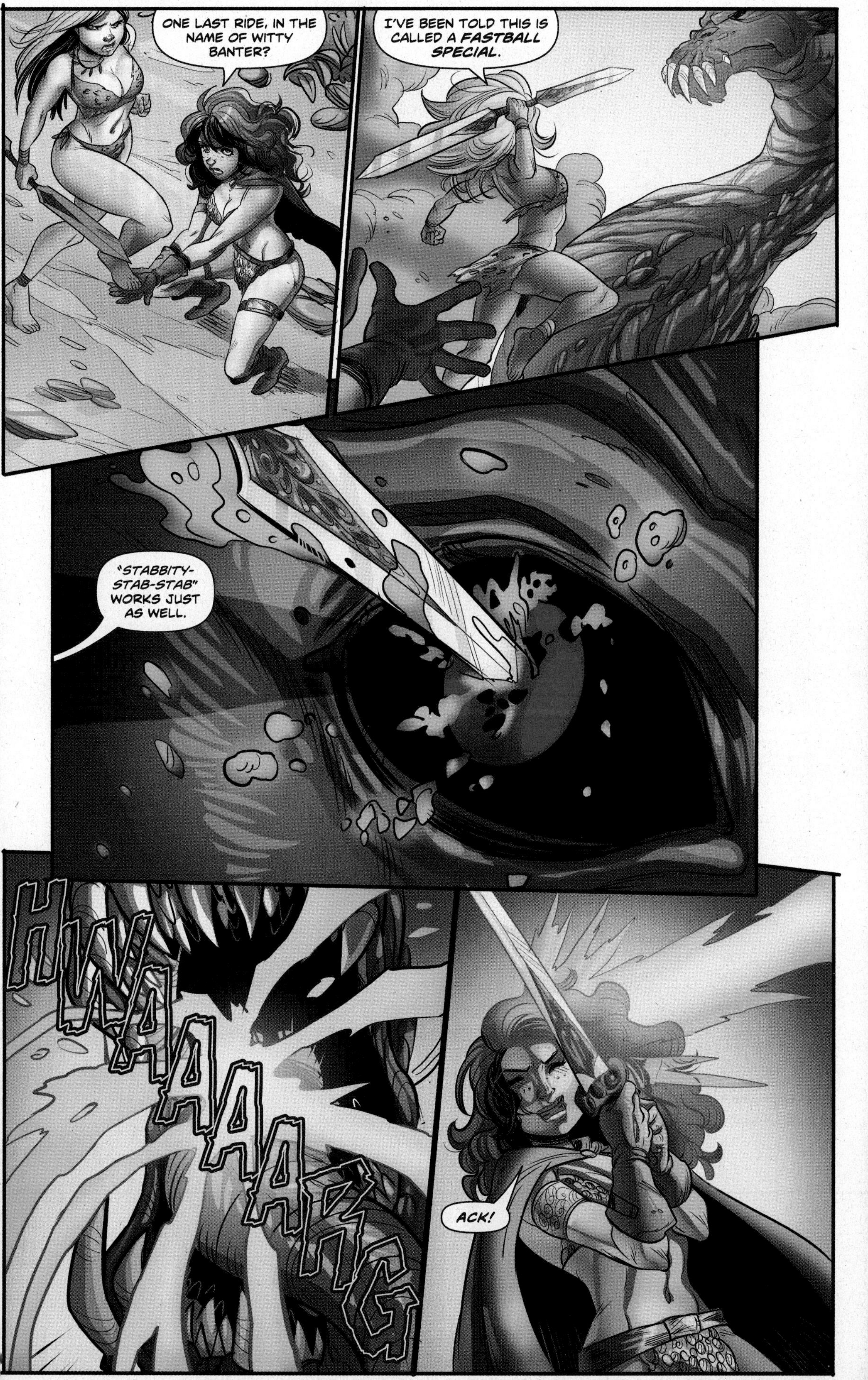
ONE LAST RIDE, IN THE NAME OF WITTY BANTER?
I'VE BEEN TOLD THIS IS CALLED A *FASTBALL SPECIAL*.
"STABBITY-STAB-STAB" WORKS JUST AS WELL.
HWAAAAARG
ACK!

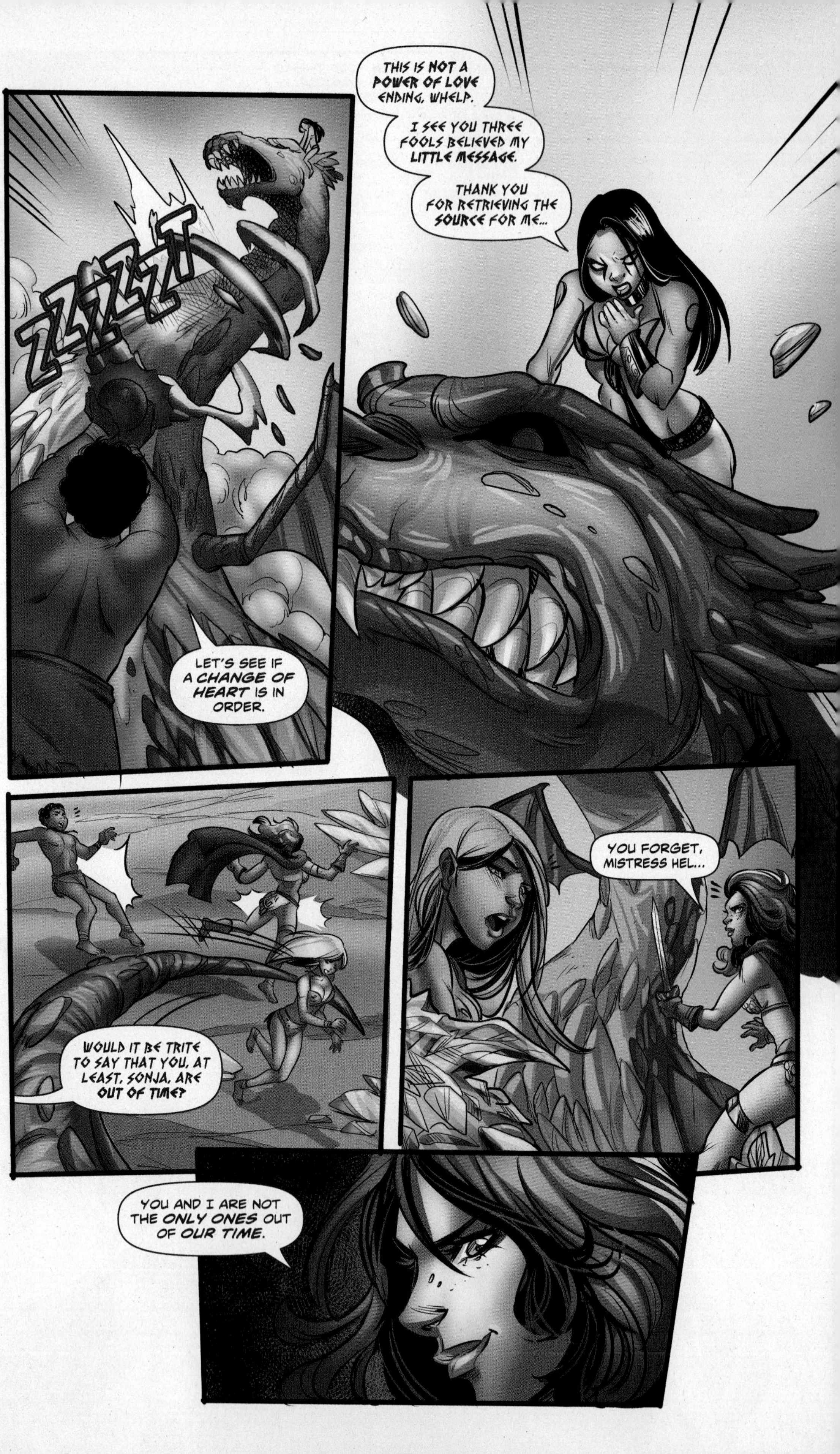
ZZZZZZT
THIS IS NOT A POWER OF LOVE ENDING, WHELP.
I SEE YOU THREE FOOLS BELIEVED MY LITTLE MESSAGE.
THANK YOU FOR RETRIEVING THE SOURCE FOR ME...
LET'S SEE IF A CHANGE OF HEART IS IN ORDER.
WOULD IT BE TRITE TO SAY THAT YOU, AT LEAST, SONJA, ARE OUT OF TIME?
YOU FORGET, MISTRESS HEL...
YOU AND I ARE NOT THE ONLY ONES OUT OF OUR TIME.

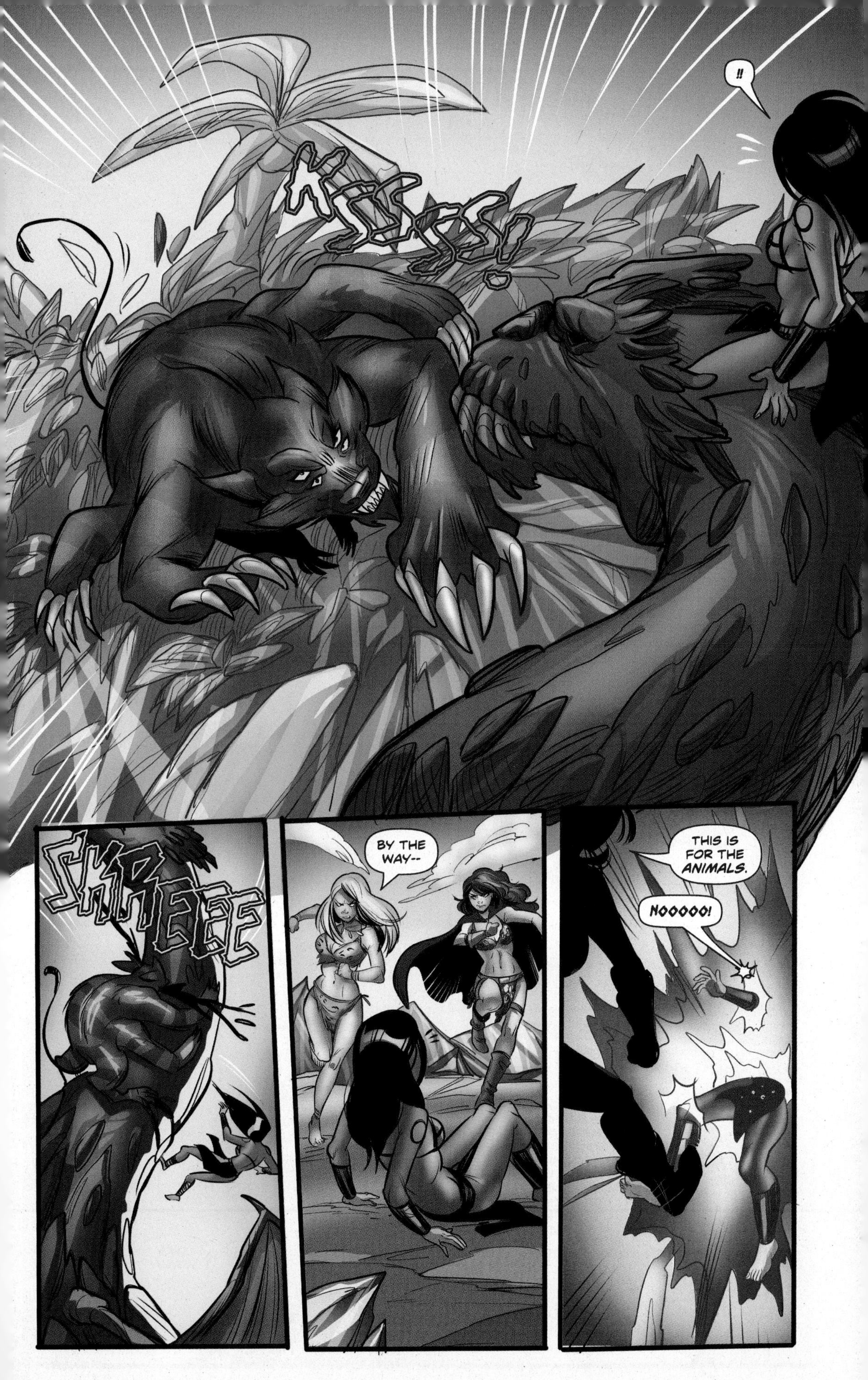
!!
HSSSS!
SKREEE
BY THE WAY--
THIS IS FOR THE ANIMALS.
NOOOOO!

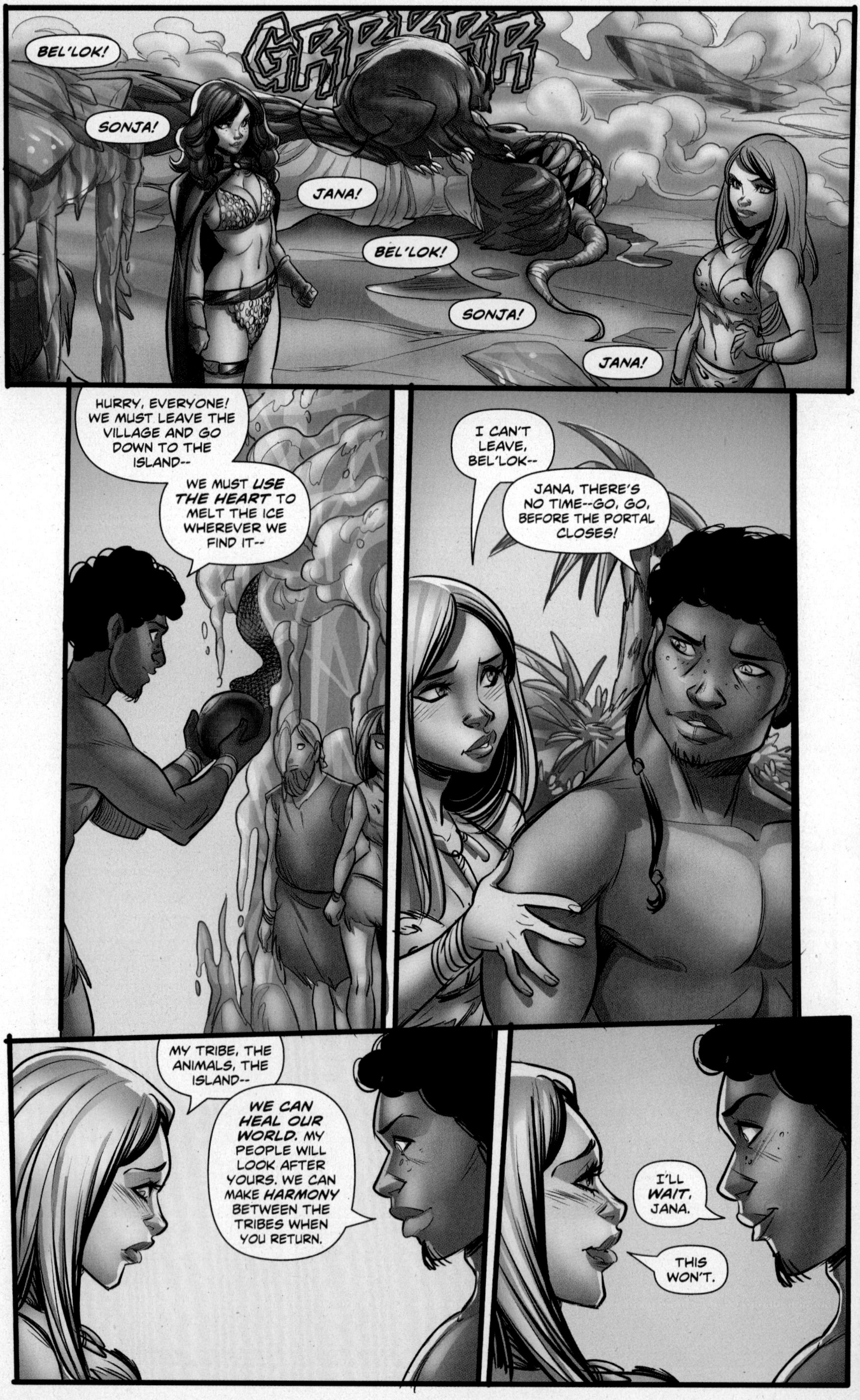
GRRRRR
BEL'LOK!
SONJA!
JANA!
BEL'LOK!
SONJA!
JANA!
HURRY, EVERYONE! WE MUST LEAVE THE VILLAGE AND GO DOWN TO THE ISLAND--
WE MUST ***USE THE HEART*** TO MELT THE ICE WHEREVER WE FIND IT--
I CAN'T LEAVE, BEL'LOK--
JANA, THERE'S NO TIME--GO, GO, BEFORE THE PORTAL CLOSES!
MY TRIBE, THE ANIMALS, THE ISLAND--
WE CAN HEAL OUR WORLD. MY PEOPLE WILL LOOK AFTER YOURS. WE CAN MAKE ***HARMONY*** BETWEEN THE TRIBES WHEN YOU RETURN.
I'LL ***WAIT,*** JANA.
THIS WON'T.

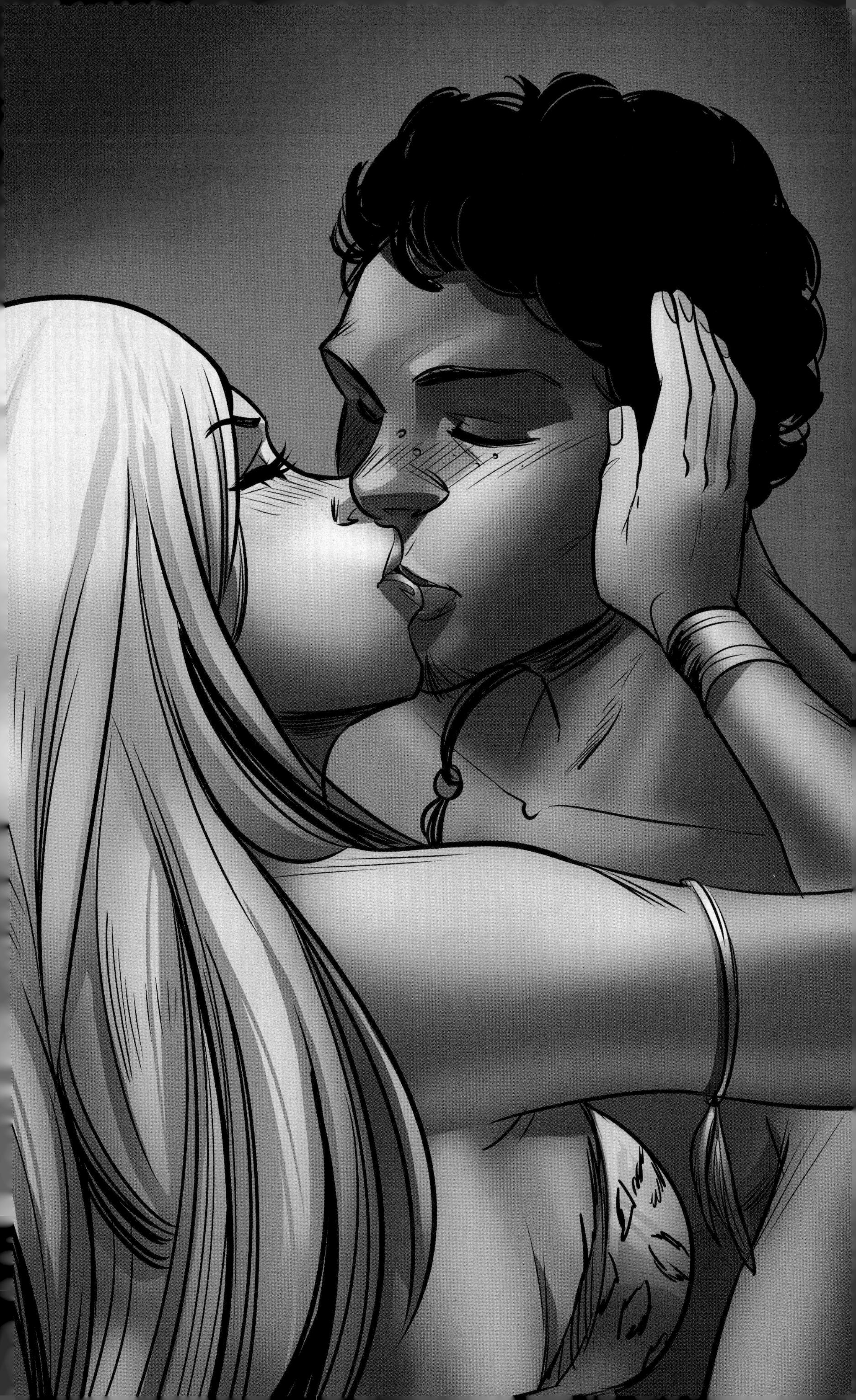

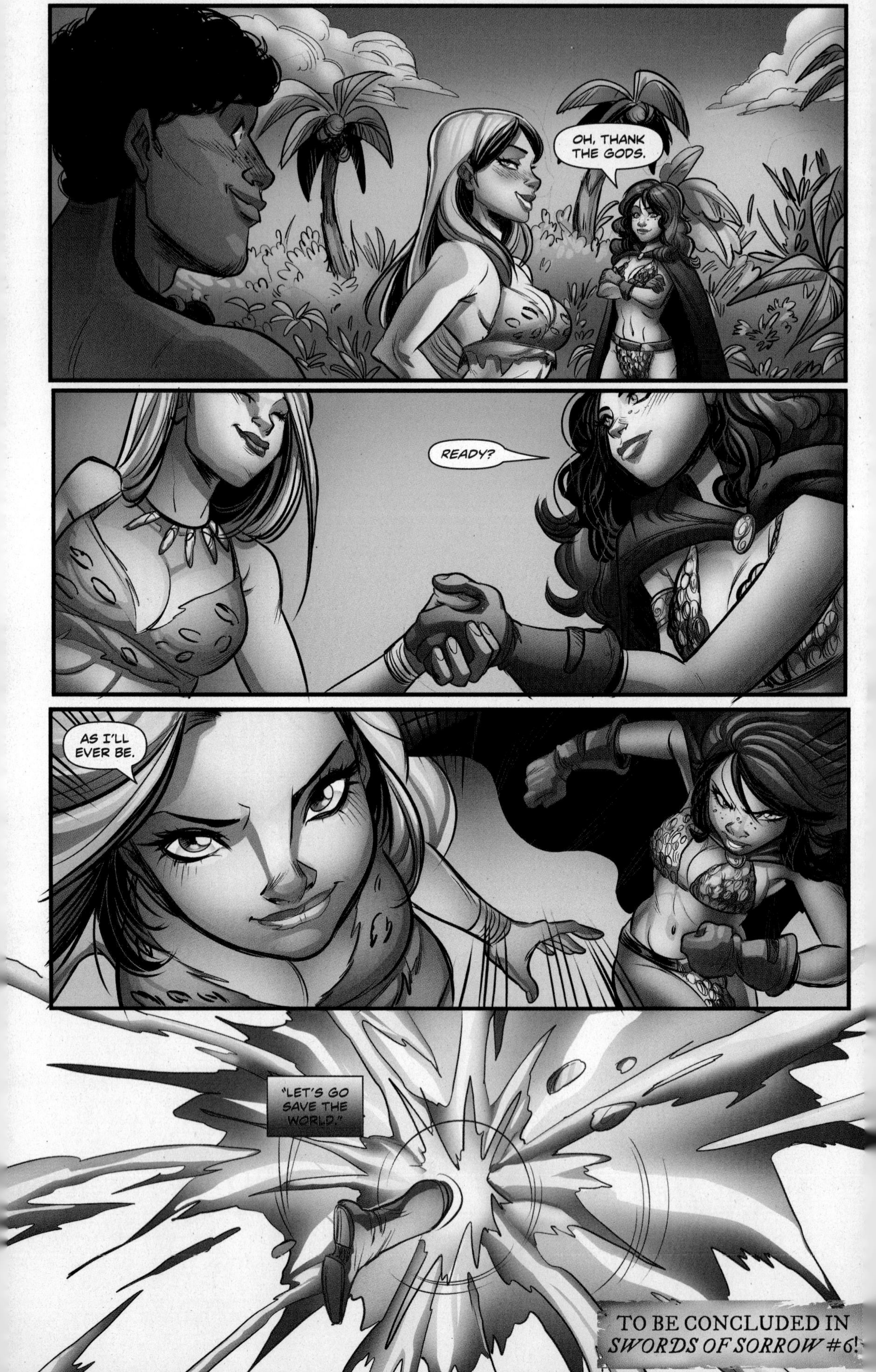
OH, THANK THE GODS.
READY?
AS I'LL EVER BE.
"LET'S GO SAVE THE WORLD."
TO BE CONCLUDED IN SWORDS OF SORROW #6!

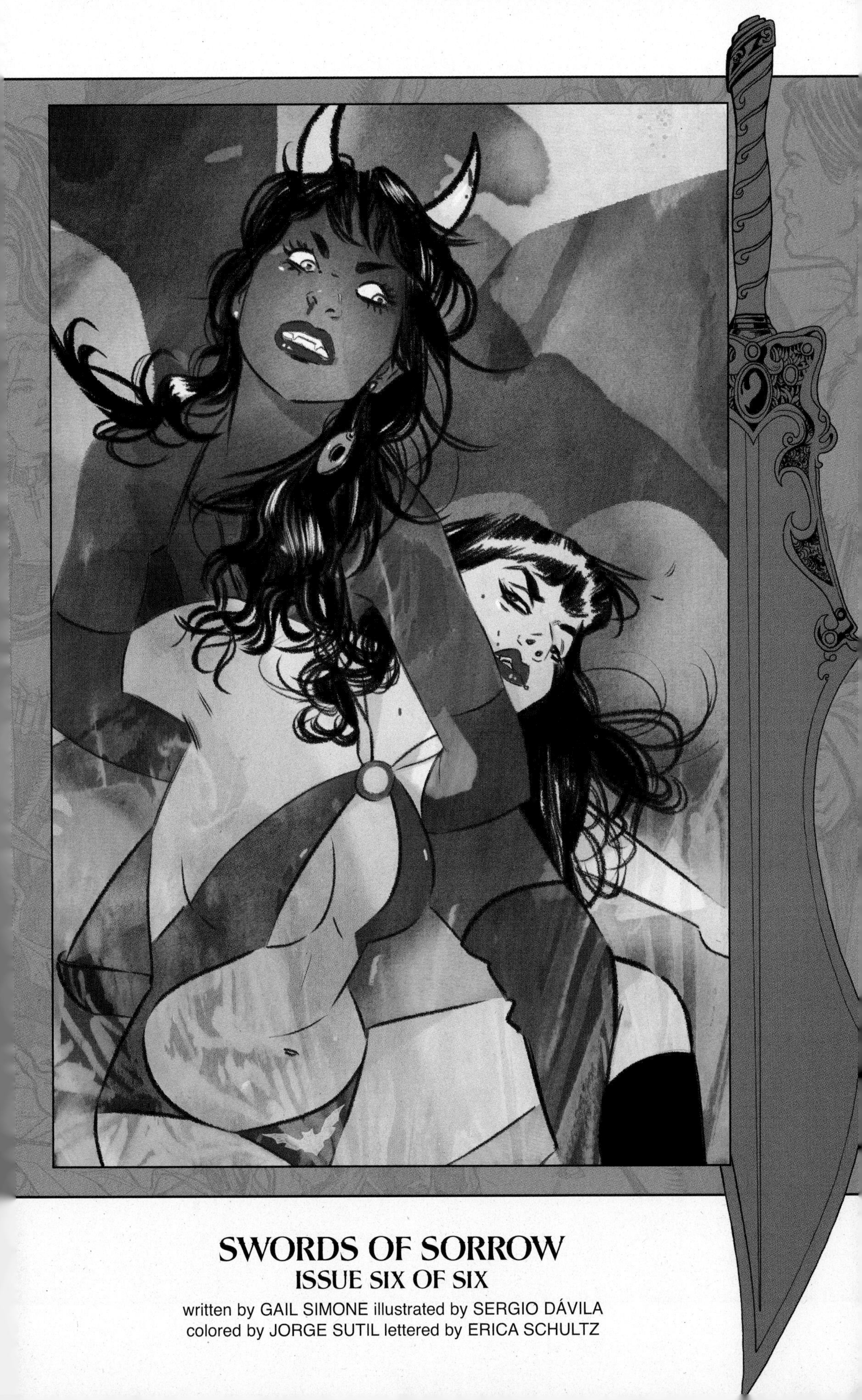

SWORDS OF SORROW
ISSUE SIX OF SIX

written by GAIL SIMONE illustrated by SERGIO DÁVILA
colored by JORGE SUTIL lettered by ERICA SCHULTZ

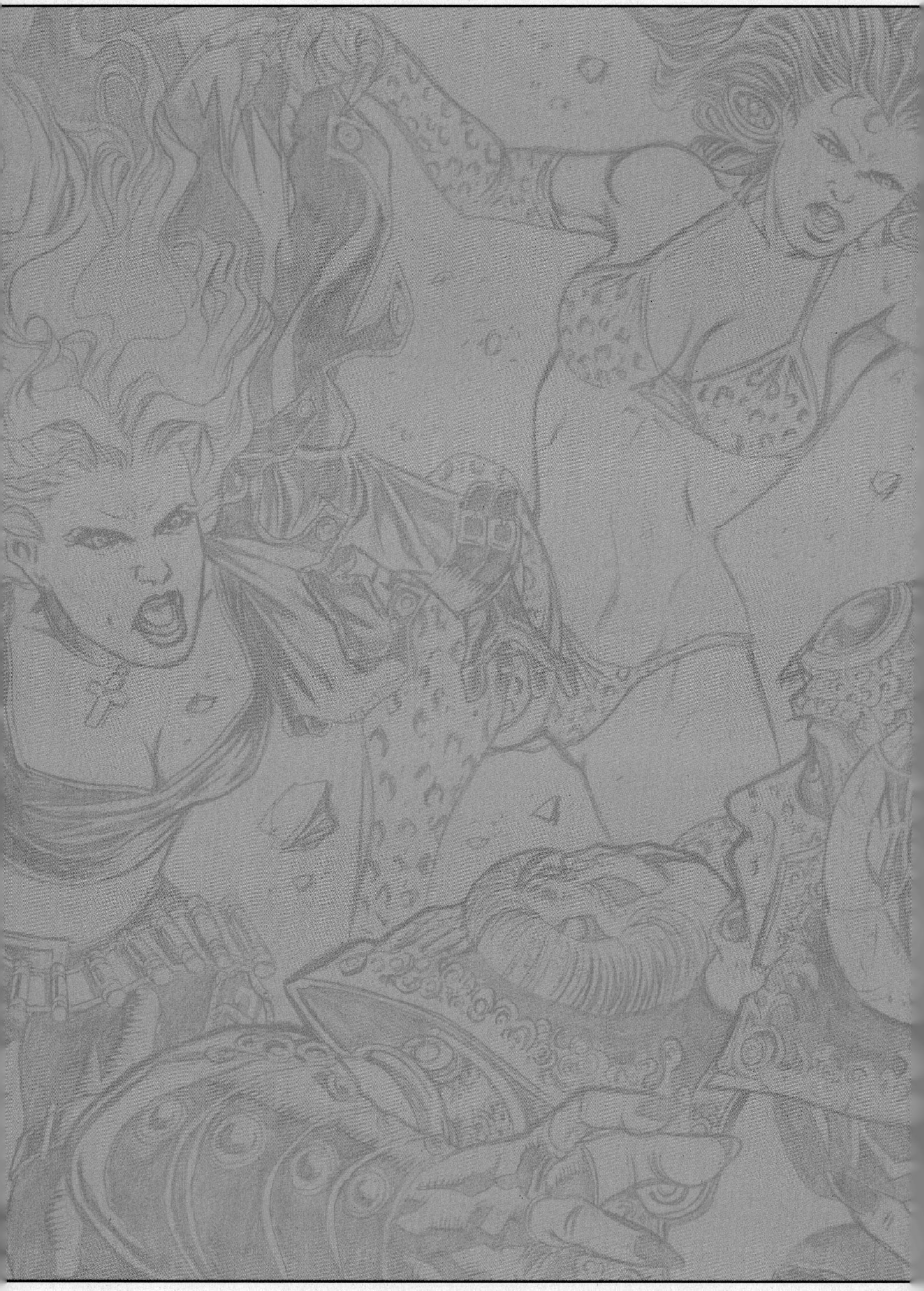

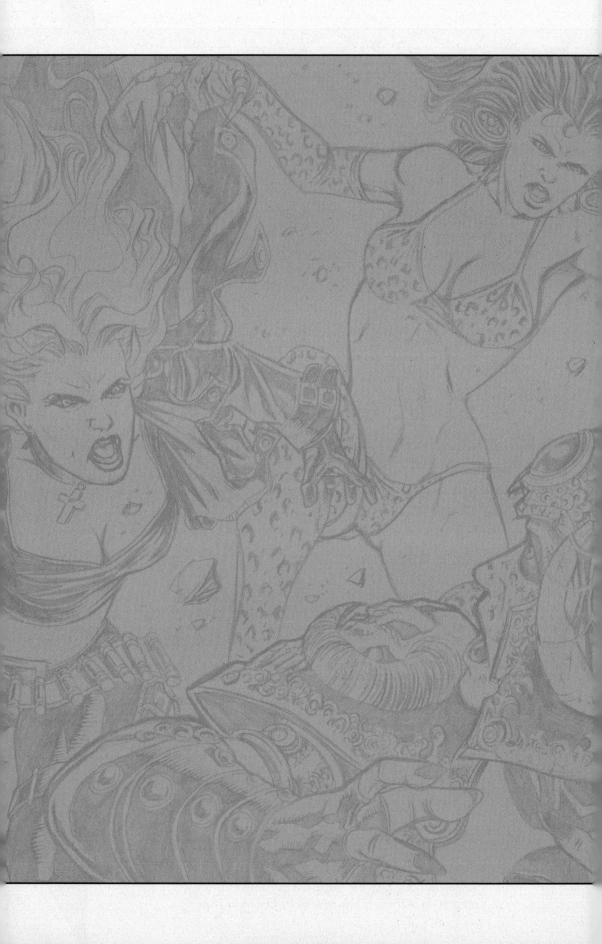

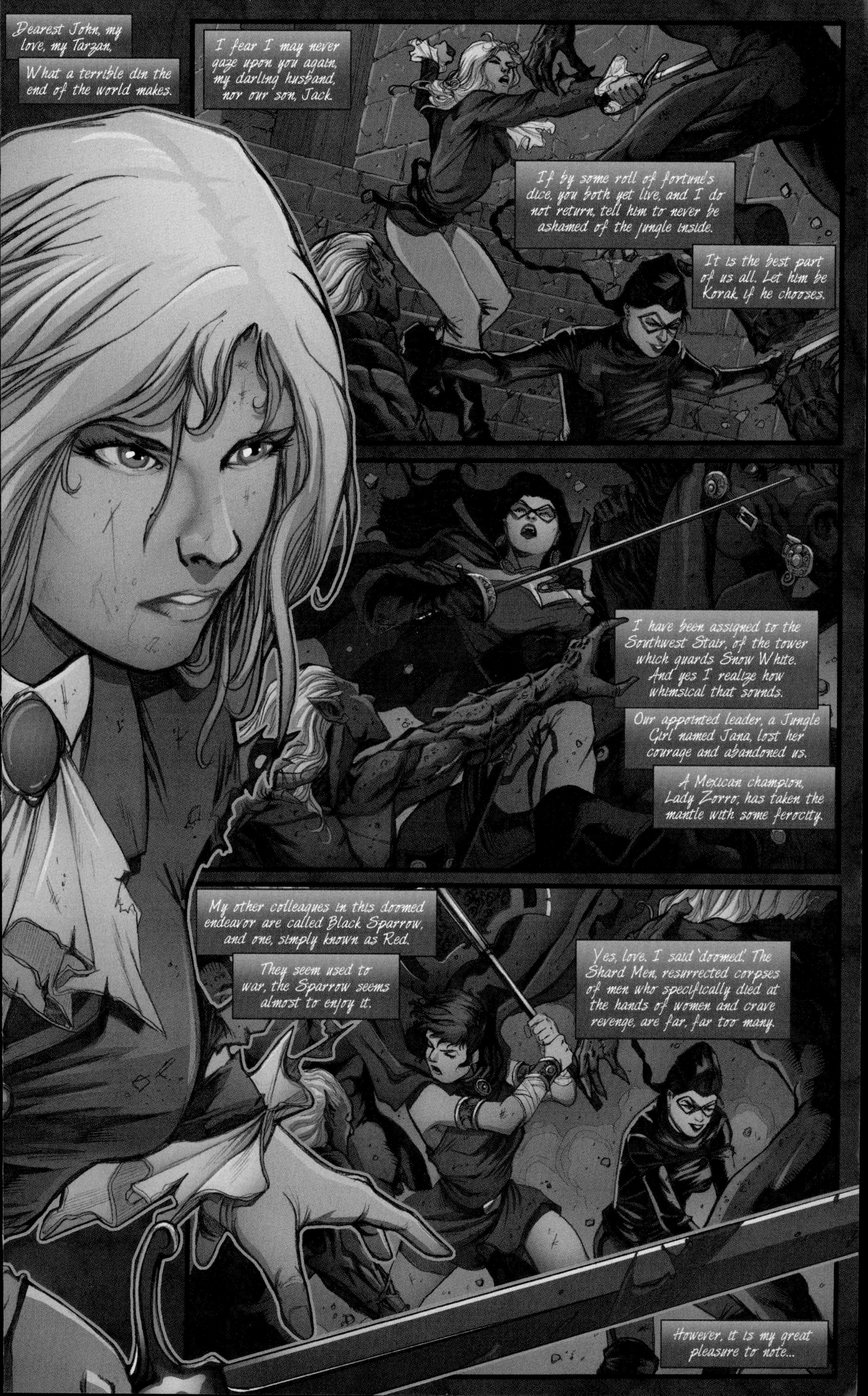
Dearest John, my love, my Tarzan,
What a terrible din the end of the world makes.
I fear I may never gaze upon you again, my darling husband, nor our son, Jack.
If by some roll of fortune's dice, you both yet live, and I do not return, tell him to never be ashamed of the jungle inside.
It is the best part of us all. Let him be Korak if he chooses.
I have been assigned to the Southwest Stair, of the tower which guards Snow White. And yes I realize how whimsical that sounds.
Our appointed leader, a Jungle Girl named Jana, lost her courage and abandoned us.
A Mexican champion, Lady Zorro, has taken the mantle with some ferocity.
My other colleagues in this doomed endeavor are called Black Sparrow, and one, simply known as Red.
They seem used to war, the Sparrow seems almost to enjoy it.
Yes, love. I said 'doomed.' The Shard Men, resurrected corpses of men who specifically died at the hands of women and crave revenge, are far, far too many.
However, it is my great pleasure to note...

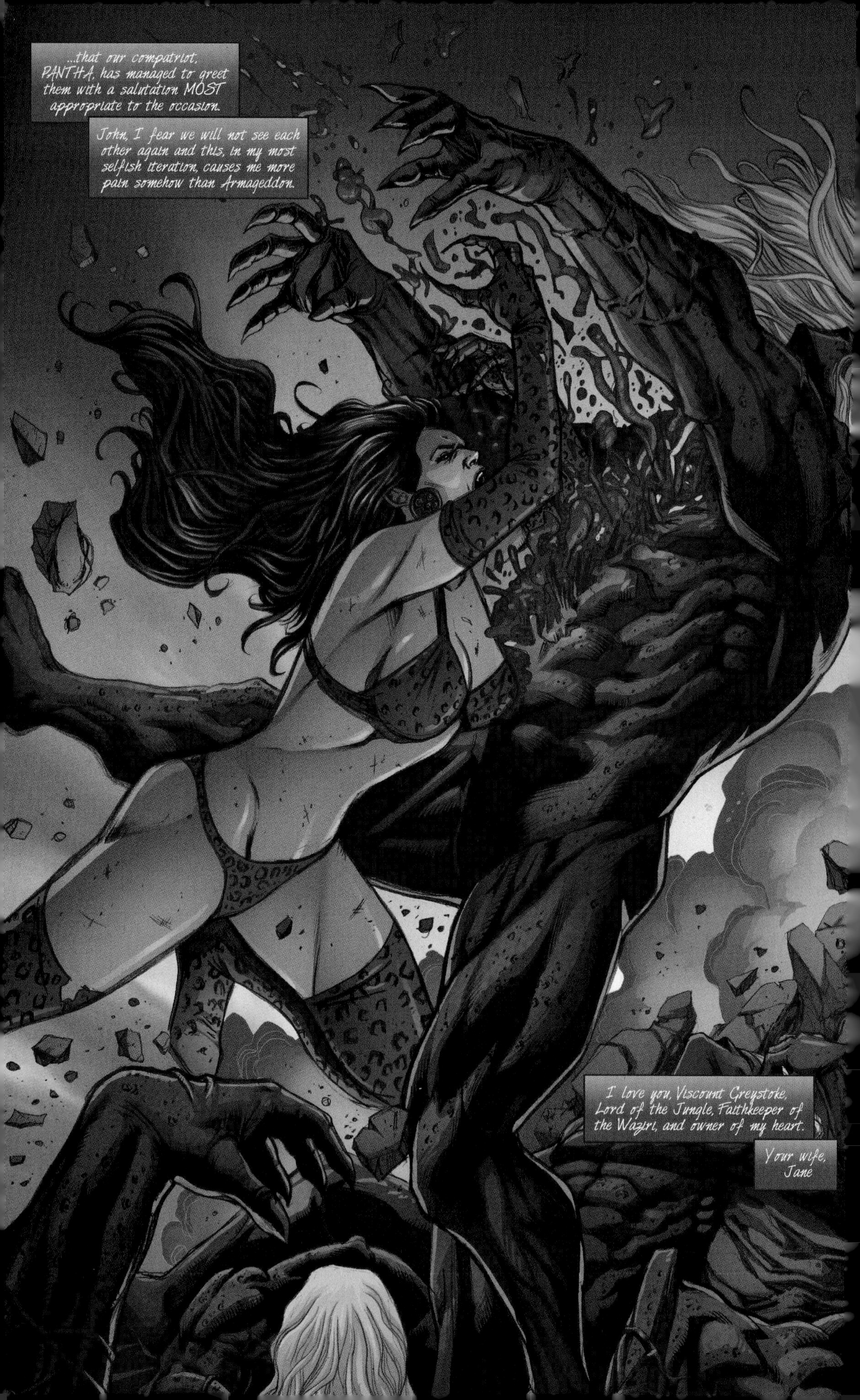
...that our compatriot, PANTHA, has managed to greet them with a salutation MOST appropriate to the occasion.
John, I fear we will not see each other again and this, in my most selfish iteration, causes me more pain somehow than Armageddon.
I love you, Viscount Greystoke, Lord of the Jungle, Faithkeeper of the Waziri, and owner of my heart.
Your wife, Jane

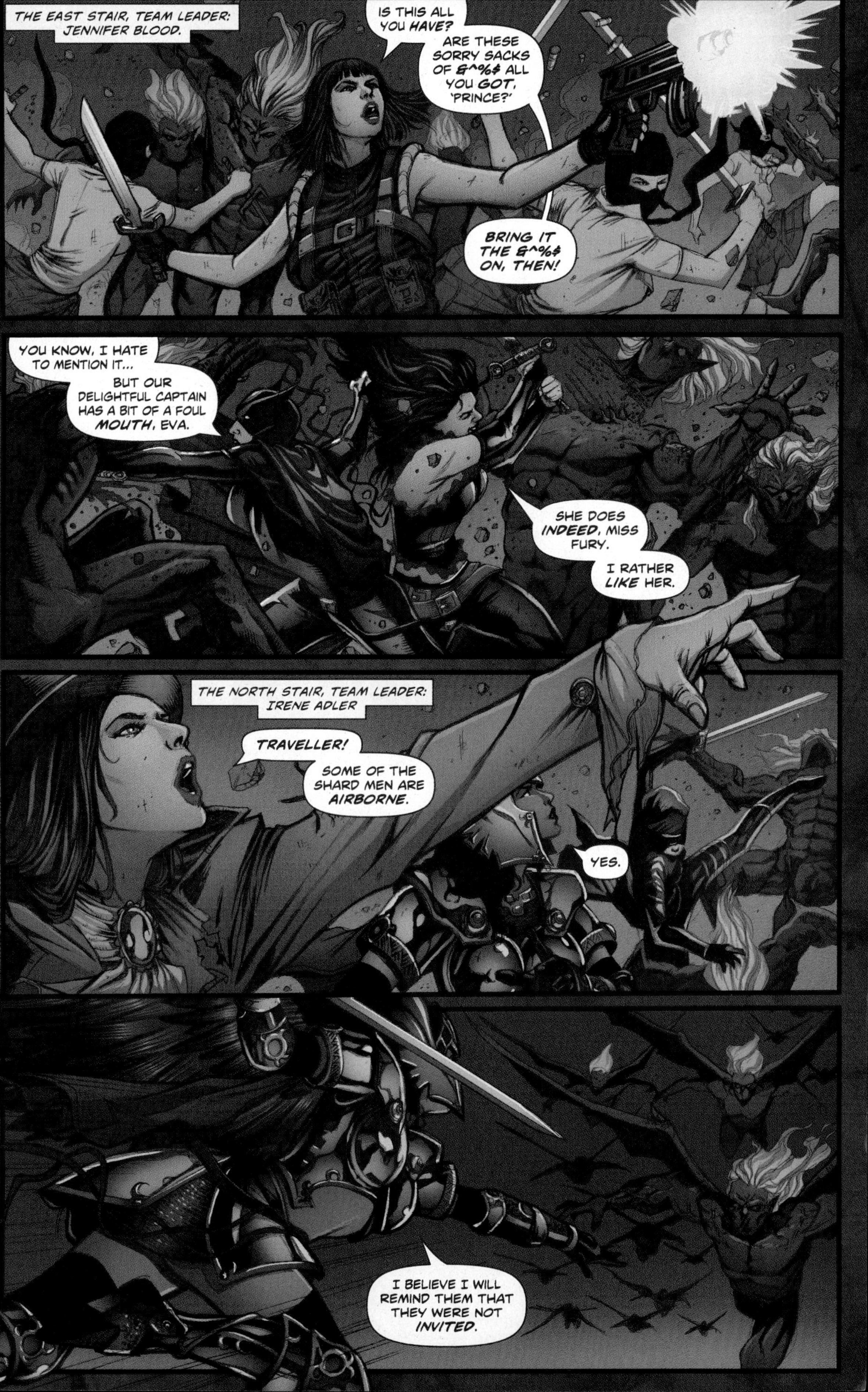
THE EAST STAIR, TEAM LEADER: JENNIFER BLOOD.
IS THIS ALL YOU HAVE?
ARE THESE SORRY SACKS OF &^%$ ALL YOU GOT, 'PRINCE?'
BRING IT THE &^%$ ON, THEN!
YOU KNOW, I HATE TO MENTION IT...
BUT OUR DELIGHTFUL CAPTAIN HAS A BIT OF A FOUL MOUTH, EVA.
SHE DOES INDEED, MISS FURY.
I RATHER LIKE HER.
THE NORTH STAIR, TEAM LEADER: IRENE ADLER
TRAVELLER!
SOME OF THE SHARD MEN ARE AIRBORNE.
YES.
I BELIEVE I WILL REMIND THEM THAT THEY WERE NOT INVITED.

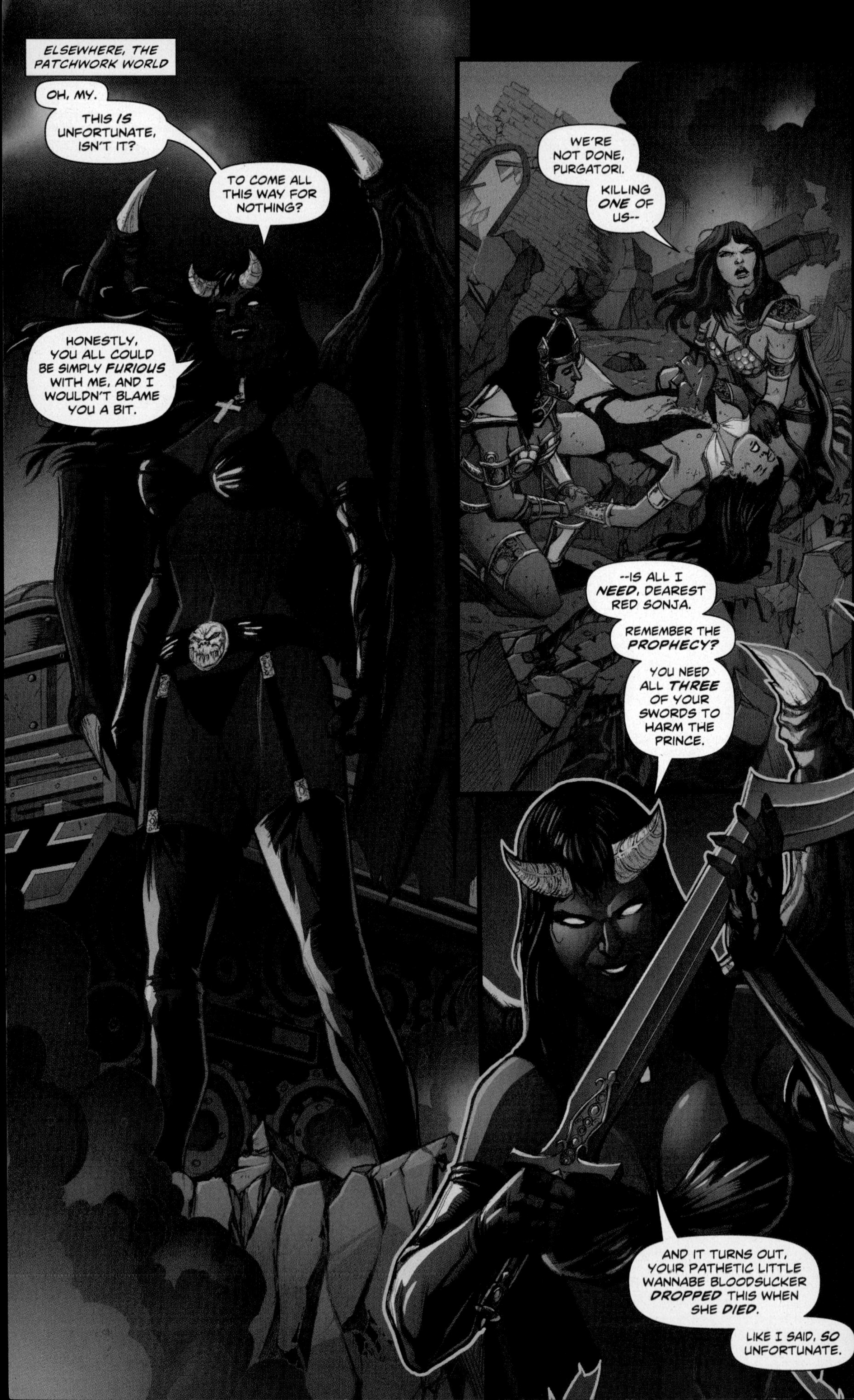

ELSEWHERE, THE PATCHWORK WORLD
OH, MY.
THIS IS UNFORTUNATE, ISN'T IT?
TO COME ALL THIS WAY FOR NOTHING?
HONESTLY, YOU ALL COULD BE SIMPLY FURIOUS WITH ME, AND I WOULDN'T BLAME YOU A BIT.
WE'RE NOT DONE, PURGATORI.
KILLING ONE OF US--
--IS ALL I NEED, DEAREST RED SONJA.
REMEMBER THE PROPHECY?
YOU NEED ALL THREE OF YOUR SWORDS TO HARM THE PRINCE.
AND IT TURNS OUT, YOUR PATHETIC LITTLE WANNABE BLOODSUCKER DROPPED THIS WHEN SHE DIED.
LIKE I SAID, SO UNFORTUNATE.

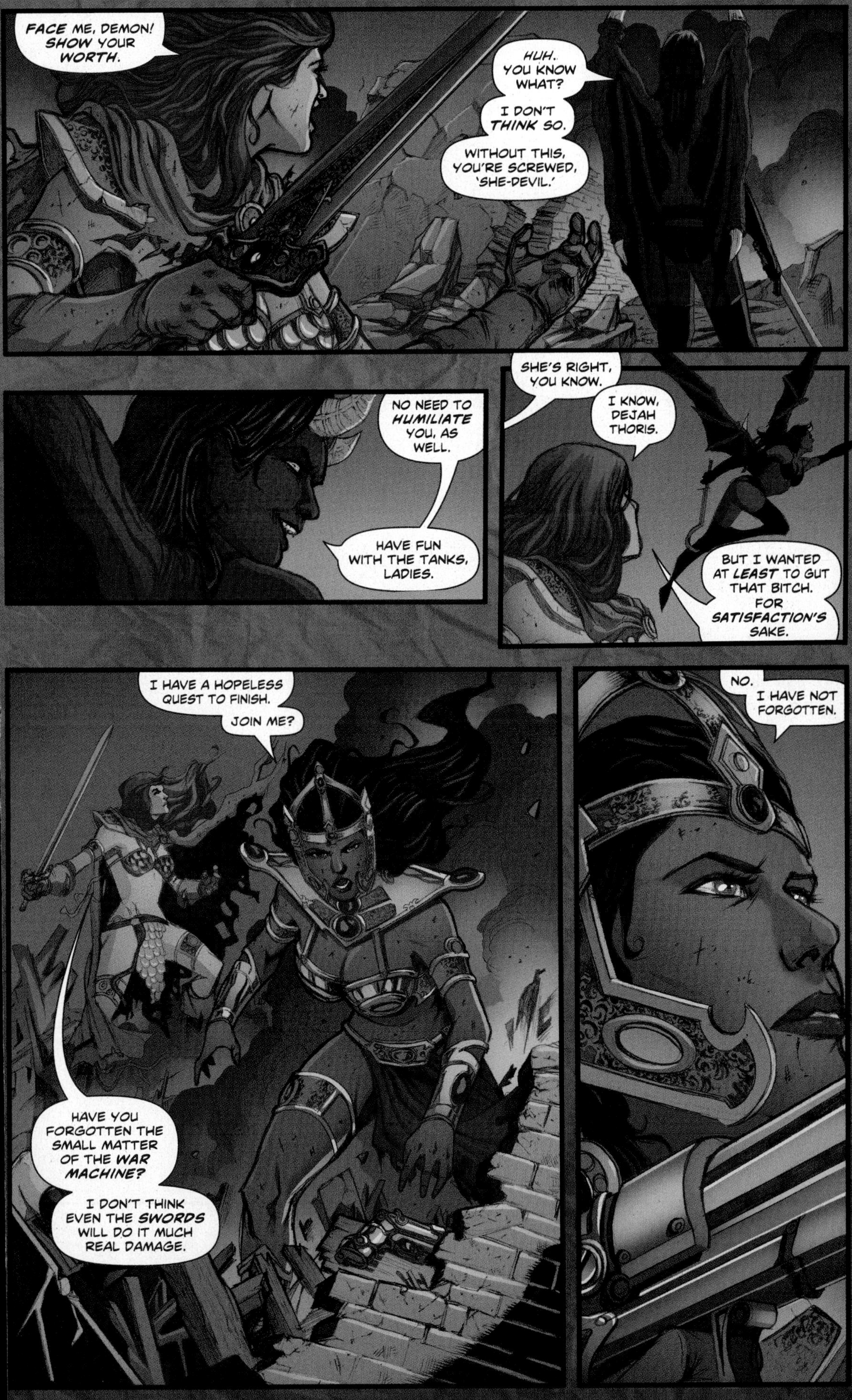
FACE ME, DEMON! SHOW YOUR WORTH.
HUH.. YOU KNOW WHAT?
I DON'T THINK SO.
WITHOUT THIS, YOU'RE SCREWED, 'SHE-DEVIL.'
NO NEED TO HUMILIATE YOU, AS WELL.
HAVE FUN WITH THE TANKS, LADIES.
SHE'S RIGHT, YOU KNOW.
I KNOW, DEJAH THORIS.
BUT I WANTED AT LEAST TO GUT THAT BITCH. FOR SATISFACTION'S SAKE.
I HAVE A HOPELESS QUEST TO FINISH.
JOIN ME?
HAVE YOU FORGOTTEN THE SMALL MATTER OF THE WAR MACHINE?
I DON'T THINK EVEN THE SWORDS WILL DO IT MUCH REAL DAMAGE.
NO.
I HAVE NOT FORGOTTEN.

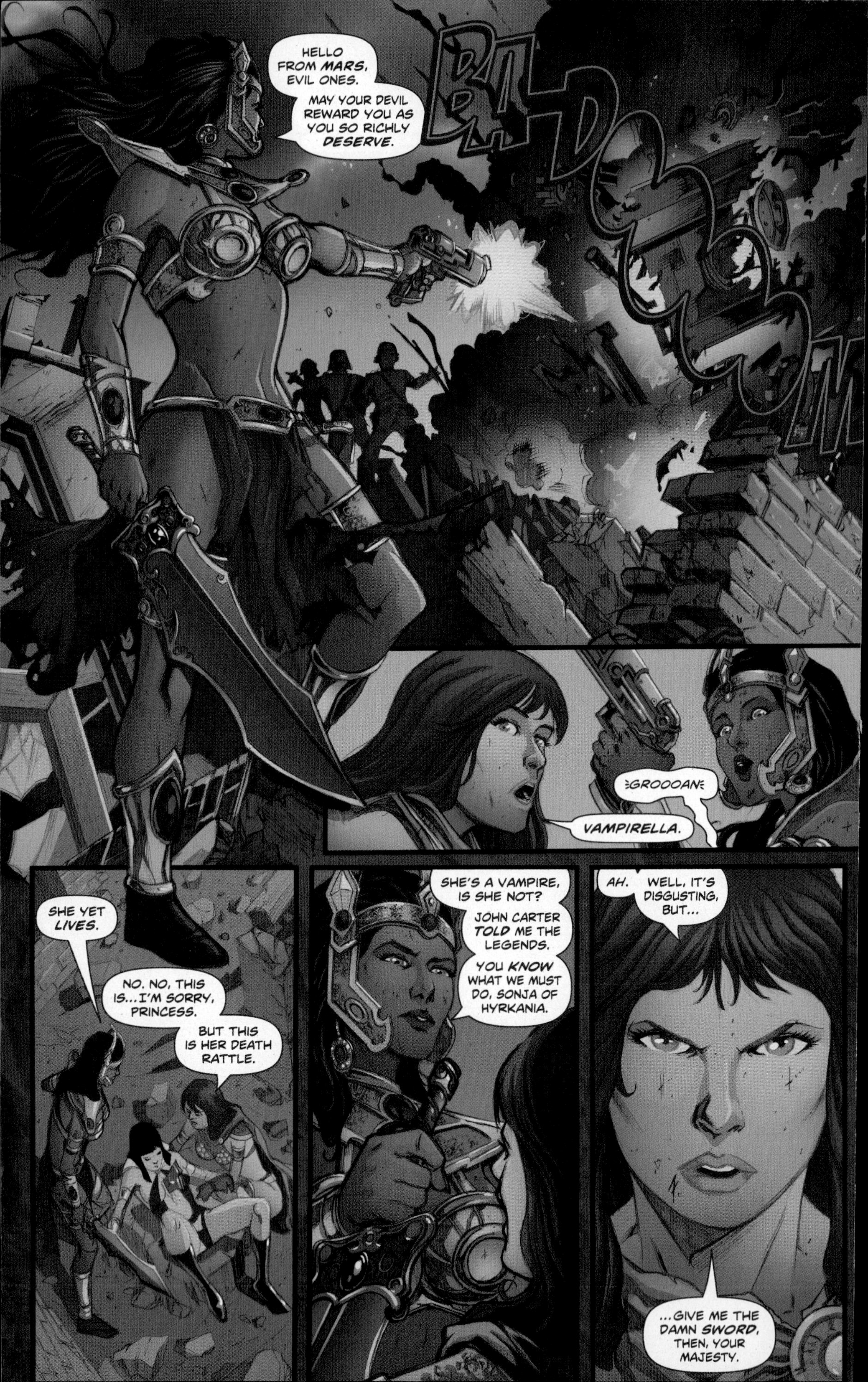
HELLO FROM MARS, EVIL ONES.
MAY YOUR DEVIL REWARD YOU AS YOU SO RICHLY DESERVE.
BADOOOOM
GROOOAN
VAMPIRELLA.
SHE YET LIVES.
NO. NO, THIS IS... I'M SORRY, PRINCESS.
BUT THIS IS HER DEATH RATTLE.
SHE'S A VAMPIRE, IS SHE NOT?
JOHN CARTER TOLD ME THE LEGENDS.
YOU KNOW WHAT WE MUST DO, SONJA OF HYRKANIA.
AH.
WELL, IT'S DISGUSTING, BUT...
...GIVE ME THE DAMN SWORD, THEN, YOUR MAJESTY.

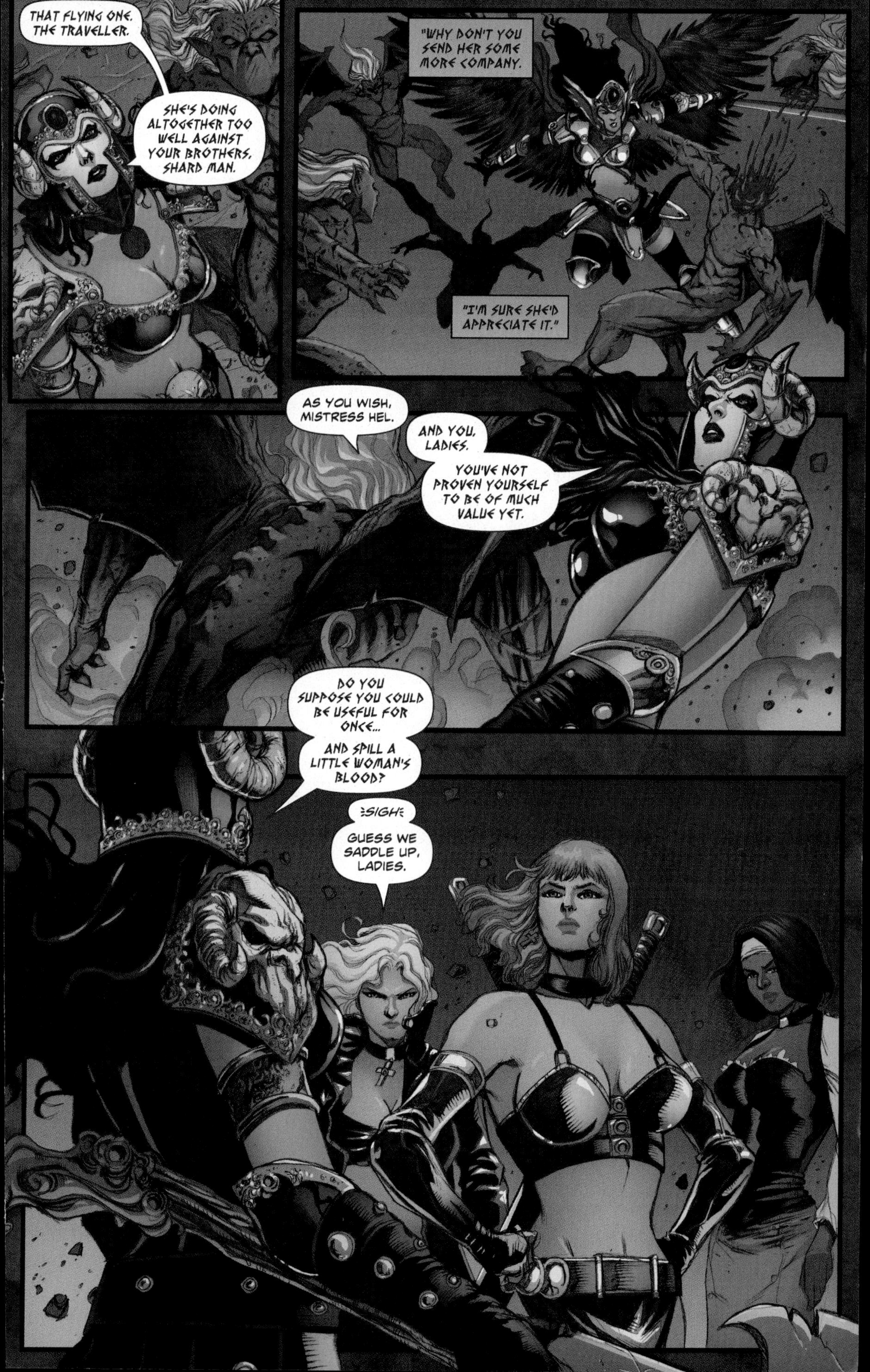
THAT FLYING ONE. THE TRAVELLER.
SHE'S DOING ALTOGETHER TOO WELL AGAINST YOUR BROTHERS, SHARD MAN.
"WHY DON'T YOU SEND HER SOME MORE COMPANY.
"I'M SURE SHE'D APPRECIATE IT."
AS YOU WISH, MISTRESS HEL.
AND YOU, LADIES.
YOU'VE NOT PROVEN YOURSELF TO BE OF MUCH VALUE YET.
DO YOU SUPPOSE YOU COULD BE USEFUL FOR ONCE...
AND SPILL A LITTLE WOMAN'S BLOOD?
SIGH
GUESS WE SADDLE UP, LADIES.

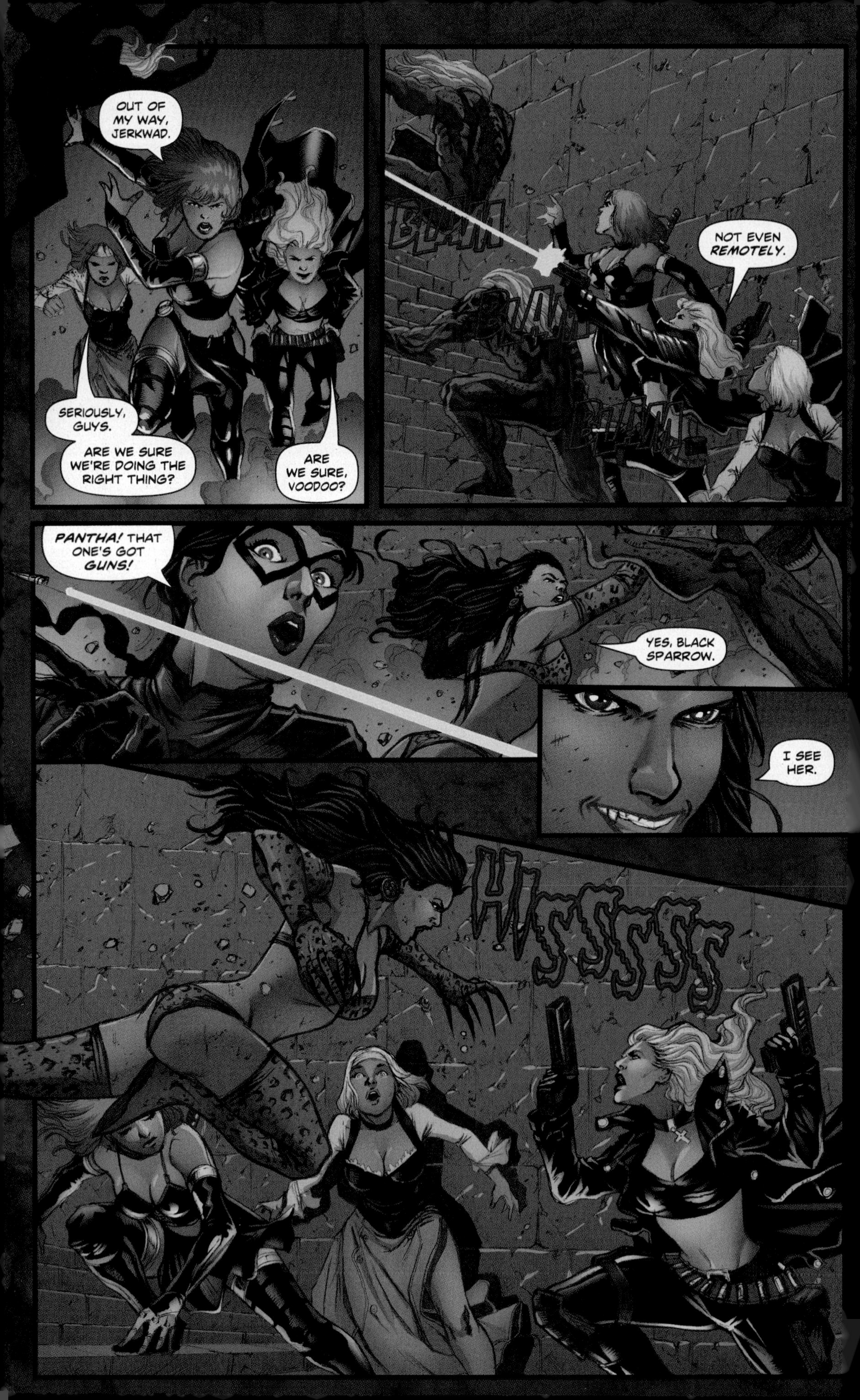

OUT OF MY WAY, JERKWAD.
SERIOUSLY, GUYS.
ARE WE SURE WE'RE DOING THE RIGHT THING?
ARE WE SURE, VOODOO?
BLAM
BLAM
BLAM
NOT EVEN REMOTELY.
PANTHA! THAT ONE'S GOT GUNS!
YES, BLACK SPARROW.
I SEE HER.
HISSSSSS

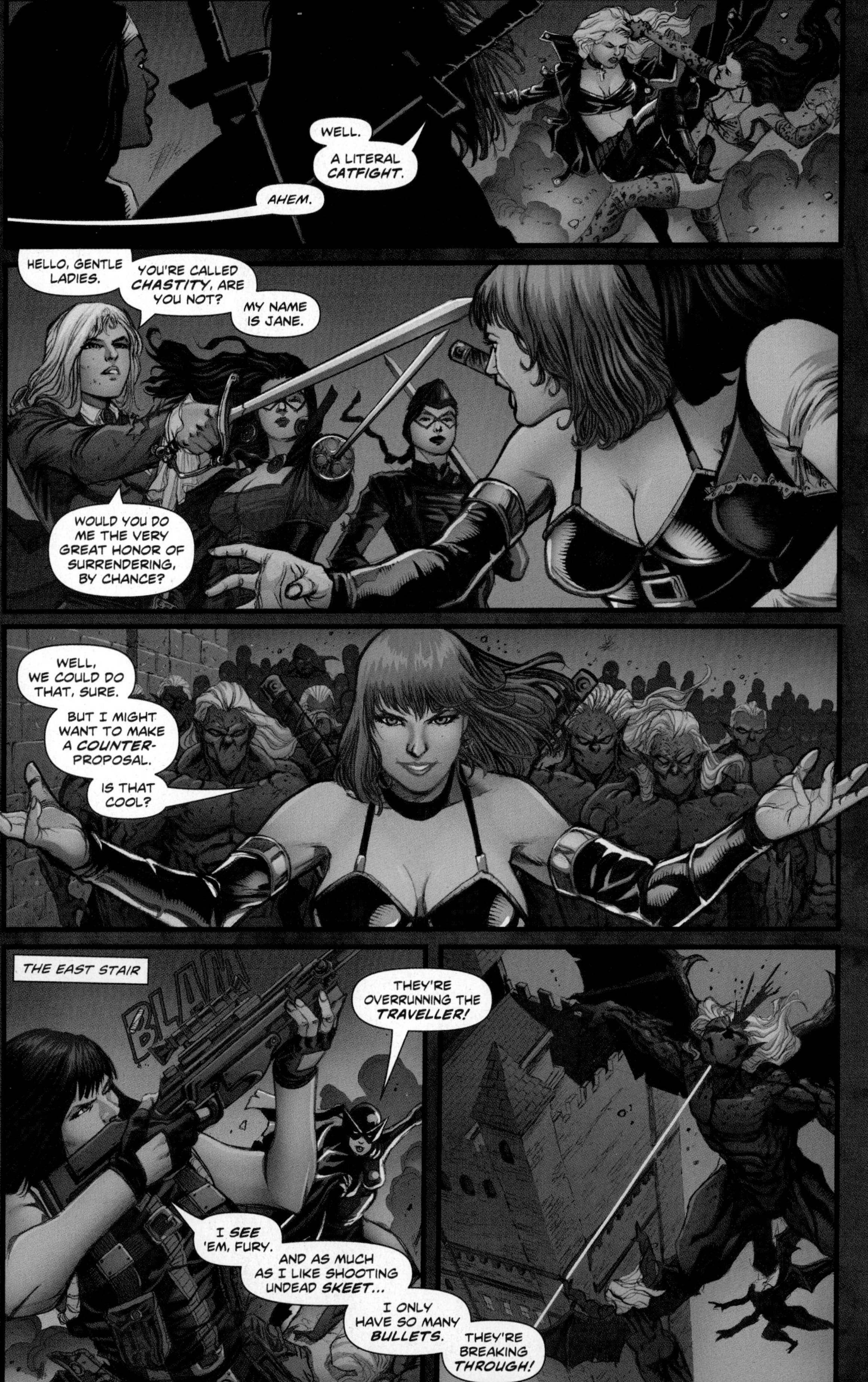

WELL.
A LITERAL CATFIGHT.
AHEM.
HELLO, GENTLE LADIES.
YOU'RE CALLED CHASTITY, ARE YOU NOT?
MY NAME IS JANE.
WOULD YOU DO ME THE VERY GREAT HONOR OF SURRENDERING, BY CHANCE?
WELL, WE COULD DO THAT, SURE.
BUT I MIGHT WANT TO MAKE A COUNTER-PROPOSAL.
IS THAT COOL?
THE EAST STAIR
THEY'RE OVERRUNNING THE TRAVELLER!
I SEE 'EM, FURY.
AND AS MUCH AS I LIKE SHOOTING UNDEAD SKEET...
I ONLY HAVE SO MANY BULLETS.
THEY'RE BREAKING THROUGH!

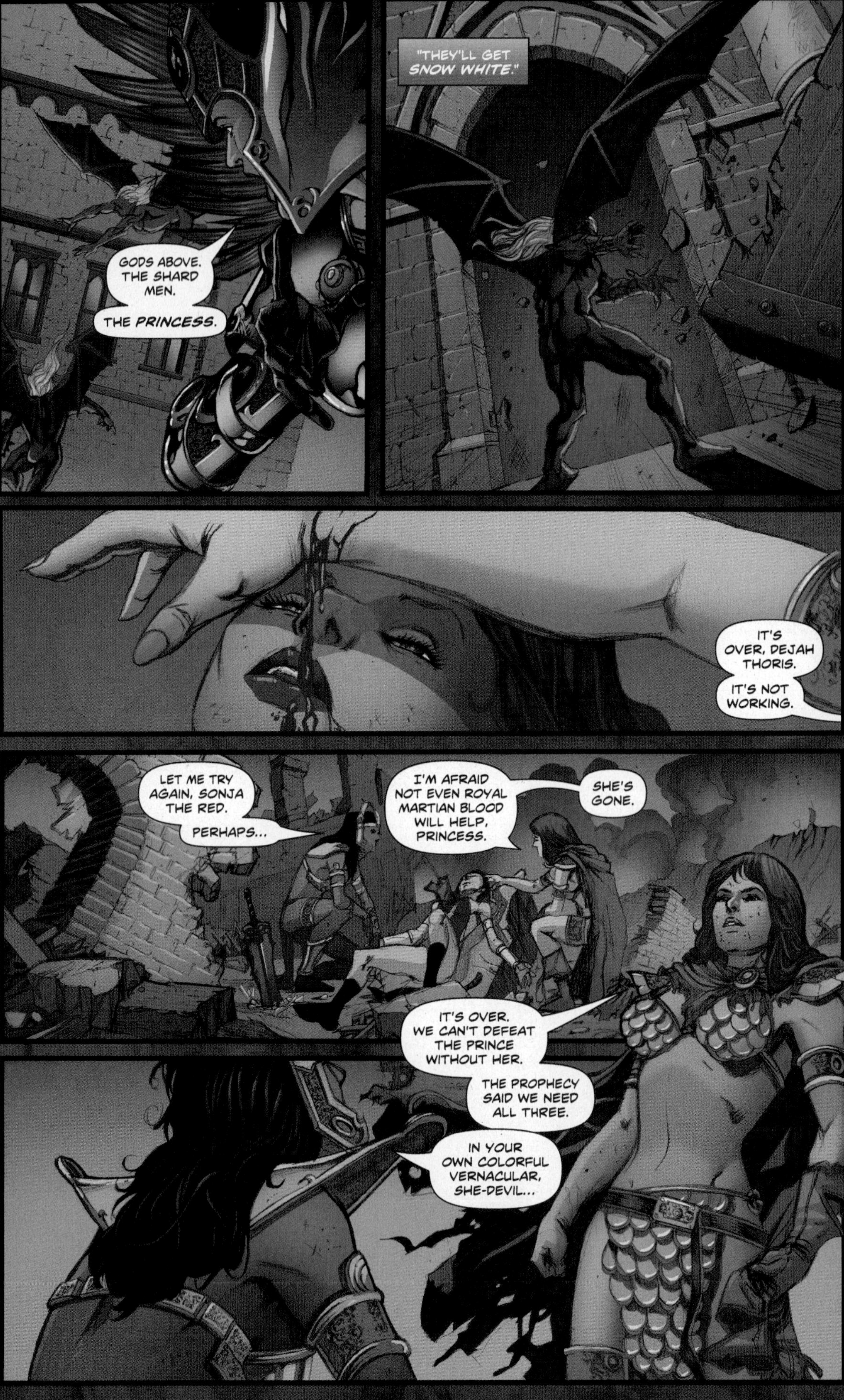

"THEY'LL GET SNOW WHITE."
GODS ABOVE. THE SHARD MEN.
THE PRINCESS.
IT'S OVER, DEJAH THORIS.
IT'S NOT WORKING.
LET ME TRY AGAIN, SONJA THE RED.
PERHAPS...
I'M AFRAID NOT EVEN ROYAL MARTIAN BLOOD WILL HELP, PRINCESS.
SHE'S GONE.
IT'S OVER. WE CAN'T DEFEAT THE PRINCE WITHOUT HER.
THE PROPHECY SAID WE NEED ALL THREE.
IN YOUR OWN COLORFUL VERNACULAR, SHE-DEVIL...

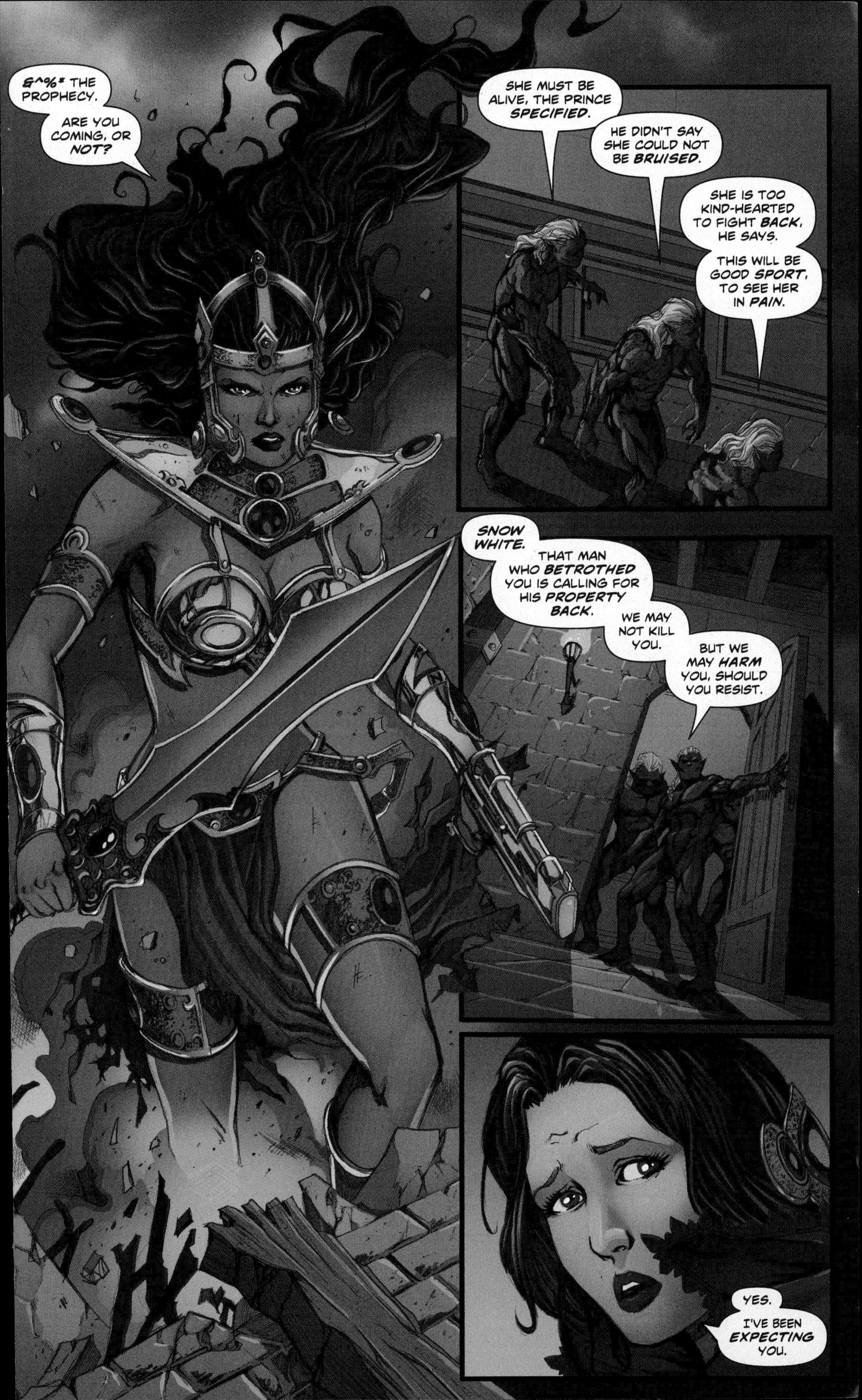
&^%* THE PROPHECY.
ARE YOU COMING, OR NOT?
SHE MUST BE ALIVE, THE PRINCE SPECIFIED.
HE DIDN'T SAY SHE COULD NOT BE BRUISED.
SHE IS TOO KIND-HEARTED TO FIGHT BACK, HE SAYS.
THIS WILL BE GOOD SPORT, TO SEE HER IN PAIN.
SNOW WHITE.
THAT MAN WHO BETROTHED YOU IS CALLING FOR HIS PROPERTY BACK.
WE MAY NOT KILL YOU.
BUT WE MAY HARM YOU, SHOULD YOU RESIST.
YES.
I'VE BEEN EXPECTING YOU.

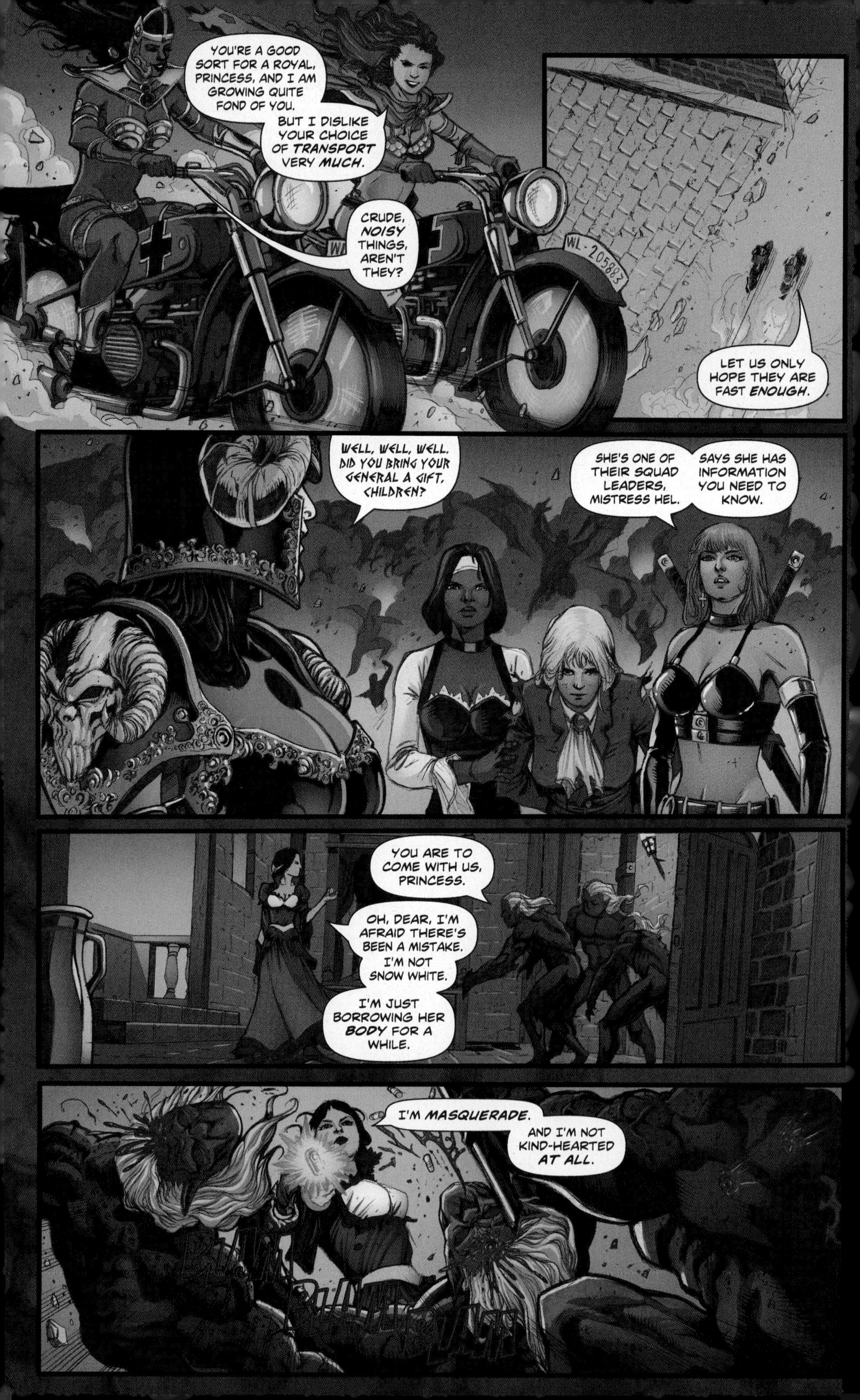

YOU'RE A GOOD SORT FOR A ROYAL, PRINCESS, AND I AM GROWING QUITE FOND OF YOU.
BUT I DISLIKE YOUR CHOICE OF TRANSPORT VERY MUCH.
CRUDE, NOISY THINGS, AREN'T THEY?
WL-205883
LET US ONLY HOPE THEY ARE FAST ENOUGH.
WELL, WELL, WELL. DID YOU BRING YOUR GENERAL A GIFT, CHILDREN?
SHE'S ONE OF THEIR SQUAD LEADERS, MISTRESS HEL.
SAYS SHE HAS INFORMATION YOU NEED TO KNOW.
YOU ARE TO COME WITH US, PRINCESS.
OH, DEAR, I'M AFRAID THERE'S BEEN A MISTAKE. I'M NOT SNOW WHITE.
I'M JUST BORROWING HER BODY FOR A WHILE.
I'M MASQUERADE.
AND I'M NOT KIND-HEARTED AT ALL.

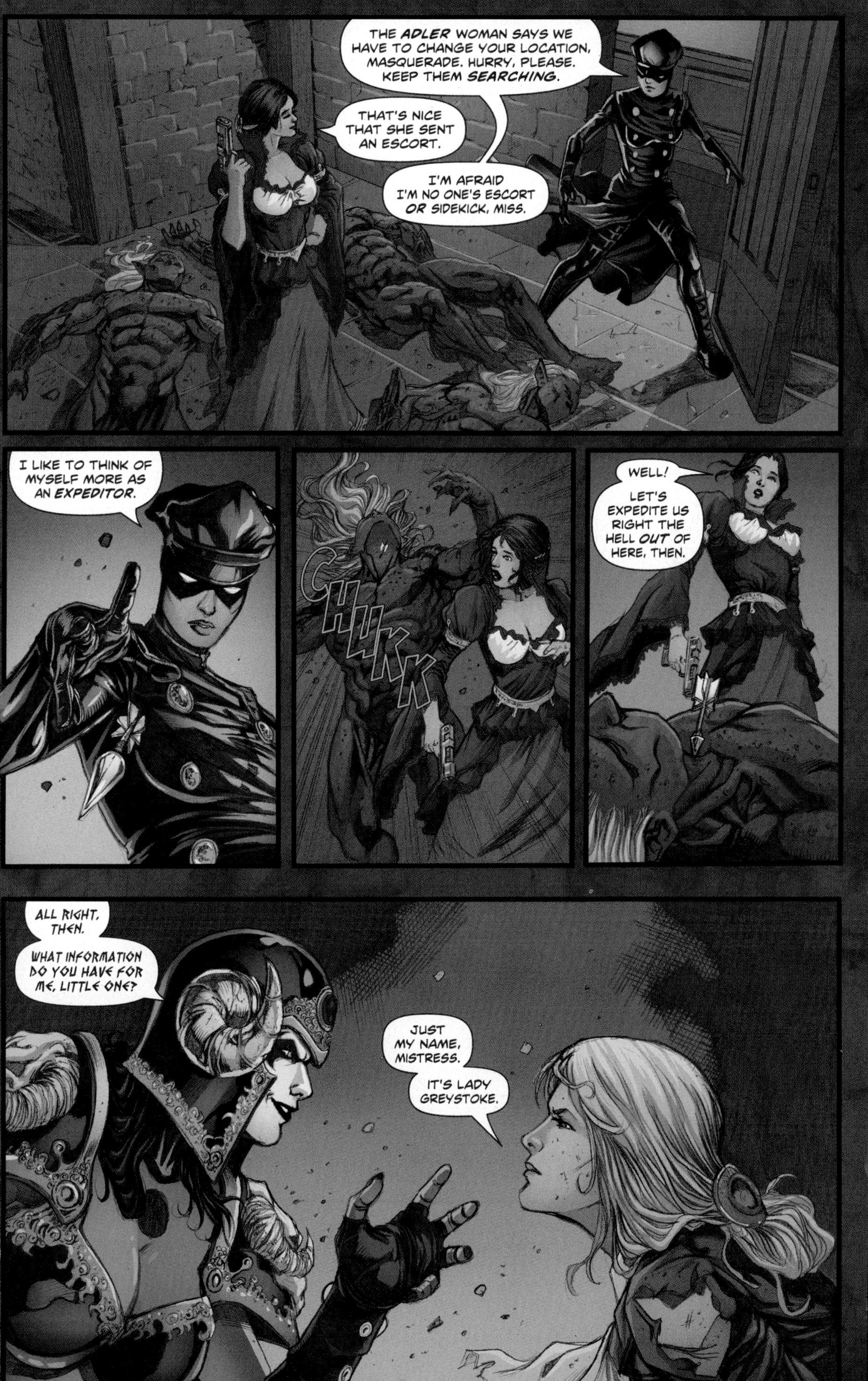
THE ADLER WOMAN SAYS WE HAVE TO CHANGE YOUR LOCATION, MASQUERADE. HURRY, PLEASE. KEEP THEM SEARCHING.
THAT'S NICE THAT SHE SENT AN ESCORT.
I'M AFRAID I'M NO ONE'S ESCORT OR SIDEKICK, MISS.
I LIKE TO THINK OF MYSELF MORE AS AN EXPEDITOR.
CHUKK
WELL!
LET'S EXPEDITE US RIGHT THE HELL OUT OF HERE, THEN.
ALL RIGHT, THEN.
WHAT INFORMATION DO YOU HAVE FOR ME, LITTLE ONE?
JUST MY NAME, MISTRESS.
IT'S LADY GREYSTOKE.

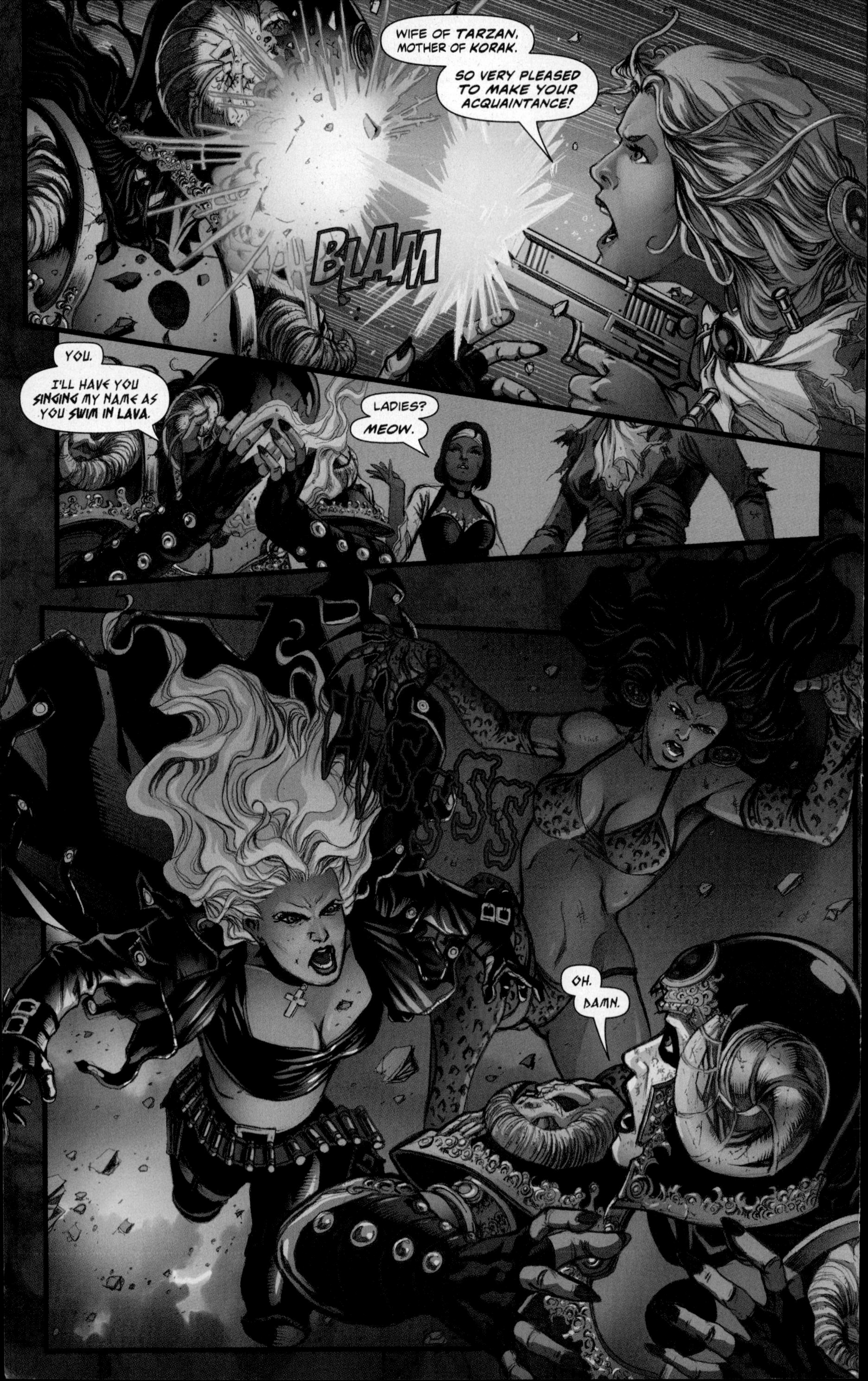
WIFE OF TARZAN, MOTHER OF KORAK.
SO VERY PLEASED TO MAKE YOUR ACQUAINTANCE!
BLAM
YOU.
I'LL HAVE YOU SINGING MY NAME AS YOU SWIM IN LAVA.
LADIES?
MEOW.
OH.
DAMN.

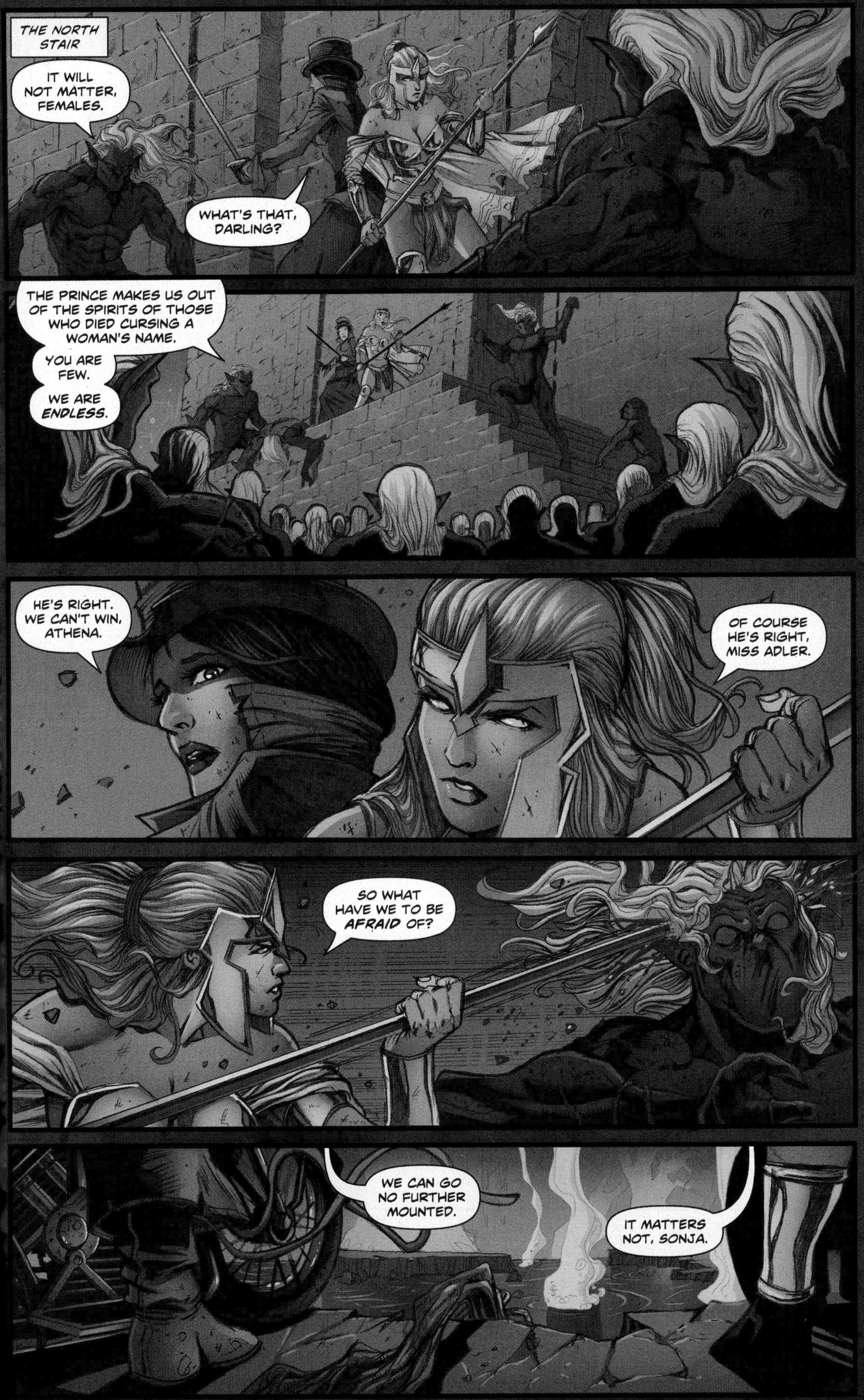
THE NORTH STAIR
IT WILL NOT MATTER, FEMALES.
WHAT'S THAT, DARLING?
THE PRINCE MAKES US OUT OF THE SPIRITS OF THOSE WHO DIED CURSING A WOMAN'S NAME.
YOU ARE FEW.
WE ARE ENDLESS.
HE'S RIGHT. WE CAN'T WIN, ATHENA.
OF COURSE HE'S RIGHT, MISS ADLER.
SO WHAT HAVE WE TO BE AFRAID OF?
WE CAN GO NO FURTHER MOUNTED.
IT MATTERS NOT, SONJA.

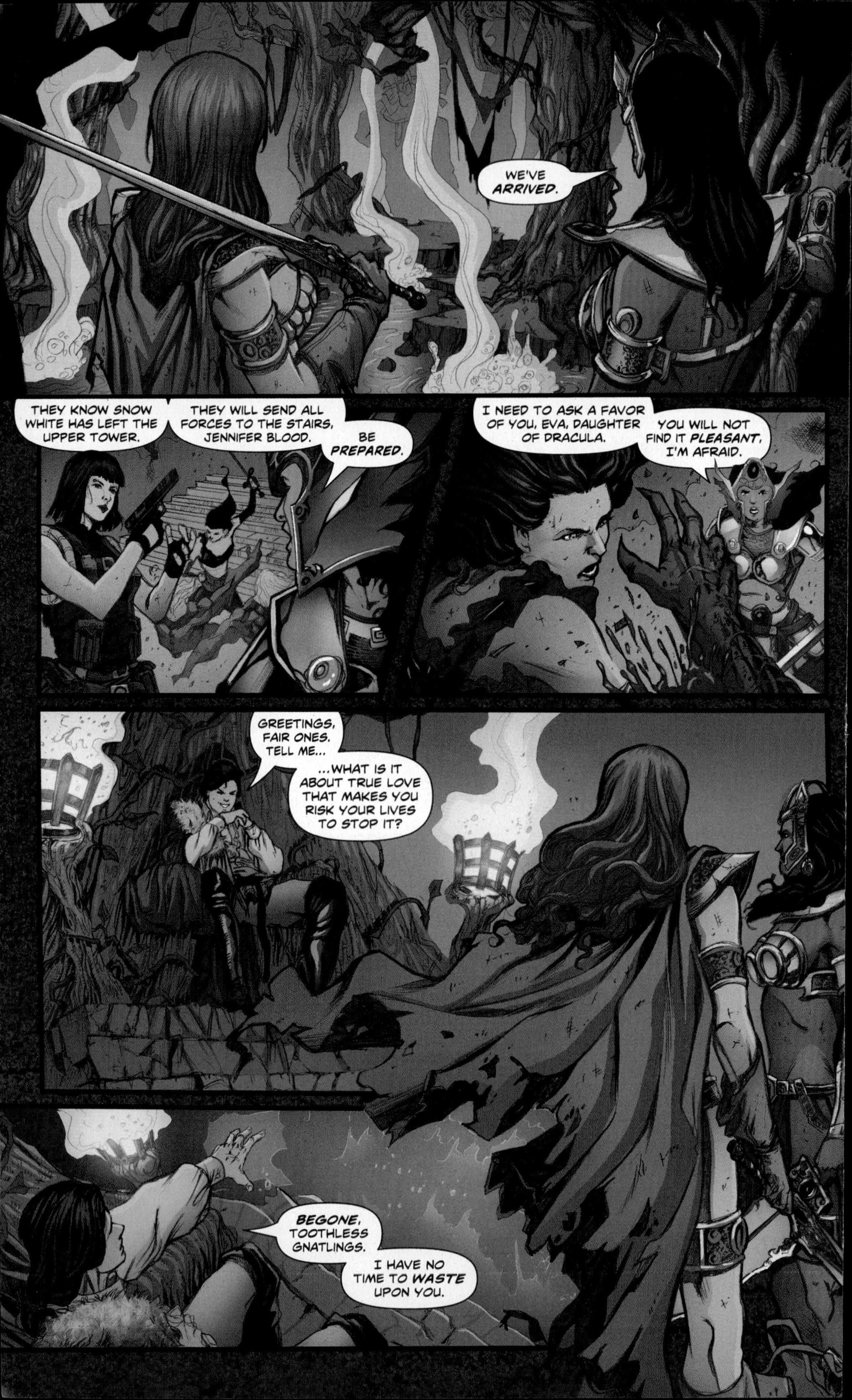

WE'VE ARRIVED.
THEY KNOW SNOW WHITE HAS LEFT THE UPPER TOWER.
THEY WILL SEND ALL FORCES TO THE STAIRS, JENNIFER BLOOD.
BE PREPARED.
I NEED TO ASK A FAVOR OF YOU, EVA, DAUGHTER OF DRACULA.
YOU WILL NOT FIND IT PLEASANT, I'M AFRAID.
GREETINGS, FAIR ONES. TELL ME...
...WHAT IS IT ABOUT TRUE LOVE THAT MAKES YOU RISK YOUR LIVES TO STOP IT?
BEGONE, TOOTHLESS GNATLINGS.
I HAVE NO TIME TO WASTE UPON YOU.

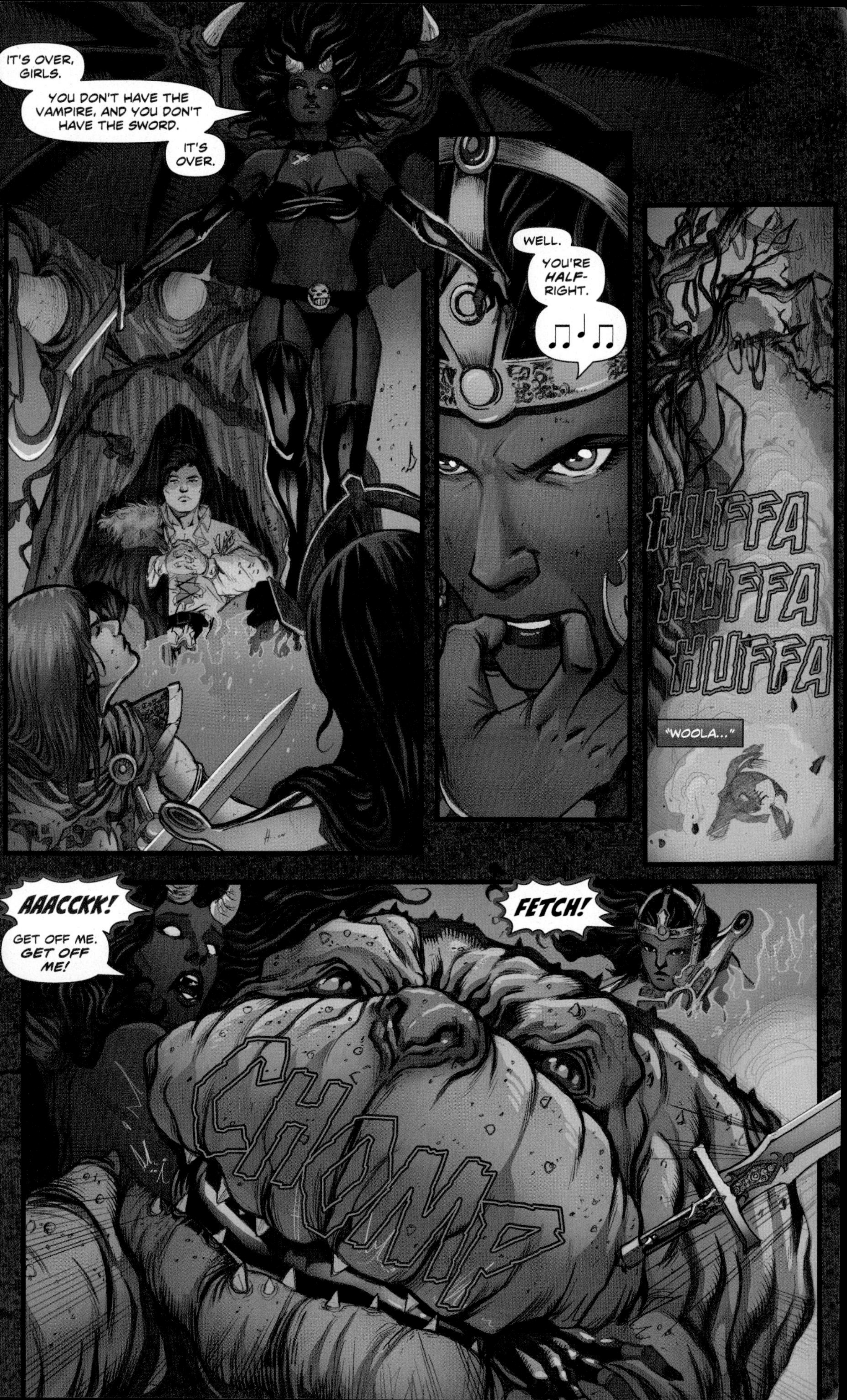
IT'S OVER, GIRLS.
YOU DON'T HAVE THE VAMPIRE, AND YOU DON'T HAVE THE SWORD.
IT'S OVER.
WELL.
YOU'RE HALF-RIGHT.
♫♩♫
HUFFA HUFFA HUFFA
"WOOLA..."
AAACCKK!
GET OFF ME. GET OFF ME!
FETCH!
CHOMP

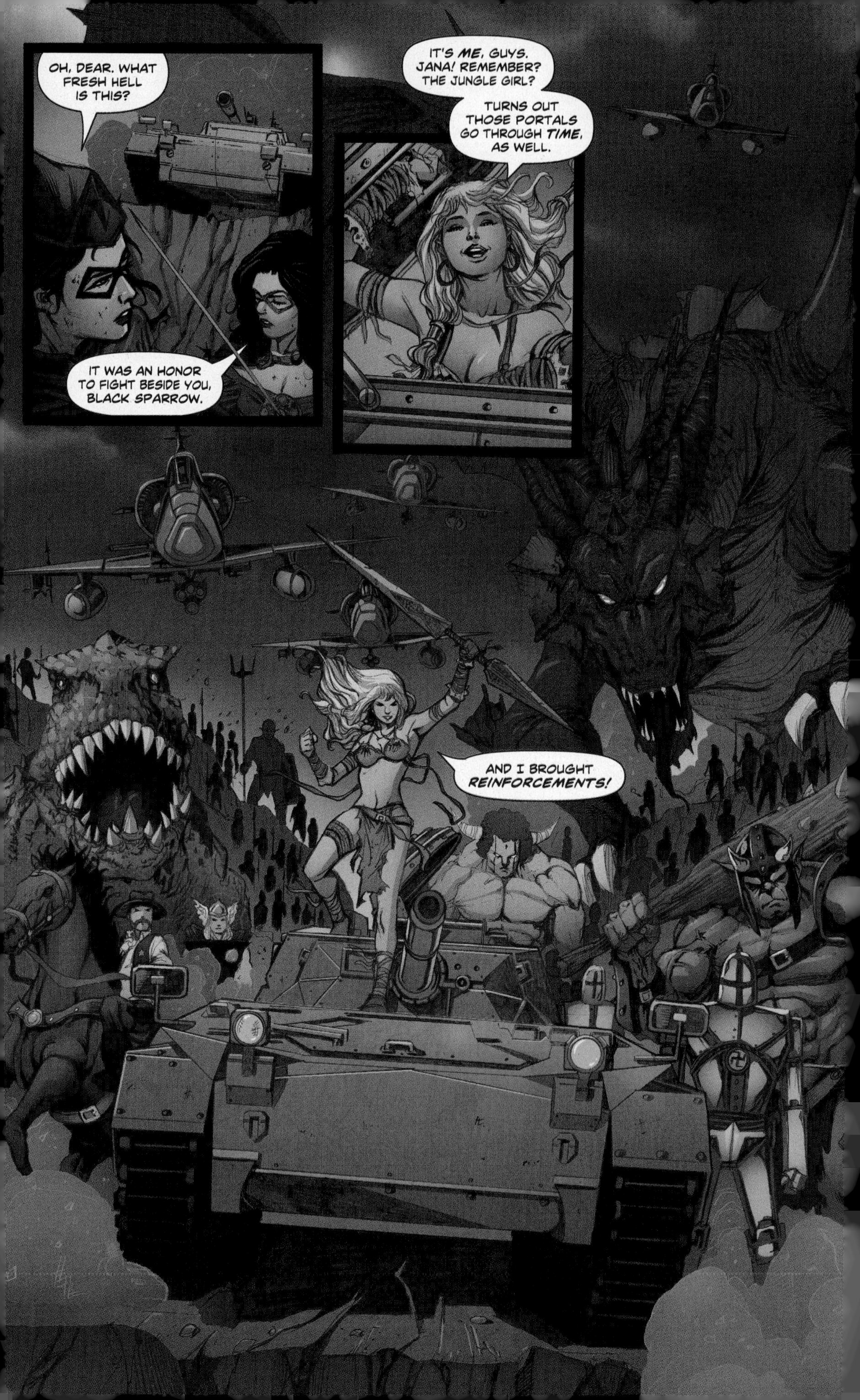
OH, DEAR. WHAT FRESH HELL IS THIS?
IT'S ME, GUYS. JANA! REMEMBER? THE JUNGLE GIRL?
TURNS OUT THOSE PORTALS GO THROUGH TIME, AS WELL.
IT WAS AN HONOR TO FIGHT BESIDE YOU, BLACK SPARROW.
AND I BROUGHT REINFORCEMENTS!

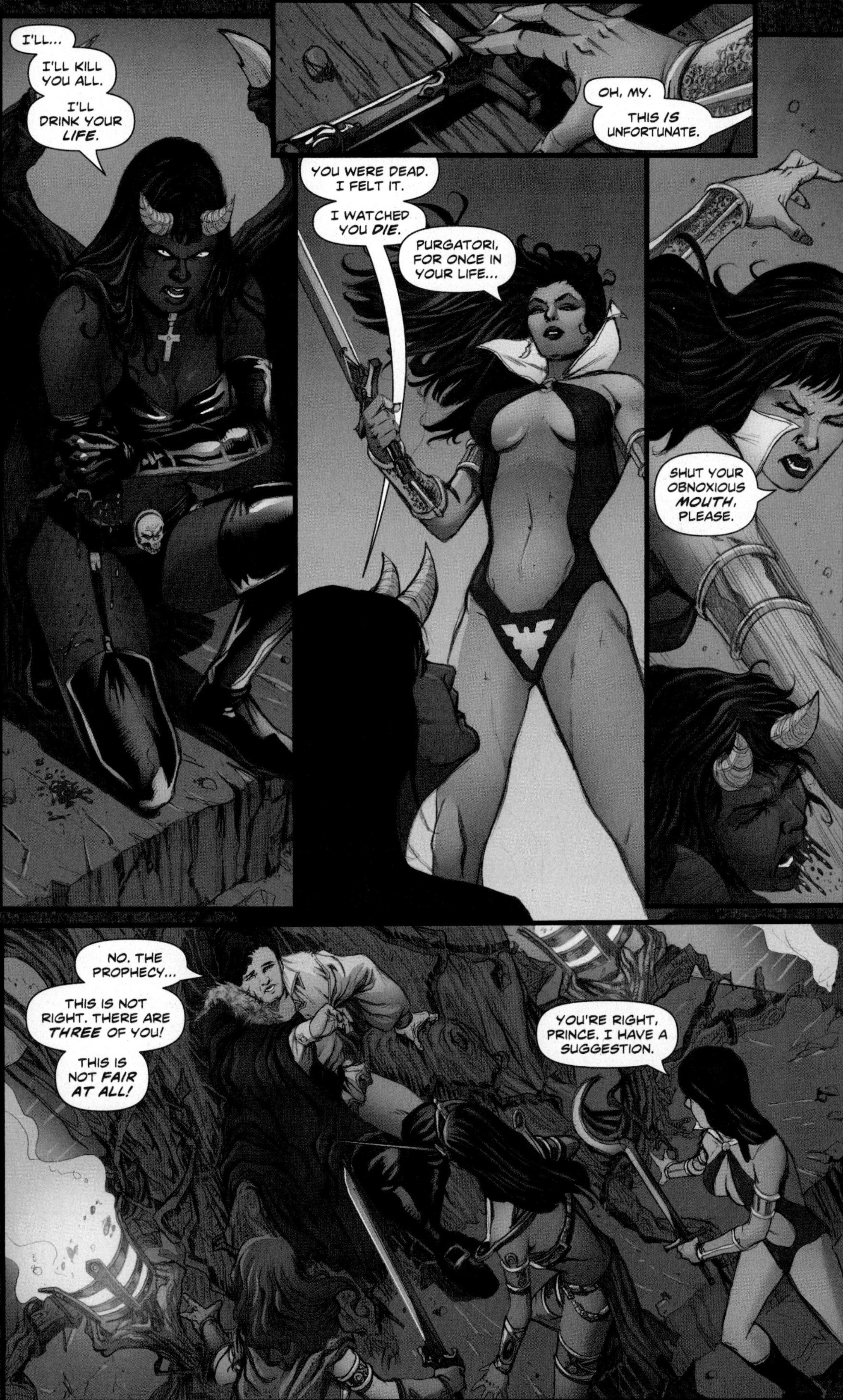

I'LL...
I'LL KILL YOU ALL.
I'LL DRINK YOUR LIFE.
OH, MY.
THIS IS UNFORTUNATE.
YOU WERE DEAD. I FELT IT.
I WATCHED YOU DIE.
PURGATORI, FOR ONCE IN YOUR LIFE...
SHUT YOUR OBNOXIOUS MOUTH, PLEASE.
NO. THE PROPHECY...
THIS IS NOT RIGHT. THERE ARE THREE OF YOU!
THIS IS NOT FAIR AT ALL!
YOU'RE RIGHT, PRINCE. I HAVE A SUGGESTION.

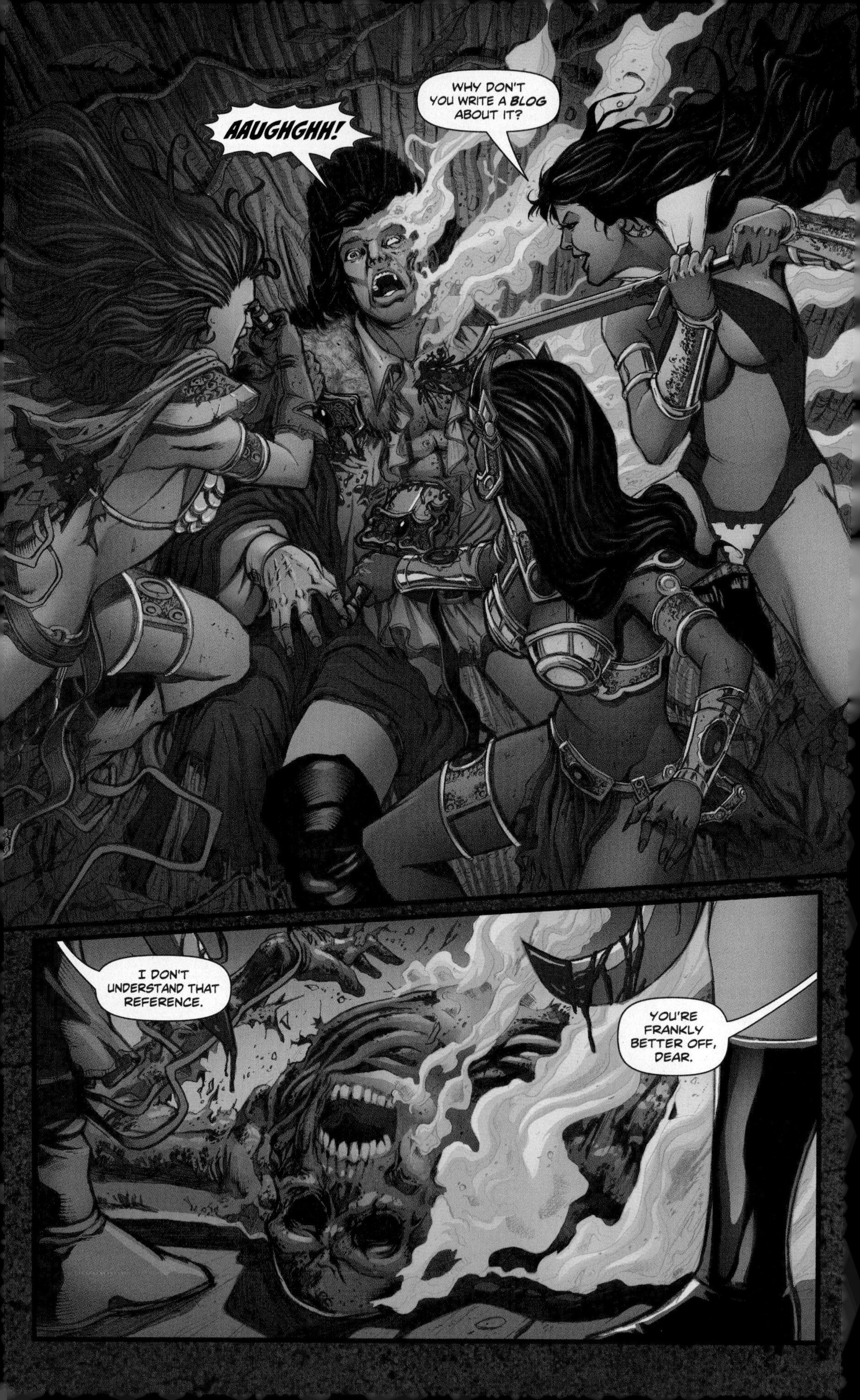
AAUGHGHH!
WHY DON'T YOU WRITE A BLOG ABOUT IT?
I DON'T UNDERSTAND THAT REFERENCE.
YOU'RE FRANKLY BETTER OFF, DEAR.

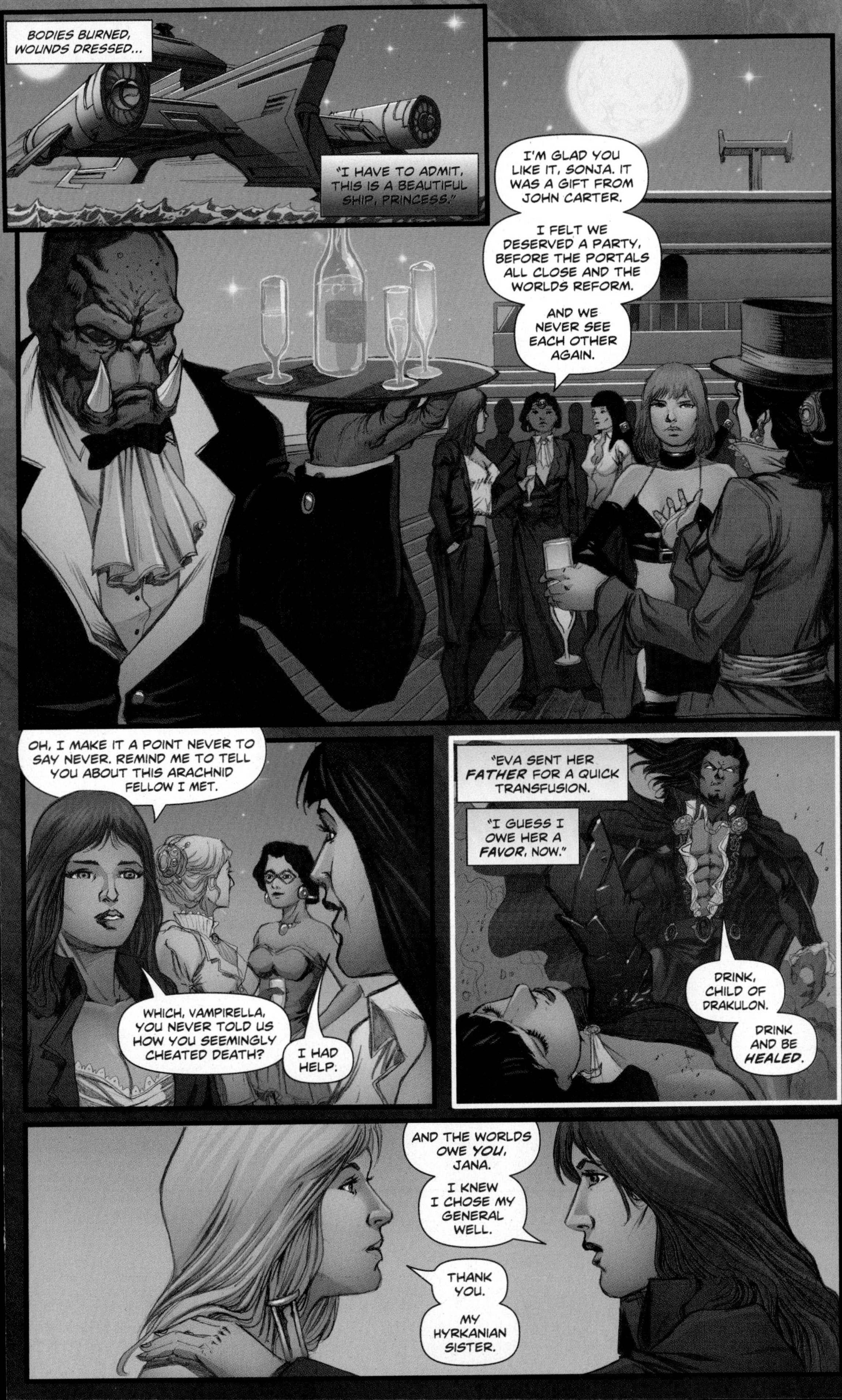
BODIES BURNED, WOUNDS DRESSED...
"I HAVE TO ADMIT, THIS IS A BEAUTIFUL SHIP, PRINCESS."
I'M GLAD YOU LIKE IT, SONJA. IT WAS A GIFT FROM JOHN CARTER.
I FELT WE DESERVED A PARTY, BEFORE THE PORTALS ALL CLOSE AND THE WORLDS REFORM.
AND WE NEVER SEE EACH OTHER AGAIN.
OH, I MAKE IT A POINT NEVER TO SAY NEVER. REMIND ME TO TELL YOU ABOUT THIS ARACHNID FELLOW I MET.
WHICH, VAMPIRELLA, YOU NEVER TOLD US HOW YOU SEEMINGLY CHEATED DEATH?
I HAD HELP.
"EVA SENT HER FATHER FOR A QUICK TRANSFUSION.
"I GUESS I OWE HER A FAVOR, NOW."
DRINK, CHILD OF DRAKULON.
DRINK AND BE HEALED.
AND THE WORLDS OWE YOU, JANA.
I KNEW I CHOSE MY GENERAL WELL.
THANK YOU.
MY HYRKANIAN SISTER.

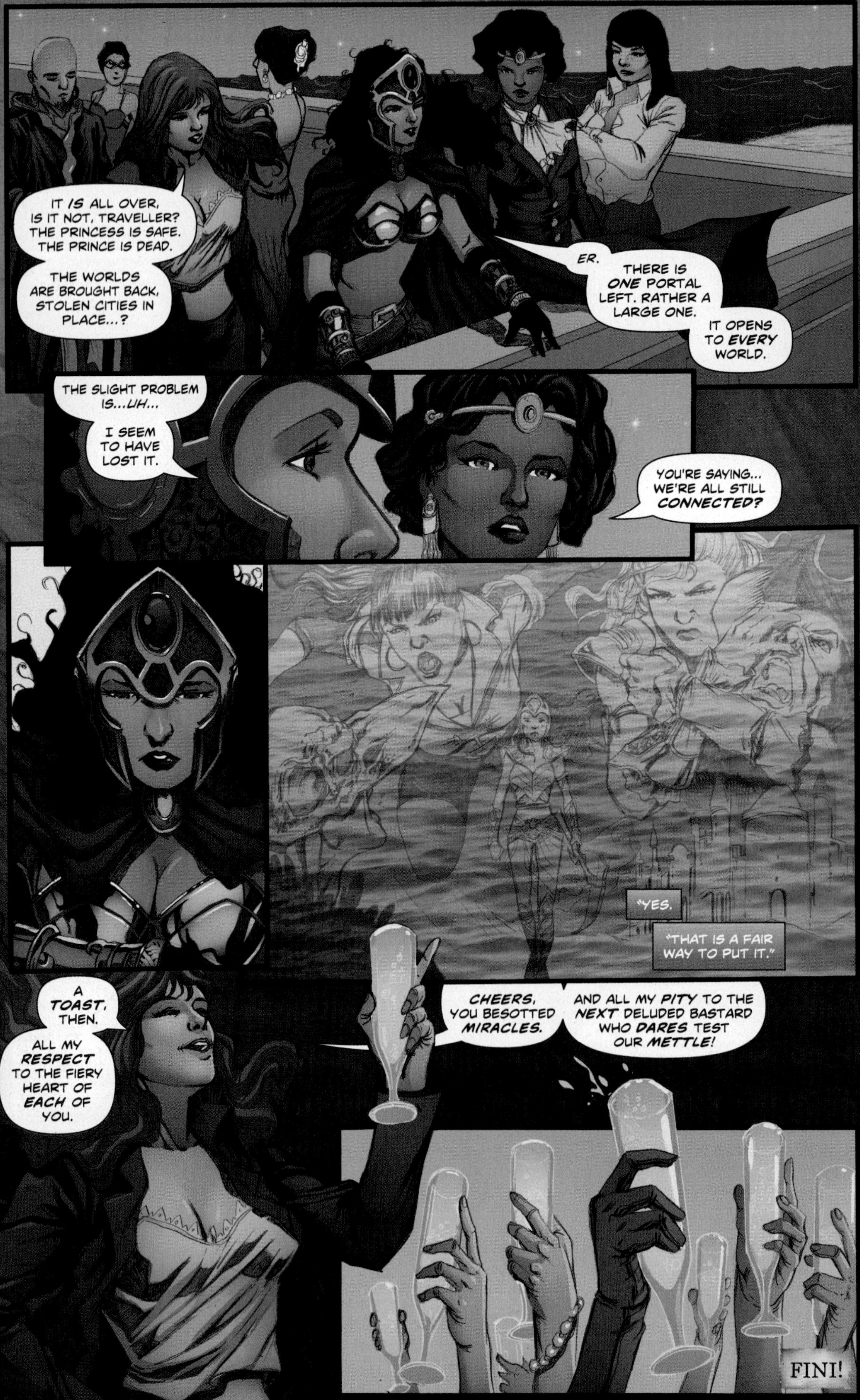
IT IS ALL OVER, IS IT NOT, TRAVELLER? THE PRINCESS IS SAFE. THE PRINCE IS DEAD.
THE WORLDS ARE BROUGHT BACK, STOLEN CITIES IN PLACE...?
ER.
THERE IS ONE PORTAL LEFT. RATHER A LARGE ONE.
IT OPENS TO EVERY WORLD.
THE SLIGHT PROBLEM IS...UH...
I SEEM TO HAVE LOST IT.
YOU'RE SAYING... WE'RE ALL STILL CONNECTED?
"YES.
"THAT IS A FAIR WAY TO PUT IT."
A TOAST, THEN.
ALL MY RESPECT TO THE FIERY HEART OF EACH OF YOU.
CHEERS, YOU BESOTTED MIRACLES.
AND ALL MY PITY TO THE NEXT DELUDED BASTARD WHO DARES TEST OUR METTLE!
FINI!

MAIN SERIES COVERS

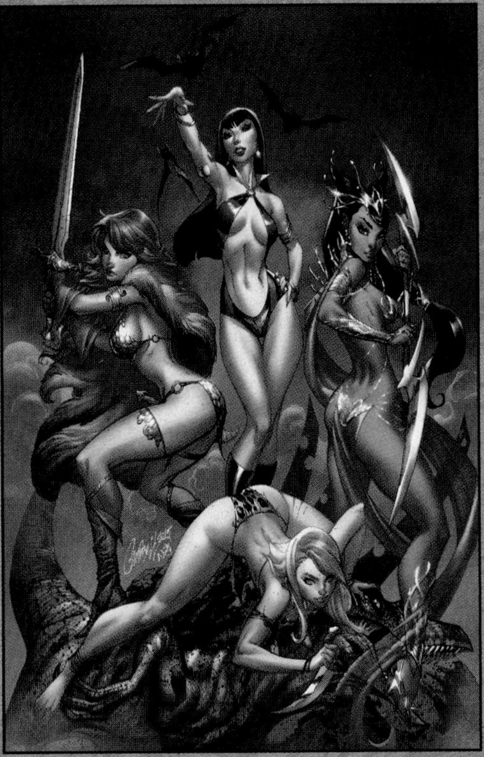

issue #1 cover
art by J. SCOTT CAMPBELL
colors by NEI RUFFINO

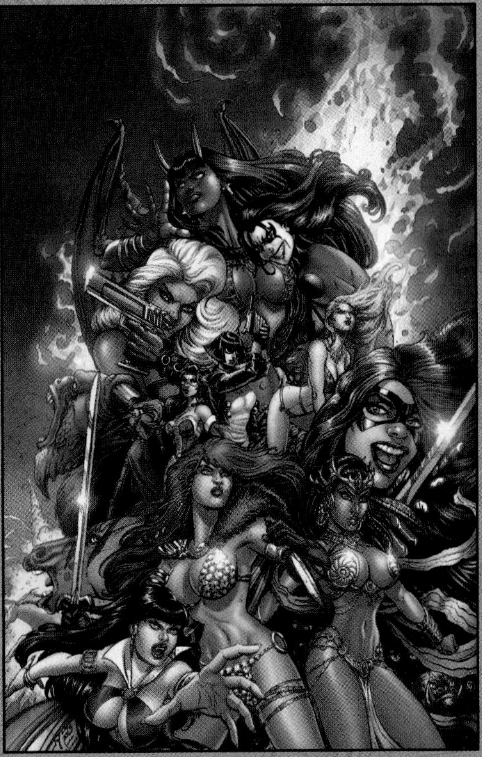

issue #1 cover
art by JOYCE CHIN
colors by IVAN NUNES

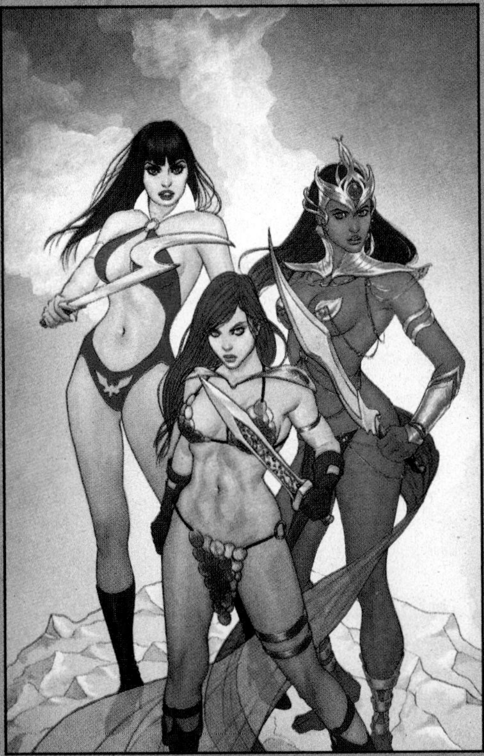

issue #1 cover
art by JENNY FRISON

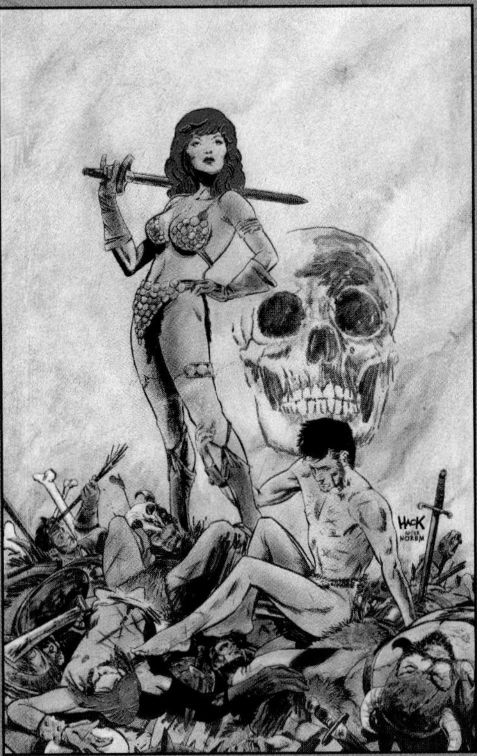
HACK

issue #1 cover
art by ROBERT HACK

MAIN SERIES COVERS

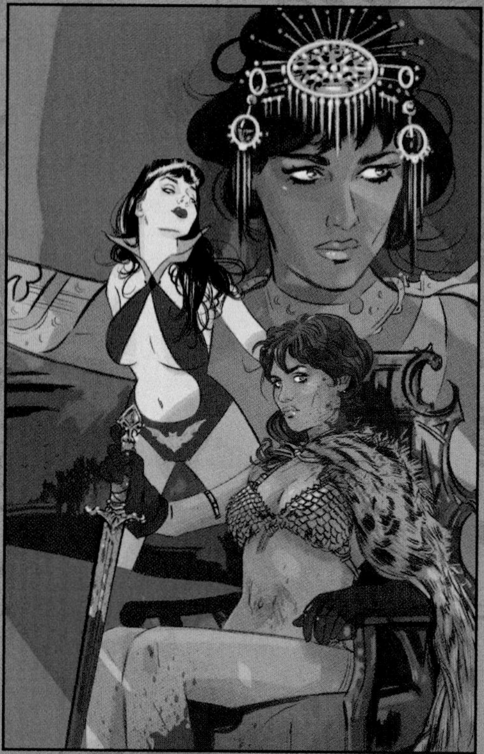

issue #1 cover
art by TULA LOTAY

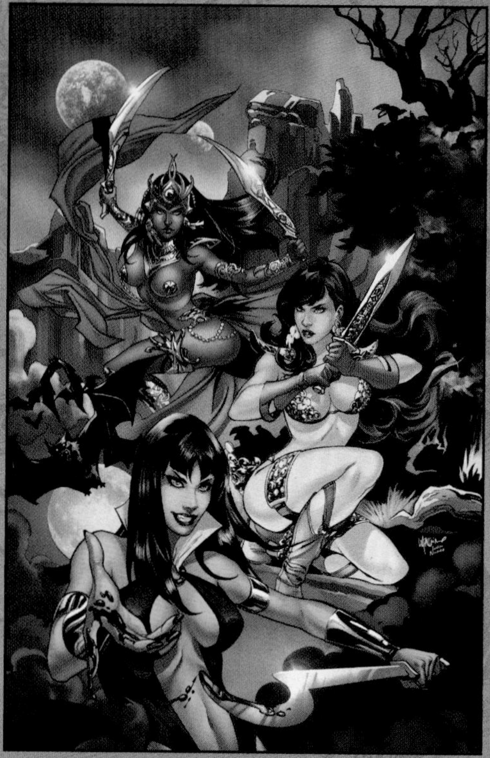

issue #1 cover
art by EMANUELA LUPACCHINO
colors by IVAN NUNES

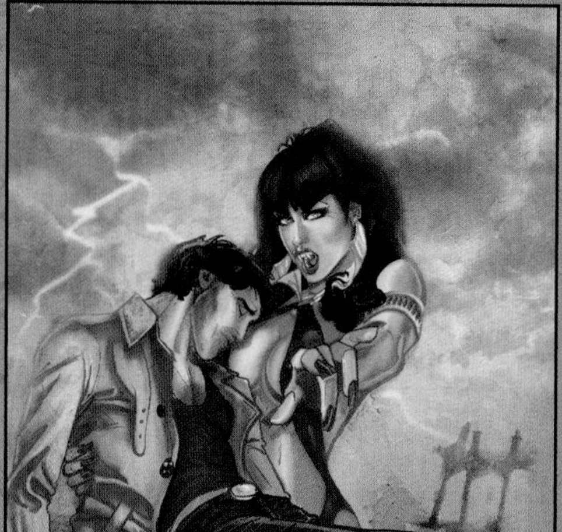

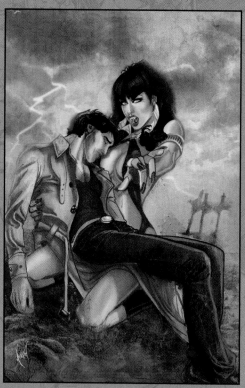

issue #1 cover
art by CEDRIC POULAT

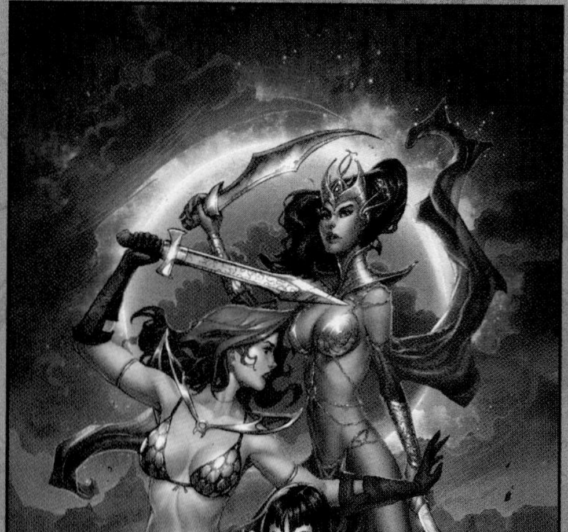

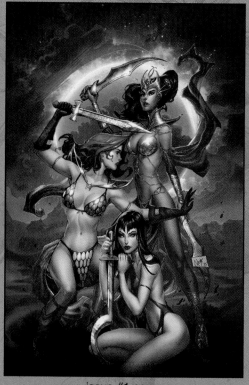

issue #1 cover
art by NEI RUFFINO

MAIN SERIES COVERS

issue #2 cover
art by ROBERT HACK

issue #2 cover
art by TULA LOTAY

issue #2 cover
art by EMANUELA LUPACCHINO
colors by IVAN NUNES

issue #3 cover
art by ROBERT HACK

MAIN SERIES COVERS

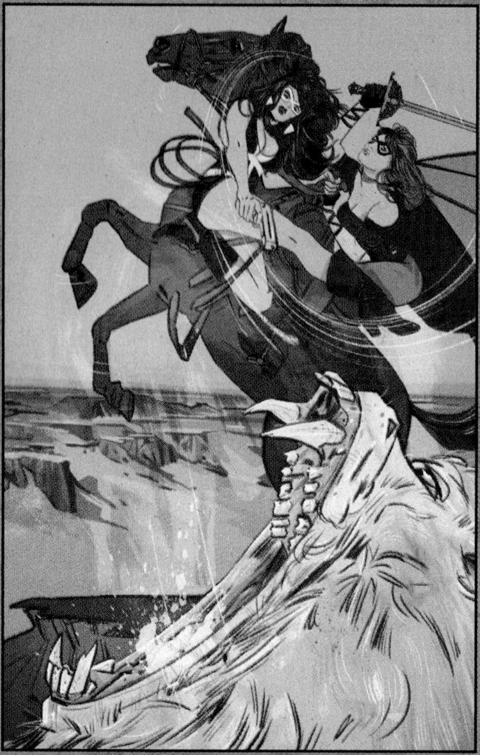

issue #3 cover
art by TULA LOTAY

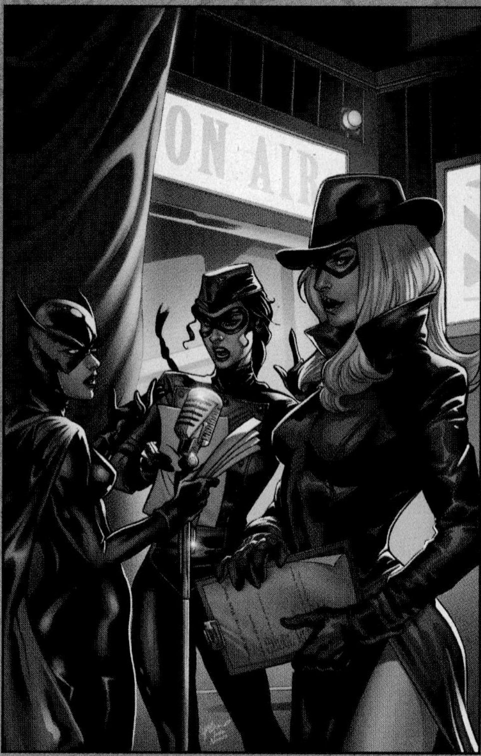
ON AIR

issue #3 cover
art by EMANUELA LUPACCHINO
inks by MARY SANAPO colors by IVAN NUNES

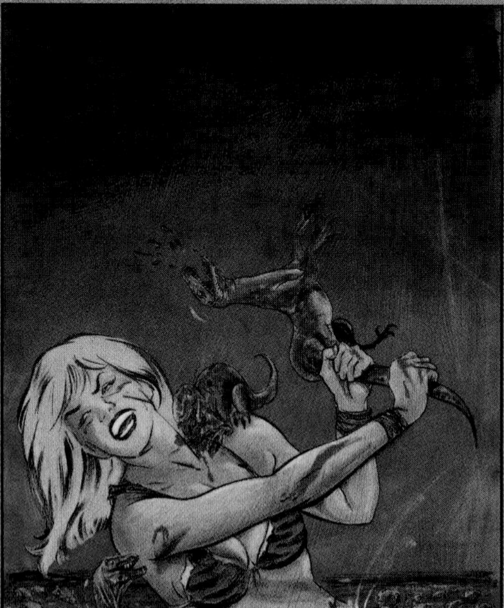

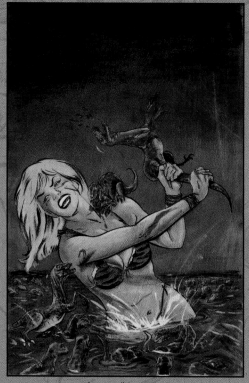

issue #4 cover
art by ROBERT HACK

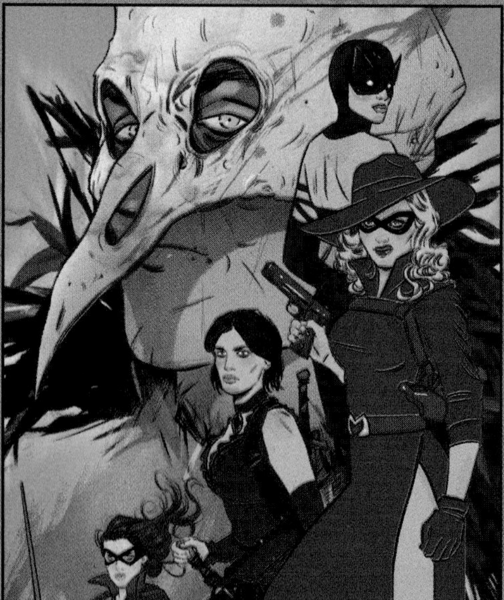

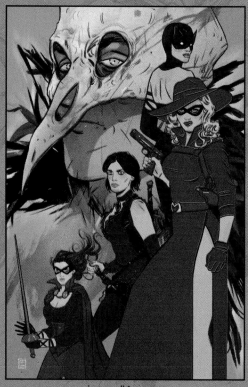

issue #4 cover
art by TULA LOTAY

MAIN SERIES COVERS

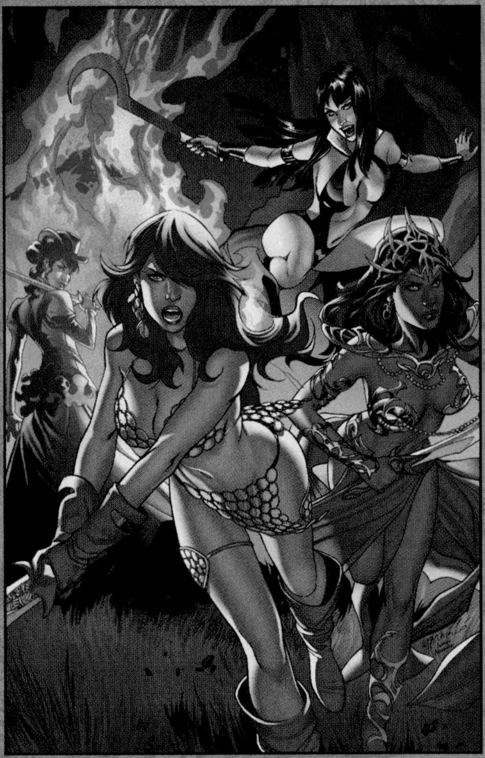

issue #4 cover
art by EMANUELA LUPACCHINO
colors by IVAN NUNES

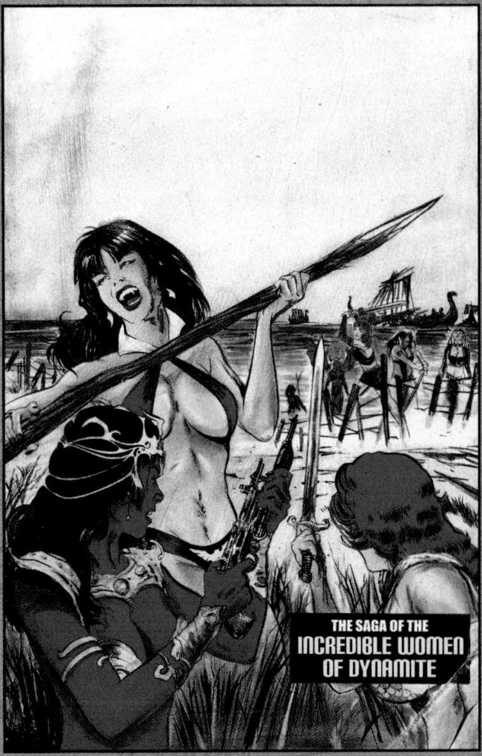
THE SAGA OF THE
INCREDIBLE WOMEN
OF DYNAMITE

issue #5 cover
art by ROBERT HACK

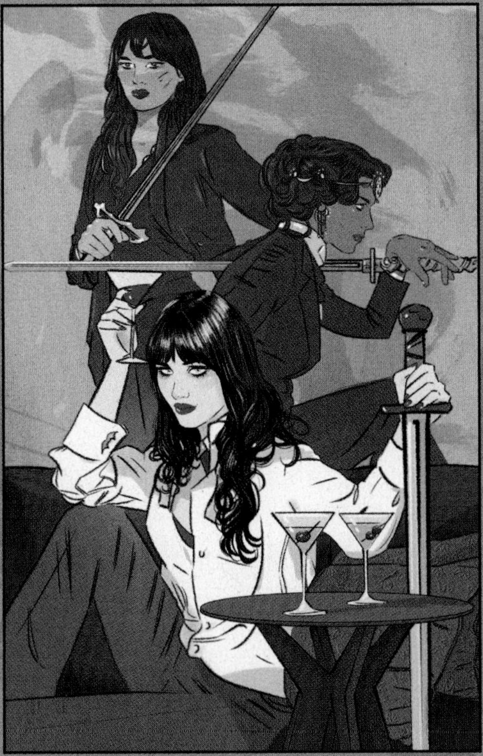

issue #5 cover
art by TULA LOTAY

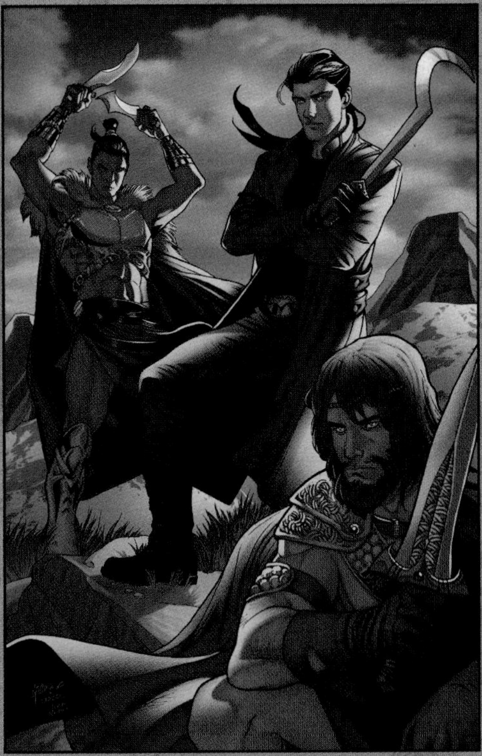

issue #5 cover
art by EMANUELA LUPACCHINO
inks by MARY SANAPO colors by IVAN NUNES

MAIN SERIES COVERS

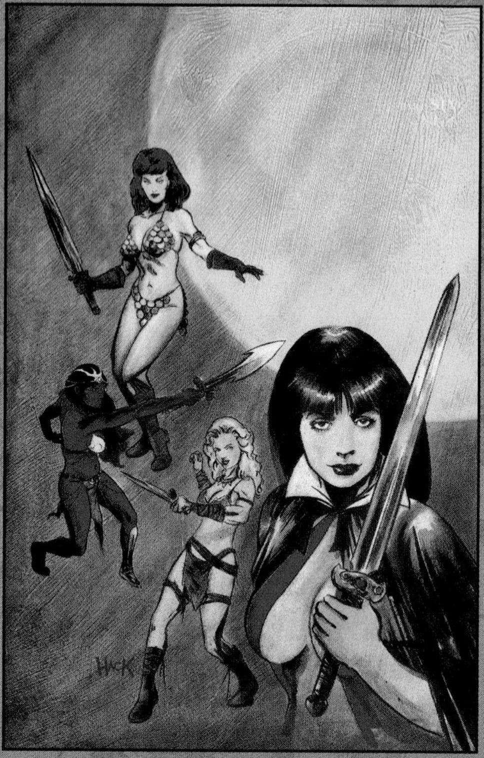
HACK

issue #6 cover
art by ROBERT HACK

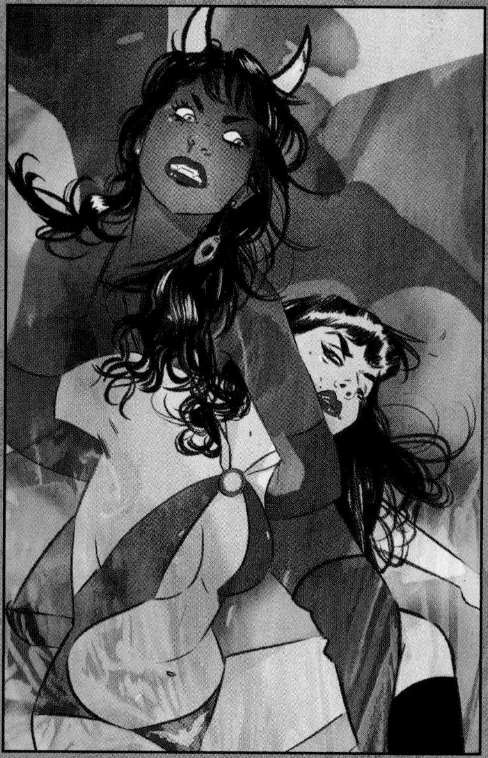

issue #6 cover
art by TULA LOTAY

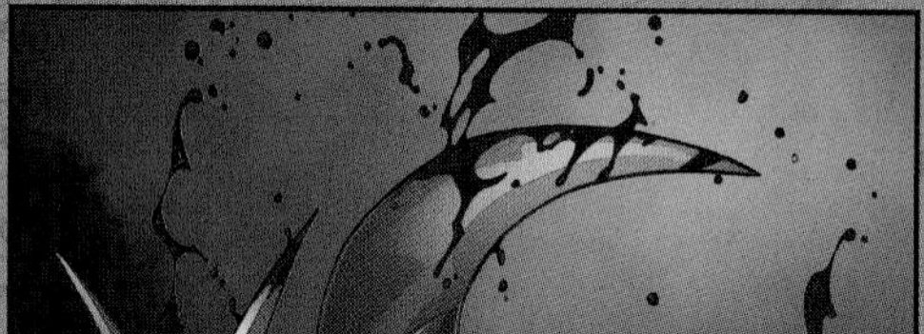

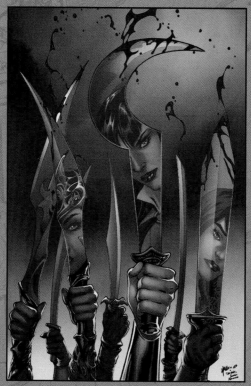

issue #6 cover
art by EMANUELA LUPACCHINO
inks by MARY SANAPO colors by IVAN NUNES

MAIN SERIES EXCLUSIVE COVERS

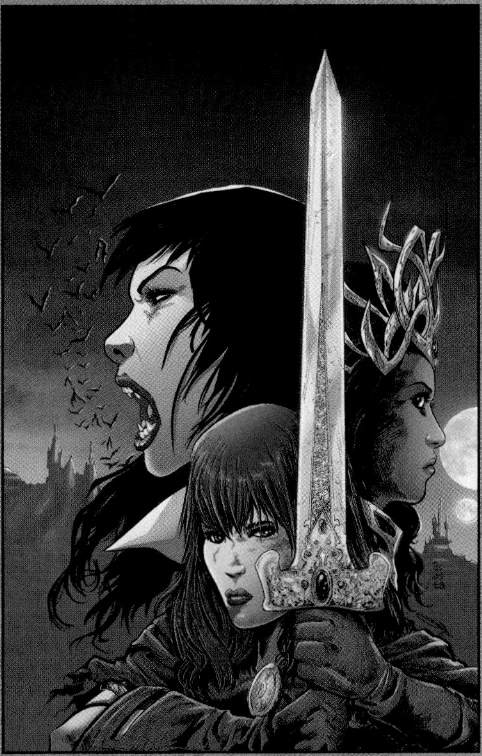

issue #1 Green Brain Comics cover
art by DAVE ACOSTA
colors by DIJJO LIMA

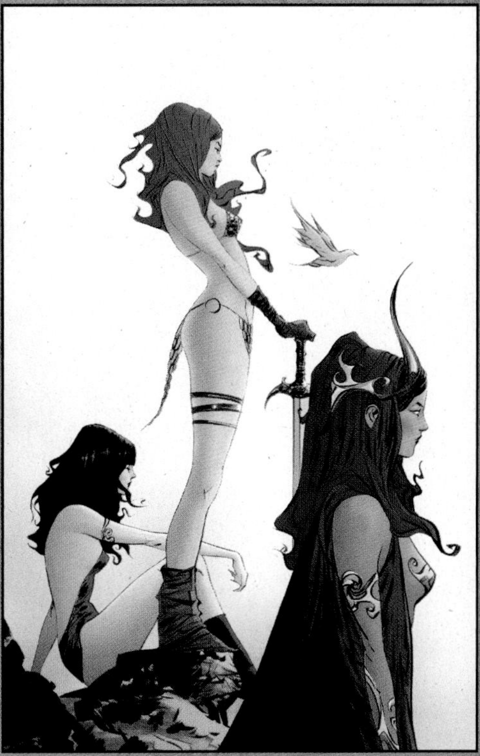

issue #1 Books-A-Million cover
art by JAE LEE
colors by JUNE CHUNG

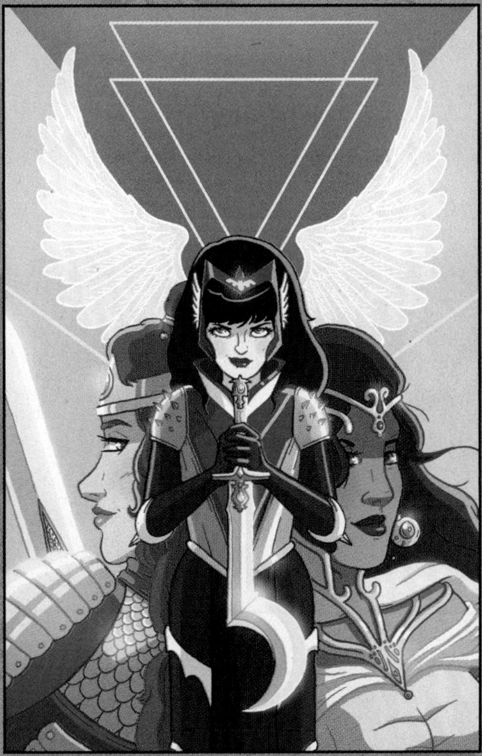

issue #1 Beware the Valkyries cover
art by KATE LETH
colors by PAULINA GANUCHEAU

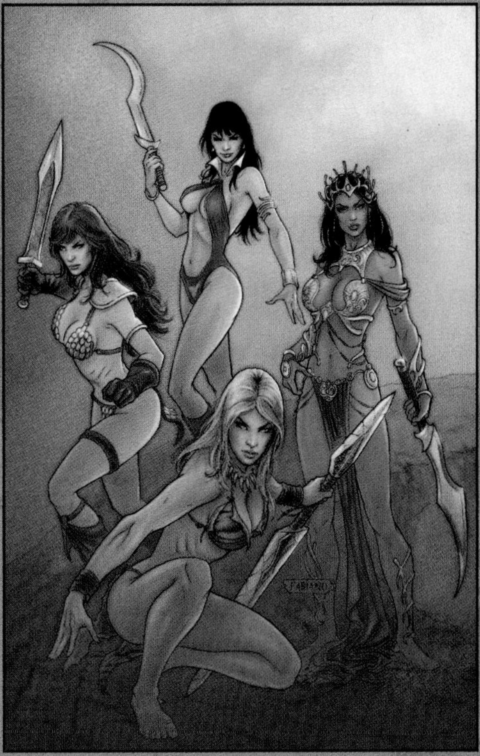

issue #1 Noble House cover
art by FABIANO NEVES

MAIN SERIES EXCLUSIVE COVERS

issue #1 ComicXposure cover
art by NEI RUFFINO

issue #2 ComicXposure cover
art by NEI RUFFINO

issue #3 ComicXposure cover
art by NEI RUFFINO

issue #1 Comics and Friends cover
art by CRAIG TUCKER
colors by DIJJO LIMA

issue #1 I Like Comics cover
art by PETE WOODS

MAIN SERIES EXCLUSIVE COVERS

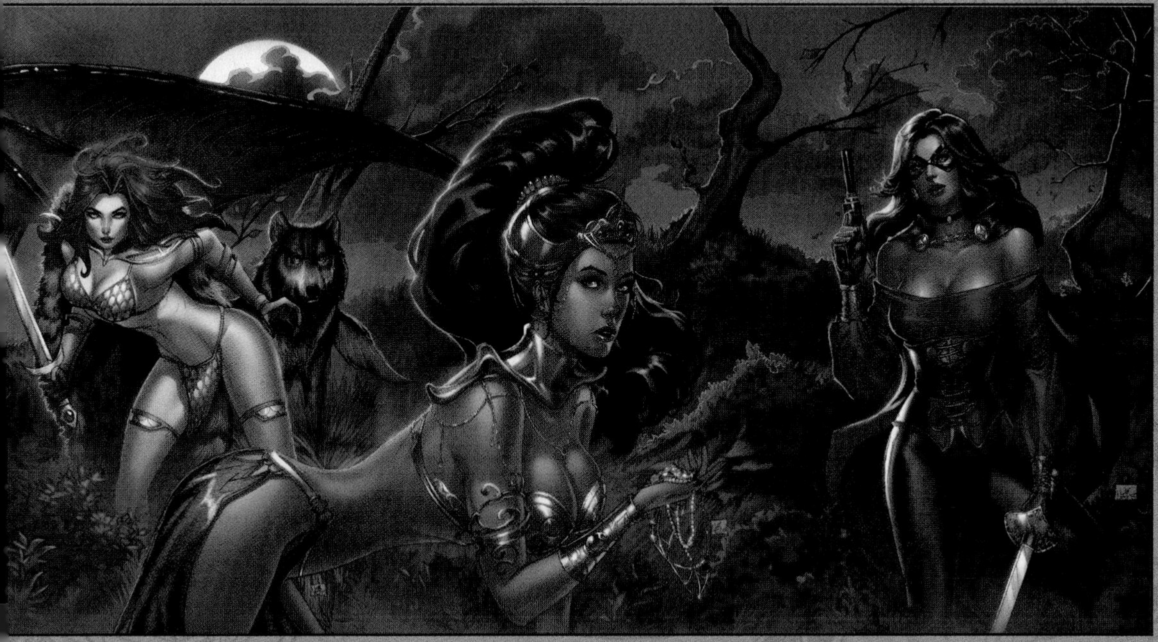

issue #4 ComicXposure cover
art by NEI RUFFINO

issue #5 ComicXposure cover
art by NEI RUFFINO

issue #6 ComicXposure cover
art by NEI RUFFINO

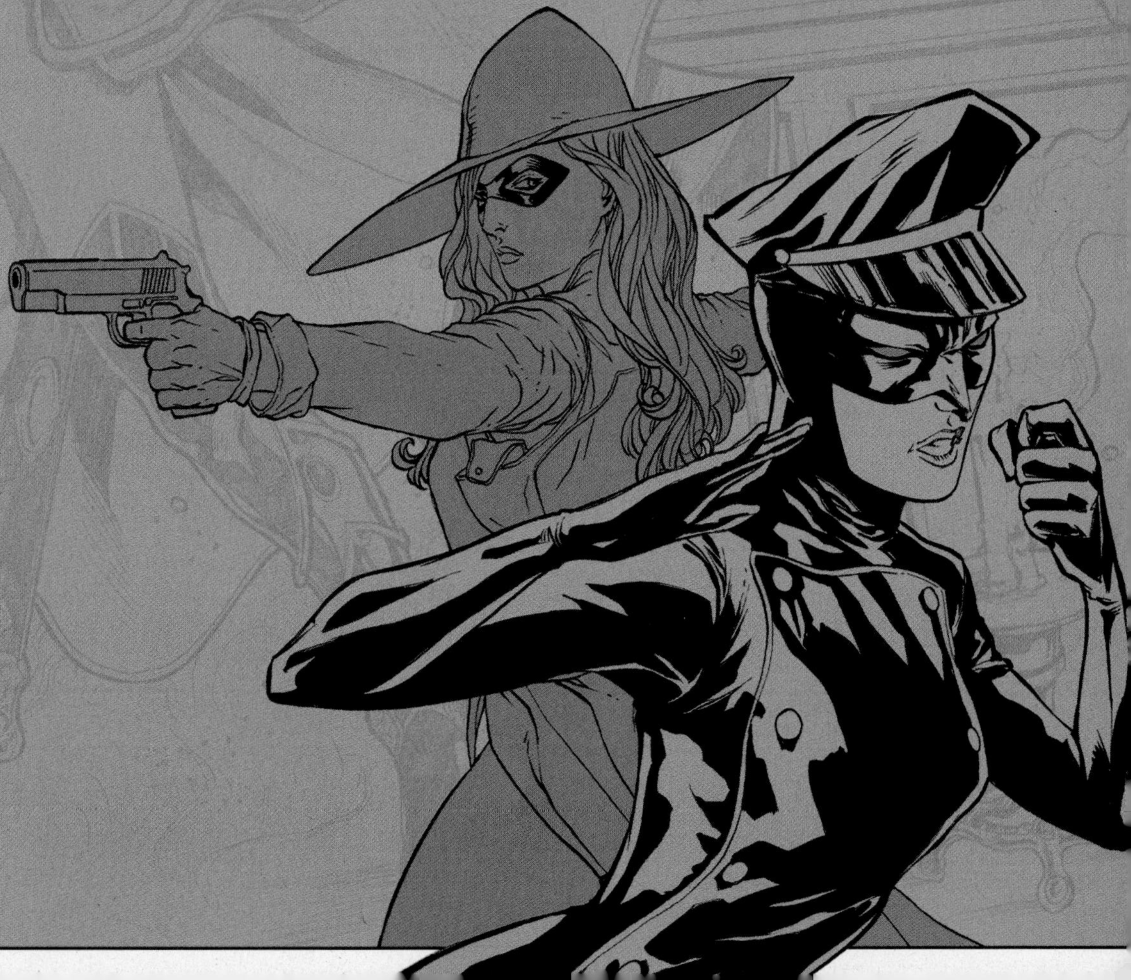

MAIN SERIES COSPLAY COVERS

Photographer Andrew Dobell of Creative Edge studios teamed up with some of the most Bad-Ass Cosplayers we've ever seen. Check out Tabitha Lyons as Red Sonja, Mojo Jones as Vampirella, Tasha Mackenzie as Dejah Thoris, and Chiquite Cosplay as Jungle Girl!

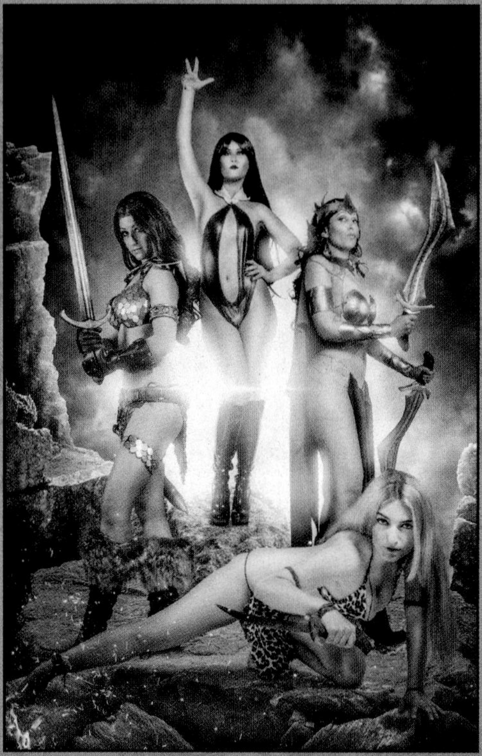

issue #3 cover

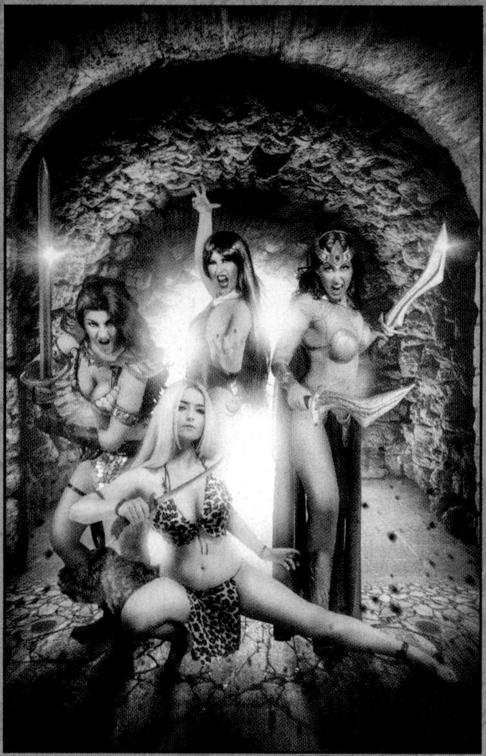

issue #4 cover

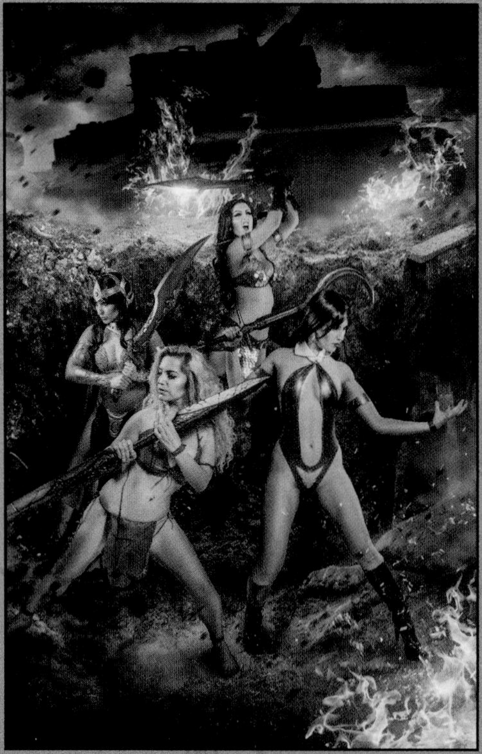

issue #5 cover

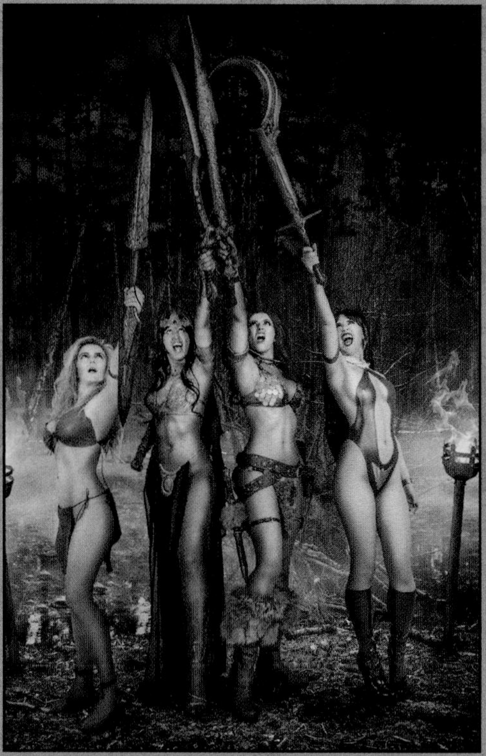

issue #6 cover

MINIS & ONE-SHOT COVERS (alphabetical)

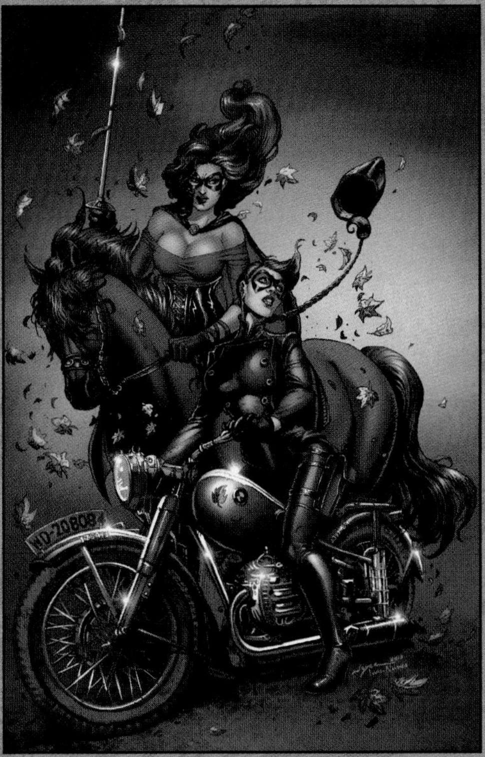

Black Sparrow & Lady Zorro cover
art by JOYCE CHIN
colors by IVAN NUNES

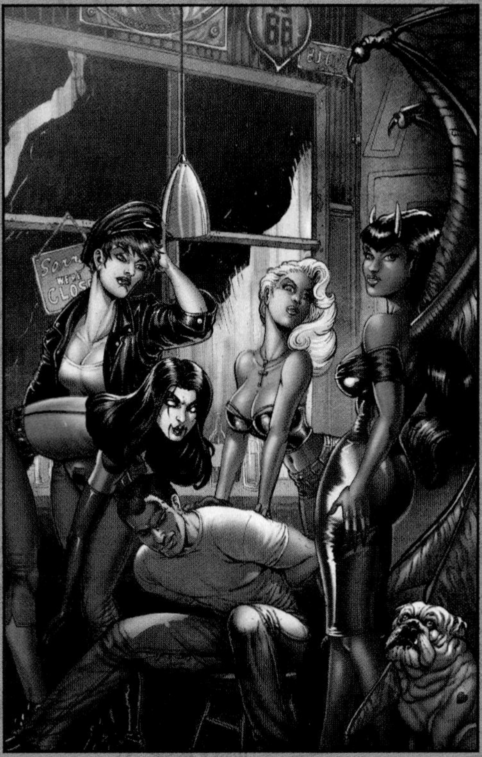

Chaos¡ Prequel cover
art by JOYCE CHIN
colors by IVAN NUNES

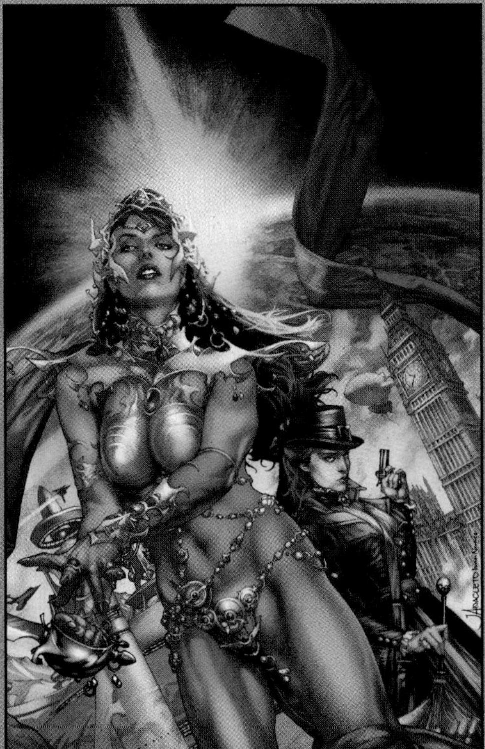

Dejah Thoris & Irene Adler #1 cover
art by JAY ANACLETO
colors by IVAN NUNES

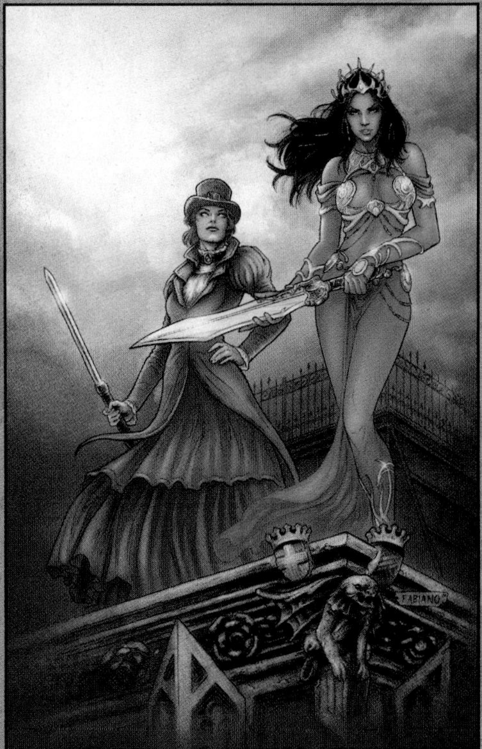

Dejah Thoris & Irene Adler #1 cover
In Your Dreams exclusive cover
art by FABIANO NEVES

MINIS & ONE-SHOT COVERS (alphabetical)

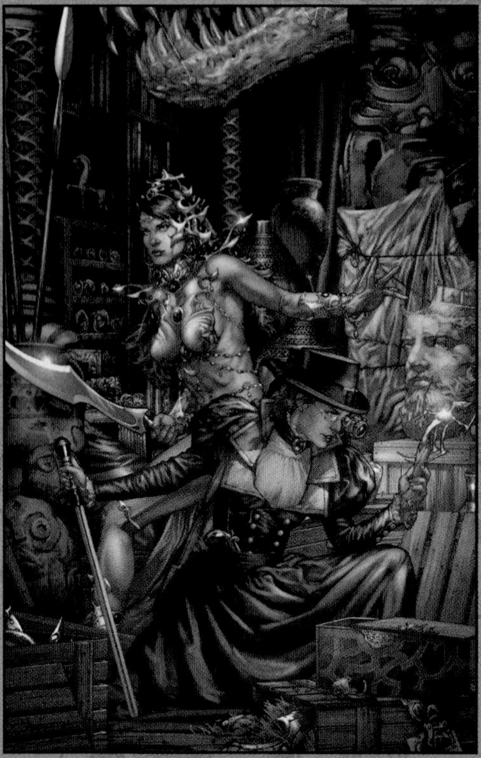

Dejah Thoris & Irene Adler #2 cover
art by JAY ANACLETO
colors by IVAN NUNES

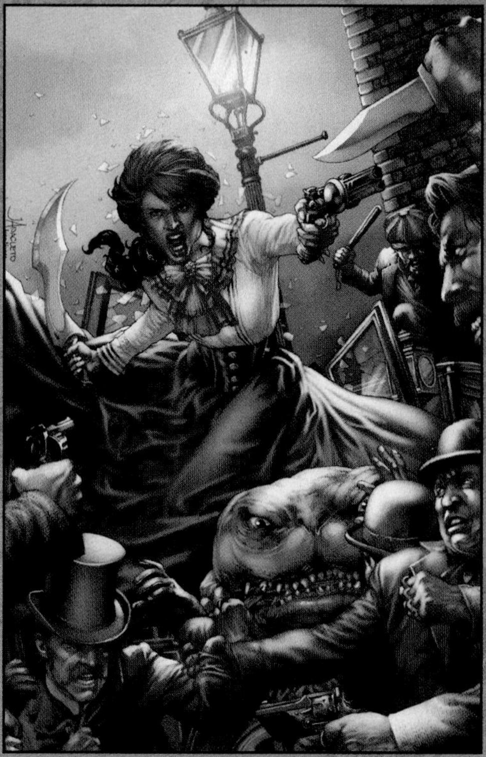

Dejah Thoris & Irene Adler #3 cover
art by JAY ANACLETO
colors by IVAN NUNES

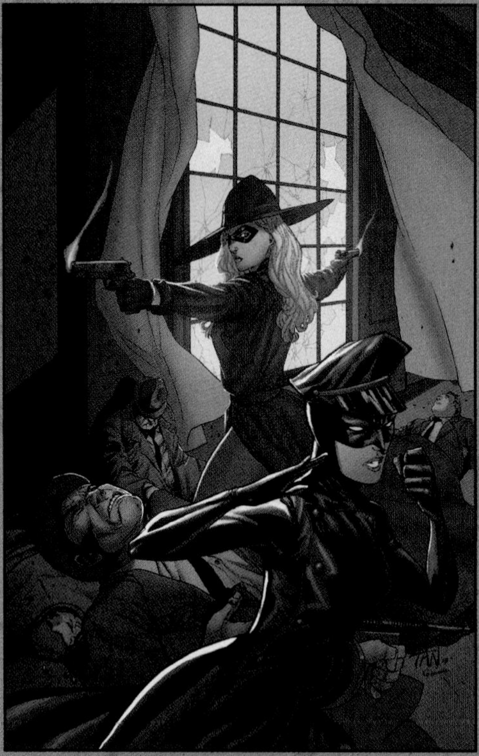

Masquerade & Kato cover
art by BILLY TAN
colors by ALEX GUIMARÁES

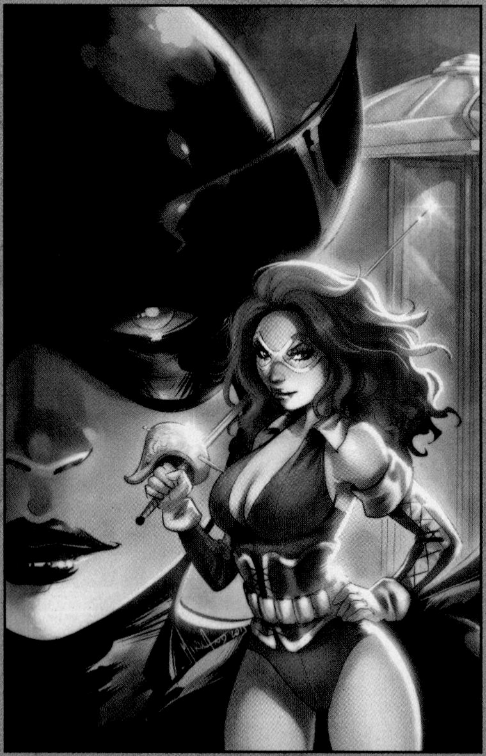

Miss Fury & Lady Rawhide cover
art by MIRKA ANDOLFO
colors by VINCENZO SALVO

MINIS & ONE-SHOT COVERS (alphabetical)

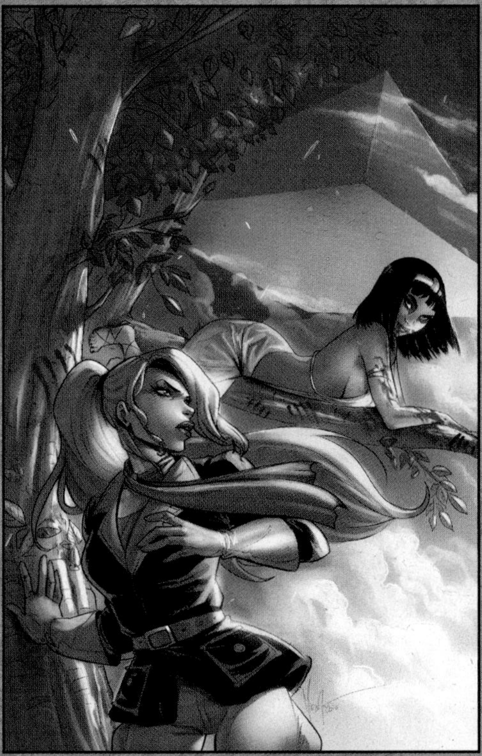

Pantha & Jane Porter cover
art by MIRKA ANDOLFO

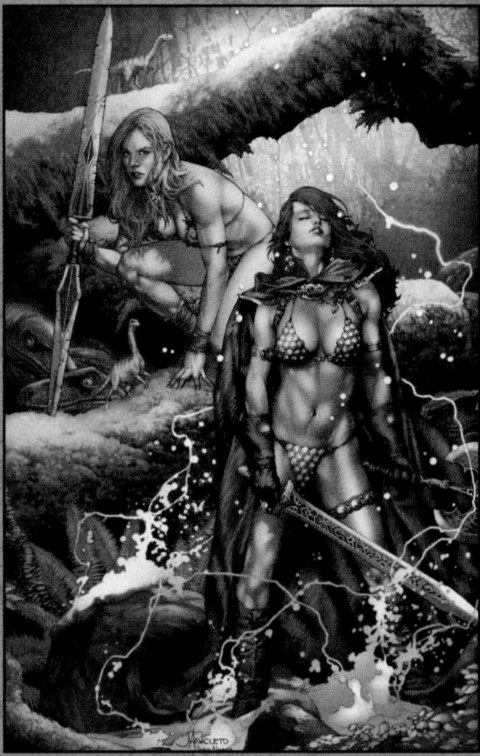

Red Sonja & Jungle Girl #1 cover
art by JAY ANACLETO
colors by IVAN NUNES

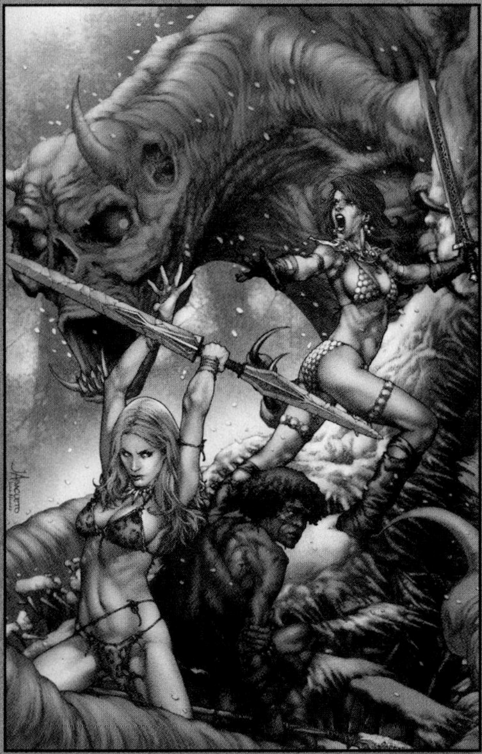

Red Sonja & Jungle Girl #2 cover
art by JAY ANACLETO
colors by IVAN NUNES

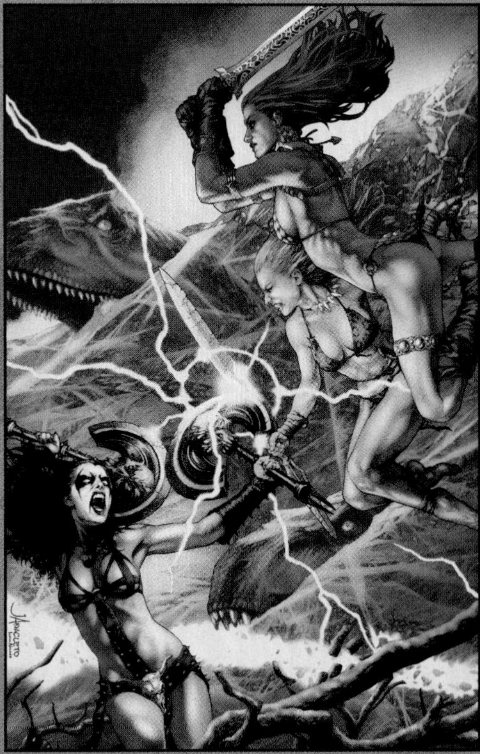

Red Sonja & Jungle Girl #3 cover
art by JAY ANACLETO
colors by IVAN NUNES

MINIS & ONE-SHOT COVERS (alphabetical)

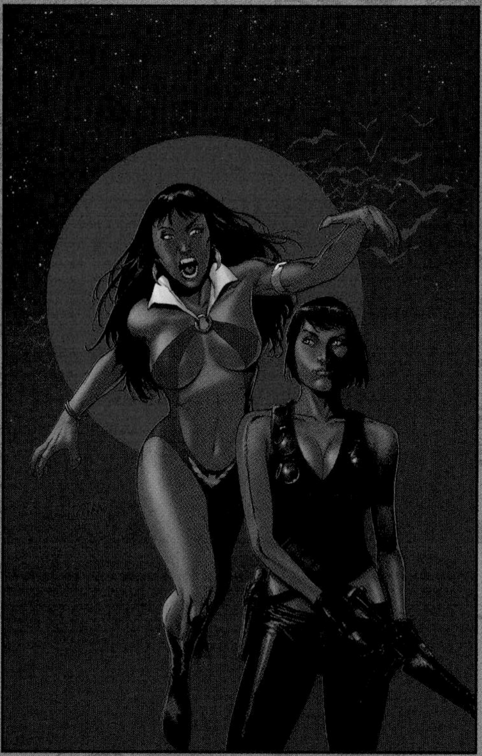

Vampirella & Jennifer Blood #1 cover
art by JAY ANACLETO
colors by ALEX GUIMARÁES

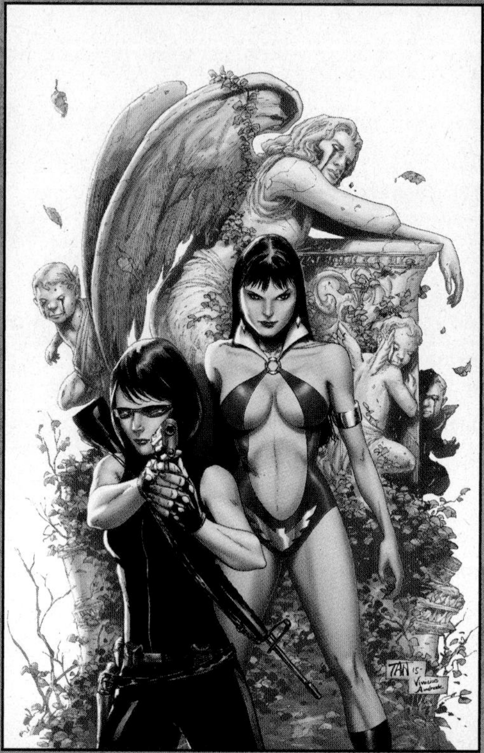

Vampirella & Jennifer Blood #2 cover
art by JAY ANACLETO
colors by VINICIUS ANDRADE

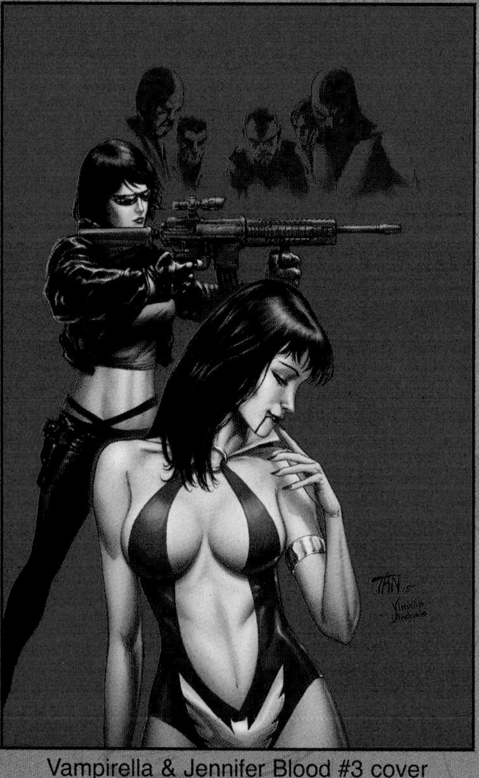

Vampirella & Jennifer Blood #3 cover
art by JAY ANACLETO
colors by VINICIUS ANDRADE

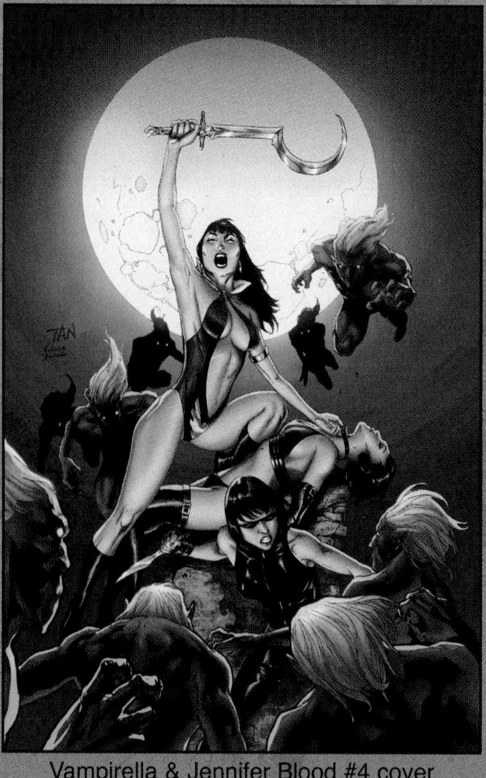

Vampirella & Jennifer Blood #4 cover
art by JAY ANACLETO
colors by VINICIUS ANDRADE

SWORD DESIGNS BY SERGIO DÁVILA

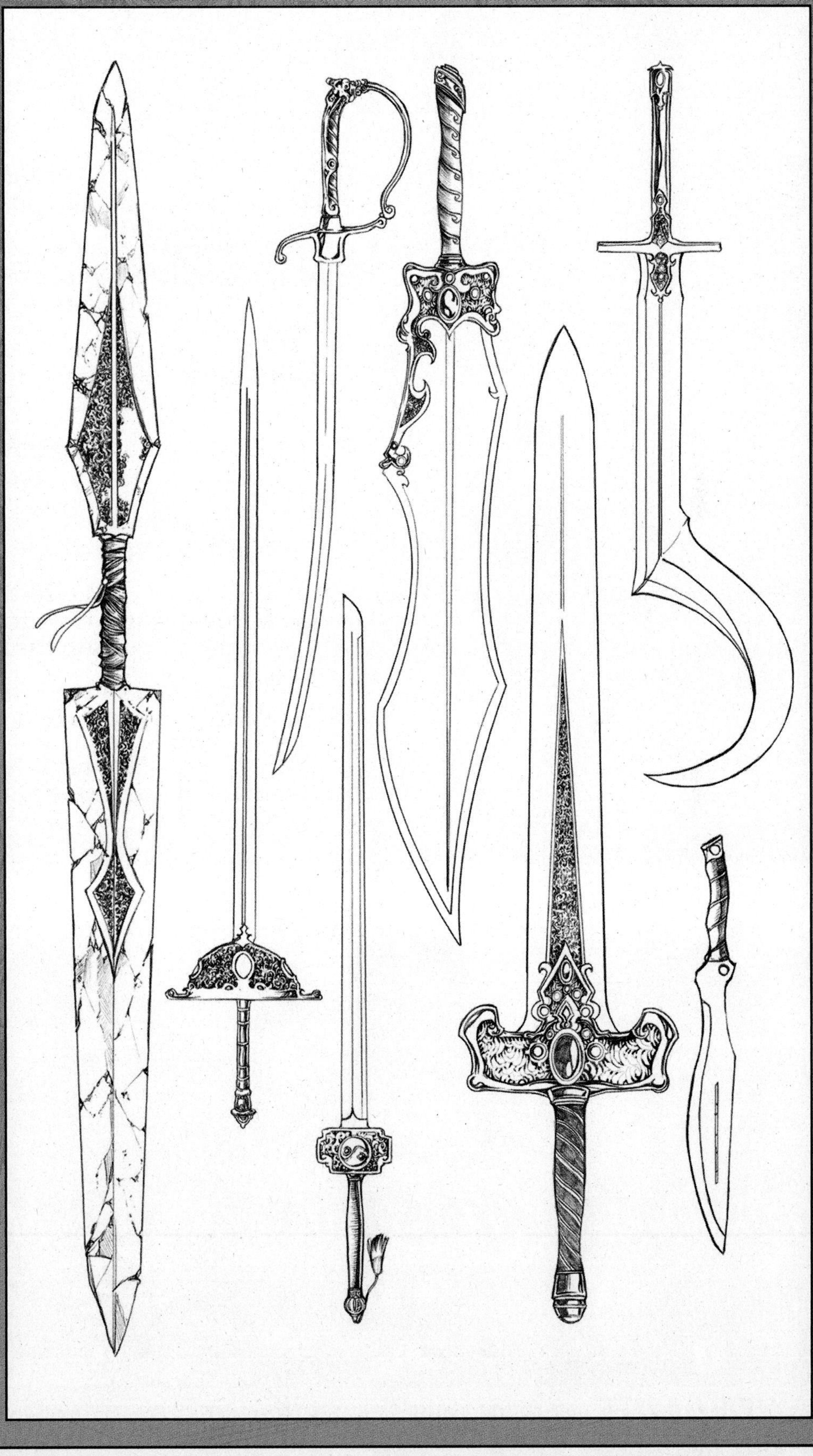

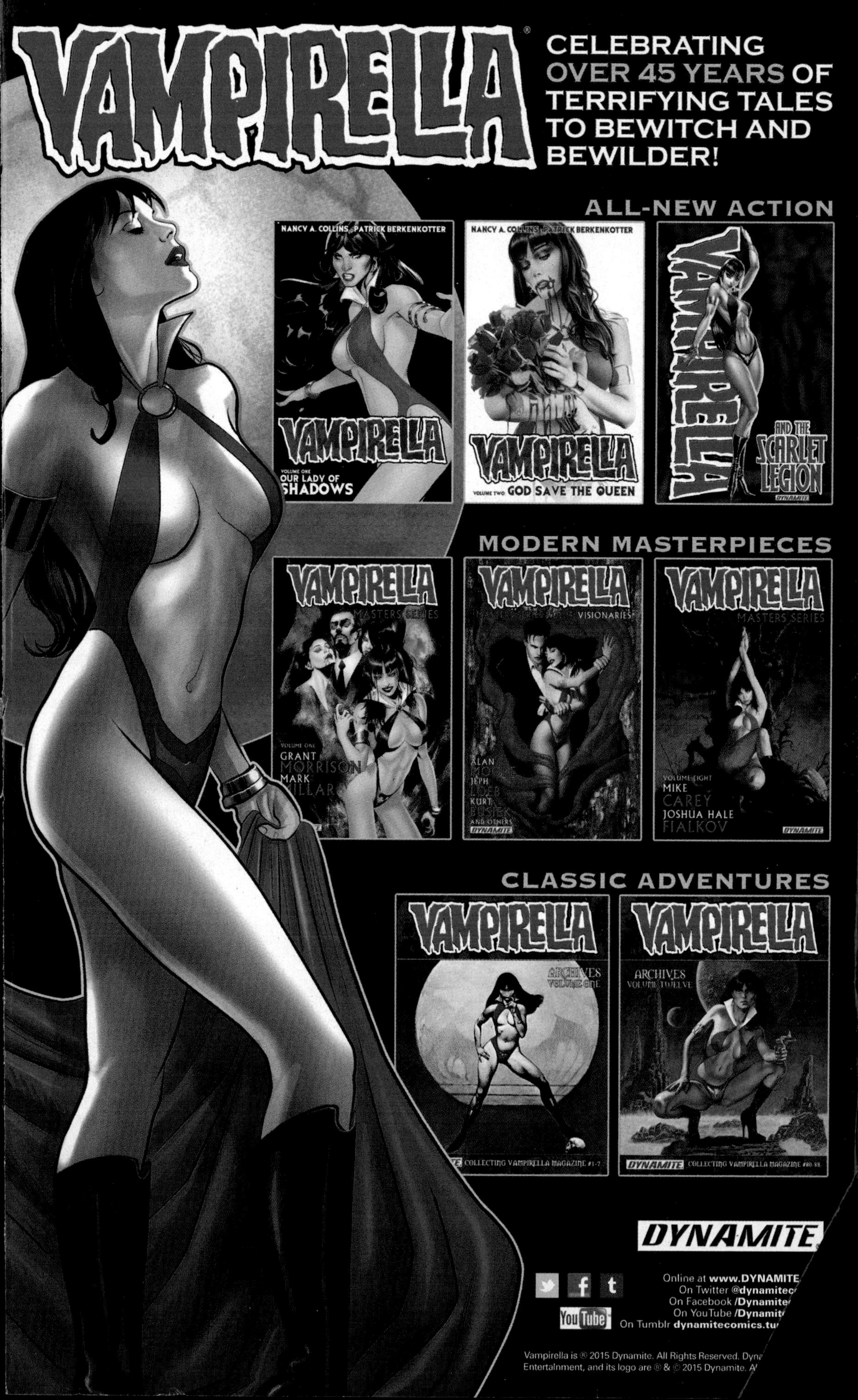

VAMPIRELLA
CELEBRATING OVER 45 YEARS OF TERRIFYING TALES TO BEWITCH AND BEWILDER!
ALL-NEW ACTION
NANCY A. COLLINS · PATRICK BERKENKOTTER
VAMPIRELLA
VOLUME ONE OUR LADY OF SHADOWS
NANCY A. COLLINS · PATRICK BERKENKOTTER
VAMPIRELLA
VOLUME TWO GOD SAVE THE QUEEN
VAMPIRELLA AND THE SCARLET LEGION
DYNAMITE
MODERN MASTERPIECES
VAMPIRELLA
MASTERS SERIES
VOLUME ONE
GRANT MORRISON
MARK MILLAR
VAMPIRELLA
VISIONARIES
ALAN MOORE
JEPH LOEB
KURT BUSIEK
AND OTHERS
DYNAMITE
VAMPIRELLA
MASTERS SERIES
VOLUME EIGHT
MIKE CAREY
JOSHUA HALE FIALKOV
DYNAMITE
CLASSIC ADVENTURES
VAMPIRELLA
ARCHIVES VOLUME ONE
COLLECTING VAMPIRELLA MAGAZINE #1-7
VAMPIRELLA
ARCHIVES VOLUME TWELVE
DYNAMITE
COLLECTING VAMPIRELLA MAGAZINE #80-88
DYNAMITE
Online at www.DYNAMITE
On Twitter @dynamitec
On Facebook /Dynamite
On YouTube /Dynamit
On Tumblr dynamitecomics.tu
Vampirella is ® 2015 Dynamite. All Rights Reserved. Dyna
Entertainment, and its logo are ® & © 2015 Dynamite. A

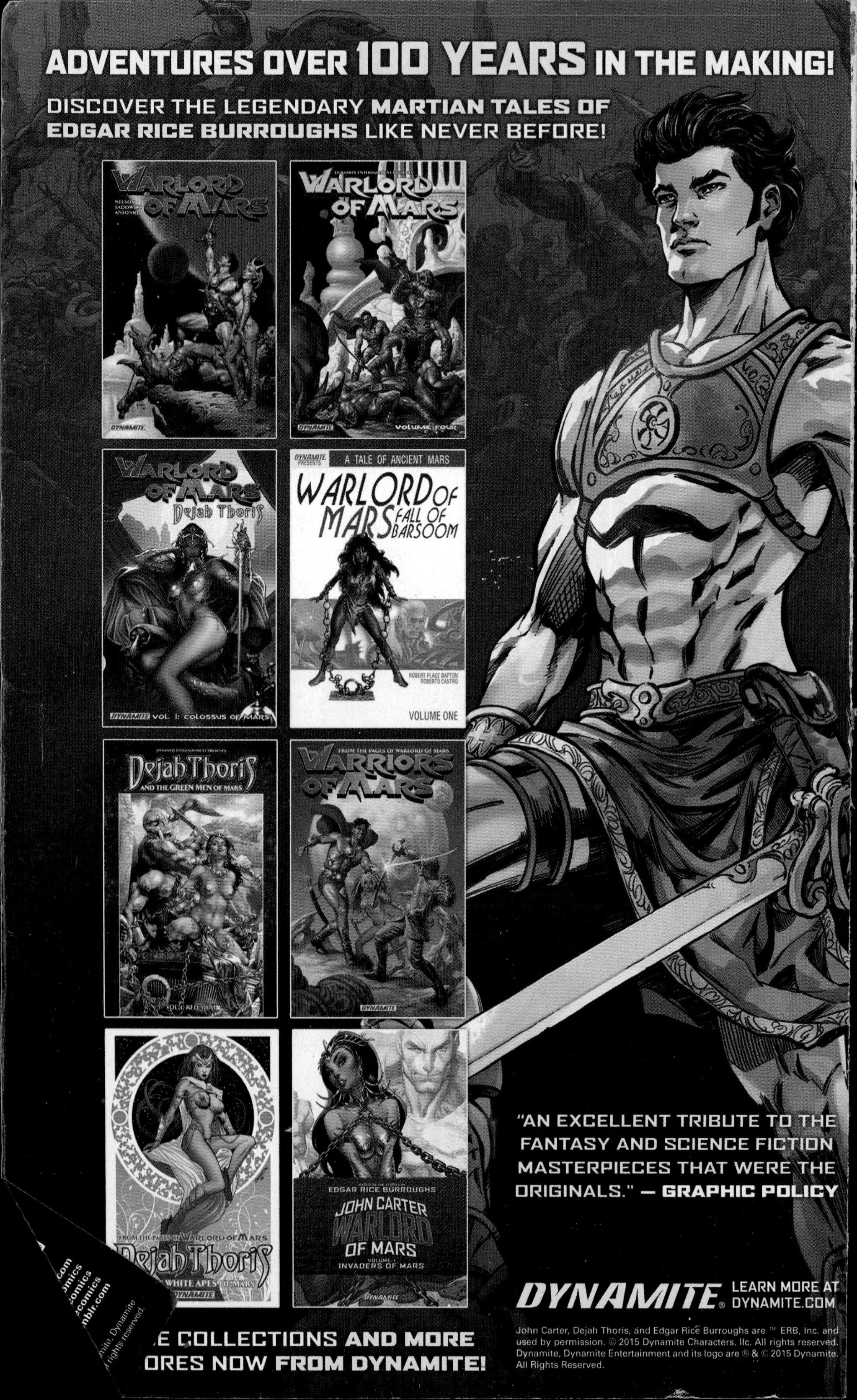
ADVENTURES OVER 100 YEARS IN THE MAKING!
DISCOVER THE LEGENDARY MARTIAN TALES OF EDGAR RICE BURROUGHS LIKE NEVER BEFORE!
WARLORD OF MARS
WARLORD OF MARS
VOLUME FOUR
WARLORD OF MARS Dejah Thoris
vol. I: COLOSSUS OF MARS
A TALE OF ANCIENT MARS
WARLORD OF MARS FALL OF BARSOOM
ROBERT PLACE NAPTON
ROBERTO CASTRO
VOLUME ONE
Dejah Thoris
AND THE GREEN MEN OF MARS
FROM THE PAGES OF WARLORD OF MARS
WARRIORS OF MARS
FROM THE PAGES OF WARLORD OF MARS
Dejah Thoris
WHITE APES OF MARS
EDGAR RICE BURROUGHS
JOHN CARTER
WARLORD OF MARS
VOLUME 1
INVADERS OF MARS
"AN EXCELLENT TRIBUTE TO THE FANTASY AND SCIENCE FICTION MASTERPIECES THAT WERE THE ORIGINALS." — GRAPHIC POLICY
DYNAMITE® LEARN MORE AT DYNAMITE.COM
E COLLECTIONS AND MORE
ORES NOW FROM DYNAMITE!
John Carter, Dejah Thoris, and Edgar Rice Burroughs are ™ ERB, Inc. and used by permission. © 2015 Dynamite Characters, llc. All rights reserved. Dynamite, Dynamite Entertainment and its logo are ® & © 2015 Dynamite. All Rights Reserved.